A
GENEVA SERIES
COMMENTARY

COLOSSIANS

Garner. sc.

After the Original Picture in Queens College Cambridge.

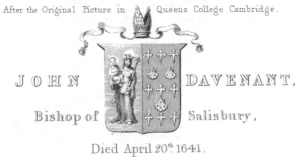

JOHN DAVENANT,

Bishop of Salisbury,

Died April 20th 1641.

LONDON

Published for the Proprietor by Hamilton Adams & Co. 1831.

AN

EXPOSITION

OF THE

EPISTLE OF ST. PAUL

TO THE

COLOSSIANS,

BY

THE RIGHT REV. JOHN DAVENANT, D.D.

LORD BISHOP OF SALISBURY;

PRESIDENT OF QUEEN'S COLLEGE, AND LADY MARGARET'S

PROFESSOR OF DIVINITY IN CAMBRIDGE:

ORIGINALLY DELIVERED, IN A SERIES OF LECTURES, BEFORE THE

UNIVERSITY.

TRANSLATED FROM THE ORIGINAL LATIN;

WITH A LIFE OF THE AUTHOR,

AND NOTES

ILLUSTRATIVE OF THE WRITERS AND AUTHORITIES REFERRED TO

IN THE WORK:

BY JOSIAH ALLPORT,

MINISTER OF ST. JAMES'S, BIRMINGHAM.

Quæ Pauli Epistola non melle dulcior, lacte candidior?—Ambr. Serm. 68.

VOL. I.

LONDON:

HAMILTON, ADAMS, AND CO.

BIRMINGHAM:

BEILBY, KNOTT, AND BEILBY.

MDCCCXXXI.

THE BANNER OF TRUTH TRUST
3 Murrayfield Road, Edinburgh EH12 6EL, UK
P.O. Box 621, Carlisle, PA 17013, USA

*

First Latin edition, Cambridge, 1627
First Banner of Truth edition 2005
(Reprinted from the English translation
by Josiah Allport, 1831)
Reprinted 2009

*

ISBN: 978 0 85151 909 8

*

Printed in the U.S.A. by
Versa Press, Inc.,
East Peoria, IL

TO

HIS MOST GRACIOUS MAJESTY

KING WILLIAM IV.

SIRE,

IT is a cause of joy to your grateful subjects to behold your Majesty uniformly evincing a lively interest in, and attention to, whatever is adapted to promote the welfare and increase the happiness of your subjects. Her Majesty the Queen, your Royal Consort, also proves herself a help-meet indeed in all that can second your beneficent aims—can render your Court exemplary in character, beneficial in influence, and attractive to the virtuous, the patriotic, and the good—and can secure to you both the affections of your subjects, and the protection and blessing of heaven.

Sire, it is the operation and the love of true Religion, with obedience to that Righteousness which is its essence, that exalts a nation—ennobles its princes—and will be the safeguard of them and their people. That Religion and Righteousness were never elucidated, at large, in a human composition, with greater excellence of manner, or power of argument, than in the Volumes here presented to your Majesty's approbation ; the matter of which was put forth two centuries ago in the Latin language, and has never before been published in English.

In presuming to lay before your Majesty's subjects, in their vernacular tongue, this incomparable
Exposition of a most interesting portion of the
Word of God, to whom could the individual who
has ventured on the hardy task, under all the considerations connected with it, crave permission to
dedicate this Edition, but to your Majesty, whom
the Providence of God has placed as a Nursing-
Father over the Church of which he is an unworthy
Minister.

Should your Majesty, and your Royal Consort,
deign to give any countenance to the performance
of one, who rests all his claim thereto on the unri-
valled merits and the unspeakable utility of his
Author, and who would not permit himself to aspire
to it on any lower grounds, your Majesty may, by
such condescension, be instrumental in promoting
the welfare of the Church; for your countenance
will commend to the attention of many, a work
singularly adapted to impress upon the judgment
those principles, which will be influential, where
reason is under any due subjection to an humble
desire to receive and obey the truth: thus will be
ensured the practice of those duties which we all
owe to God, to our Country, to Religion, and to
each other.

That Peace, Prosperity, and Happiness may
attend your Majesty's reign, and bless you and her
Majesty the Queen, for years to come, is the earnest
desire and prayer of,

SIRE,

Your Majesty's most unworthy,

But devotedly faithful,

And most obedient Subject and Servant,

THE TRANSLATOR.

BIRMINGHAM, *May* 1, 1831.

TRANSLATOR'S PREFACE.

HAVING been urged about three years ago, by a very dear Friend, who well understood the value of Bishop Davenant's Exposition, to undertake a Translation of it, with the view of rendering its excellence of more public use, I then declined, on the score of other pressing engagements and occupations. But, a short time afterwards, taking down the volume, during the agitation of Roman Catholic affairs, in order to ascertain the Bishop's opinion on a certain point, I was struck with the frequent bearing of his remarks, not more on the tenets and practices of the Romanists, than upon many specious errors which have crept into the Protestant communities, and some of which are, unhappily, in our own day, producing effects equally injurious to the integrity of doctrinal truth, to the efficiency of the ministerial office, and to the preservation of Christian unity. Hence, it appeared to me that a re-publication of this Exposition, in the vernacular language, would prove of utility to many of the Clergy, and to the Church at large. In the hope of rendering a profoundly argumentative work on Divinity more useful to general Readers, and observing the number of Fathers and Schoolmen constantly cited in it, many of whose names are now almost forgotten in the Church, I resolved to give short biographical sketches of each as they should occur. Finding, moreover, that no Memoir worthy of Davenant had been written, and that various misrepresentations had gone abroad respecting him and his opinions, I also came to the resolution of announcing in my Prospectus, a Memoir of the Bishop. Little did I then think what a task I was imposing upon myself: for the difficulty of getting at the truth amidst the various conflicting accounts given of antient authors, according to the party views, prejudices, or bigotry of their biographers, while it magnified the importance of eliciting the truth, induced considerable toil and expensive exertion.

As respects our Author himself, when collecting materials for some suitable account of him, it became requisite to search the lives and writings of his contemporaries, and wade through the histories of their time ; and I soon discovered, that, however neglected in the present age, he enjoyed, in his own, a reputation among the first : and, anxious to do justice to his merits—an anxiety augmented by the efforts of some modern opponents of him, and of his faith, to revive and propagate old misrepresentations, in order to disparage the value of his works,—my investigation and research were redoubled.

In the course of such efforts, another important circumstance arose. It became expedient to take a survey of the proceedings, and to examine the various opinions respecting the Synod of Dort, at which he was one of the

English deputies of no inferior consideration. When the
mist in which a great portion of the proceedings of that
extraordinary Council are involved, and the mis-statements
that have been published of them, and which have been
revived and iterated under the sanction of great names,
are recollected, it will be perceived that no light difficulty
was to be surmounted in this department of my undertaking.

These investigations, which could only be encountered
amidst arduous Clerical duties and other employments, if
duly borne in mind, will convince my friends that I have
not been forgetful of my pledge, nor remiss in my efforts
to redeem it to the best of my ability; and this will prove,
it is hoped, a sufficient apology for the delay of publication; a delay that has been painfully increased by severe
domestic afflictions and bereavements, and by an unex-
pected change of situation. Such unavoidable impediments
will, however, be found to have produced advantage to those
numerous friends who have honoured me with their names
as Subscribers to my undertaking, and encouraged me
from time to time by procuring more; for the period that
has elapsed, by protracting the date of carrying my volumes
through the press, afforded me opportunity to extend my
reading and inquiries, and has brought me into an acquaintance with several better informed individuals, to
whom I was before unknown, and am now greatly indebted
for much valuable intelligence and aid. To them I would
here take occasion most gratefully to tender my best and
sincerest acknowledgments; and to the Clergy and public

A 2

at large I would *humbly*, as it respects myself, but *earnestly*, as it respects my Author, commend my performance, trusting that it will not altogether prove unsatisfactory or without benefit to either.

As to my Translation, it is not for me to speak further than to state, what seems due to myself, that fidelity has been my great object; and to this I have sacrificed style, rather than, by giving a more engaging turn to a sentence, lay myself open to the charge, from any quarter, of having put a gloss upon the sense of the original.

Nothing further is requisite than to state, that in my limited space for the Life, it was necessary to use compression; and that much more might have been added in various parts. As some mis-statements may be corrected, some misapprehensions obviated, and much prejudice against those who hold the views of Bishop Davenant be removed, by the addition of documents and incidents in connexion with the facts adduced in the Memoir; it is my purpose, if God permit, and it should hereafter be deemed desirable, to revise, and take a more extended survey of the Bishop's life and writings, the period in which he flourished, and the sphere in which he moved. In the mean time, any communication of facts, records, or sentiments, from any individual qualified to impart what might be regarded new and important, will be thankfully accepted, and employed in a manner, which, it is presumed, will not be otherwise than grateful.

J. A.

Birmingham, May 1, 1831.

LIFE

OF

BISHOP DAVENANT.

THE DAVENANTS were a family of great antiquity and respectability, residing, from the time of Sir John Davenant, in the reign of Henry III., on a domain called Davenants' Lands, in the parish of Sible-Heningham, in the county of Essex. Our Prelate was born, May 20, 1572, in Watling-street, London ; his father being an eminent merchant of the city. He was one of a numerous family ; and some detailed account of his connexions will be given at the end of this biographical sketch. He was " remarkably born," says one of his biographers, " in the seventh month of his conception, and, as remarkably preserved in the first half seven years from his birth, falling down a high pair of stairs, and rising at the bottom with so little harm that he smiled."* " When a child," says his nephew Fuller, " he would rather own his own frowardness, than another's flattery, and when soothed by servants that ' not *John*, but some one of his brothers, did cry,' he would rather appear in his own face, than wear their disguise, returning, ' it was none of his brothers, but *John* only did cry.' "

In 1587, at the age of fifteen, he was admitted of Queen's College, in Cambridge, where he took his degree of A. M. in 1594, after giving such testimony of future eminence, that the profoundly learned Dr. Whittaker, Master of St. John's, and Regius Professor of Divinity, pronounced that he would, in time, prove an honour to the University. In that year a fellowship was

* Lloyd's Memoirs, p. 281.

offered him, which his father would not permit him to accept, on
account of his plentiful fortune; which course our Bishop afterwards adopted, when President of the College : for, having given
his vote against one of his own rich relations, (afterwards Sir
John Gore,) he said, " Cousins, I will satisfy your father that
you have *worth*, but not *want* enough, to be of our Society."
However, in 1597, he was elected Fellow against his will: the
President replying to his objections with the remark, that " preferment was not always a relief *for want*, but sometimes an encouragement *for worth*." In 1601, he took his degree of B. D., and
proceeded, in 1609, to D.D., and was the same year elected,
against seven competitors, Lady Margaret's Professor of Divinity ;
which he appears to have owed in a great measure to the high
testimony of Dr. Whittaker. He was also presented by Archbishop
Abbot, to the Rectory of Cottenham, Cambridgeshire.

In 1613—14, a Royal party visiting Cambridge, on occasion of
the marriage of the Princess Elizabeth with the Prince Palatine
Frederic, and an entertainment being given to them, Davenant
was selected as Moderator, in the Theological Disputation, which,
according to the custom of the age, then occurred. In the following year, on a similar occasion, another Public Disputation
took place, between some chief divines of England and of the
Palatinate, among whom the great Heidelburgh Professor, Abraham Scultetus, distinguished himself. The Margaret Professor
was then also appointed Moderator. The questions discussed, as
we learn from Nicholl's Progresses of James I., were these
three : *Nulla est temporalis Papæ potestas supra reges, in ordine
ad bonum spirituale. Infallibilis fidei determinatio non est an-
nexa cathedræ papali. Cæca obedientia est illicita.*

It is amusing to hear the *con amore* animation with which the
excellent, but pedantic Bishop Hacket, in his Life of Archbishop
Williams, p. 26, records these academical feats. Speaking of
one super-eminent disputant, Dr. Collins, he thus proceeds :—" He
was a firm bank of earth, able to receive the shot of the greatest
artillery. His works in print, against Eudæmon and Fitzherbert,
sons of Anak among the Jesuits, do noise him far and wide. But
they that heard him speak would most admire him. No flood can
be compared to the spring-tide of his language and eloquence, but
the milky river of Nilus, with his seven mouths all at once disem-
boguing into the sea. O how voluble ! how quick ! how facetious
he was ! What a Vertumnus when he pleased to argue on the

right side, and on the contrary. Those things will be living to
the memory of the longest survivor that ever heard him. In this
trial, wherein he stood now to be judged by so many attic and
exquisite wits, he strived to exceed himself, and shewed his cunning marvellously that he could invalidate every argument brought
against him with variety of answers. It was well for all sides,
that the best divine, in my judgment, that ever was in that place,
Dr. Davenant, held the reins of the disputation. He kept him
within the even boundals of the cause; he charmed him with the
Caducæan wand of dialectical prudence; he ordered him to give
just weight, and no more. Horat. l. 1. Od. 3. *Quo non arbiter
Adriæ major tollere, seu honore vult freta.* Such an arbiter as he
was now, such he was and no less, year by year, in all comitial
disputations; wherein whosoever did well, yet constantly he had
the greatest acclamation. To the close of all this Exercise, I come.
The grave elder opponents having had their courses, Mr. Williams,
a new admitted Bachelor of Divinity, came to his turn, last of all.
Presently, there was a smile in the face of every one that knew
them both, and a pre-judging that between these two there would
be a fray indeed. Both jealous of their credit, both great masters
of wit; and as much was expected from the one as from the other.
So they fell to it with all quickness and pertinency; yet, thank
the Moderator, with all candour; like Fabius and Marcellus, the
one was the buckler, the other the sword of that learned exercise.
No greyhound did ever give a hare more turns upon Newmarket
heath, than the replier with his subtleties gave to the respondent.
A subject fit for the verse of Mr. Abraham Hartwell, in his *Regina
Literata,* as he extols Dr. Pern's arguments made before Queen
Elizabeth : *Quis fulmine tanto tela jacet? tanto fulmine nemo
jacet.* But when they had both done their best with equal prow-
ess, the Marshal of the Field, Dr. Davenant, cast down his war-
der between them, and parted them."

In 1614 he was chosen President of his College. And standing now in the highest rank of English Divines for learning, eloquence, and judgment, he was selected, in 1618, by King James
I., with four other theologians of the first name in the kingdom,
to represent the British Church, and assist at the deliberations of
the Synod of Dort; to which assembly his Majesty had been invited to send deputies. And here it will be necessary to take a
brief survey of the circumstances which led to the convening of
this famous Council.

xii LIFE OF BISHOP DAVENANT.

The States of Holland had no sooner established their freedom from the Spanish yoke, than they were embroiled in theological contentions, which soon became intermingled with political cabals. The awful doctrine of the Divine decrees had been placed by the Belgic Confession and Catechism, in common with most of the other Creeds of the Reformed Churches, in the sacred and undefined simplicity of the Scriptures. But, in the period immediately subsequent to the Reformation, the prying curiosity of men, anxious to be wise above what is written, proceeded to the attempt of accurate and precise explanation of what is evidently inexplicable. When, therefore, the supralapsarian scheme began to take place of the moderate system hitherto adopted, it was opposed, on the other side, by those who, in their eagerness to sustain the freedom of human will, dangerously entrenched upon the freedom of Divine grace.

These disputes, however, led to no important consequences, until, in 1591, they centered, as it were, in James Arminius, professor of Divinity in the University of Leyden, a man who joined to unquestionable piety and meekness of spirit, a clear and acute judgment; and who had obtained no slight eminence by the talent with which he had extricated the doctrines of Christianity from the dry and technical mode in which they had hitherto been stated and discussed. His celebrity placed him in a situation ill-suited to his habits and temper. As a pupil of Beza, he had embraced the extreme views to which that divine had carried the tenets advocated by the powerful pen of Calvin. It happened that one Coornhert had advanced some opinions, which, if not loose in themselves, were, at least, expressed in a very unguarded way. The Ministers of Delft published a reply: in which the moderate and generally received sublapsarian hypothesis was sustained; which gave little less offence to the high Calvinists than did the heterodox language of Coornhert. Arminius, therefore, as the most talented Divine of the day, was applied to, in order to take up the pen, on both sides. On the one hand, his friend Martin Lydius, solicited him to vindicate the supralapsarian views of his former tutor, Beza, against the reply of the Ministers; and, on the other, he was invited by the Synod of Amsterdam, to defend this same reply against Coornhert. Placed in this remarkable situation, Arminius felt compelled to enter into an examination of the whole question, and was induced to change his sentiments, and to adopt that view of the Divine Dispensations which now

bears his name. His change, however, was very gradual; but appears to have been hastened by the publication, in Holland, of the *Aurea Armilla* of Perkins, a very powerful supralapsarian divine of the Church of England. This alteration of opinion would not have led to any serious consequences, had Arminius, and the moderate part of the Church, been left to themselves. The fundamental point of Justification by faith, with the doctrine of assurance, and even of final perseverance, were held by him to his death ; and his exemplary piety and humility secured for him the attachment even of those who, when the dispute subsequently extended, became his most zealous opponents. The heat, however, of the less discreet part of the Church, and the dangerous opinions of some who leaned to the Socinian and Pelagian heresies, (among whom may be designated Episcopius, Grotius, Limborch, &c.) being, as is no uncommon case at present, confounded with the tenets of Arminius, led to angry and uncharitable controversies, by which the peace of the Church was grievously broken in upon. Still, the questions might have been amicably settled, but that, at the annual Meetings of the Synods, in 1605, the Class of Dort unwisely fanned the embers into a flame by transmitting the following grievance to the University of Leyden :—" Inasmuch as rumours are heard that certain contro-
" versies have arisen in the Church and University of Leyden,
" concerning the doctrine of the Reformed Churches, this Class
" has judged it necessary that the Synod should deliberate respect-
" ing the safest and most speedy method of settling those contro-
" versies; that all the schisms and causes of offence which spring
" out of them may seasonably be removed, and the union of the
" Reformed churches preserved inviolate against the calumnies of
" adversaries."

When this officious document reached Leyden, it gave offence to the moderate men of both sides; and met with the following reply from the Professors there : " that they wished the Dort
" Class had, in this affair, acted with greater discretion, and in
" a more orderly manner ; that, in their own opinion, there were
" more disputes among the Students than was agreeable to them
" as Professors; but, that among themselves, the Professors of
" Theology, no difference existed that could be considered as
" affecting, in the least, the fundamentals of doctrine; and that
" they would endeavour to diminish the disputes among the
" Students." This was signed by Arminius, then Rector of the University, by Gomarus, and others.

From the signature of Gomarus to this reply, it is evident, that
his subsequent bitterness against the Remonstrants at the Synod
of Dort, was the result of that acrimony which controversy so
often engenders ; and that, at the period before us, he neither
considered the views of his Colleague as affecting the vitality of
the faith, nor even interrupting their private friendship ; although,
unhappily, afterwards, he denounced the former, as upsetting the
basis of the Gospel ; spoke of the latter, when deceased, in terms
the most harsh and uncharitable, and fomented those persecuting
measures against his followers, which have rendered the name of
the Synod of Dort so odious.

This meddling interference of the Class of Dort, having
brought the whole question before the public, kindled a flame
through the United Provinces. In the heat of this, in the year
1609, Arminius died, with a spirit completely broken by the calumny and rancour with which he was assailed. His followers
abandoned many of the views which he held in common with
Calvin, particularly on the vital point of Justification. They became universally lax both in their opinions and in their society ;
and, as has too often been the case, aversion from Calvinism became a general bond of union. Having presented a strong remonstrance to the States-General in 1610, they obtained the name
of *Remonstrants,* and their opponents having presented a counter-
remonstrance, were termed *Contra-Remonstrants.*

To settle these disputes, the Remonstrants demanded a General
Council of the Protestant Churches. This the States refused ;
but it was at length determined by four out of seven of the United
Provinces, that a National Synod should be held at Dort—a town
eminent for its hostility to the Arminians ; and letters were sent
to the French Huguenots, and to the different Protestant States of
Germany and Switzerland, requesting them to send deputies to
assist at the deliberations. Among others, the King of England,
James I., was solicited in the same manner. And he, partly from
political motives, and partly from his love of theological controversy, complied with the request, and selected for this purpose
five of the most eminent theologians in his realm, viz. Dr. George
Carleton, Bishop of Landaff, Dr. Joseph Hall, Dean of Worces-
ter, Dr. Davenant, Dr. Samuel Ward, Master of Sydney Sussex
College, and Walter Balcanqual, a presbyter of the Church of
Scotland ; and when Hall, on account of ill health, returned
home, his place was filled by Dr. Goad, Precentor of St. Paul's,
and Chaplain to the Primate, Abbot.

These divines, having received their directions from his Majesty at Newmarket, and from the Archbishop, proceeded on their journey.

On their arrival in Holland, and first public audience, Bishop Carleton addressed the States-General and the Prince of Orange, in an eloquent and impressive speech, urging them to the preservation of truth, and the cultivation of peace and unity. In all the documents and histories of this Synod, it is allowed that the British divines conducted themselves with equal talent, dignity, and judgment. It had been strictly enjoined them before their departure, both by the King and Archbishop Abbot, to allow of no meddling with the doctrine or discipline of the English Church, and to be peremptory on the point of introducing into the decisions of the Synod, the Universality of Christ's Redemption. To this they religiously adhered; and were extremely tenacious of the honour of their own Church, enforcing her moderation as a model on these subjects. With respect to *discipline* there was little difficulty. When the Belgic Confession was read, as that which was to prove the conformity or non-conformity of the Remonstrants, the articles concerning Church government were expressly excluded. Nevertheless, as the thirty-third article maintains, that " *all ministers have equal power and authority, because all are equally ministers of the one only universal Bishop and Head of the Church,*" Carleton, having consulted with his Colleagues, entered unexpectedly into a direct refutation of it; observing, that the assertion was in opposition to the example of Christ, and to the precedent of his age, of that of the Apostles, and of every subsequent period; and that the argument by which it was defended was singularly inconclusive; for the twelve apostles, and the seventy disciples were " *all equally ministers of Christ,*" yet the latter had not " *equal power and authority* with the former," and though " *all men are equally men,*" yet it follows not that one man has not " *justly power and authority over another.*" To these observations no reply was made.[*] Upon *doctrines*, the difficulty was greater. The determination of the British deputies to have general Redemption admitted into the decrees, or else to withdraw from the Synod, led to some heated

---

[*] As it is so often deemed justifiable, by party writers, to confound what is called *Calvinistic doctrine*, with attachment to *Calvinistic discipline*, the Editor not only refers his readers to pp. 374—5 of this volume for Davenant's views, but has also annexed to this Memoir, a translation of *Quæstio* xlii. of his *Determinationes*, which is an admirable summary of the episcopal argument.

discussions. Carleton came into direct collision with Gomarus
upon the subject of our seventeenth Article and upon other points ;
and the testy Hollander could not help exclaiming, *Reverendis-*
sime Præsul, non auctoritate sed ratione agendum est : for which intemperance an apology was afterwards exacted. However, the
doctrine of Redemption as a blessing to be universally proposed
and offered to all men, was so little relished by the Synod, that
it is clear, nothing but the threatened loss of the English deputies
induced its insertion. In fact, it led to so much unpleasant discussion, that it appears the Bishop would have given way : but
Davenant declared he would sooner cut off his hand than rescind
any word of it ; in which he was supported by Ward ; and it was
ultimately agreed to. Our Author assigned his " Reasons" at
length ; and they are printed in John Hales's " Golden Remains,"
at the end of the " Letters concerning the Synod of Dort."* In
fact, Davenant appears to have been peculiarly eminent in these
proceedings. " What a pillar he was," says Bishop Hacket, " in
the Synod of Dort, is to be read in the judgments of the British
Divines, inserted among the public acts : his part being the best
in that work ; and that work being far the best in the compliments
of that Synod."

At the close of the business, they received the *public* thanks of
the States-General and of the Prince of Orange ; and having travelled a short time in different parts of the Dutch territories, they

---

* It has been said, (see Carwithin's Hist. of the English Church, vol. 2)
that " *they held that the Redemption of Christ was universal, and conse-*
quently, that salvation was attainable by all." If this be *a consequence,*
it is certain that neither Davenant nor the Synod allow it. His " Reasons"
expressly maintain the contrary ; and the articles of the decrees which admit the one, are immediately followed by an article which denies the other.
The two articles, for which the Synod is indebted to our divines, run thus :
(Cap. 11. art. 5, 6) " The promise of the Gospel is, that whoever believes
in Christ crucified shall not perish, but have eternal life. Which promise,
together with a command to repent and believe, ought to be announced and
offered, promiscuously and indiscriminately, to all men and people, to whom
God, according to his good pleasure, sends the Gospel. But that many who
are called by the Gospel, do not repent, nor believe in Christ, but perish
in unbelief, this comes not from the deficiency or insufficiency of his sacrifice on the cross ; but from their own fault." Art. 8, then says, " It was
the most free counsel and gracious will and intention of God the Father,
that the quickening and saving efficacy of the most precious death of his
Son, should appear in all the elect, to endow *them alone* with saving faith,"
&c.

returned home, and were very graciously welcomed by the King, and with high approbation of their conduct. It is evident, however, that their labours in softening the decrees, and the general moderation of their conduct, had rendered them objects of suspicion to many in the Synod. Dr. Ward, in a letter to Archbishop Usher, says, " We had somewhat to do, when we came to frame canons, with the provincials, and some of the *exteri*, touching some points, especially touching the second article. Some of us were held by some half Remonstrants, for extending the oblation made to the Father to all, and for holding sundry effects thereof offered *serio*, and some really communicated to the reprobate. I had somewhat to do with a principal man on this point: somewhat passed between us privately. We were careful that nothing should be defined which might gainsay the Confession of the Church of England, which was effected, for that they were desirous to have all things in the canons defined *unanimi consensu*. We foreign divines, after the subscription of the canons, and a general approbation of the Belgic Confession, and Catechism, which is the Palatine's, as containing no dogmata repugnant to the word of God, and a decree against Vorstius's doctrine, chiefly that in his book *De Deo*, were dismissed. In our approbation of the Belgic Confession, our consent was only asked for doctrinals, not for matters touching discipline. We had a solemn parting in the Synod, and all was concluded with a solemn feast."

We have neither leisure, nor inclination, to enter largely into the proceedings of an assembly, whose results were alike disgraceful and injurious to the cause it was designed to support. The Synod was objectionable in its constitution, and overbearing and persecuting in its proceedings. The Remonstrants were summoned, not to be heard, but to be condemned; and this was scarcely attempted to be concealed. The council consisted of those alone whose views were well known. The President, Bogerman, had long been distinguished for his extreme bitterness against the followers of Arminius; and the official details of the Synod are palpably regardless, not merely of charity, but of candour. Whilst this is fully allowed, for truth requires no less, it must also be admitted that the Remonstrants gave their opponents every advantage, by insisting that the doctrine of Reprobation should be first discussed, and that they should afterwards proceed to the doctrine of election. Persisting in this demand, they were driven out with great choler and violence. The Synod then proceeded to frame their decrees, with the rejection of the opposite errors. And here the share of the British deputies happily terminates, as they had no part in the subsequent transactions. The Synod immediately followed up its decisions by a sentence against the Remonstrants, depriving them of all their offices, interdicting them from all ecclesiastical services and academical functions, and finally exhorting the States-General to enforce these Canons with the secular arm. Nor did this recommendation slumber. Politics had intermingled with all the proceedings. Maurice, Prince of Orange, was aiming at despotic authority, and found the Arminians his most powerful opponents. Hence, though an Arminian himself, he sided with the Synod, and, from secular motives, seconded their views. A series of disgraceful persecutions followed, in which some of the most virtuous and patriotic blood of Holland was shed; and this, doubtless, contributed to render the Synod generally odious, and to promote that decline of doctrinal Calvinism in England, which is so commonly said to have resulted from this convention.*

Of all assemblies, Religious Councils are most likely to be misrepresented. As few were more open to attack, so there are scarcely any which have been more grossly and unfairly assailed, than the Synod of Dort. By a series of authors in succession, a treacherous copy of its decrees, under the shape of an abridgment, has passed current. For instance, the Synod, cap. 1, art. 1, asserts, that " *God hath elected out of the common mass of sinners, a certain multitude of men—quorundam hominum certa multitudo,*" &c. but that he hath left the rest to condemnation, " *not only on account of their infidelity, but also their other sins—non tantum propter infidelitatem, sed etiam cetera omnia*

---

* Of an assembly of which so little commendable may be said, it must be noted, that they ordered a new Translation of the Bible for the United Provinces, with Annotations: " In which work they were assisted by many eminent and able divines from most of the Reformed Churches, and particularly from England by Dr. G. Carleton, Bishop of Chichester; Dr. J. Davenant, Bishop of Sarum; Dr. Hall, Bishop of Exon; and Dr. Samuel Ward, of Cambridge; by whose great and assiduous labour, jointly for many years together, the said Annotations were completed, and came forth in print, first, ann. 1637." A. Wood's Athenæ. 4to. iv. 279. This Bible, with the Notes, was translated into English, and published in 1657, in two vols. folio, by Theodore Haak, under the title of " The Dutch Annotations upon the whole Bible; together with the Translation, according to the direction of the Synod of Dort, 1618."

peccata, &c. The popular copy thus states this ; that God hath elected to salvation " *a very small number of men,*" &c. and appointed the rest to condemnation, " *without any regard to their infidelity and impiety.*" This garbled statement, or rather " deliberate falsehood," as it has been correctly termed, originated with Daniel Tilenus, who, being a Remonstrant, and harshly used in common with his friends, repaid his sufferings by falsifying the documents of his enemies, and publishing his desperate effort under the cloak of a " *favourable* abridgement." From him it was copied by Bishop Womack, from Womack by Heylin, and from Heylin by Bishop Tomline ; and thus passing current through so many hands, it continued to exasperate the enemies of the Synod, and even to excite the unqualified condemnation of its friends. Thus the late Mr. Scott, in the first edition of his reply to Dr. Tomline, not doubting the genuineness of the decree, exclaims, " Who told these presumptuous dogmatists that the elect were ' a very small number of men?' " However, in 1804, the University of Oxford published the SYLLOGE CONFESSIONUM, being a collection of Confessions made about the period of the Reformation ; at the end of which are subjoined the genuine Canons, in full, of the Synod of Dort, as a contrast to the moderation of the early Protestant Churches, and of the length to which " men, even publicly and solemnly assembled, may proceed, when enflamed by long controversy and embittered hatred." From this publication the corruption was discovered, and exposed. Yet, in a much later publication, by Dr. Copleston, now Bishop of Landaff, viz. his " Enquiry into Necessity and Predestination," the forged copy is given, with the observation, that " In order " that the wide disagreement between these (i. e. the Calvinistic) " doctrines and the articles of the Church of England may be " seen at one view, I have subjoined in a Note the Lambeth Ar- " ticles, together with that summary of the decrees of the Synod " of Dort which Heylin has given from Tilenus, as the most mo- " derate and impartial account of their proceedings." This is evident enough, that the interpolation is not yet sufficiently public, since it had escaped the notice of this learned and candid Prelate. And here, we cannot but feel surprise that Mr. Nicholls, whilst discussing these points in the Notes to vol. 1 of his Edition of the Works of Arminius, and inveighing against every flaw in the conduct and opinions of antient and modern Calvinists, should not utter a single sentence of disapprobation of one of the most audacious corruptions (abundant as they are) which literary history presents; but should complain of the "querulousness of Mr. Scott" on a subject which ought to excite the indignation of every honest man, especially the advocate of one who was himself the victim of calumny and injustice.

On the other hand, it ought not to be concealed, that the account of the Synod of Dort published by Mr. Scott, is a mere translation of the Synod's own narrative of its proceedings; and their whole conduct entitles them to little respect when stating their own cause, even were it less evident that truth is not very strictly adhered to. The venerable Editor was probably not deeply acquainted with the history of the Council, nor well versed in the volumes of Carleton, Hales, and others, who were present; or in the detailed, though, perhaps, somewhat prejudiced, account of Brandt. Yet, agreeing, as he undoubtedly did, in the main, with the Canons of the Synod, and receiving their statement with a partial eye, his concluding observations are characteristic of the piety and good sense of that admirable man. Speaking of the persecuting conduct of other churches, he finally remarks, "The proceedings of the Synod of Dort, and of the rulers of Belgium at that season, were more exceptionable than those of any other; at least as far as I can judge." It is, in truth, a melancholy reflection, that in reading the history of religious convocations, as well antient as modern, Protestant as well as Papal, we cannot but observe how little equity, not to say sacred truth, has been regarded in their proceedings; how few proofs appear of the presence of the Holy Spirit in such assemblies; and how difficult it is for a candid mind to avoid approving the conclusion of an antient father of the Church, "*I never saw any good in Ecclesiastical Councils, and am well nigh inclined to attend no more.*"

To compress the whole of our Author's concerns with the Synod together, we have to notice an attack made upon him and his Colleagues some time after, for their conduct; himself being then in the See of Sarum, Carleton in that of Chichester, and Balcanqual in the Deanery of Rochester. It is well known that King James, in the decline of life, became much changed in his theological views; inclining towards Romanism, which he had once so stoutly opposed, and, of course, declining from the tenets of Dort, which he had once as stoutly advocated. Among the rising divines of that period, was Dr. Richard Montague, a very learned and able theologian, but as zealous against Puritanism as Laud himself.* Having fallen into controversy with the Papists, he had made some severe reflections on the doctrines advocated at Dort. In consequence of this, two Clergymen, Wood and Yates, gathered out of his books certain propositions, and presented them to the House of Commons, as impugning the Established Faith, savoring of Popery, Arminianism, and what not. Montague was summoned before the House, and held to bail. He then applied to James, who was quarrelling with the Commons, and obtained leave to appeal from them to his Majesty. In consequence, he prepares a defence; but the King dying before the book was published, permission was obtained from Charles I.: and it came out, addressed to him, with the title of " *Appello Cæsarem, or a Just Appeal against two unjust Informers.*" In this work, not content with inveighing against the doctrine established at Dort, he positively asserts, with an attempt at proof, that " the discipline of the Church of England was condemned in that assembly." To this gross and unprovoked attack, Bishop Carleton instantly replied; but as the charge affected the whole of the British deputies, they united in a distinct denial and refutation of it. This was printed with their several signatures, and, being a scarce document on an important subject, we have thought it would not be unacceptable in this place, being copied *verbatim* by a friend out of the Bodleian Library.

" *A joint attestation of several Bishops and learned Divines of the Church of England, avowing that her doctrine was confirmed, and her discipline was not impeached, by the Synod of Dort.*

" IT behoveth him that pretendeth to frame a '*just appeal from unjust informers,*' therein to keep himself clear from the just imputation of unjust informing. Yet the author of the Treatise styled *Appello Cæsarem*, hath rashly, and without ground, cast a foul blot upon the Synod of Dort in general; and consequently, in common reputation, upon all the Members thereof : among whom those Divines that were by King James sent thither, and concurred in the conclusions of that National Synod, are particularly aimed at, as having betrayed or impeached the government of their reverend Mother. ' The discipline of the Church of England,'

---

* He was, however, a moderate Calvinist, having declared himself ready to assent to Bishop Hall's Via Media.

a

saith he, ' in that Synod is held unlawful:' and again, ' the
Synod of Dort, in some points condemneth, by the bye, even the
discipline of the Church of England.'

" Was that distressed Church,* in the midst of her distractions
about matter of doctrine, so wily in her intentions, as to make
preposterous use of their neighbour's assistance, and to draw
them in for concurrence, in matter of discipline, with a foreign
sister, against their own Mother? Were those that then aided
that Church *tam naris obesæ*, so dull of apprehension as not to
perceive the interest of their own? or did they demean themselves
tam sublesta fide, so perfidiously, as to suffer the government of
this renowned Church, so much as ' *by the bye*,' to be condemned
by others there, and to sit down by it?

" Had there been any color for such surmise, it might have
pleased the Appealer or Appeacher, before he recorded in print
such his odious information, tendered to his Majesty's own hands,
to have demanded, in private, such a question of some of those,
from whom, in all likelihood, he might have received particular
satisfaction. Civil correspondence required no less of him, towards those whose persons he professeth to respect, for ancient
acquaintance, and other causes.

" The best is, though himself, for his own part, doth often
salute that Synod with the compliments called in Rhetoric
χλευασμὸς and μυπτησιασμὸς, ' non equidem invideo,' and such flow-
ers strewed along his treatise; yet, in his indulgence, he giveth
others as cause, so leave, to speak in their own behalf; ' let them
look to it, and answer for it, whom it concerneth:' and again,
' let them that are interested plead for themselves.' We, therefore, who have hereunto subscribed our names, being ' interested'
in that Synod, and withal deeply in this crimination of ' Puritanism,' can do no less than answer, and clear, in some public manner, this slander published against us.

" And first, *in general*, to remove the often objected suspicion
of complication between ' Foreign Doctrine' and ' Foreign Discipline;' whereby is intended that there is a kind of natural con-
sanguinity between that Doctrine which odiously he styleth ' Foreign,' subscribed unto by that Synod, and the Presbyterian Discipline established in that and other Foreign Churches;—

" We answer, that, in the Netherlands, the party opposite to

* Meaning the Belgic Church.

that Synod, and most aggrieved with the conclusions thereof, concerning the points controverted, are, notwithstanding, as vehement and resolute maintainers of *Ministerial Parity*, as any that concluded or accepted the judgment of that Synod.

" Moreover, in our private conversations with the most eminent of the Ministry there, we found, divers times, upon occasion of our declaring to them the order and manner of our Church Government, that they were more ready to deplore than defend their own condition ; and wished, rather than hoped, to be made like the Church of England. Nor were these, therefore, the less ready to concur for the Dort conclusions, but were rather of the principal and forward actors therein.

" Secondly, *In special*, we plead against a supposed act of condemning our own episcopal discipline; which indictment, in a fair accusation, should have been laid more particularly. What action, what session, what conclusion now are we put to seek, not so much our defence, as our fault ? And for such surmise, we can find no other footing, than possibly, in the approbation of the Belgick Confession, propounded to the consideration of the Synod, about a week before it broke up.

" This Confession, composed Anno 1550, and received in their church, and in the Walloon churches, ever since the first Reformation of Religion, is unto them, for consent in doctrine, a rule, not much unlike to our Articles of Religion here established. Which, as it was formerly, Anno 1583, accepted and approved by the French Church, in a National Synod at Vitry, so upon the opportunity of this National Synod, the State and Church there recommended the same to more public judgment for further establishment.

" And, because two or three articles thereof concerned Church discipline, and avowed a parity of ministers, they, prudently foreseeing that the British divines would never approve, but rather oppose the same, did, therefore, provide that, before the examining or reading thereof, protestation should be made by the President of the Synod, that nothing but the doctrinal points was to be subjected to their consideration and suffrages. And, for the surer preventing opposition or dispute, the articles concerning discipline were accordingly retrenched and suppressed in the reading of that confession to the Synod.

" If, therefore, the British College had, in their suffrages, only answered *ad quæsita* concerning doctrine, and uttered no opinion

a 2

at all *de non quæsitis* concerning discipline, they think they had
not herein been wanting to their Synodical duty and calling:—the
rather for that,

" 1. They were sent to endeavour the peace and composure of
that distracted church, by expressing their judgments in the points
there already controverted, not by intruding in matters not at
all questioned among them.

" 2. Among the instructions given them by his Majesty, they
had none to meddle with the discipline there established ; but had
charge to use moderation and discretion, and to abstain from
multiplying of questions beyond necessity.

" 3. In that subject, there was no hope or possibility of prevailing by argument or persuasion; especially in that church,
where the civil government is popular, and so complieth more
easily with ecclesiastical parity.

" Yet we thought not fit to content ourselves with warrantable
silence; but, upon our return from that Synodical Session to the
place of our private collegiate meeting, we diligently perused the
confession, not only for points of doctrine referred to our judgments, but also for those accepted (excepted) articles touching
discipline : and consulting together what was fit to be done in
delivering our opinions next day, we jointly concluded, that,
howsoever our church discipline had not been Synodically taxed,
nor theirs avowed, yet it was convenient for us, who were assured
in our consciences that their presbyterial parity and laical pres-
bytery was repugnant to the discipline established by the Apostles
and retained in our church, to declare, in a temperate manner,
our judgment, as well concerning that matter, though by them
purposely excepted, as the other expressly referred to us.

" Accordingly, the next morning, when suffrages were to pass
concerning the doctrine comprised in that confession, we, having
by our place the prime voice in the Synod, gave our approbation
of the substance of the doctrinal articles, with advice touching
some incommodious phrases ; and withal, contrary to the expectation of the whole Synod, we added express exception against
the suppressed articles, with some touch also of argument against
them.   Which our contestation, or protestation, for so it may be
styled, was principally performed by him, whom for priority of
age, place, and dignity, it best became ; and from whose person
and gravity it might be the better taken, by the civil deputies of
the States there present.

" Therein he professed and declared our utter dissent in that point; and further shewed, that by our Saviour a parity of Ministers was never instituted; that Christ ordained 12 apostles and 70 disciples; that the authority of the 12 was above the others; that the church preserved this order left by our Saviour; and therefore, when the extraordinary authority of the Apostles ceased, yet their ordinary authority continued in Bishops who succeeded them; who were, by the apostles themselves left in the government of the church to ordain ministers, and to see that they who were so ordained should preach no other doctrine; that, in an inferior degree, the ministers that were governed by Bishops, succeeded the 70 disciples: that this order hath been maintained in the church from the time of the Apostles; and herein he appealed to the judgment of antiquity, or of any learned man now living, if any could speak to the contrary, &c.

" In giving our several suffrages, the same exception was seconded by the rest of us Colleagues, partly by other allegations, and partly by brief reference to this declaration, made *communi nomine* by our leader. To this our exception and allegation, not one word was answered by any of the Synodicks, either strangers or provincials: so that herein we may seem to have had either their consent implied by silence, or, at least, approbation of our just and necessary performance of our bounded duty to that church whereunto they all afforded no small respect, though differing in government from their several churches.

" Herein, perhaps, by some we might be deemed rather to have gone too far in contestation and upbraiding, *quasi in os*, the Civil Magistrate and Ministry there, with undue form of government of that church, whose doctrine only was offered to our opinions.

" But, on the contrary part, it hath been suggested here at home by some, that herein we came short of our duty; that we ought to have stepped yet further, by exhibiting in writing a formal Protestation, to be entered and kept by the actuary of the Synod:—whereto we answer,

" First, that the course there taken, for the manner of delivering our judgments, was not, as in the fifth question, controverted by subscription, but only by vocal suffrage; which gave no opportunity of putting in a written protestation; whereas if we had subscribed our names unto that confession, we would infallibly have added, with the same pen, our exception against the articles concerning discipline.

" Secondly, in that vocal proceeding, had we been overborne
by the multitude of their voices, or received any grievance or affront from them, touching discipline, we would have relieved our
just cause, either by written protestation or better means. But,
whereas neither the civil magistrate, in whose hearing our exceptions were constantly uttered, did gainsay us, nor any of the
divines in the Synod once opened their mouths, either in offence
of our government or defence of their own, what needed we to
redouble our stroke upon those that turned not upon us.

     ' Rixa suum finem, cum silet hostis, habet.'

  " Peradventure, some hot spirits would not have rested in a
formal recorded protestation neither, but would have charged those
churches to blot those articles out of their confession, and forthwith to reform their government ; otherwise not have yielded approbation to any article of doctrine, as there comprised ; but renounced the Synod, and shaken off from his feet the dust of
Dort,—' I have nothing to do with your conclusions ; I have no
part nor portion in them : what ends you have, how things are
carried, I cannot tell, nor care.'

  " We confess, we were and are of another mind ; our own
dispositions, and the directions of our blessed peace-making
King, kept us from kindling new fires where we had work enough
to quench the old. We then thought, and so still in our consciences are confident, that we forgot not our duty to our venerable and sacred Mother, the Church of England, but took a
course conformable to the rules as well of filial obedience, as of
Christian moderation.

  " And even then, according to our custom of weekly transmitting into England brief narrations of the proceedings in each
several session, to be imparted to his Majesty, we, by the next
messengers, sent our relation hereof, as no whit ashamed of our
deportment herein ; which, because it was then framed when we
did not imagine that any quarrel would be picked against us, for
more impartial and impassionate attestations, is here inserted, as
much as concerneth the particular.

    " ' 1619. April 29, Stilo novo ; Sessione 144, Pomeri-
    diana.'

    " ' Gregorius Martin, unus ex politicis ad Synodum delegatis,
' Hagâ jam recens reversus, narrat quanto Domini ordines gaudio
' afficiantur de singulorum in canonibus sanciendis unanimi con-
' sensu. Eo nomine Theologis cum exteris tum provincialibus

' gratias habere eorum Dominationes ob labores Synodicos exant-
' lantos. Proximo in loco postulare ut Confessio Belgica perlus-
' tretur: ita tamen ut sine gravi causa nihil immutetur, nec phra-
' sium grammaticarum argutiis curiose insistatur. In eadem
' judiciis synodicorum subjiciuntur tantum ea quæ doctrinam
' spectant, omissis prorsus eis quæ disciplinam. Intercurrit
' quæstio de authentico exemplari; sumitur illud quod in ecclesi-
' arum reformatarum confessionibus habetur. Totum perlegitur
' prætermissis qui disciplinam ecclesiasticam attinent articulis.'
    " ' Sessio 145, April 30, Antemeridiana.
    " ' Rogantur de hac confessione suffragia. Dom. Episcopus
' Landavensis omnia doctrinæ capita probat, interea tamen de dis-
' ciplinâ paucis monet; "nunquam in ecclesia obtinuisse Ministro-
' rum paritatem; non tempore Christi ipsius; tum enim duode-
' cim Apostolos fuisse discipulis superiores : non Apostolorum
' ætate, non subsecutis sæculis : nec valere rationem in hac con-
' fessione usurpatam, nempe quia omnes sunt æque ministri
' Christi: nam et 70 discipuli erant Ministri Christri æque ac
' Apostoli, non tamen inde Apostolis æquales; et omnes omnino
' homines sunt æque homines, non inde tamen homo homini non
' debet subesse." Hæc non ad harume ecclesiarum offensionem, sed
' ad nostræ Anglicanæ defensionem, se substurnuisse professus est.
' Et reliquis Britannis non nulla alia sunt subnotata, de libero ar-
' bitrio, de passivâ Christi obedientiâ; præsertim vero de phrasi
' nimis durâ et generali, cum dicatur de canonicis libris nullam un-
' quam fuisse controversiam; quæ quidem incommoda phrasis
' vitio interpretis irrepserat, cum originale *Gallican** bene se
' habeat. Item exceptioni de disciplinâ adjicitur a reliquis Bri-
' tannis similis exceptio, siquid contra legitimos ritus externos
' generaliter ibidem statuatur. Britannorum interpellationi a sy-
' nodicis responsum ne γρυ quidem.'

    " About a year after our return, the acts of the Synod were
published in print; wherein, among other particulars, the Belgic
Confession is at large set down in 37 articles, whereof two or three
contain matter of discipline received in those churches: these
belike our censurer viewing, *prout jacent in terminis*, thereupon,
without any further search, concluded that Synod guilty and condemnable, as concerning ' the discipline of the Church of England.' But still we hold ourselves to stand clear, and therefore

---

* Evidently the Latin original of our Articles is the document referred
to.

prosecute our appeal from the rash sentence of this Appellant ;
alleging for ourselves

" 1.   Though all and singular the articles there comprised had
passed Synodical scrutiny, and been approved canonically, yet
will it not follow that all and every one of the Synodicks there
gave consent thereto.   For this approbation might have passed by
the votes of the major part, *etiam reclamantibus Britannis,* who
for number were not considerable, among so many others, both
strangers and provincials.   And so a favourable construction
might have exempted the British Divines from being thought to
reach forth their hand to the striking their mother.

" 2   We deny, that, upon view of those Synodical acts, we,
by presumption in law, need to be put upon purgation herein, as
members involved in a capitular decree of the whole body.   For,
in point of discipline there passed no act at all ; there was no
proposition made ; as evidently appeareth by the same book of
the Synodical Acts, in the narration of the proceedings about this
Belgick confession ; where the matter subjected to deliberation, is
recorded with limitation ; first, *positive,* ' quæ ad dogmata & doctrinæ essentiam pertinerent; *points dogmatical and pertaining to
the essence of doctrine :'*—then *exclusive,* ' Monitum proinde fuit
eo tempore articulum trigesimum primum et secundum non esse
examinandum, quia in utroque de ordine ecclesiastico quem exteri
nonnulli a nostro diversum habent, ageretur.   *Declaration was
accordingly made, at the same time, that the thirty-first and second articles were not to be examined ; because in them ecclesiastical order, or church government, was handled ; wherein some
strangers,'* namely, the Church of England ' *differ from ours,*'
namely, from that of the Church of the Netherlands.   This recorded testimony of so express withdrawing from the eye of the
Synod all view of church discipline, might demonstrate, to any
indifferent peruser of those acts, that whereas no possibility of
Synodical condemning, so much as ' *by the bye,*' the discipline of
the Church of England, in such examining the Belgick Confession.

" As for our manner of examining and judging thereof, though
it be not so particularly set down in the said printed acts as we
could have wished, and would have provided for, had we been
made acquainted with any intent of their publication ; yet is it in
some sort touched in the same page, in that very narration of the
next session, testifying a cautelous delivery of our judgments,

' Declarant clarissimi Magnæ Britannicæ Theologi, se Confessionem Belgicam diligenter examinasse, nihilique in ea deprehendisse, quod ad fidei quidem dogmata attineret, quod verbo Dei non consentiret. *The Divines of Great Britain declared that they had diligently examined the Belgick Confession, and that therein, for as much as concerned Dogmatical points of faith, they found nothing that agreed not with the word of God;*' which reservation implieth that somewhat else which did not ' concern points of faith,' but other matter, received not their approbation. It may be said, and so we ourselves say, that the disposers and publishers of these Synodical acts had done more right to the British Divines, if special mention had been made of that other matter not approved by them, and of their particular exceptions against the articles which concerned church government.

" But it seemeth, as in most other local passages in this Synod, the actuary here intended abridgement, in what he set down; and meant not to express in particular what was said by any, concerning points not propounded to Synodical deliberation, especially touching upon so tender a thing as the open impeachment of their own established discipline : and so they think that they have given us our due herein ; partly by thus pointing afar off to what we did in our own defence, leaving the reader to find it by implication; and partly by recording that all Synodical proposition and approbation of this confession was confined to matter of doctrine only.

" According to reserved form of expression, the President of the Synod, in the Great Church of Dort, immediately after the publication of the Synod's judgment upon the five controversies, notifying the approbation of this confession, said, not that the whole and every parcel was approved, but ' Doctrinam in confessione comprehensam, in Synodo relectam atque examinatam, ut orthodoxam, &c. fuisse approbatam.' Which style of speech excludeth whatsoever is there comprised not concerning doctrine but discipline, whatsoever was not examined Synodically, nor so much as read in the Synod, whatsoever in common understanding admitteth the title of Orthodox, which attribute is proper to dogmatical points. In this sense, and of this subject, they did and well might there alledge the concording judgments, ' omnium tam exterorum quam provincialium Theologorum.'

" Nor had we cause to expect that in such publication of the whole Synod's doctrinal consent, they should trouble their own people, with expressing the dissent of some few of the exteri in a matter of church discipline ; which dissent of ours, they have delineated in this second of their acts, though over-veiled for their own peace, yet transparent enough for their own defence.

" But it was our misfortune perhaps that he who turned over all the leaves of the Belgic Confession there set forth, to find the articles concerning discipline, could not extend to cast his eye upon the page next foregoing that confession, to view the limited manner of both propounding and approving that body of articles. Which limitation had he seen and considered, so confident are we of his ingenuity, he would not have cast this hard imputation upon us.

" And now, being better informed by this our true account of the carriage of that business, he that hath traduced us will, we hope, make us some competent satisfaction, by acknowledging his oversight, and recalling what he hath unadvisedly written to our prejudice.

" As for ourselves, in the ingenuity of our conscience, we herein do not decline the judgment of any indifferent impassionate man ; and such we hope this true and plain narration will satisfy. But above all, according to our duty and desire, we humbly submit this and all other our actions, concerning our calling, to the judgment of our most venerable mother the Church of England, from whose sacred rule we avow we have not swerved, nor any whit impeached her discipline, or authorized doctrine, either abroad or at home. And as in that Synod our special care and perpetual endeavour was, to guide our judgments by that sound doctrine which we had received from the Church of England ; so were we far and ever shall be from usurping our mother's authority, or attempting to obtrude upon her children any of our Synodical conclusions, as obligatory to them ; yet remaining ourselves nevertheless resolved, that whatsoever there was assented unto, and subscribed by us concerning the five articles, either in the joint synodical judgment, or in our particular collegiate suffrage, stiled in the acts of the Synod, ' Theologorum Magnæ Britannicæ sententiæ,' and at large extant there, is not only warrantable by the Holy Scriptures, but also conformable to the received doctrine of our said venerable mother ; which we are ready to maintain and

justify against all gainsayers, whensover we shall be thereunto
called by lawful authority.

> " GEORGIUS, Cicestrensis Episcopus.
> " JOHANNES, Sarisburiensis Episcopus.
> " GUALTERIUS BALCANQUAL, Decan. Roff.
> " SAMUEL WARD, Pub. Profess. Theol. in Acad.
>   Cant. & Coll. Sid. Prefect.
> " THOMAS GOAD, Sacræ Theol. Doctor."

DAVENANT's elevation to the Episcopate was the necessary result of his Theological eminence. " He had," says his animated
eulogist, Dr. Hacket, " been public reader in Divinity in Cambridge, and had adorned that place with such learning as no Professor in Europe did better deserve to receive the labourer's penny
at the twelfth hour of the day." Accordingly in 1621, he was
nominated to the See of Salisbury, vacant by the premature decease of his brother-in-law, Dr. Robert Townson, who is said to
have been a man of singular piety, eloquence, and humility ; and
who died a few months after his consecration, leaving a large family of fifteen children, and being the fourth Bishop of that
Diocese who had been cut off in the space of seven years. It was
probably on account of the domestic burthen that thus devolved
upon him, rather than from his merit, that our Bishop was excused
the payment of the introductory fees, and of the annual pension,
which was then, it seems, customarily paid to the crown on all
similar appointments, proportionate to the wealth or poverty of the
individual :* and when introduced to the King, his Majesty enjoined him not to marry.

But though elected in July, his consecration was delayed by an
unhappy event, which befel the Archbishop of Canterbury, Dr.
Abbot; who, as he was using a cross-bow in Lord Zouch's park,
accidentally shot the keeper. Four Bishops-elect were then wait-
ing for consecration. Of these, Williams, elect of Lincoln, who,
as Heylin says, had an eye to the Primacy in case it had been declared vacant; and Laud, elect of St. David's, who had a personal
hatred to Abbot, stated an insuperable aversion to being consecrated by a man whose hands were stained with blood. Davenant
did not join in this unworthy cavil ; but kept altogether aloof, lest
he should be thought to act from private feelings of obligation to

---

* History of the Court of King James, by an Eye-witness.

XXXii   LIFE OF BISHOP DAVENANT.

the afflicted Primate : but despising the groundless objection of those who, from motives of personal pique and ambition, were willing to give up their own high views of the indelibility of the Episcopal character, and act upon the principle that it became vitiated and abortive in its operations, by an accident which, as the King justly remarked, might have happened to an angel. The rest, however, made so much of their scruples, that a commission was at length granted to the Bishop of London and four others, to discharge the Archiepiscopal function in this case ; and by these, Williams was consecrated on Nov. 11 : and Davenant, Laud, and Cary of Exeter, on Nov. 18.

Having resigned his Margaret Professorship, in which he was succeeded by his friend Dr. Ward, he took his leave of College ; and in bidding farewell to his old servant there, one John Rolfe, with his characteristic humility and piety he desired him to pray for him Rolfe modestly replied that *he* rather needed his lordship's prayers. " Yea, John," said he, " and I need thine too ; being now to enter into a calling wherein I shall meet with many and great temptations."

His discharge of his episcopal functions is allowed, on all hands, to have been most exemplary ; and it would not be easy to find a more decided testimony than that afforded by the Lord Keeper Williams, a man eminent for his learning and official attainments ; for his long exercise in all the functions of public business ; and for his penetration in diving into the characters of men. Upon resigning the great seal, and retiring to the more consistent duties of his See of Lincoln, he took Bishop Davenant for his pattern, and framed his measures upon what he deemed the most wise and successful example in these times of peculiar difficulty and danger ; and it is confessed by his enemies, that the episcopal conduct of Williams was remarkably temperate, discreet, and conscientious.

Though benevolent and cheerful, Davenant never lost sight of the consistent dignity and gravity of his character. Upon one occasion, as Fuller records, being invited to dine with Field, Bishop of Hereford, and not well pleased with the loose company he met there, he embraced the earliest opportunity of departing ; and when Field would have lighted him down stairs, " My lord, my lord," said he, " let us enlighten others by our unblamable conversation." At the same time he is spoken of as remarkably devoid of harsh or unkind judgment, as " more sensible of his own infirmities than others, being humble, and therefore charitable." Upon no occasion does he appear to have forgotten CONSISTENCY. Being once summoned to attend the King at Newmarket, he refused to travel on the Lord's-day; and upon arriving a day later than required, he assigned the simple cause; and James, much to his credit, gave him a cordial welcome, not only accepting his excuse, but also commending his seasonable forbearance.

In the intervals of episcopal duty, Davenant turned his attention to the revision and publication of his different writings. His *Expositio Epistolæ D. Pauli ad Colossenses*, had been delivered in a series of Lectures to the Students at Cambridge, as Lady Margaret's Professor. This, as it is his most valuable work, so was it the first he issued. It was published at Cambridge in 1627, republished in 1630, and went into a third edition in 1639; each edition being in small folio. There is also a quarto edition, printed at Amsterdam in 1646. The character of this book has been happily expressed by a popular writer in the following terms: " For perspicuity of style and accuracy of method; for judgment in discerning and fidelity in representing the Apostle's meaning; for strength of argument in refuting errors, and felicity of invention in deducing practical doctrines, tending both to the establishment of faith, and the cultivation of holiness, it is inferior to no writing of the kind; and richly deserves to be read, to be studied, to be imitated, by our young divines."* We may also subjoin the testimony of an invaluable living writer, who in a letter to the translator, observes, " I know no exposition upon a detached portion of Scripture (with, perhaps, the single exception of Owen on the Hebrews) that will compare with it in all points. Leighton is superior in sweetness, but far inferior in depth, accuracy, and discursiveness."† Nor can we avoid adverting to an anonymous testimony, if it were only to illustrate the utility of occasionally annexing notices in the front of valuable and rare books. A copy was received some time since by a Clergyman, (the Rev. J. Garbett, Rector of St. George's, Birmingham,) from one of his Parishioners, who having bought it with a lot of other old vo-

* Hervey's Theron and Aspasia, Let. iii.

† The Rev. C. Bridges, author of the " Christian Ministry," the most invaluable practical book that has ever yet been published on this weighty subject; and which, next to his Bible and Prayer Book, should be the study and application of every divine of the Church of England.

lumes, and not being able to read it, had been repeatedly on the
point of tearing it; but was as often deterred by the following
monition on the title-page; and, at length, conscientiously sur-
rendered it safe into the hands of his Pastor. " *Don't abuse this
good old book: for it is an extraordinary piece, and the best
Exposition upon St. Paul's Epistle to the Colossians that ever was
published to this present year* 1749, *and I am afraid there will
never be a better so long as the world endures.* H. C.   *Idem
testor, J. E.*"

In the following year, our Author printed, in London, a Sermon on Jeremiah iii. 22, on the occasion of a Fast; but of this
the Editor has vainly endeavoured to procure a sight, and probably
there is no copy now in existence.

About this time, Bishop Hall published his excellent treatise,
the " Old Religion," in which he had, in common with every other
considerate divine, admitted that the Church of Rome, though
miserably corrupt, was still a true visible Church. The extreme
Puritans took great umbrage at this Concession, as they deemed
it. Hall, therefore, appealed to the judgment of some of the
most eminent theologians of the day, and among others, addressed the following letter to our Author:

> " To the Right Reverend Father in God, John, Lord
>   Bishop of Salisbury.
> " My Lord :
> " I send you this little pamphlet for your censure. It is not
> credible, how strangely I have been traduced, every where, for
> that, which I conceive to be the common opinion of Reformed
> Divines; yea, of reasonable men : that is, for affirming the True
> Being and Visibility of the Roman Church. You see how clearly
> I have endeavoured to explicate this harmless position; yet I per
> ceive some tough understandings will not be satisfied.
> " Your Lordship hath, with great reputation, spent many years
> in the Divinity-Chair of the famous University of Cambridge. Let
> me, therefore, beseech you, whose learning and sincerity is so
> thoroughly approved in God's Church, that you would freely, how
> shortly soever, express yourself in this point: and, if you find
> that I have deviated but one hair's breadth from the truth, correct
> me: if not, free me by your just sentence.
> " What need I to entreat you to pity those, whose desires of
> faithful offices to the Church of God are unthankfully repayed with
> suspicion and slander? Whose may not this case be? I had

thought I had sufficiently, in all my writings, and in this very last book of mine whence this quarrel is picked, shewed my fervent zeal for God's truth against that Antichristian Faction of Rome; and yet, I doubt not, but your own ears can witness what I have suffered.

" Yea, as if this calumny were not enough, there want not those, whose secret whisperings cast upon me the foul aspersions of another sect, whose name is as much hated as it is little understood.

" My Lord, you know I had a place with you, though unworthy, in that famous Synod of Dort : where, howsoever sickness bereaved me of the honours of a conclusive subscription ; yet your Lordship heard me, with equal vehemency to the rest, crying down the unreasonableness of that way. God so love me, as I do the tranquillity and happiness of his Church : yet can I not so overaffect it, that I would sacrifice one dram of truth to it. To that good God do I appeal, as the witness of my sincere heart to his whole truth, and no-less-than-ever-zealous detestation of all Popery and Pelagianism.

" Your Lordship will be pleased to pardon this importunity, and to vouchsafe your speedy answer to

　　　　　　" Your much devoted and faithful Brother,
　　　　　　　　　　　　" JOSEPH EXON."

This Letter drew from Davenant the following reply, which is truly characteristic of his cautious and scholastic mode of discussing such topics.

　　　" To the Right Reverend Father in God, Joseph, Lord
　　　　　Bishop of Exon, these.
　　" My Lord :
　　" You desire my opinion concerning an assertion of yours, whereat some have taken offence. The proposition was this, ' That the Roman Church remains yet a True Visible Church.'

" The occasion, which makes this an ill-sounding proposition in the ears of Protestants, especially such as are not thoroughly acquainted with School Distinctions, is the usual acceptation of the word ' true ' in our English Tongue : for, though men skilled in metaphysics hold it for a maxim, *Ens, Verum, Bonum convertuntur ;* yet, with us, he, which shall affirm such a one is a true Christian, a true Gentleman, a true Scholar, or the like, he is conceived not only to ascribe trueness of being unto all these, but those due qualities or requisite actions whereby they are made commendable or praise-worthy in their several kinds.

" In this sense, the Roman Church is no more a True Church in respect of Christ, or those due qualities and proper actions which Christ requires, than an arrant whore is a true and loyal wife unto her husband.

" I durst, upon mine oath, be one of your compurgators, that you never intended to adorn that Strumpet with the title of a True Church in this meaning. But your own writings have so fully cleared you herein, that suspicion itself cannot reasonably suspect you in this point.

" I therefore can say no more respecting your mistaken proposition, than this, If, in that Treatise wherein it was delivered, the antecedents or consequents were such as served fitly to lead the Reader into that sense, which under the word True comprehendeth only Truth of Being or Existence, and not the due Qualities of the thing or subject, you have been causelessly traduced. But, on the other side, if that proposition comes in *ex abrupto*, or stands solitary in your Discourse, you cannot marvel though, by taking the word True according to the more ordinary acceptation, your true meaning was mistaken.

" In brief, your proposition admits a true sense; and, in that sense, is, by the learned in our Reformed Church, not disallowed: for, the Being of a Church does principally stand upon the gracious action of God, calling men out of darkness and death unto the participation of light and life in Christ Jesus. So long as God continues this Calling unto any people, though they, as much as in them lies, darken this light, and corrupt the means which should bring them to life and salvation in Christ; yet, where God calls men unto the participation of life in Christ by theWord and by the Sacraments, there is the true Being of a Christian Church, let men be never so false in their exposition of God's Word, or never so untrusty in mingling their own traditions with God's Ordinances.

" Thus, the Church of the Jews lost not her Being of a Church when she became an Idolatrous Church.

" And thus, under the Government of the Scribes and Pharisees, who voided the Commandments of God by their own traditions, there was yet standing a True Church, in which Zacharias, Elizabeth, the Virgin Mary, and our Saviour himself was born, who were members of that Church, and yet participated not in the corruptions thereof.

" Thus, to grant that the Roman was and is a True Visible Christian Church, though in Doctrine a False and in Practice an Idolatrous Church, is a true assertion; and of greater use and necessity in our controversy with Papists about the perpetuity of the Christian Church, than is understood by those who gainsay it.

" This in your ' Reconciler' is so well explicated, as if any shall continue in traducing you in regard of that proposition so explained, I think it will be only those, who are better acquainted with wrangling than reasoning, and deeper in love with strife than truth. And, therefore, be no more troubled with other men's groundless suspicions, than you would be in like case with their idle dreams.

" Thus I have enlarged myself beyond my first intent. But my love to yourself, and the assurance of your constant love unto the truth, enforced me thereunto. I rest always

" Your loving Brother,

" Jan. 30, 1628.   " JOHN SARUM."

Three years after this, Davenant, whose principles had long placed him out of favour at Court, fell under the open displeasure of the head of it. A new king had arisen. Great changes had taken place in men and measures. Laud was now supreme in ecclesiastical affairs, and was pursuing that course of rash and tyrannical conduct which spared neither Puritan nor Prelate, and was rapidly hastening the downfal of both crown and mitre, which, perhaps, the most wary and cautious demeanour could scarcely have averted. To silence all disputes upon the Predestinarian controversy, Charles, under Laud's advice, had prefixed " His Majesty's Declaration," which still remains at the head of the Thirty-nine Articles, requiring " all curious search" on that subject to be laid aside. During the Lent of 1630—1, our Bishop preached in his turn at Whitehall before the King; and his discourse was a continuation of a Sermon which he had delivered the preceding year on Rom. vi. 23. Charles testified extreme displeasure; and the Bishop was summoned before the Privy Council to answer for it, brought upon his knees, and treated by Harsnet Bishop of York, and Neile, in the presence of Laud, in a manner alike regardless of his station, age, or reputation. To this examination of Davenant, Dr. Ward thus alludes in a letter to Archbishop Usher : " I suppose your Grace hath heard of my Lord of Sarum, how he was questioned before his Majesty in the

b

beginning of Lent last; the particulars of which you shall understand by the enclosed parcel of a letter he wrote me. I am right
sorry the delivery of the established doctrines of our Church
should be thus questioned." The details of this whole affair are
given at length by Fuller and other writers. The Bishop was afterwards admitted to kiss the King's hand, but enjoined not to
offend in the same way again !

Davenant, however, was not the only prelate who was annoyed
by the Court at this time. Not to mention the long and bitter
persecution with which Laud for so many years harrassed Williams,
who had been *his* original benefactor, and which is detailed in all
its disgraceful features by Bishop Hacket; who can hear without
indignation, one of the most illustrious ornaments of the English
Church, Bishop Hall, complain, that he was brought three several times on his knees before the Council, to answer false and idle
criminations; and that he only escaped further worrying by
plainly telling the Archbishop that he would rather resign his mitre
than be subject to such persecutions ?

During this year, our Author published at Cambridge *Prælec-
tiones de duobos in Theologia controversis capitibus: De Judice
Controversiarum, primo : De Justitia habituali et actuali, altero.*
These points are discussed in a most ample manner, and form a
thick folio volume, much more considerable in size than his Exposition. This work he dedicated to the King. In 1634, he published *Determinationes Quæstionum quorundam Theologicarum.*
It is a small folio, and is often found bound with the second edition of the *Expositio.* It consists of a discussion of forty-nine
subjects controverted between Romanists and Protestants, or between Protestants of different views. They are all handled with
great acuteness, learning, and moderation. To one of these,
Quæstio xi., Archbishop Williams referred upon a memorable occasion, a short time after Davenant's decease. A Bill having
been introduced to deprive Bishops of their seats in the house of
lords, it was so ably opposed by Williams, as to lead to its rejection for that time. In this masterly speech, he refers to our
Prelate as an authority entitled to veneration in that assembly.
" The civil power," said he, in the course of his address, " is a
Divine ordinance, set up to be a terror to the evil, and an encouragement to good works. This is the whole compass of the civil
power. And therefore, I do here demand, with the most learned
Bishop Davenant, that within a few days did sit by my side, in

the eleventh question of his Determinationes, *What is there of impiety, what of unlawfulness, what unbecoming either the holiness or calling of a Priest, in terrifying the bad or comforting the good subject; in repressing of sin, or punishing of sinners? For this is the whole and entire act of civil jurisdiction. It is in its own nature repugnant to no persons, to no function, to no sort or condition of men : let them hold themselves never so holy, never so seraphical, it becomes them very well to repress sin and punish sinners ; that is to say, to exercise in a moderate manner civil jurisdiction, if the Sovereign shall require it.*" This is by no means an exact quotation of the passage of Davenant ; its language is considerably softened ; and perhaps, of the whole volume, it is the *Quæstio* which we should least readily accede to at present. It is needless to say the subject of civil right and jurisdiction was by no means distinctly understood at that period. But the Archbishop's allusion to Davenant on such an occasion, and his citing him in such an assembly, proves the opinion then entertained of his worth, his character, and learning.

In 1638, was published a little volume in 24mo. entitled, *De Pace inter Evangelicos procuranda Sententiæ quatuor ; &c.* It consists of the opinions of Bishops Morton, Davenant, and Hall,* and of certain eminent French Divines, on the subject of Catholic Unity. They were addressed to Duræus, a Scotch Divine, who had laboured to unite the Lutheran and Calvinistic Churches, and had solicited the opinions of these Prelates on the subject. Having been previously published at Amsterdam, they were now reprinted, with a list of authors who had written upon the same point. Of this little book, the opinion of Davenant forms the principal part, and is, in every respect decidedly superior to either of the others : it is written with great force of argument, and in a very spirited style.

In this unhappy period, when every thing was a subject of contention, and the Church was gasping for breath in her struggles with enemies, Laud was fomenting internal dissention by enforcing conformity in every trifle ; among which, few points occasioned more dispute than his insisting upon the communion-table being placed universally at the east end of the Church : " an evil beginning," says Bishop Hacket, " to distract conformists, who

* This letter of Hall has escaped the notice of Mr. Pratt, and is not contained in any Edition of the Author's works.

were at unity before, and to make them fight like cocks which are
all of a feather, and yet never at peace with themselves." Yet
Davenant, when the question came officially before him, decided
in favour of the Primate's injunction on the subject. " Nor," says
Heylin, " did the Archbishop stand alone in point of judgment as
to these particulars. He had therein the testimony and assent of
two such Bishops,* than which there could be none more averse
from Popery, or any thing that tended to it. A difference hap-
pening between the minister and churchwardens, in a parish of
Wilts, about the placing of the table, which the minister desired
to transpose to the end of the Church, and the churchwardens to
keep as it stood before, the business was referred to Davenant,
then Bishop of Salisbury, who, on a full consideration of the
matter, decided in favour of the Incumbent ; and, by a decree
under his episcopal seal, settled the table in the place where the
altar stood, as the minister desired to have it. In which decree
there are these two passages to be observed : First, that, ' by the
injunction of Queen Elizabeth, and by Canon xxxii. under King
James, the communion-table should ordinarily be set and stand
with the side to the east wall of the Chancel;' and, secondly,
that ' It is ignorance to think that the standing of the holy table
in that place doth relish of Popery.' "† Here we perceive the cool
judgment of Davenant opposed, in a point of discipline, to those
with whose doctrinal tenets he agreed, and supporting Laud, whose
views and conduct he doubtless disapproved. Few measures were
more unpopular than this enforced conformity about the position
of the Lord's table ; and when Laud first introduced the alteration in Gloucester Cathedral, upon being appointed Dean, his
Diocesan, the venerable and learned Miles Smith, never entered
the Church afterwards.

One of the last occasions in which we hear of Davenant in public, was in 1640, the year before his death : when the convocation
under the direction of Archbishop Laud, passed certain Canons,
principally for the enforcement of uniform discipline ; which, although unobjectionable in themselves, were extremely ill-timed ;
being at a moment when the Church was scarcely able to sustain
even her existence : and so it was that the passing of these Canons
was made a handle to hasten her destruction. All the Prelates

* The other was Morton, Bishop of Durham.
† Life of Laud.

and Clergy present signed their approbation of the new Constitutions, with the exception of Goodman, Bishop of Gloucester,
who, being a Papist in heart, refused to sign, on account of one
of them being directed to the suppression of Popery. The Primate,
with his characteristic impetuosity, thrice called out to him, " My
lord of Gloucester, I admonish you to sign." Upon his persisting in his refusal, he was immediately suspended ; and would
have been summarily deprived, but that Bishop Davenant, with
his accustomed judgment and knowledge, observed, that before
they proceeded against a Prelate of the Church, they should act
upon legal advice and direction : and that it was not customary for
the threefold monition of an authoritative superior to be uttered at
the same moment, but at due intervals, allowing time for the offending party to reflect The Archbishop thanked him for his
opinion, and acquiesced in its propriety. The result was, that
Goodman, to avoid consequences, signed the Canons ; and, as it
has been remarked, " Under these he conformed as long as the
Establishment had wealth and honour to bestow ; but when her
inveterate foes had accomplished her destruction, he threw off the
mask of hypocrisy and equivocation ; and died avowedly, as he
had lived secretly, a Roman Catholic."*

In 1641, our venerable Author published a treatise in support
of his former views on the subject of Predestination, and in reply
to a work which had appeared some years before. Samuel Hoard,
B.D., Rector of Morton, in Essex, sent forth a tract, in 1633,
entitled " *God's Love to Mankind, manifested by disproving his
absolute Decree for their Damnation :*" and it appears to have
been the earliest treatise in this country, in opposition to what is
called the Calvinistic opinion.† Davenant penned a reply entitled
" *Animadversions written by the Right Rev. Father in God, John,
Lord Bishop of Salisbury, upon a treatise intituled, God's Love
to mankind.*" Why he published it no earlier than after a lapse of
eight years, we know not. It is written with all the powers of his
mind. The whole of Hoard's book is incorporated in it, and he

* Garbett's Letter to the late Right Rev. Dr. Milner.

† Thus Whiston, in his Memoirs, vol. i. p. 11, speaking of his father,
says, " I also remember his observation on Mr. Hoard's book concerning
' God's love to mankind,' as the first that began to set aside the Calvinists'
unhappy scheme of election and reprobation in England, which, till then,
was the current opinion of the members of the Church of England, as it is
still the doctrine of the thirty-nine Articles."

appears to have been no contemptible adversary. His work is in
the form of an Epistle ; from which we find, he had originally
held the views which he there took up his pen to refute : for he
commences with this remark, " I have sent you here my reasons
which have moved me to change my opinion in some controversies of late debated between the Remonstrants and their opponents." These treatises, thus united in one publication, seem to
compress all that has been said in so many volumes on this subject. Hoard accumulates every argument in opposition to the
Calvinistic views, and presses them with considerable energy : but
in no work is the acuteness of Davenant's powerful mind more
exhibited than in his reply. He maintains, with extraordinary
force and eloquence, the unconditionate decree of election ; and
whilst he contends that this admits of sufficiency of grace given
to all ; he likewise maintains that Reprobation is of necessity involved in Election :* and his view of it is thus expressed, " Reprobation is not a denial of sufficient grace, but a denial of such
special grace, as God knoweth would infallibly bring them to
glory." The book abounds with striking passages : yet, who that
duly appreciates the simplicity of inspired truth, does not, after
reading this or any other treatise of the kind, gladly return to the
sacred volume, and feel his mind relieved and comforted with the
plain *infallible* assurance that " GOD IS LOVE," that salvation is his
free gift, and that He " *will have all men to be saved, and come to
the knowledge of the truth ?*" The Bishop closes his book with what
he conceived to be the " USES" of election ; and, doubtless, speaks
the result of his own experience, with these, which may be
deemed almost his final, words : " If we will shew that we have
not a fleeting or uncertain conjecture only, but a true and solid
knowledge of our election, we must have recourse to the fore-
named uses, and by them make trial whether our conceit of our
election be a deceitful illusion, or a true persuasion springing from
faith. We are to account it false and deceitful, if it prove idle
and unprofitable ; much more, if we find it to be the pernicious
mother of presumption. But, if it hath taught us to conceive
worthily of God ; if it hath inflamed our hearts with the love of
Him ; if it hath kindled in us a zeal of true godliness ; if it hath
beaten down our pride, and begot in us true humility ; if it defend
us against despair ; if it stir us up to frequent prayer ; if it encou-

* Whitby's book on the " Five Points" opens with a memorable extract
from this work of " good Bishop Davenant," as he styles him.

rage us to patience under the cross : then we may be assured of our predestination, and of our future possession of eternal life through Jesus Christ our Lord."

Our Author's final work was well suited to his life and character. It was a small volume written with a view of uniting the Evangelical churches ; under the title of *Ad pacem Ecclesiæ adhortatio*, &c. which was translated into English with the title of *An Exhortation to Brotherly Love*, &c. Of this beautiful little work, Bishop Hall, in his " Peace-maker," laying down the principles of Church Unity, says, " None hath so fully cleared the point, as the late honour of our schools, the learned Bishop Davenant, in that last Golden Tractate which he wrote, now breathing towards the gates of his heaven ; his pious and pithy Exhortation of the Evangelical churches to a happy peace : wherein the fundamentals of our faith are so evidently laid open, that it is not hard to judge by that unfailing rule, whom we may and must admit to the communion of Christ's Church, and whom we ought to exclude from that holy society."

On the 20th of April, 1641, Bishop Davenant was summoned to his rest, in the full vigour of his faculties and piety, at the age of 71, having presided over the See of Salisbury twenty years. The immediate cause of his decease was an asthma, with which he had been long afflicted ; but his death is said to have been hastened by the melancholy forebodings of his mind, as to the sad prospects of the nation. " The righteous is taken away from the evil to come." He died, as it has been correctly said, at " a truly convenient season ; that he might neither see nor suffer those bitter calamities which speedily overwhelmed both Church and State ;"* and which his old friend, Dr. Ward, keenly experienced, being persecuted with great severity for his steady adherence to the Church and King, by the Puritan leaders, notwithstanding his piety and the soundness of his doctrinal views. Similar was the treatment also experienced by their colleague Balcanqual, now Dean of Durham, who literally fell a victim to the fury of the Puritans ; being driven from all he possessed, and dying at Chirkcastle, Denbighshire, in consequence of the severity he met with. The like persecutions, though in a slighter degree, involved our Author's Nephews, Archdeacon Davenant and Dr. Fuller, whose benefices were sequestered. The Bishop was interred in the South

* Bp. Godwin de Præsulibus, Richardson's.

Aisle of the Choir of his own Cathedral ; where is a tablet to his memory. He bequeathed £200 for the benefit of the Cathedral : and he left to Queen's College, the perpetual advowson of the Rectories of Cheverill Magna and Newton Toney, Wilts ; and a rent charge of £31. 10s. per annum, to found two bible-clerkships, and buy books for the Library of the same College.

The following is the inscription on his monument :—

Monumentorum omnium
JOHANNIS DAVENANTII
Minime perenne, quid loquatur audi.
Natus Londini Anno Christi 1572 Maii die 20
Cantabrigiæ in Collegio Reginali
bonis literis opeam fælicem dedit,
Cujus cum Societate esset meritissime donatus
Ætatemq. et doctrinæ et morum gravitate superaret,
Cum nondum plures quam 36 annos numerasset,
D. Margaretæ in S. Theologia Professsr est electus
Celebremque prius Cathedram longe ornatiorem reddidit.
Intra quadriennium mox Collegii sui Præsidens fectus est
Cui dubium Rector an Benefactor profuerit magis
Tum vero a serenissimo et in rebus Theologicis
Perspicacissimo Rege, Jacobo, honorifice missus
Synodo Dordracensi magna pars interfuit,
Tandem hujusce Diocæseos Saribⁿˢ· Episcopus
Anno 1621 die Novembris viii* consecratus est.
Cui velut vivum exemplar antiquitatis venerandæ
Universas Primitivi Præsulis partes explevit
Atque ita per 20 pene annos huic Ecclesiæ præfuit
Summo tum bonorum omnium tum etiam hostium,
Consensu optimus & vel inde felicissimus
Quod ruinam sedis, cum superesse per ætatem non potuit,
Priusquam oculis conspiceret, vivere desierit,
Anno scilicet Christi MDCXLI. Aprilis die xx.

* Rectius xviii.

The following extract from Dr. Plume's Life of that zealous Churchman,† and excellent Christian, Bishop Hacket, prefixed

† Dr. Hacket is recorded as the last man in England who persisted to read the Liturgy in public, after it had been proscribed by the Parliament ; and the following well-known anecdote is given by his biographer, illustrative alike of his attachment to the Church, and of his holy courage. " One Sunday, while he was reading the Common Prayer in his church, a soldier of the Earl of Essex came, and clapt a pistol to his breast, and commanded him to read no further. The Doctor smiled at his insolency in that sacred place ; and, not at all terrified, said, ' he would do what became a Divine, and he might do what became a Soldier :' so the tumult for that time was quieted, and the Doctor permitted to proceed."

to his sermons, is worthy of citation, as well for its good sense, as for the testimony it bears to our Author. " In matters of doctrine, he (Hacket) embraced no private and singular opinions, as many great men delight to do, *in vetere via novam semitam quærentes*, says the father, (Jerome); but was in all points a perfect Protestant, according to the Articles of the Church of England; always accounting it a spice of pride and vanity to affect singularity in any opinions or expositions of Scripture, without great cause; and withal very dangerous to affect precipices, as goats use, when they may walk in plain paths. In the Quinquarticular Controversy, he was ever very moderate; but, being bred under Bishop Davenant and Dr. Ward, in Cambridge, was addicted to their sentiments. Bishop Usher would say, Davenant understood those controversies better than ever any man did since St. Austin. But *He* used to say, he was sure he had three excellent men of his mind in this controversy, 1. Padre Paulo,* whose letter is extant to Heinsius, anno 1604: 2. Thomas Aquinas: 3. St. Austin:—but, besides and above them all, he believed in his conscience, St. Paul was of the same mind likewise : yet would profess withal, he disliked no Arminian, but such a one as reviled and defamed every one that was not so : and would often commend Arminius himself for his excellent wit and parts, but only tax his want of reading and knowledge in antiquity : and ever held it was the foolishest thing in the world to say the Arminians were Papists, when so many Dominicans and Jansenists were Anti-Arminians : and so again to say the Anti-Arminians were Puritans or Presbyterians, when Ward, and Davenant, and Prideaux, and Brownrig, were Anti-Arminians, and also stout champions for Episcopacy ;† and Arminius himself was ever a Presbyterian :—and, therefore, he much commended the moderation of our Church, which made not any of these nice and doubtful opinions the *resolved doctrine* of

* The famous Historian of the Council of Trent.

† To which might be added Hooker, Whitgift, Bancroft, Hall, Saunderson, Beveridge, and innumerable others. In fact, the ablest defences of our Church have proceeded from the pens of writers of these views. So true is the remark of Bishop Horsley : " If we would look for warm advocates of Church authority in general, and for able writers in defence of our own form of Church government in particular, such we shall find among those Divines of our Church who were called in their day the Doctrinal Calvinists." Charge at Rochester, 1800. It may be permitted us again to refer the Reader to Davenant's sentiments on this subject in the Question given at the end of this life.

the Church : this, he judged, was the great fault of the Tridentine and late Westminster assemblies : but our Church was more in-genuous, and left these dark and curious points to the several apprehensions of learned men, and extended equal communion to both."

That the views of Davenant were such as bear the name of sub-lapsarian Calvinism, all his writings prove.* It has, however, been said, that with respect to the doctrine of Universal Redemp-tion, he was led by Abp. Usher. This is distinctly stated by Baxter; and from this it has been inferred by many, that the views of Davenant underwent a change, and that he declined to the opinion that redemption is *attainable* by all. In fact, the extraor-dinary endowments of the Irish Primate, his stupendous and uni-versal erudition, his extreme moderation, humility, fervent piety, and judgment, placed him in correspondence with all the learned men of Europe of all churches, who appealed to him for infor-mation and advice upon almost every topic of learning and theo-logy.† When in London, " the most eminent divines were wont to apply themselves to him as a father."‡ Among others, Dave-nant was on close terms of intimacy with him ; and to this the following passage of Baxter refers, in the year 1658, seventeen years after our Author's death : " In the time of my abode at Lord Broghill's, fell out all the acquaintance I had with the most

---

* Yet, Mr. Cassan tells us (Lives of Bishops of Salisbury, part ii. p. 113) " Davenant had adopted the supralapsarian hypothesis, i. e. of un-conditional predestination in the utmost sense." This gentleman's definition of the doctrine is well-suited to his accuracy of assertion. He has, how-ever, favoured the world with more than one choice specimen of his theo-logical attainment ; suited, indeed, to what might be expected from a man, who, in narrating a witty story of Bishop Thomas, concerning a Lutheran divine who refused to bury a Calvinist, sagely observes : " Although the Calvinism of the dead be not *contagious*, it may fairly be doubted whether a *known heretic* is entitled to have the service read over him, and to receive the same honours with one dying in the true faith of the Church. In this case, no doubt, the Clergyman was acting in conformity to the spirit of the Rubric. For a Calvinist must, *ipso facto*, be ' excommunicate :' and such, we know, are not entitled to Christian burial." The Reader will positively find this delectable passage in part ii. p. 316, of the above-mentioned vo-lume.

† We need go no farther than a mere glance at the invaluable selection of letters which his Chaplain, Dr. Parr, selected from the vast mass of his correspondence, and published at the end of his life.

‡ Dr. Bernard's Funeral Sermon on Usher.

reverend, learned, humble, and pious Primate of Ireland, Abp.
Usher, then living at the Earl of Peterborough's house, in St.
Martin's-lane. Sometimes he came to me, and oft I went to him.
And Dr Kendal, who had wrote pettishly against me, about
Universal Redemption and the specification of Divine grace, de-
sired me (when I had answered one of his invectives, and had
written part of the answer to the other), to meet him at Bishop
Usher's lodgings, and refer the matter to him for our reconcilia-
tion and future silence; which I willingly did. And when the
Bishop had declared his judgment for that doctrine of Universal
Redemption which I asserted, and gloried that he was the man
who brought Bishop Davenant and Dr. Preston to it, he persuaded
us, who were both willing, to silence for the time to come."
(P. 205.) In the same book, referring to the same conference, he
delivers the opinion more fully : " In my book called *R. B.'s
Judgment about the Perseverance of Believers*, I shewed the variety of opinions about Perseverance, and that Augustin and
Prosper themselves did not hold the certain perseverance of all
the elect; but held that there are more sanctified than are elect,
and that perseverance is affixed to the elect *as such*, and not to
the sanctified *as such;* which Bp. Usher averred to Dr. Kendal,
before my face, to be most certainly Austin's judgment, though
both he and I did incline to another. From hence, and many
other arguments, I inferred that the sharp censures of men against
their brethren, for not holding a point which Austin himself was
against, and no one author can be proved to hold from the Apostles' days till long after Austin, doth argue less of judgment and
charity than many of the censurers seem to have."

Upon a topic so important, a few observations may be made.
That Usher became less partial to the strict points of Calvinism
in later life, rests upon evidence too distinct to be questioned ;
and Mr. Todd, in his life of Bp. Walton, has given some interesting letters on the subject. Nevertheless, so early as 1617, when
yet a private divine, he maintained Universal Redemption, and
his correspondence contains two powerful letters on the subject.
But, perhaps, he would not then have so fully allowed what he
afterwards maintained in one of his last conversations, when,
having preached what he called " a soul-saving sermon," upon
the words " *Whom he called, them he justified*," and being asked
by Walton, whether " God, with his word, doth give internal
grace to all that are called by it, that they may repent if they

will ; and that they certainly *can* will?" he answered, " Yes, they
all can will ; and that so many will not, is because they resist
God's grace:" adding, " Bishop Overall was in the right, and I
am of his mind."

It is from this, that a supposed change in Davenant's opinion
has been inferred. Hence Mr. Jackson, in his able life of the
great Puritan divine John Goodwin (the most profound Arminian
theologian that this country has produced,) tells us, (and Mr.
Nicholls, in the Preface to his works of Arminius, repeats the remark,) that " Bp. Davenant appears to have undergone a change
of sentiment similar to that of Baxter."—There is no difficulty in
refuting this ; but there is much difficulty in reconciling Baxter's
remark with the fact.   Davenant's views at the Synod of Dort,
prior to his acquaintance with Usher, are distinctly stated in his
" Reasons," and in many of his works: and his reply to Hoard,
just before his death, is in strict accordance with them.   He held
Universal Redemption, as we have seen, at Dort ; but he held it
as inseparable from Reprobation, or Preterition ; and he maintains against Hoard the same doctrine, and the same inseparable
Reprobation.   The truth, or error, of the doctrine is, of course,
not affected by this : but, as a matter of fact, the evidence is too
distinct to be doubted for a moment, that not a shadow of change
occurred in his opinions.   How, therefore, to understand Baxter's
remark I know not.

In 1650 was published a thin folio, containing *Dissertationes
Duæ ; prima, de Morte Christi ;* (of which a translation is annexed to this work,) *altéra, De Prædestinatione et Electione, &c.* ;
to which is appended, *Sententia de Gallicana Controversia, de
gratiosa et salutari Dei erga homines Peccatores voluntate, &c.*
These treatises, selected from our Author's papers, had been sent
to Abp. Usher, by Dr. Edward Davenant, for the purpose of publication.   But the wretched state of the times prevented their
appearing for some years ; and it does not seem that the Archbishop was the Editor : for the preface is signed with the initials
T. B.   The French Controversy had arisen upon the opinions of
Cameron, a divine of the Gallican Protestant Church : Davenant's
sentiments were applied for, and are here given.   At the end of
this volume, but not named in the title-page, is *Sententia Ecclesiæ
Anglicanæ de Predestinatione et capitibus annexis, ab eodem (ut
fertur,) Authore, jussu Regis Serenissimi conscripta.*   How this
can be imputed to Davenant, and received as such by the Editor,

is inexplicable. It is manifestly the production of an inferior pen, and is decidedly adverse to his views, as stated through the rest of the volume. The Editor, T. B., I conceive to be one Thomas Bedford, who, in the same year (1650), at the suggestion of Archbishop Usher, published, along with two divinity Theses of his own, a letter of Bishop Davenant's to Dr. Ward, entitled *Epistola de Sacramentis.*

In sending up the two *Dissertationes* above-mentioned to Abp. Usher, Dr. Edward Davenant says, " I have sent up that elaborate work of the Bishop of Salisbury, which, being committed to my charge, your Grace has done me unspeakable favour to undertake the publishing of it....The short answer of his unto the French Divines, which I found scattered among his papers, is sent up in this book."* The regard of Usher and Davenant appears to have been reciprocal. The former, in writing to Dr. Ward, says, " For the Arminian Question, I desire never to read more than my Lord of Salisbury's Lectures, touching Predestination and Christ's Death." And again, " I thank you most heartily for communicating my Lord of Salisbury's Lectures. They are excellent; learnedly, soundly, and perspicuously performed ; and, I hope, will do much good for the establishing of our young divines in the present truth."

Few men appear to have been more honoured and venerated by all parties than Bishop Davenant. In all the works of friends or opponents, there is not to be found a single sentence approaching even to disrespect, much less any thing that can tend to cast the slightest reflexion upon his deportment in any measure of his public or private life. His profound learning, acuteness of intellect, catholic spirit, active benevolence, and meekness, are constantly adverted to ; and the phrases—" the good Bishop Davenant," the " excellent Bishop Davenant," the " learned Bishop Davenant," &c. &c. are the usual appendages to his name, even in the writings of those who took up the pen in express hostility to certain of his theological views.

---

* In 1641, the year of the Bishop's decease, the learned Dr. Gerard Langbaine published, at Oxford, a book, entitled " *Episcopal Inheritance,* or a reply to the humble examination of a printed Abstract, and the answers to nine reasons of the House of Commons against the Votes of Bishops in Parliament. To which is added a Determination of the late learned Bishop of Salisbury, Englished." This was reprinted in 1680, in London, but I have not been able to obtain the book.

A distinguished Nonconformist, Dr. E. Calamy, in the Memoirs of his own Life, recently published, gives an account of a conver-sation which he had with Bishop Burnet, who particularly re-quested to know the opinion of the Dissenters upon his explana-tion of the seventeenth Article in his " Exposition of the Thirty-nine Articles."—" I told his Lordship," says Dr. C. " that as for those whom his Lordship particularly inquired after, though they were very thankful to his Lordship for his pains, and for his charity to those of different sentiments ; yet, on the head of Pre-destination, which he had so laboured, they could not but be surprised to find that, when he had been at such pains nicely to state the two extremes, he should quite overlook the middle way, where truth commonly lies. He told me, that the true reason of that was, because he could not see how that called the middle way differed from one of the extremes. I freely told him this seemed more strange to several among us, because the learned DAVENANT, one of his Lordship's predecessors in the See of Sarum, had not only vigorously asserted and defended that middle way in the Synod of Dort, in opposition to Remonstrants and Supralapsarians, but had also been at no small pains to sup-port it in several of his writings ; of which his Lordship took not the least notice. This led into a pretty close discourse of two hours' length, in which his Lordship endeavoured to convince me, that such as declared for the middle way, must at last, when pressed, fall into the Arminian scheme : while I, on the contrary, asserted, and endeavoured to prove, that such as were in that way of thinking, were no more obliged to fall in with the Remon-strants than with the rigid Predeterminants." (Vol. i. p. 276.)

In 1703, Dr. Calamy, preaching in the lecture-room at Salter's Hall, discoursed from the text Rom. ix. 16, " *So then it is not of him that willeth,*" &c. and afterwards published his discourse, at the request of the auditors, under the title " *Divine Mercy exalted ; or Free Grace in its glory :*" in the preface to which, he com-plains, that " Some have given themselves a liberty to reflect on their brethren who adhere to the suffrages of the British Divines in the Synod of Dort ;" and recommends those " that would see the doctrine of particular election maintained, consistently with a general love of God to the world, to consult the learned and peaceable Bishop Davenant's ' *Animadversions upon Hoard's Treatise ;*' a book not valued according to its worth."

OUR notices of the Bishop's connexions must be very concise. He was one of many children. His elder brother, Edward, was a Merchant; but is spoken of by Aubrey " as an incomparable man;" a profound scholar, and a great mathematician. His Son, Dr. Edward Davenant, of whom Aubrey gives a long account, was promoted by his Uncle to the Vicarage of Gillingham, Dorset, and the Archdeaconry of Berks, which he resigned for the Treasurership of the Cathedral of Salisbury. He was pronounced by Sir Christopher Wren to be the greatest Mathematician of his age. He died in 1679, having been Vicar of Gillingham 53 years. He had one Son, Ralph, who was Rector of Whitechapel, London; and another, John, who was Fellow of Oriel College, Oxon; and also a daughter, Anne, who married W. Ettrick, Esq. of Wimborne; and another, Catharine, married to Dr. Lamplugh, Abp. of York. In the Bishop's will, he names three other of his brothers, viz. William, James, and Ralph. Of his Sisters, one was married to Thomas Fuller, Rector of Aldwincle, Northamptonshire, and was mother to the admirable Author of " Worthies of England," &c. and who was promoted by his Uncle to the Precentorship of Sarum, and the Rectory of Broad-Windsor, Dorset. His appointment to a Bishopric was frustrated, at the Restoration, by his decease. A second sister, married, as we said before, Dr. Ralph Townson, Dean of Westminster, 1617, and Bishop of Sarum, to which he was consecrated in July, 1619, and died May the 15th following; leaving a family of fifteen children, poorly provided for; he is spoken of as a very hospitable and disinterested man. To his family, our Bishop, who succeeded him, was a father. His widow resided in the palace to the day of her death, having, as her epitaph records, found with him " consolation and a home." Of this numerous family, it is very remarkable, that two of the daughters married divines who were also successively Bishops of Salisbury; the See occupied by their Father and Uncle: Ellen being married to Bishop Henchman, author of the " Gentleman's Calling," and one of the numerous persons to whom the " *Whole Duty of Man*" has been ascribed; and Mary to Bishop Hyde, a Cousin of the Lord Chancellor Clarendon, and whose lineal descendant, by the female line, is the present Sir William Parker, Bart.: his daughter, Margaret, having married Sir Henry Parker, Bart.; a third daughter, Margaret, was married to John Rives, Archdeacon of Berks; and a fourth, Gertrude, to James Harris, Esq. of the Close, at Salisbury, from whom descend the present Earls of Malmsbury. There was probably some connexion, though I have not been able to trace it, between our Prelate and Sir William Davenant, the profligate Poet-laureate of Charles I.; for *his* brother Robert was Chaplain to the Bishop, and presented to a Stall in Salisbury Cathedral.

Lloyd, in his Memoirs, has given an Epitaph on our Bishop, which, as exhibiting a good summary of his genius and character, we here subjoin.

> " Hic jacet omnigenæ eruditionis modestæ
>   Epitome. Cui judicium asservit
>   Maxime discretiorum,
>   quicquid uspiam est literarum Hebraicarum
>   Ethnicarum, aut Christianarum
>   Omnes linguas, artes et historias
>   quicquid prædicarunt
>   patres, disputarunt scholastici
>   decreverunt consilia
>   in sobriam pacificam, et practicam concoxit
>   Theologiam.
> Quæ in concionibus dominata est, Scholis
>   Imperavit, et Synodis* leges dedit
>   Prudens pariter ac simplex,
>   ille, ille cui severior vita quam
>   opinio ; ut pote strictius vitam
>   agens, quam sententiam, (Doctrina
>   magna lux Ecclesiæ, exemplo major)
>   Cujus libri omnes una hac notabantur
>   Inscriptione PRÆFUIT QUI PROFUIT,
>   qui Regem venerebatur, sed et timebat
>   Deum) non tam suo, quam publico morbo
>   succubuit Aprilis 3, 1641, extremam
>   in hæc verba agens animam :—
>   ' Tantum religio potuit suadere malorum.' "

---

* " Bogerman confessed that Dr. Davenant's experience and skill in the laws and histories, gave them directions for the better ordering of their debates and votes."

END OF THE LIFE.

AN

EXPOSITION

OF THE

EPISTLE OF ST. PAUL

TO

THE COLOSSIANS.

THE AUTHOR'S DEDICATION.

TO

HIS BENIGNANT MOTHER,

THE UNIVERSITY OF CAMBRIDGE,

AT ALL TIMES HELD IN HIGHEST RENOWN FOR VIRTUE,

PIETY, AND THE ACKNOWLEDGMENT OF SOUND

DOCTRINE;

THESE FIRST-FRUITS OF

HIS THEOLOGICAL PROFESSORSHIP,

ORIGINALLY COMPOSED THEREIN,

AND NOW AGAIN REVISED,

ARE WILLINGLY AND DESERVEDLY GIVEN,

DEDICATED, AND INSCRIBED,

IN TOKEN OF AFFECTION AND HONOUR,

BY

HER MOST DEVOTED SON,

JOHN DAVENANT.

CHRISTIAN READER.

RECEIVE with indulgence these Commentaries on the Epistle of Paul to the *Colossians*, which I formerly delivered at the commencement of my Theological Professorship in the celebrated University *of Cambridge*. I have with difficulty brought myself, among such a number of very learned interpreters, to permit this my feeble performance to go before the Public : but at length the importunity of friends, who thought that some benefit might accrue from this my work to the Church of Christ (to which it is fit that myself, and all that is mine, should be subservient,) overcame me. Use now (if it seem good to thee), kind Reader, this labour of mine ; but on condition that thou neither expect any highly wrought diction from the expounder of an Apostle who avowedly renounces all enticing words ; nor, in the Exposition itself, require any thing remarkable from him, who acknowledges himself to be but one Expositor among many, and desires rather to be hidden in the thick crowd, than stand conspicuous. If I shall have brought any light to the clearer understanding of the mind of the Apostle ; if in any way I shall have aided Tyros in Theology, by this my lucubration, my design, and (I imagine) thy expectations, are answered. Whoever from this my writing shall derive any profit, let him render all the glory to God ; from whom we have freely and gratuitously received our *sufficiency* (however much or little it may be) to accomplish this work. To this supreme God, the Giver of all good, commend me in thy prayers, and fare thee well in the Lord.

———

IN compliance with custom, *I* have a few things to premise, which may render the access to the explication of the context itself more easy ; and these *I* shall refer to four heads : First, *I* shall say something of the Colossians, to whom this Epistle was written ; next, of the occasion or cause of this writing ; then, of the particular design of the whole Epistle ; and lastly, of the distribution of it into its parts. We now proceed to these points in the order in which they are proposed.

Some seek for Colosse at Rhodes, induced by this argument, that it is evident the great Colossus of the Sun was in that Island ; from which they will have the Colossians to have derived their name. But the opinion of Jerome and Chrysostom is far more probable, who write that this city was situated in Phrygia, not far from Hierapolis and Laodicea. This St. Paul himself seems to intimate, since in the fourth Chapter he commands this Epistle to be read in the Church of Laodicea ; whence we may be allowed to conjecture that these two Churches were near each other : but no one places the Laodiceans among the Rhodians. Moreover, Xenophon bears attestation to this, who, in lib. 1, De Expeditione Cyri, writes, that after he had entered Phrygia, he went direct to Colosse, a populous, wealthy, and great city. Besides, Eusebius, in his Chronicles, relates that three cities of Asia, (Laodicea, Hierapolis, and Colosse,) fell by the same earthquake. Add to these testimonies Pliny, who, in lib. 5, Natur. hist. cap. 32, has not placed Colosse in any Island, but reckoned it among the Towns of the Continent. But we need not anxiously inquire

d 2

after those things which are the province of another, and may be sought from Geographers. Whoever the Colossians were, we may be firmly persuaded of this, that the benefit of this Epistle ought to extend to ourselves as well as to them.*

Now, as to the occasion of the writing, we must recollect that the Church of Colosse was founded in purity, and rightly instructed in the mystery of the Gospel by Epaphras, and other faithful Ministers of the Word. But there soon sprang up ministers of Satan, whose great aim was to obscure the Gospel, and trouble the Church. Some of these, as though the simplicity of the Gospel were unworthy the wisdom of man, obtruded philosophical subtleties upon the Colos-

---

* There seems no doubt that Colosse was situated in Phrygia, in the neighbourhood of Laodicea and Hierapolis, in whose destruction it is said, as above, to have participated. The Rev. F. Arundel, in his recent " Visit to the seven Churches," made a point of investigating the actual scite of Colosse, whose scanty ruins he seems to have clearly ascertained in the immediate vicinity of the present Town of Khonas, which appears to have sprung up from its ashes, for we find the Bishop of Chonæ present at the second Nicene Council. The Translator cannot forbear quoting the following interesting scene, which was presented to Mr. Arundel, when taking his farewell of this district. " Having crossed," says he, " a small river, (probably the Asopus,) flowing down to the plain, about half past two, our course nearly west, we were overtaken by a heavy shower, or rather a torrent, which lasted a full half hour. Nothing could exceed the grandeur of the scene just before the rain began to fall, and at the moment when it ceased. On the left were the lofty peaks of Mount Cadmus, of the darkest hue, with a few streaks of snow along their sides; clouds of a whitish colour rolling beneath those peaks, whilst the atmosphere above them was one mass of condensed clouds, black as night. On the right hand was the ridge of mount Messogis, partly in dark shadow, and partly bright with patches of sunshine; while the terrace on which were the ruins of Hierapolis, glittered with the reflexion of the white masses of incrustation, resembling sheets of water, or of ice falling over the edge. A rainbow of the most vivid colours I ever beheld, with an outer one as vivid as rainbows commonly are, extended over the whole of the scites of Hierapolis and Laodicea. This said, or seemed to say, ' Dark and gloomy as the prospect now is, and has long been, in these once highly favoured regions, the bow of mercy is again shining; and soon shall the rays of the Gospel-sun dispel all recollection of the days of pagan darkness.' "

sians; others, as though Christ were not sufficient for
salvation, recalled the abrogated ceremonies of the Law.
Thus, whilst they attempted to confound Theology with
Philosophy, Christ with Moses, they threw that Church
into the greatest danger. The devout Minister of
Christ could not patiently bear these troublers; he
hastens, therefore, to Paul, then a prisoner at Rome;
he gives an Epitome of the Evangelical doctrine which
he had been preaching; he shews the errors and impostures of the new teachers   Upon that, the Apostle,
under the impulse and direction of the Divine Spirit,
confirms the doctrine of Epaphras by his own authority, and exhorts the Colossians to persevere constantly
in the same, despising the foolish subtleties and absurdities of all heretics.—Such was the occasion of his
writing.

THE DESIGN of the whole Epistle is this, That all
hope of human Salvation is to be reposed in Christ
alone; therefore, that we must rest entirely on the
faith of Christ, and live according to the rule of the
Gospel, rejecting Mosaic Ceremonies, and Philosophical speculations

Of the parts of this Epistle it would be out of place
to say much. When we come to particulars these will
be developed more advantageously; I will now exhibit
only a cursory view of them. If, therefore, we set
aside the title or inscription, the Epistle contains five
parts: A congratulatory exordium, in which he commends the faith and other virtues of the Colossians, and
desires for them advancement in faith and holiness.
To this he immediately subjoins a lively description of
Christ and his benefits; declaring him to be the true
Son of God, the only Head and Saviour of his Church.
Having firmly established this doctrine, in the third

place, he attempts a refutation of the seducers who were thrusting philosophical fooleries and antiquated ceremonies upon the Colossians. The fourth part contains instruction in morals; wherein he roots out vices, inculcates virtues, and, lastly, forms the life of Christians, both in duties common to all, and to their domestic relations in life. The conclusion contains some private matters and salutations directed to different persons.

CORRIGENDA ET EMENDATA.

In the course of inspecting the Sheets previous to their being done up, a few typographical errors in single letters have been observed, which it was difficult to detect in the proofs, especially in the Greek sentences ; as, for instance, ſ for ς, in two or three places, and mostly at the end of a word : these the observing and learned Reader will correct for himself.

Page 93, line 22, for *access may be had*, &c. read, access to the Gospel is open to all nations.

Page 95, the passage from Tertullian about the middle ought to read thus, *When we have believed the Gospel, we require nothing farther; for we have beforehand believed, that there is not any thing which it is our duty farther to believe.*— Mr. Craig has given a paraphrastic version of this passage, in conjunction with another, in his " Refutation," which may throw light on the quotation, obscure in itself: " When we have believed the Gospel, there is nothing further necessary to be believed ; because from it we know every thing necessary to be known. This being the rule of faith which brings salvation, we have no further article, except that there is nothing further to be believed."—The passage of Tertullian is from the treatise De Præscript. Hæret. cap. 7, the last words of the Chapter.

Page 146, line 10 from the bottom, for the Θ, read O.

Page 149, line 6 from the bottom, for *inwardly*, read outwardly.

Page 166, line 10, dele *straightway.*

AN EXPOSITION

OF THE

EPISTLE OF ST. PAUL TO THE COLOSSIANS.

CHAP. I.

1. *Paul, an Apostle of Jesus Christ by the will of God, and Timotheus our brother,*

2. *To the Saints and faithful Brethren in Christ which are at Colosse : Grace be unto you, and peace, from God our Father and the Lord Jesus Christ.*

THERE are four parts of this first Chapter. The first is completed in these two short verses which I have read ; and contains the inscription or title prefixed to the Epistle itself. The second comprises a preface adapted to conciliate good-will; from the 3d to the 12th verse. The third part embraces an exposition of doctrine concerning Christ and his benefits; to verse 23. The last part to the end of the chapter, exhorts to advancement and constancy in the same doctrine.

In the title three things are to be observed : the subscription ; the inscription ; and the salutation. The terms *subscription* and *inscription* are derived from our custom in letter-writing. For it is usual for the name of the sender to be *sub*scribed to the letter itself; and the name of him to whom it is sent to be *in*scribed on the back of it. Of these in order.

The Subscription contains three things : the Names of those who send this Epistle, *Paul* and *Timotheus :* their different descriptions; the one *an Apostle of Christ,* the other *a brother :* the Founder of the apostolic office, *Jesus Christ by the will of God.* We shall now follow the thread of the context.

Paul.] I shall say but little concerning the Name, because nothing can be advanced which is either very necessary, or that is not very trite and frequently repeated. It is evident that he had been called *Saul.* Some therefore allege that he changed his name when he embraced the Christian Religion, that he might declare his change of mind by this circumstance ; for from being a proud and haughty Pharisee, he became a lowly and humble disciple of Christ. This opinion is favoured by Augustine in his Exposition of Ps. lxxii. where he thus comments, *At first he was Saul, afterwards Paul ; first proud, afterwards humble ; not as though he changed his name from any vain glory, but because from a proud man, he became lowly ; for the word Paulus means little.* Others think the Apostle assumed this name after he had brought Sergius *Paulus,* the Proconsul, to the faith of Christ, as a memorial of so great a conquest. But Luke himself discountenances this, who, in Acts xiii. 9, calls him *Paul* before the conversion of the Proconsul. A third opinion is that of Origen; who writes that this our Apostle was distinguished from the first by two names; *Saul* being his family name given him by his parents, to intimate his religion and his origin ; *Paul* being added to shew that he was a citizen of Rome. He uses this latter name in his Epistles, because it was better reputed, and more acceptable among the Gentiles. Indeed the same father shews in the same passage, that it was a common practice among the Jews to take two names. Now if any one wishes for a *personal description* of Paul, let him consult Nicephorus, lib. ii. c. 37 ; his *life* and *manners* let him seek from Acts viii. ix. xxii. and xxvi.; from Gal. i.; and 1 Tim. i.; his *praises* from Eusebius, who terms him, *the most learned of the Apostles, most powerful in* *speech and understanding* : from Jerome,* who calls him *the trumpet of the Gospel, the thunder of the Gentiles, the stream of eloquence,* &c.   But Chrysostom sets forth his praises most amply, in his discourses, De Pauli laudibus.†

An Apostle.] This is a title of office or dignity. It denotes, if we regard the origin of the term, any man whatever sent by another with a commission ; for it is derived from the Greek αποστελλειν : but if we attend to the common application of it, it denotes certain select ambassadors of Christ.   But, as Thomas‡ says, in *terms* we must regard not so much *from what they are derived,* as *to what purpose intended.*

The name, then, of Apostle, according to the use of sacred Scripture, belongs to those only, First, who had received an immediate call from God to preach the Gospel: *He chose twelve, whom he named Apostles,* Luke vi. 13, and John xx. 21 ; *As my Father hath sent me even so send I you.*

* Ad Pammach. advers. errores Joan Hierosol.

† The characters referred to in this section were either illustrious Fathers of the Christian Church who flourished in the third, fourth, and fifth centuries; or eminent writers of their day, whose productions have gained them celebrity and become standing authority. Augustine, Eusebius, and Chrysostom were Bishops of the early Christian Church; the former of Hippo, in Africa; the second of Cæsarea, and the third of Constantinople. This latter acquired the surname of Chrysostom, on account of his singular eloquence, the term meaning " golden mouth." He was an admired rhetorician and orator, and the praises of Paul were a fine subject for his powers to descant upon. Eusebius became celebrated by his numerous writings, but especially as an early historian of the Church of Christ. Jerome was particularly distinguished as a man of profound learning and extensive information ; he was an able critic and a voluminous writer ; the author of the Latin version of the Scriptures commonly termed the Vulgate, and from which Davenant in this Exposition generally cites his Scripture authorities. The Nicephorus referred to, is Nicephorus Callistus, a Monk of Constantinople of the fourteenth century, who wrote, in Greek, an Ecclesiastical History, in 23 books, 18 of which are still extant, containing the transactions of the Church from the birth of Christ to the death of Phocas, in 610. It was considered of such worth as to be translated into Latin by John Langius, and attained such celebrity as to have passed through several editions.

‡ Our Author means Thomas Aquinas, whom he often cites, sometimes under one name, sometimes the other.

Secondly, who had received a certain and infallible knowledge of evangelical doctrine, by the immediate inspiration
of the Holy Spirit. Christ promised this to them, John
xvi. 13, *The Spirit of truth shall guide you into all truth;*
this he fulfilled in Acts ii.* Thirdly, who had received an
authority, not restricted to one place, or to a certain
church, but plenary and universal; *Teach all nations,* Matth.
xxviii. *Preach to every creature,* Mark xvi. Now it is evident that Paul possessed all these. His immediate call is
proved from Acts ix. 15, *The Lord said to him* (i. e. to Ana-
nias, who had hesitated to seek Paul) *Go thy way, for he
is a chosen vessel unto me*; and Gal. i. 1. His immediate
inspiration of the mystery of the Gospel, from Gal. i. 12,
I was not taught it, but by the revelation of Jesus Christ.
His universal authority, from Acts ix. 15, where he is called
*a chosen vessel to bear the name of God before the Gentiles and
the Children of Israel.* And elsewhere he is termed *the
teacher,* not of this or of that church, but *of the Gentiles,*
Rom. i. 5.

We have thus proved the Apostleship of Paul. Now let
us inquire why in this place, and several others, he makes
mention of *this* his office. First, he does it that he might
silence the false Apostles, who whispered in the ears of the
people that he was not one of the Apostles, because he
had no intercourse with Christ whilst he dwelt upon earth,
and because he was not among them when the Holy Spirit
in the likeness of tongues of fire sat upon each of them.
But notwithstanding this, he styles and proves himself *an
Apostle,* because he was directly called and instructed by
Christ, although not at the same time as the rest.

Secondly, he claims the title of *an Apostle,* that he might
make known to the faithful themselves the certainty of his
doctrine. For it is absolutely necessary that it should be
known whence that doctrine proceeded which is delivered
to the Churches; if from human opinion, it cannot be sure
and infallible; but if from the ambassadors of God himself, and men inspired by the Holy Spirit for this work of

* By the outpouring of the Holy Spirit on the day of Pentecost.

preaching, then we can safely repose faith upon it. *All
created truth is liable to error, unless so far as it is rectified
by that which is uncreated,* Aquinas, quæst. disp. de fide,
art. 8.

Lastly, Paul affixes the name of his office, that he might
excite and stir up himself, to fulfil the work of an Apostle.
For, in calling himself *an Apostle,* he owns that the duty
of preaching the Gospel was entrusted to him; and woe
unto him, if he did not perform it.

Of Jesus Christ.] He dignifies his Apostleship from its
Founder.

By the will of God] i. e. Not only by the authority of
Christ as man, but by the gift, ordination, and approbation
of God. What is here spoken concerning God is to be
attributed not to the Father alone, but to the Son, and to
the Holy Spirit: for Apostles are appointed by the will
and authority of these also. *Christ gave Apostles,* Ephes.
iv. 11. The Holy Ghost said, *Separate me Barnabas and
Saul,* Acts xiii. 2. Neither can the will of these, whose
essence is one, be dissevered. Paul therefore was called
and chosen to the Apostleship; the sacred Trinity so willing, ordering, and ordaining it. The Apostle adduced
this that the Colossians, to whom he was personally unknown, might understand that he did not write these
things rashly, or intrude himself into the concerns of that
church; but that he did it in virtue of his apostolic office
and authority, whereby the care of all the churches rested
upon him. And so he was able, though absent, to direct
the faithful, to reprove seducers, and to support the sink-
ing state of that church. For all these things were enjoined and imposed upon him *by the will of God.* Thus
much concerning *Paul.*

And Timotheus our Brother.] Concerning Timothy very
excellent testimonies are found in the Scriptures. He was
descended from pious ancestors, as appears from Acts xvi.
and 2 Tim. i. 5. He himself also was pious and faithful, as
this our Apostle in many places testifies. He calls him *his
work-fellow,* Rom. xvi. 21; *a Son dearly beloved and faith-*

ful in the Lord, 1 Cor. iv. 17 ; *most learned in the Scriptures*, 2 Tim. iii. 15 ; and he honours him with many other
commendations. But in this place he calls him *Brother*,
either on account of his agreement in religion and true
doctrine with Paul, or from that common respect whereby
all Christians call one another *Brethren ;* because they are
presumed to be children by adoption of the same heavenly
Father.

It may be objected, Paul was the instrument of the
Spirit in delivering the doctrine of this Epistle : why
then does he associate Timothy with himself?

We answer ; Three causes are alleged, why, in the title of
this Epistle, he chose to join the name of Timothy with his
own.

First, to shew that he did not preach any other doctrine
to them than that very doctrine which Timothy approved,
who was in repute among them. For although the doctrine of Paul does not require any outward recommendation, yet the agreement and concord of ministers in the
same doctrine contributes much to persuasion. Secondly,
to render Timothy more acceptable to that church, whilst
in this subscription he unites him to himself as an equal.
Lastly, because perhaps Timothy was his amanuensis in
writing this Epistle.

Thus far we have explained *the subscription.* Now let us
unfold the doctrines.

Paul calls himself *an Apostle of Christ*, and that *by the
will of God :* What do we gather from hence?

1. That faith is to be yielded equally to these writings
of Paul, as if Christ himself or God were speaking from
heaven. For an Apostle is the ambassador of God, the
amanuensis of the Holy Spirit. Among believers, therefore, they are received on their own authority, nor need
any external or human testimony, any more than Christ
himself needed it. If any one should enquire, Whence do
you know these Scriptures to have proceeded from men
inspired by Divine illumination, and not from impostors?
I answer : This principle applies to all other things, That

you should understand what it behoves you to believe : but this faith is the gift of God.   Thus says Augustine,* Confess. lib. 6. cap. 5, *Thou hast persuaded me, O God, that not those who have believed thy books, but those who have not believed them are to be blamed; neither should they be listened to, if any by chance should say, Whence do you know these books to be furnished to the human race by the Spirit of the only true God?*

2. That it is useful and necessary for all ministers of the Gospel oftentimes to bring to mind, what office and what station they hold in the church; that having their vocation continually in remembrance they may endeavour to fulfil their duty to the utmost of their power.   For he

---

* Though Augustine has been already noticed, yet such readers as are not familiar with the ancient fathers may wish to know more of him ; and especially as it will be found that our Expositor often refers to him. A few remarks, therefore, in addition to what was observed (page 3) may be allowed here.   At an early age Augustine was instructed, by his pious mother, in the principles of Christianity ; but being a youth of great vivacity, he was led into extreme dissipation, and gave himself to licentious pleasure without restraint.   For this, however, he afterwards made ample reparation to society, in the most ingenuous manner, by his book of Confessions, cited above.   Moving from place to place, in the study and profession of rhetoric and polite literature, and having taught at Carthage and Rome, his mind in the mean while thirsting after truth, he came at length under the preaching of St. Ambrose, at Milan ; a circumstance which led to a thorough conversion at the age of 32.   Soon after this his life became devoted to piety and religion ; and, says a competent judge of his writings in the present day, " the humility, devotion, and unction of this father ; the acute, lucid, and happy way in which he meets his objectors ; and the heavenly wisdom running through his remarks, will always, notwithstanding the excess of allegorical interpretation and the defect of a clear statement of justification, make his writing valuable."   Bickersteth's Christian Student·   Perhaps, as Milner has remarked, " the doctrine of justification was never fully and clearly exhibited to the Church (after the times of the Apostles) until the days of Luther ;" yet it is somewhat remarkable that, excepting this defect, Augustine has been deemed to accord mostly in doctrinal sentiments with Calvin.   But another critic (Mr. Conybeare, in his Bampton Lectures) has observed, " he who is insensible to the beauty, the piety, and the devotion and spiritual feeling which are to be found in almost every page of Augustine's Commentary, must be, to say no more, both uncandid and fastidious."   Augustine was ordained Bishop of Hippo in 395, and died in 430, aged 76.   His works form 10 vols. folio.   His " City of God," his " Confessions and Meditations," have been translated into English.

who is always reminding himself, I am a Bishop, I am a
Presbyter, must needs at the same time understand, that it
s not allowable for him to indulge in idleness, or natural inclination, but that he must keep his eye on his flock. It
is scandalous to be compelled to say of ministers what
Tacitus (Hist. 3) writes of Licinius, *Such a torpor had in-
vaded his mind, that unless others reminded him that he was a
prince, he himself would have forgotten it.*

3. That it is incumbent upon those appointed to ecclesiastical dignity, not only to discharge the duties of their
office, but to defend the authority and respectability of that
office against obstinate and schismatical revilers. For so
Paul claims to himself apostolic dignity not from self-con-
sequence, but lest the contempt of his authority should
bring into contempt that of the Church : for contempt of
religion itself always follows contempt of those who are at
the head of the church and direct the affairs of religion.*
Hence Paul advised Timothy so to conduct himself, as that
no one should despise his youth, 1 Tim. iv. 12.

It would be easy to deduce from these instructions many
things adapted to form and correct the manners; but that
may be left to your own industry and prudence.† I shall
add two things only, which, from the declaration that Paul
was made *an Apostle by the will of God,* conduce greatly to
the comfort of the godly. It hence appears,

1. That God cannot but prove efficient when those
means are used for the salvation of men which he himself
hath ordained for that purpose. Although, therefore, the
preaching of the Gospel by men weak, despised, defiled
by sin, may seem an insignificant means to the attainment
of human salvation ; yet, since it is the ordinance and will of
God, it will prove most effectual : for *the foolishness of God
is wiser than men, and the weakness of God is stronger than
man,* 1 Cor. i. 25. There will be no need therefore to ex-

---

* Here we are reminded of the well known opinion of Dr. Johnson, that
" Malevolence to the Clergy is not far removed from irreverence for Religion." The coincidence of sentiment is singular.

† It should be borne in mind that this Exposition was delivered as Lectures to Divinity Students in the University.

pect either an angel from heaven, or extraordinary visions and divine revelations; we have only to hearken to apostolic doctrine, and it will be *the power of God to salvation to all that believe.*

2.   It also follows, that this appointment of Apostles *by the will of God,* discovers to us the wonderful love of God towards mankind, and his inexpressible desire of our salvation.   For what else is sending Apostles into the world, than sending ambassadors who should pray and intreat men that they would be reconciled to God; that they would embrace the offered salvation?   Hence Paul calls the apostolic work *the ministry of reconciliation,* and says, 2 Cor. v. 20, *Now then we are ambassadors for Christ, as though God did beseech you by us, we pray you in Christ's stead, be ye reconciled to God.*   Behold the *goodness* and *loving-kindness* of God, and that *spontaneous,* not *called for,* as Tertullian says, *by us.*

Now, in the last place, it will not be foreign to our purpose to scrutinize that apostolic dignity which the Pope claims to himself.   For on all occasions he vaunts about the *Apostolic See, Apostolic Benedictions, Apostolic Anathemas;* in short, boasts of every thing Apostolic.   Wherefore from what has been explained above concerning the nature of an Apostle, this question arises, Whether the Pope of Rome has, or has not, the apostolic dignity and authority?

Bellarmin,* De pontif. Rom. lib. 1. cap. 9, asserts the apostolic authority to be permanent in the successor

---

* Bellarmin. The greatest champion of the Church of Rome, whose folio volumes have been an exhaustless armoury whence her modern defenders have supplied themselves with weapons, though they have found it convenient seldom to imitate his ingenuousness; for his works are honourably distinguished for the full and candid way in which the Protestant views are stated. The celebrity of his labours may be evinced by the circumstance that all the most learned and eminent of the Reformed Advocates deemed it right to direct their powers against this famous controversialist. Yet notwithstanding his pre-eminence among her vindicators, it has been rightly observed by a living Prelate, that " Bellarmin was not in the best odour with the See of Rome ; his notions of the Papal prerogative not being sufficiently high to reach the views there entertained of the Pope's supremacy." (Bp. Van Mildert's speech before the House of Lords, 1825.)—

of Peter alone, because supreme and universal power was
given to Peter as to an *ordinary Pastor*,* who should have
successors; but to the other Apostles, as to delegates, who
should not. The Pope of Rome is therefore alone the
Apostolic Pontiff, his only the *Apostolic* See, and his office
that of *an Apostle*.

But on the contrary, the nature of an Apostle demands
that a man be immediately called by God to that office;
that he be also instructed in evangelical truth immediately,
by the infallible inspiration of the Holy Spirit: but this is
more than the advocates of the Papacy themselves dare
arrogate to the Pope. He is not immediately called by
God, but chosen by the Cardinals, and that very often
through the intervention of intrigue and the basest fraud.
His knowledge of sacred learning (if he has any) is acquired by study and industry, not inspired like that of the
Apostles. Therefore although they may call him *an Apostle*, we shall conclude with Tertullian, advers. Marc. lib. 1,
*The name is assigned in mockery to him to whom the nature im-
plied in the name is denied.*

Bellarmin was a Jesuit of Tuscany raised first by ClementVIII., in 1599, to a
Cardinalate, and afterwards to the Bishopric of Capua; which See he resigned to be near the Pope's person, and devote himself entirely to the affairs of the church. He died in 1621, in his seventy-first year; " bequeath-
ing one half of his soul," says Du Pin, " to the Virgin, and the other to
Jesus Christ!" thus affording a melancholy testimony of the power with
which the superstition of the Church of Rome enchains her members: for
this same strenuous defender of the doctrines of his Church, in the tranquillity of private meditation, comes to this conclusion in his book, De just.
lib. v. c. 7. prop. 3, " Because of the uncertainty of our own righteousness,
and the danger of vain-glory, it is the safest way to place our entire trust
in the alone mercy and benignity of God." His devotional writings evince
him to have been a man of undoubted piety; and, at his death, so impressed were the people with the idea of his sanctity, that it was necessary to
place guards to keep off the crowds which pressed round to touch his body,
or procure some relic of his garments.

* It is necessary for the reader, not versed in technical terms, to bear in
mind here the Ecclesiastical meaning of the word " *Ordinary*." Williams,
in his " Laws of the Clergy," thus defines it: " Ordinary, ordinarius (which
is a word we have received from the Civil law) is he who has the proper and
regular jurisdiction, as of course and of common right; in opposition to
persons who are extraordinarily appointed."

Secondly, an Apostle is bound to the preaching of the Gospel (*Woe is me, if I preach not the Gospel*), and that not in any one particular church, but every where: but the Roman Pontiffs do not think themselves obliged to preach through all the world, neither do they exercise that office at all: therefore they either lie when they call themselves Apostles, or act wickedly in neglecting to discharge the peculiar functions of an Apostle.

But perhaps it will be said, they send out preachers by their authority, and gather new churches in the Indies, and in the most remote parts of the world; and this property belongs to apostolic authority.

I answer, Nothing is less apostolic than to remain at home at ease, and send out others to labour: the Apostles indeed had inferior ministers under them, whose assistance they made use of; but they themselves in the mean time did not omit the preaching of the Gospel. Since therefore the apostolic work is not found in the Pope, neither is the apostolic nature: *for every thing evinces its own proper nature by its operations.** Add to this that he hath neither the power of working miracles, nor of conferring the Holy Spirit; and yet these were united in all who received apostolic authority from Christ. When the advocates of

---

* It may be seen by a reference to the history of the proceedings of their Missionaries in China, since Davenant wrote the above, and by the report of the Abbé Dubois, more recently, as to the result of his preaching in Hindostan, both on what anti-apostolic principles their preachers proceed, and what a different success attended them; and late statements from South America exhibit a woful description of their Priests and churches there. It has been asserted lately that the present Pope expends more money from his own coffers in promoting Missionary efforts of one kind or other than is raised by all the Missionary Societies among Protestants. If this be the case, whilst the above allusion to the results should satisfy Christians of the want of the main thing, yet such zeal, and sacrifice, and effort should, at the same time, reprove our lukewarmness and niggardliness.—For an ample account of Popish zeal, see " Adams's Religious World Displayed," vol. i. p. 323. A statement of Dr. Milner of America, given in the Missionary Register for June, 1830, and an article in the Christian Examiner for August, 1830, p. 611, both on the subject of papal zeal at the present time, are worth the reader's consultation. They contain important and instructive details.

the Pontiffs are pressed with these clear reasons, they are
compelled to shuffle, and to attribute a sort of half and
mutilated apostolic authority to their Pope. So Bellarmin, lib. ii. de Rom. Pont. cap. 12, says, Three things are
comprised *in the Apostleship :* First, that a man be immediately called and taught by God; and this he confesses
that his Romish Apostle hath not: Secondly, that he
should establish churches in those places where they never
were: Thirdly, that he should have the chief power over all
churches, and be the Ordinary of the whole Church: and
he says these two marks of the Apostleship do meet in the
Roman Pontiff. But Cajetan, in tract. 3, de Rom. Pont.
institut. confesses, *If we must speak formally and exactly,
Peter had no successor in his Apostleship more than the rest of
the Apostles : but beyond this Apostleship he was the ordinary
Pastor of the whole world : in this office of superintending the
universal Church the Pope succeeds him, and so far his chair is
called Apostolic.**

But neither must we concede this to the defenders of
the Papacy. First, because God doth not set over the
Catholic Church any universal Bishop fortified with apostolic authority, who may err, and draw those under him
into errors. With this argument Gregory checked the
pride of John of Constantinople. He says, Epist. lib. 4,
cap. 76, *The Catholic Church must needs miscarry, when he
falls who is called Universal.*† But it is agreed amongst the

* Cajetan ; otherwise Thomas de Vio, of Gaeta, another eminent defender of the Papacy, who flourished prior to Bellarmin. Besides the work
above-mentioned, he wrote notes on Aristotle and Aquinas, and an Exposition on almost all the Books of the Old and New Testament, which Mosheim describes as brief and judicious. Though an amiable man, he entertained such lofty ideas of papal authority, that in his efforts to reclaim Luther, he became a strenuous opposer of that Reformer; and in his proceedings both greatly lost his temper, and threw a cloud over his other excellencies. He was made a Cardinal, and afterwards Archbishop of Palermo ;
and accounted by Papists the oracle of his day.

† The well-known letter in which this sentence was given by Pope Gregory, commonly styled the Great, may be found at the end of all the complete copies of Brent's Translation of F. Paul's History of the Council of
Trent. It must be admitted, that, viewed with reference to his character,
there appears as much of personal ambition as of piety in this famous Epis-

defenders of the Papacy themselves, that the Pope may become an heretic, and in such case ought to be deposed. Distinct. 40, Can. Si Papa.

Secondly, he is not the universal Pastor of the Church, who, by virtue of his ordination, is bound to his own particular See: but the Roman Bishop, like any other, is bound down to his See, and to his Church of Rome; or, if he hath any more extended prerogative, he hath it by human, not by Divine right. And yet it is not of men, but of God alone to confer apostolic authority. So Cyprian: *No one of us appoints himself a Bishop of bishops. Be he whom you will, he has but the free control over his own jurisdiction.* Afterwards he subjoins that *the authority of*

tle; for Gregory was remarkable for his earnestness in exalting his See. Hence it has been justly remarked, that " there is no word in all the writings of Gregory wherein he more proudly boasts of the greatness of his Supremacy, than where he says, that he knew no Bishop who was not subject to the See Apostolic." Nay, this very letter is filled with assumptions of the same lofty kind; as where he asserts, that " to St. Peter was given the care and principality of the whole Church;" and that " the title of Universal Bishop was offered to the Bishop of Rome, by the Council of Chalcedon, and refused;" which appears to be altogether untrue. It is evident, however, that although pride and ambition were beginning to work in the Church on either hand, the grand principle on which all is built that has since brought the Church of Rome into such melancholy distinction was not, up to this period, admitted; for Gregory, in arguing with John of Constantinople against his adoption of the obnoxious title—Œcumenicus, or Universal—urges, that *it* was never given to St. Peter; none of the Bishops of Rome had ever assumed it; it was contrary to the Canons, to the Decrees of the Fathers, and an affront to Almighty God himself." But, in fact, through the letter, whilst he quarrels with the usurpation of the *Name* by his rival prelate, Gregory unreservedly claims the *Thing* both for himself and his See; to secure which he did not scruple to stoop to base flattery of the bloody usurper Phocas. Mr. Blanco White, in his interesting "Practical Evidences against Catholicism," imputes to Gregory that neglect of ancient literature, and the substitution of scholastic learning, by which the corruptions of Popery and the religious darkness of the world were fostered; and gives some extraordinary instances of his illiterateness; and it is the testimony of Ridley concerning Gregory, in his treatise against the errors of Transubstantiation, that " in his days both corruption of doctrine and tyrannical usurpation did chiefly grow." He was the inventor of the magnificent and pompous ceremonies attending the celebration of the Mass, if not of the Mass itself. The Translator cannot avoid adducing here the existing evidence of a fact communicated to him by a friend, who, on visiting Rome

the African Bishops is no less than that of the Roman.* If however they will not hear Cyprian, yet they will not reject the Council of Nice, which restricts that Œcumenical Bishop within his own limits; vide Can. 6.†

Lastly, an universal and apostolic Bishop may every where ordain Bishops and Pastors of his own right: but if the Pope should ordain a Bishop out of his own province, that would not be a lawful ordination; for so it was held by the Synod above-mentioned. It is quite clear that if any one be made a Bishop without the consent of the Metropolitan, that Synod determined him not to be a Bishop.‡ Cajetan meets this argument ridiculously, by

in 1825, observed in the Church of St. Maria della Modestia (formerly a Temple of Romulus), in the Via Sacra, an inscription in Italian literally thus: " The portrait of the most blessed Mary over the high altar spoke to Pope St. Gregory saying, ' Wherefore dost thou no longer do me reverence?' The Saint asked pardon, and granted to those who celebrate Mass at this altar the liberation of a soul from purgatory, *i. e.* of that soul for which the Mass is said." It is thus the Church of Rome has drawn to herself that wealth whereby she has maintained her power. Gregory was most severe in the point of celibacy of priests; but *dis*couraged the persecution of the Jews.

* Cyprian was Bishop of Carthage about the middle of the third century. The whole passage from which the above sentence is cited runs thus: " Neque enim quisquam *nostrûm* Episcopum se Episcoporum constituit, aut tyrannico terrore ad obsequendi necessitatem collegas suos adiget." It contains, as Bishop Kaye, in his Ecclesiastical History, p. 239, well observes, " remarkable expressions," and is evidently " aimed at some Bishop who had called himself *Episcopus Episcoporum.*"

† Council of Nice: Canon 6. " Let ancient customs prevail ; as for in-
" stance, those in *Egypt, Lybia,* and *Pentapolis :* That the Bishop of Alex-
" andria have power over all these, since the same is customary for the
" Bishop of *Rome.* Likewise in Antioch and other provinces, let the pri-
" vileges be secured to the Churches. This is as manifest as any thing at
" all, that if any be made a Bishop, without the consent of his Metropoli-
" tan, this Great Synod has determined that such an one ought not to be
" a Bishop. If any two or three, out of affectation of dispute, do contra-
" dict the Suffrage of the Generality, when duly passed according to Eccle-
" siastical Canon, let the Votes of the Majority prevail."
From a Translation of the Canons from the original Greek, by John Johnson, M.A. Proctor for the Clergy of the Diocese of Canterbury, in the Clergyman's Vade Mecum by him. 1714.

‡ The celebrated Translator of Josephus and Eusebius from Greek into Latin, *Ruffinus,* a Priest, who flourished a little after this period towards

saying, *It is one thing to speak concerning authority, and another thing concerning the execution of it: that the Pope hath the authority of ordaining in the provinces of other Bishops; but that custom has established his non-exertion of this authority.* If he hath this authority by right, it could not be so abolished by custom as to make that ordination actually unlawful which he might effect without the consent of the Metropolitan ; for *custom does not prescribe where a thing is forbidden by an express law,* says Hostiensis.* We do not deny that prerogatives have been con-

the close of the fourth century, in giving his sense of the 6th Canon of this Synod, is admitted to have stated it truly and clearly ; viz. That the ancient custom be kept both in Alexandria and Rome; that he (the Bishop of Alexandria) have the care of Egypt; the other (the Bishop of Rome) of the Suburbicary Churches, i. e. over all those places in Italy, Sicily, Sardinia, Corsica, &c. over which the Præfect, or the Vicar of the City of Rome, had jurisdiction in temporal affairs. And even the old *Latin* paraphrastical Version of these Canons confines the jurisdiction of the Bishop of Rome to the Suburbicary Churches. And not only these two Editions of the Canons, but those of other writers on them, call the several districts in which the Bishops of Rome and Alexandria exercised their jurisdiction, *Provinces;* whereas the district of a Patriarch was always called his *Diocese,* that of an inferior Bishop his *Parish:* And therefore by Metropolitans here must be meant those who had the largest Provinces, or were the most remarkable on account of the largeness of cities, and had a proportionable deference paid to them. The reason why such particular care was taken of the privileges of the Bishop of Alexandria was, that Meletius, Bishop of Lycopolis, being deposed about twenty years before this Council, by Peter, Bishop of Alexandria, in a *provincial* Synod, for idolatry and other crimes, did yet ordain several Bishops and Clergymen in *Egypt,* without the consent, and in opposition to the sentence passed against him by the Bishop and Synod. Against this the 4th Canon of the Council was probably framed :—" A Bishop ought to be *constituted* by all the Bishops that belong to the Province ; but if this be not practicable, by reason of urgent necessity, or the length of the way, Three must by all means meet together, and when they have the consent of those that are absent, signified by letter, then let them perform the ordination ; and the ratification of what is done must be allowed to the Metropolitan in every Province."

Let it further be observed, that the authority of Metropolitans must have been much older than this Synod ; for here their privileges are called *ancient customs.* Vide Johnson's Clergyman's Vade Mecum.

* Hostiensis. The author here cited by Bishop Davenant is Henry de Suza, a celebrated Civilian and Canonist of the 13th century, of such repute as to have been called " the source and splendor of the Law." He

ceded to the Roman Church, and to the Bishop of Rome,
by the ancients; but not because of his being the ordinary
Pastor of the whole Church, and armed with apostolic
authority by right Divine, but on account of the sobriety,
the consistency, and the distinguished learning of those
who, in the earliest times, were set over that Church; on
account of the dignity of the city of Rome, which was
the seat of empire; and, lastly, as Gerson says, by the
gracious and voluntary concession of other churches.

Now let us sift a few arguments of our opponents.

1. Pellarmin, lib. 2, De Rom. Pont. cap. 12, says,
Peter had the government of the whole church committed
to him; but some one ought to succeed therein as supreme
head by Divine right; and this successor can be no other
than the Pope.

I answer, there is nothing solid in this argument. First,
as it regards Peter, to whom they say the government of
the whole church was committed when it was said to him
alone, John xxi. 15—17, *Feed my sheep.* I confess, in his
character of Apostle, the power of feeding the flock of
Christ every where was given to Peter; but this was common to him with the rest of the Apostles, to whom also it
was said, *Go, teach all nations,* Matth. xxviii. 19. Secondly,
we deny that successors were appointed in this apostolic
power either to Peter or any one of the Apostles; for not
fresh Apostles, but Bishops, succeeded to Apostles.
Thirdly, if we allow a successor to Peter in apostolic
power, he will not be, by Divine authority, the Roman Pontiff; because no Divine authority appropriated the Roman
See to Peter. Whence even Cusa* does not hesitate to

---

was first created Archbishop of Embrun, and then Cardinal-Bishop of
Ostia in 1262; whence he derived the appellation of Ostiensis, or Hostiensis; under which title he is frequently cited, and by Davenant in the latter mode of orthography.

* Cusa was a profound Lawyer and Divine, created a Cardinal by Pope
Nicholas V. in 1448, and afterwards Bishop of Brixia. It is said that he
was the author of a Refutation of the Koran, addressed to Pius II. and
highly esteemed as a very learned production. A treatise of his concerning
" Learned Ignorance," in which he aimed to correct and reform the disor-
ders and abuses which the Scholastic Divines had introduced into the Semi-

confess, that, *if a Bishop of Treves should be chosen for the head of the Church, he would be more properly the successor of Peter than the Roman Bishop.*

2. They argue, the Church is one body, and hath one head on earth besides Christ : but any other head on earth besides the Pope is assigned by no one ; therefore he is the head and sovereign of the whole Church. And that it has a head on earth, he (Bellarmin) proves from those words, 1 Cor. xii. 21. *The head cannot say to the feet ye have no need of me;* but Christ can say this ; therefore there is a head in the Church besides Christ.

I answer; Although the Church be one body, and militant here in earth, yet no necessity obliges us to confess any earthly head of the whole Church; because Christ, who is ascended into heaven, is also in the world by his Spirit, and quickens and rules the whole Church ; but he forms particular churches, and governs them by particular prelates and ministers. The plea, however, which he brings from the Scripture is futile and childish : for the Apostle means not by *the head* and *the feet,* the Pope and the Church; but by *the head,* any man in the church endowed with eminent gifts ; by *the feet,* any humble or inferior person. This will readily appear if we weigh the scope of the passage. For he is not cautioning Peter against lording it over the Church; but he is warning those who were distinguished by spiritual gifts among the Corinthians, against despising their inferiors ; as Chrysostom, Ambrose, and Aquinas explain it.*

naries, is still extant. Yet this erudite man, notwithstanding the bold admission also above made, in order to sustain the Papacy set up the notion of a *running sense* of Scripture, which might be suited to the various *occasions* of the Church, and *adapted* to every *new rite.* Vide Dr. Wright's Sermon at Salter's Hall, in 1734—5, on " Scripture and Tradition."

* Though the champions for the Papacy in former ages of comparative darkness might think to impose upon the ignorant and unwary by such " futile and childish" modes, as even Bellarmin for want of better could employ in the plea here refuted ; yet in these days one would hardly imagine they would have the effrontery to risk it. However, in 1810, a Roman Catholic Priest in Lancashire, sent forth two octavo volumes of " Sermons ;" and in one of them, in support of Papal Supremacy, revived an old gloss upon

3. The Church would not be governed in the best way unless it were governed by one supreme spiritual head; but Christ left the Church instituted and governed in the best manner; therefore by one.

I answer; Christ alone is the spiritual Sovereign of the whole Church; but to institute an earthly sovereign, on whose will the whole Church should depend, would be the worst mode of governing the Church; because no mortal can discharge that office even moderately well. For how shall the Pope sitting in the Vatican, take care of the churches of the Indians or the Ethiopians? But that Pontiff does not aim at the care of churches, but at empire.

4. The Church is always increasing, and it must increase until the Gospel be preached in all the world: but this cannot be done unless there be one chief president, on whom the apostolic charge and trouble of preserving the whole Church and of extending it, may devolve; for no one ought to preach unless he be sent; and no particular Bishop can send beyond his own province.

Scripture, much akin in fallacy and plausibility to the one above, but managed with more ingenuity. For, with the most artful sophistry, carried on through two pages, he labours to prove that the words of our Lord to Peter, recorded John xxi. 15—17, " *Feed my lambs; feed my sheep,*" were a commission to Peter, in the first place to govern the faithful intended by *the lambs;* in the next, a jurisdiction over the pastors of the faithful, conveyed in the words "*Feed my sheep.*" The consequence, he concludes is, that " since Christ gives Peter a superintendence over his whole flock, he confers upon him a jurisdiction distinct from that of the rest of the Apostles—a jurisdiction more enlarged than theirs—a jurisdiction reaching over the whole body of the Church, over the taught and the teachers, over the governed and the governors." So that, as the Rev. Joseph Fletcher, in his excellent volume of " Lectures on the Principles and Institutions of the Roman Catholic Religion," justly observes, " according to this arguing the ' lambs' mean the ' sheep,' and the ' sheep' mean the shepherds!!!" It is to be believed, that this is the *general* mode of Popish instruction. The recently published discourses of a neighbouring Priest, under every cautionary restraint, might be adduced as containing abundant evidence of the truth of the assertion; and, more recently still, a distinguished Papal Orator, in the town where the Translator writes, was heard, in his ordinary pulpit exercises, labouring to establish his auditory in the belief of the doctrine of Transubstantiation, by attempting to prove, that it was *the uniform and universal belief of the Christians of the first four centuries of the Christian era!!!*

I answer; To send preachers to infidel nations is not now the work of apostolic power, but of Christian charity. Every Bishop therefore in the vicinity of any heathen nation, may, from the duty of charity, either by himself, or by others, preach the Gospel to them; and, if they should embrace the Christian faith, what is to hinder Bishops and ministers being set over them (if they require it) legitimately ordained by any other Bishop? To extend the Church therefore there is no need of a new Apostle.

We conclude, then, since the Pope of Rome is not immediately called by Christ—nor embued with Evangelical knowledge by direct and extraordinary inspiration of the Holy Spirit—nor endowed with universal power over the whole Church, he can by no mode of reasoning be styled *an Apostle,* or *Apostolic Bishop.**

Ver. 2.   *To the saints and faithful brethren in Christ, which are at Colosse.*

In these words is contained the second part of the title, which we call the Inscription, in which the Apostle describes both the place where they dwell, and the characteristics of those to whom the Epistle is sent: and this is entitled the *superscription* or *inscription* according to our custom, who are in the habit of inscribing these circum-

---

* The *grand* point at issue between Rome and her opponents, is the question of Infallibility : therefore, to the refutation of this from the actual history and tendency of her doctrines, Mr. Garbett's " powerful and valuable work" (as it has been justly styled) the " Nullity of the Roman Faith" is directed, and contains in its pages a refutation of the main arguments of their most famous modern defence, Bishop Milner's " End of Controversy." Upon the whole *Difficulties* of their system, it seems almost needless to refer to the well known volume of Mr. Faber in answer to the Bishop of Strasburg. For the recent attempts to remove the mass of crime that lies against their Church, Mr. Townsend's " Accusations of History" is quite sufficient. The present revival of this great Controversy, and the modern garb in which their advocates have cloaked the Papal tenets, have induced the Translator to refer the uninformed reader to works which appear to him to meet more especially the *existing* state of the discussion ; and the study of which will leave him void of excuse if he be entangled in the mazes of this never-slumbering and artful enemy.

stances on the back of our letters, as we have before remarked.

The persons saluted then have a threefold description;
First, from the place in which they live; 2. From three especial properties, *holiness, fidelity, brotherhood;* 3. From
the Author of all, viz. *Christ Jesus:* for they are *saints in
Christ, faithful in Christ,* and *brethren in Christ.*

Concerning the Colossians we have spoken already in
the preface; nor is it necessary to add more. This only
we shall observe by the way, that although the Catholic
Church can never wholly perish, yet each particular church
may fall away from the true religion. This happened to
these Colossians; and to all the churches which Paul honoured with his Epistles: for either they were entirely
swept away by Mahometan perfidy, or corrupted by some
foul superstition. All boast about local succession, therefore, is empty, unless a succession of true doctrine be
likewise proved. *They are not the children of saints,* says
Jerome, *who hold the place of saints, but they who practise
their deeds.* Disease succeeds to health in the same person, darkness to light; so, in the same land, superstition
may succeed to Religion, unbelief to faith. But let this
suffice here.

Saints.] That is, sanctified by the laver of baptism.
Whence, says the Apostle, 1 Cor. vi. 11, *Ye are washed, ye
are sanctified.* But when the Apostle calls all baptised
persons *saints,* he speaks according to the rule of charity,
which directs us to presume good of every one, unless the
contrary be shewn. And for the very best reason baptised
persons are called *saints.* For saintship imports two
things : First, cleansing from impurity : whence Isidore
writes, That *a saint is so called from two words* sanguine
tinctum; i. e. *to be as it were tinged with blood; because anciently they who wished to be purified, were sprinkled with the
blood of the sacrifice.** Secondly, it denotes a special de-

* Isidore : usually stiled Isidore Pelusiota, to distinguish him from two
other eminent divines and writers of the same name, in the fourth and fifth
centuries. He was a distinguished disciple of Chrysostom, a Monk, and

dication to the Divine worship: whence we call not only men, but temples and vessels, holy; because they are set apart to sacred uses in the worship of God. In both these respects a baptised Christian is rightly called *a saint.*

For, first, he is in baptism cleansed from original corruption, and the imputation of all sins. Whence it is called, in Titus iii. 5, *the laver of regeneration.* And in Acts ii. 38, it is said, *Be baptised every one of you for the remission of sins.* Hence also that saying of Nazianzen, *The water cleanses the body visibly; the Spirit accompanying it also invisibly cleanses the soul.* Hence also that ancient custom of putting white robes upon baptised persons; by which ceremony they signified the purification of their souls effected by virtue of holy baptism, as Lactantius expresses in that line, De Pascha v. 93,

Fulgentes animas vestis quoque candida signat:

Likewise the white raiment betokens their resplendent souls.

Neither does this purification consist alone in the washing away of sins, but in the combined infusion of spiritual graces; of which subject Parisiensis elegantly writes,* *Like as a royal treasurer gives the gifts promised by the king to him who produces the royal signet; so the Holy Spirit, the*

Priest of Damieta, anciently called Pelusium, in Egypt. He left 2012 letters, said to be written in a very superior style, on Scripture doctrine, discipline, and morals. Mosheim commends him as avoiding the allegorical mode of interpretation, so prevalent in that age; and asserts that his epistles discover more piety, genius, erudition, and wisdom, than are to be found in the voluminous productions of many other writers. An edition of his letters in Greek and Latin, in folio, was published at Paris, 1638. Might he not have had in view, in the above remark, the rite of ceremonial cleansing under the Law, as dwelt upon in Heb. ix. 12—22?

* The person here quoted under the epithet ' Parisiensis,' was William of Auverne, created Bishop of Paris in 1228. He was one of the most learned schoolmen of his time; being eminently skilled in theology, philosophy, and mathematics; he was also distinguished for his piety; and was moreover perhaps the most useful writer of the thirteenth century; for whilst his contemporaries were occupied in verbal quibblings and metaphysical intricacies, his works were directed to the promotion of practical godliness, the least understood of all sciences in that age of erudite ignorance and theological wrangling.

*dispenser of spiritual gifts, imparts spiritual graces to those
whom he beholds bearing the sign of holy baptism.* Peter
promises this to the baptised, Acts ii. 38, *Be baptised every
one of you in the name of Christ,* AND YE SHALL RECEIVE
THE GIFT OF THE HOLY GHOST. And this is the first
reason why Paul calls baptised persons *saints.*

Secondly, they are called *saints,* because in baptism they
are in an especial manner dedicated to the service of God.
For in baptism a covenant is entered into with God. He
receives us under his protection; we acknowledge him for
our Lord, and renounce all other lords, viz. the world, the
flesh, and the devil. We are therefore, as it were, certain
consecrated vessels, set apart from profane uses to the
sacred service of God. In this respect Nazianzen calls
baptism, *the covenant of a more holy life with God;* and
Peter, 1 Epis. iii. 21, *the answer* (επερωτημα) *of a good conscience towards God.*

From the consideration of this characteristic many inferences might be deduced ; we shall deduce three.

1. Whereas the Apostle calls not this or that good
man, but the Colossians promiscuously, saints, as many as
put on Christ by baptism; hence we learn, that we must
think and speak well of all who profess religion, unless by
clear and manifest deeds they shew themselves to be ungodly and hypocrites. For the Apostles always, when
they descend to particular men or churches, presume every
Christian to be elect, sanctified, justified, and in the way
of being glorified, until he himself shall have proved himself to be wicked or an apostate. So Paul writing to the
Corinthians affirms indiscriminately concerning them, *Ye
are washed, ye are sanctified, ye are justified,* 1 Cor. vi. 11.
For as in those things which relate to faith, we must speak
and think according to Scripture, which is a certain and
infallible rule : so, in other things which relate to charity,
it is sufficient to think and to speak according to the probability of appearances. This rule may deceive ; yet not
by any fault or hazard of him who thought better of another than he truly deserved, but rather of that hypocrite,

who was a different and much worse man than he appeared or seemed to be.*

Secondly, Whereas all of us who have been baptised are called *saints,* we are admonished of our duty, which is to SERVE GOD IN HOLINESS AND RIGHTEOUSNESS ALL THE DAYS OF OUR LIFE. For if we are without the life of saints, the name of saints will profit us nothing. *The participation of names or titles,* says Tertullian, *determines not the real state of things.* Although therefore hypocrites may be classed under the same denomination with true saints, yet they shall not receive the same rewards from Him who searches hearts.

Lastly, Whereas we are called *saints* because we have been consecrated to the service of God in baptism, it plainly follows, that every Christian who serves the devil, the flesh, or the world, is guilty of sacrilege ; for he perverts vessels consecrated to God, i. e. his body and his mind, to profane, nay to devilish uses. Well spake the Orator, *It is established by the common law of nations, that mortals may not appropriate to their use that which is consecrated to the service of the immortal gods.* But how much

* How different *Roman Catholic* principles are to this rule of Christianity let the following fact determine, taken from Gauntlet's preface to his " Lectures on the Apocalypse." Speaking of the prevailing sentiments of Papists in regard to Protestants, he says: " Some years ago I was in the habit of frequent intercourse with several emigrant French priests. In my conversation with one of them, who subsequently held an eminent situation in a Roman Catholic College, our discourse turned on the salvability of individuals without the pale of the Romish Church. My opponent, for such in this point he was, strenuously argued on the negative side of the question. In order to bring his views to a practical bearing, and to try how far personal feelings might be a barrier to his creed, I remarked, ' Then you consign me among the other heretics to eternal damnation ?' The substance of the firm and consistent reply was, ' I can make no exceptions; there is no salvation out of the Catholic Church.' My antagonist, it will be seen, was a genuine son of Rome—a true Papist, who was neither afraid nor ashamed to maintain the doctrine of that anti-catholic and anti-christian Church, of which *he* was a consistent and zealous minister." Doubtless instances of an opposite character and sentiment exist, and the Translator could give some ; but they are rare ; and, as Mr. Gauntlet well observes, those who take more becoming views of the subject dissent in an essential point from the *infallible* Church : they are not true Papists.

more shameful and abominable is it, that the devil should
be allowed to take for his use a Christian, holy, and dedicated to God by baptism.*

So much concerning the first property.

Faithful.] This is the second property wherewith the
Apostle dignifies the Colossians. Some would have this
title to be an explanation of the former; as though the
Apostle had said, We, by the law of charity, judge all
Christians holy; but they alone are accounted saints before
God who are truly faithful: For *God purifies the hearts of
men by faith,* Acts xv. 9. For although the sacraments are
not only signs representing, but also offering grace,† yet
unbelief spurns and repels the grace offered by God.
Hence that very remarkable saying of Augustine, *Whence
is there so much virtue in the water, that it should but touch
the body, and cleanse the heart, except by the word making it
so; not because it is spoken, but because it is believed?* And
Tertullian reproves those who think that the ungodly and
unbelievers are made partakers of the grace offered in the
sacraments: *Certain persons,* says he, *so think, as though
God were bound to perform even to the unworthy what he hath*

* The Translator would here take occasion to recommend most earnestly
to every reader who should not have seen it, whether an enquirer or a controversialist on the subject under treatment, the speedy and careful perusal
of a work by the Rev. H. Budd, entitled, " Infant Baptism the means of
National Reformation." If duly weighed it is a volume pre-eminently calculated to settle disputation on the question, or, as the Author states his
design, in the opening of the first letter, " to compose our differences;"
but especially is it adapted to lead to practical and beneficial results of a nature highly to be prized and desired in the present age. Whilst his pen is
thus occupied, the writer would also beg leave to commend in a similar
manner to general perusal, three volumes of " Essays on the Liturgy and
Collects" of our Church, by the Rev. T. T. Biddulph, as suitably displaying the principles avowed by every baptized Churchman, and enforcing the
correspondent character and conduct that should, as a consequence, be
maintained and exhibited by all such. Indeed, for sterling divinity, and
Christian learning, and for all the purposes of the Christian life and experience, as well as for admirable practical illustration of the most important
parts of our invaluable Liturgy, those Essays cannot be equalled, whilst
they are written in a fervid and most elegant style.

† " Non sunt tantum repræsentativa signa, sed etiam exhibitativa."

promised, and they make his liberality to be compulsory. But God watches over his treasury, nor suffers the unworthy to steal in.

Others by *faithful,* understand those who persevere in faith received. For it is very probable that some were drawn away from evangelical doctrine by those who, in the place of the Gospel, obtruded philosophical speculations and Jewish ceremonies. By this term therefore he both commends those who remained stedfast in the true doctrine of faith, and obliquely rebukes others, who, following those new teachers, turned aside from the faith of the Gospel to errors and superstitions; and he points them out as unworthy his salutation. Therefore to be initiated into the Christian profession by baptism avails nothing unless there be a stedfast continuance in the same. *Not faith received, but faith retained, quickens,* says Cyprian, Epist. lib. epist. 5.*

---

* Epist. xiii. p. 29, edit. Oxon. 1628, or Epist. vi. p. 11, edit. Paris, 1726.

Cyprian could with peculiar propriety and emphasis deliver such a principle as the above, since, during the severity of the persecution under Decius, about the years 249 and 250, he had witnessed and proved the results of a mere profession of the faith, and the effects of its abiding influence in the heart. He too had experienced in himself all its power, and at last died a martyr to his stedfastness in the succeeding persecution under Valerian and Gallienus. His parents were heathens, and he himself had continued such to an advanced period in life. His conversion was brought about by one Cœcilius, a priest of the Church of Carthage, whose name he afterwards took ; and who entertained so high an opinion of Cyprian's character as to commit to him the care of his family at his death. Cyprian had often employed his rhetoric (of which science he had been long an able teacher) in defence of Paganism ; but on his conversion, as a proof of his sincerity, he composed a treatise entitled " De Gratia Dei," which he addressed to Donatus : he next composed a piece, " De Idolorum Vanitate." His behaviour both before and after his baptism was so highly pleasing to the Bishop of Carthage, that he very soon ordained him a priest, when he consigned over all his goods to the poor, and gave himself wholly to divine things. The Bishop dying the year after, none was judged so proper to succeed him as Cyprian. Compelled soon afterwards to flee from Carthage, to avoid the fury of the persecutors whom Decius had let loose, and whose cry was " *Cyprian to the lions,*" he wrote in the place of his retreat, pious and instructive letters to his flock, and also to the Libellatici, or those pusillanimous Christians, who procured certificates of the heathen magistrates to shew that they had

Brethren.] The Colossians, and so indeed all Christians and faithful are called *brethren* for many reasons :

First, on account of their profession of one Religion, and the worship of one and the same God. For Scripture calls all those *brethren* who profess the same Religion. So Deut. xviii. 20, *Let not the king's heart be lifted up against his brethren*; and Matth. xxiii. 8, *Be not ye called Rabbi; for one is your Master, and all ye are* BRETHREN. Secondly, faithful and godly men are called *brethren*, because of the fraternal affection and love which ever flourishes among them. This fraternal charity the Apostles every where inculcate. Thus Rom. xii. 10, *Be kindly affectioned one to another with brotherly love.* This brotherly love Tertullian calls, *the jewel of the Christian name :* for true love is the heritage of Christians. Thirdly, we are called *brethren*, because we have one and the same father, i. e. God. For all the godly are by regeneration and adoption children of God himself, and thenceforward brethren with one another. *He gave them power to become the sons of God,* John i. 12. Lastly, we are called *brethren*, because we are grafted into the same mystical body of Christ, and are quickened by one and the same Spirit. As therefore they are brethren naturally, who have derived natural life and descent from the same parents; so they are brethren spiritually who derive their spiritual life and origin from the same principles.

Hence we are taught how great ought to be the concord among Christians; how far they ought to be removed from hatred and envy; how wicked it is to rejoice in the evil or

complied with the Emperor's order, in sacrificing to idols. At his return to Carthage, he held several Councils for the correction of evils which the persecution had introduced, for settling the course to be pursued towards such as professed repentance, and for the due regulation of the Church. But ere long he fell a sacrifice to that fidelity with which he *retained* and laboured to commend the faith of the Gospel, being beheaded in the persecution in 258. How important, then, does the principle adduced by our Expositor, from him, appear, in considering the life and the times of Cyprian ! Should such periods for " the trial of the faith" of professors now arise, how many Libellatici would soon be discovered ! It is a matter of serious inquiry how many Cyprians would be found to exhibit, as well as enforce, the *quickening* efficacy of faith, and a stedfast adherence to it ?

disgrace of another; and various lessons of the same kind. For *among brethren there ought to be a common feeling of fear, joy, grief. They ought not to raise themselves upon each other's ruin, nor by the fall of one to seek their own elevation.**

In Christ Jesus.] The Apostle has dignified the Colossians with the brilliant titles of *holiness, fidelity, brotherhood :* now he shews from whence they obtained these so eminent endowments, viz. from *Jesus Christ,* the author and giver of them all.

First, as to our holiness : we are rightly called saints in Christ Jesus, because only by the Spirit of Christ, and by virtue of his blood, are we cleansed from our sins, and sanctified in the sacrament of baptism. The water represents externally the pledge of grace ; but the Spirit internally works the works of grace, August. Epist. And upon Psalm lxxxvi. *Preserve my soul for I am holy,* the same Father says, *If thou shalt say that thou art holy of thyself, thou art proud; Again, being a believer in Christ, and a member of Christ, if thou shalt not acknowledge thyself to be holy thou art ungrateful.-- Say unto God, I am holy, for Thou hast sanctified me.* Moreover we are called *saints in Christ,* because not only does he effect our sanctification, but by a gratuitous imputation he communicates to us his righteousness and perfect holiness, Phil. iii. 9.

Secondly, we are also called *faithful in Christ Jesus ;* as well because true faith always looks to Christ Jesus, and acknowledges him the only Mediator and Saviour of the human race, as because that Christ by his Spirit works in us both our holiness and our faith.

Lastly, as to our brotherhood ; we are also called *brethren in Christ Jesus.* For whether we be called *brethren* on account of our agreement in faith and religion, Christ is the only Teacher of the Christian faith and of religion ; or on account of brotherly affection, Christ hath shed abroad this love in our hearts ; or on account of God being the common Parent of us all, we are adopted through Christ

---

* De alterius ruina attolli, et prostrato superscendere haud oportet.— Tertull. De pœnit. cap. 10.

and in Christ among the children of God ; or, lastly, on account of our being grafted into one mystical body; Christ is the Head of this body.

Hence we learn, that there is no sanctity, or faith, or brotherhood of any avail to salvation, unless it be grounded in Christ. For Jews, Mahometans, Heretics, have a certain sanctity of their own, a faith of their own, and also a brotherhood of their own : but all these they have apart from Christ. A Jew wishes to be *sanctified;* but by the rites of Moses, not by the blood of Christ. A Mahometan wishes to be accounted *faithful;* yet not in Christ, but the most wicked impostor Mahomet. A Papist wishes to be a *brother ;* but a Fraciscan, a Dominican, and any thing rather than a Christian brother ; which name among them is base in comparison with those novel fraternities.

And thus far as to the *Inscription.*

Here the Translator must be permitted to observe, if such be the doctrine of the Gospel, as hath been thus shewn by our Expositor—if such the obligations entailed and required by Baptism, and by our taking upon us the Christian name through that sacramental rite; then, from what have we fallen in the last century ? What have multitudes in this Christian country been doing; in reviling the *saints* of God and pouring contempt upon that holy Name ; plunging into all the pomps and vanities they pledged themselves to renounce ; abandoning their first principles and plainest duties; breaking the unity of the household of faith ; neglecting the service of God ; and so, bringing into contempt the Religion to which they had sworn subjection, and which they ought to have cherished, adorned, and promoted to the utmost of their power ! And if these things have constituted the national guilt of this Country, can any wonder that God should have permitted us to be subjected to our enemies, and exposed again to the influence, and perhaps, the domination of Infidelity and Popery ?

We come now to the latter half of the second verse.

Grace be with you and peace from God our Father, and from the Lord Jesus Christ.

In these words is contained the third part of the title, which we call the Salutation; wherein two things are to be remarked : the blessings which the Apostle desires for the Colossians ; viz. *grace and peace ;* and the authors of these blessings, *God the Father and Christ.*

Grace be with you.] In the first place we may make this general remark, that the Apostles changed or rather amplified the ancient salutation of the Hebrews. For their usual salutation was, *Peace be to thee :* but after the mystery of human redemption was revealed, in which God opened the fountain of grace to mankind, they also added *grace.* And these two blessings are thus united for the best possible reason. For *grace* is introductory good ; *peace* is final good : he therefore who wishes these two blessings to any one, includes also every intermediate benefit. But let us consider them separately.

The term *grace* denotes three things : First, the gratuitous act of the Divine will accepting man in Christ, and mercifully pardoning his sins. This is the primary meaning of this word, which the Apostle every where enforces. *By grace are ye saved,* Ephes. ii. 5. *Being justified freely by his grace,* Rom. iii. 24. This gratuitous love of God is *the first gift,* says Altissiodorensis, *in which all other gifts are bestowed.* Aquinas acknowledges this grace of acceptation, Quæst. disp. de grat. art. 1. Secondly, under this term *grace* the Apostle comprises all those habitual gifts which God infuses for the sanctification of the soul. So faith, love, and all virtues and salutary endowments are called *graces.* The words of the Apostle in Ephes. iv. 7. have this sense : *To every one of us is given grace according to the measure of the gift of Christ.* The Papists acknowledge this inherent grace almost exclusively ; and in the mean time think too lightly of that accepting grace which is the fountain and well-spring of it. Lastly, *grace* denotes the

actual assistance of God, whereby the regenerate, after
having received habitual grace, are strengthened to perform good works, and to persevere in faith and godliness.
For to man renewed and sanctified by grace, the daily aid
of God is still necessary for every single act.　When therefore the Apostle wishes *grace* to the Colossians, he desires
for them the gratuitous favour of God, the habitual gifts
of sanctification, and the unceasing actual assistance of
God.　The union of all these is necessary : inherent grace
is not given unless the grace of acceptance has preceded
it ; neither being given is it available to the production of
fruits, unless also the efficacious help of God follow and
accompany it through every individual action.

And peace.]　The Hebrews used this expression as we
use the expression health or joy : it signifies a state of
things prosperous, and flowing according to our wish,
marked by no calamities either public or private.　So Gen.
xliii. 27, *Is there peace to your father?* or, as we render it,
Is your father well?　According to Tremellius,* *Is he doing
prosperously ?*　And in Psalm cxxii. 6, *Pray ye for the peace
of Jerusalem* (i. e. Ask for those things which pertain
thereto).　But with the Apostles it is used in a more extensive sense, and comprehends, in a more especial manner,
spiritual joy and prosperity.　Therefore under this term
peace Paul, in the first place, desires for them internal
peace, or peace of conscience, which arises from the grace
of God accepting us for Christ's sake : hence said Christ,
John xiv. 27, *My peace I give unto you;* and the Apostle,
Rom. v. 1, *Being justified by faith we have peace with God.*
This is that *peace which passeth all understanding,* and it for-

---

* Tremellius:—A learned Jew of the sixteenth century ; a native of
Ferrara, in Italy ; first converted to Christianity in the Church of Rome,
and afterwards to the Protestant Religion, and some time settled in Cambridge as Professor of Hebrew ; but driven again to the Continent on the
predominance of the Roman Catholic party upon the accession of Mary.
He is celebrated for a Translation of the Bible, simple and perspicuous,
and closely adhering to the Hebrew, published first in 1575, and again, with
corrections, in 1587.　It was very popular with the Reformed Divines.—
Vide " Horne's Introduction," &c. vol. ii. under the head " Modern
Latin Versions."

tifies and guards the heart of a good man as with a military garrison; so Phil. iv. 7, φρουρήσει τὰς καρδίας ὑμῶν, *it shall keep your hearts.*

Secondly, as Jerome explains it, he wishes them brotherly peace; for so he means in that passage, *Pacem rumpentes gratiam excludunt—breaking peace they exclude grace.* And this peace is both a great and desirable good, and very frequently celebrated by the Apostles, and acknowledged as the special gift of God; whence it is said, 1 Cor. xiv. 33, *He is the God of peace and not of confusion,* and elsewhere (2 Cor. xiii. 11), *the God of peace and love.* The seeds of schism had been scattered abroad; there was need therefore of peace.

Lastly, he wishes also that external peace, viz. the well-being of the Colossian Church, and of all the individuals in it; but yet only so far as it does not militate against their spiritual good: for sometimes it conduces more to the welfare of the faithful that they be afflicted than that they enjoy external peace and tranquillity.

This is the sum of the apostolic wish: from whence we may gather many things worthy of observation.

From the order itself we are taught three things:

1. Inasmuch as he places *grace* before *peace,* he teaches us that this is first of all to be desired, that we may have God propitious. If he be hostile, even blessings will be turned into a curse.

2. He teaches besides, that true peace cannot belong except to those only who are in favour with God. *There is no peace to the wicked,* i. e. to the man not reconciled by Christ.

3. Lastly; from the very order in which these benefits are placed, he shews that all good things which fall to the lot of the godly, are as it were streams from this fountain of divine grace.

From the thing itself desired;

4. Paul shews us by his own example the duty of every minister of the Gospel; which is, not only to preach grace and peace to his people, but from their inmost souls to

intreat and implore the same from God by incessant prayer: neither is sufficient of itself.

5. He reproves the folly of this world, in which almost all wish for themselves and their friends, health, riches, and honours ; but grace, peace, and other spiritual good things, they neither regard, nor think of. But Christ commands us to *seek first the kingdom of God*, Matt. vi. 33.

6. He comforts the godly and faithful by shewing them that the grace of God, and the peace of God *they* always possess ; in comparison of which good things whatsoever fall to the wicked are filth and refuse—σκύβαλα. *A God appeased*, says Bernard, *tranquillizes all things, and to behold him at peace is to be ourselves at peace.* Bernard, in Cant. 33.*

And so far as to the blessings desired. We shall now speak of the Authors of them, whom the Apostle designates in these words following,

From God our Father and from the Lord Jesus Christ. In which words he points out both the fountain and the channel of all grace, and he describes both by their relation to us :

From God our Father.] The fountain of grace is God

---

* This Bernard is termed the last of the Fathers of the Church ; he was a Monk of the Cistertian order, and Abbot of Clairval, born in 1091, and who died in 1153 ; after having acquired the greatest authority in the Church of any person in his time, even surpassing that of the Pope himself. " No emergency of importance in Religion occurred in which he was not consulted as an oracle; his free censures were received with awe and reverence in the remotest parts of Europe ; and his example rendered the new order of the Cistertians so popular, that he lived to see the foundation of one hundred and sixty Convents, which acknowledged him as their second head." He was equally distinguished in his controversies against various heresiarchs, and especially the famous Abelard, and by his successful encouragement of the second Crusade ; for " through his commanding eloquence he put in motion princes, nobles, and people throughout the European Continent," and descended to the grave followed by the title of ' The Great St. Bernard.' Such sentiments, however, as those quoted from his writings by our Expositor constitute his truest greatness, and these, it seems, abound in his works, often republished in 2 vols. folio : the Paris edition of 1690 being esteemed the best.

himself. For if by *grace* we understand the gratuitous love of God towards us, this love flows immediately from the Divine will, is not called forth by human merit : Hence says God, Jerem. xxxi. 3, *I have loved thee with an everlasting love ; therefore with loving-kindness have I drawn thee.* And most divinely does Bernard speak, in Cant. Serm. 59, *And God loveth : not that he derives this from any other source, but from himself the fountain of love ; and therefore his love is the more intense, not so much because He hath love, as because he is himself love.* 1 John iv. 16. The love of God does not find us worthy, but makes us worthy of his love.—If we understand by *grace* the habitual gifts of holiness, it is manifest all these emanate from God alone to our souls. *Every good gift and every perfect gift is from above, and cometh down from the Father of lights,* James i. 17 ; which the Schoolmen shew by many reasonings ; viz. That nothing can be a physically operating cause in the production of grace but God alone. 1. The infusion or the production of grace is analogous to the manner of creation ; inasmuch as it neither has any innate cause in the subject in which it acts, nor any materials by whose capabilities it might be educed by a natural agent : it is therefore of God alone, who out of nothing made all things, to infuse and impress grace : *God will give grace and glory,* Ps. lxxxiv. 12.

2. Grace arises out of the supernatural participation of God ; but it is the work of the divine goodness only to communicate himself in this gratuitous manner to his creature.

3. Grace is not imprinted on the soul, unless by that cause which is able to work immediately in the soul itself; but it is the privilege of God alone to be able to glide into the human soul, and to change and incline it by internal operation : Therefore God is the fountain of grace. Hence the error of Thomas,* with Bellarmin and his other follow-

---

* Thomas Aquinas, noticed by our Author sometimes under the one name and sometimes under the other, was born at Aquino, in Italy, in 1224. The number of his works is prodigious, amounting to seventeen volumes folio ; though he died as early as the age of 50. He is stiled " The

ers appears evident, who attribute to external sacraments a physical causation of grace.

Our Father.] God, as God, as Creator, wills good to all his creatures, but not all good. For he wills the communication of the good things of nature not only to wicked men, but to the very brutes; because he bestows them as the Author of nature: but the good things of saving grace he communicates to his children alone; because these he dispenses as the Father of mercy. And for this reason the Apostle added *Our Father.* On this account the Saviour when he prescribed a form of prayer, taught us to invoke *Our Father;* because there is no hope of obtaining the good things of grace unless we are adopted among his children. And from this paternity of God he

Angelical Doctor;" and his authority among the Schoolmen was almost decisive in Theology. Like our own Hooker he was little less eminent for his self-denying humility, than for his wide erudition and deep reasoning powers. It is said that when Pope Clement IV. shewed him a vast heap of wealth, observing, ' You see the Church cannot now say, Silver and gold have I none;' ' True,' replied the great Schoolman, ' neither can she now say to the sick, Take up thy bed and walk.'—Though, like other fallible men, and especially voluminous writers, he is sometimes found in error, yet Protestant Divines and Scholars have done justice to the vast attainments of this wonderful man. Our Expositor frequently quotes him as authority in points of importance. Dean Philpotts says, " I do not affect to be deeply versed in his writings; but I have read enough of them to bear testimony to the uncommon vigour and astonishing acuteness of his mind." (Letters to Charles Butler, Esq.) And Mr. Southey speaks of him, as " a man whose extraordinary powers of mind few persons are competent to appreciate." (Vindiciæ Ecc. Aug.) As calculated in an especial manner to stamp the character of the man, and as a hint to those who forget that, *Bene orâsse est bene studuisse,* it may not be improper to insert here,

The Prayer of Thomas Aquinas before commencing study:—

" Ineffably wise and merciful Creator! illustrious Source of all things! true Fountain of light and wisdom! Vouchsafe to infuse into my understanding some ray of Thy brightness; thereby removing that two-fold darkness under which I was born, the darkness of sin and ignorance. Thou, that makest the tongues of infants eloquent, instruct, I pray Thee, my tongue likewise: and pour upon my lips the grace of Thy benediction. Give me quickness to comprehend, and memory to retain: Give me a facility in expounding, an aptitude in learning, and a copious eloquence in speaking. Prepare my entrance into knowledge; direct me in my pursuits, and render the issue of them complete: through Jesus Christ our Lord. Amen."

concludes, whatever good is necessary to the pious shall be bestowed upon them by God; *How much more shall your Father who is in heaven give good things to them that ask him?* Matth. vii. 11.—Let these things suffice concerning the fountain of grace, viz. *God.*

And from the Lord Jesus Christ.] The Apostle here points out the channel of grace, viz. *Jesus Christ,* the Mediator between God and men. God the Father himself is the fountain of grace; but he chooses that it should be derived to men through and for the sake of his Son: For as by the first Adam sin is derived to those who, after the flesh, are descended from him; so by the second Adam, viz. Christ, grace is derived to those who are spiritually regenerate. Therefore Christ is said to convey grace to his people, either by the efficacy of his operation—or the benefit of his intercession—or the merit of his passion. As he is the Head of the Church, it is his peculiar office effectually to quicken his members, and to communicate grace, i. e. spiritual life and motion to them. Being a Priest, he prays and intercedes for this grace. Having offered himself a sacrifice acceptable to God, he meritoriously acquired the favour and grace of God for the Church. Hence it is that in the Holy Scriptures all grace and spiritual blessedness is set forth as given to us in Christ: as in Ephes. i. 3, 4, *Blessed be the God and Father of our Lord Jesus Christ, who hath blessed us with all spiritual blessings in heavenly places in Christ: according as he hath chosen us in him before the foundation of the world, that we should be holy and without blame before him in love:* iv. 16, *From whom the whole body fitly joined together and compacted by that which every joint supplieth, according to the effectual working in the measure of every part, maketh increase of the body unto the edifying of itself in love;* John i. 16, *For of his fulness have all we received and grace for grace.*

The Lord.] Christ is designated by the relation which he bears to us; for he is Lord of us, and indeed of all creatures. And this title belongs not only to the divine nature, but also to his assumed nature: For God the

Father would have *all things to be subject unto him;* and *made him to sit above all powers,* Ephes. i. 20, 21, and Heb. ii. 8, *He put all things under him.* But he is *the Lord* of the godly, not only by right of Sonship, but also by right of redemption and deliverance.

Ye see whence grace flows to us, *From God our Father, through our Lord Jesus Christ.* Hence observe

1. They who are estranged from God through obstinate perseverance in sin, are destitute of quickening grace; and, if we speak of spiritual life, they are dead carcases, not men. For as a man who turns himself away from the sun, deprives himself of light and heat; so he who turns himself from God through sin, deprives himself of the influence of saving grace: for *grace is from God.*

2. They who are not adopted children, assuredly cannot either ask or expect any grace from God. In order therefore that we may approach the throne of grace with the assurance of faith, God must be intreated that *He would send the Spirit of adoption into our hearts, whereby we may cry unto him, Abba, Father.* For this grace is not simply from *God,* but from *God the Father.*

3. Let him who seeks grace implore neither the saints, nor even the blessed mother of Christ; but ask it from the Father in the name of Christ his Son: for that which the Son requires, who is the medium of grace, is easily obtained. Therefore the Papists err, who say that no grace comes from heaven to earth without passing through the hands of Mary.

4. Since Christ is our Lord, let us conduct ourselves as good and faithful servants. It is the duty of servants to frame their life and manners according to the will of their master; diligently to discharge the duty assigned them by their master; to form no friendships with the enemies of their master; if they err humbly to submit themselves to their master; and innumerable other things of the like nature; which, so long as we neglect, we deny that Christ is our master not by our lips, but by our lives.

And thus far we have unfolded the apostolic salutation. From the consideration of which arises an important controversy between us and the Papists, which we shall briefly touch upon. The Apostle, as you have heard, desires for the faithful *grace and peace from God, and from the Lord Jesus Christ ;* i. e. gratuitous acceptance for Christ's sake, adoption among the children of God, and assurance of the remission of sins : Hence it is enquired Whether the faithful can or cannot assuredly determine with themselves that they are in favour with God, and that their sins are remitted them for Christ's sake, in whom they have believed ?

Our opinion is that every faithful and truly justified man may, and ought, infallibly to believe,* that his sins are remitted to him as an individual, and that God is reconciled to him; i. e. that he hath this *grace and peace,* which the Apostle desired for the Colossians.

The opinion of the Papists is, That they who are truly justified and in favour with God, yet neither can nor ought to believe that they are reconciled to God and justified; but to hope and conjecture only that they are in a state of grace, and have obtained remission.

We establish our opinion by these arguments :

1. From the nature of faith. He who is endued with true faith sees, by the very light of that faith kindled in his heart through the Holy Spirit, that he believes in Christ, and is justified by faith : but he who sees this, at the same time is able to conclude that he is in favour with God, and that his sins are remitted him. For Scripture plainly states, *Being justified by faith we have peace,* Rom. v. 1. *He that believeth on the Son hath everlasting life,* John iii. 16 and 36. Therefore the whole difficulty lies in this, To shew that a believer is authorised to say, not from conjecture and opinion, but from conviction, I believe in Christ. This is proved from Augustine, De Trin. xiii. 1, *That which we are commanded to believe we are not able to see; yet faith itself when it is wrought in us, we know to be in us.* So Thomas, *Whosoever hath knowledge or faith, is sure that he hath it ;*

---

* An expression corresponding to this opinion in one of the Collects of our Church is " perfectly and without all doubt." Vide Collect for Saint Thomas's day, a striking and godly prayer, that, as Churchmen, it may be even so with us.

because it is of the nature of faith, that a man should be certain of those things of which he hath faith   To which purpose also Cajetan thus writes, *By the certainty of faith any one knows that he hath the gift of faith infused into him, and he believes this, as he believes other things which he does believe, as for instance, the incarnation of Christ,* &c.   Durandus* also writes, *He that hath faith is as certain that he hath it, as he is certain of any thing else: For, believing, he experiences that he believes,* Lib. iii. dist. 23. qu. 7.   Thomas alleges this reason; *Because every state of the intellect itself is the proximate cause of its own recognition, since its very essence exists in the mind.*†   It may be confirmed by many testimo-

---

* Durandus: one of the most learned Lawyers of his time, who flourished in the thirteenth century, and whom Davenant often quotes. He was a pupil of the celebrated Henry de Suza, after quitting whom, and taking his Doctor's degree, he taught Canon law at Bologna and Modena, and published a famous work entitled " Speculum Juris," which gained him the surname of " Speculator."   Being introduced by his former Tutor, now Cardinal-Bishop of Ostia, at the Court of Rome, he was employed by Clement IV. and four succeeding Pontiffs, in important and honourable charges.   Among other posts of distinction assigned him, he was made Master of the sacred palace.   The person holding this office was " a kind of Domestic Chaplain, or preacher of the Pope."   A part of his jurisdiction in this capacity " referred to the printing of books, and the power of prohibiting them."   Of this office Mr. Mendham has given a full and interesting account in his valuable work on the " Literary Policy of the Church of Rome," Ch. i. pp. 11—13.   In the progress of his preferments and honours, Durandus was created Bishop of Mende, and employed as Legate to Gregory at the Council of Lyons.   Being recalled to Rome, he was afterwards created Marquis of Ancona, and then Count of Romagna, which provinces he governed during the tumults of the Guelph and Ghibelline factions.   The " Rationale Divinorum Officiorum" is, however, the best known of his works, and has been the most frequently reprinted.   It is a detailed view of the rites and worship of the Roman Church, and contains a competent portion of fable.   He died at Rome in 1296.

† On account of its ambiguity and the difficulty of translating this passage, the original extract is here adduced : " Quia omnis habitus intellectivæ partis, ex hoc quod per essentiam suam in mente consistit, est principium proximum suæ cognitionis."   *Recognition* seems to the Translator to be the sense of " *cognitio*" in this place, as including the mind's assent and confession of its own perceptions.   In the verses subjoined 1 Cor. ii. 12, and 2 Cor. xiii. 5, we may observe the nicety of the Apostle's expression ; in the first ειδω'μεν, simple perception ; and in the second επιγινωσκετε, the acknowledgment of this perception.

monies of Scripture, that the regenerate know that they are born again of the Spirit, and the faithful know themselves to be the faithful: Thus 1 Cor. xi. 12, *We have received the Spirit which is of God, that we may know the things which are given us of God;* 2 Cor. xiii. 5, *Know ye not that Christ is in you except ye be reprobates?* 1 John iv. 13, *We know that we abide in him, and he in us, because he hath given us of his Spirit.* For faith, as light, not only makes other things, but itself visible.

2. From the nature of the promises. The promises of gospel grace and the remission of sins, through the reconciliation of Christ, are to be so believed by us as to afford firm and solid consolation: but unless I in particular believe that I am reconciled, and that I am absolved from sins, they cannot yield this consolation. The former is evident, because the very end of gospel grace and of the divine promises is, that *we may have strong consolation,* Heb. vi. 18. But that general faith of the Papists, that every one who believes truly and lives piously, hath remission of sins; or that conditional faith, I, if I am faithful, am in the grace of God, does not yield *strong consolation,* because it may consist with despair. *It is necessary,* says Bernard, *to believe that you cannot have forgiveness, unless by the mercy* of God; but at the same time believe this, that your own sins are forgiven you through him.* Bernard, De annunt. Serm. 2. And the reason is because promises of God do not take effect until they have been accepted by us; although, therefore, remission of sins, upon condition of faith, be offered to all, yet it must of necessity be accepted by men individually and singly, that it may be useful and salutary to each one. Promises are not accepted by those who do not, but by those who do know, and understand, and feel, that they apprehend and accept them.

3. The Holy Spirit specially seals each particular believer, and makes him sure of his adoption, by a certain wonderful and secret testimony: for he is given to every

---

* The *Indulgentia plenaria, plenior* and *plenissima,* with other expressions, shews that the Scholastics gave the force of forgiveness to *Indulgentia,* as if in opposition to absolute justice.

believer as a pledge of divine love; and he, finally, pronounces in the hearts of the godly, that they are in favour
with God : which testimony they both may and ought to believe. Therefore they do believe in particular that they are
in the grace of God, and that their sins are remitted them.
The authorities from which all this is proved are well
known : Rom. viii. 16, *The Spirit beareth witness with
our spirits that we are the children of God;* Gal. iv. 6,
*Because ye are sons, God hath sent forth the Spirit of his Son
into your hearts, crying, Abba, Father;* and Ephes. i. 13,
14, *Ye were sealed with that Holy Spirit, after that ye believed, which is the earnest of your inheritance.* Nor is this
testimony fallacious or conjectural, but certain and infallible in all in whom it is found. For the word is *the ministration of the Spirit,* 2 Cor. iii.; and faith conceived by the
ministration of the word, is always joined with the witness of the Spirit itself. Therefore the impression of faith
by the Holy Spirit, in the heart of a particular man, is, as
it were, a particular testimony that he is in grace, and that
he is a child of God. So Bernard, Serm. 5, De dedicat.
ecclesiæ, *Who can tell whether he is worthy of love or hatred?
Who hath known the mind of the Lord?   Here it is necessary
that faith should come to our aid ; that what is concealed concerning us in the heart of the Father, may be revealed to us by
his Spirit ; and his Spirit bearing witness may persuade our
spirits that we are the children of God.* But he persuades
by calling and justifying us freely through faith.

Bellarmin replies, that the Holy Spirit witnesses to our
spirits only by some experience of an internal suavity and
peace which produces nothing better than a conjectural
certainty. De justif. lib. iii. cap. 9.

But Bernard rejects this jesuitical comment : for he says
this testimony is received by the act of faith ; and that the
Holy Spirit persuades our spirit that we are the children of
God, by faith, not by fallible conjectures. So Chrysostom in viii. ad Rom. *When the Spirit testifies can any doubt
remain ?*

4. From the effects of faith. True believers have *boldness, and access with confidence to God the Father by faith;*

Ephes. iii. 12, and Heb. x. 22. But he who continues doubting, and ignorant whether he be a child of God or not; whether he be in a state of enmity or reconciled; he cannot approach the throne of grace with this confidence; he cannot call God his Father, but with the greatest hesitation; much less can he confidently ask those things which are necessary for salvation from him, as from a Father.

Bellarmin rejoins, For enabling us to approach the throne of grace with confidence, it is not necessary that we be certain of our justification in particular; a positive assurance from the Catholic faith, that Christ suffered for us, died, rose again, and intercedes with the Father, is sufficient.

But this reply is invalid; because although it may be a general truth that the death of Christ was sufficient for all; yet is it also true, that the fruit of the death, of the resurrection, and of the intercession of Christ, actually belong only to those who are implanted into Christ; that I should be sure, therefore, the benefits of Christ belong to me, it is necessary I should be sure also, that I am become a member of Christ, i. e. am justified and reconciled to God. For, if I doubt whether I am effectually called and justified, I must also doubt, whether I am *without Christ, without God, an alien to the commonwealth of Israel, and a stranger to the covenants of promise,* or not, Ephes. ii. 12. When all these things are left in doubt, what place is there for confidence?

These are our arguments: several others we shall omit for the sake of brevity. Now let us proceed to

The arguments of the Papists.

Bellarmin, De justif. lib. iii. cap. 4, endeavours to prove the uncertainty of grace and of the remission of sins,

From the Scriptures.

1. From Prov. xx. 9, Who can say I have made my heart clean, I am pure from my sin? Although therefore some may be clean from sin, yet they themselves do not know it, neither have they an infallible testimony of their purity and righteousness.

I answer, that no one can say this : neither are any clean from indwelling sin, as Bellarmin fancies ; but this does not forbid the assurance of the remission of sins and of a state of grace. For Paul acknowledges indwelling sin ; and yet believes that he was freed from condemnation, and from the imputation thereof, Rom. vii. Therefore though his argument may be good with the Papists, who place their hope in works and inherent righteousness ; yet it is frivolous among the orthodox, who seek justification from faith and grace, not from the law and their own righteousness.

2. *No man knoweth whether he is worthy of love or hatred, but all things are held doubtful as to the future.* Eccl. ix. 1.

For the version I contend not with our adversaries. It is clear that Solomon spake of the judgment which is formed from external events; for he subjoins, *because there is one event to the righteous and to the wicked,* ver. 2. He does not therefore deny that the godly may be certain, through faith, of the favour of God, but by events. Which exposition Bernard approves, who says, that *faith here comes to our help, and reveals to our hearts that we are the children of God.* as we have before shewn.

3. *Concerning propitiation be not without fear, to add sin unto sin: And say not His mercy is great ; he will be pacified for the multitude of my sins.* Ecclesiasticus v. 5, 6. This place strangely galls the heretics.

Perhaps it does gall heretics, but it does not in the least affect the orthodox ; for it leads to no conclusion against the assurance of remission. In the first place, because the passage may be understood of those who thought that their sins were taken away by the expiatory sacrifices, although they continued in the intention of sinning, and added sins to sins daily : such people as these who without true conversion of heart, thought their sins were expiated by victims, it does direct to be not *without fear of their sin being propitiated,* or (as it is in the original) *of the propitiation of their sin.* And this exposition those words following confirm, (ver. 7) *Thou shalt not delay to turn to the Lord ; for suddenly his wrath shall come forth,* &c. But we may allow it to be understood concerning those whose sins, upon true repentance, have been remitted : They ought not to be without fear concerning propitiation and remission of sins ; for instance, adultery, theft, drunkenness, or any other : but that fear is, not lest the sin should not be remitted, but lest the same and greater imputation should return if it be again committed. *For sins remitted return through ingratitude, not as it regards the act, but inasmuch as he who falls again is for his ingratitude rendered liable to much greater punishment than if his sin had not before been absolved.* Durand. lib. iv. dist. 22. q. 1.

4. A fourth argument Bellarmin draws from those passages where justification and remission of sins is proposed under a condition. *If the wicked man shall repent for all his sins, he shall live,* Ezek. xviii. *Ye shall be my friends if ye do what I command you,* John xv.; and the like. But no one can be certain by the assurance of faith, that he is turned to the Lord with all his heart, and hath true faith and penitence such as is required ; since no where in Scripture is a testimony of this kind found concerning our faith and penitence in particular.

I answer ; To receive the grace of remission, the condition of faith and true penitence is necesssry on our part; but what he adds, That no one knows whether his faith and repentance be such and so great as is required by God, is most false. For justification does not depend on the degree or measure of faith or penitence, but upon the genuineness : And every man who hath received faith and repentance by the gift of the Spirit, has experienced that his faith and penitence are true, and not hypocritical, as was before shewn. Whence that saying of Augustine in Ps. cxlix. *There is a mode of glorying in the consciousness that you have ascertained your faith to be sincere, your hope certain, and your love without dissimulation.* As to his plea, that a testimony concerning *our* faith, or *our* remission in particular, is not found in Scripture, we will explain it when we come to the reasonings of Bellarmin; for there this will recur.

5. He endeavours to find a fifth testimony from those passages where remission is proposed to the penitent under the form of a doubt: Joel ii. 12, 14, *Turn unto me with all your heart. Who knows if God will return and repent?* And Acts viii. 22 (in reference to Simon Magus), *Repent, if perhaps the thought of thy heart may be forgiven thee.* These, and like passages, says Bellarmin, signify an uncertainty of remission, not in respect of the divine promise, but in respect of our disposition.

To the first testimony another Jesuit shall answer this Jesuit. Thus then Ribera* upon this passage, *Who knows if God will return and repent?* says, *That is, perhaps he will not suffer the Chaldeans to come into your land, nor that ye shall be led captives, if ye will repent.* The prophet, then, does not direct them to doubt of the remission of their sins if they turn, nor does he command the truly penitent to doubt the fact of their penitence; but he shews that he himself is not certain concerning the removal of external judgments, although they turn: respecting this, therefore, they might hope, concerning the other they might be certain. Moreover, he shews from Ambrose, that this phrase is not always expressive of doubt; and from Gregory, that it sometimes indicates the difficulty of a thing, and the scarcity of instances in which it has been done.

To the second likewise Ribera answers; That *Peter had no doubt of his sin being remitted, on his repentance; but he doubted if the penitence of Simon would be real.* That may

---

* Ribera (Franciscus de): A Spanish Scholar of the sixteenth century; who acquired a high reputation for his intimate acquaintance not only with the Latin, but also the Greek and Hebrew Languages; at the same time being considered one of the most excellent Divines of his age. Being ordained a Priest, Ribera retired to his Alma Mater at Salamanca, to pursue his theological studies in uninterrupted privacy, and was then persuaded to enter the Society of Jesuits; a member of which body he continued till his death in 1591, after having filled the Chair of Professor of Divinity in the University of Salamanca for thirty years. He wrote Commentaries on the Minor Prophets and on St. John's Gospel, with other works, mostly published after his death, and eulogised in high, but evidently deserved and just terms, by his Roman Catholic Biographers.

be also added which Tremellius has observed : *This is not the phrase of one who doubts, but of one rising above his doubts and difficulties.*

6.   He, lastly, brings forward those passages which recommend diffidence to the godly and faithful themselves; as, *Happy is the man that feareth always,* Prov. xxviii. 14. *Work out your salvation with fear and trembling,* Phil. ii. 12. Therefore we ought not confidently to believe (says he) the remission of our sins.

I answer; Filial fear does not exclude certainty concerning reconciliation and the remission of sins; on the contrary, it is necessary that he who believes that he is reconciled to God, should so much the more fear, lest by giving the rein to his lusts he should fall into fresh guilt.   These quotations do not direct us to be doubtful about the remission of sins, but to be careful and fearful of offending God.—And so much concerning the testimonies that are brought from the Scriptures.

Those which he has brought from the Fathers are of no value; for they prove only this, that although a man may not be conscious to himself of any sin, yet this affords no certainty of his being free from sin ; which we readily confess.   But it is one thing to be absolved *from* sin, and quite another to be *free from* sin.

But let us come to the reasonings of Bellarmin, which he promises us shall be no common ones :*

1.   Nothing can be sure by the certainty of faith, unless it be either directly contained in the word of God, or, by evident consequence, may be deduced from the word of God : but that such, or such a man, hath his sins remitted him, is not contained in the word, nor evidently deduced from it; therefore it is not sure with the certainty of faith. The Minor is proved by the word of God testifying only in general that sins are remitted to the faithful and penitent: but that Peter or John may believe or may repent, is not revealed in the word, nor can it be correctly inferred from it ; because there is no other inference than this, The word of

* Egregias rationes—conclusives !

God testifies, that they who truly believe and are converted obtain remission of sins : I am sure that I am a true believer and penitent; therefore I have obtained remission of my sins.   The Minor, says Bellarmin, is not only false, but also impossible without a special revelation.

Answer.   Before I come to the Minor, I will premise a few words in explanation of the Major.   What Bellarmin says, That nothing can be sure with the certainty of faith, unless it be propounded or deduced from Scripture, must be understood concerning the doctrine of faith which we believe, not concerning the habit or act of faith by which we believe.   For example : That God is three in one is a doctrine of faith; of this therefore we are sure because it is thus written in our Bible; but my believing in the Trinity in Unity, is an act of my faith, the certainty of which is not written in the Scriptures, but on the tablets of my heart.   Certainty of the former respects the whole Church ; therefore it is revealed in Scripture, which lies open to the whole Church : but the certainty of the latter, that is to say, of the habit or act of faith dwelling in the heart of this or that man, respects him alone, and is therefore discovered to him alone by a reflex act of the mind itself, and still more clearly by the internal operation of the Holy Spirit, who, together with faith and grace, gives a consciousness of that faith and grace being received, as we have before proved.   Here we may adduce Scotus, who, 3 dist. 23, says, *Like as I believe that God is three in person and one in essence; so also I believe, that I have faith infused, by which I believe this.**

* Davenant here cites from Duns Scotus, a famous Scholastic Divine who flourished in the fourteenth century ; a Briton by birth, educated first in the Convent of Franciscan Friars at Newcastle, and then sent to Oxford, where he made rapid progress and was soon distinguished.   It is said that not less than 30,000 students came to Oxford to hear his Lectures : This led to his transfer, by his Order, to Paris, where he was appointed Regent of the Divinity Schools.   He was considered one of the first wranglers of his time, and was an indefatigable writer.   Such was his acuteness and ability as to obtain for him the epithet of Doctor Subtilis ; but differing with his Master Aquinas about the efficacy of divine grace, he gave rise to a controversy which engaged the learned in eager and trifling disputes for

Another observation must be added which also pertains to the Major; viz. that every conclusion is of faith which is drawn from one proposition contained in Scripture, and another following by fair consequence; whether it be known by sense, or by reason, or in any other mode. This Gerson teaches, De vita spirit; and Medina.

Now I come to the Minor; and I deny that it may not be maintained by evident inference from the word that this or that believer hath his sins remitted. For Scripture speaks to individuals; Rom. x. 9, *If thou shalt confess with thy mouth the Lord Jesus, and shalt believe in thine heart that God hath raised him from the dead, thou shalt be saved.*

But Bellarmin urges that the Minor proposition is as yet wanting, viz. I confess, and I believe : therefore the conclusion, I shall be saved, cannot be derived from faith.

I answer, as above, that this Minor does not respect any general doctrine of faith, but the particular act of the believer : it must not therefore be sought in our Bibles, but in our hearts. But now if by any spiritual perception, or certain experience, or, lastly, by the testimony of the Holy Spirit, or by all these, the Minor proposition be established, the conclusion will be of faith, because the Major proposition was of faith. And we have before proved from the Fathers, from the Schoolmen, and from the Scriptures, that believers have a clear knowledge of their faith and reconciliation : the same things therefore we shall not again repeat.

Still our adversary urges ; We see many to be really deceived, thinking they have faith and grace when they have not. For many heretics boast the assurance of faith ; many also think, though not renewed, that they have obtained faith, and the remission of their sins from God : therefore they have not this certainty of which they make such a parade.

I answer; all this is nothing to the point. For we do not maintain that every man who dreams that he has faith, grace, and the remission of sins, is really possessed of

years; and of the twelve folio volumes which resulted from all his labour and study, how small a portion would probably repay the trouble of perusal!

these gifts; but that every one who is indeed possessed of them, knows also that he truly believes, and is in favour with God, &c. The Jesuit concludes affirmatively from the Major to the Minor, in this manner : An heretic and carnal man is deceived, in judging concerning faith and grace; therefore the truly faithful and renewed man may also be deceived. Like as a man is deceived, who in a dream thinks not that delusions but realities are presented to his mind, yet it follows not from thence that he is, or can be deceived, when he is satisfied that he is not asleep, but sees the things placed before his eyes : so the heretic and carnal man, dreaming about faith and grace, is deceived, fancying that he possesses the realities; but the truly re-newed man beholds these things presented as it were to his mental eyes, in the watchfulness of open truth, not in the vision of dreaming vanity; he therefore cannot be deceiv-ed. At last he asks, By what mark shall we prove that we are not deceived, and that others are? Foolish question! By what sign will you prove to one sleeping, that he is not awake, but that you are? By the experimental certainty of watchfulness itself, which hath a clearer and stronger perception, I do not think, but I know that I am awake : the dreamer thinks the same, but he is deceived. So by a certain experimental proof the faithful know that they have faith; yet they are not able to prove this to others, who do not perceive the internal emotions of their hearts : Neither can they persuade those dreamers that they have not faith, be-cause indeed they adhere, if not more confidently, yet more pertinaciously to false notions than to true ones.

2. This article of faith, *I believe that my sins are remit-ted me*, is laid down in no summary of faith; therefore it is not proper to believe it.

The conclusion is utterly invalid; however I shall not stop to repel it; but I answer, that the article is laid down in all creeds. First, by evident consequence. For when I say, *I believe in God*, (as Augustine, and after him all the Schoolmen have it), I say not only that I believe that there is a God, or that I believe his words; but *that I myself love him, and through believing in God go to him, and am in-*

corporated among his members. For all these things are implied in the words, *I believe in God.* Compend. theol. 5. 21. Secondly, it is laid down expressly by that article, *I believe in the forgiveness of sins.* For that which Bellarmin pretends is not the sense, I believe that remission of sins is given in the Church; which the devil and any reprobate may believe: but I believe remission of sins to be given me through Christ, because I believe in him. This Aquinas himself seems to grant, De justif. art. 4, where he says, *In the justification of a sinner, it is not necessary that all the articles of faith be in actual contemplation at the time, but only that God be contemplated as justifying and remitting sins; in which the other articles are implicitly included.* In quæst. disp. in respon. ad 9mo. Here I ask, To whom is God regarded as forgiving sins? Is it to any undefined individual, or to the justified person himself? Beyond doubt, to that man himself, who is then meditating on the remission of his sins.

But again he objects, If we are bound to believe the remission of our sins, then whoever does not believe this is an heretic: but he neither can nor ought to believe this, who offends wilfully and remains in mortal sin: therefore every such sinner is an heretic; which is contrary to reason.

Bellarmin is deceived in two points: First, in this, that he determines him to be an heretic who does not believe whatsoever he ought to believe: for not the defect of faith, whether of act or of habit, constitutes an heretic, but a pertinacious opposition to the doctrine of faith. For, if every one be an heretic who does not believe the mysteries of the Christian faith, all Gentiles would be heretics; even all Christians who are not renewed would be heretics: for no one believes any article of faith by scriptural and infused faith, before he has received the gift of faith in regeneration. Secondly, that is not by any means sound, which he says, That a wilful sinner is not bound to believe the remission of his sins. For he is bound to surrender his will; he is bound to repent, and also to believe God, who promises remission to the penitent. We say not, therefore,

That he, voluntarily remaining in grievous sins, can believe that sins are remitted him, or ought in his present condition so to do: but we say, that he, by the help of God, may, and is in duty bound to come out of that state, and to believe this.

3. It is not expedient that men should have certainty concerning the remission of their sins and special grace; for he who is confident that he is justified, easily becomes proud as a Pharisee.

I answer, He who is confident that he is justified by inherent righteousness and his own works, is easily puffed up: but he who believes that he is justified freely, thenceforward glories in God, in himself is abased: For, *what hath he which he hath not received?*

4. God hath revealed the remission of their sins to some by special favour, as Authors testify concerning St. Anthony and St. Francis. But why should he reveal that to certain persons by special grant, if the assurance of it be common to all the faithful?

The credit of these narrations rests with the authors. But I answer; There is nothing to prevent that which is believed through faith, from being more distinctly and evidently shewn by special revelation, if such be God's will. Paul believed through faith the bliss of the future state; yet God was pleased to communicate to him in a trance a brighter vision of the celestial happiness. So, although they believed the remission of their sins, yet God would impart to them a more manifest assurance of it.

5. The most perfect and holy men have trembled and doubted concerning their state and the remission of their sins: how therefore is an assurance of special grace and remission set before all believers?

Answer. We do not maintain that true believers never doubt either the remission of their sins, or the state of their reconciliation with God; but we contend that these doubts arise from the flesh, not from faith. This, therefore, is the difference between us and the Papists: They commend doubt in the faithful themselves, and attribute it to the virtue of humility; we recognise it as sin, and say

that it is a remnant of sin : they leave a believer in perpetual doubt; we say that he at length breaks through it, and
is convinced by faith that his sins are remitted, not by
conjecture, or hope only, into which, as the Papists suppose, deception may enter. But that, whilst we are in
this frail body, faith may abide in a man who is subject to
frequent doubts, is evident from Matth. xiv. 31, *O thou of
little faith, wherefore didst thou doubt?*—This the Schoolmen
also grant. *In a believer, an idea may spring up in opposition
to that which he most firmly holds,* Aquinas, De fide, art. 1.
And in another place, *The certainty of faith implies the stedfastness of adhesion, not the quiescence of the intellect.* So
Durandus, Lib. iii. dist. 23, qu. 7, *Faith may be subjected to
some degree of doubt, and yet be sound.*

It is not, therefore, necessary, that the assurance of faith
exclude all doubts, but that it prevail.

And these are Bellarmin's extraordinary conclusives,
with which he opposes the assurance of faith, conceding
in the mean time the assurance of hope to the faithful ;
concerning which distinction I shall also add a few remarks,
and conclude.

I ask of the Papists, then, whether they mean human
hope, i. e. hope arising from probable conjectures and the
deduction of human reason ; or divine and scriptural hope,
i. e. a virtue inspired by the Holy Spirit. If they say that
the godly are assured of grace and the remission of sins
by human hope, they allow nothing more to the godly, than
what the unbeliever may have; if by inspired hope, let
them hear their own friend Durandus,* Lib. 3 : *That which
depends upon inspired hope cannot but come to pass.* Scripture
also assigns the same certainty to this hope as to faith.
Rom. viii. 24, *We are saved by hope;* and xv. 13, *The God
of hope fill you with all joy and peace in believing, that ye
may abound in hope, through the power of the Holy Ghost.*
Faith, therefore, is the eye of this hope ; and this hope is
excited and established by the Holy Spirit, whose gift it

* Vide Note p. 38.
E 2

is : unless, therefore, faith be blind, and the Holy Spirit excite to false persuasion, there will be the same certainty in inspired hope as in faith. For inspired hope not only comprehends that pleasing expectation of future good, which lies in the will; but the undoubted assurance of obtaining those things which subsist in the realising and self-appropriating act of the mind ; so also faith : as Parisiensis, De mor. cap. 3, rightly observes.

Finally, I add the confession of adversaries : of Catharinus,* who in the Council of Trent, maintained that *the faithful have the assurance of divine faith as to their own grace*

---

* Ambrose Catharinus, of Siena, a Dominican Friar ; a celebrated Divine of the sixteenth century, who was one of the Theologians deputed to the Council of Trent in 1545, where he displayed remarkable ability. He is represented by Roman Catholic Biographers, as having, in that Council, " distinguished himself as much by the singularity of his opinions, as by his profound learning." The fact seems to be, that along with his defence of some peculiarities of Popery, he commented freely upon the distinctions which the Romish Church draws between Divine faith, and the faith of the Church ; and in the various discussions in which he took a part, he proved himself not only an able Divine and Rhetorician, but he boldly maintained and defended some scriptural truths alleged against Luther as heretical. Vide Father Paul's History of the Council of Trent.—He was, however, soon afterwards created Bishop of Minori, and from thence translated to the Archbishopric of Conza in 1551 ; and died suddenly at Rome in 1553.

Since writing the above, the Translator, as he had some difficulty at coming to what appeared to him the truth relative to Catharinus, has been pleased on finding that the Rev. Mr. Scott, in his survey of the Council of Trent, vol. 2 of the " Continuation of Milner's Church History," corroborates the view he had taken. Page 272, he observes ; " On the nature of justification knowing how much the Church of Rome confounds it with sanctification—making it to include an infused habit of grace, and not simply to be acceptance to the favour of God—we are surprised and gratified to find some leading characters openly asserting the forensic sense of this term." Then p. 276 : " On Free-will, Catharinus maintained, that without God's special assistance man cannot do what is morally good ;" p. 279, " We may add, that Catharinus avowed the same sentiment which was adopted by our own Milton (viz. with respect to election), and by Dr. John Edwards."

No wonder he should have been represented by his Biographers as " maintaining singular opinions ;" or that F. Paul, the faithful historian of the Council of Trent, who disclosed all its secrets, should have been pronounced by such writers, " a *Calvinist* in a Friar's frock !"

and justification: of the Divines of Cologne, who write in Enchirid. Christ. institut.* *That it is necessary for justification that every one should assuredly believe that his sins are remitted him:* of Bellarmin himself; who is forced to confess that the hope of Christians should be most sure, as well on the part of the will as of the understanding; and that by reason of a peculiar disposition only, it is accompanied by any fear. But we have before shewn that these fears and doubts do not take away assurance, but oppose it, and at length are put to flight by faith resisting, and cleaving to the divine promises.

We conclude, therefore, that every true believer hath, and believes that he hath that *grace* and *peace* of God which Paul wishes for the Colossians.

---

* Cologne long held a conspicuous rank among the Papal cities of Germany, and was noted for its University and the zeal of its Clergy. In 1536 Herman de Meurs, its then Archbishop, having embraced Lutheranism, and adopted the Reformation in his Archiepiscopate, sent for Beucer and Melancthon to preach in his province, assembled a Council of his Bishops and Clergy, and drew up a new code of laws for their regulation. Probably this *Enchiridion* was one of the results of their sittings on this occasion: for the writer is informed, that in Seckendorf's Comm. de Lutheranismo ad Indicem 1. Hist. Schol. &c. mention is made of such a book as written in German under the title *Enchiridion Plebeii,* in 8vo. The Papists in Cologne were offended at it as containing the Lutheran doctrine, and wrote against it. Most likely it was translated into Latin. The Papal answer might adopt the title of the book intended to be answered. But the above-cited proposition, adduced as from an adversary, is hardly consistent with any modification of Roman doctrine on the subject. Herman was deprived of his Archbishopric in 1547, and his successor Adolphus summoned a Council of the Bishops and Clergy, which, according to Du Pin, sat from March 11, of that year, to April 6, 1549, to restore matters that had been unsettled, and adopt such regulations as were deemed necessary to adjust the affairs of that church; and doubtless every thing was *revised* which Herman had introduced, though the Bishops and Clergy that had concurred with him might guard against much Popish restoration. But the Translator has not been able to trace out any thing corresponding to the work in question. In Howell and Co.'s Catalogue for 1829, there is mentioned, under the title Colon, *Canones,* &c. with *Enchiridion Christianæ Institutionis,* appended; date 1538, and in *folio:* but the latter work may have been in another *form* and date, and bound up with the former.

Verses 3, 4.

3.   *We give thanks to God and the Father of our Lord
Jesus Christ, praying always for you.*

4.   *Since we heard of your faith in Christ Jesus, and of
the love which ye have to all the saints.*

We have dismissed the inscription or title to this Epistle.
Now follows a preface or exordium, adapted to conciliate
their good will ; which is the second portion of this chapter, and extends from this third verse to the twelfth.   Its
parts are three, 1. A congratulatory proposition, in verse
3d.   2. The causes of this congratulation narrated and illustrated, from the 3d to the 9th.   3. A solemn prayer for
the increase of all spiritual good things, from the 9th verse
to the 12th.

1.   The congratulatory proposition ; *We give thanks to
God, and the Father of our Lord Jesus Christ,* &c.

We give thanks.]   The persons congratulating are denoted
in this first word, and also the mode of congratulation.

The persons who rejoice and congratulate, on account
of the faith and love of the Colossians, are Paul and Timotheus, preachers of the Gospel.   Whence it appears
how godly ministers are affected towards the people of
God ; viz. that they rejoice not so much because they receive temporal fruit from their flock, as that the flock of
Christ reap spiritual fruit from their preaching.   This is a
mark of true love and pastoral affection, that he rejoices
in their good as much as in his own ; especially in their
spiritual good.

The mode of congratulation, and of expressing apostolic
joy is by giving thanks, 'Ευκαριστοῦμεν.   To give thanks, is
to declare oneself grateful for a kindness received, by
acknowledging it, and by proclaiming the author of it.
For in this the apostolic congratulation differs from civil or
ordinary congratulations : in the latter, we are wont to celebrate the fortune, or the industry, or the prudence of
those to whom, because some great good has happened,
we are glad ; but the congratulations of the Apostles are
nothing else than simple renderings of thanks, in which

they celebrate the benignity of Him who bestows spiritual gifts on men. Now who that is, is declared;

To God and the Father of our Lord, &c.] Here the person is described to whom thanks are presented by the Apostle. And he is described as well by his absolute name, that it is God; as by his relative title, that it is *the Father of Christ.* The Apostle employs both with the best design.

In the first place, he gives thanks to God because He is the Giver of all good: but although he designates the first person in the Trinity, yet he does not exclude the rest. *For the works of the Trinity, as it respects things external, are undivided.* Therefore what God the Father gives to the creature, the same the Son gives, and the Holy Spirit. But because the first person is the fountain of Deity, therefore the rest are understood where he is named.

Observe, 1. From the apostolic example, we here learn, in all our joy for good things bestowed either upon ourselves or others, that the recollection of God ought instantly to occur to us; because whatever is *joyful* and *salutary* comes of his beneficence.

2. We are admonished of this, that it behoves us, as often as we observe any one adorned with remarkable gifts from God, to break out into the praises of God and to giving of thanks: for God will have this payment of praises and thanks to be rendered to him, by all those who hold his benefits, as a recognition of his supreme dominion. So the Psalmist, cxvi. 12, 13, says, *What shall I render unto the Lord for all his benefits towards me? I will take the cup of salvation, and will call upon the name of the Lord.* Every man is bound in the debt of honour (as the Schoolmen say), to render something to that person who has done him a favour. But God needs not our good things; we should therefore render to him what is his own, i. e. the glory of his benefits. If we are unwilling to do this, as he who does not acknowledge his feudal lord, by this crime of ingratitude loses his copyhold; so he who does not acknowledge God, the Author of his good, may in justice be deprived of that good.

And the Father of our Lord, &c. These words are not so
to be understood, as though God were one, and the Father
of Christ another ; but are to be explained in this manner;
to God and the Father of Christ, i. e. to God, which God is
also the Father of Christ: or so, *We give thanks to God and
the Father of Christ,* i. e. to Him who is both the God of
Christ, and at the same time also the Father of Christ.

He is called *the God of Christ* in regard of his human
nature. For the human nature of Christ, like other creatures, hath God for Creator and Preserver; whence Christ
hanging upon the cross, cried to the Father, *My God, my
God, why hast thou forsaken me?* Matth. xxvii. 46 : and in
John xx. 17, said, *I ascend to my God and your God.*

But he is called *the Father of Christ* also in respect of
each of his natures. For the Father by an eternal and ineffable generation hath communicated to his Son his Divine
essence. I say by an eternal generation : because we must
not think in divine things that God the Father is prior to
his Son, as among creatures the father always is. Well
spake Damascenus,* Ἐπὶ μὲν οὖν τῆς τοῦ Ὑιοῦ γεννήσεως ἀσεβὲς
λέγειν χρονον μεσιΐευσαί: *with respect then to the generation of
the Son it is impious to say that there was interval of time.*
For the Son is not brought into existence from a state of
non-existence, but always was with the Father, and in him
from all eternity, and without beginning begotten by him.

---

* Johannes Damascenus, or John of Damascus, so called from his being
born at that place, where his father, though a Christian, was Counsellor of
State to the Caliph of the Saracens. He was educated by a Monk of Jerusalem, from whom he imbibed the religious opinions of the times, and
became one of the most distinguished writers of the eighth century. On
the death of his father he succeeded him in the situation he had held, and
occasioned great troubles and vexations to the Emperor of Constantinople,
by becoming an active defender of image worship. Yet, though thus heterodox, he left a treatise, from which the above citation is quoted, on the
orthodox faith, against all heresies, which seems of value. The two kinds
of Theology, which the Latins termed scholastic and didactic, were united
in this laborious performance. The book, says Moshiem, was received
among the Greeks with the highest applause, and was so extensively admired, that at length it came to be acknowledged among that people as the
only rule of divine truth ! It was published with his other works in Greek
and Latin by Lequien, in 2 vols. folio, in 1712.

Whence John xvii. 5, the Son says to the Father, *Glorify me with that glory which I had with thee before the world was.* But concerning the Divine nature of Christ, we must speak more largely hereafter. In respect also of the human nature, Christ, by special privilege, is called the Son of God; and God, the Father of Christ: Luke i. 32, *the Son of the Highest:* Luke xxiii. 46, *Father, into thy hands I commend my spirit:* John x. 36; and in many other passages.

But it may be asked, Why, in this place, it was not sufficient for the Apostle to say, *We give thanks to God,* but he should also add, *and to the Father of our Lord Jesus Christ?*

I answer, first, he adds this for our consolation: for in the verse preceding he had called God *our Father;* in this he calls the same God *the Father of Christ.* He intimates, therefore, that we and Christ are brethren; and thence that our true Brother always intercedes with God the common Father, for his brethren; and that is easily obtained from the Father which the Son requests; especially when he requests any thing for his brethren, not for strangers, Heb. ii. 11.

Secondly, to distinguish Christian invocation, from the invocation of Heathens and Jews. For an Heathen invokes and praises *God Almighty, who made the heaven and the earth;* a Jew invokes *the God of Abraham, and Isaac, and Jacob;* but Christians alone invoke and acknowledge *God the Father of our Lord Jesus Christ.*

Lastly, that he might shew that the benefits of God the Father are derived to us through his Son and our Brother Jesus Christ. For unless God were the Father of Christ, and of us through Christ, we should have no hope of obtaining the benefits of God.

Praying always for you.] The Apostle here shews for whom he gives thanks, viz. for the Colossians; and when, *praying always,* i. e. always when we do pray.

Observe 1. In that the Apostle gives so frequent, so regular thanks to God for benefits conferred upon others, he shews the nature of Christian love, which *rejoices with*

them that do rejoice, weeps with them that weep, and finally
reckons the happiness and misery of its friends as its own.
Parisiensis well terms *love the most trustworthy and innocent
of thieves, because it makes all the goods of its neighbour its
own, and yet takes away nothing from him.* Nay out of
another's good things it finds a gift which it may present
truly acceptable to God, viz. the praising of God and giving of thanks.

2. The Apostle by his conduct reproves the envy and
jealousy of this age: in which, so far from men being willing to give thanks to God for the distinguished and excellent gifts of others, they are rather ready to turn the
same to evil, and revile them with malevolent detractions.
From which this disadvantage always happens, that they
who, by rejoicing in the prosperity of others, would have
found their own benefit, by envying it do but torment
themselves : for *set aside envy, and what I have is thine ; set
aside envy, and what thou hast is mine,* as says Augustine in
Psal. cxxxix.

Praying always.] I join these [two words], because they
were not always in the act of giving thanks ; but they always gave thanks then when they prayed. Therefore the
latter word is a limitation of the former ; and it is customary among the Greeks to explain a participle by the sub-
junctive.

Observe 1. The time of praying is therefore the most
convenient time for rendering thanks to God ; for prayer
is *the elevation of the mind to God;* and then especially
thanks are to be given to God when the mind glows with
pious affections. For thanks are accounted dry and sterile
before God, which proceed only from the outward lips ;
they must be drawn from the bottom of the heart, which,
becoming fervid by prayer, is fain to celebrate the glory
and the praises of God, not for form's sake, but seriously.

2. Hence also, we gather this, that the giving of thanks
for benefits received, is the most suitable introduction to
petition for new benefits, whether for ourselves or for
others. For this is Paul's method : he gives thanks to
God for the good bestowed on the Colossians ; then he de-

sires from God a confirmation of those gifts; as ye shall
hereafter hear.

And so far concerning the congratulatory proposition.
The narration and the illustration of the cause of this giving of thanks follows; the narration in the 4th verse; for
there he names those good things which had excited him
to give thanks to God, viz. their *faith and love.* The illustration follows to the 9th verse.

Ver. 4.   *Since we heard of your faith in Christ Jesus, and
the love which ye have to all the saints.*

In this fourth verse, the Apostle explains (as I have said)
the cause of his joy and congratulation: and he does it by
the enumeration of certain spiritual gifts which were conspicuous among the Colossians. Here he specifies two;
viz. *faith* and *love:* and each gift he illustrates by annexing, not its adequate, but its primary and principal object;
faith in Christ, love towards the saints.

Your faith.] By *faith* here he means the profession of
the Christian religion, which the Colossians had embraced,
through the ministry and preaching of Epaphras and
others; not indeed the external profession of faith alone,
but an internal and sincere faith dwelling in the heart: for
by the rule of charity, the latter is always to be presumed
in the former, unless hypocrisy and impiety be discovered
to evince the contrary.

He places this faith in the foreground, and puts it before
other spiritual gifts, because it is in its nature prior to the
rest. For it is the foundation and root of godliness and
religion; it is the gate of life, through which God first enters into the human mind; it is the basis of the spiritual
building. For as in the creation light preceded the other
creatures; for God said, *Let there be light, and there was
light on the first day:* so in the work of regeneration, God
says, Let there be the light of faith, and it first shines in
the mind, then other virtues follow. The very first *approach to God* is made *through faith,* Heb. xi. 6. The first
purification of the human *heart* is effected *by faith,* Acts

xv. 9. That our works may be pleasing to God, faith is in the first place required, Heb. xi. Whence Prosper, De vita contemplat. iii. 21, excellently writes, that *faith is the foundation of righteousness, which no good works precede, but from which all proceed: it purges us from all sins, illuminates our minds, reconciles to God,* &c.*

Hence it appears, whatever is done by unbelieving men, however holy and pious it may seem, is yet the dead carcase and image of a good work, not a good work, nor to be recompensed by any reward which is promised to true godliness.

We will adduce a few testimonies of the Fathers, because the Papists, who decry faith upon all occasions, and extol works, ascribe a certain merit to these works of unbelievers.

1. Clemens Alexandrinus,† Strom. 1. says, *When life is ended it will be of no avail to men to have done rightly now, unless* [*in conjunction with all this laudable morality*] *they have faith.* Augustine says, *Whosoever hath not a right faith towards God, with all his laudable deeds, departs from this life into condemnation,* lib. iii. contra duas epis. Pelag. cap. 5.

* Prosper :—An Ecclesiastical writer of the fifth century, of great excellence and eminence, and who at that early period ably opposed the Pelagian heresy: he died about the year 463. There is an edition of his works in 8vo. so recent as the year 1732.

† Clemens Alexandrinus :—a distinguished Father who lived in the third century. He was employed as a Catechist, and afterwards made a Presbyter in the church of Alexandria. Under him arose many eminent men; though, from the manner in which his mind was evidently imbued and warped by the mystical philosophy of his time (in which he had acquired an extensive knowledge, as any of his writings would shew), his statements of Christian doctrine were defective. He was a copious writer; but of all his works only the following appear to remain, viz. his " Proetrepticon, or an Exhortation to the Pagans;" " Pedagogus, or the Instructor ;" the fragment of a treatise on the use of riches, entitled, " What rich man can be saved ?" and his " Stromata," the work cited above by our Expositor. This title is borrowed from Carpet-work, and intended to denote the miscellaneous nature of the philosophical and religious topics of which the work treats. It is considered valuable, as containing many quotations from ancient books, and recording several facts which are not be met with elsewhere.

All the life of the unbelieving is sin: Prosper, Sent. 106.
*When the acknowledgment of God is wanting, all righteousness
is like the human body without a head,* Lactantius, vi. 9.—I
bring forward no more: these sufficiently shew why the
Apostle in the first place gives thanks to God for the faith
of the Colossians, viz. because without faith nothing can
be grateful and acceptable to God.*

So much concerning the first gift.

In Christ Jesus.] The Apostle shews the object of Christian faith; not the general, or adequate object, but the
principal; and, if we regard the act of justification, the
peculiar object.

The general and adequate object of faith is, all the truth
revealed by God in the Holy Scriptures. There is a sort of
general faith which answers to this description, and which
by a sure persuasion resolves that whatever things are
made manifest in the word of God, are most true. But
this general assent of faith cannot justify; because justification brings with it peace of conscience, purification of
heart, free access to God, and many other privileges, of
which, doubtless, any one may be void, nothwithstanding
his firmly believing the whole Scripture to be true and in-

---

* On this use of the Fathers by Davenant, it may be permitted the
Translator to adduce a passage from Bishop Douglas in their behalf. Speaking of Dr. Middleton on Miracles, he observes, what may justly be applied
to some other writers respecting those ancient witnesses to many important
truths: " He has justly provoked the indignation of every serious Christian, by the indecent contempt with which he treats the earliest Fathers of
the Church, whose names have been venerable in every age, and whose labours in defence of Christianity, for the truth of which most of them laid
down their lives, ought to have secured them from insult, if they could not
procure his esteem. And if there be any superstitious conceits, or weak
prejudices to be met with in their works, a veil ought to have been thrown
over them, as these are faults not of their own, but of the times in which
they lived; and which, if they disgrace the pages of the Fathers of the
Christian Church, detract equally from the merit of their cotemporaries,
the Philosophers of the Platonic and Pythagorean schools." Douglas's
" Criterion;" or " Rules by which the true Miracles recorded in the New
Testament are distinguished from the spurious miracles of Pagans and Papists." Edition by the Rev. William Marsh; a work deserving of every
enquirer's perusal in this age of rebuke and blasphemy.

spired by God: For the devil himself knows the Scriptures, and acknowledges them to have proceeded from the Author of truth. Therefore in this general object of faith, viz. the word of God, there is one special and main object which is principally to be considered by a believer, and to which all other things that are delivered in the Scriptures have a certain relation and reference, as Durandus speaks, in Prolog. Sent. And this object is, Christ Jesus in the character of a Mediator and Saviour, which is intimated under his very names ; for *Christ Jesus* means nothing else than—*anointed Saviour.*

Now it is clear from the Scriptures that he is the principal object of faith, and that all other things which are delivered in the Scriptures regard Christ as their end and aim. John v. 39, *Search the Scriptures, they testify of me;* and a little after, *Moses wrote of me.* So in Luke, ult. ver. 44, *All things must be fulfilled which are written in the law of Moses, and in the Prophets, and in the Psalms concerning me.* So it is affirmed concerning the whole law, that it was *a Schoolmaster to bring us to Christ.* Him the prophets described ; Him the ceremonies of the law shadowed forth ; Him, in short, with all his benefits, the Gospel offers and exhibits to us. The Apostle, therefore, has rightly placed, as the special and principal object of faith, not the Word of God in general, but Christ Jesus our Saviour and Mediator, who is principally regarded by a believer, and to whom all things in Scripture have reference.

Now from hence it follows, that the proper and principal act of justifying faith, is the apprehension and particular application of the gratuitous promises which are offered to believers in this Mediator, Christ. Which particular and justifying faith includes general faith ; for if it should waver in general concerning the truth of the divine word, it could not confide in particular concerning the promises made to us in Christ the Mediator ; but it justifies, not so far as it assents in general to the divine word, but so far as it is applied to this its principal and peculiar object, viz. to the promises of grace in the Mediator.

Which is evident, first, because as Thomas expresses it,

1 quæst. 45, art. 6, *the justification of a sinner pertains to the goodness and the mercy of God superabundantly diffusing itself.* But we neither can, nor ought, to seek or apprehend the goodness and mercy of God, independently of the promises of grace, which are made and ratified to us in Christ the Mediator : therefore in these alone, as in the proper object, the act of justifying faith is exercised, when and as far as it justifies.

Secondly, it is evident from the distribution of the Scripture ; for it is divided into the Law and the Gospel : but justification is not sought or contained in the doctrine of the Law. Not in that part which prescribes obedience and promises a recompence to those fulfilling its commands ; because the conscience of every one witnesses, that we cannot be justified by the legal covenant. Much less in that other part which contains the threats and punishments due to those who violate the law ; because this doctrine affords not the hope of salvation, but inspires the dread of hell. It remains, therefore, that justification be sought in the Gospel, i. e. in the promises of grace ; and the act of faith, as far as it justifies, should be especially directed to these promises.

Thirdly, we shew this from clear testimonies of Scripture. Acts xiii. 38, 39, *Through Christ is preached the forgiveness of sins ; and by him all that believe are justified from all things from which ye could not be justified by the law of Moses,* And Rom. iii. 21, 22, *But now the righteousness of God without the law is manifested, being witnessed by the law and the prophets ; even the righteousness of God which is by faith of Jesus Christ unto all and upon all them that believe.*

I argue these points the more at large, because Bellarmin, De justif. lib. i. cap. 8, &c. says, that justifying faith is a general assent to all things which are contained in the word of God ; and makes, not the promises of grace, but the whole revelation of God, the object of this faith. If he intends, that justifying faith assents to the whole divine word, we willingly concede it : but if he denies that it has a certain principal object in the word which it regards before all others in the act itself of justifying, viz. Christ the Mediator, and his gratuitous promises concerning the

remission of sins, he is opposed to St. Paul, who, in a
hundred places, names Christ as the principal object of
faith, not the word in general : he also opposes even Aquinas, who says, that *faith in the act of justifying does not
even regard and contemplate all the articles of faith alike,
much less the whole word of God, but only God as remitting
sins.*—But here a doubt which is raised by the Schoolmen
may be briefly solved.

They ask, How Christ can be the object of faith, when
faith has for its object an enunciation or proposition revealed by God ? Christ is a thing, and (as the Logicians
say) an incomplex term, not a proposition in which truth
or falsehood is perceived.

It is answered, That is called an object of faith which is
either believed itself, or concerning which any thing is believed. The thing itself which is believed is a proposition
or enunciation; that concerning which it is believed is a
thing signified by a simple term, as Durandus says. Aquinas more plainly remarks ; The object of faith is regarded
in a twofold manner : either on the part of the thing believed ; and so the object of faith is always something incomplex, viz. the thing itself concerning which the propositions of faith are formed, as Christ, the resurrection,
the final judgment, creation, and the like : or on the part
of the person believing ; and so the object of faith is that
enunciation which faith apprehends concerning the thing,
as that Christ is the Mediator and Saviour, that our bodies
shall rise again, and that Christ will come to judge the
world, that God created the world, and the like.—Thus far
concerning the first gift, i. e. faith, and its object, viz.
Christ.

And love to all the saints.] This is that other gift, from
which the Apostle has taken occasion to give thanks to
God in the name of the Colossians ; and to which also is
joined a certain special object of this virtue, viz. *the saints.*

Respecting this gift itself we must first enquire what it
is. Lombard* thought (lib. i. dist. 4), that love was

* Peter Lombard, commonly known by the title of Master of the Sentences. He was born at Novara, in Lombardy, but brought up at Paris,
in the University of which place he distinguished himself so much, that he

nothing else than the Holy Spirit himself immediately moving the will to the act of love.   For he put this difference
between love and the other virtues, that the Holy Spirit
moved the soul to acts of other virtues, by the intermediate infusion of certain habits, but to the act of love immediately by himself, without any other habit being created or infused.   And he grounded this opinion especially
upon that passage of John, 1 Epis. iv. 8, *God is love ;* and
again in vers. 16, *God is love, and he that dwelleth in love,
dwelleth in God, and God in him.*   But this opinion can by
no means be supported : for as faith and hope are created
gifts, so also love is a habit created by God, by which the
will is inclined to love God above all things for his own
sake, and all other persons for the sake of God.   For if the
act of love were an immediate motion of the will by God,
without a habit infused, it would follow, First, that the
act of love would not be voluntary, because it proceeds
neither from the will naturally (for love is above nature),
nor from the will as perfected by supernatural habit; but
only from the will as it is moved as the instrument of a
superior cause ; just as the hand or the foot may be moved
by something else.   Secondly, it would follow, that man
would not have any promptitude in love, or delight in the
exercise of love : for promptitude and delight in actions,
argue a habit either acquired or infused.

The Scripture itself also opposes this comment of Lombard, and clearly teaches that 'αγάπη, or our love, is not
the Holy Spirit, but *a fruit of the Holy Spirit,* Gal. v. 22.
The Fathers also testify against it.   'Αγαπη 'εστί διάθεσις
ψυχης 'αγαθη, *it is a disposition of the mind by which it is made
to prefer nothing to God,* Maxim 1. centur. sentent. tom. 7.

was first appointed Canon of Chartres, afterwards Tutor to Philip, son of
Lewis VI., and finally Bishop of Paris.   He died in 1064.   His great work
of the Sentences is looked on as the source of the Scholastic Theology of
the Latin Church, as that of Damascenus had been of the Greek.   Of the
occasion and nature of this work, of so much importance in the conduct of
Papal Theology, Du Pin has given a full and interesting account in his Ecclesiastical History, Cent. 12. Chap. xv.   Lombard also wrote Commentaries on the Psalms, and on St. Paul's Epistles.

And Prosper; *Love is a rectified will turned from all earthly
things, and inseparably united to God, kindled by a certain
fire of the Holy Spirit ;* De vita contemp. iii. 13. He says
that love is *inspired* by the Holy Spirit, not the Holy Spirit
himself. To the passage cited from John, *God is love,* the
answer is easy ; For God is called love causally, not formally (as the Schoolmen say), i. e. inasmuch as he causes
love in us ; for he is the eternal fountain whence our love,
and all other virtues, flow to us. Or God may be called
love essentially, in the same manner as God is said to be
wisdom, and justice ; because these attributes are not accidents in God, but one and the same essence with God.
But this does not in the least prevent the possibility of our
love being a created gift; as our prudence, and righteousness, and holiness are created gifts, although God may be
rightly called prudence itself, and righteousness itself, and
holiness itself.

We see what love is. Now, in the second place, since
it is connected by the Apostle with faith, let us enquire
concerning the connexion of faith and love, viz. Whether
true faith can exist without love ?

First, we grant that the mind of man can be so enlightened as to believe God, i. e. to assent to the divine word
in general, and yet at the same time, be destitute of love.
The Schoolmen call this *fides informis ;** we, *historical faith,*
or *general faith.* So the very ancient Schoolman of Altissiodorum, lib. 3, *We believe God by informal faith, i. e that
God is, and that God is Almighty, and many other things.*
Concerning this also James speaks, Chr. ii. 14, *What doth
it profit though any one say he hath faith, but hath not works ?*
Then a little after, *The devils believe and tremble.*

But there is also another faith, which we call *justifying
faith,* the Schoolmen *fides formata,†* which not only believes
God, but in God, i. e. which apprehends God as appeased
and reconciled in Christ ; and this we say is never separated from love. The former is a simple irradiation, not a

---

* That is, indefinite or crude faith.
† That is, formed or definite faith.

theological virtue ; this latter is the first among these three celebrated theological virtues.* And the perpetual connection of this with love is proved by many reasons :

1. Because this faith apprehends God as good and merciful, and the Author of salvation to a man's self through Christ; and this apprehension produces necessarily the love of God : For so Altissiodorensis, *The estimation with which any one regards God through faith to be his chief good, engenders the desire of that good ;* lib. 3.

2. Because justifying faith sanctifies and purifies the heart ; but a heart void of love is not sanctified or purified.

3. Because every one who believes with true and justifying faith, has a right to eternal life : For so the Baptist, *He who believes in the Son hath eternal life.* And Paul to the Galatians, *Ye are all the children of God by faith.* But these things are united in no one who is void of love.

4. The Schoolmen themselves shew that these three theological virtues are always joined. So Altissiodorensis ; *All the virtues are united : for faith is the necessary cause of hope and love,* lib. 3. But concerning the connection of faith and love in the very act of believing, thus Parisiensis writes ; *Living faith is not only a light to shew the things believed ; but a life exciting us to do or to decline those things, to*

---

* The " lively" or living faith of the Church of England, defined in her 12th Article, which alone interests the soul in Christ for justification, it has been well observed, is not to be confounded with the " formed" faith of the Church of Rome—i. e. a faith clothed in all the fruits which it is to produce, and justifying us by means of its fruits ; " They say that the Scriptures which speak of justification by faith ought to be understood of *a formed faith ;* i. e. that our justification is to be ascribed to our faith, only on account of our love" and other fruits of it : " nay they make love to justify, and not faith. But what else is this than to abolish the promises again, and return to the law ?" Melanc. Apol. Confess. p. 52, ed. 1537. " The Papists say that man is justified by a *formed* faith. They mean, not by faith, but by other virtues." I. Op. 1, 373.—In the Council of Trent, Marinarus " liked not that it should be said, that *faith* is *formed with charity,* because that kind of speech is not used by St. Paul, but only that faith *worketh by* charity" or love. F. Paul. 183. Conv. 1. 306. Vide Scott's Continuation of Milner's Church History : and also Bellarmin's conclusion noted in this vol. p. 10 : Note.

seek or avoid them.   And Durandus, *To believe in God is not simply an act of faith, but the act of faith and love together.*

From these considerations it is manifest, when the Papists argue that true faith may be separated from love, they are either playing upon words, or opposing their own Schoolmen. For that faith which is void of love, differs in kind from that which is justifying; for the last is a theological virtue, the other is not : they differ in the object; for this apprehends God reconciled to us in Christ; that is not able to apprehend any such thing : they differ also in their effects; for this brings peace to the conscience, that fear: they differ, lastly, in their acts ; for the act of this is to believe in God, the act of the other is only to believe God, as we have before shewn.

The last question, which has respect to faith and love, remains ; viz. Whether love be so conjoined with faith that it is the form of faith ? So it appeared to Thomas, to Durandus, and to others of a more recent date. For they imagine faith by itself to be a certain dead and inanimate thing, and whatever it hath of life or merit, to be borrowed from love as from its soul and form.

But on the other hand, Altissiodorensis (whom I have often named)* opposes this, lib. 3, where he maintains, that true and formed faith naturally precedes love; and he adduces the following reasons :

1. *The just lives by faith;* therefore he loves by faith; therefore living faith is prior in its nature to love, and hence it is not formed and enlivened by love.

2. From 1 Tim. i. 5, *The end of the commandment is love out of a pure heart, and of faith unfeigned :* therefore true faith, and that which purifies the heart, produces love ; and by consequence it is not formed from love.

3. The motion of true faith precedes the motion of

---

* The person often cited by Davenant under the epithet of " Altissiodorensis," was William Bishop of Auxerre, whose Theological Summary is far superior to the general style of Divinity of the twelfth century, in which he flourished. Though little is recorded of him, his character and excellence as a Writer and a Christian, are quite evident by Davenant's quotations from him here, and especially under the 18th verse.

love; therefore the habit itself of true faith naturally precedes the habit of love. For we believe and repose our
faith on God before we are able to love him.

4. From the Apostle to the Galatians v. 6, *In Christ
Jesus neither circumcision availeth any thing, nor uncircumcision,
but faith which worketh by love:* therefore faith is the efficient cause of love, and hence love is not the form of faith,
but its daughter or handmaid.

But when they (the Papists) are driven to straits, they
endeavour to explain their opinion in this way: That love
is the form of faith, not in such manner as in natural
things, a form is said to give the shape to material; but
only in this respect, that by love the act of faith is perfected: for faith hath its entire efficacy and merit from love.
Thus Aquinas, Q. 2. quæst. 4, art. 3. and qu. disp. de fide,
art. 5. And Durandus, lib. 3. dist. 33. quæst. 8, *Love is
not the inherent, but extrinsic form of faith; neither does it
become a form of faith as being of its nature, but as far as it
is meritorious.*[*]

But all these things are fallacious and weak. For, first,
love does not elicit nor perfect the proper act of faith;
because although they are simultaneous, yet naturally the
act and even the habit of faith precedes the act and habit
of love.

Secondly, love does not, as they think, render the act
of faith meritorious, or acceptable to God: but on the contrary, the power of meriting (as they speak) i. e. of rendering our actions acceptable, is placed more especially in
faith than in love. For without faith it is impossible that
the act of loving can be acceptable to God. Also the regenerate man renounces his own understanding through
faith, before he does his own will through love. Love
therefore is not the form, but the offspring of true faith.

Hitherto we have considered the gift itself of love: Now
let us come to the object.

To all saints.] Where two things are to be remarked:
the object of love, specified in this place, *the saints;* and
the extent of the object, *all* saints.

[*] " Nec informat fidem quoad esse naturæ, sed quoad esse meritorium."

By *saints* the Apostle understands the baptised, and those who profess the Christian religion, as we have before shewn;* for love presumes such to be true saints.

As to the object of love we must know, that the saints are neither its only nor primary object. For, as Augustine writes, De doctrin. Christ. i. 25, *There are four objects of our love; one, that which is above us, viz. God; another, that which is ourselves; the third, that which is near to us, viz. our neighbour; the fourth, that which is beneath us, viz. our own body.* Concerning each of these we shall speak somewhat briefly.

1, First, then, the principal, and also the formal object of love, is God himself: for he is loved for himself, all other things in their relation to him, and as far as they participate, or are able to participate the Divine likeness and blessedness. When, therefore, the Apostle celebrates the love of the Colossians to the saints, he does not exclude, but necessarily supposes love to God. For as a colour is not seen without light, because light is the medium of seeing colour: so our neighbour is not loved without the love of God, because God is the medium of our loving our neighbour. Hence the Saviour in those two great commands places foremost the love of God, as the cause and fountain of the love of our neighbour. Matth. xxii. 37—39. Hence also Augustine, Confess. lib. 10, cap. 29, observes, *He loves thee less than is right, who together with thee loves any thing else for any other cause than because he loves thee.*

2. Augustine places oneself as the second object of love to every one, and that rightly. For as the Philosopher (Aristotle) has observed, Eth. ix. cap. 8, 'Aπ' αυτου πάνla τα φιλικὰ καὶ πρὸς τούς ʼαλλους διηκει: *All kindly feelings proceed from oneself towards others.* And God himself in the command of loving our neighbour includes the love of oneself; *Thou shalt love thy neighbour as thyself.* Plain reason also evinces this. For since love is founded upon the communication of the divine fruition or blessedness,

* Vide p. 20, 21.

every one, so far as he understands that he can be a partaker of the divine fruition, is bound to love himself, and
to desire that divine good to himself which is the proper
subject of love.

Nay, we may moreover add, that no one is able to love
God truly,* who at the same time does not truly love himself: for he who loves God, wishes to enjoy the divine blessedness; but to wish this good to himself is to love himself truly. Furthermore, every one wishes the enjoyment
of God to himself first, and more intensely than to another; so that if it could not be vouchsafed to more, every
one had rather it should be communicated to himself by
God than to another. And the reason is, because more
causes concur to make him in this manner love himself
rather than another. For another may fall from this divine
good without my loss or fault, but I myself cannot.

But it may be asked, if every one is bound to love himself, and that more intently than another with this kind of
love, why is there no express and direct precept concerning the loving oneself? Nay, why is the love of oneself
condemned, 2 Tim. iii. 2, *Men shall be lovers of themselves.*

It is solved thus : Since to love God is to love oneself,
therefore when it is commanded that we love God, it is
commanded in effect that we love ourselves. For he who
loves God wishes to enjoy God, desires to be united to
God; he wishes therefore the chief and greatest good to
himself, and hence he loves himself as much as possible.
Also, it may be replied, that the written law was given in
aid of the law of nature, which was obscured through sin;
yet was not so obscured, but that it might move any one
to love himself: therefore an express command concerning
the love of oneself was not necessary. But as to what is
said that the love of oneself is condemned in Scripture, it
must be understood concerning an inordinate love which
respects sensible good, not of that kind of love which has
respect to divine good. For no one can too much love, or

* Ex charitate.

too much desire for himself spiritual good things; but
sensible and transitory ones he may; and in this consists
that love which is to be blamed.

3.   I now come to the third object of love, which our
present design has chiefly in view; and this is that which
is *near to us* (as Augustine says), i. e. *our neighbour.**

But a person is called a neighbour not *from consangui-
nity* only, but from *a mutual participation of reason,* as the
gloss has it.   So also Justin Martyr, *A man's neighbour is
nothing else, but a being participating in a similar condition
and in rational faculties.†*   But this must be observed by
the way, that a neighbour is loved by us with true
love, not simply as he is a partaker of rational nature, but
so far as that rational nature may be a partaker of the divine blessedness : for love is founded in the mutual participation of the divine fruition, as was before observed.
Among neighbours therefore, i. e. among men, the especial
objects of our love are holy men, as the Apostle both here
and elsewhere teaches; as in the Epistle to the Galatians,
vi. 10, *Let us do good unto all men, especially unto them who*

---

* A couplet from Augustine, which it is said he caused to be inscribed
upon his table, is worthy of being cited here ; it is a practical testimony
that *he* was not actuated by the " bitter and unchristian spirit" recently attributed to those supposed to hold Calvinistic tenets :—
      " Far from this table be the worthless guest
      Who wounds another's fame though but in jest."

+ *Justin,* or *Justinus,* surnamed the *Martyr*; one of the earliest writers
in the Christian Church, was born at Neapolis, the ancient *Sichem* of Palestine, in the province of Samaria.   His father Priscus was a Greek Gentile, and he himself was deeply versed in the Platonic Philosophy, when he
was led by a conversation with a Christian convert, to inquire into the merits of that Religion which he afterwards embraced in 132, and supported
both by preaching and writing until he was called upon to seal its truth with
his blood.   He was beheaded, after having been scourged, according to the
imperial edict, in the reign of M. Aurelius, A.D. 165.   Among his works
(a good summary of which has lately been given to the public in a small
8vo. volume, by Bishop Kaye), the best known are his ' Dialogue with
Trypho the Jew,' and his first and second Apology for the Christians; the
former of which he presented to Antoninus Pius, and the latter to his successor, Aurelius.   Specimens from these will be seen as we proceed, and
evince the power of the Gospel, in the ennobling of the mind, above all
Philosophy.

are of the household of faith. So Augustine, *The more holy members are to be embraced with a greater love.* And the venerable Bede ; *The union of hearts is more sacred than that of bodies.** But it is easy to assign a reason, why the saints are more to be loved by us than others, viz. because that which is the formal reason of love, is more visible in them than others : For as those objects are better seen, which are placed more in the light, because light is the formal object of vision; so those men are more loved, who are more united to God, because God is the formal and proper object of love.

The last object of love Augustine makes to be, *the human body :* which he has therefore done, because love being

---

* Bede, justly named the Venerable, was born about the year A.D. 670, in the country between the mouth of the Ware and the Tyne. His works make eight folio volumes, and consist principally of Commentaries on the Scriptures, chiefly drawn from the Fathers: and abounding with allegorical interpretations. From his writings it is evident that he had acquired all the learning, philosophical and theological, that could be attained. His information, surprising as it may seem for a person in this country, at that age, had been derived from his access to a library collected at the Monastery at Jarrow, by Benedict Biscop, a Monk who had been encouraged under Alfrid, King of Northumberland, to collect books in France and Italy. The volumes he got together contained the concentrated wisdom of ages ; and from these treasures were Bede's productions gathered. His most valuable work is his Ecclesiastical History, which, though abounding in legendary fables, the natural result of the credulity of the age and the sources of his resort, is an inestimable record of the early history of the Anglican Church.—Mr. Southey in his Vindiciæ Ecclesiæ Anglicanæ, has given a very interesting view of the character and productions of this eminent and holy man. He was employed at the period of his dissolution, and during a long and painful illness, in dictating to Wilberth, a young disciple, a translation of St. John's Gospel. Just as this was being brought to a close, he said, " It is now time that I should be released, and go to Him who created me. I have lived long and my merciful Judge hath ordered my ways well. The hour of my freedom is at hand ; and my soul desires to behold Christ in his glory." The young disciple then said to him, " Master, there is yet one sentence more." " Write quickly, then," replied the adoring saint. Presently Wilberth said, " Now it is done." " You have said truly," rejoined the dying man : " It is finished. Take my head between thy hands. and place me so that I may look towards my oratory, and then call upon my Father." Being then laid on the pavement, in the position which he directed, he expired presently, chaunting the doxology with his latest breath.

founded upon the communication of divine blessedness,
whatever may participate that blessedness may be the object of love. But now, although our body cannot enjoy
the divine blessedness in knowing and in loving God, yet
it may be the instrument in many works of piety of a soul
that does know and love God; whence from the beatifica-
tion of the soul redounds a certain incidental blessedness
to the body, viz. the blessedness of immortality and inca-
pability of suffering.—So much concerning the objects of
love. Now let us consider the extent of that object which
is here expressed by the Apostle. He would have love to
extend to *all* saints, i. e. professors of true religion.

All.] When the Apostle extends love to *all saints*, he is
to be understood, not only concerning the internal affection, but the external exercise of love, which is discerned
in liberality and beneficence towards those who stand in
need of our aid, For, as much as in us lies, we ought to
be beneficent towards all, not only our neighbours or relations, but strangers, nay enemies and wicked men.*
Concerning strangers we have the practice of the apostolic
Church: The Macedonians and Achaians made a collection for the poor saints that dwelt at Jerusalem, Rom. xv.
26. So the Corinthians are excited to supply the wants of
others from their abundance, 2 Epis. viii. 13.† So Gaius
is praised for his love toward strangers, 3 Epis. John, ver.

---

* Who can forget the exemplifications given us of this by our Redeemer
in the parable of the good Samaritan, and as implied in Rom. v. 6—10?

† Tertullian in his " Apology," cap. 39, gives a fine illustration of the
effects of the Gospel in inducing this Christian love : " Every one," says
he, speaking of the conduct of the early Christians, " pays something into
the public chest once a month, or when he pleases, and according to his
ability and inclination; for there is no compulsion. These gifts are, as it
were, the deposits of piety : Hence we relieve and bury the needy, support
orphans and decrepit persons, those who have suffered shipwreck, and those
who, for the word of God, are condemned to the mines or imprisonment.
This very charity of ours has caused us to be noticed by some :—See, say
they, how these Christians love one another !"—The world had not before
witnessed the like; and surely these persons had learned of him whose benevolence " excludes no persons from its tender regards ; which disdains no
condescension, grudges no cost, in its labours of love." Luke xix. 10 ; 2
Cor. viii. 9.

5. Well spake Lactantius, *What we give to our relatives through affection, we should give to strangers from philanthropy.* It is a saying of a Grecian poet, *That a good man, if he abound in riches, is a common treasure.* The Scripture in many places enjoins that enemies should be loved : *Do good to them that hate you,* Matth. v. 44 ; and Rom. xii. 10, *If thine enemy hunger, feed him;* Whence that saying of Tertullian to Scapula, *It is the custom of all to love their friends; but it is the peculiarity of Christians to love their enemies.** And this especially points out the power and

* Scapula, the President and Proconsul of Africa ; to whom Tertullian wrote in consequence of his improper conduct towards the Christians in his Province, pleading their cause in as admirable an address as he had before composed in their behalf under the persecution of the Emperor Severus. The Romish Church, *professing* the Religion of Jesus Christ, yet seems to have always retained the character of her Pagan ancestors, and not content with retaining a barbarous hostility towards her enemies in principle, has ever evinced the same towards those, partakers indeed of faith and love, but unable to comply with her superstitions.   Hence her principle and conduct towards all those, whom *she* deems heretics, is hatred, persecution, and—if possible—extermination; and she has ever gloried in the effects, the more appalling they have been to humanity.   For historic evidence of this, let the Reader look into " Townsend's Accusations," p. 248.   In addition to the statements there given of the exulting commemoration of the massacre of St. Bartholomew's day, the writer may add, on the testimony of a friend before referred to, p. 13, who recently visited Rome, and communicated the fact to him, that two scenes of that massacre were painted in Fresco by the famous Vasari, on the walls of a noble chamber in the Vatican !   One is the murder of Coligny.   The figures are of the natural size, and the scientific painter has fully represented the horrors of the scene. This chamber forms the communication between the Pauline and Sistine Chapels, where the great mysteries of the Roman Catholic Church are celebrated by the Pope in person ; and when the Pontiff carries ' the body of Christ' every Easter, from one to the other, he passes within two yards of the representation of the dead body of Coligny, preserved as a triumph of Holy Mother Church !!

As facts of this kind are often most disingenuously denied, when it is supposed *proof is not at hand*, the following confirmation must be deemed decisive and important by all who would not abjure common sense.   It is the spontaneous and express testimony of the Jesuit Bonanni, in his Numis Pont. Romæ 1699, Tom. 1, under Greg. XIII. p. 336, where he is describing the notorious medal struck on the occasion HUGONOTTORUM STRAGES.   He not only particularly relates the public rejoicings which then took place at Rome, but affirms with relation to the painting in the

efficacy of love. For as that fire is hotter and stronger which not only is able to warm things that are near, but such as are far remote ; so that love is the more perfect and lively, which not only extends to neighbours, but to those most distant, i. e. to enemies. Neither ought we to think this love of enemies to be a matter of advice, but of command ; for he loves not God above all things, who does not love an enemy : which may be thus demonstrated :

In every enemy of ours two qualities are found : one which is a ground of love, viz. a participation of the divine likeness, and the possibility of his participation of blessedness : another which is the ground of hatred, viz. that he inflicts an injury upon us, and opposes us : if therefore, setting aside the ground of love, we are altogether converted into hatred, our enmity outweighs divine love. Now, as to men openly wicked, such as are given to drunkenness, adultery, perjury, Christian love does not desert even these. For *love hopeth all things;* 1 Cor. xiii. 7 ; it therefore hopes that these may be converted to God ; and

Vatican, executed by command of the Pope—" Colinii et Sociorum cædem in Vaticanæ Aula describi coloribus jussit a Georgio Vasaro Religionis vindicatæ monumentum, et de profligata hæresi trophæum, sollicitus indequàm salubris ægro Regni corpori tam copiosa depravati sanguinis emissio esset profutura." The whole passage would be worth the attention of the Readers of Dr. Lingard, if the credit of the Papal historian had not been sufficiently disposed of by Dr. Allen.—On the subject which it is here wished to impress upon the consideration of the thoughtful Reader, if he still doubt of the true character and tendency of Popery, let him only peruse the last chapter of Mendham's " Literary Policy of the Church of Rome." Indeed the Translator would intreat every one who has not read that volume, and who desires to come to a right conclusion about the real character of the Infallible and unchangeable Church, to procure it for that purpose. It is of vital importance to a decision in the mind of a wavering Protestant, as to the light in which he should view Romanism and its efforts at the present time. It is more than probable, that on closing the volume, after perusal, his mind would recur to recent events in France as affording a practical demonstration of the reflections with which its statements close. It is a fact, moreover, pretty well accredited, that the recent Revolution there was occasioned mainly by the intriguing of the Priests with the Court party, and by their attempts to introduce that system of things, which in this country, and in Ireland, they are ever and anon insinuating that the Protestant Clergy are interested in upholding.

that they may become partakers of the communion of
saints and of eternal blessedness : Therefore the godly
man hates the wicked man, but with *a perfect hatred:* but
a perfect hatred is that which is neither defective in justice,
nor knowledge, i. e. that you neither hate the men on account of their vices, nor love the vices on account of the
men.

From these considerations, therefore, it is manifest, that
Christian love embraces every rational creature except
devils and the damned ; because all either are, or at least
as far as we know, may be partakers of holiness and blessedness.   But devils and the damned love forsakes, because
God has forsaken them : therefore we cannot desire to them
the good of eternal life, to which love chiefly has respect;
because this would be repugnant to love, which approves
the justice of God, and acquiesces in his revealed will.

And these things may suffice concerning the virtue of
love, the object, and the extent of the object : and having
dwelt so long upon these heads, we must pass over the inferences which might be drawn either for instruction, or for
direction, or even reproof, and proceed.

Verse 5.

For the hope which is laid up for you in heaven ; whereof ye
heard before in the word of the truth of the Gospel.

In the former verse the Apostle has explained the causes
of his giving of thanks, viz. the faith and love of the Colossians : now he proceeds to illustrate and confirm the
same, from the final and instrumental causes.   The final
cause, *the hope laid up in heaven :* the instrumental cause,
the word of the Gospel.   But because the connection and
even the sense of these words is disputed, these doubts
must be cleared away, before we proceed to treat the subject matter.

Some connect these words, *because of the hope which is laid*
up for you, with that expression, *we give thanks,* which is
placed in the beginning of the third verse, in this sense ;
We give thanks to God having heard of your faith and

love, because from hence we understand you to be of the number of those for whom an eternal reward is laid up in heaven. So Athanasius.

Others refer these words to the verse immediately preceding in this sense ; We give thanks to God having heard of your faith and love, which faith and love ye have embraced, and persevere in, on account of the hope laid up in heaven, i. e. on account of celestial blessedness. For hope here is put for the things hoped for, as faith is often taken for those things which are believed. So Chrysostom and Theodoret. Now let us return to the words of the Apostle.

For the hope which is laid up, &c.] Some one of the Colossians might ask from Paul, Why do you give such thanks to God for our faith and love? What good shall accrue to us from thence? Do you not see plainly that the faithful and godly are despised and trodden upon by all? Paul answers, I give thanks not on account of the temporal advantage which you are about to derive, but on account of the heavenly felicity, which from thence I know to be reserved for you.

And here three things must be observed : The name of the heavenly reward ; it is called *hope, our hope.* The manner: the reward is not said to be conferred immediately, nor only proposed and offered, but *laid up,* set apart for us. Lastly, the place must be remarked, *in heaven.*

For the hope.] Under the name of hope is comprehended whatever of good is to be expected in the life of glory. And by this word he intended to point out celestial happiness ;

First, that from hence we may understand that this reward is to be expected by us with patience : for so the Apostle in writing to the Romans viii. 25, says, *If we hope for that we see not, then do we with patience wait for it.* A patient expectation is the proper effect of hope, and therefore very necessary ; because whatever is hoped for, is deferred : and delay by its very nature is distressing, unless patience attend us to sustain the mind. And this is the language of patience, which Tertullian expresses in his book De Animâ; *Some one may I ask, When shall I come to this hoped for joy? Patience answers, When God shall be pleased to give it: for no delay of that which will certainly come is long.*

Secondly, The promised blessedness is called our *hope,* i. e. the thing which we hope for: through an Antonomasia;* that hence we may be led to consider that this object alone is worthy of our hope; and that other frail and transitory things which are commonly hoped for and sought after, are, in comparison with this heavenly prize, rather to be trampled under foot than hoped for or sought after.

Lastly, By this term the carnal and worldly are reproved, who neither care nor hope for future blessedness; they covet only the pleasures of the present life, and into those they plunge themselves. But as Cyprian speaks, De bono patient, *The very fact itself of our being Christians is the substance of hope.* If you find not comfort and pleasure in the things hoped for, you are a Christian in vain. Thus far concerning the name of this treasure.

Laid up, αποκειμένην.] Here he intimates the manner of the reward, that is to say, the way in which it concerns us in the present time. It is not given to us nor are we brought into the possession of it immediately: for this would subvert the nature of hope, and of the thing hoped for. For the present possession of any thing is enjoyment, not hope. Whence the Apostle, *Hope that is seen is not hope: for what a man seeth, why doth he hope for it?* Rom. viii. 24. Neither is it said that this prize is only offered to us, and proposed; for it would weaken our hope, if the certainty of the things hoped for should depend upon ourselves and our disposition, so as either to be given to us or denied, according to the merit of our works. But it is said to be *laid up for us,* i. e. hidden in reserve with God our Father. But if any thing be in reserve for us, even with a good and honest man, we entertain no doubt concerning its future recovery; nay, our goods are placed for that end with ano-

---

* Antonomasia: a figure of rhetoric, in which for some proper name is put the name of some office, possession, or dignity; or to one object the name of any other which nearly resembles it.

ther, through fear of their not being in safety with ourselves. When therefore the Apostle calls the kingdom of
heaven *the hope laid up for us,* he shews that the godly
ought to be certain of the attainment of life eternal; because it is as a treasure kept in store for his children by
God himself their Father. Hence that saying of Christ,
Luke xii. 32, *Fear not little flock, for it is your Father's good
pleasure to give you the kingdom.* Admirably writes Clemens Alexandrinus concerning the certainty of the godly.
*A faithful man hath the God whom he has loved; and by faith
has received what is uncertain to others; and he obtains the
promise* κρατει επαγγελίας *; he possesses future things as present:
nay he hath so certain a persuasion, that he makes more sure of
them than of present things.* But whence this so great certainty, unless because he knows that this treasure is laid
up for him?

In heaven.] Behold the place where this treasure is!
From which we learn that such is the nature of this treasure, that when once possessed it never afterwards can be
taken away. For so says the Saviour, Luke xii. 33, *Hither
thief approacheth not, nor moth corrupteth any thing here :* as
though he would say that all things laid up in heaven, are
beyond the toss of fortune, and the danger of loss.

Secondly, from the fact that the reward hoped for is laid
up *in heaven,* we are given to understand, that it is not any
thing low or mean, but divine, magnificent, and plainly
celestial. Concerning all earthly things, Prudentius
(Hymno ad Galli cant.) hath well said,

> Aurum, voluptas, guadium,—opes, honores, prospera,
> Quæcunque nos inflant mala,—fit mane, nil sunt omnia.*

But as these earthly things pass away and vanish, and
have nothing fixed or permanent about them ; so *heavenly*

> * Or gold, or pleasure, wanton mirth,
>   Wealth, honours, or prosperity ;
>   Whatever evils chafe on earth,
>   When morning dawns,—as nought they be.

Prudentius was a Poet of the fourth century, a Spaniard by birth, born
at Saragossa about the year 348, author of several poems on devotional subjects, first published at Venice, in 1501, in 1 vol. quarto, and afterwards in

things stand on the solid basis of their perpetuity, and have nothing fading or transitory : Parisiensis de retribut. sanctorum.

Lastly, if our hope be laid up in heaven, there ought our mind to be perpetually directed : *for where the treasure is, there is the heart,* Luke xii. 34. That saying of Paul is the saying of every true Christian ; *We have our conversation in heaven, from whence we look for the Saviour,* Phil. iii. 20. Upon this, Clemens has elegantly observed that *every faithful person, even upon earth, verges upon a celestial nature and life.* Strom. 2. But such a forgetfulness of heavenly things hath taken possession of us, that that saying of Prudentius may justly be turned upon us,

Nemo animum summi memorem genitoris in altum,
Excitat, ad cœlum mittit suspiria nemo.*

In Hamart.

And these things concerning the prize hoped for, concerning the manner in which it respects us in the present life, and also concerning the place where it is lodged. It remains that we say something of that interpretation of Chrysostom and Theodoret, which we adverted to above.

These words, *for the hope laid up for you in heaven,* Chrysostom refers to the love and faith of the Colossians ; as though he would say, Ye have believed, and have exercised love towards the brethren on account of the hope laid up for you in heaven, i. e. on account of the reward of celestial blessedness. It is necessary to say something concerning this interpretation, inasmuch as the words bear it, and many interpreters follow it.

a Variorum Edition at Hanau, and a third In usum Delphini, 4to. at Paris, in 1687.

* Surely this *was* a Christian Poet, who in this couplet had in view Isaiah lxiv. 7 ; and may not the Apostolic appeal, Col. iii. 1, be allowed us *here*, " If ye be risen with Christ, seek those things which are above."
The sense of the above quotation is thus attempted for the advantage of the mere English reader :—

Regardless of its lofty birth, the mind
Ne'er wakes a thought th' Almighty Sire to find ;
Ah ! who with ardent longings soars on high
To gain th' eternal realms beyond the sky !

But because it agrees in other respects with the former
interpretation, while in this one it differs, that it makes the
hope reserved in heaven, the motive, not in respect of Paul's
giving thanks, but of the faith and love of the Colossians ;
we shall discuss only this one question ;

Whether it is lawful to do good works, such as to believe in Christ, to love the saints, with a view to, or for
the sake of the reward reserved in heaven ?

Against this is objected John x. 12, where the Saviour
reprehends hirelings, who propose to themselves their own
advantage in feeding the sheep of God.

To this we answer, They are not blamed because they
expect the eternal reward promised by God to well-doers,
but because they had respect to temporal reward, and that
alone ; and in the mean time neglected the work commanded by God : *he is a hireling, and cares not for the sheep,*
verse 13.

It is objected, secondly, that it is the way of servants,
not of sons, to work for the sake of reward : but we
are sons ; therefore we ought not to regard the reward in
our work.

I answer, to work for the sake of reward, as he does
who would not serve God without reward, is truly sordid
and servile, neither becomes a son loving his father ; but
whilst labouring, to have respect to the reward promised
by our father, is neither servile nor sordid.

Thirdly, to believe in God, or to love God (or one's
neighbour) on account of the reward of blessedness, is to
love for the sake of something else : but we ought not to
believe in God, or to love God on account of any thing
else, but for his own sake ; consequently not because of
the reward of blessedness.

I answer, God himself is the reward promised to the
faithful ; therefore whilst they expect and regard an
eternal reward, they expect nothing but God. But if we
understand the reward to be not God himself, but the very
act of enjoying God ; then it must be answered otherwise,
viz. that this reward is not to be so regarded, that it should
be the end for which we love God, but only that it should

be the end of our action, i. e. of our affection and love: And this is allowed; because a less good is lawfully made subordinate to a greater, as to its end; yet the enjoyment itself of God at home is a greater good than faith or the love of God by the way; therefore faith and love are lawfully subordinate to that as to the end.

Even some Fathers are quoted against this opinion. Clemens Alexandrinus, Strom. 4, asserts, *that a good and perfect man does no good, either through the fear of punishment, or because of the hope of reward, whether from men, or from God himself.* Bernard, in his book De amore Dei, is cited by Durandus in support of this opinion, *Though God cannot be loved without reward, nevertheless he is not to be served with a view to the reward.*

The same answer may be given to both; viz. that the reward ought not to be regarded as the only, or even as the principal motive, but God and his glory is to be regarded as the ultimate end: whilst our heavenly felicity is to be regarded as an end subordinate to that: for we aim at the reward of blessedness, that we may love God more securely and ardently for ever.

These objections being answered, the truth must be established by reasons drawn from Scripture.

1. What was done by the saints and commended in the Scriptures, it is lawful to do; but the saints had respect to this reward, and it is recited to their praise. David in Ps. cxix. 112, says, *I have inclined my heart to perform thy statutes, even unto the end.** Moses, Heb. xi. 26, is said to have *looked to the recompence of reward,* ἀπέβλεπεν εἰς μισθαποδοσιαν. Paul to the Philips. iii. 14, *I press towards the mark for the prize of the high calling.*

2. Right reason directs the agent to regard the end of his action: for it is of the nature of an end that it should be aimed at, and from the desire of it excite the doer to

---

* Davenant follows the Vulgate, which is *propter retributionem*, and admits of a sense apparently more accordant with the tenor of the argument, though that of our version is the primary meaning: the version of Tremellius is *in finem usque*, id est, says he in explanation, *tota vita.* Vide Note, p. 30.

action; for the end is the principle from which in actions the practical intellect reasons concerning those things which relate to the end. But the reward of blessedness is the end proposed to faith, and love, and to all good works, as is evident from 1 Peter i. 9, *that ye may receive the end of your faith, the salvation of your souls.*

3. God himself offers this reward to those who do well: therefore he wishes that to be regarded by us; nay, he bids us to regard it. For he would have given no promises of blessedness to the pious, unless he wished that we should have respect to them whilst acting well. In Matth. vi. 33, we are commanded to *seek first the kingdom of God:* but who seeks what he is not permitted to regard? In 1 Tim. iv. 8, it is said,*Godliness hath the promises of the life that now is, and of that which is to come;* but in vain if it be not lawful to be excited to do well by the prospect of them.

We conclude, therefore, that a reward to good works is proposed by God, and that it ought to be regarded by us,

1. That hence we may learn the will and munificence of God.

2. That we may exercise hope and faith by fixing our view upon it.

3. That hence we may be excited to cheerfulness in good works.

But we ought not to regard and look to the reward;

1. So as to be unwilling to serve God if there were no reward.

2. So as to set the blessedness itself as our end in loving God.

3. So as to infer any merit in our good works from the reward being proposed.

Hitherto we have treated of the final cause of the faith and love of the Colossians: It now remains to speak of the instrumental cause in these words, *Which ye heard before in the word of the truth of the Gospel.*

The Apostle shews in these words whence the Colossians conceived the hope of obtaining this celestial blessedness; to wit, from the Gospel preached to them before by Epaphras. But here are two things to be noticed by us : the instrument of producing faith and hope in general, viz. *the word of God* heard ; in particular *the word of the Gospel*, which is distinguished by an adjunct, viz. *truth.*

As to what pertains to the first, the things which are hoped for and believed by Christians, are placed beyond human reach ; therefore that they may become known to us, there is need not only of human, but of divine instruction. But the word of God is the organ of this divine instruction, according to that appeal in Rom. x. 14, *How shall they believe in him of whom they have not heard? and how shall they hear without a preacher?*

But here we must shew more explicitly in what sense the word preached by men becomes the instrument of producing faith and hope, since faith and hope are free gifts derived immediately from the fountain of grace, Jas. i. 17.

We must know therefore, that two things concur to produce faith or hope ; a knowledge of the things to be believed or hoped for; and the assent of the heart. This knowledge arises from hearing the word : for the knowledge of salvation is not communicated to men in these times by extraordinary revelations or inspirations ; but *the word preached is the power of God unto salvation to all that believe.* Therefore as to the propounding and knowledge of the things to be believed and expected, hope and faith depend upon hearing as a necessary instrument. But then, as to the internal assent of the heart, whereby every one firmly apprehends and applies the doctrine proposed to be believed and hoped in to his own comfort, this assent arises from feelings of hope and faith infused by the internal operation of the Spirit. Therefore the doctrine of faith and hope is promulgated by man, but the habits of faith and hope are infused and implanted by God himself. Whence Clemens, Pædag. 1, ʹΗμεν κατηχησις εις πίστιν περιάγει, πίστις δὲ αγίω παιδευέται πνευματι. *Instruction indeed leads to faith, but faith is also taught by the Holy Spirit.* And here that celebrated saying of Augustine applies, *Think not that man can learn any thing from man : if there be*

*no teacher within, all our babbling is in vain.   There are cer-
tain outward assistant teachers and admonitions ; he who teacheth the heart hath his seat in heaven.** So the Apostle to the
Hebrews iv. 2, *The word preached did not profit them, not
being mixed with faith in them that heard it.*

Therefore God himself is the Creator of faith and hope
in the hearts of men : but the hearing the word of God is
the instrumental cause ; as well because it shews the object and proposes it to the mind of the person believing or
hoping; as because those habits of faith and hope are not
imparted to sleepers, or to those occupied any other way,
but to hearers of the word of God, and to those meditating in the same; on which account the word is called *the
ministration of the Spirit,* 2 Cor. iii. 8.   Contemners of the
word are void of the hope of salvation.—Thus much concerning the general instrument, viz. *the word of God.*

Through the word of the truth of the Gospel.] Now he
declares in particular whence the hope of eternal life
springs.   For the divine word is not adapted in every part
to produce hope ; nay the law serves to arouse fear.   Hope,
therefore, arises, not from the preaching of the legal covenant, *This do and thou shalt live;* but from the promulgation of the evangelical covenant, *Believe, and thou shalt be
saved.*   Well spake Tertullian, advers. Marc. iii. cap. 16,
*The possession of eternal life comes not to us through the disci-
pline of the law, but through the grace of the Gospel.*   As the
possession is through grace, not through the law, so the
hope of the possession is excited through the preaching of
the grace of the gospel, not of the doctrine of the law.
They who expect eternal life from the covenant of works,
do not hope, but presume.   But it has been shewn before
by us, that the proper object of faith and hope, is, not all
those things in general which are delivered in the word, but
the promises of grace : it is not necessary therefore to take
up more time in explanation or proof of this matter.

---

* August. tract. 4 expos. in Epis. Joan.   The original is singularly expressive : *in cœlo cathedram habet qui corda docct.*

The word of the truth.] The Apostle distinguishes the Gospel by a paraphrastic expression. Erasmus* translates it *the veracious word,* because the genitive of a substantive should be often rendered by an adjective, after the usage of the Hebrew language. But he has not sufficiently reached either the meaning or force of Paul's expression. For both the doctrine of the law is *the veracious word,* and many doctrines of the Philosophers are *true;* but *the word of truth,* is (by way of eminence) appropriated to the Gospel.

* Erasmus, well known by his philological and theological treatises as an able scholar and useful writer; the " Πρόδρομος," says Aubery, " of our knowledge, and the man that made the rough and untrodden ways smooth and passable." He was born at Rotterdam in 1467, and educated in an excellent school at Dusseldorf, in Cleveland ; and at nineteen years of age entered among the regular Canons of the Monastery of Stein. From thence he went into France, visited Paris, and studied in the College of Montaigne. Obtaining there some English pupils, he was induced to visit this country, and studied awhile at Oxford ; afterwards he travelled into Italy, and gained great reputation. He came again into England, on the express invitation of Henry VIII., at whose Court he flourished about the commencement of the sixteenth century ; and also became further distinguished by Lectures read in Greek and Theology to the students at Cambridge, in which University he was appointed Lady Margaret's Professor about 1511, and was presented to a Prebendary by Wolsey, and afterwards to the Rectory of Aldington, in Kent. But though thus naturalised, as it were, here, he returned again to the Continent, and was created Counsellor to Prince Charles of Austria. He did not, however, stay long at the Austrian Court, but withdrew to Basil, and spent his latter days in active literary employ with friends he had made there. He entered warmly into the affairs of the Reformation, and in 1516 published his celebrated New Testament, in Greek and Latin, which was received with the utmost eagerness by all those whose minds were turned to Theological pursuits: yet there were many others to whom the publication of the various Editions of the Scriptures by Erasmus and his brother Reformers, and the circulation of " THE WORD OF THE TRUTH" by their means, was most offensive. It alarmed the profligate and illiterate Monks. They declared from the pulpit, ' that there was now a new language discovered, called Greek, of which people should be aware, since it was that which produced all the heresies—that in this language was come forth a book called the New Testament, which was in every body's hands, and was full of thorns and briars—that there was also another language started up, called Hebrew, and that they who learnt it became Jews!' Besides such efforts to promote learning, Erasmus built a School at Rotterdam, endowed it, and directed the order of the Institution. But it is unnecessary to dwell upon his life, though full of interest and incident ; it has been written at length by different hands, besides the prin-

A twofold reason may be assigned for this ; First, because what is most excellent in any kind, is wont (per antonomasian*) to claim its generic name as by special prerogative. Since, therefore, among the various kinds of truths, saving truth is more excellent than the rest ; the doctrine of salvation is called the doctrine of *the truth.* The doctrine of the law, since we are become weak through sin, becomes a doctrine of death ; the doctrine of the Philosophers relates to men as citizens, not as touching their salvation ; the doctrine of the Gospel therefore remains, which alone is saving, and therefore is alone called, by way of eminence, *the word of the truth,* i. e. saving truth.

Secondly, the Gospel may be called *the word of the truth* because it is the word concerning Christ, who is *the way, the life, and the truth ;* John xiv. 6. For Christ is the true body, in comparison with which the legal rites and ceremonies were shadows and figures : whence that word, *The law was given by Moses, grace and truth by Jesus Christ,* John i. 17. And John viii. 31, *If ye continue in my word, then are ye my disciples indeed; and ye shall know the truth, and the truth shall make you free.* Since, therefore, Christ is the truth, and the Gospel hath Christ, both as its author and its object, it is most aptly called *the word of the truth.*

I must not here proceed to such observations as may be deduced from what has been hitherto advanced concerning the instrumental cause of producing faith in particular, and also from this title whereby the Gospel is distinguished, being anxious to hasten forward to the verses which follow.

---

cipal features of it being embodied in various and ample Biographical Sketches, in works either well known or easily accessible. Though an eminent promoter of the Reformation by exposing the abominations of the Church of Rome, he had not, like Luther and Melancthon, the probity or courage publicly to abjure her. That church, however, after his death, which happened at Basil in 1536, repaid whatever services he might have rendered to Religion by his ridicule of her practices, by condemning him for a heretic. This took place in a conclave held at Rome about 1655.

* Vide Note p. 79.

Verse 6.

*Which is come unto you as it is in all the world; and bring-
eth forth fruit, as it doth also in you, since the day ye
heard of it, and knew the grace of God in truth.*

Paul in the preceding verse celebrated the Gospel, inasmuch as it was the instrumental cause of producing hope
in the hearts of the Colossians : but he still advances in
his praises of the same gospel.   For it is the custom of this
Apostle, having once named the Gospel, forthwith to
launch out in commendation of it.   Which he does the
more freely in this place, because having commended the
Gospel, both the Colossians who so readily received it,
and Epaphras who so faithfully preached it among them,
are associated by him in that commendation.

Now let us come to the text.

In it the Apostle introduces three things : First, he
shews the diffusion of the Gospel, in particular—*it is come
to you;* in general—*and to all the world.*   Secondly, he
declares its efficacy, *it bears fruit ;* where the Vulgate, and
Chrysostom also add a word which is wanting in our versions, viz. *et crescit,* καὶ αὐξανόμενον, and increases.   Thirdly,
he extends this efficacy from the circumstance of time,
since the day ye heard, &c.

Which is come unto you, τοῦ παρόντος εἰς ὑμᾶς.]   Here the
goodness, and the love of God towards the Colossians
shines forth : For the Colossians had not come to the Gospel, but the Gospel to them.   The sick are wont to seek
physicians, and to provide medicines at their own expence ;
but the heavenly Physician seeks the sick, freely sends
the medicine of the Gospel to them who are neither looking for, nor thinking of it.   So the prophet, Isa. lxv. 1, *I
am found of them who sought me not.*   And the Saviour himself says, Luke xix. 10, *The Son of man is come to seek, and
to save that which was lost.*   Upon this Cyprian observes,
De Baptismo Christi, *The beloved of the Father loved us
without any desert of ours, of his own free grace bestowed on*

us the benefit of his advent, of his own free grace healed us, of his own free grace cured us.

From this also, human misery and infirmity are apparent : for we cannot live by the powers of nature and the freedom of the will, so as to merit, from the grace of congruity, the light of the Gospel. Some of the Schoolmen have fancied that a man who has turned his natural good disposition (bonis naturalibus, as they say) to good account, deserves, of congruity, that God should impart to him the knowledge of the saving Gospel and other benefits gratuitously. Whence Durandus ; *There is no one, if he does what is in his power, but God will reveal to him all those things without which there is no salvation.* And elsewhere ; *He who lives well according to the law of nature, God will aid in things necessary to salvation.* But we know that the Gospel came not to Socrates, Phocion, Aristides, Cato, Seneca, and others, who turned their natural good dispositions to better account than those Corinthians to whom it came, who were *whoremongers, thieves, drunkards,* &c. 1 Cor. vi. 10. Therefore as the Gospel came to the Colossians, not called for by their merits, but voluntarily offered by the divine goodness ; so also we must think concerning all others. *It is emphatically expressed* (says Gerson*) *in the Lord's Prayer—*

---

* Gerson, so named from the place of his birth; otherwise John Charlier, a distinguished Ecclesiastic who flourished in the latter part of the 14th and the commencement of the 15th centuries. On account of his eminence and excellence as a Scholar and a Divine, he was made Chancellor of the University of Paris ; but he became most celebrated for the parts he sustained, first, at the Synod of Pisa, in 1409, and then in the Council of Constance in 1414, where he appeared as Ambassador from the King of France, and Deputy from the University of Paris and the Province of Sens ; and obtained the titles of " Evangelical and Most Christian." At that Council, Cardinal Zabarella pronounced him to be " the greatest divine of his time." Mosheim places him at the head of the Latin writers of that period, and calls him the most illustrious ornament of it ; asserting that he was a man of the greatest influence and authority, whom the Council of Constance looked upon as its oracle, the lovers of liberty as their patron, and whose memory, he adds, is yet precious to such among the French as are at all zealous for the maintenance of their privileges against Papal despotism. In the Council he urged many things for the Reformation of the Church, besides preaching boldly on the subject ; and a Treatise

*Let thy kingdom come, i. e. let it come to us, because we are
not able by any inward power of our own to go to it.*

As also in all the world.] To the particular extension of
the Gospel to the Colossians, he adds its general diffusion
in all the world. For the Gospel is compared to the sun,
which traverses and illuminates all parts of the globe. This
light the Apostles and disciples of our Saviour spread
about. Paul himself preached the Gospel from Jerusalem as
far as to Illyricum; Mark, in Egypt; Matthew, in Ethio-
pia; Thomas, in India; Simon Zelotes, in Britain; and
others, elsewhere: And Ecclesiastical writers relate what
provinces each of the seventy disciples traversed in their
preaching. The most ancient Fathers also speak of the
Gospel as even then disseminated among the most remote
nations. We shall be content with the testimonies of Jus-

which he composed at the time on " the trial of Spirits," is said to abound
with excellent rules for the detection of feigned revelations and visions, and
contributed to prevent the canonization of some pretended saints. An observation of his on the Protestant Confession of Augsburg is worth recording here, as being in unison with the afore-cited sentiment. On that
Confession (Vide Scott's Continuation of Milner's Church History), " Gerson writes, that *many fell into despair, and some even committed suicide, because
they found it impossible satisfactorily to observe the traditions of the Church, and
had heard of no consolations from grace, and the, righteousness of faith.*" Yet
the solid learning and good sense of this man, though they had carried him
through the other official stations which he had sustained with such credit
and distinction, and his correct views of the sovereignty of divine grace
and the need of the Gospel here evinced, were not sufficient to raise him
much above the darkness of that period, or to carry him through what the
plain state of things indicated to his judgment as necessary. It is a burning zeal for the glory of Christ—the welfare of his Church—and the salvation of precious souls, which alone can conduct a man through the work of a
Reformer. Gerson retired to Lyons in the prime of life, probably out of
disgust at what he had witnessed in the discharge of his public functions, or
through vexation for having taken part against Jerom and Huss, raised up
in Bohemia to proclaim the kingdom of God, and revive again the consolations of grace and the righteousness of faith among men. He, however,
passed some years in his retirement at his Brother's, in pious and useful exercises, carrying his humility so far as to instruct youth at school; and died
in 1429, aged 66. He wrote several works, which have been justly valued, and have passed through various editions. " The Imitation of
Christ," passing under the name of Thomas a Kempis, has been attributed
to him.

tin Martyr, Clemens Alexandrinus, and Tertullian.* *There exists no race of men, whether of Barbarians or Greeks, or bearing any other designation ; either of those who use their traines for dwellings,†* *or of those who dwell in tents,‡* *or of those who know not the use of dwellings, among whom prayers are not offered up in the name of the crucified Jesus,* &c. Justin Martyr, Dialog. cum Tryphon. *The word is withheld from none, the light is common, it hath shone to all men : there is no Cimmerius§ in the word.* Clemens Alexandrinus has these words ; *Whom have all people heard of? In whom have all nations believed, unless in Christ?* Tertullian, after enumerating all nations, adds concerning us ; *The abodes of the Britons, inaccessible to the Romans, yet have been brought under subjection to Christ.*‖ And elsewhere; advers. Marc. he asserts, *That Christ had captivated the whole world by faith in his Gospel.*

* These Fathers, as living in the first ages of the Church, and becoming Apologists for the early Christians, are (next to the brief notices we gather from Scripture), the principal sources from whence information respecting them is obtained.

+ Probably alluding to the ancient Germanii or Sarmatii.

‡ The Arabians as being the most distant.

§ Nullus Cimmerius :—Alluding to Cimmerius on the Western Coast of Italy, so gloomy as to have become proverbial, and have its name used to express any condition of obscurity.

    " There, under ebon-shades, and low-brow'd rocks,
      As ragged as thy locks,
        In dark Cimmerian desert ever dwell."
                         L'Allegro of Milton.

Vide also Hom. Odyss. lib. ii.

‖ Roman Catholic writers have been accustomed to boast of the introduction of Christianity into Britain under Pope Gregory, from the well known circumstance of his being struck with the interesting appearance of some of the West Angles forced from Britain and exposed for sale at Rome ; and many Protestant writers have given currency to the assumption.¶ But the obligations of England to him by sending Augustine to the West Saxons have been strangely overrated. Tertullian, who flourished nearly four centuries before Gregory, speaks of the important event of the reception of Christianity by this country as having occurred before *his* day. It had certainly been previously introduced into the greatest part of South Britain, and was not unknown even at the Court of Ethelbert before Au-

¶ See an elegant poetical Version of this by Wordsworth.

But here a doubt is started by some, who think the Gospel could not have spread into all the world in so short a space of time, as for instance, forty or fifty years. They also urge that objection, that many nations, nay, another hemisphere is now discovered, which was unknown in the times of the Apostles.

Now to this it may be replied, first; That expression *into all the world* is to be explained (by synecdoche) for the greatest part of the world. For we must not think that the Apostles penetrated into all the corners of the known world; but into the most noted provinces, and especially preached the Gospel in the great cities, i. e. they diffused it far and wide. So Luke ii. 1, *There went out a decree from Cæsar Augustus that all the world should be taxed,* i. e. all the provinces subjected to the Roman Empire. So John xii. 19, *All the world is gone after him,* i. e. men of all kinds indiscriminately.

Secondly, the Gospel is come into all the world, inasmuch as a school of Evangelical doctrine is open to all the world, although it may not be preached in particular places. It is opposed, therefore, to the doctrine of Moses, which was open to one nation only, whereas access may be had to the Gospel for all nations. Whence that saying of the Apostle, Titus ii. 11, *The grace of God that bringeth salvation hath appeared to all men.* Not that the preachers of the Gospel, bestirring themselves in all directions, could preach to all and every one; but the preaching of Gospel grace is offered to all and every one without distinction of nations.

But as to what is objected in the last place about the New world, viz. that the Gospel was never known to those people, since they were unknown in the times of the Apostles; I

gustine was known there; for his Queen Bertha was a Christian, and had a Christian Chaplain about her person; and the arrival of Augustine was soon succeeded by the too common accompaniments of the Roman creed— tyranny and persecution. How small a portion of Britain is indebted to Gregory may be seen, among other writers, in the learned " Defence of English Orders," by Mason, translated by Lindsey. " Adams's Religious World Displayed," may also be consulted with satisfaction, vol. i. p. 393.

answer, First, that this is uncertain ; for we learn from Ecclesiastical history, that the Gospel penetrated into the far-
thest coast of the Eastern India ; and the most learned men
(among whom is Arias Montanus, in libro Phaleg.*) think
the Eastern parts of this India were contiguous to the
Western parts of America, or of the New World. Although
this also could be answered, that those regions began to be
inhabited, long after the times of the Apostles ; yet when
the Gospel is said to have come into all the world, it is
understood into those parts of the world which were inhabited by men.   It is now quite clear that the Gospel
was preached in all the world.—But why does the Apostle
introduce the mention of this thing in this place ?

First, that he might shew the prophecies of the ancients
to have been truly fulfilled, and also of Christ the Saviour,
concerning the calling of the Gentiles, and the propagation of the Gospel. *The Gentiles shall come to thy light, and
kings to the brightness of thy rising,* Isa. lx. 3.   *The people
who walked in darkness have seen a great light,* ibid. ix. 2.
This Gospel of the kingdom shall be preached in all the world,
Matth. xxiv. 14.   This could not but confirm the Colossians in the doctrine of the Gospel, when they understood
that it was destined for the Gentiles, by the divine decree,
from the beginning of the world.

Secondly, (as Chrysostom has observed), because persons
are confirmed in the faith from having many associates in
their tenets.   For although the multitude of those who err
does not procure credit for error; yet a multitude of per-

---

* Arias Montanus : a learned Spaniard, born at Frexenel, in Estrema-
dura, in 1527.   After studying in the University of Alcala, he took the
habit of a Benedictine, and attended the Council of Trent in 1562, where
he obtained considerable reputation.   On his return to Spain, he retired to
a hermitage, whence he was withdrawn by Philip II. to edite a new Polyglot, which he completed in 8 vols. folio, Antwerp, 1572.   After satisfactorily clearing himself at Rome, from a charge of corrupting the text, he
was offered a bishopric by Philip, but preferred a second retirement, from
which he was again solicited by the king to return, and become librarian of
the Escurial.   He died in 1593, aged 71.   Besides the Antwerp Polyglot,
Arias, who was one of the most learned Divines of the sixteenth century,
published several other works, which are chiefly erudite Commentaries on
the Scriptures.

sons concurring in the truth, strengthens the minds of the faithful, and as it were reproaches unbelievers with their infidelity.   Whence that remark of Augustine, *Whoever now requires miracles to establish his faith, is in himself a mighty miracle, who, in the midst of a believing world, does not himself believe.* De Civitat. Dei. xxii. 8.

Lastly, the Apostle calls to mind the propagation of the Gospel through the whole world, that the Colossians might hence understand that those new doctrines of the Philosophers and Seducers, which began to be sown in that Church, were not a part of the Gospel, because they were not propagated by the Apostles through the whole world. And with this same argument we disprove all the errors of the Papists: For they can never prove either the supremacy of the Pope of Rome, or the infallibility of his authority, or the worship of images, or the sale of indulgences, or any other dogma in which they differ from us, to have been preached through the whole world by the Apostles or their coadjutors: Theirs, therefore, are not the decrees of the Gospel, but the silliest imagination of lying dreamers; wherefore the faith of Christians is not bound by them. Shrewdly spake Tertullian, *When we believe the Gospel we have no liking for any thing further: for this we first believe, that there is not any thing beyond it that we ought to believe.**—So much concerning the diffusion of the Gospel: Now of its efficacy.

And bringeth forth fruit.]   Here we must supply, *in all the world, as it doth in you;* we may also add, (what is found in many copies), *and increaseth.*

These first words, *and bringeth forth fruit,* shew the efficacy of the Gospel in producing faith, love, and holiness in the hearts of them that hear; in regard to which, preaching is aptly compared to sowing, and the word to seed, which, *cast into the ground, bringeth forth fruit, some a hundredfold, some sixty, some thirty,* Matth. xiii.

---

* From Tertullian's piece, " De præscriptione Hereticorum," a tract in which he enumerates and censures the various heresies that had infested the Christian Church.

The Apostle, therefore, here speaks of that spiritual fruit which is perceived in conversion, and in the entire change of manners and hearts, when men overwhelmed before in vices, begin to bloom in virtue, and become resplendent in holiness.*

The Fathers every where laud this efficacy of the Gospel. Clemens Alexand. in Protrept, for instance where he says, *The Gospel of Christ hath tamed the fiercest beasts, viz. very wicked men:* and Lactantius, Instit. iii. cap. 26,†

* This was fully exemplified in the conduct and characters of the primitive Christians: the change of conduct, the mental effects which conversion produced in the early ages of Christianity, is unparalleled in the history of man: " We," exclaims Justin Martyr, " who formerly rejoiced in licentiousness, now embrace discretion and chastity : we, who resorted to magical arts, now devote ourselves to the unbegotten God, the God of goodness ; we, who set our affections upon wealth and possessions, now bring to the common stock all our property, and share it with the indigent ; we, who, owing to diversity of customs, would not partake of the same hearth with those of a different race, now, since the appearance of Christ, live together and pray for our enemies, and endeavour to persuade those who unjustly hate us, that by leading a life conformed to the excellent precepts of Christianity, they may be filled with a good hope of obtaining the same happiness with ourselves from that God who is Lord above all things." In an age of Libertinism, we see, the *Christian* was distinguished by purity. Hatred was transformed into love, and the violence of passion subsided into tenderness and peace. The proud became humble. The contemner submitted to contempt. All felt that the *Morality* of *their* Religion was a fixed and imperative Rule, and not, like the Ethics of Philosophy, mere reasoning, often too vague and imperfect to convince, and always too destitute of authority to command. But *this reform* was vital; it altered not so much the exterior appearance as THE INWARD HEART.

† Lactantius was a Christian convert of Africa, and an eminent writer of the early part of the fourth century. On account of his fine genius he was chosen by the Emperor Constantine to be Tutor to his Son Crispus; and it is recorded to the commendation of his character, that, in the midst of the Imperial Court, he lived in such contempt of earthly advantages, as to be often in extreme poverty ! His most celebrated work is his " Divine Institutions," which, whilst it powerfully refutes Paganism, is not free from many erroneous views. He is the most elegant of the Latin writers on subjects of this nature, and has been called the Christian Cicero, not only for the clearness and purity of his Latinity, but from its resemblance to the works of that Orator. His authority as a Theologian is, however, very small, many of his opinions, even on fundamental points, being extremely

observes, *The wisdom of philosophers does not extirpate vices, but conceals them: the precepts of God change the whole man, and, the old Adam being cast out, they render him* A NEW CREATURE. This is depicted in the Prophet Isaiah by an elegant similitude, lv. 10; *As the rain cometh down from heaven, and returneth not thither again, but watereth the earth and maketh it bring forth and bud; so shall my word not return unto me void, but it shall accomplish that which I please, and it shall prosper in the thing whereto I sent it.*

And on this passage, it is worth while to observe, that the Apostle immediately subjoins the bearing of fruit to the preaching and hearing of the Gospel: From which fact he teaches us that the power of the Gospel, consists not so much in the illumination of the understanding, as in the reformation of the will. If this tree be not made good, and produce not the good fruits of holiness and newness of life, in vain we glory in the Gospel; which falls upon unholy men not as a benefit, but as their condemnation. Heb. vi. 7, *The earth which drinketh in the rain that cometh oft upon it, and beareth thorns and briars, is rejected and is nigh unto cursing.*

And increaseth.] This is found in various copies, and is expressed by the Syriac translation; which words shew the efficacy of the Gospel in the multitude of those professing it. For it is said to increase when the number of those increases who embrace the Christian faith. And truly in this sense the Gospel has increased to a miracle. *The Grecian philosophy* (says Clemens) *if any magistrate prohibited it, immediately died away; but the Kings of the earth opposed the Christian doctrine, and yet it increased.* The Church had been harassed by ten continual persecutions

unsound. St. Jerome remarked with truth, that he was better able to destroy the errors of the heathen, than to maintain the doctrine of Christians; and onr learned Bishop Bull, whom no one will accuse of depreciating the ancient Ecclesiastical writers, says, " that he knew little of Christianity, was ignorant of Scripture, and was never reckoned among the doctors of the Church." Still he could judge of the *effects* of Christianity on the lives and morals of its subjects, and the citation of him by our Expositor, as a witness from an " Imperial Court," is powerful; and goes to prove, as in other instances, how conversant Davenant was with the best authors.

under the Heathen emperors, yet, for all that, it was not even impaired by so many calamities : but as Augustine writes, Epis. 42, *The Gentiles, and their idolatries, are overcome, not by the opposition, but by the death of the Christians.**

In the Acts of the Apostles, Luke in many places takes care to record this increase of the Christian Church, as a proof of the Divine protection and the power of the Gospel. Thus, ch. v. 14, *The multitude of them that believed increased;* and xvi. 5, *The churches were established, and increased in numbers daily.* It is no sign of Evangelical truth for its professors to propagate their Religion by arms (as the Mahometans do), or by fire and fraud (as the Papists); but when by preaching, or by patience, Religion prevails against those who oppose it, this is a strong argument that Divine assistance is present with its ministers. We have a clear evidence of this in the restoration of the Gospel through Luther and other pious men, in that it increased daily, whilst the Pope was gnashing his teeth, and the kings of the earth raging.—So far in regard to the diffusion and efficacy of the Gospel.

From the day ye heard it and knew the grace of God in truth.] He magnifies the efficacy of the Gospel in these words; and, at the same time, extols as well the Gospel, as the Colossians themselves, and Epaphras too, as some think : the Gospel from its peculiar doctrine; the Colossians from their mode of hearing, and Epaphras from his mode of preaching.

The efficacy of the Gospel is magnified from the circumstance of time ; as soon as it was preached it began to work, and it continues still to work : Here is double praise be-

* It was the unparalleled patience of the Christians under sufferings; the improbability that men addicted to vice should submit to the loss of all that is desirable, and deliver themselves voluntarily to the executioner, which first awakened the curiosity of the philosophic Justin; such the first reasoning which led him to embrace a Religion, for the professors of which he became such an apologist as we have lately seen, and of which he himself became subsequently a Martyr. The translator dwells upon these points as facts calculated to meet the scepticism and libertinism of the present day.— Vide Note p. 99, and the History of the Christian Church in the second and third Centuries, Encyclopædia Metropolitana.

stowed upon the Colossians ; first, for their docility, because they had immediately embraced the Gospel ; secondly, for their constancy, because they hitherto persist and
abide in the same.

Observe, Hearers of the Gospel must not procrastinate,
but from the moment of its being preached they are bound
both to believe it, and to bring forth fruit. Thus the
Apostle, Heb. iii. 8, *To-day, if ye will hear his voice, harden
not your hearts.* And truly it is the voice of the devil
which says, Give the present time to sin, the future to
God and the Gospel ; yield the flower of your age to sin,
the residue to Religion.

Nor, secondly, is it sufficient, as soon as the Gospel is
offered, to receive it with joy, and bring forth fruit ; but
it behoves us to persevere in each, viz. both in faith and in
holiness. The parable of the stony ground is well known,
which received seed, and brought forth fruit, yet to which
it is imputed as a fault, that those fruits withered away
through the heat of the sun. This inconstancy is also
blamed in the Ephesian church, Rev. ii. 4, *I have somewhat
against thee, because thou hast left thy first love :—repent, and
do the first works. The past things perish,* says Cyprian, *if
those things which were begun cease to go on to perfection.*
Cypr. De bon patient.

The grace of God.] He magnifies the Gospel from that
peculiar feature whereby it is distinguished from the Law.
For the Law declares the will of God *imperatively*, and imposes its mandates upon us ; the Gospel shews the will of
God *savingly*, and offers us grace in Christ : And these distinctions are not to be confounded by persons who would
not obscure the Gospel.

Here the error of the Papacy is detected, who promise
to the regenerate grace and salvation in the doctrine of the
Law. For they teach that men are justified by inherent
righteousness, and merit salvation by their works. If justification and salvation are by the Law, why should the
Gospel be called the doctrine of grace, and be distinguished by this title from the Law ? Let Paul decide this question, Rom. iii. *By the works of the law shall no flesh be jus-*

*tified: for by the law is the knowledge of sin. Now the righ-
teousness of God without the law is manifested—by the faith of
Christ. For all have sinned and are justified freely by his
grace,* &c. Aquinas himself, convinced by such evident
testimony, writes in this manner, *The legitimate use of the
law is, that man should not attribute to it what is not contained
in it : the hope of justification therefore does not stand in moral
precepts, but in faith alone.* In Rom. iii.

In truth 'Εν 'αληθεία.] These last words are explained
very diversely. For some would have 'εν 'αληθεία to be nothing else than *in the Gospel ;* because the Gospel is before
called *the word of the truth.* Therefore Paul here says that
they knew the grace of God *in the truth,* i. e. in the Gospel.
Of this exposition we shall say nothing now, both because
I do not much approve of it, and because I have before
spoken concerning this title of the Gospel.

The second exposition is that of those who interpret *in
the truth* to mean in truth and sincerity, free from all external
disguise and hypocrisy ; and they refer this to the Colossians, and to their praise, who, not by outward pretence,
but in reality, were embracing the Gospel.

Whence arises this clear evidence, that neither the *name* of
Christian, nor of the Gospel, can any ways profit men, if
the reality of the things themselves be wanting. For he
who is not a true Christian, is not a Christian at all ; he
who is not truly Evangelical, is not Evangelical at all. For
entity and truth are convertible terms, as the Metaphysi-
cians are wont to say. Hence that rebuke denounced
against the Angel of the church at Sardis, Rev. iii. 1, *Thou
hast a name that thou livest, and art dead.* But *a mere name
can have no place, either among the good or the bad,* as says
Justin Martyr, Apolog. 2.*

The last exposition is that of those who refer these words
to the praise of Epaphras, who had preached the Gospel
truly and sincerely to the Colossians, unmixed with the
error either of philosophical speculations, or the leven of

---

* This citation refers to the distinction of things into three classes, *the
good, the bad, and the indifferent ;* according to the philosophy of that age.

Jewish superstition. Therefore it intimates that they ought
to be persevering in the doctrine already known, nor
should allow themselves to be carried away by any wind or
new doctrine whatever; because the doctrine of the Gospel was before delivered to them in truth, but now to
depart from the truth and embrace errors, was base and
shameful.

And hitherto the Apostle has set forth the praises of the
Gospel, from its extension, from its efficacy, from the circumstances of time, from its proper object, and, lastly,
from the mode of its promulgation. In the next verse he
passes from the praises of the Gospel to the praise of Epaphras, who had preached this Gospel to them.

Verses 7, 8.

As ye also learned of Epaphras, our dear fellow-servant,
who is for you a faithful minister of Christ;
Who also declared unto us your love in the Spirit.

In these two verses the Apostle is wholly intent upon
sending back Epaphras, the minister of the Colossians, to
that church, with the strongest commendations. For it
conduces much to the promotion of religion that a people
think honourably of their prelates and ministers: for if the
priests of God begin to be despised, religion will soon be
despised, and the worship of God contemned; which we
see in the case of the Sons of Eli, 1 Sam. ii. 17. Here,
therefore, we shall note three things in general; and afterwards proceed to a particular exposition of the words.

1. By the example of Paul, ministers are taught not to
decry others that themselves alone may stand pre-eminent,
but to take as much care of the reputation and good esteem of others, as of their own: for whilst we turn our
carpings and the scourge of our revilings upon one another, we, one and all, become spurned at and trampled
upon by the laity.

2. Since the reputation of ministers is so essential to
the Gospel, let us understand that each of us must strive

to obtain a good report : therefore we ought not only to
abstain from all evil, but from all appearance of evil.
They are not to be listened to, says Augustine, *who say that
a good conscience before God is enough for them, and in the
mean time recklessly despise the esteem of men. Whoever keeps
his life from gross sin, does good to himself ; but whoever
guards his reputation, is charitable towards others. Our good
conduct is necessary for ourselves : our reputation for others*,
De bono viduit, cap. 22.

3. Since the unspotted reputation of ministers is a
matter of such moment, let those persons consider how
much guilt they fasten upon themselves, who, either by
malevolent detractions call undeservedly into suspicion, or
by witticisms and jokes expose to derision, those who,
even on the mere ground of their vocation, ought to be
honoured by men.   That Poet spake piously, whoever he
was, who said, *Reputation, integrity, and the eye cannot be
trifled with*.   Moreover, Theologians determine this detraction to be worse than theft : Both are bound to make resti-
tution, viz. the robber and the detractor : but satisfaction
is made much more easily for theft than for detraction;
because the quantity of loss in the former may be known
and estimated ; in the latter it cannot.—Let these general
remarks suffice concerning that upon which the Apostle
laid such stress, viz. that Epaphras, the minister of the
Colossians, might be acceptable and honourable among
his own people.   And now let us treat, specifically, of
those commendations which are heaped upon him by the
Apostle.

As ye also learned of Epaphras, our dear fellow-servant.]
In these words he commends Epaphras by a comparison,
or reference to himself, and that on a two-fold ground :
first, that he was *dear* to him ; secondly, that he was his
fellow-servant.

Dear.] On account of his sincerity in preaching the
Gospel : for Paul embraced all those with a wondrous love
who laboured faithfully in the Gospel.   Now this was
highly to the honour of Epaphras, that he was one of the
bosom friends of Paul : for if it be to one's honour to be

commended by those who are themselves approved among
men, then much more is it to one's honour to be both commended and loved by them. Whilst, therefore, he calls
him *his beloved,* he intimates that he ought to be beloved
by them. *The potter envies his fellow-potter, and the smith
the smith ;* but it should not be so among ministers.

Our fellow-servant.] On account of the same office of
preaching the Gospel, in which both served the same Master. But, when he calls him his *fellow-servant,* he puts the
Colossians in mind by the way, that Epaphras was no
common minister, but a general in the Gospel warfare, and
their Apostle, as it were.

And here we should mark the humility and candour of
such a man, who, placed, as he was, at the summit of
Apostolic dignity, acknowledges Epaphras as his equal.
They who, among the ministers of the Gospel, surpass
others in rank and dignity, ought to imitate this humility.
Humility is a bright ornament in all Christians; but it is
brightest and greatest when seen in those who are most
eminent and exalted.

He pursues the commendations of Epaphras still farther,
on the ground of the character and relation in which he
stands to Christ and the Colossians.

Who is for you a faithful minister of Christ.] Here is a
three-fold commendation of Epaphras : from his office or
vocation, *a minister of Christ ;* from the character of his
ministry, *a faithful minister ;* from the design or end of his
ministry, *for you,* i. e. for your salvation. Upon all these
grounds, he ought to be held in the highest esteem and
love among the Colossians.

A minister of Christ.] The word διάκονος, *Minister,* which
is used in the Greek text, is not employed in this place for
the special office of taking care of the widows of the poor,
to which duty the seven were chosen, Acts vi. 3 ; but in a
larger sense, it is put for any dispenser of the divine word ;
so that sometimes it comprehends the Apostles themselves,
as in 1 Cor. iii. 5, *Who is Paul, or who is Apollos, but ministers by whom ye believed ?* in the Greek, 'αλλ' η̈ διακονοι δι' ω̈ν
'επιστεύσατε. But waving any remark upon the word, let us

inquire into the dignity of the office itself. *A minister of Christ;* i. e. a minister of the Supreme King of heaven, of earth, and hell. Not even angels disdain to minister to and serve this Lord.

But a minister in what? (for this also adds much to the dignity of the ministry). Not in any mean or abject business, but in the dispensation of the most precious treasure, viz. Gospel grace. Among the ministers of kings, the treasurer is accounted one of the most honourable: how much honour therefore should people attach to those, through whom the treasure of the grace of the Gospel is dispensed to men? Such a minister was Epaphras; and, therefore, worthy of being loved and honoured by the Colossians.

From this title, which is given to preachers of the word, many things may be deduced.

1. That, since they are the ministers of Christ, they may not be despised, or injured with impunity, by any man. David avenged the injury done to his ambassadors by the Ammonites, in shaving their beards and cutting off their garments, 2 Sam. x.; how much more shall Christ avenge his ambassadors and ministers, if any thing be done against them injuriously or contumeliously, by Ammonites amongst us?

2. That, since they are ministers of this heavenly King, it behoves them not to set their hearts upon temporal advantages, but to look for a heavenly reward. This splendid recompence Christ promises to his servants, Dan. xii. 3, *The wise shall shine as the brightness of the firmament; and they that turn many to righteousness, as the stars for ever and ever.* Upon this crown Paul had his thoughts ever fixed, 2 Tim. iv. 8, *There is laid up for me a crown of righteousness,* &c.

Faithful.] This in a special manner conduces to the praise of Epaphras. It is a great thing to be a minister of Christ, i. e. a dispenser of the Gospel; but as the Apostle speaks, 1 Cor. iv. 2, *It is required in stewards,* or ministers, *that every one be found faithful;* this faithfulness is particularly to be noted in two things:

1. In this, that a minister should always regard the honour of his Lord, not his own glory. But he regards the
honour of God, who *so speaks as the oracles of God, that
God in all things may be glorified,* 1 Pet. iv. 11; and he
seeks his own glory who so speaks that he may please vain
men, and be commended by them either on account of
genius, or learning, or eloquence. Concerning this desire
of vain-glory, Paul says to the Galatians, i. 10, *Do I seek
to please men? If I yet pleased men, I should not be the servant of Christ.* A wholesome admonition to preachers is
that direction of Prosper; *Let them not in preaching place
their confidence in splendid diction; but in powerful effects.
Let them not be gratified by the acclamations of the people, but
by their tears: nor let them aim at eliciting applause, but sighs.*
De vita contempl. lib. i. cap. 23.

2. The faithfulness of a minister is apparent in this,
that he not only advances his Master's glory, but promotes
with all his power, the benefit and safety of the people
committed to him. This they do by watching over the
flock; by distributing to them the food of their souls seasonably; by dispensing milk to babes, and strong meat to
the more advanced; and, to sum up all in a word, by never
omitting, through indolence, to do or speak whatever may
be necessary to the salvation of the people; nor to teach
or do any thing, by any act of treachery, which may be
hostile to their salvation. We have an illustrious specimen of this faithfulness in Paul, who, with a bold confidence, could declare concerning himself, *I seek not mine
own profit, but the profit of many, that they may be saved,* 1
Cor. x. 33. But, to exhibit this faithfulness, it will be
useful for every one constantly to propose to himself these
three circumstances; Who? What? To whom?

Who he is, let him first of all carefully consider. He is
not a private man, nor free, and master of himself; but an
ambassador and servant of Christ: wherefore it behoves the
pastor not to indulge in ease and pleasure, but to prosecute, with all diligence, the business laid upon him.

What he has undertaken to handle, he should next se-

riously think with himself; viz. the Word of God, and the
Sacraments of Christ. Either to conceal the former, or in
any manner to adulterate it, is a gross impiety; to cast the
latter before dogs or swine, or deny them to the children,
is the greatest sacrilege.

To whom all these things are to be administered, let him
consider in the last place ;—To the sheep of Christ, to His
brethren, to the children of God ; to those *whom Christ redeemed, not with silver and gold, but with his precious blood.*
He who shall lose even one poor soul of these by his un-
faithfulness, *it were better for him if a millstone were hanged
about his neck, and he were cast into the sea,* Luke xvii. 2.

But here it may be asked, Why in extolling Epaphras,
the Apostle should mention only his faithfulness, not his
wisdom; when each is required in the dispensation of the
Divine word? as it is said in Matth. xxiv. 45, *Who then is
a faithful and wise servant, whom his lord hath appointed over
his household?*

It is answered, First, because these two qualities are
connected and joined with each other, so that true faithfulness cannot exist unless wisdom also be with it, which
teaches and shews what is required from a faithful man :
for wisdom is *the eye of every virtue.*

Secondly, that by the way he might check those new
and false teachers in the church of the Colossians, who
affected a shew of wisdom, whilst at the same time, they
divested themselves of all regard for fidelity. He therefore
calls Epaphras *a faithful minister of Christ,* that he might
oppose him to those in whom an opinion of their own wisdom predominated, when, nevertheless, they were unfaithful towards Christ.

For you.] After the Apostle had recommended Epaphras on the ground of his vocation itself, that he was *a
minister of Christ;* and on the ground of the character of
his ministry, that he was *a faithful minister;* he now adds
what greatly conduced to conciliate their love to him, *for
you,* i. e. for your good, for your salvation.

From the design, therefore, and end of the ministry, he

shews that honour is due to a minister from his flock: for
Epaphras is not a minister of Christ for himself, but for
others, viz. the Colossians.

It was a true dogma of the Philosopher (Aristot. Pol.
22), that there are two properties in every thing which excite the love and care of men, τὸ ἴδιον, καὶ τὸ ἀγαπητόν, i. e.
it is their own, and it is beloved by them. Both of these are
found in Epaphras; τὸ ἀγαπητὸν, worthy of love, for he was
a minister of Christ, and moreover faithful; τὸ ἴδιον, for he
was peculiarly the minister of the Colossians. Hence
arises a useful and necessary lesson, and which can never
be sufficiently learnt by the laity.

Although a Christian people are bound to love and honour all ministers, yet each flock ought to cherish with
especial love and honour those who are set over them in
particular. So Paul, 1 Thess. v. 12, *We beseech you, brethren, to know them which labour among you, and are over you
in the Lord, and admonish you; and to esteem them very
highly in love for their works' sake.*

Whence it appears how defective and blamable is that
affection in many who prefer to hear, and more love, any
one rather than their own proper settled minister. If Paul
had written to men of this sort concerning any one—*Who
is a minister of Christ for you,* he would have excited, not
their love of him, but their contempt. These are they,
who, *having itching ears, heap to themselves teachers after
their own lusts,* as the Apostle writes 2 Tim. iv. 3.

So much for the commendation of Epaphras from his
office, from his fidelity in the execution of it, and from the
peculiar design thereof, viz. that he was appointed to the
Colossians.

Verse 8.   *Who also declared unto us your love in the
Spirit.*

Paul has commended the faith and love of the Colossians, when yet he was unknown to them by face, as appears from Ch. ii. 1 : Therefore some one might have asked,
Whence, Paul, could you have this knowledge of us and
of our affairs ?   He meets this question, and shews that he
has not commended them rashly, but he had discovered
and ascertained all by the relation of Epaphras, a most
competent witness.

Who also declared.]   He shews the author of the relation, which he does in order that he might gain favour for
Epaphras among them : for it is natural to all to love those
whom they have understood to think and speak honourably
concerning them.

And here it is to be observed, how faithful a minister of
Christ Epaphras was, not only in preaching the Gospel,
but in exciting the minds of men to mutual love.   For, as
it is likely he had declared to the Colossians, how great
an Apostle Paul was, with what admirable knowledge,
with what singular zeal, he was distinguished; and thus
excited in their minds an admiration and wondrous love of
Paul ; then he goes to Paul and explains how much affection there was in the Colossians towards him.   This, then,
is the duty of an ingenuous and pious man, to promote
love and charity among all ; not to sow the seeds of hatred
and strife.

Your love.]   Here the Apostle touches upon the chief
head of his relation : for he had said many good things to
Paul concerning them, but had particularly extolled their
love.   Some refer this their love to all the saints ; but inasmuch as he had commended that in the fourth verse, the
opinion of Chrysostom is the more probable, who refers it
to the Apostle Paul ; which also the following words seem
to intimate.

In the Spirit, or, *through the Spirit.*]   Two reasons are
assigned by interpreters, why he states their love to be *in
the Spirit.*

The first, a general one, which regards the very nature of love: to wit, because the Holy Spirit is the author of it ; and also because love flows from a spiritual heart, i. e. from a heart regenerated and renewed.

Hence observe the dignity of Christian love. For natural love, or predilection, arises from those inclinations which they call στοργὰς φυσικάς, natural affections. Worldly love arises either from views of interest or from conformity of manners ; carnal, from the appetite for pleasure : To all these something corrupt, sordid, and vicious always adheres. But Christian love arises from the *Holy Spirit,* and is altogether full of holiness and purity.

The other reason why the love of the Colossians is said to be *in the Spirit,* is special, and hath respect to Paul himself; For, as we have before said, they had never seen Paul, but had only heard of him through Epaphras and others : because, therefore, they had loved him whom they never saw in the flesh, they are said to love *in the spirit.* Therefore the word *spirit* is taken in the same sense as in 1 Cor. v. 3, *Being absent in the body, I am present with you in the spirit,* &c.

Hence observe, that the duty of every good man is, to embrace with spiritual love all good men, although known only by report. That any one may be esteemed worthy of our love, it is sufficient if he be known in respect to his virtue, although he be unknown in person.

And thus far we have been employed in explaining the first and second part of the exordium. The last remains, which is comprised in the three following verses, 9, 10, 11.

Verses 9, 10, 11.

*For this cause we also, since the day we heard it, do not
cease to pray for you, and to desire that ye might be filled
with the knowledge of his will in all wisdom and spiritual understanding;* &c.

In this verse and the two following is contained the last
part of the exordium; which consists of a prayer for the
increase of spiritual blessings, of which the Colossians had
been made partakers in some measure.

But the Apostle desires for them three kinds of blessings: the first, those which respect the perfect knowledge
of the truth, ver. 9; The second, those which respect the
exercise of godliness and purity, ver. 10; The last, those
which respect patience and the enduring of the cross, ver.
11.

In this 9th verse, from which we must begin, we may
observe three things:

The motive which excited Paul to this prayer, *For this
cause we also,* &c.

The manner of the prayer itself, *cease not to pray for you
and to desire.*

The sum of the prayer, *that ye may be filled,* &c. to the
end.

Since the day we heard it.] Here he intimates the motive
to his prayer, viz. the relation of Epaphras about their
faith, love, &c. For these words refer to the whole narration concerning their faith in Christ, their love to the saints,
their hope laid up in heaven, and also their love in particular towards the Apostle: for because so many good
things had been told him of the Colossians, *he ceased not
from that day to pray for them,* &c.

Observe 1. The best method of declaring our love and
affection consists in this, that we pray for those whom we
love, and desire these *spiritual* and *salutary* blessings for
them from God. For to love, is to wish good to another
not for our own, but for his sake; and truly to love is to

wish real blessings to another; but real blessings are these spiritual ones, which render the possessors good.   Hence, though the Apostle most tenderly loved all those to whom he sent his Epistles, yet we no where read that he sought honours or riches for them from God, but faith, love, holiness, patience, and other things of the like kind.

2.   It ought especially to stir us up to pray for our brethren, when we perceive in them the first fruits of the Spirit and of renovation, and, as it were, the seeds of piety.   For so Paul, because he understood the fundamentals of Religion to have been laid in the Colossians, *on this very account*, more earnestly sought from God the increase of the same graces.   We may observe the like in his Epistle to the Ephesians, i. 15, 16, *Having heard what faith and love is in you, I cease not to give thanks for you, making mention of you in my prayers*, &c.   Chrysostom illustrates this by an elegant similitude : *As in the race, says he, we especially wish well to, and excite by our encouragement and our cheers, those who are not far from victory ; so in this race of the Christian life, we ought chiefly to favour and assist with our prayers those whom we perceive pressing with alacrity to the destined goal.**—And so much concerning the motive.

* John Chrysostom flourished toward the close of the fourth century. He was a native of Antioch, born of a noble family in that city about the year 354 ; and became, as he advanced in years, so celebrated and admired for his attainments and virtues, (being, by the care of his mother, like Augustine, instructed in Christianity), that at an assembly of Bishops, it was resolved to enrol him among their body.   On hearing this, Chrysostom retired to the summit of a mountain, in company with an old man, and afterwards entirely secluded himself in a dreary cave, from all converse with mankind.   But his health suffering in this state, he returned to Antioch, the Bishop whereof soon promoted him to the office of a Presbyter; and his reputation as a preacher became so great, that, on the death of the Patriarch of Constantinople, he was, by general consent, elected to that dignity ; but to proceed to his See he was obliged to leave Antioch privately, the people being unwilling to part with him.   At Constantinople he commenced a reform of the abuses among the Clergy, who had been suffered to relax through the negligence of his predecessor: he retrenched a great part of the expences in which Nectarius had lived, in order to feed the poor and build hospitals ; and he preached with the utmost zeal and plainness against the pride, luxury, and avarice of the great.   His attention to the condition of his Clergy, led to his justly admired discourses on the Priesthood.   His

We cease not to pray and desire for you.] The Apostle now expresses the manner of his praying, which is perceived in two things : in its importunity, *we cease not ;* in its fervid devotion, *to pray and desire.*

freedom of speaking against reigning vices, and especially in declaiming against the gaiety, impiety, and corruption that prevailed at the Court of Arcadius, raised him many powerful enemies. Theophilus of Alexandria first obtained his deposition and banishment ; but so great was the tumult of the people, that the Emperor was compelled to send him letters of recal. Eudoxia, however, soon after had him banished again to a most inhospitable and barbarous place in Armenia. But there he gained such respect that the jealousy of his enemies was further excited, and an order was procured for his removal to a still worse station, the very shore of the Black Sea ; when, as he was being removed, the soldiers (no doubt suitably instructed) treated him so roughly that he died by the way, A. D. 407, in the 60th year of his age. Chrysostom, if not so Evangelical in his views as some of the Fathers, yet confined himself more to the literal and historical sense of the divine word than others ; and is justly ranked among the most eminent Christian orators : his eloquence was manly, and his fidelity as a minister of God's word unbending ; his genius was uncommon, and his erudition extensive. He exhibited himself both as a moral and controversial writer ; composed a great number of homilies ; and his works were so abundant as to form thirteen folio volumes. His treatise on the Priesthood has been translated into English : and we are further indebted, if not to his own pen, yet to a Greek Liturgy commonly ascribed to him as the compiler, for that most excellent prayer at the close of our daily service, than which it would be difficult to conceive one more suitable to the conclusion of our prayers and supplications.

The Translator is informed, that in the service of the Greek Church as performed in Russia, no less than five prayers of St. Chrysostom are retained, of which the following is one ; and, as a testimony of that Church's holding the essentials to salvation, and as corresponding with the statements already given in this work of the doctrine of the sacred Trinity, the insertion of it in this place may not be deemed impertinent :

" It is just and right to praise Thee, to magnify Thee, to worship Thee, in all places of thy dominion ; for thou art, O God, unspeakable, unknown, unseen, incomprehensible ; Thou art the very same from eternity ; Thou and thine only Son, and thine Holy Ghost. Thou broughtest us out of nought into existence, and when we were fallen through our disobedience, thou liftedst us up again, in that thou didst every thing to bring us to heaven, and to give us an inheritance in thy kingdom which is to come. For these and all other benefits, known and unknown, seen or hidden, we give thanks to Thee, and thine only Son, and thine Holy Ghost. Accept our humble thanks that thou hast vouchsafed to receive this service at our hands : Thou who art surrounded with thousands of archangels, and ten

Importunity in prayer is commanded in Scripture; *We ought always to pray, and not to faint;* Luke xviii. 1. *Pray without ceasing,* 1 Thess. v. 17. *The constant prayer of a righteous man availeth much,* James v. 16.

But it may be said, How is it possible that Paul should never desist from prayer, when the weakness of human nature will not sustain continual praying? nay, the Euchitæ, or Messaliani, who made constant prayer the pretext of indolence and sluggishness, are reckoned among heretics. Theodor. lib. 4. Augustine, tom. vi. De hæres.

I answer, We are said not to cease from prayer, or not to leave off praying for any thing, when we have a fixed desire of that thing in our heart. So Augustine, in Psalm xxxvii. *Thy desire is thy prayer; if there be a continual desire, there is continual prayer.*

Secondly, we are said not to faint, or not to cease from praying, when we exercise it in its proper time and place. For it is idleness in a man, and he ceases from his work, which he does not perform when he can and ought.

In either respect, therefore, Paul said truly, *We cease not to pray for you.* For there was both a perpetual desire in his mind (at least as to the habit) of promoting their good; and that also, as much as in him lay, he did promote by his prayers, as often as opportunity of praying offered itself to him.

Observe, then, the duty of the pastor is not only to teach his flock, and to commend them to God in public prayers, but also in his private prayer he ought never to be unmindful of the people committed to his care. Thus Samuel was actuated towards the people of God, *Be it far from me to sin against the Lord in ceasing to pray for you;* 1 Sam. xii. 23. So our Apostle, *God is my witness, whom I*

thousands of angels, who, together with the many-eyed Cherubim and six-winged Seraphim, sing, and declare and proclaim this song of triumph."

From the Holy Liturgy of our holy Father John Chrysostom, Archbishop of Constantinople; as given in the German of Yasnowsky, Chaplain to the Grand Duchess of Saxe Weimar, and Minister of the Greek Chapel of her Imperial Highness.

serve, that without ceasing I make mention of you always in my prayers, &c. Rom. i. 9.

Neither let any one here object, that men of remarkable holiness, such as were Samuel and Paul, might help the people of God by their constant prayers; but that other ministers who are destitute of this holiness, cannot: For well hath Augustine taught, *that even wicked priests are heard when they pray for their flocks, although they are not heard when they pray for themselves,* contra Epist. Parmen. lib. ii. cap 8. And so much concerning the importunity of the Apostle's prayer : What follows is concerning its vehement devotion.

To pray and to desire.] In these two words the Apostle intimates the devotion and even the vehemency of his prayer for the Colossians. Some by the word προσευχόμενοι, understand the desire of the mind ; by that other, αἰτούμενοι, the expressed petition of the lips. But here, by προσευχην, I not only understand the internal elevation of the mind, but that part of prayer which especially paves the way for our petitions, in which we adore and glorify God, commemorating his majesty and goodness, and those other attributes which excite love and devotion in the minds of those who pray. But αἴτησις, is the petition itself of the things desired, which follows this προσευχην, or devout direction of the mind and of the prayer to God. When, therefore, the Apostle says that he prayed, προσευχεσθαι, for the Colossians, he seems to me to intimate that he commended them to God, whenever he felt his mind at all devoutly inflamed towards God: indeed, the prayer of a mind kindled and inflamed is most efficacious, so as to penetrate the very heavens. But when he says that *he desired*, αἰτεῖσθαι, for them, he signifies the vehemence of his petition: for ἄιτησις, *desire*, is the entreating for necessary things. He therefore so prayed to God for the spiritual progress of the Colossians, as men are wont to intreat others for the things which they greatly need.

Observe 1. Devotion and a pious affection towards God ought always to open the way to our particular petitions, whether we seek necessary things for ourselves or for others.   For he who rashly, and without regard to the Divine Majesty, dares to launch forth to make any petition, provokes God to indignation, not to beneficence.

2.   We should seek benefits from God, not coldly, neither for form's sake; but we ought to be actuated by a clear perception and an earnest desire of those things which we seek from God.   For he who requires that with his mouth which he disregards with his heart, does not pray to God, but mocks him.

We have explained the cause, and the mode of the Apostle's prayer; it now remains that we consider the sum of the petition itself, comprehended in the words immediately following :

That ye may be filled with the knowledge of his will, in all wisdom and spiritual understanding.]   Now the Apostle begins to unfold the sum of his prayer.   And here two things are to be noted : the quantity of the blessings sought, and their quality.

That ye may be filled.]   The Apostle has before shewn that the Colossians were endowed with faith, hope, and love, and all other spiritual gifts ; but now he asks something greater from God, viz. that they may be *filled* with the same.

It may be said, we are not able to obtain full and perfect knowledge, or love, or holiness, whilst we carry about this mortal body.   For so the Apostle, 1 Cor. xiii. 9, *We know in part, and we prophecy in part,* &c.   Why, then, does the Apostle pray that they may be *filled* with knowledge, which he himself knew could not be attained?

I answer, there is a twofold plenitude of knowledge and of every grace : a plenitude for the inheritance, and a plenitude for the way.   The plenitude of the inheritance is the greatest measure of grace which the mind of every one is able to contain : this is not to be had before we are introduced to the state of glory.   But the plenitude of the way is the greatest measure of grace which God has determined to impart to every one of the elect in this world : and this is had by all the elect before they remove from this life.

Concerning this the Apostle speaks, Ephes. iv. 7, *To every one of you is given grace, according to the measure of the gift of Christ.* And Augustine, in Psalm xxxviii. *There is a certain perfection, according to the measure of this life; and it belongs to that perfection, that each knows that he is not yet perfect.* This perfection and plenitude of grace the Apostle desires for the Colossians in this prayer.

Hence we are taught that we ought never to think that we have attained the fulness of any grace destined for us in this life; but we ought always to strive and to seek from God, that we may be filled more and more with all spiritual gifts.

We are, whilst we live here, as children who are not yet arrived at maturity : whence the holy Scriptures excite all to a constant advance in every gift of divine grace. Lest I should be tedious, I will only note the places, I will not recite them. To the increase of faith, 2 Cor. x. 15: of hope, Rom. xv. 13: of love, Ephes. iv. 15: of knowledge, Ephes. iii. 19 : of all grace, 2 Pet. iii. 18. Many passages from the Fathers might be adduced for this opinion. Nazianzen, for instance, says, *A Christian either advances or falls back; he cannot remain in the same state.* Bernard says, *He is by no means good who does not wish to be better; and where you begin to be unwilling to become better, there you leave off to be good.**

* This renowned Romanist—Bernard (vide Note page 32)—engaged against the uncorrupted Christians of Cologne (who had settled there from among the persecuted Albigenses, to the great annoyance of the Papists,) when he came to describe those followers of Arnold, said : " If you ask me " of their faith, nothing can be more Christian ; if you observe their con- " versation, nothing can be more blameless ; and the sincerity of their lan- " guage they prove by the consistency of their deeds. In testimony of his " faith you may see a man of this order frequent the church, honour its " elders, offer his gifts, confess his sin, and partake of the Communion: " and what can be more expressive of the Christian ? In life and manners " also, he circumvents no man, defrauds no man, does violence to no man. " His fasts are frequent, his bread is not that of idleness, his labour pro- " cures him his support."—Such is the testimony of an opponent to the Protestants of Piedmont. Would to God that as honourable a report could invariably be borne of modern Protestants, or that different practices could not be affirmed of them, nor *their* enemies ! At all events, the foregoing

We must therefore always seek and labour that we may be filled more and more with spiritual gifts.

Thus much as to the quantity.

The knowledge of his will.] In these words and the following the Apostle explains what are those blessings which he desires for the Colossians, and of what kind. *Abundant knowledge* is one blessing, επιγνωσις, i. e. knowledge upon knowledge: a cumulation and fulness of knowledge. But of what kind? Not any whatever, but that which is here described by its object and its cause, viz. *the knowledge of the divine will* flowing from *wisdom and spiritual understanding.* *The knowledge of the divine will* denotes the act with the object: *Wisdom and understanding* mark the habits infused, whence this actual and efficacious knowledge flows. As to the object of this knowledge, we must know that the divine will, in itself, is of infinite consideration, and inscrutable to men : This knowledge, therefore, must be limited and restricted to the revealed will; for knowledge *(agnitio)* presupposes a manifestation of the thing to be known.

But now, this revealed will, the full knowledge of which the Apostle seeks for the Colossians, is referred to two kinds : a knowledge of the things to be believed, and of those to be done; or of faith, and new obedience. With respect to faith, *This is the will of God, that every one who seeth the Son, and believeth on him, may have everlasting life,* John vi. 40. As to holiness and obedience, *This is the will of God, even your sanctification, that every one should know how to possess his vessel in sanctification and honour,* 1 Thess. iv. 3, 4. The knowledge, therefore, of the divine will embraces in itself the knowledge of the Law and of the Gospel : of the Law, which shews us the abyss of our misery, and also proposes to the regenerate a rule of new life; of the Gospel, which opens to us the depths of divine mercy, and also teaches the method of obtaining salvation.

passage, if no other could be produced, would of itself alone be sufficient to crush the foul slanders which, even at this day, continue to be discharged by the ignorant and malevolent against a most exemplary and brutally persecuted community. But calumny naturally follows persecution.

Neither is the bare apprehension of these things called *the knowledge of the divine will,* but the efficacious apprehension which applies Christ to ourselves, and expresses the rule of the law in our life and actions, as far as in us lies. *Hereby we know that we know him, if we keep his commandments,* 1 John ii. 3; the commandments as well concerning faith as obedience.

Ye see the object of this knowledge: now let us proceed to the cause or fountain of it.

In all wisdom and spiritual understanding.] The Apostle shews whence that efficacious knowledge of the divine will arises, or in what it is grounded, viz. *in wisdom and spiritual understanding.* What is expressed in the Greek by ενσοφια, some render *per sapientiam ;* others *cum sapientiâ:* but it comes to the same thing; for all understand that that knowledge of the divine will is not from us, neither by human learning, but by infused wisdom.*

Let us, therefore, inquire into two things : What is wisdom and understanding? and whence derived?

Lombard, and after him, all the Schoolmen have indulged in many speculations respecting these points, where they dispute about the seven gifts of the Holy Spirit: the ground of which disputation is sought from Isa. xi. 2, where, however, only six are enumerated. But, omitting all other, let us enquire what is their opinion of these two gifts.

Wisdom, says Lombard, quoting the passage above-mentioned, *is a habit infused for the contemplation of, and delight in, eternal truth alone ; understanding, for the consideration of the Creator and invisible creatures.*†

---

* Or by wisdom imparted from above, according to John Baptist's declaration, John iii. 27, " A man can receive nothing except it be given him from heaven ;" and our Lord's to his disciples, Matth. xiii. 11, " It is given unto you to know the mysteries of the kingdom :" Hence St. James testifies, i. 17, " Every good gift and every perfect gift cometh down from the Father of lights."

† The celebrated Peter Lombard, vide Note p. 64. His Sentences, from which the subjoined definition is cited, are a collection of ancient authorities in defence of primitive truth, illustrating especially the moral condition

Parisiensis says, that *the gift of wisdom is opposed to childishness; and the proper office of this is to produce in the mind a contempt of vain and temporal things, and to cause it to take knowledge of such as are heavenly, and to embrace them with delight; but the gift of understanding is opposed to stupidity; and its property is to penetrate the secrets of things and their signs; to see clearly into what are veiled in mysteries, or shadowed forth in any manner; not to cleave to, or be deceived by the external appearances of things.* It is therefore, as it were, the acute and polished light of wisdom itself, and without some measure of this gift, he says, no one can attain unto salvation.

Altissiodorensis says, *Wisdom is the knowledge of God absolutely, understanding is the knowledge of God relatively, viz. in reference to the creatures.* He adds, that *wisdom is the knowledge of God by spiritual taste, because by means of wisdom, the graciousness of God is tasted.*

Gerson says, That *understanding is a certain spiritual light, infused into creatures for the knowledge of God;* that *wisdom is a light infused, under, or by which, divine things are perceived experimentally.*

But these descriptions of the Schoolmen do not seem to me sufficiently ample : for they restrict, as well wisdom as

of man, and the articles of the Christian salvation : they were so far appreciated by the Clergy of the time as to call forth a succession of Commentators, whence " Theology assumed a new aspect, and instead of the divine " truths of the Gospel being presented to the mind, as they originally " were, in their native purity and excellence, they were involved in so- " phism and the intricacies of metaphysical subtilty. Thorny and perplex- " ing arguments superseded the artless simplicity of primitive instruction. " The Aristotilian Philosophy itself was resorted to, and was so intimately " blended with the system, that the Stagyrite, and not St. Paul, became " the standard of authority in the Schools. The advantages accruing to " the See of Rome from this revolution in Theology were numerous; and " the Canon law, which was brought into existence about the same time, " while it added to the influence of the Roman See, tended to establish the " reign of superstition. So far was the Gospel removed out of sight at " this time, that it was impossible for men to see how much its beautiful " simplicity was disfigured ; or what a wide departure from ' the faith once " delivered to the saints' had now taken place."—Vide Grier's Epitome of the General Councils of the Church ; p. 182.

understanding, to a contemplative life ; whereas both equally regard an active one.

Wisdom, then, is the infused knowledge of those things
which pertain to faith and a good life, with pious affections
inclining to the application and practice of the same.

For spiritual wisdom consists not of the illumination of
the intellect alone, neither of the renovation of the affections alone, but of both conjointly.   Which may be
proved from many testimonies of Scripture : *The fear of
the Lord is wisdom ; and to depart from evil is understanding,*
Job xxviii. 28.   *Whoso keepeth the law is a wise son,* Prov.
xxviii. 7.   From which and similar places, it is manifest,
that this wisdom, although as to its essence it is a certain
perfection of the intellect, yet as to its matter and use, is
also practical and moral.   Wisdom, therefore, is not only
the light of the soul, but a certain healthiness and perfection of it.   The light of mere knowledge is sometimes
communicated to the wicked ; for many know the will of
God, but they do it not, nay, they plainly hate it : but the
light of wisdom always renders a man pious, because it at
once inclines the will to that good which is apprehended
by the intellect.   Such wisdom Paul supplicates for the
Colossians.

As to what pertains to the understanding or intellect,
συνεσιν, I do not think it to be a gift in reality distinct from
the afore-mentioned wisdom ; but to be a more eminent
degree ; and, as it were, the pinnacle of wisdom.   It is,
therefore, a certain ripeness of wisdom, by which any one
is fitted to judge of truth and falsehood, good and evil,
when they are involved in some special difficulty, from particular circumstances.   Hence the disciples of the Saviour
are said to be 'ασύνετοι, *without understanding,* Matth. xv. 16,
because they understood not the doctrine of Christ clothed
in parables.   And Paul wished for Timothy, *an understanding in all things,* 2 Tim. ii. 7.—But we shall render these
points more plain by adducing examples ; and first in
things to be believed, then in things to be done.

Let a question be proposed, Whether the only Mediator
of God and men be the man Christ Jesus ; every one en-

dued with the gift of divine wisdom will immediately affirm that he is. Now let it be involved in special difficulties, Whether he is *so* our only Mediator, that he has not communicated the office of interceding to his glorious mother and to other saints; or whether he is *so* our Mediator, that he alone hath made satisfaction for our sins, having left no part of the satisfaction to be made by us. Now there will be need of understanding, i. e. of the clearness of wisdom, which, if wanting, we shall easily fall into error.

Let it be also enquired, Whether it is lawful for subjects to bear arms against their Sovereign; even every Papist will immediately answer it is not lawful. Now let particular circumstances be added: Is it lawful by force of arms to oppose their king when condemned for heresy, and excommunicated by the order of the Pope? If the gift of understanding be wanting, every Papist will doubt and vacillate; nay, he will break out into open rebellion, as we have seen testified by experience.—You perceive what wisdom is, what understanding, and what is their difference.

Now, in the last place, is it asked Whence these gifts come to us? The Apostle points out that in one word, when he adds *spiritual.*

Spiritual.] But it is called so, because it is produced by the Spirit of Christ, not acquired by our ability. For the uncreated Wisdom of God, is the Author of this created wisdom.* In Aristotle, Plato, Socrates, and the rest of the heathen writers, that wisdom in which they excelled was an acquired habit; but in the faithful, saving wisdom is an infused habit. *If any lack wisdom, let him ask of God, who giveth to all men liberally,* Jas. i. 5. Whence says Clemens, *Wisdom cannot be bought with earthly coin; nor is it sold in the market, but in heaven,* Pædag, lib. ii. cap. 3.

From these considerations we deduce some inferences.

---

* It may be permitted to refer the Reader to a splendid illustration of the nature and excellencies of this wisdom in Ecclesiasticus xxiv.

1.   Whereas the Apostle intreats a full knowledge of the divine will for the Colossians, we gather that a blind ignorance, however devoted, is not pleasing to God. *For that is not good which is not rationally good;* as Tertullian intelligently remarks against Mare. lib. i.

2.   Whereas he wishes wisdom and understanding for the Colossians, we learn that that trust in the faith of their prelates, which the advocates of Popery every where extol, is not sufficient for the people; for he who hath wisdom and understanding, sees with his own eyes, not the eyes of others.

3.   They are led not by an Apostolic, but an anti-Christian spirit, who deny to the people the ordinary means of obtaining wisdom and spiritual understanding, viz. the reading and understanding of the divine word: For *the law of the Lord is undefiled, converting the soul; the testimony of the Lord is sure, making wise the simple,* Ps. xix.

And thus much concerning the first part of the Apostle's prayer, for those good things which regard the perfect knowledge of the truth.

Verse 10.

That ye might walk worthy of the Lord unto all pleasing, being fruitful in every good work, and increasing in the knowledge of God.

We have dismissed the first part of the Apostle's prayer, where he seeks for the Colossians those good things which conduce to the perfect knowledge of the truth.   Now I come to the second, where he earnestly desires for them the perfect exercise of piety and holiness.

And, in the first place, it may be observed, from the order itself of this prayer, That wisdom and spiritual understanding are poured into the minds of men from God, not for barren knowledge and idle speculation, but for the practice and exercise of holiness.

The Apostle in the verse before us does two things: He proposes, in general, the sum of this his desire, *That ye might walk worthy of the Lord.* Then he draws it out into parts, and explains how we may walk worthy of God: First, as to the intention and scope, if we refer all things ἐις ᾽αρέσκειαν, to the pleasing of God; secondly, as to the two-fold operation, if we be fruitful in works, and increase in the knowledge of God.

That ye might walk worthy of the Lord.] To walk is an Hebrew phrase, often put in the Scriptures for beginning and keeping to a course of life : as *to walk deceitfully,* and *with simplicity,* in many passages of the Proverbs of Solomon; and *to walk in the ways and in the statutes of God,* as is frequent with David in the Psalms. So in the New Testament, *to walk according to the flesh,* and *according to the Spirit,* i. e. to live and to converse. By this form of speaking, we are admonished that Christianity consists in a perpetual journey towards the celestial country, and that no one must halt by the way, but must perpetually walk and go forward. But how is he to walk?

Worthy of the Lord.] What these words mean we shall readily understand, if we compare them with similar forms of speaking, which occur elsewhere in this our Apostle; so Ephes. iv. 1, *I pray that ye walk worthy of the vocation.* Phil. i. 27, he exhorts them to conduct themselves *worthy of God.* He walks worthy of the Lord, therefore, who so lives as becomes him who is called by the Gospel to the adoption of the sons of God, and to the lively hope of the inheritance of heaven.

Here some may ask, How is it possible to walk in a manner worthy of the Lord, or of God, or of the Gospel, or of our vocation; since nothing adequately corresponds to the high excellency of all these things, except perfect and immaculate righteousness and holiness, such as is not found in men who retain this body of sin?

I answer, the word *worthy,* in the Scriptures, does not always denote the exact proportion of equality of one thing to another, but a certain accordance or suitableness, which takes away repugnance, though it does not establish absolute condignity. So Matth. iii. 8, *Bring forth fruits* WORTHY *of repentance,* i. e. according with and befitting, not repugnant to the repentance which ye profess. He, therefore, walks worthy of God who flees from the baseness and folly of carnal men, who carries himself as a faithful soul, loving God and his brethren, although he often slides and sins through infirmity. For this our worthiness does not depend upon our absolute perfection, but upon the gratuitous condescension of God, who accounts, as worthy his favour, those who follow the guidance of his spirit; and those unworthy who yield themselves slaves to the flesh and sin.

Hence is to be noted,

1. The infinite goodness and compassion of God, who accounts us children, worthy of adoption and of the heavenly inheritance, although we are very far from perfect holiness; provided we *walk not in the counsel of the ungodly, and stand not in the way of sinners, and sit not in the seat of the scornful; but delight in his law, and meditate therein continually,* Ps. i.

2. Hence also appears the pride of those who, from this divine loving-mercy, attempt to establish the merit of *condignity;* as though *to walk worthy of God* was to merit heavenly felicity by their works. But the Apostle dreamt no such thing; only he would have them strive after holiness, that it might thence appear they did not receive the knowledge and the grace of God in vain.—And this is the sum of his desire in general.

Unto all pleasing, or *compliance;* or *That ye may please in all things.*] What the Apostle had proposed in general, he now begins to explain particularly; and first he shews how we may walk worthy of God, as to the intention and universal scope of our life; if, forsooth, all our actions have reference to pleasing God.

Therefore the word ἀρέσκειαν, pleasing, I think is to be taken, in this place, not so much for the result of pleasing, as for the desire and intention of pleasing. For so the word itself is often used: Rom. xv. 2, *Let every one of you please his neighbour.* And Gal. i. 10, *If I pleased men I should not be the servant of God.*

But as the Apostle adds a note of universality, *that ye may please in* ALL *things,* so the Greek Scholia explain it by distribution into λογοις, εργοις, και δογμασι, *words, works,* (as well internal as external) and *also doctrines.*

The reason why the Apostle emphatically requires this general intention of pleasing God, is this; Because the end determines the quality in moral things, as the form does in natural things. *Our duties are to be judged of, not by the beginning but by the end,* says August. in Ps. cxviii. And, lib. iv. contr. Julian, cap. 3, *Whatever good is done, and is done not on this account, because it ought to be done, although it seems good in the view of its being a matter of duty, yet the end itself not being right, it is sin.* So Clem. Strom. 6. *The action of every heathen is foul, because he has not the right end in view.* The scope therefore of our whole life ought to be this, that we may please God, and may glorify him thereby.

But here, in regard to the intention of pleasing God, it behoves us to resolve some doubts.

It is asked, 1. Whether in every good work, the actual intention of pleasing God be necessary through the whole course of the work? For instance; A dutiful son obeys his parents with the intention of pleasing God; I ask, whether he sins in any particular instance of duty, if he should not always actually keep this intention in mind?

I answer; It suffices if that intention should have preceded, and be habitually retained, although it be not thought upon in every single act: for many operations proceed by virtue of some primary intention, although the actual intention hath ceased to accompany them. As a dart, by the single impulse of him who throws it, is borne through an intermediate space to a point, although he thinks not either of the space or the point; so a good work proceeds from a single impulse of the will to its mark, when the performer no longer actually thinks of the mark and of his first intention. The same may be illustrated by

the similitude of a traveller, who does not actually, every
step he goes, think of that place whither he is going, and
yet proceeds straight thither, by virtue of his primary intention.

But here we should be admonished of two things : First,
that we must endeavour, as much as possible, to retain the
actual intention of pleasing and of glorifying God in each
particular work.   Secondly, we must take care, lest, after
the first good intention, some bad and inordinate intention
insinuate itself: for this latter does not derive rectitude
from the former; but the former will by this latter be
marred, corrupted, and defiled.

2.   It is asked, Whether it be possible for a regenerated
man always to retain this habitual intention of *pleasing God
in all things,* although in the mean time he fails in many ?

I answer ; That not only is it possible, but necessary, if
he wishes to retain faith and a good conscience : for these
cannot consist, neither remain in the same heart with the
design of sinning and of displeasing God.   Therefore every
believer constantly keeps in mind the purpose of pleasing
God and of abstaining from sin, according to that saying
of Paul, *The good that I would I do not ; but the evil which I
would not, that I do.   Now if I do that I would not, it is no
more I that do it, but sin that dwelleth in me,* Rom. vii. 19.
He who chooseth good, and not evil, retains the design of
pleasing God, although, being allured by evil concupiscence, he sometimes does that through infirmity which
displeases God, he makes it his main business to please
in all things, whilst he studies to avoid every single sin.

Lastly, it is asked, Whether a believer retaining this design of pleasing God, is always acceptable and pleasing to
him, notwithstanding those his failures and infirmities?

I answer, first, That the person of a godly and faithful
man is always pleasing and acceptable to God, because he
is regarded by God not as he is in himself, but as a member under Christ the head ; *But there is no condemnation to
them who are in Christ Jesus,* Rom. viii. 1.   Secondly, The
good works of the faithful, although imperfect, are nevertheless pleasing to God, because they are regarded by him

as by a loving Father, not as an austere judge ; as covered
and adorned with the most perfect obedience of Christ, not
as naked and alone.   Lastly, The failings and sins of the
faithful are indeed hateful and displeasing to God, but out
of a simple hatred, not redounding upon the person.* And
therefore God hates sin in the regenerate, and for that reason declares war against it, through the Spirit of grace ;
but the regenerate themselves, in the mean time, are acceptable to him, and on that account he favours and
blesses them.   And so much concerning the intention of
those who walk worthy of the Lord.   We must proceed to
the working.

Being fruitful in every good work, and increasing, &c.]
Good working ought to follow a good intention, if we wish
to walk worthy of God, and to please him.   But he names
two kinds of working : the first is practical working, which
tends to labour : the other is theoretical working, which
labours for the acquisition of knowledge itself.   In the
first, two things are to be observed : What he requires,
fruitfulness ; What is the matter about which this fruitfulness is exercised, *Every good work.*

Fruitful.]   This is a metaphorical expression taken from
a tree ; not every tree, but one bearing fruit.   For the
godly are compared to *trees planted by the rivers of waters,*
which bring forth fruit in their season, Psal. i.   They are
compared to branches grafted in the fruitful vine : *I am the*
vine, ye are the branches : he who abideth in me bringeth forth
much fruit, John xv. 5.   From this comparison three things
may be noted :

1.   As no tree can bear fruit, unless it hath a certain
life-giving seed in itself, and is moreover nourished daily
with good sap ; so no one can bear spiritual fruit, unless
he hath in himself the seed of the Spirit, and is daily watered with the outpourings of divine grace.   *Without me*
ye can do nothing.   If a man abide not in me, he is cast forth
as a branch, and is withered.   Hence it is said, 1 John iii.
9, *Whosoever is born of God doth not commit sin ; for his seed*

---

* Vide page 77, on the meaning of " a perfect hatred."

remaineth in him : and he cannot sin because he is born of God.
The Holy Spirit is called seed, because by his power, as a
certain life-giving seed, men are rendered fruitful in good
works. Not much unlike this similitude is that of Parisiensis, when he says, that *virtues are called fruits, because the
mind of the regenerate man is like a field sowed with the life-
giving seed of the wo'd of God; which conceives and brings
forth all kinds of virtues, from the gratuitous and spiritual
embrace of its eternal Spouse, i. e. God.*

2. As that tree is pleasing to God, which does not occupy the ground in vain, neither dissipates the moisture
which it draws on leaves and blossoms alone ; but produces
good fruits : so he alone is pleasing to God, who does not
uselessly occupy room in the Church, neither wears the
appearance and form of godliness alone, but puts forth its
power and virtue by fruitfulness. Very remarkable are the
places of Scripture on this point : in Luke xiii. 7, the Lord
says concerning the fig-tree, *I seek fruit and find none: cut
it down; why cumbereth it the ground?* On the other hand,
a fruitful tree is pleasing to its Lord, and is customarily
his care and delight: *My Father is the husbandman : every
branch which beareth fruit he purgeth it that it may bring forth
more fruit,* John xv 2.

I therefore say with Nazianzen, *Let no Christian be indolent or unfruitful, but let every one from the things which he
hath bring forth fruit to God : the sinner, penitence ; he who
runs well, perseverance ; the youth, chastity ; the old man,
prudence ; the rich, mercy ; the poor, thankfulness,* &c.*

---

* Gregory Nazianzen :—Our Expositor has cited this Father before, with
advantage to his readers (vide p. 21 and 116) though it was not convenient
there to insert a sketch of him : But the beauty of this quotation induces us
to enquire into his character ; because it is not always the case, that the main-.
tenance of Christian truth is an evidence of consistent conduct and fair pretensions to Christian integrity.—Gregory, surnamed Nazianzen, from Nazianzum, a town of Cappadocia, of which his father was Bishop, was born
A.D. 324, at Azianzum, a village near it, and was one of the most illustrious ornaments of the Greek Church. He was made, much against his inclination, Bishop of Constantinople in 379 ; but was scarcely seated in his
Episcopate, than his tranquillity was disturbed by a schism in his Church,
occasioned by the attempts of Maximus, a Cynic Philosopher, whom he

3. As a tree lives and bears fruit, not for itself, but for the owner, and for others to whom he sees fit to impart of its fruits ; so a godly man ought not to live to himself alone, nor to care only that his life be honourable to himself, but that it may be especially honourable to God, who is *his* Lord, and beneficial to all his brethren ; for this is to resemble a fruitful tree.—And thus much concerning the fruitfulness required : It remains to speak of the matter of this fruitfulness.

In every good work.] Behold the very broad and spacious matter in which the fruitfulness of a godly man is exercised : And truly in this he differs from a tree : For no person seeks different fruits from one and the same tree ; but God expects that every one of the faithful and regenerate should produce every kind of good works. And the reason of this dissimilitude arises from this circumstance, that since the fruit of any thing answers to its seed, a tree produces only one sort of fruit, inasmuch as the virtue and power of the seed planted is limited to one ; but the seed which is sown in the hearts of the pious (viz. the Grace of the Holy Spirit) avails to the producing equally of every spiritual fruit : Unless, therefore, they

had baptised, to supplant him in the See : Supported by the Emperor Theodosius, he defeated his opponent, and his election was confirmed in the Council of Constantinople, held in 381. The difficulties of his situation, however, induced him shortly after to resign it ; when he retired to his paternal estate at Nazianzum, and there lived in seclusion till 389, the period of his decease. He was not only a man of piety, learning, and talent ; but also in other respects an estimable character, displaying on most occasions more moderation and liberality than was usual among the Divines of his age. As a Divine he so far outstripped the rest of his day, that " he was " entitled *'ο θεολόγος κατ' 'εξοχην* ; and a difference from his doctrine was " identified with Heresy. A dutiful son, a faithful friend, and universally " beneficent, he would have been a model for society, had he not been too " sensitive, and, perhaps, too ascetic. Humble, though full of energy ; " despising worldly advantages unless he could apply them to the advance- " ment of Religion ; untainted by immorality, forgiving injuries, and in- " defatigable in his Ministry, he may be accounted the most exemplary, " as well as the most able Christian on record in the fourth century." Vide Encyclop. Metropol. under Ecclesiastical Writers of the fourth Century. His works are extant in 2 vols. printed at Paris in 1609. His style is said to be equal to that of the most celebrated orators of ancient Greece.

produce every fruit, they do not answer the nature and efficacy of the seed. For *the fruit of the Spirit* is not one alone, but manifold ; viz. *love, joy, peace, patience, long-suffering, goodness, benignity, and the like ;* Gal. v. 22. There are, therefore, two things to be noted in the matter of the fruitfulness :

The first, that God does not approve of every kind of fruitfulness, but restricts it *to good works.* But those are called good works which are commanded and directed by God. They, therefore, who by their own inventions, and a certain superstition, 'εθεχοθρησχεία, a will-worship, attempt to please God, are judged not to grow fruitful, but wanton. For so speaks the Psalmist, cvi. 39, *They were defiled with their own works, and went a whoring with their own inventions.* Wisely and piously spake Cyprian, *The exercises of righteousness are to be chosen not by our own will, but by the will of God,* De singul. cleric. And in Isaiah God complains of the Jews, that they *worshipped him by the precepts of men,* ch. xxix. 13.

The second, that fruitfulness of any one kind is not sufficient, but we must be fruitful in *every good work.* If any one produce the good fruit of alms deeds, and mingle with them the impure fruits of lewdness ; or if any one be conspicuous for chastity, and defile himself by avarice ; he would not answer the divine will, or the Apostle's desire of being fruitful in every good work : nay, he is accounted by God bad and unclean. For who shall say that any one is clean, who is wont to wallow even in a single sewer ? Hence the Apostle bids us *abstain from all appearance of evil,* and wishes us to be *sanctified wholly* ὁλοτελεῖς, wishes *spirit, soul, and body to be preserved blameless,* 1 Thess. v. 22, 23.

And so much concerning that practical working whereby we please God.

Increasing in the knowledge of God.] This is that other working of those who walk worthy of God, and study to please him. As they are fruitful in good works as far as respects an active life, so they increase and advance in the knowledge of God as far as respects a contemplative life.

The Apostle alludes to that increase in our spiritual stature, concerning which he also speaks in Ephes. iv. 13,
where he shews, that we must increase *till we all come in
the unity of the faith, and of the knowledge of the Son of
God, unto a perfect man, unto the measure of the stature of
the fulness of Christ.*—We observe,

1. Increase in knowledge is no less necessary to a
Christian man, than fruitfulness in works ; because we are
bound to both by the divine command, and we are taught
to seek both from God by Apostolic example.

2. From the circumstance of the Apostle joining these
two, he wishes to intimate that fruitfulness in works cannot exist, without this progress in wisdom ; nor progress in
wisdom and the true knowledge of God, without fruitfulness.

The reason of the former is this ; Because wisdom so
directs the operation of virtue, as sight does the walking
faculty.   Take away sight, and no one can walk aright ;
take away wisdom, and he cannot be fruitful as he ought.
For that action is bad which is not directed by knowledge,
although it belong to the class of the good.*   And the reason of the latter is, because the desire and the practice of
holiness is, by the divine œconomy, a certain preparation
for obtaining more abundant knowledge from God ; and on
the other hand, the neglect of holiness and good works, is the
cause why God inflicts spiritual blindness, and gives men
over to a reprobate mind.   *I understand more than the ancients, because I keep thy precepts,* Ps. cxix. 100.   *Into a malicious soul wisdom shall not enter ; nor dwell in the body which
is subject unto sin.*   Wisdom i. 4 : And Rom. i. 21, 28, *Because when they knew God, they glorified him not as God,
their foolish heart was darkened, and God delivered them over
to a reprobate mind.*   As therefore from true knowledge,
arises the study of holiness and the practice of good
works ; so again from this fruitfulness knowledge itself
takes a new increase : as also from ignorance arises an
abandoned life ; so again, from this abandoned life, igno-

rance and spiritual stupidity is increased.—But let it suffice to have said thus much concerning the second part of the Apostle's prayer.

Verse 11.

Strengthened with all might, according to his glorious power, unto all patience and long-suffering with joyfulness.

This is the last part of the Apostle's prayer for the Colossians, and has especial respect to the enduring of the cross. And there are three things to be noted in it :

1. The good itself which is sought, strengthening ; *being strengthened with all might.*

2. Whence this good is expected and obtained : from *the glorious power of God.*

3. To what end this good of being strengthened subserves ; *unto all patience and long-suffering with joyfulness.*

Strengthened with all might.] These words are connected with the 9th verse ; *We cease not to pray for you, that ye may be filled with all knowledge,* &c. *that ye may walk worthy of the Lord....being strengthened with all might,* &c.

This strengthening fortifies the mind as well to endure as to abstain ; for it impresses that fortitude on the mind, *which,* as Prosper says, *not only being beaten by divers troubles remains unshaken, but also yields, through being enfeebled, to no allurements of pleasure,* De vita contemplat. iii. 20. It is most properly, therefore, the business of this strengthening to invest a man with that spiritual power, by which he may act virtuously and live religiously, notwithstanding those difficulties and dangers which restrain him from godliness.

The School doctors affirm somewhat more explicitly that this might exercises its energies in five things ;

1. In attempting good works, however arduous. 2. In striving against vices. 3. In despising earthly things. 4. In resisting temptations. 5. In enduring afflictions. And here it is proper to observe the order of the Apostle's

prayer. He entreated for them, in the first place, an infused *knowledge* of the divine will ; secondly, *fruitfulness* in
works of holiness : now, lastly, he desires for them *might,*
from some special strengthening, because the cross awaits
all those who will live godly in Christ, 2 Tim. iii. 12.

Observe ; Even after a knowledge of the truth is infused,
and the grace of holiness imparted, yet the regenerate remain infirm and weak to undertake any spiritual good, to
strive against vices, to resist temptations ; unless they are
further strengthened and sustained.   This Paul confesses,
*To will is present with me, but how to perform that which is
good I find not,* Rom. vii. 18. This was manifested in
David and Peter, who, by reason of this infirmity of our
nature, fell in the day of temptation.

This infirmity of the regenerate and sanctified man, Parisiensis illustrates by some beautiful similitudes in his
book of Temptations and the means of resisting them ; of
which it will not be foreign to our undertaking to adduce
a few, that it may be understood what wisdom the Apostle
evinced in desiring strengthening also for them after sanctification.

1.   He compares *the regenerate and sanctified man to a
knight splendidly armed, who proceeds to battle mounted upon
a prancing and refractory horse : for he is often thrown by the
movements of his steed, unless some other person come to his as
sistance : so the regenerate man, having in himself a concupiscence resisting and fighting against the Spirit, will ofttimes be
thrown to the earth, unless he be supported and strengthened
from another quarter.*

2.   He compares *the regenerate and godly man to a building, the upper part of which consists of firm and solid materials, the lower is dry and combustible : for so the renewed
man, as to his regenerated part, viz. his spirit, consists as it
were of endowments and graces that are divine, which possess
in themselves stability ; but as to his inferior part, viz. the flesh,
he consists of lusts and evil inclinations : as therefore that
building, so the renewed man, being easily inflamed in the inferior part, will be wholly destroyed, unless he be protected and
succoured from some other quarter.*

3. *As a Virgin, although she be adorned with remarkable chastity and modesty, yet if she pass her life in the midst of corruptors, will need assistance lest she be overcome by their blandishments or threats; so the human soul adorned with grace and holiness, nevertheless requires constant strengthening, because it exists among corrupting men and evil spirits, and also inbred lusts.*

Ye see the necessity of strengthening on account of the infirmity of the flesh. But why does the Apostle say, *strengthened with* ALL *might?*

First, to intimate that we fight not against one enemy, neither are opposed by weapons on one side only, but by many, and on every side. There are three chief adversaries, the flesh, the world, the devil; under each of which, as leaders, there are innumerable bands of troops. Secondly, to signify that it profits us little, if we conquer any one or some of these enemies, unless we bravely tread them all under our feet. For, as Cyprian speaks, *if avarice be overthrown, lust rises: if lust be subdued, ambition succeeds: if ambition is spurned, wrath incenses, pride inflates,* &c. Unless we overcome these enemies one and all, we are conquered : There is therefore need of *all might* against every kind of enemy.—Thus much concerning the good which is sought.

According to his glorious power, Κατὰ τὸ κράτος τῆς δόξης αὐτοῦ.] This is an Hebraism ; for the genitive case of the substantive is put instead of an adjective, *vim gloriæ,* i. e. *vim gloriosam, the power of God* for *glorious power.* Now in these words the Apostle shews whence the strengthening and might of the godly comes, namely, from the glorious power of God. Three things are to be considered : What this strengthening power is; Why it is called glorious power ; How it comes to us, and whence it is derived. As to the first : The strengthening power is the Holy Spirit himself, with his gifts; who breathes wonderful might into our infirm minds. For so Christ himself speaks, Luke xxiv. 49, *Tarry ye,* said he to the Apostles, *in the city of Jerusalem, until ye be endued with power from on high ;* i. e. until the Holy Spirit enter into you from heaven : For so

Paul when writing to the Ephes. iii. 16, *May God grant you, that ye may be strengthened mightily by his Spirit in the inner man.*

We are here taught

1. That no one ought to confide in his own strength, as though by his own power he could resist temptations, or endure griefs and afflictions for Christ; but he should seek strengthening from this Spirit.   Piously and wisely spake Augustine, *A presumption of stability keeps back many from stability: no one will be strong by God, but he who perceives his weakness in himself,* De verbis Domini. serm. 13.

2. That when temptations are overcome, it behoves us to ascribe the glory to God, not to ourselves, or to our own power. *Not unto us, not unto us, but to thy name give the glory,* Ps. cxv. 1.   For it is a species of pride when any one would seem to have that from himself which he borrowed from another.

Lastly, when we see heretical and impious men confidently undergoing pains and torments, we must know, that it is not might, but madness; not strength, but stupidity: for true courage is the gift of the Holy Spirit, and is given to the sanctified alone.   For the things which seem to be done by heretics and the wicked with a certain fortitude, argue not so much their strength, as the violent impulses of the devil: *for the deeds of heretics are as the deeds of dæmoniacs,* as says Parisiensis, De moribus.

Thus it appears whence this *strengthening might* comes. Let us enquire why it is called *glorious.*

Glorious.]   The Apostle could have said, we are strengthened by God, or by his power; but he adds this epithet, *glorious power,* or *glorious might;*

1. That we may place the greater confidence in this divine power : Because this very word contains in itself an earnest, or rather a promise of victory and triumph: for this could not be glorious power, if it might be overcome by an evil spirit and sin. *In all these things we are more than conquerors through him who hath loved us,* Rom viii. 37.

2. It is called *glorious power* on account of the admirable mode of conquering the devil, the world, and the flesh. For the Spirit of God not immediately, by his absolute power, beats off these enemies of our salvation ; but by inspiring us with strength causes even ourselves to trample them under. Moreover that power must necessarily be very admirable and glorious, which makes feeble man, clothed with sinful flesh, to overcome the insults and wiles of devils, the alarms and solicitations of the · flesh, the hatred, snares, and injuries of the whole world. Of this glorious power God himself speaks, *My strength is made perfect in weakness,* 2 Cor. xii. 9. Vide 1 Cor. i. 27.

Only one thing now remains to be explained : How this glorious power of the Holy Spirit comes to us. It is derived unto us by the gracious mediation and intercession of Christ sitting at the right hand of the Father. Concerning the gift or sending of his Spirit into the hearts of believers, we have the promise of Christ, John xvi. 7, *It is expedient for you that I go away, for, if I go away, I will send the Comforter unto you.* Christ, therefore, as God, together with the Father and the Holy Spirit, gives this glorious power of the Holy Spirit to his people. God alone gives God. Christ, as man, intercedes with the Father, and by his intercession obtains this Spirit of fortitude for all the elect : John xiv. 16, *I will ask the Father, and he will give you another Comforter, that he may abide with you for ever.*

Hence we gather that Christ, although seated in heaven, is yet the living head of, and really united to, the Church which is on earth. For as the natural head diffuses sense and motion through its body ; so Christ, the spiritual head of the Church, communicates the vital power of his Spirit to all his members.

Here we see the real practical use of that article, *He sitteth at the right hand of the Father :* For we do not believe as we ought the sitting of Christ at the right hand of the Father, unless we believe that he so reigns in heaven, as far more effectually to protect and strengthen his people

by this his glorious power, than if he continued to be yet
present upon the earth in the body, and stood by each one
of us.

We have unfolded what, and what kind of good that
strengthening is which the Apostle intreated for the Colossians ; we have explained also whence it is derived, and
by whose mediation it is conferred upon us : It remains
that we now explain what end it subserves.

Unto all patience and long-suffering with joyfulness.] He
shews the use and end of our divine strengthening and of
our spiritual fortitude, viz. that it may beget in us *patience*
or *endurance,* and *long-suffering ;* then he annexes the characteristic of Christian patience, viz. *joyfulness.* Let us
inquire, first, what is the nature of these virtues.

Interpreters are not sufficiently agreed what is ὑπομονη,
patience, and what μακροθυμία, *long-suffering.* Some refer
ὑπομονη, i. e. *patience* or *endurance,* to those evils which are
inflicted by God ; μακροθυμια, to those which are laid upon
us by men. Chrysostom so distinguishes them, as to say,
that *endurance* is to be exercised towards those whom we
are not able to punish ; *long-suffering* towards those whom
we may. He endures, therefore, who bears with equanimity that evil which he cannot repel : he is long-suffering,
who, being offended by an equal or an inferior, takes not
revenge though he has it in his power.

But these expositions appear to me to restrict both
words too much. It is more probable, then, that we
should say 'ὑπομονη, or *endurance,* respects that load and
weight of affliction visited upon us, either by God, or by
men ; (for this word is derived ἀπὸ τοῦ ὑπομένειν, which signifies *to remain under* a load of afflictions, and not to be
overwhelmed by their weight) ; but μακροθυμίαν, or *long-suffering,* respects the length and duration itself of the incumbent evil. Therefore, he who is not broken either by the
deferring too long our deliverance from evil, or by the protracting too long our reinstatement in good, the same hath
this *long-suffering,* because his mind duly extends its view
to the end which is far distant. (Tit. ii. 3 ; 2 Pet. iii. 12 ;
Jude, 21).

These two virtues are the inseparable companions of
that strength and fortitude which the Spirit liberally bestows upon us; for they are joined to that *fortitude,* as
secondary virtues to the primary one. But they differ in
this principally, that *fortitude* arms us against the fear and
dread of evil approaching and attacking us, and does not
allow us to flee and decline the fight : *endurance* and *long-
suffering* support the mind itself against the perception of
evil which has already come upon and arrested us, and
does not permit us to sink under grief and sadness, but
teaches us to bear it without any immoderate or unbecoming passion.—We see now what is the nature of endurance
and long-suffering.

Let us consider, secondly, the necessity of these virtues ; and first of patience. Now this virtue is very necessary to all the godly, because occasion of exercising it occurs on every hand.

1. If we regard God himself, he exercises their patience
in chastising them. *Whom the Lord loveth he' chasteneth ;
and scourgeth every son whom he receiveth,* Heb. xii. 6. This
chastisement, if patience be present, works with it for
salvation ; if absent, produces murmuring, desperation,
and finally, condemnation.

2. If we regard the world, patience is very necessary
to the godly : for *in the world, and from the world they will
have tribulation ;* and *as many as will live godly in Christ Jesus
will suffer persecution.* He, therefore, who is destitute of
patience, is exposed naked to the iron storm of all weapons.

3. Lastly, if we regard other virtues, patience is necessary. For to faith, righteousness, chastity, punishment is
often held out with infamy : Here patience unfolds its
strength, and exhibits itself, as it were, a shield to the
other virtues ; for

The virtue which patience does not sustain is a widow.

                                              Prudent.

Patience is so ordained in the things of God, says Tertullian, *that no one who is a stranger to patience can perform any
precept.* Whence that saying of Paul to the Romans ii.

6, 7, *God will render to every one according to his deeds ; to those who endure, the glory of good works.*

Now let us observe what relates to *long-suffering ;* nor is there less necessity for this :

First, by reason of the promised good ; for *hope which is deferred afflicts the soul,* Prov. xiii. 12. There is need therefore of long-suffering to those to whom the blessedness of heaven is promised, lest they grow remiss, and, through despair of the reward, cast off the exercise of godliness. For the flesh murmurs and rebels, and accuses God of delay and slackness, because he does not immediately confer what he promised : but this spiritual long-suffering says, *For yet a little while, and he that shall come will come, and will not tarry.* Heb. x. 37.

Secondly, there is need of long-suffering, by reason of the incumbent evils. For that which Epicurus was wont to say consoles not the godly : *All grief, if long, is light; if heavy, is short ;*[*] for their afflictions are both heavy and protracted : The whole of their life is a warfare ; all this life is to them a vale of tears. *Ye shall weep and lament,* says Christ, John xvi. 20, *but the world shall rejoice.* Where, then, is the comfort of the godly ? *In quietness and in confidence shall be your strength;* as Isaiah beautifully says, cap. xxx. 15. And Jerome, Lament. iii. 25, 26, *The Lord is good unto them that wait for him. It is good that a man should silently wait for the salvation of God.*[†]

---

[*] The Philosopher, whose maxim is here cited, the Leader of a Sect well known by the name of ' Epicureans,' flourished about three hundred years before Christ ; he maintained notions respecting the gods which bordered on Atheism ; and made *pleasure* the end of his doctrine. His followers became divided into two kinds, the rigid and the remiss ; the latter illustrated the leading principle of the system abundantly in their practice. It was such who said, " *Let us eat and drink, for to-morrow we die,*" and against the spread of whose pernicious errors the Apostle directed that pungent corrective, 1 Cor. xv. 33 : " *Be not deceived ; evil communications corrupt good manners : awake to righteousness and sin not, for some have not the knowledge of God.*" How could such offer any consolation to the afflicted and miserable !

[†] *Bonum est præstolari cum silentio salutari Dei.* Davenant in loc. from the Vulgate.

We have seen the nature and necessity of patience and long-suffering : Now let us ponder the fruit and admirable effects. And this is first to be premised, that the benefits which arise from afflictions, whatever they are, do not arise but through the medium of this patience : therefore they are the rather to be ascribed to patience than to that affliction, which is most hurtful to those who are impatient.

1. Patience discomfits and overthrows all its enemies, without inflicting or returning a wound; it does not deign to aim a weapon at them, nevertheless it achieves a conquest even by quietude. *The heathen and their idolatries,* says Augustine, Epist. 42, *are overcome not by resistance, but by the martyrdom of Christians.*

2. Patience causes all its enemies to serve itself, and contribute innumerable advantages : to say nothing of the rest, it occasions its persecutors to prepare for it the crown of the eternal kingdom. *Blessed are they who suffer persecution for righteousness' sake, for theirs is the kingdom of heaven,* Matt. v. 10. Whence that saying of the martyr Vicentius to Dacian his tormentor, *Never hath any one so well served me as thou hast.*

3. Our patience confounds the devil, causes angels to rejoice, glorifies God himself, and, lastly, sometimes melts and converts the most inveterate enemies. Tertullian, captivated by the great advantage of this good, exclaimed, De patient : *Let me lose all the world, provided I am enriched by patience.**

With joyfulness.] These last words determine the character of true and christian patience; for hereby it is distinguished from that which is philosophical and hypocriti-

---

* Next to the displays of this grace as given by the primitive Christians, and the martyrs at the time of the Reformation, the conduct of the Waldenses under their severe and long protracted persecutions, affords the most instructive illustrations of its excellence and advantage on a large scale. Vide " Authentic details of the Waldenses, collected during a residence among the Vaudois of Piedmont and Wirtemberg, in 1825," Hatchards ; a volume, it is apprehended, not sufficiently known on account of its unpretending merits, and the profits of which are intended for the benefit of the Vaudois.

cal. That which is philosophical, (such as is celebrated in
the instance of Socrates) had not this spiritual joy united
with it ; that which is hypocritical hath inward repining :
that alone which is Christian possesses joy and spiritual
cheerfulness in the midst of calamities. *They departed from
the presence of the council, rejoicing that they were counted
worthy to suffer shame for his name.* Acts v. 41.

But an objection is raised from the passage before adduced, viz. *Ye shall lament, but the world shall rejoice :* therefore the afflictions of the godly (it is said) do not produce
gladness, but grief and tears. That opinion of the Philosopher in his Ethics, (Ethic 3) is also well known, That
fortitude is occupied about a troublesome and unpleasant
object, and therefore it is sufficient if a brave man be not
sad, although he may not be joyful.

I answer, This gladness is not concerning the object of
patience, for that inflicts pain; but concerning the act,
the advantage, and the end ; for the consideration of these
produces gladness. To rejoice concerning an object is not
suitable to every virtue; for there is some kind of virtue to
which it pertains to grieve about its object, viz. penitence :
but to rejoice concerning its own act pertains to every
virtue ; because to every one endued with virtue, it is delightful to exercise himself according to the habit of that
virtue. Whence even the penitent himself rejoices, though
it be at his own sorrow : so the brave and patient are made
joyful by the very exercise of fortitude and patience, although from the objects of these virtues they feel grief and
pain.

But this joyfulness, which arises from the consideration
of its own virtuous and praiseworthy employ, is not that
which the Apostle chiefly regarded ; but rather that which
arises from confidence of the divine love ; from a sure
knowledge that all our afflictions work together for the
good of our souls ; from the certainty of deliverance, and
the hope of glory. For so says the Apostle, *All things
work together for good to them that love God,* Rom. viii. 28.
And in the Epistle to the Philip. i. 28, *In nothing terrified
by your adversaries ; which is to them an evident token of per-*

dition, but to you of salvation. And the Saviour, Matth. v.
11, 12, *When ye shall be persecuted, rejoice; because great is
your reward in heaven.* Gregory says, *The more severely I
am oppressed by present evils, the more certainly I anticipate
future joys.*

And thus much concerning the third part of the Apostle's prayer, with which he concludes his exordium, or second part of this Chapter, and of the whole Epistle : We
proceed to the third.

Verse 12.

*Giving thanks unto the Father, which hath made us meet to
be partakers of the inheritance of the saints in light.*

Having explained the title of the Epistle, and the preface, we come now to the third part of this Chapter, which
extends to the 23d verse ; and contains the sum of Evangelical doctrine concerning the redemption of the human
race.

Now in this part of the chapter the Apostle accomplishes three things.

1. He sets forth the benefit itself of redemption, from
verse the 12th to the 15th.

2. He describes the person of the Redeemer, from that
verse to the 20th.

3. He explains the manner of the Redemption, or of
the procuring of our salvation, to verse 23d.

The benefit of Redemption contains in itself many other
benefits, which we shall discuss in their order one by one.
But we may reduce the sum of the Apostle's discussion to
this proposition, viz. We are saved by the merit and passion of Christ alone, who is sufficient to procure human
salvation, without Jewish ceremonies and the other means
which were foisted in by the false Apostles.

Let this in general be observed and premised : The best
preservative against error is to hold aright the benefit of
redemption ; as also the sufficiency and efficacy of the Re-

deemer. For why does the Apostle undertake to unfold this doctrine? Doubtless that by the understanding of it all seductive subtleties may be dissipated.

By laying down the same foundation concerning the sufficiency of Christ the Redeemer and Mediator, we shall be able to expose and crush the errors of the Papists, respecting the invocation of saints, the necessity of human satisfactions, the granting of indulgences, and many others with which they have contaminated the Christian Religion. Most truly said Calvin, *Popery stands not except with ignorance of Christ.**

* Our Expositor has here cited an authority, a reference to whom is, in the minds of some well-meaning and otherwise sensible and intelligent persons, more odious than an exhibition of sin itself. But none, surely, will object to, or take offence, at the sentiment adduced, so truly in point, except those who favour the dominance of that noxious and blighting system justly animadverted upon. The Translator, however, cannot refrain from taking occasion to observe, that whilst we are to yield deference to names, or parties, only so far as they speak the language and follow the steps of Christ, we should still not stand aloof from the admission of truth, on account of a name ; and though he is no admirer of Calvin's peculiarities, or, rather, the excrescences grafted upon truth as his opinions, by ultra and anti-Calvinists ; yet, as a receiver of those doctrines which Calvin held and well maintained, in common with all *true* Believers, from the first shining of the Sun of Righteousness upon this earth, he thinks it well to lay before his readers a few remarks upon the subject adverted to, judiciously selected from various competent judges by the pen of another. That excellent Author, the Rev. T. H. Horne, in his admirable work " The Introduction to the Critical Study of the Scriptures," vol. ii. Append. No. vi. Sect. 14, " on the principal Commentators," &c. art. 2 ; has some citations well worth the knowledge and the consideration, of every fearful and prejudiced person, in reference to the character under notice. " The Commentaries and other expository writings of this great man" [Calvin], says he, " have always been deservedly celebrated and admired ; though it has been the fashion, with some modern divines, to depreciate them, on account of those peculiar dogmas which Calvin deduced from the Sacred Writings." " Calvin's Commentaries," says the learned Matthew Poole, in the preface to the ' Synopsis Criticorum Sacrorum,' " abound in solid discussions of theological subjects, and in practical improvements of them. Subsequent writers have borrowed most of their materials from Calvin ; and his interpretations adorn the books, even of those who repay their obligation by reproaching their master." The great critic Scaliger said, " that no Commentator had better hit the sense of the Prophets than Calvin :" and another eminent

Now we will follow the thread of the context, and begin from this 12th verse, in which three things are to be observed :

1. The primary cause of salvation, or of our redemption, the mercy of God ;

2. The primary effect of this mercy, ἱκανότης, a certain new and supernatural faculty and fitness in us ;

3. The end of this new faculty or meetness, that we may participate in the heavenly inheritance.

Giving thanks to the Father.] These words are connected with the 9th verse, where the Apostle says, *We cease not to pray for you, and to desire that ye might be filled with all knowledge,* &c.; now he subjoins, *Giving thanks to the Father who hath made us meet.* This third part of the chapter, which relates to the benefit of redemption, the Apostle beautifully and wisely opens by the giving of thanks : By which conduct of his he would intimate to us these two things;

1. That this benefit of human redemption is so great that it would be impious not only to discourse, but even to think of without the utmost gratitude of soul. Scarcely ever does the Apostle mention this, but forthwith he breaks out into praising and blessing God. Ephes. i. 3, *Blessed be*

critic of our own time (Rosenmüller), has remarked, " that although Calvin was not deeply versed in Hebrew, yet, as he possessed an acute and subtle genius, his interpretations of Isaiah in particular, contain many things which are exceedingly useful for understanding the Prophet's meaning." Nothing, indeed, can more satisfactorily evince the high estimation to which the Commentaries of Calvin are still entitled from the Biblical Student, than the following eulogium of one of the most learned Prelates that ever adorned the Anglican Church—Bishop Horsley. " I hold," says he, " the memory of Calvin in high veneration ; his works have a place in my library ; and in the study of the Holy Scriptures, he is one of the Commentators whom I most frequently consult." To this testimony may be added that of another accomplished Scholar lately deceased, the Rev. J. J. Conybeare. " The Commentaries of Calvin," he observes, in his Bampton Lectures for 1824, p. 237, " though in the exercise of our Christian liberty we may freely question and dissent from many points, both of doctrine and discipline, maintained by their illustrious author, are yet never to be perused without admiration or instruction."

the God and Father of our Lord Jesus Christ, &c.   So Zacharias, Luke i. 68, *Blessed be the Lord God of Israel, who hath redeemed,* &c.

2. That we ought to give all diligence to be certified through the Spirit of faith, that we are in the number of those whom God hath made meet for the participation of eternal life. For it is absurd and preposterous to give thanks for a benefit received, when you are not yet sure whether it has been received or not. He therefore who, by his own example, wishes the Colossians and other Christians to give thanks to God for having obtained the benefit of salvation, wishes all to labour, that, by a true and lively faith, they may attain to this knowledge, being most full of comfort, and very needful to the Christian in this vale of tears. But to whom are thanks given? To God *the Father.*

To the Father.] *To God and the Father,* in some copies. The Apostle points out the primary cause of human salvation, viz. the unmerited goodness and mercy of God the Father. He names the Father, because as he is the fountain of Deity, so also is he to be understood as the fountain of all spiritual benefits. James i. 17. But we must not exclude either the Son or the Spirit : for their will and operation are conjoined in the salvation of the elect. As, however, there is an order in the procession of the divine persons, so that the Son proceeds from the Father, and the Holy Spirit from the Father and the Son : so also a certain order is to be understood in their operation ; the Father worketh from himself, the Son from the Father, and the Spirit from both. We say that God the Father, or the whole Trinity, is the primary cause of our salvation from a twofold consideration ;

First, because *from the mere good pleasure of his own will, before the foundations of the world were laid, he predestinated us to eternal life;* as it is said Ephes. i. 4 and 5. For this, therefore, eternal thanks are to be given to God ; for, without this, assuredly we should be altogether excluded from heaven. Rightly spake Prosper, *No other shall come into the fellowship of the inheritance of Christ, but those who were chosen before the foundation of the world,* De lib. arbitr.   So the Saviour himself, Matth. xxv. 34, and Luke xii. 32, ευδοκησεν, &c.

Secondly, because in time, through effectual calling, he draws the elect to himself, who, if left to their own inclination, would never embrace the salvation offered.   *No man, says Christ, cometh unto me, except the Father draw him,* John vi. 44.   But he draws by special, secret, and efficacious grace, which is communicated to those alone, but is denied to all others.   Whence that observation of Augustine, In Epist. Joan tract. 4, *Many hear, but those only are persuaded to whom God inwardly speaks.*

Thus far concerning the primary cause of our salvation, viz. the mercy of God predestinating and effectually calling us; for which cause thanks are to be given to him.

Who hath made us meet.]   Now let us weigh the primary effect of this divine goodness and mercy.   And that is a certain spiritual *worthiness* or *fitness,* whereby we are, and are accounted meet to participate in the spiritual benefits which are communicated to men in Christ.   But that this fitness or condition of new worthiness be found in us, presupposes two things on God's part; powerful operation and merciful acceptance.   For it is by the Divine operation and acceptance we are made *meet* to participate in the lot of the saints.

The divine operation is necessary, because we must be changed and become new creatures, before we can be partakers of celestial benefits.   For there is in us nothing but an entire unfitness either to understand, or do, or, finally, to receive, spiritual good.   'Ουχ ικανοὶ 'εσμεν.   *We are not sufficient of ourselves,* 2 Cor. iii. 5.   *Flesh and blood cannot inherit the kingdom,* &c.: 1 Cor. xv. 50.   *Except a man be born again, he cannot see the kingdom of God,* John iii. 3.   Therefore that these obstacles may be removed, and we may be rendered meet, God renews us by the Spirit; he breathes into us the new life of grace; finally, he pours into our minds, faith, hope, love, and those other virtues which are required for the participation of the heavenly promises.   *For this divine grace* (as Aquinas has well said,

Quæst. disput. de virtut. art. 10,) *is therefore communicated to the elect, that they may perform the actions ordained unto the end of eternal life.* For it confers upon the soul a certain new principle of a spiritual and divine nature, whereby it is rendered meet for the participation of things that are spiritual and divine. *For the nature of the human soul, how perfect soever in natural gifts, is, without grace, not susceptible of glory.* Parisiensis, lib. de virt. cap. 11. Therefore the grace of God alone makes us *meet* for the participation of divine things, in effectually calling us, justifying, and sanctifying us by a certain internal operation of his Spirit.

But besides this operation of God, which renders us meet by changing and regenerating us, the merciful acceptance of God is also required, to cover our infirmities and reckon our feeble endeavours in the room of perfect obedience. For as there is nothing good in us, unless we have been renewed by the divine operation; so the good things of the renewed would be even as nothing worth for the enjoyment of the heavenly heritage, unless they were accepted by the most indulgent Father for the sake of the transcendent worthiness of Christ. Therefore, that there may be in us the least spark of good, the power of God in working it is required; and that that good, whatever it be, may make us *meet* to be reckoned among the children and heirs of the kingdom, his fatherly clemency is requisite in accepting it.

Nor need we look far for a reason why we think this acceptance necessary, since it is certain, that in the regenerate themselves, after the operation of the regenerating Spirit, there is not perfect newness: but as in wine diluted, the water as well as the wine is mingled in every part; so in the whole renewed man, the qualities of regeration and the remains of corruption, are found blended together. *No one in this life is thoroughly perfect: for the infirmity of the godly is not yet healed, but is daily being healed,* Prosper, De vit. contempl. i. 9. Whether, then, we regard the inward qualities, or the external acts of the godly, they are not *meet to participate the lot of the saints in light,* without this merciful acceptance. *Woe to the commendable life of man, if thou sift it without mercy,* says Augustine, Confess. lib. ix. cap. 13. And the Psalmist, cxliii. 2, *Enter not into judgment with thy servant, for in thy sight shall no flesh be justified.* Beautifully writes the Apostle to the Ephes. i. 5, 6, *God hath adopted us according to the good pleasure of his will. He hath accepted us by his grace in the beloved.*

These things being established concerning the Divine operation and acceptance, we may deduce a few corollaries :

1. It is not in the power of fallen and corrupted man to make himself meet for the participation of spiritual gifts, such as grace, faith, blessedness : God alone, who imparts the gifts, gives with them the disposition also for their reception. Wherefore what some of the Schoolmen assert about the preparations and dispositions which proceed from the power of free-will in the state of corrupt nature, are to be received with caution : Such as that saying of Durandus, In Sentent. lib. i. qu. 6, *Although it be not in the power of man to produce in himself love or grace, yet it is in his power so far to dispose himself, as that God will give grace to him.* And that of Albert, Compend. v. 2,*

* Albert, styled the Great, a German, of the Dominican Order, and a follower of Peter Lombard ; " a man," says Mosheim, " of vast abilities, and an universal dictator in his time." His celebrity, however, is so clouded with the legendary tales related of his acquirements and performances in occult philosophy, that it is impossible to say what portion of it is duly merited : and of the twenty-one folio volumes attributed to him, it has since been ascertained that many pieces which are there inserted were not composed by him. Still the distinction he obtained for his extensive acquaintance with the subtle philosophy and obscure theology of the times was so great, that, in 1248, he was called to Rome by Pope Alexander IV. and appointed Master of the Sacred Palace (vide Note *, p. 38). In 1260, he was elected Bishop of Ratisbon ; but finding his episcopal duties inconsistent with his love of retirement and study, he resigned his Bishopric, and returned to Cologne to enjoy the leisure of Monastic life. He was, however, drawn from his retirement by Pope Gregory X. who sent him into Germany and Bohemia to preach the Crusade. He afterwards attended the Council of Lyons, and then returned to Cologne, where he remained until his death in 1280.

Grace is not given unless to those who have an aptitude for grace.

But to these we oppose plain Scripture, which everywhere teaches that God ἱκανῶσαι, i. e. *renders us sufficient and meet* for spiritual and heavenly things, since of ourselves we are most unmeet, either to receive or perform them. Against these also we place in opposition the more sound of the Schoolmen : *Free-will,* says Aquinas, *is not the cause of grace, by means of an adequate disposition.* God, observes Parisiensis, *previously confers upon us our efforts and preparations, that he may afterwards render them more profitable.* And again, *Although I am moved towards thee, O Lord, but faintly and weakly; yet am I not moved at all, but by Thee, when drawn towards Thee.* Idem.

2. The general offer of grace which is propounded to all by the ministry of the Gospel, is not sufficient to procure salvation; but, that it may become efficacious, there must needs be added the internal operation of God, which renders us meet to receive grace and salvation. The offer of grace and salvation is common to all through the preaching of the Gospel; but that internal efficacious operation, which fits and qualifies us to lay hold upon salvation, is peculiar to the elect. *All that the Father giveth me, shall come to me,* John vi. 37. *The world cannot receive the Spirit of truth,* John xiv. 17. Whence also that in Acts xiii. 48, *As many as were ordained to eternal life believed.* Augustine acknowledges this peculiar operation of God in the case of the elect, De prædest. sanct. lib. i. cap. 16, *They who attain to the vocation according to the purpose, must all be taught of God, neither can any one of them say, I have believed, that thereby I might be called: for I have been called by the mercy of God to believe.* God does not work in us to will and to do good, because by precepts externally given he speaks inwardly upon our senses, but because he inwardly sheds abroad his love in our hearts. Idem, De Spirit. de lit. cap. 25.

3. No one from the merit of inherent righteousness, or of his good works, can claim to himself the lot of the saints : For how can we force our righteousness upon God,

or urge our good works as meriting heaven, when we have nothing good of ourselves? But as Augustine well said, *Whoever reckons up his deeds of righteousness to Thee, what does he enumerate, but Thine own gifts?* Confess. lib. ix. cap. 13.

Let us therefore be content to be called, through grace and by Divine acceptance, to the enjoyment of the heavenly heritage, and humbly confess that of ourselves we are most unworthy of so great a favour. God has made us meet, by regenerating us through the Spirit, and by accepting us for Christ's sake. And thus much concerning this primary effect and benefit of Divine mercy, viz. *that He makes us meet for eternal life.*

To partake of the inheritance of the saints in light.] The Apostle here shews the end or fruit of the Divine operation in the regenerating and sanctifying of the elect. For it may be asked, What profit arises to us hereby, that we are renewed and enlightened? that we become imbued with faith and love? that we are received into the favour of God? The answer is, By this Divine work we are *made meet to be partakers of the inheritance of the saints in light,* 'εις την μεριδα του κληρου.

In all these expressions there is something ambiguous and obscure. The word *sors* is taken in two ways, either for a state and condition, or for a portion and inheritance.* It is used for state and condition by the poets. *Sors tua mortalis,* says Ovid, *Your mortal lot:* so in Horace, *Nemo dicitur vivere contentus suâ sorte, No one is said to live contented with his lot,* i. e. his state and condition. If we adopt this meaning, the Apostle says that he gives thanks to God, because He had translated himself and the Colossians from the state of children of wrath, into a new state and the condition of children of God. For God, in regenerating the elect, and infusing into them faith and holiness, gives them this dignity, *that they may become sons of*

---

* Davenant here, as elsewhere, quotes the Vulgate, where the Greek του κληρου is rendered *sortis,* of the lot; in our translation, *of the inheritance.*

God, John i. 12, 13; that from being *strangers and foreigners,* they may become *fellow-citizens with the saints, and of
the household of God:* Ephes. ii. 19.   So Acts xxvi. 18.

But this, although it be a true, is not the full exposition.
I annex, therefore, that other concerning the portion and
heritage to be participated by all the godly.   For, as the
Israelites divided the land of Canaan by lot, it hence came
to pass that that inheritance which had been assigned to
each tribe, was called its lot.   Hence *the lot of Ephraim,*
and *the lot of Judah,* &c. Josh. xv. 1.   Here the Apostle,
alluding to the heavenly inheritance, calls it also *the lot of
the saints.*   He would therefore have the Colossians made
meet not only for participating the condition of children
now, but also for their future inheritance.

In light.]   And because he adds *in light,* some explain
this of the light of faith; others, of the light of glory:
but the Apostle, methinks, would include both with reference to the respective periods.   For,

1. God renders all his children meet to partake of life
eternal by a participation of the light of hope and faith commenced in this life; even as it is said in John vi. 47, *He
that believeth in me hath eternal life:* he does not say *shall
have,* but hath.   A *true believer,* says Clemens, *rejoices because of those things which are promised, as already present;
and being certainly persuaded of them, he already possesses
them, though future.*   Strom. 7.

2. But it must also be added, that they are likewise
made meet to partake of the lot of the saints in the light
of glory, as to the future world.   For grace is given to the
faithful, that they may be led on to glory; according to
those words of the Apostle, Rom. viii. 30, *Whom he predestinated, he called; whom he called, he justified; whom he justified, he glorified.*   God, therefore, in effectually calling
and justifying the elect, makes them meet to obtain glory,
i. e. *to partake of the lot of the saints in light.*   We are now
in possession of the meaning of the Apostle: hence let us
deduce some observations.

1. Inasmuch, as the Apostle says that we are made
meet εἰς μερίδα, not εἰς μερίδας, for *a portion of the blessed,* not

for portions, he would have us to understand the wide distinction between this heavenly and an earthly inheritance. For an earthly inheritance the more it is divided among several, the less is possessed by each: but the heavenly kingdom is possessed entire by innumerable saints; yet so that the number of the participants hinders not the most perfect and full participation to each.

2. But because he calls eternal life *a lot,* he intimates under the name of *a lot* that this kingdom is not to be attained by our own strength or virtues, but is bestowed upon us by divine Providence; as we have it in Prov. xvi. 33, *The lot is cast into the lap; Jehovæ autem est ratio ejus,* as Tremellius renders it; *but the Lord is the disposer of it.*

3. It is called the lot *of the saints,* not of all persons indiscriminately, that the unbelieving and unholy may understand this lot belongs not to them. For so the Apostle, 1Cor. vi. 9, *Know ye not that the unrighteous shall not inherit the kingdom of God? Neither fornicators, nor idolaters, nor adulterers, &c.* The ungodly have their lot, but it lies in earthly gains and pleasures; as they themselves confess, Wisdom ii. 7, 8, 9, *Let us fill ourselves with costly wine and ointments; let us crown ourselves with roses; for this is our portion, and our lot is this.* Far more excellent is this lot of the godly: for *God is their portion,* Lamen. iii. 24. They who *have* obtained this lot, are called saints in heaven: they who *would* obtain it, must live as saints upon earth.

4. Lastly, this inheritance of the blessed is said to be laid up *in light,* that we may understand it to be something lovely, delightful, and comforting in the highest degree; for nothing can be more lovely or more pleasant than light. That region of the saints shines not by the light of the sun, *for the glory of God doth lighten it, and the Lamb is the light thereof,* Rev. xxi. 23. By this metaphor then, the kingdom of heaven is contrasted with that place of torment which is said to be filled with thick darkness, that the mind may conceive of it, as a place most horrible, hideous, and loathsome. He would therefore inflame us with a love of this lot of the saints, which is illumined with such light; and fill us with horror at that opposite

lot of the wicked, which is enveloped in darkness and deep gloom.

Verses 13, 14.

Who hath delivered us from the power of darkness, and hath translated us into the kingdom of his dear Son :
In whom we have redemption through his blood, even the forgiveness of sins.

The Apostle has been hitherto employed in enumerating and enlarging upon those saving benefits which have been bestowed upon us by God the Father: for the benefits of our redemption are so united, that he who is a partaker of one is a partaker of all. *Who hath made us meet to be partakers of the inheritance of the saints in light,* is the verse preceding. Now, in verse 13, the Apostle connects two other benefits, without which that preceding one cannot stand; and these are, *deliverance from the power of darkness,* and *translation into the kingdom of his dear Son.*

Who hath delivered us from the power of darkness.] In explaining this benefit, three things are to be shewn by us : 1. *Who* hath delivered ; 2. *Whom*, or what sort of persons ; 3. *From what.*

1. Who ? *God the Father ;* for these words are immediately connected with the foregoing, *Giving thanks to God the Father, who hath made us meet—Who also hath delivered,* or *hath forcibly plucked us away.** But the Father being spoken of, we ought to understand the whole Trinity in these external operations ; as we have before observed. Wherefore the original author of man's deliverance is the Triune and One God, who purposed this from eternity, and in the fulness of time sent his Son to accomplish this work which he had decreed. *So God loved the world,* &c.

---

* Ἐρρύσατο, eripuit. " Not simply liberavit, sed eripuit. The word signifies by main force to deliver, or pluck away, even as David pulled the lamb out of the bear's mouth."—Vide Leigh's *Critica Sacra.*

John iii. Therefore it is properly said by the Schoolmen, *The whole Trinity redeemed man by an act of power ; the incarnate Son redeemed him by the effect of his humiliation.* And no one else ought to, or could, deliver man, except God alone ; of whose power and will he was created out of nothing. None other ought, because (as Tertullian well observes) *by this act he would forcibly take away from the Creator his own servant.* For so great is this benefit of deliverance, that it binds us more than the benefit of creation itself. If, therefore, one had made us and another had delivered us, we should have been more strictly bound to that other deliverer than to God the Creator. Hence also another remark of Tertullian, *Who ought to seek the lost sheep ? Ought not he who lost it ? Who lost it ? Was it not he who possessed it ? Who possessed it ? Was it not he who created it ?* But neither could any other deliver. For he must necessarily be stronger than the devil who could wrest his prey from him : For *no one can enter into a strong man's house and seize his goods, unless he shall have first bound the strong man, and then he shall spoil his house ;* Matth. xii. 29. But who could overcome and bind this prince of darkness who was holding us captive, except the mighty God alone ? It was he, therefore, who plucked us from him.

Us.] We must consider, in the second place, *Whom,* or what sort of persons God delivered. And this consideration may be twofold ; of those who were to be delivered, or of those who have been delivered.

While we were to be delivered, i. e. previous to our deliverance, we were not only diseased and weak, but were openly and secretly opposed to our own deliverance. Œcumenius,* describing the infirmity of fallen man, says, *He was without strength, and having need of great help.* Also, shewing his rebellion, and hostile mind, he says, *he was*

---

* A Greek Father, who was Bishop of Tricca, in Thessaly, towards the close of the tenth century, celebrated for Commentaries on the Acts of the Apostles and the whole of the Epistles, which are said to be judiciously compiled from Origen, Chrysostom, Eusebius, and others.—Vide Horne's Introd. vol. ii. append. p. 195, 6th edit.

even impious, having rejected the helper.   The Apostle himself paints man in the condition of corrupt nature in these
same colours, in Rom. v.

1. Observe here the immeasurable love of God, who
would deliver such persons : for no one cares to redeem a
thing of no value.

2. Observe the infinite power of God, who delivered
man in spite of the devil, and against the will of man himself ; as the angel did Lot out of Sodom.

And now the other thing is respecting those who have
been already delivered : for after they have been set at liberty, they are faithful and holy who were before rebels
and unholy.   If therefore it be asked, What sort of persons
are they whom the mercy of God hath delivered?   The
answer is, that they now are new men, shining in faith and
godliness. *Us,* says the Apostle, *hath he delivered ;* i. e.
us who believe; us who love the brethren ; us who walk
worthy of the Lord, bringing forth the fruit of all good
works : such he hath delivered.

Hence it is manifest,

1. Whatever carnal men dream about their deliverance
and salvation, is most vain.   For as the Israelites, whilst
they served Pharaoh, and lusted after the Egyptian flesh-
pots, were not in the enjoyment of liberty ; so Christians,
whilst they obey the devil, whilst they wallow in the delights of sin, are not delivered from slavery and a state of
condemnation.

2. Hence also we infer, for the consolation of the
godly, That the faithful and godly alone are free, are honoured, are unspeakably precious with God; whilst, on
the other hand, the ungodly, although they glitter in the
eyes of men, are accounted for slaves the most vile and
abject.   Truly said Clemens, Strom. viii. *The most excellent
thing in the earth is the man who most serveth God.*

From the power of darkness.]   Who the deliverer is, what
sort of persons they who are delivered had been and are,
has been shewn : it now remains to explain from what they
have been delivered, *From the power of darkness ;* i. e. from
the power of the devil, of sin, and of hell ; or, in one

word, from the state of corrupt nature, under which all
those things are comprehended ; or, as others are accustomed to say, from the darkness of ignorance, of unrighteousness, of misery.   All these come to the same point:
we need not, therefore, labour for words.

We are said to be delivered *from the power of darkness,*
because we are delivered from the power of the devil, who
is *the prince of darkness,* and labours more and more to
darken and to blind his subjects.   We all are born under
his kingdom and power, so that before our deliverance he
worketh in us according to his own will.   Thus in Ephes.
ii. 2, *Wherein in times past ye walked according to the prince
of this world,* Wherefore one of the Fathers said, *That a
throne, as it were, was erected for the devil in the heart of every
ungodly man :* and those who are not yet liberated he
terms, *the horses of the devil; because he drives them hither and
thither at will.*   But this *prince of darkness* is bruised under
the feet of the faithful, Rom. xvi. 20, to whom, by the
Spirit of God, new strength is administered to trample
upon this unclean spirit.

2.   God hath delivered us from the power of sin, which
hath blinded the understanding, corrupted the will, and
placed us in a condition of darkness both as to knowledge
and to spiritual and saving practice.   *Ye were sometime
darkness,* Ephes. v. 8.   So John i. *The light shineth in darkness;* iii. *but men have loved darkness,* viz. the darkness both
of ignorance and wickedness.   Now from this darkness
God has rescued us, whilst he pours in the light of faith,
whilst he imparts the Spirit of holiness ; which blessings
being bestowed, this power and dominion of sin is dissolved.   Ἁμαρτια ὑμων ϗ κυριέυσει, Rom. vi. 14, *The body of
sin is destroyed, that henceforth ye should not serve sin,* ver. 6.

Lastly, He hath delivered his people from the power of
hell, i. e. from the miseries and calamities which arise from
the guilt of reigning sin.   For hell is described as a place
of darkness, Matth. xxv. 30, *Cast ye him into outer darkness.*   From the power of this infernal darkness they are
delivered by the Divine mercy, *for there is no condemnation
to them who are in Christ Jesus,* Rom. viii. 1.   In every case,

therefore, God hath delivered his people from the power of darkness. We touch upon these points lightly now, because all of them are to be treated again.

1. Observe for instruction; that the whole world is involved in darkness under the devil, neither is there a spark of saving light to be found in us before deliverance; for we are in *the power of darkness;* that is to say, spiritual darkness hath dominion over us.

2. Observe for caution; that the godly, being delivered, ought to have no fellowship with the works of darkness: for they are rescued from the power of the devil and of sin, and therefore by serving these they shew themselves to be deserters. *Let us therefore cast off the works of darkness,* &c. Rom. xiii. 12.

3. Observe for consolation; that although the godly are often oppressed by temporal calamities, yet they are delivered from that great misery which consists in the horror and guilt of eternal death, in comparison of which misery, all external evils are light and trifling.

And hath translated us into the kingdom of his dear Son.] The Apostle annexes a new benefit, which much enhances the loving-kindness of God. For it seemed a light matter to him to deliver us from the power of darkness, i. e. from a condition of the deepest misery, unless he translated us from thence into the kingdom. i. e. into a state of the greatest felicity and joy.

From which conjunction of these benefits we may infer; That there is no middle state; but all men are either most wretched slaves under the dominion of Satan, or translated into the kingdom of Christ. There is no third kingdom; neither can the same person be a subject to both. But let us come to the express words of the text.

There are three points to be well considered in these words: What is the nature of this translation? What may be understood by the kingdom into which we are translated? Why it is called *the kingdom of his dear Son,* and not *of God,* or *of heaven,* or *of light?* which regard to the contrast seems to have required.

And hath translated us, μετεστησε.] This word seems to
have been borrowed from those who plant colonies and
compel people to migrate from their native soil, in order to
inhabit some new region : for so God has translated us
from the kingdom of darkness, which is the native soil of
us all, into the kingdom of the pious and blessed.

But how hath he translated us? We may understand
that from the contrast. We are living in the kingdom of
darkness, in consequence of our blindness, infidelity, and
impurity ; but from this kingdom to that other we remove
by means of effectual knowledge, faith, and holiness.
Acts xxvi. 18. Unrighteousness and wickedness constitute us the servants of the devil ; faith and godliness constitute us the household of God.

God translates us then from that melancholy and gloomy
kingdom, when he illuminates our hearts by pouring into
them faith, when he changes and restores our will by imparting grace ; for, being enlightened and sanctified, a
man is by that very act translated from the power of darkness into the kingdom of his Son ; because he cannot possibly be at the same time a citizen of two cities, which observe contrary laws and institutions.

Here observe, To be delivered from darkness it is not
enough that we be called to this kingdom, and admonished
to desert that other; but it is necessary that we be translated and changed by the mighty working of the Holy
Spirit from our former condition into this new one.

Here the error of the Pelagians is detected, who would
have grace to be nothing else than that which acts as a
monitor of free-will.* But from this passage and innu-

* Our Expositor has here alluded to an heresy universally prevalent in
the benighted heart of fallen man, and which has been a greater barrier
with multitudes to the reception of the humbling religion of Jesus, and
more injurious to the welfare of the Church, than, perhaps, any other ;
having been maintained openly, or taught covertly, either from design, or
through ignorance and negligence, in all states of the Church. The primary advocate of the baleful delusion implied under the title of Pelagianism, and which begins in a denial of original sin, and proceeds, consistently
with this denial, to dispute the necessity of the grace of God to quicken,

merable others, it is manifest that we have need not only of such admonishing grace, but of that which changes, heals, liberates, and translates ; for without such grace no one gets out of the kingdom of Satan.

Therefore He is to be regarded with the highest and unceasing honour who has translated us into this kingdom : for so are colonies accustomed to honour their founder.

Into the kingdom.] Let us inquire now what is intended by this word *kingdom*. *The kingdom of God,* or *the kingdom of Christ,* or *the kingdom of heaven,* in sacred Scripture denotes many things.

1. First, it is put for the state of glory and blessedness : as when we are commanded to *seek the kingdom of God,* Matth. vi. 33 ; when [it is said] the ungodly *shall not inherit the kingdom of God,* 1 Cor. vi. 9. If we understand *the kingdom of the Son* in this manner, then God must be said to have translated his people into this kingdom, inasmuch as they have a right to it, and possess it in hope, although not in reality. But this does not seem to me to accord with the design of the Apostle in this place.

enlighten, and sanctify the soul, was one Morgan, (a name of the same signification as Pelagius,) said to be a native of Wales, born in 354, and educated in the Monastery of Bangor, of which he became Abbot. In the early part of his life he went to France, and from thence to Rome ; where, about the year 400, he commenced formally and systematically to promulgate his opinions. His morals being irreproachable, he gained many disciples ; but his errors were promptly and ably met and exposed by Augustine, who flourished at the same period, being born in the same year, and who, on account of the zeal and eloquence with which he supported Evangelical truth, was emphatically called, ' The Doctor of Grace.' The heresy, however, made a rapid progress after Augustine's death ; and, under one modification or another, it is still widely operative in the visible Church, to the present day ; opposing the most important truths of the Gospel, and destructive of vital religion in the heart. It would be well for every one, who is not alive to the effects of this error, to examine into the nature and tendency of it ; and to reflect on the aptitude of the human heart, through love of self, and pride of intellect, to receive and maintain its doctrinal theory. For a satisfactory elucidation thereof, the Reader is referred to the Dissertation on the Death of Christ, appended to the second volume of this work ; in the opening chapter of which our excellent Expositor has given an extended view of the subject.

2. Secondly, it is put for the promulgation and knowledge of the Gospel: as, *To you it is given to know the mysteries of the kingdom of heaven,* Matth. xiii. 11. *The kingdom
of God shall be taken from you,* &c. Matth. xxi. 43. *These
only are my fellow-workers unto the kingdom of God,* Coloss.
iv. 11. In this sense God is said to translate those into the
kingdom of his Son, whom he plucks from the darkness
of ignorance and idolatry, and enlightens with the knowledge of the Gospel. Thus the Colossians, thus all Christians, are *translated from the power of darkness into the kingdom of Christ,* which is *the kingdom of light.* But this
translation denotes only the external and apparent state of
a Christian; whereas the Apostle speaks of the internal.

Lastly, it is taken for a state of grace, i. e. for the acquisition of remission of sins, of renovation, and of divine
favour on account of Christ the Messiah and Mediator:
also for the whole multitude of those who are in this state.
The kingdom of God is within you, Luke xviii. 21. *The
kingdom of God is not meat and drink, but righteousness, and
peace, and joy in the Holy Ghost,* Rom, xiv. 17. I deem
this to be the peculiarly proper sense of this expression.
For God is said to have translated us into the kingdom of
his Son, because he hath communicated to us those spiritual gifts, and wrought in us that spiritual condition, which
makes us subjects and members of Christ. Therefore, by
the kingdom of Christ we must understand all the benefits
of grace which are obtained through union with and subjection to Christ our spiritual King. You now understand
what the kingdom of Christ is.

From what has been said, observe now the contrast of
these kingdoms, that ye may be able to hate the one, and
long after the other. The kingdom of Satan is the kingdom of darkness, i. e. of ignorance, of wickedness, of
misery: the kingdom of Christ is the kingdom of saving
knowledge, of righteousness, of happiness. Who would
not deliver himself by flight from that doleful kingdom,
and shift his abode to this blessed one? But we find that
it happens far otherwise; for all are desirous of remaining

in the kingdom of the devil, almost even to their latest breath, and then only to be translated into the kingdom of Christ.

The kingdom of his dear Son; or *of the Son of his love.*] It remains that, in the last place, we consider well why the Apostle calls it *the kingdom of his Son,* not *of God,* or *of heaven,* or *of light,* as in other places.

1. It is very aptly called the kingdom *of the Son,* because God admits no one to this kingdom, be it understood either of grace or of glory, except through his Son as Mediator. He is the channel of grace; through his mediation its streams flow to us, and we are planted in this spiritual kingdom ; as is evident from Ephes. i. 3, 8.

2. This kingdom is called *the kingdom of the Son,* because Christ the Mediator received it from the Father to order the government and administration of it to the end of time. He is the Head and the Saviour of his Church ; he confers both *grace and glory* after his own good pleasure : *I appoint unto you a kingdom, as my Father hath appointed unto me,* Luke xxii. 29.

3. The Apostle probably called it the kingdom *of the Son,* rather than *of God,* or *of light,* because he wished to open the way and make an easy transition for discoursing on the person of the Son. For he immediately enters upon that doctrine, which he could not so aptly have proceeded to unless he had expressly named the Son.

Now since this kingdom of grace and glory may be truly called the kingdom of Christ, we must strive to be one with Christ, and to be grafted in him: For those who are plucked away from Christ, are the withered branches of the vine, and exiles from this kingdom, although they seem to dwell in it, and even to enjoy its privileges.

Of the Son of his love, or his beloved Son, της ἀγάπης ἀυτȣ.] This is an Hebraism : The Son of his love, i. e. his Son most beloved ; as, *the Son of perdition, the most abandoned.*

Christ is rightly called the Son of the Father's love, because he hath the Father's whole and entire love communicated to him, even as he had his essence. This God himself hath manifested by a voice from heaven, *This is my beloved Son in whom I am well pleased,* Matth. xviii. 5. But it is mentioned in this place, that from hence we may understand that we are loved by God in Christ the well-beloved.

This is a great consolation to the godly man, when he calls to mind that he is not merely a subject, but a member of Christ so beloved of God. For hence he derives the hope of obtaining from God whatever is necessary to salvation. For how can he refuse his subjects, his friends, the brethren of his Son whom he loves with singular love?

Hence, if any one being planted in Christ is seduced through his infirmity, or the temptation of Satan, to commit sin, he takes confidence of pardon; for God, who with such a supreme affection loves Christ himself, cannot hate those who are in Christ, and enjoy the having him for their intercessor with God. 1 John ii. 1.

To conclude, in a word: The love of God towards Christ, is the cause and most certain earnest of his kindness towards all those who are translated into the kingdom of Christ.

Verse 14.

In whom we have redemption through his blood, even the forgiveness of sins.

The Apostle descends from God the Father to Christ *the God-man,* the Mediator, the instrumental cause of our salvation: For God hath delivered us from the power of darkness, God hath translated us into the kingdom of grace; but by the mediation of his Son.

Therefore in this short verse he accomplishes three purposes: he shews, 1. Who is our Redeemer; the incarnate Son of God, *In whom we have redemption.* 2. What, and what sort of redemption it is of which he speaks; viz. such as consists in *the remission of sins.* 3. With what price this redemption was acquired and purchased, *through his blood.*

In whom we have redemption.] These words are connected with the last in the former verse : *In whom,* viz. in his beloved Son. Here, therefore, it is proper to consider the person of the Redeemer.

Christ the Son of God, *the God-man,* is our Redeemer. This work required God, that he might overcome death : and man that he might die for us. As God, by right of property he undertook this work of redeeming his creatures ; as man, by right of relationship he undertook to redeem his brethren.

To accomplish this work of redemption, not the Divinity alone, not the humanity alone was necessary ; no, not an angelic nature ; but the Son of God alone ; who, as the Apostle says, Phil. ii. *when he was in the form of God, made himself of no reputation : and took upon himself the form of a servant, and was made in the likeness of men.* Whence also that declaration that *the Church was purchased with the blood of God,* Acts xx. 28. Well spake Augustine, *that which mediates between divinity alone, and humanity alone, is the human divine nature, and the divine human nature.* Nor was it ill said by Aquinas, *The humanity of Christ is the instrument, the divinity is the chief agent in fulfilling the work of our salvation,* Quæst. disp. de verb. art. 5.

From this consideration of the person who redeems us, we may observe the infinite guilt of sin ; agreeable to that remark of Bernard, *Acknowledge, O man, how grievous are those wounds for which it is needful the Son of God should be wounded.* This ought to strike us with horror and detestation of sin.

It demonstrates also the infinite love of God towards the human race, who willingly sent his own Son to redeem miserable mortals. Let this inflame us with reciprocal love ; let this excite us to every kind of obedience.

It must also be observed, that the Apostle does not say we have redemption by the Son of God, but *in* him. For *by* Christ the whole world is said to be redeemed, inasmuch as he offered and gave a sufficient *ransom* for all ; but *in* him the elect and faithful alone have effectual redemption, because they alone are *in* him.

Hence we learn that no one hath, or can have, any fruit of the redemption procured by Christ, unless he be in Christ. But we are engrafted in Christ through faith by the Holy Spirit. Therefore salvation is not derived to us unless from Christ our Head ; for when he becomes our Head, and we his members, then we are in him, then his saving virtue extends to us ; but not before : For *he is the Saviour of his body*, Ephes. v. 23.

Here also we must briefly resolve a doubt. For, when the Apostle says, *In whom we have redemption*, viz. we Christians, through the one oblation of the Son of God our Redeemer; it may, I say, be asked, Whether the Fathers under the Old Testament enjoyed this redemption? Christ not being then born, not to say offered, for the expiation of the sins of men.

We answer, the faithful under the Old Testament enjoyed redemption in Christ through his blood which was to be shed, like as we have through his blood having been shed : because this sacrifice of Christ had a saving efficacy, not only by the actual offering, but by the eternal decree of God, and the eternal efficacy of the same sacrifice, as well before as after it was offered. *Jesus Christ the same yesterday, to-day, and for evermore*, Heb. xiii. 8. *The Lamb slain from the foundation of the world*, Rev. xiii. 8. Therefore all the faithful under the Law, by faith in the Son of God, had Redemption even as we under the Gospel. *Abraham saw the day of Christ and was glad*, John viii. 56. He saw it, not by carnal but spiritual vision. Augustine, and the rest of the Fathers concur in this most true opinion. *All the just before Christ lived by the same faith as ourselves*, Contr. Epist. Pelag. lib. iii. cap. 4. *In ancient times there were spiritually righteous men; faith in a Christ to come dwelt in them*, Contr. adversar. leg. et proph. lib. i. cap. 17. *Their faith and ours was the same, because they believed that would be done to him which we believe hath been done*, ad Optat. Epist. 157.

Thus much concerning the Redeemer, viz. Christ the
Son of God, incarnate and dead as concerning us; but
who was to become incarnate, and to die, as concerning
the ancient Fathers.

The forgiveness of sins.] The Apostle summarily comprises and explains what he understands by *redemption :* for
these words are connected by apposition with those, *In
whom we have redemption*, i. e. *the forgiveness of sins.*
The Apostle adds this explanation with the best intention: for we have not as yet entire and full redemption,
but we expect *it* in the day of the resurrection. We have
that redemption which consists in the forgiveness of sins ;
and having obtained it, we are delivered from the bondage of the devil, of sin, and of hell. The devil cannot
any longer detain us as captives, rule us as his slaves, and
drive us here and there as he pleases ; sin itself which
cleaves to us cannot reign in us ; finally, even hell cannot
torment us with perpetual fear, or claim any lordship over
us : For, our sins being remitted, the power of the devil
is broken, the wrath of God is removed, the condemnation
of eternal death is taken away. From all these things,
therefore, we have redemption at the same time that we
have forgiveness of sins. But there is yet another bondage, viz. that of the corruption of our bodies, and of eternal sufferings, from which the elect are not yet redeemed,
but shall be redeemed at the coming of Christ. Luke xxi.
28, *Lift up your heads, for your redemption draweth nigh.*
The Apostle calls this ἀπολύτρωσιν περιποιήσεως, *the redemption
of the purchased possession*, Ephes. i. 14. This also Christ
merited for us : but he would not bestow upon believers at
once this incorruption of their bodies, and deliverance
from present external miseries, and from the remains of
sin, for the following reasons ;

First, lest the condition of the head and of the members
should be plainly dissimilar. For Christ himself was *a
man of sorrows*, having endured every kind of misery : he
did not at once sit down at the right hand of the Father
in glory, but first underwent hunger, thirst, crucifixion,
and death : it is therefore but consistent, that the members

of Christ should pass likewise through sufferings and death itself to glory.

Secondly, they are not fully redeemed from these bodily afflictions, neither from the remains of sin, that they may have matter for glorifying God, whilst they endure them with the greatest constancy and patience, whilst they resist with all their might all the lusts of sin ; that God, even as a just judge, may confer upon them, after having well fought this fight, the unfading crown.

Lastly, he would not straightway deliver the faithful from this bodily misery instantly, lest Christians should seem to embrace Christ on account of this temporal deliverance, rather than on account of that spiritual one.

To conclude, therefore, when the Apostle explains redemption by *the remission of sins*, he wishes to shew what part of the benefit of redemption is granted to believers now, and what is reserved for them in another world.

Through his blood.] We have already treated of the person of the Redeemer, and also of the blessing of redemption itself. The last branch only of this verse remains, concerning the price or method of redemption, *through his blood*, i. e. this redemption was procured through his bloody death. The Apostle states the price expressly, because captives are redeemed or liberated from bondage in many other ways :

1. By free manumission : as when a master voluntarily dismisses his slave from his bondage and declares him free. But this mode was unsuitable ; because God had determined otherwise ; and because the devil, who held us captive, never would have voluntarily dismissed us.

2. By exchange ; so we read it was often practised in wars, as when the Carthaginians sent to Rome, ten Romans who had been taken in battle, upon condition that the Romans should restore as many taken from the Carthaginians. But neither in this way could the redemption of man have been accomplished : for by no exchange of any creature could the reproach brought upon God by man be compensated.

3. By violent abduction : as when David by force of

arms delivered his men, and recovered them from the hands of the Amalekites, 1 Sam. 30.   But neither in this manner ought the human race to have been delivered : for although Christ might justly wrest from the devil, by main force, the prey which that robber had acquired by wicked craft; yet could not man, guilty as he was of treason against God, be reconciled in that manner.

4.   The last and only ground therefore of redeeming us remained, viz. that which might be effected by way of justice, all our debts being paid by our Surety, Christ Jesus. But by the payment of what ransom did he discharge so vast a debt ?   *Not with gold and silver, but his precious blood,* 1 Pet. i. 18.

Through blood.] He points at Christ's bloody death : not that the previous acts and sufferings of Christ did nothing to merit human salvation ; but that by pouring out his blood, i. e. in death, there was a completion of satisfaction. *Although,* as Aquinas truly says, *any one act of Christ was meritorious in our behalf, yet to make satisfaction for the guilt of human nature which was under the bond of death, it was necessary that Christ should sustain death ;* Quæst. disput. de grat. Christi, art. 7.   But we are redeemed by this *blood,* or by this death, of Christ, inasmuch as it expiated the wrath of God, inasmuch as it dissipated the power of the devil.

Christ averted the wrath of God from us, by undergoing the penalties due to it, that he might liberate us from our debts.   *He without any evil deserts* (says Augustine) *underwent punishment, that we without any that were good might obtain grace.*   And the Apostle, Gal. iii. 13, affirms, *Christ was made a curse for us, that he might redeem us from the curse.*

Here therefore we must observe, that although the devil held us captives, yet the price of our redemption, that is to say, the blood of Christ, was offered as a satisfaction to God, not to the devil : therefore it rested with God either to condemn or to absolve : and God being reconciled, and sin remitted, the power of the devil immediately vanished. And God is abundantly satisfied in the death of Christ for

the sins of the whole world, because the death of Christ
was the death of God; the blood of Christ, the blood of
God : Therefore from the infinite dignity of his person, the
price of his blood and his flesh which he offered for us was
infinite. So Cyril, De recta fide ad Regin. lib. 2, *If God
incarnate and suffering in his own person be understood, every
creature is trifling in comparison of him, and the death of his
one body suffices for the redemption of the world.**

Thus, then, satisfaction has been made to God and our
sins expiated. Now we must shew how the shedding of
the blood of Christ, not only hath reconciled God to us,
but also utterly destroyed the power of the devil: for from
him hath this bloody death of Christ delivered us.

Now to understand this, in the first place it must be admitted, that the power of the devil over man was upheld
by the sin of man. For if we suppose that man is free
from sin, then by no pretext of right whatever could the
devil exercise any power over him. When, therefore, the
devil attacked Christ our Saviour who was free from sin,
and by his satellites, the Jews, put him to a most painful
and ignominious death, he lost, by the judgment of God
himself, the power which he had over us the guilty, through
having exercised that which he had not over Christ the innocent. For, by this injury offered to Christ, and endured
patiently by him, God adjudged to him power over the
devil, and over all that he had possessed; so that he might
take from him the spoil at his pleasure, and rescue out of

* Cyril, Patriarch of Alexandria, the writer here cited, flourished in the
fifth century, and " distinguished himself by his zeal against Nestorius,
Bishop of Constantinople; who, in some of his homilies, had asserted, that
the Virgin Mary ought not to be called the Mother of God. The dispute
at first proved unfavourable to Cyril, whose opinion was not only condemned, but himself deprived of his Bishopric and thrown into prison. But he
was soon after released, and gained a complete victory over Nestorius ; who,
in 431, was deposed from his See of Constantinople. Cyril returned to his
See at Alexandria, where he died in 444. He also wrote against Theodorus
of Mopsuestia, Diodorus of Tarsus, and Julian the Apostate. He composed Commentaries on St. John's Gospel, and wrote several other books.
His works were published in Greek and Latin, in 1638, in 6 vols. folio."
Platt's Univer. Biogr. Vide Pearson on the Creed, in Notes from Cyril.

his hands whomsoever he might think fit. Therefore after that the devil was overcome by the death of Christ in a way of justice, and deprived of his possessions by the Divine decree ; then Christ, having triumphed over him, took from him, by an irresistible arm, his own elect, and trampled him not only under his own feet, but under the feet of all his people. Thus the devil was vanquished by the death and blood of Christ, and we are rescued from his jaws.

To this doctrine both the Scriptures and the Fathers bear testimony. God foretold this victorious death of Christ, Gen. iii. 15, *I will put enmity between thy seed and between the seed of the woman : It shall bruise thy head, and thou shalt bruise his heel.* And in Isa. liii. 12, *He shall divide the spoils of the strong,** *because he hath poured out his soul unto death.* He suffered his innocent soul† to be forced from him, that he might deliver our guilty souls from the power of the devil. Augustine, lib. xiii. De Trin. cap. 14, *What is the righteousness by which the devil was conquered? What but the righteousness of Jesus Christ? And how was he conquered? Because, though he could find in him nothing worthy of death, nevertheless he slew him. And verily it was just that he should let go the debtors whom he held, because they believed in him whom, without owing any debt, he slew.* And cap. 15, *In redemption, the blood of Christ is given as a ransom, as it were, for us ; which being accepted, the devil is not enriched, but bound, that we might be freed from his bonds.* Similar expressions are to be met with in Theodoret, De Provid. Serm. 10, and in Leo, Serm. 5. De passione Domini.‡

* " Dividet spolia fortium :" Davenant here quotes from the Vulgate, which follows the Septuagint on this text.

† Vide Isa. liii. 10—12, to justify the adoption of this word, and support the doctrine conveyed by it.

‡ Theodoret, Bishop of Cyrus, a town in Syria, an Ecclesiastical Historian, who was a native of Antioch, and a disciple of the celebrated John Chrysostom. He was raised to the See of Cyrus A.D. 420 ; and after having favoured the opinions of Nestorius, he wrote against that heresiarch, and indeed opposed all the different heretical sects of the time. His zeal

From what has been thus said concerning the method of our redemption, various passages of Scripture apparently opposed to each other, are reconciled : Some of which assert that we are justified and saved *freely,* as Rom. iii. 24 ; others teach that we are redeemed with *a price,* as 1 Cor. vi. 20. Some declare that by *the might* and *power* of Christ, we were delivered from the power of the devil, and that he was *spoiled, triumphed over,* and *destroyed,* as Col. ii. 15, Heb. ii. 14. Now all these passages are equally true. For we are redeemed and saved *freely,* as it respects ourselves ; since we ourselves contributed nothing to our redemption. We are redeemed with *a price,* as it respects God ; for Christ offered his own blood to him for our redemption. We are delivered by *power and might,* as respects the devil ; whom, being previously conquered by Christ, and delivered over to him by right, He spoiled by force of arms.

From this redemption obtained by the death and blood of Christ alone, we deduce these inferences ;

1. We are not our own masters, but the servants of the Redeemer : we ought not therefore to serve our own lusts, but to yield obedience to his commands.

2. Neither our own satisfactions, nor merits, nor the sufferings of martyrs, could redeem us from the penalties

for the *Catholic* Faith rendered him obnoxious to the Eutychians, by whom he was deposed in the Synod which they held at Ephesus ; but he was restored to his diocese by the Council of Chalcedon in 421. Nothing is known of his future history, except that he was alive till after A.D. 460, and was renowned for the sanctity and simplicity of his manners, and as an eloquent, copious, and learned writer, remarkable for his acquaintance with all the branches of sacred erudition. He wrote, besides his Ecclesiastical History from the time of Constantine to that of Theodosius the younger, and his Discourses on Providence above adverted to, Commentaries on the Scriptures ; Epistles ; Lives of famous Anchorites ; Dialogues ; and Books on Heresy. In his ingenious and learned treatise, De curandis Græcorum affectionibus, " he opposed," says Mosheim, " with fortitude and vigour, those that worshipped images ;" and in his first and second dialogues occur some remarkable passages, bearing decisive evidence that the doctrine of transubstantiation was not then known to the Church. The Jesuit Sirmond gave at Paris, in the year 1642, a noble edition of the works of this prelate, in four vols. folio. Garnier published an edition in 1648, to which he added a fifth volume.

due to our sins: but the blood of Christ only, who was without sin. Well spake Tertullian, *If thou hast offended in no instance thyself, then by all means suffer for me: but if thou art a sinner, how shall the oil of thy poor vessel suffice for thyself and me?* De Pudicitiâ. cap. 22.*

---

* Our Author has frequently quoted Tertullian before, and no wonder he should have done so; for the glory of God, and the increase of Christianity, were the objects which influenced the conduct, and appear prominent in the writings, of that distinguished man; and induced him to devote his life to the study of the Holy Scriptures; the elucidation of truth; and, generally, the exposure of error. He was a Presbyter of Carthage, born there about the middle of the second century. His father was a Centurion under the Proconsul of Africa, and had his son well educated in all the accomplishments and learning of the Greeks and Romans; and he grew up intimately conversant, as well with all that was ornamental, as instructive in general literature. It is uncertain how he was occupied previous to his embracing Christianity, though some persons have supposed he was an advocate. His conversion took place not long after the commencement of the reign of Severus, and a little before the conclusion of the second century. Being a man of a strong and vigorous mind, and dissatisfied with Paganism; observing the efficacy of the Christian Religion over the lives and minds of men; considering its great antiquity, as it regarded its main principles through the promises and prophecies of revelation; the harmony and truth of the predictions recorded in the books of the Christians; the frequent testimonies which the heathen deities gave to its truth and authenticity; he, by such means, was brought to profess Christianity. The cruel conduct which, about this time, was manifested towards the Christians by Severus, induced Tertullian to undertake the vindication of their cause. To accomplish this object, he published his celebrated " Apology," which has been referred to at page 74, dedicating it to the magistrates of the Roman Empire. In this work, with great learning and eloquence, he pleaded the cause of the persecuted Christians; complained of the injustice of their enemies, and the methods of their proceedings; and demonstrated the falsehood of the crimes with which they were charged: he proves the meekness and innocency of the devoted followers of Christ; their temperance and sobriety; their piety to God, and obedience to their prince; the reasonableness of their principles, and the holiness of their lives, beyond contradiction. The result of this was very satisfactory, as it certainly, in some degree, mitigated the enmity of the Emperor; and for some time the persecutions ceased. Tertullian also kindly and usefully engaged in writing to the martyrs in prison, to comfort them under their afflictions, and exhort them to perseverance. About the year 205, the Bishop of Rome published a constitution, by which he admitted persons guilty of adultery and fornication to a place among the penitents. Against this constitution, Tertullian wrote his book, cited by Davenant, as above—De Pudicitiâ. For this he was excommuni-

Verse 15.

*Who is the image of the invisible God, the first-born of every
creature.*

In the three foregoing verses we are told of the benefit
of redemption itself. In these four which follow we have
an accurate delineation of the Redeemer. And the Apostle introduces this excellent personal description of Christ
that it may more evidently appear with what security we
can repose all our hopes of salvation in such a Redeemer;
and that all other methods of salvation foisted in by seducers ought to be rejected as most palpable fables.

Now the Redeemer is described by a threefold relation:

1. By his internal relation to God; he is *his image.*

2. By his external relation to the creature formed; he
is *the first-born of creation,* its Creator and Preserver.

3. By his relation to the creature renewed, that is to
say, to the Church: for he is *the Head*—the origin, &c.

Who is the image of the invisible God.] The Apostle
commences the description of the Redeemer, from his internal relation to God. And here we have to consider
three particulars:

1. How many things enter into the consideration of an
image, i. e. what is considered to constitute an image.

2. What sort of an image of God, Christ is, or in what
sense he is called *the image of God.*

---

cated: the ill usage which he received from the Ecclesiastics of the Church
of Rome occasioned his becoming a Montanist; and whether he was ever
reconciled to their communion is uncertain. He lost hereby the title of
saint; but, as Dr. Jortin has well observed, Charity bids *us* suppose that he
lost not what is infinitely more important. Besides his writings before noticed, he composed and published many other books and tracts, on various
subjects of divinity and matters of controversy of his time, to the amount,
it is said, of 50. But for further and ample particulars respecting his writings, opinions, and character, the Reader may refer for satisfaction to
Bishop Kaye's " Ecclesiastical History of the second and third centuries,
illustrated from Tertullian."

3. Why God, of whom Christ is the image, is called *invisible*.

As respects the first point: in the consideration of *an image* there are these three particulars : First, that what is called an image must possess the likeness of some other thing. For if no likeness subsist between them, it is absurd and contrary to all reason to call it an image : for it cannot represent the other; which is the peculiarity of an image.

Secondly, it is required in an image, that that which is properly understood by this term should be in some way drawn and derived from that of which it is called the image. For a mere resemblance where there is no deduction or derivation of the one from the other, does not constitute a proper character of an image: as, for example, we do not call milk the image of milk, or an egg the image of another egg; because the one is not derived from the other.

Lastly, it is required, that the likeness which exists between the image itself, and that of which it is the image, should pertain to the specific nature of the prototype, as far as to its participation in, or, at least, its designation of the species. When it pertains to the very nature of the species, it is called an essential and natural image, or an image of equality : when it extends only to the outward designation of the species, it is called an accidental or artificial image, or an image of imitation. In the former way, the image of a king is said to be in the prince his son : In the second, the image of a king is said to be impressed upon his coin, or painted on a picture. Having laid down these principles, let us now enquire, What sort of an image of God Christ our Redeemer is, or in what sense he is called *the image of God.*

And here a twofold consideration occurs. For Christ is to be regarded either as he was the eternal and invisible image of the Father before the foundation of the world, or as he was the visible and manifest image of the invisible Father, viz. after the assumption of the flesh.

Christ, then, was from all eternity, and always will be, the uncreated WORD, the perfect, essential, and invisible image of his invisible Father.   Before either angels or men existed, to contemplate this image by mental vision, yet even then, he was the image of his Father:

1. Because he possessed the exact likeness of him, for he was χαρακτηρ της ὑποστάσεως 'αυτοῦ, Heb. i. 3, *the express image of his person.*

2. He moreover had this likeness drawn and derived from God the Father through that wonderful and ineffable generation from the Father.   For the eternal Father, knowing himself from eternity, begets the Word, the consubstantial image of himself.   If any one expects aught from me concerning the mode, he shall have that sentiment of Ambrose : *Thou art commanded to believe : it is not permitted thee to discuss,* De fide lib. i. cap. 5.*

---

* Ambrose, Archbishop of Milan in the latter part of the fourth century. He was son of a Prætorian Præfect in Gaul, and appointed at an early age, on account of his talents and learning, first, to be Assessor to Probus, and the Governor of the Provinces of Liguria and Æmilia, about the year 370. He was chosen from hence, to the eminent station he afterwards occupied in the Church, by the unanimous call of the people, on his entering an assembly of the Milanese, by virtue of his authority as Governor of the Province, on an occasion of a popular contest between the Catholics and Arians, about a new Bishop; when he pleaded for peace and subordination with such singular suavity and wisdom, that a cry was raised—' Let Ambrose be Bishop.'   But he was exceedingly averse to accept a function to which he had been so unexpectedly but honourably chosen.   No person, indeed, could ever be more desirous to rush into the office of a Bishop, than he seems to have been to avoid a post of such distinction and responsibility : but, when induced to accept it, he entered upon its duties with equal assiduity and diffidence.   He preached every Sabbath, and attended to every thing incumbent upon him in such a station, with evident sincerity and the most undeviating fidelity and justice.   He had succeeded to Auxentius, an Arian ; but he soon effected the expulsion of Arianism from Italy.   He became no less eminent for his eloquence as a Divine, than he had been as a Lawyer ; and, on various occasions, had to display it ; which he did with the greatest success, both on behalf of the truth against the Arians, and of the church, against Maximus and Justinia the Mother of Valentinian. He gave a remarkable evidence of firmness in refusing the Sacrament to Theodosius, and even denied him entrance into the church of Milan, on account of cruelties the emperor had exercised at Thessalonica ; representing to him

3. Lastly, it is not a shadowy image of the Father that he bears, in a nature dissimilar, but in the same essence and Divine nature.

It may be asked, How is Christ called the image of God, when he himself is God; for it is impossible that the same thing should be called the image of itself?

We answer, The word *God* is, in this place, taken with reference to person, not to essence; for it designates the Father only, not the Divine nature in general.   Christ,

---

his guilt in such forcible and pathetic terms, as to induce his remorse, contrition, and repentance.   Ambrose died in peace at the seat of his Bishopric, at the age of 64, after having been twice compelled to leave it through the troubles and wars of his time.   Amidst every other fluctuation, he evinced a simple dependance on the mercy and grace of the Lord Jesus ; and left behind him a bright example of indefatigable exertion, and of zealous devotedness to the duties of his sacred calling.   His character and conduct, however, have been variously judged of, and as diversely represented, according to the partialities and prejudices of men who have undertaken to canvass his active habits ; to scrutinize his ardent zeal in the cause of religion, and on behalf of the church ; or to criticise the numerous writings he left behind him.   On a careful and repeated review of every account of this Father which the present writer could obtain, he is disposed to adopt the concluding remarks of Dr. Adam Clarke's notice of Ambrose and his writings, as affording the fairest representation : " Having been bred up in the " midst of State affairs till advanced in life, his knowledge of *Theology* must " necessarily have been both limited and superficial ; hence we find him " flying to allegory for interpretation—the easy resource of an uninformed " mind but a lively conception, as requiring no argument to prove it, and " no study to frame it.   His works on *Morals* are, undoubtedly, his best " performances, and evince the strong conceptions of an upright character : " in *Doctrine* he is all that Rome could wish him, and a mysticising fancy " could make him : as a *Disciplinarian* he has the noble fortitude of a man " conscious of rectitude, and yet not austere where circumstances appeared " to call for lenity, *(Epist. to Sinagrius)*."   There is reason, however, from the very numerous conflicting opinions respecting Ambrose, to apprehend, that a *correct* opinion of what he was, can hardly be formed from his works as now extant ; since Papal expurgators and emendators, seeing what might be made of them, may have turned them to as good an account in their favour as Cyprian's : For what will not Jesuitical policy and authority, intrigue and ingenuity effect, where it has the power and influence, and as the circumstances of the *infallible* Church require ?   Ambrose was a composer of *Hymns*, and is understood to have been the first who introduced regular choral music into the Christian Church.—Vide " Clarke's Succession of Sacred Literature," and Encyclop. Metropol. under " Ecclesiastical Writers of the Fourth Century."

therefore, is the image of the Father, not of the Godhead. The person of the Son bears the likeness of the person of the Father; but the Essence or Divine nature in the Son is altogether the same as in the Father: *I and my Father are one.* Christ therefore cannot be the same *in person* with Him of whom he is the image; but there is no reason why he may not be the same *in essence.*

It may again be asked, Why is the term image appropriated to Christ, since the Holy Spirit also is of the same essence with God the Father?

To this we answer, Not because he lacks the reality of the Divine nature; for the Spirit is also of the same essence with the Father and the Son : but because the Spirit proceeds by mode of the will, the Son by mode of the nature ; and because he proceeds not from the Father alone, but likewise from the Son ; but an image ought to be the representation of one definite person.—These things being explained, let us now deduce some observations from this declaration of the Apostle, *Christ is the image of God.*

Observe, 1. The error of Arius is disproved, who denied that Christ is of the same essence with the Father : for if he is the image of the Father's person, he is co-essential with the Father; because a creature cannot be the *eternal image* of the Creator, but only after the image, through the communication of free endowments.

2. The contrary error of Sabellius is also refuted, who affirmed that the Son is the same with the Father, nor to be personally distinguished from him : but nothing can be more manifest, than that an image is something distinct from that of which it is the image. There is the Father; and there is also the Son, because the image of the Father is the Son.*

---

* When the numerous express declarations of Scripture respecting the person of the Saviour are borne in mind, and when the almost unanimous testimonies of the early Fathers are called to recollection, it seems marvellous that such errors, as those above-mentioned, should ever have occurred ; especially among men professing to take the word of God for their guide. Arius, the celebrated propagator of the heresy first adverted to, arose in the beginning of the fourth century. He was a man of family and educa-

3. We are instructed by whom we are to be formed again to the image of God which we have lost; viz. through this perfect and essential image of God, whom God sent

tion, and owing to his being encouraged, and his heresy espoused by Eusebius, Bishop of Nicomedia, and by the sister of the Emperor Constantine, it soon spread. But there were too many in that age valiant for the truth, for adherence to which the Church had undergone ten persecutions; and such a resistance was made by those who knew the truth as it is in Jesus, to an error so awful as the denial of the supreme and co-eternal Godhead of Christ, that a Council was speedily convened—the *first general* Council of the Christian Church, viz. that of Nice; at which 318 Bishops, from all parts where Christianity had been established, were assembled, with numerous Presbyters and others, to the number, it is said, of above 2000 persons. At this Council the anti-Christian doctrine was condemned, and that Creed drawn up, which, something enlarged and confirmed at another Council about fifty years afterwards, is held by the Church of England to this day; and in which it is the glory of a fallen sinner believing in Christ for salvation, to confess Him the Redeemer and Saviour, the Son of the living God, one with the Father, co-equal and co-eternal; and the Holy Ghost as the author and giver of life.—The opinions of those who rejected this faith, once delivered to the saints, have undergone material changes since Arius's time. The two Socini, theological speculators in the sixteenth century, were the chief agents in these mutations; and since their emendations, Christ is held to be, by the followers of men of such superior wisdom, information, discernment, and *rationality*, not what even Arius taught—" the first and most glorious production of creative power, who, though he had a beginning, existed before, superior to all other creatures, and the instrument by whose subordinate agency the universe was formed;" but he is sunk in dignity and worth to a mere peccable creature, without any existence before his birth of the Virgin, or other prerogative besides the excellence of his moral character, and his mission from the Father; so far does one fundamental error lead to another; those who adopt the first lie generally proceeding further, and raising up other sects that are still more remote from the truth. " The radical mistake," as a modern writer of great utility on the subject has justly observed, " in all these systems, whether heretical or orthodox, " proceeds from the disposition, so natural in man, of being wise above what " is written. They are not satisfied with believing a plain declaration of the " Saviour, ' I and my Father are one.' They undertake, with the utmost " presumption and folly, to explain in what manner the Father and the " Son are one; but man might as well attempt to take up the ocean in the " hollow of his hand as endeavour, by his narrow understanding, to comprehend the manner of the Divine existence." The great work of Bishop Bull, " Defensio Fidei Nicænæ," upon which his renown permanently rests, remains a tower of strength upon this point. Bishop Horsley's tracts dispersed the shadows of Dr. Priestley's raising. But, perhaps, to those who would have the summary of the early opinions concisely, but decidedly, ex-

into the world on purpose that he might renew man, fallen
and shamefully corrupted.   *Only by this image of God can
you be conformed to the image of God,* says Ambrose, De
fide, lib. i. cap. 4.

Now let it suffice to have spoken thus much concerning
the Son, as far as in himself he is the invisible, eternal,
and natural image of God the Father before the foundation
of the world.   But Christ must also be regarded as far as

pressed, the recent admirable volume of Dr. Burton on the " Testimony of
the Fathers," may be strongly recommended.   We cannot, however, but
regret, that this able writer should have dismissed a subject of such vital
importance, without an exhibition of the *practical* efficacy of the orthodox
system.

Sabellius was an African Presbyter or Bishop, who lived in the century
preceding Arius, and gave name to the heresy next adverted to by our Expositor.   The notions said to have been maintained by him in systematizing
and vindicating errors previously broached, and to account for the glorious
declarations of the Gospel and the great Mystery of Godliness which it unfolds, are curious indeed.   But his history and opinions are involved in
great obscurity.   He is generally stated to have held, as the foundation of
his heresy, that, (in the words of Bishop Bull), " God was but one person ;
and that there was no real distinction, much less division of persons, in the
Divine essence ;" and against this the arguments of Davenant are levelled.
The learned Mosheim, however, does not hesitate to pronounce, that " this
is in great part false."   In his " Commentaries" he has entered copiously
into the whole review of what is to be gathered from the ancients concerning this heresiarch ; and seems to have proved that his heresy has been confounded with that of Noetus.   The summary of his investigation is, that
" the opinion of Sabellius is not the same with that of Noetus ; for the
former did not suppose, as the latter seems to have done, that the person of
the Deity was in entire simplicity one, and that it had assumed and joined
to itself the human nature of Christ ; but that a certain energy, emitted
from the Father, or rather a part of the person and nature of the Father,
was joined to the man Christ ; and that this virtue, or part of the Father,
was the Holy Spirit," (p. 688).—But these, and the above-mentioned errors
and subtleties, are not befitting us to dwell upon.   They are evidently not
to be sustained by the Word of God ; and our Expositor, from that fountain of truth, overturns them at once ; and, if the foundations be destroyed, what shall the foolish builders do ?   It need only be added, that the
reader who desires farther information, as to the history and progress of these
or other errors, and has not more ample means of obtaining it, or who
would find the works mentioned in the preceding article of a literary character beyond his attainments, will in Grier's " Epitome of the General
Councils of the Church," and Douglas's " Errors of Religion," meet with
suitable satisfaction.

he is the visible and manifest image of the invisible God
since his incarnation, and that with respect to ourselves,
because he represents God to us.

And to this also the Apostle seems to me to have had an
eye, inasmuch as he does not barely say, Christ is the
image of God, but τοῦ Θεοῦ 'αρράτου, of *the invisible God;*
where an implied antithesis is to be understood ; as though
he had said, that Christ is now become the visible image of
the invisible God. For that substantial image of God
shone forth in Christ incarnate, and represented to us, as
in a glass, God the Father, when he shewed himself to us
in the flesh, as the mighty and present God, and gave us
to behold in that flesh the justice, mercy, truth, and power
of God. For in the man Christ shone forth the most bright
image of the Divine perfection : Ὁ Θεὸς 'εφανερωσθη 'εν σαρκί,
God was manifest in the flesh. And Christ himself says,
John xiv. 7, 9, *If ye had known me, ye should have known
my Father also. He that hath seen me hath seen the Father.*
Here we behold the Divine wisdom and goodness, for he
who is the invisible God proposes to mankind the visible
Son and God manifest in the flesh, that by him who is *the
light, the way,* and *the truth,* we may more easily approach
to him who is *invisible* and *incomprehensible.*

From this most wise Divine appointment we gather, that
it is not fit for us to know God out of Christ, or, passing
by Christ, to proceed directly to God. For this kind of
knowledge or approach to God, would rather strike horror
into us miserable mortals defiled by sin, than afford comfort.* *The sight of God,* says Nazianzen, *instils fear into
men ; because God drawing nigh to us convicts the soul of its
disease.* Orat. 4. [Isa. vi. 5.]

Wherefore, in like manner as they who are unable to fix
their eyes on the blaze of the sun itself without pain, may
yet look upon its reflex image even with pleasure ; so we
who are not able to behold the Divine Majesty in itself,
contemplate the living image of it in Christ with the highest joy.

* It was a wise saying of Luther, " Nolo Deum absolutum."

N 2

This may suffice concerning Christ *the image of God.*

It remains that we attend to that last observation; viz. why God is called *invisible.* And that is to be considered either in respect of the Divine nature in itself [absolutely], or in the person of the Father.

Invisible.] First in respect of the Divine nature considered absolutely; because neither by the eye of the body, nor even of the mind can it be beheld, whilst we sojourn here. *Ye cannot see my face,* Exod. iii. 20. *No man hath seen God at any time,* John i. 18. *He dwelleth in the light inaccessible,* 1 Tim. vi. 16. It is impossible that we should see God with our bodily eyes, because the act of seeing pre-supposes a visible object: but in God there is neither corporeal light, nor colour, nor form; nor, in short, any thing that hath the nature of a visible object. Whence the folly of the Anthropomorphites is evident, who attributed to God a human appearance, and bodily lineaments, not unlike our own.* If God were such, he could not be invisible.

But neither in this life are we able to behold the essence of God with our mental eyes. *No one hath seen that fulness of divinity which dwells in God, no one comprehends it in his mind,* says Ambrose, in Luke lib. i. cap. 1. Which will easily appear if we consider the modes of our knowledge whilst we are in this pilgrimage.

---

* These were a sect of ancient heretics, whose doctrine proceeded from taking every thing spoken of God in the Scripture in a literal sense. Locke seems to think that this prejudice is almost inherent in the mind : it was entertained by the whole sect of the Stoics, and examples of its influence may easily be traced, not only in the writings of many of the Fathers, but also among modern Divines. Other writers, however, have fallen into the opposite extreme ; and supposed that God is not only a stranger to human affections, such as pity, love, joy, &c., but that even the ideas of wisdom, justice, mercy, and the like, are different in the Divine mind from what they are in our conceptions, not merely in degree, but even in kind. This opinion was embraced by Hume, and admitted by Archbishop King, though on different principles of reasoning; and has latterly received the sanction of a learned and able writer of the present day. As Socinianism has of late assumed much of its cast from these notions and principles, there is the greater propriety in adducing these remarks, and in drawing the attention by them to the refutation deduced by our Expositor, and in requesting the consideration of the young to the first article of our Church.

For we know God either by causality, or by remotion, or by eminence.* By *causality ;* whilst we contemplate the Creator, through the creatures of which God is the cause. But notwithstanding this knowledge, the essence of God remains invisible : because an effect shews not the essence of its cause, unless when it is of the same species with the cause, or demonstrates the whole virtue of the cause.

We know God by *remotion ;* when we consider the imperfections of the creatures, and perceive them to be remote from God; as conceiving him to be immortal, not susceptible of suffering, and incapable of sin. But this knowledge does not extend to the Divine essence : for considerations of remoteness indicate negatively what God is not; they do not shew positively what he is. For no privation belongs to the essence of a positive existence.

We know God by *eminence,* when, after considering the perfections of the creatures, we ascribe them to God in the highest degree of excellency; thus, because wisdom, strength, holiness, are perfections in the creatures, therefore we judge God to be perfectly strong, perfectly wise, perfectly holy. But neither in this way do we rise to a perception of the essence of God, because none of these things are predicated of God, and of the creature univocally. Aquin. Quæst. disput. De simp. div. essen. art. 4.

To this threefold way of knowing God add also that knowledge which we have by faith ; and yet then the divine essence remains invisible. For so Paul himself confesses, 1 Cor. xiii. 12, *We see now through a glass darkly.* For faith shews rather what sort of a being God is towards us, than what he is in his own essence. Therefore God in himself is to us invisible.

2. But we must also add that God in the person of the Father may be said to be *invisible* by a certain special mean-

---

* " Cognoscimus enim Deum vel per causalitatem, vel per remotionem, vel per eminentiam." It is scarcely needful to observe how impracticable it is to render these and other technical phrases of the School divinity, which occur in this work, into English, with any thing like precision. They become sufficiently perspicuous, however, by the tenor of the passages in which they are employed.

ing ; for in this place, the name of God (as we have before
suggested) is to be taken with respect to person rather
than to essence.

God the Father, then, is called invisible, because (as the
Fathers with reason held) he never appeared to the Patriarchs : but the Son, who also was invisible as to the divine nature, chose to appear to them by assuming some
created form. So Tertul. in lib. De Trin. et alibi : *He who
spake to Moses was the Son of God, who always also appeared to the Patriarchs.* So Prudentius, in Apotheosi. *Whoever is recorded to have seen God, saw the Son sent forth from
him.* In this manner the Son of God chose, as it were, to
give a prelude of his incarnation ; the Holy Spirit also we
read of as having appeared in the visible form of a *dove,*
and of *tongues of fire ;* but the Father never took any visible appearance, but was always in every respect invisible.

Now the first use of this is, since God hath made it clear
that he is *invisible,* the heathen and papists who worship him
under the likeness of man are hence convicted of idolatry.
For God himself, inasmuch as he hath not shewn himself
visible, hath decided that he is not to be worshipped under
a visible image, Deut. iv. 15. This base idolatry of the
Church of Rome, all the Fathers, and some even among
the Papists themselves, have condemned. *To worship the
divine essence in material things, is to dishonour it by the senses,*
Clem. Strom. 6. *No image of him ought to be worshipped,
unless that which is the same as himself,* August. Epist. 119.
It is foolish to make images to represent God, or to adore them.
Durand.   But they do make them for worship : Cajet. in
3 quæst. 25. art. 3.*

* Vide page 14.—The Papists sometimes attempt to deny that they do
this, or else excuse themselves, saying, that " to paint or grave any of the
three persons, or the three persons, as they appeared visibly and corporally,
is no more improper or unlawful, than it was indecent for them to appear
in such forms." To this we may oppose the opinion of Tertullian, who, in
his Treatise De Idololatriâ, shews that *making idols,* no matter of what *substance,* or in what *form,* was idolatry ; and that building their temples or
altars, or adorning their shrines, though even to gain a living, was idolatry
also. But the Romish Church not only enjoins the adoration of such
images, but goes farther, and by the ninth article of Pope Pius IV. main-

Secondly, Since God is invisible to us in this life, and
yet our happiness consists in seeing him ; we ought to sigh
for that other life : and we ought so to frame our life that
we may at length attain to the beatific vision of the invisible God.   It behoves us, therefore, to guard our heart
against all defilement : *Blessed are the pure in heart, for they*

tains " that the images of Christ, and the mother of God, are to be had and
retained, and that due honour and worship is to be given to them." It was
the grossness of this constant practice of image worship—" the reverential
bowings and bendings of the knee, and prostrations practised before the
images and relics in the public worship of the church of Rome," says the
Rev. James Smith, " that first led me to the suspicions I conceived of the
erroneousness of the church of Rome, as contrary to the express words of
the Second Commandment." This took place whilst he was a student in
the Romish College at Lisbon, and eventually led to his separation from the
church of Rome, and becoming a Clergyman of the church of England.
His volume on " the Errors of the Church of Rome" is a publication well
worth attention, containing a fund of information on the subjects at issue
between us and them. This is what constitutes Protestantism. Papists
are wont to assail Protestantism as a *new* Religion, and to brand *us* as heretics ; whereas true Protestantism is a return to the true, and ancient, and
orthodox faith—" the faith once delivered to the saints," and from which
THEY have swerved. They are fond of reverting, as it respects us in
England, to Henry the Eighth's time. But the case is parallel to the one
just adverted to ; only differing as to magnitude and numbers. As Sharon
Turner in his Modern History, vol. i. p. 573, has well observed : " All
" Henry's Court, and Parliament, and Nation, were born and educated in
" the Romish faith, and all they did was therefore the act of Catholics. A
" different state of things began in Edward VI. and Elizabeth's time. They
" were trained up to Protestant principles ; and so were the children of most
" of the subjects of Henry VIII. The acts of these were therefore those
" of Protestants. If any of the preceding Catholics threw off opinions and
" habits, which they thought wrong, they were still Catholics who so act-
" ed, and their decisions were the decisions of Catholics discerning what
" was erroneous, and preferring what their reason and conscience perceived
" to be preferable. Their children being educated as Protestants, acted on
" different principles ; they judged as Protestants, as their fathers had
" judged as Catholics. This distinction is important. The change of Ca-
" tholics into the new opinions, was the verdict of Catholics in their fa-
" vour ; who met them with a Catholic mind, and examined them with
" Catholic prepossessions. The English Reformation was thus the wise and
" good work of the Catholics themselves, correcting the abuses of their own
" church, and establishing a purer system of Catholic Christianity. Pro-
" testantism is Catholic Christianity reformed from its papal corruptions.
" Romanism is sectarianism, compared with Apostolical Christianity."

shall see God. Matth. v. 8.   It behoves us to *follow peace and holiness, without which no one shall see the Lord.*   To conclude, in one word : If any hope or desire dwell in us of ever seeing him who is invisible, always let us bear in mind that of St. John, 1 Epist. iii. 2, 3, *When God shall appear, we shall see him as he is: And every man that hath this hope in him, purifieth himself, even as he also is pure.*

And so far concerning the comparison of Christ to God.

The first-born of every creature.]   Here the Apostle describes the Redeemer by comparison with the creatures, and asserts that he is begotten of God before any creature existed.   But in this place it must not be concealed, that these words are expounded in different ways by interpreters.

Some make them apply to the human nature of Christ, and explain *the first-born of every creature* to mean, the Lord of every creature ; and think the Apostle alludes to the prerogative of *the first-born* under the Old Testament. For he who was *the first-born among many brethren*, was honoured by the rest as head : he discharged the office of king and priest in his family : upon him, therefore, the other brothers depended; from him was derived blessing and sanctification to all.   Since, therefore, the man Christ is constituted the Lord of the whole world, Psalm viii. and Heb. i.; since by him his brethren are sanctified, Heb. ii. 11, he is most fitly called *the first-born of every creature*, because he hath the right and prerogative of the first-born over every creature.

Augustine, in many places, applies the word *first-born* to the human nature of Christ.   In lib. De fide, et symb. tom. 3.   And against Secundinus, Manich. tom. 6.   *He is called*, says he, *the only begotten Son, because without brethren; the first-born, because with brethren.   You will not find in what manner you may understand both expressions concerning him with respect to the same divine nature.*   This sense has no disadvantage, and some embrace it, that they may more easily meet the cavil of the Arians.

But almost all the Greek Fathers, and many of the Latin, interpret the word *first-born* of Christ, in his divine nature. Therefore they would have this to be the sense of these words : *the first-born of every creature,* i. e. begotten before any thing was created, τεχθεὶς πρὸ πάσης κτίσεως, because begotten from eternity. Let us adduce a few of their testimonies. Tertullian, in libro de Trin., says, *How could he be the first-born, unless because, according to his divinity, the Word proceeded from God the Father before every creature?* Ambrose, De fide, lib. i. cap. 4, says, *He is called the first-born, not the first-created, that he may be believed in, as begotten in respect to his nature, and first in respect to his eternity.* Chrysostom in this place observes, Ου πρωτόκτιστος, 'αλλὰ πρωτότοκος ; *not first-created ; but first-born.*

But it may be said, Why is he not called *the first-born of God,* instead of *the first-born of every creature?*

The construction is somewhat harsh, when we explain *the first-born of every creature* to be begotten of God before every creature : but the Apostle chose to connect the mention of the creature with the eternal generation of Christ, that from thence he might be understood to have been so begotten by God the Father from eternity, as in time to become the efficient beginning, and even the basis and foundation of the whole creation, which, unless it depended upon him, would fall into nothing.

Thus says Basil,* *He is called the first-born of every creature, because he is the cause of creation, coming into existence from things which were not.*

---

* This eminent Father is placed by Erasmus among the greatest orators of antiquity ; he is admitted by all to have been one of the most learned and eloquent doctors of the Greek Church. He was born of highly respectable Christian parents, who spared no pains in his instruction. After studying at Athens, returning to his own native place Cæsarea, and teaching rhetoric there with success for some time, he travelled into Syria, Egypt, and Lybia ; but finding there was no true rest or enjoyment to be had but in the privacies and exercises of Religion, he returned home to give up himself thereto. The reputation he obtained for learning and piety, occasioned at length his being chosen Bishop of Cæsarea, about the year 370, which station he held about nine years. He was much persecuted by the Emperor Valens, because he refused to embrace the Arian doctrine. Besides Expository, Homiletical, and Moral works, Basil left upwards of 400 Letters, which, it is said, are models of epistolary style, and replete with valuable information

But here two things are to be avoided: First that we do not, from its being said that Christ is *the first-born* in respect of the divine nature, infer, that this ineffable generation took its origin from some beginning of time.   Christ hath a beginning of origin, viz. his Father of whom he is begotten : but he hath not a beginning of time; for he is begotten by the Father from eternity.   Well spake Thomas, *The Son hath not so received from the Father as though receiving afterwards what he had not before : but because he hath his being from the Father even from all eternity : according to that Scripture, The Lord possessed me in the beginning of his way,* Prov. viii. 22.   *His goings forth have been* a diebus eternitate, *from the days of eternity,* Micah v. 2.   *In the beginning,* John i. 1.   Therefore this word *first,* when it is spoken concerning God, does not impute a temporal beginning to God, of whom it is affirmed; but only excludes the priority of other things : *I am the first and the last,* Rev. xxii. 13.   Nor hence must we infer that God either had a beginning or will have an end ; but we must from hence deny that any thing either existed before him, or will continue after him.   So, when Christ is called the *first-born,* we are not to infer that therefore he had a temporal beginning of his existence : but we must therefore deny that any thing was co-eval, or more ancient than He.

Secondly, we must be aware of inferring with the Arians, from Christ being called *the first-born of every creature,* that therefore Christ is a creature.   For thus they argue ; As the first-born of brethren is of the number of the breth-

respecting the history of the eventful times in which he lived; evincing also, that, " to a capacious and powerful understanding, richly stored with original conceptions and acquired knowledge, Basil united great activity, presence of mind, and moral courage ; and was neither disheartened by difficulties, nor intimidated by dangers.   In a variety of ardent contests, and most trying circumstances, he is seen universally acquitting himself with dignity and firmness; and even when unsuccessful, maintaining the respectability of his character and station."   The opinions of a man like this—being founded in truth, tried by experience, and guarded by intelligence, learning, and principle—are to be regarded ; and whilst the value of them is thus evident, the propriety of our Expositor's frequent reference to him is apparent.

ren, and the first-born of the flock are of the flock : so the first-born of every creature is of the number of the creatures.   But in the passage before us, we must understand no numbering of him among the creatures, but only a precedency to them.   In the case of first-born, they who are second-born have the same nature with the first; because they take their origin from the same person : But Christ is so termed *the first-born,* that he is also *the only begotten :* for he alone is begotten of God the Father ; creatures are not begotten, but created by God.   Therefore the first-born of every creature, signifies nothing else than begotten before any created thing.

Christ is the true God, because begotten not made ; because begotten before every creature.   For whatever exists is either Creator or creature.

Verses 16, 17.

For by him were all things created, that are in heaven, and
that are in earth, visible and invisible, whether they be
thrones, or dominions, or principalities, or powers : all
things were created by him and for him.
And he is before all things, and by him all things consist.

The Apostle proceeds in describing the Son of God by a comparison with the creatures ; and proves and illustrates what he had laid down in the preceding verse, viz. that *Christ was the image of God, and the first-born of every creature ;* in other words, that he is the Son of God according to nature, begotten of him before any creature was made, i. e. from all eternity.   This he proves by reasoning from the nature of cause and effect : and he shews that Christ is the efficient, the preserving, and final cause of all creation ; and on that account prior both in dignity and time to every creature.   And this argument he illustrates from the various divisions of creation.   But each of these will be more conveniently discussed by following the order of the context.

For by him were all things created.] He here gives the
reason why he had termed Christ *the first-born of every
creature.* And his reason, as the Schoolmen will have it,
is derived *à causa exemplari;* from his being the ideal
cause, or the cause as a model. And they infer this because it is said, 'εν 'αυτῷ, *in him;* not δι''αυτοῦ, *by him.* And
here they philosophize at large about the eternal idea of all
things in the Word. Nor, indeed, do we ourselves deny
that the Maker of the world, had in himself from all eternity, the plans of all things ready described, so that all
things were present *to* the Word, though not present *in*
themselves. For as the Philosopher says, 7 Metaph. de
rebus artificialibus, *The form of those things must have existed in the mind of the workman, before they could have been
exhibited in the workmanship; as every material house is always built according to the immaterial pattern which was already planned in the mind of the architect:* so concerning the
system of nature, we may with truth assert, that the plan
or scheme of all things must have existed in the Divine
mind and arrangement before they were actually produced.

Now if in this manner we explain the words of the Apostle, 'εν 'αυτῷ 'εκτιθη πάντα, *in him were all things created,* we
obtain the strongest proof of Christ being prior to, and
more excellent than all creatures; inasmuch as the ideal
cause is always prior to that which is made according to
it. I have chosen to notice this interpretation of the
Schoolmen, because there is no fallacy in it: but I am myself much more inclined to the opinion of Chrysostom. and
our writers, who regard this expression as a Hebraism, and
say that 'εν 'αυτῷ and δι''αυτοῦ have the same meaning, so
that the reason is derived from the efficient cause. For
this preposition *in* is often taken for *per* in the Scriptures.
Hoc genus dæmoniorum non ejicitur nisi in jejunio;* *this
kind* (of evil spirits) *can come forth by nothing but by fasting.*
So 1 Cor. xii. to speak *in* the Spirit, and to receive gifts *in*
the Spirit, are certainly used in each case for *by* the Spirit
[as expressed in our English Bibles]. And I the more wil-

* Vide Vulgate, Matth. xvii. 21; Mark ix. 28.

lingly concur in this opinion because the Apostle himself says, *condita*, not *cognita ;* i. e. *made*, not *designed ;* and also because in the end of the verse, resuming what he had said after a long parenthesis, he uses the word δι᾽ αυτοῦ, *by him,* thereby plainly shewing that he considered these words equivalent.

The argument therefore is most valid—Christ is not a creature, but before all creatures ; because by him they were made. For that which makes is before the thing made, *not only in cause, but in time also,* as the Philosopher rightly observes, De part. animal. i. 1.

But here some person may object that we are solving one obscurity by the introduction of a still greater ; inasmuch as it may be disputed, whether Christ is the Maker of all things, or not.

I answer, The Apostle is writing to the Colossians, not to Pagans, but to Christians; and therefore takes it for granted that they allow Christ to be not a mere man, but the incarnate Word ; which being allowed, it follows that he is the Maker of all creatures, John i., *The word was in the beginning with God :* ALL THINGS WERE MADE BY HIM, AND WITHOUT HIM WAS NOT ANY THING MADE.

That are in heaven, and that are in earth, visible and invisible,] What he had just asserted, that *all things were made by Christ,* he now illustrates by a twofold division of things created : the former of which is drawn from the different locality of the things created ; the latter, from their different qualities.

In heaven and in earth.] In this division he comprehends the whole creation. For under the term *heaven* he understands, as is customary in Scripture, the Highest Heaven, the abode of angels and of the blessed ; the starry sky also, in which are fixed the heavenly orbs ; and the atmosphere, in which meteors and other volatile bodies do move : When he says *in earth*, he means not only all things which are on the surface, but those also which are subterraneous ; such as are laid up in the bosom and bowels of the earth, and in the sea likewise, which surrounds the earth, and with it makes up one sphere. Thus Moses himself speaks, Gen. i.

In the beginning God created the heaven and the earth:
under which two names the whole fabric of nature is comprised.

Visible and invisible.] This is the second division, drawn
from their qualities, which also includes all created things.
The visible things of heaven are the sun, moon, and stars;
the invisible, are the angels: The visible things upon earth
are the plants, the animals, the elements; the invisible are
the souls of men. These, as well as all other things whatever, were created by Christ.

Now this statement that Christ is constituted THE *Creator of the things which are in heaven and in earth, visible and
invisible,* refutes at once the foolish aberrations of many
Philosophers and heretics:

First of the Peripatetics,* who fondly imagined that the
world must be eternal. Consequently they admit of no
creation, but lay down that there is an eternal motion in
the heavens, and an eternal succession of generation and
corruption in sublunary bodies. But they are convicted of
error, not only by the Apostle's authority, but even by
plain reason. For if motion had been eternal, time also
must have been infinite. But how then has the whole of
it passed away and ceased to flow, if it hath been infinite?
for what is infinite cannot pass or flow away. If the heavens have existed from eternity, then the sun has performed an infinite number of revolutions, and an infinite number of years are gone by. But this is impossible, since
the days that have elapsed are by the known laws of proportion, greater than the number of years: for no other
number greater by a certain and known proportion than
that which is infinite is admissible; for this would of itself
evince that both were finite. As to generation and corruption, it cannot be so much as imagined to be eternal, unless it be granted that there is in causes either an infinite
progression or circulation. Besides, the possibility of

---

* The well known sect of Philosophers which arose from Aristotle, and
were so named from their habit of walking when giving and receiving instructions in their tenets.

coming into existence, and of going out of existence, is repugnant to every idea of eternity; but in every thing created there is implied this possibility of decay.   These, however, are very thorny topics, nor does an over inquisitive debate concerning them belong to the Theological chair.   Justin Martyr, in his Quæstionibus, and William of Paris,* in lib. de Universo, part. ii. cap. 11, may be consulted on these subjects.

2.   As to the dreams of those other Philosophers, who think that the angels were created by God, and this material world by the angels, which error the followers of Apelles have adopted; vide Tertullian de carne Christi ;† I answer, to create is the work of Christ, and not of angels.   For it is an admitted axiom among Divines, that the act of creation cannot be conceded to a creature, not even as the instrumental cause, much less as the principal: First, because in the process of creation, there is a bringing forth from non-existence into existence; but between non-existence and entity there is plainly an infinite distance, impassable to the powers of any created thing. Secondly, because every action of a creature is an accident; but accident has no admission, except in a subject already existing : therefore the creature cannot possess the creative accident; for then it would possess an accident, when there was nothing in which the acting power could inhere as its subject.   Finally, because in creation the entire being of a thing is imparted; but the entire being is only imparted by Him who is entirely one act; for a finite and natural cause can never form any thing out of nothing. But the authority of Scripture is sufficient for us, which teaches that the whole fabric of the world was made, not by the ministry of angels, but by the power of the Word.

3.   Of the Marcionites and Manichæans, who scout the works of creation, especially those of a material and vi-

---

* Vide page 21, Note *.

† In the present day, Bishop Kaye's " Ecclesiastical History," illustrated from Tertullian, 1 vol. 8vo. may be referred to, for information on this subject, with every requisite advantage.

sible nature, as if unworthy of God's operation ; vide Tertullian advers. Marcion, lib. 1.*

The Apostle, however, testifies of these very works, that they were created by Christ; and God himself pronounced that they were in their kind *very good*, Gen. i. Nor is it true that a thing which is inferior to another, is therefore bad and imperfect, provided it possess all those properties which belong to its species. Therefore, although earthly and material substances may be inferior to the heavenly and spiritual, yet are they in their kind good, and worthy of Christ as their Creator. Even this very world, in that it consists of both substances, is in reality more complete than it would have been, if containing the invisible alone.

Fourthly, Of the Sadducees and Atheists, who reject invisible substances altogether ; for they neither admit the existence of angels or immortal souls. But these rob

---

* Marcion was a heresiarch of the second century, born at Sinopia, a town of Paphlagonia, upon the Euxine : he was the son of a Bishop of that place, and being excommunicated by his father for an act of immorality, he went to Rome, joined the heretic Cerdon, about the year 143 ; and these two erected, on the foundation of the Gnostics, a structure of considerable extent, embracing those doctrines adverted to by our Author, with others of an extraordinary character ; and they were soon spread over Italy, Egypt, Palestine, Syria, and the adjacent parts. Marcion seems to have been the chief promulgator of their opinions, and gave the denomination to the sect. This heresy may be seen more at large, together with a refutation of the various notions it comprises, in Bishop Kaye's Early History of the Church.

The Manichæans were a sect which arose in the latter half of the next century ; so called from the opinions they derived from Manes, or Manichæus—a Persian, and educated among the Magi, being himself one of that number before he professed to have embraced Christianity, which he sadly corrupted ; and spread the seeds of his heresy, or rather of his motley mixture of some of the doctrines of Christianity with the ancient philosophy of the Persians, principally in Arabia, Egypt, and Africa. Besides inculcating the dogmas of the two eternal principles of light and darkness, so prevalent among the Magi, and the other notions opposed by our Expositor, Manes represented himself as the Comforter promised by Christ ; not identifying him, as our Lord does, with the Holy Spirit, but understanding an Apostle sent by the Spirit, to complete what the Saviour had left imperfect. The inquisitive Reader, who wishes for more particular information respecting these men and their various notions, will find much curious and interesting matter about both in Bower's " Lives of the Popes."

Christ of the chief glory of creation : for those invisible substances are far more dignified than the visible. They lop off the most noble part of the creation. They oppose the most evident experience, which hath concluded upon the existence both of good and evil spirits, from the various effects that cannot be produced otherwise than by spiritual beings.

Let us, therefore, rejecting at once all these errors, confess that *by Christ were all things created,* &c.

Whether thrones, or dominions, or principalities, or powers.] The Apostle had before asserted that Christ was the Maker of all things, as well visible as invisible : Now he illustrates and extends that assertion by a new sub-division of the invisible creatures. But it must be observed, that the abstract is here put for the concrete : for by *dominions, principalities,* and *powers,* we are to understand angels appointed to dominion, principality, and power; that is, governors and princes.

Melancthon thinks, that under these denominations, not only all orders of invisible angels, but all governments, and the whole range of created things, of civil and domestic polities, are included. According, therefore, to his interpretation,* the Apostle teaches, that all the creatures were not only made, but arranged by Christ ; so that those which presided over others, both in heaven and in earth, are still in subjection to him, because all degrees of pre-eminence and command are arranged and appointed by him.

* *Mosheim* says of Melancthon, that " by his example, influence, and instructions, many were greatly animated ; and that his sentiments relating both to sacred and profane erudition, were so universally respected, that scarcely any had the courage to oppose them." The annals of antiquity indeed, present few worthies that may be compared to him. With a mind stored with every species of learning, and competent to engage in any disquisition on literature or religion, he rendered more signal advantages in his time to each than, perhaps, any of the other doctors of the age. Though most intrepid when the cause of religion was in peril, and of unshaken constancy in the hour of trial, yet he was pre-eminently distinguished by a love of peace and concord. A fellow labourer with Luther in the Reformation, his remains were deposited close by that Champion's, and an elegant epitaph was inscribed on his tomb by the learned Beza; which, as a compendium of his character, a summary of his excellences, and a testimony

But the exposition of those who apply the terms used in
this passage exclusively to heavenly and invisible beings, is
both more general and, in my opinion, more just. For
thus says the Apostle himself in Ephes. i. 20, 21, *God hath
set Christ at his own right hand in the heavens, far above all
principality, and power, and dominion;* where without doubt
he understands what is heavenly. In the third chapter, indeed, he openly states that sentiment in these words, *principalities and powers in heavenly places,* verse 10. Let us,
therefore, take it for granted that he is speaking of invisible beings.

In the next place, we must enquire what kind of distinction amongst the angels the Apostle has laid down in
these words. Dionysius,* and the Schoolmen who follow
him, from this and other passages, in which angels are
spoken of under different names, so describe their various
orders, duties, and properties, as if they had themselves
been conversant with heaven for many years, and had had
learnt precisely their whole polity. And though I have no
vast fondness for their fine spun comments, yet, because it
is proper for the Divine to be acquainted with the errors
of Theologians of any name, I shall give a summary of the
points which are copiously handled by them.

of the estimation in which he was held, may be permitted a place here, as
translated in " Coxe's Life of Melancthon."

> Here then, Melancthon, lies thy honoured head,
> Low in the grave amongst the mould'ring dead!
> In life 'twas thine to make all others blest,
> But to thyself denying peace or rest:
> Thine was the holy toil, the anxious tear,
> Lov'd Philip—to the good for ever dear!
> O Earth! let lilies here profusely spring,
> And roses all around their odour fling!
> For rose and lily each their glories blend,
> The sweet, the fair, in our departed friend!
> Soft let him sleep, and none disturb his rest;
> None *he* disturb'd while living—none opprest!

* Davenant refers to the treatise of the Celestial Hierarchy, which,
though not of an earlier origin than the fifth century, was falsely pretended
to have been written by Dionysius the Areopagite, the Convert of St. Paul;
and is commonly quoted, as here by our Expositor, under his name; which
is the case with the other forged writings imputed to him.

Hugh de St. Victor,* in Sum. Sentent. tract. ii. cap. 5,
distributes the heavenly angels into three classes or hierar-
chies, which he terms the highest, the middle, and the
lowest. Each of these he subdivides into three orders.
In the highest are *cherubim, seraphim,* and *thrones :* In the
middle class are *dominions, principalities,* and *powers :* In the
lowest are *virtues, archangels,* and *angels.*

Now these titles they are pleased to attach to the angels,
as characteristic either of the qualities in which they excel, or of the offices assigned to them by God. Thus they
choose to call those *Cherubim* which excel in the splendour
of knowledge ; *Seraphim* those which are most ardent in
divine love ; *Thrones* those which contemplate the glory and
equity of the Divine judgments. The *Cherubim,* they say,
enlighten others with wisdom ; the *Seraphim* inspire with
love ; the *Thrones* teach to rule with judgment. Those of
this first class they suppose never to be sent forth to discharge any office, but to wait upon God continually. In
the middle class (as hath been said) they place the *dominions, principalities,* and *powers.* The *dominions* regulate the
duties of the *angels ;* the *principalities* preside over people
and provinces ; the *powers* are a check upon evil spirits.
In the last class they put the *virtues, archangels,* and *angels.* The *virtues* have the power of working miracles assigned to them ; the *archangels* are sent as messengers in
matters of most importance ; *angels* in those of less conse-

* Hugh de St.Victor, or Cardinal Hugo : a Divine who lived in the early
part of the twelfth century ; a native of Flanders, a Monk of the Dominican order, and the first Monk that was made a Cardinal. He settled in
Paris, where he became Prior of St. Victor, and, with the assistance of 500
other Monks, formed a Concordance of the Bible ; but died at the early
age of 44, distinguished by his learning and genius, and obtaining such reputation by his works (consisting of Commentaries on Scripture, Sermons,
Dialogues, &c.), as to be called a *second Augustine,* and sometimes, from his
close adherence to the doctrine and imitation of the style of that Father,
the tongue of Augustine. He held the Protestant doctrine respecting the Apo-
cryphal books : "Non ad probationem fidei, sed ad morum instructionem ;" and
he defended the Canon of Scripture against those who would introduce apo-
cryphal books as true ! His works were printed at Rouen in 1648, in three
vols. folio.

quence. These opinions are collected from Dionysius,
from Gregory the Great (hom. in Evang. 34), and from the
Schoolmen; and in collecting them together I have followed their more generally received opinions ; for they are
by no means agreed among themselves on these subjects;
some of them referring *the virtues* to the second class, and
the principalities to the last; others again opposing this arrangement.

Our Divines treat this subject with a more becoming reserve. For though they admit these different titles, which
are found in this passage and others, as marking distinctions
both of order and dignity amongst the angels themselves;
yet, inasmuch as the Scriptures do not explain what these
distinctions are, or in what they consist, they do not presume to discuss and define them. So Augustine before
them observed, *What is the actual distinction between these
titles, let those say who can ; at the same time, let them prove
what they say : for myself I am content to confess my ignorance
of them.* Enchirid. cap. 58.   And in another place, ad
Oros. contra Priscill. cap. xi. tom. 6, *That there are distinctions of some kind, I believe, but what those distinctions are I
know not.*   Therefore, passing by these speculations, we
will infer the following corollaries :

1. As for the angels, even the most perfect of them, to
whatever degree of dignity advanced, Christ is above
them all; being himself their Creator and their Disposer.
Whence that observation, Heb. i. 6, *Let all the angels worship him.*

2. Neither the offices of Christ are to be attributed, nor
divine worship paid, to the angels ; since they are the servants and creatures of our Redeemer.

3. The different titles by which they are distinguished,
do not so much express their inequality in natural dignity,
as the difference of offices which they seem to discharge
in the affairs of men. For from this difference of offices,
some of which are more dignified than others, they receive
those titles of *angels, archangels, principalities, powers,* &c.
Nor are we able to state, for a certainty, whether the same
angels always perform the same duties, and retain the same

titles, or not : indeed, the more probable supposition is, that different names are given them, according to the different offices to which they are commissioned.

But a question remains to be resolved, viz. When were these angels created ?   The Apostle says, they were created by Christ; but Moses does not mention angels among the works of the creation.

Dismissing those Philosophers who insist upon the eternal existence of these spiritual substances, the opinions of Divines on this point are twofold.   Some think they were created before this visible world ; and in this opinion almost all the Greek Fathers coincide.   Basil says that before this world there was another ἀθεωρῆτον καὶ ἀνιστόρητον, *invisible, and undescribed by Moses,** *on account of the stupidity of the Jewish nation :* and he affirms, that in this more ancient world, those *thrones, dominions,* and *powers* existed, of which the Apostle speaks.   Chrysostom and Nazianzen are of the same opinion ; and among the Latin Fathers we may reckon Jerome and Hilary.

To confirm this notion, that expression of Job xxxviii. 4, 7, is first alleged, *Where wast thou when I laid the foundations of the earth—when the morning stars sang together, and all the sons of God shouted for joy ?* By *the Sons of God* they understand the angels, and hence infer their existence before the foundation of the world.

But it is answered, We are not authorised to conclude from this expression, that angels were created before the visible world, but before the earth was founded, i. e. before the dry land was formed.   Moreover, it may be said, that though the angels were created at the same time with the world, yet they might very possibly be enabled to praise the Creator of the world from the first moment of their existence.

And therefore their opinion is the more probable, who suppose that the angels were created at the same time with the heaven of the blessed ; and they say that there is a synecdoche (a part put for the whole) in those words of

---

* " Intelligibile et a Mose non descriptum."

Moses, *God created the heaven,* meaning thereby, both heaven itself and all those blessed existences which that heaven contains :

1. Because the angels are parts of the universe : but
if they had been created apart, before this visible world,
they must be totally distinct from the order of material
creatures, and of themselves have constituted a distinct
intelligible universe.

2. Because Moses expressly states, *In the beginning
God created the heaven and the earth;* i. e. both those bodies and every thing else which heaven and earth contain :
In the beginning, viz. of *time* or *creation,* as Lyranus correctly expounds it.* Therefore angels were not created
before that beginning. This, however, is more plainly asserted, Exod. xx. 11, *In six days the Lord made heaven and
earth, and all that in them is :* and therefore also the angels.
Whence the Schoolmen affirm (Aquin De creat. art. 18),

---

* Lyranus, or Nicholas de Lyra, so called from the place of his nativity,
Lyre, a small town in Normandy. He was descended from Jewish parents,
but embracing Christianity, entered among the Franciscans at Verneuil, in
1291. Having remained there some time, he was sent to Paris, where he
applied with the greatest diligence to his studies, and was admitted to the
degree of Doctor. He was author of " Postills," or a Compendium of the
whole Bible, which occupied him seven years in accomplishing. The Rev.
James Smith, a man of considerable learning, first educated for the Romish
Priesthood, at Lisbon, but who afterwards became a Protestant Clergyman,
in a valuable work published by him in 1777 on " The Errors of the Church
of Rome," says, that Lyra " was one of the most celebrated Commentators on the Scripture of the fourteenth century." " It is no inconsiderable
praise that, by the general soundness and justness of his expositions, he at-
tracted the admiration, and contributed, probably, in some measure, to the instruction of Luther, and of his great co-adjutors in the work of Reformation." Luther said of him, in reference to his work, " Ego Lyranum ideo
amo, et inter optimos pono : quod ubique diligenter retinet et persequitur
historiam, quanquam auctoritate patrum se vinci patitur, et nonnunquam
eorum exemplo deflectit à propriétate sententiæ ad ineptas allegorias." The
best edition of Lyra's Commentary is that of Antwerp, 1634, in six vols.
folio : it is also found in the *Biblia Maxima,* edited by Father De la Haye,
in 19 vols. folio. Lyra was also the author of *Moralia,* or Moral Commentaries upon the Scriptures."

For further account of this Author, his work, and the principles that
guided him, vide Conybeare's Bampton Lectures for 1824, pp. 210—215,
and " Horne's Critical Introduction."

that there are four first-formed and coeval things, viz. the angelic nature, the empyreal heaven, shapeless matter, and time.

3. Because Jude says, verse 6, That *the angels who kept not their first estate, but left their habitation, are reserved for judgment.* Here heaven is called the *habitation,* or dwelling-place of *angels;* and it is not very likely that angels should have existed many ages without a dwelling-place peculiarly their own. We conclude, therefore, that Moses when asserting, *In the beginning God made the heaven and the earth,* and the Apostle when affirming that *all things were made by Christ which are in heaven and in earth, visible and invisible,* had both exactly the same meaning.

All things were created by him and for him, και εις αυλον.] The Apostle here, by repetition after a long parenthesis, resumes his first position, that *all things were made by Christ.* On these words, I need add nothing further than my former observation, that εν αυτω, and δι αυτου are synonimous terms, and are henceforward put one for the other in this resumption of the statement.

The Apostle, however, was not content with the plain and simple repetition of the former assertion; but in order to amplify the dignity of Christ, he adds, that not only were all things made *by him,* but *for him,* or *on his account.*

For him.] Here then he shews that Christ is not only the efficient, but also the final cause, on whose account all creatures were made.

But how were all things created *for Christ?* That they might minister to his glory; inasmuch as they shew forth his Divine power and infinite goodness, and inasmuch as all things are subservient to him. For God does not act from a wish destitute of an end, as men do, but from love of an end to be accomplished, which, as far as is possible, he is pleased to communicate to his creatures. Christ possesses, and in all fulness, infinite glory from all eternity ; but in creating the world he manifested this his glory to us, and laid on all his creatures the obligation of glorifying him. Hence the Psalmist, in Ps. cxlviii. beginning with the angels, runs through the whole scale of creation,

and calls upon all to glorify God, because *at his word they
were created.* Christ, therefore, in creation intended this
his glory, not indeed as the price of his labour, nor as private advantage to himself; but as being proper, decorous,
strictly his due, and beneficial to the very creature itself.
For every creature as it hath come forth from God, so it
returns to him as far as it can, as Boethius has expressed
it in those lines, De consol. lib. iv. metr. 6,

>Hic est cunctis communis amor,
>Repetuntque boni fine teneri :
>Quia non aliter durare queant,
>Nisi converso rursus amore,
>Refluant causæ, quæ dedit esse.*

Thus translated by Duncan,

>" This love to all is common, and they seek
>To be confined within the bounds of good ;
>Because no otherwise can they endure,
>Unless, by love attracted, they return
>To that First Cause which gave them to exist."

Duncan's Boethius, 1789.

---

* Boethius, Anicius Manlius Torquatus Severinus, the author of the
above lines, was a prose as well as a poetical writer, descended from one of
the noblest families in Rome, and born about the year 479. At an early
age he discovered excellent parts ; and to enrich his mind with the study of
philosophy, as well as to perfect him in the Greek language, he was sent to
Athens. Returning to Rome, he was soon distinguished, and promoted to
the principal dignities in the State, being chosen to the Consular dignity
three times, created a Patrician, and made Master of the Offices. Though
living in great affluence and splendour, he studied theology, mathematics,
ethics, and logic ; and his success in each of these branches appears from his
works still extant. The great offices which he bore in the State, and his
consummate wisdom and inflexible integrity, procured him such a share in
the public councils as to give rise to jealousies, which led to plots and intrigues to effect his ruin. But the employment of his pen in the defence of
true Religion, and against the Arian heresy, which then prevailed in Italy,
appears to have afforded those who felt his influence and hated the
truth, the strongest ground against him. Three chiefs among the Arians,
whose errors he had exposed in a treatise, ' De Unitate et Uno,' and who
were in that period a persecuting body, with whom Theodoric took part,
at length succeeded in turning the mind of the Monarch against him.
Whilst he was engaged in a distant part of the western empire, they alleged
against him a treasonable correspondence with Justin the Emperor of the East ;

Hence observe,

1. Since all things made by Christ are also formed for the glory of Christ, it is incumbent upon us not to dishonour our Creator, for the manifestation of whose glory we were created. For if that instrument be accounted useless and good for nothing, which does not answer its end; then is that one evil and execrable which is in opposition, and, as far as possible, detrimental to the purpose intended by it.

2. Since the angels themselves were created for the glory of Christ, they must not be so united with him in the work of salvation, as to (detract from, much less) oppose the glory of their Creator.

---

and the Senate, without summoning him to his defence, condemned him to death. Theodoric, however, apprehending some bad consequences from the execution of a sentence so flagrantly unjust, mitigated it to imprisonment in a solitary tower at Pavia. In that forlorn state he endeavoured to derive from philosophy and religion, those comforts which they were capable of affording to one in such a situation; sequestered from his friends, in the power of his enemies, and at the mercy of a capricious tyrant; and, accordingly, he there composed that " golden volume," as a great historian has termed it, from which the foregoing lines are quoted. About two years after his banishment, viz. in Oct. 526, Boethius was put to death, and it is asserted, in a most barbarous manner. Thus perished, owing to the spirit of the times, the first Philosopher, Orator, and Theologian of the sixth century; and, perhaps, the most generous, liberal, and noble-minded man. His tomb is to be seen in the Church of St. Augustine, at Pavia, but his bones were removed some years after, by order of Otho, to a more honourable receptacle.

Boethius wrote several philosophic works, besides the one on Divinity already mentioned. But his most celebrated performance is " The Consolations of Philosophy" above cited. Few works have undergone so many editions, and it has been translated into all cultivated languages. There are two versions by British Sovereigns; one in Anglo-Saxon by Alfred the Great, and an English Translation by Queen Elizabeth. It is to be regretted, however, that it does not embrace the range of Christian consolations which, from Boethius's knowledge of Christian Theology, might have been expected; though probably he would have added a book on those firmer supports under the " afflictions of the present time," had he been spared a little longer; since his work is evidently unfinished, and there is an order in the topics leading to that supposition.

Verse 17.

And he is before all things, and by him all things consist.

The Apostle in this place dignifies Christ with two pre-rogatives : He is before every creature; and is, as it were, the foundation and support of all creatures.

The point of priority has been explained and proved above ; for we have shewn that Christ was begotten of God, and that the world was made by Christ : each of which proves that he has the precedency of all creatures, as well in dignity as in time. For he whom God begat, must of necessity be both co-eternal and co-essential with God. *All other things,* as Aquinas properly observes, *are such as God was pleased to make them; but the Son is such as God himself is.* Now he who made the world must have existed before the world : for he made it by imparting existence to that which had no existence previous to its being created. From these two considerations therefore, both that he was begotten of God, and that the world was made by him, it is proved that *he is before all things.*

This declaration of the Apostle clearly refutes those who deny Christ to have had a personal existence, ὑφιστάμενον, be-fore his incarnation. For how could he have been *before all things* if he was not before his incarnation ? How could he frame all things who was not himself in existence ? Tertullian, in Praxiam, says, *He who came forth from so great an essence, and made such great existences, could not but himself have a personal existence.**

---

* Tertullian against Praxeas :—" The schisms and commotions that arose in the Church, from a mixture of the Oriental and Egyptian Philosophy with the Christian Religion, were, in the second century, increased by those Grecian Philosophers, who embraced the doctrine of Christ. The Christian doctrine, concerning the Father, Son, and Holy Ghost, and the two natures united in our blessed Saviour, were, by no means, reconcileable with the tenets of the Sages and Doctors of Greece; who, therefore, endeavoured to explain them in such a manner as to render them comprehensible. Praxeas

By him all things consist.] This is a new and excellent privilege of Christ, that he not only made all things at first, but that he also sustains and supports them by his Divine energy, in such a manner that, if he should withdraw it, they would again sink into their former nonentity.

This, therefore, is the doctrine of this passage; Every creature, whether earthly or heavenly, visible or invisible, would sink back again into its former nothingness, if the Divine preservation were withdrawn. This proposition of the Apostle is by no means easy to be understood; therefore we will endeavour to support it both by argument and authorities, as well as clear away what is wont to be advanced against it.

1. No acting force of the agent remains in the effect, when the action of the agent has ceased, unless in some way or other that force be converted into the very nature of the effect, so as to be inherent in it as its own property : but if it be a something transcending the nature of the effect, and a property peculiar to the agent alone, then it must cease when the action ceases. Since, therefore, *self-existence* is the peculiar property of God alone, it can remain in no created body, even for a moment of time after this action of Divine conservation has ceased. Theologians illustrate this argument by comparing the action of God on the creature, to that of the sun on the atmosphere ; for the essence of every creature has the same relation to God, as the light of the atmosphere to the sun.* The sun derives its light from its own proper nature, the atmos-

[a Philosopher of Phrygia, in Asia], a man of genius and learning, began to propagate these explications at Rome. He denied any real distinction between the Father, Son, and Holy Ghost; and maintained that the Father, sole Creator of all things, had united to himself the human nature of Christ. Hence his followers were called Monarchians, because of their denying a plurality of persons in the Deity ; and also Patropassians, because, according to Tertullian's account, they believed that the Father was so intimately united with the man Christ—his Son, that he suffered with him the anguish of an afflicted life, and the torments of an ignominious death !"—Mosheim.

* Aquinas cont. Gent. iii. cap. 64.

phere by participating in the influence of the sun : so God
has his existence from his own nature ; all other things by
participating in existence from him.   As, therefore, the
brilliancy of the atmosphere immediately ceases when the
bright shining of the sun ceases ; so the existence of every
creature instantly vanishes when God's conservating power
is withdrawn.

2. In reference to God, the action is the same with the
preservation as the creation of his creatures; the only difference between them is, that creation exhibits the acting
power of God in the original production of a creature ;
preservation shews the same action in not deserting the
creature when produced.   A creature has the beginning of
its existence from the energy of God ; the continuance of
its existence from the same God, not withholding that
energy.   Durandus, therefore, has not hesitated to assert
of every creature, that, *as long as it is in existence, so long it
is being created by God, because as far as God is concerned, the
work of creation and the preservation of creatures is the same.*
Hence it follows, that by whomsoever all things are formed, by the same also are they preserved ; for *preservation is
not by a new act, but by the continuance of that act which originally gave existence.*   Durand. lib. ii. dist. 1. quæst. 2.

3. As every work of art presupposes a work of nature
for its foundation ; so every work of nature presupposes a
work of God : for as every artificer borrows his materials
from nature, so nature herself does from God.   In the
same manner, therefore, as the existence of all works of
art is preserved by virtue of the natural substance of which
they are composed ; so the essence of natural substances
continues by virtue of the preservation of God, who created
them.

4. Every effect depends upon its cause, as far as it is
its cause ; as a house depends upon the architect for its
construction : although for its duration it depends upon the
solidity of the wood and stones.   The architect is the
cause of its having been made ; therefore for *its making,*
i. e. for *the structure itself* it depends upon him : but the
nature of its material is the cause of its actual existence ;

therefore upon the material it depends for *its durability*. Now to apply this to our argument : God is the cause of things, not only as to *their formation*, but as to *their being : In him we live, and move, and have our being*, Acts xvii. 28. Therefore all things depend upon him, not only as to their first production, but as to the continuance of their essence ; since he is the cause both *of the being* and also *of the formation* of all things.

To confirm these arguments I will adduce but two passages of Scripture : The first from John v. 17, *My Father worketh hitherto, and I work.* Which passage interpreters apply to this continual operation of God and of Christ in the preservation and government of the creatures. For *God rested on the seventh day* from making new creatures ; but he never rests or ceases from the preservation of, and administration to, the creatures that are made. The other authority is taken from Heb. i. 3, where Christ is spoken of as *upholding all things by the word of his power.* Which expression intimates that the Divine power of Christ is the support* and the foundation, as it were, of all creatures, which would presently fall at once into annihilation unless sustained by him.

And now let us draw some testimonies from the Fathers :

1. Justin Martyr, De decret. Aristot. reprehens. says, *As that which sprang into existence never would have existed unless God had pronounced his Fiat : so neither would they continue in existence, unless the same God had commanded those things which are not subject to decay, to stand for ever ; and that those things which spring up and decay, should constantly increase and multiply.* Here, by the way, I may be permitted to remark, what I had before passed over, viz. That Christ not only sustains and preserves every individual thing, by the virtue which flows from him, which we have already likened to a continued work of creation : but also, that by virtue of this primary blessing, he propagates the various species of things by successive generations.

---

* The Fulcrum, as it were ; as a friend remarked, ' Here is the very desideratum of Archimedes.'

Augustine, sup. Genes. ad lit. lib. 4. cap. 13, says, *The power and energy of an Almighty and All-sustaining God, is the cause of subsistence to every creature; and if that energy which created them should at any time cease from ruling them, their species would all at once cease, and all nature fall to nothing.* If, therefore, we credit Augustine, no creature whatever could exist without this Divine upholding, or *manutention,* to use the scholastic term.

Gregory, Moral. 16. cap. 18, on those words of Job, xxiii. 13, *He alone is,* observes, *But why does he say, He alone is? All these things (says he) are, and yet fundamentally they are not, because in themselves they have no subsistence; and unless they were upheld by the hand of their Governor, they would by no means exist. For all things subsist by him who created them. Inasmuch as all things were made of nothing, and their being would again fall into nothing, unless it were retained by the hand which made them all.*

Gerson, De vit. spirit. lect. 1. says, *As a vessel contains water and gives it its shape, so that it is prevented from flowing away rather by the help of the vessel than by its own nature; so God in his own nature prevents the defectible principle of the creature from acting, and preserves it by his agency from falling back again into nothing.*

Let us now meet some objections to the contrary.

1. A created agent communicates to the work made, the power of holding together when his operation has ceased, as we continually see in an architect and his building: Therefore God, whose operations are far more perfect than those of any artificer, must impart this property to his works.

We answer, There is no parity of reasoning. For a created agent is the cause of that work being *constructed* only, and not of *its continuance in existence.* A house, for instance, depends upon the architect only as long as it is *in building;* but when *it is actually built,* it depends for its existence, as I have before shewn, upon the nature of the materials. But with God the case is very different; because (as we have proved) he is the cause of the *original existence* as well as of *the formation* of all things. It involves a contradiction therefore, that God should communicate to any creature an existence independent of himself: for this would be, in fact, to place it above the condition of a creature.

2 It is objected, There are some created things which cannot but continue, inasmuch as they have in themselves neither the power of assuming a new form, or the contrary; of this kind are all the heavenly bodies: these, therefore, at least, may continue in their state, even if the Divine conservation were withdrawn.

We answer, The consequence does not hold: because although the heavenly bodies have no natural power whatever of assuming a new form, neither is there any thing external which may effect their dissolution, yet would their very form and substance cease and vanish away, if the Divine conservation were to cease. For this liability of created things to dissolution (or non-entity) depends neither upon the nature of the material, or of the form, but upon God's withdrawing his influence. This objection may also be answered by a distinction in the mode of conservation. For there is an *indirect* conservation, viz, by removal of the destructive principle: this the heavenly bodies do not require, but only the elementary and corruptible things. As far as this is concerned the objection is allowed. But there is a *direct* conservation of which we are now treating, through the immediate upholding of the Creator: and of this preservation, both the heavens, and every other being dependant on the First Being, stand in need.

3. They object, Every creature hath an innate earnest desire of its own preservation: but no natural desire is either vain or impossible: therefore every creature has the power of self-preservation.

It is answered, The creature seeks its own preservation, but not to be preserved of itself and by its own powers, but by that very Cause which gave it its existence. Therefore the desire is not *vain;* for it gains its end by the proper means.

4. It is said, Such is the state of angels and of men in happiness as no longer to require a preserving Providence; for happiness (as Boethius, lib. 3, De consolat. defines it,) is *a state perfected by the assemblage of all good things:* but the power of self-preservation is one of those good things especially, without which all the rest are frail and uncertain: therefore the spirits in blessedness have this power, and so do not require other preservation.

We allow that happiness is a state of perfection, and that among the assemblage of blessings in which it consists, the power of preserving itself in this state of happiness must be found. The blessed Spirits, therefore, have this self-preserving power, as far as they have the power of inseparably cleaving to God; but not so far, as that if they were separated from God, they could preserve either their own happiness or existence. If any one wishes any thing further on this subject, let him consult Aquinas, 1 quæst. 104. art. 1; and quæst. disput. De conserv. rerum, art. 1; and also contra Gentiles lib. 3, cap. 64.*

From what has been said we may gather the following remarks for our own benefit.

1. For the support of our confidence; for we may rely fearlessly on this Redeemer, and the preciousness of his blood, who is a person of such infinite power and majesty that he did create all things, and still upholds all things, which would otherwise relapse into nothing.

2. To produce within us humility. For if we cannot retain our natural existence even for a moment without his preserving power, how much less our supernatural and freely given existence? With Gerson (Par. 2) I will unhesitatingly assert; *In whatever degree a man is more accomplished than ordinary in natural or gratuitous endowments; in the same degree is he more liable to fall short and fall away, when this special sustentation by the arm of Christ is withdrawn. We may form a conjecture on this point from the case of Lucifer,*

* The Reader may profitably consult our own Hooker, who has much that is very excellent, and quite to the point, on this and the preceding topics, in his first Book of the " Ecclesiastical Polity."

Adam, and others, whose perfections, when left to themselves, what were they, but an increase of the weight to their downfall?

3.   For persuading us to obedience ; since it is but reasonable that all our life should be devoted to serving Him by whom we were both brought into this life, and are sustained in it.   Thus the Psalmist reasons, Ps. c. 2, *Praise the Lord with gladness ; come before his presence with a song ; be ye sure that the Lord he is God, for He hath made us, and not we ourselves.*

Lastly, let us add this consideration : that these things are not so to be appropriated to Christ, as to exclude either God the Father, or the Holy Ghost, from the preservation of the creature.   For, as they said at the creation of man, *Let us make man ;* so could these three persons say, *let us preserve man.*   And what has been said of man the same might be said of all creatures; viz. that all were both at first created, and are still preserved by the united operation of the whole Trinity.   For that saying of Augustine, De Trinit. lib. i. cap. 4, is most true, *The persons are inseparable, and operate inseparably.*

And thus much concerning the character of the Redeemer, derived from a comparison of him with the creature formed : We must come to the last part of this character, derived from his relation to the creature renewed, i. e. to the Church.

Verses 18, 19.

And he is the head of the body, the Church; who is the be-
ginning, the first-born from the dead ; that in all things
he might have the pre-eminence.

For it pleased the Father, that in him should all fulness
dwell.

We have explained that description of Christ which was
drawn from his relation to the cteature in general. It now
remains to explain that which is derived from his relation
to the creature redeemed, that is to say, the Church.   In
these two verses he does two things: First, he sets forth
Christ by titles peculiar to him, *the head, the beginning, the*
first-born.   Secondly, by certain arguments he demonstrates
that these titles are his indefeasible right : the first is taken from the final cause, *that in all things he might have the*
pre-eminence; the second, from the efficient or ordaining
cause, *for it hath so pleased him,* viz. the Father; the last
from the formal cause, because in him is *all* that *fulness,*
which can constitute him *the head of the Church,* &c. Let
us begin by an explanation of the titles ; and first let us
set forth this of *the head of the Church.*

The head of the body, the Church] i. e. of *his* body, which
body is the Church; for so the word *Church* is joined with
the word *body* by apposition. And here there are three
things to be discussed by us respecting this *head* and
body.

First, we shall enquire, In which of his natures Christ
is the head of the Church.

Secondly, in what respects this title of *head* is assigned
to him.

Thirdly, who they are of whom this body of Christ consists.

As to the first; we say Christ is the head of the Church
in each of his natures.   For here he is called *the head of*
the Church, who had before been called *the image of the in-*

visible God. But that image was the eternal Son of God, the incarnate Word : Therefore Christ, *the God-man,* is the head of the Church. For the Church ought to possess such a head as might have a natural conformity with the rest of the members to be incorporated in it. Now this conformity suits Christ according to his human nature; whence Christ and the Church are called *one flesh,* Ephes. v. 31. But it was also necessary that the Church should have such a head as could infuse into it spiritual life. Now this is the province of God alone ; whence God is plainly called *the husband* and *the head* of the Church, Psalm xlv. 10, where, under the representation of the marriage of Solomon with Pharaoh's daughter, the espousals of Christ and the Church are prefigured ; *Hearken, O daughter, and consider, and incline thine ear : forget also thy father's house : so shall the king greatly desire thy beauty ; for he is thy Lord God.*

It is, however, objected, That Christ was not the head of the ancient Church in each nature, because he had not yet assumed human nature. But it is the office of the head to impart and communicate its excellencies to the body ; and the human nature of Christ could not benefit the Church before his incarnation ; because that which does not exist cannot operate. Therefore he was not the head of the Jewish church as to his humanity.

We answer, Although Christ had not yet actually united the human nature to his own ; nevertheless, as to the Divine decree respecting his future incarnation and passion ; as to the eternal efficacy thereof ; and as to the living faith of the Patriarchs ; even the human nature of Christ, and that which he was to do and suffer in human nature, although not actually undergone, produced many benefits to the ancient Church. All believers, being elect in Christ, *from the foundation of the world,* are, through Christ, adopted into the family of God, Ephes. i. 4, 5. God, therefore, by reason of his eternal purpose concerning the incarnation of Christ, even then accounted as members of his body all who believed in him. He was *the Lamb slain from the foundation of the world ;* why not then also the living head of the

P 2

Church from the foundation of the world? Things are
present to God and to faith, which are not present to nature. Aquinas, quæst, disp. de gratia Christi, art. 4. ad.
9m. says, *That Christ, according to his human nature, was the
head of the Church before his incarnation, by the operation of
faith, which apprehended his future incarnation; and so acquired the benefit of justification.* But that Divine of Altissiodorum speaks much more clearly, lib. 3. tract. i. quæst. 3.
de dignitate Christi capitis, &c. He asks, *Whether Christ,
as to his human nature, was the head of Abel and of the rest of
the faithful; and whether they were members of the body of
Christ?* He answers, that *there was then the same faith respecting his future incarnation, as there now is concerning his
past incarnation; and the same efficacy in their faith as in ours.
As, therefore, faith in Christ who is now come, makes a man
a member of Christ incarnate; so their faith in Christ to come,
made them members of Christ who was to be incarnate. Christ
then was, even as to his humanity, the head of Abel and of the
rest of the faithful; not indeed according to his humanity as
actually existing; but according to his humanity as existing in
their faith. For faith looks beyond time. By this faith blessings flowed to them from the fulness of Christ, even as they do
now to us.* Thus far Altissiodorensis.

But it is also further objected; that Christ is not the
head of the Church in his Divine nature, inasmuch as according to that he hath not a conformity of nature with
the rest of the members; nor yet according to his human
uature, because in respect of that he has not the power of
infusing spiritual life to his members: therefore in no way
is it the case.

We answer, first, generally; If there be found in the
person of Christ the perfect quality of a head, this is sufficient for his being in strict truth called the head, although
neither in one nature nor the other, separately considered,
all the conditions of headship may meet. To that which
was objected concerning the humanity not infusing life and
spiritual motion, we answer by a distinction. The life of
grace is infused either by the primary agent, who creates
grace in the soul in the way of its original source; and in
this sense grace flows from the Deity alone; or by an in-

strument attached to the primary agent; and so the humanity of Christ is said to infuse grace and spiritual life instrumentally. As, therefore, it derogates not from the nature of a *corporeal* head, because it infuses life and motion
to the other members not immediately of itself, but by
means of some secret power ; so neither is it any detraction from the honour of the *mystical* head, that it infuses
life and grace, not primarily from itself, but by means of
the indwelling Deity.   Christ is, therefore, notwithstanding these things, the head of the Church in each nature.

You see what kind of a head the Church has ; not God
alone, nor a mere man ; but Jesus Christ, God and man.
Hence many observations arise :

1. Whereas the head of the Church is God, we infer
that the Church will abide for ever, neither *shall the gates
of hell prevail against it ;* for *if God be with us who shall be
against us ?* A less than God would indeed have been incompetent to the protection of the Church : for the devil,
and almost the whole world wage constant war against it.
Herein, then, is the consolation of the Church, that *Christ,
the head of the Church, is greater to protect it, than the devil,
the enemy of the Church, is to oppose it ;* Cyprian, De exhort.
martyr. cap. 10.

2. If the head of the Church be God, the members of
the Church ought, with all fear and reverence, to obey its
head in all things.   For there is an infinite obligation which
binds every creature to obey its God ; but that obligation,
if possible, surpasses infinite, whereby the Church redeemed and sanctified, is bound to be subject to *its* God,
its mystical and life-giving head.

3. If the head of the Church be God, then the ascension of Christ into heaven has not deprived the Church of
its head : nay, he is present, and will be always present,
with his whole Church, by the presence and power of his
Divinity, although he may not appear to our eyes by his
bodily presence.   This he himself promised, Matth. xxviii.
ult. *I am with you always, even unto the end of the world.* The
error of the advocates for the Papacy, therefore, concerning an earthly head is to be discarded ; who, as the Israel-

ites heretofore said to Aaron, *Make us gods which shall go
before us, for as for this Moses we wot not what is become of
him ;* so say they, Let us make to ourselves some visible
head of the Church, for we know not what has become of
Christ.* Moreover also, inasmuch as our Head is a man,
we infer two things,

1. On account of this alliance of nature, he must of
necessity intimately love us, and have such a keen sense of
our miseries, as to be most ready to succour us (Judg. x.
16). This the Apostle himself infers, Heb. ii. 17, 18,
*Wherefore in all things it behoved him to be made like unto his
brethren, that he might be a merciful and faithful high priest in
things pertaining to God, to make reconciliation for the sins of*

---

* It is worthy of remark, that on a Papist—a Jesuit of learning and distinction—a Professor of Rhetoric, History, and Philosophy in the Univer-
sities of Rome, Fermo, and Macerata, and, in the latter place Counsellor
of the Inquisition—being employed about the middle of the last century to
prove the Pope's supremacy, by shewing from century to century, that since
the Apostle's time to the present, it had ever been acknowledged by the
Catholic Church, he soon found that he had undertaken more than it was
possible to perform ; viz. on coming to the close of the second century.
" Nay," says he, " while, in order to support and maintain this cause, I
" examined, with particular attention, the writings of the Apostles, and of
" the many pious and learned men who had flourished in *the three first centu-*
" *ries* of the Church, I was so far from finding any thing that seemed the
" least to countenance such a doctrine, that, on the contrary, it appeared
" evident, beyond all dispute, that, during the above-mentioned period of
" time, it had been utterly unknown to the Christian world. In spite,
" then, of my endeavours to the contrary, reason getting the better of the
" strongest prejudices, I began to look upon the Pope's Supremacy, not only
" as a prerogative quite chimerical, but as the most impudent attempt that
" had ever been made : I say, in spite of my endeavours to the contrary ;
" for I was very unwilling to give up a point, upon which I had been
" taught by Bellarmin, that THE WHOLE OF CHRISTIANITY DEPENDED ;
" especially in a Country where a man cannot help being afraid of his own
" thoughts, since upon the least suspicion of his only calling in question
" any of the received opinions, he may depend upon his being soon con-
" vinced by more cogent arguments than any in *Mood* and *Figure*. But
" great is the power of truth ; and at last it prevailed : I became a proselyte
" to the opinion which I had proposed to confute ; and sincerely abjured,
" in my mind, that which I had ignorantly undertaken to defend."

The Reader is referred to *the Preface* to " the History of the Popes," by
Archibald Bower, Esq. in seven vols. 4to.

the people. For in that he himself hath suffered being tempted,
he is able to succour them that are tempted.

2.   Whereas our head was a man we have this comfort,
that every ground of triumphing over us is taken from the
devil.   He overcame the first Adam, the head and beginning of the human race ; but the second Adam, the head
of the Church, overcame him.   Nay, in Christ, we who
are his members conquer, just as in Adam we were conquered.   The victory of our head makes us conquerors.

Thus far concerning the first question, viz. In which nature Christ is the head of the CHURCH.

Now, secondly, it is proper to consider in what respects
Christ is called the HEAD.   But since this mystical head is
so called by a metaphor borrowed from the natural head,
the appellation will be obscure, unless we understand in
what respects this similitude between Christ and the natural head, between the Church and the natural body, consists.   Well said the Philosopher, Topic vi. cap. 2, *A me-*
taphor, by similitude, manifests to us the thing treated of ; for
all who use metaphors draw them on the ground of some resem-
blance they bear to the point to be illustrated.   Let us then
take into consideration the similitude in the text.

A natural head is regarded in a twofold relation to its
members, that is to say, of difference and of agreement ;
so also this mystical head : Aquinas, quæst. disp. de gratia
Christi, art. 4.

The head differs and is distinguished from its members in
three ways :

1.   In way of eminence or dignity.   For the head possesses more fully and perfectly all the senses than the subordinate members : so Christ, the mystical head, possesses
all spiritual grace much more abundantly than all other
men and angels put together : *The Spirit was given to him*
without measure, John iii. 34.

2.   In way of direction or government.   For the head
regulates and directs : the members are ruled and directed
by the head in their operations : so Christ has the absolute
dominion and government over the Church : It obeys his
nod, and submits in unreserved conformity to his will.

Thus the Apostle teaches, Ephes. v. 22, 23, *Wives submit yourselves unto your own husbands as unto the Lord; for the husband is the head of the wife, even as Christ is the head of the Church: Therefore the Church is subject unto Christ,* &c.

3. In way of causality or influence. For the head imparts and communicates sense and motion to all its members: the members are devoid of all motion and sense if separated from the head: So Christ sends forth spiritual life and the motion of grace into his members which are otherwise insensible, dead, and destitute of all spiritual motion. *Without me ye can do nothing,* John xv. 5; but, on the other hand, *I can do all things through Christ which strengtheneth me,* Phil. iv. 13.

Therefore the appellation of *head* is most fitly applied to Christ, in respect of all those particulars in which the head must differ and be distinguished from all the members. Now, then, let us consider those things in which the agreement of the head and the members is perceived: And these are three:

1. The natural head hath a natural conformity with the rest of the members: for as the Poet hath rightly said, it would be monstrous and ridiculous,

*If a painter should form a design of uniting a horse's neck to a human head.**

Thus monstrous would it be, if the head of the Church had not a natural conformity with the Church. But Christ hath this, as is shewn, Heb. ii. *He took not on him the nature of angels, but he took on him the seed of Abraham. Forasmuch as the children are partakers of flesh and blood, he also himself likewise took part of the same.*

2. The head and the members have a conformity in their destination to the same end, viz. the preservation and safety of the whole person: thus Christ, and the members of Christ, which are one person, are ordained to the attainment of one end, viz. eternal glory and happiness; and to the accomplishment of this end both head and members assiduously co-operate. This is the care of the head, to

---

* Horace, De arte poetica, l. 1 : Smart's translation.

lead its members to final blessedness.　So spake Christ, John xvii. 12, *Those that thou gavest me I have kept, and none of them is lost.*　Hence he is called *the Saviour of his body*, Ephes. v. 23.　This also is the object proposed to all the members of Christ, to attain to the participation of this blessedness together with their head.　For what was the purpose and sentiment of Paul, the same is that of all the faithful, *One thing I do, forgetting those things which are behind, and reaching forth unto those things which are before, I press towards the mark,* &c. Phil. iii. 4.

3.　The head and the members of the natural body agree in the circumstance of their having a continuous union with each other, and all of them deriving their motion and intellectuality from the same soul.　So this mystical head, and all the members of it, have a certain mutual continuity, and have their spiritual intellectuality and vivifying principle from the same source.　For there is between Christ and all the members of Christ, a certain uninterrupted union by means of the Holy Spirit, who, in all its plenitude, dwelling in Christ the head, being one and the same numerically, is shed forth among all his members, quickening each separately and uniting all in one body.　Thus most clearly does the Apostle speak, Ephes. iv. 16, *The whole body fitly joined together, and compacted by that which every joint supplieth, according to the effectual working in the measure of every part, maketh increase of the body unto the edifying of itself in love.*

These are particulars in which there is agreement of the head with the members.　And hence it follows that Christ is the true and living head of the whole Church, both in those respects in which the head ought to differ from, as well as in those in which it ought to agree with, its members.

Of the body, the Church.]　It remains that we inquire, in the last place, who and what they are, out of whom this body of Christ is composed, which in this place is called *the Church.*

The term *Church* is derived from a word signifying *to call out;* it is therefore an assembly or multitude of those

called out : And this calling is effected by the ministry of
the Gospel, and other means which God has appointed for
bringing men out of a state of ignorance and misery, and
leading them to a state of glory. In this sense we call any
assembly of men whatever, professing the doctrine and religion of Christ under legitimate pastors, a church. Such
were those seven churches to which John sent his Apocalypse; such the Roman, Corinthian, Colossian, and all
other visible and local churches. These assemblies are
called churches, and those who live in them are members
of those churches, and are to be regarded, in the judgment
of charity, as members of the Holy Catholic Church, as
well because those means are offered to them on God's
part, by which men are called to the participation of eternal life ; as because on their part, in outward act and profession, those means are received and employed for salvation.

This external vocation through the proffered grace of the
Gospel, and this external adoption and profession of Christianity under legitimate pastors, constitutes the outward
and visible Church ; and the professors of it are visible
members of the Church. But there is also another more
effectual vocation joined to this external one, in some persons, namely, by grace implanted and impressed through
the power of the Spirit in the hearts of the called ; by
means of which they not only enter upon the external profession of Christianity, but are joined to Christ himself by
the internal bonds of faith and the Spirit : *Many are called,
but few chosen,* says the Saviour.

These things being settled and allowed by the opinions
of all, as well Papists as of our own communion, we come
to what is before us, and comprise our opinion in this proposition ;—The Catholic Church, which is called the body
of Christ, consists of such as are truly sanctified, and
united to Christ by an internal alliance ; so that no wicked
person, or unbeliever, is a member of this body, solely by
the external profession of faith, and participation of the
sacraments. We oppose this position to Bellarmin, who,
(Lib. 3. De eccles. militant. cap. 2, § atque hoc interest.)

ventures to assert, *For any one to be called absolutely a member of the true Church no internal virtue is required, but only an external profession of faith, and communion of the sacraments, and union with the Roman Church.* Hence he manifestly places among the true members of the body of the Catholic Church, ungodly men, disguised hypocrites, and infidels; provided they abide in outward communion with the Church of Rome. On the other hand, observe what is elsewhere said by this very Bellarmin.

1. They who stand related to the Church as evil humours to the human body, are not true members of the Church. This proposition is manifestly true : for each sound body desires the preservation of its members ; but it does not desire to preserve evil humours, but to expel them. *Now they who are void of faith and internal virtues, are, in the Church, as evil humours are in the human body.* Bellarm. De eccles. milit. lib. 3. cap. 2.

2. Nothing is truly and formally that which it is said to be, having a diminutive term annexed to it ; as a dead man is not truly a man, a city in a picture is not truly a city. Boys know this who have entered only upon the first steps in logic. But the wicked and infidels are not *living members* of the body of Christ, by Bellarmin's own concession, cap. 9 : nay, he expressly calls them *dead members* in the same chapter; where he moreover adds, *I say that as it pertains to the design of a member to be a certain part of a living body ; a wicked Bishop and a wicked presbyter are dead members, and therefore not true members of the body of Christ.* But now mark the dullness of this disputant. The question proposed in the beginning was, Whether wicked men and infidels were true members of the Catholic Church which is the body of Christ, on account of their outward communion and profession of faith ? The Jesuit undertook to defend the affirmative part ; and now he is compelled to confess, that they are not *living* but *dead members ;* that *they are not true members so as to answer the purpose of a member.* But what is neither living, nor true, nor answers the purpose of a member, how will Bellarmin maintain to be nevertheless a true member ? Hearken ; *He*

is not a true member so far as answers the character of a member, but he is a true member as far as regards the character of an instrument. This is mere trifling! For nothing can be understood of which the formal cause is denied; neither does the genus determine the species.

3. Those whom the Church itself would not acknowledge as members or its parts, if it knew what they are, Christ, who knows all things, does not acknowledge. Nay, Bellarmin asserts, cap. 10, *that the Church intends only to collect the faithful, and if she knew the wicked and unbelieving, she either never would admit them, or, if they accidentally were admitted, she would cast them out.* Who, then, in his senses would affirm, that the wicked and unbelieving, whom Christ would condemn, and whom the Church, if she knew them to be such, would cast out, are true members of Christ, and of the Catholic Church?

4. The Church which is the body of Christ, hath no member which doth not receive a vital influx from the head: for (as we have before shewn) the same Spirit is diffused from the head to all the members: *He who hath not the Spirit of Christ is none of his,* Rom. viii. 9. But infidels, and the wicked have not this vitality of grace flowing from the head. That which Bellarmin is compelled to answer is childish; viz. Although they have neither an internal union with the head, nor an influx of grace, yet they have external union, which suffices to constitute them true members of the Church, i. e. of the body of Christ. This subterfuge is vain: for (as Aquinas rightly speaks, quæst. disp. de grat. Christi. art. 7. ad. 11m.) *Christ and his true members are one mystical person, whence the deeds of Christ, the head, are in some manner those of the members:* But that external union neither makes a man one person with Christ, nor a partaker of the obedience and righteousness of Christ; therefore it does not make him a member of Christ.

5. The same man is not at the same time a member of Christ and of the devil: but wicked men are numbered amongst the servants and the children of the devil, John viii. 38 and 44; therefore they are not to be reckoned among the members of Christ.

It is not my purpose to heap together more arguments, or refute those of Bellarmin.   I will only add some testimonies extracted from the Fathers and the Schoolmen, that from them ye may be able to see clearly how entirely these novices, the Jesuits, have departed from the truth of the Scriptures, from the authority of the Fathers, and from the doctrine of the ancient Schoolmen.

1. Clemens, Strom. 7, cap. 5, says, that the Church is 'αθροισμον των ἐκλεκτων *the congregation of the elect;* and a little after, *The true Church is one, and in its registry all those are inscribed who are just according to God's purpose.*

Cyprian, De dupl. martyr. *In vain does a man mix in the assembly of the saints in the temple made by hands, if he be excluded from the universal mystical body of Christ.* Cyprian is speaking of the wicked.

Augustine, De baptis. contra Donat. lib. 4. cap. 2, *They do not all belong to the Church who are within its pale, but they who are living piously within it.* And cap. 4, *In the body of this beloved dove, neither heretics nor the wicked are reckoned.*   Ad Orosium, quæst. 52, *As the ark was constructed of hewn timbers, so the Church is built up of the saints.*

But let us come to the Schoolmen who also coincide with us in this instance.

William of Altissiodorum, lib. 3, says, *As the natural body of Christ consists of the purest members; so the mystical body of Christ, which is the Church, consists of most holy believers: and thus the natural body of Christ is the emblem of his mystical body.*

Hugo de St. Victor, De sacram. lib. 2. par. ii. cap. 2, says, *The holy Church is the body of Christ animated by one spirit, and united in one faith and sanctified: of this body each and all the faithful are members.   They are all one body by reason of one Spirit and one faith.*

Hales;* *the wicked are not of the body of the Church, although they are of the Church,* parte 3. quæst. 12. memb. 3. art. 3.

---

* Alexander Hales, a Scholastic Divine, supposed to have been a native of Gloucestershire, who died in 1245.   He was designated the Irrefragable

Gerson, par. 1, *The congregation of the Church is united to
Christ the head, by the bond of the Holy Spirit ; being joined
to him by certain qualifying dispositions which give a lively
harmony to this mystical body.*

But enough of testimonies. We conclude, therefore,
that this body of the Church, of which Christ himself is
the head, does not consist of any unfaithful and wicked
members, but of the pious and holy alone ; whom God delivers from the power of darkness, and translates into the
kingdom of his dear Son. Hence we may learn,

1. It is not sufficient for salvation to be a visible member of any visible church by an outward profession of faith,
unless you are a mystical member of the Catholic Church
by a true faith and the Spirit dwelling in the heart *What
does a treacherous soul in the house of faith?* says Cyprian.

2. It is not befitting Christians to envy those who are
endowed with the more excellent gifts ; because they are
members of the same body : what, therefore, is conferred
on one, *that* should be esteemed as given to all, according
to that remark of Augustine in Psalm cxxxix. *Lay aside
envy, and what I have is thine; lay aside envy, and what thou
hast is mine.*

3. Since godly members are of the same body, it behoves them to be ready to assist each other ; and they
ought to feel equally affected with the good or evil which
fall to others, as with their own. So says the Apostle, 1
Cor. xii. 26, *If one member suffer, all the members suffer with
it ; or if one member be honoured, all the members rejoice with
it.* Thus far concerning the first title of Christ.

The beginning and the first-born from the dead.] These
words are variously read and expounded. In the Greek
they stand thus, ἀρχη πρωτότοκος ἐκ τῶν νεκρῶν. Some, there-

Doctor, and Fuller stiles him " the first of all Schoolmen," placing him at
the head of eight other distinguished British School Divines, and stating
that he was master to Thomas Aquinas and Bonaventura. He wrote a
' Commentary on the four books of Sentences,' or ' Sum of Divinity,' at
the command of Pope Innocent IV.; Nuremberg, 1482, and often reprinted. Other works have been attributed to him, but incorrectly. This
would seem to be the one from which Davenant has quoted.

fore, expound them, *The beginning, the first-born from the dead.* Others supply the copulative καὶ, *The beginning* AND *the first-born from the dead*: so Beza. Athanasius, and after him Calvin, interpret them by supplying the causal conjunction, *The beginning,* BECAUSE *the first-born from the dead.* Chrysostom reads, not ἀρχη, as it stands in our copies, but ἀπαρχη, *the first fruits and first-born,* &c. But this is of little importance to the main point. For according to all, the Apostle signalizes Christ with these titles to shew that he not only rose first, but that he is to his Church, i. e. to all his members, the beginning and fountain of salvation and of grace in this life; of glory and of blessedness in that which is to come. For the Church hath a twofold state : of grace and of a spiritual resurrection in this life; of glory and of a beatified resurrection in the other : The Apostle, therefore, in this place, declares Christ to be the author of both.

Two things, then, are here to be explained : 1. That Christ himself was the first in the glorious resurrection : 2. that Christ was the first in such manner as to be to all of us the cause, as well of the spiritual resurrection, whereby we rise again from the death of sin, as of the corporeal resurrection, whereby we rise to the life of glory. For Christ was both the first in the order of rising as it respects himself, and the beginning as it respects us.

As to the first point ; Christ is rightly called *the beginning and the first-born from the dead ;* for he alone hath risen as the beginning of his resurrection, raising his body by the power of his Godhead. He also alone hath risen to spiritual life and glory, no more to die. That he rose by his own power, not by that of another, is clear : John ii. 19, *Destroy this temple, and in three days I will raise it up. I have power to lay down my life, and I have power to take it again,* John x. 18. Although, therefore, we read both in the Old and in the New Testament, that some rose from the dead before Christ, this does not strip Christ of these titles ; for no one hath risen as the beginning of his resurrection, but all were quickened by the efficacy of another. Besides, none of those arose to the immediate enjoyment

of glory, but to the present manifestation of the Divine
glory. For truly spake Cyprian, in lib. De resurrectione
Christi. *These rose indeed,* says he, *before Christ, but in the
name and the faith of Him: one through Elijah when he was
living; one by Elisha in his lifetime, and another after his
death; but then they again returned to death which they had
thus tasted. Lazarus also rose at the command of Christ, and
some others; yet all these only enjoyed the gift of life for a
time, then again returned to the grave. But Christ being
raised from the dead, dieth no more,* as it is said Rom. vi. 9.
The resurrection, therefore, of these few preceding the resurrection of Christ, does not in the least oppose his being
called *the beginning and the first-born from the dead:* since
they rose neither by their own power, nor to everlasting
life; Christ both by his own power and for ever.

2. Now let us come to the second reason of his being
called *the beginning and the first-born from the dead;* viz. because he not only, as we have before shewn, quickened
himself, and that to life immortal; but because he is the
effective beginning and cause of the rising again of all his
members; whether we regard the resurrection to grace from
the death of sin, or the resurrection to glory from the
death of nature. I join them together, because, although
Christ never rose from the death of sin, inasmuch as he
never was subject to sin, nevertheless this one resurrection
of Christ is the cause of both in us; and these two resur-
rections are so intimately united, that whoever does not
rise beforehand by the power of Christ from the death of
sin, will never rise to the life of glory. Let us, therefore,
first shew that Christ's rising again is the cause of our spiritual resurrection.

Christ is the beginning of our spiritual resurrection, by
his death and resurrection, 1. as the *meritorious* cause; for
he merited this spiritual quickening of his members: 2. as
the *efficient* cause; for, by the same power wherewith he
raised himself from the dead, he both raises all that are his
from the death of sin, and regenerates them to the new life
of grace. So says the Apostle, Rom. vi. 11, *Reckon ye
also yourselves to be dead indeed unto sin, but alive unto God*

through Jesus Christ our Lord. 3. Lastly, as the *exemplary* cause; for the resurrection of Christ is every where proposed to us as a type and pattern of our spiritual resurrection : *Like as Christ was raised up from the dead, so we also should walk in newness of life,* Rom. vi. 4.

If Christ were not in us *the beginning* of this spiritual resurrection, there would be no hope of the blessed and glorious resurrection, as it is written in Rev. xx. 6, *Blessed is he who hath part in the first resurrection; on such the second death hath no power.* For the Spirit of regeneration is the earnest of the blessed resurrection, giving the commencement of spiritual life, and the right to that resurrection which is unto life eternal. Hence Tertullian (in libro, cap. 47, De resurrectione) beautifully says, *that by regeneration our bodies are inaugurated for this resurrection.* And Aquinas, in Epist. ad. Rom. upon those words, chap. viii. 11, *If the Spirit of him who raised up Jesus from the dead dwell in you, he that raised up Christ from the dead shall also quicken your mortal bodies by the Spirit that dwelleth in you;* says, *Our bodies shall be quickened for glory on account of the dignity which they have obtained from the circumstance of their having been the temples of the Holy Spirit.*

Thus, then, it appears that Christ is the beginning and the cause of our spiritual resurrection by his corporeal death and resurrection.

Now as to that corporeal resurrection which we expect; of this also Christ is *the beginning*, in all those ways which we have touched upon in the spiritual resurrection. 1. As the meritorious cause : For by his passion and victory he won for his people a glorious resurrection : *He was delivered for our offences, and was raised again for our justification,* Rom. iv. 25. *But whom he hath justified, he will glorify,* Rom. viii. 30. *Who is gone into heaven, and is on the right hand of God,* 1 Pet. iii. 22.*

2. As the efficient cause : For he himself by his Divine power will raise up all his people to glory ; John v. 28, *The*

---

* Our Author's words under this reference are, " Deglutiit mortem, ut vitæ æternæ hæredes efficeremur," which are borrowed from the Vulgate, and seem to be an addition to the text, as an interpretation.

*hour is coming in which all that are in their graves shall hear
the voice of the Son of God, and shall come forth,* &c. and 1
Cor. xv. 20, *Christ is risen from the dead, the first-fruits of
them that slept.* Why *the first-fruits?* Because, like as
under the law, the offering of the first-fruits was the cause
why the rest of the fruits should be blessed ; so the resurrection of Christ is the cause why the rest of the members
shall rise again. *I am released from my death ; I rise again
by the power of Christ,* says Prudentius, in Apoth.

Lastly, As the exemplary cause. For the glorious resurrection of Christ the head, holds out to us an example of
our resurrection and future glory : *He shall change our vile
body, that he may make it like to his glorious body,* Phil. iii.
21.

It is therefore evident that Christ is most deservedly distinguished with these titles by the Apostle, viz. of *the beginning* and *the first-born from the dead ;* as well because he
quickened himself to the life of glory, as because he
quickens all that are his, both from spiritual and corporeal
death.

Observe, 1. From the circumstance of Christ being said
to be to us *the beginning* both of the life of grace and of
the life of glory, we conclude that they who are not united
to this beginning, are neither partakers of grace in the present life, nor will be of glory in the life to come : but this
union is effected by faith and the Holy Spirit : they who
are destitute of these will also be destitute of the other.

2. Since Christ is called *the first-born from the dead,* we
understand that death is not now to be feared by Christians; who are entitled to expect by-and-by a certain new
and glorious resurrectional birth. For as Christ, on rising
again, is called *the first-born from the dead ;* so all we, after
rising again, shall obtain a certain new nativity. *He hath
begotten us again unto a lively hope by the resurrection of Jesus
Christ from the dead, to an inheritance reserved in heaven.*
1 Pet. i. 3, 4. *Death doth not take away life, but renews it,*
as spake Prudentius wisely.—Thus much respecting the
titles themselves.

That in all things he might have the pre-eminence.] The Apostle is now engaged in shewing that the titles above-mentioned belong to Christ by the best possible claim.

Some refer these words to every thing which had preceded them in his description of Christ the Redeemer : as though the Apostle had said, *He is the image of God, the first-born of every creature, the head of the Church, the beginning and first-born from the dead,* to this end, *that in all things he might have the pre-eminence,* i. e. that it might be proclaimed to the whole world, that he is the Lord of all creatures, and placed above all things which are either in heaven or in earth.

Others refer them to this last clause, in which Christ is declared to be *the first-born from the dead,* in this sense ; Not only is Christ the Creator and chief of all things which live, but also, by his death and resurrection, he is *the first-born,* he that again quickens *the dead :* this only was wanting to him ; therefore, that in all things he might have the pre-eminence, he chose to die, he chose to rise again *the first-born from the dead.* If any other had overcome death, and quickened us, then Christ would not have had the pre-eminence in all things ; for that other would have been the chief in respect of the dead.

Here it is proper to remark the wonderful wisdom of the Apostle in divine things, who, in the death of Christ, which appeared full of infirmity and ignominy, finds an argument for augmenting his glory and majesty. For although this circumstance *of dying,* if considered in itself, is a mark of infirmity ; yet for any one *so to die,* as to raise himself again, as to deliver all others from death, by the power of his death and resurrection, i. e. to be *the beginning and the first-born from the dead,* is pre-eminently honourable and glorious.

Verse 19.

For it pleased the Father that in him should all fulness dwell.

The Apostle still proceeds in confirmation of those titles which a little before he had bestowed upon Christ. But in this verse there are two reasons complicated and involved together, which we shall separate for the sake of perspicuity. The first is taken from the efficient, or ordaining cause, in this manner; *it pleased* God the Father (for these words must be supplied) that Christ should be *the head of the Church, the first-born from the dead,* &c. therefore, on the best possible ground, we attribute these titles to him. So Peter, Acts ii. 36, said, *Let all the house of Israel know assuredly, that God hath made that same Jesus both Lord and Christ:* i. e. God the Father himself hath given the Church to Christ, and in turn Christ to the Church, and hath constituted him its head and Saviour, by his eternal ordinance.

But how was this *good pleasure* of God made evident to Paul, or how can we be assured of it?

1.   From the testimony of God himself in his word ; for *Moses and the Prophets bear testimony* to Christ the Redeemer. *Had ye believed Moses, ye would have believed me, for he wrote of me,* John v. 46, &c.   2. From the whole life of Christ, from his death and resurrection ; in all which his Divinity shone forth, and proclaimed to the whole world that he was sent from God the Father, to gather together the Church, and accomplish the salvation of man.

It is not without just reason that the Apostle, in speaking of the Redeemer of the human race and the head of the Church, puts us in mind of the good pleasure of God ; because no one could take this honour to himself without the Divine will and decree.   For which reason God himself revealed this his good pleasure by the prophets, as in Isaiah xlii. 6, *I the Lord have called thee, and have given thee*

for a covenant of the people, for a light of the Gentiles. And
Christ himself, on every occasion, enforces this decree of
God, and this his mission from God the Father, Luke iv.
18, *The Spirit of the Lord is upon me, because he hath anointed me, he hath sent me to preach the Gospel to the poor, to
heal the broken-hearted,* &c. Isa. lxi. 1.   And John iv. 34,
My meat is to do the will of him that sent me.

Two things are to be noted here:

1. That salvation and grace are not to be sought in any
other than in Him in whom it hath pleased God they should
be sought.   But concerning his will respecting it, we are
to judge from the word of revelation.   In the whole business, therefore, of our salvation, this thought ought always to be present to Christian minds, What is the good
pleasure of God?   For if we turn aside from his will, in
vain do we expect any good.   For example: I desire the
remission of sins, or deliverance from some impending
evil, or some spiritual grace: I hesitate about what must
be done to obtain the object of my desire: The orthodox
direct that I should flee immediately to Christ, and plead
his intercession alone with the Father; the Papists direct
that I should flee to the blessed Virgin, or to other saints.
Here, then, what is to be done? You must enquire, What
hath been the good pleasure of God the Father? You
must obey his will.   We easily shew you that it hath
pleased God that we should use the intercession of Christ
our head: but the whole tribe of Papists never will prove
from the Scriptures, that it hath pleased God that we
should approach him by the mother of Christ, or through
the saints.

2. Since it hath pleased God that Christ should be our
perfect and absolute Redeemer, it is manifest that they
undermine the eternal purpose of God, who have devised
new modes of salvation, of which it cannot be said, that it
hath pleased God we should seek remission of sins by
them.   Hither we may refer human satisfactions, papal in
dulgences, and whatsoever is blended in the business of
salvation without the ordinance of the Divine will.   All

these, as much as in them lies, set aside the eternal decree of God respecting human salvation.

2. *All fulness dwell.*] This is that other reason why Christ is most properly called *the head of the Church ;* and it is taken from the formal cause, in this manner ; God, whom it pleased that Christ should be *the head of the Church,* not only so ordained by decree, but, besides, furnished him with all the gifts which were requisite to render him the *suitable head of the Church.* This title, therefore, most especially befits him.

By *fulness* in this place some understand a fulness of Deity ; others, a fulness of habitual grace.* It is certain each fulness dwells in Christ; and perhaps the Apostle desired to comprehend each. For doubtless he asserts, that there is in Christ whatever is requisite to render him the perfect Redeemer of mankind, and *the head of the Church :* but for undertaking these offices, both a fulness of Divinity and a fulness of habitual grace are requisite. Concerning the Deity of Christ we have before spoken : of the fulness of habitual grace we shall only shew these three things briefly.

1. That this fulness of grace was in Christ.

2. Adduce some reasons why it was befitting that a fulness of grace should be in Christ.

3. We will shew that this fulness of grace was the privilege of Christ alone.

1. As to the first; when we say that there was in the man Christ a fulness of habitual grace, we mean not that this grace was infinite : for, since it is a created quality, and is inherent in the soul of Christ, which also was created, it cannot be infinite. But by *the fulness of grace* we understand all those perfections to which the term grace extends itself. For whereas a certain measure of grace is found in other men, so that one man may be endowed with some gift of grace in which another is wanting; in Christ

---

* Vide our Expositor's other great work, " Dissertatio duo de Justitia actuali et habituali, &c."

there is a concurrence of all the gifts of grace. Besides, whilst other men obtain grace in an inferior measure; Christ not only possesses all grace, but also hath it in the highest degree. Whence some say that this habitual and infused grace of Christ, may in some sense be termed infinite : viz. inasmuch as it is not limited in kind or degree ; but contains in itself whatever falls under the term grace : As if any one should say the light of the sun is infinite, not as far as regards the essence of that attribute, but as far as the nature of light alone is considered ; because whatever appertains to light is found in the solar light in the highest degree. But this is an incorrect mode of speaking. The Scriptures every where affirm this fulness of grace to be in Christ, John iii. 34, *The Spirit was given to him without measure.   In him are all treasures,* Col. ii. 3.

Ye see then that all fulness of grace is in Christ.

2. Now, in the second place, let us consider, Why it was necessary this fulness of grace should be in Christ. First, *the fitness of things* required it, on account of the union of his soul to the Word. For it is just and proper that in proportion as any thing is nearer to the influential cause, so much the more abundantly should it partake of the influence itself : Since, therefore, God himself is the fountain of grace, the soul of Christ, so near to God, cannot but abound in grace. Secondly, *necessity* requires it, from consideration of the end, on account of the relation of Christ himself to the human race. For grace was to be bestowed on him not as on a private person, but as the universal fountain from whom it might be transfused into the rest of men. But in this fountain all the parts ought to be full and combined. The Evangelist shews that grace is shed abroad in us from Christ, John i. 16, *Of his fulness have all we received.* And the Apostle, Ephes. iv. 7, *To every one of us is given grace according to the measure of the gift of Christ.*

3. It remains that we shew, in the last place, that this fulness of grace is peculiar to Christ alone. To prove

which we employ this one argument.   In the saints *mili-tant* here on earth there is not a fulness of grace; for it cannot consist with so many remains of the old man as are found in them : for a fulness of grace leaves no room for sin.   But not even in the very saints *triumphant* is there this perfect fulness of all grace which is in Christ: For if one star differeth from another star in light and magnitude, then how much more does it differ from the sun?   All the blessed have the greatest measure of grace and glory which the mind of each individual can contain ; but the mind of any mere creature hath not that capacity, either of grace or of glory, which Christ hath.   There is *fulness* in him alone.

But an objection is raised, that the Virgin Mary, for in-stance, is said to be *full of grace*, Luke i. 28; and Stephen also *full of grace and power*, Acts vi, 8 : and that therefore a fulness of grace is not peculiar to Christ.

I answer, the fulness of grace is twofold : One may be regarded on the part of grace itself, when a man hath it in the greatest extent, both as to every kind of grace, and in the greatest perfection as to degree.   This is the fulness of Christ alone.   The other regards grace on the part of the possessor, when a man hath it as fully and as suffici-ently as his state and condition can contain : And thus a fulness of grace is compatible to Mary, Stephen, and others : For the Virgin Mary had full and sufficient grace for that state and condition to which God had chosen her.

And thus briefly have we dispatched those three points which we proposed to explain : That all fulness of grace was in Christ; Why all fulness ought to dwell in Christ; and that this fulness is found in Christ alone.

Hence observe, that God is not accustomed to impose an office upon any one, without at the same time, conferring upon him all those powers which are necessary for the dis-charge of it : He lays upon Christ the office of *head of the Church ;* but he also imparts to him *a fulness of grace.* Therefore, whoever thrust themselves into offices, for the administration of which they are altogether incompetent, are not called to them by God, but are impelled either by avarice or ambition.

2. For any one to be accounted the *head of the Church*, he must necessarily have *a fulness of grace.* In whom this *fulness* is wanting, it is well with him if he be numbered among the members of the Church ; he cannot assume to himself the name and the honour of *head* without the greatest arrogance or folly, as Gregory hath shewn, Epist. lib. i. epist. 82.

3. Since there is a *fulness* of grace in Christ alone, we must expect its streams to flow to us from him alone : they who seek grace elsewhere *commit two evils ; they forsake the fountain of living waters, and hew them out cisterns, broken cisterns that can hold no water,* Jer. ii. 13.

And now we have gone through the description of Christ our Redeemer.

Verse 20.

And, having made peace through the blood of his cross, by him to reconcile all things unto himself ; by him, I say, whether they be things in earth, or things in heaven.

Our Apostle has, up to this point, been occupied in explaining the doctrine of Redemption. The blessing of redemption itself he has slightly glanced at in verses 12, 13, 14. From that 14th verse to this place, he has described the Redeemer, and dignified him with various titles. Here, in this verse, and the two following, he again returns to the subject of redemption, and more copiously expounds the mode of it, having before but briefly touched upon that topic. But of the work of redemption, or reconciliation, he speaks first, *generally,* as far as it relates to all, in this verse : then, in the two following, *specially,* as far as it pertains to the Colossians themselves.

Now in the words before us there are many things to be observed :
1. That the reconciliation is effected.
2. By whose decree and authority it took place.
3. With what it was effected.
4. By whom.
5. In what manner.
6. On whose behalf.

1. The Apostle takes it for granted that the work of reconciliation is accomplished. He does not, therefore, apply himself to prove that mankind *is* reconciled to God, but to present to our view the very method of reconciliation. Now *to reconcile* is nothing else than to renew a friendship broken asunder by some grievous offence, and so to restore the parties at enmity to their former concord. And here we must bear in mind, that, before the fall, all rational creatures were in close familiarity with God ; but by that apostacy there took place, as it were, a violent separation of the creature from God, and a turning away of God from the creature : so that the same God who had loved man, when created, as a son ; hated him, when fallen and corrupted, as a traitor. But notwithstanding this fall of man, and this hatred of sin on God's part, it pleased God to reconcile fallen man to himself.

From this certain persuasion of reconciliation being accomplished, arises our great consolation in that spiritual struggle which the conscience experiences under the horror of sin.* For if we had to treat with a God hostile to us, who, under the load of so many sins, could raise his eyes towards heaven? who could think think on the Divine Majesty without trembling ? But when we recollect that we have to do with a God propitiated and reconciled, we approach the throne of mercy with great confidence. For he will not deal with us in strict justice, as with enemies ; but, as if treating with friends and children, he will pass

* Vide Note, p. 91.

by our sins, he will call to remembrance his fatherly pity
and compassion; and that, indeed, because the reconciliation is accomplished.

2. In the second place it is to be inquired, By whose
decree, counsel, and authority this work of reconciliation
hath been undertaken and accomplished? We answer at
once, that it was done by the authority and appointment of
God the Father. This we gather from the connection of
this verse with the preceding; *It hath pleased him* (that is
to say, the Father) *that in Christ should all fulness dwell;
And by him to effect the reconciliation.* Here, therefore, it is
also proper to substitute that word 'εὐδόκησε, *it pleased* the
Father *to reconcile,* &c.

In many other places the work of reconciliation is ascribed to God the Father: But that remarkable one, 2 Cor. v.
18, 19, contains the sum of them all, *God hath reconciled us
unto himself: God was in Christ, reconciling the world unto
himself.* Although, therefore, (as we shall presently shew)
the work of reconciliation is attributed to Christ, as the
proximate and immediate agent; yet it is proper to ascribe
it to God the Father; and, by consequence, to the whole
Trinity, as the primary cause: For the whole Trinity, which
foresaw from eternity the fall of the human race, pre-or-
dained this way of effecting reconciliation by Christ, and
inspired the man Christ Jesus with the will to suffer for the
redemption of mankind. So it is said in Isaiah xlii. 6, *I,
the Lord, have called thee in righteousness, and will hold thine
hand, and will keep thee, and give thee for a covenant of the
people,* &c. In which place the prophet teaches us, that
Jehovah himself had ordained and called Christ to this
work of reconciliation, and strengthened and upheld him
during his whole accomplishment of human salvation. It
is evident, therefore, that God was the primary author of
this reconciliation, and was induced to devise this plan of
our redemption entirely from his own good pleasure, and
from free love. The Apostle here employs this particular
term 'εὐδόκησε, *It pleased him well.* And in Jeremiah xxxi. 3,
we read, *I have loved thee with an everlasting love.* And in
all parts of Scripture, this gratuitous love of God is de-

clared to be the cause why the Father sent his Son into the
world to obtain salvation for us, John iii. 16, *God so loved
the world that he gave his only begotten Son.* And in Ephes.
ii. 4, 5, *For his great love wherewith he loved us, even when
we were dead in sins, he hath quickened us,* &c.   For, as Altissiodorensis well observes, *love is the first gift in which all
others are given.*

But here a doubt meets us concerning this eternal love
of God. For it may be asked, What need was there of
reconciliation, if God loved us from eternity? since reconciliation is not needed among friends, where there are no
enmities.

We offer an answer from the venerable Bede :* Thus,
says he, in Rom. v. *God loved us in a wonderful manner,
whilst he hated us : in every one of us he hated what we had
done ; he loved what he himself had done :* i. e. as the Schoolmen say, he loved the human race as far as respects the
nature which he himself had made ; but he hated it as far
as respects the guilt which men had contracted.   Therefore
the love of God towards the being created by himself, moved him to devise this reconciliation : the hatred of God towards sin, prohibited by him, but committed by us, subjected us to the necessity of reconciliation.   Aquinas,
therefore, 3 quæst. 49. art. 4, rightly states the matter ;
*We are not said to be reconciled, as though God began to love
us anew ; for he has loved us with an eternal love : but because
by this reconciliation all cause of hatred is removed, as well by
the remission of sin, as by the re-payment of a more acceptable
good.*

Hence we are taught that our salvation is not the wages
of our merit, but the free gift of God.   For this original
decree of human redemption proceeded from ευδοκία *Divinâ,*

---

* In the account of Bede given on page 73, by inadvertence, a remark intended to have been inserted respecting his History, was omitted, and the
Translator takes occasion to introduce it in this place.   It is, that that
work, though drawn from such stores of learning as existed in the cotempo-
rary Italian church, abounds with evidence, that many dogmas which the
Papacy has of late years obtruded upon the world, were not known in the
Church up to Bede's time.

the good pleasure of God, and from his eternal love, whereby us, who were fallen and sunk in sin, he hath voluntarily saved and reconciled to himself: according to that saying of Ambrose in Epist. 11, *God called us to salvation when we were straying from him, and not even desiring the right way;* and Paul to Titus, ii. 11, *The grace of God which bringeth salvation, appeared unto all men,* Ἐπεφάνη η χάρις ; as it were, shone upon us suddenly and unexpectedly, when we were neither seeking or looking for such a thing.

3. Let us proceed, and see, in the third place, to whom we are reconciled. *To himself,* says the Apostle, i. e. to God the Father, and, consequently, to the whole Trinity. So he speaks in many places : Rom. v. 10, *When we were enemies we were reconciled to God by the death of his Son :* and in 2 Cor. v. 19, *God was in Christ reconciling the world:* To whom ? *To himself.* It is plain we must understand in these places, by the word God, *God the Father,* because of the correlative *Son* which is subjoined.

But here we must beware not so to consider ourselves reconciled to God the Father, as to deny that we are reconciled also to the Son and to the Holy Spirit. For since all sin is committed against the Divine Majesty, it follows of necessity, that the three Persons who possess the same essential Divinity, and were equally offended by the commission of sin, should be equally appeased by the expiation and remission of it.

But two reasons are assigned by Zanchius,* (De trib. Elohim,) why the Scriptures usually teach that we are re-

* Jerome Zanchius, born of an illustrious family at Bergamo, in 1516, became a member of the congregation of canons regular of St. Giovanni di Laterano, when only fifteen years of age, and while in that society formed a close intimacy with the celebrated Peter Martyr, also an associate of their community. The conversation and example of this distinguished convert to the reformed church, made a great impression upon Zanchius, as well as upon many of his brethren, which was farther increased by the lectures which Peter subsequently delivered at Lucca. The result, though not immediate, was decisive ; and Zanchius, after having worn the monastic habit nearly twenty years, at length threw it off, in conjunction with eighteen of his companions, and openly seceded from the Romish communion. This abjuration necessarily induced him to quit Italy ; and accordingly, in 1550,

conciled to the Father, rather than to the Son or the Holy
Spirit. First, Because the Father is the fountain of the
whole Godhead, and of all the Divine counsels and operations : on which account also it happens, that he is, in order, the first of those against whom our sin is committed ;
and, in order, the first of those to whom we are reconciled.
Scripture therefore usually states, that we are reconciled to
the Father, rather than to the Son, or the Holy Spirit, that
it may indicate the fountain whence reconciliation flows,
and against whom sin is first committed. The other reason is, Because the Scriptures would point out the peculiar office of each Person. For although the acts of the
Trinity are ad extra indivisible, yet certain of them are
appropriated to each Person peculiarly. It is, therefore,
the property of the Father, as the fountain from whence
grace flows, to receive us into favour: and hence the Scrip-

---

he took refuge at Geneva, where he remained two years; and then, declining an invitation to England to fill a Divinity professorship at Oxford, he
proceeded to Strasburg. Here he obtained the Theological professorship,
and read lectures both in Divinity and in the Aristotelian philosophy, with
great reputation, till 1563, when, owing to the increased annoyance and
persecution he had to endure at Strasburg, he removed to Chiavenna, in the
Grisons, in the capacity of Pastor to a reformed congregation there. During his residence here, he had to witness the devastation of a dreadful pestilence among his flock, which almost depopulated the place. The Divinity
Chair at Heidelberg becoming vacant in 1568, he was induced to accept of
it, and settled there under the immediate patronage of Frederic III. Elector
Palatine, at whose instigation he composed two celebrated treatises, the one
entitled *De Dei naturâ ;* the other, the one quoted above, *De tribus Elohim
uno eodemque Jehovâ.* The treatises were directed principally against the Socinian heresy, the advocates for which were exhausting every artifice to de-
grade the Son, and Spirit of God, to the level of mere creatures. His amiable and enlightened Patron had urged Zanchius to be very particular in
canvassing the arguments made use of by the Socinians; and Zanchius gave
himself to the work in a truly Christian spirit; producing two treatises
fraught with the most solid learning and argument; and breathing, at the
same time, genuine candour and sterling piety. The death of the Elector
in 1578 occasioned his resignation of the Professorship at Heidelberg: but
although he took up his abode after this event at Newstadt, he returned to
Heidelberg in 1585, and there passed the remainder of his days, dying in
that place in 1590.—He was the author of several other important controversial treatises, of which one " On the Doctrine of Predestination," has
been translated into English.—Vide Middleton and Gorton.

tures are wont to say, that we are *reconciled to the Father.*
It is the property of the Son, as Mediator, to intercede,
and fully to pay λύτρον, the ransom-price of reconciliation :
hence they say that we are reconciled *by the Son.*   It is the
property of the Spirit to set the seal to this confidence of
reconciliation in our hearts.   We are reconciled, therefore,
to the Father, and we are reconciled also to the Son and to
the Holy Spirit, inasmuch as they are one God in three
Persons.

But here it is objected : If Christ reconciles us to the
whole Trinity, then he reconciles us to himself : but no one
is called a Mediator in regard to himself, but with reference to another.

I answer, The Son must be viewed in a twofold light :
In one with reference to the Divine essence and nature, in
regard to which he also is offended : in the other with reference to the Divine economy, whereby this Person, although offended, was willing to take human flesh, and, by
a voluntary engagement, to be the medium of reconciliation between God and men.   The same Christ, therefore,
received the sacrifice of reconciliation, as God offended in
his nature ; but he *offered* it as Mediator, the God-man, in
the Divine economy, or voluntary dispensation of grace.—
This is the opinion of Junius.

Ye now understand to whom we are reconciled, viz. to
the whole Trinity.   Let us then enquire,

4.   In the fourth place, by whom this reconciliation is
effected.   *By him,* says the Apostle ; i. e. By him whom he
had before called *the image of God, the first-born of every
creature, the head of the Church, endowed with all the fulness
of grace;* by Christ Jesus, the incarnate Son of God.
*There is none other name under heaven whereby we can hope to
be saved,* Acts iv. 12.   No creature either could or ought to
reconcile us to God ; not an angel ; nor a mere man ; but
Christ the Θεανθρωπος—the Son of God.   An angel could
not reconcile us, because the rule of Divine justice required, that satisfaction should be given by the same nature that had sinned and was to be delivered.   Neither, indeed, was it fit that man should owe his salvation and re-

demption to any other than to him to whom he owed his creation. Bernard, De passione Dom. cap. 46, gives as a reason, *Because redemption more excites us to love than creation.* If, therefore, we had been redeemed by any other than he who created us, we should have loved him more than our Creator. I even affirm, finally, that an angel could not perform this work. For an angel owes to God whatever he hath, and can do on his own account: he has no superabundant merit, which he can afford to expend for the redemption of man. But if an angel could not effect this work of reconciliation, much less could a mere man, guilty of sin, and obnoxious to Divine wrath. For, as the Apostle says, Ephes. ii. 3, *All are by nature the children of wrath.* Nay, if we could suppose any man entirely free from sin, he nevertheless would not be a fit redeemer and reconciler for mankind. For the redemption and reconciliation of the human race requires a mediator whose obedience is of infinite merit, whose humility is as pleasing to God as the pride of our first parents was displeasing. But the obedience of any mere man, however holy, is due and required by God; is finite, and hath nothing whereby it can answer for and expiate an infinite offence. Therefore Christ alone, the God-man, could and ought to reconcile us to the Father: he alone could, in respect of his Divine nature: he ought, in respect of his human, which he assumed for that very end, that he might deliver man and bring him back to God. Whence the Church, Acts xx. 28, is said to be *purchased with the blood of God.*

Hence we infer, that Christ alone is the bond of our union with God; so that, out of him, we are miserable, because not yet reconciled to God.

Hence also we refute their error who seek reconciliation with God either by the aid and intercession, or by the merits of angels or of saints. For since Christ is called *our reconciler,* this title, even as all the former ones, is to be understood exclusively and by way of contrast, as though the Apostle had said, He, and no one besides him, is *the head of the Church;* He, and no one besides him, is endowed with *a fulness of grace;* He, and no one besides him, hath the office *of reconciliation* assigned to him by God the Father : By Him, and by Him alone, *it hath pleased God to reconcile all things to himself.*

5.   Now let us consider, fifthly, how Christ hath reconciled us to the Father : *Having made peace,* says the Apostle, *through the blood of his cross,* i. e. through the blood shed on the cross ; or, through that bitter and bloody death which he endured on the cross.

Two things, then, are here to be discussed :

1.   Why God willed peace and reconciliation should be made through the blood and death of his Son ; and

2.   Why by the death of the cross.

As to the death of Christ considered in itself : Some other possible mode of redeeming mankind was not wanting to God ; but no one was more congruous than this, as Augustine writes, De Trin. lib. 13. cap. 10.   This mode was the most consistent with respect to God, because it accorded as well with the Divine justice as with the Divine mercy.   God shewed his justice in exacting a full satisfaction ; the death of an infinite person for infinite guilt.   He shewed his mercy, in exacting it not from us miserable creatures, who were incapable of paying it, but from Christ, who could pay it.   But when we say that another mode of reconciliation was possible, we wish to be understood as speaking of absolute possibility, as it respects the nature of the thing itself : For if it had seemed fit to God, he could have forgiven man all his sins without accepting any ransom ; or he might have been content with the least measure of suffering from Christ, although he had not yielded himself to death.   But if we regard the eternal decree of God, concerning the deliverance of mankind by the death of his Son, then, upon this hypothesis of the Divine pre-ordination, the death of Christ was necessary to human redemption : for it is impossible either that the Divine fore-knowledge should be deceived, or that the Divine decree should be changed.   Hence that prayer of Christ to the Father, Matth. xxvi. 42, *Father, if this cup may not pass from me except I drink it, thy will be done.* The event shewed it could not : not because it was absolutely impossible, but because God had decreed from eternity, that the benefit of our redemption should arise from the passion and death of Christ; which decree it was impossible to abrogate.

But even as to us, Divines are used to adduce many reasons to prove that this mode of redeeming mankind by the death of Christ was most congruous. And, in the first place, they lay down this principle, That any mode is more suitable and adapted to the attainment of any end, in proportion as there is in it a greater concurrence of expedients to that end. This being admitted, it is easy to shew that in this mode of redemption by the death of Christ, many expedients concur which must altogether contribute to advance our salvation.

1. By this death of Christ, man most clearly discovers the infinite love of God towards him, and is thus inflamed to love God in return, than which nothing more conduces to human salvation. So says the Apostle, Rom. v. 8, *God commendeth his love towards us, in that whilst we were yet sinners Christ died for us.* Now, truly, upon this view of the love of God, ungrateful and inhuman is that man who is unwilling to return that love.

2. By this death of Christ we are constrained both to avoid and to abhor sin. For that must of necessity be deadly which could be healed in no other way than by the death of Christ. Who, then, seriously reflecting that his sins could not have been expiated in any other way than by the blood of the Son of God himself, does not shudder to *trample under foot* this most precious blood by his daily trangression? as the Apostle speaks in Heb. x. 29.

3. By this death of Christ, an example of righteousness, humility, obedience, patience, and of all virtues, is set before us. For the godly rejoice to suffer for righteousness sake, when they reflect that Christ Jesus, the Captain and Author of their salvation, underwent death itself. For as it is honourable of the soldier to drink of that cup which his general had tasted before him ; so is it to Christians, to taste of that cup of affliction which Christ himself drank of for them. Therefore this mode was most

suitable, because it especially excites to the love of God, to hatred of sin, and to the practice of godliness.

But now it remains for us to shew why he chose to suffer this ignominious death of the cross ; for both in this place, and frequently elsewhere, this is urged by the Apostle, as in Phil. ii 8, *He became obedient unto death, even the death of the cross.* This kind [of death] not only serves to aggravate his sufferings, but also to confirm our faith.

1. This kind of death shews that Christ took upon himself the curse which was due to us, and freed us from the same : for God hath therefore pronounced the death of the cross accursed, Deut. xxi. 23, because he had determined for our deliverance to inflict this shameful kind of death upon his Son. The words of the Apostle, Gal. iii. 13, refer to this ; *Christ hath redeemed us from the curse of the law, being made a curse for us : As it is written, Cursed is every one that hangeth on a tree.*

2. Because this kind of death corresponded to many types and figures. For the sacrifices which prefigured Christ were placed upon wood, and were raised aloft before they were burnt. The brazen serpent, suspended upon a pole, shadowed forth, according to Christ's own interpretation, his crucifixion ; *As Moses lifted up the serpent in the wilderness, even so must the Son of Man be lifted up*, John iii. 14. *I, if I be lifted up, will draw all men unto me*, John xii. 32.

3. That the pious may understand from thence, that no kind of death for righteousness sake is shameful, or to be dreaded by those subjected thereto. For many who by no means dread death itself, yet shun it when coupled with shame and ignominy : but the cross of Christ arms his disciples against this fear ; which was manifest in the martyrs, who avoided not death, however ignominious.

To these reasons we might add others from the Schoolmen ; which we shall only name, because they seem partly trifling, and partly too curious.

Because Adam sinned by the fruit of the forbidden tree, therefore this second Adam was willing to suffer punishment upon the tree of the cross.

Because by being lifted up at his death, he seemed to prepare an ascent for us into heaven.

Because being stretched upon the cross, he seemed to call the whole world *to look for* salvation hidden in him.

Because, by his blood running down upon the earth, he would not only purify the earth; but also by his body hanging in the air, he would purify the air.

This, and much more of the same kind, occurs in Aquinas, part. 3. quæst. 46. art. 4.

All things, whether they be things in earth, or things in heaven.] In this work of redemption it is, in the last place, to be considered, how widely this benefit reaches, how far its virtue and efficacy extend. *It pleased God,* says the Apostle, *by him to reconcile all things, whether they be things in earth, or things in heaven.*

This passage is very difficult to be explained : interpreters, therefore, torture it, and are in return themselves tortured by it.   In the first place, we must admit that the Apostle is speaking of the efficacy of the reconciliation made by the blood of Christ, as far as this ransom is considered in itself, and in its peculiar value; as far also as the benefit of it is offered to all, by the preaching of the Gospel on the part of God : for he must not be understood as speaking of the actual reconciliation of particular persons; since many are not reconciled to God by the blood of Christ, for want of application.

But yet a doubt remains, on account of the Apostle's distributing his sentence into two members, derived from the places spoken of.   He says that God willed to reconcile *all things* to himself by Christ; and then he employs this division, *whether they be things in earth, or things in heaven.*   It is asked, in what way does reconciliation relate to heavenly things ? for where there is no sin, where there is no breach, there needs no reconciliation.

Chrysostom expounds this passage of the angels; whom he states to have been our enemies by reason of the fall and rebellion of man against God their Lord, but to have been made friends and well-disposed towards us after we were reconciled to God by Christ.   And in this sense he

supposes Christ to have reconciled the things which are *in
earth* and which are *in heaven.*   But this interpretation does
not remove the difficulty.   For although it be true that the
angels became more kind towards us from the period when
we were redeemed by Christ; yet the Apostle does not
speak of *that* in this passage; but he manifestly speaks of
a reconciliation of earthly and of heavenly things which is
made to God, not which is effected between themselves :
It pleased him to reconcile to himself, &c.

Others, by *all things which are in heaven,* understand all
the faithful who died before Christ's passion; and by the
all things which are in earth, all the rest of the faithful.
But it is not at all likely that the Apostle regarded men
alone : for he would then have said, ᵉιτε τοὺς ἐπὶ τῆς γῆς,
ᵉιτε, τοὺς εν τοῖς ὀυρανοῖς, *whether they be persons in earth or in heaven;* and would have used πάντας, *all persons,* not πάνlα, *all
things.*

The Apostle, therefore, seems in this distribution to have
intended to comprise divers objects, viz. men and angels ;
nay, the whole fabric of the heavenly and earthly creation ;
all which in their proper measure participate in this benefit
of redemption; according to that expression of this same
Apostle, Ephes i. 10, where he says, *That God purposed in
the dispensation of the fulness of times,* ἀνακεφαλαιωσασθαι *to gather together in one, or to renew all things in Christ, both which
are in heaven and which are in earth.*

When, therefore, the Apostle says, that it pleased God
*to reconcile all things to himself, as well things in heaven, as
things in earth, by the blood of Christ,* we say this reconciliation, taken *strictly,* refers to men alone.   For since *to reconcile* is to renew a friendship broken off by offence, we
alone, from among his enemies, are restored unto the love
and favour of God, which we had lost by sinning.   If we
understand it for *effectual* reconciliation, it regards the elect
alone, who constitute, as it were, a community : as says
Ambrose, De voc. gent. i. 3, *Among the elect there is a certain special universality to be reckoned.*   But if we may understand it *analogically,* it may be extended to the blessed
angels themselves, and to all creatures.

With respect to angels; as far as they are confirmed in grace and established in the Divine favour through Christ, so that now it is clearly impossible that any enmity should occur between them and God; therefore the establishment of angels in Divine grace through Christ, is the same thing as the reconciliation of men by the same.

Neither may we doubt that the angels themselves need the grace of Christ the Redeemer, that is to say, the grace of *confirmation* and *exaltation,* though not the grace of *reconciliation.* For, as they are creatures, they cannot of their own nature be beyond danger of falling. Moreover, that heavenly and glorious union with God, which the blessed angels enjoy in eternal life, is a benefit which surpasses the deserts of any creature whatever; therefore, not even the angels themselves are admitted into this ineffable bliss of the Divine fruition, but so far forth as they are enrolled under Christ, the head both of angels and men: Whence the Apostle calls the blessed angels *the elect;* 1 Tim. v. 21, *I charge thee before the elect angels.* But the election, whether of men or of angels, out of Christ, cannot be understood. To this, I think, refers that passage of Job (Job xxxviii. 7) where good angels are stiled *sons of God,* not because they are begotten of God (for Christ is the only Son of God) but because they are adopted as sons of God for Christ's sake. Hence, therefore, it is evident, that the grace of Christ the Mediator is necessary for the happiness even of angels; not that by it they should be justified and absolved from sin, but that by it they may be confirmed in the Divine love, and exalted to the glorious and abiding participation of God, which transcends the power and dignity of created nature.

Now, in the last place, as to what pertains to the fabric of the world; it is certain, as all things were created for man, so by the sin of man all things were in a manner overturned, and subjected to vanity and misery. For so the Apostle expressly teaches us, Rom. viii. 19, &c. *The whole world waited for the manifestation of the sons of God: For the creature was made subject to vanity under hope, because the creature itself also shall be delivered from the bondage of*

corruption, into the glorious liberty of the children of God.
To whom, therefore, will this whole fabric of the world
owe its restoration and renovation? Doubtless to Christ
the Son of God, our Creator and Restorer, who, dying
without sin, won the privilege of being the restorer of all
things which were fallen to ruin by sin. It may not, therefore, be improperly said, that Christ hath reconciled *all
things to God, as well the things that be in earth, as the things
that be in heaven :* men *peculiarly,* by taking away their sins,
and the wrath of God occasioned by sin : angels *analogically ;* by taking away the possibility of their falling and of
incurring the Divine anger : the fabric of the world *metaphorically;* in delivering it from the bondage of corruption,
and restoring it to its native purity and beauty, when the
fulness of the time shall come ; according to that declaration, 2 Pet. iii. 13, *We look for new heavens and a new earth,
according to his promise.*—And thus much concerning the
extent of this benefit.

Observe then, Since such is the efficacy of the blood of
Christ to establish peace between God and men, we must
earnestly labour that we may obtain an interest in the
blood of Christ, and partake of that peace which passeth
all understanding. The only means of applying to ourselves this quickening and saving blood of Christ, is true
faith ; *Being justified by faith, we have peace,* Rom. v. 1. Let
us seek faith from God, that laying hold on the blood of
Christ, thereby, that blood may bring peace to our consciences.

Verses 21, 22.

*And you that were sometime alienated and enemies in your
mind by wicked works, yet now hath he reconciled,
In the body of his flesh through death, to present you holy,
and unblamable, and unreprovable in his sight.*

The Apostle descends from the proposition to the particular application of it; and what he had stated generally
concerning the reconciliation made by Christ, he applies
particularly to the Colossians themselves.

Where we have to observe by the way, That general
doctrines are of very little avail to influence the minds of
men, unless a special application of them be made to the
hearers. For that maxim of the Philosophers, *Every action
is accomplished by contact,* especially applies to the sacred
action of preaching. Every doctrine proposed generally,
is occupied, as it were, in a remote object, nor can it reach
to the soul itself; but when it is specifically applied, it
comes in a manner into the very interior of the mind, and
touches and penetrates it. But let us examine the words
of the text.

In these two verses four things are to be taken notice
of;

1.   The miserable condition of the Colossians under the
state of a corrupt nature ; *ye were sometime alienated and
enemies.*

2.   The cause of this misery, viz. their actual wickedness; *the mind being intent upon wicked works.*

3.   Deliverance from this misery under a state of grace ;
now he hath reconciled you in the body of his flesh.

4.   The end or effect of this deliverance ; *to present you
holy, and unblamable, and unreprovable,* &c.

1.   *And you that were sometime alienated and enemies.*] He
begins by a description of their miserable condition under
sin, in order that they might entertain a greater gratitude

for the benefit of deliverance. First he says that they were *alienated.* From whom? From God, from Christ, from the Church, from all hope of obtaining salvation. For this was the condition of the Gentiles whilst they sat in the darkness of nature, void of the grace of the gospel; as the Apostle fully shews, Ephes. ii. 11, 12, *Remember that ye, when ye were Gentiles, were without Christ, aliens from the commonwealth of Israel, strangers to the covenants of promise, having no hope, and without God in the world.* This is the misery of those that are alienated. Such were the Colossians; such all the heathen before they were illuminated by the Gospel.

Observe, 1. Clemens Alexandrinus, therefore, has grievously erred, who writes, that the heathen, by virtue of their philosophy, may please God and obtain salvation, Strom. 6.* Augustine more truly says, *that salvation is to be granted to no one but him to whom the one Mediator between God and man, Christ Jesus, hath been revealed from heaven.* De Civit. 18. 47. Why is salvation granted to no one without this? Verily because he remains alienated.

2. Certain also of the Papists are deceived, who talk about merit of *congruity,* such as they suppose may be found in persons who are not in a state of grace. But whoever is alienated from God and Christ, merits nothing either of *condignity* or *congruity,* but the wrath of God and hell: For *by nature we are the children of wrath.*

Lastly, we must observe, that the Apostle says of the

---

* The Translator has often been perplexed, in the progress of his undertaking, by the contradictory opinions of Divines and Historians relative to the Fathers; and it has cost him much toil and painful investigation to trace out the truth. In reference to the work of Clemens here alluded to, Dr. A. Clarke, in his " Succession of Sacred Literature, vol. i. p. 125," most highly extols it, representing Clemens as describing in it the true Christian; and asserting that " the whole book is worthy of serious regard, as it points out the pure manners of the Christians who lived in the second century." It is possible Dr. Clarke may thus speak from a consideration of the facts which the book contains, and Davenant with reference to the doctrines. But it is not often that such a favourable view of differences of opinion can be entertained; too frequently they appear to have arisen from envy and party feeling, and to have been sustained by the malignant passions of prejudice and bigotry.

Colossians, that they were ἀπηλλοτριωμένους, *alienated.* Therefore, both they and all men were united to God according
to the law of creation; but they became aliens afterwards
by their own fault. Which refutes the foolish notion of
Valentinus concerning certain men, whom he calls men of
wood and earth, whom he imagined were alienated from
God and incapable of salvation, being evil by nature; as
Irenæus tells us, lib. i. cap. 1. *But,* Isa. lix. 2, says, *your
iniquities have separated between you and your God, and your
sins have hid his face from you that he will not hear.*

And enemies.] He proceeds in his description of their
former misery : They were not only *alienated* from God as
to outward condition, but were *enemies* by internal disagreement. Now they are called *enemies* as well in the active as
in the passive signification of the term, i. e. they hated
God as *an enemy,* they were hated by God as *His enemies.*
This tends very much to augment the misery of the Colossians under that former condition : For if it be the height
of felicity to be united to God through love ; then is it the
depth of misery to be separated from God by hostile enmity.

That men in the state of a corrupt nature hate God, and
therefore in this sense are his *enemies,* is plain from Rom.
i. 30, where among other characteristics of the heathen,
this is reckoned by the Apostle, that they are *haters of God.*
The Saviour, John xv. 18, charges the whole world with
this crime, *If the world hate you, ye know that it hated me
before it hated you ;* and a little after he subjoins, *He that
hateth me hateth my Father also.*

But here it is asked, Since God is goodness itself, and
since it is of the nature of goodness that it be loved and
desired by all, how are men called *enemies of God?* and in
what sense are they said *to hate God?*

It is answered, first, that as *the peculiarity of friends is
to like and dislike the same things,* so that of enemies is to
like and dislike contrary things. *By way of interpretation,*
therefore, (as the Schoolmen say) he is accounted an enemy whose will is opposed to the will of another in all
things. But so is the carnal man towards God; Rom. viii.

7, *The carnal mind is enmity against God ; for it is not subject to the law of God, neither indeed can be.*   Secondly, the heathen and the wicked are said to hate God, even *directly ;* not in that they conceive him to be the Creator and Preserver of the universe (for that is impossible), but to be a lawgiver, a judge, and an avenger.

But man under sin is said to be *an enemy to God* in another sense, viz. inasmuch as he is odious and hateful to God : *For the ungodly and his ungodliness are both alike hateful unto God,* Wisdom xiv. 9.   Therefore, whilst the Colossians were under a state of sin, they were under the divine wrath and hatred.   Rightly said Augustine, on those words of our Saviour, John iii. 36, *He that believeth not the Son, the wrath of God abideth on him : not, it will come upon him, but it abideth on him, for long since it fell upon all the children of Adam, the burden of it lies upon them, until it be removed by Christ the Mediator.*

Nor is it wonderful that wicked and unholy men should be accounted *enemies to God,* since God himself is most holy and pure.   *We consider one thing friendly to another, which bears a resemblance to it in its virtues,* says Plato, De leg. 8. Since, therefore, after the fall, so great dissimilarity took place between God and men, they were of necessity *alienated* and *enemies.*   Therefore,

1.   Since as many as are not yet reconciled to God by Christ, are lying in so miserable and grievous a condition, we should hasten to get out of this state of perdition, and strive with all labour and prayer that we may be translated into a state of salvation.

2.   Since God alone hath power to rescue us from this state of condemnation ; as many as perceive that they are delivered and received into Divine favour, should give continual thanks and render unceasing obedience to their Deliverer.

Thus much with respect to the misery of the Colossians, and, consequently, of all men under sin.*

* What a powerful argument arises from these observations for Christian Missions to the heathen !   But even the good Davenant does not appear to have been alive to this consideration.

2. *The mind being intent upon wicked works,* Τῆ διανόια 'εν τοῖς 'εργοις τοῖς πονηροῖς; i. e. *the mind cleaving to, or existing in evil works.* For the mind is said *to be in* that thing which it always meditates upon, to which it is borne, and inclined by its desire ; as the mind of a hungry man is said *to be in the dish,* so the mind of the wicked is said to be in wicked works. I conceive with the learned Beza, that this is the genuine sense of the words, although they are taken in a different meaning by other interpreters. Here, therefore, the Apostle shews the cause of the enmity between God and men who are not yet called, as the Colossians were aforetime, namely, that corruption and depravity inherent in the mind, and breaking forth and shewing itself in wicked works ; according to that declaration of God concerning the fall of man, Gen. vi. 5, *Every thought of his heart is only evil continually.*

This corruption of the human mind is perceived in the understanding, the will, and also in the inferior faculties and the affections.

1. The understanding is *clouded* by the darkness of ignorance. Whence that assertion of the Apostle concerning the Gentiles, Ephes. iv. 18, *Having the understanding darkened,* &c. Hence the worship of devils prevailed for true religion among almost all nations ; hence they committed many abominable things without shame, as the Apostle amply states, Rom. i. That this blindness of the understanding is a just cause of Divine hatred, is evident from the Divine nature : for *God is light, and in him is no darkness at all,* 1 John i. 5. And according to the primary law of creation, man was made in the likeness of God.

2. As to the will, it is infected with the poison of wickedness ; which was not unknown to philosophers themselves. For Plato, in his Sophists, expressly asserts, that the mind of every man labours under two diseases ; *ignorance* and *wickedness.* Hence that observation in Job xv. 16, *Abominable and filthy is man : he drinketh in iniquity as water.* The many adulteries, thefts, murders, and wickedness of every kind openly committed by men, do but too plainly prove this inward perversion of the will. We have here therefore, in the human mind, another cause of this enmity.

3. The last remains, which is ἀταξια disorder in the affections, and rebellion in the inferior appetites against right
reason.   Hence that saying of the Poet, *I see and approve
the better course ; but I follow the worse.*   The human mind
is so hurried away by corrupt affections, that although it
perceives what is good and ought to be done, what is evil
and to be avoided, yet it cannot restrain itself from being
borne away in a contrary direction.   This depravity of the
human mind Augustine bewailed and wondered at, Confess.
viii. cap. 9, *Whence this strange thing ? the mind commands the
body and it is obeyed ; it commands itself and it is resisted.*
And the Apostle to the Romans, vii. 19, *The good that I
would, I do not, and the evil that I would not, that I do.*
Such and so great depravity exists in *the mind,* i. e. in the
understanding, the will, and the affections of every man
not yet called to Christ Jesus : on which account he is
most deservedly reckoned by the Apostle *an enemy of God.*
Hence we conclude,

1. That the fault of original sin does not consist alone
or chiefly (as some of the Schoolmen would have it) in the
inferior faculties of the mind, but has pervaded all the
powers of the soul, and fixed its chief seat in the noblest
part of it, that is to say, *in the mind itself.*   For not in this
place only, but in many others also, the Apostle teaches
that *the mind* itself is wholly corrupt by sin.   Whence, Rom.
xii. 2, he says, *Be ye transformed by the renewing of your
mind.*   And concerning the whole man under a state of sin
he asserts, 1 Cor. ii. 14, *The natural man receiveth not the
things of the Spirit of God.*   Most truly said Parisiensis,
De sacram. baptismi, *The human mind not having obtained
grace, is nothing better than a dead body.*   We are not to
suppose, therefore, that sin arises solely, or chiefly, from
the motions of the sensitive appetite.

2. Amongst the heathen, or whatever others are not yet
sanctified in Christ, although there may be found sometimes
those who evince an appearance of holiness, of righteousness, chastity, and other virtues ; yet *the mind* of all of
them is corrupt and defiled by internal impurity.   For, although their hand does it not, yet *the mind* is bent upon

and exercised in wicked works. Or if *the mind* shrinks
from adultery, murder, drunkenness, and the like; yet is
it full of pride, infidelity, vanity, and many other spiritual
sins, which, for the most part, are more *culpable,* although
carnal vices are more *infamous.* Well spake Tertullian,
*There is no truth in those who are ignorant of God, the Head
and Lord of truth.* Augustine also says shrewdly, in his
preface to Ps. xxxi. *Although their hands are employed in useful operations and they seem to steer the vessel very well, they
are nevertheless hurrying it among the rocks.*

3. That all those are still *enemies to God,* and in a state
of enmity, whose *minds are occupied in wicked works.* The
minds of the godly are often carried away to many sins,
lust drawing them aside ; but to cleave to, and, as it were,
live in wicked works, this is peculiar to such as are not yet
rescued from *the power of darkness.*

Verse 22.

*Now hath he reconciled in the body of his flesh through
death.*

The Apostle, after he had set before the eyes of the
Colossians their former misery in being *enemies to God ;* and
had stated the cause of this misery, and of their enmity,
viz. their corrupt *mind :* immediately presents to them the
contemplation of their present happiness, in that they were
received into the favour of God ; and he subjoins the end
or effect of this reconciliation, viz. their *sanctification* and
newness of life, *that he may present you holy.*

Now hath he reconciled.] That is, after the gospel was
preached to you and received by faith; after your mind,
which was wholly given to evil works, was purified. And
here three things are to be weighed by us.

1. We gather from this place that a twofold reconciliation is to be seen in the Scriptures: The one *general,* accomplished by the sacrifice upon the cross, concerning

which the Apostle speaks in a former verse, *It hath pleased God to reconcile all things to himself by the blood of the cross.* And John i. 29, *Behold the Lamb of God which taketh away the sin of the world.* This I call *general,* because it is considered according to the value of the sacrifice, which is not only general, but infinite ; because also it is considered according to the mode of proposing it, the preaching of the Gospel, which mode is indefinite and general ; for this expiatory sacrifice is proposed and offered to all by God, according to that declaration Tit. ii. 11, *The grace of God which bringeth salvation hath appeared unto all men.* But besides this reconciliation accomplished upon the cross, and *generally applicable* to all, the Scripture also shews us a *particular* and *applied* reconciliation, effected in the heart and conscience of individuals ; that is to say, when that sacrifice of Christ, which hath in itself an universal power of reconciling all, is actually applied to reconcile this or that man. Of this the Apostle speaks in saying *You hath he now reconciled.* He had before said, *On the cross he hath reconciled all things to God, both which are in heaven and which are in earth,* i. e. he hath paid an adequate price for the deliverance and reconciliation of all ; but *now he hath reconciled you* by this particular and applied reconciliation.

2. We are also taught when, and in what way, men become partakers of this reconciliation, which we call *particular ;* viz. by the exhibition of faith in the Gospel. For in the fourth verse, the Apostle gives thanks to God for the faith of the Colossians. This faith, therefore, is the reason why the Apostle asserts that those who were heretofore alienated from God, *are now reconciled.* In Rom. iii. it is clearly taught that this application of the sacrifice of atonement to the reconciliation of every believer, is effected by faith : *The righteousness of God by faith of Jesus Christ is unto all and upon all them that believe,* verse 22. And a little after, *Whom God hath set forth to be a propitiation through faith in his blood.* From which words it is clear, that Christ is proposed to the world by God as an *universal* atonement or propitiation ; but that He renders

the Father propitious to this or that man, then only when he is *specially* apprehended by them through faith.*

Lastly, We see from these words how Christians may shew themselves to be of the number of those who are truly and effectually reconciled to God, namely, by the change of their mind, will, and works. For from this the Apostle concludes that they were reconciled to God, because that when they were enemies to God, they had their mind occupied by wicked works; but now they manifest themselves to be the servants of God, whilst they strive to please God in all things, and to bring forth the fruit of every good work, as it is said in verse 10, *Now hath he reconciled you.* The other points which might be noticed concerning this reconciliation, having been explained above, we omit; and pass on to the following words.

In the body of his flesh through death.] That is, *in his fleshly* and truly human *body.* The Apostle speaks of the material cause of reconciliation and salvation; and shews that this sacrifice of the body of Christ, was that true and only sacrifice which was shadowed forth by those legal sacrifices which did not avail to expiate sin, as Paul plainly declares, Heb. x. 4, *For it is not possible that the blood of bulls and of goats should take away sins. Wherefore when he cometh into the world he saith, Sacrifice and offering thou wouldest not, but a body hast thou prepared me.* But what kind of body? *A fleshly,* i. e. a human body, and of the same nature with our bodies. But how was his fleshly body the instrument of our reconciliation? In dying; *through death,* says the Apostle. Vide Iren. lib. iv. cap. 74.*

---

* For ample elucidation of the doctrine glanced at in this and the preceding Section, see our Expositor's Dissertation on " the Extent of the Death of Christ," appended to the second volume of this work.

* Irenæus :—a Christian Bishop and Martyr of the second century, born in Greece, and educated by Polycarp, who sent him on a mission into Gaul, where he became a distinguished member of the church at Lyons, under Photinus. On the martyrdom of this prelate, Irenæus was appointed his successor in the diocese in 174, and presided in that capacity at two Councils held at Lyons, in one of which the Gnostic heresy was condemned, and in the other the Quartodecimani. He also went to Rome, and disputed

It is not necessary to repeat what we said about the death of Christ when explaining the 20th verse. From these words of the Apostle we shall note only two things subversive of the foolish notions of certain heretics:

1. That the body of Christ was *fleshly,* i. e. truly human, not heavenly, or a phantasm, as Marcion and Valentinus formerly fancied, whom Tertullian clearly refutes, *If the flesh of Christ were a phantasm, then also all his works which he did by the flesh were so. The form of his existence was suppositious ; the act was suppositious. He was an imaginary worker, and his works were imaginary.* And what they commonly adduced in support of this error, viz. that a fleshly body is unworthy of God, the same Father well clears away, by answering, *That there is no substance worthy for God to assume ; but whatever he shall assume, he himself renders worthy.* Which may be illustrated by the similitude of a king taking a consort to himself from among his subjects.

2. That Christ himself truly suffered and underwent death in this flesh. Which refutes the absurd heresy of Basilides, who taught that Simon the Cyrenian, being transformed into the resemblance of Christ, was crucified by the Jews; but that Christ himself stood by in the likeness of Simon and derided the Jews. Perhaps these extraordinary assertions of heretics do not require a refutation ; for they who thus argue that all things are imaginary, are themselves in truth *imaginary Christians,* as Tertullian, cap. 27, learnedly argues against the Valentinians.* Thus much concerning the deli-

there publicly with Valentinus and other heresiarchs. He turned his pen against all the internal and domestic enemies of the Church, by attacking the monstrous errors which were adopted by many of the primitive Christians, as appears by his five books against heresies, which are considered as one of the most precious monuments of ancient erudition ; yet, though several editions of them have been given in Greek and Latin, no translation has appeared in our own language. Irenæus suffered death in the fifth persecution of the Christians under Septimus Severus, A.D. 202. He was a very humble, modest man, and amidst all his zealous exertions for Christian truth, evinced that he was, agreeable to his name,—" a lover of peace."

* Basilides, referred to in this Section, was an heresiarch of the second century, the chief of the Egyptian Gnostics ; a species of arrogant Philo-

verance. What remains has respect to the end and effect of this deliverance.

To present you holy, and unblamable, and unreprovable in his sight.] He thus shews the end of our redemption and reconciliation, viz. the obtaining righteousness and holiness; which in many other places the sacred Scriptures signify. Luke i. 74, 75, *That we being delivered out of the hands of our enemies, might serve God without fear, in holiness and righteousness, all the days of our life.* And Tit. ii. 14, *Who gave himself for us, that he might redeem us from all iniquity, and purify unto himself a peculiar people zealous of good works.*

But here the Apostle seems to comprehend a twofold holiness of those that are reconciled; one which consists in the remission of sins, and the imputation of Christ's righteousness; the other which consists in our renovation, and in the fruits of holiness. For in both ways Christ presents all his people holy before God. They are now strictly saints by imputation, because they are regarded as one mystical person with Christ their head; but as to inherent holiness, that is not effected instantly, but increases daily, and acquires not the summit of its perfection before we are translated from this life to the life of glory.

Yet we maintain that this incipient sanctification is real, although not complete. And therefore the Apostle adds these words, *before God.* For he is said to be just and holy before God, who is so in reality, not in appearance only; *in rectitude of intention, not in fictitious imitation,* as Lyra not inaptly remarks on these words.

sophers, who entertained the most extravagant and insane opinions respecting a succession of derivative fountains of being, or existences proceeding from the Deity, through which the stream of life flows onward to the utmost verge of the universe. These they call Æons, one of whom they made the Creator of this world. Basilides attempted to blend Christianity with the monstrous absurdities of this system. He wrote twenty-four books upon the Gospel, and in these broached such impieties and blasphemies of the shocking character of which our Expositor has adduced a specimen.— Valentinus, (to whose absurdities reference was made at page 250) was likewise an Egyptian Gnostic of the same period, who, if possible, exceeded Basilides in his insane vagaries and blasphemies—notions to which one can hardly imagine nothing but the brain of a maniac could have given birth.

But concerning the distinction of those words which are here brought together, we have forgotten to observe one thing. The expression, then, *to present us holy,* some refer to God, in this sense, to present us such as God may acknowledge for holy and dedicated to him. That next, *unblamable,* they refer to the private conscience; that is to say, that he may present us such as our own conscience does not condemn; according to that word, Rom. viii. 1, *There is no condemnation.* Finally, that expression ἀνεγκλητους, *unreprovable,* they refer to others: to wit, that we be such as our neighbours cannot deservedly blame.—But we need not lay much stress on the distinction of the words, since it is the custom of the Holy Scriptures to bring together synonimous words merely for the sake of amplification: and perhaps the Apostle intended nothing else by collecting and uniting these three words, than to make known that Christ the Mediator imparts his perfect righteousness to all his people. But now let us gather some observations:

1. By his saying, that *He may present us holy,* not *that we should present ourselves holy,* it is evident that those who are reconciled and renewed have obtained their holiness from Christ, whether we speak of it as actual, or inherent, or by imputation. For we make no attempts at good, if they be not excited; and they are vain, if they be not assisted. Whence that declaration of Paul, *By the grace of God I am what I am: I laboured more abundantly than they all; yet not I, but the grace of God which was with me.* Infused righteousness remains not, neither is operative without Christ: and imputed righteousness covers us only so far as we are accounted in Christ, as members under the head.

2. By his saying that Christ hath reconciled us that *he might present us holy,* we readily understand that they are not yet reconciled to God, who abide in their former impurity; for whomsoever Christ hath delivered from divine wrath, them also hath he freed from the service of sin. We must therefore beware, lest we flatter ourselves with a false hope of reconciliation, without this evidence of sanc-

tification and renewal. This is fully proved from Rom. vi.
18, *Being made free from sin, ye were the servants of righteousness.*

3. Whereas he adds, To present you *holy before God,*
he shews that no semblance of piety and religion can profit men, *if by external duties they cover over the secrets of impiety,* as Tertullian says. For he who is commended by
men, when blamed by God, shall not be acquitted by men
when condemned by God.

And thus far we have explained the benefit of redemption described by the Apostle, as well in general with respect to all, as in particular in regard to the Colossians.
The last part of this chapter yet remains, in which he exhorts them to perseverance in this most true doctrine, which
recognizes all the means of human salvation as placed in
Christ only.

Verse 23.

*If ye continue in the faith grounded and settled, and be not
moved away from the hope of the Gospel, which ye
have heard, and which was preached to every creature
which is under heaven; whereof I, Paul, am made a
minister.*

Our Apostle has before unfolded and applied to the Colossians, the sum of Evangelical doctrine concerning the
person of Christ, and the benefit of redemption and reconciliation by Him. From hence to the end of the chapter
he exhorts them to perseverance in this most true doctrine,
which Epaphras had preached to them, which he, Paul,
also had now confirmed by his approbation and concurrence: Because *not that faith which is only received, but that
which is retained quickens,* as Cyprian speaks, Epist. lib. i.
epist. 5.

In this verse he stirs them up by three arguments to a
stedfast faith in this Evangelical doctrine. The first is de-

rived from the utility and necessity of constancy and perseverance in the right faith : for without this no fruit of the redemption by Christ is obtained ; *If ye continue in the faith,* &c. The second is derived from the multitude of believers, or from the common consent of all Christians ; for this same gospel was preached and received through the whole world ; therefore it is folly to leave this and embrace the new doctrine of seducers. The third is derived from Paul's own ministry : Paul, who was an Apostle called of God, and taught the mystery of the faith by the Holy Spirit, had preached this doctrine everywhere ; therefore the Colossians ought to abide in this doctrine, and not hearken to those new teachers, who drew them from Christ, and would have them seek salvation elsewhere.

If ye continue in the faith grounded and settled, and be not moved away from the hope of the Gospel which ye have heard.] This is the first incentive to perseverance in the true faith, derived, as before said, from the utility and necessity of it : From the *utility* in this manner, *If ye continue in the faith,* &c. then *Christ will present you holy, unblamable, and unreprovable before God :* therefore it is highly useful to continue. From the *necessity* in this manner, *If ye do not continue in the faith,* then ye cannot be partakers of the power of those benefits which are offered in Christ : therefore it is equally necessary to continue. For this verse connects with the former, and unites with it the condition which God imposes upon us, if we would enjoy the redemption and reconciliation procured by Christ. There are many things to be noted in this argument of the Apostle.

1. That by faith we are constituted holy, unblamable, and unreprovable before God. This is deduced from the very connection of this verse with the foregoing. The Apostle had affirmed in *that,* that Christ *had reconciled the Colossians to God,* in order to *present them holy :* here he adds the condition *of faith,* by which they apply and acquire this holiness to themselves. Therefore, not an incipient renovation, not the works which we do, constitute us righteous and unreprovable before God ; but faith, apprehending Christ and seeking daily the forgiveness of sins.

So it is regarded Rom. iii. 22, *The righteousness of God, by faith of Jesus Christ, is unto all and upon all them that believe.* And Gal. ii. 16, *We know that a man is not justified by the works of the law, but by the faith of Jesus Christ.* Whence said Augustine, De civit. lib. 19. cap. 26, *The perfection of our righteousness is placed rather in the remission of our sins than in the perfection of our virtues.* And, Contra duas Epist. Pelag. lib. 3. cap. 5, *Our faith determines that of unjust we are become just, not by the law of works, but by the very law of faith.*

2. The kind of faith of those who are truly reconciled to God which constitutes them holy and unreprovable in his sight, is not an uncertain, temporary, and illusory faith ; but a rooted, solid, and stable one.   For the Apostle requires us to be τεθεμελιωμένοι κὰι ἑδραῖοι, *grounded and settled.* The former of these words is taken from buildings, whose foundations are laid in solid, not in sandy, or miry ground : the other from seats, upon which those who have sat down remain immoveable.   This, therefore, the Apostle intends, That the true and living faith which reconciles to God, and constitutes a man just, is not volatile, but, as it were, founded upon a rock, and fixed in a firm place by deep roots.   Admirably said Cyprian, Lib. De simpl. prælat., *Let no one account that the good can depart from the Church. The wind does not disperse the wheat ; nor the tempest overturn the tree fixed by strong roots.   Empty chaff is driven about by the storm ; feeble trees are beaten down by the gust of a whirlwind.   They went out from us, but they were not of us : for if they had been of us, they would have remained with us.* 1 John ii. 19.

3. Upon what foundation this faith rests ; even upon the free promises of God which are offered in the Gospel. This the Apostle shews in saying, *and be ye not moved from the hope of the Gospel :* for *the hope of the Gospel* denotes the expectation of those rewards which the Gospel promises to believers.   For there is this difference between the Law and the Gospel : the Law puts the hope of eternal life under the condition of works and of perfect obedience ; *He that doeth these things shall live in them,* Levit. xviii. 5 : but the

Gospel inspires the hope of salvation in us, through the mercy of God alone, on the condition of faith; *He that believeth hath eternal life.*

Therefore the Papists, who find the hope of their salvation in the law, and trust to their own merits for justification, overturn, and, as much as in them lies, extinguish the grace of the Gospel. We do not exclude the pursuit of good works, but the merit thereof; neither do we deny that those who are reconciled should do good works; but we maintain that these works are not such, as can present us holy and unreprovable before God: This is the peculiar province of faith, as it apprehends Christ the Mediator and Redeemer. Although, therefore, we have not a *legal* hope which arises from the special merits and perfect observance of the law; yet we are not moved away from *Evangelical* hope, which is founded on the gratuitous promises of God, and his fatherly compassion by Christ.

Lastly, from all these considerations we conclude, that there are two sorts of men altogether excluded from the benefits of Christ: one, of those who are wholly devoid of faith, of whom it is said, *He that believeth not shall be damned;* the other, of those who have acquired a certain appearance or shadow of faith, yet prove, by falling away, that it was either a loose opinion, or a certain sudden light; not a true and justifying faith, rooted in the recess of the heart, united with sanctification and regeneration. Tertullian, De præscript. advers. hæret. cap. 3, says concerning these, *Let the straws of light faith fly away as they will at any blast of temptation; the heap of corn will be laid up the purer in the garner of God.* And a little before, *They are neither to be regarded as prudent or faithful whom heresies have been able to draw aside. He is no Christian unless he persevere even unto the end.* Since, therefore, *the utility* and the *necessity* of true and abiding faith is so great, the Apostle, by this consideration, exhorts the Colossians, and all Christians, to continue in the faith and the doctrine of the Gospel.—Thus much as to the first reason.

Which ye have heard, and which was preached to every crea-

ture under heaven.] This is the second reason why it behoved the Colossians to continue in that doctrine of the
Gospel which they had learned of Epaphras ; namely, because it was the same with that which the Apostles had
disseminated through the whole world. For although the
truth of the Gospel does not rest upon human authority or
approbation, or the number of believers, yet the consent
of all the churches in receiving the same doctrine, contributes much to the confirmation of our faith.

But what the Apostle here says, that the Gospel was
preached *to every creature,* is taken in various ways by interpreters ; yet in this they agree, that under the designation *creature,* should be understood only the rational creature, viz. mankind ; because they alone can comprehend
and need the doctrine of the Gospel. And so the Saviour
himself speaks, Mark xvi. 15, *Go ye into all the world, and
preach the Gospel to every creature.* Therefore this epithet is
appropriated in common to the human race by the figure
antonomasia, because man is the chief of all the creatures.
Gregory, in Moral. vi. cap. 7, seems to me to assign a reason for this, more ingenious than solid : *By* EVERY CREA-
TURE (says he) *man alone is understood, because existence is
common to him with stones, life with trees, sensation with animals, discernment with angels: he is, therefore, rightly expressed by a title of universality, under which, in a certain degree, the universe itself is comprehended.*

But it being admitted, that by *every creature* we must
understand all men, yet some doubt may arise how the
Gospel can be said to have been preached to all men, since
it is very probable, that in the time of the Apostles, many
existed who were not made partakers of the Gospel.

Some, therefore, reply, that there is a certain hyperbo-
lical synecdoche in these words, nor could the Apostle
mean any thing else than that the doctrine of the Gospel
was disseminated far and wide. Others think that the pre-
terite is put for the future, which was customary in prophetical predictions, to denote the certainty of future
things. Because, therefore, the Gospel was at that time

preached among many nations, and to be preached in due time to all, it is spoken of as preached *then* to every creature.

But they seem to me to explain this passage best, who say, that *every creature,* or *the whole world,* is opposed to the single Jewish nation : so that the sense will be, that the Gospel was proposed not to the Jews alone, as the Mosaic law was ; but also to other nations without distinction. Therefore there is nothing else signified by this kind of expression, than (what Paul sets forth in Galat. iii. 28) that in the Gospel *there is neither Jew nor Greek, neither bond nor free, neither male nor female ;* but that Christ is equally offered to all in the preaching of the Gospel. This Gospel then, in the faith of which he wished the Colossians to continue, is the same as was preached to all other people. But we spake of this universal extension of the Gospel when we explained the sixth verse ; therefore it is not necessary to add more : We only deduce from hence a few observations.

1. We hence infer against the Papists, That it is sufficient for salvation if we yield credence to that Gospel which was openly preached to all, although we may be ignorant of, and reject those doctrines, which they foist upon the faithful under the title of *traditions.* For Paul clearly teaches, that the Colossians would be holy and unblamable, if they continued in the faith and the hope of the Gospel which was preached to every creature. In vain, then, do the Papists cry out, that there are certain traditions not written, but privately committed to certain perfect men, to which, however, they would have the faith of all Christians bound under the pain of anathema. Of this character are those opinions concerning purgatory—indulgences—the adoration of images—the Supremacy of the Pope ; to which if any one does not give credit, he is put as much beyond a state of salvation by them, as if he denied altogether the fundamental articles of the faith. But we affirm with Tertullian, Præscript. Hæret. cap. 22, *It is not to be believed that the Apostles either did not know the fulness of the Gospel, or gave not a complete rule to all.* Nay,

Paul himself deprecates this perfidy which the Papists
palm upon all the Apostles : Acts xx. 26, *Ye are my wit-*
nesses that I am pure from the blood of all men. For *I have*
not shunned to declare unto you the whole counsel of God.

2. Hence we also infer, That the word of God is not to
be withheld from the laity, but that all men are to be invited to the reading, hearing, and meditating on it. For if
the Apostles have promulged to all people, all things necessary to salvation; if they committed the same to writing, that from the knowledge thereof *the man of God may*
be perfect, thoroughly furnished to every good work, 2 Tim.
iii. 17, why is that Gospel now pertinaciously denied to a
Christian people, which was preached to every creature
from the beginning ? Whatever they insist upon in opposition to the reading of the Gospel, the same might have
been alleged against the preaching of it : For many understood not the Apostolical declarations ; many, misunder-
standing them, perverted them to establish errors. But
notwithstanding these things, the Apostles invited all to
hear ; therefore, we also ought to call upon all to read.
But, on the other hand, the Papists fear lest their people
should be injured by reading the Scriptures, though they
have no apprehension lest they should be injured by reading foolish and lying fables. The orthodox Fathers have
both judged and spoken otherwise about the Scriptures.
Chrysostom frequently exhorts the people to read the
Scriptures *with all diligence.* Hom. 9. in Epist. ad. Coloss.
He hath the like in Hom. 3, De Lazaro, and elsewhere.
Augustine, De utilitate credendi, ad Honor. cap. 6, says,
The doctrine of Scripture is so adapted, that every one cannot
but draw from thence what is sufficient for him, if he only
comes to draw devotedly and piously. It will not be tedious
to add to these that most admirable testimony of Damascenus, De fide orthod. lib. iv. cap. 18: Κάλλιστον καὶ
ψυχωφελέστατον, &c. *The best and most useful thing for the*
soul, is to search diligently the Scriptures : For as a tree planted
besides the running waters, so the soul watered with the divine
Scriptures is enriched, and bears perfect fruit, viz. sound faith ;
and is always adorned with verdant leaves, i. e. deeds pleasing

to God. But to what purpose are these things ? That ye may understand that that wholesome doctrine which God would have to be preached through the whole world, is unjustly withheld from Christian people.

Lastly. When the Apostle directs us to continue in the Gospel which was preached by the Apostles in all the world, he delivers to us the rule of the true and catholic faith, viz. the apostolical preaching, which we now have committed to us in writing. If we can shew the doctrine of our Church to correspond with this, we are Catholics, although we dissent not only from the church of Rome, but from many other churches. For we ought to continue firm and grounded in that faith which was from the first preached to every creature, not in novel dogmas which afterwards crept into the Church. Rightly and wisely said Gerson, De vit. Spirit. par. 3, *The doctrines of the Apostles are of another authority than those of their successors; even as the authority of the primitive Church was greater than that of the present. It is not, therefore, in the power of the Pope, or of councils, to change the doctrines delivered to us by the Apostles: nor have they equal authority with respect to this point, viz. to make any thing to be clearly an article of faith.* Thus testifies Gerson. But Paul himself speaks much more pointedly, *If we, or an angel from heaven, should preach any other Gospel unto you, than that we have preached, let him be accursed,* Gal. i. 8. Since, therefore, our church acknowledges and receives the apostolic doctrine heretofore preached in all the world, let us not regard the railings of Romanists, who call us heretics and schismastics because we continue not stedfast in certain papistical errors.

Thus much concerning the second reason why we should continue in the doctrine of the Gospel.

Whereof I, Paul, am made a minister.] This is the last argument for continuance in the doctrine received. For in these words it is shewn, that the Gospel preached to the Colossians by Epaphras, was the same with that which was every where disseminated by Paul himself. Moreover, Paul, although he was personally unknown to the Colossians, was yet of great celebrity among all the churches : for his wonderful conversion and his call to the Apostleship were matters of great notoriety among them. If, therefore, *every man in his own calling is worthy of credit,* then ought Paul, who was set apart for the preaching of the gospel, to be credited concerning the truth of the Gospel rather than the false Apostles : But this Paul approved the doctrine of Epaphras ; therefore ought the Colossians to continue in it. Three things are here to be observed.

1. Christians must not lend their ears to those who undertake the office of preaching when they have not a legitimate call to it. For the Apostle seems in this place to oppose his lawful ministry to that of those seducers who had crept into the church of the Colossians, relying upon their own temerity not upon the Divine appointment. No wonder, therefore, if those who possessed not lawful authority to teach at all, should teach falsehood. Such were they who wished to lead away the Colossians from the Gospel ; but, nevertheless, they must continue in it.

2. That no one can exercise the public office of the Ministry, unless he can say with Paul, that *he is made a minister of the Gospel.* Therefore a call is to be looked for, *from the authority either of God giving a special revelation, or of a superior giving a mission, or of inevitable necessity ;* as Gerson properly asserts, par. 3. Upon those who act otherwise, that sentence of Jeremiah, xxiii. 21, is deservedly launched, *I have not sent these prophets, yet they ran ; I have not spoken to them, yet they prophesied.*

Lastly, That legitimate Pastors themselves are to be only *ministers* of the Gospel, not *lords;* according to that saying of Paul, 2 Cor. i. 24, *We have not dominion over your faith, but are helpers of your joy.* The true Apostles, *content with ministering only,* left *all authority* in matters of faith to God. But our well known self-erected apostle in sheep's clothing arrogates to himself the authority of creating new doctrines of faith, and of imposing them upon Christian people under anathema : nay more, that whatever he happens to dream when placed in his chair of authority must be regarded as oracular through Christendom. But no one is bound to believe a minister, only so far as he proves to us that he speaks according to the mind of the Lord. So Aquinas, quæst. disp. de fide, art. 10, *We do not believe the successors of the Apostles only so far as they announce to us what the Apostles left to them in the Scriptures.* This is the case with all who are made *ministers of the Gospel;* we are not bound to repose faith in them only so far as the testimony of God is considered to be in them. We receive the voice of God himself with undoubting faith ; but we prove the doctrine of ministers by judging whether it agrees with divine truth, before we yield credence to it : and for this end, to every believer the faculty of judging is given by the Holy Spirit, as to every man is given by nature and reason the faculty of judging in human affairs.

Thus much concerning these three arguments with which the Colossians are excited to constancy.

Verses 24, 25.

Who now rejoice in my sufferings for you, and fill up that which is behind of the afflictions of Christ in my flesh, for his body's sake, which is the Church :

Whereof I am made a minister according to the dispensation of God, which is given to me for you to fulfil the word of God.

In the preceding verse the Apostle had said, that he was made *a minister of the Gospel* by God : here he expatiates on those afflictions which he underwent on account *of the Gospel* and *of his ministry* therein : and in so doing he seems to anticipate an implied objection. For the Colossians might be inclined to say, Why do you exhort us to perseverance in the doctrine of the Gospel ? They who profess it are daily oppressed by innumerable calamities. You, yourself, are now living in bonds in consequence of your professing and preaching the Gospel. The Apostle, therefore, anticipates this objection, and argues, that because he is now enduring persecution on account of the Gospel, they, for that very reason, ought to persevere in it; for unless its doctrines were both true and saving, he never would undergo such numberless inconveniences for the promulgation of it.

Here, therefore, two points are to be considered :—How the Apostle conducts himself under these afflictions; namely, with a placid, and even a joyful mind, *I rejoice in my sufferings for you.* What reasons he had for this joy and for such endurance : and he assigns three,

The Apostle rejoices in these his afflictions, first, because of conformity with Christ; *I fill up that which is behind of the afflictions of Christ.*

2. Because of the advantage redounding therefrom to the Church ; *for his body the Church.*

3. Because of the nature of the office assigned to him by God, to which these afflictions were subservient; *whereof I am made a minister,* &c.

Who now rejoice in my sufferings for you.] Here he shews how he conducts himself in his afflictions ; not only with fortitude, but with joy and cheerfulness. He therefore wishes, by this his example, both to encourage the Colossians to stedfastness in the Gospel, and even to strengthen them to the endurance of any suffering for the Gospel's sake. This personal fortitude, indeed, and promptitude to encounter afflictions of every kind for the benefit of the Church, he professes on all occasions : vid. Acts xxi. 13 ; 2 Tim. ii. 10 ; and 2 Cor. xii. 15. *Most willingly will I spend and be spent for your sakes,* i. e. their souls' sakes. Now from this disposition in St. Paul, we infer,

1. That the ministers of the Gospel ought to be ever ready to bear their cross : *The servant is not greater than his Lord; if they have persecuted me, they will also persecute you,* John xv. 20. The ministers are leaders, as it were, in this Christian warfare; and the devil is sure to harass the leaders more than the private soldiers. Cyprian speaks

correctly when he says, De singul. Cleric. *The enemy aims more at the officers in an engagement than the men; and the higher the pinnacles of buildings, the more violently are they beaten by the winds and storms.* If, therefore, patience be requisite for all Christians, however humble their station, ministers of the word, who, of course, are exposed to injuries and reproaches of all kinds, and from every quarter, have the more need of it. Christ himself has apprised them of this in these words: *Ye shall be hated of all men for my name's sake. But in your patience possess ye your souls,* Luke xxi 17, 19.

2. It is not enough merely to bear the cross, it must be done without reluctance of spirit, or inward repining; nay it ought to be made our joy and glory when we suffer indignities for the sake of the Gospel, and of our sacred ministry. It is therefore said of the Apostles, *They departed from the presence of the council rejoicing that they were counted worthy to suffer shame for the name of Jesus,* Acts v. 41. *That is a bad soldier,* says Prosper, *who follows his General sorrowing. If you have done any good in a reluctant manner, you are rather the sufferer of the action than the agent of it.* We should, therefore, ever place before us the example of Paul, who rejoices in the things which he suffered.

Thus we see how the Apostle behaved in his afflictions: Let us now investigate the causes of such exemplary patience and joy. The first is derived from the conformity which we have to Christ through sufferings and afflictions, conveyed in these words which immediately follow.

And fill up that which is behind of the afflictions of Christ in my body.] In this place the conjunction serves instead of a causal particle. For the Apostle is giving his reason why he ought to rejoice in his sufferings, viz. because by this means he fills up in his body that which remained of the afflictions of Christ. And here two questions arise for explanation: 1. Why the Apostle assigns his sufferings to Christ himself. 2. Why he says that he *fills up,* ὑστερήματα, *that which is behind,* or *the remains,* or, as it is in the Vulgate, *those things which are wanting* in the sufferings of

Christ. For these words seem at first sight to imply that the passion of Christ was imperfect.

Now as to the first question; the sufferings of Paul, and of all other true believers, are called the sufferings of Christ himself on two accounts:

1. Because of the mystical union that subsists between the Head and the members, in respect of which not only the Head, but the whole body of the Church, is comprised under the name of *Christ.* For this statement we have the clearest authority, 1 Cor. xii. 12, *For as the body is one and hath many members ; so also is Christ.* In which expression, the term Christ denotes both the Head itself, and the Church united to this Head. Now it is customary for every one to attribute to himself those injuries which are inflicted upon any part of his body. Thus wounds of the hand or foot are properly said to be the wounds of the man himself; and it is usual for him to exclaim that he is wounded in the hand or in the foot. So also, in the same manner, the Apostle, because he is himself a member of the body of Christ, calls his afflictions *the afflictions of Christ.* This, then, is the first reason : Because Christ and all his members constitute one mystic person.

2. The second reason is; because of the sympathy Christ feels in the afflictions of his members, and which is the result of the union before spoken of. For as we are accustomed to consider the privations and sufferings of those with whom we are most intimately connected as our own, because we are as much afflicted with their distresses as we should be by our own; so Christ accounts the sufferings of his brethren as his own, because he is not less affected by them than when he himself suffered. Virgil introduces Mezentius crying out that he was wounded, when his son was slain by the sword of Eneas.

> ......*heu, nunc misero mihi demum*
> *Exilium infelix, nunc altè vulnus adactum.**
>
> Æneid. x.

* ....Ah ! now at length
On wretched me my exile lies,
Now the deep wound is driven home.

So Christ himself exclaims from heaven, Acts ix. 4, *Saul! Saul! why persecutest thou me?* The afflictions of the godly, therefore, are called the afflictions of Christ, by reason of his union and joint sufferings with them.

Now then let us enquire, Why the Apostle not only ascribes his sufferings to Christ, but also adds, that he himself *filled up that which was behind of the afflictions of Christ in his body.*

And first of all, we must beware of inferring from hence that the passion of Christ was imperfect, or that any thing was wanting in it for the full liberation of the human race, and satisfaction for their sins. For the whole volume of Scripture declares the contrary. *He was wounded for our transgressions; and by his bruising we are healed,* Isa. liii. 5. *By one offering of himself he hath for ever perfected them that are sanctified,* Heb. x. 14. As far, therefore, as satisfaction for sins is concerned, there is no deficiency in the passion of Christ.

Therefore, that we may clearly understand this subject, we must know that God not only decreed by his eternal counsel what sufferings Christ on his part should in his body undergo for the redemption of the Church; but also what each member of the Church should in his flesh be subject to for the name of Christ: But both these sufferings, as well of the Head as of the members (as we have already shewn), are called *the sufferings of Christ,* and make up, as it were, one body of sufferings; with this distinction, however, that he suffered for the redemption of the Church, which sufferings of his may be called προτερηματα *the preceding sufferings:* we suffer on other accounts, and our sufferings should be called ὑστερηματα, *the succeeding sufferings;* for we do but slightly taste of that cup of afflictions, which Christ first drank deeply of and commended to us. But all his sufferings he submitted to for the atonement of sins; we are subjected to them for other reasons.

Any Christian, therefore, may be said *to fill up that which remains of the sufferings of Christ,* when he takes up the cross of Christ and bears patiently those afflictions which

God has allotted to be borne by him after the pattern of Christ, though for another purpose. Upon this passage Lyra makes no bad comment: *The sufferings of Christ are taken in a twofold sense; in one, for those which he actually sustained in his own body, in which nothing remains to be completed; in the other, for those which he should sustain in his mystical body, even to the end of the world; and thus there remains the residue of many sufferings still to be completed.*

What has been thus observed upon the sufferings of Paul, and, by parity of reasoning, of all the faithful, viz that they are accounted the sufferings of Christ himself, tends

1. To strike terror into the ungodly. Whilst they are afflicting the Church, they think that they are only vexing a few pitiful and contemptible men. But the real fact is far otherwise; for they are wounding Christ himself (who is the Head of all believers) in his members. Vengeance, therefore, the most inevitable and bitter, awaits them; seeing that they are provoking the Lord of glory himself, to whom *all power is given in heaven and in earth,* Matth. xxviii. 18.

2. To the honour and dignity of the godly. For surely an honour and dignity it is to be received into the fellowship of the sufferings of Christ. Therefore we read in Acts v. 41, *They rejoiced that they were counted worthy to suffer shame for the name of Jesus:* And in Phil. i. 29, *To you it is given not only to believe in him, but also to suffer for his sake.* Nazianzen says, reason prescribes that we rather *honour* than *despise* the afflicted. And why should we not regard them as highly honoured who are preferred above others to a participation of Christ's sufferings, as it were to a participation of the royal cup; and who drink of that cup, indeed, of which Christ drank first?

3. To the great consolation of the pious. Because it confirms their hope of obtaining future blessedness. *This is a faithful saying, If we be dead with Christ we shall also live with him; if we suffer with him we shall also reign together with him,* 2 Tim. ii. 11, 12. Whence Gregory remarks; *The more sorely I am borne down by present evils, the*

more assuredly do I anticipate future joys. *Blessed are they which are persecuted for righteousness' sake; for theirs is the kingdom of heaven,* Matth. v. 10.

And thus much of Paul's first reason for rejoicing in his sufferings, viz. because of his being made like to Christ.

For his body's sake which is the Church.] This is the second reason which the Apostle gives for rejoicing in his sufferings, viz. because great benefit would arise to the Church from them. For so he speaks to the Philippians, i. 12, *I would ye should understand, brethren, that the things which happened unto me have fallen out rather unto the furtherance of the Gospel.* And again, 2 Tim. ii. 10, *Therefore I endure all things for the elects' sake, that they may also obtain the salvation which is in Christ Jesus.* But in what sense is Paul said to suffer *for the Church,* or *for the Elect?*

He is said to suffer *for them,* not to effect their redemption, or to expiate their sins; but for their edification and confirmation in the doctrine of the Gospel. For he suffered imprisonment and bonds, not for any actual sins of his own, but for preaching the Gospel: hence he says that *he suffered trouble for the word even unto bonds:* 2 Tim. ii. 9. Nor did Paul ever suppose for a moment that his sufferings could purchase remission of other men's punishment; but only that his example might confirm others in a similar constancy. For which reason in a passage above cited he said, that *he endured all things for the elects' sake;* not that they should look for satisfaction to be made for their sins by the merit of his sufferings; but that *they might obtain the salvation which is in Christ Jesus.* In this very passage also, immediately after mentioning his sufferings for the Church, he adds, *of which I am made a minister;* not, *of which I am made a Mediator,* or *a Redeemer:* giving us thereby to understand that he did not speak of his sufferings as affording satisfaction, but as tending to edification. For his sufferings had this end in view, the building up of the Church by preaching the word and enduring persecution.

But since the Papists pervert this passage, to ground their doctrine of indulgences, it will not be at all irrele-

vant to my purpose briefly to glance at the controversy on
this point.

Cajetan, in his tract, De indulgent. quæst. 3, in order to
prove that the sufferings of the saints can make satisfaction for the temporal punishment due to the sins of their
fellow men, provided they be applied to them by a Papal
Indulgence, alleges this passage, and has these words :
*That it was the intention of the saints to suffer for us, the
Apostle testifies when he says, I fill up those things which are
wanting of the sufferings of Christ for his body which is the
Church.   Whence it appears clearly, that the divine Providence
had ordained some sufferings of the saints should have respect to
the completion of the sufferings of Christ, for his body ; and
that the saints did complete this ordinance by the superabundance
of their sufferings.*   Catharinus takes occasion from this
passage to descant upon indulgences copiously.   The
Rhemish annotators also collect from these words that the
sufferings of the saints do make satisfaction for others, and
may be communicated to those who need them on the score
of that communion which subsists between all the members of the same mystical body; and in this communication consists, as they say, the dispensation of indulgences.
Let us, therefore, in a few words, propound what they on
the one side, and we on the other, have stated on this
point ; and then we shall confirm our doctrine, and refute
theirs.*   Now the Papists, for enabling them to legalize
this scandalous trafficking in indulgences, prepare the way
by four preliminary deceptions.

---

* It is scarcely needful to remark that this refers to the Translation of
the New Testament, published by the English Papists at Rheims, in opposition to the authorised Protestant Translation in England, and with a regular series of Annotations in defence of their own tenets, and in refutation
of those of the Reformed Churches.   It was reprinted in this country in
1601, by Dr. Fulke, with the English Version annexed, and a confutation
of the above arguments, in a series of counter-annotations; a work which,
containing, as it does, almost every thing that has or can be said on both
sides, is, perhaps, one of the most valuable volumes of such a nature in the
English language.   It was reprinted, with considerable additions, in 1617
and in 1633 ; the reprints are, of course, more valuable than the early copies.   Though not scarce, it has of late years much risen in price, and will

First, they pretend that though God does remit all the guilt to the truly penitent, yet that he does it only by commuting the eternal punishment into a temporal one; so that those sins must either be expiated and redeemed by certain satisfactory works, or they must be atoned for in purgatory.

In the second place, they lay it down as a maxim, that some few, as, for instance, the blessed Virgin, John the Baptist, and many of the martyrs, had suffered much heavier punishments than were due to their own individual sins, and had wrought more good works than were necessary for ensuring their own salvation.

Thirdly, they assert, that these superabundant sufferings of theirs, being duly mixed up with those of Christ, are laid up in the common store-house of the Church.

Lastly, they assert, that this treasure is placed by the Almighty in the hands of the Roman Pontiff, to be disposed of at his pleasure; so that he has the power of bestowing these superabundant sufferings of the saints upon any penitent whatever, who shall, by their potency, be released from all temporal punishment due to him, either from ecclesiastical injunctions, or even from the dispensation of divine justice. And upon these deceptions, as upon a

probably ere long become rare. The student, in purchasing it, should take care to procure a copy which contains his able Defence of the English Translation, annexed.

In 1816 an edition of the Rhemish Testament was published in Dublin, under the sanction of Dr. Troy, the titular Archbishop of Dublin; and on some Notes in it being brought forward in the House of Lords in 1824, on the Examination of the Irish Bishops, the question was taken up in the Catholic Association, the book denounced, and the leader of that body threatened to quit the Catholic Church unless it was suppressed. As a specimen of the charitable doctrines inculcated by those zealous Divines, one of the Notes is subjoined; *Ex uno disce omnes.* It is under the text Matth. xiii. 29, in the Parable of the Tares, " *The good must tolerate the evil, when it is so strong that it cannot be redressed without danger and disturbance of the whole Church, and commit the matter to God's judgment in the latter day. Otherwise where ill men (be they Heretics or other malefactors) may be punished or suppressed without disturbance and hazard of the good, they may and ought, by public authority, either spiritual or temporal, to be chastised or executed.*"

foundation, is built the whole system of Indulgences so profusely vended by Papal bulls.

We, on the other hand, contend ;

1. First, that to all believers and true penitents, as well the expiatory punishment, as the entire guilt, is remitted, for the sake of the passion and satisfaction of Christ.

2. We deny that any of the saints ever possessed superabundant merits in themselves, or suffered severer punishments than their sins deserved.

3. If we allow that those saints were harassed and afflicted more than their sins deserve, yet we utterly deny that any accumulation of merits can arise from thence, to be drawn upon for the remission of other men's punishments, which they have incurred from divine justice.

Lastly, if there be a store of merits and sufferings attached to the Church (which, as respects the merits and sufferings of Christ, we willingly acknowledge,) yet we deny that it is committed to the Pope's custody, or that he has any power by his bulls of assigning the sufferings of Christ and his saints to men. And now for the proofs of these positions.

1. Christ the Mediator hath taken upon himself both the guilt and the punishment due to us, and, by his passion, hath delivered us from both ; therefore there can be no need either of our own satisfaction, or of those of the saints, to be applied to us by papal bulls. The antecedent is easily substantiated by the clearest Scripture authorities. *My blood is shed for many for the remission of sins,* Matth. xxvi. 28. But *the remission of sin implies nothing more,* as Durandus properly observes, lib. 4, *than that it is not imputed to us for punishment. There is no condemnation to them who are in Christ Jesus,* Rom. viii. 1. But condemnation has reference properly to the punishment imposed for guilt in conformity with the sentence of the judge. Whenever, therefore, condign punishment is inflicted, the sentence of condemnation has most assuredly preceded. *Their iniquities will I remember no more,* Jer. xxxi. 34. But he who executes punishment after the guilt has been forgiven,

plainly shews that he keeps the guilt itself in remembrance. Moreover, when the guilt and the punishment are proportioned, as the measure to the thing measured, then, whatever quantity of expiatory punishment is required, the same quantity of sin committed is imputed. Therefore the first proposition, which supposes that Christ hath obtained for us a half remission, is false. *Christ,* says Augustine, *by imputing to us the punishment which he suffered, without any guilt of his own, hath cancelled both the guilt and the punishment.*

2. None of the saints either had superabundant merits, or bore sufferings greater than their sins deserved. Therefore it is absurd to look to them for a borrowed satisfaction for those punishments which we deserve from the justice of God. They had no superabundant merits, because no man ever yet hath perfectly satisfied the divine law *Enter not into judgment with thy servant, O Lord,* said the Psalmist, cxliii. 2, *for in thy sight shall no man living be justified.* Again, Ps. cxxx. 3, *If thou, Lord, shouldest mark iniquities, O Lord, who shall stand.* And Bernard, in his comment on Ps. xci. 14, observes, with equal nobleness of sentiment and piety of heart, *The sum total of man's merit is this, to fix all his hopes on him by whom salvation is complete,* Tom. 1. To this you may add, that the merits of even a holy man are in no way equal to the purchase of eternal happiness; and, therefore, most foolishly do the Papists look for a superabundance, in those in whom it is impossible to find an equivalent. Nor, indeed, did any of the godly at any time suffer punishment more extensive than their sins. For God always inflicts punishment *short* of what the Schoolmen call *condignity;* because infinite punishment is due, as the Papists themselves admit, for a single mortal sin, even of the least degree. The second opinion, therefore, of the Papists, which ascribes penal sufferings to the saints, severer than the demerits of their own sins, falls to the ground.

3. The merits and sufferings of the saints cannot be communicated to others in such a manner, either by imputation or application of them, as to free them from the punish-

ment of their offences : In vain, therefore, do the Papists
attempt to establish a treasure upon these grounds. And
this we prove,

1. Because, by the general consent of Theologians, no
man's merits, save those of Christ alone, extend beyond
the man himself. To this the Papists readily answer, that
the works of the saints, as to their merits, do not extend
beyond the individual himself, nor are transferable to other
men ; but that in respect of their satisfactory virtue, they
may be both imputed and imparted to others. But we shall
easily get rid of this distinction. For whatever has been
already most highly rewarded in the saints themselves, cannot still remain to be rewarded, or in any way to be imputed to others for their remission; but both the sufferings
and all the good works of the saints, as well meritorious
as satisfactory, are most abundantly rewarded by that single gift of bliss eternal. For these works are, (as they
maintain) meritorious as far as they originate in love; and
satisfactory as far as they have penalty attached to them;
But whether we consider love, or penalty, or any thing
else as the condition of works, that single prize suffices
for a most ample remuneration; nay, further, *the sufferings*
of this present time are not worthy to be compared with the
glory which shall be revealed. Rom. viii. 18.

2. Secondly, No man can make satisfaction for another
in respect of an injury done to a third person, unless by permission of the person to whom the injury is done. Wherefore Aquinas, in commenting upon those words in Rom.
iii. *Ye are justified through the Redemption which is in Christ*
Jesus, whom God has set forth as a propitiation, has thus expressed himself; *According to this, the satisfaction made by*
Christ was effectual both for justification and redemption; be-
cause God had ordained him to this according to his purpose.
But God never ordained, according to his purpose, that
any of the saints should make satisfaction for us; therefore no satisfaction of theirs delivers us from punishment.
No man can deliver his brother, Psal. xlix. 8. *Was Paul cru-*
cified for you? 1 Cor. i. 13. *We have an advocate with the*
Father, Jesus Christ the righteous ; and he is the propitiation

for our sins, 1 John ii. 1, 2, viz. he himself alone and no other than he.   Leo, writing on the sufferings of the martyrs, and all the saints, well observes, *They have received crowns, they have not bestowed them ; and their fortitude has afforded examples of patience, not rewards of righteousness.**

* Pope Leo I. surnamed the Great ; elected Bishop of Rome in 440, and deservedly reckoned among the Fathers of the Church.   He is allowed on all hands to have been a man of great energy of character, and of decided piety ; and very strenuous for the authority of his See.   He did not, however, claim for it that supremacy over others which was subsequently assumed ; yet it was not a little enhanced in its pretensions by the great respect paid to his personal merits.   Soon after his elevation his episcopal zeal was called into action against the Manichæans, who, fleeing from those provinces in Africa which were at that time ravaged by the Vandals, repaired to Rome in great numbers, and soon infected many with their strange doctrine, and corrupted others with their more strange practices.   And it is worthy of remark, that in opposing their idolatrous worship of the sun as the throne of God's power, and the moon as the seat of his wisdom, Leo was led to aim at suppressing the custom that had long obtained among the Christians, of turning to the east when they prayed.   He alleged two reasons why the custom should be suppressed, and both deserving of particular notice : the first, because men may easily pass from worshipping God in the sun, to worship the sun itself ; for he supposes some, who in his time used to kneel down to the sun, to have paid that respect, not to the sun, but to God in the brightest work of his hands.   The second reason he alleged is, because it is a wicked profanation of the worship of the true God to use the same ceremonies in worshipping him, that are used by the Pagans, when they worship their idols.   By the first of these reasons, as Bower in his life of Leo, has justly observed, images ought to be banished from all places of worship, at least for the sake of the gross and ignorant vulgar, who may easily, and commonly do, pass from the worshipping of God, or our Saviour, in an image or statue, to worship the image or statue itself ; and it may safely be said, that among the *Roman* Catholics there is scarce one in a thousand, who does not immediately address in his prayers the image itself, which is rank idolatry.   By Leo's second reason, the far greater part of the ceremonies used at present by the Church of Rome, are evidently condemned, as a wicked profanation of the worship of the true God ; since most of them have been borrowed of the Pagans, as is notorious, and has been demonstrated by Dr. Middleton, in his " *Exact Conformity between Popery and Paganism,*" and more recently in Gray's " *Connection of Sacred and Classical Literature.*"   By Leo's exertions some of the Manichæans abjured their errors, and having first performed the due penance, were received by him into the church.   Against those who continued obstinate the imperial laws were put into execution, and they were condemned to perpetual banishment.   They deserved, says Leo, a more severe punishment ; but to punish them more severely was repugnant to the spirit of the Church, and to that lenity

3. Lastly, the intention of the person making satisfaction is required, where the sufficiency or satisfaction of one is to be applied to the remission of another : but it can never be shewn, that either Peter, or Paul, or any other saint suffered with the intention of our receiving remission of our sins (as to punishment) by their sufferings. Therefore the third proposition, which supposes a store of satisfactions of the saints transferable to us, falls to the ground.

Argum. 4. If there were a store of merits and sufferings in the Church, (which, as to the merits and sufferings of Christ, is most true, for *in Christ there are all treasures)* yet

in which she places her chief glory, abhorring to shed the blood even of the most detestable heretics. How different the spirit of that church is now (remarks the Biographer of Leo, from whom we here borrow), those too well know who have ever had the misfortune to be any ways concerned with that tribunal, of all that ever was heard of, the most cruel and sanguinary— the Tribunal of the Inquisition. And, we may remark, what different doctrines appear to have been inculcated, as well as different conduct practised in the church of Rome in Leo's time, to what has been since taught and enforced by the Papal See ! At the fourth General Council at Chalcedon, in 451, assembled to condemn the heresy of Eutyches, who, virtually at least, denied the human nature of Christ, the Legate of Leo delivered a letter from him, in which he defended the Scriptural doctrine on the subject, with a perspicuity so extraordinary at that period, that his Epistle was received as a rule of faith, was called emphatically the *Columna Orthodoxæ Fidei,* and constantly read, during Advent, in the Western churches. Leo suppressed the custom of publicly confessing private sins, but recommended auricular Confession, which had been abolished, about 70 years before, by Nectarius, at Constantinople ; and which has since been magnified into a Sacrament. But Leo's most material achievement was the stop which his personal interference put to the ravages of Attila in Italy, whom he persuaded, when at the very gates of Rome, to withdraw his forces. With Genseric he was afterwards, in 455, scarcely less successful ; as, although he could not prevent that barbarian from taking and plundering Rome, he yet so far prevailed as to divert him from his design of burning it. Du Pin, who seldom loses an opportunity of striking at the arrogance and presumption of the head of his own church, observes, " The church of Rome never had more true grandeur and less pride than in this Pope's time. The Bishop of Rome was never more honoured, more considerable, and more respected than in this Pontiff ; and yet never carried himself with more humility, wisdom, sweetness, and charity." He died in 461, having occupied the papal Chair 21 years : His works, which consist of Sermons and Letters, were published by Father Quesnel, in two vols. folio, in 1700.

it is no privilege of the Pope to distribute and dispense this treasure, by his bulls, to individuals expressly named : and that for the following reasons :—

1. The blood, and the passion of Christ, and the store of his merits, is applied to particular persons by the sole operation of the Holy Spirit producing faith, and by the internal operation of faith laying hold on Christ ; but no papal bulls produce faith, nor stir up a man to apprehend its object; therefore they apply neither the blood nor the merits of Christ to men, nor are of any service in the remission of sins. The Pope, then, can do no more for the remission of sins than any other priest : but what is the duty of ministers Paul teaches in 2 Cor. v. 19, *God was in Christ reconciling the world unto himself, and hath committed unto us the word of reconciliation.* He did not grant the power of remitting the punishment of men by bulls even to the Apostles themselves ; but he commanded them, by the word and preaching the Gospel, to encourage men to seek for reconciliation and remission in Christ. Indulgences can be of no use to unbelievers, and to believers they are unnecessary ; because their faith applies the merits and sufferings of Christ to their souls.

2. The dispensing of Christ's blood, and the actual application of his saving merits to a particular person, is entrusted to no man who does not know the person to whom those spiritual benefits are to be imparted; but neither the Pope, nor indeed any other mortal knows this ; for God alone *knows who are his :* therefore God alone bestows indulgences by the application and acceptance of the sufferings of Christ.

3. Real repentance and true contrition of heart, in conjunction with true faith, is more effectual with God in obtaining perfect remission, than any papal indulgence can be; for God himself is far more bountiful than any Roman Pontiff : but, if we believe the Papists themselves, neither the ordinary penitence of the faithful can obtain, nor is the benevolence of God wont to grant, any other forgiveness than from guilt only : it is not, therefore, very likely, that the Pope by virtue of his indulgences should be able to absolve a man forthwith from the penalty.

4. Whatever a limited agent does, if he exceeds the bounds of his commission, goes for nothing: but the Pope, in pretending to remit by his bulls, those temporal punishments which divine justice requires them to endure, exceeds the bounds of his commission; for God never delegated such authority to him. Punishments of his own imposing for discipline's sake, he may relax; but those which the Divine justice has determined to exact, he cannot.

5. The Pope cannot de facto absolve any man from those penal chastisements which God is pleased, not uncommonly to inflict, after true repentance; again, therefore, he boasts falsely of his power by bulls to free men from the temporal punishment of their sins. For when God has determined to chasten any man by disease of body, death of children, or loss of property, no plenary indulgence of the Pope can deliver him at all from these temporal afflictions.

6. The remission of sins is fully set forth in Holy Scripture; but this remission by means of indulgences is (as the Papists confess) authorised neither by the Scriptures or the ancient Fathers, but has been brought into repute merely by the act of the Roman Pontiffs. *The Scripture does not speak expressly of indulgences,* says Durandus, lib. 4. disp. 20. qu. 3, *nor do the holy Fathers say a word about them.* Silvester Prierias,* the master of the sacred palace

* Silvester Prierias; so called from his birth-place, Prierio, a village in Montserrat: but his proper name was Mazolini (vide Biographie Universelle, tom. xxviii. p. 30). He was a Dominican Monk, who flourished at the beginning of the 16th century. The date of his birth has not been ascertained; but it is known that he embraced the Monastic life while very young. He studied theology, civil and canon law, and geometry; and, for some time, was a Professor at Bologna. Called to Rome to teach theology, he was soon after nominated Master of the Sacred Palace. He was one of the earliest writers against Luther; but, notwithstanding the lavish commendation bestowed upon his labours by most Italian Biographers, he was not equal to contend with the great Reformer, and Leo X. prohibited Mazolini from continuing to write on the points under discussion; a principle upon which the Roman See has often found it convenient to rest, in order to avoid the bringing out of the whole truth. He, however, nominated him one of Luther's judges; an inconsistency which was severely and justly

(as they call it), says, *the system of indulgences is no where set forth in Scripture.* And further, neither Gratian* himself, nor the master of the sentences, makes any mention of these empty bulls of the Roman Pontiffs.

Lastly, the Schoolmen themselves cannot agree as to the intrinsic value of indulgences ; wherefore almost all of them advise those who have procured them, to fulfil all the prescribed penances notwithstanding ! And they furthermore add, that to render them effectual there must be a

reprehended by the Protestant writers. The time and place of Mazolini's death are equally unknown ; but it is asserted his morals were very relaxed. He was the author of 47 works in Latin, or in Italian, on theology, philosophy, and mathematics: these have long since fallen into oblivion. One of the most popular (for it passed through several editions in the 16th century) was his Summa Silvestrina, seu Summa de Peccatis aut Casuum Conscientiæ, vel Summa Summarum : Bologna,⹂1515, 2 vols. 4to. This, most probably, is the work cited by Davenant. With respect to the admission made by the author as adduced above, Craig, in his " Refutation of Popery," has given it with an amplitude which the Translator cannot withhold from his Readers. He introduces it thus: " Sylvester Prierias, in his controversy with Luther, says, That indulgences have not been made known to us by the authority of the Scripture, but by the authority of the Roman Church, and of the Roman Pontiffs, which is greater. Indulgentiæ auctoritate Romanæ Ecclesiæ, Romanorumque Pontificum quæ est major. Thereby constituting the authority of the Pope superior to that of revealed Scripture. As his partisans have elevated his personal authority in the Church, far above the authority of revealed Scripture, this has a direct tendency to render Christianity, like Mahometanism, a system of human institution—an invention of man."—Our Expositor might have added farther, in confirmation of the position in his last Section, an admission of Aquinas, Sum. part. 1. Qu. 1. art. 8 et 10, " Our faith is founded upon revelations made by prophets and apostles. The church has instituted nothing except such things as are not essentially necessary to salvation."

* Gratian :—a Benedictine Monk of Bononia, in Italy, of the 12th century, was a native of Chiusi, and was the author of the first portion of the " Decretals," or " Concordantia discordantium Canonum ;" in which he attempts to reconcile those Canons which seem to contradict each other. One mode of doing this was by maintaining the dogma of Infallibility. The following is his doctrine on the subject, Cap. 6. dist. 40, " Si papa infinitas animas secum in infernum traherit, tamen nemo dedit ei dicere, quid facis ? Though the Pope should draw with him innumerable souls to hell, yet no man ought to say to him, What doest thou ?" Gratian was, however, guilty of some errors, which Anthony Augustine endeavoured to correct in his work entitled " De emendatione Gratian." Gratian's Decretal forms the first part of the Canon law.

reasonable cause for them : but if they applied to men the merits of Christ, *they* would procure remission of sins, let the cause of their being granted be ever so trifling. Vid. Gerson, par. 2. tract. de indul.

But now let us meet the arguments of our adversaries. And here they discover a singular hardihood; for though they themselves acknowledge that indulgences cannot be proved from Scripture, yet do they endeavour to wrest many parts of Scripture to this purpose. As for instance,

1. *I will give unto thee the keys of the kingdom of heaven; and whatsoever thou shalt bind on earth shall be bound in heaven, and whatsoever thou shalt loose on earth shall be loosed in heaven,* Matth. xvi. 19. What was given to Peter was given to the Pope; and from this passage it is evident, that ample powers of absolving, as well from the guilt as the punishment, were given to Peter : Therefore, &c. Cajetan. opusc. tract. 8.

I answer. This power of absolution, if we speak of a man's own conscience, is exercised by ministers, not in dealing out indulgences, but in the preaching of the Gospel ; and that not *authoritatively*, but *declaratively ;* which, indeed, the Papists themselves are forced to confess : for they acknowledge that when a man is truly contrite and penitent, his sins are forgiven him, before the form of absolution has been administered.

2. *For what I myself forgive, if I have forgiven any thing, for your sakes forgave I it in the person of Christ,* 2 Cor. ii. 10. From which passage Aquinas argues thus : *I have forgiven, in the person of Christ,* signifies the same as if Christ had forgiven. But Christ is able to remit the punishment due to sin, independently of any satisfaction of our own by indulgence : therefore, Paul *could,* and therefore, also, the Pope *can,* whose authority in the Church is not a whit less than Paul's was. Aquin. Suppl. 3. part. q. 25. art. 1.

I answer, The Apostle is here speaking of a certain Corinthian who had committed incest; and he exhorts the Corinthians, who had referred the case to him, to receive him back again into the Church, though he had been excommunicated, because he had professed sincere repen-

tance ; and he encourages them to do so by his own example. But Aquinas here seems to imagine that certain penances had been imposed upon this incestuous person for
the satisfaction of divine justice, which Paul by his authority had relaxed ; which is altogether foreign to the plain
sense of the passage.

3. *I am a partaker of all them that fear thee,* Ps. cxix.
63. Therefore satisfactory works done by one may be
transferred to others for the remission of sins, Thom. 3. in
suppl. quæst. 71. art. 1.

I answer, The prophet is here saying nothing more, than
that he endeavours to separate himself from the ungodly,
and to associate with the godly and faithful : nor did the
communication of works of satisfaction enter his mind.—
The Schoolmen are in the habit of bringing many other
arguments of this sort to confirm this doctrine of indulgences, and of transferring satisfactions from one to another ; but they are adapted so ridiculously to this purpose,
that they are not worth the trouble of refutation. Passing
over their *testimonies,* therefore, let us come to their *arguments.*

1. The common blessings of the Church are at the disposal of the head of the Church : but the store of merits
of Christ and the saints are the common blessings of the
Church, and the Pope of Rome is the head of the Church ;
therefore, he may dispense those blessings by his indulgences.

I answer, We admit that the spiritual blessings of the
Church are dispensable by the ministers of the Church ;
but not in any way they please. Therefore they are said to
dispense these common blessings by preaching, and by administering the sacraments ; but not by the sale of indulgences. As to the store, or treasure spoken of, we answer,
that it consists of the sufferings of Christ alone, and
not in the smallest degree of the sufferings of the saints.
And as to the Pope, he neither is head of the Church, nor,
if he were, can he, by any vested right, dispose of this
store or treasure. For what Cajetan here says is very true,
The store of the merits of Christ cannot be interfered with by

the Pope, unless to be dispensed in a lawful manner. Cajet.
de Indulg. tract. 9. quæst. 1. But the dealing them out by
bulls is no lawful act, because it is not built upon the command of the Supreme Lord, who directed his Apostles to
dispense the merits of Christ to the faithful by preaching
the word and administering the sacraments, &c.

2. They who are reconciled to God remain still, after
the remission of their guilt, bound to make satisfaction for
the remission of the temporal punishment they have deserved ; and this we see proved by many convincing examples in the Scriptures. God forgave David the crimes of
adultery and homicide, yet he adds, *Because thou hast given
much occasion for the enemies of the Lord to blaspheme, therefore the child shall surely die,* 2 Kings xii. 14, So in Numb.
xiv. *I have pardoned the sin of the people: nevertheless not one
of them shall see the promised land.* So again, after God had
forgiven David the sin of numbering the people, he nevertheless punished him by sending a pestilence to lay waste
the kingdom. From this sort of expressions the Papists
conclude that the divine justice exacts satisfaction from us
for the ends of punishment, after the forgiveness of the
guilt itself; and then they add of themselves, that this
satisfaction may be fully made, not only by our own sufferings and merits, but by those which are dealt out at the
Pope's pleasure, from the common treasury.

In answer to all this ; I admit that the faithful do experience much chastisement at the hand of God, after he has
forgiven their guilt; but I deny that the intention of these
chastisements is to satisfy divine justice. Although God
absolves all true penitents from all satisfaction by punishment, for the sake of Christ's death, yet he does not excuse them from all salutary and chastening visitations.
There is then a fallacy in the *consequence,* when the Papists
draw this inference—The faithful, after their sins are forgiven them, endure temporal punishments ; therefore they
endure them to satisfy the wrath of God. Another end,
therefore, being assigned, this sophism is solved. Augustine specifies three purposes, viz. *The exhibition of the misery
due to sin, the amendment of our sinful lives, and the necessary*

trial of our patience; Tractat. in Joan. 124. But now what the Papists have been pleased to set forth in addition, viz. that men may by indulgences be absolved from these temporal punishments, which otherwise, by every rule of divine justice, they ought to have been subjected to, is very plainly refuted from the above cited passages. For the Pontiff, by all the powers of his bulls, can neither defend the true penitent from the death of children, nor from a general pestilence, nor inflict any other chastisement than such as is according to the good pleasure of God.

3. From that communion of saints, which is an article of our Creed, they argue, that the satisfactory works of the saints which were not immediately wanting for their own individual expiation, are laid up in store for the public benefit, and from thence may be dispensed by the Pope, who is appointed treasurer of this fund.

I answer, They assume two false hypotheses ; one, of the superabundance of the merits and sufferings of the saints ; the other, of the power of the Pope; both of which we have already refuted. As to the foregoing inference from the communion of saints, we assert, that this communion consists in our participation of one God, one Christ, one baptism, one spiritual life, and, finally, of the same mystical union with one Head, and with each other; and not in the communication of satisfactions. And the reason is evident, because to make satisfaction for another, and to liberate him from the punishment which divine justice requires, is a work of mediation, not of simple love. The offices of charity are indeed common amongst all the members of the same body ; the offices of a Mediator can be performed by no one member to another, but proceed from the Head alone to all the other parts ; for he alone is the Mediator between God and men.

In the last place, to return from our digression, from this passage of Paul which we are now considering, and which was the occasion of my discussing this controversy, Cajetan argues as follows; Holy men suffered with the very view and intention of making satisfaction thereby for others ; for Paul expressly says, that he was *filling up that which remained of the sufferings of Christ, for his body's sake which is the Church.* And the Rhemish doctors infer from it that the penal works of one member do make satisfaction for others.

I answer, Paul's real meaning we have already explained, viz. that he bore his many afflictions for the Church, not to expiate sins, but for its edification and confirmation in the doctrine of the Gospel. When, therefore, they argue that from the circumstance of Paul having suffered many afflictions for the Church, he did so to make satisfaction to God for the Church, their argument is absurd ; for we have assigned other causes for it. But we will confirm this our interpretation by the testimony of Anselm, and then conclude. *I fill up, says he, those things which are wanting. But to whom (or where) are they wanting? In* MY *body. For in the body of Christ, to which the Virgin gave birth, no suffering was wanting ; but in my body a part of his sufferings yet remain, which I endure daily in behalf of his universal body, which is the Church. For if I ceased to teach the faithful, I should not sustain these sufferings from those who are without faith : but inasmuch as I am always endeavouring to benefit the Church, I am always forced to endure afflictions.* Such is Anselm's interpretation.* From which it appears

* Anselm; Archbishop of Canterbury in the eleventh century, who, though distinguished for his anxiety to uphold the power of the Roman Pontiff, deserves to be remembered as a learned and devotional writer, and as one of the principal revivers of literature after the prevalence of profound ignorance for three centuries. He was a native of Piedmont, first Prior and then Abbot of Bec, in Normandy. Invited over to England by Hugh, Earl of Chester, he was made Archbishop of Canterbury in 1092, but soon manifested his high Church predilections by refusing to consecrate bishops invested by the king, denying it to be the king's prerogative. His obstinacy on this and many such points, has laid his memory under much obloquy ; as he was thereby engaged in perpetual broils with William Rufus and Henry II. respecting the affairs of the Church ; and much of his time was spent in travelling backwards and forwards between England and Rome, to obtain the advice and direction of the Pope. He died in 1109, aged 76. His works, with all his faults, bear certain testimony that his piety was sincere and fervent.

that Paul suffered those afflictions for the Church, that he
might thereby continually instruct the Church, not that he
might make satisfaction for the sins of its faithful members.

But let us leave these Papists to their dreams about human merits, and their delusions of Papal indulgences, and
return to the explanation of the context.*

Verse 25.

Of which CHURCH *I am made a minister according to the
dispensation of God which is given to me for you to fulfil the word of God.*

This verse is a continuation of the foregoing one, in
which the Apostle professed the state of mind in which he
endured the afflictions laid on him for preaching the Gos-

---

* The Translator cannot refrain from adding, in this place, a few remarks
to what were made at page 285, on *Indulgences.* The subject is the finest of
all those connected with the system, for illustrating one regular Canon in
the logic of Romanism—that of assuming that the same word signifies the
same thing in the primitive, and in the modern papal use of it; or, in the
present instance, that the *relaxation of canonical penance,* as existing to the
third century and onwards, is the same thing as—a treasury of merits contributed by the Redeemer and the saints, and at the disposal of the Pope—
the release of human souls a pœna et culpa—the remission of sins, full,
fuller, and fullest—pardons, in particular, for tens, hundreds, and thousands of years—all of them facts, not denied, but explained away, by Romanists who know their own religion, and who have some conscience remaining.
Proof enough is in readiness to be produced for all these points; and of the
millenary pardons, the brass tablet in the Chapel of St. Michael, Maccles-
field, is an existing testimony. But perhaps the most satisfactory is derived from the unwilling admission of R. CHALLONER, Bp. of Debra, and
V. A. in his " *Catholic Christian instructed,*" &c. 1788. At page 117, he
writes of these elongated Indulgences, " And thus, if it be true that there
ever were any Grants of *Indulgences* of a thousand years, or more, they are
to be understood with relation to the punishment corresponding to the sins,
which, according to the Penitential Canons, would have required a thousand
or more years of penance"—" as by their sins they (the sinners) had incurred a Debt of Punishment proportionate to so long a time of Penance, these
Indulgences of so many years, if ever granted (which some call in question)

pel ; viz. that it was composed and cheerful ; and for which
he assigned two reasons. The former derived from his conformity with Christ ; *I fill up in my body that which remains
of the sufferings of Christ ;* i. e. by suffering I am made like
unto Christ : therefore *I rejoice in those things which I suffer.*
The other reason is derived from the benefits accruing to
the Church by his sufferings, I endure afflictions *for his body
the Church;* therefore I must and will rejoice in these my
sufferings. Now in this verse 25, he adds a third reason
why he should be so ready and willing to bear any thing
whatever for the Church ; and it is derived from the nature
of his office, *I am made a minister of the Church by God's
ordinance;* therefore, so long as I can be of use to the
Church, I ought to rejoice in my afflictions.

In explanation of this verse there are four points to be
considered :

1. The office itself to which Paul was appointed, described in these words, *of which I am made a minister.*

2. Who assigned this office to him ; viz. God himself :
he was appointed, κατα την οικονομίαν Θεȣ̃, *according to the dispensation* or arrangement *of God.*

3. Those whom this office of Paul regarded ; viz. the
Gentiles, and amongst them the Colossians ; *it is given to
me for you,* &c.

4. What was the scope and purpose of this appointment, viz. *to fulfil the word of God.*

Of which Church I am made a minister.] Minister, or
διακονος, is sometimes a general term, designating any person discharging any office ; sometimes a particular one,
restricted to those who had the care of the revenue of the
Church and of the poor committed to them ; such were those
seven who were set over that business, Acts vi. 3.

---

were designed to release them from this Debt."—Nothing but conviction of
the fact, which it is puerile to dissemble, could have wrung this unwilling
testimony from so bigotted a writer. And it may be inferred from his own
statement, and on his own principles, that if no such Indulgences had existed hitherto, it is high time they were established, particularly in heretical England.

In this verse it is used in that more extensive signification ; yet so as not to express any thing less dignified than
the Apostolic ministry : for the office committed to Paul
was the apostleship, as appears from the words. For he
does not say that he is made a minister of this or that particular Church, but of the Church universal, namely of
that which in the foregoing verse he had called *the body of
Christ.* Now from this mention of his office, and this title
of *minister* which Paul assumes, let us deduce a few observations.

1. The circumstance that Paul, who was constituted an Apostle, should speak of himself as a Minister of
the Church, is an excitement to those who have obtained
the higher situations in the Church, to activity ; and admonishes them to think more of their duties than their honour ; and of the task imposed upon them, rather than the
dignity attached to it. We, alas ! on the contrary, *are
more willing to be called pastors, than studious to be such : we
avoid the labours of our office, but are eager to obtain its honours,* as Prosper lamented of old, De vit. contemp. lib. i.
cap. 21. But we should always recollect, that the very
term *minister,* is rather a title of labour than of dignity.

2. We also infer hence, that those who have the superiority in the Church, have but a ministry, and not an absolute dominion. *I am made* A MINISTER *of the Church,*
says the Apostle, not, *a lord.* Ministers should not, like
earthly potentates, lord it, either over the persons or the
consciences of Christians. This Peter forbids in 1 Epis.
v. 2, 3, *Feed the flock of God which is among you, not as being
lords of the heritage, but being examples to the flock.* And
Paul expresses his aversion to it, 2 Cor. i. 24, *Not that we
have dominion over your faith, but are helpers,* &c. The Roman Pontiff, therefore, who makes himself, not the *minister,* but *the lord* and *God* of the Church, is no successor
either of Paul or of Peter. For, he desires to rule, at least
by an indirect dominion, over both the persons and property of all Christians, and even of kings themselves ; and
by a direct dominion over their faith and consciences, as
far as he imagines that he is constituted a spiritual monarch.

Hence came those extravagances of the Papists, that the
Pope is superior to all councils; that the Pope is infallible
in matters of faith; that those who do not submit to the
Roman Pontiff are not in a state of salvation; that all interpretation of Scripture is to be derived from the repository of his breast; with many other absurdities of this nature. From all which it is clear that he claims not for himself *the pastoral office* in the Church, but assumes *kingly
dominion.*

3. Inasmuch as Paul assigned the ministerial office laid
upon him, as a reason why he ought to rejoice in his afflictions; he wished to impress upon all ministers of the Gospel, that nothing can be more joyous, or truly honourable,
than unjust persecution, whilst they are discharging, and
because they do discharge the duties of their calling. For
as wounds, and even death itself, are glorious to a soldier
in defence of the post in which his commanding officer has
stationed him; so is it the glory of a minister, to suffer
afflictions, nay even death itself, in the discharge of that
ministry which Christ has committed to him.

But here we must always remember that consolation at-
tends upon those afflictions, of which we may say with
Paul, *I suffer these things for the Church, and because I am
a minister of the Church.* But it is a very different thing
indeed, when a man must confess, I suffer these things
from the Church, and because I am a disturber of the
Church. *Let none of you suffer*... *as an evil-doer, or as a
busy body in other men's matters: but if any man suffer as a
Christian, let him not be ashamed, but let him glorify God on
this behalf,* 1 Pet. iv. 15, 16. And thus far as to the office
itself: It next follows as to the Author of the office.

According to the dispensation of God.] The Apostle shews
in these words the authority by which he was made a minister of the Church, viz. by the ordinance of God himself.
In this place, then, by the words, the dispensation of God,
he understands a lawful and defined power given to him by
God for dispensing and administering the spiritual things
pertaining to the Church. For the Church is the household
of God; nor has any person a right to interfere in it in any

way ; but all things are to be done *according to the arrange-*
ment of God himself. So the Apostle observes to the Hebrews, v. 4, *No man taketh this honour unto himself, but he*
that is called of God, as was Aaron. We learn, therefore,
from this word οἰκονομίας, that the Church is like a family ;
that God is the master of this family ; that the apostles,
the bishops, the presbyters, and deacons are the servants
and ministers of God in carrying on the business of the
family.

Hence observe,

1. Since the Church is the household of God, no one
ought to exercise any function in it but by the legitimate
calling of God himself. Now a legitimate calling is either
extraordinary, such as that of the Apostles was formerly ;
or ordinary, such as that of bishops and ministers is now ;
and this ordinary calling ought to be given, under some
visible sign, by those who have ecclesiastical and rightful
jurisdiction, that it may be known to the Church : which is
observed by all Churches in the ordination of ministers.
They who receive orders in this manner have a right to affirm, that they are made ministers *according to the dispensa-*
tion of God. They who have not received this ordination
are but intruders into the concerns of another man's family
without either the appointment or the approbation of the
master.

2. Since ministers are appointed in the Church according to the dispensation of God, we are to understand, that
what they both teach and do is not valid from their sole
command and mere arbitrary authority, but by the delegated authority and approbation of the supreme Lord, i. e.
of God himself. For that which a minister does contrary
to the will of the Lord, can never stand good ; for he is
bound to dispense such things, and in such a manner as the
Lord hath directed.

3. Since in every *arrangement* and the management of
any family, it is requisite there should be order, not only
with respect to the service itself, but also with respect to
the servants themselves, if they are numerous ; it is evident
that those are disturbers of the Church of God, and de-

range *this economy* who endeavour to introduce equality of ministers into the Church. For *order*, according to the correct definition of the Schoolmen, *is the distribution of similar and dissimilar things, assigning to each its proper place;* and wherever there is a plurality without order, confusion immediately arises. Now, according to this arrangement and economy of God, one is appointed a bishop, others are ordained priests, others deacons; nor ought those who are placed in inferior situations to assume those functions which belong to their superiors. For the Lord himself of the family *gave some Apostles; and some Evangelists; and others Pastors and teachers,* Ephes. iv. 11 ; and in place of those, it was his will that ministers should be substituted for ever, distinct in their proper orders.

4. Since God has shewn such care in regulating the administration of the Church, it is the duty of each individual in it, both to know and to do what belongs to his department, by virtue of this divine arrangement. For, as Durandus rightly observes, Lib. 2. disp. 9. quæst. 1, *Without order, action is presumption ; without action, order is negligence; but without knowledge, both action is dangerous and order useless.* Hence also that saying of the Saviour, Matt. xxiv. 45, *Who then is that faithful and wise servant, whom his Lord hath made ruler over his household,* &c. This dispensation of God committed to his ministers, requires both faithfulness *to will,* and wisdom and knowledge *to perform,* the duties assigned to them in this *economy* of God.

And thus far concerning this ministry, and the Author and Ordainer of it, viz. God himself.

Which is given to me for you.] Now, in the third place, we must explain to whom this ministry, or dispensation, which was delegated to Paul by God himself, had relation. *It is given to me,* he says, *for,* or *on account of you;* i. e. *you Gentiles;* amongst whom the Colossians are included. The Apostle seems desirous of shewing, that he taught them in his own right, as a part of the Gentile Church, which was particularly entrusted to him. That this ministry of instructing *the Gentiles* was indeed entrusted to Paul, is evident from many passages of Scripture : As Acts xxii. 21,

Depart, for I will send thee far hence unto the Gentiles. And
Rom. i. 5, *We have received the Apostleship for obedience to
the faith among all nations.* Whence he says, 1 Tim. ii. 7,
*that he is ordained a preacher, and an Apostle, and a teacher of
the Gentiles.*

But here it may be questioned how this dispensation of
God can be said to be given to Paul towards or for the
Gentiles, and not for the Jews also, and so not for all mankind; since the Apostolic office includes plenary and universal power, unbounded and unlimited. For this is assigned by express commands to the Apostles, *Teach all
nations; Preach the Gospel to every creature.* This is resolved as follows:

The Apostles were not confined by virtue of their Apostolic vocation to particular districts or nations; but as it
was very inconvenient for the same men to traverse all
countries; one undertook the management of this, and
another of that province, either by Divine intimation, or by
a private arrangement among themselves. Thus, in the
Epistle to the Galatians, ii. 7, *the Gospel of the uncircumcision* is said *to have been committed to Paul, the Gospel of the
circumcision to Peter;* because Paul was employed in declaring the Gospel to the Gentiles, Peter to the Jews; and
that by a certain special appropriation from God.

But here it is necessary also to add, that this *appropriation,* as we call it, did not at all diminish the Apostle's authority, or prevent Paul's preaching to the Jews, or Peter
to the Gentiles, if occasion should offer itself. Of Paul,
indeed, it is expressly said, that he was *a chosen vessel to
bear the name of God before the Gentiles and the children of
Israel;* and he taught the Hebrews by an Epistle, as is
commonly held.*   Nor is there any doubt but that Peter,
both at Antioch and in other places, instructed not only
the Jews, but also the Gentiles in the doctrine of the Gospel. The general Apostolical power, therefore, respected
all nations alike, but the convenience of the Church re-

* Alluding to doubts which some entertain about the genuineness of this
Epistle.

quired that particular persons should be assigned to certain provinces.

And here let us observe how useful and even necessary is this institution of the Church, that certain ministers be attached to certain places and congregations. For if it pleased God that the Apostles, who, by virtue of their calling, might exercise their pastoral charge equally over the whole world, should nevertheless be especially set over certain particular provinces ; how much more proper is it for those pastors who have not the calling which the Apostle had, to be destined to particular churches marked out for them, that they may be able to say, in superintending that flock, *a dispensation is given to me for* YOU ?

Those, therefore, who would encourage a vagrant and itinerant ministry, in direct opposition to the canons of the ancient Church, which have decreed that no man shall be ordained without a specific title, outrage all reason. Let every man, therefore, understand towards whom a dispensation of the Gospel is given to him, that he may *be able to attend to that flock over which the Holy Ghost has made him an overseer*, as we read in Acts xx. 28. And thus much as to the object of the Apostolic ministry.

To fulfil the word of God.] In these words the Apostle states the end or design which God intended in assigning to him this dispensation of the Gospel towards the Gentiles. But these words are explained by interpreters in two ways. Some say, that *to fulfil the speech*, or *the word of God*, means, fully to expound the whole doctrinal system of salvation, and to promote it to the last moment of life. As if the Apostle had said, *I must not be deterred either by afflictions, or bonds, or even death itself, from preaching the Gospel; for God hath laid on me this charge of the Gospel for the very purpose of my striving unto death in defence of it.* If we adopt this meaning, there are two things to be learnt from it :

1. That a minister is bound not to preach the word vaguely, but πληρωσαι τον λογον, *fully* to explain and to teach every thing that concerns the salvation of his flock.

2. That to preach the whole counsel of God is not suf-

ficient, without our persevering in the discharge of this duty even to the end. Many are fervent and constant in their preaching at the beginning of their ministry, but afterwards grow cold and self-indulgent ; but this is not to *fulfil*, but only to begin the preaching of the word.

Others explain *to fulfil the word of God*, to mean the completing those promises concerning Christ and the calling of the Gentiles which the ancient prophets had foretold. As if the Apostle had said, God has made me an Apostle to you Gentiles, that he might *fulfil* what he had promised by the prophets, to wit, the offer of salvation by Christ. Such was that word of God, Isa. ix. 2, *The people who walked in darkness have seen a great light ; upon them that dwell in the land of the shadow of death, hath the light shined.* And of the same nature is that passage in Zech. ii. 11, *Many nations shall be joined unto the Lord, and shall be my people ; and I will dwell in the midst of thee.* To make good this word of God, a dispensation of the Gospel was given unto Paul for the Gentiles. If we follow this interpretation, we are thence enjoined, that as God, by calling us Gentiles to the knowledge of the Gospel, hath fulfilled his part ; so we, in return, are bound to make good our part by believing, by obeying, and by walking in the light of the Gospel.

Verses 26, 27.

Even the mystery which hath been hid from ages and generations, but now is made manifest to his saints ;
To whom God would make known what is the riches of the glory of this mystery amongst the Gentiles, which is Christ, in you the hope of glory.

These verses have the same end in view as the foregoing, viz. to confirm the Colossians in the doctrine of the Gospel ; and this the Apostle executes by highly extolling its dignity. In the former of them he magnifies it, and at the same time excites them to embrace it, by two considerations : 1. By its antiquity and rarity ; *the mystery hidden from ages and generations.* 2. By its manifestation and the present opportunity ; *but now is made manifest,* &c.

In the latter verse he accomplishes two objects. He shews the cause of this manifestation, viz. *the will of God.* Then he explains more fully what was manifested : first generally ; *the riches of this glorious mystery :* then he explains particularly, what are those riches, or, as it is in the Greek, τίς ὁ πλοῦτος τοῦ μυστηρίου τούτου ; *what is the riches of this mystery,* viz. *Christ* himself dwelling in us by faith ; for thus he becomes to us *the hope of glory.*

Let us begin, then, with the former verse.

Even the mystery which hath been hid from ages and generations.] Here let us consider, 1. What the Apostle understands by *a mystery.* 2. Where it was *hidden.* 3. From *whom* it was hidden.

1. *A mystery* is a religious secret containing some concealed meaning. And a thing is concealed from us, either by the intervention of some other object, or by its positive distance from us. We must moreover know, that the word *mystery* is sometimes applied, in the Scriptures, to express the summary of our Christian faith in the person, the nature, and the offices of Christ ; as, for instance, in 1 Tim. iii. 16, *Without controversy great is the mystery of godliness. God was manifested in the flesh, justified in the Spirit, seen of angels, preached unto the Gentiles, believed on in the world, received up into glory.* Sometimes also it is used, by the figure synecdoche, to express a part only of this mystery, viz. the calling of the Gentiles, and their incorporation into the Church without either circumcision or the other works of the law. The Apostle is speaking of this, Ephes. iii. 3, 5, 6, *God hath made known to me the mystery, which in other ages was not made known to the sons of men; that the Gentiles should be fellow heirs, and of the same body, and partakers of his promises by the Gospel.* In this sense Paul uses the word *mystery* in the passage before us, viz. for the secret counsel of God concerning the salvation of the Gentiles by the grace of the Gospel in Christ : and this is that

mystery for the promulgation of which Paul *was made a mi-nister.*

2. But where and how was this mystery concerning the salvation of mankind by Christ *hidden?* It was hidden, as was slightly touched upon before, in the secret and eternal purpose of God ; for God himself decreed, even from all eternity, to conceal and hide from us this mystery, even until the fulness of the time should come. Therefore was it laid up and removed to a great distance from us. For what can be further removed from human sight, than that which is hid in the secret repository of God's will? Hence it is termed by the Apostle, in Rom. xvi. 25, *the mys-tery kept secret since the world began.* But there was also an interposed veil, as it were, of the legal ceremonies, under which the mystery of future redemption was but darkly intimated even to the Jews themselves.

3. And now, in the third place, if it be enquired *from whom* was this mystery hidden; we do not hesitate to answer, that the clear knowledge of it was hidden, not only from the Gentiles and the Jews, but even from the angels themselves. As to the Gentiles, who, before the coming of Christ, *were sitting in the shadow of death,* there is no doubt but that they neither understood nor expected this eternal life, which Christ brought with him for his people. How indeed could they, when the predictions of the Messiah which was to come, were sealed up from them in the sa-cred Scriptures, and these divine oracles themselves regard-ed as the peculiar property of the Jews? David, therefore, says, in Ps. cxlvii. 19, 20, *He sheweth his word unto Jacob, his statutes and his judgments unto Israel : He hath not dealt so with any nation, and as to his judgments they have not known them.* From the Gentiles, therefore, was this mys-tery absolutely and totally hidden.

With respect to the Jews also, who lived under the Old Testament, this mystery was *partly* and *comparatively* hid-den from them. *Partly,* because, with the exception of the prophets and a few inspired men, the general mass of the Jews, though they did expect the Messiah, expected him only as coming to themselves ; they never thought of

his being intended for the Gentiles. The calling of the
Gentiles, therefore, was a mystery altogether hidden from
the greatest part of the Jews. Then, as to those very prophets and more enlightened Jews, to them also this grace
of the Gospel was a hidden mystery, speaking *comparatively.* For those prophetical revelations were but like a
candle shining in a dark place, in comparison of the declarations of the Evangelists, which are like the shining of
the mid-day sun. They looked to this future calling of the
Gentiles, but only, as through the twilight, very indis-
tinctly ; we look directly upon it in the clear and open
daylight. To this it must be added, that they had only a
general notion of the Gentiles receiving some sort of blessing in the promised seed, at some future time ; but they
had no notion whatever of their being admitted into the
covenant of the sons of God in this manner, that is, without circumcision, and without any kind of obedience to
the Mosaic ritual. And this we are authorised to conclude
from the circumstance of the Apostles themselves not immediately comprehending this great mystery, even after
they had received their commission to preach the Gospel
to every creature. For Peter would not have ventured to
go in to the uncircumcised, unless God had previously
communicated this mystery to him, and given him the
knowledge of it by a supernatural revelation. For thus he
expresses himself, Acts x. 28, *Ye know how it is unlawful
for a man that is a Jew to go in to one of another nation ; but
God hath shewed me that I should not call any man common or
unclean.*

In the last place, not even the angels clearly understood
this mystery of Gospel grace. *For to the principalities and
powers in heavenly places, hath been made known by the Church
the manifold wisdom of God ; according to the eternal purpose
which he purposed in Christ Jesus our Lord ;* Ephes. iii. 10, 11.
This body of the Church, therefore, composed of Jews and
Gentiles, of circumcised and uncircumcised, inasmuch as
it was a mystery concealed from all eternity in the secret
will of God, was to the very angels a new and wonderful
thing.

Observe 1. The doctrine of the Gospel is a sacred mystery; therefore it ought to be received with reverence and purity both of heart and ears. The Gentiles drave all profane and impure persons from their sacred mysteries; how much more becoming is it that every kind of impurity should be discarded from these saving mysteries? *The law commands all men*, says Cicero, 2 De legibus, *to approach the sacrifices with purity:* But the Gospel is, indeed, a sacred secret; therefore, let both the preacher and all his hearers approach it in purity both of mind and body.

2. The Gospel was a mystery concealed from all eternity; therefore it had existed from all eternity; and, consequently, is not a new invention of the Apostles, as the Athenians called it when they took Paul to task for preaching it, saying, Acts xvii. 19, 20, *May we know what this new doctrine whereof thou speakest is? for thou bringest certain strange things to our ears.* The Gospel might indeed sound *new* in the ears of the Athenians; in itself, however, it was not new, but eternal: for in religion nothing but what is false is new. Wherefore, in the Apocalypse, xiv. 6, it is called *the everlasting Gospel*.

3. Since it pleased God that this saving Gospel should be concealed from the whole world for so many ages, the very novelty of its manifestation ought to stimulate us to a serious contemplation of it; for if *other jewels derive their value from their rarity only*, as Tertullian observes, surely this jewel of the Gospel, which not a single being had a clear view of during a period of almost four thousand years, is much more valuable.

Thus far, then, as to the Gospel having been a hidden mystery from all eternity: now let us discuss its revelation and manifestation.

But now is made known to his saints.] Three points may here be remarked upon. 1. Why this mystery was manifested. 2. When. 3. To whom.

1. The Apostle says, that this mystery was *manifested*, not discovered, or brought forth to the light by our labour; to the end that we might understand that no human inge-

nuity was ever able to penetrate or gain access to this mystery of human salvation. Unless, therefore, God himself, who at first concealed it, had thought fit spontaneously to reveal it, the whole human race must have lain in endless night ; no man could have known, none would have sought for the Redeemer of the world.

A twofold reason may be assigned for the necessity of this manifestation, arising on the one hand, from the nature of the things revealed, on the other, from the nature of the human understanding. The things revealed, viz. the mysteries of our salvation in Christ, are supernatural, and dependant entirely on the mere will and dispensation of God. As, for instance, the incarnation of God, the atonement made for sin by his death, salvation by grace through faith in this Mediator, are all of a nature that never could have entered into the human mind, unless God himself had manifested his intention of delivering mankind by these means : for they were all dependant on the free will of God, and not upon any connexion of natural causes.

Now, as to the human understanding; so entirely is it obscured in the thick darkness of sin, that it is not merely dim-sighted, but totally blind to all spiritual perceptions. *The natural man perceiveth not the things of the Spirit of God,* 1 Cor. ii. 14. There is, therefore, a necessity of a Divine manifestation. Augustine, Hypog. 3, beautifully remarks, *Let no man boast of having engendered faith in his heart by the soundness of his own reasonings ; but let him acknowledge that both before the Law, and under the Law, and since the abrogation of the Law, the faith which is in Christ Jesus is savingly revealed to every man by the illumination of grace, which is from God the Father.* For, as Gerson correctly observes, par. 3, *The eye of the soul is become turbid through the infection arising from sensuality, through the cloudiness in the animal faculties, and through blindness in the intellectual.* Therefore, to sum up the whole ; The mystery of the Gospel is above nature ; it depends on the eternal and secret counsel of God. The human mind, through sin, is deteriorated beneath its natural sphere ; its eye is stained,

overclouded, and totally blinded : Therefore this mystery
could never have been comprehended by us, unless it had
been made manifest by God.

From this I shall draw only one conclusion :

It is the extreme of folly to construct a Christian creed
out of philosophical principles; since the doctrine of salvation revealed by the voluntary act of God, could not
have been discovered by any acuteness of human intellect.
Here, then, the Scholastic doctors, and the Papists who
tread in their footsteps, have erred most egregiously, ob-
truding many dogmas, derived not from divine relation, but
from the arguments of blind reason, as articles of the
Christian faith.   Of this nature are free-will, inherent
righteousness, the merits of works, and a great many more,
all to be found in the Ethics of the Philosopher; none
in the Epistles of Paul.   Here, then, that warning of the
Apostle, Col. ii. 8, may properly be introduced ; *Beware
lest any man deceive you through philosophy.*   For, as Tertullian, advers. Marc. lib. 1, truly asserts, *All heresies have
drawn existence from the brains of Philosophers.*

Thus much, then, as to the manifestation itself: Now
let us proceed to notice the time when it was made.

Secondly, the Apostle says, *Now* this mystery is made
manifest.   By using this adverb of time, the Apostle takes
occasion to press upon the Corinthians the present opportunity, which he much wished them to seize; as though he
would say, That which was concealed from all the past
ages, could neither be known, nor received by them, to
their salvation ; but being by the free grace of God, manifested and revealed to you, through the Apostles, at the present time, it both ought, and may be, at the present time,
acknowledged and received by you.

Observe 1.   It is incumbent on all Christians to take
advantage of present time and opportunity, according to
that exhortation, Heb. iii. 15, *To-day, whilst it is called to-
day, if ye will hear his voice harden not your hearts.*   For if
we reject the Gospel, the condemnation which awaits us to
whom it has been manifested, will be greater than that of

those who lived in the past times, and from whom it was concealed.

2. Inasmuch as the Apostle says, it is now *made manifest,* he at once stops the objections of all who exclaim that the doctrine of salvation is a difficult and dark doctrine. Time was when the mystery of the Gospel was hidden, but now it is plain to be seen, and even courts observation : *If our Gospel be hid, it is hid to them that are lost,* 2 Cor. iv. 3. We admit, indeed, that certain passages of Scripture are difficult of comprehension ; but whatever is laid down as necessary to salvation, is plainly and clearly revealed by the Apostles to the whole world. So thought all the Fathers, whatever Sophists may prate to the contrary. We shall select a few testimonies out of many. Clemens Alexandrinus, in Protrept. calls the Scripture, *the sun of the soul. The light,* says he, *is common to all, and the word is hidden from none. There is no Cimmerius in the word.** Augustine, lib. 2, De doctr. Christ. cap. 9, says, *Every thing which pertains to faith and moral practice, is found in those parts of Scripture which are plainly expressed.* Chrysostom, Hom. 3. De Lazaro, says, *The Philosophers wrote with obscurity ; but the Apostles and Prophets, on the contrary, set forth all things openly and clearly, and as general teachers of the world, brought them down to the level of all capacities, that every man might be able to learn for himself what was spoken by merely reading them.* To these testimonies of the Fathers we may also add that of Gerson, par. 1 : *The literal sense of Scripture expresses plainly enough every thing necessary for salvation.* From these extracts, then, we may collect, what enormous guilt the Popish Prelates bring upon themselves, who, under the lying pretext of obscurity (as if really the mystery of salvation were not laid open) snatch the Evangelical books out of the hands of the people, and thrust their own wild fantasies and traditions into their places. But we assert that the mystery of salvation is now laid open in the doctrine of the Apostles, and that no man

---

* Vide Note p. 92, for Cimmerius.

has a right either to conceal the Gospel, or to force new mysteries of salvation in its place.

To his saints.] The Apostle in these words points out *to whom* the Gospel was manifested.

Now some understand the word *saints* to mean those whom God decreed to be consecrated in Christ Jesus, i. e. the elect. Others restrict its meaning to the Apostles, the Evangelists, and such like, gifted with the spirit of prophecy ; to whom God directly manifested this mystery, that they might be his Ministers in revealing the same to all the world : They suppose that these are called *saints* by way of eminence. If we adopt the first sense and interpretation, we must not apply it to every kind of revelation, but only to that which is effectual, and brings salvation home to the hearts of the hearers ; which produces not a mere knowledge of Christ, but, at the same time, a real trust in Christ thus known. For in this way was the Gospel manifested to the saints alone, according to the words of Isaiah, liii. 1, *Who hath believed our report, and to whom hath the arm of the Lord been revealed?* Which words are accordant with that declaration of the Saviour, Matth. xiii. 11, *To you it is given to know the mysteries of the kingdom of heaven, but to them it is not given.* To hear, indeed, is given and granted to all ; but to know unto salvation, is given only to the saints and the elect. Hence we may deduce two points of doctrine :

1. It is no disparagement to the dignity or the truth of God, that the numbers of those who really believe, and in their hearts embrace the truth, is small; for though, like seed, it is sown universally, yet it strikes root only in the hearts of the elect, in which the Holy Spirit powerfully operates. For *all men have not faith,* 2 Thess. iii. 2. But *if any man be of God, he heareth God's words,* John viii. 47 ; because he himself *opens the hearts* of the elect, that *they give heed* to the Gospel, Acts xvi. 14. Gregory says, *Unless the Holy Spirit be in the heart of the hearer, useless are the words of the preacher.* And in the same strain Augustine remarks, *Many hear, but those only are persuaded to whom God speaks inwardly.*

2. Wisdom unto salvation belongs only to the saints and to the godly : the ungodly and the unholy have the mystery of salvation preached to them, but they do not receive it, unto salvation ; for hearing they do not hear, and understanding they do not understand. *Wisdom does not enter into a wicked heart, nor will dwell in a body that is subject to sin. For the Holy Spirit of discipline will flee deceit,* Wisdom. Ch. i. ver. 4. True wisdom in the mysteries of God is ever accompanied with sanctity, but iniquity with folly.

But, as was before stated, others understand by the word *saints,* the Apostles, &c. to whom that hidden mystery was manifested in some extraordinary manner. If we admit this explanation, we must understand an extraordinary and immediate manifestation by the Holy Spirit; for the Holy Spirit revealed the mystery of salvation to the Apostles immediately, that through the medium of their ministry it might be revealed to all others. *But the Comforter, which is the Holy Spirit, whom the Father will send in my name, he shall teach you.* John xiv. 26.

That we, then, may obtain the full meaning of the Apostle, let us unite these separate interpretations in one, and conclude thus : This mystery is manifested *primarily* to the Holy Apostles, and *secondarily* to other saints ; *immediately* to the Apostles, *mediately* to all the servants of God.

Verse 27.

To whom God would make known what is the riches of the glory of this mystery among the Gentiles, which is Christ in you, the hope of glory.

Having treated in the foregoing verse on the concealed and manifested mystery of salvation, let us now proceed with the Apostle, who does three things in this one verse :

1. He adds the reason why that mystery, hidden from so many ages past, should now be revealed to the saints.

2. He distinguishes this mystery of salvation, as he proceeds, with new encomiums, viz. *riches* and *glory*.

3. He states specifically what are the riches and what is the glory of this saving mystery; namely, *Christ* himself dwelling in us by faith.

As for the first; the Apostle adds the reason of this divine dispensation, for the purpose of answering an implied objection. For it might be asked, If this doctrine of the Gospel be the doctrine of salvation, why was it not made known to the world during so many ages? Why even now is it made known effectually only to the elect and to those who are sanctified by the Spirit? The Apostle gives no other reason for this distinction than the will of God: *This mystery was made manifest to those to whom God was pleased to make it known.* The same will of God, therefore, is the cause both of that *concealment*, by which the Gospel was hidden from the ages gone by; and of that *revelation* by which it is now made manifest to his saints.

Some persons fondly pretend, that that barbarous age was not fit to receive such mysteries; but that in this its more matured period, the world became wiser, and more capable of receiving the doctrine of salvation. But this supposition is grounded on a false hypothesis; for the grace of God does not *find*, but *make* men fit for receiving grace. Others again imagine, that God in mercy refrained from revealing the doctrine of salvation to those ancient times, because he foreknew that they would reject it. But this reasoning also is refuted by experience; for the foreknowledge of human pride and infidelity does not stop the promulgation of the Gospel. Nay more, God suffers it to be preached expressly to many to whom it is *the savour of death unto death*, 2 Cor. ii. 16. So that it is useless to seek for, or to give any reason why the mystery of salvation was so long hidden from so many nations, and why it was afterwards revealed, beyond that of God's will, *Who in times past suffered all nations to walk in their own ways*, Acts xiv. 16. Hence then let us learn,

1. How rash is that maxim of the Schools, viz. That it is a part of Divine Providence to provide for every man

the necessary means of salvation. For since the revelation
of a Mediator is absolutely necessary for salvation, and yet
no provision was made for the revelation or knowledge of
this Mediator for so many generations of mankind ; either
their assertion is false, or the Providence of God defective.
For, as Augustine truly observes, De civit. lib. 18. cap. 47,
*Salvation is not to be granted to any man except to him to
whom has been revealed, by the will of God, the one Mediator
between God and man—Christ Jesus.*

2.   That notion of the Schools is also of very dubious
import, viz. *That there is no man who does the best in his
power to whom God will not reveal what is necessary for his salvation,* Durand. lib. 2. As is also this, lib. 3, which is nearly
akin to it : *If a man lives well according to the law of nature,
God will supply what is necessary for his salvation.* Both
these axioms of the Schools are faulty in two respects :
First, in the supposition that a man in his natural corrupt
state either is able to live well, or to seek after grace.
Secondly, in the supposition that a revelation of saving
grace is due to those natural works and exertions. Prosper had learnt better things when he said, Ad capit. Gall.
resp. 8, *It is the part of impiety to teach that the grace by
which we are saved, is conferred upon us as the reward of our
good works, or is withheld from us by reason of our bad ones.*

Lastly, as the will of God was the only acknowledged
cause why the Gospel, after being concealed for so many
ages, was afterwards manifested to the whole world ; so
the same will of God is the cause of its being known effectually to the saints ; and of its striking on the ears of the
reprobate without fruit. So Paul states in this very passage, *It is made manifest to his saints, to whom God would
make it known.* So also testified the Saviour himself, Matt.
xi. 25, *I thank thee, O Father, Lord of heaven and earth,
because thou hast hid these things from the wise and prudent,
and hast revealed them unto babes. Even so, Father, for so it
seemed good in thy sight.* This will of God in the effectual
illumination of the elect is *operative,* and, as the Schoolmen express it, has respect to his intention ; and therefore
performs what he approves. But the case is very different

with the unbelieving : for in offering to them the doctrine
of salvation, God is also willing that they should receive
it ; but he wills it with a will *approving ;* not with a will
operating and *producing.*   Under this persuasion, Prosper,
ad Capit. Gall. respons. 5, observes, *The effect upon those
whose outward ears are saluted by a bodily voice, is a different
thing from the effect upon those whose inward sense God hath
opened, and in whose hearts he has laid the foundation of faith
and the fervour of love.*—And thus far as to the cause of
concealment and of the manifestation of this mystery of
salvation, viz. *the good pleasure of God.*

2. *What is the riches of the glory of this mystery amongst
the Gentiles.*]   The Apostle here proceeds to set off the
mystery of the Gospel now offered to all nations, but effectually made manifest only to the saints, with fresh encomiums, ascribing to it *riches* and *glory :* it is a mystery
rich, abundant, and withal *glorious.*

First, as to what pertains to *the riches* of this mystery,
God, in this calling of the Gentiles, has unfolded his spiritual treasures, and offered to men the vast and admirable
riches of his mercy, his goodness, and his grace ; as it is
expressed, Ephes. ii. 7, *He shews to the ages to come the exceeding riches of his grace.*   Nor are they only offered to us
on the part of God ; but if we are enrolled amongst his
saints, we have actually received those most desirable
riches of *wisdom, righteousness, sanctification,* and *redemption ;* 1 Cor. i. 30. Speaking of these riches, Christ says,
Rev. iii. 18, *I counsel thee to buy of me gold tried in the fire,
that thou mayest be rich ; and white raiment, that thou mayest
be clothed, and that the shame of thy nakedness do not appear.*
With these riches this mystery of the Gospel is filled.

1. Learn hence, that were it not for this grace of the
Gospel, the whole world would be in misery, in want, in
beggary. Men, being blind, do not perhaps feel this their
spiritual indigence ; but that insensibility does not lessen
their want ; as it is said Rev. iii. 17, *Thou sayest, I am rich,
and increased with goods, and have need of nothing ; and
knowest not that thou art wretched, and miserable, and poor,
and blind, and naked.*   Such is the condition of all those

who have not yet been made partakers of the riches which the Gospel brought to light.

2. Hence we learn what sort of riches we ought to thirst after, and pursue even with insatiable desire; not, forsooth, the dirty ore dug up from the dirty earth, but those heavenly and spiritual treasures sent down from above. For this grace contained in the mystery of the Gospel, is that *pearl of great price,* which a wise merchant, when he has once seen, will immediately sell all he has in the world to buy, Matth. xiii. 46. As, then, we should consider the heir of some king, or other rich man, to be mad, who, thinking nothing of all his hereditary property, employed himself in scraping together the ordure from his father's stable as his riches; so ought a similar suspicion of madness to attach to any man, who can disregard these riches which his heavenly Father has offered him in the Gospel, and give up his whole heart to scraping together gold and silver, which, in comparison with the other, are to be accounted as dung. Phil. iii. 8.

Lastly, from the Gospel mystery containing such great riches, an argument may very seasonably be derived in favour of the dignity of the Gospel ministry: For what office can be conceived more honourable than that of Ministers, who are entrusted with the power of dispensing such great and valuable riches? Whoever, therefore, despises these Ministers, does but too plainly prove his contempt of God himself; and, like swine, trample the Gospel pearl under his feet.

Thus much as to the riches of this mystery.

But, as if this were too little in so great a matter as the mystery of our salvation, the Apostle adds, that it is not only a *very rich,* but also a very *glorious* mystery; τίς ὁ πλοῦτος τῆς δόξης, &c. *What is the riches of the glory.* Indeed, it is well worthy of observation, that not only in the verses before us, but almost every where else, when he speaks of the riches of this Gospel mystery, he adds something about its *glory.* Thus Rom. ix. 23, *That he might make known the riches of his glory,* &c. And Eph. i. 18, he wishes *the eyes of their understanding to be enlightened, that they might know what is the hope of the calling of the Gospel, and what the riches of the glory of his inheritance in the saints.*

The Apostle introduces the word *glory* that he may obviate the scandal which men pretend arises from the contemptibleness of the Gospel : for in the estimation of carnal men, the doctrine of the Gospel seems contemptible. That all men, therefore, may be assured that there is nothing really contemptible in the Gospel, he employs these splendid eulogies to exalt its dignity ; nay more, to shew that it is altogether so glorious as deservedly to claim every kind of honour.

This mystery of salvation, then, contained in the Gospel, is properly called *glorious* for two reasons ; one of which may be considered on God's part, the other on ours.

On God's part, because nothing so properly shews forth the divine glory, as does the manifestation of the grace of the Gospel in Christ Jesus. From whence arose that hymn of the angels, Luke ii. 14, *Glory to God in the highest, and on earth peace, good-will towards men.* For as true glory arises from the manifestation of virtue, all the divine virtue and goodness shone forth in the free calling of the Gentiles to salvation by the Gospel. For in it the truth of God, his compassion, his justice, his wisdom shine forth ; as might be abundantly proved were we inclined to descant more at large on this general topic. But let us fix upon only one of these virtues, viz. the divine compassion : of which Cicero has well remarked, De Offic. 2, *It most redounds to our glory, if ever we have opportunity, of helping a man who appears to be surrounded and borne down by a powerful enemy.* To which we may add, that it is more eminently glorious to exert this kindness when neither called upon so to do by the deserts of the individual relieved, nor induced to it by any prospect of remuneration. Now let us apply this observation to the case before us. The whole human race lay prostrate under the tyrannous oppression of that most powerful of all enemies, the devil ; but the mystery of the Gospel teaches us, that through the aid of the Divine compassion, and without any previous merit of our own, we are snatched from under the burden of their oppression and set at liberty ; therefore, it best illustrates the glory of God, and most correctly, in this respect, is it called a *glorious* mystery.

On our part, moreover, it may be called *a glorious mystery,* because it ensures to believers real and eternal glory ; nay more, by the power of faith it puts them into present possession of it. On this account it is preferred to the law of Moses, 2 Cor. iii. 7, 8, *If the ministration of death was glorious, how shall not the ministration of the Spirit be rather glorious?* And in the Epistle to the Hebrews, xii. 18, *Ye are not come to the mount that might be touched, and that burned with fire, nor unto blackness, and darkness, and tempest; but ye are come unto mount Zion, and the city of the living God, the heavenly Jerusalem, and to an innumerable company of angels.* To this glory the Gospel calls and conducts those who are sanctified and faithful, and, therefore, there is the best of reasons for its being called *a glorious mystery.*

Now there are two sorts of men which stand reproved by this divine attribute : First, they who endeavour so to interpolate and mutilate the doctrine of the Gospel, as well nigh to obliterate *the riches* and *glory* of the divine compassion contained in it. And here it is that the Papists have sinned most grievously ; ascribing, as they do, the power of washing away sin and procuring salvation, to their own merits and satisfactions, free-will, and other absurdities of this sort, and thus concealing this glory of the compassion and free mercy of God, which constitutes this mystery *glorious.* For this mystery of the Gospel is no longer glorious to God if we may be allowed to boast of our own good works, and to obtain salvation through their merits.

They also are glanced at who, in the profession of the Gospel, neither regard nor look for any thing better than external peace, worldly honours, and temporal accommodations of this kind. This mystery of the Gospel is indeed fruitful, honourable, and glorious ; but it promises fruits of another kind, other honours, and glory of a very different description. It brings with it fruits, not of money, but of righteousness ; honours, not of the world, but of heaven ;

glory, not of fleeting vanity, but of eternal blessedness.
It is, therefore, our business to seek for glory in the way
of this glorious mystery; according to the exhortation of
Christ, Matth. vi. 33, *Seek ye first the kingdom of God and
his righteousness, and all these things shall be added unto you.*
Ye see, then, that the treasures of riches and glory are
offered to us in the Gospel : And now let us consider in
whom these riches and this glory are vested, and how they
are derived to us.

Which is Christ in you, the hope of glory.] The relative
which has *riches*, not *mystery*, for its antecedent.   For the
Apostle had been, in the foregoing verses, celebrating *the
riches*, or *the abundance* of this Gospel mystery; and now
he adds, by way of explanation, *which riches*, or *abundance
is Christ himself*, whose indwelling *in you* produces *the hope
of eternal glory*.   Here, then, two points arise for consideration :

1.   That *Christ* himself is that treasure of spiritual
riches which is offered to us in the Gospel.

2.   That Christ confers these treasures upon us, as far as
he is in us; for thus is he *the hope of glory.*

There can be no necessity for our taking much trouble to
prove that we have *in* Christ the hidden treasures of all the
spiritual goods which are offered us in the Gospel : For in
the third chapter of Ephes. vers. 8, they are spoken of
under the title of *the unsearchable riches of Christ.*   And in
Col. ii. 3, the Apostle distinctly asserts, that *all the treasures
of wisdom and knowledge are hid in Christ.*   The reason of this
is evident ; viz. because Christ is the head of the Church ; and
from the head, as from a fountain, all life and spiritual motion
in the inferior members is derived.   Nor do we only derive
every indwelling grace from Christ, but also the grace of
Divine acceptance into life eternal, as far as we are reckoned in Christ the Head, and are found clothed with the garment of his perfect righteousness.   In Christ, therefore,
all our riches are laid up ; in Christ is all our *hope of glory.*

But inasmuch as it is but too clear and evident, that all
men are not made partakers of these riches ; therefore, in
the second place, the Apostle adds how Christ is made the

treasure of the riches of salvation to men; by what means they have in Christ their hope of glory; namely, as far as *he dwells in them,* so far they have the hope of glory. But Christ is said *to be,* or *to dwell* in any man, when he, by the Holy Spirit exciting faith in the heart, attains to a true knowledge of him, and a living trust flowing from that knowledge. He, therefore, who truly believes all the doctrines concerning the natures, and the union of the natures, and the peculiar offices of Christ; his being, for instance, very God and very man, the Mediator and Redeemer of the human race, and the other points which are revealed in the Word; who, by the inspiration of the same Spirit, is fully persuaded that Christ is so to him as he is in himself, i. e. his God, his Mediator, Redeemer and Saviour; the man, I say, who implicitly believes these things, dwells in Christ, and Christ in him, and by the operation of his Spirit and of faith, receives all the riches of Christ. Upon this ground, Christ himself plainly declares, in John xv. that when separated from him we are dead as to spiritual life; *I am the Vine, ye are the branches: he that abideth in me and I in him, the same bringeth forth much fruit. He that abideth not in me, is cast forth as a branch, and is withered.* But now, we abide in Christ when bound to him by faith and the Spirit. Now the uses of this are these;

1. Since so long as Christ is not in us we cannot be partakers of his spiritual blessings; let us labour, by faith in him, to induce him to take up his abode with us: for, as Cyprian truly says, *It is by faith, and not by personal contact, we are united to Christ in this life.*

2. Since we can have no hope of obtaining glory, either in ourselves, or in angels, or saints, or any where out of Christ alone; much less let us look for it in our own works. It is an excellent remark of Gerson, in a Poem which he calls " Testamentum Peregrini," part. 2;

> *Seek not the robe of works:—By blood*
> *And by pollution stained, they will but bring*
> *Confusion too and shame of face.*

Let this discussion suffice for those three points which in this verse I proposed to consider; viz. the cause of the concealment and of the revelation of this mystery which bringeth salvation: the commendations of this mystery ; that it is rich, and glorious : and the person by whom and in whom we are made partakers of all spiritual blessings, viz. by Christ, and in Christ, through the agency of the Spirit, and faith the gift of the Spirit.

Verse 28.

Whom we preach, warning every man, and teaching every man in all wisdom, that we may present every man per-fect in Christ Jesus.

The Apostle has already brought forward many argu-ments to confirm the Colossians in the doctrine of the Gospel which they had received : here he adds another, drawn from his own labour in advancing it : as if he meant to say, That very same Gospel which Epaphras preached among you, I myself am announcing to the whole world ; which I should not do, were I not certain that it is the only doctrine of salvation: Take care, therefore, that ye be not driven away from it.—But I proceed to the exposition of the words themselves by observing, that the Apostle effects three objects :

1. He shews the main subject of his preaching ; *whom we preach,* &c.

2. He points out the manner of his preaching ; *warning every man,* &c.

3. He declares the aim and intention of his preaching; *that we may present every man,* &c.

1. *Whom we preach.*]   *Whom,* namely Christ, the image of God, the Head of the Church, the source of all fulness, the only Mediator and Redeemer of mankind, dwelling in you by faith, and ensuring to you the hope of eternal glory ; this Christ, I say, we preach to you.

In these words, then, the Apostle marks the distinction between his doctrine and that of false Apostles. They were joining angels with Christ, and the works of the law with faith, in the business of salvation : but Paul was teaching that Christ alone was competent to fulfil every part of the office of a Mediator and Redeemer ; and that faith in Christ, not obedience to the law of Moses, procured our salvation. The doctrine, therefore, of this passage is this ;

That they only preach Christ aright and as they ought to do, who teach that all hope of salvation for mankind is laid up in him alone, and who acknowledge that we receive the riches of divine grace through him alone. The other Apostles also preached such a Christ : For Peter, Acts iv. 12, says thus ; *There is salvation in no other ; for there is none other name under heaven given among men whereby we must be saved.* So Paul declares, Gal. v. 4, *Christ is become of none effect to you, whosoever of you are justified by the law; ye are fallen from grace.*

Hence it appears that the Papists do plainly deviate from the purity of the Gospel doctrine, who unite angels and saints with Christ in the Mediatorial office ; intermix their self-righteous works with the perfect righteousness of Christ in the matter of justification ; and incorporate masses, indulgences, and satisfactions of their own contriving, with the blood of Christ in the work of reconciliation. He who makes Christ a sort of half-way Saviour and Mediator, does not in fact preach him, but the chimera of his own brain : for this is a fundamental error in the principal subject of Gospel preaching.

2. *Warning every man and teaching every man in all wisdom.*] Here the Apostle proceeds to describe the manner of his preaching, upon which we must make three observations.

The *first* is, that the ministry of the Gospel recognises two separate offices, viz. Warning, and Teaching. The word νουθετεῖν, which the Apostle adopts in this place, seems to me more extensive in its meaning than the Latin word admonendi, *warning* or *admonishing*. For it is literally, *to*

put a good mind into a man; which is effected, not only by
warning, but by rebuking, comforting, and many other
means.   Labour, therefore, and attention of every description in a Minister, which is calculated to regulate the affections, and is found practically conducive to that effect,
so that the doctrine of salvation may take deep root in
men's hearts, is included under the term νουθεσιαν.   Whether,
therefore, we would correct the transgressor, or rouse the
negligent, or cheer the desponding, or in short, work upon
the will and the affections in any manner, all is included in
this first part of a Minister's duty, viz. νουθέτησιν.   Wherefore Clemens, Pædag. lib. 1. cap. 8, says, that νουθετησις *is
the prescribed diet for a diseased soul, counselling it to take
what is salutary, and cautioning it against what is injurious.*
This part, therefore, of the ministerial office, is chiefly
conversant with the reformation of the morals of men :
Nor is it to be despised on the ground of the topics being
common and ordinary which are urged by ministers in their
exhortations and rebukes.   For Seneca wisely observes,
*What is the use of shewing that which is evident?   Much every
way.   For sometimes we know but pay no attention.   Admonition teaches not ; but it warns, it excites, it keeps the memory
alive, it prevents the thing from gliding out of sight.   We pass
by many objects that are before our eyes ; to admonish is a kind
of advice.   The mind often neglects what is plain before it ;
therefore the notice of things most notorious must be suggested
to it.*   Senec. Epist. lib. 14. Epist. 94.

Another part of Gospel preaching is observable in teaching.   But διδασκειν, *to teach,* relates to the *understanding,* as
νουθετεῖν, *to warn,* does to *the will* and *affections.*   It is, therefore, a Minister's duty not only to correct depraved affections and bad morals, but also to enlighten the blind understanding.   He ought to be both *like salt,* to dry up the
corrupt humours of the affections ; and *like light,* to dispel
the darkness of the mind : the one is done by warning and
rebuking ; the other by teaching and instructing.

The doctrine itself also is twofold ; viz. of *the law,* and
of grace: and it belongs to the ministerial office to explain
each, and to bring forward all those passages of Scripture

which are essential to the full understanding of each, as
well as to refute all conflicting errors. As to the doctrine
of grace, no one doubts but that it is the special duty of a
Minister of the Gospel to unfold all its mysteries; and as
to *the law,* it is evident that he ought to instruct the people of God in the true knowledge of it. For the law is the
dictate of the Divine mind, and the rule of the human will
and operation; and every one is bound to make himself
acquainted with that rule to which his life ought to be conformed.

But in teaching on this point it is so easy to err, that
some cautions may be useful. We must be careful, then,
in setting forth the doctrine of the law, not to suffer men's
minds to rest upon it, as if they were to obtain salvation
by obeying it; but they must be led to the throne of
Christ's mercy by the rigours of the Law: for *the Law is
our schoolmaster to bring us to Christ.*

We must observe also, that the doctrine of the Law is
adapted in one way, to those who are faithful and truly penitent, and in another to the reprobate and rebellious. To
the godly it should be set forth only as a rule of holy life,
by walking in which they obey God; but not that they
should justify themselves thereby: to the ungodly it must
be set forth not only for the direction of their lives, but to
strike terror into their minds, and shew them the justice of
their condemnation, unless they repent and flee to Christ
their Mediator.—Thus have we considered the twofold
duty of *warning* and *teaching.* Now, in the second place,
let us see how far this office extends.

Every man.] The Apostle appears to me to reiterate
these words for three reasons:

1. To display his Apostolic authority, and the right of
which he is possessed, to warn and to teach not only the
Colossians themselves, but also those teachers who made it
their business to corrupt the purity of the Gospel doctrines.

2. To shew that every distinction between Jew and
Gentile was removed, and that the Gospel was open not to
one nation only, but to all. Wherefore he says, Rom. i.

14, *I am debtor to the Greeks, and to the Barbarians, to the wise and to the unwise.*

That he might avow his zeal, and declare how his affections were bent upon the salvation not of this or that man, but of all mankind. For as a physician makes it the business of his profession to cure not this or that individual only, but all that he can ; so the Physician of souls exerts himself (as much as in him lies) to give relief to all.

This example of Paul must be imitated by all Ministers of the Gospel; who, though not commissioned like him to teach all nations, yet should be animated with the apostolic purpose of bringing to Christ all those who are committed to their superintendance. This very purpose they ought to exhibit in warning and teaching every man placed under their ministry. They are not to think lightly of the poor, nor to be intimidated by the great, so as to shrink from their bounden duty both of teaching and warning. *Whoever*, says Augustine, *disobeys the commands of God and disregards reproof, is on that very account to be reproved, because he will not bear reproof.* De corrept. & grat. cap. 5.

In all wisdom.] This is the last expression we have to consider as to the manner of apostolic preaching ; viz. that he had concealed nothing, but had instructed every man in all wisdom. The expression *all wisdom*, however, is not to be stretched beyond the limits of the present subject ; but only to be applied to all wisdom of a saving nature, or such as is necessary for salvation. He does not profess to teach worldly wisdom, which is attained by the light of reason ; but heavenly and spiritual, which is discerned by the light of faith, and is contained in the doctrine of the Gospel. Whatever, then, was necessary to be understood for obtaining salvation through Christ, that the Apostle openly expounded before all men. That this was Paul's meaning in this passage, is evident from the collation of other places in which he also declares the same persevering zeal in instructing the Church. In Acts xx. 18, &c. *Ye know how I have kept back from you nothing that was profitable to you ; but have shewed you and taught you publicly, and from house to house ; testifying both to the Jews and also to the Gentiles, repentance towards* **God**, *and faith towards our* **Lord** *Jesus* **Christ**. Immediately after which he adds, *I take you to re-cord this day, that I am pure from the blood of all men; for I have not shunned to declare unto you the whole counsel of* **God**; ver. 26, 27.

Hence many inferences might be deduced.

1. The whole sum of Christian wisdom consists in depending upon Christ alone, and understanding the counsel of God concerning our salvation obtained by him. He who sincerely holds this doctrine is accounted as furnished with all wisdom.

2. The Apostles have publicly set forth every thing which is necessary for obtaining salvation in Christ; the obscure traditions, therefore, of which the Papists have so many fables, are no part of that wisdom which is unto salvation. And the reason is obvious: For the wisdom which is necessary to salvation was preached by the Apostles openly to all men; but these traditions of theirs, according to their own account, were not entrusted to all, but only to their prelates, or other eminent men among them. Therefore the knowledge of them is not necessary for the salvation of a Christian. If we consult the Fathers, though they allow of some traditions as to external ordinances, and the indifferent usages of the Church, yet, in all matters concerning faith and salvation, they, one and all, hold that the doctrines of Scripture which the Apostles preached, and afterwards committed to writing, are sufficient. Tertullian, De præscript. says, *Since the coming of Christ, there has been no need for speculation; nor for inquisitiveness since the promulgation of the Gospel.* And Augustine, in his comment upon John xi. tract. 49, observes, *Those things were selected to be written down which seemed sufficient for the salvation of those who believe.* I add no more on this topic now, having touched upon the error before more than once.

3. The man who is not apt to teach, nay more, who is not able to instruct God's people in all spiritual wisdom, is not a fit minister of the Gospel. To this end Paul (Tit. i. 9) requires in a spiritual pastor not only the knowledge

of *sound doctrine,* but also *the holding it fast,* that *he may be able to instruct others in sound doctrine, and to convince the gainsayers.* But let those who neither can nor will do this, *see the heavy guilt that they bring upon themselves by withholding the word of instruction from their brethren, and by depriving dying souls of the remedy of life;* as Gregory remarks in Pastorali.

Thus, then, have we discoursed of the primary object, and also of the manner of apostolical preaching; in which the Apostle embraces three things, viz. the *warning* and *doctrine:* the persons who ought to be taught, viz. *all men:* and lastly, the matter which ought to be preached to people, viz. *all* saving *wisdom,* And now we will pass on from the manner to the aim or purpose of the Gospel Ministry.

That we may present every man perfect in Christ Jesus.] Behold, then, the end and aim of Paul, and so, indeed, of every other Minister of the word; viz. that they may bring all kinds of people to that saving knowledge of Christ in which Christian perfection consists. Now to avoid confusion herein, let us make two separate explanations. The first as to the intention of Paul; the other as to Christian perfection, or the character which constitutes it.

In respect of the first, then, it is asked, Is not this intention of Paul either extravagant or absurd, it being most certain that the greater part of mankind will not be brought to Christ after all the efforts of the Gospel ministry? For though many are called, yet few come, i. e. are chosen. Why, then, does he profess an intention which never can be fulfilled?

I answer, Neither is the Apostle's intention of bringing all men to Christ, though few will in reality be brought, nor are his endeavours to fulfil it extravagant or vain. That it is not extravagant there are two reasons: 1. Because it is in conformity with the rule of Charity, for according to that rule we are to presume favourably of every man until the contrary is shewn : But Ministers have no evidence against any particular man being saved; therefore they are bound to entertain a good hope for every man, and to do every thing they can for promoting his salvation.

2. This desire is not extravagant, because it is in perfect accordance with the revealed will of God. For that revealed will in the promulgation of the Gospel offers salvation to every man without respect of persons ; and no man is excluded, unless he exclude himself by his unbelief. Agreeable to this statement is 1 Tim. ii. 4, *God will have all men to be saved, and to come to the knowledge of the truth.* What, therefore, God himself hath declared to be his will in offering the Gospel, the same also ought to be the will of his Ministers in preaching it.

But here another question is raised from the foregoing : If God would have all men to whom he sends the Gospel of salvation to be saved, why are not all saved ; since the will of God, neither in itself nor in the means by which it acts, can be hindered in producing the effect intended ?

A common answer to this question is taken from Augustine : When God is said to will that all men should be saved, we must make a distribution of individuals into classes, not of classes into individuals ; so that the sense will be, God wills that some should be saved of every class of men. But to me the commonly received distinction of the Schoolmen between the will of his *good pleasure* and his *visible will* (voluntate *signi*), is better suited to this passage. We therefore reply, that the will of his *good pleasure* is always effectually fulfilled, because it is formally and essentially in God, and is his practical absolute will, when employed concerning any future good. But his visible will is not always fulfilled, because it is not formally and essentially in God, and is not his absolute and practical will ; but, it is his declarative or approbative will (if I may be allowed such a word) towards us. God is, therefore, said to will, by his *visible will*, the salvation of all, to whom he proposes and offers the Gospel, which is the ordinary means of effecting salvation. Moreover, we are not to inquire into the secret will of God ; but all our actions must be directed according to his revealed will : and we ought, therefore, to wish and aim at the salvation of all those to whom God vouchsafes to grant the saving Gospel.

Neither is the endeavour of the Ministry, in drawing those to Christ who will never come, vain. In the first place, because, whilst they are performing their duty, they are relieving their own consciences. Secondly, because, though the exertions of the ministry in behalf of the reprobate, fail of their intended effect, they abundantly answer their purpose in all those fore-ordained to salvation. Lastly, because by this means infidels and reprobates will be condemned in the day of judgment, and deprived of every excuse for their sins ; having disobeyed the calling through the perverseness of their own evil affections.—And thus far as to Paul's intention.

Now (in the last place) let us consider Christian perfection.

The Schoolmen hold two sorts of perfection ; one of the *way*, the other of the *country*, to which the way leads. In this passage the Apostle has the former more particularly in view ; and this is the first point to which the Ministers of the Gospel endeavour to lead their people, that by means of it they may be brought to the attainment of the second.

This perfection of the *way* may also be considered in a twofold manner. For a man is called *perfect* who is in possession of every thing which is necessary for a state of salvation ; and so every believer is perfect. A man is called *perfect* also, who has attained to every degree of grace and virtue ; and in this sense no man is perfect : for every Christian always may be, and ever ought to be, growing and advancing in grace and holiness.

But what constitutes the character of Christian perfection ? The Apostle seems to insinuate the answer by adding *in Christ Jesus ; that we may present every man perfect in Christ Jesus.* When, confessing our own imperfection and corruption, we take refuge in Christ, and by faith lay hold of his perfection, and are renewed by the Holy Spirit into his likeness, then, and not till then, are we *perfect in Christ Jesus.* The Apostle, therefore, does in effect say, that he labours, by preaching the Gospel, to impress true faith and earnest piety on the hearts of all men.

Hence we infer,

1. That the Ministry is, as it were, the hand of God himself reforming and perfecting men in spiritual life; which, if we speak of the subject of degrees of perfection, is done very gently and gradually. For, as Prosper says, De vita contempl. 1. 9, *no man is in this life completely perfect; for the infirmities of the godly are not yet healed, though they are under the daily process of healing.* Hence that address of Paul, Gal. iv. 19, *My little children, of whom I travail in birth until Christ be formed in you.*

2. Hence also is shewn the empty pride of the Monks in claiming to themselves alone that state of perfection which is within the reach of every true Christian. For it is quite absurd to suppose that a good Christian cannot be in the way of perfection without turning Franciscan or Dominican; when Paul, who wished to present all men perfect in Christ Jesus, yet never attempted to persuade one to bind himself down by any sort of monastic vows and rules. But let us hear that grave theologian John Gerson, who beats down this pride of the Monks upon all occasions. In his work Contra assert. Matthæi de Grabbon,* part. 1, he maintains the following propositions: 1. *The Christian religion may be observed perfectly, yea, most perfectly, independently of any vow obliging to counsels of perfection.* (This he proves by the example of Christ, the Apostles, and the saints in the primitive Church, who were under no vows or monastic discipline whatever). 2. *It is the height of impropriety, perversion, and, I scruple not to add, arrogance, to call these factitious religious institutes, states of perfection, when it is certain the most imperfect men are professors of such obligations.* 3. *The religion of Christ may be and ought to be observed by the prelates of the Church more perfectly than by the Monks.* And in the third part of his work, he brings many arguments to prove that the perfection of a Christian does by no means consist in the vow of

---

* Grabbon appears to have been a Monk of the 15th century, who maintained some peculiar notions on this subject, which were condemned in the Council of Basil. Vide Du Pin, cap. viii. Cent.xv.

celibacy, and poverty, and obedience to the monkish rules,
but in the observance of the Divine precepts. Whence
also Clemens Alexandrinus, Strom. 7, says, *that there is as
much perfection to be found in the conjugal as in the monastic
life.** We therefore conclude, that the perfection of which
the Apostle is here speaking, does not consist in monastic
observances, but in faith, in charity, and in sanctity of
life; in all which he who has the greater firmness, ardour,
and strength, is to be accounted the most perfect.

Verse 29.

*Whereunto I also labour, striving according to his working,
which worketh in me mightily.*

The Apostle amplifies his ministry by a twofold argument: 1. By his great labour, which he intimates under
the words *labouring* and *striving*. 2. By the effectual assistance of Christ, which he expresses in adding, *according
to his working, which worketh in me mightily.* He employs
both these arguments for confirming the Colossians in the
doctrine of the Gospel. For if Paul propagated this doctrine with all diligence, it ought also to bind the Colossians
with equal constancy: If Christ promoted this doctrine by
Divine aid, the Colossians ought to adopt the same as the
word of God.

Whereunto I also labour, κοπιῶ.] This Greek word does
not simply mean *to labour*, but *to labour vehemently, and even
to weariness.* He therefore shews, first, from the labour
annexed to it, both the difficulty and the dignity of his
ministry: for a difficulty which arises from labour increases
its value.

---

* Clemens in his 3d Strom. refutes the notions of the Marcionites about
abstinence from Marriage, from the saying of St. Paul, 1 Tim. iv. 1—3,
" that those who forbid marriage propagate the doctrine of devils:" and
also by the example of Peter and Philip, who were both married and had
children.

How many and how great labours Paul underwent in preaching the Gospel, we may ascertain from the Acts of the Apostles. No one visited more people in preaching ; no one contended more strenuously with the enemies of the Gospel in disputation ; in short, no one in any work of the ministry exercised himself more earnestly by labour. Whence he did not fear to assert, *that he had laboured more abundantly than all the other Apostles,* 1 Cor. xv. 10. This labour of Paul, then, I refer to all those acts whereby he studied to extend the Gospel. But the Apostle adds, *I labour striving.*

'Aγωνιζόμενος.] I conceive that this refers to the dangers and sufferings of Paul, which he was often compelled to sustain in the discharge of his Apostolic office. For the metaphor is derived from those wrestlers who contended in the public games, and underwent many severe and arduous struggles in those contests.

If any one would see a catalogue of those sufferings which Paul sustained, let him look into 2 Cor. xi. 23, &c. where he glories that *he was in stripes, in prisons, in deaths oft : that he was beaten with rods, stoned ; was three times shipwrecked : that he was in perils of waters, of robbers, of the Jews, and of the Gentiles : that he passed his life in watchings, in hunger, in thirst, in cold, and nakedness.* Paul contended with all these opponents, and overcame them all by enduring : Whence in 2 Tim. iv. 7, 8, he triumphantly exclaims ; *I have fought a good fight, I have finished my course, I have kept the faith : Henceforth there is laid up for me a crown of righteousness.*

Here learn,

1. That they who propose to themselves ease, pleasure, riches, or honour, are not suited for the Ministry of the Gospel. For if the pastors of cattle undertake a laborious life, so that Jacob could truly say concerning the pastoral life, *In the day the drought consumed me, and the frost by night ; and my sleep departed from mine eyes,* Gen. xxxi. 40, then how much more does it behove the pastors of souls, from whom God will require whatever shall be lost through their indolence, to shrink from no labour ? *If any one de-*

sire the office of a Bishop, he desireth a good work, 1 Tim.
iii. 1 ; *work, not honour ; labour, not pleasure ;* says Jerome.
They are wicked prelates, says Gregory, *who retain the chair
of government to enjoy pleasure, not to exercise labour,* Moral.
lib. xi. cap. 10.

2. That ministers ought to make up their minds, not
only to labour in the word, but even to labour for the word
under the cross. For the cross is the portion of all the
godly, but especially of ministers. Hence said Christ to
his Apostles, John xvi. 2, *The time will come that whosoever
killeth you will think that he doeth God service.* And in the
last verse, *In the world ye shall have tribulation.* A certain
one said, *It is princely to have a bad character for doing well :*
but I should rather say, It is *priestly* to suffer cruelty for
doing well. Hence Paul writing to Timothy unites both,
in 2 Epis. iv. 5 ; *Do the work of an Evangelist ;* there is labour in execution ! *endure afflictions ;* there is firmness in
suffering ! He who has learnt these two lessons, the same
knows with Paul how to labour and strive ; to sustain labour *in* the word ; afflictions and dangers *for* the word.
These cannot be separated : for he is defective in his vocation who dreads to suffer for the truth. *Patience in the
things of God is so inculcated,* says Tertullian, in his treatise, De patient. cap. 1, *because he who is a stranger to patience can obey no precept, can perform no work pleasing to the
Lord.* For this is the shield of every virtue.—So much
concerning the labour : now let us consider the Helper.

According to his working, which worketh in me mightily]
i. e. according to the effectual working of Christ. This is
that other argument whereby the Apostle enhances his ministry, and shews at the same time his modesty and humility. He had affirmed that he laboured and strove to present every man perfect in Christ Jesus : Now he adds that
he did this not relying upon human strength or his own
powers, but upon the divine assistance of Christ, strengthened and aided by his might.

Concerning this *efficacy,* or *might* of Christ, we shall consider three things : the origin of it ; the mode, and the
effect.

1. Every operation flows from some origin: it is proper to inquire, therefore, in the first place, what is the origin of this most effectual working; according to which Paul says that he laboured and strove with so much constancy and fortitude.

We answer, that Christ himself, or the Spirit of Christ, is the efficient principle of this working: For thus Christ himself promised, Luke, ult. 49, *Behold I send the promise of my Father upon you; but tarry ye in Jerusalem until ye be endued with power from on high,* i. e. until the Holy Spirit descends upon you, who will be the fountain and the principle of all might and spiritual strength in you all. Hence that glorying of the Apostle, Philip. iv. 13, *I can do all things through Christ who strengtheneth me.*

2. We must inquire, how the Holy Spirit effects this sufficiency in Ministers to fulfil the work of their ministry. Not only by the concurrence and aid of his might, but by the communication and influence of his grace. For he creates in the minds of godly Ministers certain new and supernatural qualities, whereby they are rendered adequate to do and suffer all those things which devolve upon Ministers of the Gospel. So Paul expressly declares, 1 Cor. xv. 10, *By the grace of God I am what I am; and his grace which was bestowed upon me was not in vain: but I laboured more abundantly than they all: yet not I, but the grace of God which was with me.* And in 2 Cor. iii. 5, 6, *Our sufficiency is of God; who hath made us able ministers of the New Testament.* How hath he made them so? By his Spirit as the effective principle; by the grace of the Spirit as the formal principle.

Lastly, we must speak concerning the effects of the Spirit and of his grace strengthening us. Whereas, then, it is required in a Minister that he both do and suffer all those things which are necessary to further the Gospel, we say the effects of this Spirit and grace are of a twofold division. Some are to render the Minister fit for the duties of his calling: of this kind are the illumination of the mind, the sanctification of the will, love and regard for the flock, and many other such endowments, with which the internal

working of Christ, operating in his mind, adorned and enriched Paul.   Others are to render a Minister firm and
ready to endure any thing for the Gospel : of this kind are
fortitude, constancy, patience, zeal for the Divine glory,
and all those other virtues with which the soul is upheld
and sustained in undergoing afflictions.   We are able also
to add a third kind of effects, which are to promote the
success of the Gospel, and to procure for the Apostles
themselves extraordinary authority : namely, the power of
working miracles, which some interpreters think to be intended when the Apostle says, *according to his working, which
worketh in me mightily ;* for this they apply to the *power* of
miracles.   From all these things, therefore, it appears that
Paul both performed and endured all things for the advancement of the Gospel, not in his own strength, but *according to the power of Christ working in him.*

Hence we infer,

1. That no one should undertake the ministry relying
upon his own ability or strength, but suppliantly to seek
the aid of Divine grace.   For no one is competent by himself for such a duty : but as Cyprian piously remarks, De
nativ. Christi, *The Spirit infusing himself into the minds of
the humble, enlarges the contractedness of the human intellect,
and opens the mental eyes to behold invisible things.*   Thus also
no one is ready and strong in himself to suffer for the Gospel : but as *it is given to men to believe the Gospel,* so also
the ability *to suffer for the Gospel* is derived from God, Phil.
i. 29.

2. No one should be deterred from the pastoral office
on account of those injuries and reproaches which are wont
to be heaped upon Ministers : for the Spirit of Christ will
be with them strengthening them to endure all things even
with joyfulness.   *In the world ye shall have tribulation, but
in me ye shall have peace,* says Christ, John xvi. 33.   There
shall be from me an inward consolation to revive you, as
long as there shall be an outward tyranny from the world to
crush you.

3. They are not strengthened by the Spirit of Christ,
but hurried along by that of the devil, who, when pressed

by afflictions, do not think upon patience, but seek revenge. And here it will repay our trouble to consider what a difference there is between Paul, Peter, and the rest of the Apostles, and the Roman Pontiffs. The Apostles were armed against the persecutions of tyrants by fortitude from God, constancy of mind, and patience: but the latter proclaim, that they are armed by treachery, sword, and fire. For Bellarmin teaches, that God had not provided all things necessary to his Church unless he had granted power to the Pope of changing kingdoms, deposing kings, and absolving subjects from the oath of allegiance, if it should happen that any king should resist the Church. God, however, is not wanting to the Church, although he granted not to the Pope power of deposing kings, because he has given to the Church the power and the will to suffer for righteousness, and because by these sufferings the religion of Christians is increased; according to that remark of Tertullian, in his Apologet. cap. 50, *The more we are cut down by you, the more we increase; for the blood of Christians is the seed of the Church.*

Lastly, it is hence manifest that all the labour of Ministers is lost, as it respects their hearers, unless the powerful working of Christ produce the effects in the minds of the one as well as of the other. *Paul may plant, and Apollos may water; but God giveth the increase,* 1 Cor. iii. 6. *It is necessary that the Holy Spirit should work internally, that the remedy may be effectual which is offered externally: Unless he is present in the hearts of the hearers, the word of the speaker is useless,* as Augustine has well said.

We have now completed the first Chapter, in which the foundations of the whole of the Apostolic discussion are laid down, the titles of Christ explained, and the doctrine of our redemption by Him settled and established. In the following Chapter the Apostle encounters those seducers who attempted to withdraw the Colossians from Christ.

END OF THE FIRST CHAPTER.

EXPOSITION

OF

THE SECOND CHAPTER.

OF this whole Chapter a few things may be premised generally; and then, according to our custom, we shall proceed to a particular elucidation of the text.

In this general dissertation we shall briefly point out three things, viz. the Apostle's object in this Chapter; the state and sum of the controversy to be discussed; and the arrangement or distribution of the whole Chapter in its parts.

As to the design of the Apostle: he aims directly in this whole discussion, to retain the Colossians and all other Christians firm and stedfast in the truth of the Gospel, which places all the ground of our salvation in Christ alone; and to fortify them against the deceptions of all seducers, who would blend with Christ, in the business of salvation, either the doctrine of philosophy, or the Mosaic ceremonies, or even traditions of their own invention. Therefore, as a wise physician, in the preceding Chapter the Apostle had exhibited to them the sustenance of wholesome doctrine; in this he points out the food to be avoided as noxious and dangerous to the souls' health. In the former, as a *good* husbandman, he sowed the good seed in the field of the Colossian Church; in this, as a *provident* husbandman, he warns them, lest, falling asleep, they should admit for wheat the tares sowed meanwhile by impostors. This, then, is the scope of this Chapter, viz. that the Colossians may be retained and confirmed in the true doctrine, and fortified against novel corruptions.

Now from these remarks it is easy to reduce the sum of the whole controversy to two points. First, that in Christ alone, according to the Gospel doctrine, we have every thing sufficient to salvation. Secondly, whatever traditions, ceremonies, and philosophical speculations are obtruded in the business of salvation, in addition to Christ, are altogether vanity and imposture. These propositions the Apostle so treats through this whole Chapter, that he does not dismiss the one before he proceeds to the other; but indiscriminately and alternately, and often by varied turns, he lays down, proves, and illustrates sometimes the one, and sometimes the other. And it seems to me that the Apostle adopts this method with the design that by frequent discussion and repetition of both, he may fix each of them deeply in the minds of Christians.

Finally, we have to speak of the division of this Chapter into its members; and it seems that the whole may be aptly divided into four parts :

1. The exordium or preface, comprised in the first seven verses.

2. The proposition of the subject to be treated, briefly laid down in the eighth verse.

3. The confirmation of the Apostle's judgment, extended as far as to the seventeenth verse.

4. The conclusion of the question, amplified and illustrated, to the end, as is common in conclusions.

OF THE EXORDIUM.

Let us now enter upon a view of the Exordium, comprehended (as I have stated) in the seven first verses : and that consists of three parts;

1. In a narrative proposition, in which he shews both his conduct and his mind towards the Colossians; in the first verse.

2. The statement of his reasons or the occasion; in which he gives many reasons for his procedure, and proposition; from the first verse to the sixth.

3. An hortatory conclusion; in which he advises them to obey the truth, nor suffer such great solicitude of an Apostle for their salvation to be in vain; in verses six and seven.

From the construction of this Exordium I venture to assert, that there is no rule laid down by Aristotle, Cicero, and other masters of eloquence, concerning the framing of introductions, which is not adhered to in this brief opening. For three things are required by them in a legitimate Exordium : That it be adapted to render the hearer *attentive*, and *docile*, and to *conciliate his affection*. We render our hearers *attentive* when we shew them that we are about to speak of great and unusual things, or which relate to those who hear. The Apostle excels in all these respects : for what is either greater or more excellent than *the mystery of God, the treasures of Christ?* What either to be more wondered at, or more dangerous than the *speeches* and *deceivings* of impostors and their arts? Lastly, What more properly concerned the Colossians than that spiritual consolation, and *the riches of understanding*, which is promised to them at the threshold of this address? These things, therefore, are sufficient as to *attention*.

Now as to what pertains to *docility ;* Rhetoricians direct that in an Exordium, the sum of the subject to be treated, and the points of proof, should, as it were, be scattered by the way : for it ought to be ὁδοποιησις τῶ 'επιοντι λογω, *a paving of the way for the discourse that is to follow*, as Aristotle wisely says in Rhetor. 3. 14. This the Apostle effects in verses 3 and 4. In the former he lays down the ground of his defence; in the latter he confutes the reverse by stigmatizing it with the name of *imposture*.

Concerning the great art of conciliating their *good-will* much need not be said ; it abundantly shines forth in every sentence. He conciliates their *good-will* to himself from his own personal character, by relating what labours he had undertaken for them, and what benevolent feelings he always entertained towards them; from the personal character of his adversaries, by reciting their impostures and frauds ; and from the personal character of the Colossians themselves, by declaring their order, their stedfastness in the faith, and by importuning them to constancy and progress in these good qualities; and, lastly, from the facts themselves, by teaching that he strives for the treasures of Christ, but his adversaries for dross instead of gold, i. e. for doating schemes and impostures.

Although these technicalities are not immediately in connexion with our undertaking, I was nevertheless desirous to glance at them by the way for two reasons. One was, lest we should despise the sacred Scriptures and their writers as devoid of eloquence and human literature. For that remark of Ambrose, Epist. lib. 8. ep. 63, is true: *The writers of the divine books, although they did not write them according to the rules of art, but according to grace, which is superior to art; yet they who have written concerning this art, have discovered the rules of it in their writings.* And that also of Augustine, 4 De doctr. Christ. cap. 7, *The sacred writings possess, but do not affect eloquence.* For God, who hath formed the voice, the mind, and the tongue, however he would have their discourses to be wanting in disguise, was yet unwilling that they should be in any wise deficient in useful and solid art. Vide Rupert, lib. 7, concerning the works of the Holy Spirit, as largely proving this.*

The other reason why we have just touched the skilful disposition of the Apostle's writing was, lest unskilful and unlearned men, when they write or preach whatever comes uppermost, exhibiting no study or art, should flatter themselves, as though they trod in the steps of the Apostles. They, being extraordinarily assisted by the inspiration of the Holy Spirit, wanted not the ordinary aid of art; but

* Rupert, Abbot of Duyts or Deutch: he was born at Ypres, in Flanders, in 1091, and died in 1135. He is commonly known and cited as Rupertus Tuitiensis, and is one of the three famous Commentators of the 12th century noticed by Du Pin: but besides his Commentaries on parts of the Bible, he wrote several other Theological Treatises, among which was the one cited above. He was a learned and a pious man. But Bellarmin and other late Roman writers disparage his works, because, forsooth, he entertained opinions about the Eucharist differing from the novel Popish doctrine of Transubstantiation.

us, to whom it is not permitted to expect this full power to work miracles, it behoves to seek aid as well in writing as in preaching, by study, by industry, and every suitable means. But quitting these things, let us proceed to the text.

CHAP. II.   Verse 1.

For I would that ye knew what great conflict I have for you, and for them at Laodicea, and for as many as have not seen my face in the flesh.

In this short verse is contained the first part of the Exordium, viz. the narrative proposition ; in which he shews his conduct and his good-will towards the Colossians, Laodiceans, and all others imbued with the Christian faith. These words are connected with the two last verses of the first Chapter, as appears by those words, *for I would,* which look back to the preceding in this manner : He had said that he strove and laboured, that he might teach and present every one perfect in Christ Jesus ; now what he had spoken universally concerning all, he applies specially and expressly to the Colossians : As though he had said, ' Ye have heard with what care and solicitude, with what conflicts I have spread the Gospel among others; I have defended it when spread, and have withstood seducers : I wish you to understand, moreover, that you have not been overlooked by me ; whom, although I have never seen or visited, yet I have sustained the same conflicts for you also, I have had the like care and solicitude on your account.' This is the connection of these words with the foregoing : In the explication of them we shall have to examine three things :

1. What the Apostle has an eye to in so often repeat-

338 AN EXPOSITION OF ST. PAUL'S *Chap.* ii.

ing and enforcing his labours and conflicts undertaken for
the Churches; viz. their benefit, which he intimates by
saying, *For I would that ye knew.*

2. What, and of what sort, was this conflict which the
Apostle underwent.

3. For whom this conflict was undertaken: which he
shews specially and definitely, *for you; and for the Laodiceans;* and then indefinitely, *and for as many as have not
seen my face,* &c.

For I would that ye knew.] The Apostle shews what was
his meaning in commemorating this his conflict; viz. he
does not seek empty glory to himself from thence, but he
regards the gain and utility accruing to the Colossians
from this knowledge of his conflicts. And this gain is
manifold,

First, When a people understand what labours and conflicts their salvation demands from the Pastor, hence arises
the fruit of mutual affection and kindness: for he is truly
ungrateful, who does not love that man in return, who loves
him and strives with all diligence for his salvation. In order, therefore, that the hearts of a people may be inflamed
with love for their Minister, it is useful that they should
know, what they do and what they endure for their sakes.

Secondly, hence springs the fruit of mutual solicitude
and diligence; for if any spiritual sense exist in them,
they are excited to the care of their own salvation, which
they perceive to be the subject of such earnest care to
another.

Lastly, hence is produced the fruit of like constancy and
patience; for loyal soldiers are animated by the example
of their leader; and boldly (when occasion offers) they
commence that fight which they observe to be bravely and
successfully fought by their pastors. Hither, especially,
all ecclesiastical histories tend, which propose the deeds
and sufferings of the Martyrs to be contemplated by all,
that from thence their minds may be prepared to take up
the same cross. The Apostle, therefore, regarded these
advantages as he intimates in saying, *For I would that ye
knew what great conflict I have,* &c.

Hence we derive two lessons :

1. It must not be deemed boasting, if Ministers sometimes freely talk of the labours and toils of their ministry
among the people : for Paul very often did this ; it is very
proper for the people to know this ; it is done with a view
to their spiritual good.

2. They who do not know, or are unwilling to know and
acknowledge the labours, watchings, and conflicts of Ministers for their salvation, oppose themselves and their own
advantage : for from this knowledge they reap much fruit,
as was before shewn.

Thus much concerning the first point.

2. *What great conflict I have.*] Ye have heard why the
Apostle wished his conflicts for the Colossians to be
known ; now, in the second place, we shall explain what
kind, and in what things that conflict consisted. Erasmus
and the ancient interpreter* translate ἀγωνα, *solicitude,* with
little appositeness : for any one may be solicitous about his
own or another's affairs, although there may be no one who
opposes and resists him : but no person is said to have a
conflict except he who has strife and contention with an
adversary. Every conflict requires solicitude ; but all solicitude does not always pre-suppose a conflict. We, therefore, receive the interpretation of Beza.

But what was this conflict ? with whom, and on what
account sustained ?

It was a conflict as well of mind as of body ; with Satan,
with deceivers—the members of Satan, with various kinds
of afflictions ; it was undertaken for the edifying, confirming, and retaining the members of Christ in the faith.

Conflict *of mind* consists either *in affections* or *in actions.*
Contrary *affections* strove in the mind of the Apostle, arising from different causes. For sometimes he rejoiced and
exulted, and was full of hope, through witnessing the
faith, and love, and other virtues of the godly ; Rom. xvi.

---

* Davenant probably means the Vulgate, for Beza translates ἀγωνα
certamen, with this note, " Vulg: et Erasmus ἀγωνα vertunt solicitudi-
nem non satis expresse."

19. Sometimes he mourned, grieved, and feared by beholding their dissensions, errors, or afflictions. *Who is
afflicted, and I am not afflicted?* &c. 2 Cor. xi. 29.   *I fear,
lest as the serpent beguiled Eve, so,* &c. 2 Cor. xi. 3.   As to
what relates to *actions,* the mind of the Apostle was
scarcely ever free from conflict.   He had continual conflicts of prayer against Satan, and his satellites, for the
salvation of the faithful, Rom. xvi. 20.   And 2 Thess. i.
11, *We pray always for you,* &c.   He moreover contended
by writing and preaching, with false apostles, detecting
and refuting their errors ; with all ungodliness of men,
restraining, and dispersing it, as appears in 2 Cor. x. 4,
&c.   Lastly, he contended with the infirmities of the faithful themselves, reproving, instructing, and consoling them ;
as is every where to be seen in the writings of Paul.
These were the conflicts of *mind* by which Paul was daily
distracted.   But neither was *the body* of the Apostle free
from its own tortures : it had to encounter fatigues, watchings, hunger, thirst, fastings, inclemency of weather, and
racks, 2 Cor. xi. 23, &c.   Whether, therefore, we regard
the labours he sustained, or the griefs he underwent, in
each respect the Apostle was distinguished by divers bodily conflicts.

If now it be asked, What advantage could result from
this commemoration of so many of the Apostle's conflicts
of mind and body ?   It is answered, That the Apostle proposed to himself no other end than the good of the
Church.   For that he might bring men to Christ, present
them perfect in Christ, keep them stedfast and persevering
in the faith of Christ, and lead them at last to the kingdom of Christ, he sustained the conflicts before-mentioned.
So he himself declares, 2 Tim. ii. 10, *Therefore I endure all
things for the elect's sake, that they also may obtain the salvation which is in Christ Jesus with eternal glory.*   From these
things various arguments touching Ministers may be
gathered.

1.   A good Pastor ought to be affected with the good or
evil of his flock, as much as with his own.   For *the Pastor,*
as Cyprian, speaking De lapsis, observes, *is wounded by*

the hurt of his flock, and he likewise is revived by the health of his flock. *I draw each to my bosom, I participate of its sorrow and joy by turns,* says the same Father.

2. A good Minister is never less idle than when he is idle. The rude peasant thinks that saying of the Poet may be turned against Ministers, *to the idle it is always a feast:* for they suppose that we make holiday the whole day long; nor have any occupation after we have left the temple; but if we are such as we ought to be, a conflict devolves upon us of praying, meditating, studying—I had almost said unceasingly, certainly daily and assiduously.

3. It behoves Ministers to be of such a mind as not only to pray for their flock, but to be ready to submit to the cross, nay, even to death, if it should be required: 2 Cor. xii. 15, *I will very gladly spend and be spent for your souls.*

4. Ministers ought, in all their cares, labours, and conflicts, to have this in view, not that they may gain empty glory, or any earthly advantage; but that the people may obtain salvation. For Clemens well says, *It is the duty of a Theologian to lend his assistance for the preservation of those who desire to be preserved, not to put together the ornaments of elocution.*

All these lessons affecting Ministers arise from the example of Paul.

LESSONS AFFECTING THE PEOPLE.

1. There is that inaptitude in the people to spiritual things, that without great conflicts on the part of Ministers they cannot be brought to God, nor be kept in the true religion; therefore it is proper that they should submit themselves to those who have the care and labour of seeking their salvation.

2. It is fit duly to honour Ministers, who are vexed by so many cares, worn by so many watchings, bruised by so many conflicts for their sakes. For if the leaders of an earthly warfare are honoured among all men, how much more fit is it that the leaders of the spiritual warfare should be honoured! according to that injunction of the

Apostle, 1 Thess. v. 12, *Know them which labour among you,
and are over you in the Lord, and admonish you, and esteem
them very highly in love for their work's sake.*

3.   They are reproved to whom it is a pleasure to contend against, and strive about matters of no moment with
their Ministers, who, on their account, undergo so many
laborious conflicts : for what is more unworthy than that
he should be harassed and wounded by his flock, who
daily fights for the flock against their spiritual enemies?
Thus much concerning the Apostle's conflict.

3.   *For you, and for them at Laodicea, and for as many as
have not seen my face in the flesh.*]   It has been shewn why
the Apostle calls to remembrance his conflict, and what
this conflict was; it remains, in the last place, that we
consider the persons for whom it was undertaken : and they
are described (as hath been said) both definitely and indefinitely.

For you, and for them at Laodicea.]   Here the Apostle
expressly professes that his afore-mentioned conflicts were
undertaken for the Colossians and Laodiceans; where we
must explain why he expresses these by name, and why he
joins them together.

He mentions them by name that he may anticipate an
implied objection; for it might occur to them to say, You
have, indeed, sustained heavy labours, you have endured
remarkable conflicts ; but for the Romans, Corinthians, and
Galatians; and for others, to whom you have personally
preached the Gospel; but your voice *we* never heard ; nor
have we even beheld your face.   Paul anticipates these
surmisings, and shews them that he sustained his conflicts
of prayer, of solicitude, and of writing also for them, although he had not exercised the office of preaching among
them.   Yea, he entered the lists for them in this his Epistle, to encounter their seducers.

But why does he unite the Laodiceans also?   Because
this Epistle (according to his direction Chap. iv. 16) was
to be recited publicly in the church of Laodicea; therefore
he wished to mention them also, lest they should suspect
that they were overlooked by the Apostle; besides, it is

very probable that the Laodicean Church, on account of its vicinity, was assailed and attempted by the seducers in the same manner as that of the Colossian : in order, therefore, that they might understand the doctrine of this Epistle to relate to them in some especial manner, he expressly introduces them.

And as many as have not seen my face in the flesh.] That is, as many as have not seen me present in body, nor have heard me preach by word of mouth : for Paul was well known by reputation, and by his written Epistles to all the Churches.   The Apostle adds this indefinite clause (as Œcumenius observes) lest he should seem to insinuate against them a suspicion of carelessness, thus earnestly exciting them to constancy and perseverance in the truth of the doctrine of the Gospel.   He does this, not because he doubted of their stedfast faith, but because the nature of lovers is such, that they are more solicitous about absent than present friends : that he, therefore, being absent, might intimate this as the cause of his anxious care, rather than his distrust of their faith, he declares that he was so affected towards all the rest among whom he could not be present.   For what the Poet remarks concerning the bird and its young, may much more truly be said of the Pastor and his people : This bird, if she leave her unfledged young ever so little, thinks of, and fears, the approach of serpents much more anxiously than when she sits by them.   (Hor. Epod. od. 1.)   So the Pastor, if he is compelled to be absent from his flock, is much more solicitous than when he is watching over them, lest they should fall from their faith, be corrupted in their manners, or their salvation should in any measure be endangered.

Hence we learn,

1.   There is another sort of aspect that conciliates love among the servants of God, than that of flesh and the eyes ; viz. the aspect of the mind.   For Christian love does not conceive friendship and affinity to consist in local nearness, but in spiritual unity.   There is, therefore, a certain mutual benevolence and solicitude among the godly about their spiritual proficiency, although they have never

beheld, and are absolutely unknown to each other by face.

2. The care and solicitude of a faithful Minister is not lightened, but is increased, if at any time he should be withdrawn from his flock. For he who is absent in body ought always to be present with the flock in spirit, and to help them in the meanwhile by his prayers, and by any other means, with all his might.

3. Also it behoves him, with Paul, to exert himself to the utmost, that from his deeds all should understand that he is neither unmindful or neglectful of the people committed to him.

Let these things suffice concerning the first part of the Exordium, viz. the narrative proposition.

Verse 2.

That their hearts might be comforted, being knit together in love and unto all riches of the full assurance of understanding, to the acknowledgment of the Mystery of God, and of the Father, and of Christ.

We have now gone through the first part of the Exordium, which consisted of a narrative proposition ; for the Apostle relates in it how great a conflict he had sustained, that he might retain the Colossians, Laodiceans, and other Christians whom he had never visited, firm in the truth of the Gospel, against all the machinations and deceptions of seducers.

We now come to the second part of the introduction ; a statement of successive reasons of the actions and purposes of the Apostle. For he accumulates many arguments, from which he proves that his advice in persuading them to constancy in the doctrine they had received, was excellent, and that they would best consult their own salvation by following it, i. e. by perseverance, for these have a mutual connexion.

In this verse the argument is drawn from the triple fruit of true and Evangelical doctrine. The Apostle contends that they should persist in it; and that it is expedient for them to persist in it. Why? First, *that their hearts might be comforted;* This is the first fruit. Secondly, *that they might be knit together,* and, as it were, cemented *in love;* this is the second fruit. Thirdly, *that they might attain a more enlarged, more certain, and more evident assurance of understanding :* and here he finally declares, by apposition, what understanding or knowledge he means; not that of worldly things, but *of God the Father and of Christ.*

That their hearts might be comforted.] These words may be referred to the Apostle's conflict for the Colossians, and his earnest persuasions to perseverance in the received doctrine; for from this conflict for them they might receive twofold comfort.

1. Since they saw from it that they were highly regarded, and greatly beloved by the Apostle. For it is the greatest consolation to men in danger to perceive that others care for them, especially those who are able to assist them; which the original word itself shews, for παρακαλειν is to excite the mind of a person in difficulty by encouraging him, or applauding; as in single combat, or battles, men encourage by their shouts those friends whom they wish should conquer. Thus does the Apostle comfort the Colossians, contending with their seducers, by his good wishes, his advice, his encouragement, and his instruction.

2. They were comforted by this conflict of the Apostle, since they clearly saw from it that the doctrine they had drawn from Epaphras was approved by the Apostle, and its reverse rejected and condemned. For, as Epaphras was not one of the Apostles, they might entertain some doubt respecting the certainty of doctrine delivered by him; especially when many were introducing new doctrines with great appearance of wisdom. This scruple is therefore removed from their hearts; for the Apostle, directly taught of the Holy Spirit, confirms the same doctrine by his suffrage, and contends for retaining it.

But these words may and ought to be referred to the
thing itself to which the Apostle endeavours to persuade
the Colossians, viz. Perseverance in this true doctrine : for
from this perseverance their hearts were about to receive
especial comfort:

1. Because the doctrine of salvation by faith alone in
Christ Jesus, brings tranquillity and peace to troubled consciences. For as the modulations of harmony are wont to
be applied to revive and arouse the mind when sorrowful ;
so are the gratuitous promises of God in Christ, to bring
fresh warmth and tranquillity to men's hearts and consciences. Hence that saying of the Apostle, Rom. v. 1,
Being justified by faith, we have peace with God. And hence
every solid consolation is every where shewn by the Apostle to be founded on the doctrine of grace ; 2 Thess. ii. 16,
Hath given us consolation through grace. And Phil. ii. 1, *If
there be any consolation in Christ.* They, therefore, who
embrace this doctrine, thence obtain consolation.

2. They will be comforted from persevering in the doctrine of the Gospel, because the doctrine of innovators (by
establishing a necessary observation of ceremonies, by introducing the worship of angels, and other vain and uncertain traditions) harassed men's hearts and minds with various scruples and anxieties. Now to be exempt from these
is a great part of spiritual consolation.

Observe 1. When the doctrine of the Gospel is attacked, it behoves a Minister who has any regard for the
consolation of the Church, to defend his fellow-soldier,
and to repress the audacity of heretics : unless he shall
have done this, he will be considered to have failed in his
duty, both to the people of God, and to the glory of the
Creator. As, therefore, Paul vindicates Epaphras from the
calumnies of seducers, and confirms the Colossians in the
truth of the Gospel ; so should we do when the same occasion occurs. For when the truth of the Gospel is in danger, it behoves all to assist, as if to extinguish a confla-
gration.

2. If we would receive consolation from the Gospel in
the business of our salvation, we should not mingle the

commentaries and decrees of men with divinely delivered
doctrine. For as water mixes not with fire, but fire is extinguished when water is poured upon it; so the doctrines
of men cannot coalesce with the saving word of God; but
when these are tacked to it, the fervour of the word (i. e.
the spiritual efficacy in gladdening the heart) is quenched.
Hence the Apostle says to the Galatians, v. 4, in opposition to the teachers of the law, who taught that the works
of the law were to be joined to faith in Christ for justification, *Christ is become of no effect unto you, whosoever of you
are justified by the law.*

The Papists snatch from men's hearts every comfort of
the Gospel, whilst they tread in the footsteps of these seducers, and mingle with the doctrine of the Gospel their
own doctrine of indulgences, expiatory masses, and meritorious works; in which they place the hope of obtaining
remission of sins, justification, and glorification; while
the grace of Christ is neglected, or retained for form's
sake only. It is, however, worthy of remark, that although
many, whilst idly disputing, thrust their masses, indulgences, merits, and such like things on God and man; yet,
when their consciences contend in earnest with Divine justice, they are constrained to fly to Christ alone, and in
very deed confess, that their hearts cannot be comforted, if
this doctrine be departed from. Of this we will adduce
some testimonies:

Anselm, in his meditations, says, *Place thy whole confidence in the death of Christ alone; commit thyself wholly to
this death; with this death cover thyself; and involve thyself
entirely in him. If the Lord would judge thee, say, Lord, I
place the death of my Jesus between me and thee and thy judgment; otherwise I contend not with thee. I bring forward his
merit for my merit, which I ought to have; but, alas! have
not.* Parisiensis, in Lib. de Rhetor. divina, says, *Ye must beware, in contending with God, lest you rely on a frail foundation; which he does who confides in his own merits. For as he
who strives on his own merits, deprives himself of the aid of
God; so he who altogether distrusts himself, and relies on grace
alone, attracts to himself the aid of God.* Gerson, in his

Sermon De nuptiis Christi et Ecclesiæ, part. 1, teaches
that we must trust in the merits of Christ alone before the
Divine tribunal : also, in his treatise De distinctione vera-
rum Visionum à falsis ; and in a Sermon De verbo Dom.
part. 2 ; and De consolat. theolog. part. 3. Bellarmin himself, lib. 5. De justific. cap. 7, says, *It is safest to repose
our whole confidence in the mercy of God alone, on account of
the uncertainty of our own justification.*

But to what purport are these things adduced ? That ye
may understand, that if we would have our hearts receive
true and sound comfort, we must persevere in that doctrine
which enjoins us to repose our hope in Christ alone ; and
that *that* must be exploded which would mingle with it
merits, ceremonies, indulgences, &c.

Being knit together in love, Συμβιβασθεντων.] Συμβιβάζω is *to
knit, to bring to adherence,* as carpenters fit together two
pieces of wood, so that they adhere in indissoluble union.
By this word, therefore, the Apostle shews another fruit
budding forth from this perseverance in the truth of the
Gospel doctrine which they had learnt from Epaphras; viz.
mutual love, and the indissoluble concord of minds. But
this concord of minds not only is *the fruit* of constancy
and stability in true faith, but also it is *the condition* without which the afore-mentioned comfort cannot be possessed : the first cannot, therefore, be had without the second.

1. It is *a fruit ;* because the intellect is the leader of
the will ; as, therefore, discord in the intellect brings with
it discord in the will ; so concord in the intellect (particularly in matters of faith) brings with it concord in the will.
This is every where observable in the Sacred Scriptures.
*The multitude of them that believed were of one heart and of
one soul,* Acts iv. 32. This unity of minds is truly the result of unity of faith ; for unity of faith is the firmest bond
of unity of mind. This Nazianzen excellently shews, Orat.
10, De reconcil. ad Mon. *Nothing so much conciliates concord among those who have at heart the things of God, as
agreement concerning God ; and nothing more tends to discord
than disagreement concerning Him : since he who in other*

things is most modest, in these becomes most fervent, &c. Love
is, therefore, the fruit of unanimity in faith, which so binds
the minds of the godly, as it were, in covenant, that though
some light offences may intervene, yet, as the boughs of
the same tree, driven asunder by the wind, immediately
come together again because they are fixed steadily in one
and the same root; so something similar takes place as it
regards the minds of the faithful, because they are still
rooted in the same faith. On this account, therefore, he
would have them persevere unanimously in the faith, that
they may be united also, *being knit together in love.* Concord of minds is, therefore, the fruit of perseverance in
the doctrine of the Gospel.

Yet it is also *a condition* without which the above-named
spiritual comfort is not obtained. For comfort is not had out
of Christ: if any one lives without love, he is without
Christ, as says John, *He who dwelleth in love dwelleth in
God.* And, vice versa, he who casts off love is rejected
of God. For as no member can be recruited and nourished, if its union with the rest of the body be dissolved; so
no one can participate in that full influx of comfort from
Christ, if that unanimity which ought to exist between
himself and the rest of the brethren be destroyed.

DOGMATICAL THESES.

1. It is folly to hope for any firm union between those
who differ on the chief points of religion and fundamental
doctrines of the Christian faith. When Joram enquired of
Jehu, *Is it peace?* he replied, *What peace, so long as the
whoredoms of thy mother Jezebel and her withcrafts are so
many?* So do those of the True Religion reply, and justly
too, to such as maintain a false religion, *What peace,* &c.
i. e. while the errors and corruptions of the church, which
ye acknowledge as your mother, are so many?

2. Pious Princes should endeavour in their dominions
to establish the one true religion, if they look forward to
the salvation of their subjects, or to peace and public concord, however false politicians may scoff at it. For they
cannot have subjects *knit together in love,* unless they have

them of the same opinion in religion. We were very near being taught how true this is, by the extinction of the king, nobles, prelates, and, indeed, the whole government.

3. Those who would in this life enjoy spiritual consolations ought to preserve the bond of love, and agreement of faith with their brethren; for when these are present, all things are full of love, repose, and consolation; let these be removed, every thing abounds with and is debased by suspicion, animosity, and calamity.

So far concerning the second fruit of perseverance and unanimity in the truth received.

And unto all riches of the full assurance of understanding.] This is the third fruit to be participated in by the Colossians, if they should remain in the truth of the Gospel. For not only will they become more firmly bound together in love, but they will more abundantly increase in faith itself: for their faith will be triply augmented; *in richness, in abundance, in intelligence or clear-sightedness.* *Riches* refers to the matter embraced by faith; *full assurance and intelligence,* to the mode of embracing it.

As to the first; the faith of Christians is augmented in *richness* when they who have learnt only the principles and elements, as it were, of salvation (God blessing, and the Divine Spirit enlightening their minds more and more) proceed to farther attainments, and deduce from these principles many other particular propositions, and thus are enriched in a manner with new furniture in the knowledge of religion. For, as in other sciences, the principles are few, but in these few, innumerable conclusions lie virtually hid, which afterwards are drawn out by the intellect when it is employed on these principles; so in this science of Theology, some few principles, absolutely necessary to be known, are presented to tender minds just approaching the Christian faith; and afterwards a rich treasury of sacred knowledge is collected for every purpose of salvation, by assiduous meditation, and by hearing, and chiefly by the internal operation and teaching of the Spirit. They, therefore, who constantly persevere in the doctrine of the Gospel, thence obtain *all riches.* For *the Lord, who hath laid the foundation of this spiritual edifice, in his mercy daily builds it up until he finishes it,* August. De præd. sanct. lib. 1. 7. *He who hath begun a good work in you will perform it,* Phil. i. 6.

Hence spring forth various doctrines.

1. The laity themselves should not be content with an elementary knowledge in religious matters, but ought to press forward from easy principles to a particular and richer knowledge of those things which have more difficult explications and require a deeper research. Thus the Apostle to the Hebrews, vi. 1, says, *Therefore, leaving the principles of the doctrine of Christ, let us go on unto perfection.*

2. When these riches are sought, it is certain that the means also necessary to their attainment should be sought out. He who would have a treasure must dig in the earth. He who would have riches in the knowledge of divine things, must search the Holy Scriptures, carefully hear Ministers, and perform all those other things ordained by God for the acquirement of these riches. So much of the *riches* of faith.

I come now to the *full assurance* (πληροφοριαν): by which word is denoted that firm and certain adherence to what is believed, which springs from the internal operation of the Spirit illuminating the intellect, inclining the will, and, lastly, (if I may so express it) firmly stamping the impress of the things believed upon the mind itself. And this *full assurance* is at length attained by those who remain firm in the doctrine of faith ; for as trees as soon as they are planted, are not so firmly fixed in the earth but that they are driven from side to side by the wind ; so the faith of the godly at the commencement wavers with many doubts : but as the same trees in course of time fix their roots deeper, so faith also daily shoots its roots deeper into the mind, and at length, by the grace of the Spirit, acquires that steadiness which cannot be overthrown by the craft of seducers, the violence of tyrants, or any other machination of the devil.

I remember to have read a little tale told by Gerson which is well adapted to illustrate this. He relates that he once knew a pious man, vexed and harassed by doubts, even in the article of faith ; who, nevertheless, at the last, was led to such a light of truth and assurance, that no trace of wavering dwelt in his mind ; nor, indeed, did he doubt more of that than he did of his own existence. He adds, moreover, that this assurance did not spring from any new reasonings or demonstrations, but from humility, and the captivation of his intellect, and some wonderful illumination of God from the eternal hills. Worldly men do not believe that such illuminations do occur, and that such a *full assurance* is impressed on the minds of the faithful ; but the godly, who constantly persevere in the Gospel, have experienced them. The Apostle requires this undoubting persuasion in the doctrine of faith, Ephes. iv. 14. *That we henceforth be no more children, tossed to and fro and carried about,* &c.

Hence we learn,

1. The faith of a Christian man ought not to depend upon others, but be settled in the believer by the efficacy of the Spirit; so that if prelates and ecclesiastics, nay, even the whole world, should depart from sound faith, yet should every one of the laity hold to the received faith. *If we, or an angel from heaven should preach unto you any other Gospel than that ye have received, let him be accursed :* Gal. i. 9.

2. Hence it is evident how greatly Romanists err, who think that the assurance of our faith lies enshrined in the papal breast of the Pope ; not for every one in his own breast. Now it is most certain, that the determination of a Pope cannot give *full assurance* to my heart; but the operation of the Spirit both can, and is accustomed to do so, in the case of true believers. *The anointing which ye have received of him abideth in you ; as the same anointing teacheth you of all things, and is truth, and is no lie,* 1 John ii. 27.

3. Their complaint also is unjust, who aver, that we cannot now arrive at assurance in matters of faith, since Christians are separated into different sects, and there are divisions and controversies every where. Notwithstanding

this, the godly have this *full assurance* of Gospel truth.
Clemens, Strom 7, rightly says, *Truth is to be found, by
those who wish it, from a diligent search of the Scripture.*
And Lactantius, Institut. lib. 7. cap. 2, asserts what is very
much to our purpose : *We do not attain truth by thinking
and disputing, but by hearing and learning from Him who
alone can both know and teach ;* i. e. (as I interpret it) from
the Holy Spirit, speaking outwardly in the Scriptures, and
inwardly in the heart of each believer.   Thus far of *full
assurance.*

Lastly, that we should weigh what the Apostle adds,
that they would have not only a *full assurance,* but a *full
assurance of understanding,* i. e. *the understanding fully assured.* The mind, therefore, is not only inclined firmly to
adhere to what is believed by the power of the will when
softened by grace; but the intellect, at the same time, is
so brightened by supernatural light, that it can clearly
contemplate the certain and indubitable truth of these
things. Thus Parisiensis, in his Tractat. de fide. cap. 1.
writes, *No power can effect any thing either contrary to or
above itself.* Consequently the human intellect cannot believe of itself; and it is therefore necessary that it should
be enlightened by a stronger light and greater illumination.
It is by this light, then, that the intellect conceives a proposition which is behind, and at the same time sees the
formal reason why it is believed. Now this reason is neither a scientific, nor demonstrative medium, but Divine authority. For infused faith shews the intellect that the
doctrine it believes is derived from God. Gerson excellently sets forth this in this treatise on errors in regard to
faith. *An infused faith is requisite,* says he, *for every one's
assent to Catholic truth, which points out and shews the reason
of belief; viz. that God hath delivered this truth.* This is,
therefore, to have a full assurance of the understanding,
both to perceive the truth itself and its Author. It appears
from Scripture that this enlightened understanding is always joined with faith. Thus Ephes. i. 17, *The Father of
glory may give unto you the Spirit of wisdom and revelation
in the knowledge of him, the eyes of your understanding being*

enlightened, &c. And 1 Pet. ii. 9, *Who hath called you out of darkness into his marvellous light.*

Hence we learn,

1. That that is not a divine but a brutal animal faith, which has no understanding or comprehension of those things which are believed. Such a faith Staphylus extols in the collier who professed that he believed what the church believed, and the church believed what he himself held, whilst he was ignorant all the time what either the church or he himself held.* But the true faith has *full assurance of the understanding;* this implicit and blind faith has not a grain of understanding.

2. Whoever assents to the belief of a doctrine only on account of the authority of its teachers, the multitude of its believers, or some such external motive, while he is in the mean time without that internal light in which the mind beholds the formal reason of its belief; such an one has not the attribute of infused faith, but a light notion in matters of faith. *For no one believes any thing to be true, merely because he wishes to believe it is true.* Picus Mirand. tom. i. p. 94.†

---

* Fredericus Staphylus, who first broached the above sentiment, afterwards immortalized by Bellarmin, was a native of Osnaburg, born in 1512. He was at first a Lutheran, a Greek Professor at Breslau, and Theological Professor at Konigsberg. He attached himself to the Romish Church in 1553, and was at the Council of Trent in the following year; became Counsellor to the Emperor, and the Duke of Bavaria; but died at Ingoldstadt, the 5th of March, 1564, after having published some works, among which are the following :—De Desidiis Hæret. which was translated by Stapleton, and printed at Antwerp, in 1565, in 2 vols. 12mo.; Apologia de Germano Script. Sacr. intellectu, &c. The Archbishop of Salzbourg was commissioned by the Pope to transmit to him a Cardinal's Hat from Rome, to appoint him Doctor in Theology, and elevate him to the Episcopate. Vide Annals of the University of Ingoldstadt, cited in Dictionnaire Universelle, Paris, 1812. Vide also, Aub. Miræi Scriptores, Sæc. xvi., Sect. cxvi. in Fabricii Biblioth. Ecclesiast. Hamburgii. 1718.

† Picus (John) or Giovanni Pico di Mirandola, one of the celebrated Italian literati of the fifteenth century, who contributed to the revival and diffusion of learning in Europe. He was born in 1463, third son of the Prince of Mirandola and Concordia, and almost from his childhood displayed an eager attachment to literature. Deprived of his father when young, his mother paid assiduous attention to his education, and at the age of fourteen

From the whole we gather how disgracefully the Papists err, who say that we cannot believe the doctrine of faith revealed in Scripture, otherwise than because the church confirms it by its suffrage. That blasphemous saying of Hermanus is well known: that the Scriptures were worth just as much as Æsop's fables, unless the testimony of the church were added to them. But if *the full assurance of understanding* arises from internal light and secret persuasion of the Spirit; then all the elect will recognise the

he was sent to the University of Bologna, to study canon law, but after spending two years there, he set out to visit the most celebrated schools in Italy and France. He went to Ferrara, where he was kindly received by his relation Duke Hercules I. and studied under Batista Guarino. He had a great readiness in acquiring languages, and is said to have been master of twenty-two when he was but eighteen years of age. Trithemius, his contemporary, says he was master of all the liberal arts, that he cultivated with success, Latin, Greek, and Hebrew literature, was an admirable poet, and the most learned philosopher and skilful disputant of the age. Settling at Florence, he addressed a panegyric to Lorenzo de Medici, whose patronage he obtained. In 1486 he went to Rome. There he posted up 900 propositions appertaining to dialectics, morals, physics, mathematics, &c. challenging any antagonist whomsoever to dispute with him upon any one of them. But instead of opponents such as he expected, he encountered an accusation of heresy, and thirteen of his propositions being accused before Pope Innocent VIII. he was silenced, and thought proper to leave Rome. He then returned to Florence, where he composed an apology for his opinions; and was at length acquitted of all blame. The effect, however, of the anxiety produced by this business, caused a total change in his course of life; and though young, rich, elegant in person and in manners, and in some degree habituated to pleasure, he gave himself up to devotion, and confined his studies to theological subjects. These induced a most enthusiastic desire to be useful, and he resolved to distribute all his property among the poor, and travel barefooted through the world to preach the Gospel. An early death, at the age of 32, put an end to his projects. His principal works are—" Hexaplus, or an Explanation of the Six Days of the Creation;" a book on the Psalms, another, " Adversus Astrologiam Divinitricem, & Epistolarum, lib. viii." He also wrote on the Jewish Cabala, which was in great credit in the sixteenth century. He was one of the learned men whom Naudé has thought it necessary to vindicate from the charge of being a Magician. The writings of Picus, it is said, " display an acute genius, and a vast extent of learning." He is admitted on all hands to have been a very extraordinary person, and was denominated the Phœnix among the geniuses of his time. But his works added very little to true science, notwithstanding his attainments and erudition.

A a 2

voice of Christ in the Scriptures, although the Roman church, or any other visible church disclaim it.   Therefore we do not reject the external voice of the church, or consider its ministry at all unnecessary; but we hold that *the full assurance of the understanding* in matters of faith arises from internal light and the testimony of the Spirit, without which, if the church were a thousand times to inculcate the belief of this or that, yet no one should believe it.

To the acknowledgment of the mystery of God, and of the Father, and of Christ.] These words are connected with the former ones by apposition, as it is termed: For they explain what, and of what kind, is that *full assurance of the understanding* which they will acquire: It is not of human things, or philosophical or Jewish fables; but the knowledge *of the mystery of God, and of the Father, and of Christ.*   Two things are to be examined: What he understands by *mystery;* and why that mystery is called *of God, and of the Father, and of Christ.*

The *mystery* Chrysostom interprets to be our reconciliation and access to God the Father by the incarnate Son, not by angels.   Cardinal Hugo says, that this mystery is nothing else but the saving death of Christ.   But these interpretations are too restricted.   Under the word *mystery* then, the Apostle includes the whole doctrine of the Gospel, which was revealed through the Apostles for the salvation of the human race.   The Gospel is with good reason called a *mystery,* since it is impervious to human reason, which never could have formed even the slightest notion of that mode of acquiring salvation which is proposed in the Gospel; but would have wearied itself in vain in seeking salvation in the visionary schemes of the human imagination.

But why is the Gospel, or Evangelical doctrine, called *the mystery of God, and of the Father, and of Christ?*   On two accounts:

1.   Because the triune God was the Author and Framer of the doctrine of the Gospel; and Christ was sent by the Father as a herald and promulgator of the same.   It therefore flowed from them as from its efficient causes, and

hence it is appropriately termed the Gospel *of God and of Christ.*

2. Because God, and the Father, and Christ are the principal objects of the doctrine of the Gospel. For the Gospel lays open to us the majesty, the will, the nature, and, finally, the attributes of God; it teaches, moreover, that this God has a paternal affection for us as adopted for his sons, through and on account of Christ his incarnate Son, Gal. iv. 5. Lastly, it depicts Christ to us as the Mediator uniting and reconciling us to God ; together with all his offices, operations, and other functions which relate to the full knowledge of Christ. Therefore, from this threefold doctrine, which respects the nature of God, his paternal affection for the human race, and Christ the Mediator, the Gospel is called, as from its more noble part, *the mystery of God, and of the Father, and of Christ.*

Hence we learn,

1. As the law was enacted, not only by the Father, but also by the Son, (for the Apostle says, Gal. iii. 19, *it was ordained in the hand of a Mediator ;)* so the Gospel is to be attributed not to the Son alone, but to the Father, nay, and the whole Trinity : for it is the mystery of God, and of Christ *effectively.* It was extreme dotage, therefore, in Marcion to imagine that one God was Author of the law, and another of the Gospel : whom Tertullian thus refutes in lib. 5. vers. Marc. *Distinguish,* says he, *the law for one God, and Christ for another God, if thou canst divide a shadow from its substance.* And again : *The liberty of the Gospel was to be promulgated by the same by whom the servitude of the law was ; for no one can emancipate the servants of another.* Joachim the Abbot* was also mad in his conjecture, for he taught that a triple doctrine proceeded from the three per-

---

* A Cistertian Monk, Abbot of Corazzo, and afterwards of Flora, in Calabria ; he was born at Celico, near Cozensa, in 1130 ; travelled on a pilgrimage to the holy land, and after founding several monasteries, died in 1202. His works were published in folio at Venice, in 1516, and his life was written by Gervaise, a Dominican, in 2 vols. 12mo. 1745. As he advanced many heterodox notions in his works, he wrote a Declaration of his faith two years before his death, in which he desired that they might under_go the revisal of the Abbots of his Order, and whatever was censurable

sons; the doctrine of the old law from the Father; the
doctrine of the Gospel, as we have it delivered to us in the
sacred Scriptures, from the Son; and a third Gospel still
to be looked for from the Holy Spirit, which he terms *the
eternal Gospel.* But if the Gospel which we have, is the
Gospel as well of God as of Christ, either the Holy Spirit
is denied to be God, or this Gospel must be ascribed to
him, and no new one expected from him.

2. As the Gospel proceeded from God and from Christ;
so does it every where discourse of God and of Christ, and
of those benefits which we obtain from God the Father
through Christ. Whatever doctrines cannot be referred to
these heads, such as those of heretics, scholastics, and the
like, are not to be accounted Theological mysteries, but
human inventions. This should have been considered by
those who *have devised a Platonic and Aristotelian Christianity,* as Tertullian somewhere says: who, as Gerson writes,
*should justly be called Sophists and Matæologists,** not Evangelists or Theologists;* since, leaving the useful and intelligible instructions concerning God and Christ, they betake
themselves to logical, mathematical, metaphysical, and
such like speculations. 2 Lect. super Marcum.

Thus far concerning *the mystery of God and of Christ,* the
full knowledge of which the Apostle promises to the Colossians abiding in the faith they had received.

might be submitted to the censure of the Church. Agreeably to this declaration, his Commentary on the Proverbs was condemned by Innocent III.
and two other works were afterwards condemned by Alexander IV. in 1256,
and by the Council of Arles in 1260, without, as is said, reflecting on the
orthodoxy of the author. It is, however, not to be wondered at that Joachim's writings should have been thus condemned, he was renowned for
learning and piety, and asserted that Antichrist was born in the Roman
state, and would be exalted to the Apostolic See. Vide Milner, vol. iii.
p. 425.

* Ματαιος from Ματην—frustra; meaning teachers of idle vanities; or,
as Theodoret explains the word in Psalm cxviii. *that which is useless and
without profit.*

Verse 3.

In whom are hid all the treasures of wisdom and knowledge.

In the last words of the preceding verse the Apostle had mentioned Christ: and seizing this occasion, he runs off into the praises of Christ, yet so that he does not advance beyond the limits of his subject. For this slight digression contains a most weighty reason why they should not depart from the doctrine which Epaphras had preached to them, and derived, in fact, from the completeness of the same, as what was amply sufficient for salvation. Having, therefore, laid this ground-work, he paves the way for the contest with the seducers.

But first it must be observed here, that these words *in whom*, are referred by some to the whole phrase of *the knowledge of the mystery of God, and of the Father, and of Christ*, in this sense; that in the investigation of this mystery, i. e. of the Gospel, all the treasures of our wisdom and saving knowledge are placed. But they are referred by others to that last word *Christ ;* in which Christ—our Master, and the Author of the Gospel (say they)—exists as in the most copious fountain, an inexhaustible store of wisdom and knowledge.

The difference between these two interpretations is great. For the former makes the Apostle speak of our wisdom and knowledge, which we attain, by rightly knowing Christ, or the mystery of Christ : therefore, they would have all these treasures, viz. all the fulness and perfection of our wisdom to be in Christ *objectively*, i. e. in the knowledge of Christ, according to that saying of the Apostle, *I determined not to know any thing save Jesus Christ*, 1 Cor. ii. 2. But the latter would have him to speak concerning the wisdom and knowledge residing habitually in Christ; they therefore

conclude from this place, that all wisdom and knowledge
reside in Christ *subjectively.* I dare not reject this opinion, since there is neither falsehood in it, nor does it depart
from the words themselves : But I think that the Apostle
rather had regard to the former, nor spake so much concerning the wisdom with which Christ is wise, as concerning that, by the apprehension of which, we become wise.

2. And it is also to be noted, that these words *wisdom
and knowledge* are not explained in the same manner by all.
Some would have that there is no difference between them,
but that they are introduced and repeated for the sake of
amplification only ; as if the Apostle had said, that in
knowing Christ, we have the most absolute and perfect
knowledge. Others say, the term σοφια (wisdom) designated an acquaintance with God, or divine things; γνωςεως
(knowledge) denotes the comprehension of human affairs,
or of creatures. But there is a third opinion, which I prefer : it is that which explains the former term (which they
render *sapientia)* to mean an acquaintance with those doctrines which relate to faith ; but the latter *(scientia),* the
understanding of those that relate to the Christian life.
Wisdom, therefore, embraces the things to be believed ;
knowledge, the things to be done. Both these are known,
when Christ, or the mystery of Christ, is properly understood.

In the last place, we must remark, that it is said these
treasures are not merely placed or situated in the knowledge of Christ, or the Gospel of Christ, but *hidden.* By
which word is intimated, that what is precious and magnificent in Christ, or the Gospel of Christ, is not conspicuous,
or directly meets the eyes of carnal men; but is so concealed, that it is discovered only by those to whom God
has given a quick sight, i. e. spiritual eyes to see. So
Christ himself said, Matt xi. 25, *I thank thee, O Father,
that thou hast hidden,* &c. And the Apostle, 1 Cor. i. 23,
shews that Christ is no treasure to carnal men, but an offence and object of ridicule; *We preach Christ crucified, to
the Jews a stumbling-block,* &c. This opinion, therefore,

being adopted, which would have all these treasures in the mystery of Christ to be understood *objectively,* we hence derive these instructions :

1.　He is truly wise, who has learnt the Gospel; he is altogether unwise who seeks saving knowledge elsewhere for here are *all treasures.*

2.　He who places secular knowledge, and the things of the world, before this study and sacred knowledge, prefers rubbish to treasure : for the mystery of the Gospel is *treasure ;* all else is *dung and dross.*

3.　It is not to be wondered at that almost all the world errs both in faith and practice.　They err, in things to be believed, because they take not the rule of faith from the Gospel, but from human authority : in things to be done, because they take not the rule of life from hence, but from the custom of the ungodly,　But in this both *wisdom* and *knowledge* should be sought.

4.　If we would gain saving knowledge from the Gospel, we must attend to it not lazily, and in a perfunctory manner, but we must labour and toil in acquiring this treasure.　For this treasure is not placed in open view, it is *hidden.*

5.　We must not confide in our industry or discernment ; but diligently intreat God, that he would quicken our sight, and permit this hidden treasure to be seen by us : *Open thou mine eyes, that I may behold wondrous things out of thy law,* Ps. cxix. 18.

Up to this point in the Exposition of these words, *In whom are hid all the treasures of wisdom and knowledge,* we have followed that opinion which explains them *objectively,* respecting that perfect knowledge which we have in the true knowledge of Christ.　But because (as was before said) these words are explained by some, of that perfect wisdom which Christ hath in himself *subjectively,* we will discuss their interpretation and opinion, and refute their erroneous inferences.　But both the Schoolmen, as well as the Ubiquitarians, follow this opinion : for from this passage both conclude that omniscience is an attribute of Christ, even in regard to his human nature.　But the Schoolmen, although they differ from our Divines *verbally,*

yet they concur with them *virtually.* For what they call
omniscience, they nevertheless include within certain limits : whence it is evident they ascribe to the soul of
Christ an omniscience, not indeed absolute, which is the
property of the Divine nature, but a certain similitude of
it, and, as it were, the thing itself in a certain relation.
But the Ubiquitarians much more boldly teach that the
very Divine omniscience was really communicated to the
human nature of Christ, in the same manner as the omnipotence; Jacobus Andreas, Colloq. Mompelg. tract. de
persona Christi ; where also he brings forward this passage.
We shall set forth the opinion of the Schoolmen, and refute that of the Ubiquitarians, but very briefly.

The Schoolmen, besides the uncreated wisdom of Christ,
allege a manifold created wisdom to be in him. Alexander
Hales, part. 3. qu. 13. memb. 1 et 2, laid down a fourfold
knowledge in the soul of Christ : The first he calls *a knowledge by the grace of union;* the second, *a knowledge by the
grace of comprehension ;* the third, *the knowledge of a perfect
nature ;* the fourth, *the knowledge of experience.* Aquinas,
part. 3. qu. 9. art. 1, omits the first : for he does not think
any new species of knowledge ought to be supposed in the
soul of Christ on account of union ; only he grants that
the knowledge of comprehension is much more clear and
excellent in the soul of Christ because of this union, than
in any of the blessed, whether angels or men. He, therefore, attributes a triple knowledge to the soul of Christ ;
viz. a *blessed,* an *infused,* and an *acquired* knowledge. But
now (to come to the point) they ask, whether the soul of
Christ knows all things according to this created wisdom ;
whether he hath an equal knowledge of all things with
God ; and they answer in the affirmative. But when they
attempt to explain their opinion, they say that the knowledge of God is to be considered in a twofold manner ; in
respect to *God himself,* and in respect to *creatures.* As to
God's knowledge of *himself,* the soul of Christ does not
know, neither can it know, all things which God knows ;
for it does not know all that God can do ; because this
knowledge would comprehend the divine Godhead, which

is incomprehensible. But as far as regards *the creatures,* they say that Christ in the Word knows all things which are, and which will be, whether things spoken, done, or thought by any mortal; because he is to be the judge of all. They affirm, moreover, that he knows all the essence, and power, and acting of every creature, because he is the Lord of all. They, therefore, conclude, if we speak concerning knowledge as it respects the creatures, that the soul of Christ, as to *the number of the things known,* has a knowledge equal with God; because he knows all the creatures even as God; but as to the *means of knowing, and the mode of knowing,* his knowledge is far inferior : For because God knows all things by himself as by the cause; the soul of Christ [knows them] not by himself, but by the Word; God knows all things in a more clear and profound manner. But this universal knowledge of the creatures, is not that omniscience which is the attribute of the Divine nature; because all the creatures taken together, which are, which have been, or shall be, are not in fact infinite. Therefore, according to the Schoolmen, the soul of Christ, or the human nature, is not capable of omniscience, neither likewise of omnipotence.

Now to proceed with the Ubiquitarians; they think that, like as the other attributes of Godhead, so omniscience is really communicated to the human nature of Christ; and they abuse this passage to establish their error, *In whom are hid all the treasures,* &c.

We answer, nothing can be concluded from this passage in favour of that absolute omniscience of the soul of Christ, on many accounts. First, because it is much more likely that the Apostle speaks concerning our saving wisdom, which we have in rightly knowing Christ, than concerning the wisdom of Christ himself. Secondly, because if it be granted that he speaks concerning the wisdom and knowledge with which the soul of Christ is endued, we may interpret this of that highest fulness of created and infused knowledge, in which there is nothing wanting that is required to perfect the soul of Christ, although there may not be omniscience, of which the creature cannot properly

be said to be capable. Thirdly, let us assume the omniscience of Christ to be proved from this passage, yet they
will not immediately make out from this that that is in the
soul or human nature of Christ: for the Apostle does not
say, *in which* soul, or nature ; but *in whom,* i. e. Christ, *are
all treasures:* they are, therefore, in Christ, because in *the
Word,* not because in the human nature. So Ambrose
places the treasures of omniscience in the person of Christ,
not in the human nature : he says, *it is just that the knowledge of all things should be in the Author of all things.* But
the Word, not the human nature of Christ, created all
things. So Aquinas in his Commentaries refers this omniscience to the Word, not to the soul: *Whatever,* says he,
can be known concerning God, all THAT *the Word has abundant knowledge of in himself ; whatever can be known concerning the creature, he knows pre-eminently in himself ; and therefore in the Word are all treasures.*

We have thus vindicated this passage from the cavils of
the Ubiquitarians : We shall now refute their error by a
few arguments ; and that from their own principles.

1. They concede that each nature in Christ possesses
and retains its own properties, so that the property of one
nature can never become the property of the other : thus
James Andreas, Colloq. Mompelg.* But what is really
communicated to one, that becomes the property of the
other : Omniscience, therefore, being really communicated
to the human nature of Christ, does not remain the property of the Divine nature alone ; because it is found in the
other nature.

2. The attributes of the Divine nature are not communicated *essentially* to the human nature ; for were this the case,

* Andreas ; was a celebrated Lutheran Divine of Wirtemberg, eminent
as a Reformer, and distinguished by the part he took in the controversies of
his day ; being engaged in the public conferences at Worms, Ratisbon, Augs-
berg, Meming, Torgau, &c. The work above referred to is the discussions
at Mompelgard, with Beza, concerning the Lord's supper, the person of
Christ, predestination, &c. He was Chancellor to Gustavus Vasa, and
employed by that Monarch to translate the Scriptures into the Swedish
Language. He died in 1590, strong in the faith, which, through an active
life, he had laboured to maintain and defend.

the human nature, upon the acknowledgment of Chemnitz
himself, would turn out Divine :* for since the properties of
Divinity are not accidents, but the essence of God himself,
they cannot belong to, neither are they communicated, i. e.
formally, habitually, or *subjectively.* But no other mode besides
the essential and *accidental* can be desired : therefore the attributes of Divinity, among which our opponents themselves
assign omniscience, are not communicated to the human
soul. But they say they are communicated by an hypostatical union. Yet this is nothing to the purpose. For the
attributes of the natures are not transferred from one to the
other by virtue of the hypostatic union ; but the attribute
of one nature is ascribed to the other in the concrete, for
the sake of the identity of the thing supposed. As when
we say that God suffered, or was crucified, or was born of
a virgin ; that the man Christ was omniscient, omnipotent,
the Creator of the world : predications of this kind are
true, not because the Divine nature in itself in any manner
admits the possibility of suffering ; or the human nature
the attribute of omnipotence and omniscience : but because
that man who suffered was God ; and God who is omnipotent, was also man in unity of person.

3. He who says that the human nature of Christ is omniscient, and is so by that omniscience which is the attribute of the Godhead, he assigns one and the same know-

* Trac. de duabus naturis, cap. 22. Martin Chemnitz was another eminent Lutheran Divine, who flourished about the same time with Andreas,
in the Duchy of Brandenburg, to the Prince of which he became Librarian.
To the learned Martin Chemnitz's examination of the Decrees of the Council of Trent, the history of Religion, says Mosheim, is more indebted than
many are apt to imagine. He died in 1586, at Brunswick, leaving behind
him several important works, especially the ground-work and commencement
of an elaborate Harmony of the four Evangelists, with a Commentary on
the same, which was afterwards completed by other hands, and is held in
high repute on the Continent. Of this harmony and his other theological
writings, Leigh, in his treatise on learning, asserts, " they are most profitable, especially that excellent work, or rather most rich bibliotheque, which
contains both a refutation of the Council of Trent, and also an explication
of the whole doctrine of the Church ; to be read daily by all to whom the
knowledge of the truth is welcome."

ledge to the human soul and to the Divine nature.* But our opponents themselves condemn the Monothelites,† who ascribe the same will of Deity and humanity in Christ; why are they not also to be condemned, who hold that there is the same knowledge in both?

4. That rule of Leo which is contained in his tenth Epistle, viz. that either nature can perform what is peculiar to it with the concurrence of the other, is proved by the Ubiquitarians themselves: But if omniscience be communicated to the human nature of Christ, then the human nature performs what exclusively belongs to the Godhead; for it comprehends all things by the infinite power of the communicated omniscience.

In short; There is in the human nature of Christ, all that fulness of infused and created knowledge which is required for the ministration of our salvation; in his Divine nature absolute omniscience is found: and, consequently, *In him are all the treasures of* created and uncreated *knowledge.*

---

* Chemnitz, de duabus naturis, cap. 23.

† The opinion of the Monothelites here adverted to had its rise in 630. The Sect were condemned by the sixth general Council in 680, as being supposed to destroy the perfection of the humanity of Jesus Christ, depriving it of will and operation. The account which Milner gives of the rise, spread, and opposition to this heresy by Sophronius Bishop of Jerusalem, is interesting and instructive.

Verses 4, 5.

And this I say, lest any man should beguile you with en-
ticing words.

For though I be absent in the flesh, yet am I with you in the
Spirit, joying and beholding your order, and the sted-
fastness of your faith in Christ.

In these two verses the Apostle assigns two reasons why
he laboured so much in confirming the Colossians. The
first is derived from the danger which threatened them ; *lest*
any one should beguile you, &c. The second from the love
dwelling in the Apostle's heart ; *For though I be absent,*
&c.

And this I say.] These words are referred by some to
the verse immediately preceding, concerning all the treasures of wisdom hid in Christ ; which the Apostle affirmed
with this view, lest being seduced by impostors, they
should think that the means of salvation should be sought
elsewhere. By others they are referred to all those things
which had been before stated in this Chapter ; as though
the Apostle had said, I would that ye knew my conflict
with those false teachers to have been undertaken for this
end, lest ye should be beguiled by their sophistical conceits. It is of no importance to the main drift of the subject. For this is the meaning, that the Apostle strenuously
defends the true doctrine concerning our salvation reposed
in Christ alone, and on this account, lest the Colossians
attaching themselves to the vain devices of men, this saving doctrine should be neglected.

Hence we learn,

1. That to preach and fully teach Christ and the benefits of Christ, is to stop the way against all the idle and
superstitious inventions of men : for when Christ is rightly
known, those beggarly elements are held in contempt.

This is clearly taught in Philip. iii. 8, *1 count all things but loss for the excellency of the knowledge of Christ Jesus,* &c.

2. Where the treasures of wisdom laid up in Christ alone are not known, there the people easily fall into errors, into superstitious worship, and finally into the very pit of perdition. For as weak women who lack children, are wont to amuse themselves with lap-dogs and birds ; so weak, unhappy souls, destitute of the knowledge of Christ, in vain seek comfort in the silly trifles of human contrivance.

3. Here, then, we see why in the Papacy so much regard is paid to masses, indulgences, pilgrimages, satisfactions, invocations of the dead, and other things of that kind ; viz. because, forsooth, they know not that all the treasures of wisdom and knowledge are laid up in Christ : for this being admitted, that crude mass of superstition falls to the ground, which Christ and his Apostles never contemplated, except with abhorrence.

Lest any one should beguile you with enticing words.] See the danger in which the Colossians were ; that is to say, of the circumvention of false teachers ! Behold also the instrument with which they endeavoured to create this danger for them; viz. enticing words !

Παραλογιζεσθαι, or *to beguile,* is *by a false reason,* which hath the semblance of truth, to deceive the unskilful. Whence Aristotle draws a parallel between it and spurious gold, or die, which counterfeit the real nature of those things they have not in them. Under this word, therefore, the Apostle would comprehend whatever is introduced in any manner under the appearance of Religion, against the simplicity of the doctrine of the Gospel. For although the impostors seemed by specious reasons to establish the worship of angels, the observance of ceremonies, and certain philosophical vanities ; yet they could not effect it by legitimate arguments derived from the word of God, but by paralogisms and sophistical deceptions.

And, indeed, these sophisms of seducers proceed either from *malice,* or of *ignorance.* From malice, when wicked men oppose acknowledged truth, either for their own

glory and advantage, or that they may occasion trouble and
dislike to true teachers. So the Scribes and the Pharisees
opposed Christ and his doctrine, that they might establish
their own vain traditions, and that they might obtain honour among the unthinking multitude. These impostors
are the most wretched of all mortals; for, as Cyprian
writes, Epist. lib. 2. epist. 1, *the souls* of all those to whom
by their deceivings *they have been the authors and leaders to
perdition, will be required at their hands in the day of judgment.*

There are others who deceive the people by their sophisms from ignorance; for their own minds, too, are ensnared by the same devices with which they endeavour to
ensnare others. And these sophisms for the most part prevail among those in whom a preposterous zeal, void of
knowledge, predominates. In this catalogue we may
reckon those who, inflamed with a certain pious affection
towards the saints of God and holiness itself, were at
length so far carried away by a singular blind zeal, as to
imagine and require that the saints should be worshipped
and invoked; to contend that even the kingdom of heaven
is acquired by the fruit of their good works; and to hawk
about these their sophisms every where with the greatest
ardour for true doctrine. Among this number even they
also are to be accounted, who, burning with a just hatred
against all superstitious worship, because God will not be
worshipped by the commandments of men, are hurried away
with such a zeal as to maintain that all rites, all the ordinances of the Church, even concerning things indifferent,
are to be rejected and exterminated. But we should take
care not to be imposed upon either by the one or the other:
for both attempt to ensnare others, being deceived by their
own sophisms. *Honey is good,* says Gerson, *with the honey-
comb; that is to say, the savour of devotion, with the moderation of discretion.* And thus much concerning the danger
threatening the Colossians, the repelling of which is the
object of the Apostle.

With enticing words, εν πιθανολογια.] This is that instrument or means which the seducers employed in order to

deceive. Under this word the Apostle comprehends rheto-
rical and flattering insinuations, sophistical and intricate
subtleties ; with which they endeavoured either to insinuate or force an entrance into the minds of men. In short;
whatever is so flattering to human reason, by its specious
colouring, as to lead a man from Christ, is to be referred to
the pernicious *enticing words.* This deceitful sophistry the
Apostle condemns in 1 Cor. ii. 4. Not that *persuasiveness
of words* is in itself condemnable, for it is a great excellence of speech; but the abuse of it, when it acts by apparent, but false reasons, and is employed to impose upon
men.

Concerning that insinuating *persuasion,* Tertullian, in
writing against Valentinus, clearly speaks, *Impostors have
the art to persuade before they teach ; but truth persuades by
teaching, not teaches by persuading.* Concerning that sophistry, Prudentius formerly complained ;

> Fidem minutis dissecant ambagibus,
> Ut quisque linguâ est nequior ;
> Solvunt ligantque quæstionum vincula
> Per syllogismos plectiles,
> Væ captiosis sycophantarum strophis,
> Væ versipelli astutiæ.*

But [it may be said] how can there be such enticement
in those in whom there is no truth? For (if we believe the
Philosopher) things which are true are *more easily reduced
to the shape of argument, and more persuasive,* than false ones
are. Rhet. i. 6.

This is the solution : They are so indeed, both in themselves and in their nature; but as it regards the unskilful
and external appearance, many false things seem more probable than many true ones. And that happens, because

---

* Thus attempted—

> Faith into nicest subtleties is split,
> As each is furnished with more wicked wit ;
> The Casuists' knot alike to tie or loose,
> The tortuous syllogism's found of use:
> Shame on the quibbling turns of arts untrue !
> Shame upon fallacies of varying hue !

false things are connected to true ones by their great likeness : whence it comes to pass that they are not distinguished by the unskilful, especially when aided by the art
of impostors, which is accustomed to draw the colour of
truth over false things.

DOGMATICAL OBSERVATIONS.

1. In theological subjects it is not proper rashly to give
credit to reasonings, however plausible, which are not
built upon the word of God as their foundation : for very
often they have a wonderful *persuasiveness*, when, nevertheless, they have no truth. That remark of Tertullian [in
his treatise] De anima, should be borne in mind, *Build up
faith from thy foundation.*

2. As the Spirit of Christ is to be acknowledged the
inward teacher of those who preach the Gospel uncor-
ruptly; so a crooked serpent is their master who impose
upon men by sophistical subtleties and this counterfeit
persuasion. For that deceiver first employed this *enticing
mode* in Paradise, in beguiling the woman.

3. This is the aim of sophists in treating divine things,
To put forth their own opinions, not the word of God; to
beguile men, not to edify them; to obtain the victory for
themselves, not that truth may conquer; according to that
remark of Clemens, Strom. 1, *Opiniativeness is the beginning of contention, strife the effect of it, victory the end.*

Thus far concerning the impostors and their weapon, viz.
false and counterfeit *persuasion.*

Verse 5.

*For though I be absent in the flesh, yet am I with you in
the spirit, joying, and beholding your order, and the
stedfastness of your faith in Christ.*

This is the other reason of the Apostle's solicitude for
the Colossians, taken from his inward affection towards
them; and contains in it an implied anticipation. For

B b 2

they might say, You are far distant from us ; you are moreover ignorant of our affairs : you are not, therefore, solicitous about us ; neither if you would, can you recommend
those things which will conduce to the welfare of our
church. He removes each objection : the former by a distinction, I am distant from you, but in *body*, not in *mind*
and *affection:* the other by a negative, I am *not* ignorant of
your affairs, for *I perceive your order and faith:* I am able
to advise you therefore, equally as if I were present.

But that we may proceed in order, it will be proper to
observe, in the illustration of the words, two things : 1.
After what manner he is influenced, or the mode of the
Apostle's affection towards the Colossians ; 2. Wherefore
he is so influenced, or the cause of his affection. The
mode consists in two things : as well in unceasing thought
about them, and meditation on their affairs, &c. as in rejoicing on their account.   But now as to the cause why he
so often thinks of them, why he rejoices in this contemplation, he assigns a double one; viz. their order and stedfast faith.

*For though I be absent in the flesh, yet am I with you in the
spirit.*] Here he shews that he was never so far absent
from the Colossians, but that in mind, in care, and thought
he was present with them.

1. Because he never put the recollection of them out
of his mind.   For it is the peculiarity of the lover not to
be severed in mind from those whom he loves, although
separated by distance of place.

But Ambrose, and some modern interpreters also, explain these words, *I am with you in the Spirit*, not only of
that thought and remembrance of them, but of some extraordinary presence of the Spirit granted to the Apostle
by Divine power : such as Elisha had, who perceived in
his mind those things which were done by his servant,
equally as though he had stood before him ; which is gathered from those words of the prophet, 2 Kings v. 26,
*Went not mine heart with thee, when the man turned again
from his chariot to meet thee?* The prophet remained in his

house, and yet he says that his heart went with his servant, because he saw as clearly his act, as they who were present when he met them. And these words, *Beholding your order,* &c. favour this interpretation. We do not, therefore, deny, that what was granted to the prophets, could have been granted to an Apostle also : since the care of all the churches was laid upon him, it is very likely the state of all the churches was also known to him, not only from the vague report of men, but from the revelation of the Divine Spirit; to the intent that he might better consult and provide for the necessities of the churches. We, therefore, admit and unite both interpretations, stating that the Apostle was with the Colossians as well in the meditation of his mind, as in the revelation of the Spirit, although absent in body.

Joying and beholding.] That is, joying because I behold: for the conjunction has the force of the causal particle. But this disposition of his mind the Apostle wished to express, lest they should suppose that he doubted their constancy, inasmuch as he so earnestly excited them to perseverance : nay, he does this because he greatly desires that they should continue in the same, that this his joy may likewise continue; like as he does with the Philippians, iv. 1, *My Brethren, dearly beloved, my joy and crown, so stand fast in the Lord.*

Ye see after what manner the mind of the Apostle, being absent, was affected ; viz. so, that he always thought about the Colossians, that he beheld their state, that he rejoiced in this contemplation and observation.

Hence we infer,

1. That a faithful Minister never ought to be wholly absent from his flock : therefore, by care, by thought, and by prayer to God he should be present with them, when he cannot be present in body.

2. The true joy of a minister arises from the circumstance that the people continue and increase in spiritual blessings, not from the circumstance of himself being enriched with temporal ones.

3. That state of the people which affords an occasion of joy to the minister, ought likewise to afford occasion of greater solicitude; for Paul, in consequence of his joy at beholding their present state, laboured the more earnestly lest they should be cast down from the same by the deceit of impostors. For he knew the malice of the devil, *who rages mostly when he sees a man liberated from his chains; is then most wrathful, when he is dispossessed.* Tertull. De pœnit. 7.—Thus much concerning the mind and affection of the Apostle towards the Colossians : Now let us proceed to the causes.

Beholding your order, and the stedfastness of your faith in Christ.] The first reason why Paul had so much pleasure, rejoiced so exceedingly concerning the Colossians, is their *order ;* the second, their *stedfast faith ;* on account of which they are deservedly praised. But this, by the way, is to be remembered ; that this praise is a most skilful and strong inducement to perseverance in the things praised. For he who praises what you do, declares, first, that it is good ; for otherwise it would not be fit to be praised : secondly, he declares that it is easy to you ; because you have long effected it : lastly, he intimates that it would be base and disgraceful if you desist ; because praise earned is never lost without shame being incurred on the other hand. But let us consider the things themselves.

Your order.] Under the term *order* he seems to me to denote three things : the settled manners of the individuals ; the well-appointed discipline of that church ; and their agreement and concord. Goodness of manners is constantly included under the term order in the Scriptures ; just as, on the contrary, they who are of bad manners are said to walk *disorderly : Withdraw yourselves from every brother that walketh disorderly,* 2 Thess. iii. 6. When, therefore, he praises their order, he intimates this, that they individually walk soberly, righteously, and godly in their vocation. Moreover, public discipline is also to be included under this term, as what promotes and preserves it ; For this teaches prelates to rule well, subjects to obey duly; and compels the negligent and refractory to perform their duty. Concerning this the Apostle speaks, 1 Cor. xiv. 40, *Let all things be done decently and in order.* For this he commends his Timothy, Epis. i. cap. 3. He now, therefore, praises the Colossians because this Church discipline flourished among them, which, if neglected, all things would be in shameful confusion, sedition, errors, and crimes.

Lastly, he comprehends agreement and unity in religion under the word *order :* for τάξις is a military term, and denotes a compact body of soldiers marshalled in due order : Thus, then, the Apostle, when he says that he beheld their order, intimates that he regarded them as a well arranged phalanx of soldiers, united and cleaving together in the unity of the faith, and therefore invincible.

Hence we may lay it down,

1. That there is nothing more beautiful or useful than order, nothing more shameful or injurious than confusion. Admirably does Nazianzen write concerning this matter, Orat. 26. *Where order prevails, there beauty shines brightly ; where there is want of order, there arise in the air storms, upon the land commotions, by sea inundations, in cities seditions, in bodies distempers, and among souls sins. Order comprehends celestial and terrestrial things ; there is order among rational beings, order among irrational ones ; order among angels, order in the stars, order in all things.* No wonder, since God him-self is not the author of *confusion,* but of *harmony,* and that especially in the churches of the saints, 1 Cor. xiv. 33.

2. Since order is *the arrangement of equals and unequals, distributing their proper places to every one ;* they who introduce equality of ecclesiastical ministers subvert order. For it is the polity of Cyclops, not ecclesiastical discipline, where *no one recognizes another.**

3. Since from that order which flourishes among the people, their pastors derive such joy, it follows that they who despise and trample upon the legitimate orders of the Church, undeservedly vex and injure with great sorrow

the prelates of the Church, in opposition to that direction of the Apostle, Heb. xiii. 17, *Obey them that have the rule over you, and submit yourselves to them.*

4. Order is as the fence opposed to seducers : therefore, they seldom are plunged into errors who observe the order of obedience due to those set over them; on the other hand, where the order of commanding and of obeying is neglected, there a breach is easily effected, as through a routed army. So much concerning order.†

And the stedfastness of your faith in Christ.] This is the second cause of joy to the Apostle. He saw the Colossians attacked by the seducers, he saw tares every where scattered by them ; but, at the same time, he perceived that the faith of the Colossians could not be overcome, that those tares were not approved by them for wheat, but were despised and rejected ; hence that joy. *This stedfastness,* or solidity *in the faith,* therefore, denotes two things : first, that they suffered not the true doctrine to be wrested from them, but remained firm and immovable in it, like soldiers at their post: the other, that they did not permit strange and foreign doctrines to be mingled with it; but filled their minds with sacred doctrine, the inventions of men being excluded from the business of faith. For that is properly said to be *solid,* which is *full of itself alone,* that is, which does not receive any thing heterogeneous into it. That is, therefore, a stedfast faith, which not only embraces the true doctrine, but which admits no mixture of that which is false and foreign to it. Which, also, the Apostle himself afterwards intimates, when he restricts faith to Christ ; as though he would say, What they proclaim for the doctrines of faith without Christ, are to be rejected.

Hence we learn,

1. When the mind wavers and vacillates between various opinions, that is not a stedfast faith, but an empty

---

* Euripid. There is an allusion in this passage in the play which cannot be preserved in the English Translation.

† May every Reader be duly impressed by the force of these arguments against schisms and divisions !—Translator.

shadow of faith. It is the will of God, therefore, that our assent to the cause of Religion and the faith, be firm, and without any hesitation. For he hath no stedfast faith who inclines sometimes to one side, sometimes to the contrary. A faith suspended between conflicting opinions is reproved 1 Kings xviii. 11, *How long halt ye between two opinions? If the Lord be God, follow him; but if Baal, follow him.*

2. That faith also which, together with the faith of the Gospel, admits the traditions and inventions of men, is not stedfast, but hollow: if it were stedfast, there would not be a void place in it for those heterogeneous things. Tertullian admirably expresses himself in this sentence, *Cum credimus evangelio, nihil desideramus ultrà credere. Hoc enim priùs credimus, non esse quod ultrà credere debeamus.** De praescript.—So much concerning the causes of the Apostle's joy.

We have dispatched the two parts of this preface: that is to say, the narrative proposition, in which the Apostle declared what a conflict he sustained for the Colossians; and the statement of his argument, in which he brings many reasons of the fact itself. The last part remains, which contains the hortatory conclusion.

---

* See this same passage employed, and translated, p. 95.

Verses 6, 7.

As ye have therefore received Christ Jesus the Lord, so walk
ye in him;
Rooted and built up in him, and stablished in the faith, as
ye have been taught, abounding therein with thanks-
giving.

We have said that the Exordium of the Apostle is composed of these three members; a narrative proposition, the
statement of his reasons, and an hortatory conclusion. We
are arrived at this last, included in these two short verses.
In which he shews, first, what is to be done by them;
namely, to cleave unto Christ, even as they had received
him from Epaphras; ver. 6. Secondly, he teaches them
how to cleave unto him. And the mode consists in three
things : in the stability of faith; in its fulness; and in
gratitude of mind for it.

We commence with the sixth verse; in which he teaches
what he wishes to be done by them, 1. by proposing a rule
to their observation, *As ye have received Christ Jesus the
Lord;* 2. by requiring action, or obedience to this rule, *so
walk ye in him.*

As ye have therefore received Christ Jesus the Lord.] The
rule of faith and of life which he proposes to the Colossians, is the doctrine of Christ preached by Epaphras, and
received by them; to which he would have them adhere
constantly. We must, therefore, understand, what doctrine he had promulgated respecting Christ. He had,
doubtless, taught, that all the grounds of our salvation are
placed in Christ alone; that Christ is the Lord of our faith
and of our life; and that both are to be directed towards
the Gospel of Christ, as to the brighter polar star; the
Mosaic ceremonies must not be joined with the faith of the

Gospel : This rule Epaphras had prescribed to them : to
this rule they were bound ;

1.   Because they received and approved of it : For when
the Apostle says, *as ye have received* (as Chrysostom well
observes) he binds them, as it were, by their own testimony : for he intimates that it is not his object that they
should now receive some new doctrine, but that they should
continue in what they had received ; that not to do so, argued either folly or levity in them.

2.   Because, although they must not of necessity persevere in every doctrine received, as, for instance, in an
erroneous one ; yet they must remain in this, because, this
doctrine being received, Christ Jesus the Lord himself was
received ; *Ye have received Christ Jesus the Lord.*   In this
form of speaking there is great force, which it is proper
to examine.   We must observe, therefore, that he does
not say, *As ye have received the doctrine of Christ,* or *concerning Christ ;* but, *As ye have received Christ himself.*   For
we not only perceive the doctrine of Christ by faith, but
we receive our quickening Saviour, and we hide him in the
heart for our salvation.   And, indeed, that saying of the
Poet is known and approved by all,

   It is more shameful to eject than not to admit a guest.
They could not, therefore, without great baseness reject
the doctrine or the faith received, because by that same
act they would reject Christ himself.

But that also must be noted, that he affirms they had
received *Christ the Lord :* for (as the most learned interpreters will have it) the Apostle lays a stress upon this word.
For the false apostles preached Christ, and their disciples
received Christ : but *those* neither preached, nor did *these*
receive *Christ the Lord,* but the fellow-servant of Moses ;
therefore they joined his doctrine with the ceremonies prescribed by Moses.   But the Colossians, and so all true
Christians, received *Christ the Lord,* both of their faith and
their life : nor will they suffer rules of faith and Christian
life to be imposed upon them by any one else.   For the
servant cannot manumit himself, or make himself over to
a new lord ; because he is not his own master : neither

could the Colossians subject themselves either to the Mosaic ceremonies, or the maxims of philosophers, because they had received *Christ the Lord.* From what we have said we may deduce the following instructions :

1. The true faith is not to be changed, although the prelates and doctors of the Church should begin to strike out a new one ; because *as we have received,* so we must persevere. The Romanists, therefore, in vain thrust upon us their novel opinions ; it is sufficient to answer, We have not so received from the Apostles.

2. We must not persevere in every doctrine received from our elders : but if they have received Christ, then we must abide in the same doctrine ; but should they have imbibed the poison of Antichrist, we are not bound to do the same. In vain, therefore, they also heap their old errors upon us : we say with Cyprian, *In things which regard religion it does not behove us to follow the custom of men, but the truth of God.*

3. The Gospel is to be received with the greater reverence, because *that* being received, *Jesus Christ* is received. The doctrines of men, however true, bring nothing else to the mind than knowledge : but the doctrine of the Gospel brings salvation, nay, the Saviour himself.

4. He is a Christian in vain, nay, to his great loss, who resolves not to direct both his faith and his life by the rule of Christ : for it is to mock Christ, if he is not worshipped as *Lord* by those who receive the Gospel.—Thus much concerning the Rule.

So walk ye in him.] He requires from them obedience to the rule proposed. When he says, *we must walk in Christ,* he shews by implication that Christ is the royal way to God and to eternal blessedness ; *I am the way, the truth, and the life.* Chrysostom hath made this observation, who immediately adds, *We must walk in Christ, because He is the way, and not angels, which leads to our heavenly Father.*

To walk in Christ denotes two things : to *persevere* and to *advance* in the doctrine and the faith of Christ; to live according to this rule and the guidance of the Spirit of Christ. As to the first ; faith hath a progressive motion :

Whence we are said with propriety enough to walk, when we proceed in the faith itself. *They shall go from strength to strength,* says the Psalmist lxxxiv. 7. And Paul, Rom. i. 17, *from faith to faith.* But this term of *walking* is much more often accommodated to progress in a course of holiness. Hence *to walk in the ways,* or *in the commandments of God,* is in frequent use by David; and with Paul, *to walk after the flesh,* or *after the Spirit; to walk in newness of life,* or *as children of light;* and in many like passages.

Therefore two things are required: that they should abide and proceed in the faith; that they should conform their life to the rule of faith. Now let us deduce some inferences.

1. As Christians are rightly said *to walk in Christ,* because they regulate both their faith and their life by the rule prescribed by him; so the Monks walk in the respective founders of their sects, who seek perfection in the rule invented by them.

2. Since Christ is the only way to heaven, he who aims at heaven out of Christ, wanders about blind and miserable, and will never arrive thither.

3. He who thinks he can walk in Christ by a solitary faith, attempts to walk with one foot, which is impossible. *To walk in Christ* is to proceed as well in holiness as faith; for the Spirit of Christ stirs up to both or neither.

4. The life of a Christian man is in constant motion. He departs from sin and the world, and advances in holiness of life, and towards the heavenly state, by Christ as by the way, faith and love inclining him to this new motion as inherent qualities; but impelled and directed by the Spirit of Christ as the principal agent and mover, who also himself imparted both faith and love.

And thus we have briefly explained what the Apostle required to be done in this his hortatory conclusion; namely, that they would cleave to Christ; to which he draws them, 1. By proposing the rule itself to their contemplation; 2. by requiring their submission to this rule. Now it follows, that we explain how we are to abide in Christ; which we learn from the following verse.

Verse 7.

Rooted and built up in him, and stablished in the faith, as
ye have been taught, abounding therein with thanks-
giving.

That the Colossians should cleave to Christ, the Apostle
advises in the foregoing verse : now he shews somewhat
more explicitly how they are to cleave to him. And the
mode consists,

1. In the stability of that faith which adheres to Christ
and the doctrine of the Gospel; *Rooted, and built, and*
stablished.

2. In that fulness, or sufficiency, which faith in Christ
acknowledges; *abounding therein,* &c.

3. In gratitude for this fulness which we have through
the faith of Christ; *with thanksgiving.*

Rooted and built up in him.] The stability of faith is described by two metaphors : The former borrowed from trees ;
the latter, from buildings. The metaphor *being rooted,* is
borrowed from trees. For as trees cannot have stability
unless they send forth roots into the earth, and that earth
not miry, but firm : so our faith cannot have stedfastness
unless it fix its roots in Christ, as in the firmest soil. The
other metaphor is borrowed from buildings. For as a house
hath no stability unless it be built upon a firm foundation ;
so neither faith, unless it rest upon Christ alone. Whence,
likewise, the Saviour Christ commends his prudence who
built his house upon a rock, but reproved his folly who
preferred to erect his upon sand, Matt. vii. 24. By these
two metaphors, therefore, the Apostle points out to us that
we should cleave to Christ as closely as possible.

And stablished in the faith as ye have been taught.] What
he has before represented figuratively, he now expresses in
direct terms, as interpreters will have : But he seems to me
to do even something more than that. For in those figurative terms he expresses that stedfastness of which our
faith partakes from having placed its roots in firm soil,

(viz. in Christ) and resting upon a due foundation : but here he touches on that stability which we are said to have from the strengthening of faith itself, after that it shall have been rooted in this soil, and built upon this foundation. This difference it is easy to observe in trees, which as soon as they are planted have their stability hence only, that they are planted in firm soil : but when they shall have increased in height, they have also other strength in themselves : So a tender faith hath its stability in Christ; but being increased and advanced, it acquires new strength as to the internal habit itself. The Apostle, therefore, wishes the faith of the Colossians, not only to be built upon a firm foundation, but also to be strengthened and grow in itself daily.

And whereas he joins by a parenthesis *(as ye have been taught)*, it tends to the greater caution, so to speak. For he had advised them concerning the same matter before in the foregoing verse ; saying, *As ye have received him, so walk ye in him :* here he again requires stedfastness of faith, and shews in what faith they must continue ; viz. in the very faith which they had been taught by Epaphras, not in the novel faith of false apostles.

He twice inculcates the same counsel, that he may correct a wrong inclination prevailing very much among the common people : For they were wont to grow weary of the received doctrine, and eagerly to desire new teachers, who led them away from the truth to their own dreams. He, therefore, reproves their itching ears, when he bids them remain in the faith as they had heretofore been taught, and forbids them to yield to the new faith of the seducers.

We have explained what stability the Apostle requires in the doctrine of the Gospel. Now from what we have said we may draw these instructive lessons ;

1. It is not enough to be planted in Christ, unless we are so established in him, and cleave so entirely to him, that we neither rest on any other, as the foundation of our faith, nor suffer ourselves to be detached from this by any devices. *For other foundation can no man lay than that is laid, which is Jesus Christ,* 1 Cor. iii. 11. Those vacillating

persons, therefore, are reproved, who, seizing every occasion, flee away from Christ to Antichrist: but, as Chrysostom says, *that which is grounded and rooted, is not easily
moved away.* They also are censured who cleave to Christ
only externally, when they have their roots in the mean
time fixed elsewhere. Among these we may reckon all
who retain the name of Christians, yet have their hope
placed chiefly upon saints, monastic observations, or other
idols of their hearts, but not on Christ. Against such, that
rebuke of the prophet Jonah, ii. 8, may be levelled, *They
that observe lying vanities forsake their own mercy.*

2. Faith is that which secures our walking in Christ as
in the way, without error, our abiding in him as in the
root with fruit, our standing upon him as a foundation
without being shaken. Therefore, all seducers who labour
to injure our faith are to be shunned and avoided; for by
that means they attempt to separate us from Christ.

3. Since Paul restricts Christians to that faith which
they have been taught by Apostles, we gather, that the
rule of Apostolical doctrine, viz. the Holy Scriptures, is
not to be removed out of the sight of the people. For it
is unjust to demand that any one should act or believe according to a prescribed rule, and yet be unwilling to allow
him the knowledge of this rule. But like as wicked boys,
when they are bent upon mischief, shut out the schoolmaster; so the Papists, when they would make a traffick of
their own trumpery among the people, take special care
that the word of God should be withheld from them. But
let us proceed.

Abounding therein.] He has described the stedfastness
of faith: Now, in the second place, he touches that abundance, or sufficiency, which he requires in the faith of the
Colossians, or rather, that which he states to be in the
faith of Christ alone. This abundance interpreters refer to
that perpetual increase which is required from believers in
matters of faith. Therefore, they think that the Apostle
exhorted them, that they should not only not abate, but
daily grow in the abounding knowledge of evangelical doctrine. Yet I think (which I would say with the permission

of the good), that another sense is included in these words
in this place. Therefore I explain περισσεύοντες ἐν αὐτῇ, feeling assured that you *abound* in that faith which rests on
Christ alone, i. e. that you are rich, overflow, and possess
abundantly all things necessary to salvation. It is not,
therefore, to the increase of our knowledge I refer this
abundance; but to the thing known, viz. the doctrine of
the Gospel concerning Christ.

Never ought it to seem wonderful or novel that we explain
abounding—knowing or determining that ye abound: for,
in the Holy Scriptures, words very often denote a supposition of our knowledge of those things which they really
signify. As 1 Cor. iv. 8, *Ye are full, ye are rich, ye have
reigned as kings without us;* i. e. Ye think ye are full, ye are
rich, ye have reigned, &c. And in Rom. v. 20, *The law
entered that sin might abound;* i. e. that ye might know the
magnitude of sin. Therefore, I so explain *abounding*, in
this place, knowing, or determining with certainty that ye
abound.

I follow this interpretation, because it especially agrees
with the purpose of the Apostle's exhortation. For he
wishes them to remain rooted in the faith of Christ alone:
but that which especially conduces to their doing so is,
that they should make up their minds that by this faith
in Christ they *abound*, i. e. that they had all things which
are necessary to be known for salvation.

Moreover, this especially opposes the opinion of the
false teachers. For they thought that they had discovered
poverty, and defects, in faith and the doctrine of the Gospel, and therefore they patched upon it philosophical speculations, and Mosaic ceremonies, and innumerable other
traditions: but, on the contrary, the Apostle says, we
abound in it, we have in that doctrine all abundance of
saving knowledge.

Lastly, this best connects with the following words, *with
thanksgiving.* For this ought especially to excite us to
gratitude, because in Christ alone God hath administered
to us abundantly all things necessary to salvation.

This sense of the words being granted, we learn that the

tales of the Monks, about the perfection of the monastic state, are mere folly; as though the doctrine of the Gospel had not prescribed to all the most perfect instruction as to the attainment of life eternal, but that this had been delegated to Dominic and Francis. But if in this doctrine we are abundantly supplied with all things necessary to salvation, it follows, that what is added, to what is already abundant, must be vain and superfluous.

With thanksgiving.] This is the last thing to be observed in the mode in which we cleave to the doctrine of the Gospel. We ought to cleave to it firmly, that is to say, being rooted in Christ himself; we ought to cleave to him in such a manner as to acknowledge that in Him is all-sufficiency to salvation: now, in the last place, we ought so to cleave, that we may shew gratitude of mind for this abundance of saving grace opened and offered to us in the Gospel and in Christ. And that is rightly required from us,

1. Because the magnitude of the benefit claimed it. For in the Gospel a store and accumulation of the benefits of God, nay, the whole treasure of Divine munificence is set forth and offered to us; it ought, therefore, especially to excite us to gratitude.

2. Because the danger of its contrary—ingratitude, urges it. For God is wont to withdraw his benefits from the ungrateful: unless, therefore, we wish to be deprived of the Gospel of salvation, we ought to accept it with all thanksgiving.

3. Because the nature of true faith impels to it. For true faith, embracing Christ as the Saviour, is wont to warm the heart itself with gratitude towards God, and to melt the icyness which is found in the hearts of unbelievers.

Hence we learn,

1. True faith does not consist with ingratitude. For he who, through faith, sees himself delivered from the jaws of hell, and designed for the glory of heaven, cannot but be grateful to the Author of his felicity.

2. They who make no account of the Gospel, are not

as yet partakers of the benefits of Christ : if they were, surely they would break forth into thanksgiving for this saving light so mercifully communicated by God.

3.   God justly withdraws this benefit from those who do not receive it with thanksgiving.   For this gratitude is as a certain tribute, and special service, which God requires in acknowledgment of his supreme dominion from all his feudal subjects : they who refuse to pay this are rightly expelled from their heritage.   And these things concerning thanksgiving.

We have now dismissed this exordium of the Apostle. He proposes the question itself in the verse next following ; then confirms his own opinion, and refutes the contrary.

Verse 8.

Beware lest any man spoil you through philosophy and vain deceit, after the tradition of men, after the rudiments of the world, and not after Christ.

The Exordium now dispatched, the second part of this Chapter follows : In which is proposed the state of the question to be discussed, which he had lightly touched in verses 3 and 4.   And if it be reduced to a logical proposition it stands thus :— In the business of salvation, neither philosophical speculations, nor traditions of human invention, nor Mosaical ceremonies ; but the pure, genuine doctrine of the Gospel is to be received.   This is the Apostle's judgment.   But in order that he might produce more effect upon the minds of the Colossians, he preferred, instead of proposing it in that mode, to direct his discourse to them by the figure apostrophe, and converse as it were with them.   And so in this verse the Apostle effects three things. 1. He excites them to beware of impostures. 2. He reduces these impostures to three kinds. 3. He lays

down a general reason or rule whereby it may be understood that they are to be rejected.

Beware lest any man spoil you.] Here he directs his discourse to the Colossians, and endeavours to render them
cautious in a twofold manner:

1. By this particle of attention, *Beware lest.* For this
strikes the mind much more pointedly than if he had said,
All the patches of men which are woven upon the Gospel
are to be rejected by Christians: For he who so speaks
seems to treat with the understanding alone; but he who,
with the Apostle, calls upon his hearer to take care that he
be not deceived by these fictions of men, he not only in-
structs the understanding, but moves the will and affections to hatred of the false doctrine. For by this form of
speaking he points out, as with a finger, the plots laid for
them, and the approaching deceiver: and thus sentinels,
when they have discovered the enemy, exclaim, Beware!
Take care; the enemy is upon you!

2. He excites them to the greatest caution by the elegant metaphor of spoliation. For συλαγωγειν is *to drive away
the booty;* as robbers are accustomed to carry away men
and cattle with them, when they have prevailed in fight:
So the Amalekites, having plundered Ziklag, bore away
the men and all their goods, 1 Sam. xxx. By this word,
therefore, he shews the great danger that threatened them
from the seducers, who attacked them with the design to
bring them into bondage, as spoil taken in war; viz. whilst
they led them from the Gospel to their impostures. This
mode of speaking, therefore, is very powerful to excite
their minds to attention and caution.

Hence we derive some observations;

1. We are not to believe all who undertake to teach in
the Church: but must take care, and weigh with serious
examination, whether their doctrine be sound or not. This
the Popish teachers forbid, because they doubt of their
doctrine. This Apelles the heretic* heretofore forbade, as
it is stated in Euseb. lib. v. cap. 13, for he said, *it was not*

---

* He broached his opinions about the middle of the second century.

proper to inquire into doctrine; but that every one should hold fast that which he received and believed. But the Apostle in this place speaks otherwise ; and in 1 Thess. v. 21, and Acts xvii. 11.

2. It pertains to the duty of the pastor, not only to instruct his flock in sound doctrine, but to prepare and arm them against the designs of seducers. For he holds the place of a sentinel ; he ought, therefore, to admonish them of the approach of the enemy ; he ought to point out the snares laid for them : which, unless he shall have done, *whatsoever through indolence is left unguarded, will be required from the pastor,* Cyprian, De sing. cler.

3. The doctrine of the Gospel is as the sheepfold of Christ. The sheep are safe whilst they abide within this fence : but when they wander to new and strange doctrines, as straggling sheep, they fall a prey to robbers, i. e. to heretics and seducers. By this treachery the papacy hath spoiled so many churches ; for it hath withdrawn them from the doctrine of the Gospel ; then it hath led them whither it would, as its own slaves.

Through philosophy and vain deceit.] After the Apostle had forewarned the Colossians to beware of impostures, he enumerates the various kinds of impostures. The first is what he has designated by the name *philosophy :* then terms are subjoined in apposition, which explain what philosophy he intends, namely, *false and vain.* But since inquiry is often instituted among theologians concerning the use of human reason and philosophy in the matter of religion : and since also mutual criminations arise hence between us and the papists, whilst we charge upon them the crime of corrupt theology, because, in the article of justification, free-will, and many other things, they follow Aristotle, rather than Paul ; they, on the other hand, saying, that we, in the question of the presence of the body of Christ in the Lord's supper, cleave to philosophical principles, and reject the manifest word of God ; on these accounts, I say, we shall treat somewhat more largely of this matter ; and shall bring all those points which we are about to mention under these heads :

1. We shall shew that true philosophy is not condemned by the Apostle.

2. We shall explain what we ought to understand under the word *philosophy* in this place.

3. We shall shew wherein the use, wherein the abuse of philosophy consists, as far as relates to divine matters.

1. As to the first ; Whether we speak concerning moral or natural philosophy, whether concerning any other branch of philosophy, or of the whole as a certain entire body ; it is certain that that cannot be condemned, lest God himself be called into judgment. For philosophy is the offspring of right reason : and this light of reason is infused into the human mind by God himself, according to that remark of Tertullian, *Reason is of God.* We, therefore, judge, not the discipline of the Stoicks, nor Platonists, nor Aristotelians, to be true philosophy : but whatever among all these, or others, shall have been discovered, spoken, or written, by the light of right reason ; all this taken together we call *philosophy.* Therefore, not the dreams of philosophers constitute philosophy, but the principles of every one, which agree with truth and good morals. For as the errors of Theologians do not pertain to theology as parts of it, but as disease ; so neither do those of Philosophers pertain to philosophy. We scruple not, therefore, to call philosophy, with Clemens Alexandrinus, Strom. 1, *a morsel of eternal truth.* They, therefore, who desire philosophy itself to be exploded from the schools of Christians, are either altogether ignorant, and have it in view to hide their ignorance among the common ignorance of all ; or they are wicked, and desire to expose us stripped of all advantage from learning, untaught and defenceless, to artful and armed enemies; which wicked purpose of Julian, Nazianzen discovers and reproves, Orat. 1. in Julianum.

I might in this place speak of the various advantages of physics, ethics, and logic. For not only does common life derive assistance from all these, but even divine Theology, by the admission of Tertullian, a bitter enemy of philosophers ; *In what way could any one be trained to human prudence, or to any action whatever, without learning, since*

*literature is an help to every department in life? How will
you reject secular studies, without which there cannot be divine
ones?* Tertul. De idol.   If, therefore, the Apostle had
condemned and rejected philosophy, he would verily have
rejected the light of reason, and would have cast great injury upon God, the author of it.   As often, then, as what
relates to human and eternal affairs is slighted and rejected
by divines, it is to be understood, not of true and genuine
philosophy, but of the errors and fancies of philosophers.
For tares are sown in philosophy as they are in our religion:
and truth is nearly excluded from it by the pernicious
things diffused in it.   To conclude then, in a word, If the
errors of philosophers, or their crabbed subtilties, are
marked out under the term *philosophy,* then we are free to
reject and condemn *such* philosophy : but if we may call
the knowledge of the truth, discovered by the light of natural reason, by this term, we judge that is not to be condemned, but to be cultivated.

2.   It is clear that true and genuine philosophy is not
condemned.   Let us enquire, in the second place, of what
kind that is which is excluded by the Apostle ; viz. that of
vain deceit, to which he affixes the ignominious brand of
κεῖνης ἀπάτης.   This philosophy condemned is, then, both *vain*
and *deceitful.*

Now, truly, philosophy, or human reason which is the
mother of philosophy, is always found *vain* and *deceitful*
when carried beyond its proper bounds, that is, when it
attempts to determine concerning those things which cannot be judged of by *the criterion* of natural reason ; and of
this kind are those which concern the worship of God and
the salvation of men.   Philosophy is, therefore, to be listened to when it pronounces about things subject to itself,
according to the light of right reason : but when it would
determine concerning human justification, reconciliation
with God, the mode of Divine worship, or of other matters
relating to faith, it is to be exploded ; because, in those
things which are beyond the grasp of reason, and depend
wholly on the revealed will of God, it brings nothing solid
or true, but betrays itself to be altogether *vain* and *deceit-*

ful. The Apostle hath elsewhere alleged the cause of this; viz. Because the *natural man receiveth not the things which are of God; for they only are discerned by the Spirit of God;* 1 Cor. ii. 14. But a philosopher, considered as a philosopher, is nothing more than a natural man; and reason itself, not illuminated by faith, pertains to this natural condition: it cannot, therefore, extend to the knowledge of salvation; and, if it should attempt, it miserably spends itself in vain. Here, then, we renounce philosophy and human reason, and confess with Justin Martyr, a theologian and philosopher, Paræn. ad Græcos, that *Neither poets nor philosophers are fit authors for instituting a Religion, but God alone by revelation.* Which also Prudentius has expressed in very elegant verse, which it will not be irksome to annex. In lib. 2. cont. Symmach. he is shewing that reason cannot but fail if it intrude itself into divine things;

> Quippe minor natura aciem si intendere tentet
> Acriùs, ac penetrare Dei secreta supremi;
> Quis dubitet victo fragilem lassescere visu,
> Vimque fatigatæ mentis sub pectore parvo
> Turbari, invalidísque hebetem succumbere curis?
> Sed facilis fidei via, &c.*

Vide Hilar. 1. de Trinit.

Neither ought this to seem wonderful. For if brute animals can judge very well concerning things which relate to sense, such as their meat and drink, yet cannot judge of human affairs: then, by a parity of reason, neither can men pronounce by natural light respecting heavenly doctrine and Divine worship, although they may determine by the aid of it, what is good and right in human concerns.

---

* Thus translated for his friend, by Mr. J. F. Pennie, of Lulworth, author of the " Royal Minstrel, Rogvald, Scenes in Palestine," &c. &c.

> " Should man, inferior in his nature, strive
> Into the secrets of his God to dive,
> O, who can doubt his feeble sight would fail,
> And his weak pow'rs of mind confounded quail
> Beneath the vain attempt! 'Tis faith alone
> Can easy make her way—"
> to mysteries yet unknown.

That we may, therefore, accommodate these points to the matter in hand ; The false Apostles, under the pretext of a certain secret wisdom, endeavoured to obtrude upon the Colossians certain new doctrines about the worship of angels, the expiation of souls, and other things of that kind, drawn, no doubt, from the writings of the Platonists. What says Paul to these things? Believe not; he replies : fallacious and vain is philosophy when it prescribes about religion. It behoves you to learn how God the Father would be approached, how your sin can be expiated, not from Plato and human reason, but from God and his word. Let us explode, therefore, and condemn philosophy promulgating directions concerning these things.

But it is objected, that divine and spiritual things are known to human reason, and that by the natural light of the same : for thus says the Apostle, Rom. i. 19, 20, *That which may be known of God is manifest in them ;—The invisible things of him from the creation of the world, being understood,* &c. If reason comprehends divine things, then may it determine respecting them, neither will it, therefore, be called *vain.*

It is answered ; The natural knowledge of spiritual things is obscure and feeble, extending only to the *existence* of those things.   As, for instance, that there is a God, that there is a worship of God, that there is a blessedness for souls, reason and philosophy perceives; but how God is to be worshipped, how happiness is to be obtained, it discovers not : whilst, therefore, it attempts to determine respecting these things and the like, it is *vain* and *deceitful.*   This knowledge may render a man *inexcusable,* but it cannot render him a competent teacher, unless knowledge infused by grace be added.

3.   Let us approach to what we proposed to treat of in the last place, viz. to shew the abuse and use of reason or philosophy in the business of religion.   For they who perpetually cry out for the exclusion of human reason from treating of sacred things, without discrimination, seem to require that men should engage in the greatest affairs without reason ; when, indeed, they cannot rightly manage the least, if that natural light of reason be extinguished.

The abuse of natural reason, or philosophy, in the cause of religion is manifold.

1. When it attempts to deduce the fundamentals themselves of religion from its principles. For although the principles of right reason are true in themselves, nevertheless there cannot be elicited from them what is to be determined concerning the mystery of the Trinity, the incarnation of Christ, the justification of a sinner, invocation of God, and his worship; all which things are to be deduced from higher principles, namely, from the will of God revealed in the Word. Reason is *the discursive power which proceeds from principles to conclusions:* but it does not possess in itself the principles of those things which are apprehended by faith; therefore, it daringly builds conclusions upon the sand of its own opinions.

2. When it opposes its own principles, which are true in the order of nature, to theological principles, which are far above the order of nature. For example; it is true, that *out of nothing, nothing can be made;* it is true that *dissimilar species cannot be predicated of each other, and cannot unite in the same subject;* it is true *there is no return from privation to possession:* but all these things are to be understood according to the course of nature and the power of a finite agent. Philosophers therefore err, when they think that they can hence conclude against the creation of the world, the incarnation of God, and the resurrection of the dead; all which the Scriptures teach as done, or to be done, not by virtue of natural causes, but by the Almighty power of God. Here, therefore, that rule of Aquinas, Quæst. disp. de fide, art. 10, is to be retained, *Theology can never contradict true natural reason, but often rises above it, and thus* APPEARS *to oppose it.* For true reason does not affirm that those superior things cannot be effected absolutely; but cannot be effected by any finite power; and this theology likewise confesses. In those matters, therefore, which are of this kind, *philosophy,* as says Clemens, Strom. 1, *should submit itself to theology, as Agar to Sarah; should allow itself to be advised and corrected: but if it be unwilling to become obedient, cast out the handmaid.*

3. When it obtrudes for legitimate conclusions its er-

rors, drawn sometimes by false consequences from true premises. Thus the Stoics, Epicureans, Aristotelians, and as many as come under the denomination of philosophers, do not always teach the dictates of right reason, but the dreams of their own fancy. But, truly, if any one should attempt, under the name of philosophy, to introduce these errors into theology, he commits a double sin : first, inasmuch as he resolves the corruptions of philosophers into the dogmas of philosophy itself; next, because he even thinks to subject theology to the rules of philosophy. And the Fathers appear to me strictly to have reproved this abuse in the antient heretics, and sometimes to have declaimed severely, on that account, against true philosophy and philosophers. Nothing is more frequent in Tertullian : *A philosopher is the creature of boasting. They affect truth, and in affecting it they mar it. Every heresy is engendered by the devices of philosophers. All heresies consist of the maxims of philosophers. All the dogmas of heretics, when they grow frigid and stiff, and therefore cannot take wing, find a place of settlement and repose among the thorns of Aristotle.* Nor is Lactantius more mild towards them; for in Institut. lib. 3. cap. 2, and in many subsequent places, he continually attacks philosophy and philosophers. But, as I have said, these respect not true and sober philosophy, keeping within its bounds ; but that bold and deceitful counterfeit, which dares to mingle itself with things beyond its reach, or which publishes the opinions of private men for the decrees of truth itself. You perceive the abuse ; now let us shew the use of true philosophy : And this is manifold.

1. The knowledge of philosophy is useful, nay, necessary to the clear understanding and perspicuous elucidation of many passages which every where occur in the sacred Scriptures. For although the principles of our Religion are derived from God, not from human reason, or any philosophical science ; yet many forms of speaking occur in the books of holy Scripture, many examples and illustrations, which cannot fully be understood and stated with perspicuity, without the aids of human literature. Of this kind are those passages which speak of the motion, the

influences, the obscuration of the heavenly bodies, which, to be understood rightly, require the knowledge of astronomy. Of this kind also are those which allude to the properties of certain animals, as of the wolf, sheep, lions, bears, doves, and eagles; all which need the light of natural philosophy. To this also may be referred those which relate to the nature and temperature of countries; as when forms of speech are derived from heat or drought, when from shade, or water, or cooling winds, and are often applied to illustrate spiritual things: for these are not rightly explained unless by him who shall have well investigated and examined the nature of those places; but this he shall not be able to do without the knowledge of geography. Lest our discourse should become too diffuse by an enumeration of particulars, we may truly say, there is no part of philosophy, or of human learning, which may not at times, be called in to his aid, by the interpreter of sacred literature, in order to contribute what falls within its province. This, therefore, is the first use of philosophy.

2. Philosophy, especially that which teaches the rules and the art of reasoning rightly, is particularly necessary, and to be employed by all, in discriminating between, and treating all controversies relating to religion. For although reason receives the principles of religion by the light of faith, yet this light, proceeding first from these principles, according to the laws of good and necessary consequence impressed by God himself upon a rational creature, is both wont, and ought to judge, how the parts of heavenly doctrine cohere together and mutually establish each other; what is consistent, what inconsistent with them. Our faith ascends above reason; but yet not rashly or irrationally. For reason herself is aware that the object of our faith is deduced from the principles of sacred Scripture. For instance; I believe the resurrection of the dead. How? Because reason itself proves this doctrine to be delivered in the Holy Scriptures: for I should not believe it unless I understood it to be founded in the Scriptures. On the other hand; I do not believe purgatory. Why? Because reason can collect from no part of Scripture, according to

the rules of good and sound logic, the truth of this doctrine. This use of reason and logic in sacred things, God
is so far from condemning, that he requires it of all : nay,
for this end he plants in human minds certain laws of judging, and of discerning truth from falsehood, certainty from
uncertainty, consequential from inconsequential reasoning,
that we may use this light of reason in all things, and especially in Divine matters. Ephes. v. 17, *Be not unskilful,
but understanding what the will of the Lord is:* and iv. 14,
*That we should be no longer children, carried about with every
wind of doctrine,* &c.; and 1 Thess. v. 21, *Prove all things,
hold fast that which is good.* This is commended in the Bereans, who, on hearing Paul preach, *Searched the Scriptures daily, whether those things were so or not,* Acts xvii. 11.
But there cannot be this investigation and examination of
doctrines, unless the judgment of men be employed, which
determines of the truth of conclusions by its own principles, and of the truth of things, not by relying upon principles known to it without the word of God, but delivered
in the sacred Scriptures, as was before said. Tertullian,
De resurrect. carnis, has well spoken in regard to this opinion : *It is the part indeed of common sense to be wise in the
things of God, but for testimony of what is true, not in aid
of what is false ; this is not contrary, but according to the Divine economy.*

3. The knowledge of philosophy is necessary, as well
for the instruction of those who have not yet enrolled themselves under Christ, as for resistance, if they should obstinately oppose our Religion. He who has been born and
constantly educated in darkness, is not directly to be drawn
into the clear light of the sun, lest it should happen that
by so much light he should be overpowered rather than enlightened : so they who have been educated from childhood
in the darkness of Paganism, cannot immediately bear the
light of the Gospel, but are first to be awakened by reasons drawn from natural light, to contemplate this light.
So Paul acted with the Athenians, Acts xvii. 24. Clemens Alexandrinus, Strom. 1, illustrates the reason of this

by a happy similitude : *As they who would address the people do this most commonly by a public crier, that the things which are said, may be heard by all; so when discourse is to be held with men ignorant of the Christian Religion, the opinions and expressions of nature itself, which may be perceived and understood by them, are to be employed.*

But now as to what belongs to the conflict with philosophers speaking against Religion, who does not see that it is necessary to be armed with philosophy? For it is like a trench and rampart against their inroads ; it is a sword wherewith to thrust them : which, although it renders the truth in no ways more powerful, yet it is very useful in this respect, that it repels sophistry, and weakens its force against it. The saying of Julian the Apostate is remarkable, *We are caught by our own wings.* He uttered this lament when he saw the Gentile philosophers and their errors overthrown and routed by Christians through the advantages of human learning and philosophy itself. And truly this was very honourable to the teachers of the Church, because the enemy were cut off by them in their own camps, and *overcome by those weapons in which they were wont to delight and confide,* as says Lactantius, lib. 3. cap. 1.

4. The use of philosophy and of literature is also valuable among Christians ; since men's minds are prepared and rendered more acute by these studies for the treatment and reception of a more sublime science ; because we are able to adorn and enrich our dissertations on sacred things with the good sayings of philosophers. *For the good sayings of philosophers,* says Justin Mart. Apolog. 1, *are the heritage of Christians.* For I agree not with those who think that not only the remarks of philosophers, but of the most holy Fathers, should be altogether withheld from sacred discourses. Prosper, in Præfat. ad 2, lib. de vita contemplativa, seems to me to decide much better : *Truth,* says he, *from what quarter soever it shines, is not to be ascribed to human wit, but to God; neither ought it to be believed to be the property of some, but of all, which is such and so great of*

itself, that it is not then great when the great shall have taught it, but rather itself makes them great by whom it could have been taught or learned.

5. In the last place, I also add this ; that it may even be employed to the moderate and useful delight of the hearers, as a certain seasoning, as it were, drawn from polite literature. For, if the Divine benignity shall have granted us bodily food, not only necessary to repel hunger, but sweet and pleasant to delight the taste ; why should we not also account this same to be granted us in regard to spiritual food? especially since this delight hath usefulness joined with it. For it occasions those things which are pre-eminently the doctrines of faith to flow into the mind more easily and pleasantly. Hence says Clemens, *The truth which is sought from the holy Scriptures is as necessary to life as bread; but that which is sought from other instruction, is but as sauces and sweetmeats.* I would not by this be understood to approve the affected vanity of those who crowd their discourses with short sentences collected from all quarters, in the meanwhile being altogether unmindful of the Scriptures; but I wish to shew that philosophy, and, therefore, all polite literature, hath its place and use, even in sacred things, if employed with address.

After the tradition of men.] The Apostle has reduced all the impostures of false teachers to three kinds. The first was placed in the curious speculations of the conclusions of philosophers concerning the worship and the will of God, drawn from the judgment of reason not from the revealed word : This philosophy, although it wears the appearance of secret and sublime wisdom, yet Paul condemned and exploded it as *vain* and *deceitful.* Now he censures a second sort of false doctrine, which he calls *the tradition of men.* But he does not intend those curious and abstruse speculations which he has before glanced at under the name of philosophy (for those doctrines had a certain shadow of wisdom), but superstitious and foolish observances, founded in external things, which rested upon custom and antiquity alone, but were confirmed very much either by the pretended visions of impostors, or by the

stratagems and power of dæmons themselves. Of this
kind were those traditions of the Pharisees about trifling
matters, as the washing of cups, and many other such like
things ; in which, however, they would have that great
sanctity consisted. Of this kind were the rites and observances of the Gentiles in sacrifices, marriages, and funeral
solemnities. Hither also appertained the observances and
modes of averting of all presages, of hours, days, and of
things of invention; all which abounded in the most vain
and foolish traditions and rites. Lastly, it is proper to refer hither the ridiculous ceremonies and superstitious rites
of the Papists, which they have transplanted from the Heathen themselves into the Christian Religion, by the acknowledgment of Gerson, part. 3, De direct. cor. *The Church,*
says he, *hath changed many rites of the Gentiles, not by the
abolition of them, but directing the attentions of the faithful
about things of this kind to a good end.* Neither will it be
beside the matter to give some examples of these superstitious traditions, and that upon the authority of this Romanist, lest we should seem to charge the Papists falsely.
*The worship of saints seems to abound with superstition : for
instance, the offering such a gift to such a saint ; as a cock for
boys, a hen for girls ; the invoking one saint in preference to
others for the cure of some particular disease ; the thinking
that in one church more than another, the virtue of some one
saint will be found more powerful and more prompt.* He labours much that he may free these rites from superstition.
The same writer, in his book De erroribus circa artem ma-
gicam, says, *Magicians charge us likewise, and weary themselves to draw us into the same case. Are not such things, say
they, done or tolerated by the Church, in certain pilgrimages,
in the worship of images, in blessing of candles and water, in
exorcisms? Is it not said daily, If any one should remain nine
days in this church, If he should be sprinkled with that water,
If he should devote himself to such an image, he shall be healed
forthwith?* These things he acknowledges to be practised
by the Papists, and that under the pretence of Divine worship, and to be approved, or at least tolerated by their prelates. But it is worth while to hear how he endeavours to

excuse this manifest superstition ; *They are endured,* says he, *because they cannot be utterly eradicated, and because the faith of the common people is regulated, and preserved by the faith of their superiors.* But what is that regulated faith of their superiors concerning these things ? Hear ye, *This is the intention of the church, that such things be done, not as necessarily efficacious, or as though the chief hope were placed in such things, preferring them to their obligations to God; but that the piety of faith may be nourished and increased by these things.* But we shall refer both these, and monastical observations also, and all external rites, which are obtruded upon God as parts of Divine worship, to those condemned traditions of men, upon the authority of Paul, and of Christ : *In vain they worship me teaching for doctrines the commandments of men,* Matth. xv. 9. For in the cause of Religion, that rule of Tertullian is ever to be retained, *It is not permitted us to follow any thing from our own humour, nay, not even to choose what any one shall have introduced of his fancy.*

But here it may be asked, Whether it behoves us to reject and abolish all traditions and external rites adopted by men, as condemned by the Apostle, or not ?

We answer, Nothing less : For it behoves us to yield the power of instituting rites, to be observed for the sake of good order and decorum, to the rulers of the Church, upon the authority of the Apostle himself, *Let all things be done decently and in order,* 1 Cor. xiv. 40. And elsewhere, *Obey them that have the rule over you.* Concerning rites or traditions of this kind, the rule of Augustine is to be commended ; *In these matters there is no better discipline for a grave and prudent Christian, than to demean himself after that manner in which he sees the church, whatever church it be to which he has conformed himself, demean herself. For whatever is enjoined that does not violate faith nor morals, is to be accounted as indifferent.* Epist. 118. ad Januar. cap. 2. To this may be referred ecclesiastical laws respecting the time of fasts and festivals, the difference of garments, and, in fine, the whole external order which is observed in performing sacred offices. Whoever rejects rites and traditions of men of this kind, when they do not oppose the word of

God, is a disturber of public order, and a despiser of the power ordained of God. But here it is fit to add certain cautions.

1. That men should not prescribe any rites or external works with the design of obtaining by them righteousness, the remission of sins, or acceptance with God without a Mediator: for, as to what pertains to all these matters, Christ is sufficient, nor does he require any additions of human invention. Traditions of this kind (and such are almost all those of the Papists) are overthrown by that denunciation of the Apostle, Gal. v. 4, *Whosoever of you are justified by the law ye are fallen from Christ.* How much more are they fallen from Christ, who seek justification and salvation in human commands? Prosper hath well decided concerning these observances : *Fastings, abstinences, vigils, almsdeeds, and other things of this kind, are not to be offered for righteousness, but with righteousness to God,* De vita contempl. lib. 3. cap. 10.

2. We should take care that these traditions concerning things indifferent in their nature, should not be so enjoined as to bind the conscience equally with the laws of God; i. e. so that this guilt of condemnation should be incurred by any violation of them, although that should happen without contempt of those who enforce them, or scandal to any. Wisely and truly says Gerson, part. 3, *They abuse their power who wish that all their ordinances should have their validity under the sanction of eternal punishment.* And part. 1, in conclus. Matth. Grabb. *That every one who does any thing contrary to the canonical injunctions sins mortally, is in error.*

3. We should take care lest traditions concerning things indifferent should be so multiplied as thereby to impose a servile yoke upon Christians, and bring them again, as it were, under a Jewish bondage. For this the Apostles themselves carefully avoided, Acts xv. 10, *Why tempt ye God to put a yoke upon the neck of the disciples, which neither our fathers nor we were able to bear?* Augustine, Epist. 119, says, *this exuberant abundance of ceremonies is to be retrenched, because they load Religion with servile burdens.* And reason necessarily requires that. For this superfluous occu-

pation about human traditions always begets ignorance
and contempt of the Divine precepts, Matth. xv. 6. It
might be proper here, therefore, to discuss this sink of
Papistical traditions; but I had rather ye should hear an
inquiry concerning this matter from some one among themselves than from me. Gerson, part. 1, De nuptiis Christi
et Eccl. asks, *What means such a multitude of constitutions
whilst the Gospel is neither known nor regarded? Let the
Gospel be in the first place known and maintained.* And, De
vita spirit. coral. 14. part. 3, *Such is the multitude of this
kind of constitutions, that if they were kept in their rigour,
the greatest part of the Church would be damned.*

And thus ye have what the Apostle would understand
under the name of *traditions;* how far they may be approved, how far rejected. Now let us proceed to the
third kind of false doctrine which is here reproved by the
Apostle.

After the rudiments of the world.] This is that last species of imposture, or of false doctrine of which the Apostle advises us to beware. Some refer these words to that
idolatrous worship of the sun, the moon, the sea, the
earth, fountains, and floods, which the Gentile philosophers taught. For they divided the power of the one God
into the particular virtues of the elements and creatures;
and assigned a certain portion of the Divinity to each of
these, and, consequently, a part of the Divine worship.
Therefore, both Augustine, in Epist. ad Galat., and some
from among modern interpreters, think the doctrine of the
worship of creatures to be glanced at in this passage. But
I rather embrace the interpretation of those who understand by *the rudiments of the world,* those introductory lessons by which God instructed the Jewish church; namely,
the Mosaic rites, the legal ceremonies, and the shadows of
Christ to come: for the Divine wisdom was pleased to imbue the infancy of his Church with these, as with certain
first principles of Religion, and to prepare it to receive
Christ, and the perfection of the doctrine of the Gospel,
when it should arrive at full age. I come over to this opinion the more willingly because Paul himself, Gal. iv. 3, by

elements of the world designs that ceremonial worship which was in force under the old Testament, *Even we, when we were children, were in bondage under the elements of the world.* And in verse 9, *How turn ye again to the weak and beggarly elements,* &c.   But Paul contends in this Chapter and the following, with those who attempted to bring circumcision and the other Mosaic rites into the Church, and to mix them with the doctrine of the Gospel.   This, therefore, the Apostle says, that they are to be avoided as impostors who, though the ceremonies enjoined by God himself under the Old Testament are now abrogated by the coming of Christ and the Gospel, would, nevertheless, force them upon Christians.   For *the* old *law had a shadow of good things to come, not the express image of the things,* Heb. x. 1. In this text, therefore, we may see an intimation of the doctrine of the abolition of ceremonies.

The Schoolmen are accustomed to adduce a threefold cause why it is proper that the legal ceremonies should cease after the coming of Christ ; because they were *obscure* as to their signification, *imperfect* as to their efficacy, and *burdensome* as to their observance : for in all these points they opposed the grace of the Gospel.   But this reason seems to me most valid, That the legal ceremonies had a certain profession of faith annexed respecting the Messiah who was to come, and expiate the sin of the human race.   As therefore, he would sin greatly who should declare his belief that Christ is to come and to suffer, by professing it in words ; so he sins who does it by his deeds, i. e. who by those legal observances professes the same. This Augustine shews in his treatise contra Faustum, lib. 19. cap. 16,* *Christ is not now promised to be born, to suffer, to rise again ; which the sacraments of the old law typified : but he is announced as born, as having suffered, and risen again ; which these sacraments that are observed by Christians now typify.*   Therefore the practice of the Jewish ceremonies now would be a profession of a false faith.

* Faustus was an Englishman, first a Monk of the Monastery of Levins, then Abbot of the same, and afterwards Bishop of Ries.   Vide Milner, vol. ii. A.D. 594, p. 546.

But it is objected, that the Apostles after the passion of
Christ observed, and directed to be observed, some legal
institutions.   Paul circumcised Timothy, Acts xvi. 3.   By
the decree of the Apostles it was ordained that the Gentiles should abstain from blood, and from things strangled,
Acts xv. 29, and this abstinence related to the observance
of a ceremonial law.   By what right, therefore, are they
who lay upon Christians *the rudiments of the world,* i. e. the
ceremonial law, accounted as impostors?

We have one sufficient answer to both objections.   As
to what pertains to the observance of ceremonies, it is
proper to distinguish with Augustine, Epist. 19, ad Hieron.
three periods.   One was before the passion of Christ, in
which the legal ceremonies were *alive :* the other, after his
passion, but before the full developement of the Gospel, in
which they were *dead :* the third, after that the truth of the
Gospel shone clearly, in which they were *dead* and *buried.*
We say, therefore, that Paul circumcised Timothy, and the
Apostles put forth that decree in the intermediate time in
which the legal institutions were *not buried.*   But it is meet
to add two other points : First, that the Apostles in this
intermediate time observed and retained these legal ceremonies, not, however, as parts of the Divine worship, not
as figures of spiritual things; (for as to faith and conscience, they were abrogated by the passion of Christ) but
only in a manner for public utility, and for the sake of
avoiding offence, they observed those, as any other ceremonies whatever, left at the discretion of the godly.   For
so we see Timothy was circumcised by Paul, because he
thought it of advantage to the Church ; Titus was not circumcised, because he judged it not expedient.   Timothy
received circumcision, therefore, not as a necessary Sacrament (as Isaac, Jacob, and others had aforetime) but as an
indifferent ceremony.   The same was the case with the
Apostolical decree about abstaining from blood and things
strangled ; which was not imposed upon Christians as a
certain matter established by the Divine law, but as suited
to those times, namely, that the Jewish and Gentile

churches might coalesce more easily with each other. But it is proper to add that other point also, That the case was not the same with all the legal ceremonies. For whereas they are divided by the ancient Schoolmen into sacrifices, sacraments, sacred things, and observances; it was not lawful after the passion of Christ to call in the aid of sacrifices for propitiating God, nor sacraments for spiritual sanctification, nor those legal rites for the worship of God without a Mediator; but it was lawful for a time (especially to Jews embracing the Christian religion) that they should retain certain of these observances for this end, lest they should give offence to their weak brethren, Acts xxi. 26. Now then from these things which have been stated, we may collect the difference between the Apostle's retaining certain legal institutions, and seducers urging the Mosaic law. The Apostle did that from respect to the weak before the Gospel was fully published; the seducers urged it to be done for a continuance: The Apostles allowed certain things to be observed with freedom of conscience, for the sake of charity, and of avoiding offence; the seducers recalled the whole Mosaic law, and that as necessary to justification and salvation. Thus much may suffice respecting these three forms of impostures; viz. philosophical speculations, human traditions, and legal rudiments.

And not after Christ.] In these last words is contained the general reason why the three aforementioned doctrines of the seducers are to be avoided and rejected; viz. because neither those curious speculations, nor those superstitious traditions, nor those abrogated ceremonies, are after Christ.

1. All these things are denied to be after Christ, because they are not after the doctrine made known by Christ himself, and his Apostles by the inspiration of the Spirit of Christ.

Where we must observe, that this is the strongest of all ways of concluding that this is not after Christ, i. e. not made known in the Gospel of Christ, therefore not to be admitted in the business of our justification and salvation.

Thus the Apostle exploded the doctrines of seducers; thus we explode the traditions of Papists, which they urge as necessary to salvation.

2. These things are denied to be after Christ, not only because they did not proceed from him, but because they lead Christians off from him. And they lead them off in two modes :

1. By exercising and detaining the mind elsewhere. For through its innate curiosity, the human mind more readily engages in these new and strange doctrines than in Evangelical simplicity, especially when they are obtruded under the pretext of Religion. He, therefore, who shall have brought his mind to these new doctrines, begins forthwith to grow weary of the Gospel; according to that saying of the Apostle, 1 Cor. i. 23, *We preach Christ crucified, to the Greeks foolishness.*

2. They also lead it off by offering a hope of salvation in other things. For because it is much more easy to perform some external works than to believe truly in Christ, and as soon as a hope is afforded of obtaining justification, the remission of sins, and eternal salvation in these works of human tradition, Christ is forthwith forsaken, and the greater part agree to run to these external aids. This is too clearly perceived in the papacy, where almost all hasten to saints, to indulgences, to expiatory masses, to personal satisfactions, whilst there are few who flee to sincere penitence and faith, i. e. to God in Christ; for these traditions, which are not after Christ, have led almost all from Christ.

Verse 9.

For in him dwelleth all the fulness of the Godhead bodily.

In a foregoing verse you have understood the state of the controversy, namely this,—The doctrine of Christ made known in the Gospel is sufficient for salvation; neither is it needful to join thereto either the maxims of philosophers, or the inventions of any men whatever, or even the Jewish ceremonies (formerly enjoined by God himself). Paul undertook to demonstrate this against the false apostles; and he proves it by several arguments.

The first is drawn from the perfection which is in Christ, and, by consequence, in his doctrine. Now thus the case stands: Additions are needed to supply some defect or imperfection; but He in whom *dwells all the fulness of the Godhead bodily,* is not an imperfect Mediator, Saviour, or Teacher of the Church; therefore, in the business or doctrine of salvation we ought not to join any thing to Christ or his doctrine. As though he had said, Perfect Deity dwells in Christ our Saviour and Teacher, with all Divine attributes, wisdom, power, mercy, &c.: what need is there, then, to seek other means or helps to salvation out of Him? Will Philosophers instruct thee better than Wisdom itself? Will Angels lead thee sooner to God than Mercy itself? Will those ceremonies and legal shadows justify thee better than Christ himself, the scope and fulfilment of those ceremonies? Rest thyself in him alone, therefore, in whom alone *dwells all the fulness of the Godhead bodily.*

But the better to understand the force of this argument and also the signification of those words, because the reason is drawn from the indwelling Divinity, let us consider these three things; the dwelling, *In him;* the inhabitant, *all the fulness of the Godhead;* the mode of inhabiting, *bodily.*

In him dwelt.] That is, in the man Christ, or in that human nature in which he undertook and administered the business of our salvation : In that human nature, I say, so mean and despicable in the eyes of unbelieving men, all the fulness of the Godhead dwelt and perpetually dwells ; Phil. ii. 6, 7.   The Apostle employs this metaphorical term *indwelling*, to shew that the Deity abode in the man Christ, not separately, but as in a fixed and proper residence.   We must beware, therefore, not to push this metaphor beyond the design of the Apostle : For that rule of the Schoolmen is true, *In metaphorical statements it is not proper to take the similitude in all points.*

But here it is worth while to enquire why God himself chose to himself this dwelling of human nature, when he would promulgate the doctrine of the Gospel and procure our salvation ?   As to the preaching of the doctrine of salvation, it behoved that not a mere man, but God inhabiting human nature, should promulge the Gospel ;

1.   Because the Gospel could not be carried on without the abrogation of the Mosaic law and the Levitical priesthood : But it was not equitable for this to be abrogated except by him who was far superior to Moses ; viz. by the Son of God, not by any fellow-servant of Moses himself. This is demonstrated in the third Chapter to the Hebrews, where a comparison is made between Moses and Christ. Moses is said to be *a servant in the house of God ;* Christ, *a Son and constituted Lord over the house of God.*   It is not therefore wonderful if Moses yield *to Christ,* and the law *to the Gospel;* since *in Christ dwelt all the fulness of the Godhead.*

2.   It was requisite for the Gospel to enter as an eternal doctrine, never to be changed ; but it mostly conduces to this, when we understand that it was promulgated by the eternal God himself.   For if Deity itself had not dwelt in Christ in some special manner, what should hinder, but that as the Mosaic law gave way to the Gospel, so the Gospel should give way to some other third doctrine ?   But when it appears that Christ was the Author of the Gospel, and that he assumed human nature to make known this

doctrine to men, no one may dare to think of its abrogation.

3. The Gospel is to be received by all the faithful, not
only as perpetual doctrine, but as certain, as perfect, as
saving; but as soon as it is known that in him who
brought the Gospel into the world the Godhead dwelt in
that mode in which it is here asserted, it is immediately
understood that in the doctrine of such a person, certainty,
perfection, and salvation are found. For they who receive
the rule of faith directly from truth itself, can in no wise
be deceived. Well said Clemens Alexandrinus, Strom. 6,
*Men, speaking as men about God and divine things, are not
worthy of credit ; but the voice of the Lord is more worthy of
credit than any demonstration.* Neither can the doctrine
fall under the suspicion of imperfection, which He, all
whose works are perfect, would not divulge by his Ministers, but by himself. Lastly, that must necessarily be
saving, which He taught who is the only way to salvation.

It was fit that the doctrine of salvation (as you see)
should be promulgated not by a mere man, but by God
dwelling in human nature. We will now also shew that the
very work of our salvation required this indwelling of God
in our nature.

1. Because human nature being severed from God, and
alienated from the life and communion of God through sin,
is most suitably restored to the communion of God, and
most firmly preserved in the same, by this mode. The Fathers commonly assign this reason. Iræneus, lib. 4. cap.
59, says, *How can the Ebionites be saved, if he be not God
who wrought out their salvation upon earth? and how shall
man pass over unto God, if God pass not over unto man?**

* Ebionites, the followers of Ebion, an Heresiarch of the first Century,
who, though he rejected, with Cerinthus, that portion of the Gospel of St.
Matthew containing an account of the miraculous conception, yet invented
a modification of Cerinthus's error, that Christ was born of human parents
in the ordinary way ; but still considering him no more than a mere man.
Against this heresy Iræneus particularly wrote : and in what a dangerous
case he viewed those who imbibed the heresy, under any form, may be
judged from the quotation adduced above. Dr. Priestley attempted to set
aside the force of Iræneus's testimony against it ; with what grounds for his

Athanasius, Orat. 3, says, *Unless Christ be the real Son of God, man is not firmly united to God: For what a mere man hath received may be lost, as was the case with Adam. There-fore, that grace and the gift might remain firm, God assumed our nature; that thereby all spiritual good might be delivered to us in firm possession.* Cyril, De Incarn. Verbi, cap. 1, says, *The Word was made man, that in him, and in him alone, the nature of man being crowned with the endowments of in-nocence, might be enriched with the Holy Spirit, not to depart now, as was the case with Adam, but to remain therein.*

2. God chose to dwell in our nature, that thereby we might be sure that all his merits pertained to us as brethren and co-heirs. So says Athanasius; *The Son of God took our nature upon him, that henceforth we, being constituted of earth only, should not come to the earth; but being joined to heaven by the Word, should be conducted to heaven by him.* Fulgentius observes, *God hath saved that in us which he assumed for us; and made that nature a partaker of salvation, which he joined to his own;* ad Thrasimund, lib. 1.*

efforts let the Reader decide from Dr. Burton's Bampton Lectures, lect. 7, and from his " Testimonies of the Ante Nicene Fathers." Horseley's Tracts against Priestley may also be well referred to ; and Townsend's New Testament Harmony, in his Notes on the commencement of St. John's Gospel.

* Fulgentius was an ecclesiastical writer of some eminence in the early part of the sixth century, and equally deserving of notice for his distin-guished humility and piety. Du Pin gives an interesting account of his parentage, the remarkable events of his early years, the distinctions he gained, and his singular self-denial and devotedness to a religious life ; his being made Bishop of Ruspa, and brought under the notice of Thrasimond, King of the Vandals, at whose instigation he wrote a Treatise in three books against the Arian heresy, from which the above quotation is probably derived. Through the influence of the Arians, Fulgentius, with all the other Catholic Bishops of Africa, was banished into Sardinia ; and in that retirement he wrote several other pieces, the orthodox sentiments main-tained in which, as well as in the afore-mentioned, as reported by Du Pin, are deserving the consideration of all who regard such sentiments when held and enforced in the present day to be novelties. On Thrasimond's death, Fulgentius and his companions in exile were recalled by his successor, on which he returned to his Bishopric, and spent his remaining years in the duties thereof as an exemplar of all that was excellent, dying in the year 533.

3. It behoved the Divine nature to be joined with the human, that men might have access to God with confidence, and that Divine grace might have a channel by which it should be derived to men. For since God assumed a nature allied to, and consubstantial with us, we can approach him with boldness; *For no man hateth his own flesh, but nourisheth and cherisheth it,* Ephes. v. 29. We can also draw grace from this our mystical Head, as the members of the natural body receive sense and motion from the natural head.

All the fulness of the Godhead.] That is, not some portion of the Divinity, which the Gentiles had an erroneous persuasion of concerning their false gods; neither excellent endowments of Divine grace and munificence only, which are common to angels, and prophets, and other holy men : but the Λόγος itself—true and perfect God, with all his Divine attributes, namely, infinite wisdom, power, goodness, dwells in this human nature of Christ. And the Apostle seems to allude to the ark of the covenant : for God promised that he would dwell there, hear them from thence, and be propitious to them : and, furthermore, the Apostle intimates, that the ark and the propitiatory, or mercy-seat, were types of Christ, and that the Deity dwelt in a much more excellent way in his human nature, than he did formerly in the tabernacle, concerning which it is written, Exod. xxix. 44, 45, *I will sanctify the tabernacle of the testimony, and I will dwell among the children of Israel,* &c. As, therefore, the Jews, who had an appointed place whence God uttered his oracles, and made known his will, could not, without sin, enquire elsewhere about things pertaining to God; so we, who have the fulness of the Godhead dwelling in the body of Christ, cannot seek either the will of God or our salvation elsewhere, without the greatest folly and impiety.

Hence we learn,

1. As often as seducers endeavour to lead us away from the Gospel and from Christ, to their traditions and inventions, we must seriously reflect what kind of Saviour and Teacher Christ Jesus was ; viz. one in whom dwelt *all the*

fulness of the Godhead; and it is the height of madness to require new teachers after him.

2. Whoever, therefore, wanders out of Christ, or mixes any other thing with his doctrine as necessary to salvation, he accuses Christ of imperfection, and denies the fact that *all the fulness of the Godhead dwelt in him.*

3. This we observe in the Turks and Jews, who are not content with the Gospel doctrine, because they do not believe that *all the fulness of the Godhead dwelt in him* who proclaimed the Gospel. As to Papists, who, being fascinated with novel and marvellous error, acknowledge that *all the fulness of the Godhead* is *in Christ,* yet deny that all the fulness of salvation is contained in his doctrine, I know not what to say.

Before we proceed to the *mode* of this indwelling, let us briefly resolve a doubt which may arise in the mind of some, from the Apostle's words. For when he asserts that all the fulness of the Godhead dwells in Christ, he seems to say that the entire essence of the Deity assumed to itself this habitation of the flesh of Christ, and, therefore, that not only the Son, i. e. the second person in the Trinity, but the Father also, and the Spirit, were incarnate.

The Samosatenians,* who deny a Trinity of persons, think that they can drive us to this difficulty, viz. that if we affirm a Trinity, we shall be also compelled to admit that the three Persons were incarnate, because the fulness of the Godhead, i. e. the entire and perfect Divine essence, dwelt in Christ incarnate.

* Samosatenians, or Paulianists, so named from Paul of Samosata, Bishop of Antioch in the latter part of the third century. These heretics maintained that the Son and Holy Ghost exist in God as the faculties of reason and activity in men; that Christ was born a mere man; but the Reason of the Father descending into him caused him to be called the Son of God, and did by him work miracles and instruct the people. Alas! how many Heretics of this cast, or of the grades mentioned in the two preceding Notes, exist among us and distract the Church in the present day. The theological Student, however, would do well to ascertain the way in which these heresies were met at the time of their first rise, by consulting Dr. Burton's invaluable work before referred to, " The Testimonies of the Ante-Nicene Fathers to the Divinity of Christ."

I answer, that the whole Divine nature was incarnate, not because it is incarnate in all the Persons, but because none of the perfection of the Divine nature is wanting to the Person of the Son. For since the Divine nature, or essence, is spiritual, it can neither be supposed nor allowed to have parts ; but wherever the Divine nature is found, there it is found entire and perfect. The whole Divine nature, therefore, was incarnate, but not as considered absolutely and in itself common to all the Persons, but as it is considered in its personal properties, or mode of being, limited in the person of the Son. *God entire, is one person,* says Luther, tom. 2.

But against this, that saying of Augustine, in Enchir. cap. 38, is urged ; *The works of the Trinity are indivisible :* therefore, if the second person assumed and adapted the human nature to himself for a dwelling, then both the Father and the Holy Spirit did the same, and, by consequence, not the Son alone, but the three persons are incarnate.

I answer, to assume flesh imports two things : the act itself, or the uniting of this flesh; and the end of this act, viz. the person to whom this flesh is united and adapted. As regards the act, it is common to the three persons ; for the Father and the Holy Spirit jointly effected the incarnation of Christ. But as regards the end, it is peculiar to the Son alone. As, for instance, if a father gives a wife to his son, but the son himself marries her, both are rightly said to have contracted the marriage ; yet with this difference, that the father married the bride to the son, and the son married her to himself; so, in the incarnation of Christ, both effected this conjunction of the human nature with the Divine; but yet so, that God the Father joined this flesh to his Son, the Son took it to himself. As, therefore, in the former example, not the father, but the son is said to be married, although the will and the action of both concurred in choosing and taking that wife : so in this latter, not the Father, but the Son only is said to be incarnate, although both concurred in creating and uniting this body. And what is affirmed respecting the

Father, must also be understood of the Holy Spirit. It
would be easy to shew this from the Scriptures. For *the
Word* alone is said *to be made flesh*, i. e. to be incarnate,
John i. Yet the work of incarnation is ascribed to the
whole Trinity: to the Father, who is said *to have prepared
this his salvation*, Luke ii. 31, and Heb. x. 5: to the Son
himself, who is said to have taken the seed of Abraham,
Heb. ii. 16: and, lastly, to the Holy Spirit, who in the
conception of Christ, is said to have *overshadowed the Virgin*, Luke i. 35. Thus far concerning the dwelling, viz. the
human nature of Christ; and the inhabitant, viz. the Λογος,
or the Son of God : Now let us enquire about the *mode* of
inhabiting.

Bodily, σωματικῶς.] Because God is said to be present
with his creatures in many ways, the Apostle shews that he
dwelt in the human nature of Christ in a certain special
manner. For God, by his universal presence, is at hand
with all things, so as to preserve and uphold them ; he is,
moreover, present with the saints and faithful by the special efficacy of his Spirit, so as to sanctify and enrich them
with the endowments of his grace : but God is not only
present in these ways with the human nature of Christ, the
fulness of the Godhead besides, i. e. the Λόγος, the full, true,
and perfect God, dwelt in it bodily ; not that the spiritual
and incorporeal nature of the Word is changed (for that is
immutable), but that the manner of existing was new, although the nature of the Word existing remained the same.
By *bodily,* therefore, we ought to understand *personally ;*
i. e. not by efficacy or assistance alone, but by hypostatical union : so that the Λογος inhabiting or assuming, and
the nature inhabited or assumed, should be one person, or
one ὑφιςταμενον, *one substance.* Whence it happens that the
Word is declared incarnate, and *that* man is not *a mere
man*, sanctified and upheld by the Divine Spirit, but *the
God-man.* This Augustine briefly and perspicuously explains in these words, *God took the temporal substance of the
flesh into the Eternal person of the Divinity.* What is *he took
it in person*, but that he united it personally to himself, so
that what is assumed becomes one with the person assum-

ing? In this place, then, *to dwell bodily,* is nothing else than to join to himself *personally.*

Neither should it seem a strange interpretation, when we explain this word σωματικῶς, ὑποςτατικῶς, *bodily, personally :* for as the Hebrews put *souls* for *persons* (Gen. xiv. 21, *Give me the souls, and take the goods to thyself;* Acts vii. 14, *Jacob with three score and fifteen souls went down into Egypt.* And Ezek. xviii. 20, *The soul which sinneth it shall die ;* i. e. the person) so, among the Greeks, σῶμα signifies *person.* Thucydides, lib. 1, says, *many poor persons are more ready* σωμασιν η χρημασι πολεμεῖν, i. e. *to go to war in their own persons,* (as they say) *than to contribute money for the war.* So Demosthenes said, σωμάτων και χρημάτων πληθος, abundance of bodies, i. e. of *men,* or *persons,* was on *the side of the Athenians,* when he wished to excite them to war. And so this word is used in the well-known epigram,

Σωματα πολλὰ τρέφειν, και δωματα πολλ᾽ ἀνεγείρειν, &c. *to nourish many bodies, and raise up many houses,* &c.

The Apostle, therefore, when he says that the Godhead *dwells* in Christ *bodily,* means, that the eternal Son of God united the human nature to himself, so that the person of the Word, which subsisted in the Divine nature alone, now also subsists in the human nature, and imparts personality to it, which the human nature possessed not in itself. There are not, therefore, two persons in Christ, one of man, and the other of the Son of God ; but the Divine nature is so united to the human, that it subsists in it σωματικῶς, i. e. σεσαρκω μενως και ὑποςτατικῶς, *incarnate and personally.* Hence the sacred Scriptures call the Son of Mary *the Son of the Highest,* Luke i. 32 ; and it is affirmed, verse 35, *that Holy thing which was born* of Mary, was *the Son of God.* On account of this personal union, *the Branch of David* is called *Jehovah,* Jerem. xxiii. 5, 6; and *the blessed God,* Rom. ix. 5. Hence Hugo de St. Victor, Erud. theol. de Verb. incarn. collat. 2, says, *The Son of God did not take the person man, but took man into the person.* The personal Word assumed man ; not a person, but the nature. It is said he assumed man, because a human soul and body were assumed. It is not said that he assumed the person of man (or a human person), because that soul and body which he assumed, were not previously united together personally, but they derive their personality from the Word dwelling bodily in that human nature.

And this may suffice as to the mode of this hypostatical union; for the human mind is not able to fathom the whole depth of this mystery. If any doubt remain, *Apply faith,* as Justin Martyr speaks, *which will render the solution easy.* Piously and modestly does Chrysostom remark on this matter: *I know that the Word was made flesh, but how he was made so I know not. Do you wonder because I know it not? Every creature is ignorant of it.* We are not, however, so entirely ignorant of the mode, but that we can, out of the Scripture, stop the mouths of heretics who deny it. Let us, therefore, briefly solve the objections which they are wont to allege against this personal union. And those objections are advanced either as to the Divine, or as to the human nature.

1. As to the Divine nature they object: The Son of God or the person of the Λογος, was a perfect substance from all eternity: but nothing can be added to a perfect substance; therefore the human nature was not taken into personal union with the Word.

We answer, Nothing can be added *to the constitution* of the essence of a perfect substance; as to *communion* with its complete essence somewhat may be added. For although the hypostasis of the Word was perfect by reason of his *nature,* yet for the perfection *of the end,* which is to redeem the Church, there could, nay there must be something added to this perfect substance, namely, the human nature, in which the Son of God by his blood might purchase the Church to himself. But here we must beware not to think that the human nature is so added to the Divine hypostasis, as to be an equal part of it, by a mutual union constituting this hypostasis, but that it is ενυποϛτατον, i. e. *subsisting in the person,* not as an equal part, but as *an instrument pertaining to the unity of the hypostasis,* as Damascenus expresses it; or as a thing subsisting in its principal. And from this it appears how we should receive what is contend-

ed for by the Schoolmen, viz. that the hypostasis, or person
of Christ was compounded after the incarnation. For this
is asserted by them, not with respect to *parts,* as though
the person of the Word were compounded of the human
nature and the Divine, as of parts; but with respect to
number, because *that* now subsists in two natures, which,
before the incarnation, subsisted solely in the Divine. Thus
Aquinas 3. part. qu. 2. art. 4, says, *The person of Christ is
considered either according to what it is in itself, and so it is
simple; or according to the natures in which it subsists, and so
it is said to be compound, inasmuch as that simple person subsists in two natures.* Thus much as to the first objection.

2. It is objected, that to become incarnate, or to take
to itself human nature, is to be changed : but the eternal
Deity cannot be the subject of any change : therefore he
could not become incarnate, and, therefore, he does not
dwell *bodily* in the human nature of Christ.

We answer, That to be incarnate, as also to become
man, occurred to the Word not by transmutation, but by
union; which is a species of relation: but what is predicated
anew of any subject relatively, does not, therefore, presup-
pose a change of the thing to which it is ascribed, but of
the other which it connects with it. For instance; God,
who was not a Creator from all eternity, became a Creator
in time; but yet this new appellation does not imply a
change in God, but in the creature, which is brought into
being by God from nothing : So the Son of God, who was
not man, neither incarnate from all eternity, is made man,
and becomes incarnate; yet is not changed in himself, because a change takes place in the human nature which is
assumed, and not in the Divine which assumes. The Son
of God was not man, or incarnate, when he did not impart
personality to the human nature; he is pronounced man,
and incarnate, when he did impart personality to that nature; but this he did, not by changing his Divine nature,
but by uniting this human nature to himself. To be made
man, imports absolutely a real change in the subject acquiring human nature, as when man is made from the earth
or seed ; because here the subject which is made man loses

its former nature : but when the person of the Son of God
is incarnate and made man, that is not understood to be
done by transmutation, but (if it may be permitted to frame
a word) by a new personation of human nature. And thus
the Word was made flesh *substantially, not by conjunction,*
yet without a change of his nature ; by creating and uniting the human nature to himself, not by changing the Divine nature.

With respect to the human nature, it is objected,

1. If the human nature of Christ subsists in the person
of the Λογος, not in its own proper personality, then the
man Christ will be more imperfect than all other men : because all others have human personality, and are subjects
existing in that nature ; Christ alone, in as far as he is
man, hath not this personality, but subsists in the Divine
person of the Logos by the hypostatic union.

I answer ; Proper personality is not wanting to the human nature, on account of the defect of any thing which
is required to its perfection, but on account of the addition
of something which far excels its nature, viz. its union to
a Divine person. Christ, therefore, is not more imperfect,
but more eminent than other men ; because our human nature subsists in us in its proper personality, but it subsists
in Christ in that which is Divine ; and it is much more
noble and honourable to subsist in God by hypostatic union
than to subsist by itself. For if we say the sensitive part
is more noble in man than in a brute, because it is joined
to a more noble *form,* although in a brute the *form* is complete, and in man it is not, but is joined to what is complete : then, by parity of reason, the human nature is more
worthy and more excellent in Christ, on account of its
union with the Divinity, than in us, although in us it subsists in proper personality, in Christ otherwise.

2. It is objected, If the human nature of Christ subsists in the person of the Logos, then he hath two perso-
nalities : for since *a person* is *an individual substance of a rational nature* (according to the definition of Boethius) and
Christ, in as far as he is man, is a single rational being ; it

E e 2

follows that there are two persons in Christ ; and so we fall again into the Nestorian heresy.

I answer ; For personality more is required than to be constituted an individual or single being : for a person supposes not only a singular and rational substance, but, moreover, one existing by itself, and not joined to another more worthy. We, therefore, admit that the human nature of Christ, or Christ as far as he is man, is an individual or singular ; but we deny that he is a person. And the reason is obvious; because in the moment in which the soul of Christ was created, and his flesh conceived, in that same moment they were united to the Divinity. If they had existed apart from the Logos, they would have had their own personality : but because they began to exist together, and to be united to the Word at the same time, there was a necessity that this human nature should draw its personality from the Word. For any thing is called a person from what it hath of the greatest excellence : Since, therefore, the Divinity is incomparably more excellent than the humanity, the human nature deservedly takes its personality from thence.*

* It may be permitted the Translator to observe here, that Pope Gelasius, the fiftieth Bishop of Rome, in defending the true doctrine of the Union of the two natures in one person, against the Eutychians, employed an argument which, whilst establishing the truth here contended for, at once overturns the doctrine of Transubstantiation, and proves that it was unknown to the Church up to his time—the close of the fifth century. The Eutychians were supposed to believe the human nature in Christ to have been, by its union with the Divinity, absorbed by, and transformed into the Divinity ; so that Christ could not be said to have two Natures after the union. Against these, Gelasius undertakes to prove the *reality* of the two natures in Christ, notwithstanding the union ; and he argues thus :—" *The Sacraments of the Body and Blood of Christ, which we receive, are certainly a divine thing, and by them we are made partakers of the Divine nature ; but yet* THE SUBSTANCE OR NATURE OF BREAD AND WINE DO NOT CEASE TO BE IN THEM. *Indeed,* THE IMAGE *and* SIMILITUDE *of the body and blood of Christ is celebrated in the mysterious action : we are, therefore, to believe the same thing in our Lord Christ, as we profess, celebrate, and take in his* IMAGE, *viz. That, as by the perfecting virtue of the Holy Ghost the elements pass into a Divine Substance, while their nature still remains in its own propriety ; so in that principal mystery* (the union between the Divine and human natures), *whose efficacy and power these represent, there remains one true*

3. It is objected; If the human nature of Christ be hypostatically united to the Divine, then each is united with the other entirely ; because it is without parts : but if this be granted it follows, that wherever the Divine nature is, there is also the human ; and so we pass into the camp of the Ubiquitarians.

We answer; the consequence is denied ; because it is a personal union with the properties of both natures preserved.   Since, therefore, it is a property of the human nature to be circumscribed by certain limits; it loses not this property by virtue of this union to the infinite nature.   For as the natures united are not analogous, they are not made so by the personal union; since the union only joins together, but does not change the natures.   Since, therefore, the finite nature and the infinite are not analogous, the Divine is not circumscribed by this personal union, nor the human extended to the infinite.   We, therefore, confess, that the human nature is inseparably and indivisibly united to the Divine, and that the Divine is in no place separated from the human : not that the humanity is in all places where the Divinity is, by local position ; but that by a real and hypostatical union it is joined to the Divinity wherever existing.   The union, or conjunction, is circumscribed by no distance of place, because it consists in this, that the Deity sustains the humanity as its own and peculiar pro-

and perfect Christ ; and both natures, of which he consists, remain in their properties unchangeable."—We may well unite, in the words of Bower, who gives us this Specimen of the Theology of the early part of the Church, in his life of Gelasius, " He must be quite blind, who does not see that the whole strength of the Pope's argument rests upon this, That the bread and wine in the Eucharist retain the nature and substance of the bread and wine, notwithstanding their sacramental union with the body and blood of Christ. This he does not prove, but supposes as a truth, not questioned either by the *Eutychians* or the Catholics, and from thence argues the human nature in Christ, to retain, in the same manner, its own substance, though united with the Divinity.   Should we suppose the bread and wine in the Eucharist to be changed into the body and blood of Christ, this argument had been of no force against the *Eutychians*, but might have been by them unanswerably retorted against the Catholics."   See also The History of Transubstantiation by Bishop Cosins, 1657, in which Treatise the above passage from Gelasius is adduced in Cap. 5.   This fact has given much exercise to the Jesuitic screw of Roman criticism.

perty, and yields subsistence to it; and thus the Word, omnipresent in heaven, earth, and every where, sustains the humanity existing in the heavens alone : But the actual position of the body of Christ is included in certain space, because the nature of a body requires it.   Some illustrate this by the example of the Sun and the solar Sphere.   For as the Sun is inseparably united to its orb, yet the property of the sphere, to be in East and West at the same time, does not accord to the globe of the sun ; so the humanity is inseparably united to the Divinity, but will not be, on that account, wherever the Divinity is.   But some perhaps may say, that the sun is not united to his orb as a whole, but as a part only ; but humanity is united to the entire Word.   We acknowledge a dissimilarity of the similitude in this respect; but it tends more to confirm our opinion. For every spiritual nature, wherever it is, is a whole; because it is without parts, or indivisible, and its entireness is considered in the perfection of its essence, not in the extension of quantity.   The Word, therefore, as far as it is a spiritual substance, is whole, and entirely in the human nature united to it, for it cannot be detached from it : and the same Word, as far as it is an infinite substance, is equally whole and entire without the human nature, for its immensity cannot be included in such narrow limits : But whether considered in the body united to itself, or out of the human nature of Christ, it no where exists disunited from the human nature, because every where it sustains it as its own.

Verse 10.

And ye are complete in him, which is the head of all princi-
pality and power.

That we must adhere to Christ and his doctrine alone, is
concluded in the foregoing verse from the infinite perfection of Christ; which neither requires nor admits any additions of philosophy, or traditions, or ceremonies. The
Apostle now shews that same thing by two other arguments.

The first is drawn from the effect; *Ye are complete,* or
consummate, or *perfect in him;* i. e. Christ himself is not
only perfect in himself, inasmuch as *in him dwells all the ful-*
ness of the Godhead; but he brings it to pass that we are
complete through him, namely, having all things in him,
and his doctrine, which are necessary to our salvation :
Therefore it is not needful to seek salvation apart from
Christ and the Gospel.

The second is taken from the office of Christ. Christ is
the head, not only of men, but of angels also ; by him,
therefore, both men and angels have their perfection. Men
ought not to seek or expect salvation from angels, but both
should depend upon Christ, who is *the head* of both. Now
let us examine these reasons separately.

And ye are complete in him.] Two things are here to be
noticed : 1. What it is to be *complete,* or in what things
our completeness, consummation, or perfection consist.
2. How this perfection may be obtained or held by us;
which the Apostle intimates when he says, *in him.*

As to the first; *To be complete* is nothing else than to be
furnished with all things necessary to salvation : which we
may severally refer to these three heads; 1. perfect wisdom, or saving knowledge : 2. righteousness : 3. sanctification : possessing which things in this life, happiness and
glory will follow in the life to come.

1. In Christ we have perfect wisdom; because by the right knowledge of him, according to the doctrine of the Gospel, what is sufficient to salvation is known : *This is life eternal, to know thee the only true God and Jesus Christ whom thou hast sent,* John xvii 3. Hence the Apostle (1 Cor. ii. 2) desired *to know nothing but Christ and him crucified.* For that which is full admits nothing beyond. Hence the mind filled with Evangelical knowledge, desires not any new knowledge in order to salvation ; because this is consummate, full, and perfect doctrine. *I admire the fulness of Scripture,* says Tertullian, adversus Hermogenem. HEAR HIM ! *I will hear thoroughly ; nor will I hear any one besides Him,* says Hilary, De Trinit. 6.*

2. In Christ we have complete righteousness ; because he has fully satisfied both the Divine law, and even God himself for our sins : according to that declaration of Isaiah (liii. 11) *By the knowledge of himself shall my righteous servant justify many, for he shall bear their iniquities ;* and of the Apostle, Rom. iii. 22, *The righteousness of God by faith of Jesus Christ is unto all and upon all them that believe ;* and Rom. x. 4, *Christ is the end of the law for righteousness to every one that believeth.* In this respect, therefore, principally, we are *complete,* because being destitute of any righteousness of our own, Christ enriches and adorns us with his. Chrysostom, Hom. 17. in 10 ad Rom. observes, *That if thou shalt believe in Christ, thou hast both fulfilled the law, and much more than the things which it had commanded ; forasmuch as thou hast truly received much greater righteous-*

---

* Hilary, a Christian prelate of the fourth century, one of the early fathers of the Church, born at Poictiers, of which city, after his conversion from heathenism, he eventually became the Bishop in 355. His zeal in favour of the Athanasian doctrine respecting the Trinity, which he defended with much energy at Bezieres, drew on him the persecution of the Arian party, with Saturninus at its head, who prevailed on the Emperor Constantius to exile him into Phrygia. After four years spent in banishment, he was permitted to return to his See, where he occupied himself in committing the arguments for his side of the question to writing, and produced a work on the Trinity in 12 books, which has been much celebrated. He continued to distinguish himself as an active servant of the Church till his death, in 367.

ness. More briefly and explicitly says Bernard, Serm. ad
milit. temp. 11, *Death is put to flight by the death of Christ ;
and the righteousness of Christ is imputed to us;* and Epist.
190, *The righteousness of another is assigned to man, because
he had none of his own.* We have saving righteousness,
therefore, in Christ.

3. In Christ we have sanctification, or indwelling righteousness. For what else is sanctification than a cleansing
from sins and iniquities, whereby we were separated far
from God; and a reception of gifts and graces, whereby
we are brought nigh to him to serve him? Truly it is now
manifest, that we are daily both cleansed from the pollution of our sins, and adorned and enriched with all the fulness of Divine gifts, so far as, being united to Christ, we
are quickened by his Spirit; by whose efficacy the remains
of the flesh are mortified, the image of holiness is restored,
and our life is directed towards the attainment of happiness. Whence this Spirit is called *the Spirit of holiness,*
Rom. i. 4. No one hath Christ, but he hath together with
him, this Spirit of Christ; the Apostle affirming, *If any
one hath not the Spirit of Christ, he is none of his,* Rom. viii.
9. No one hath this Spirit but he is strengthened by his
aid to serve God in good works, to resist the world and the
lusts of the flesh. For as the needle, being touched by
the magnet, turns itself to the arctic pole ; so the human
heart being touched and quickened by this Spirit of Christ,
turns itself to God and the commands of God, and rests
in them.

Ye now perceive how much the Apostle comprehends in
saying that we *are complete* in Christ : for by this one word
he shews that we have in Christ whatever is required for
saving knowledge, justification, and sanctification : And
by the same means he crushes all the errors of false Apostles : For if we have complete wisdom in Christ, there is
no need of philosophical additions; if complete righteousness, there is no need of legal ceremonies ; if sanctification, there is as little need of angels for purifiers or en-
lighteners of our souls. Ye observe in what things this

completeness consists ; let us enquire how it is obtained
and held.

In him.] We are declared to be complete not *from him,*
or *by him* only, but *in him:* that we may understand that
we have that aforesaid wisdom, righteousness, and holiness, not as far as we look to Christ, as though he were
distant from us ; but as far as we are incorporated into
Christ, as far as we have Christ dwelling and abiding in us.
For although it is most certain, that all the fulness of the
Godhead and of saving grace is in Christ, so that he is
like a copious fountain whence abundance of living water
flows, yet this is the difference between him, the spiritual
fountain, and a natural one : There is no necessity that
they who wish to drink of a fountain should enter the
fountain itself; because, standing without that, they may
draw from thence to quench their thirst : but it is not so
with Christ, who is the fountain of grace and righteousness to us, for we cannot receive of his fulness unless we
are in him.   For, as the old Adam in us is the cause of
corruption and death ; so this new Adam dwelling in us is
the cause of righteousness and salvation.   And it is the
same whether we affirm that Christ dwells in us, or that we
dwell in Christ ; for these are united : John xv. 4, 5, *Abide
in me, and I in you.   As the branch cannot bear fruit of itself,
except it abide in the vine ; no more can ye, except ye abide in
me.   I am the vine, ye are the branches : he that abideth in
me and I in him, the same bringeth forth much fruit.*   Whatever, therefore, men hope concerning grace, righteousness,
and sanctification, for obtaining eternal life and glory, it
will be found mere dreaming and delusion, if they are not
in Christ, and Christ in them.   And, indeed, Christ is in
us, and we are in him, when, by the power of the Spirit,
and of faith wrought in our hearts by the Spirit, we are
united to this our Head, and are grafted in him as branches
in the vine.   Concerning the Spirit, the Apostle, Rom.
viii. 9, declares, *If any one have not the Spirit of Christ, he
is none of his.*   Concerning faith, it is said, John iii. 36,
He that believeth on the Son hath everlasting life ; because *life*

is in this Son, 1 John v. 11.   Upon this Durandus well observes, lib. 4. qu. 8. dist. 1, *No one can be justified unless
through union with Christ ; but the first union with Christ is
through the Spirit.*   And Cyprian, De cardin. oper. Christi ;
By faith, not contact, we are joined to the Spouse.

Thus we have explained these two things : what it is to
be complete ; and that no one is complete or perfected by
Christ, but he who is in Christ.   Let us deduce some instruction thence.

1.   Since we have complete justification in Christ, it is
plain they know not Christ, or at least treat him with contumely, who, not contented with him, seek higher righteousness and perfection in their own works and inventions.
From this error flowed the superstition of the Monks, and
presumption about the merit of works.

2.   All the godly derive great consolation on account of
their being complete in Christ : For when they regard
themselves, they find that many corruptions still lie concealed within them ; that in many things they daily fall and
sin ; but that, notwithstanding these things, they are acceptable to God, they are justified before God, because
they are united to Christ by faith and the Spirit : *There is
no condemnation to them who are in Christ Jesus,* Rom.
viii. 1.

3.   The wicked and unbelieving are excluded from the
benefits of Christ, because they are separated from Christ
himself, inasmuch as they are void of the Spirit and of
faith, without which no one is in Christ, and Christ abideth
in no one.   And thus much for the first reason derived from
the effect : I proceed to the other.

Which is the head of all principality and power.]   This argument is drawn from the office of Christ, and his prerogative above all angels, whom the Apostle intends under
the words *principality and power,* as in the 16th verse of the
preceding Chapter.   The false apostles threw out many
things respecting these angelic principalities and powers :
The Apostle, therefore, inculcates that Christ is not only
the Head of the Church with respect to men, but of the
angels also ; and that men and angels are the fellow-ser-

vants of this our Lord Jesus Christ. Whether, therefore, we consider the angels in reference to Christ, or in reference to ourselves, from either consideration the doctrine of the false Apostles is overturned. For they taught, 1. That angels are to be worshipped; 2. That by them access to God is opened for us; 3. That by them we derive spiritual blessings.

1. Now, that the angels are not to be worshipped, is evident from their relation to Christ: because worship is due to God alone; but the angels are not only inferior to God, but even to Christ as man, inasmuch as he is *the Head* and Lord of all angels. Hence, Heb. i. 6, it is said, *When he bringeth in the first-begotten into the world, he saith, And let all the angels worship him.* Hence we perceive that the angels are nothing more than creatures, although lofty and noble; But *the Catholic Church directs that God alone is to be worshipped; it advises us that no creature is to be worshipped;* says Augustin, De morib. Eccl. lib. 1. cap. 30.

2. Hence also it is inferred, that the angels are not mediators between God and the human race: For if Christ be *the Head* of angels, then they cannot invade the office of Christ, nor make themselves equal to him in this respect. But *there is one Mediator between God and men, the man Christ Jesus:* who is *the Head,* not the colleague of angels.

3. Whereas the angels are, under Christ *the head,* united to the rest of the Church, we readily understand that saving grace, and those excellent gifts of faith, of love, and the like, are not impressed upon human souls by the power of angels, but of Christ himself. For the more noble members do not impart a vital stream to the inferior ones; but the head emits sense and motion equally to these as to the other.

All these things will be equally evident, if we consider the relation of angels to ourselves. For they are our brethren, and fellow-servants; they are members of one and the same Church; because the same Christ is *the head* both of men and angels.

1. If, then, they are our fellow-servants, and members of the Church together with us, they are not to be worship-

ped or adored by us, upon the confession of an angel himself; Rev. xxii. 8, 9, *I fell down,* says John, *to worship before the feet of the angel: but he said unto me, See thou do it
not; for I am thy fellow-servant, and of thy brethren: Worship God.* That saying of Augustine to this effect is well
known; *We honour them by love, not servitude,* De vera relig. cap. 55. And that of Parisiensis, De legib. to the
same purport; *The angels are to be honoured, but with honour
due to the servant, not the lord.*

2. Whereas we and the angels are fellow-citizens, and
members of the same body, it is inferred that angels are
not mediators between us and God. For the whole Church
is accepted of God on account of one and the same Mediator: but to attribute it to one member, that the rest are
accepted on his account, is contrary to reason and the
Scriptures. Whence says Augustine, Contr. Epist. Parm.
lib. 2. cap. 8, that *he alone is a Mediator for whom no one interposes, but he himself for all.* And the Apostle, Rom. viii.
34, places the hope of our salvation in him, not because
we have an angel our fellow-servant, but the Son of God
seated at the right hand of the Father, an intercessor for
us: *Who is he that condemneth? It is Christ that died, yea,
rather, that is risen again, who is even at the right hand of God,
who also maketh intercession for us.*

3. Since the angels are members of the same Church,
it follows from this relation of angels to men, that faith,
love, and holiness, are not gifts of the angels, but of Christ.
For as in corporeal generation, one part does not form and
frame another, but all are formed by one and the same
power: so, *in spiritual regeneration,* as Albert properly observes, *our mind, in the formation of grace is not fashioned by
the angels, but by the Spirit of Christ.** But here two
things may be objected against what is said respecting
Christ as the head of angels, and men as fellow-servants
with the angels.

1. If Christ be the head of the angels, and angels be-

* It appears there were men worthy to be heard among the Papists, who
could exalt Divine grace, and give the proper place to angels. Oh! si sic
omnes. Vide p. 169, Note.

long to the body of the Church, then he is also the Saviour
of the angels; for he is *the Saviour of the body*, Ephes. v.
23: But the angels need not the benefit of a Saviour or
Mediator; therefore it does not seem that Christ is the
head of angels, as to this procuring of salvation and eternal happiness.

I answer; the angels had no need of Christ as a Saviour
to deliver them from sins committed, for they stood stedfast in obedience to God; neither did they need the favour
of a Mediator to snatch them from a state of wrath, for
they never had God for their enemy: but they needed
Christ the Saviour, they needed the favour of Christ the
Mediator, that they might retain fixed their condition in
righteousness, that they might have sure and inviolable
peace with God, that they might be accounted worthy of
the eternal and glorious fruition of God; which beatific
vision of God surpasses the nature and desert of any creature. This Augustine intimates, De fide ad Petrum diac.
cap. 23; *This very thing*, says he, *that the holy angels can
by no means be changed from that state of happiness in which
they are fixed to a lower, is not naturally implanted in them :
but after they were created, they were placed in it by the
bounty of Divine grace.* But grace is bestowed on no creature except through the Mediation of Christ, who is the
channel of grace. Here seems to apply the Apostle in 1
Tim. v. 21, in calling the blessed angels *the elect angels.* But
election, whether of men or angels, shews that the salvation of those who are elected is to be attributed alone to
God in Christ. For this also Christ is said, as in Ephes.
i. 10, αναχεφαλαιωσασθαι, *to have gathered all things together ;*
and in Colossians i. 20, αποχαταλλάξαι, *to have reconciled all
things to God the Father, whether they be things in earth, or
things in heaven.* The most learned interpreters expound
each of these texts to relate to this benefit of Christ the
head which is derived to the angels : and although that
word *to reconcile*, in its proper and primary signification,
cannot apply to the angels, yet in its broader and analogi-
cal application, they have shewn that it may be extended
even to them. In which they follow Bernard, who, in Serm.

22, in Cantica, after he had proved that *Christ was made to men, as he had been before to the angels, wisdom, righteousness, sanctification, and redemption*, objects as to the angels in this manner, *How there could have been redemption for the angels I do not see: for Scripture does not teach us that they were captives through sin, or obnoxious to death so as to render redemption necessary to them.* He then answers, *He who raised fallen man, granted to the standing angel that he should not fall; thus delivering the one out of captivity as he defended the other from captivity : And on this ground there was redemption to both, liberating the one, and preserving the other.* From these considerations, therefore, the first objection is done away, and it is proved that Christ is truly called *the head of the angels*, not only by reason of his ruling power, but on the score of saving grace, although the angels never were in a condition of sin and condemnation.

2.   Since because Christ is *the head* of the angels, we affirm that the angels are our fellow-servants, not mediators, or dispensers of grace ; it is objected that we rob the angels of their dignity, and snatch from them the ministry delegated to them by God : for they are *ministering spirits sent forth to minister for them who shall be heirs of salvation*, Heb. i. 14.   And in Psalm civ. 4, it is said, *He maketh his angels spirits, and his ministers a flame of fire.*   By which terms they suppose that some angelic virtue for the illumination of the human mind, and for exciting the will to the love of God, is intended.

I answer ; We confess that God employs the ministry of angels for many things ; but especially in guarding the elect and promoting their spiritual safety.   For as the bodily as well as the spiritual welfare of men is attacked by evil spirits ; so it is clear from the Scriptures that in both respects we are defended and assisted by good angels.   To omit examples which might be drawn from the old Testament ; we read that the Apostles were brought out of prison by the ministry of angels, Acts v. 19, and xii. 17.   And Christ himself impresses terror upon those who shall offend one of his little ones, by this argument, that they have angels assigned to them by God the Father, Matt. xviii.   But as

to our souls, it may also be granted; because, although to
pour the light of faith and the fire of love into human
minds, is the prerogative of God; yet, as he employs the
external ministry of men to enlighten the minds of the
elect, and excite their wills to piety; so likewise he employs the invisible and internal ministry of angels. Whence
the Schoolmen admit, that the angels cannot create or infuse, yet they can enkindle, and excite spiritual knowledge,
good thoughts, and pious affections in the mind and will.
And they say that this is done in a threefold manner: 1.
by removing impediments, driving away evil spirits, and
bad illusions; 2. by exciting and directing visions, by representing to the mind good thoughts; 3. by moving the
passions duly in the sensitive appetite, in inclining the will
to its proper office. But to what purpose do we urge so
many of these things? That it may be understood that we
do not disparage the office delegated to the angels by God,
as to the *promotion* of the salvation of the elect: and that
it may also be understood, that the ministry of the angels
in bringing about our salvation being admitted, yet they
are not to be worshipped by us, but to be acknowledged
for ministers of Christ, and our fellow servants, although
somewhat more honourable. For the same Christ who is
the head of the elect, is also *the head of all principality and
power*, i. e. of all angels. Therefore, as we are not to worship with religious adoration, either earthly kings or ministers of the word, although those protect our goods and
our bodies by their external rule, and these direct our souls
in the way of salvation by their ministry: so neither ought
we to worship the angels, although they render the same
offices in a secret and invisible manner. But there will be
occasion to treat concerning the worship of angels when
we come to the 18th verse; now let it suffice that we hold
ourselves *complete in Christ, who is the head of all principality
and power.*

Verse 11.

In whom also ye are circumcised with the circumcision made without hands, in putting off the body of the sins of the flesh by the circumcision of Christ.

Hitherto the perfection of Christ having been the subject of consideration, the Apostle taught in general that there was no need for the additions of the seducers : Here he withstands those particularly who imposed the Judaical ceremonies upon Christians. Now, among the Mosaic rites, circumcision held the primary place ; because by submitting to this, men bound themselves to observe the rest, Gal. v. 3, *I testify to every man that is circumcised, that he is a debtor to do the whole law.* Therefore this being done away, it follows that Christians are also delivered from all the rest. On this account, then, he insists on circumcision, since it is his intention to shew, and to conclude, that all the Mosaic rites are now abrogated. And this verse is so connected with the foregoing, that it aptly meets the objection which those teachers of the ceremonies doubtless urged. For the Apostle had affirmed in the preceding verse, that Christians are *complete in Christ;* ' But, nay,' says some Jewish doctor, ' you are mistaken, Paul, and you would endeavour to mislead Christians : they are not yet complete, because they are not yet circumcised : and without circumcision they are not accounted the holy people of God, they are not received into the covenant which was entered into with Abraham and his posterity.' Therefore that he might crush this objection, after that he had stated that we *are complete in Christ,* he subjoins, *In whom also ye are circumcised.*

With respect to the interpretation of the words ; those alone seem to contain any difficulty, *in putting off the body of the sins of the flesh.* Beza translates them thus, corpore

peccatis carnis exuto, *the body of the flesh being freed from
sins.* He, therefore, takes the word *body* properly, and
says, this our body is freed from the sins of the flesh by
the circumcision of Christ. But Erasmus, and almost all
other interpreters thus ; *whilst ye have put off the body of the
sins of the flesh;* or, *in the putting away of the body of the
sins of the flesh.* They, therefore, take the word *body* metaphorically, for that mass of native corruption in which
we are involved : and they think the word flesh is added
that he might signify whence that body of sins hath its
origin and motion; namely, from carnal generation, and
from the carnal part of man, that is to say, from that part
which is not yet regenerated. This interpretation, as it is
less forced, I rather embrace : which the Apostle himself
elsewhere favours; Rom. vi. 6, *that the body of sin might be
destroyed;* so likewise in the 3d Chapter of this Epist. ver.
5, he calls particular sins, *members.* He, therefore, seems
to use the same metaphor in this place also.

Let us dismiss words, and proceed to the point. The
argument of the Apostle is this, They who now have circumcision, even that which is more excellent than the Mosaic, are not to be compelled to the latter : but Christians
are circumcised with a circumcision far more excellent and
efficacious, &c. This he shews in a threefold manner ; 1.
From the Author of our circumcision : They were formerly
circumcised by Moses, or by other men inferior to Moses ;
but we are circumcised *in Christ,* or *by Christ:* for *in* and
by have the same meaning. 2. From the mode of the
Jewish circumcision and of ours : *they* had a circumcision
made by hand; *we, the circumcision of Christ.* What is
this ? An inward circumcision wrought by the Spirit of
Christ. These two clauses are, therefore, to be joined, *the
circumcision made without hands,* and *the circumcision of
Christ;* and both are to be referred to the mode of our circumcision. 3. From the different effect : the Jewish circumcision cut off the foreskin of the flesh ; ours, the whole
body of sin.

In whom also ye are circumcised.] The Apostle lays a
stress upon it, to teach the Colossians they had no need of

the Mosaic circumcision. The reason is drawn from the
excellence of our circumcision, which he shews first from
its Author : *in Christ,* i. e. by Christ, or by the efficacy and
virtue of Christ, *ye are circumcised;* in vain, therefore,
would ye receive the Mosaic circumcision. The force of
this argument is clear, if we recal what has been said by
the Apostle about Christ. For he has extolled Christ as
the only begotten of God, the Head of the Church, the
storehouse of grace, and, finally, as enriched with the fulness of the Godhead itself: it would, therefore, tend to
bring reproach upon Christ, if any one being circumcised
by him, should desire to be circumcised by any one else ;
for the desire of another indicates that there was some defect in the circumcision of Christ himself. For as it would
be both injurious to himself and to his king, should any
one, being adorned with the dignity of a knight by the
king himself, desire to receive the same honour after another manner by some inferior minister : so he who is circumcised by Christ, our King and Lord, proceeds to diminish his majesty, if in this same thing he should desire the
ministry of another. Thus much concerning the Author :
I pass on to the manner.

*With the circumcision made without hands, by the circumci-
sion of Christ.*] I unite these, because both may be referred to the manner of this circumcision which we have obtained in Christ, or by Christ. For it might be said, that
Christ circumcised no one. Nay, says the Apostle, we are
circumcised in him. But in what way ? *With the circumcision made without hands,* i. e. not bodily and sensibly; but
with the circumcision of Christ, i. e. spiritually, inwardly,
and invisibly, such as it behoves us to expect from our
heavenly Priest. The mode of this circumcision is described then, 1. Negatively : It is *not wrought manually,* for
it is *made without hands.* By this he opposes the Mosaic
circumcision, which consisted in an external operation administered by the hands of men. 2. It is also described
positively; since it is called *the circumcision of Christ,* i. e.
a certain internal circumcision effected by the power of the
Spirit of Christ himself. And by this it is far preferred to

the Mosaic circumcision : which, if it be compared to this,
is plainly a thing of no worth, Rom. ii. 28, and Phil. iii. 3.
But here it is to be observed by the way ; that the Apostle,
when he disputes about circumcision and the other Mosaic
rites, speaks of them, for the most part, as they are considered in themselves, apart from Christ, and not related
to Gospel grace ; because they were so urged by the false
apostles with whom he disputed. For they sought righteousness and sanctification in the ceremonies themselves,
neither did they acknowledge that there was concealed in
them the shadows of Christ to come ; on that account they
would not allow them to be abrogated by the advent of
Christ : The Apostle, on the contrary, argues, We have
that spiritual circumcision which the bodily one shadowed
forth ; therefore, that ought now to cease, lest, while we
would retain the shadow, we deny that the body itself is
come.

It is objected, The Apostle's reason does not seem solid :
for he thus concludes, Ye are circumcised with the circumcision *made without hands,* therefore ye need not that which
is made with hands : Any one from among those teachers
of the ceremonies might rejoin, Nay, we need both : for
Abraham was circumcised in heart by faith and the Spirit,
yet he did not decline to undergo external circumcision
besides.

We answer ; The case is not the same. For Abraham
by virtue of the Divine command was bound to corporeal
circumcision ; Christians are not bound : Abraham by submitting to this sign declared and confirmed his faith concerning Christ, to be born of his seed, free from all sin ;
but we do not look for Christ to be born, but believe that
he is born : finally, Abraham had no other sign of the covenant entered into with God ; we have, namely, baptism,
substituted by God himself in the place of circumcision.
From what, then, has been said concerning the Author and
the mode of our circumcision, we may derive some instructions.

1. Christ being taken away, there remains nothing in
the sacraments but an empty shew, and a ceremony strip-

ped of all salutary efficacy: for Christ is the substance of
the sacraments; the virtue and operation of Christ is the
very life of the sacraments. That saying of the schools is,
therefore, a sensible and sound one, *Sacraments represent by
similitude; signify by institution; but sanctify by the virtue of
Christ.*

2. If, as an outward administration of the sacraments
is made by the hands of men, so an inward operation is
wrought by the sole power of Christ; then it is vain to
seek grace as though it were hidden in the signs themselves, or attached to the performance of them, i. e. to the
outward administration of the sacraments: for it is to
Christ alone, not to those external rites. Parisiensis has
learnedly written on this matter in Tract de sacram. bapt.
cap. 2, where he shews that the external solemnity of the
visible signs is nothing more than a book, in which is read
the virtue and grace which proceed from God himself. This
Prosper also teaches in Epist. ad Demetriadem; *That which
is visibly performed in the sacraments is one thing, what is invisibly celebrated is another: nor is the form in the sacrament
the same thing with the virtue: since the form is applied by the
assistance of a human ministry, but the virtue proceeds through
the efficacy of a Divine work.* More succinctly does Cyprian
state it, De bapt. *The Spirit alone imparts the reality of the
sacrament to us.*

3. We must not glory because we are made partakers of
the external sacrament, unless we obtain besides the internal and quickening work of Christ: for if this be wanting,
as it was heretofore said to the Jews, Acts vii. 51, *O ye
uncircumcised in heart,* so it may be justly said to us, *O ye
unbaptized in heart.*

4. The external administration of the sacraments is not
to be despised, although the quickening and saving effect
is to be expected neither from the human ministry, nor
from the external signs, but from the Spirit of Christ: because Christ concurs with his institution, nor wills us to
seek that grace from him which he promised, if we despise the sacraments of grace which he has directed to be
used by us.—And thus much concerning the mode or qua-

lity of the circumcision which we have in Christ; namely,
that it is not outward and bodily; but inward and spiritual.

In putting off the body of the sins of the flesh, or *in spoiling,* &c.] The last thing which we proposed to be considered in the circumcision of Christ, was the remarkable
effect of this circumcision, viz. *the putting away of the body
of the sins of the flesh.* See how the spiritual circumcision
which we have in Christ excels the bodily and manual circumcision! That external rite cut off a small portion of
the body: this internal operation is wont to abolish the
whole body of sin, not the body itself, or the flesh itself,
but *the body of the sins of the flesh,* i. e. the mass of vices
and sins which spring from the flesh, that is to say, from
our inbred and original corruption, with which flesh the
soul of every one is no less surrounded than with its natural flesh.

We have here, then, a brief and perspicuous description
of inward, i. e. of true circumcision: It is a *putting off the
old Adam with his deeds,* or the corrupt likeness derived to
us from our parents, infected with sin; or, as Origen remarks in Epist. ad Rom. cap. 2. lib. 2, *It is the cleansing the
soul, and casting away the vices.*

Neither is it to be wondered at that this spiritual circumcision should have a different effect from that corporeal
one, since it has a different agent, and different instruments. For the Agent in this spiritual circumcision is our
Lord God himself; Deut. xxx. 6, *The Lord thy God will circumcise thy heart, to love the Lord thy God with all thine heart,
that thou mayest live.* Behold the Agent, God; the effect,
new motions in the heart itself, even spiritual life. But in
corporeal circumcision the agents were men: Abraham circumcised Isaac the eighth day, Gen. xxi. 4; so Joshua
circumcised the children of Israel, Josh. v. 3. But will
you expect from men any thing beyond man? Yet further,
the instruments also are far different: for men perform corporeal circumcision with corporeal instruments; according
to what is said Josh. v. 2, *Make thee sharp knives, and circumcise the children of Israel:* But God circumcises the heart

with the sword of the Spirit and the word ; for *the word of God is sharper than any two-edged sword, piercing even to the dividing asunder of soul and spirit,* &c. Heb. iv. 12. It is quite reasonable, therefore, that the effect of this circumcision should be the putting away of the body of the sins of the flesh, i. e. the cleansing of the soul, not the impressing of a bodily sign.

Hence we learn,

1. That Christ is a Saviour not only by the merits of his passion, but also by the efficacy of his internal operation; for he has not only expiated our sins by his blood ; but he hath renewed our hearts, and washes away the body of sins which cleave to our souls, by his Spirit.

2. Since this spoiling of the body of sins is the work of the Spirit of Christ, we ought not to resist this Spirit, but commit our whole selves to be renewed and directed by the same. The reins of the flesh are, therefore, not to be loosened, but we must walk in the Spirit. *Walk in the Spirit, and ye shall not fulfil the lusts of the flesh,* Gal. v. 16.

3. It is not sufficient for the Christian, as it were, to cut off one or other member of this body of corruption; but he must needs prune, strip off, and cast away the whole : for this spiritual circumcision does not pertain to one member only, but to all. Ears, tongues, eyes, heart, mind, in short, the whole man must be circumcised, because the whole is defiled by sin. Rightly says Parisiensis, De virtut. cap. 22: *He is not cleansed, except he hath renounced all sin. For who will call a man clean that rolls in one sewer only ?*

But here a doubt arises concerning the effect of this internal circumcision : For it seems that that whole body of sins is not put away from regenerate Christians, as well because they perceive in themselves yet the motions and lusts of indwelling sin, as because Scripture commands the spiritually circumcised, i. e. the truly renewed, daily to mortify more and more the old Adam, to put off the old man, and to put on the new : Ephes. iv. 22, 24.

I answer; the whole body of sins is put away and abolished totally from all the regenerate, 1. As to its guilt; for *there is no condemnation to them that are in Christ Jesus,* Rom. viii. 1. 2. As to its dominion; for as many as are in Christ Jesus are ruled not by the desires of sin, but by the Spirit of Christ: 3. As to the Sacrament itself of regeneration; for in it, not this or that, but all our sins are washed away and mortified sacramentally. In these modes, therefore, sin is deposed and abolished in this life. Yet, again, *sin* is not totally put away; 1. As to the nature of sin: whence that injunction of the Apostle, Rom. vi. 12, *Let not sin reign;* He does not say, Let it not lie hid, let it not cleave ; but *let it not reign in your mortal body.* 2. It is not put away as to its motion and act: whence that saying of the Apostle, Rom. vii. 23, *I see another law in my members warring against the law of my mind.* The act, therefore, of the laying aside of sin, or of natural corruption, if it be referred to the very nature of the thing, is not perfected in a moment, but is continued in all the godly until the last breath.

Verse 12.

Buried with him in baptism, wherein also ye are risen with him, through the faith of the operation of God, who hath raised him from the dead.

It has been proved in the foregoing verse, that circumcision is by no means necessary to Christians, inasmuch as they are circumcised in Christ with an inward and spiritual circumcision. But as yet room is left for doubt: for some one might perhaps say, The outward sign by which the minds of the godly may be confirmed and persuaded that they are truly made partakers of the spiritual benefits in Christ is wanting. The Apostle, therefore, shews, that

not even that is wanting; nay, that Christians have a more
excellent and express sacrament than circumcision, viz.
baptism; *Buried with him in baptism.*

Three things are to be noted, 1. The spiritual benefits
which are received in baptism : viz. the burial of the old
man, which we usually call mortification ; the raising again
of the new man, which we term vivification. 2. From what
fountain these benefits flow, viz. from the death and resurrection of Christ ; which is intimated in those words,
With him, in him, or *by him.* 3. By what instrument these
benefits are applied to us ; viz. *by faith.*

Buried in baptism.] This burial of the body of sins, or
of the old Adam, is signified in baptism, when the person
to be baptised is let down into the water ; like as the resurrection is when he is raised out : For in the ancient
Church they not only sprinkled, but immersed in the water
those whom they baptised.

But in what sense are we said to be συνταφεντες, *buried together?* For the natural body of Christ was truly buried,
but is it to be thought that our bodies are buried in the
same manner in the administration of baptism? The Apostle does not assert that : but, as Chrysostom has rightly
observed in Rom. vi. *That which is done in Christ by nature,
is understood to be done in us by analogy and comparison.* The
body of sin, then, is buried, when its power is weakened,
repressed, overwhelmed, and, as a corpse buried in the
earth, can move no more and impel the man whithersoever
it would, or hinder our salvation. And this is said to be
done in baptism in a twofold respect :

1. In respect to Christ ; in whom, when we are engrafted by baptism, the benefits of the death of Christ are conferred upon and sealed to us : but he being dead and buried, it is clear that our sins were also dead and buried with
him ; because *he bare them in his own body,* 1 Pet. ii. 24.
This is what is urged by the Apostle in Rom. vi. 3, *As many
of us as were baptized into Christ, were baptized into his death.*
In looking back, then, to the person of Christ our Head,
our sins are rightly said to be indeed dead and buried in
his death and burial ; and we are said to be buried in bap-

tism as to the body of sin, because we are endowed with
this benefit obtained through the death of Christ: and
thence it comes to pass that our sins are not imputed to
us, but are accounted as dead and buried.

2. Not only in the person of our Head, but even in our
ownselves our sins are said to be buried in baptism: because that mortification and burial of sin is not only performed sacramentally in one moment in the act of baptism; but really also is carried on by the spirit of grace
received in baptism, through the whole life of a Christian.
For the case of bodily death and burial is different from
that which is spiritual. The former hath no degrees, because it is pure privation; he, therefore, who is dead, cannot daily die more and more. But the latter is in process,
not in act past: therefore it hath degrees, so that he who
is dead to sin, may die more; he who is buried may be buried more, inasmuch as the work itself is to be perfected
in man, although as to the sacramental representation and
sealing of it it wanted nothing.

Ye are also risen.] This is the second effect of baptism,
which is shadowed forth when the baptized person, after
immersion in the water, is drawn out of it, But the Apostle, under this word *resurrection,* comprehends that new
life which the regenerate began to live after they were dead
and buried with Christ. And I call it new, because it hath
both a new beginning, and new motions, or operations.
The new beginning is not a soul living, but a spirit sanctifying; not desire innate, but grace imparted. The new
fruits are, not those *works of the flesh,* Gal. v. 19, &c. *adulteries, strifes, envyings, murders, drunkenness, and the like;*
but *love, joy, peace, gentleness, goodness, faith,* &c. These
two benefits are always linked and joined together. For
as Christ himself did not abide in death, but rose again;
so, by virtue of his death and resurrection, we not only die
to sin, but also so rise again, that we *live unto righteousness,*
1 Pet. ii. 24. Thus it is in Rom. vi. 5, *If we have been
planted together with him in the likeness of his death, we shall
be also in the likeness of his resurrection.*

Hence we may infer,

1. A Christian living in sin and serving his lusts, is a horrible sight, nay, is deemed a monster before God. For the dead to walk or move is plainly a prodigy : But a Christian either is, or ought to be, not only dead, but buried, as to the old man.

2. A Christian growing torpid in indolence, i. e. not bearing the fruits of righteousness, nor aiming at newness of life, although he abstain from acts of sin, yet shews that he is forgetful of his baptism. For baptism is *a covenant of a more pure life with God :** care should, therefore, be taken, that what hath been once done in baptism sacramentally, should always be carried on in life really.

3. External washing cannot yield solid comfort to a Christian, unless he discovers besides, these internal effects of mortification and vivification. For baptism, considered as the mere washing of the body, conduces nothing to salvation, unless it is also made to us *the washing of regeneration,* Tit. iii. 5. For rightly said Cyprian, De zelo, *To put on the name of Christ, and not to proceed by the way of Christ, what else is it than a forgery of the Divine name?* We put on the name of Christ when we undergo external baptism ; but we enter the way of Christ, when we die to the world that we may live to God.

4. They who walk after the lusts of the flesh, can neither accuse God nor the inefficacy of baptism ; but themselves, who resist the Spirit ; whom, if they would obey, sin would be weakened in them daily, the image of righteousness would be renewed, and, finally, that would be accomplished in reality which in baptism was done sacramentally.

And thus far concerning the two effects of baptism; namely, our spiritual burial and resurrection : It remains that we enquire into the cause and fountain of these benefits: which the Apostle briefly indicated in these particles, *With him, In whom.*

We are said to be buried *with Christ* in baptism, and also to have risen *in Christ,* or *by Christ,* that we may not attri-

---

* Vide page 22.

bute these supernatural effects either to the external ele-
ment, or to our own strength.   Therefore, the death, burial, and resurrection of Christ is the cause of our mortification and spiritual vivification.   1. It is the cause *meritoriously*, as was before contended for by us at the 18th verse
of the first Chapter ; because, by his death and resurrection, he merited for us this mortification and spiritual rising again, as it is said Isaiah liii. 10, *If he shall lay down
his soul for sin, he shall see a lasting seed.** For because he
laid down his natural life, he merited to raise up a spiritual
seed to himself, and to communicate spiritual life to them.
2. The death and resurrection of Christ is also the cause
effectively of our mortification and resurrection ; inasmuch
as rising again from death, by that same power with which
he effected his own bodily resurrection, he effects also
this our spiritual.   For, as by the power of the Word he
raised from death the humanity united to the Word ; so
also by the same power he quickens us, who are united to
and planted in him, to a new life of grace.   Rom. vi. 11,
*Reckon yourselves to be alive unto God through Jesus Christ
our Lord.*   3. Lastly; the death, burial, and resurrection
of Christ, is the cause of this our death, burial, and resurrection by way of *example :* For thus it is every where
propounded to us by this Apostle ; *Like as Christ was raised
from the dead, so we also should walk in newness of life,* Rom.
vi. 4.   On these accounts, then, the Apostle rightly affirmed,
that we were dead and risen again *with him,* and *in him;*
because, *by the merit, efficacy, and example* of his death
and resurrection, we have obtained mortification and spiritual resurrection.

   Hence we observe,

   1. Christ is not dead, buried, and raised again for himself alone; but for us : for in his death and burial he hath
mortified and buried our sins, and in his resurrection he

---

   * Davenant gives the Vulgate version of this passage ; *Si possierit pro
peccato animam suam, videbit semen longævum.*   Bishop Lowth, whose translation of Isaiah liii. was the result of close critical examination, thus renders
the quotation from the aforementioned text, " *If his soul shall make a propitiatory sacrifice, he shall see a seed which shall prolong their days.*"

hath raised us up together with himself, as though he had
taken us by his hand. When, therefore, you meditate on
the death and resurrection of Christ, contemplate not only
what was done in him, but likewise what is done in thyself.
For as the Apostle divinely speaks, Ephes. ii. 5, 6, *When
we were dead in sins, he quickened us together with Christ, and
hath raised us up together and made us sit together in heavenly
places in him.*

2. It is incumbent upon every Christian, not only to
believe the death and resurrection of Christ, but to have
and perceive them in himself, that he may exhibit also to
others a real and lively testimony of the same; and this he
does who renounces sin and lives to God. Nearly to this
effect Origen wrote, In Genes. xvii. hom. 3, *What does it
profit if I believe that Christ came in that flesh only which he
received from Mary, and do not shew that he also came in this
my flesh?* We may add; What does it profit if I believe
that Christ died and rose again in the flesh which he received from Mary, and do not shew in my flesh that he is
dead and raised again, i. e. that I am dead and raised again
in him and with him? All the godly may gather from
hence that they are true and living members of Christ;
namely, if they aim with their whole soul at mortification
and newness of life. For whoever does this, does it not in
his own strength; but he is buried with Christ, he is risen
again in Christ; and, therefore, he is planted in Christ,
and quickened by the Spirit of Christ. Thus much may
suffice respecting the cause, or fountain of our mortification and vivification. It follows that we notice the medium
or instrument by which these benefits are apprehended.

*Through the faith of the operation of God, who hath raised
him from the dead.*] We come now to that instrument by
the help and assistance of which the above-named benefits
of baptism are apprehended and possessed. For if this
faith be wanting, although the treasures of grace in the
sacrament are offered on God's part, yet they are not received on our part, but repelled by infidelity. But the
sense of the words must be considered before we inquire
into their subject matter. These words, then, *through the*

faith of the operation of God, are used to be explained by
interpreters in two ways. Some give the meaning thus;
through the faith of the operation of God, i. e. by the faith
which God works in every one of the faithful, by the faith
which springs from the Divine operation. But others explain them thus; *through the faith of the operation of God,*
i. e. by that faith which is directed to that wonderful operation of God which raised Christ again for our justification.
Whether we follow this latter or the former interpretation,
three things are to be noticed in these words of the Apostle : The instrument by which we apprehend the treasures
of grace offered in baptism ; viz. *faith:* the Giver or the
worker of this faith, *God,* or *the operation of God;* the particular object which faith most especially regards in this
business, *the power of God raising Christ again from the dead
for our salvation.*

Through faith.] As to this first; it is not in vain that
faith is required by the Apostle, that we may obtain the
benefit of spiritual resurrection. For, as in the baptism of
adults previous faith is required, according to that declaration of our Saviour, Mar. xxi. 16, *He that believeth and is
baptized shall be saved ; and he that believeth not shall be
damned;* so, from those who are baptized in infancy, subsequent faith is required ; which if they do not exhibit afterwards, they retain only the outward sanctification of
baptism, the internal effect of sanctification they have not.
Whence says Augustine, Quæst. ex N. Test. qu. 59. *He
who imagines baptism to consist in the carnal form, is not spiritual ; neither can he obtain the celestial gift, who trusts that
he can be changed by water, not by faith.* We have a strong
and perspicuous reason for this ; viz. because the substance
of the sacraments is Christ himself; all the virtue and vitality of them is from Christ : but, indeed, Christ is not
approached by unbelievers; for men of this kind, whilst
they receive the sacraments, because *their hearts are dry
and their minds barren, they indeed lick the rock, but suck
thence neither honey nor oil,* as Cyprian somewhere says.

By way of profit, let us learn not to confide with Papists
in the opus operatum ; but enquire farther, whether we

possess all the other things without which the inward effects of baptism are not secured. So much concerning the instrument of faith.

Of the operation of God.] The Apostle points out the Author or Giver of faith; namely, God himself. For since the salutary efficacy of baptism depends upon faith, it is proper that faith itself should be expected from God alone, lest we should have some occasion of glorying in ourselves. Hence that affirmation of the Apostle, Ephes. ii. 8, *By grace are ye saved through faith ; and that not of yourselves; it is the gift of God.* We ought not, therefore, as the Pelagians would wish, to allege that faith springs from the human will; nor that it is natural, as Basilides thought, according to the statement of Clemens, Strom. 2 ; but as Augustine has stated, that it is bestowed upon us by the free gift of God : for although *good works are done by man, yet faith is wrought in man,* Epist. 105, ad Sixtum.

Who hath raised him from the dead.] Some contend that this clause is added by the way, to intimate that God stirs up faith in the human heart by that same infinite power with which he raised up Christ from the dead. For since our hearts are dead in sins and unbelief, there is need of the same Almighty power to quicken them which shewed itself in the revival of Christ, as it is said in Ephes. i. 19, 20. Let us not reject this sense : But we also add this ; that the Apostle here wished to point out, as with the finger, what kind of faith he required from us ; viz. that whereby we believe in God, who, by his wonderful operation, raised Jesus from the dead for our justification, as it is in Rom. iv. 24, 25. Therefore, lest our faith should wander in any confused and indefinite speculation about God, he, as it were, moderates this infinite object to us, since he would have faith not contemplate the efficacy of God simply, but as far as it raised up Christ; for thus it became a saving efficacy to us.

And very suitably in this place, where he treats of faith united with our spiritual resurrection, he directs it to look at that power of God which raised up Christ from the dead ; viz. for two causes, which we have before touched

upon : 1· Because that same power which raised up Christ
from the dead, infuses strength into us for this spiritual resurrection. 2. Because this resurrection of Christ is the
cause of ours, as also was before shewn. But now two
things remain to be cleared up which yield occasion for
doubt.

1. The first arises from hence, that in these last words
Christ is supposed to be raised by the power of another;
whereas it is certain that he raised himself by his own
power ; according to that prediction of his, John ii. 19,
Destroy this temple, and in three days I will raise it up. Christ
speaks *concerning the temple of his body,* by the interpretation of John himself.

I answer, In statements of this kind, in which divine
operations are referred to God the Father, neither the Spirit nor the Son is excluded, but the order of operation is
noted. For that saying of Christ is most true, John v. 19,
*Whatsoever the Father doeth, those things also doeth the Son
likewise.* Therefore, both by the Father's power and his
own, was he raised up; because the power of both is the
same. Whence says Hilary, De Patr. and Fil. unitat. *He
himself performs the works of God the Father by a nature not
differing from God.*

2. The other doubt, which is strongly urged by the
Anabaptists, is somewhat more difficult. For since in this
whole disputation of the Apostle, mortification, newness
of life, and, finally, faith itself, is connected with baptism ; but infants can neither mortify the flesh, nor produce
the fruits of a new life, nor, in short, believe; they conclude that those of that age should not be baptised.

We answer ; If they speak of actual faith, of actual desire, and the profession of mortification and vivification,
we say those places of Scripture which require these
things in baptized persons should be restricted to adults :
But with respect to infants, because they are sinners not
by their own proper act, but by hereditary habit, it is sufficient that they have mortification and faith, not exerting
itself by a proper act, but included in an habitual principle
of grace. But that the Spirit of Christ can, and is wont

to effect this habitual principle of grace in them, no sane person will deny.   Moreover, it is not necessary that the sacraments, in that very moment in which they are administered, should effect all those things which they represent; nay, upon the concessions of the Schoolmen themselves, *A covenant admitting of delays is allowable when a bar is placed in the very act of undertaking it.*   But now the very defect of reason in infants as to acting, is an impediment to their possessing actual faith, or actual desire of mortification.   Besides, although faith and actual penitence are required from an adult before he receives the sign of the covenant, yet it is not required as to the act from the infants of believers; because to be in covenant is a sufficient reason for receiving the sign of the covenant: but infants are included in the same covenant with their parents; *I will be the God of thee and of thy seed,* Gen. xvii. 7.   This we see in Abraham, who first believed and afterwards was circumcised; but his Son Isaac, inasmuch as he was already in covenant, he circumcised before he was of age to believe. This, in the case of the infants of Christians, is done duly and after the example of the Apostles, who did not baptize adults except they made a profession of faith; but when the parents embraced Christianity, then they baptized their whole families, and no one is ignorant that (in the Epistles) infants are also comprised under the name of a *family.*   The passages are manifest; Acts xvi. 15 and 33, 1 Cor. i. 16.

Let it suffice to have noticed these things about infant baptism against the Anabaptists.

Verse 13.

*And you, being dead in your sins and the uncircumcision of
your flesh, hath he quickened together with him, having
forgiven you all trespasses.*

A new reason is propounded to shew them that we have
no need of circumcision, and those other legal rites ; because in Christ we have not only sanctification, or regeneration, but perfect justification from sins, and that by
gratuitous remission. But that this benefit may be recog-
nized with more glorious evidence, he does three things :

1. He places before our eyes the miserable condition of
our nature ; *And you being dead,* &c.

2. He points out our deliverer ; namely, God by Christ ;
he hath quickened together with him.

3. He declares the mode of deliverance, by the gratuitous remission of sins ; *having forgiven,* &c.

*And you being dead in your sins and the uncircumcision of
your flesh.*] In these words the state of man in corrupt nature is depicted, by shewing both the evil and its cause.
The evil with which he is afflicted, death itself; *and you
being dead.* The twofold cause of the evil: actual sins,
which are here termed παραπτωματα, or offences, and original corruption, which is signified by the epithet *uncircum-
sion.*

With respect to the evil itself; All the children of Adam
are reckoned as dead, 1. Because they lie under the state
of spiritual death, having lost the image of God in which
they were created ; and Divine grace, which was, as it
were, the soul of the soul, being withdrawn, and a pollut-
ing mass of deadly vices succeeding in their room. 2.
Because they lie under the sentence of eternal death,
having become obnoxious to Divine wrath, and to that
punishment which must be expected from an incensed

God : for *we are by nature the children of wrath,* Ephes. ii.
3. Death, therefore (as you see) hath seized upon us all ;
spiritual death, actually ; eternal death, by sentence ; and
in each respect we are justly said to be altogether undone.

In sins] i. e. In actual transgressions of the Divine law :
This is one, and a clear cause of our death. For *the wages
of sin is death* by the Divine ordination. *The soul that sinneth it shall die; the death of grace,* inasmuch as sin, by its
impurity, dissolves that gracious union of the soul to God,
in which our spiritual life consists ; according to that declaration of the prophet, Isa. lix. 2, *Your iniquities have separated between you and your God, and your sins have hid his
face from you,* &c.: and *the death of hell,* inasmuch as Divine justice requires that a punishment adequate to the offence should be imposed on sinners ; but an offence against
infinite Majesty deserves infinite punishment : *Tribulation
and anguish upon every soul of man that doeth evil;* Rom. ii.
9. Whoever, therefore, lives in sin, is in death.

And the uncircumcision of your flesh] This is the other
cause of our death. Some take these words literally, and
think that there is denoted not the cause itself of death,
but the sign of the cause. For as circumcision by itself
did not avail to life ; so neither did uncircumcision by
itself extend to death ; but they are said to be *dead in uncircumcision,* inasmuch as that was a symbol of alienation
from the Divine covenant, out of which they could expect
nothing but the curse and destruction, as is concluded by
the Apostle, Ephes. ii. 11, 12. But I incline to their opinion who take this word figuratively, and by *uncircumcision
of the flesh* understand that original sin which is derived to
all by carnal propagation, and renders the very soul itself
as though it were carnal. For although this word may properly signify a particular part of the body, yet, figuratively,
it may be transferred to many other things : Sometimes it
denotes the Gentiles themselves, as circumcision does the
Jews, as in Rom. iii. 30, *It is God who justifies the circumcision by faith, and the uncircumcision through faith.* Sometimes it denotes Heathenism, or the condition of the Gentiles, as in Ephes. ii. 11, 12. But in this place (as it has

AN EXPOSITION OF ST. PAUL'S

been said) it signifies that natural depravity which adheres to all the children of Adam from their mother's womb. Neither is this signification of the word unusual. Thus it is said in Deut. x. 16, *Circumcise the foreskin of your heart.* But more plainly in Jerem. ix. 25, *Behold the days come that I will punish all them which are circumcised with the uncircumcised,* i. e. every one who, though outwardly circumcised, yet bears within him the native depravity of the heart.

Retaining, then, this signification of the word, we say that every natural man is dead in this his native corruption; as well because no part of the soul can exercise any vital action in spiritual things, as because, on account of this corrupt nature, it is subject to Divine wrath and the punishment of eternal death.

1. The understanding, which is the eye of the soul, is darkened and wholly blinded as to spiritual things; *the natural man receiveth not the things of the Spirit of God, neither can he know them,* 1 Cor. ii. 14. But another evil also arises out of this darkness: For the mind which cannot receive spiritual things on account of this darkness, rushes also headlong into vain speculations, into errors, heresies, and finally into innumerable deceivings. Hence heresies are reckoned among the fruits of the flesh, Gal. v. 20. In this condition, then, of corrupt nature, the understanding lies dead; deprived of its spiritual and salutary light; corroded, moreover, by vanity and error, as though it were preyed upon by worms.

2. The will also is most sadly depraved; so that it has lost all the desire of a good man, and burns with the constant thirst for vain, nay, for unlawful things. Hence that complaint of God, Gen. vi. 5, *Every imagination of the thoughts of man's heart is only evil continually;* and of David, repeated by the Apostle, Rom. iii. *There is none righteous, no not one: there is none that seeketh after God. They are all gone out of the way, they are together become unprofitable.*

3. The inferior powers of the soul are disordered, so that they refuse to obey the mind, nay, endeavour to govern it: *I see a law in my members warring against the law of my mind,* Rom. vii. 23. Hence all the affections follow not

the controul of reason in depraved man ; they restrain it,
they bind it, and lead it captive whithersoever they are inclined.

Now let us sum these points together. The mind has
lost its light, and is buried in darkness ; the will has lost
its rectitude, and is filled with perversity ; the affections
have lost their subjection, and are pleased with rebellion :
and all these evils derive their origin from the uncircumcision of our flesh, i. e. from the infection of corrupt nature :
we are, therefore, rightly affirmed by the Apostle to be
dead in the uncircumcision of our flesh. To all which it
must also be added, that this original sin involves us in the
condemnation of eternal death, equally as that actual guilt
concerning which we have before spoken. For thus says
the Apostle, Rom. v. 12, *Wherefore as by one man sin entered
into the world, and death by sin ; and so death passed upon all
men, for that all have sinned.*

Ye perceive the miserable condition of the human race
without Christ, and the causes of the misery. Let us now
also deduce some additional lessons from the parts discussed about this our spiritual death and its cause.

1. Since every man in the state of corrupt nature is
spiritually dead, it is not in the power of free-will, by its
own strength, to prepare himself for his conversion ; even
as a dead man cannot dispose himself for his resurrection.
Admirably spake Gerson, part. 2. in Serm. de Spiritu
sancto, *It is the most foolish presumption for any one to think
that he can anticipate God, as though he were like a slave to
follow the will of man.* And Parisiensis is of the same opinion in his treatise De virtut. *God first bestows efforts and
preparations, that afterwards he may confer more.* Each of
these divines had been taught by the prophet, who denies
that conversion is in the corrupt will of man, but depends
upon the Divine compassion : *Turn thou us unto thee, O
Lord, and we shall be turned,* Lament. v. 21.

2. Since every man is spiritually dead, he not only cannot dispose himself to quicken his own soul, but he cannot dispose himself to any motion to quicken and convert
himself either external or internal, unless his mind be

formed to the life of grace by God. For as every natural
motion and operation presupposes a natural power; so
every spiritual motion (such as is conversion to God) presupposes a spiritual power. That opinion of Bellarmin,
therefore, De grat. et lib. arbitr. i. 12, and iv. 11, is not to
be borne, who would have the efficacious grace of God to
be nothing else than the implanting of such a perception,
whereby the human will is rendered apt to be persuaded to
obedience. The prophet Ezekiel, xi. 19, speaks otherwise,
*I will give them a new heart; I will take away the heart of
stone.* And Augustine, De spirit. et lit. cap. 30, *The healing of the soul is by grace: the freedom of the will by the
healthiness of the soul.* And Aquinas himself, quæst. disp.
de virtut. art. 10, says, *For performing actions suited to the
attainment of eternal life, grace is first divinely imparted, by
which the soul hath as it were something of spirituality.*

3. Since the cause of death both spiritual and eternal
is the transgression of the Divine law (for he says that the
Colossians *were dead* in their sins) the madness of almost
all men is discovered, who have delight in that which is a
deadly poison to the soul. He who should give poison to
another, is deservedly adjudged guilty of murder; what
shall we say of him who causes the death of his own soul
by this poison of sin? I would say with Lactantius, Institut. 3. 18, *If a murderer is base, because he is the destroyer
of man; he lies under the same wickedness who kills himself,
because he kills a man.* But I will affirm that he has more
truly slain a man who has destroyed his own soul in sinning with delight, than if he had only taken away bodily
life from himself.

4. Since *the uncircumcision of the flesh,* i.e. original corruption, has pervaded and extinguished the spiritual life of
the soul, and all its spiritual faculties, we infer that Bellarmin (lib. 5. cap. 6, de grat. et lib. arb.) and the rest of the
Jesuits, who assert that human nature is not absolutely
less healthy than it would be if created in natural holiness,
too much extenuate this evil. They draw this notion from
Durandus, who, lib. 3. dist. 3, quæst. 1, thinks nothing
more was done to human nature by the first sin, except that

it was deprived of original righteousness; and now, left to itself, follows the principles of nature.   But, on the contrary: The darkness of the understanding, the depravity of the will, the rebellion of the inferior passions, are not the dispositions of the nature ordained by God: not *of the nature*, I say; for although God had not added supernatural grace to nature, yet it would not have been without natural order and beauty, of which, through sin, it is now destitute.   Whence Parisiensis, in tract. de vitiis et virtut. cap. 5, says, that they undoubtedly err, who determine original sin to be nothing else than a defect of grace: And he says that it is a positive brutality innate in us, and the cleaving of pollutions alien to our souls and not belonging to them.   What else does the Psalmist confess in Psal. li. 5, *I was shapen in iniquity, and in sin did my mother conceive me?*   I believe these words will not bear that Jesuitical comment, *I was conceived in pure nature, and in no worse a condition than Adam in his state of innocence would have been, if God had not further conferred upon him the supernatural gift of righteousness.*

Last of all, the very words themselves on which we are occupied, *dead in the uncircumcision of your flesh,* denote more than a mere withdrawing of supernatural grace.   For be it that original righteousness was an armour, put upon our first parents by God, for resisting all the darts of temptation; this being withdrawn, they would indeed be unarmed and exposed to danger; but not immediately wounded or diseased, much less dead.   But what has been said is enough concerning this condition of death, and its cause.   Let us proceed to the notice of the Deliverer.

Hath he quickened together with him.]   That is, God the Father who raised Christ from the dead, hath also quickened us likewise with spiritual life, on account of his death. Here, then, we see our Deliverer, namely, God in Christ, by Christ, and with Christ.   Nor must we wonder that this work is to be attributed to God and Christ: for it is the work both of Almighty power and goodness to quicken man dead in sins; and it surpasses the power of all

creatures. God alone could impart animal or corporeal life
to this fragment of earth; he alone, therefore, can impart
spiritual life to earthly and carnal man. It is a greater work
to quicken an ungodly man dead in sins, than to create
heaven and earth. For whether we are quickened by the
forming again of the image which we have lost, or by the
removal of the guilt which we have incurred, either operation is the work of God. He quickens the soul by renewing it, and by cleansing away the filth of sin : *For we are
his workmanship created in Christ Jesus unto good works,*
Ephes. ii. 10. He also quickens the soul (which the Apostle has especial respect to in this place) by taking away
the deadly guilt of our sin. For we were *dead,* inasmuch
as the sentence of death was passed against us by reason
of our sins : we are said to be *quickened,* inasmuch as this
sentence is done away through the death of Christ, and we
are delivered from the guilt of punishment, and reconciled
to God. Hence,

1. We may learn the eternal love of God the Father towards us, who is not so averse to us wretched mortals dead
in sins, but that he vouchsafes to quicken and revive us
from the death of sin. We shudder to touch the dead bodies of our friends : but God is not only ready to touch
our dead souls, but to embrace them; and not only that,
but would even restore them to life. This should inflame
us with mutual love towards God.

2. Let us consider the infinite guilt of sin, which could
not be acquitted, except by the death of the Son of God
for our sins, and his being raised again for our justification.
For this the Apostle intimates, when he says, *he hath quickened us together with Christ.* He delivered Christ to death,
then he quickened him, that he being quickened, we,
through, and on his account, might be restored to spiritual
life. That was, doubtless, deadly sin, which could not be
expiated but by the death of Christ : we were dead indeed,
who could not be quickened otherwise than by the life of
the Son of God. This should excite us to hatred of and
avoiding sin.

You see our Deliverer, God in Christ, or with Christ; now let us consider the mode of this deliverance from the most wretched condition of sin and death.

Having forgiven you all trespasses.] He now explains what was stated in the preceding words, that God had quickened the Colossians together with Christ, by shewing how it was done; viz. by the free forgiveness of all their sins. But we must also add; that with this forgiveness of sins which quickens the soul, there must be understood to be always united at the same time, the infusion of sanctifying grace, which also quickens in another sense : as is evident from the foregoing verse. For when sin is remitted, guilt is not only taken away, but the will, disordered and marred through sin, is quickened and restored through grace. Therefore the infusion of grace is always joined with this forgiveness of sin.

In this forgiveness of sins two things are to be noticed: that it is *gratuitous,* and that it is *universal.*

That it is *gratuitous* the word χαρισαμενος shews, being derived from the word *gratia—grace* itself. But we are to understand that it is *gratuitous* on our part : for we are absolved without any price paid by ourselves ; but on the part of Christ we are redeemed with a price, namely his most precious blood. This the Schoolmen themselves acknowledge ; *Remission of sin,* says Durandus, lib. 4. dist. 1. quæst. 7, *is nothing else than the not imputing it as to punishment.* This the Apostle teaches, Rom. iii. 24, when he affirms that we are *justified freely by the grace of God, through the redemption that is in Christ Jesus :* then Chap. iv. verses 7 and 8, he shews that this grace consists in this, that God is willing to remit, and unwilling to impute, sin to us. And, indeed, if we seriously examine the matter itself, either a gratuitous remission, or no remission at all, must be admitted. As to ourselves, we are not able to pay ; since the debt is infinite, and we, and all that belongs to us, finite. We cannot make any satisfaction by doing ; because our good deeds are gifts of God, are due to God, are few and imperfect: nor can we blot out our sins by suffering, because no punishment of guilty man is deletive of

sin ; therefore, he who, notwithstanding punishment, remains a sinner for ever, will remain to be punished for ever.
Therefore, the mode of gratuitous remission alone remains
for our deliverance ; according to that parable of Christ,
Luke vii. 41, *There were two debtors, the one owed fifty pence,
the other five hundred.* How were they liberated? It immediately follows, *When they had nothing to pay, he frankly,
or freely and gratuitously, forgave them both.*

All trespasses.] Remission is not only *gratuitous*, but
universal. For it does not accord with the Divine majesty
and goodness, freely to remit some part of our debts, and
to require the other part from us ;

1. Because he remits to no one even a single sin, unless on the account that he has received the blood of Christ
as *a ransom:* but this being received, he would be unjust
if he did not remit all things, because it outweighs all.

2. Because to forgive is an act of paternal love, which
cannot dwell with hostile enmity : but enmity does remain
whilst any sins remain unremitted ; they, therefore, who
admit of a partial and half-remission, make God at once a
father and an enemy, reconciled and hostile.

3. Because, unless we reckon upon an entire and full
remission of sins, remission would be in vain, nor comprise its primary object ; but nature does nothing in vain,
much less the Author of nature. And this is evident,
because the end of remission is the attainment of life
eternal ; but a partial remission cannot yield the hope of
life eternal, because death is the wages even of one sin.

If we consult the Scriptures, we shall find that remission
of sins is either entire and universal, or none is given and
promised. Jer. xxxiii. 8, *I will cleanse them from all their
sins ; and I will pardon all their iniquities.* Mic. vii. 19, *He
will cast all our sins into the depths of the sea.* 1 John i. 9, *He
will forgive us our sins, and cleanse us from all unrighteousness.*
Ye see, then, that remission of sins is *gratuitous* and *universal.* Hence we derive these Corollaries.

1. To forgive sins is the property of God alone : for
who can forgive another his debt, whilst the will of the
creditor is not yet understood ? *I, even I, am he that blot-*

teth out thy sins for my name's sake, Isa. xliii. 25, Now,
forgivenesses of sins which are said to be made by men,
are either remissions of injuries, or abatement of satisfaction, or of other things which are in the power of man, or
evangelical promises of the remission of sins on the previous supposition of faith and true penitence : but forgiveness of eternal punishment is not in human power. The
papal priests may sprinkle holy water upon sinners, but
(as Parisiensis learnedly remarks, de Universo 2. 2. cap.
148) *they have not the water of divine grace in their power, by
which alone the washing away of sins is effected.* The ministers of the Gospel also may use their keys to absolve men
from their sins : but how ?   Hear Durandus, out of Lombard, lib. 4. dist. 18, *God puts away sin by himself, by washing the soul from its stain of guilt, and by relaxing the debt of
punishment ; priests absolve, by shewing that the remission is
made or not made.* The sacerdotal absolution, therefore,
hath then force, when it is made by the *unerring key,* as
the Schoolmen rightly observe.

2. The Papists err, who would have the punishments
due to sin, according to the Divine righteousness, to be
expiated either by the proper satisfactions of the individuals, or to be relaxed by papal indulgences : for these devices oppose gratuitous remission. For, if *to remit* be not
to charge with punishment, gratuitous remission is not
granted us where just punishment or satisfaction is required from us. These additions of human satisfactions also
oppose the dignity of the satisfaction exhibited by Christ ;
for Christ, by submitting to punishment without any fault,
hath delivered us both from the guilt and the punishment.

3. As universal remission of sins is always granted on
God's part, so also there ought to be in us an universal
detestation of sin. And, doubtless, that is most true, that
there is always found in every truly reconciled man an
hatred of all his sins, and also a purpose and aim henceforward to abstain from all. For he who hath received remission of all, hath received at the same time the infusion
of grace, which arms and fortifies him against all. He,
therefore, who cherishes, as it were, in the bottom of his

heart, the love of any sin, and resolves to continue in the
same, flatters himself in vain about his sins being remitted.

4. Troubled consciences have here wherewith they may
sustain themselves ; for the Apostle said not, You hath he
quickened, *having destroyed* all sins, but *having forgiven.*
Therefore, although we may perceive sin lurking in us, and
opposing the Spirit; yet, if it is not pleasing to and ruling
us, it does not exclude this spiritual quickening. For the
universal remission of sins takes away the guilt of all our
sins ; and the infusion of grace joined to this takes away
the dominion of them all : but neither remission nor grace,
whilst we bear this mortal body, takes away the nature, or
the motion of indwelling sin.

Verse 14.

Blotting out the hand-writing of ordinances that was against
us, which was contrary to us, and took it out of the
way, nailing it to his cross.

The Apostle illustrates the benefit of the remission of
sins, concerning which we have discoursed above ; and in
doing so he teaches that Christians are not now, after all
their sins are remitted, to be brought again under the obligation of the law, especially of the ceremonial law. And
the reason is derived from the removal *of the thing* to the
removal *of the sign*, for the legal rites were as so many
hand-writings, or appendixes to hand-writings, to signify
the guilt of the human race ; therefore, guilt being taken
away by the blood of Christ, it is right this hand-writing
also should be abolished.

But that we may the better arrive at the meaning of the
Apostle, we shall lay down three points to be explained,
which being explained, we shall perceive both the sense of
the words, and the matter contained in them.

1. What the Apostle understands by *the hand-writing in ordinances, or decrees.*

2. How this hand-writing was *contrary to us, and against us.*

3. How it is now *made void:* Which *making void* he amplifies by three words ; it is *blotted out,* it is *taken out of the way,* it is *nailed to his cross.*

1. Concerning *the hand-writing of ordinances,* or confirmed and sealed as it were *in ordinances,* the opinions of interpreters are various; yet all agree in this, that they suppose something to be intended under this word, which may, by force of testimony, prove us guilty before God. And indeed, rightly : for this is the use of a hand-writing or bond, that to this the creditor may appeal, and convict the debtor, if he attempt to evade or disavow the debt : the very purport, therefore, of the metaphor, compels us to find out some such meaning.

Some of the Fathers assert that this *hand-writing* is nothing else than that covenant of God with Adam, Gen. ii. 17, *Of the fruit of the tree of the knowledge of good and evil thou mayest not eat ; for in the day in which thou eatest thereof thou shalt surely die ;* for this being violated, both Adam himself and his posterity were held guilty of death as by a bond. Others refer it to that stipulation of the Jewish people, promising that they would perform all things which God commanded by Moses: for so it is written, Exod. xix. 7, 8, *When Moses had laid before them all the words which the Lord commanded him, all the people answered together and said, All that the Lord hath spoken we will do.* By this promise, therefore, they bound themselves, as by a hand-writing, to the perfect obedience of the law ; which, nevertheless, they performed not ; and, therefore, might be justly condemned from this their own hand.—Some, by *the hand-writing,* understand the remembrance of our sins, written, as it were, in the Divine mind and each one's own conscience ; whereto the prophet alludes, saying, *I will blot out thy transgressions, and will not remember thy sins,* Isa. xliii. 25. When, therefore, they are not blotted out, we may be convicted, as by a bond, from the testimony

either of the Divine knowledge, or of our own conscience.
Melancthon interprets *the hand-writing* to be that sentence
of condemnation which, from the decrees of the Divine
law, conscience infers against itself: for instance; The
Divine law hath decreed, *Thou shalt love God with all thy
heart : Thou shalt not covet,* &c.   *If thou continuest not in
these things, thou shalt be cursed.*   These are the decrees of
the law.   Now conscience suggests, I have not loved God
with all my heart; I have coveted : therefore, I am cursed.
He calls this conclusion, arising out of the decree of the
law, *the hand-writing :* he says this is *blotted out,* when the
law loses its power of condemning; but, as will be hereafter shewed, it loses this upon our sins being forgiven
through the death of Christ.   Some modern writers understand the ceremonial rites; which they would have to be
called *a hand-writing,* because they were the testimonies of
human guilt: for circumcision testified innate depravity ;
the purifications admitted the filthiness of sin ; sacrifices
indicated the heinousness of the guilt of the offerer.   And
this is, indeed, truly asserted : for the ceremonies, as far
as they are considered not as sacraments of Gospel grace,
but as appendages of the law, were nothing else, as Beza
properly remarks, than a public confession of human misery.   Those words, τοῖς δόγμασι *ordinances,* seem to confirm
this opinion, (for by *ordinances* the Apostle was wont to
denote the Jewish rites ; as in Ephes. ii. 15 ;) also the very
design of the Apostle in this place; because he here contends against those who endeavoured to restore Judaism,
as is plain from the inference in verses 16 and 20.   According to the opinion of those, then, *the hand-wriing* is
said *to be blotted out,* i. e. the ceremonial rites are now
abrogated, because the debt itself being paid by Christ, it
is not just that the bond should remain, which would testify that we are still debtors, and that the guilt of our sin
is not yet done away.

The two last opinions come nearest to the mind of the
Apostle : but both these and the former also seem to me to
be defective in this, that they restrict this hand-writing too
much, the one to the *moral law* alone, the other to the *cere-*

monial ; whereas the Apostle wished to comprehend both. For the benefit of the hand-writing being blotted out has respect to all, as well Gentiles as Jews : therefore it is proper to understand the hand-writing to be of that kind, whereby, in some measure, all are bound : but the Gentiles were never bound to the ceremonial law.

I therefore explain *the hand-writing in ordinances* to mean the force of the moral law binding to perfect obedience, and condemning for any defect thereof; laden with the ceremonial rites as skirts and appendages.   The Apostle, then, states two things ; viz. that the law itself as to the power of binding and condemning, is abrogated ; and the rites or ceremonies, in which was founded, as it were, a public confession and confirmation of this obligation and merited condemnation, are, at the same time, abolished. And this best agrees with the Apostle's design : For he here contends against those who urged the Mosaic rites, and especially circumcision : and he concludes, that that hand-writing being done away, the rites also in which the acknowledgment of the debt was contained, ought likewise to be done away.   Thus much concerning *the hand-writing in ordinances.*

2.   We must explain how this *hand-writing in ordinances* is said *to be against us ;* and a little after, to be *contrary to us :* And since as we have interpreted *the hand-writing in ordinances,* of both laws, the moral and ceremonial, these things are also to be applied to each.

As to the moral law ; that is, indeed, in itself *holy, just,* and *good ;* nevertheless, by accident it is become hostile and *deadly* to us, namely, by the introduction of sin and our corruption ; (as the Apostle shews, Rom. vii. 12, 13.) 1. Because the law propounds decrees plainly contrary to human nature : for that is spiritual, but we *are carnal, sold under sin,* Rom. vii. 14.   2. Because it arraigned, and convicts, and brings us in guilty of sin : for to summon to judgment, and to arraign of guilt, is the office of an adversary ; and this the law does in the tribunal of every man's conscience : *For by the law is the knowledge of sin,*

Rom. iii. 20. 3. Because, after it hath proved us guilty of sin, it denounces against us the sentence of condemnation and of malediction : For this is the sentence of the law, *Cursed is every one that continueth not in all things which are written in the book of the law to do them,* Gal. iii. 10. Therefore, on all these accounts, the law of God considered in its rigour, and as far as it hath the power of binding to perfect obedience, and of condemning, is hostile to mankind, and, as it were, a bond attesting our infinite debt, and giving power to the creditor of condemning us, and of casting us into prison, whenever it shall be his pleasure.

Now, with respect to ordinances, or the ceremonial law, which were annexed to this hand-writing, those legal institutions were also contrary to men :

1. Because they were almost infinite as to number, and most burdensome as to the observance. Whence that remark of Tertullian, advers. Marcion, 2. cap. 19, *God loaded the Jews with those legal disciplines, that he might subdue their obstinacy, and mould them by toilsome duties.* And on this account we are admonished in Gal. v. 1, to stand fast in our liberty, and not to be again entangled with that yoke of bondage.

2. They were also contrary to men by their signification and testimony. For although they seemed to promise the destruction of sin, yet there entered into them a confession rather than an expiation thereof; especially if any one regard them not as *seals* of Gospel grace, but as appendages of the law itself, and parts of legal righteousness. But in this sense they were pressed by the false apostles with whom Paul contends ; as manifestly appears from this, that they would not allow they were abrogated by the coming of Christ and the fulness of the grace of the Gospel.

Ye perceive, therefore, in what sense those ceremonies were contrary to us ; viz. because they were both burdensome, and also signified and admitted that the hand-writing of the law had been violated by us. On these accounts it was the height of folly to impose those ceremonies upon Christians, and, after the debt was paid and the guilt expiated by Christ, to compel them to a public confession of it, as though it yet remained due.

3. Lastly, it remains that we consider, How this *handwriting in ordinances* is *made void;* which is expressed in these three forms of speaking, *it is blotted out, it is taken out of the way, it is nailed to his cross;* By all which expressions this one thing is shewn, That by virtue of the passion of Christ dying upon the cross, the condemning force of the moral law was taken away, and all the rites of the ceremonial law were likewise abrogated. For the handwriting of the law bound us to obedience, and to the penalty of disobedience. Christ, therefore, our Surety, by yielding the exact obedience which the law demanded, and undergoing the punishment which was required from violators of the law, did that to which *we* were bound by this hand-writing, and so blotted out the hand-writing itself. For, as says Augustine, *shedding his blood without sin, he blotted out the hand-writing of all sin.　Christ was made under the law, that he might redeem them that were under the law,* Gal. iv. 4, 5.

But it must be observed, that this hand-writing may be said to be blotted out in two ways : First, *universally* and *sufficiently* as it respects God : because by the blood of Christ such satisfaction is made to God, that he cannot require that hand-writing of the law from any debtors, when they flee by faith to this Deliverer ; but according to the order of his own justice is necessarily engaged to acquit them.　Secondly, *particularly* and *efficaciously,* when, in fact, it is blotted from the conscience of all believers who lay hold on Christ by faith ; according to that declaration of the Apostle, *Being justified by faith we have peace with God.* But, truly, he cannot have peace who sees himself overwhelmed with debt, and, moreover, entangled by a bond : but as soon as any one takes hold of Christ by faith, thenceforth this hand-writing is blotted out, and his conscience enjoys a blessed peace.　And Paul in the most admirable manner hath provided for trembling consciences by a certain beautiful gradation.　For, not content with having asserted in the foregoing verse, that *all our sins are forgiven us;* he subjoins, that *the hand-writing itself is blotted out :* but lest any one should think that it is not so blotted out, but that a new charge may be raised, he therefore adds, it is moreover *taken out of the way :* and lest it should be thought to be preserved hidden somewhere, and may be preferred against us hereafter; nay, says he, *it is nailed to his cross,* i. e. it is torn and rent in pieces by those nails wherewith Christ was affixed, and lacerated upon the cross. And, indeed, the guilt of our sins being expiated, and the condemning power of the moral law ceasing, the ceremonies must necessarily be abolished which proclaimed human guilt, and shadowed forth that expiation which was to be made : And thus *the hand-writing of ordinances is blotted out.* I add no more concerning this abrogation of rites, because we have treated the same matter in verse 8. From what has been said about the hand-writing itself, and its contrariety to us, and its abrogation, it remains that we elicit some instructions.

We learn, from the hand-writing itself;

1. Since every mortal man is, through the hand-writing of the law, guilty of death, how dreadful is the condition of the ungodly and unholy, who trample under foot that blood of the Son of God whereby alone this deadly hand-writing can be blotted out. They will fall, therefore, into the hands of the living God, who will at last require from them the uttermost farthing of the debt.

2. We here see the insane pride of Pharisees and Papists, who think that they themselves can satisfy God when he deals with them according to this hand-writing of the law ; yea, pay more than is due to him from the hand-writing, by counting up works of supererogation, as they call them : but what need, then, for the blotting out of the hand-writing by the cross of Christ ?

From its contrariety, we learn,

1. Since this hand-writing is said to be contrary to, and against us : we gather from hence, that our nature is depraved and corrupted : for, according to the terms of the first institution, the law of God was not contrary to us, but

friendly and wholesome. Let us, therefore, acknowledge, that it is not by the fault of the law, or of the Lawgiver, but our own, that this hand-writing is rendered deadly to us.

2. As to the rites and ceremonies : Since the Apostle pronounces them to be contrary to us, they are reproved who would restore Judaism, and burden the Church with useless and unprofitable ceremonies, and beguile Christians of the liberty acquired by the cross of Christ.

From the abolition, we learn,

1. Since this hand-writing of the law is abrogated and blotted out as to its condemnatory power, we infer, that it yet retains its directing force. We may not, therefore, take from hence a licence of sinning, but alacrity in serving God ; for we are delivered from all our sins, and from all our enemies by the death of Christ, not that we may grow wanton in sin, but that we may *serve God without fear in holiness and righteousness all our days,* Luke i. 74, 75.

2. Since the comfort of a troubled conscience consists in the blotting out of this hand-writing; we must labour to maintain, by a sure faith, not only that Christ has procured the blotting out of this hand-writing, but, moreover, that in fact it is blotted out as respects ourselves. Since, as in a case of debt, no one thinks himself sufficiently safe until he sees with his own eyes, or, at least, knows for certain, that his bond is cancelled : so, in this case of sin, we shall not be at peace, till we see by the eyes of faith that the hand-writing of our sins is blotted out by the blood of Christ.

Verse 15.

And having spoiled principalities and powers, he made a shew of them openly, triumphing over them in it, or *in himself,** i. e. by the power of himself alone.

The Apostle proceeds to amplify the foregoing benefit; and shews not only that all our sins are forgiven, and the hand-writing blotted out by the blood of Christ, but moreover that all our spiritual enemies who could have done us any injury, are trodden under foot, triumphed over, and stripped of all their arms, strong holds, and forces, by Christ dying upon the cross. But to render this illustrious victory of Christ apparent to our mental view, he employs remarkable metaphors, taken from the custom of commanders in their triumphs. For that word *having spoiled,* alludes to that custom whereby conquerors were wont to deprive the conquered of their arms, and to fix them for a trophy of the same in the spot where their enemies had been put to flight. And what he adds of *making a shew,* and *triumphing over them,* has respect to that pomp of victors in which they were accustomed to lead their captives ignominiously chained together before their triumphal chariot, in the view and amidst the shouts of the populace. Cicero, Orat. in Pisonem, describes this manner of the antient triumphs in these words, *What is there in that chariot? in those princes led before it in chains? in those representations of towns? What is there in that gold? in that silver? in those lieutenants and tribunes on horseback? in those shouts of soldiers? What in all that pomp,* &c. And now, as to those last words, 'εν 'αυτῷ, *in it,* or (as some copies have it) 'εν αὐτῷ, *in himself,* they set forth that Christ con-

---

* " In semitipso." Vulgate.

quered and triumphed, not by the valour and the exertions
of others, as earthly conquerors do; but by his passion
alone, or in his own individual power.

Let us proceed, however, to a more explicit treatment of
the words themselves ; in which these two things may be
considered : 1. Who were these enemies, whom the Apostle asserts, were *spoiled, made a shew of,* and *triumphed ovei* ?
Principalities and *powers.* 2. Of what kind this *spoiling,
making a shew,* and *triumph* were.   For since these words
are figurative, they must be reduced to some proper and
perspicuous sense.

1. *Principalities and powers.*]   By these two titles he
designates the enemies conquered by Christ, namely, wicked dæmons, enemies of our salvation.   And they are termed
principalities and powers, because they have usurped the
chief power and rule over men ; as appears from Ephes. vi.
12, where they are called *the rulers of this world.*   And 2
Tim. ii. 26, *the devil* is said *to hold men ensnared and captive
at his will.*   Hence he is compared in Luke xi. 21, to a
strong man armed, who, having expelled another from his
house, holds whatsoever he finds there by force.   They are
denominated *principalities and powers,* therefore, in this
place, for this reason in particular, because mankind are
held, afflicted, and harassed under their tyrannical rule.
But inasmuch as commanders and generals are never conquered alone, but we understand by *their* being conquered,
that their army was likewise overcome and put to flight:
as when we say that Hannibal was vanquished by Scipio, or
Pompey by Cæsar, we should be understood to mean not
them alone ; but that with them the Carthaginians and the
forces of Pompey were all vanquished.   These spiritual
principalities and powers, therefore, being subdued, whatever with them militated against human salvation is likewise
laid prostrate ; the old Adam, death, hell, the world, and
our sins ; for all these were enemies to us, being troops
confederate with the devil.   The Scriptures, then, affirm,
that not the devil alone was vanquished by Christ, but also
all those other foes who supported his kingdom, and were
accustomed to promote our bondage under him.   Concern-

ing the Prince himself being vanquished, we may, to omit
other places, advert to the passage before us, and to Heb.
ii. 14 ; Christ *by his death destroyed him who had the power
of death, i. e. the devil.* Respecting the slaughter and conquest of the army of the devil, Hosea prophesied, Chap.
xiii. 14, *O death, I will be thy plagues ; O grave, I will be
thy destruction.* And Paul, 1 Cor. xv. 55—57, triumphs in
the fulfilment of this by Christ, *O death, where is thy sting?
O grave, where is thy victory ? The sting of death is sin ; and
the strength of sin is the law. But thanks be to God, which
giveth us the victory through our Lord Jesus Christ.* You see
among the enemies subdued by Christ were death, the
grave, the law, and sin. Therefore, to sum up all in a
word ; this our chief adversary the devil, together with
whatever held man in bondage, or opposed human salvation, was conquered and overthrown also. And thus is it
briefly shewn who were the enemies spoiled by Christ,
made a shew of, and triumphed over ; viz. the devil, with
all his satellites. Now let us examine what this *spoiling of
principalities and powers,* what this *making a shew, and triumphing over* them, might be.

I find three opinions about this matter. The first is that
of Liranus, Aquinas, and many Romanists : who explain
this place thus ; *spoiling principalities,* i. e. the infernal
powers or dæmons ; by leading Abraham, Isaac, and Jacob,
and the rest of the Old Testament fathers from the place
which they call *Limbus,* he *led them,* viz. the same fathers,
to heaven ; *triumphing over them in himself,* i. e. making them
triumphant. But every thing by this interpretation is distorted ; here is nothing accordant either to the mind of the
Apostle, or to truth : we reject this opinion, therefore, as
palpably false. The interpretation does not agree with the
context, because the Apostle asserts that they who were
led, and triumphed over, were those who were spoiled : if,
therefore, they account that the dæmons were spoiled, they
ought also to account that they were led and triumphed
over. Add to this that the word ἐδειγμάτισε, does not denote a glorious leading to heaven, but an ignominious leading, such as of captives in triumphal pomp, as was before

shewn. But neither does the exposition agree with the truth of things itself; because that *limbus,* placed at the borders and brink of hell, in which they think the fathers were kept, as in a dark dungeon, till the death of Christ, is a mere fiction. For howsoever the Schoolmen, in 3. Sent. dist. 22. obstinately maintain, that the ancient fathers were excluded from heaven, and thrust into *limbus;* and Bellarmin, De Christi anim. cap. 16, asserts, that Christ by his descent into hell conferred upon the fathers that *bringing them forth out of that prison,* and *leading them to heaven;* nevertheless we, relying upon truth itself, deny this fictitious place; we deny the devil to have been spoiled in this sense, viz. that the patriarchs were translated out of his dominion to heaven by Christ after his passion.

Although I would not rashly affirm that *the bosom of Abraham* (which they likewise call *limbus)* was the very seat of the blessed, to which the souls of the pious pass, since Christ by his blood hath consecrated *a new way,* Heb. x. 19, 20 ; yet that it was not a part of hell, but a celestial place, and full of blessedness, is gathered from Luke xvi.— 1. Because the good angels are said to have *carried* the soul of Lazarus into this place, ver. 22. But it is more likely that a pious soul was carried to some part of heaven, than thrust down to the borders of hell. 2. Because it is said, *Dives being tormented in hell lift up his eyes, and saw Abraham afar off, and Lazarus in his bosom,* ver. 23. It was, therefore, a place situated above, not beneath. 3. Because it was a place most full of consolation : for thus Abraham addressed the rich man, ver. 25, *Remember that thou in thy lifetime receivedst thy good things, and likewise Lazarus evil things ; but now he is comforted, and thou art tormented.* But *limbus* is affirmed by the Papists to be a dismal place, most remote from essential blessedness. Lastly, because *a great gulph is fixed* between this place and hell, ver. 26 ; but between hell and limbus, i. e. the mouth, and, as it were, the nearest part of hell, there cannot be said to be a great gulph fixed.

The passion of Christ had the eternal fruit of salvation as to all believers : therefore, the patriarchs, who believed

that Christ was to suffer, were saved from hell and the
devil by the virtue and merit of his death, like as we also
are who now believe Christ to have suffered. *They looked,*
therefore, after this life, not for limbus, but for *that city
which hath foundations,* Heb. xi. 10, *an heavenly country,*
ver. 16, even already *prepared for them.*

Although Christ himself died in the fulness of time, yet
he first became a Surety to his Father that he would die for
the deliverance of the human race : therefore, this security
being accepted of the Father, there was no impediment why
the patriarchs, being freed from their debts, should not be
put in possession of salvation, before the price itself was
actually paid. For if among men, culprits and debtors are
accustomed to be liberated upon just satisfaction being
made, why should we not think God the Father to have
done the same of his goodness ? Not any reason, therefore, obliges us to determine that the patriarchs were shut
up in the prison of limbus, and were brought out and delivered a long time after upon the coming of Christ.

Moreover, although the fathers speak doubtfully concerning this thing, yet testimonies are not wanting from
among them whereby this papistical limbus may be overturned. Tertullian, advers. Marcion, 4, cap. 34, says ;
The mouth of hell is one thing, the bosom of Abraham another.
And a little after ; *There is a temporary receptacle for the
souls of the faithful, where they have a foretaste of happiness
till the resurrection.* This father differs from the Papists in
two things ; 1. Because, although he does not think the bosom of Abraham to be the celestial place, yet he thinks it
to be elevated far above hell : 2. Because he thinks the
souls of the pious to be preserved there till the resurrection ; whereas the Papists acknowledge their limbus to be
long since spoiled.* Augustine, in lib. quæst. super Genes.
qu. 168, explaining those words written of Jacob, Gen. xlix.
33, *He died and was gathered to his people,* refers them *to*

* The inquisitive reader may find the opinions of Tertullian on this subject, and the other notions here adverted to, more fully stated in Bishop
Kaye's interesting " Ecclesiastical History illustrated from Tertullian."
But the most copious and learned view of the whole question will be found
in Archbishop Usher's answer to the Jesuit.

the people of the blessed angels, viz. of that city which is called by St. Paul *mount Zion, the city of God, and the heavenly Jerusalem,* Heb. xii. 22. Augustine follows up the same opinion in lib. 2. contra Pelag. & Cœlest. cap. 30. Here, then, he placed the fathers, immediately after death, among the angels, although elsewhere he determines otherwise about this matter; as De civit. Dei. lib. 20, cap. 15. But let us dismiss these architects of limbus,* who suppose Christ to have spoiled the dæmons in this sense, that he had emptied limbus, and taken the patriarchs away.

The second opinion is that of Jerome Zanchius ; who thinks these words may be explained of a real and visible spoliation, exhibition, and triumph celebrated over the dæmons, in the presence of God, the angels, and blessed spirits. For although Christ might earn a triumph upon the Cross, yet he conceives that it was completed when the conqueror penetrated by his Spirit into the infernal kingdom, and brought out the dæmons thence, and led them through the air ; all the angels, and souls of the pious dead, being witnesses : and he imagines that this triumph was afterwards continued from the resurrection to the ascension of Christ. It is my intention neither to confirm nor oppose this opinion : but, as it is doubtful, and cannot be corroborated by manifest testimonies of Scripture, I pass it by.

The third opinion, and which pleases me best, is that of Origen, Œcumenius, and of almost all of our time ; who interpret this whole passage of a spiritual spoliation, a leading forth, and triumphing openly accomplished upon the Cross. He spoiled dæmons then, he made a shew of them, and also triumphed over them upon the Cross, when, to carnal eyes, he seemed to be conquered and triumphed over by them : For, as the kingdom of Christ is not of this world, neither sensible ; so the victory and triumph of Christ over our enemies, is not proposed to be surveyed by the eye, but to be contemplated by the mind by faith.

---

* " Now had they brought the work by wond'rous art
Pontifical, a ridge of pendant rock
Over the vex'd abyss."   MILTON.

Now faith easily conceives that the devil was *spoiled* by
the death of Christ; because mankind are plucked from his
jaws, and his dominion is broken and diminished.   For he
held us bound *with the chain of our sins:* his bonds, therefore, being broken asunder, he is stripped of his prey, and
we are delivered.   Hence Augustin, De Trinit. lib. 4, says,
*From whence the devil received the power of externally wound-
ing the flesh of the Lord, from thence his inward power, which
held us captive, was slain.*   So also we in like manner say,
that he was *made a shew of,* i. e. treated with the completest
shame and ignominy, as captives are wont.   Neither is he
without reason said to be made *a shew of,* i. e. to be overwhelmed with shame like those who are led captive : for
when he hoped utterly to have devoured Christ, he himself
beyond all expectation was devoured by the death of Christ.
Therefore, as when gladiators engage, if he who has laid
the other prostrate, and almost dispatched him by wounds,
should receive a deadly thrust, and be overcome by him
who was wounded, and just ready to die, becomes loaded
with the greatest dishonour; so Christ loads the devil with
the greatest ignominy, because, being crucified and dead,
he, notwithstanding, in like manner overcame and subdued
him.   And this he is said to have done εν παρρησία, i. e. as
some translate it, *openly;* because Christ died openly upon
the Cross, and thus, as in the sight of the whole world,
conquered the devil : or, as others translate it, *boldly;* because he intrepidly engaged with the devil, and subdued
him by his death, knowing for certain that he, by this
mode, should overturn the kingdom of the devil.

To come now to the last words, he is also said *to have
triumphed over the devil* 'εν 'αυτω̃, *in it,* i. e. *upon his cross;*
because, as Origen very properly remarks, *two are understood to have been affixed to the cross; Christ visibly, of his
own will, for a time ; the devil invisibly, against his will, and
for ever.*   The eye of faith, therefore, regards Christ, sitting on the summit of the cross, as in a triumphal chariot;
the devil bound to the lowest part of the same cross, and
trodden under the feet of Christ.   Or, if we read 'εν αυτω̃,
in himself, it must mean, *by his own power,* with no military

aid, as commanders are accustomed to conquer in battles; according to what is said in the prophet Isaiah lxiii. 3, *I have trodden the wine-press alone.* Thus you see how Christ, by his death upon the cross, spoiled the devil, made a shew of him, and finally triumphed over him most gloriously, *accomplishing a noble triumph,* as Œcumenius aptly remarks on this passage.

But it may be asked, How are the dæmons said to be spoiled, disarmed, and led in triumph, when it appears by the declaration of the Apostle, Ephes. vi. 12, that they are yet exceedingly powerful to attack the faithful themselves; *for we wrestle* even now *against principalities and powers,* so that we need the strongest armour.

I answer, they are spoiled and disarmed of all power whereby they could deprive the elect of salvation; but for the exercise of these, and that they also may triumph over them after the example of their Leader, they are permitted to tempt and oppose believers, but they shall never overcome them. For he who *bruised Satan* under his own feet, *shall also bruise him under ours,* Rom. xvi. 20.*

We may add:

1. Since Christ hath spoiled and taken away the powers hostile to us, we have an argument whereby afflicted consciences may be comforted in the conflict: For although the devil, sin, and our other foes, may appear to press upon us; yet they cannot conquer, because they are restrained by the authority of Christ our Leader; they lie crushed and trodden under his feet.

2. We are animated, therefore, to the spiritual warfare against these enemies, who are already overcome and routed, nay, triumphed over by our Captain: for those who are vanquished are always more angry than powerful. He, therefore, who despairs of being able to overcome the devil and all his satellites, seems to deny the victory of Christ, who, through his triumphing, causes us to triumph.

* Some important remarks and useful criticisms on the subject which has been discussed in the few last pages, and well worth the Student's consideration, will be found in Horne's Critical Introduction, vol. iii, p. 216, et ubi.

3. Since Christ hath obtained this splendid victory by dying upon the cross, this glorious effect of the cross ought ever to be revolved in our mind against the scandal of the cross. For it was heretofore objected by the heathen that Christians were the most foolish of all mortals, inasmuch as they expect salvation from him who was nailed to the cross, and cut off with an ignominious death by his enemies. But we who, by the eye of faith, see the devil trodden under foot and spoiled by this death of Christ, can say with the Apostle, Gal. vi. 14, *God forbid that I should glory save in the cross of our Lord Jesus Christ.*

4. Since Christ hath overcome not only the devil, but all his satellites, as death, sin, and the rest of our foes, upon the cross; we must beware lest we so live, that they may appear not broken, but reigning over us. *The world is crucified unto me, and I unto the world*, says the Apostle, Gal. vi. 14. We may truly say this, if we despise the pleasures of the world, and sin; but if not, that word will be applicable to us, *Many walk, of whom I have told you often, and now tell you even weeping, that they are the enemies of the cross of Christ: whose end is destruction; whose God is their belly; and whose glory is their shame: who mind earthly things;* Phil. iii. 18, 19. Epicureans are rightly called *enemies of the cross of Christ,* for they seem to wish to restore their kingdom unto those whom Christ spoiled on the cross.

Verses 16, 17.

Let no man, therefore, judge you in meat or in drink, or
in respect of an holy day, or of the new moon, or of
the sabbath days,
Which are a shadow of things to come ; but the body is of
Christ.

We have finished the third part of this Chapter, viz the
confirmation of the Apostolic sentence, which Paul has
proved and supported by many and cogent arguments ; the
heads of which it is proper now to repeat, that it may be
evident how aptly this conclusion is drawn from those premises.

The proposition to be confirmed, as is manifest from
verse 8, was this : In the business of salvation neither philosophical speculations, nor Mosaical ceremonies, nor any
traditions of human invention are to be received ; but the
doctrine of the Gospel alone is abundantly sufficient for the
salvation of every believer.   This is proved first, from the
excellence of Christ our Saviour and Teacher; verse 9.
Secondly, from the perfection which we obtain in Christ
alone ; as also from the office of Christ ; verse 10.   Thirdly,
from the benefits which Christ, by his Spirit and his death,
confers upon us ; verses 11, 12, &c.   And the spiritual
benefits are, circumcision (i. e. regeneration), remission of
sins, the blotting out the hand-writing of the law, and the
spoiling of all our enemies.   Since we obtain all these benefits by Christ, this conclusion admirably follows, *Let no*
man, therefore, judge you ; &c.

We come now, then, to the fourth and last part of this
Chapter, viz. the conclusion or inference arising from the
preceding argument : which consists of three particulars,
according to the three kinds of impostures which the

Apostle in the eighth verse advised us to beware of; for against all these respectively he draws the conclusion ;

1. Against the Mosaic ceremonies, which were urged by the Judaizers ; verses 16, 17.

2. Against curious and superstitious doctrines about angels ; which were propounded by philosophizers ; verses 18, 19.

3. Against rites and human traditions, which were devised by doting men, verse 20, &c.

Let us begin with the Mosaic ceremonies; against which he places a conclusion in verse 16, and annexes the reason of the conclusion in verse 17.

Let no man judge you] i. e. Do not regard, fear not, the judgments of those persons who condemn you for neglecting ceremonies, since Christ himself hath delivered you from them. For the seducers assumed to themselves judicial authority, and, as judges, praised and absolved those who observed the Mosaic rites ; on the other hand, they condemned as guilty all who neglected these ceremonies. The Apostle, therefore, advised the Colossians, that although they could not avoid these preposterous judgments, they would, nevertheless, cease to regard them. For, as lawyers say, *A sentence given by any but its proper judge is no sentence in law :* but these men had not the power of recalling ceremonies abrogated by Christ, and of imposing them as necessary to salvation upon Christians, who were now delivered from this yoke by the death of Christ : *Let no man therefore judge you,* i. e. acknowledge no man to have this power.

In meat or in drink.] He instances in certain particular rites, in the observance of which the Jews placed a great part of their holiness; but since there is a like reason for those which are here named by the Apostle, and for all others, he would have us understand that all were abrogated together. As to *meats;* it is certain from Levit. xi. that there was a distinction of meats to the Jews under a precept, so that by virtue of the Divine appointment they were compelled to abstain from some. In *drink* also, they

had their rites and observances : for they who wished to be
accounted more holy, were accustomed to abstain from
wine and all manner of strong drink ; as we see among the
Nazarites, Numb. vi. 3, and in the mother of Samson,
Judg. xiii. 4. If any one also should drink out of a cup to
which there was not a cover, he was considered unclean,
Numb. xix. 15. These and other things of this kind the
Apostle concluded were of no importance to salvation, nor
were Christians to be condemned for the neglect thereof.

*Or in respect of an holy day, or of the new moon, or of the
Sabbath-days.*] With the Jewish abstinence from meats he
joins the observation of stated times. But the Jews had
many festivals, as you may read in Levit. xxiii. and Exod.
xxiii. &c. It was necessary to celebrate some yearly ; as the
feasts of the Passover, of Pentecost, and of Tabernacles :
some at the beginning of every month ; as of the new
moons, Num. xxviii.: some every seven years ; as of the
sabbaths. All these are noticed by the Apostle in this
place ; from these he wished a judgment to be formed respecting the rest. But what he says *in part of an holy day*,[*]
some explain *in regard of an holy day;* some *of holy days
by turns ;* others simply *in part of a holy day,* i. e. on account of some part of a festival being violated ; for some
festivals lasted many days, and with many ceremonies :
All these no one was permitted to violate in any part : but
the Apostle on the contrary concludes that no one is necessarily to be observed in any part. This, therefore, is the
sense of the Apostle's conclusion ; namely, that Christians
are not to be condemned as though they were transgressors of the Divine law, or guilty of the violation of conscience, because from henceforth they did not abstain
from meat or drink forbidden by the ceremonial law,
or because they did not observe the feasts enjoined by
the same law, whatever false apostles had superstitiously
determined to the contrary. From these things the following observations arise :

1. It is the peculiar character of seducers to load the

---

[*] *In parte diei festi ;* the Bishop here, as usual, follows the Vulgate.

consciences of men with ceremonies, as things necessary to salvation, and to condemn them for the omission thereof: thus did the false apostles heretofore ; thus do false Catholics of the present day, who make the chief worship of God consist in the observance of their traditions, and the omission of the same to be the damnable guilt of eternal death. A grave author, Gerson, Chancellor of Paris, continually complains of this tyranny of the Popish Prelates, and torturing of consciences. Part. 3, De vita spirit. anim. lect. 4, he says, *They abuse their power, who wish whatever they ordain to have force by an obligation to eternal punishment.* And a little after ; *No law is to be enacted as necessary to eternal salvation, which is not in some degree after the Divine law.*

2. It is the duty of Christians, when ceremonial rites are imposed upon them under the plea of necessity, of righteousness, or of merit, to reject the same, and to despise those masters of ceremonies : For so the Apostle directs, both in this place and in Gal. v. 1, *Stand fast, therefore, in the liberty wherewith Christ hath made us free, and be not again entangled with the y ke of bondage.* But those are entangled with the yoke of bondage upon whom any ceremonies whatever are imposed as necessary, and meritorious, and saving. As, therefore, Christian modesty enjoins us to obey prelates, when they prescribe decorous rites for the sake of order ; so Christian liberty enjoins us to withstand the same when they obtrude their traditions under the plea of worship, or of necessity for salvation. For here that saying of Cyprian, De hæret. baptizandis, ought to have weight, *It is dangerous for any one to surrender his right in Divine things.*

3. Distinction of meats or of days is not now to be retained by Christians upon the opinion of necessity, of holiness, of righteouness, or merit. *The kingdom of God is not meat and drink,* &c. Rom. xiv. 17. *Whatsoever is sold in the shambles, eat,* &c. 1 Cor. x. 25. *Ye observe days, and months, and times, and years,* Gal. iv. 10. *Every creature of God is good and nothing to be rejected if it be received with thanksgiving,* 1 Tim. iv. 4. *Meats have not profited them that*

have been exercised therein, Heb. xiii. 9. Well spake Prosper, De vita contempl. lib. 3, cap. 19, *It is a miserable thing to condemn others for receiving meat or drink, or to arrogate sanctity to ourselves for abstinence.* And Tertullian, De cib. Judaic. *Evangelical liberty has taken away the observances of meats. The true and pure meat is a conscience undefiled.*

Here, therefore, we blame a double error of the Papists. First, in this they grievously err, and approach very near the Tatians* and Manichæans, because they forbid certain meats at certain times, on the ground that they think them more cursed and less holy than others. For when they would assign a reason why it is not lawful to eat flesh at the time of fasting, although it is permitted to feed upon fish; they pretend that the earth is cursed by God, and, as a consequence, all earthly animals are so; that the water, with the fish, was not put under the curse; that Christ was accustomed to eat fish, not flesh; by which arguments they affirm that they believe fishes to be in themselves more holy and clean than flesh. Secondly, they further err in this, that they place the merit of I know not what extraordinary perfection in abstinence from meat: whence it comes to pass that to the Carthusian monks, who would be accounted more perfect and holy than the rest, the use of flesh is forbidden for ever, and to all others during Lent. That remark of Augustine, Serm. De tempore 157, may fitly be brought against them, *There are certain observers of Lent more delicate than religious; seeking rather new delicacies, than chastising old lusts. They shudder at the vessels in which flesh is cooked, as though these were unclean; but they dread not the luxury of the appetite and gluttony.*

---

* The disciples of Tatian, a heretic of the second century. Regarding *matter* as the source of all evil, he contended, that the body ought to be severely mortified; and urged his disciples to abstain from wine and animal food. They acted upon his notions to such a degree, as to reject with a sort of horror all the comforts and conveniences of life, and abstained from wine with such a rigorous obstinacy as to use nothing but water even at the celebration of the Lord's supper! Hence they were also denominated Encratites, or Temperate; Hydroparastates, or Water-drinkers; and Apotactites, or Renouncers.—The Manichæans held some similar notions, vide art. Note, p. 226.

For if we look into the Schoolmen they place the whole
argument of ecclesiastical fasting in a difference and choice
of meats, not in abstinence and moderation. Hence Hales,
part. 4. quæst. 28. memb. 3. art. 2, contends, that we are to
abstain in the time of fasting not so much from *quantity* as
from *quality* : for he asserts, that during the time of fasting,
it is a greater sin to eat a little flesh, than to devour much
fish. And Durandus, lib. 4. dist. 7. quæst 4, writes, *That
a Popish fast is not broken by one meal, however great, provided they abstain from the meats prohibited,* i. e. from flesh,
eggs, and milk. Hence it comes to pass that the Papists
feel no scruple to taste wine or fish, however delicate, during Lent, or figs, dates, and almost all other articles which
are accounted delicacies, provided they religiously take
care not to eat flesh. No wonder fasts are so pleasing to
them to whom it is holiness to fast in this manner.

But now let us meet certain doubts, which may arise
from this apostolic doctrine, concerning the abrogated
difference of meats and days.

1. It is objected that Christian magistrates have commanded abstinence from meats at certain times; and on
this account, those who violate this command are criminal,
and may be judged : therefore, Christians are judged on
account of meats ; which seems to oppose the apostolic
conclusion, *Let no man therefore judge you*, &c.

It is to be answered, first, that the Apostle blames those
who introduce a difference of meats for the cause of sanctity ; viz. that so they may condemn as transgressors of the
law, those who do not observe this choice of meats : but
he blames not those who decide that, for the sake of public utility, the one may be taken at this time, or the other
at that : so that they may offer no scruple to men's consciences, as if it were a thing unlawful in itself to do
otherwise. Secondly, we say that the magistrates themselves wish that laws of this kind, in which the fate of the
commonwealth is not involved, may be accepted and observed *after the manner of citizens*, not rigorously ; that is,
they would have subjects to be bound not to contravene
statutes of this kind with contempt or scandal ; but they

are unwilling so to bind their consciences, that if by accident, or infirmity, or any other reasonable cause, they
should act contrary, they should be accounted despisers of
the magistracy, much less violaters of the Divine law.
Gerson, in Regulis moralibus, observes, *No man is bound
by the fasts of the Church when under known infirmity of body,
scandal being excluded.*   And Erasmus, in Tract. De ami-
bili ecclesiæ concordia, says, *The constitution of the Church
by no means binds those who incur danger from eating fish, or
who find that fasting injures the health of the body, or the vigour of the mind.*   In fine ; it accords not with ecclesiastical or magisterial polity, to prescribe choice of meats at
certain times, upon the plea of necessity, or sanctity, or
merit ; but because it is consistent either with public good,
or reason, or the example of the saints, that certain persons should abstain at certain times.   With respect to
public utility, politicians may see to that : but I affirm
it is consistent with reason and the examples of Scripture.
For as it is allowable and accordant with reason, that in
festivities of public joy, we use more dainty food and allowable gratifications ; according to that direction of the
prophet, Nehem. viii. 10, *Eat the fat and drink the sweet ;
for this day is holy unto our Lord :* so also is it lawful and
decorous, when there is cause of signifying public grief or
penitence, to abstain from delicate food, and from those
other things whereby the body is wont to be cherished and
delighted.   This we find observed by Daniel, chap. x.
verses 2, 3 ; *I was mourning three full weeks.   I ate no pleasant bread, neither came flesh nor wine in my mouth.*   This
also was the use in the primitive Church, yet so that, as
Augustine testifies, *no one should be urged to severities which
he could not bear ; nor that be imposed upon any one which he
refused,* De morib. eccl. lib. 1. cap. 33.

Let these things suffice for resolving the first doubt.

2.   As to festival days ; it is objected that the Jews were
even bound to the observance of them after they had embraced Christianity, because God commanded the festivals
instituted under the old Testament to be observed for ever.
It is expressly said concerning the Passover, *Ye shall keep it*

as a feast to the Lord throughout your generations for ever,
Exod. xii. 14. The same command is given concerning the
Sabbath, Exod. xxxi. 16. And of every other feast it is
said, Levit. xxiii. 21, *It shall be a statute for ever in all your
dwellings throughout your generations.*

I answer, That Hebrew word, *Gnolam,* which interpreters sometimes render *eternal,* sometimes *everlasting,* and
sometimes *an age,* denotes perpetuity either *absolute,* or for
a period; i. e. limited according to the nature of the thing.
It denotes an *absolute* eternity, when it is predicated of
God, or of other eternal things : as when it is said, *The
truth of God abideth for ever,* or when God himself is called
eternal. It denotes *a period,* or *a circumscribed* perpetuity,
in regard to the condition of the subject, when it is predicated of things in their nature frail and mutable : As in
Deut. xv. 17, concerning a servant who did not wish to go
free, *Thou shalt take an awl and thrust it through his ear, and
he shall be thy servant for ever.* So 1 Sam. xxvii. 12, Achish
said concerning David, *He hath made his people utterly to
abhor him, therefore he shall be my servant for ever.* Latin
authors speak after the same manner. Thus Horace,

" Who sells his freedom in exchange for gold,
(Freedom, for mines of wealth too cheaply sold,)
Shall make *eternal* servitude his fate,
And feel a haughty master's galling weight."

Francis's Hor. Ep. x. L. 1.

Thus the Schoolmen are accustomed to affirm that ungodly
men are justly punished in *the eternity of God,* because they
have sinned *in suo æterno, in their own eternity.* In all these
places by the word *eternal* we are to understand nothing
else than the longest duration of a thing according to its
nature and condition. So, then, with respect to the feasts
and other Jewish ceremonies, which God enjoined to be
observed for ever, that the eternity was not absolute, but
is to be received in a limited sense, according to the condition of the subjects. And this limitation extended to
the advent of Christ and the revelation of the Gospel.
This Jeremiah foretold, Chap. xxxi. 31, *Behold, the days
come, saith the Lord, that I will make a new covenant with*

the house of Israel, and with the house of Judah. So Moses
himself, Deut. xviii. foretels the coming of a new prophet.
St. Paul, in Heb. ix. 10, asserts that those legal ceremonies
were *imposed until the time of reformation :* and in Galat. iii.
24, 25, he says, that the law was *a Schoolmaster to lead to
Christ,* after whose coming we were to be no longer under
this School discipline. Since, therefore, holy days and
other ceremonies had a limited condition, in the purpose of
God, their eternity (as it is called) is for a period, and
limited.

Lastly, it is objected, that Christians are not yet freed
from the observation of days : For in the Church we celebrate the feast of Easter, of the Nativity of Christ, Pentecost, and some others : we appear, therefore, not yet to
have shaken off the yoke of Jewish ceremonies.

We answer ; In the Jewish festivals there was something
moral, something ceremonial. In that they had a certain
portion of time set apart for the public worship of God,
and for the solemn testifying of gratitude for benefits received ; this was moral, and natural, and common to them
with all other nations : but as to their being bound to observe this or that special season, and the peculiar ceremonies which were significative of things to come, this rested
on the obligation of a Divine command : and these and the
other things of the same kind were ritual, temporary, and
belonged to the Jews alone, in reference to their times.
We, then, are delivered from the *ceremonial* observance of
days, but not from the *moral.* Whatever, therefore, some
are wont to adduce to the contrary, it was piously and prudently provided by the ancient fathers, that those great benefits of the Incarnation, the Passion, the Resurrection,
and Ascension of the Son of God, and the Descent of the
Holy Spirit, should be celebrated annually in the Church :
the remembrance of all which we consecrate by stated an-
niversaries ; *lest,* as Augustine says, *in the rolling wheel of
time an ungrateful forgetfulness creep upon us.* De Civit.
Dei, lib. 10. cap. 4.

First, the duty of gratitude towards God demands it :
for public benefits are to be acknowledged publicly, and

to be celebrated by a public offering of thanks : which
cannot be conveniently done, unless they who govern the
Church or the State prescribe appointed days in which we
may assemble ; See Joel ii. 15.

Secondly, Reason admonishes us, that to render the remembrance of past benefits more efficacious, they should
be recollected (if it can be commodiously done) at that
very time in which they were originally bestowed : for a recollection of the day itself excites the mind to a more attentive consideration of the benefit.   Hence that injunction of God to the Jews, Exod. xiii. 3, 4, *Remember this
day in which ye came out of Egypt,* &c.   *This day, I say,
came ye out, in the month Abib.*

Thirdly, the interest of the people recommends it; By
occasion of these festivals, the chief mysteries of our salvation are opened to them; which we may see in the sermons of the Fathers, who always treated those subjects
which were connected with the institution of the feasts
themselves.   Thus Nazianzen, in sanct. Pentecost. says,
*Our feasts are celebrated in a spiritual manner ; for each solem-
nity hath its peculiar tendency ; as the word hath to those who
attend upon the word: but that is the most powerful out of the
word, which is best suited to the time.*

Fourthly, the examples of the pious confirm it.   For in
the old Testament besides the festivals appointed by God,
we read that others were introduced on occasion of new
mercies : the feast of Purim, or *of lots,* instituted by Mor-
decai, and approved by the Church, Esth. ix. 27 : the feast
of Dedication, in memory of the reparation of the temple,
and of the deliverance from the tyranny of Antiochus, 1
Maccab. iv. 59.   Which feast Christ himself honoured by
his presence, John x. 22 ; and, doubtless, he never would
have done that, if he had considered a feast appointed by
man for the recognition of Divine benefits to be unlawful.
Therefore the Church, relying upon these reasons and examples, hath rightly judged that certain holy days should
be appointed for the public worship of God, and for the
public celebration and acknowledgment of benefits received
from God.

But here, that all superstition may be avoided, we must apply certain cautions.

1. We must not think that there is more of holiness in one day than another; but must understand that, on account of the order and regulation of the Church, and for the other reasons above-mentioned, we assemble upon one day rather than another for these exercises of holiness.

2. We must not think that the Christian Church is bound by any necessity to the constant observance of holy days; but must conclude that these days appointed by human authority, may be done away and changed by the same authority if the advantage or necessity of the Church should require it: For (by the rule of law) *Any thing may be dissolved by the causes which may originate it, be they what they may.*

3. Neither must we conclude that private Christians are bound by such necessity to the celebration of festivals, but that they may omit the public solemnization of them, if either necessity or charity require it: but let them take heed lest, upon a false pretext of necessity or charity, they violate the order of the Church, and abuse their Christian liberty. Hostiensis, De feriis.

4. Although certain festival days are distinguished by the names of Apostles or Martyrs, yet we must not think that they are appointed for the worship of them, or are to terminate in the honour of these. For that error of Bellarmin is to be exploded, who, lib. 3, De cultu sanct. cap. 16, asserts that the honour of feast days immediately and determinately pertains to the saints. The holy Fathers judged otherwise: Eusebius, in lib 4. cap. 15, observes, *We do not worship the Martyrs, but we love them as followers of Christ, of whom we also wish to become followers.* Basil, in Asceticis, cap. 40, says, *It is not proper that Christians should appear together in remembrance of the Martyrs for any other cause than to pray, and by a rehearsal of the constancy of the Martyrs be stirred up to an imitation of like zeal.* These festivals, then, are referred to the remembrance of the saints, by whom Christ hath edified his Church for our own benefit; but for the worship and honour of God alone,

who bestowed upon Apostles and Martyrs whatever they either had or did, or endured, worthy of praise. This is clear by the practice of our Church. For in those festivals which are distinguished by the names of the Apostles, we do not worship the Apostles, or offer incense to them, or, finally, invoke them ; but we invoke God alone, and offer thanksgivings to God for those benefits which we have received by the ministry of the Apostles.

5. We must not imagine that the outward performance is a worship acceptable to God, so that nothing else is required by the law of feasts than to cease *from daily works,* and *attend the sacred rites;* as Bellarmin, De cultu sanct. lib. 3. cap. 10, would have it; but we must much rather consider that internal operations are required ; namely, cessation from the works of sin, elevation of the mind to God, grateful recollection and consideration of those benefits in remembrance of which festivals were instituted : If these things be wanting, we mock God by the outward solemnity of a holy day. Thus spake Ambrose, De natal. Dom. ser. 14, *Whatever polluted character be present at the festival, although he may be there in body, he is separated in mind; and whilst he would be serviceable, he is really injurious.*

Lastly, we must beware, lest we pervert holy days to idleness, luxury, and base pleasures altogether unbecoming Christians. For although in publicly observing sacred rites, it is not unlawful to relax the mind, yet we must take heed that that saying of Tertullian, in Apologet. be not rightly applied to us ; *Is public rejoicing to be thus expressed by public disgrace? Do these things become solemn days; which are unbecoming other days? Shall license in evil be piety? Shall an occasion of luxury be accounted religion?*

Verse 17.

Which are a shadow of things to come; but the body is of Christ.

The Apostle concluded in the preceding verse, that Christians are not to be judged or condemned because they do not observe the ceremonial law concerning the difference of meats and appointed festivals. Lest this should seem impious to the Jews, who knew that these ceremonies had been sanctioned by God himself, he meets their secret thoughts, and demonstrates the afore-mentioned conclusion by the most solid reason. His reason is derived from analogy : As the shadow hath relation to its body, so have the ceremonies of the law to Christ and the Gospel : but where the body is, it is ridiculous to catch at and embrace its shadow : therefore, since we have Christ and the Gospel, it is foolish to retain ceremonies. But to proceed in order we shall here consider three things :

1. That the rites of the Mosaic law concerning meats, holy days, and other matters were shadows of future things ; *they are shadows of things to come.*

2. That the things shadowed out are exhibited and clearly manifested to us in Christ and the Gospel ; *but the body is of Christ.*

3. That since it is so, it is meet that these shadows should be abolished ; which the Apostle intended to shew by this contrast.

1. *Which are a shadow of things to come.*] That is, Which ceremonies obscurely delineate the offices and benefits of Christ, and the doctrine of the Gospel; for these are those things to come of which the Apostle speaks. Whence Augustine (contra Faustum) calls the Mosaic ceremonies *prenunciative observations.* And Paul says that they *are*, not that they were, shadows of things to come,

although Christ had then been exhibited, and the Gospel
laid open; because he speaks of them as considered in
their nature, abstracted from the circumstances of time:
for this is the custom of disputants. So that if any one
should now be asked, What the legal ceremonies were?
he might answer, They are shadows of things to come; not
that they now actually exist, or did shadow forth things to
come, but that this may be the definition and nature of the
ceremonies considered in themselves.

But it may be shewn that the things to come, viz. Christ,
and grace, and the doctrine of the Gospel, were shadowed
forth in all: but we shall only insist upon those that are
particularized by the Apostle in this place, namely, meats
and holy days. Concerning meats, that saying of Christ
appears most true; *Not that which goeth into the mouth de-*
fileth a man; but those things which come out of the mouth, and
the heart, they defile the man; Matth. xv. Therefore, that
certain meats are forbidden as unclean, is not to be referred
to the nature of the things, but to the signification, and to
the shadowing forth obscurely of the moral doctrine, which
now is clearly taught by the Gospel. The law forbad le-
vened bread to be eaten, in the seven first days of the Passover, Exod. xii. 15; but what was shadowed forth by this
ceremony St. Paul shews, 1 Cor. v. 7, *Purge out the old le-*
ven that ye may be a new lump, &c. In Levit. xi. various
kinds of animals are prohibited as unclean; but it is the
fixed opinion of all Divines, that that was done, not on account of any natural uncleanness, but either on account of
a moral signification, or for an express distinction of the
Jewish church from other nations. The antients for the
most part follow that moral signification in their commentaries; and shew in the several animals prohibited, the depraved affections and habits that are to be avoided. Thus
Origen, Hom. 7, in Levit. So Tertullian, De cibis Judaic,
from whom it will not be wearisome to quote a few words;
That men might be cleansed, beasts are branded: viz. that men
who possess the same vices, might be accounted on a level with
cattle. And a little after, *Human habits, actions, and desires*
are depicted in animals: they are clean if they chew the cud,

i. e. if they always have the divine precepts in their mouth, &c.
*When the law forbids swine to be eaten, it reproves a life filthy,
and polluted, and delighting in the impurity of vice.* Tertullian makes these and many more such remarks. Theodoret
follows the same argument, quæst. 11, in Levit. and Augustine embraces the whole matter in these few words, *The
meats,* says he, *which the Jews avoided in cattle, it behoves us
to avoid in morals.* More recent commentators think that
God had not respect to the particular properties of the animals in those prohibitions ; but rather wished to distinguish
the body of the Jewish Church by this ceremonial from the
Egyptians, Chaldeans, and all other nations. By these
rites, therefore, they publicly professed themselves to be
the peculiar people of God, both washed and sanctified ;
whereas all other nations were deemed unclean. The vision
of St. Peter, and the application of it, contained in Acts
x. verses 11 and 23, favours this opinion. From which it
is easy to gather, that by that distinction of animals was
shadowed forth the distinction of the Jews from other nations, which is done away through Christ. Whether, therefore, we follow the antient or the more recent opinion, or
(which may fitly be done) join them together, it is plain
that those distinctions of meats were only shadows of
things to come, which are made manifest to all by the Advent of Christ.

Now, as to holy days, the argument is the same. For
although they were instituted as a memorial of past benefits ; as the Passover, in commemmoration of the deliverance from Egypt ; the feast of Pentecost, in remembrance
of the benefit of the giving of the law ; the feast of Tabernacles, in memory of the Divine protection in the wilderness ; the Sabbath, in memory of the creation ; and so of
the rest : yet there was conjoined with them, a shadowing
forth and promise of the spiritual benefits to be exhibited
in Christ. The deliverance from Egypt, and the Passover
of the Jews, shadowed forth our deliverance from the powers of hell, and the death of Christ : the feast of Pentecost, and that celebration of the giving of the law shadowed forth the descent of the Holy Spirit, and the writing of

the law in the tables of the heart by the same Spirit. The feast of Tabernacles delineated the pilgrimage of a pious man through the desert of this world to the heavenly country; the Sabbath represented the spiritual gladness and rest imparted to the conscience by Christ; and the feast of the New Moon, the enlightening of the Church by Christ, *the Sun of righteousness,* or the sanctification of a new life. Not to trace every instance, we may say with the Apostle, Heb. x. 1, This ceremonial *law was a shadow of good things to come, not the very image of the things.* But the substantial benefits themselves are now bestowed upon us Christians, the shadows being taken away.

But here it may be asked whether the pious under the old Testament, before the appearance of Christ and the revelation of the grace of the Gospel, enjoyed only these empty shadows; or were also made partakers of Christ and his substantial blessings. For since in these ceremonies there was not salvation, righteousness, or the remission of sins, they were the most miserable of mortals if their salvation depended upon these alone. For *it was impossible that the blood of bulls or of goats,* or any external ceremonies, *should take away sins,* Heb. x. 4.

We answer, that they used these shadows according to the Divine command; but they penetrated by faith even to the substance itself, viz. to Christ veiled under these ceremonies. They were, therefore, partakers of spiritual good things like as we; but those good things which were proposed obscurely and sparingly under the old Testament, are exhibited clearly and fully under the New. Whence Clemens, in Strom. 6, observes, *There is one Testament of salvation from the beginning of the world, although there seems a difference in the mode of bestowing it.* And Augustine, in Evang. John tract. 25, remarks, *To the antients temporal things were promised; spiritual things were figured. They waited for the promises by Moses, and they waited for the promises by Christ.* And more plainly, contra Adimant. cap. 16, *Types and shadows did not impart salvation; but those things which were signified thereby.* And upon those things the Patriarchs fixed the eye of faith: as is expressly said of Abraham, John viii. 56, *He saw the day of Christ and was glad;* and it is shewn of all, Heb. xi. 13, *These all died in faith, not having received the promises; but having seen them afar off.*

2. *But the body is of Christ.*] That is, In Christ we have those true and solid benefits which were shadowed forth and figured in the aforesaid ceremonies. It will not be necessary to run through the ceremonies minutely: For whether they shadowed forth moral purity, this Christ clearly taught, perfectly exhibited; whether they engaged for the expiation of sin, this Christ merited for us upon the Cross; or promised the participation of heavenly blessings, this also Christ communicated to all his people by the Gospel: to sum up all in a word; Whatever good was concealed in the legal shadows, that we have revealed and held forth by Christ and the Gospel. Upon this, Tertullian, De Trinit. remarks, *The authority of the Old Testament totters not, whilst it is upheld by the revelation of the New; nor is the power of the New Testament cut off, whilst it is rooted on the Old.* And Lactantius, in Instit. 4, cap. 20, says, *The Testaments are not different; for the New is nothing else than the completion of the Old, and in each there is the same Testator—Christ.* The time, therefore, of the Old Testament was the time of signifying; but this, of manifesting: that was a time in which the good things to be exhibited were prefigured by shadows; this is the time in which the truth itself, and the body of things so prefigured, is exhibited, according to that word of John, *The law was given by Moses, but grace and truth came by Jesus Christ,* John i. 17. On many accounts, therefore, the Mosaic rites are compared *to shadows;* but Christ, and the grace of the Gospel exhibited with Christ, *to the body:*

1. Because as the body is the cause of the shadow, not vice versa; so Christ was the cause of the Mosaic rites; and he, therefore, had power to abolish the same by his coming.

2. Because as the shadow is the sign of the body; so the types and figures were the signs of Christ to be exhibited.

3. Because as the shadow represents the body very obscurely and imperfectly ; so those legal ceremonies represented Christ.

4. Because as the shadow by itself avails nothing, neither can ; but it is the property of the body to act, and to
exert its own power : so those ceremonies by themselves
could avail nothing to the remission of sins, sanctification, and salvation; but all the efficacy of salvation is
from Christ.

These things being established, viz. that the ceremonies
were shadows, it remains, in the last place, to shew, that
Christ having exhibited the body of these shadows, it is
right that they should now be done away :

First, Because, as Augustine properly remarks, *The method to be observed in our obedience towards God, is, that whatever God directs in appointing particular times, is so to be observed as he directs it.* Now God, in his wisdom, so directed
times, that he would have shadows, and the discipline of
a tutor, to prevail until the coming of Christ; but when
Christ, the Sun of righteousness, arose, he would have
those shadows to flee, and the meridian light of the Gospel every where to shine. So the Apostle argues in Gal.
iv. ; *When we were children, we lived under those elements as
under tutors : but since God hath sent his Son to deliver us, we
ought not to recur to these weak and beggarly elements.*
Therefore, as it would have been contemptuous, not to use
these ceremonies under the Old Testament, when enjoined
by God himself, so it is folly to desire to use the same now
under the Gospel, when they are done away by Christ
himself.

Secondly, because means are used in order to an end ;
and the end of the ceremonies was the utility of the signification, which has now ceased and that for two reasons :
first, because the things which were signified as future, are
no longer future, but accomplished : therefore, they would
be false shadows, since they would assume that to be future, which is past. Secondly, because the doctrine of the
Gospel now clearly propounds all those mysteries which
were only obscurely suggested by the ceremonies. Let the

carnal celebration, therefore, now end, when the spiritual signification shines forth : for what need is there of a little lamp in the splendour of the sun?

Thirdly, it is not now proper to retain the ceremonies, because far better things are substituted in their places· For Christ hath abrogated the ancient rites, not by condemning them, but fulfilling them ; for he so removed the shadows and representations, as to exhibit to men the substantial and real body in their room. Whence that declaration of Augustine, Advers. Judæos, *The people of Christ are not now compelled to observe what they observed in the times of the prophets, not because those things are condemned, but because they are changed for the better.*

And here just occasion presents itself for reproving those who, notwithstanding this abrogation of the ceremonies, are so delighted with shadows, that they place more holiness in following rites and human traditions than in obeying the Gospel. But of this superstition we shall have occasion to treat hereafter. Let it now suffice to have spoken thus much concerning the argument of the Apostle derived from analogy, or the relation of the body to the shadow.

Verse 18.

Let no man beguile you of your reward in a voluntary
humility and worshipping of angels ; intruding into those
things which he hath not seen, vainly puffed up by his
fleshly mind.

We shall inquire first into the sense of these words, and
then proceed to the subject matter.

Let no man beguile you of your reward.] This word κατα-
βραβενέτω, which is here translated *beguile you of your re-*
ward, is taken from the gymnastic contests, in which the
judge and umpire of the contest is called βραβευς, or βραβευτης :
hence βραβευειν means *to regulate the contest, to dispense the*
rewards, &c.   But from this special signification it is transferred to a general one, and denotes him who regulates and
defines any act or matter in that mode in which those umpires were accustomed to do.   But καταβραβευειν, as here used,
means to discharge this office perversely, and unjustly to
decide, not on the ground of right, but according to his
own will, to withdraw and take away the prize.   Hence
Beza translates it, *Let no umpire determine concerning you.*
Erasmus, *Let no one intercept the prize from you ;* others,
Let no one defraud you of your reward.   But to confess the
truth, that Greek word cannot be expressed in a single Latin one : Every interpreter, therefore, adopts what best
pleases him, since, indeed, by this one word, all those
things are denoted which different interpreters adduce.

The participle θελων *willing* some join with the preceding
words, and take it to be the same with 'εθελοντης, *voluntary,*
in that sense in which Cicero, in his Philippics, called
Asinus *a voluntary Senator,* and *chosen by himself :* so these
seducers were umpires, but *voluntarily,* and chosen by
themselves ; for this power of judging and dispensing they

arrogated to themselves without any right. *Let no one be a voluntary umpire,* says Beza. Others think that this word ϑελων is placed with an ellipsis, and supply the words *to do this,* i. e. *to defraud you,* or *exercise the authority of a judge over you.* So the Greek Scholiast, and Calvin. Tremellius follows the Syriac, as though it were to be read, Μηδεις ὑμᾶς καταβραβευειν ϑέλοι, translating it, *Let no one be willing to render you blamable.* I embrace the first interpretation; because the second is forced to supply something by conjecture, and the third is opposed to the Greek manuscripts.

In worship of angels,] Some take this to be spoken of a certain new worship, or of new articles of religion, which the seducers boasted that they had received by extraordinary visions from angels : by *the worship of angels,* therefore, they understand the worship delivered or revealed by angels. But others apply it to the doctrine of the seducers concerning angels being worshipped : which opinion appears to me the more probable, as well because Paul himself, at the beginning of the Epistle, so studiously made angels subordinate, and subjected them to Christ as their Creator ; as because it is evident from history, that the worship of angels prevailed in those regions of Phrygia, and on that account was afterwards condemned in the Laodicean council, as Theodoret writes.

Intruding into those things which he hath not seen.] Erasmus thinks that the original term ἐμβαλευειν, means to walk in a stately manner, as the gods and kings were accustomed to do in tragedies ; for the buskins worn by tragedians, were called εμβαδες; from which he would derive ἐμβαλευειν. But Budæus,* with more truth, and more according to the use of the Greek language, shews that the word means

* Budæus, or William Bude, a Frenchman ; celebrated for his acquaintance with classical literature in the sixteenth century. He was a native of Paris, the son of John Bude, lord of Yere and Villiers, and studied at Orleans to qualify himself for the legal profession, when, after a while, conceiving an ardent desire for literature, he devoted himself to it with such ardour, that he became one of the most learned men of his time. His first

nothing else than *to place the foot upon*, or *to enter into possession of* any thing : For thus did the false apostles thrust themselves into things the most unknown and obscure, as into a house very familiar to them, or in their own possessions, where they governed and determined as they pleased, and imposed upon Christians according to their own will.

Those last words, *vainly puffed up by his fleshly mind*, are explained in different modes, but with no difference of sense. For whether we render it by *the sense of his flesh*, or by *the mind of his flesh*, or by *his fleshly mind*, or, lastly, by *the persuasion of his flesh;* it speaks the same thing, viz. that the seducers drew their doctrine, not from the revelation of the Divine Spirit, but from the presumption of human reason. But we dismiss the explanation of the words and proceed to the matter itself.

In these 18th and 19th verses is contained the second part of the Apostle's conclusion, which is an inference from the discussion already considered. And here he rejects that corruption of religion which had its origin from a deceitful philosophy. For as the Jews (whom he had refuted in the two preceding verses) obtruded the Mosaic ceremonies ; so others introduced curious speculations from the schools of the philosophers, and particularly the worshipping of angels, which is found among the dogmas of the Platonists. For Plato, in 4. De legibus, prescribes, that, after the tutelary gods, dæmons are to be worshipped. And in Epinomide, he says, *that dæmons ought to be worshipped because they hold the middle place between the gods and men ; and discharge the office of interpreters :* they are therefore to be worshipped χάριν τῆς εὐθήμου διαπορειας, *for their propitious and happy intercession between God and men.*

work was a translation of some treatises of Plutarch ; and in 1508, he published notes on the Pandects. But his great reputation as a critic depends on his treatise " De Asse," relating to the weights, coins, and measures of the antients ; and his " Commentarii Linguæ Græcæ," a rich treasure of Philological science. He was employed on embassies by Louis XII. and by Francis I., the latter of whom made him his Secretary and Librarian. He died in 1540, in the 73d year of his age.

In this verse the Apostle does three things.

1. He deeply brands those seducers, and concludes that no regard is to be paid to them; and that on two accounts: First, because they usurp the authority of judges to themselves; secondly, because they abuse the same to defraud the people. Both these are intimated in the words, *Let no man beguile you of your reward, according to his will.*

2. He shews in what instance they abused the authority usurped, and endeavoured to deceive the people, viz. whilst they suggest to them a foolish humility, and the worship of angels; *in a voluntary humility and worshipping of angels.*

3. He reproves this erroneous doctrine on a double charge, viz. that of ignorance and pride. It arises from ignorance; for *they intruded into those things which they had not seen;* and from pride, for these things they prated about, not being taught of the Spirit, but relying upon their own wit, *vainly puffed up by their fleshly mind.*

Let no man beguile you of your reward.] He rebukes those seducers, and shews they were not to be accounted of: 1. Because in sacred things which had respect to the worship of God, and the salvation of men, they arrogate to themselves, by no right whatever, an imperious power of determining and decreeing, even as the judges were accustomed in contests. For these voluntary umpires decreed the reward of eternal life to be granted to no one who was unwilling to subscribe to their novel doctrines. But whence did they derive this authority of defining? Who made them lords over the faith of Christians? Who gave them the power of framing new doctrines? They truly usurped to themselves this office, and became voluntary judges by their own suffrages. Therefore, inasmuch as the Apostle strikes at this usurped authority of seducers, we must understand that such power is granted to no mortal man, that he should determine any thing in matters of faith and religion of his own will; but is bound to judge according to the rule of law, i. e. according to the sacred Scriptures: *If they speak not according to this word, it is because there is no light in them,* Isa. viii. 20. *Prating without the authority of*

Scripture is of no credit, says Jerom, in Cap. 1. ad Titum.
And Lactantius, Instit. lib. 3. cap. 13, observes, *A man, be
he who he may, if he trusts in himself, that is, in a man, is
certainly arrogant, since he presumes to claim for himself what
human condition does not admit.* It is, then, above the condition of man to be an absolute judge in matters of faith.
Hence estimate Romish tyranny, which has claimed to
itself for a long time this very power over all Christians.
What pleases them, either must forthwith be believed, or
they brandish their anathemas. If you require the testimonies of Scripture to support the faith, they say that they
are judges of all controversies, and of the Scriptures themselves; nay, that they can prescribe articles of faith from
unwritten traditions. But what else is this than to rule
over the churches, and the consciences of men in the same
manner in which umpires were accustomed to do in the
games and contests?—Thus far concerning the first mark
of seducers, which they possess in common with our
Papists.

Secondly, those seducers are reprehended and rejected,
not only because they usurped to themselves undue and il-
legal power, but also because they abused the same to deceive Christians. How? Namely, whilst they exercised
them in vain worship and toil, from which they could derive no profit; and whilst they led them from the straight
course, and from the mark set before them in the word, to
their own inventions. For as a director of the games, if
he should order any one to run (as they say) without the
course, would defraud him of his prize; because he never
would arrive by that way at the goal: so they who direct
Christians to seek salvation apart from Christ, endeavour to
beguile them of their reward; because they never could gain
the prize of their high calling: For *we are made partakers
of Christ, if we hold the beginning of our confidence stedfast
unto the end,* Heb. iii. 14. Therefore, be it established, that
whoever endeavour to lead us from the simplicity of the
Gospel and from Christ, do, by the same effort, endeavour
to beguile us of our reward. Therefore, let them be despised and withstood; for they are *voluntary judges,* they are

deceitful impostors.—Thus much concerning the two marks which are branded on these seducers.

In humility and worshipping of angels.] Some explain these words of the pretended humility of the seducers themselves, and of a certain new worship which they feigned to have been made known to them by angelic revelations. But (as we noted at the beginning) the opinion of the antients is the more probable, which most of our own writers, and even of the Papists, follow; viz. that the Apostle spake of a certain preposterous humility, and worship of the angels themselves, to which they attempted to persuade Christians.

But these words, *in a humility and worshipping of angels,* are connected; because, under the pretext of humility, they introduced that worship. For they argued, that we were unworthy to approach God directly; therefore, the intercession of angels was to be solicited, and that they were to be invoked to conduct us to God. As to the *humility,* then, or *lowliness of mind,* we must understand that it was not a true and laudable, but a preposterous and superstitious humility, forced upon the minds of Christians, by those seducers. Now I call that preposterous which makes a man dejected in what he ought to be joyful; or which diminishes and lessens his confidence in those things in which it is laudable to have the greatest confidence. Such a humility, then, they induce, who wish us on account of our unworthiness, not to implore forthwith the power and assistance of our *God-man* Mediator, but to go first to angels or saints.

But this foolish lowliness of mind is rightly reproved, because Christ himself is more united to us both by nature and love than the angels; and the Scriptures command us to go unto him with boldness, and to no other Mediator: Rom. v. 2, *By whom we have access;* and Ephes. iii. 12, *In whom we have boldness, and access with confidence by the faith of him;* and Heb. iv. 16, *Let us come with boldness unto the throne of grace.* For he, therefore, humbled himself, and took our nature, that we might approach him the more boldly as our elder brother: *I can speak more safely,* says

Augustine, *and more cheerfully to my Jesus, than to any of the holy spirits of God,* De vis. infirm. lib. 2. cap. 2. That humility, then, which leads us from Christ the Mediator is to be renounced : *If any man sin, we have an advocate with the Father, Jesus Christ the righteous : and He is the propitiation for our sins,* &c. 1 John ii. 1, 2.

And worshipping of angels.] That improper lowliness of mind begets superstitious worship. The Latin word *colo,* commonly used for *worship,* is of a general signification; and we are rightly said *colere*—*to revere,* not only God, but parents, or any other superiors. Thus speaks Cicero : *Du'y is that by which we reverence, and* colimus, *worship superiors;* and elsewhere, *Thy Father, whom* colui—*I worshipped and loved.* But the Greek word, Ѳρησκειας, which the Apostle uses, is wont to be referred to religious or Divine worship : For it is derived (as Plutarch writes) from the Thracians, among whom Orpheus first taught the worship of the gods. Therefore, the Colossians in this place are admonished, lest, being deceived by impostors, they should give Divine or religious worship to angels.

But because, from this and similar places, there arises between us and the Papists a great controversy about the worship of angels, and deceased saints, who are ισαγγελοι, *equal to the angels,* Luke xx. 36 ; in order that it may be seen with whom the truth lies, we shall briefly dispatch these three points. First, we shall shew a distinction of worship : Secondly, demonstrate that religious worship is due to God alone : Thirdly, prove that this worship rendered formerly by these seducers to angels and saints, and now by the Papists, is forbidden.

1. As to the first; *Worship* is *obedience rendered to any one on account of his excellence.* But under the word obedience I include the act of the mind, whereby we apprehend the excellence of the person, or of the thing honoured ; the act of the will, whereby we submit inwardly to him, and are ready to acknowledge it by suitable offices; and the act of the body, whereby we shew the outward sign of our humility. But now this worship is exercised with a threefold difference, according to a threefold excel-

lency of the things which are worshipped. There is a certain worship of civil subjection which is offered to a person by reason of a particular eminence and dominion which he hath over another; with this civil worship we worship magistrates, parents, preceptors, &c. There is another worship of moral reverence, which is offered to persons or things on account of their excellence considered in themselves, by reason of virtue, station, or any dignity apart from authority in the person honoured, or subservience in the person honouring. We worship learned, pious, and wise men with this moral worship, although we are not subject to them by any political subordination: we venerate saints and angels with this same worship, yet in a higher degree, because they are endowed with more excellent gifts, virtues, and graces : *We honour them with love, not with service.* August. De vera relig. cap. 55. And, lastly, there is the worship of sacred religion, or *latria,* which is rendered to him alone whom we apprehend as the author of creation and of our blessedness. Thus much concerning the difference of worship.

2. Now let us shew that religious worship, whether it be called latria or dulia, is to be given to God alone, not to angels or saints.*

It is shewn, first, from the interpretation of the word itself, and that by the concurrence of the Heathen, the Fathers, and Schoolmen. *Religion,* says the Orator, *is that which produces regard and service to some superior nature,* which he calls *divine ;* and elsewhere ; *Religion is that which is comprised in the pious worship of the gods.* Lactantius, in his Instit. lib. 4. cap. 29, remarks, *We are tied and bound to God, by the bond of piety, whence Religion itself derives its name.* So Augustine, De civit. Dei, lib. 10. cap. 1. *If we merely call it worship, it does not appear due to God alone ; but if we more distinctly call it Religion, it signifies not any worship, but that of God.* So Aquinas, Q. 2. qu. 81. art. 1,

---

* For some readers it may perhaps be well to observe, that *latria* and *dulia* are terms adopted by the Romish Church in reference to divine worship ; that latria means the highest kind of religious invocation, and dulia is intended to designate what they regard of an inferior character.

Religion hath reference to God : and art. 8, *Religion is a virtue exhibiting service to God in those things which especially pertain to God.* Hilary, 8 De Trinit. says, *Religion paid to the creature is accursed.* From all these testimonies it is plain that religious worship is to be paid to God alone.

Secondly, the same is evident from clear testimonies of Scripture. From Deut. vi. 13. *Thou shalt fear the Lord thy God, and him only shalt thou serve.* From Gal. iv. 8, *Ye did service unto them which by nature are no gods;* εδȣλευσατε. Religious service δȣλεια *dulia*, therefore, is due only to him who by nature is God. In Rev. xix. 10, the angel would not be adored by John : *See thou do it not ; I am thy fellow-servant. Worship God.*

Thirdly, the same is proved by reason. For the foundation of religious worship, whether you call it *latria* or *dulia*, is infinite excellence apprehended under the consideration of our first cause and chief good : it is not a sufficient reason, therefore, for offering to them, that angels and saints are endowed with supernatural gifts, or procure for us many good things, unless they are the first and chief cause to us, and of our chief good : So says Augustine, tract. 23, in Evang. John, *This is the Christian religion, to worship but one God ; because only the one God renders the soul happy :* and lib. 22, contr. Faust. *We worship the martyrs with the worship of fellowship and love, whereby they also in this life worshipped holy men,* Where it is to be observed, that dead saints are worshipped with the same worship with which they were whilst alive, and, therefore, not religious worship.

3. In the third place we must shew, that the Papists ascribe to angels, and even to saints, supreme religious worship, no less than these seducers, who are censured for introducing the *worshipping,* θρησκειαν, of angels. For Bellarmin says, that the heresy of Simon Magus is reproved in this place, who taught that certain angels were to be adored as lesser gods, because they made the world ; and prescribed sacrifices to be offered to the same, and, in fact, paid to the angels the highest worship of adoration ; but that this does not affect the Papists, who only render to them *dulia,*

i. e. worship inferior to that which is Divine. But this jesuitical tergiversation avails nothing. For the Apostle forbids not this or that, but *all worshipping* of angels, i. e. all
religious worship not founded in the word of God, whether
that used by the followers of Magus, or the Papists. It
is, then, ridiculously said, That he forbids that religious
worship which Simon Magus paid to angels, therefore, not
that which the Papists render : for he forbad both. Moreover the Platonists themselves, or the heretics did not
worship the angels as in their apprehension first causes,
but as ministers under God ; they, therefore, might use
that distinction of latria and dulia, as well as our Papists.
Lastly, the Fathers in this place testify that the same worship is forbidden which the Papists daily render, viz. the
worship of invocation, whereby they acknowledged the
angels as Mediators between God and man. For so Theodoret and Chrysostom assert; the former of whom declares
that oratories were built to the angel Michael by those
idolatrous worshippers of angels ; which every one knows
is also done by the Papists.

But since the Papists, whatever worship they pay to
angels or saints, always escape through this loop-hole, viz.
That they do not render it with the intent of worshipping
them with *latria*, as the first cause and authors of good,
but with *dulia*, as servants most pleasing to God, by whose
assistance they more easily obtain whatever they require
from God, the fountain of all good ;—we shall clearly shew,
that they do render that to angels and saints, which pertains
to that highest worship of *latria*. Laying aside, therefore,
all that tacit mind and intention of theirs, which God alone
knows, we shall deliver our judgment upon this point from
the external actions, which meet our eyes and ears.

1. Prayer, or religious invocation, is an act of latria, or
of the highest worship: for when we pray religiously, we
acknowledge that he upon whom we call can hear us, that
he can deliver us, that he can give us those good things
which we ask; Whence that declaration in the Psalms,
Psal. l. 15, *Call upon me in the day of trouble; I will deliver*

thee, and thou shalt glorify me. But the Papists call upon
angels and saints; they think that they can be delivered by
their aid ; and, finally, they honour them for their deliverance. Now, truly, all these things are proper to God
alone; to be every where present, and to hear the prayers
of all that call upon him, to deliver supplicants from impending evils, to bestow gifts, and, lastly, to be adored
with religious honours for this his compassion. Since,
therefore, in the very act of invocation, these things are
ascribed to saints and angels, *latria,* or Divine worship, is
paid to them. Upon this, Tertullian, De orat. cap. 1,
writes, *that Christ taught us that our religious intreaties should
be offered to him alone whom we believe every where to hear and
to see us.* And advers. Marcion, 4, *They who supplicate
another god, and not the Creator, do not pray to him, but dishonour him.*

2. To make a vow to another, is an act of *latria,* due to
God alone. Isa. xix. 21, and Psal. l. 14, *Offer unto God
thanksgiving, and pay thy vows unto the Most High ;* and Psa.
lxxvi. 11, *Vow and pay unto the Lord your God.* Aquinas
himself, Q. 2. quæst. 88. art. 1, thus defines a vow, *A vow
is a promise made to God, by which we dedicate the things promised to the Divine service.* But now the Papists cannot
deny that they *may* make vows to angels and saints.
Whence, in the profession of the Friars Predicate, that
formula of vowing is customary, *I vow to God, and to the
blessed Mary, and to all the saints,* &c. Nay, when in any
danger, they utter some vow to the saint whose aid they
implore. What does Bellarmin say to all this? *The vow
is made to God for a token of gratitude towards the first cause
of all good things ; but to saints or angels, as a token of gratitude towards the intercessors by whom we receive benefits from
God.* But this does not excuse the idolatry; because,
whatever be the intention or reference, an act of latria
cannot be offered to creatures. For what Bellarmin says
of vows, might be said of sacrifices under the Old Testament, viz. That sacrifice was to be made to God alone, in
token of gratitude and obedience towards the First Cause ;

but that sacrifices might be offered to angels or departed
patriarchs in token of gratitude and obedience towards
mediators and intercessors.

3. To erect a temple (i. e. a house of prayer and of
religious worship), to raise altars, and offer incense in
honour of any one, is to pay Divine honour to him. Concerning temples, Augustine, Contra Max. Arian, remarks,
If we were to erect a temple to an angel, we should be anathe-
matized from the truth of Christ and the Church of God. So
concerning altars; *An altar is that which testifies that he to*
whom it is erected is accounted a God. Concerning incense
it is evident as well among the heathen as the Jews, that it
was a token of Divine honour ordained for his own worship
by God, Exod. xxx. 37. All these the antient heretics assigned to angels; these the Papists assign to angels and
saints. Concerning temples, Bellarmin says, De cultu
sanct. lib. 3. cap. 4, *Sacred houses are rightly erected and de-*
dicated, not only to God, but also to the saints: and this that
there he may be worshipped and invoked as a patron to whom it
is dedicated, for instance, Peter or Paul. But God claims
this honour to himself, M Y *house shall be called the house of*
prayer, Matth. xxi. 13. Concerning altars, the same author
confesses, they are dedicated to saints, but not with the
purport of an altar, but of a monument or sepulchre.
But what madness is this to refer those things to other
respects and inferior worship which God himself in his
word, hath confined to the worship of latria? Lastly,
concerning incense, the same Bellarmin concedes, that
sweet odours are burnt to the images whether of angels or
of saints: But these ceremonies (as hath been said) refer
to the outward acts of latria. We conclude, therefore, with
the Apostle, as well against antient heretics as these new
ones, *Let no man beguile you into the worshipping of angels*
or of saints; for what is peculiar to God is rendered to
creatures by both. Let us proceed, and dismiss the rest
briefly.

Intruding into those things which he hath not seen.] He rejects this doctrine of the worshipping of angels on a two-

fold account. First (as ye perceive) because it proceeded
from those who are accustomed rashly to invent and boldly
to speak about matters altogether unknown to them. For
when he says *intruding into those things which he hath not
seen,* his meaning is, *Determining or decreeing concerning
those things the certainty of which he neither sees to be revealed
in the word of God to the eye of faith, nor has investigated by
the judgment of a sound reason, nor comprehended in a way of
certain knowledge.* Towards these, that remark of the
Apostle, 1 Tim. i. 7, applies, *Desiring to be teachers, understanding neither what they say, nor whereof they affirm.* For
if you ask those who would have angels and saints to be
worshipped by us with invocations, dedications of temples
and altars, promising of vows, and other religious ceremonies, whence they learn that this worship is to be paid
them; they cannot say that they learn it from the word of
God, or from the example of prophets or apostles, or from
any certain ground, but that they only so determine of their
own will concerning things altogether unknown to them.
Proceed and ask them, since they would have saints and
angels to be invoked by us, how they can persuade us that
they hear always and receive the prayers of all those who
supplicate them: Some will answer, that angels and saints,
from the beginning of their happiness, see all things which
are performed by us, in the mirror of the Divinity; others
think that our prayers are revealed by God himself to those
whom we invoke, from the very instant we utter our
prayers; some suppose that the saints know the prayers of
men from the relation of angels. But of these things they
have nothing established by sound reason. So Cajetan, in
Qu. 2. qu. 88. art. 5, ingenuously confesses, *We are not certain that the saints hear our prayers, though we piously believe
it.* They intrude themselves, therefore, into those things
which they know not.

Hence we may infer:

1. That their bold curiosity is not to be endured who
intrude themselves into the determining of things the investigation of which surpasses human wit. For, as the

Apostle prudently advises, Rom. xii. 3, *Let no one think more highly than he ought to think; but let him think soberly. Where an obscure matter exceeds our measure, and the holy Scripture does not clearly help us, human conjecture rashly presumes to determine anything.* August. ad Optat. Epist. 157.

2. Concerning things relating to religion, nothing should be determined without a sure foundation; but that foundation is the word of God; for whatever things we see relating to our salvation we see in this. He who obtrudes any thing which he did not find there, hath not seen it, but imagined, as in a dream, that he hath seen it.

3. Our Church is not to be condemned because she does not receive those dogmas about purgatory, indulgences, the worship of saints, and other things of the same sort: since (if we should allow, which, however, we cannot allow, that they are not repugnant to the word of God,) it is certain, neither the Fathers nor the Papists found any of these in the Scriptures. And we are not bound to believe men when they intrude upon us those things which they have not seen.

4. They, therefore, exercise tyranny over the Church, who pronounce as heretics, and anathematize, all who will not hold those comments of men for articles of faith.

Thus far concerning the defect of certain knowledge in these seducers.

Vainly puffed up by his fleshly mind.] Here again the Apostle reprehends the aforementioned doctrine; because, not only do the authors of it labour ignorantly, but, moreover, are puffed up with pride, and thence presume that their inventions are the dictates of truth itself. For *the fleshly mind* denotes the reason of the animal man, or perspicacity not enlightened by the Divine Spirit. Therefore, they rashly think that they can discover truth in the business of religion by their own acuteness of understanding, whereas *the natural man cannot receive the things which are of God,* 1 Cor. ii. 14. Whence Athenagoras, in his apology for Christians, rightly observes, *Although the philosophers did as much as reason could, yet they found not out* *the truth concerning God, because they would know it, not from God, but each for himself.**

Three properties of impostors may, therefore, be observed in this place.

1. In Divine things to have confidence in the acuteness of their reason, and to think that they can find out the mysteries of religion by the light of nature. This was the fault of the antient heretics, this is the fault of the Papists, who in matters of Religion and faith hold as many dogmas derived from human reason, as from the Scriptures.

2. To love these inventions of their own brain with a certain foolish self-complacency, and to exhibit, like apes, this most deformed offspring of their own conceit, for the highest and fairest wisdom. This was the custom of all heretics, who despised, in comparison of these their inventions, the doctrines clearly delivered in the Scriptures, as things placed before their feet.

3. Not only to love and to extol these doctrines springing from their fleshly mind, but, moreover, to be so puffed up as to account these their dreams for the revelations of the Holy Spirit himself. They, therefore, imagine, that they are filled with the Spirit, when they are inflated and puffed up with empty wind. I might confirm all these things by examples from the antient heretics; but it is not needful to repeat old things: consider the Papists, who in all those points which they thrust upon Christian people without the authority of the word, blush not to usurp that affirmation of the Apostles, *It seemed good to the Holy Spirit*

---

* Athenagoras:—This Author was an Athenian Philosopher of the second century. Removing from Athens to Alexandria, he was there converted to Christianity, and some time afterwards made master of the Christian Cate-chetical School in that city, and became equally remarkable for his zeal for Christianity, as for his great learning; both which are apparent from the Apology above-mentioned, which he addressed to the Emperor Aurelius and his son Commodus. He distinguished himself also by another work upon the Resurrection. These pieces are written in a style truly Classical, and have been several times printed together: the last and best edition is that of Deehair, in Greek and Latin, with the Notes of various Critics, published at Oxford, in 1706.—Clement of Alexandria and Pantænus were among the Scholars of Athenagoras.

and to us.—Thus much concerning the second species of impostures, which hath its foundation in the cunning of human wit.

Verse 19.

And not holding the Head, from which all the body by joints and bands, having nourishment ministered, and knit together, increaseth with the increase of God.

The Apostle proceeds in refuting the doctrine of the seducers concerning the worship of angels ; and does it by a new argument, and the weightiest of all : But thus his instruction would run : Those are not to be heard by you who endeavour to draw you away from Christ your Head : but this they do who intrude the worship of angels ; therefore both they and their doctrine are to be rejected. He omits the major proposition because it is clear of itself : He expresses the minor in deep terms, *Not holding the Head.* For these words must be connected with the preceding, in which those who introduce the worship of angels are censured because they intrude themselves into unknown things ; because they are puffed up by an opinion of their wisdom ; and now he adds, in the last place, because they hold not Christ the Head. Then he joins an amplification of this argument, borrowed from the effects of the head, and their fruit. Two effects are touched upon: The first ; this Head supplies all things necessary to its members. The second, it binds and knits together the same as well to itself, as to each other. Lastly, he notes the fruit; the spiritual augmentation of the Church itself. Therefore, we must not depart from such a Head.

And not holding the head.] This is that capital crime of seducers ; Whilst they would have angels to be worshipped, they proceed to diminish the dignity of Christ; for they take away from him the prerogative of the Head. They

hold not the Head, because they themselves neither rightly
judge of the virtue and sufficiency of this Head, nor preach
it to others. For Christ, *the God-man*, is the Head of the
Church : If they acknowledged him to be *God*, they would
seek from him alone grace and salvation ; if to be *man*,
they would not solicit angels or other men to intercede
with God for them; since they have Christ our elder brother, sitting continually at the right hand of God. Although, therefore, as far as words go, they concede the
name of the Head of the Church to Christ, yet they take
away from him the reality and the prerogative itself of the
Head, whilst they hope more easily to obtain mercy, grace,
righteousness, and remission of sins by the meditation of
saints or angels, than of Christ; and, therefore, they offer
the worship of invocation to them more frequently and
more earnestly than to Christ.

Hence we may infer,

1.   The primary object of Satan is, by seducers, who are
his ministers, to withdraw Christians from Christ the Head,
and to persuade them to rest for salvation upon other aids,
not upon Christ alone.

2.   They who feel concern for their salvation ought never
to turn their eyes from their Head : for if they are plucked
away from him by the wiles of seducers, there is an end
of salvation.

3.   Christians are plucked away, and do not hold the
Head, whenever they embrace new doctrines, new worship,
new means of salvation, never prescribed or delivered by
Christ and his Apostles. *If any man teach any other doc-*
trine, and consent not to wholesome words, even the words of
our Lord Jesus Christ, he is proud, knowing nothing. 1 Tim.
vi. 3, 4. Thus far concerning the crime of seducers, viz.
that *they do not hold the Head;* by which argument the
Apostle proves that they are to be rejected.

Now, if it be enquired, *Why* they are to be avoided who
hold not the Head, or Why it is so necessary for us to adhere to the Head ; the Apostle shews it from the effects
which flow from the Head, and the fruit of the same;
which are comprehended in these words,

*From which all the body by joints and bands having nourish-
ment ministered, and knit together, increaseth with the increase
of God.*] He illustrates the effects of Christ the Head by
metaphors borrowed from the natural head and body. For
as the members, whilst they are joined to the Head, receive
life, motion, and sense from it, by arteries, veins, and
nerves, and are also connected with each other by certain
ligaments : so, whilst Christians cleave to Christ the Head,
they receive and draw from him spiritual life by spiritual
joints and bands, and, moreover, are united to each other
by the strongest ties.

All those things which bind us to Christ, and by which
celestial benefits are supplied to us, are called *commissuræ*,
or ʼαφιὰ, *joints;* and all those things by which the members
cohere together under this Head, and communicate mutual
advantages to each other, are termed *juncturæ,* or σύνδεσμοι,
bands. The phrase *nourishment minis'ered,* must, therefore,
be connected with *joints ;* and *knit together,* with *bands.*
The former has respect to the union of the members with
Christ ; the latter to the union and binding together of the
members with each other ; and from both the increase of
the Church results. Which two things, for the sake of
perspicuity, we shall consider apart.

First, then, the effect which is obtained from cleaving
to Christ our Head is this, that *the whole body,* cleaving
indeed to him, hath *by joints nourishment ministered.*

Now, truly, the joints by which we are united to Christ
the Head, and by which the influence of Christ is derived
to us, are the Spirit of Christ, and the gifts of the same
Spirit, especially faith, which is the hand whereby spiritual
benefits are apprehended. Without the Spirit of Christ,
no one is joined to Christ : *If any man have not the Spirit
of Christ, he is none of his,* Rom. viii. 9. Therefore, that
we may be quickened and united to Christ, first of all
God pours into us the Spirit of Christ. For as that member is not truly united to the head which is not animated
with the same essence as the head itself; so neither is that
Christian united to Christ who lacks the Spirit of Christ.
This Spirit, therefore, is the primary *joint* by which we

touch Christ, Christ us, and one another mutually, and by whom all gifts are derived to us. And among these gifts faith obtains the primary place, by which, as a secondary mean, we are united to Christ, and by which we receive the righteousness of Christ, the remission of sins, and all the grace promised in the Gospel by Christ. *I am the bread of life; he that cometh to me shall never hunger, and he that believeth on me shall never thirst,* John vi. 35. Faith, therefore, is that other *joint* by which we are united to Christ, and by the operation of which the grace of the Gospel is derived to us. For the whole body which thus adheres to Christ the Head by the Spirit and by faith, *hath nourishment ministered,* as we translate ʼεπιχορηγεῖται. What is the force of this term? The Greeks call him χορηγὸν who supplied all the apparatus to the leaders of the antient sacred dances. By a metaphor derived from this, he is said χορηγεῖν, *to supply the expenditure,* who furnishes to another the things necessary for any particular object: and ʼεπιχορηγεῖν, the word used by the Apostle, signifies the doing of this copiously and abundantly. When, therefore, it is said, that the whole body of the Church hath, by the *joints* afore-mentioned, *nourishment ministered,* the Apostle intends that all things necessary to its salvation are by Christ abundantly supplied to his Church cleaving to him. For whether (to use the terms of the Schools) we regard grace making grateful, or grace gratuitously given, Christ abundantly communicates both to his Church by his Spirit; so that every thing is supplied to it by its Head which it can even wish in order to life eternal. Of that grace which has respect to the justification and sanctification of any particular person, the Apostle testifies, in Rom. viii. 10, and 2 Cor. viii. 9, that it is ministered to all his members by Christ. As to that which relates to the edification of the Church, those gifts of grace are likewise abundantly ministered to the Church; 1 Cor. xii. 7, &c. and Ephes. iv. 11, 12. Thus much as to the prior effect. We may here observe,

1. In the whole body of the Church is not found a single dry member, but all are watered by the streams of grace flowing from Christ the Head.

2. To adhere to the Roman Pontiff as a visible head,
does not constitute a true member of the Church ; but to
adhere to Christ the Head. Therefore, hypocrites, and the
ungodly, are not true members of the Catholic Church, to
whatever visible church they may join themselves, unless
by the joints of the Spirit and of faith they are united to
Christ.

3. As to doctrine and saving grace, the whole body of
the Church is supplied from its head, not one member by
another. Whence Theodoret, on this text, says, *The
Church receives both the fountains of doctrine, and the matter
of salvation from Christ the Lord.*

4. The Papists err, who will have the Church to draw
the doctrine of salvation, not alone from Christ the Head,
but from human traditions ; who will have her also to receive the matter of salvation, viz. holiness, merit, and satisfactions, not from Christ alone, and the passion of
Christ, but from angels, from saints, and the sufferings of
saints. If this be true, this statement of the Apostle is
not true, that his whole body *hath nourishment ministered,*
i. e. is abundantly supplied and furnished for the attainment
of salvation by Christ the Head. Thus much concerning
the first effect, which is obtained by those who cleave to
Christ the Head.

The second effect of the Head is, that by virtue of it *the
whole body is by bands knit together.* These words, as hath
been said, respect the union and binding of the members
not only to their Head, but to one another : for, as it is
said in Rom. xii. 5, *We being many are one body in Christ,*
&c. And the bands, or σύνδεσμοι, by whose power we are
knit together in one body, are the same of which we have
before spoken ; the Spirit, and the gifts of the Spirit. For
the same Spirit which unites us to Christ, is that principal
band by which we are united to one another : for *by one
Spirit are we all baptized into one body,* 1 Cor. xii. 13. Now
after this Spirit is infused into all the ligaments of the
Church, it enkindles in every one that excellent gift of
charity which is also the firmest bond of cohesion. There
are also other ties by which the members of the Church are

bound to one another, viz. the diversity of gifts and call-
ings emanating from the same Spirit: for *God gave some,
Apostles; and some, prophets; and some, evangelists; and
some, pastors and teachers; for the perfecting of the saints, for
the work of the ministry, for the edifying of the body of
Christ;* Ephes. iv. 11, 12. These, then, are those eminent
effects which are found by all who cleave to Christ the
Head ; but which are lost by those who do not obtain the
Head ; for to those who are separated and plucked away,
there is no place in this body, where all things are knit
together.

It remains now that we speak of the fruit which springs
from this union of the members to the Head, and their being
knit with one another, and the consequent effects: He expresses this in these words;

Increaseth with the increase of God.] Whilst they continue united to Christ the Head by true faith, and knit
together by love, the whole body of the Church *increaseth,*
&c. He calls the spiritual growth of a Christian in faith,
love, holiness, and all saving grace, *the increase of God.*
This growth is said to be *of God,* as well because it is from
God, as the primary agent; *(for Paul may plant, and Apollos may water, but God giveth the increase,* 1 Cor. iii. 6) as
because it tends to the glory of God, as its ultimate end;
and as a certain divine and spiritual increase, not carnal or
earthly.

We may observe of this increase of the Church,

1. As there is a growth in the natural body in all its
parts ; so in the mystical body of the Church, all and
every member of it increaseth spiritually : Therefore, that
is not a living member of this body which does not increase.

2. Not every increase is approved, but that which proceeds from God. For as a member of the natural body is
not properly said to increase when it is inflated with any
bad humour: so the faith or piety of a Christian man is
not increased when his mind is filled with human traditions and will-worship ; because those things are not from
the Spirit, but from the empty wind of ignorance and
pride.

3. Hence we learn not to be deceived by that incongruous mass of opinions of the Romish Church. That kingdom of the Pope may be increased, extended, and spread in every part of the earth; yet it is not proved to be the body of Christ. Why? Because it is increased by an external increase of splendour and temporal things; it is increased by a heap of traditions, and by an accession of many superstitions; not by the true knowledge of God, not by sincere piety; in a word, it is not *the increase of God.* That which the Poet spake of Cyclops may, therefore, be truly said of this Church:

Monstrum, horrendum, informe, ingens, cui lumen
ademptum,

The light, I say, of the Divine word, by being deprived of which, churches do not increase, but are puffed up.

And thus much for this second member of the Apostle's conclusion, in which he rejects and condemns curious speculations and doctrines, springing from the force of natural reason, not from the revelation of the Divine word.

Verses 20, 21.

Wherefore, if ye be dead with Christ from the rudiments of the world, why, as though living in the world, are ye subject to ordinances;
Touch not, taste not, handle not?

From this twentieth verse to the end of the Chapter, the Apostle concludes against the last appearance of false religion, or imposture, which consists in those external ordinances that are imposed upon the consciences of men under the plea of necessity, of worship, or of righteousness. We must observe the order itself of the refutation: For first he concluded that the Jewish ceremonies instituted by God himself, did not bind Christians: he began with these

as the more noble, because they had the appearance of
Divine authority : Secondly, he rejected those new doctrines which derived their origin from philosophical
subtilty : now, in the last place, he contends against those
superstitious observances which, being invented by men,
are obtruded, not under the plea of a Divine command, but
of supererogation, humility, mortification, &c. as appears
from the last verse. As to this third and last part of the
Apostle's conclusion, it seems to consist of four parts :

1. A general argument against these ordinances introduced by men is proposed ; verse 20.

2. What ordinances are here condemned by the Apostle
is shewn in particular instances ; verse 21.

3. Two arguments against the same ordinances are
comprised : one derived from the nature of the things
themselves about which these prohibitions are made ; the
other from the origin of the prohibitions ; vers. 22.

4. Under what colour seducers are accustomed to gloss
over these their mandates is exposed ; and notwithstanding
these, it is concluded that there is nothing of true wisdom
or piety in these ordinances; vers. 23.

If ye be dead with Christ from the rudiments of the world,
&c.] *To be dead* in this place, is *to be delivered from the
rudiments of the world,* so that they may have no more authority over you than worldly laws over the dead.

Why as living in the world, &c.] That is, why, as though
subject to these worldly rudiments, do ye seek the worship
of God and righteousness by things of this kind? For
men are subject to the laws of that place in which they
live ; but they are free from the laws of those countries in
which they have ceased to live.

Are ye subject to ordinances.] That is, to new ordinances
devised by men, or to old ones revived by human authority.
For the original word, δογματίζεσθαι, means to be held or
bound by the decrees of our masters : as the Academics
were bound to adopt the dogmas of Plato : the Peripatetics, of Aristotle ; and all the rest, the opinions of those
to whose sects they join themselves. Paul, therefore,
would have the Colossians, in the business of salvation,

whether in faith or practice, not *be bound* in this manner. This is the verbal meaning : let us next examine the force of the argument itself. The argument, then, proceeds from the less to the greater ; Ye have been delivered from those ordinances which God himself prescribed : therefore, ye must be delivered from the burthen of traditions invented by men. Let us consider two things ; the cause of this deliverance, and from what we are delivered.

If ye be dead with Christ.] The death of Christ delivers us from the ceremonial worship : which was before expressed by the Apostle in other words, when he said that by this death *the hand-writing of ordinances was blotted out.* For first, the death of Christ merited that all his people should be freed from the bonds of ceremonies : Secondly, he not only merited that, but, a new covenant being confirmed, he actually abolished the old with its appendages, viz. the Mosaic ceremonies : Thirdly, he brought to believers those very blessings which were shadowed forth by the rites ; namely, the expiation of sin, righteousness, holiness, and all others : we ought not, therefore, to grasp the shadow in ceremonies, when we have the very substance in the death of Christ. But we have often treated of this point ; therefore, it may suffice lightly to glance at it.

Let us, then, consider, from what Christians are delivered. First, they are delivered, by the death of Christ, from the rudiments of the world, i. e. from those ordinances, or from that school discipline by which God himself formerly instructed the world by Moses, and which consisted in weak and elementary matters : This is now supposed, because it was proved above. Secondly, they are delivered from the bondage of rites and human decrees : This is gathered and inferred from the former deliverance : for that interrogation, *Why as living in the world are ye subject to ordinances ?* is as if he had said, It is most unjust to impose this yoke upon you ; and ye will be most foolish if ye submit to it ; for God would not have abrogated the ceremonial worship instituted by himself, that a new one should be devised by men.

From the foregoing remarks these observations arise :

1. They who have given their names to Christ are bound to follow the doctrine of the Gospel alone as to righteousness and salvation. For Ambrose on this passage rightly says ; *Every one who is baptized into Christ, renounces all superstitions, that he may exercise faith alone in Christ.*

2. They who force Christians to Jewish ceremonies, exercise tyranny over the people of God, and require tribute, as it were, from the dead : for the dead are not more delivered from the sway of magistrates, than Christians from the law of Moses. Whence holy Scripture sometimes says, that *we are dead, and delivered from these rudiments ;* sometimes, that *the law itself is made void and dead ;* that it may be understood by all, that the consciences of Christians ought in no way to be subject to them.

3. If not to those, then much less are consciences to be ensnared by ordinances of human invention, so as to be driven to seek holiness, righteousness, and salvation in them. For if they are obtruded for this end, they are crushed by that bolt, *In vain do they worship me by the commandments of men.*

4. Therefore, not only do they sin who invent new decrees in religion, but they who subject themselves to the same, and suffer the liberty procured by the blood of Christ, to be snatched from them. Why are ye subject to ordinances? says the Apostle : As though he had said, It is your duty to refuse this yoke, and *to walk in the liberty wherewith Christ hath made you free,* as he advises, Gal. v. 1.

But here, by the way, it is proper to give this admonition; that all these things are to be understood of those rites and ceremonies which are obtruded as parts of Divine worship, as necessary duties of sanctification and righteousness, as obligatory upon the conscience in themselves. For if ordinances are instituted by those who preside over the Church, for the sake of order; as about the becoming apparel of ministers, the time of public fasts or festivals, and, finally, of all that external discipline which ought to be observed in the performance of sacred offices; these do not pertain to superstition, but to the legitimate authority of those who are set over the Church, and for avoiding confusion.—Thus much concerning the general argument, whereby it is proved that Christians are freed from rites.

Verse 21.

Touch not, taste not, handle not.

The Apostle had condemned the audacity of the seducers, who, when God himself would have us to be freed from the ceremonial law, yet dared to load the consciences of Christians with human rites and traditions. He now shews, by particular instances, what those rites were for which the false apostles contended : and this he does in the way of mimickry, by introducing their very words and decrees, *Touch not, taste not, handle not.* Ambrose explains this passage, as though Paul were speaking in his own person, and deterring Christians from all desire after the things of the world. But without doubt the figure of speech escaped him : for these things are brought forward by the Apostle *mimically,* or *by way of recitation,* not *dogmatically*; as Augustine and all the later interpreters acknowledge. But among these, likewise, there is a disagreement about the sense of the words. Some refer them to different things, in this manner: *Touch not,* for instance, a dead body, because it is unclean ; *taste not* this or that food, because it is forbidden; *Handle not,* for instance, sacred vessels, because they are consecrated. But some refer all these things to meats, in this sense ; Μη ἅψη, *Eat not,* i. e. however slightly ; (for this Greek signifies not only *to touch,* but *to eat often*). *Taste not,* i. e. Put not either this or that food to the mouth, although ye swallow not any of it; Lastly, *handle not,* i. e. touch it not, even with the hands, although all desire of tasting be absent. The

progress of the false apostles in their ordinances is, therefore, described by this gradation. For as soon as they
had ensnared the consciences of men, they always proceeded to more rigid things. First, they forbad them to
eat of certain meats; then, if they succeed in this, they
forbid them even to taste; and, if here you resist them not,
then, lastly, they will enjoin you not even to touch.

And the Apostle rather insists upon these ordinances of
the difference of meats, than upon others, because in this
point has the superstition of misemployed men exerted
itself: always in this abstinence from particular meats
have they imagined that some sanctity consists. This may
even be inferred from the Apostle attacking it in so many
places; *The kingdom of God is not meat and drink, but righteousness, and peace, and joy in the Holy Ghost,* Rom. xiv.
17. *Meat commendeth us not to God; for neither if we eat
are we the better; neither, if we eat not, are we the worse,* 1
Cor. viii. 8. *In the latter times, some shall depart from the
faith; commanding to abstain from meats,* 1 Tim. iv. 1, 3.
Unless this error had taken deep roots in the minds of men,
the Apostle would not have been compelled so frequently
to strive at eradicating it.

But here it may be asked, what difference is there between this imposture, and that which he had reproved
above at verse the 16th? for in each place, they who
wished a difference of meats to be observed by Christians
are reproved.

I answer, The former urged a choice of meats by virtue
of the Divine command and the law of Moses, which they
supposed not yet abrogated: but these latter employed
another pretence, as will be evident when we arrive at the
last verse. Both, then, urged the same thing; both would
ensnare the consciences of men; both sought holiness and
righteousness in these external rites: but the former would
have this abstinence from certain meats to be a thing commanded by God; the latter, to be a voluntary worship, and
therefore of greater merit with God. That the Apostle,
then, might the better expose their folly, he employs irony;

intimating, in this manner, that that in which those hypocrites would have the all in all of holiness to consist, was altogether a thing ridiculous.

From what hath been said these instructions follow :

1. There is no end of ceremonies and traditions, if once they are admitted with an opinion of merit and holiness : for the authority of seducers always will proceed to the imposition of severer matters. Wittily said Calvin, *They tie you up at the beginning, that they may strangle you afterwards.*

2. We must resist the ordinances of hypocrites of this sort, not only because they are full of error in themselves, but also on account of the dangerous consequence. For God hath prescribed certain and fixed things in his worship : but if you allow men this power to prescribe their traditions, under the notion of worship, they will daily heap on more and heavier ; neither is there any end of their burden.

3. They who make holiness to consist in difference of meats, or in external observations of this kind, however they may seem to themselves to philosophize wisely, are, nevertheless, contemptible, and to be derided for their pains.

4. Seducers for the most part prohibit, by their authority, things allowed by God, and very necessary, as meat, drink, marriage ; they impose and enjoin superfluous and ridiculous matters, as the worship of images, long pilgrimages, muttering of prayers not understood, according to a certain calculation, and other charms, not only abhorrent from all religion, but even reason itself.

We conclude, therefore, that the consciences of Christians are not to be burdened either by these rites, which relate to differences of meats, or by any which consist in the observance of external things, as though they were parts of sacred worship or religion.

Verse 22.

Which all are to perish with the using ; after the command-
ments and doctrines of men.

The Apostle proves by two other reasons, that neither
the true worship of God, nor the justification or sanctification of a Christian man is placed in the observance of
rites, regarding the choice of meats, or any other external
things. The former is derived from the very nature and
condition of these things; *which all are to perish with the*
using. The other from the origin or authority of such
rites ; *after the commandments and doctrines of men.*

Which all are to perish with the using.] We have in these
words a clear and solid reason why it behoves us not to
make the worship of God, or our holiness, to consist in
these external rites. First, because the very nature and
condition of these things oppose it. For godliness, righteousness, holiness, are spiritual things lighted up in the
human heart by the aid of the Holy Spirit. The choice of
meats, therefore, neither begets holiness and righteousness
in the soul, nor evinces it. For whether you eat flesh, or
fish, or fruits, you use earthly and transient things, in
which there is no spiritual power to purify or defile the
soul. Secondly, because the end or use of meats is designed by God himself for bodily sustenance, not for the
sanctification of souls ; for it was his pleasure that they
should be consumed in the very use, not that we should
expect from them the spiritual fruits of righteousness, holiness, merit, &c. Hence the sacred Scriptures every where
disprove the false opinion of those who thought that men
become more holy by abstinence from certain kinds of
meats, or worse by the indifferent use of meats of whatever kind. Christ himself, in Matth. xv. blamed the Pharisees for this error, and admonishes his disciples, in ver

11, lest they also should be deceived by the same; *Not that which goeth into the mouth defileth a man ; but that which cometh out of the mouth, this defileth a man.* And when the Pharisees, having heard this discourse, were offended, Christ confirmed his opinion from the very condition and corruptible nature of all meats ; *Do ye not yet understand, said he, that whatsoever entereth in at the mouth goeth into the belly, and is cast out into the draught ?* ver. 17. As though he had said, It is foolish to seek holiness or righteousness in those frail, earthly, and corruptible things, or to fear any pollution and contamination of sin from them : for all things of this kind are neither good nor evil in themselves, but are to men just as are the minds of those who use them. This, then, is the sentence of Christ himself concerning meats. Moreover, Paul, not only in this place but many others, invalidates their opinion, who thought that some religion consisted in a difference of meats ; and, for the most part, he uses this very argument, taken from their earthly and corruptible nature. Thus, 1 Cor. vi. 13, *Meats* are intended *for the belly, and the belly for meats ; but God shall destroy both it and them.* He does not say that meats are intended for sanctifying the mind ; but for filling the belly. And Rom. xiv. 17, 18 (which passage we have before cited), *The kingdom of God is not meat and drink, but righteousness, peace, and joy in the Holy Ghost : For he that in these things serveth Christ is acceptable to God.* He, therefore, who imagines that he serves Christ, inasmuch as he abstains from certain kinds of meats, or because he binds himself to the observance of certain rites as to external things, deceives himself, neither does he on these accounts become more acceptable to God ; but if he cherishes peace and righteousness in the Holy Spirit, then he will at length be acceptable to God. Well spake Prosper, De vit. contempl. 3. 10, *Fasts, abstinences, and other things of this kind, are not to be offered to God for righteousness, but with righteousness.* If, then, there is no righteousness in fasting, how much less in abstaining from this or that sort of meat, when, meanwhile, other meats are taken, and that perhaps with no very strict moderation?

The instructions are these :

1. When any thing is proposed to us for observance, the nature of the thing itself is to be considered : if the observation consist in bodily and transitory things, such as in food, raiment, or the like, we ought not to suppose that the immediate worship of God, righteousness, or holiness consists therein.

2. Commandments of this kind, therefore, if they are prescribed by those who have legitimate authority, and that in a legitimate manner, they must be received in that sense, that they wish them to be observed, either for the sake of external order, or as far as they may be referred and directed to some useful end : not that they are parts of Divine worship in themselves, or that by the performance of the work itself, they add to our righteousness, holiness, or merit with God.

3. If sometimes those observances which consist in these transitory things are violated, provided contempt and scandal be shunned, the soul is not defiled by the mere act of omission, or involved in deadly guilt ; because (as we have before shewn) the nature of these things is not of a kind to reach to the sanctification or defilement of the soul.

4. Hence we gather the error and folly of the Monks, who think that they are more perfect and holy than all other mortals, because they have bound themselves to abstain from certain external things which they could lawfully use, as, for instance, from meats, from elegant clothing, from the private possession of goods, &c. ; whereas, all these are of the number of earthly and corruptible things, by the use of which, in itself, no one can be defiled or rendered worse ; and by the abstaining from which, no one can be made more righteous or holy.

5. Whatever is worthy of praise in abstaining from these indifferent things, or in the use of the same, when they are prescribed by men endowed with authority, the whole depends, not on the nature of the things themselves (for they are earthly and corruptible), neither on the work or action itself, but upon the mind of the person obeying,

and the useful end to which these observations are referred.

Thus much concerning the former reason, derived from the nature and condition of the things themselves.

After the commandments and doctrines of men.] This is that other reason why the religion, righteousness, or salvation of Christians is not placed in those decrees, *Touch not, taste not, handle not,* and such trifles ; viz. because they derive not their origin from God, but from men. For although God himself imposed upon the Jews, under the old Testament, ceremonial ordinances of this kind, that they might possess in them shadows of spiritual and future things ; yet, under the Gospel, he commanded the same to be abrogated, so that now they are imposed by the commandments of men, not by the authority of God. It is, therefore, rightly said, that all those things are now *after the commandments and doctrines of men.*

But let us weigh the force of this argument ; This is after the commandments and doctrines of men : therefore, it is not one of the things necessary to salvation, or to the worship of God, or for the acquiring of righteousness and holiness ; for the following reasons :

1. Because God retains to himself alone this honour of appointing what he will have directly and immediately to pertain to Religion and his worship. *Ye shall not do every man whatsoever is right in his own eyes : but what thing soever shall be commanded you of the Lord, observe to do it ; thou shalt not add thereto, nor diminish from it ;* Deut. xii. 8, 32. Hence that remark of Christ, Matth. xv. 9, *In vain ye worship me, teaching the doctrines and commandments of men.*

2. Because if these commandments of men pertained to the worship of God as parts of it, it would follow that the worship of God might be abrogated by human authority : for all these decrees may be either taken away or changed by the authority of those by whom they were ordained from the beginning : but that men have this power over the worship of God is most absurd.

3. Because if it be conceded that the observance of human decrees is a necessary part of worship or holiness

in itself; it would thence follow, that God may be worshipped in ways not only different, but plainly contrary to one another, according to the will of men. For these human commandments are not only different, but sometimes opposed to each other. You may see this in the different orders of Monks among the Papists, on whom different commandments are imposed, such as relate to food, and raiment, and almost all other external observances. You may observe it also in the different rites of churches: for, in administering the sacraments, in ordaining ministers, in fasts, in feasts, and in almost all external rites, the ceremonies of different churches are different. And, as Irenæus is quoted in Eusebius, lib. 5. cap. 23, *The very difference of churches in these things, the more illustrates the harmony of the faith.* But if these observances and ceremonies of human command pertained in themselves to the worship of God, and to holiness, there could not be any difference in them, they could not bind some, and not bind others, according to diversity of places, but would be the same among all, and would equally bind all. For that rule of Parisiensis, De fide, cap. 2, is most true: *The worship due to God is not a worship which may be refused to him without injury, by any person who is capable of worshipping him: for the Religion by which God is worshipped, and by which he is pleased and served by men is uniform and universal.* From these things it is clearly evident, that the commands and traditions of men are not to be obtruded upon the Church under the notion of *worship* and *righteousness,* because they are the commandments of men and not of God.

Hence we derive the following Instructions:

1. That alone immediately and properly concerns Religion and the worship of God, which hath the testimony of the Divine will. *It so behoves us to worship God in the way in which he himself has prescribed that he is to be worshipped,* Augustine, lib. 1. De consensu Evang. cap. 18.

2. They who would have religion, righteousness, and holiness to consist in observing their commands and traditions, arrogate that to themselves, and their inventions, which is peculiar to God and the Divine commands. *Men*

as men, speaking concerning God, are not worthy of credit;
Clemens Alexandrinus, Strom. 6.

3. Since salvation and righteousness is not placed in
the commands of men, they grievously err who so multiply these burdens of human traditions as thereby to hinder
Christians in the exercises of true righteousness and godliness : For, *it commonly happens, that when a thing is paid
where it is not due, it is neglected where it is due,* Tertull. De
pœnit. This Christ himself complained of, that the people of God were drawn away from the observance of the
Divine commands, whilst they were entirely employed
upon the traditions of the Pharisees, Matth. xv. 6. Gerson, De vita Spirit. part. 3, reprehends this in that heap of
ceremonies and traditions of the Papists ; *Unnecessary occupation in human traditions begets ignorance of the Divine
precepts.*—Thus much concerning the second argument from
the origin of these commands.

Verse 23.

*Which things have indeed a shew of wisdom in will-worship
and humility, and neglecting of the body ; not in any
honour to the satisfying of the flesh.*

In these words of the Apostle we have a censure of
human rites and traditions which are obtruded upon Christians under the notion of necessity, righteousness, or the
Divine worship. The passage is well worthy of being
diligently considered. For hence we may perceive that the
Papists can allege nothing for their traditions, which was
not alleged by antient impostors, and refuted by Apostles ;
that we do nothing else, when we oppose the same, than
what Christ himself, what his Apostles before us have done,
and what they would have us to do for the sake of retaining Christian liberty.

In this verse, therefore, which puts a conclusion to the refutation, there are three things to be observed and explained, as to those rites prescribed by men:

1. We must observe the Apostle's concession: for he concedes to them λόγον σοφίας. *Which things have indeed a shew of wisdom.*

2. Three pretences are to be noted, by which for the most part human traditions are covered to wear the appearance of wisdom: These are, *will-worship, humility, and neglecting of the body.*

3. We may observe the censure of the Apostle, who, notwithstanding these pretences so fair, accounts these commandments of men for things of nought: *not in any honour to the satisfying of the flesh.*

Which things have indeed a shew of wisdom.] The Greek word λόγον, some translate *reason,* some *shew,* and others *pretence;* with little difference of sense. For the Apostle means this: The aforesaid commandments of men have a shew, or external appearance of wisdom, they have not the reality and truth. There is, then, in these words, a prolepsis, or anticipation, which, whilst it concedes to the adversaries what they could allege in pretence, at the same time would have them understand that it was of no value. But when the Apostle says, these doctrines of men *have a shew of wisdom,* he means, they have the appearance of some excellent doctrine, rather brought from heaven than excogitated by human counsel: for thus the word *wisdom* is used by Paul, as Beza hath rightly observed.

1. And they have this shew or pretence, First, on the part of the impostors. For these, for the most part, pretend, that they do not bring forward any thing of their own mind, but promulgate those things, being enlightened by the Spirit of wisdom himself. Under this pretence, Montanus formerly vaunted his prophecies, and imposed upon many: for thus Tertullian, De præscript. before he was a Montanist himself, writes, *They assert that the Paraclete spake more things to Montanus than Christ delivered in the Gospel; and not only more, but even better and greater.* Those who are a little more modest, venture not to pre-

tend immediate revelations of the Holy Spirit; yet, that
their notions may not appear destitute of a shew of Divine
wisdom, they are wont to affirm, as it is stated in Irenæus,
lib. 3. cap. 2, *that their doctrines were not indeed consigned in
writing by the Apostles, but delivered to them viva voce; according to that saying, ‘ We speak wisdom among the perfect :’
and their own fictions every one asserts to be this wisdom.* Thus
says Irenæus. Therefore human traditions have this shew
of wisdom on the part of the impostors.

2. On the part of superstitious and carnal men, they
have a shew of wisdom, because carnal things are suited to
the taste of carnal men, but spiritual things are not esteemed. Whence that saying of the Apostle, Rom. viii. 7,
The wisdom of the flesh* is enmity against God; and 1 Cor.
ii. 5, *Your faith should not stand in the wisdom of men, but in
the power of God.* For that seems full of wisdom to a carnal man, which accords with the nature and disposition of
the flesh ; and nothing is more pleasing to the carnal mind,
than to have salvation, righteousness, and holiness in rites
and external things. You see, therefore, how human traditions *have a shew of wisdom ;* namely, 1. From the fraud
of impostors, who always boast that they flowed from the
Spirit of wisdom : 2. From the carnal nature of superstitious men, whom it always pleases to seek salvation and
righteousness in rites and external exercises. But, nevertheless, we must hold, that they have the shew only, and,
as it were, a vain shadow of wisdom, not the reality. For,
as Lactantius has truly said, Instit. lib. 4. cap. 1, *where the
repute of foolishness appears, there wisdom is chiefly to be
sought ;* so we may truly affirm, where to the carnal man
the repute of wisdom appears, there folly is always to be
found. *For this wisdom descendeth not from the Father of
lights, but is earthly, sensual, devilish;* James iii. 15.

Instructions :

1. They are to be accounted for impostors who, in the
business of salvation, obtrude upon us doctrines under the
pretence of revelation or tradition, without the testimony

---

* “ Sapientia carnis.” Vulgate.

of the word. For whatsoever shew, or rather shadow of wisdom there might be in these human inventions, yet true and saving wisdom will never be found in them.

2. In the worship of God we ought not to run after and embrace those things which are most approved by human reason; for if we use this guide, we shall, instead of true wisdom, embrace some shew, and painted shadow of wisdom.

3. Hence infer what you ought to conclude about popery, viz. whether it possesses that genuine wisdom, or only *the shew of wisdom*. It obtrudes its doctrines, and its innumerable commandments, as necessary to salvation : but under what pretence? The same with all impostors; viz. that all its decrees flow from the Holy Spirit directing and inspiring the Church; that they do not bring in human commandments, but those unwritten traditions which the Apostles left as a deposit to Rome. Behold a wonderful shew of Divine wisdom! But if I further ask, How will it be proved to me that these your ordinances have flowed from the Spirit of God and from the Apostles? Forthwith they retort against you, Either believe, or be accursed : but in the mean time they produce no testimony from the word of God. They who thus confirm their dogmas, may display among the unskilful a *shew of wisdom*, but among the sober, and the prudent, they will be accounted to have lost the thing itself.

Thus much concerning the Apostle's concession, that there is only a *shew* of Divine wisdom in the doctrines and commandments of seducers.

In will-worship, 'εν 'εθελοθρησκεια.] He begins to shew with what colours seducers were wont to paint this false wisdom. The first is, as you may call it, *voluntary worship;* i. e. not commanded or prescribed by God himself, but offered to him by human will and choice. This, then, is urged by impostors, He who performs only those things which are bidden and commanded by God himself, does nothing but what is common; but he who goes beyond those precepts, and worships God by certain voluntary works, to which he is not bound, he becomes as an angel

among men, he lays up to himself merits of supererogation ;
he finally makes God a debtor to him. And this *will-
worship* is very pleasing to human nature. For since there
is a double will-worship; one, when a person of his own
accord chooses any creature to whom he offers the worship
due to God ; the other, when he worships the true God,
but not in that manner, neither by those acts whereby he
hath defined his worship, but by others, chosen of his own
will : the former species of *will-worship* is condemned by
almost all, because it clearly detracts from God what is
his own, and transfers it to the creature ; but this other is
commended by many because it seems to offer to God what
is his own, and something beyond it ; it has, therefore, as
it were, the appearance of a certain free-will offering. This
colour imposed upon the Monks, who think that they, inasmuch as they worship God by certain works not commanded by God himself, are in a higher and more perfect
condition than other men who endeavour to perform only
those things which are enjoined. Hence, also, they have
dreamed, that they so overflow with merits, that they hesitate not daily to bestow out of their great treasure upon
others. Hence, also, the ignorant multitude are not only
accustomed to beg, but to purchase at any price the superabundant merits of the Monks. Nay, for this end, they
say monasteries are instituted, *that they may make satisfaction for the sins of their founders, and of all in general,* Gerson, part. 2. serm. De abstinent. Carthus. But lest we
should be deceived by this same pretext, we ought to
remember, That God, indeed, loves the willing worship-
per, i. e. him who joyfully and willingly does that which he
hath commanded to be done ; but that he hates will-worship, i. e. those acts which are offered to him as the immediate worship of God, when they were not prescribed and
commanded by him for this end : for this is *to go a whoring
with their own inventions,* Psalm cvi. 39. We must also
know ; that abstinence from certain meats, celibacy, voluntary poverty, and other things of that kind, in which impostors place this voluntary worship of God, and I know
not what merit of supererogation, are nothing else than

things and actions indifferent, which, to certain persons at
certain times, may be instruments, or means availing in the
worship of God, as also their contraries may be: But,
neither in the one nor the other, ought we to imagine, that
there is any worship or merit.

And so far as to the first pretext, wherewith seducers are
wont to gloss over their commandments.

And humility.] This is the second colour with which the
commandments and doctrines of men are painted. For all
seducers endeavour to persuade the people, that there is
nothing more pleasing to God than humility, and devoted
submission of mind; which they would have to consist in
this, that Christians should submit themselves simply and
absolutely to those who are set over them, and to their
traditions and commandments, believe whatever they propose to be believed, and do whatever they direct to be
done. This humility they babble about as being of the
greatest merit with God, because he has enjoined all, *Obey
them that have the rule over you,* Heb. xiii. 17; because he
himself has plainly said concerning this matter, *He that
heareth you, heareth me,* &c. Luke x. 16. They, moreover,
add, that this especially conduces to the salvation of
Christians, that they should not discuss the commands of
those who are set over them (such as the worship and faith
recommended by them to the Church), but receive and
observe them; because it is most safe for the ignorant to
follow the opinion of the more wise. When, by this artifice, they have procured for their rites and doctrines an
authority plainly Divine, the submission and obedience of
Christian people seems to have *a shew of wisdom,* so that
by this their subjection, they think not only thus to act
piously, but prudently. Ignatius Loyola, the father of the
Jesuits,* deceived by this pretence, advises in that Epistle

---

* The history of the Founder of the Sect here adverted to, though
highly curious and interesting, is too extensive, even in its more important
features, to be entered upon in the limits of a biographical Note. From
distinction as a Spanish officer, in the wars between Charles and Francis, in
the early part of the sixteenth century, he became as distinguished as a
Religious devotee, and for the origin of that body which emerged at this

which is read at table in the College of the Jesuits every
month, and seriously commands, that those things which
the Superior enjoins, they should simply perform with
a blind obedience, not considering whether what is

eventful æra.   The change in his views which led to this, resulted on his
pondering over the lives of some of the Romish Saints, during a long confinement under wounds, received at the siege of Pampeluna, against the
French, in 1521.   On his recovery, he hung up his arms in the Church of
Montserrat, and dedicated himself to the blessed Virgin.   The character of
the man, and the circumstance which so affected his subsequent proceedings, by his mind taking a direction for Religion, was thus described by the
celebrated Vieira (one of his Order), in a Sermon which he preached in
Lisbon in reference to him some years after.   " The Cids, the Pelayos, the
Geryons, the Hercules who had figured in Spain, roused his spirit to covet
an heroic resemblance.   Their celebrity stimulated him.   Navarre seemed
a small point of defence; the Pyrenees but inferior walls; and all France
but a petty conquest.   He considered that he was a captain, a Spaniard, and
had been conquered.   Weary with combating thoughts so vast, he called
for a book of chivalry to amuse himself, but he could only find a volume of
the lives of saints.   If it had been what he wished, it would have led him
to be a famous knight ; but, being what it was, it made him a great saint.
Instead of being a cavalier of a flaming sword, he became the saint of a
burning torch.   At first the contents displeased him, but he became asto-
nished, as he read, to find that there was in the world another scene of sol-
diership, quite new, and unknown to him before : and he resolved to become one of its most zealous members.   He took off his noble collar, he
laid down his helmet, he stripped off his armour, and offered up the sword
which he had valued above all things, as the first tribute of his new feelings, on the altar of Montserrat.   After passing through various scenes as
a mendicant, a student, and a preacher, he became at last the founder of
that sect which assumed the name of the Company of Jesus ; a sect which
arose to uphold the Popedom, till its final consummation of iniquity, just at
the time that the temporal power of the Pope received a blow, from which
it has never recovered, by the attack of the Duke of Bourbon upon Rome,
and the sacking of the great City, in 1527, by his Colleague in arms, and
successor in that extraordinary event—the Prince of Orange.   The Order
was organized about 1530, and on its resolving upon a vow of submission to
Pope Paul III., he, in 1540, established it by a Papal Bull, under the title
of " the Society of Jesus."   Hence they received the epithet of Jesuits ;
and thus was created an Order, when, as Hume justly remarks, " the
Court of Rome perceived that the lazy Monks and Mendicant Friars, who
sufficed in times of ignorance, were no longer able to defend the ramparts
of the Church, assailed on every side ; and that the inquisitive spirit of the
age required a Society more active and more learned to oppose its dangerous
progress."   The Papacy was not disappointed ; for the Society has been
proverbial for their intrigues in nearly every State on the face of the Globe.

enjoined is good or useful, since every thought of the kind takes away the merit and weight of obedience. It is also the common opinion of the Romanists that there ought to be such a humility among Christians, that they should not

The able corrector of Mr. Dallas, in his history of the Order, has well summed up their extensive operations. " The Jesuits," says he, p. 374, " had no sooner appeared, than they overran the universe with surprising rapidity : they became the Instructors of Youth ; the Masters of Seminaries ; the Confessors of Kings; the distributors of favours ; and the nominators to every office, civil and ecclesiastical, and sometimes even to crowns ; in a word, the arbiters of every great event: they acquired immense wealth in freehold estates, and in the benefices which they procured for their houses : they formed the most substantial and brilliant establishments; and laid the foundations of a monarchy, calculated to resist the most powerful princes."—All this was effected, to use the appropriate terms of Sharon Turner, " through a remarkable combination of ability, enthusiasm, benevolence, intelligence, craft, ambition, piety, and superstition." Under the semblance of vows of poverty and chastity, together with that IMPLICIT OBEDIENCE TO THE CHIEF OF THE ORDER, as above-mentioned by Davenant, it has always been taught among them, that *oaths might be falsified!* Their statutes, in fact, have been denounced as " a complete code of perfidy, immorality, and revolt ;" and, wherever they have gained a footing, this body has established itself as an arbitrary power over the legal and regular authorities of the State. Loyola lived to see the diffusion of his Order over the greatest part of the Old and New worlds ; and its attainment of a new spiritual empire for the Popedom, in Asia and South America especially. In less than twenty years, owing to its Missionary activity, it included twelve large provinces possessed of one hundred Colleges. Within two centuries after, their number was found to amount to 20,000. This was ascertained in consequence of the inquiries instituted about them owing to the Provincial Letters of Pascal, laying open their detestable casuistry and diabolical intrigues. In 1554, long before Pascal's time, and only fourteen years after their establishment by Paul III., the Faculty of Theology in Paris, whose advice the Parliament had sought, pronounced, that " the " Society, withdrawn from the obedience and submission due to authorities, " unjustly deprived both temporal and spiritual lords of their rights: " brought discord into every form of government, and occasioned among " the people many subjects of complaint, many law-suits, altercations, " schisms, and jealousies ; that it appeared dangerous to all that concerned " the Faith ; calculated to disturb the peace of the Church ; to overturn " the Monastic orders; and more fit to destroy than to build up." The formidable body, however, proceeded in its career of iniquity, till, in 1773, Pope Clement XIV. pronounced its extinction in a Bull dated July 21 of that year. Since the restoration of the Monarchy in France, the Order has been revived, and in 1830, at the breaking up of the Jesuit Establishment at Montrouge, among their archives was found the following statement rehave the least doubt about those things which are set forth by the Romish Church, as to faith or practice in Religion and the worship of God.   But we, notwithstanding, may truly assert, that this blind obedience and humility is not only foolish, but impious and irreligious.   And the grounds for this are,

1.   Because we are bound to obey superiors only in cases in which they are *our* superiors.   Now, as to the framing doctrines of faith, or instituting the worship of God, God alone is our Superior : if, therefore, men attempt to devise doctrines of faith, or to introduce a new worship, they step beyond the limits of the power granted them, and are not to be acknowledged as superiors in this matter.

2.   Because the command of an inferior authority does not oblige to obedience when it is contrary to the command of a superior,   Hence that remark of the Apostle, Acts v. 29, *It is meet to obey God rather than man :* and of Cyprian, De sing. cler. *It is not allowable to please men where the will of men includes not the will of God.*   But admonitions of this kind would be vain, if a blind obedience in all things was due to our superiors.

3.   Because no one subjects himself knowingly to the peril of mortal sin, but he thereby sins mortally, as the Schoolmen say : but whoever vows, or performs absolute subjection and blind obedience to men, subjects himself to manifest peril ; for every man may err, as well in command-

specting the Society : The Government is divided into 5 assistances, which comprehend 39 provinces, 24 professed houses, 669 colleges, 61 noviciates, 176 seminaries, 335 residences, 223 missions, 22,787 Jesuits, of which 11,010 are priests.—In England, 19 noviciates, 299 Jesuits, 28 priests. For specimens of Popish intrigue, and influence, by means of this body, so devotedly submissive to the Chief of their Order, the Reader may consult Sharon Turner's Modern History of England.   As evincing itself more recently, let him consider the late Records of Ireland, and the investigations in our houses of Parliament ; let him bear in mind the late Revolution in France (vide Note, p. 76) : above all, let him reflect on the well-known boast of Cardinal Gonsalvi, that *they* (the Papists) had such influence with the Turkish Court, as to suppress the further spread of Heresy there : This was manifested by the Papacy succeeding in procuring a Firman against the proceedings of the agents of the British and Foreign Bible Society, and the progress of the Protestant Missionaries in Turkey ! !

ing to do things which are evil, as in prescribing to believe
things which are false.

4. Because to attribute to men what is the peculiar
right of God, is great impiety : but absolute dominion
over our bodies and our minds, is the property of God
alone. The human will owes absolute obedience to him;
the understanding owes to him prompt assent in all things :
but to yield to any mortal such subjection of the will, and
of the understanding, incurs the crime of treason against
the Divine Majesty. For that saying of Tertullian concerning God and the Divine commands is true, *I esteem it
audacity to dispute about the goodness of a Divine precept : for
we ought to obey it, not because it is good, but because God
hath commanded it ;* De pœnit. And that is no less true of
the Apostle, when men order us to do or to believe any
thing, *Prove all things ; hold fast that which is good,* 1 Thess.
v. 21.

But they who require this preposterous humility and
blind obedience from the people, are wont to object, That
it is not the duty of subjects to judge of the doctrines or
commands of their superiors; but it rather pertains to the
prelates and superiors, to judge of the faith and actions of
subjects : therefore, they seem to recede from their duty,
when they doubt whether those things are true and lawful
which are promulgated and confirmed by the authority of
those who are set over them.

I answer, Subjects neither ought, nor can judge of the
decrees of superiors by a judgment of authority ; but they
can, and ought to judge of those things with a judgment
of discretion, as far as they concern themselves. Aquinas
very well explains the reason of this, Quæst. disp. de
consens. art. 5. *Every one,* says he, *is bound to examine his
own actions according to the knowledge he has from God, whether it be natural, or acquired, or infused ; for every man
ought to act according to reason.* Thus speaks Aquinas.
This is confirmed by the example of all the pious; who,
although they arrogated not to themselves a judgment of
authority over their prelates or magistrates, yet they used
a judgment of discretion about the things proposed to

them. We see this done by Daniel, who judged that the
edict of Darius, concerning not praying to God, was not
to be observed by him. We see it in the Apostles, who
judged that they could not, consistently with piety, obey
the commands of the priests, Acts iv. 20. Finally, this
was done in the reign of Mary, by all our martyrs ; who
judged rightly that they ought neither to believe those
things which were then proposed by the prelates to be
believed, nor to do what they commanded to be done.

From these things, then, it is evident, that even the
second colour also of submission and meritorious humility,
whereby human decrees are commended to the people, is
vain, and has nothing of true wisdom in it.

And neglecting of the body, ἀφειδία σωματος, *not sparing the
body,* or *severity to the body.*] Behold the third colour with
which human decrees being painted and glossed over, wear
the appearance of piety and wisdom. For since carnal
men are mostly employed in an inordinate care of the flesh,
they who afflict by fasting, waste by watchings, or subdue
by flagellating this frail body, which others unduly cherish,
are supposed to be spiritually wise, and careful of their
salvation above others. Therefore, all those decrees which
have for their object this subduing of the flesh, so strike
the eyes of the ignorant by that mask of sanctity and mortification, that they do not meanwhile observe the poison-
ous errors which are customarily concealed under them.
For in all these, impostors always present an outward mortification of the flesh, but cherish within, mental pride and
hypocrisy. But for the better understanding of this whole
matter, we will bring forward, first, a few examples of
those who exercised this *severity to the body :* secondly, we
will expose the errors which usually lurk under decrees
and exercises of this kind : finally, we will shew what is to
be determined concerning these exercises of carnal mortification.

1. Evagrius, Historiæ eccl. lib. 1. cap. 21, reports, that
the Monks of Palestine sometimes fasted for more than
five days together, and afflicted themselves with such labours and watchings, that they seemed to be dead, and

lying unburied upon the earth, and relates many other extraordinary things about them; yet so as to exalt them to
heaven, account this plan of life, and term it, *a most holy
and divine kind of life.* The same author, lib. 3. cap. 49,
writes that others, on account of their continued watchings, were called ἀκοιμήτους, the sleepless.* Bernard, Serm.
6. cap. 49, in Psalm xci. writes, that certain Monks, by
various exercises of the body, and abstinences, were worn
down beyond their strength, beyond nature, beyond custom. Jerome, in his epitaph on Paula, relates, that when
she had recovered from a burning fever, she was altogether
unwilling to use the weakest and smallest quantity of wine,
although her Physician, and Jerome himself, earnestly advised her to it, and shewed her the imminent danger of a
dropsy from continually drinking water. But the most
celebrated of all for this mortifying of the body were,
the Flagellantes, *whose order arose in the year* 1260, *at Pe-
rusia, in Tuscany, when the whole world suffered from a dreadful famine. These men, wandering about, beat themselves publicly almost to death, and exercised these bloody rites for thirty-
three days; then they thought that they had expiated their
sins and were reconciled to God, and at length they returned
to their homes.* Hospin. pag. 271.* It would be easy to
collect more examples of those who exercised this *severity
to the body;* but these may suffice.

2. We will now, in the second place, lay open the

---

* Our Expositor here refers, I presume, to the work De Monachatu, of
a distinguished Swiss divine, Rodolph Hospinian, who flourished towards
the latter part of the sixteenth century, being born at Altdorf, in the Can-
ton of Zurich, in 1547. Having received a liberal education at Zurich,
Marpurg, and Heidelburg, he entered the Church in 1568, and three years
afterwards obtained the freedom of the city of Zurich, and the superintendance of the Abbey School there. He was considered the only Scholar
capable of refuting the Annals of Baronius, then Confessor to Clement
VIII. and afterwards Cardinal, and very near succeeding to the Popedom
in 1605, a celebrated, but partial historian of the Church, whose work,
though of vast learning, is entirely perverted to the interests of Rome.
Hospinian gained universal applause by the portions of his work against
Baronius, printed occasionally under the title of " the History of the
errors of Popery." Besides this elaborate work, he wrote a history of the
Jesuits, and several other pieces.

errors to which they, who are wont either to order or to practise these things, are commonly obnoxious.

1. They err as to the very nature of Christian mortification : for they consider the afflicting and injuring of the body to be true mortification ; whereas, that pertains chiefly not to the flesh, or the inferior part of the soul, but chiefly to the mind and will : for the mind and will of a man not yet renewed are carnal. They foolishly dream, therefore, that they are mortified persons, through the body being weakened and almost destroyed, when, in the meanwhile, the soul, which is the seat of sin, is filled with incredulity, pride, envy, and other spiritual vices. See Mirandulanus, De fide et ord. credendi ; and in Exposit. orat. Dom.

2. They err as to the means themselves, or, at least, as to the mode of applying these means. For it is one thing to subdue the flesh by moderate fasts and watchings, lest it should rebel against the spirit ; another, so to afflict and wear down the natural powers, that they cannot advantageously serve the spirit. For *whilst the flesh is unduly restrained, it is enervated for the exercise of good works: and whilst they endeavour to stifle entirely the incentives to vice, it is rendered too feeble to preach or pray,* Gregor. Moral. 30. cap. 28. Whence Aquinas, in xii. ad Rom. writes, that *he loses the dignity of a rational man, who prefers fasting or watching, to the full use of his senses.* And Gerson, part. 3, remarks, *There have been many who, to merit the fame of contemplation, have endeavoured to imitate Elias, or Daniel, or John the Baptist ; but who, by this abstinence, have become, not prophets, but fanatics.*

3. They err, because they bind themselves to these external services by the notion of a necessity so absolute, as not to allow the violation of them even for the sake of health. We see this in the example of Paula ;* we see it

---

* This person, before alluded to, was a learned Roman Lady, of a noble family, who added to the brightest qualities of the mind, the virtues of Christianity. But superstition corrupts the fairest things ; and under its influence, this Lady, with others of her time, became famous in Papal history, by countenancing and promoting the monastic life. She was well versed in the Hebrew Scriptures, and the intimate friend of Jerome, dying a few years before him, A.D. 407.

in the Carthusian Monks, who dare not even taste flesh,
though bodily infirmity demand it; we see it in all who are
brought under the government of the Church of Rome,
who imagine that they commit mortal sin, if they do not
fast according to the Papal statutes. But since it was just
that the ceremonial law itself should yield to the love of
God, how unjust is it that human mandates should refuse
the same subjection in things indifferent?

4. They err because they judge that the worship of
God, the merit of salvation, and the expiation of sins,
stand in these outward exercises. Thus says Peter Soto,*
*To deny that fasting is a work by which we merit eternal life,
and make satisfaction for our sins, is a most manifest error.*
Alensis, part. 4. quæst. 28, tells us, *A fast, whether enjoined
or assumed, is satisfactory for sins.* Thomas, Q. 2. quæst.
147, *A fast is assumed for three things: to repress the lusts of
the flesh, to raise the mind of man to higher things; and to
make satisfaction for sins.*—These are the errors in which
almost all are implicated who exercise this *neglecting of,*
or *not sparing,* the body.

Now, in the last place, that we may not appear to reject
outward exercises of mortification, we shall briefly shew
what is the opinion of our church respecting these things.

We very much approve the remark of Athanasius, *That
these bodily exercises are praiseworthy, if they are united with
knowledge and moderation.* Fastings, then, and watchings,
and other things of this kind, we confess, have their utility, if we understand their use and end; i. e. if they are
referred to the chastening of the body, lest by excess, or
sloth, it should be excited to sin; if they are referred to
the external testifying of internal penitence; if, lastly, they
are referred to this, that being assisted by those helps, we
may more ardently call upon God. For rightly spake

---

* More commonly called Dominic Soto, was a learned Spanish Dominican, born at Segovia, in 1494, where his father was a gardener. He distinguished himself as a Theologian, and was one of the most active and
esteemed members of the Council of Trent; proving himself there, as well
as in his writings, a true Romanist. He was appointed Confessor to
Charles V., and died in 1560, aged 66. His works were numerous.

Tertullian, advers. Psychicos, *When fasting, we possess a stronger mind, and a heart more active to these spiritual things, than when that mansion of the inner man is glutted up with food, or drenched with wine.* But if we think there is any merit of satisfaction or justification in these external exercises, then they are not used *with knowledge,* and, therefore, are rejected by God; as we may see Isa. lviii. 3, where they obtruded upon God this very opus operatum in these words, *Wherefore have we fasted, and thou seest not? Wherefore have we afflicted our soul, and thou takest no knowledge?* God answers, *It is not such a fast as I have chosen,* &c. So Zech. vii. 5, 6, he denies that they fast for him who place holiness and the worship of God in an external work. But the Apostle most clearly distinguishes in 1 Tim. iv. 8, between *bodily exercise* and *godliness,* or true worship. We, therefore, ought to know, that all these things come under the head of external discipline, not of works of divine worship.

Besides this knowledge, there is also required a due moderation in all these things; for that abstinence or chastening of the body, which hath no regard to its peculiar infirmity, is foolish. Hence we read in Eusebius, lib. 5. cap. 3. that Alcibiades was reprehended because he would not use the creatures of God, but took only bread and water for the sustenance of his body. We see also Timothy himself advised by Paul, 1 Tim. v. 23, no longer to be too abstemious, but to *use a little wine for his stomach's sake and his often infirmities.* These free and moderate fasts were in use in the primitive Church : but those necessary and rigid ones beyond the strength of the body, were always condemned by the wiser men. Thus Augustine, 1 De mor. eccl. cath. cap. 33, testifies, *No one is compelled to severe things which he cannot endure; nothing is imposed upon any one which he refuses.* Prudentius, 1 Cathemer. hymn. post jejun. says, *An open and free mode of abstinence is set before all; neither are we impelled by severe terror : it is his own will binds every one.* Prosper, De vita contempl. lib. 2. cap. 24, says, *We ought so to fast that we may not be subject to the necessity of fasting, lest, not with devotion, but un-*

willingly, we perform an act that is really voluntary. And
thus you find that *neglecting* or *chastising* of the body,
which is full of superstition, is to be exploded, although
that chastising of the body which is joined with true knowledge and due moderation, is to be retained. And thus
much of the three pretences whereby impostors are accustomed to gloss over their commands and superstitious doctrines. Now let us hear what is the Apostolic censure of
mandates and things of this kind.

Yet *they are of no value,* since they respect *those things
with which the flesh is filled.*] Thus Beza. [*Not in any honour* (supply, *do they hold the body*) *to the satisfying* or
contenting *of the flesh.*] Thus others.

They who approve this latter interpretation, think that
the Apostle, in these words, explains what is that *neglecting* of the body which he reprehends ; namely, when the
body is had in no honour to satisfy or fill it. In this place,
therefore, they interpret the word *honour* by *care;* as 1 Tim.
v. 3, *Honour widows,* i. e. have a care and consideration of
them : therefore *not to have the body in honour,* is to bestow
no due care upon it. But by what is added—*to the satisfying of the flesh*—they mean *the filling of it,* which is opposed
to that inanition whereby the strength of the body is les-
sened and impaired ; and they think that the Apostle used
this fuller word to reprove those hypocrites who defrauded
the bodies of their necessary food, as if it were a fault to
satisfy the body; whereas surfeiting and gluttony are vices,
not sufficiency. But the care of just sustentation is due
to this earthly body, not only because it is the necessary
organ of the soul, but because it is the temple of the
Holy Spirit, because it is a member of the body of Christ;
nay, if it be esteemed in the place of a beast of burden,
still it is proved that sufficient aliment is due to it : for *a
righteous man regardeth the life of his beast,* Prov. xii. 10.

We ought, then, to understand, that the care of the body
is twofold : one which tends to the fulfilling its unlawful
desires, which is evil and forbidden, Rom. xiii. 14 ; the
other, good and lawful, which has the more concern to
afford the body food and necessaries for life, lest strength

and health should fail it to undergo the duties which devolve upon us in our vocation. He who rejects this latter
care, holds his body in no honour; and some think that
this kind of person is reproved in this place.

This is a probable interpretation : But neither do I think
the interpretation of Beza is to be despised; who refers
those words, *not in any honour*, to the very rites and commandments of abstaining from and choosing meats, and
thinks they are answered from the contrary. *Which indeed
have a shew of wisdom, yet are not of any worth.* Beza supplies the word *yet*, because it is usual with those who adopt
the Hebrew idiom (as Paul occasionally does), to understand the adversative particle. But now, if it be asked,
Why are not those commandments of men of any value,
the Apostle gives the cause, *for the satisfying of the flesh*,
they refer, *ὄντα* or *συντείν ὄντα, to the satisfying of the flesh*, i. e.
they rest in meat and drink, and things earthly and vain,
in which the kingdom of God does not consist, but in
those which relate to spiritual sustenance and life eternal ;
as was shewn in the foregoing verse. But the Apostle asserts commandments of this kind to be of no value or
moment, not because they are void of all utility, if proposed and observed *with knowledge* and *moderation*, as
Athanasius advises; but they are in themselves of no value
and moment for justification, sanctification, satisfaction for
sins, and the worship of God, as the seducers would contend they were.

It is not needful to add more concerning this censure of
the Apostle, which relates to these ordinances referring to
external things ; for we have often treated sufficiently of
this matter. The fourth part of this Epistle yet remains ;
which contains instruction in morals, roots out vices, inculcates virtues, and, finally, forms the life of Christians, as
well in respect to their common duties, as to their social
relations.

THE END OF THE SECOND CHAPTER.

ADDENDA TO VOL. I.

For Note *, p. 14.

It was probably Stephen, the 22d Bishop of Rome, raised to that See on the Martyrdom of Lucius, in 253, who was intended ; and to whom, as well as to Cyprian, Bishop of Carthage, in consequence of Marcion, Bishop of Arles, having embraced the Novatian heresy, the rest of the Gallican Bishops wrote, for their mutual advice on the subject. Stephen was, on this occasion, backward to interfere ; but afterwards, in a similar case of Basilides, interposed with such arrogance, as would have involved the churches in Spain in endless calamities, had not Cyprian and the other Bishops of Africa zealously interposed also to counteract his assumption. Cyprian, perceiving his disposition to usurp undue authority, advanced the following five arguments against appeals to the See of Rome :—

First, Such appeal was contrary to an Ecclesiastical Canon.

Second, Unjust ; because it prejudiced the rights of particular Bishops.

Third, Because the Clergy and people should not be compelled to leave their own homes and go beyond sea.

Fourth, Causes could be better decided on the spot, when the proper witnesses were at hand, and could be easily produced.

Fifth, Because there is a competent authority every where in the Church.

Vide *Craig's Refutation of Popery*, Vol. ii. Dissert. v. p. 18.

The insolence, ambition, and arrogance now *beginning* to work in the See of Rome, led to the decisions subsequently adopted at the Council of Nice, as adverted to in the Sixth Canon of that Council, given below on the same page to which this refers. In what light Cyprian, and his Bishopric, ought to be regarded in contradistinction to the church of Rome, let the enquiring Reader examine and judge from Bower's History of the Popes, vol. i. under " Stephen."

Note to close of Section at top of page 16.

This (the voluntary concession of other churches) took place in the Council of Chalcedon, in 451, and the decree which embodied it was signed by 630 Fathers ; and, as hath been well observed by Craig, the arguments used by this great Council, demonstrate, as plainly and clearly as such a proposition admits of demonstration, that neither Constantinople, nor Rome, nor any other See, had, or ought to have, any superior authority whatever by Divine right, but merely from Ecclesiastical Constitution, founded on political reasons of State, according to the relative dignity of the Sees in the Empire.

The words used by the Fathers are these following :

" Whereas the See of old Rome had been, not undeservedly, distin-
" guished by the Fathers with certain privileges, *because that city was the*
" *seat of the Empire*—the Fathers of Constantinople were induced, by the
" same reason, to distinguish the most holy See of new Rome with *equal*
" *privileges*, thinking it FIT that the *City* which they saw *honoured* with the
" *Emperor* and *Senate*, and *equalled* in *every civil privilege* with *old Rome*,
" should likewise be equalled to her in Ecclesiastical matters."

If there were no other document but this to confute the pretended supremacy of the See of Rome, by Divine right, surely this Canon of so
great a Council as 630 Fathers composed, held not till the middle of the
fifth century, with the reasons alleged for its enactment, ought, of itself,
to be sufficient. In this there is no mention made of, nor any reference to
St. Peter ;—no allusion to any supposed dignity derivable from him ;—
every thing connected with rank, or pre-eminence, depends on civil or political considerations, because (as the Fathers allege) the two imperial cities
enjoyed equal civil rights, they should enjoy equal Ecclesiastical privileges.
Hence it incontrovertibly follows, that in the Church of Christ, as every
thing originally was equality, whatever pre-eminence subsequently was
possessed by any particular church, or see, it was derived from a civil source ;
i. e. from human institution ; for, according to the ordinance of the Messiah, all his *Apostles* were equal ; none, according to Him, was to be Master.—Vide Craig's Refutation.

For Note p. 26.

Cyprian's works, edited by Bishops Fell and Pearson, are among the
prohibited books in Pope Benedict's Index Expurgatorium. The reason is
obvious; those Editions contained passages which the papal Inquisitors had
blotted out, or omitted, in former editions, as standing in honest array
against the prerogatives and usurpations of Rome, and excluded such as
they had obtruded into the Text to maintain her assumed supremacy.
Those Editions were printed, in fact, from genuine copies of Cyprian's
works ; but the diffusion of them would not suffice for that Church which
had the power of accomplishing *its* ends by other means.

For Note p. 53.

Since the Note in this page went through the press, the writer has observed the work there referred to, among the prohibited books in the Index
of Benedict XIV. dated 1708, under the Latin title.—The Divines of
Cologne were esteemed by ours, in the seventeenth century, to have been
most clear on the doctrine of Justification and the imputation of Christ's
Righteousness.—Vide " Morning Exercises" at Southwark, edited by
Vincent, in 1675.

For Note p. 93.

The persecution there alluded to arose from the great aversion of the Britons, the Scots, and the Picts to the Anti-christian rites which Austin wished to introduce among them. They were so shocked at the many Pagan superstitions and ceremonies introduced by him into the Saxon worship, that they looked upon it as no better than Paganism, and avoided the communion of those who came from Rome to establish it, as they avoided the Pagans ; nay, so great was the aversion, which the *Scots* in particular bore to all the *Roman* Missionaries, that Dagamus, a Bishop of that nation, not only declined sitting with them at the same table, but would not even lodge with them under the same roof. Popery soon resented this in its well known manner.—Bede, Eccl. Hist. l. 2. c. 4.

END OF THE FIRST VOLUME.

AN

EXPOSITION

OF THE

EPISTLE OF ST. PAUL

TO THE

COLOSSIANS,

BY

THE RIGHT REV. JOHN DAVENANT, D.D.

LORD BISHOP OF SALISBURY;

PRESIDENT OF QUEEN'S COLLEGE, AND LADY MARGARET'S

PROFESSOR OF DIVINITY IN CAMBRIDGE:

ORIGINALLY DELIVERED, IN A SERIES OF LECTURES, BEFORE THE

UNIVERSITY.

TRANSLATED FROM THE ORIGINAL LATIN;

WITH A LIFE OF THE AUTHOR,

AND NOTES

ILLUSTRATIVE OF THE WRITERS AND AUTHORITIES REFERRED TO

IN THE WORK:

BY JOSIAH ALLPORT,

MINISTER OF ST. JAMES'S, BIRMINGHAM.

Quæ Pauli Epistola non melle dulcior, lacte candidior?—Ambr. Serm. 68.

VOL. II.

LONDON:

HAMILTON, ADAMS, AND CO.

BIRMINGHAM:

BEILBY, KNOTT, AND BEILBY.

MDCCCXXXII.

EXPOSITION

OF

THE THIRD CHAPTER.

WE have now finished the two former Chapters of this Epistle; and shall proceed, with the Divine assistance, to the explication of the third Chapter. But, in the first place, we must premise, what the scope of the Apostle is; for it is useful, nay, necessary to have this before our eyes, that we may understand what an apt and suitable bearing all his observations have upon it. The whole discussion, then, of the Apostle has respect to this, viz. that after the doctrine of the faith of the Gospel had been established, and the impostures of false apostles exploded, he might stir up the Colossians to exercise holiness of life, and avoid corrupt morals. For it is customary with St. Paul, in all his Epistles, to subjoin to disputations concerning the faith, exhortations to newness of life: For he would have a good tree to bear good fruit, namely, a sound faith to yield a holy life. You perceive the scope. In the second place, then, it is easy to elicit the sum or argument of the whole Chapter, and, as it were, to include it in a few lines. This, then, is what is here inculcated by the Apostle, viz. that the Colossians, and so all true Christians, are made partakers of the death and resurrection of Christ; and on this account it behoves them to die to sin, to live to God, to put off the old man with his deeds, and to put on the new man. The sum, then, of the Apostolic exhortation is contained in these two propositions : 1, A

new and heavenly life must be entered upon by those who
are risen again with Christ. 2, The indwelling corruption
of our nature must be mortified by those who are dead with
Christ.

It remains that we proceed to the parts of this Chapter.
And here we have a two-fold exhortation : A *General* one
which regards all Christians alike, from the beginning of
the Chapter to verse 18. A *special*, or personal one, which
is directed to certain orders of Christians, namely, to
wives and husbands, children and parents, servants and
masters ; from the 18th verse to the end of the Chapter.
The *general* exhortation is distributed into three branches.

The first, comprehended in the four first verses, teaches
us how, and stirs us up to seek the true end, that is to say,
heaven, and Christ dwelling in heaven.

The second exhorts to the practice of those things
which are ordained to this end. And this practice consists in mortification, i. e. the laying aside of vices; and
vivification, i. e. the exercise of all virtues : concerning
which he discourses largely from the 5th to the 16th
verse.

The third calls to the meditation and study of the Divine
Word, and likewise prescribes a general rule to be observed
in all our actions, vers. 16 and 17.

I conceived these things should be premised, because we
are led more easily by parts to the knowledge of the whole.
I shall not follow out more of this sort, because (as Seneca
has well observed) *there is in too many divisions as great a
fault as in no division.* It is useful to distribute a subject
matter into parts ; it is frivolous to mince it : for to take
in the minutest points with the same care as one would the
greatest, is mere toil. Therefore, we shall observe the
parts and smaller matters of the divisions as they offer
themselves in the explanation of the context, which, relying upon the Divine aid and the illumination of the Holy
Spirit, we forthwith enter upon.

CHAP. III. Verses 1, 2.

*If ye then be risen with Christ, seek those things which are
above, where Christ sitteth on the right hand of God.
Set your affection on things above, not on things on the
earth.*

Having established the doctrine of the Gospel, and vanquished the seducers, the Apostle comes to the business
of exhortation, that he might train to holiness of life those
whom he had brought to hold the truth of faith. But this
exhortation arises and is deduced from the twelfth and thirteenth verses of the preceding Chapter, where these words
occur, *Buried with him in baptism, who hath also raised and
quickened you:* hence he now infers, *If ye be risen with
Christ, seek those things which are above.* We have said that
the first branch of the general exhortation is included in
the four first verses; and has for its object to excite the
Colossians to aim at and desire the true good, viz. what is
spiritual and divine; and, moreover, to beget in them a
contempt of apparent good things, viz. corporeal and
earthly ones. And the Apostle acts prudently in prescribing and defining, in the first place, the thirst for the true
end: since inordinateness of the will as to the end, engenders inordinate and monstrous actions through the whole
course of our life; for as the form is the principal in natural things, so the end is in morals.

But to come to the matter itself, here are two things to
be observed by us.

1. The duty to which we are excited by the Apostle,
comprehended in three precepts: Seek those things which
are above; φρονεῖτε, i. e. *think upon and love the things above;
seek not after, neither mind, earthly things.*

2. The inducements, or motives (as they say) to the
performance of this duty. For the seeking and loving the
things above, two inducements are brought: one taken
from our resurrection; vers. 1, *Ye are risen with Christ:* the

other from the exaltation of Christ; *where Christ sitteth at the right hand of God.* For the despising earthly things two others are used; the first derived from our spiritual death ; *Ye are dead, and your life is hid with Christ,* vers. 4 ; the latter, from the expectation of our life of glory ; *When Christ, who is our life, shall appear, then shall ye also appear with him in glory.*

1. Of the duties.

Seek those things which are above.] The word *Seek* indicates labour and effort; and, to use the scholastic phrase, excludes *sluggish willingness.* By the *things which are above* we must understand, in the first place, the kingdom of heaven, or the beatific vision of God, and those pleasures to be hereafter enjoyed with Christ our Head and the blessed angels, which *neither eye hath seen, nor ear heard, nor have entered into the heart of man,* 1 Cor. ii. 9. But, secondly and consequently, we must understand those gifts of grace which are the seeds of this desired glory, as faith, love, holiness, and all those means by which, as by an intermediate path, God would have us proceed to this mark of heavenly glory. For Augustine hath properly remarked, that these things may also be called *things which are above,* because *as to the excellency of their worth they far surpass earthly things;* as, furthermore, because all things of this kind *are bestowed from above, and come down from the Father of lights,* Jas. i. 17. When, therefore, the Apostle exhorts to *seek those things which are above,* he would have us to understand, that we ought not only to seek celestial pleasures, but so to live that we may at length attain to them. For he who does not advance in faith, love, and holiness, he does not, by the whole course of his life, seek heaven, but hastens to hell.

Hence we infer,

1. That heaven is not given to the indolent, but to those who seek it by great labour, *Seek ye the kingdom of God, and his righteousness,* Matt. vi. 33. And elsewhere, *the violent take it,* not those who slumber.

2. Celestial pleasures are not possessed in this life : we should, therefore, long after and patiently expect those

things, being certain to obtain them at last, if we seek
them as we ought to do.

Τὰ ἄνω φρονεῖτε, *Mind the things above, think upon* or *savour
them.*] The word φρονεῖτε, in our translation *set your affections,* embraces two acts ; the act of the mind or of the
understanding reflecting about any thing; and the act of
the will and affections approving and loving any thing:
Therefore, the Apostle would have us raise our minds to
heaven, and perpetually have those things above at heart ;
neither that alone, but that we should ardently love those
things, and fix our affection upon them. Unless we join
these two, no one will prepare to seek heavenly things ;
for *there is no desire of a thing unknown:* it is, therefore,
necessary to know, and frequently to revolve in mind, these
heavenly things ; for no one seeks that about which he
thinks not : But neither is it sufficient to think, unless it
is done with love and affection ; for nothing is sought by
us except that which is desired and loved. Bernard truly
observed, *The understanding and the affection in men are
sometimes opposed to each other, so that the one knows and approves the things which are above, although the other is found
to desire the things on the earth.* When that happens, the
mind is distracted and torn away, not excited to seek.
Hence it is that Paul exhorts us not only to know, but to
savour the things which are above.

Hence we learn :

1. That it is the duty of a pious and Christian man,
always to have in mind that heavenly kingdom, and those
heavenly good things which relate to the attainment of it.
We observe this in Abraham, the father of the faithful, of
whom the Apostle testifies, Heb. xi. 10, that *he looked for a
city which hath foundations.* This we read of the Christians
of the primitive Church, who had this kingdom above so
frequently in their minds and discourse, that from thence
they fell under the suspicion, among the heathen, of aiming
at the sovereignty. Just Martyr. Apol. 2. ad Antoninum.

2. It is also their duty who hope they shall obtain eternal blessedness, to order the course of their life according
to heavenly considerations ; and to judge of all matters

with a constant reference to these supernal things : for this
is effectually *to savour the things above,* viz. to be so affected by their excellence and sweetness, as to thirst for
them with an insatiable desire, and refer all things to the
attainment of them. The Psalmist felt this love in his
heart, and well expressed it, Psal. xlii. 1, *As the hart panteth after the water-brooks, so panteth my soul after thee, O
God.* Hence we may conclude, that all they who promise
themselves the happiness above, when, in the meanwhile,
they do not at all savour the things above, are delighted as
by a certain pleasing dream, and never will be satisfied
with those things, because they were never wont to thirst
or hunger for them at heart. The last branch of this exhortation remains.

Not on things on the earth ; supply, *seek and savour.*] The
Apostle calls all those things, in which the kingdom of God
does not consist, *things of the earth ;* as riches, pleasures,
honours ; and I add, in fine, those ceremonies and observations which centre in things earthly and corporeal :
for this hortatory conclusion being drawn from our death
and resurrection with Christ, it shews all those things to be
of no esteem. But now they are said *to savour of* or *seek
earthly things,* who place their happiness in these things,
who by these earthly blessings (as they are called) are influenced in all their judgments and decisions. These sen-
sualities are well depicted by the Apostle, in Phil. iii. 18,
19, *Many walk, of whom I have told you often, and now tell
you even weeping, that they are the enemies of the cross of
Christ : whose end is destruction, whose god is their belly, and
whose glory is in their shame, δι τὰ ἐπίγεια φρονοῦντες, who mind
earthly things.* They were men of this kind, whom our Saviour censured in his parable, Luke xiv. because, while
they regarded fields, oxen, and wives, altogether neglected
the call of salvation.

Hence we may observe,

1. That no one can savour of things heavenly and
things of the earth at the same time. For if this could be
done, there would have been no need of this clause denying and forbidding it ; but it would have been sufficient to

have said, *set your affections on things above,* without its
being added, *and not on things of the earth.* But that saying
of the Saviour is true, *No man can serve two masters,* Matt.
vi. 24. If, therefore, we be slaves to our earthly desires,
we shall never be watchful to promote our salvation. The
poet heretofore sang, *Our bosoms do not admit two cares;* and
the Apostle said, *foolish and hurtful lusts drown men in per-*
dition, 1 Tim. vi. 9.

2. We must observe, that Paul forbids us to seek and
savour earthly things, he does not forbid us to use earthly
things, much less, indeed, to obtain them. We cannot
live without the use of earthly things ; but they would not
serve for necessary uses, unless they were before acquired.
Therefore, to *seek* and *affect* them, means in this place, to
desire them with the whole heart, with every labour and
industry : and to acquiesce in those things as in the greatest good. This carnal and worldly men do, whatever they
pretend: this is evinced by their coveting these earthly
things in every way and without measure. Now it is plain,
that that is sought and proposed as their sole end, which
is sought immeasurably : for in that which is sought on account of some end, a measure is admitted in proportion to
the end.

3. We may add a reason why it is not fit to affect
earthly things, but those alone which are above; and that
twofold, One taken from the vanity of these things; for
earthly things, as Parisiensis has well remarked, *cannot im-*
part satisfaction to him that hath them, nor support to him
that rests upon them, nor profit to him who labours for them.
What then shall it profit a man if he shall gain the whole
world, &c. Matt. xvi. 26. The other from their contrariety
to true and heavenly pleasures. For, as the heavenly man-
na failed after the children of Israel had eaten of the fruits
of the earth ; so the sweetness of spiritual pleasure is not
perceived by those who have a longing after these earthly
things. Whence said Augustine, *If the mind hath delight*
from what is external, it will remain without delight from what
is internal. Thus much for the matter of the Apostle's exhortation. Let us proceed to the inducements.

If ye be risen with Christ.] That it is our duty to seek
and affect the things which are above he argues, first from
our resurrection with Christ: For these words *if ye be
risen,* are not expressive of doubt, but the language of inference and conclusion : for the assumption, viz. *ye are
risen with Christ,* is presupposed from those things which
were contended for in the foregoing Chapter, verses 12 and
13. And this argument proceeds from the cause to the
effect : for this our resurrection which we have by Christ,
is the efficient principle of the new life, and, therefore, of
the new conversation and work. For we must know, that
Christ, by the same power wherewith he raised himself from
corporeal death, hath raised all his people from spiritual
death. Hence said Bernard, *There is a twofold resurrection;
one of the soul, which the secret coming of Christ effects ; the
other of the body, which the glorious coming of Christ will accomplish. And as the outward man will receive in its corporeal
resurrection, new life and functions: so in this spiritual resurrection, the inner man now receives new life and a new sensitive
power.* Hence that injunction of the Apostle, Rom. vi. 4,
*As Christ was raised up from the dead by the glory of the
Father, so we also should walk in newness of life.* This spiritual resurrection is effected in baptism, both sacramentally and really ; sacramentally, by the external administration of the rite ; really, by the internal operation of the
Holy Spirit. The Apostle comprehends both in Tit. iii. 5,
*According to his mercy he saved us by the washing of regenera-
tion and renewing of the Holy Ghost.* These things being
laid down, it is clear, that this ought to be the greatest
inducement to all believers to seek and savour the things
which are above. For he who is risen again is risen to
another kind of life ; but he who is risen with Christ, he,
as far as it can be done in this life, ought to imitate Christ
rising again. Therefore, like as Christ, being raised from
the dead, cared no more for earthly things, but ascended
to heaven to live a glorious and heavenly life : so Christians, who are spiritually raised, ought not to cleave to
earthly things and desires, but elevate their minds to
heaven.

Hence we observe,

1. It is the duty of Christians to imitate Christ, and to do those things spiritually which Christ did corporeally. For instance; Christ died; we ought in like manner to die to sin: Christ rose again; we ought also to rise to newness of life: Christ ascended into heaven; it is our duty to soar to heaven in mind. This is what the Apostle would have us understand in Rom. vii. 5, where he requires that we, being planted together, should coalesce together in conformity as well to the death as to the resurrection of Christ. *The Apostle,* says Chrysostom, *would have Christians to be partakers with Christ in all things.*

2. It is not only our duty to rise with Christ; but to derive power from the resurrection of Christ for this spiritual resurrection; for that virtue wherewith Christ raised himself, he communicates to all his people to raise up them also. The argument, therefore, from the resurrection of Christ is strong for our spiritual resurrection. Hence the Apostle, having laid down the death and resurrection of Christ, subjoins Ὅυτω καὶ ὑμεῖς λογίζεσθε, &c. *Likewise reckon ye also yourselves to be dead indeed unto sin, but alive unto God through Jesus Christ our Lord.* Rom. vi. 11.

3. They are now inexcusable who still are absorbed in earthly things and desires; since they have a new nature proportioned and inclined to the things which are above, communicated to them by the quickening power of the resurrection of Christ. Therefore, like as iron, which cannot raise itself aloft by its nature, yet, by the operation of the magnet acting upon it, is raised upward: so human minds, by their own aptitude being set upon earthly things, by virtue of the resurrection of Christ, can elevate themselves to high and heavenly things. Thus much for the first inducement.

Where Christ sitteth on the right hand of God.] This is that other inducement or spur to seek and affect lofty or celestial things: Christ sitteth at the right hand of God; therefore it behoves us to seek and to affect the things that are above. First we shall explain the meaning of these words; and then shew the force of the argument, or the consequence of the reason.

In the first place, then, it must be borne in mind, that this is spoken of Christ properly and especially as to his human nature, in which he rose, and ascended, and sits at the right hand of the Father, as it is stated in the Apostle's Creed : and although as to the Divine nature, we must believe that he sat at the right hand of the Father from all eternity, i. e. as Damascenus, Lib. 4. cap. 2, has expounded it, that he had an equality of Divine Majesty with God the Father : *By the right hand of the Father we mean the glory and honour of the Godhead; in which the Son of God existed, before the world began, as God, and of one substance with the Father, but became incarnate in these last days, and sitteth there bodily, his flesh being also glorified.* Therefore, passing by this Exposition of Damascenus, which respects the Divine nature of Christ and his eternal Majesty, let us inquire what is intimated under the words *to sit at the right hand of God,* when they are applied to the human nature of Christ and its exaltation effected in time.

This is the sum; Since God hath no bodily right hand, by this sitting is signified, that Christ as man, having accomplished the work of our redemption, is not only endowed with immortality and perfect blessedness, but is raised to heaven, placed above all creatures, Lord, Governor, and Judge of the whole world, and especially constituted the most glorious and powerful King and Patron of the Church. Augustine, De fide et symbolo, Tom. 3, says, *to sit, is to possess judicial power; but to be at the right hand of God, is to be in the highest blessedness; as to be at the left hand is to be in the deepest misery.* But what it is for the man Christ to sit at the right hand of the Father, is best explained by the Apostle in Ephes. i. 20, 21, and 22. It comprises, then, the exaltation of the human nature to a state of the completest happiness and glory of which it could be capable, and likewise exaltation and authority over all other creatures.

The error of certain moderns is therefore to be avoided,

who, from this sitting of Christ at the right hand of God,
endeavour to infer, that Divine Majesty, ubiquity, and all
the properties of Deity are really *communicated* to the
human nature of Christ. But they are easily refuted;

1. Because, if the Divine attributes be really communicated to the human nature, the human nature is really
God : for the Divine attributes are nothing else than the
Divine essence. We therefore acknowledge that Christ
incarnate has an equality of glory and majesty with God
the Father : but we deny that the flesh of Christ, or the
human nature, has, or can have this ; because it is not consubstantial with God, although it is hypostatically united
to God.

2. They are refuted from the circumstance of time. For
(as they will have it) a real communication of attributes
to the human nature arises from its hypostatic union with
the Divine : but this sitting of the man Christ at the right
hand of God, of which the Apostle speaks, followed his
passion and resurrection. This we learn from the order of
the articles in the Apostle's Creed : *He rose again ; he ascended into heaven ; he sat down,* &c. This Christ himself
teaches us, Luke xxiv. 26, *Ought not Christ to have suffered,
and to enter into his glory?* And the Apostle, Heb. i. 3,
*After that he had purged our sins, he sat down at the right
hand of the Majesty on high.*

3. As to the ubiquity of Christ's body ; that is manifestly refuted, not established in this place. For the Apostle says, that the minds of Christians ought to be directed
heavenward, not set upon earthly things, for this reason, that
Christ is exalted at the right hand of God in the heavens,
now no more to dwell with us upon earth in his bodily presence, although as to the presence of the Divine Majesty
he is ever with us. Thus in Ephes. i. 20, *He set Christ at
his own right hand.* Where? *In the heavens ;* and Heb. i. 3,
in the highest places. Although, therefore, the right hand
of God is every where, if thereby we understand the
Divine Majesty and power; because God is every where :
yet Christ, as far as regards his body, or his human nature,
is set at the right hand of God, not as regards his ubiquity,
but his presence in heaven.

And thus ye see briefly in what sense Christ is set at the
right hand of God : His Divine nature, or the person of
the Word, sits in the equality of Majesty and glory, and of
all the Divine attributes ; the human nature sits above all
created things, but yet beneath God, viz. endued with
majesty, and the greatest glory adapted to it, and of which
it can be capable.

Those things being explained, it remains that we shew
the force of this argument: Christ sitteth on high at the
right hand of God ; therefore we ought to seek and affect
the things which are above.   There are two reasons which
strengthen this consequence.   The first derived from the
love of all the faithful to the Head and Saviour Christ
Jesus.   It is a common saying, *The mind is where it loves, not
where its actual seat is:* and that saying in the Gospel is also
well known, *Where the treasure is, there will the heart be
also*, Matt. vi. 21.   Since then Christ, who is the love and
delight of the souls of the faithful, is placed in the heavens at the right hand of God, it is needful for every pious
and holy soul to flee towards that celestial place as by a
straight course, and in heart and mind especially to have
conversation there daily.   That saying of Paul, Phil. i. 23,
I have a desire to depart and to be with Christ, flowed from
this affection.   The inferior members can never be well if
they be disjointed and separated from their head : it is no
wonder, therefore, if all the faithful mount to heaven as
much as they can, and strive to join themselves to Christ
their Head.

The other cause is derived from the influence of the head
over the members.   For Christ sits not idle at the right hand
of the Father, but imparts saving grace to all his people, and
supplies them with strength to trample under foot earthly
things, and seek those which are above.   For Christ being
exalted hath attractive virtue, he draws all his people upward,
and suffers them not to cleave to the earth.   Even as the heavenly sun draws upwards by his power, gross and earthly va-
pours ; so Christ, the Sun of Righteousness, separates our
gross and rigid souls from the dregs of earthly things, and
by his efficacious working raises them to heavenly.   The
argument, therefore, is derived from what is possible or

feasible : as though he had said, Although ye cannot by the strength of nature seek and affect the things that are above, yet by the aid of Christ sitting at the right hand of God, and drawing you to himself by the Spirit of grace, ye are now able to accomplish that. *I can do all things,* says the Apostle, *through Christ strengthening me,* Phil. iv. 13.

Hence we infer,

1. There is no reason why we should fear the hosts of our spiritual enemies, the devil, the world, and the flesh ; because Christ our Saviour is more powerful than all these, inasmuch as he is exalted at the right hand of God, far above all creatures. *What fear of the world is there to him, who hath God for his guide through the world?* Cyprian, De Orat. Dom. *Human persecution shall not shake the mind, but Divine protection shall strengthen faith.* Idem, De exhort. martyr. cap. 10.

2. This ought to induce a perpetual exercise of faith, that as often as we are troubled with earthly desires, forthwith we should look up to heaven, we should contemplate Christ sitting at the right hand of God, and seek spiritual strength from him. Thus Stephen was even supported against the very terrors of death, Acts vii. 55.

3. They are not true and living members under Christ the Head, whose minds are not directed heavenward. *For wheresoever the carcase is, thither will the eagles be gathered together,* Matt. xxiv. 28.

So much for the inducements to seek those things which are above.

Verses 3, 4.

For ye are dead, and your life is hid with Christ in God ; When Christ who is our life shall appear, then shall ye also appear with him in glory.

That the things which are above were to be sought by the Colossians, and so by all believers, is proved by two reasons ; from our resurrection with Christ, and from the

exaltation of Christ himself. The Apostle now enters upon
that other part of his admonition, by which he forbids us
to seek and to affect earthly things; and he corroborates it
by two other arguments. The first taken from our spiritual
death ; *for ye are dead* : to which he adds a silent occupation; *your life is hid.* The latter is derived from the certain expectation of future glory. And this certainty is
shewn by the circumstance of the time assigned when this
life of glory shall be given us; namely, *when Christ shall
appear.* We shall begin from the former reason.

For ye are dead] Namely, to sin, to the world, and to
the flesh; as the Apostle constantly testifies. *Reckon ye
yourselves to be dead indeed unto sin,* Rom. vi. 11. *The world
is crucified unto me, and I unto the world,* Gal. vi. 14; And
elsewhere, *They who are Christ's have crucified the flesh with
the affections and lusts.* Here let us consider two things :
How we are dead ; and, How much this consideration prevails to the slighting of earthly things.

As to the first; They that are born again are dead to sin,
not because sin is wholly eradicated and extirpated from
their mortal body ; for this would oppose every one's experience who perceives within himself the fuel of sin : but
because its dominion is broken, weakened, and debilitated ;
because its power is gradually subdued by the operation of
grace; because at length it shall be wholly overcome and
extinguished by the perfection of glory. Whoever, therefore, are born again in Christ are dead to sin, because all
their sins are abolished, in the sacrament of regeneration,
as to the guilt; because they are sealed to be entirely abolished, even as to the act, and begin to be abolished by
the Spirit operating within; finally, because believers are
bound to mortify them, on account of the vow of mortification undertaken at baptism. Therefore, as in common
language we say that he is *already a dead man,* against
whom sentence of death is passed ; so we rightly say, that
they who are born again *are dead,* or that sin *is already dead*
in them, because in their baptism the sentence of death
was as it were passed against sin ; the execution of which
sentence is forthwith begun, is daily proceeding, and at

length completed. It was not badly said by Parisiensis, De legib. cap. 28, *All sin is reckoned to be dead that hath not extinguished the life of grace; wherefore it is accounted dead, since it is not permitted to rule.* It would be easy to confirm this by many testimonies of the Scriptures. For they every where teach, that those who are born again in baptism not only die to sin sacramentally, but also receive the Spirit of Christ, by whose virtue and efficacy the lusts of the flesh are really mortified in them. Rom. vi. 6, *We know that our old man is crucified with Christ, that the body of sin might be destroyed.* They moreover teach, that we stipulated with God, to the perpetual study of mortification and a godly life: Thus speaks Peter, Epis. i. cap. iii. 21, where he calls baptism *the answer of a good conscience towards God.* We now understand what the Apostle meant with himself, when he says that the Colossians *are dead;* and in what sense Christians are said *to be dead to sin* by their baptism.

Now it remains that we examine, in the second place, the reason of this consequence, *Ye ought not to seek, or set your affections on earthly things, because ye are dead:* Which is most forcible on many accounts.

First, it prevails from the removal of the cause to the removal of the effect. For the effects of the dominion of sin are *to savour and to seek earthly things:* but in those who are dead to sin, sin has lost this lordly power: it cannot, therefore, compel them to unlawful lusts. The Apostle affirms this in express words, Rom. vi. 7, *He who is dead is free from sin:* and ver. 14, *Sin shall not have dominion over you.* This may be illustrated from the similitude of a tyrant who formerly flourished and domineered, but was afterward wounded, subdued, and cast into prison. For as he, whilst protected by his guards, held the citadel, ruled the miserable citizens, and compelled them to obey his commands; but after he had been stripped of his defence, forced from his citadel, overcome, and bound, was derided and despised by all, neither had any one who regarded his directions: so sin, whilst it lives in the unregenerate man, urges and impels him to all wickedness; but after its dominion is broken, it can do nothing except to those who voluntarily give up themselves to it again.

Secondly, when the Apostle reasons, *Ye are dead, there-fore ye ought to savour earthly things,* an argument is dedu-ced by a *simile.* For as bodily death severs men from all commerce with earthly things, so this spiritual mortifica-tion ought to estrange our minds from the study and de-sire of earthly things. Bodily death of necessity wrests men from all worldly concerns; spiritual mortification, by a certain divine operation, withdraws us from the love of these things : To be dead, then, means this, that they who have the Holy Spirit mortifying within them the lusts of the flesh, are able, by his assistance, to despise earthly things, and desire those that are, heavenly. Paul affords a remarkable specimen of this, who was so much removed from the desire of earthly glory, as to regard as dung what-ever is desirable and glorious in the eyes of the world.

Lastly, the Apostle's conclusion is supported by what is *honourable* and *due.* It is *honourable,* that they who have died sacramentally in baptism, should shew in their life that they are really mortified. It is *due,* that they who have vowed the mortification of the flesh in baptism, should exercise the duty of mortification by a contempt of earthly things. And thus ye see this consequence, *Seek not earthly things, because ye are dead,* is most firmly sustained by the force of many reasons. Now let us deduce some ob-servations or doctrines.

1. A Christian serving the lusts of sin, is a deserter and voluntary captive. For he is delivered from the service of sin, this tyrant being weakened and smitten with a deadly wound. See the miserable and shameful condition of these in 2 Pet. ii. 19, 20 : *Of whom a man is overcome, of the same is he brought in bondage. For if after they have es-caped the pollutions of the world through the knowledge of the Lord and Saviour Jesus Christ, they are again entangled there-in, and overcome, the latter end is worse with them than the be-ginning.*

2. There is no cause why a Christian should despond, because he perceives in himself the rebellious motion of sin, unless he obeys its lusts, and is himself drawn head-long into rebellion. For, notwithstanding these entice-ments of sin, he who neither yields the consent of the will,

nor the members of his body as instruments of iniquity thereto, is accounted *dead to sin.*

3. The Apostle requires that we should duly hold the mystery of our baptism, and transfer it to the use of piety and holiness. For he derives this most beautiful exhortation, *Seek not the things that are on earth, because ye are dead,* from the consideration of baptism, as it will appear to those who look back to the 12th verse of the foregoing Chapter. So in Rom. vi. 3, *Know ye not that as many of us as were baptized into Jesus Christ were baptized into his death?* as though he had said, It is shameful and unworthy of a Christian not to know this.

4. They grievously sin who suffer their baptism to be rooted from their memory, as a transient ceremony : for this sacred mystery, although once performed, should be perpetually revolved in mind, and expressed in conduct.

Let us proceed to the next clause.

And your life is hid with Christ in God.] It has been said that there is an implied occupation contained in these words, whereby he meets a twofold objection.

1. It is objected, That the Apostle contradicts himself : he had just now said that the Colossians were risen ; but those who are risen again are alive : now in almost the same breath he affirms that they are dead ; but the dead are not alive.

This difficulty is solved by distinguishing, They are dead to the world, to sin, and the flesh, as was before shewn ; but they live to God and Christ. The same Spirit who mortifies the carnal life within us, quickens us to a new and spiritual life. And this is that life which all those live by Christ who are dead to sin.

2. It might be said that Paul opposes common experience. For all the pious perceive themselves as yet infested by the remains of sin, oppressed by various sorrows, and at length fall under death : How, therefore, can it be true, that they are risen with Christ and follow a new life ?

The Apostle answers, that this new life is, in fact, only begun, and is imperfect and obscure in the faithful themselves : but in Christ their Head it is completed, perfected,

glorious; yet hidden. Therefore, Paul would anticipate
these objections in saying, *Your life is hid with Christ in
God.* Let us now examine the words themselves respectively.

Your life.] The word *life* is taken for that supernatural
life whereby we live *to* God under a state of grace, and
whereby we are to live *with* God in a state of glory : For
the life of grace is nothing else (so to speak) than the
childhood of glory. And both these are called *your life*
by way of eminence; in comparison of which a carnal and
bodily life is considered as death : for a carnal life leads to
death, and that eternal. Whence in the holy Scriptures
they are accounted dead who live after the flesh ; *Let the
dead bury their dead:* and 1 Tim. v. 6, *She that liveth in
pleasure is dead while she liveth.* Moreover, he who lives
the life of grace according as he is led by the Spirit, he day
by day ripens for eternity, Rom. viii. 13. And as the carnal life of sinners is death, if it be compared to the spiritual life of the faithful; so the natural life of man is death,
if it is compared to the supernatural life of the blessed. For
this whole bodily life passes away and vanishes any moment, nor has it any permanency; but that whole supernatural life stands in the perpetuity of its solidity, and hath
nothing transient. Therefore, the Apostle intending this
spiritual and supernatural life, rightly and emphatically
says, *Your life.*

Is hid.] This may be applied as well to the life of grace
as to the life of glory. The spiritual life of the saints is
hid, First, as to the wicked. For the world does not discover any thing spiritual in the children of God ; but accounts them the most despicable, foolish, and miserable
beings. So says the Apostle, Heb. xi. 36—38, *They had
trials of mockings and scourgings, being destitute, afflicted, tormented, of whom the world was not worthy.* Neither is it to
be wondered at, since this spiritual life consists in those
things which meet not the eye or sense; namely, in adoption, in regeneration, in union with Christ, in faith and
love, and the other gifts of the Holy Spirit. Hence that
tardy confession of the ungodly, Wisdom v. 3, &c. *These*

are they whom we had sometime in derision and a proverb of
reproach. We fools accounted their life madness, and their end
to be without honour. How are they numbered among the chil-
dren of God, and their lot is among *the saints!*

Secondly, as to the saints and faithful themselves, their
spiritual life is hid; but partly, not entirely. I say it is
in some measure hid, because they themselves do not
always clearly perceive the life of grace in them; but sometimes, being assaulted by the temptations of the devil and
the flesh, they are half in doubt that they themselves are
indeed slain, and destitute of the Spirit of God. Hence
that word of the Psalmist li. 10, *Create in me a clean heart,*
O God; and renew a right spirit within me. Moreover, when
they perceive in themselves this spiritual life, they nevertheless acknowledge it to be very weak, languid, and obscure on account of that perpetual resistance and rebellion
of the flesh. So Paul felt that he *delighted in the law of*
God after the inner man; Here we see his spiritual life! yet
the same Paul *sees another law in his members warring against*
the law of his mind; Here we see the same life hidden and
obscured! Rom. vii. 22, 23.

Now as to the life of future glory, that is much more
hidden: For although we have the seeds of this life within
us, yet they are trodden down under this mortal body, neither are they brought into full light before the day of
Christ's coming. In the meanwhile, as it is in 1 John iii.
2, *We are now the children of God, but it doth not yet appear*
what we shall be: nay, we are not indeed able to take in
even in imagination this hidden life, 1 Cor. ii. 9.

With Christ in God.] This also fitly accords both to the
spiritual life to which we are now raised, as well as to that
glorious life to which we are to be raised; for each is hidden in Christ, as in the fountain, the root, or original.
But these words *in God,* are added, because Christ himself,
as man, hath withdrawn himself from the earth, and ascended to God the Father. Therefore, God is invisible
and hidden from the world, and Christ with God, and our
life with Christ. As to spiritual life, it is certain that
whatever small streams are derived to us, the fountain itself

lies hid in Christ; nay, the streams of spiritual life are not
derived to us, except so far as we are joined to Christ, in
whom this life is laid up. *I live*, says the Apostle, *yet not
I, but Christ liveth in me,* Gal. ii. 20. Hence is that declaration John xv. 5, 6, *If a man abide not in Christ and Christ
in him, he is cast forth as a branch, and is withered.* But our
life of glory is also hid in Christ. For as the life of the
branches is not extinct in the season of winter, but is hidden in the root of the vine itself: so the blessed and glorious life of the faithful is hidden and reserved in Christ,
the spiritual vine, in this season of their earthly pilgrimage. Nay, and we also are said, in this sense, to be already put into possession of this celestial life, namely, as
we are already raised to heaven in Christ the Head, and
endued with eternal life and immortality. This is what the
Apostle would have us to understand in Ephes. ii. 6, *He
hath raised us up together with him, and made us sit together
in heavenly places in Christ Jesus.* In Christ, therefore, as
man, our celestial life is hid, as in the modelling cause :
for he shall *change our humble body, that it may be fashioned
like to his glorious body,* Phil. iii. 21.* It is also hidden as
in the material and meritorious cause : for he hath expiated
our sins by his death in the flesh, and merited for us this
life. *In the Son,* therefore, *is* that *eternal life* which God
hath bestowed on us, 1 John v. 11. It is hidden, lastly,
in the man Christ, as in the efficient, that is to say, the
secondary and instrumental cause. Moreover all supernatural life is hidden in God, as in the principal cause and

* Our translation of this fine passage is not very happy. Bishop Horsley gives the following; which is here copied for the sake of the impressive
remark subjoined to it, and its suitability to the tenor of our Expositor's
observations :—" *Who shall cause the fashion of our body of humiliation to be
made like unto his body of glory, according to the energy of his power of subduing
all things to himself.*—This transformation of the bodies of the faithful, by the
power of our Lord, requires a previous transformation of the mind to a resemblance of him, by faith in his word, by reliance on his atonement, by
conformity to his precepts, and imitation of his example. For he that hath
this hope in him, of being transformed into the likeness of his Lord, of
seeing him as he now is, and of standing for ever in his presence ; he that
hath this hope ' purifieth himself even as He is pure.' "

chief fountain. The Apostle unites each cause, both primary and instrumental, in Rom. vi. 23, *The gift of God is
eternal life, through Jesus Christ our Lord.*

In conclusion,

1. We are hence taught, as often as we perceive spiritual grace languish within us, to seek a fresh supply from
Christ, in whom is hid the fountain of spiritual life.

2. Hence it is seen how necessary it is to be united with
Christ by faith and the Spirit : for if we are separated
from him, we are not Christians, but the dead carcases of
Christians ; because in him is hidden all our life.

3. Here we have relief under our infirmity and imperfection; because, although all spiritual things in us are
weak and imperfect, as faith, love, and holiness ; yet,
through Christ, we have spiritual life perfected in all things.
This is the consideration whereby St. Paul sustained himself, Phil. iii. 8, 9, *I count all things but dung, that I may
win Christ; and be found in him, not having mine own righteousness,* &c.

4. Here we have most suitable consolation, and the
firmest anchor to our hope in all external miseries. For
our life is laid up in God ; but God will not deny the deposit : it is hid with Christ; but it is impossible that
Christ and life be separated ; it is no less impossible that
they should perish whose life is hid with Christ. Let us
conclude, therefore, that heavenly things are to be sought
by us, earthly things to be trodden under foot; because we
are both dead to these earthly things, and have a supernatural life as well of grace as of glory hidden with Christ
in God.

Vers. 4.   *When Christ who is our life shall appear, then
shall ye also appear with him in glory.*

The Apostle proceeds still further to shew that earthly
things are not to be sought or savoured by Christians, but
heavenly ones. He derives his argument from the expectation of the glory destined for us. We shall consider

first, the matter contained in these words in itself: secondly, we shall shew the force of the consequence; that
it may be understood how it tends to establish this conclusion, Earthly things are not to be affected by us.

In the former part three things are to be considered : the
Author of the gift; the time of the bestowal; the gift
itself.

1. The Author, or the Cause of the glorious and blessed
life which we expect, is Christ himself: Whence he is
called *our life* by a causal not an essential predication; because it was he that promised this life to us, it was he that
merited it for us, it was he prepared it, he that will bestow it. He promisd it, in the name of the Father, Luke
xii. 32, *Fear not, little flock; for it is your Father's good
pleasure to give you the kingdom;* and in his own name,
John x. 28, *I give unto them eternal life,* &c.   He merited
it, 1 John iv. 9, *God sent his only begotten Son into the world
that we might live through him;* and 1 John v. 11, *God hath
given to us eternal life, and this life is in his Son.*   And he
hath prepared us for this life, and this eternal life for us.
He hath prepared us, and made us meet for the participation of this life by his Spirit; *He hath made us meet to be
partakers of the inheritance of the saints in light,* Col. i. 12.
*He hath quickened us together with Christ : by grace ye are
saved,* Ephes. ii. 5.   He hath also prepared this kingdom
for us by his ascension; *I go to prepare a place for you :
And if I go and prepare a place for you, I will come again
and receive you to myself; that where I am, there ye may be
also,* John xiv. 23.   Finally, he will bestow upon his people this crown of eternal life ; *Thou hast given him power
over all flesh, that he should give eternal life to as many as thou
hast given him,* John xvii. 2.   *There is laid up for me a crown
of righteousness which the Lord shall give me,* 2 Tim. iv. 8.
Christ, then is rightly called *our life,* i. e. the author or the
cause of our eternal life : as it is in Heb. v. 9, *And being
made perfect, he became the author of eternal salvation to all
them that obey him.*

2. Now let us consider the circumstances of time :
When he shall appear, THEN we shall obtain a glorious life.

The revealing, or manifestation, or appearing of Christ, is propounded in a threefold manner in the Scriptures:

First, he is manifested bodily in the flesh, to the bodily eyes of men, in his nativity. Whence Simeon, Luke ii. 30, congratulates himself on the bodily sight of Christ: *Now lettest thou thy servant depart in peace, for mine eyes have seen thy salvation. God was manifest in the flesh*, 1 Tim. iii. 16.

Secondly, he is manifested spiritually in the preaching of the Gospel, to the spiritual eyes of believers. Of this manifestation Paul speaks in Gal. iii. 1, *Who hath bewitched you that ye should not obey the truth, before whose eyes Jesus Christ was evidently set forth.* And in John, 1 Epist. i. 2, *The life was made manifest*, &c.

Thirdly, he remains to be manifested to the whole world in the splendour of his glory, by his coming to judge the living and the dead. Of this final manifestation the Apostle is speaking : for unto this day the glorification of his saints is deferred, doubtless to be perfected then. *I know that my Redeemer liveth, and that he shall stand at the latter day upon the earth*, Job xix. 25. And 1 Cor. xv. 52, 53, *The trumpet shall sound, and the dead shall be raised incorruptible, and we shall be changed. For this corruptible must put on incorruption ; and this mortal immortality.* This, then, is that festal day of which the Apostle subjoins a clear and most delightful promise in these words following,

3. *Then shall ye also appear with him in glory*, or *glorious*] That is, Then shall ye each be made like to your glorious Head and Saviour Jesus Christ. The promised glory of this eternal life (if I may speak with the Schoolmen) consists in a twofold array ; in the robe of the soul, and the robe of the body. The robe of the soul consists, First, in the manifest vision of God, which succeeds to faith ; according to that declaration of the Apostle, *Now we see through a glass darkly ; but then face to face*, 1 Cor. xiii. 12. Secondly, in that perfect fruition, which succeeds to hope: *They shall neither hunger, nor thirst; since the Lamb who is in the midst of the throne shall feed them, and shall lead them unto living fountains of waters : and God shall*

wipe away all tears from their eyes, Rev. vii. 16. Thirdly, in
the perfect love of God, which succeeds to our imperfect
love, and shall perfect it for ever : *Prophecies shall fail,
tongues shall cease; but love never faileth*, 1 Cor. xiii. 8. But
indeed, what of glory and of happiness shall it not comprise ? To see, to love, to enjoy God ! we are not only not
able to express it, but we cannot comprehend it in our
mind : For truly says Gregory, Moral 27. 26, *When mortal
man would discourse about eternal glory, he disputes as one
blind about light.*

That glorious robe of the body consists in the various
endowments with which it shall then be adorned : In
brightness ; *The righteous shall shine forth as the sun*, Matt.
xiii. 43 : in exemption from suffering ; *this corruptible shall
put on incorruption*, 1 Cor. xv. 53 : in agility; which, according to Augustine, shall be such, that *wherever the spirit
flies, there shall the body also forthwith be.* Other things
were likewise added by some of the Schoolmen ; but it is
not my purpose with over nicety to define any thing about
these matters; that saying of the Apostle, in 1 Cor. xv.
43, 44, shall suffice, *It is sown in dishonour, it is raised in
glory ; it is sown in weakness, it is raised in power ; it is sown
a natural body, it is raised a spiritual body.* If any one desires to see more about the state of the blessed, let him
consult Prosper, De vit. contempl. lib. i. cap. 4 ; Parisiensis, De universo ; Albert, Compend. lib. vii. cap. 23, 24,
&c. Thomæ Summ. part. iii. qu. 82. art. 1, 2, &c.

And thus much concerning the gift of glory, the time of
the bestowment, and Christ the giver thereof. Now, in the
second place, we shall consider how wonderfully all these
things conduce to the contempt of earthly, and the desire
of heavenly things.

First, then, that state of glory promised to us and daily
expected, ought to move us to despise earthly things. For
if the heirs of an earthly king should disdain to be occupied in low and abject employments; how much more does
it behove those destined for a celestial kingdom, to tread
under foot the lusts of earthly things ? That saying of
Alexander is worthy of remembrance, who, when invited

to a contest of running with certain plebeians, said, that
it was not befitting the son of a king to enter the course
except with kings. It behoves us also to maintain this
royal temper, and to resolve that we cannot, in conformity
with the dignity of our condition, engage with worldly
minded men in the contest for earthly things ; but that we
ought so to frame our course with the sons of God and co-
heirs of heaven, as to seek and obtain heavenly things.
This is what Christ advised ; *Take no thought, saying, what
shall we eat, or what shall we drink, or wherewithal shall we
be clothed ? for after all these things do the Gentiles seek : but
seek ye first the kingdom of God and his righteousness,* Matt.
vi. 31. *A saint, while he seeks after eternity alone, holds beneath him every thing transitory,* says Gregory, Moral 1.
3. 14.

Secondly, if we seriously consider who is the bestower
of this glorious crown, that likewise will excite us to despise earthly things. Christ our life, as we before shewed,
promised it, he merited it, he will assign this crown of
glory: But to whom? to those who seek and delight in earthly things? By no means; but to those who *seek the things
that are above,* and *love his appearing,* 2 Tim. iv. 8. It is
proper to expect the reward from him for whom you have
fought : if for the world, the flesh, or the devil, expect no
other reward than death : if for Christ, then, and then
only, it will be lawful to hope for glory in the end : *He who
soweth to the flesh shall of the flesh reap corruption; but he
who soweth to the Spirit shall of the Spirit reap life everlasting,* Gal. vi. 8. Admirably spake Bernard : *There is no road
to the kingdom, without the first-fruits of the kingdom; nor can
that man hope for the kingdom of heaven, who has not yet obtained the dominion over his own lusts.* So 1 John iii. 2, 3,
When Christ shall appear, we shall be like him : And *whosoever
hath this hope in him purifieth himself even as he is pure.* But
Christ was as pure from the lusts of earthly things as could
possibly be : for he would not yield the least inclination of
his body to the devil, to obtain thereby *all the kingdoms of
this world and the glory of them,* Matt. iv. Thus we ought
to be animated, if we expect life eternal from Christ our
life.

Thirdly, the circumstances of the time in which we expect this glorious life is a most powerful inducement to withdraw our minds from the love of earthly things. For when shall this crown of glory be given? *When he shall appear,* i. e. on the day of the coming of the Lord. Now this day, if we believe the Scriptures, will come both quickly and suddenly.

Quickly ; *Yet a little while, and he that shall come, will come, and will not tarry,* Heb. x. 37. And Rev. xxii. 12, *Behold I come quickly, and my reward is with me.* It ought not, then, to seem troublesome or burdensome to regulate the short period of our time, and to abstain from earthly things, when Christ is at hand, and promises us eternal glory. *The hireling, because he ponders heavily his drudgery, thinks lightly of the reward,* says Gregory, Moral, 8. 8. *Be patient, therefore, and stablish your hearts, for the coming of the Lord draweth nigh,* Jas. v. 8.

That day shall likewise come suddenly : *As the light shineth from heaven, so shall the Son of Man be in his day,* Luke xvii. 24. *The day of the Lord will come as a thief,* 2 Pet. iii. 10. Now then who does not see how dangerous it is to be involved in earthly things and desires, and so to be taken unawares ? Christ foresees this our danger, and forewarns us to avoid it ; *Be ye like unto men that wait for their Lord when he will return from the wedding,* &c. Luke xii. 36. *Behold I come as a thief.* Blessed is he that watcheth, and keepeth his garments, lest he walk naked, and they see his shame,* Rev. xvi. 15. What, then, will become of us, if we are taken unawares immersed in all these earthly things ? Hear Gregory ; *He who would not go with the stream, let him avoid the torrent ; lest by that which allures him, he be carried to that which he avoids : for he is drawn to the same point to which he inclines,* Moral 22. 2.

And thus it has been briefly shewn, that whether we consider the gift itself of eternal glory, or the giver, or the time of giving, all and every one of these considerations ought to withdraw us from the love of earthly things, and excite us constantly to seek and to meditate on heavenly things. It now remains that from the whole we deduce some corollaries, as well for instruction as for correction, and then finally for our consolation.

Instructions arising from this verse.

1. God will have Christ his Son to be the fountain and the bestower of this glorious life to all his faithful members: it is, therefore, not to be hoped for or supplicated from any others.

2. This Christ, being exalted to heaven, is removed from our sight: he is therefore to be apprehended by the eye of faith: and this ought to be the perpetual exercise of the pious, to soar towards heaven, to contemplate Christ glorified, and to render the assurance of that future glory certain to themselves.

3. The happiness of Christians is not placed in the things of the present life, but the whole depends upon the expectation of future things. *The resurrection of the dead is the confidence of Christians,* says Tertullian. Therefore there is need of special faith.

Consolations.

1. Not we ourselves, but Christ is the keeper of the eternal life promised to us: Therefore, although we are compelled to tremble, as often as we consider our frail condition in ourselves; yet, as often as we meditate on the most firm and faithful care of Christ, we send forth that triumphant voice of faith, *I know that there is a crown laid up for me.*

2. This glory in reserve for the pious is able to assuage all temporal calamities. Cyprian, writing against Demetrian, admirably treats this matter; he says, *He, whose entire joy and glory is in the world, suffers from worldly adversity: he, to whom there can be no well-being after the world, mourns under worldly misfortune.* But the faithful bravely endure the ills and misfortunes of the world, whilst they look forward to future good and happiness. Vide Habbac. iii. 17, 18.

3. Nothing that is of any moment and worth can be snatched from the pious man. Against our good things (as they are called) of fortune, even against this frail life,

the ungodly may prevail : but against the good things
promised, and our eternal life nothing can prevail.

Reproofs.

1. They are to be blamed, who, either never think, or
think not with joy of Christ and the coming of Christ.
For who can excuse their torpor who do not ardently desire
the life of his life, who do not wait for that natal day of
this new life with gladness ?

2. And they also are deservedly to be blamed who seek
the glory of this world : for what else is this than to wish
to violate this Divine decree ? He has decreed that the
glory of Christians is to be expected on the second coming of Christ. In the meanwhile, it behoves us to bear the
injuries and miseries of time, to dream not here of glory
and happiness, unless hereafter to hear with Dives, *Remember that thou in thy lifetime receivedst thy good things, and
likewise Lazarus evil things, but now he is comforted and thou
art tormented,* Luke xvi. 25.

3. They are to be derided, or rather to be pitied as the
madmen of this world, who think themselves happy because they enjoy the pleasures, the honours, the wealth of
this world ; and think the pious, on the contrary, to be
most abject and miserable, because they, for the most part,
are destitute. But those are not truly happy, for whom
eternal misery remains, nor those miserable, whom eternal
glory awaits. Well said Lactantius, Instit. 6. 22, *As we
arrive at true good through fallacious evils, so we come to real
evil through fallacious good.* And thus we dismiss the first
member of the general exhortation.

Verse 5.

Mortify therefore your members which are upon the earth; fornication, uncleanness, inordinate affection, evil concupiscence, and covetousness which is idolatry.

Having gone through that former part of the exhortation which teaches us what is to be sought without us, and what to be avoided; the Apostle proceeds, and teaches what is to be extirpated and abolished within us, what is to be nourished and cherished. That former part directed us to seek the true end, viz. celestial blessedness; this directs us to enter upon the path which leads thereto, namely, true holiness. Now of this exhortation, which calls us to the life of holiness, there are two parts. In the former, he excites the Colossians to lay aside or to put off vicious actions and affections; in the latter, to put on and exercise good ones. And the Apostle, in this and the following verse, persuades us to mortify, first, carnal vices, which immediately respect our peculiar, but unlawful pleasures; secondly, in the verses which follow, spiritual vices, which tend immediately to the injury of our neighbour. But let us come to this fifth verse.

The Apostle here does two things: First, he proposes a general exhortation to the study of mortification; Secondly, a particular enumeration of certain vicious deeds and affections which he would have to be mortified.

Mortify therefore your members which are upon the earth.] In these words you have the general exhortation to the practice of mortification. We may observe in them,

First, the connexion or dependence of the words; for the illative particle *therefore*, compels us to look to what goes before. They are thus then connected with the foregoing words: Because *ye are risen with Christ*, because *ye are dead with Christ*, because *ye have a glorious life hid in Christ*, THEREFORE *mortify your members*, &c. Hence we infer that our participation with Christ in dying, rising again, and ascending, is the strongest inducement to newness of life and holiness.

Secondly. Let us consider the act itself to which we

are invited, expressed in this word, *mortify,* i. e. make the
body of the old Adam as a dead carcase ; that, although
it may retain certain members and lineaments, yet they are
inefficacious, being destitute of life and motion; i. e. *Let
not sin reign in your mortal body, that ye should obey it in
the lusts thereof;* Rom. vi. 12. This our mortification, therefore, is nothing else than the study and the practice of repressing our corrupt nature, and restraining all unlawful
actions and affections which are wont to spring from thence.
But in this study these three things are involved : a serious
determination of resisting sin ; an avoiding of the occasions
which are wont to induce us to sin; a careful use of all
means which tend to the subduing of sin. A good determination averts the heart itself from the ways of sin; a diligent avoiding of it causes us not to return to it; the use
of means, that we should be constant in our determination,
and proceed happily.

But since the Apostle exhorts us to mortify our members, it may here be asked, 1st. Is mortification a human
work, or of the human will ?   The Apostle seems clearly
to assert it in this place: but the whole Scripture proclaims
our mortification and vivification to be the effects of the
Divine power alone, produced by the Holy Spirit regenerating and inspiring new life into men.   *Which are born not
of blood, nor of the will of man, but of God,* John i. 13.
*We are his workmanship created in Christ Jesus unto good
works,* Ephes. ii. 10. Rightly said Gerson, part. 3, *God
not only quickens the dead in sins, but stirs up the affections of
the soul to a desire for this quickening.* And Augustine, *The
freedom of the will does not prevail in those things which pertain to God, but only in the works respecting the present life,*
Contra Pelag. hypognost. lib. 3.

We shall easily solve this difficulty, if we will consider
what sort of persons those were of whom the Apostle is
here speaking. For he is speaking not of the profane and
the dead in sins ; but of Christians, i. e. those whom he
presumes to be regenerate : and he commands *them* to *mortify their members,* &c. Therefore, for the sake of perspicuity, we must admit the existence of a twofold mortification : First, that which we may call *habitual* or *internal,*

and this is the work of the Divine Spirit alone, infusing it
where he will: but this mortification he effects whilst he
infuses himself into the human soul together with the gifts
of his grace, by the efficacy of which the power and dominion of sin is mortified and overthrown. Secondly, that
which we call *external* or *practical;* and this is the work of
the renewed man himself, whilst by the aid of the Spirit,
he brings forth the fruits of that internal mortification, that
is, whilst he resists the temptations of sin, whilst he restrains inordinate affections, whilst he diligently takes care
lest he fall into unlawful deeds ; for he who does this is
said to mortify his flesh. Therefore, the act of mortification attributed to us is nothing else than the 'ενέργεια, or
operation springing from infused grace, even that which
we have called the *internal* or *habitual* mortification effected
by the Holy Spirit.

2. It is again asked, How this Apostolic exhortation
agrees with the preceding ? He had said, ver. 3, that they
were dead, now he adds, *Mortify your members :* but what
necessity is there that any one dead should be still ordered
to mortify himself ?

The solution depends upon what was before said. First,
then, we answer, that the Colossians were dead *sacramentally* by having received baptism; but are bidden to mortify their members *actually,* viz. in the conversation of life :
now these things are accordant, not contradictory. Secondly, we say that they were moreover dead by *habitual*
mortification, viz. through the effect of internal mortification infused into their hearts by the Holy Spirit: and they
ought to mortify themselves by a *practical* mortification,
exercising infused grace in opposing their lusts. Thirdly,
we also add, that the cause of natural death and spiritual mortification are different. He who has undergone
natural death is vainly commanded any more to mortify
himself daily ; because natural death is pure privation, and
admits not in the subject of it any thing contrary : but
spiritual mortification is not pure privation ; for whilst we
carry this mortal body, every thing inducing to the contrary is to be relinquished, because it must be perpetually

resisted and mortified more and more : Well spake Origen,
in Epist. ad Romanos : *The mortification of sin is not effected
in a moment, but is the work of an unceasing struggle. Sin
languishes from the commencement of our mortification, it wastes
away in the progress, at last (i. e. in our death) it shall be
abolished.* Lastly, it is not unseasonably answered, that
the dead are commanded still to mortify themselves, because if they neglect the constant practice of mortification, vices that were trodden under and subdued recover
their strength ; corruption that was broken off sprouts
anew ; and the grace of the Holy Spirit being stifled, the
man returns to his former course. This is illustrated by
Chrysostom in an elegant similitude : *As a man who has
cleansed and polished a statue which had been covered and corroded with dust and filth, may truly say that it is cleaned, and
yet properly direct it to be wiped every day, because such direction refers to that soiling which will adhere afresh to the statue
if it be neglected : so the Apostle truly said that the Colossians
were dead to sin, yet wisely admonishes them to mortify daily
the works of the flesh ; because this admonition refers to those
impure desires which will grow up afresh, and prevail, unless
repressed by constant and diligent labour.* Thus much respecting the act of mortification, to which ye see that
those who are already dead to sin are not excited in vain.

3. *Your members which are upon the earth.*] He passes
from the act to the object about which this practical mortification ought to be exercised. Let us, therefore, in the
third place, consider this object ; and since every word
here used by the Apostle hath great meaning in itself, we
shall examine each singly.

Members.] As to this first word we must point out two
things : First, what the Apostle intended by *members ;* Secondly, what is the reason of this epithet. He calls, then,
all vicious and inordinate dispositions, desires, motions,
and acts of corrupt nature, *members :* for all these are to
be mortified by us, i. e. opposed, subdued, repressed. The
primary members of this our corrupt nature are three : the
darkness and vanity of the intellect ; the depravity and
obliquity of the will ; the rebellion of the inferior appe-

tites and their proneness to sin. To these are allied innumerable inferior members, and which, as it were, depend upon them, some of these are soon after subjoined in this place, and more occur in Galat. v. 19—21, where, the name being changed, they are called *works of the flesh.*

Now let us see why they are termed *members.* It is usual to adduce three causes for this title.

First, because the old Adam, or the mass of corrupt nature dwelling in us, is compared to a body, Rom. vi. 6, or to a *man,* in the same place; therefore it was just and proper, this same metaphor being retained, to call the parts of this corruption *members.* Every one of us possesses three men, or three bodies : the natural and visible body, the members of which are also known and visible; the body of sin, or of the old Adam, the members of which are those vicious dispositions, desires, and actions which we just now glanced at : and the body of the new man, which is renewed after the image of God ; the members of which are faith, love, holiness, and other gifts of the Holy Spirit.

2. The vicious affections and acts proceeding from this old Adam are perhaps called *members,* because they cleave to and exert themselves in each of the members and parts of this natural body. Therefore, by that figure of speech which they call *metonymy of the subject,* the term *members* is transferred to signify the vicious affections and acts which are in and from the bodily members.

3. They are called *members* from the proportion, or similar use which they have, if compared with the members of the natural body. For as we use the members of this natural body to fulfil the desires and perform the operations of nature ; so the old man uses those vicious affections as instruments, for fulfilling the desires and performing the works of sin.

Ye perceive why they are called *members :* now let us look why *your* and *earthly* is added.

Your.] These members are called ours, because that whole body of sin is also properly ours. This natural body which we bear, is ours now as to its use ; but we received it from God as to its creation: Job x. 10, 11, *Hast thou not poured me out as milk, and curdled me like cheese? Thou hast clothed me with skin and flesh, and hast fenced me with sinews.* But this body of sin, and every one of its members are in every respect ours: for *God made man upright:* man has rendered himself depraved and corrupt.

Earthly.] So he calls vicious desires, because they always tend to earthly things; because they hold the minds of men to earthly things; because corrupt habits and affections dwell only among earthly things, but are excluded from heavenly ones: Rev. xxi. 27, *There shall in no wise enter into it any thing that is defiled;* and xxii. 15, *Without are dogs,* &c. This general exhortation to mortify our earthly members being now explained, we deduce some corollaries.

Mortify therefore your members which are upon the earth,

1. He is not risen with Christ who does not labour to mortify the flesh: for from the virtue of the death and resurrection of Christ communicated to us, there always follows a desire of mortification and holiness: Therefore, as many as delight in the flesh, are not mortified, but are dead in sin.

2. A true desire of external mortification cannot exert itself in men corrupt by sin, unless they have within them the effective principle of internal mortification, the grace, I mean, of the Spirit of regeneration. Therefore, the external exercises which are sometimes wrought by the wicked, and bear the resemblance of mortification, are not the genuine effects of internal mortification, but false appearances.

From the act commanded; *Mortify ye,* we infer,

3. That the regenerate themselves never attain such perfect mortification in this life, but that they must always strive to mortify themselves more and more.

4. If they relax in this desire, that which happened to holy David may happen to every one, that he be carried away by the impetuosity of his lusts, and, for a time, may be a wretched slave to sin, over which he had before triumphed gloriously.

From the object; *members,*

5. This body of sin is as natural to every one of us, as is the very body of our flesh; nor does it consist of fewer members than that other.

6. As whilst we live here we necessarily carry about this natural body, nor are able to put it off; so neither can we entirely lay aside this body of sin, which cleaves to us, although we can and ought to chasten and subdue it. There is, therefore, a perpetual, laborious, and dangerous warfare to the Christian: perpetual, because with an enemy not to be extirpated in this life ; laborious, because with a manifold enemy; dangerous, because with an internal enemy.

7. Original sin is not to be placed in a mere privation or withdrawal of original righteousness, as certain of the Schoolmen dream ; but, furthermore, in many depraved and corrupted dispositions, habits, and affections. Parisiensis hath learnedly proved this opinion in lib. De vitiis et peccatis, cap. 5 and 6. Thomas, 1. 2. qu. 82. art. 1, assents to this, whose words I shall annex : *We must assert, that as bodily sickness partly consists in privation, as far as the equality of health is taken away; and partly in positive infliction, the humours themselves being disordered : so also original sin consists in the privation of original righteousness ; and, together with this, in the disorder of the faculties of the soul : wherefore, it is not a mere privation, but a certain corrupt habit.* Thus speaks Thomas. Neither is it probable that these words which are used by the Apostle, *the old Adam, the body of sin, earthly members,* intend nothing else than mere privation.

From the epithets, *your,* and *earthly,*

8. Original sin hath its origin, neither from God our Creator, nor from the principles of our pure and upright nature, but from the voluntary sin of our first parents. Hence our members are called parts of it, i. e. of the old Adam, propagated to us, and dwelling in us.

9. If there be any thing good in us, that ought to be referred to God alone; for *What hast thou which thou hast not received?* If we would arrogate any thing to ourselves

which we might claim as peculiar to us, and our own, it is sin and corruption, not merit and righteousness.

10. The mind of sensual man lies wholly sunk in earthly things, neither is he able to raise himself heavenward before grace be infused : for the members of our soul, i. e. the inclinations and affections, are *of the earth*, earthly, or affixed to the earth *naturally ;* and, indeed, are not raised towards heaven except by *grace* exciting them.

11. We must withstand all these earthly desires, because they are members of the old Adam, to obey whom is nothing else than to rush to destruction.—Thus much concerning the general exhortation.

Fornication, uncleanness, inordinate affection, evil concupiscence, and covetousness which is idolatry.] The Apostle by a general exhortation had persuaded to a mortification of the earthly members of the old Adam : Now, that we may be certain what those members are, he adds a particular specification of certain of them, from the enumeration of which he would have all the others also, which are of the same nature and origin, to be understood, i. e. what are the effects of the old man. He begins, as you perceive, with carnal vices : to these he couples covetousness, which he then marks with a black brand, by comparing it to idolatry. As to the vices of carnal luxury, he seems to me to condemn, 1. The external actions ; for to these I refer *fornication* and *uncleanness :* 2. The internal motions and affections, which that word παθος (rendered, *inordinate affection*) denotes: 3. The very root or fountain of external and internal lust, which he calls *evil concupiscence.* Let us run over these, each in its order.

Fornication.] Augustine, Exposit. Epist. ad Gal. tom. 4, defines fornication *indiscriminate concubinage, unrestrained by lawful wedlock, and sought only for the gratification of lust.* It is wont to be restricted to those who have commerce with prostitutes, or at least with concubines : for if they violate married females or virgins, the one is deemed *adultery,* the other *ravishment.* So familiar was this vice among the Heathen, as to be accounted by most among the lawful pleasures. That saying of the comedian is well known,

It is not a crime (believe me) to corrupt a boy. And lest any one should say this was spoken in the person of Mitio, he will find the same, according to Horace, to have been the opinion of the rigid Cato; who, when he observed a youth entering a brothel, said, *Hither it is right that young men should descend;* as though that were an argument of probity and honesty. This opinion had taken deep root in the minds of almost all the Heathen, that fornication was either lawful, or at least to be tolerated. This error, therefore, the Apostle in the first place meets, and asserts that fornication should be utterly repelled by Christians ; for if this be proved, it easily follows, that other kinds of pleasure which incur heavier guilt are much more to be avoided.

As to this vice; 1. We shall shew from the Holy Scriptures how pernicious it is : 2. We shall overturn those excuses which are usually brought by the patrons of lust. It will be manifest that this is indeed a heavy sin, if it be weighed in the standard of the sanctuary.

1. Because it is always reckoned up, not among lawful pleasures, but among the most loathsome and detestable impurities. The Apostle, in Rom. i. 29, writes, that those who are delivered to a reprobate mind *are filled with all unrighteousness, fornication, wickedness,* &c. And in Ephes. v. 3, *Fornication and all uncleanness let it not be named among you,* &c.

2. Because they are judged to be excluded from the intercourse of faithful Christians who follow fornication : but no one is to be cast out of the Church for light errors. We have this broad sentence of Paul against fornication, 1 Cor. v. 9, 11, *I wrote unto you not to company with fornicators: if any man that is called a brother be a fornicator, &c. with such an one no not to eat.*

3. Because for this crime men are excluded from the kingdom of heaven, and are subjected to the Divine wrath and indignation. 1 Cor. vi. 9, *Neither fornicators, nor idolaters, nor adulterers, nor effeminate,* &c. *shall inherit the kingdom of God.* And in Heb. xiii. 4, *Whoremongers and adulterers God shall judge.*

It is very easy to add many other reasons to these, which may also demonstrate the weight of this crime.

4. Because it more especially pollutes the body than other vices : but our bodies are *members of Christ and temples of the Holy Ghost*, 1 Cor. vi. 15, &c. It is, therefore, no light crime to make the members of Christ members of harlots, or to make the temple of the Holy Spirit an abode of lust.

5. Because it peculiarly blinds the mind and understanding. The wise Solomon, being blinded by this vice, proceeded to idolatries ; *Women turned away his heart*, 1 Kings xi. 3. Neither, indeed, did this escape the philosopher. Eth. vii. 10, 'Ουχ αμα φρονιμον και ακρατη ενδεχεται ειναι τον αυτον; *Wisdom and incontinence in the same man are incompatible.* Gregory the Great, in Moral 33, says, that *blindness of the mind is the eldest daughter of luxury.*

6. Because not only does it constitute the fornicator himself guilty of eternal death, but those miserable beings also with whom he sins. This greatly augments the aggravation of this sin : for it is not so in other crimes. If a man steals the goods of a woman, if he bears false testimony against her, if, finally, he should kill her, he does her an injury ; but he does not involve her in damnable guilt, because he does not make her a partaker of his sin : but the fornicators defile them with their sins ; so that, although they themselves repent, yet they are of necessity tormented in mind, because as much as is in them they have precipitated other souls into hell by the contagion of their crime. Thus much as to the enormity of this sin.

Now let us hear, secondly, what is wont to be alleged by those who deny that simple fornication (for I would use their own words) is a mortal sin : and also by those who, when they have admitted that it is a mortal sin, yet contend that brothels and prostitutes must be retained. The former was not only an error of the heathen, but (if we believe Albertus*) of certain Christians : for he writes that the Greeks openly defended this, and that it was refuted

* Vide Vol. i. p. 148.

by the Latins in the Council of Lyons, Part. 2. tract 18,
quæst. 122. Alfonsus de Castro* relates the same from
Guido, lib. 7. tit. *Fornicatio.* The other is the error of the
Papists, who stiffly maintain that brothels are not to be removed from cities: which is inferred as well from their
writings, as from their practice (for they are not attempted
to be done away).

1. They who deny that fornication is a mortal sin, thus
argue from Acts xv. 20. The things there enumerated
seem to be placed on one footing ; but fornication is there
enumerated with certain indifferent things : *They should
abstain from pollutions of idols, and from fornication, and
from things strangled, and from blood.*

I answer, that fornication is not always reckoned in the
Scripture with things in their nature indifferent, but sometimes with things simply evil, as we have shewn. And the
reason why, in this place, it is enumerated with certain
things indifferent, is not, because they are of the same
nature, or of equal guilt; but because all these things
equally prevailed to disturb the Church, and to excite dissention between the Gentile converts, and the Jews who
were yet weak.

2. They object, that which is mortal sin, and morally
evil in itself, is understood to be so by the light of nature ;
but the Heathen, who were averse to the more flagitious
crimes, as adultery, rape, and incest, thought that fornication should be imputed to no one as a vice; viz. because
nature did not point it out as a sin.

I answer, first, we must not decide *concerning things according to the opinion of the ungodly,* as we must not *about
the taste of things according to the estimation of the sick,* as
Aquinas has well remarked. Therefore, although a corrupt
and blinded mind does not judge fornication to be sin, yet

* Alphonsus (Peter) a Spanish Jew of the twelfth Century, who became a convert to Christianity, and wrote, first, a " Dialogue between a
Jew and a Christian ;" and afterwards, a Treatise on " Science and Philosophy :" he was eminent for his knowledge of sacred and profane literature.

it is by no means on that account not to be regarded as a sin : for, by the confession of the Orator, Cic. De legib. 1, *so corrupting is the habit of evil that by it the small sparks issued from nature are extinguished, and contrary vices spring up.* But neither do we admit, that fornication was not condemned by the wiser Heathens. Alcmena in Plautus says, *With a woman whom thou judgest to be immodest thou wilt not converse, either in jest or in earnest, unless thou be the most foolish of all men.* Tacitus also observes, *There is nothing pure in a mind corrupted by lust.*

3. It is objected, Sin cannot come by a Divine command; but God commanded Hosea the prophet, *Go take unto thee a wife of whoredoms, and make to thyself children of whoredoms,* &c. Cap. i. 11. It is not a sin, therefore, to commit fornication.

I answer, the word *fac, make,* which is added in the Vulgate version, is neither in the Hebrew, nor the Greek; but the prophet is commanded to take to himself for a wife that harlot, and bring home to his house even the children which were born to her in fornication. Whether this were a true fact, or was proposed in a figure only, to express the spiritual fornication of the Jews whom God had espoused to himself; it in no way helps those patrons of fornication. If we assert with Origen, Jerome, the Chaldæ paraphrast, Tremellius, and many others, that this was done in vision only, then it is altogether irrelevant to the point. If we admit with Irenæus, Basil, Augustine, Cyril, and others, that it was done in reality; yet it argues nothing in defence of fornication: for the prophet was not commanded to commit fornication, but to take to himself a wife formerly addicted to fornication. Hence says Augustine, versus Faustus, lib. 22, cap. 80, *What is there, I ask, inimical to the Christian faith, if a harlot, abandoning her fornication, becomes a chaste wife ?* But that which follows in the Vulgate version, *and make to thyself children of fornication,* is not repugnant to this opinion, which supposes the prophet to have married this prostitute : for either those were called children of fornication whom she had had before, as appears from the original context; or, if it be referred to those whom she was to conceive by the prophet, they also were called children of fornication; because following the example of their mother they would most likely become fornicators. Lastly, whichever of these be the fact, it may be answered, That God can specially command a thing which may be forbidden by the ordinary law: thus he commanded Abraham to slay his innocent son, and the Jews to carry away the goods of the Egyptians: Therefore, by the intervention of a special and extraordinary command, the obligation of an ordinary one ceases; because the condition of the case is changed.

4. They object, Fornication is not contrary to charity; therefore it is not a sin. For thus these points are argued by Augustine, Tom. 9, De decem chord. cap. 10, *When I go to a harlot, to whom do I do what I am unwilling to suffer? How do I violate that maxim, What you would not have done to you, you should not do to another? If I lust after my neighbour's wife, I am unwilling that any one should lust after mine. If I covet my neighbour's goods, I am unwilling that he should take away mine: I do therefore what I am unwilling to suffer. But when I go to an harlot, to whom do I do what I am unwilling to suffer?*

I reply, it is repugnant to charity even in the highest degree. 1. Inasmuch as it is repugnant to the good of the offspring that may be born, whose instruction and education is neglected, seeing that it is the conception of promiscuous concubinage. 2. Inasmuch as it is repugnant to the good of the woman who is corrupted, and to the good of the fornicator himself; whilst the body and mind in each is polluted, and a deadly guilt is incurred. 3. Inasmuch as it is repugnant to the Divine love; whilst the image of God is destroyed by this foul lust, and the command of God is violated. Neither does it help them to affirm that that rule, *What you wish not to be done to you, you should not do to another,* is not violated by fornication. For what a man would wish to be done to by others is not to be regarded simply: but what he would wish in a regulated and sound will. If a man should wish his own daughter to be defloured, it will not, therefore, be lawful for him to deflour the daughter of another; because this is the wish of an evil and inordinate will.

Let us now come to the Papists, who concede that fornication is a mortal sin; but maintain, nevertheless, that brothels and public harlots should be allowed in cities, lest the inclination of lustful men should transgress against married females. *In human governments,* says Aquinas, Q. 2. qu. 10. art. 11, *they who preside, justly tolerate some evils, lest they should incur worse;* and he instances lewd women. This was the very plea of the heathen; for thus says Cato, *Young men ought to have recourse to harlots, lest they should approach the wives of others.* But Augustine also is called in to their aid, and that expression, *Take away harlots from human society, and you will disturb all things by lust,* is cited from his lib. 2. De ordin. cap. 4.

I answer,

1. The Papists favour fornication too clearly, when for the sake of avoiding adultery, they tolerate fornication, and to avoid fornication do not allow marriage. I speak of the Clergy and Monks, to whom the extraordinary gift of continence is not granted by God. For why do they tolerate fornication among the laity, which they say is a mortal sin, and not allow marriage among the clergy, which the Holy Spirit, Heb. xiii. 4, has pronounced to be *honourable in all;* unless that (whatever they contend to the contrary,) they do not cordially and sincerely determine it to be a deadly sin? Hence that observation, Dist. 82, in Gloss : *They declare that no one is now to be rejected for fornication, because our bodies are more frail than they were formerly.* And Caus. 2. qu. 7, in Gloss, *No one is at this day to be rejected for simple fornication.* It is clear, therefore, that the Papists are the manifest Patrons of fornication : nor is it to be wondered at if they so willingly abstain from wedlock.*

---

* In the Decretals of Gratian, which were upheld in credit by the Papacy, it is actually laid down on the alleged authority of a Council at Toledo, *Qui non habet uxorem, loco illius* CONCUBINAM DEBET HABERE. Dist. 39. Edit. Paris, 1512.

2. What they affirm, that brothels are to be tolerated lest married women should be violated, is contrary to the Divine command, Deut. xxiii. 17, *There shall be no whore of the daughters of Israel,* &c. It is contrary to Apostolic doctrine; which would have matrimony, not fornication, to be the remedy for lust. It is contrary to the received opinion of Theologians, who deny that a compensation of sins is to be admitted : Harlots, therefore, are not to be prostituted lest married women should be violated. Lastly, it is contrary to the duty of the Christian magistrate ; who is bound, as much as in him lies, to take care that all may live piously, soberly, and righteously : Rom. xiii. He ought not, therefore, to suffer those who openly profess whoredom.

3. With respect to the remark of Augustine, *Take away harlots from human society and you will disturb all things by lust;* we answer, it is not of much weight: because he wrote those books *De ordine,* when he was a young man, and not then baptized, as is evident from the first of his Retractations.* We also oppose to it the more serious of the Fathers. Lactantius, Instit. lib. 6, cap. 23, says, *The devil set up brothels, and published the shame of unhappy women.* Clemens, Pædag. 3. cap. 3, *Brothels are trophies of public intemperance.* Tertullian, de cultu fæminar. calls harlots *the most unhappy victims of public lusts.* But now how disgraceful to the Christian magistrate, if he defend the inventions of the devil, if he suffer that victims be publicly immolated to lust, if, in short, he do not demolish the trophies of intemperance. Besides, I say, that however diligently the magistrate may endeavour to repress fornication, yet he can never wholly remove from human society harlots or fornicators, no more than he can remove thieves or murderers. Therefore the Papists may dismiss this fear.

---

* The use of Augustine's opinion in this matter, at a time when he was no Christian, is quite in papistical keeping, as to the mode of sheltering themselves under authority, or wresting the sentiments of the Fathers to their purpose. Of this many of their modern writers furnish eminent examples, as recent controversial works amply exhibit.

Lastly we must also add; that this remedy (the toleration of brothels*) is worse than even the disease which is dreaded. For although adultery be in itself worse than fornication; yet it is worse for a whole city to be continually polluted by brothels, than if it should sometimes happen that certain wedded women be violated. But even this is by no means to be conceded; that the honour and chastity of married women can be better preserved by the permission of fornication than by the severe punishment of it. For by impunity, and the continued habit of sinning we become more daring; and if we have served an apprenticeship to lust among harlots, becoming anon veterans, we the more confidently assault wedded females. This point acquires support from the fact, that we scarcely ever have either read or heard of married women having been defiled by any other than by those who were before accustomed to practices with harlots : so admirably does the toleration of brothels conduce to the protection of the chastity of married women !—And these remarks may suffice against those who either deny that fornication is to be accounted a sin, or say that it is to be tolerated for the sake of avoiding adultery. We have dwelt the longer in opposing fornication, because it has obtained its patrons. The other vices which remain we shall remark upon more briefly.

In the second place, then, ακαθαρσια, or *uncleanness*, follows : By which term the Apostle would comprehend all the more filthy kinds of lust, as adultery, incest, rape, and especially those sins of excess which even nature herself abhors. Therefore, they who not only wallow in one kind of lust, but in different kinds, and those the most foul, are called *the unclean*. This *uncleanness* prevailed among almost all the Gentiles ; which you may easily gather from their poets, who often blame, although they sometimes approve these impurities, Rom. i. 27. Tertullian, in his book, *De*

---

* The horrid fact may not be generally known among Protestants that Public Stews, or houses of prostitution, are to this day officially licensed in Papal States, and that his Holiness derives a large portion of his revenue therefrom. Papal Rome is literally " the Mother of harlots !"

6

Pudicitia, speaks of this uncleanness : *Those impious furies of lusts,* says he, *contrary to nature itself, we remove not only from the threshold, but from the whole house of the Church ; for they are not sins merely but portentous vermin.** Therefore, because the unrestrained appetite of the lustful is wont to proceed sometimes from fornication to this uncleanness ; so, after fornication, the Apostle declares that all other uncleanness is also to be mortified.

Observe, 1. There is no sin so foul, so foreign from humanity itself, into which the inbred corruption of our nature may not impel a man not yet mortified.

2. Lesser sins pave and fence a path, as it were, to greater; this *uncleanness* always follows in the train of fornication : Hence says the Apostle, Ephes. v. 3, *But fornication and all uncleanness.*

3. To avoid greater sins, it is most safe not to tolerate the lesser, but as much as in us lies to root them out. If you resist vice at its birth there will be no growth to worse ; but if in this you indulge ever so little, the iniquity increases.† Thus far we have contended against the external acts of lust.

Πάθος.] Some translate this *effeminacy,* others *lust.*‡ The Apostle teaches that after all the external acts of lust have been repressed, the internal motion itself, and the unbridled passion must be restrained. Πάθος, then denotes that disposition of the mind whereby any one is fitted and ready for the sin of lust, when any occasion is offered ; and because this vice arises from the effeminacy of a mind unwilling to sustain the attack even of the least temptation, therefore some not improperly render Πάθος *effeminacy.* For they are justly deemed effeminate whose minds do not resist the temptations of the flesh ; but willingly and immediately yield themselves to the bonds of lust, even as Samson yielded himself up to be bound by Dalilah.

---

* Alluding probably to the abundance of particular insects as an indication of impending judgments ; as in the case of the plagues of Egypt.

† See Bishop Hopkins's most instructive and impressive Sermon on " *The great evil and danger of Little Sins.*"

‡ In our version it is translated *inordinate affection.*

The Apostle teaches that such a disposition of mind is
to be mortified and abandoned by a Christian man ; nor
may any Christian whatever refuse to do it ;

1. Because it is Heathenish to serve his own lusts ; it
is Christian to serve God and holiness.   Whence says the
Apostle, 1 Thess. iv. 3, &c. *This is the will of God, even
your sanctification, that every one should know how to possess
his vessel in sanctification and honour, not in the lust of concupiscence, as the Gentiles which know not God.*

2. Not only is it Heathenish, but it is brutish, to labour under this disease. For it is the property of brutes
to be actuated and governed by their passions ; it is the
part of a man to restrain them, and to reduce them within
the sphere of reason. He, therefore, who is drawn aside
by every appearance of pleasure presented to his mind or
his sight, becomes *like to a horse or a mule, which hath no
understanding.* Ps. xxxii. 9.

3. All holy and praiseworthy men have been accustomed to banish afar off this effeminacy of mind. The example of Joseph recorded in Genesis xxxix. stands pre-eminent, whom his mistress daily solicited with her entice-
ments to lust, yet could not prevail. If he had laboured
under this effeminacy, he would also have yielded immediately to gratify lust. But as Tertullian wisely says in his
Apologet. *A pious and chaste man beholds a woman with safe
eyes, because his mind is blind to lust.* Unless their minds
are firmly set against the allurements of sin, and strengthened by Divine grace, men become the wildest slaves of lust,
and resist not even its slightest temptations, but are led
away as captives to every vice.

Evil concupiscence.] Now the Apostle endeavours to cut
up the very root of wickedness. For *fornication and uncleanness,* as hath been said, denote evil acts ; Παθος, or *effeminacy,* that lustful and intemperate habit of mind,
whereby men are so prepared, that straightway they seize
every occasion of exercising lust, nor can restrain themselves ; such as the Greeks call κυπρομανεῖς—(Venus-mad).
But now *evil concupiscence* denotes the first motion of *inordinate desire ;* which is called *evil* to distinguish it from

natural and spiritual concupiscence. For there is a three-fold concupiscence: Natural; which comprehends the desiring power planted in the mind by God himself, and governing the ordinary motion of the same: vicious or carnal; which denotes the inordinateness and rebellious motion of this power: spiritual; which denotes a new and holy inclination of a reformed mind, of which concupiscence the Apostle speaks, Gal. v. 17, *The Spirit lusteth* or *desireth against the flesh.* Natural concupiscence, when it is carried to its due object and in a due manner, is to be gratified: spiritual, which tends to heavenly things, is to be nourished and cherished: carnal, which is likewise called evil, because it thirsts inordinately and after inordinate things, is to be mortified. Hence we may derive two lessons ;

1. A Christian man ought to aim even at that perfection which he understands he cannot attain in this life. For no sinner hath ever been able to mortify and restrain all the first motions of inordinate concupiscence; yet all are bound to attempt it: for that Divine mandate stands immoveable, *Thou shalt not covet.* Concerning which, Augustine,* Epist. 200, ad Asellicum, truly said, *The law, in declaring thou shalt not covet, has laid down not the power which we have in this particular, but the object at which we should advance progressively.*

2. Those first motions of inordinate desires are sins, though the mind does not assent to them. Bellarmin, therefore, is wrong, who concludes, in De stat. pecc. 5. 7, that that rebellious motion of concupiscence has the nature, not of *guilt*, but of *punishment.* Why does the Apostle call it *evil?* Why does he say it is *to be mortified?* He is not wont to speak thus about punishments; which he teaches us are to be borne patiently, not to be mortified or resisted. Let the Jesuit hear Paul, who in Rom. vii. not once, but often, terms inordinate concupiscence *sin*, even in the regenerate who consent to the law, and oppose these motions. Let him also hear Augustine, lib. 5, contra

* After he became a Christian ; see p. 45, Note.

Julian, cap. 3, *The lust of the flesh, against which the good
Spirit lusteth, is sin, because we yield obedience contrary to the
sway of reason.* Lastly, let him hear his own Schoolmen :
Parisiensis says, *We ought to follow with the sword the petty
thieves of first, second, and third motions, that is, the thoughts,
desires, and delights which are beyond the control of reason,* De
sacram. pœnit. cap. 15. *The whole host of the flesh which
wars against the Spirit is sinful : therefore also all the battal-
lions of that army : wherefore both the first battallion, which is
that of the first motions ; and the second, which is the delights
beyond the control of reason, are sinful.* De sacram. matr.
cap. 7. We have also Aquinas in concurrence with us,
who is compelled to confess that the first motions in unbelievers are sins : whence it is manifest that they have the
nature of sin, even in the faithful, although they have not
the guilt, forasmuch as it is remitted in baptism. Lastly,
we have Gerson also, Part. 2. in Reg. Moral. 6, *All the
first motions which are suited to follow reason, and to be regulated by it, if they precede it may be called sins ; because they
deviate from the order of nature as it was first constituted.*
Now let us proceed to those points which remain.

And covetousness which is idolatry.] Let us inquire,
1. What the Apostle would understand under the name *covetousness* or πλεονεξίας. 2. Why it is coupled with these
carnal vices. 3. In what sense it is termed *idolatry.*

1. It is the insatiable appetite of the mind seeking
riches, and confiding in them as in its chief good. That
this insatiable thirst is the property of covetousness is
shewn in Eccles. v. 10, *He that loveth silver shall not be satisfied with silver ; nor he that loveth abundance with increase.*
Now that the rich are wont to confide in their riches, and
to rest in them as their chief good, we see in the parable
of the rich man, which is contained in Luke xii. 19, *I will
say unto my soul, Soul, thou hast much goods laid up for many
years, eat, drink, and be merry.* The vice of *covetousness*
πλεονεξίας is not the simple desire or seeking for temporal
goods ; but the doing it with an insatiable desire, by unlawful modes, and with a heart acquiescing and confiding
in them. For temporal goods may be coveted in three

methods; for the necessity of life; for discharging the duties of benevolence; for enjoyment, or making them the end. This last is that vice of πλεονεξιας, to be avoided and mortified.

2. It may be enquired, Why he annexes *covetousness* to these carnal vices; for it seems rather to be reckoned among those that are spiritual. But the Apostle wisely inserts covetousness among them; and that on these accounts:

1. Because it is of a middle kind, between carnal and spiritual sins. Those vices are properly designated carnal, which have a sensible delight in a sensible object; as we see in the sins of gluttony and luxury: Those are as properly designated spiritual, which seek spiritual delight amid spiritual objects; as pride about personal excellence. Now covetousness occupies a middle place: it is carnal in respect of the object, because it seeks delight in external and corporeal things; it is spiritual in respect of the delight itself; because a covetous man hath delight only in this, that he possesses riches.

2. Because it affords incentives, causes, and occasions to both, namely, to carnal and spiritual vices. Hence spring the greatest incentives and excitements to luxury, to pride, to anger, and envy. Take away covetousness, and you will eradicate the greatest part of vices; for *it is the root of all evil,* 1 Tim. vi. 10.

3. Now, in the last place, we must see in what way it is called *idolatry.* Let Aquinas answer, *Not in kind; because a covetous man does not intend in regard to his money to account it as a God; but in similitude; because he pays to it supreme obedience.* So Ales; *A covetous man is called an idolater, because as an idolater behaves to an idol, so in a similar manner does a covetous man to his money.* Chrysostom, in Hom. 65, in xi. Joan, expatiates thus on this comparison, *As an idolater looks to, and regards with veneration, his idol: so a covetous man the riches he has heaped together: nor dares to touch them. As the one heaps together his idols in a certain corner, and shuts them up in closets and with bolts; so the other does to his money. In short, the former worships the*

idol; the latter, the gold ; this immolates oxen and sheep to his idols ; that gives up his mind and affections to covetousness. Such and many more like remarks hath Chrysostom. But it may still more perspicuously be said, That a covetous man is an idolater, because he loves his riches above all things ; because he trusts in them more than all things ; because he serves his riches more than he does God himself.

1. Because he loves them above all things : for as Clemens has rightly observed, Pædag. Q. 12, *Heaven is open, and he seeks not God; gold is hidden, and he ransacks the bowels of the earth for it.* Whence does this arise, unless because he had rather enjoy riches than God ? Therefore, he commits spiritual idolatry with the riches of the world, *not,* as Gregory somewhere observes, *by the exhibition of ceremonies, but by the oblation of concupiscence.* For to whatever the affections of the heart cling as the chief good, that is taken into the place of God.

2. Because also he places that trust in riches which is due to God alone. For, in his heart he says *to gold* (what Job, xxxi. 24, loathes) *thou art my hope; and to the fine gold thou art my confidence.* Now that in which we hope, we make our God. Therefore, the voice of all the godly is, *In the Lord have I hoped; I have made God my helper.* But the covetous man has money alone as the sponsor or surety 'εγ∫υητην of his felicity.

3. Because he altogether neglects the service due to God, and gives his whole service to the scraping together of money. *Ye cannot serve God and Mammon,* Matt. vi. 24. And, therefore, as the god of the gluttonous is their belly, because their belly is perpetually served ; so the god of avaricious men is money, because they serve money day and night.

Corollaries.

1. Nothing is more miserable or more foolish than a covetous man ; because he forsakes God, and confides in clay. But *their silver and their gold shall not be able to deliver them in the day of the Lord's wrath,* Zeph. i. 18. Therefore we ought to trust, *not in uncertain riches, but in the liv-*

ing God, who giveth us richly all things to enjoy, 1 Tim.
vi. 17.

2. Nothing also is more base and flagitious than a covetous man; because as much as in him lies, he thrusts
God from the throne of his Majesty, and sets up money in
his place.

3. This vice is to be avoided before all others : because
(to use the language of the Schools) it is most *adhesive to
the creature,* and most *aversive from God;* but all the disgrace and defilement of sin consists in turning to the creature and departing from God.

4. Scarcely any one is wholly free from this idolatry ;
for we all cleave unduly to the creature, and thus incur
some stain of idolatry. But we must withdraw the mind
from them, and return to the love and service of God.

And thus much concerning the dissuasion itself from the
vices above-named. The confirmation thereof follows in
the two succeeding verses.

Verses 6, 7.

*For which things' sake the wrath of God cometh on the chil-
dren of disobedience :
In the which ye also walked some time, when ye lived in
them.*

The Apostle confirms the afore-mentioned dissuasive by
two arguments. The first is drawn from the destructive
consequence ; for those sins enumerated provoke the Divine wrath; ver. 6. The second is derived from the removal of the cause ; for in the regenerate inbred sin formerly
lived : now it is dead, ver. 7. In the former argument
three things are to be noted : 1. The cause of the event ;
For which things' sake. 2. The event itself, viz. the outpouring of the Divine wrath ; *the wrath of God cometh.* 3.

The quality of the persons subjected to this Divine wrath : *the children of disobedience,* ’επι τους υιους της απειθείας.

1. *For which things’ sake*] namely, for *fornication, uncleanness, inordinate affection, evil concupiscence, and covetousness,* the wrath of God falleth upon sinners. These words are not to be taken in such sense, that we should conclude it is peculiar to these sins alone to excite the Divine wrath (for this meets all sins) ; but because upon those gross flagitious crimes, which especially overthrow human happiness, God is especially provoked to exercise vengeance. And on this account, the chief argument is : These sins are the occasion of heavier punishments ; therefore, from them we must abstain with all care, for *it is a fearful thing to fall into the hands of the living God,* Heb. x. 31. The Apostle wished to point out distinctly the cause of human misery, and of the Divine judgments, for two reasons,

1. That God might be cleared from all suspicion of cruelty or injustice, and might be acknowledged by all most merciful and just. For God is *the Father of mercies,* and not willing to overwhelm the human race with such calamities : but as the Poet formerly sang :

At heaven itself we aim through folly ;
And such our crimes e’en God we suffer not,
To lay aside his vengeful bolts.

Hor. lib. 1. od. 3.

Therefore our wickednesses provoke the Divine wrath against us.

2. To throw a restraint upon the wicked : For, as saith Cyprian, *it affords great power to the wicked when he can deliberately rush forward with impunity.* On the other hand, It hath great power in restraining sin, when he understands it to be the sure cause of future misery. This the Apostle intimates in these words, *For which things’ sake the wrath of God cometh,* &c.

The wrath of God.] We pass from the cause to the effect. The Fathers with almost unanimous consent explain *the wrath of God* to be the Divine punishment or vengeance. For it is not fit to assign troubled affections to God ; since, as Augustine hath truly said, in Evang. Joan,

*The anger of God is not the perturbation of an excited mind,
but the tranquil constitution of righteous judgment.* And in
Enchirid ad Laurent. cap. 33, *When God is said to be angry,
perturbation is not signified, like what is in the mind of an
angry man; but his vengeance takes the name of anger from
human motions.* Ambrose in Psalm xxxvii. *God does not lie
open to passion, so that he should be angry; since he is without passions; but because he avenges he seems to be angry.
This seems so to us, because we are accustomed to avenge ourselves with commotion.* The Schoolmen speak the same, but
more compendiously : Anger is attributed to God, not according to *the passion of inquietude,* but according. to *the
effect of vengeance.* From this common opinion of theologians, Tertullian in 1 contra Marcion, and Lactantius in
lib. De ira Dei, cap. 5, and 16, seem to differ : whose
opinion is either to be softened down by a suitable interpretation, or rejected.

We may therefore assume, that by *the wrath of God* vengeance is to be understood, or the punishment imposed
upon sinners ; and it will be easy to shew that this wrath
of God is joined and connected with sin, and especially
the sins of luxury. In Gen. vi. 11, we read, *The earth was
corrupt and filled with violence.* Here is the sin ! But directly it follows, ver. 17, *I will bring a flood of waters upon
the earth and destroy all flesh.* Behold the wrath or vengeance ! So in Gen. xviii. 20, *The cry of Sodom and Gomorrha is great, and their sin is very grievous.* Here you
have the sin. Gen. xix. 24, *Then the Lord rained upon Sodom and Gomorrah brimstone and fire.* Here you have the
vengeance. It would be tedious to go through all the examples of sacred Scripture. Let that in Job xxxi. 3, suffice : *Is not destruction to the wicked, and a strange punishment to the workers of iniquity ?* as though he had said, It
is certain, and placed beyond doubt, that God is estranged
from sinners, and provoked to destroy them.

*Seldom hath punishment, though halting in its pace, failed
to overtake the wicked striving to keep head of it.** Nay, it

---

* Horace, lib. iii. od. 2.

never fails, unless the sinner repent, and forsake his wickedness.

2. If we now inquire, Why the wrath of God is poured upon sinners, the reasons are at hand.

The first is derived from the Divine justice. For although God is not pleased with the sins of men, yet he is pleased with his own righteousness, according to which, punishment is due to sinners. Therefore, it is not evil in God to punish the wicked, because it proceeds from the love of righteousness; but the evil is in man, to deserve punishment; because it proceeds from the love of wickedness.

The second is derived from human advantage. For this is the particular end of punishments, that they may effect the amendment of sinners. *Whatever the Divinity may avenge before the last judgment, is not for the destruction of men, but is to be believed as intended for their recovery,* Augustine, contra epist. Man. cap. 1. Nor is it any objection to this argument that unbelievers are not so much admonished by these punishments to conversion, as blinded to condemnation, because this does not prevent them from sowing the seeds of a good harvest among the godly; for, as Cyprian, De zelo, remarks, *the punishments of the imprudent convey health to the prudent.*

The third is derived from the settled Providence of God : For God is the author of order throughout the universe, nor suffers any disorder to exist. But yet sin by its very nature is nothing else than mere disorder. As Aquinas has truly observed, Quæst. disp. De pecc. orig. art. 8, *Every sin is restored to order by means of punishment, in that it reduces its inequality to a certain quality.* And again, Quæst. disp. De pecc. venial, art. 10, *For it is just and determined that he who wishes to seek the pleasure of sin against the Divine will, shall be compelled to experience the bitterness of punishment against his own will.* John Gerson has spoken well concerning this matter, Part. 3, *Whatever thing deviates from one Divine constitution is driven into another ; so that which deviates from the constitution of mercy, rests in that of justice: where no less in conformity with this constitution are*

the condemned fixed in hell than the blessed in heaven.—So far
concerning the cause of the Divine wrath, and the outpouring of the same.

Upon the children of disobedience.] The quality of the
persons subjected to this Divine wrath, is described in
these words. In the Greek it is 'επὶ τοῦς υἱοὺς τῆς ἀπειθείας.
Some translate these words, *upon the children of distrust,* or
incredulity; others, *upon the intractable,* or *disobedient children.* All these come to the same point; and denote men
of that kind who can by no means be persuaded to believe
the Divine word, and renounce their sins. In this term
'ἀπειθείας, therefore, two crimes are involved; one of *unbelief,* the other of *disobedience;* this latter is the genuine
offspring of the former. Such were those who lived before
the flood in the days of Noah; whom Peter, 1 Epis. iii.
20, calls *the incredulous;** who, as Christ says, did in security, *eat, drink, marry, and knew not until the flood came
and took them all away,* Matt. xxiv. 38, 39. Such were the
people of Sodom and Gomorrha, who would not believe at
the preaching of Lot, but, as though he spake in mockery,
slighted him, Gen. xix. 14. Finally, such are all the reprobate, to whom that saying of the prophet Zechariah
vii. 11, well applies, *But they refused to hearken, and pulled
away the shoulder, and stopped their ears, that they should not
hear.* It is plain, therefore, that the reprobate and blinded
are described in this place : For although the elect may be
disobedient for a time, yet they are not *the children of disobedience upon whom the wrath of God cometh;* because,
being softened by the effectual operation of Divine grace,
they at length yield; as we may perceive in all the examples of the godly who have fallen.

But here it may be doubted, what the Apostle meant,
when he said, *for these sins,* viz. *fornication, uncleanness,* &c.
the wrath of God cometh upon the children of disobedience.
Does it not also come upon the children of God ? Who is
ignorant that David felt the arrows of Divine wrath for

---

* *Incredulous* in the Vulgate ; *disobedient* in our version, more consistently with the original.

his adultery with the wife of Uriah? and that other saints have been grievously punished for other crimes of theirs?

I answer, It is not to be denied that even the children of God, when they give the reins to the flesh, and yield themselves to sin of this sort, feel the wrath of God falling upon them : but it does not lie perpetually upon them ; because they do not continue in these sins. Yet we must distinguish concerning the wrath of God : for God sends his wrath upon his fallen children, but paternally and for chastisement; and upon disobedient children as an enemy and to cut them off. Therefore, in these latter words the Apostle preferred to hold forth examples of the Divine wrath, that thus he might, indirectly as it were, instil the fear thereof into the pious. But we must add this also : When believers rush into sins of this kind against conscience, although that bond of the eternal good-will of God which depends upon election is not loosened; yet the love of friendship is loosened for a time, or at least the perception and enjoyment of it, which depend upon faith and sanctification. Therefore, whilst they are asleep in such sins, God acts towards them as with enemies; they are not able to apprehend God otherwise than angry and hostile towards them : they cannot, therefore, approach the throne of grace with confidence, but, like Adam, they flee from God, and throw themselves into hiding-places. There is need, therefore, of stirring up their faith and love; there is need of serious repentance, to avert the wrath of God, and obtain the favour and the smile of his countenance : For that declaration of St. Paul is true, Rom. ii. 9, &c. *Tribulation and anguish upon every soul of man that doeth evil: but glory, honour, and peace to every man that worketh good. For there is no respect of persons with God.*

From these things we may draw the following instructions.

1. Under public calamities and miseries, we must not murmur against God ; but impute whatever evils we suffer to our sins.

2. As often as we are solicited to sin, we should oppose to its allurements the consideration of the Divine wrath, which closely follows sinners.

3. Nothing is more to be desired by a Christian, than
that he may retain the Divine favour; nothing is more to
be dreaded than that he should provoke the wrath of
God.
4. God is not so much provoked to vengeance by sin
itself, as by the obstinacy of the unbelieving and impenitent sinner.
5. However the children of unbelief flatter themselves,
they cannot avoid the Divine wrath ; for *wrath* now *cometh
upon them,* and *in coming it will come, and not tarry.*
6. Not only will the Divine wrath be poured forth upon
the wicked, but upon the children of God themselves, if,
quenching the grace of the Spirit, they indulge the lusts
of the flesh. Therefore, the study of mortification is incumbent upon all who dread the wrath of God as they
ought.

Vers. 7. *In the which ye also walked some time, when ye
lived in them.*

The Apostle is still occupied in confirming the foregoing
dissuasive ; and he shews the Colossians by a new argument that they must abstain from fornication, and so from
all impurity of life. Now this argument is drawn from the
removal of the cause to the removal of the effect ; and the
argument of the Apostle is thus applied : Sin is but the
living and reigning cause of a wicked and lustful life : but
sin is not living in you, but mortified : the cause, therefore, having ceased, the effect ceases. The Major is supposed : the Minor is shewn, in this verse, by a contrast of
their former state. There had been a time, indeed, when
ye lived in those sins, namely, before your conversion ;
but now it is passed, and ye do not live in them, but ye
are dead to sin by baptism. It is usual among authors,
when they say concerning any one, *That he has lived,* to intimate, He is dead, or he no longer lives : So the Apostle,

in saying *when ye lived in them, ye then walked in sins,* would intimate, Ye now live no longer in them ; therefore, ye ought not to walk any longer in them. Thus ye have the force of the argument. Now let us consider the words.

In the which.] Erasmus renders it, *among whom,* and refers it to *the children of disobedience :* but Beza better, *in which,* viz. the aforesaid vices, *for which the wrath of God cometh on the children of disobedience.*

Ye also walked.] They are said to *walk in sins,* who constantly commit sin, who resist not concupiscence, but obey it with pleasure; Ephes. ii. 2, 3. Therefore, as men are accustomed to walk here and there in transacting their daily business ; so are those occupied in sins as in their ordinary vocation, and as though they had nothing else to do.

When ye lived in them.] i. e. When the cause of those sins, viz. the old Adam, or inbred corruption, lived and reigned in you ; which corruption is now weakened and mortified. *To walk* and *to live,* then, whether the expressions are referred to the flesh or to the spirit, differ in the same manner as *power* and *operation* among philosophers : For life precedes, and operations suitable to life follow ; as in Gal. v. 25, *If we live in the Spirit, let us walk in the Spirit :* so they who live in sin, walk in sin.

The sense of the words being now explained, two things which belong to the matter, are to be weighed : 1. The former state of the Colossians living in sin ; which is expressed. 2. The new state of the same persons now dead to sin ; which is implied by the contrast.

From the consideration of their former state, these instructions arise.

1. Nothing is more unhappy than unrenewed men. For to walk in sin with pleasure, is to hasten towards hell with pleasure : *The wages of sin is death,* Rom. vi. 23.

2. The fruits of a man in a corrupt state, are not works *preparatory to grace,* or, *deserving life eternal, of congruity,* as the Schoolmen say ; but they are *preparatory to hell,* and *meritorious of eternal death, from condignity :* for he walks

in most gross and grievous sins, not in the paths of God's commands.

3. They who *appear* to walk in virtue, dazzle the eyes of men by outward and pretended shew only ; whilst they really walk in sins, in which they live : for their deeds correspond to the powers whence they derive their origin.

4. The Papists, therefore, err, who ascribe to these works of carnal and unbelieving men, not only the praise of true virtue, but the efficacy of qualifying for the reception of grace; Durandus, lib. 4. dist. 15. qu. 3. Prosper speaks otherwise; *No true virtues dwell in the minds of the ungodly :* and Lactantius, lib. 6. cap. 9, *There is no doubt but every ungodly man knows not God : and that all his virtues which he thinks that he has or holds, are found in that way of death which is full of darkness.*

Now as to that new state of the converted and regenerate, among whom the Gospel intimates that the Colossians were now placed, these things are to be observed,

1. It is not unuseful for the renewed themselves, to call to mind their former state under sin : the Apostle mentions that they formerly walked and lived in sin, who were now dead to sin ; not for the sake of upbraiding, but of encouraging them.

2. Christians that are now believers, ought not to take it amiss, when ministers bring before their eyes what they were under a state of sin in unbelief : for this is the Apostle's custom in almost all his Epistles. *Ye have yielded your members servants to iniquity unto iniquity,* &c. Rom. vi. 19. *Neither thieves, nor covetous, nor drunkards,* &c. *shall inherit the kingdom of God : And such were some of you : but ye are washed,* &c. 1 Cor. vi. 10, 11. But most manifestly, Ephes. ii. 11—13, *Remember that ye being in time past Gentiles in the flesh, were without Christ, being aliens from the commonwealth of Israel, having no hope. But now in Christ Jesus,* &c. Tertullian, De Pudicit. hath well observed to this point : *I am not ashamed of the error from which I am now free ; because I feel that I am become better.* No one need be ashamed to improve.

3. The regenerate receive a twofold advantage from a

notice of this kind. 1. They are thereby excited to gratitude : for they must needs acknowledge that they are
changed not by the power of free-will, but by the efficacious operation of the Holy Spirit. Hence the prophet;
Turn thou us, O Lord, and we shall be turned. And Jerem.
xiii. 23, *If the Ethiopian can change his skin, or the leopard
his spots ; then may ye also do good, who are accustomed to do
evil.* Hence, then, as I have said, the regenerate are excited to thankfulness to God. *God be thanked that ye were
the servants of sin, but ye have obeyed from the heart that form
of doctrine which was delivered you.* Rom. vi. 17. And
Paul speaking of himself says, 1 Tim. i. 12, 13, *I thank
my Lord, who hath enabled me, who was before a blasphemer
and persecutor,* &c. Why does he, a true penitent and believer, thank God ? Because not only is the mercy of
God necessary when we repent ; but also that we may
repent.

2. They are excited to newness of life ; for a new life
requires new habits. Since, then, from the comparison
and contrast, they find that they are now other persons
than what they were heretofore, they understand at the
same time, that of necessity it behoves them to live in
another manner. For the Christian Religion not only calls
men to believe new doctrines, but to perform new works.
Whence says Cyprian, De Zelo, *To put on the name of
Christ, and not to walk by the way of Christ, what else is it
but to prevaricate with this Divine name?* This is constantly
inculcated upon the regenerate ; as in Rom. xiii. 12, *The
night is far spent ; the day is at hand: let us therefore cast off
the works of darkness, and let us put on the armour of light :*
and Ephes. v. 8, *Ye were sometime darkness ; but now are ye
light in the Lord : walk as children of light.*

4. Here we have the difference between the regenerate
and the unregenerate : The regenerate may fall into sin,
but they do not habitually walk, neither can they live, in
sin : for those walk in sin, who freely, constantly, and
with full consent sin : he falls into sin, who rarely, through
fear, and with wrestling is drawn aside into any crime or
devouring sin, as Tertullian calls it. Therefore, they are

much deceived in their opinion, who think that they are
faithful and regenerate, when that cannot be said concerning them which is here said of the Colossians, *In the which
ye also walked some time, when ye lived in them;* but, Ye still
walk in them, and live in them.

And thus much of the two reasons whereby he confirms
his dissuasive from the sins enumerated in the fifth verse.

Vers. 8, 9, 10, 11.

But now ye also put off all these; anger, wrath, malice,
   blasphemy, filthy communication out of your mouth.
Lie not one to another, seeing that ye have put off the old
   man with his deeds;
And have put on the new man, which is renewed in know-
   ledge after the image of him that created him:
Where there is neither Greek nor Jew, circumcision nor un-
   circumcision, Barbarian, Scythian, bond nor free; but
   Christ is all and in all.

After a dissuasion from carnal vices in which special
pleasure is sought, the Apostle dissuades also from spiritual ones, in which the injury of one's neighbour is attempted. In this last part of his dissuasions the Apostle
does three things, which he includes in these four verses.
1. He lays down and enumerates the vices to be abandoned; which are those either of the heart; as *anger, wrath,
malice;* or those of the mouth; as *evil speaking, filthy communication, lying.* 2. He subjoins a reason why vices of
this kind should be abandoned by the Colossians, and that
a twofold one: namely, because *they had put off the old
man, and put on the new.* 3. He amplifies and strengthens
these reasons in verse 11 by setting aside those false causes
with which some men conceived that we are either benefitted or injured before God; these he rejects as things of

uo avail, in order to shew that human salvation entirely
depends on the Spirit of Christ mortifying and quickening
us ; and that therefore we must aim at mortification before
all other things.

As to what pertains to this eighth verse now under consideration, in it he effects two things. 1. After his dissuasion from carnal vices which render men infamous among
all the sober and prudent, he dissuades also from all spiritual ones, which are deemed lighter faults, which are not
accounted as vices among the generality. 2. He enumerates some expressly, that from these it may be understood
that others of the same kind are to be condemned and
abandoned.

1. *But now ye also put off all these.*] In this general
persuasion we must first observe the circumstance of time
denoted by the particle *now.* As if he had said, Ye were
overwhelmed with spiritual vices as long as sin lived in
you ; but now, since it is mortified and hath ceased to
live, ye ought and ye can put these things away : For God
requires from Christians in a state of grace, another life
and other manners than those to which they were heretofore accustomed in a state of sin. So the Apostle in many
places declares. Thus Rom. xiii. 12, *The night is far spent ;
the day is at hand: let us therefore cast off,* &c. And 1
Thess. v. 5, 6, *Ye are the children of the day, and not of the
night: let us not sleep as do others,* &c. Augustine, De vita
Christiana, wisely remarks, *Let us not flatter ourselves with
the name of Christians : but let us believe that this is the very
reason we shall be judged, if we falsely claim to ourselves a
name which doth not belong to us.* Cyprian also says, *We
are Philosophers not in word, but in deed; neither do we talk
great things but we live them.* Now, therefore, we especially must lay aside those vices, because we are Christians
born again.

2. Secondly, We should well weigh that act to which
the Colossians are exhorted by the word ἀπόθεσθε ; which
may be explained either to *put off,* as men put off their old
and dirty clothes, or to *lay aside,* from the sight, from the
affections, and from all the senses, as the corpses of the

dead shut up in sepulchres. And this last best agrees with the preceding word, *mortify:* as if he had said, Not only mortify your sins; but as though they were dead remove them from you, and put them away, and separate them from you altogether as dead bodies.

Now the instructions to be gathered are these :

1. Sin cleaves to the regenerate themselves, nor can it be entirely eradicated : yet we must still labour to put it off more and more every day.

2. We must not account sin a pleasure ; but a thing to be hated by a Christian as deadly poison, or to be avoided as a putrid carcase. Now what it is to put away sin, by what power it is done, and how far it can be done by us in this life, we have explained in the exposition of the fifth verse, at these words, *Mortify therefore your members which are on the earth:* What is there said of the act of *mortifying,* may be applied to this act of *putting off*.

3. Thirdly, we should consider that this object of putting off is of wide signification; as wide as the nature of sin itself: not this or that sin, but *all* sins are to be put off. For because some are enumerated just after, it is not by way of restriction to them, but by way of exemplification : for both those which are specially named, and all others besides (it is intimated) should be put off.

3. We are all prone by our nature and ready to run headlong into all sins. For original and inbred sin, although it is only one actually, yet is it virtually a whole army of vices ; not unlike a seed, which is actually single, but virtually all those which are produced from it. Their corporeal constitution, and other external causes, make some men more inclined to certain vices; but there is no actual sin into which a man may not fall, in whom the nursery and fountain of all sin exists. We must, therefore, be on our guard against and avoid them all. So much of the general persuasion. Now let us come to the specification of the particular sins, in that order in which they are adduced ; and first to those of the heart.

Anger, wrath, malice.] Anger in this place signifies an inordinate desire unjustly to injure one's neighbour for

some past offence. It is briefly defined by Damascenus,
lib. 2, cap. 16, ὄρεξις τῆς ἀντιτιμωρήσεως, *the appetite for revenge.* And in this unjust and vindictive desire of revenge
(as the Schoolmen say) the *formal* of anger is contained.
Θυμὸς, or *wrath,* denotes the hasty excitement of this passion, and that accession of blood around the heart, which
the Schoolmen call the *material* of anger.   Whence the
same Damascenus says, in the passage before quoted;
Θυμός ἐστι ζέσις τοῦ περὶ καρδίαν "αἵματος ἐξ ἀναθυμιάσεως τῆς χολῆς
γινομένη.   *Wrath is the boiling up of the blood around the
heart, which arises from the kindling of resentment.*   Κακία or
malice, as some will have it, is a general vice, and denotes
that vicious propensity which infects all the affections and
desires, and inclines them to evil.   Whence Bernard, in
his Serm. 1, De pugn. spir. says, malice is *the taste for evil:*
it is, then, the property of malice to make evil savoury
and sweet; and, on the contrary, to render good insipid
and unpleasant.   But in this place I consider κακία to denote especially that machination of evil in the heart, which
is wont to arise from anger in malevolent and incensed
minds.   We see all these in the example of Cain, Gen. iv.
5, Cain was very wroth and his countenance fell: thence
he contrives the murder of Abel, when he says, *Let us go
out:* This was the effect of his *malice.*   From the same
disease of *malice* proceeded those words of Esau, Gen.
xxvii. 41, *The days of mourning for my father are at hand,
then will I slay my brother Jacob.*

You will now see what and what kind of sins are here
reproved by the Apostle.   It follows that we should, in the
second place, offer some reasons for which these sins of
an angry mind are to be opposed and extirpated.   Gregory,
in Moral. 5, cap. 31, adduces many :

1.   Because through anger the use of wisdom is lost,
yea, reason itself is for the time extinguished.   Hence, on
that passage in Eccles. vii. 9, *Anger rests in the bosom of a
fool,* Basil, in his Homily against anger, says, *Anger renders a man altogether ferocious, nor suffers him to remain any
more a man.*   The sentiment of the Poet, *Anger is a short
madness,* is well known.

2. Because through anger, justice, the most illustrious
of all the virtues, is violated : for whilst an exasperated
mind sits in judgment, every thing which its fury may
suggest it thinks right. Hence James, i. 20, *The wrath of
man worketh not the righteousness of God.* We have an example in the sons of Jacob, who, when inflamed with anger, perfidiously and cruelly slaughtered the Shechemites,
Gen. xxxiv.; whence they merited that reproach of their
dying father, *Cursed be their anger for it was fierce, and their
wrath for it was cruel,* Gen. xlix. 7.

3. Because by anger the kindness of social life (which
is peculiar to man) is lost. Hence Solomon, Prov. xxii.
24, says, *Make no friendship with an angry man ; and with a
furious man thou shalt not go :* As if he had said, these are
entirely unfit for social life.

4. Because through anger the illumination of the Spirit
is shut out. For the God of peace dwelleth not in a disturbed and wrathful heart, but in a mild and peaceful one.
Chrysostom, in Hom. 30, ad pop. Antioch. says ; *The Holy
Spirit dwelleth not where rage inhabits.* Yea, he shews that
such men are more like those possessed with devils, than
men filled with the Holy Spirit: for as demoniacs froth
and distort their countenances ; so angry men have their
minds foaming and distorted. See also Basil, De Ira.

5. Because through anger, which has an appetite for
revenge, the remission of our sins is hindered, and the
Divine wrath is provoked against us. Matt. xi. 26, *If ye
forgive not men their trespasses, neither will your Father which
is in heaven forgive you your trespasses.* Admirably speaks
Tertullian, De orat. *How rash a thing is it either to pass a
day without prayer, or to lose a prayer by continued anger ?*

6. Because by being angry that which is the attribute
of God is usurped with sacrilegious audacity. *Say not I
will recompence evil ; but wait for the Lord and he shall save
thee,* Prov. xx. 22. *Vengeance is mine, and I will repay,*
Deut. xxxii. 35. But an angry man (as is commonly said)
makes himself the judge, and would have God to be the
executioner : Yea, most commonly he would vindicate for

himself and by himself; a property which God hath reserved for himself alone.

Now in the last place it may be inquired, whether all anger is evil and unlawful, since the Apostle advises us to lay aside anger without any distinction.   It is clear, that anger is not an affection evil in itself; both because God, who cannot be the author of evil, hath implanted in the human mind the faculty of anger; as especially because we read that Christ was moved with anger, Mark iii. 5. Hence Basil calls anger, *the very strength of the soul;* Damascenus, *the guardsman of the judgment.*   Because Eli had not this anger, he stirred up against himself the Divine vengeance, as says Gregory, Moral 5, cap. 30. Hence the Apostle enjoins, *Be ye angry and sin not.* That is to say, Be ye angry where there is a fault with which ye ought to be angry; otherwise, as Ambrose rightly says, *it is not a virtue, but weakness and remissness.*

But that we may distinguish the natural and lawful affection from the inordinate and unlawful emotion of the same, we say that that anger is good which arises from a good motive, namely, from the love of God, or of our neighbour; and which tends to a good end, as the glory of God, and the correction of our neighbour; which proceeds according to a prescribed rule, awaiting or following for instance the determination of reason.   Hither pertains that saying of Augustine, in De civit. Dei, lib. 9. cap. 5, *Under our discipline it is not so much inquired whether a pious mind may be angry, as wherefore he is angry: for no one of sound reflection would reprehend the being angry with a sinner that he may be corrected.*   And Bernard, Epist. 69, says, *Not to be angry with what one ought to be angry, is to be unwilling to amend a sin: to be more angry than one ought to be, is to add sin to sin.*   Lastly, Basil in his Homily De Ira, would have anger to be *a bridled horse, which obeys reason as a curb.* Such anger is not condemned.

On the other hand, it is clear that that anger is evil which arises from a bad beginning, or which tends to a bad end, or is exercised in an improper manner.   If it should arise from a love of praise, or hatred of one's neighbour; if it should tend to effect one's own revenge, or the injury of one's neighbour; if it should forestall the judgment of reason, or be borne headlong with a loose rein. For as Gregory in his Moral 5, cap. 33, well says, *The anger which impatience excites is one thing ; the anger formed by a zeal for justice another.* We may hence conclude that we are not to cherish *apathy,** but that tumultuous and inordinate passion is to be restrained. And thus much as to the sins of the heart: Certain sins of the mouth now follow.

Blasphemy, filthy communication out of your mouth.] The Apostle aptly proceeds from vices of the heart to the sins of the mouth; because they arise from the inordinate affections of the heart.

And first he persuades us to lay aside *evil speaking :* in Greek βλασφημια; which word is derived from βλαπτειν την φημην, *injuring or disparaging the fame* of another by reproachful and evil words. This word in its primary and principal signification in the Holy Scriptures, imports a derogation or injury by words offered to the chief and greatest Good, that is, the good and great God. Now God is blasphemed in three ways : 1. When that which is repugnant to his nature is attributed to him ; as if any one should say that God is corporeal, corruptible, subject to sinful passions; as the Poets formerly imagined and wrote. 2. When that which most befits him, is taken away ; as if any one deny that he is good, merciful, omnipotent, &c. which blasphemy has its origin from the same ignorance. 3. When that which is the property of God is attributed to the creature ; as if any one should say that the angels created this world, or that they are omnipotent; if any one say that mere† men can remit the sins of other men, can dispense with the penalties and punishments of the dead ; or that they can by infallible judgment prescribe articles of faith to Christians. From the decree of God himself we find that capital punishment was assigned to this blas-

---

* This was the maxim of the Stoics.

† *Nudos homines,* men in their natural impotence and deformity.—Trans.

phemy, Levit. xxiv. 16, which we read in ver. 23, was inflicted on the blasphemer. But since in this place the Apostle seems to point out not that blasphemy whereby the Divine Majesty is assailed, but that whereby men are injured, dismissing this blasphemy of the Divine name, let us pass on to that other.

We say, then, that to this evil speaking which assaults one's neighbour, the epithet of blasphemy is also applied not only in this but in many places of Scripture. For instance, in Rom. iii. 8, *As we be slanderously reported,* &c. 1 Cor. iv. 13, *Being defamed, we entreat,* &c. Tit. iii. 2, *Put them in mind to speak evil of no man.** This blasphemy of one's neighbour arises from that anger and wrath of the heart which the Apostle has advised us above to lay aside. For *the heart by the bitter gall of malice, cannot through its instrument the tongue, scatter any thing but bitters,* as Bernard truly says. But it has no kind of vengeance so ready as this of evil-speaking.

This evil-speaking kind of blasphemy hath a double way of injury: one secret, called *detraction;* the other open, called *railing.* Rash and angry persons take the open course of injury; the crafty and malicious prefer the secret one. Let us consider how grievously both sin. And the grievousness of this sin is evident,

First, from the magnitude of the injury done to the neighbour who is evil spoken of: For they wound his reputation, which is a principal external blessing: nor is it easy to repair this injury by any just satisfaction; since here the quantity of loss cannot be estimated, which may be done in the taking away of other external matters.

Secondly, from the magnitude of the injury done to those who hear and take up those reports of evil speakers: For by these means, charity towards their neighbour is put an end to with them; hatreds, suspicions, contentions, and sometimes strifes are the consequence. Which inconvenience we read happened to Saul and David by the ef-

---

* The same word is used in the original Greek and in the Vulgate in each of these passages. viz. *blaspheme.*

forts of evil speakers and detractors. Hence that prayer of the Psalmist, cxx. 2, *Deliver my soul, O Lord, from lying lips, and from a deceitful tongue.*

Thirdly, from the magnitude of the injury done to God himself. For as God is praised in the saints when his works which he effects in them are praised ; so when the saints are blasphemed and defamed by evil reports, God himself is blasphemed : for as a consequence, this blasphemy redounds against God who is the author of holiness : For *the servants being wounded an injury is done to their lord,* Justinianus, Instit. imp. lib. 4. cap. 4, De injuriis.

Fourthly, from the punishment due to evil speakers and detractors ; and that according to civil, ecclesiastical, and divine laws. Justinian's pandects have this passage, lib. 4, cap. 4, De injuriis ; *An injury is committed not only when any one shall have been struck with the fist or a stick ; but likewise when he shall even have been reproached.* And the punishment is awarded according to the quality of the reproach, and also to the quality of the person affected by it. Gratian, Caus. 2. quæst. 1, has this passage, *If any one of the clergy shall have offered reproach or contumely to his bishop, let him be suspended.* And Caus. 6, quæst. 1, *Let the calumniators and revilers of their brethren be held infamous* (Cap. infames). As to the rule of Scripture ; in Levit. xix. 16, there exists a law of the same kind, *Thou shalt not go up and down as a tale-bearer among thy people.* The punishment is assigned, 1 Cor. vi. 9, 10, *Neither thieves, nor covetous, nor drunkards, nor revilers, nor extortioners,* &c. *shall inherit the kingdom of God.*

We will now deduce some Corollaries from these considerations ; and first, such as respect the blasphemers themselves.

1. The passion and habit of evil speaking argues an unregenerate man, and one still in a state of death and condemnation : for it is reckoned among the principal deeds of the *old man.*

2. Nothing is more unhappy than evil speakers and slanderers : for as Nazianzen elegantly says, *It is the extreme of misery to place one's comfort not in one's own happiness, but in the evils of others.*

3. Those who exercise this art are not disciples of the
Apostle, but of the devil, and to him they give their assiduous labours : for he is called, Rev. xii. 10, *The accuser
of the brethren.* Hence Parisiensis not unwisely calls evil
speakers and slanderers, *the devil's dog-teeth*, De moribus,
cap. 11.

We will now add other Corollaries which regard those
who willingly lend an ear to these detractors.

1. If, therefore, evil speaking is so great a crime, then
to hear evil speakers with delight cannot be void of sin.
For not only they who commit the sin are worthy of punishment, but they also who applaud these sinners. *I cannot easily affirm which of these two is most censurable, to slander, or to listen to slander*, says Bernard, lib. 2, De consid.
ad Eugenium ; which is most true of *the hearing what is
agreeable* (to use a Scholastic phrase). Each hath a devil ;
this in the ear ; that in the tongue.

2. It behoves a pious man to turn away from and to reprove blasphemers and slanderers ; nay, also to defend and
to extricate his brother, when wounded by their detractions. We should withstand them ; because, *as the north
wind driveth away rain, so doth an angry countenance a back-
biting tongue*, Prov. xxv. 23. We ought to succour a
wounded brother also : *Whoso privily slandereth his neighbour, him will I cut off*, says the Psalmist, ci. 5. *I brake
also the jaws of the wicked, and plucked the spoil out of his
teeth*, was among the consolations of Job, xxix. 17.

Respecting those injured and wounded by slander, the
pious in this case have their consolation :

1. Because they may hence understand that the wicked
break out into these attacks upon the good, not so much
from their judgment, as from long-standing hereditary disease in their minds. They ought not, therefore, to grieve
so much for their neighbour, as at the disease and madness of their slanderers.

2. Because slander harms not a good conscience. Neither does any one suffer prejudice from the opinion of
those who have no judgment : nor, *if prejudice doth arise
against them in this world, will it in the judgment of God,*
as Ambrose well remarks, De interpret. lib. 2. cap. 3.

3. The opinion of good men, together with the testimony of the conscience, is sufficient for pious persons in this evil world, against the lip of those speaking lies; for as the Poet wisely sang,

False praise can charm, unreal shame control
Whom, but a vicious or a sickly soul?
                    Hor. Epist. lib. 1. Ep. 16.

4. Let not the godly ever be provoked by the example of evil speakers to speak evil again; but let them say with the Apostle, *Being reviled we bless: being persecuted we suffer it: being defamed we intreat,* 1 Cor. v. 12. *He cannot be moved by slander, who excludes the slandering of men by the gift of the Divine blessing,* Ambrose, Serm. 6, in Ps. cxviii. And the Psalmist says, cix. 28, *Let them curse, but bless thou.* Thus much concerning this first sin of the mouth.

Filthy communication] αισχρολογιαν, which the same Apostle calls *corrupt communication* λογον σαπρον, Ephes. ii. 29. And well does he call it *corrupt:* for it grows and buds forth from a corrupt root and also brings corruption, if I may so say, to the morals of men (for foul discourse is the daughter of luxury; since the libidinous, whose hearts are on fire with corrupt desires, easily break out into foul language). Hence says the Apostle, in those words cited from Menander, 1 Cor. xv. 33, *Evil communications corrupt good manners.*

This *filthy communication* is to be avoided by the Christian on many accounts,

1. Because it makes that which is most precious and peculiar to man, namely his faculty of speech, foul and ridiculous; *a gift not granted us for this purpose,* as it is well observed in Virgil, Æn. 4. 647. For obscene and scurrilous language is generally used for the purpose of raising a laugh. Against those who endeavour by obscene language *to excite the laughter of fools,* Clemens Alexandrinus gravely inveighs, Pædag. 2, cap. 5, *If no one,* says he, *would willingly assume a ridiculous bodily shape, why should we try to become ridiculous in words. Ridiculing the power of speech, the most honoured of all the possessions of man.*

2. Because it indicates and proves a corrupt mind. For

as bad fruit betrays a bad tree, so ridiculous and obscene
words, a ridiculous and obscene mind.   For as Clemens
adds (ibid) *a man's discourse is the fruit of his mind.*

3.   Because it is opposed to the sacred profession of a
Christian.   Hence says the Apostle, Ephes. v. 3, 4, *But
fornication and all uncleanness or covetousness, let it not be
once named among you as becometh saints.*   *An evil word,*
says Lactantius, *proceeds not from the mouth of him who
cultivates chaste language.*   This has reference to all Christians, but especially to those who are ministers of the
word.   *Thou hast consecrated thy mouth to the Gospel : it is
unlawful to open it for such things; sacrilege to accustom it to
them,* says Bernard.   Whence that Canon of the Council
of Carthage cited by Gratian, which runs, *We are of opinion that a minister who plays the buffoon and foul-mouthed
jester should be stript of his office.*   For *foolish sayings in the
mouth of a Priest is blasphemy,* says Bernard, De consid. ad
Eugen. lib. 2.

4.   Because they corrupt both the speakers and the
hearers.   Clemens, Pædag. 2, cap. 6, truly and eloquently
says, *that which is disorderly in words, will engender the practice of indecency also in deeds ; but to be modest in what we
say is to keep and preserve ourselves from lewdness.*   Now as to
what belongs to the hearers; we have Chrysostom's just
remark, *As dust and mud make the ears of the flesh unclean,
so does obscene and filthy communication the hearing of the
mind.*   We shall conclude with that saying of our Saviour,
Matt. xii. 36, *But I say unto you, that for every idle word
men shall speak, they shall give an account thereof at the day
of judgment.*   If, then, an idle word will receive the condemnation of a rigorous judge, how much more a foul or
injurious one?   *Think then how worthy of condemnation he
is, who does not refrain from malice, when those words are
punishable which merely are wanting in utility.*   Thus reasons
Gregory, Dial. lib. 3.   Let us, then, put away from our
mouths all malice and evil speaking, or filthy communication, as what defiles us with its foulness.

We may add to what hath been said,

1.   Those who among their friends are accustomed to

use *filthy communication* as a kind of savour to their discourse, act like Commodus, who (according to Lampridius) for the sake of a joke, had human fæces mixed with the most exquisite dishes.

2. Pious men should not quietly submit to impure conversation; for as Athanasius says with truth, *a modest and pious man would bear to have stones thrown at him with greater patience than to hear obscene words.*

Vers. 9. *Lie not one to another, seeing that ye have put off the old man with his deeds;*

10. *And have put on the new man, which is renewed in knowledge after the image of him that created him.*

We are now come to the last sin of the mouth, which the Apostle here persuades us to put off, namely, *lying:* which they are often found to be guilty of, who are most indignant when it is laid to their own charge; foolish and ridiculous people, who, while they allow themselves the liberty of sinning, would take from others that of blaming it. But let us come to the point, and inquire,

1. What lying is, and how many sorts of it there are.

I approve the definition of Augustine, De mendacio ad Consent. cap. 4. He says, *It is the voluntary setting forth of what is false, with the intention of deceiving.* To this Durandus (lib. 3. dist. 38. qu. 1) agrees, and the rest of the Schoolmen. Aquinas, Q. 2, qu. 110, art. 1, has this passage: *If the following three circumstances concur, that what is uttered be false, that it was wished to announce a falsehood; and, moreover, that it was the intention to deceive; then it has the qualities of a lie complete: for it is false both materially and formally.* So Ales, part 2. qu. 122. memb. 1, *The false meaning of a word is as the material in a lie: the completion, or formal property of it is the intention of deceiving.* The most received division of falsehoods is that taken

from their diverse objects : For one is called *pernicious;*
another, *officious;* and another, *jocose.* The first is employed for the sake of injury ; the second, for that of assistance ; the third, for diversion.

2. We shall inquire if any of these be lawful, and
without sin before God.

First, the Scripture itself denies it. Thus Revel. xxi. 8,
*Fornicators, idolaters, and all liars, shall have their part in
the lake which burneth with fire and brimstone.* And, xxii. 15,
Without are dogs, and whosoever loveth and maketh a lie. In
Prov. xii. 22, *Lying lips are an abomination to the Lord.*
Ephes. iv. 25, *Wherefore putting away lying, speak every
man truth with his neighbour.* Secondly, Right reason denies it. For what is in itself evil in its nature, (ex genere)
can by no means be good and lawful : but every falsehood
is in itself evil, since it is an act grounded upon an unlawful matter. Thus Durandus says, lib. 3. dist. 38. qu. 1,
*Language was instituted, not that men might deceive one
another by it, but that they should use it to tell their mutual
thoughts: it is therefore an unlawful act for one to utter words
to signify that which he doth not intend in his mind.* Aquinas
proves this by the same reasoning, Q. 2. qu. 110, art. 3,
Language, says he, *is the natural sign of the understanding :
it is therefore unnatural and unlawful that any one should
signify that by his speech which does not exist in his mind.*
Hence Aristotle (Eth. 4, cap. 7) concludes that all falsehood is wrong in itself, and to be avoided. Wherefore the
most sound of the Fathers held all falsehood to be sin.
Augustine, Enchirid. cap. 18, says, *Every falsehood is a
sin, although he does not sin so greatly who lies with the desire
of advising, as he does with that of injuring.* And again, in
his treatise De mendacio ad Cons. cap. 21, *No one is to be
brought to everlasting salvation by the aid of a lie.* Clemens
Alexandrinus, Strom. 7, says, *A good man neither on his own
account or his neighbour's will lie.* Gregory, Moral. 18, cap.
4, on Job xxvii. writes, *Every falsehood is sin : for whatever
is discordant with truth, disagrees with equity. Neither is the
life of any one to be defended by the fallacy of lying, lest he
should injure his own soul who endeavours to give life to the*

flesh of another. The opinion of Cassian, which he gives
in Collat. 17. cap. 17, is therefore to be disregarded, *that
to ward off any great danger it is as lawful to use falsehood as
hellebore.** And, cap. 25, he says, *that the Patriarchs had
recourse to the protection of a lie in defence of life.*† Those

---

* This refers to the use of Hellebore among the antients, which was constantly exhibited by them to control the paroxysms and abate the symptoms
of the more formidable and dangerous diseases, particularly madness.

† Cassian, to whom these two sentiments are attributed, was a Monk of
the fifth Century, a native of Scythia, but educated in the Monastery of
Bethlehem ; who afterwards wandered through Egypt and Thebais with
another Monk of the name of Germanus, for the sake of conferring with
men of similar inclinations. He was at length ordained by Chrysostom,
and settled at Marseilles, where he founded two Monasteries, one for men
and another for virgins. He composed a code of Instructions for Monks,
with the pieces above-mentioned, entitled " Collationes," or the subject of
his conferences with others on the principles of Monachism, principally derived from the discipline and manners which prevailed among the Syrian
and Egyptian Monks. He engaged in the controversy against Nestorius
respecting the union of the two natures in Christ. The conclusion of his
appeal to Nestorius as given by Du Pin, is remarkable. He says, adverting to the orthodox faith respecting the Person of Christ, " 'Tis the faith
" of this Creed which hath given you admittance to Baptism ; 'tis by that
" that you have been regenerated ; 'tis by this faith that you have received
" the Eucharist and the Lord's Supper. Lastly, I speak it with a sorrow,
" 'Tis that which hath raised you to the holy Ministry, to be a Deacon and
" Priest, and made you capable of the Episcopal Dignity. What have
" you done ? Into what a sad condition have you cast yourself ? By los-
" ing the faith of the Creed you have lost all ; the Sacraments of your
" Priesthood and Episcopacy are grounded upon the truth of the Creed.
" One of these two things you must do ; either you must confess, That
" he is God that is born of a Virgin, and so detest your error ; or, if you
" will not make such a Confession, you must renounce your Priesthood ;
" there is no middle way. If you have been orthodox, you are now an
" apostate ; and if you are at present orthodox, how can you be a Deacon,
" Priest, or Bishop ? Why were you so long in an error ? Why did you
" stay so long without contradicting others ?" Thus we see how a denial
of the supreme Divinity of the Lord that bought us was regarded in those
days. On the doctrine of grace, however, and the strength of Free-will,
as developed in his Collationes, Prosper considered Cassian himself greatly
in error, and opposed his sentiments. It would seem, indeed, as Mosheim
intimates, that in this respect he was a Semi-pelagian. His sentiments
cited by our Expositor, would, moreover, certainly lead to such doctrines
as have since been the disgrace of his Church, the occasion of many evils,
and a hindrance to Religion in the world ; and when we find them applaud-

who are of this opinion have not God, but Plato, for the author of such licentiousness : for he, in 3, De repub. says, *Falsehood is sometimes useful to men, as a medicine is : wherefore it is to be allowed to the public Physicians ; but to be meddled with as little as possible by private people.* So much for Plato ; who is, however, less indulgent to this sin of lying than Cassian. Jerome fastens this error upon Origen, lib. 1, Apolog. adv. Ruffin, where he writes, *the disciples of Origen are united among themselves by the insane mysteries of lies ; Origenistas inter se orgiis mendaciorum fœderari.** But to all these errors we oppose those things which we have already adduced, and especially that admonition of the Apostle, Rom. iii. 8, *that we are not to do evil that good may come.*

3.   Let us inquire whether parabolic and figurative expressions deserve the name of lying. For example, suppose one to say that a Heretic is a wolf; or should any one recite a parable, as that in Judges ix. 8, of the trees choosing to themselves a king, and many other such which occur in the Scriptures.

ed as they were by many subsequent heads of Orders, one cannot wonder at that Jesuitry—that sophistry and guile, which has since distinguished the Roman church, and is now clothing Romanism in a garb to suit modern sentiments and modern liberality.

    * This great man, Origen, following as he did the principles of the Platonic philosophy, and imagining that the nature and extent of the reason of all doctrines of Religion might be found in it, and engaging a number of disciples, may be stated to have been the head of such speculative notions, and the mysticism they gave rise to. For from his disciples emanated in time the Philosophic or Scholastic theology, remarkable mostly for such absurdities. Vide Mosheim, under the notices of Origen.—As to what was just before remarked, as alleged in favour of the monstrosity so insidiously maintained, Cecil has well observed, that " the instances of *artifice* which " occur in Scripture are not to be imitated, but avoided : if Abraham, or " Isaac, or Jacob equivocate in order to obtain their ends, this is no war- " rant to me to do so : David's falsehood concerning Goliath's sword argued " distrust of God. If any part of the truth which I am bound to commu- " nicate be concealed, this is sinful artifice : the Jesuits in China, in order " to remove the offence of the Cross, declared that it was a falsehood in- " vented by the Jews that Christ was crucified ; but they were expelled " from the empire : and this was designed, perhaps, to be held up as a " warning to all Missionaries, that no good end is to be carried by artifice." Vide Cecil's Remains, p. 341, 8vo. edition.

It is certain that neither the matter nor the form of lying can be found in these ; and, therefore, they are wholly void of all taint of sin.   The matter is not found ; because falsehood is not uttered, but the truth expressed in a figurative and customary manner ; for as the natural, so the metaphorical signification of words depends upon custom and the will of the speakers.   Since, then, custom permits us to call a cruel man *a wolf* or *a lion*, or a base or foundation *a rock :* the proposition is the same, whether you say *a Heretic is a wolf*, or *a heretic is hostile and injurious to the flock of Christ*: that *the devil is a roaring lion; or the devil seeks souls for his prey : Christ is a rock ; or Christ is the base or foundation of human salvation.*   The same reasoning applies to parables: For, as Augustine justly remarks, De mend. ad Cons. cap. 5, *Every proposition is to be referred to that which it sets forth ; but all that is figuratively said or done, sets forth that which it intimates to those by whom the proposition is to be understood.*   Thus the Schoolmen.   So Aquinas, quæst. disp. de prophetia, art. 10, *In metaphorical language the literal sense is attended to, and not what the metaphor expresses, but the meaning which is conveyed by the metaphor.*   Durandus, lib. 3, dist. 38, says, *A figurative expression is not true or false according to the sense which it conveys, but to that which is intended.*   So Gerson, part. 1, *In parables the literal sense is not that expressed by the words, but that pointed out by the things or the facts.*   But neither is the *form* of lying found in these : for metaphors, parables, and apologues, are not used with the intention of deceiving, but with that of teaching with the greater elegance and pleasure.   For he who asserts that *a heretic is a wolf*, or *the devil a roaring lion;* or he who puts forth a parable or apologue, does not intend to impose any thing false upon his hearers, but to represent more clearly something true, and useful to be known.

4.   In the last place, Let us glance at that Jesuitical equivocation, which is defended, truly I know not whether more ridiculously or impiously, by those master-builders and patrons of lies.   And first, we shall offer an example of Jesuitical equivocation, or (as they term it) mental re-

servation ; then we shall convict them of manifest lying. Let us then assume that any Popish priest interrogated whether he be a priest or not, should answer expressly, nay, swear if it be necessary, that he is not a priest ; he having reserved this thought in his mind, that he is not a priest of Apollo ; or, that he is not such a priest as he desires to be ; or, that he is not a priest bound to declare this to others : I ask whether he is guilty of a lie. That most lying Jesuit Parsons, in his Tract, ad mitigat. spect. &c. cap. 8, denies that he is. We affirm it, and we prove it from that definition of Augustine and the Schoolmen : For, *he voluntarily announces a falsehood, and that with the intention of deceiving*. There is the *material* of lying; for he denies that he is what he is : there is also the *form;* for by this denial he intends to impress a false opinion on the mind of his hearer. What has the Jesuit to reply to this ?*

* The history of the man here referred to, and who figured principally in the time of Queen Elizabeth, is as extraordinary as the principles which he maintained to serve *the* Church, *at that time*, were horrible, and his conduct base and mischievous. His proper name appears to have been Robert Person. He was born in 1546, at Nether Stowey, in Somersetshire, where his father is said to have been a blacksmith. He however obtained an University education, having been a student at Baliol College, Oxford, where he took his degrees in arts, and obtained a Fellowship. According to Fuller, he was expelled from his post with disgrace, having been charged with embezzlement of the College money. He then went to Rome, and entered into the Order of the Jesuits, and in 1579, he returned to England as superior of the Catholic Missionaries. Two years afterwards, he was obliged to leave the kingdom hastily, in consequence of his political intrigues, when he again took refuge at Rome, where he was placed at the head of the English College. His political sagacity and active disposition induced Philip II. to employ him in some preliminary measures at the time of his projected invasion of England by the " *Invincible Armada ;*" and, after the failure of that scheme, Parsons rendered himself formidable to the government of Queen Elizabeth by his attempts to promote insurrection, and procure the assassination of that Princess. He seems, however, to have carried on his plots with a degree of caution that argued a prudent regard for his own safety. From Camden's State Trials it appears that when Parsons came to England to head the party for pushing the treasonable practices determined on against the Queen, he at first so far proceeded without reserve to develope his schemes, that the Government was soon obliged to take active measures to counteract the proceedings of the iniquitous band ; and to avoid seizure (as some even of the Papists meditated delivering him

He answers, first, *that the enunciation mentioned above is not false, because the enunciation or proposition, which is partly expressed and partly conceived in the mind, is one: but that is true, viz. I am not a priest of Apollo, or I am not a priest obliged to declare it.*

In reply; we allow this proposition, *I am not a priest obliged to declare that I am one,* is one : but we affirm that that other also which is expressed in words is an entire proposition, and distinct from this. Therefore, by this very point in which he defends himself, he is convicted of a lie; namely, that when he conceives the true proposition in his mind, he utters a falsehood : for although the true and false one may be in the view of the internal conception of the mind ; yet the lie properly so called, regards the other, and the external declaration of the mind by the signs of words. However true, therefore, may be that which this priest has shut up in the conception of his mind, yet what he puts forth by the enunciation of a false proposition is a lie.

We may illustrate this by an example. Suppose any one being asked, Whether fire is hot, should assert and swear that fire is not hot, this distinction being reserved in his mind, that it is not hot by adventitious heat; or should any one say that man is not a rational animal, and then should defend himself on the ground that he is not a rational animal of the feathered or finny tribe ; who would

---

into the Magistrates' hands for divulging the designs of deposing the Queen) Parsons lived under the several appellations of Walley, Darcy, Roberts, Farmer, and Phillips. Well might he contend for the principles combated by our Expositor. Thus, while Garnet and others of his fraternity became the victims of their zeal, he kept himself secure from danger, and died in 1610, at Rome, where he had for twenty-three years presided over the English College. Besides his Tract above-mentioned in defence of lying, he was the author of a " Conference about the Succession to the Crown of England," which he published under the name of Doleman, with a Dedication to the Earl of Essex ; with other Tracts adapted to promote the unceasing designs of the Papal agents of his Order against Protestantism. He devoted one entire Pamphlet to the Defamation of the Earl of Leicester, an edition of which was published on the Continent, with a most mischievous and appalling title. Vide Sharon Turner's Modern History—Reign of Elizabeth, Notes.

not see that such an one is not free from the guilt of lying by these trifling reservations? For in a negative proposition, it is whatever is usually contained in the comprehension of the predicate that is removed from (i. e. denied of) the subject; not a single species only. So that he who dares to confirm propositions of this kind with an oath, relying upon his mental reservations, is guilty of perjury by the suffrages of all the antient theologians.

We only now adduce some few rules, leaving it to you to apply them to this dispute.

Rule 1. *By whatever artifice of words an oath is taken, God accepts it as he to whom the oath is made understands it.* Isidore.

2. *An oath is received according to the common usage of language.* Gerson, part. 2. But neither he to whom the oath is made, nor common usage, understands those clauses of reservation; and he who offers to make an oath knows this.

3. *No one ought to swear to any thing as certain,* says Durandus; *for an oath is calling **God** to witness for the confirmation of the truth of what the hearer doubts, and to which he will not assent on a simple assertion.* But there never was a doubt, whether that priest was the priest of Apollo: nor was it needful to profane an oath in proof of it.

4. *An oath consisting of many or equivocal words, binds in that sense which the words are wont to convey to persons rightly understanding them. If among such the words equally convey several significations, then the oath binds in that sense in which the swearer believed that he to whom the oath was made understood them at the time.* Altissiodorensis, lib. 3, tract. 19, qu. 4.

From all these instances we conclude, that notwithstanding the mental reservation, the material of a lie exists in that assertion of the priest, viz. his false proposition.

But, in the second place, the Jesuit answers, *The lie does not exist formally in this example: for he did not intend to deceive his hearer, but preserve himself from danger, in denying he was a priest, with the aforesaid mental reservation.*

But we reply, he intended both of these; for he would

preserve himself by deception, yet not likely to preserve himself unless he had first deceived his hearer by this jugglery. I conclude, therefore, with Ales, part. 2. qu. 122, mem. 1, *Although the ulterior intention be to benefit himself or his neighbour, nevertheless the immediate intention is to deceive; and as far as this is concerned a lie is told: for this last, the intention, in itself regards the language ; but the former regards the will of the party, and not the words themselves.**

Seeing that ye have put off the old man with his deeds.] The Apostle here comes to the first argument of the aforesaid dissuasion. He derives it from the removal of the cause to the removal of the effects. For the old man is the cause of the vices before-mentioned ; when he, therefore, is put off, they must be put off also.

The old man denotes the corruption inherent in our nature, the inclination of all our faculties to evil; and, moreover, that state of sinfulness which they acquired by the habit of sinning before their ingrafting into Christ. The

---

* The doctrine of the Church of Rome, concerning Equivocations, mental Reservations, and the Lawfulness, or rather Obligation, of concealing, with the most solemn Oaths, what has been revealed under the seal of Confession, has perhaps some affinity with the doctrine of the Priscillianists, which overspread and disturbed Europe in the fifth Century—a sect which inculcated on their Proselytes the dreadful maxim, " *Swear, forswear, but never betray a secret,*" and by which Cassian, as noticed at the outset of this topic, would seem to have been corrupted. The defence set up by the Romish divines for such a notion is, " That what is only known under the Seal of Confession, is not known to a man, but to God represented by a man, i. e. to the Priest or Confessor; and therefore the Priest may, with a safe Conscience, affirm, even upon oath, that he knows not what he thus knows. It is by recurring to this doctrine, that F. Daniel Bartoli, in his History of England, or rather of the *Jesuits* in England, endeavours to justify the conduct of the Jesuit Garnet, in not discovering the Gunpowder plot, to which he supposes him to have been privy. But as it was disclosed to him in confession, or at least under the seal of confession, he would have sinned grievously by discovering it, though by such a discovery he might have saved a whole nation from destruction. So that the violating such a Seal is a far greater evil than the loss of so many lives—than the utter ruin of an entire Nation :"—a doctrine evidently repugnant to the dictates both of reason and humanity, horrible in its own nature, and awfully dangerous in its consequences wherever it is held.—Vide Bower, Vol. i. p. 150.

deeds of this old man are those sins afore-mentioned, and
others of the like kind extended to acts.   He dissuades
from these in other words, but in the same sense, in Ephes.
iv. 22, *That ye put off, concerning the former conversation, the
old man, which is corrupt according to the deceitful lusts.*

He means that they *have put off* the old man sacramentally in undergoing baptism; efficaciously by the operation
of the Spirit of regeneration; totally indeed as to the guilt
and dominion of sin ; inchoatively as to the nature and act
or the motion of sin.   But having spoken at length concerning this putting off of the old man, on the 12th verse
of the preceding chapter, we will refer to that rather than
inculcate the same things over again.

Vers. 10.   *And have put on the new man, which is renewed
in knowledge after the image of him that created him:
Where there is neither Greek,* &c.

Here is that other argument connected with the former
one; for it cannot possibly happen that he who puts off
the old man, should not at the same time put on the new.
For as in physics, as soon as the old form (of existence) is
expelled, a new one immediately succeeds : So when the
old Adam is put off, a new man is at the same time put on :
but when the new man is put on, the works and conversation of the old man must cease.

Here are three things to be observed : 1. What does the
Apostle point out by this *new man*, whom he says the Colossians have put on.   2. How has the renovation taken
place; by little and little, and continuously.   3. In what
this renovation of the new man consists.

The new man.]   As to this first, it may be explained in
one word : for if the *old man* (as I have before shewn) designates the inherent corruption of our nature, with the
proneness and inclination of all our faculties to do evil;
then, by the law of contraries, *the new man* will designate

the renewing, and fresh propensity of all our faculties to
do good, infused into and impressed upon the faithful by
the power of the Holy Spirit. *I delight in the law of God
after the inner man,* Rom. vii. 22. *That he would grant you
to be strengthened with might by his Spirit in the inner man,*
Ephes. iii. 16. The Holy Spirit, therefore, strengthens the
renewed for those actions for which they before had neither
the faculty nor inclination. Two Corollaries arise out of
the consideration of this new man :

1. First, it excites to duty. It behoves those who have
put on the new man, to adopt a new method of life. *If
any man be in Christ, he is a new creature ; old things are
passed away ; behold, all things are become new :* 2 Cor. v. 17.
He who assumes the character of a king, is both foolish
and wicked if he acts the part of a buffoon ; so is it with
him who puts on the new man, if he shall act the part of
the old.

2. Secondly, it depresses pride : for it behoves us to
remember whence we obtained this newness, whatever it
may be, and good works ; namely, from the renewing Spirit. *In nothing then,* as says Cyprian, *should we boast, since
nothing is ours. What hast thou which thou hast not received?*
1 Cor. iv. 7.

2. *Which is renewed.*] This word respects the manner,
for it indicates the constant workings of the Holy Spirit
in renewing us : as if he had said, This your renewing
ceases not for one moment ; for you have so put on the
new man, that ye be more and more to be renewed daily :
which is clearly taught in 2 Cor. iv. 16, *But though our outward man perish, yet the inward man is renewed day by day.*

Now the reason why there is need of this daily renewing
is on account of the remains of indwelling sin ; which the
Divine wisdom has not seen fit to eradicate in a moment,
but would rather leave it to the day of our dissolution, for
the exercise of our virtue and the preservation of humility
within us. As, therefore, in wine mingled with water,
both wine and water are found in every part : so in the renewed man the conditions of regeneration and some corruptions of the old man are found mingled and wound up

together. Thus Augustine, de pecc. merit. et remiss. lib.
2. cap. 7 and 8, says, *Perfect newness does not exist in the
mind itself of the regenerate :* and again, cap. 28, *The law
of sin remains in the regenerate, although overcome and broken
through.* On this account, therefore, the Apostle says this
new man is still to be renewed in the sons of God.

Corollaries.

1. As the Spirit of God renews us more and more inwardly; so it behoves us, thus supported and aroused by
the grace and help of the renewing spirit, to advance outwardly in holiness and good works : for *men*, says Augustine, de correp. et grat. cap. 2, *are led by the Spirit of God,
that being acted upon they may act, not that they themselves
should do nothing. Lest ye receive the grace of God in vain,*
2 Cor. vi. 1.

2. Those who deny that sin remains in the renewed,
deny this daily benefit of the Holy Spirit renewing and re-
moulding us continually. For renewing intimates that
something of the old man remains : for the old man is
nothing else than *the body of sin*, as the Apostle elsewhere
speaks. Thus much on the manner of the renewing;
namely, that it is not effected in a moment, but by little
and little.

3. Now, in the last place, we must consider in what
things this renewing consists. The Apostle seems to place
it in two particulars ; the illumination of the mind, which
he denotes by the word *knowledge*, and the healing and
sanctification of the will, which he points out by the word
image.

In knowledge.] As to the former, it is the property of
the old man to have the mind darkened, as to what belongs
to spiritual and saving knowledge. *Having the understanding darkened*, Ephes. iv. 8. *But the natural man receiveth not
the things of the Spirit of God*, 1 Cor. ii. 14. The Holy
Spirit, therefore, when he leads us to a knowledge of spiritual things, begins this work of our renewal, by the infusion of life-giving knowledge and the light of faith.
Hence that prayer of the Apostle for the Ephesians, i. 17,
18, *That the Father of glory may give unto you the Spirit of*

wisdom and revelation in the knowledge of him; the eyes of your understanding being enlightened, &c.   The Apostle uses the word *agnition* rather than *cognition,* lest any one should think he spoke of some idle and speculative knowledge; whereas the former word always means with him a lively, efficacious, and operative knowledge.   This enlightening, then, of the understanding. and infusion of faith, and spiritual knowledge, is the first effect of a regenerating and renewing spirit.   Whence Parisiensis very properly calls faith, *the first life of the human mind, and like spiritual light in the works of the re-creation: it is the gate of life through which God first enters the human mind;* de morib. cap. 1.

I will here remark, Those who require in Christians only a blind devotion, seem to wish to build up the edifice of holiness without a foundation, and to approve of Christians only half renewed.

After the image of him that created him.] After the light of knowledge and of faith is infused, the regenerating Spirit (who is the Creator of the new man) impresses the image of God upon the will.   It is, therefore, another effect of regeneration, that when the mind is enlightened by faith, the human will should be conformed to God, and shew forth a Divine disposition in its love of holiness and righteousness.   In this sense the Apostle, in Ephes. iv. 24, says, this new man is *after God created in righteousness and true holiness.*   So 2 Pet. i. 3, 4, Christ is said to have given to the renewed *all things that pertain unto life and godliness;* and that these gifts have made us *partakers of the Divine nature,* and freed us *from the corruption which is in the world through lust.*   By this image is denoted, therefore, a certain representation, as it were, of the Divine sanctity in the human mind.   Concerning this image of God there are many disputations among the Fathers and Schoolmen.

First, they are wont to say, that the Son of God alone is the image of the Father; we are made according to this image, while irrational creatures have only the traces of the Divinity, not the image of God, not being made after this image.   As to what pertains to this distinction between the eternal and natural Son of God, and we the

adopted sons, it is not accurately remarked in Scripture. For
as he is called *the image of the Father,* Heb. i. 3; so we
also are said to be not only made in the image, but *the
image of God,* 1 Cor. xi. 7. We must, however, hold, that
Christ is the image of God the Father in one way; we in
another : He is the image by *equality,* having entirely the
same nature with the Father of whom he is the image;
every regenerated person is the image by *imitation,* partially
representing a certain similitude to the Divine nature in
some gifts of grace. Augustine illustrates this by no in-
apt simile : *As the image of an Emperor,* says he, *upon a
coin differs from that in his son; so does the image of God in
us differ from that in Christ.*

Secondly, the Schoolmen and Fathers inquire in what
this image of God after which we are created, consists;
and the consideration of this more nearly concerns our
present purpose. Tertullian, in his treatise against Marcion, lib. 2, determines it in *immortality, freedom of will,*
and *the capacity of knowledge.* Augustine, in 9 de Trin.
cap. 4, assigns the image of God in the soul as consisting
in these three things, *mind, understanding,* and *affections;*[*]
but in 1 de Trin. cap. 11, as *memory, intellect,* and *the will.*[†]
The Schoolmen for the most part say, this image of God
consists in *natural gifts;* but the likeness in *gifts of grace;*
and the Gloss upon Genesis expresses this opinion, in saying that man was made *after the image of God,* as to *natural qualities :* after *his likeness,* as to *qualities of grace.* We
allow, with the Fathers and Schoolmen, that a certain
image of God is found in the natural faculties of the mind,
which may be called the image *of the natural creation;* but
nevertheless we affirm, both in this passage and every other
of Paul, that *this* image of God (which may be called the
image of *the supernatural re-creation*) is not placed in the
powers, faculties, or qualities themselves of the native
soul; but in the re-arrangement, sanctification, and confirmation of these according to the nature and will of God.

---

[*] *Mentem, notitiam, amorem.*

[†] *Memoriam, intelligentiam, voluntatem.*

To this Ambrose seems to me to have alluded in those words, Hexam. 6, cap. 8, *Thou art painted, O man, painted by the Lord thy God; thou hast a good artist, and painter; do not thou deface a good picture, shining not with varnish, but truth; not formed of wax, but of grace.* He, therefore, places the image of God which we bear in the effects of grace. Then we are renewed after the image of God when all the powers and inclinations of our souls are enlightened and sanctified.

We derive these Instructions:

1. The end of our regeneration is, that we may be made like to God, and, like a hard and polished mirror, reflect (as far as infirmity permits) his wisdom, righteousness, holiness, &c.

2. Those who do not seek after holiness and righteousness, still bear the image of the old Adam, nay, indeed, that of the devil; they are not yet renewed after the image of God, which chiefly consists in holiness: they must be adjudged to him whose character they bear impressed on their minds.

3. God's kindness and love to man, must be considered in this work of regeneration: it is a great proof of his goodness and clemency, that he once willed that his image should be impressed upon us; and would renew and restore it again after it was obliterated and deformed. The consideration of the value God set upon this restoration will still more shew forth the Divine clemency: He created man first in his image by his voice and his word; but he restored him a second time by his death and blood. Let, then, this benevolence of God in regenerating us at so great a cost, and renewing us after his image by his Holy Spirit, be a spur to us in laying aside our vices, and pursuing godliness.

So far of the twofold reasoning by which the Apostle confirms the preceding dissuasions from vice: in the next verse we have an amplification of the same reasoning.

Vers. 11. *Where there is neither Greek nor Jew, circumcision nor uncircumcision, Barbarian, Scythian, bond
nor free ; but Christ is all and in all.*

The Apostle has excited the Colossians to renounce their
carnal and spiritual vices, by this argument chiefly ; that
they *had put off the old man and put on the new.* He now
seems to polish and point this very argument itself : 1. By
discarding the false opinion of those, who, neglecting this
renewing of themselves, confided in external privileges,
and despised those who were without them. 2. By substi-
tuting a true one, viz. that all external things which are
esteemed excellent and honourable, avail nothing to salvation without this renewal : on the other hand, what is esteemed vile and base, in no respect hinders it, because
Christ is all in all.   Let us examine the words in their
order.

Where there is neither Greek nor Jew.] That is, where
there is considered no difference of nations in respect to a
new or renewed man, or the state of regeneration ; so that
any one should hope he is more acceptable to God because
he is a Jew, or fear that he is despised because he is a
Gentile : Nay, If thou art a Jew, and art without this renewing, thou art a dog, and no son ; if thou art a Gentile
and hast it, thou art a son, and no more a dog.

We thus prove it.   The difference of nation does not
promote the salvation of any one if he be without sanctification, nor hinder his obtaining it if he have it : we must,
therefore, seek after holiness.   Hence it is that in the
Scriptures the pride of the Jews, who plumed themselves
on the privileges of their nation, is always rebuked. Thus
in Matt. iii. 9, *Say not within yourselves, we have Abraham
to our father :* and John viii. 39, to the Jews who boasted,
We have Abraham to our father, Christ says, *If ye were
Abraham's children, ye would do the works of Abraham.   But*

ye are of your father the devil, &c. vers. 44.   On the other
hand, if the Gentiles were renewed and sanctified, they are
shewn to be acceptable to God.   See Acts x. 34, *Of a truth
I perceive that God is no respecter of persons; but in every
nation he that feareth him and worketh righteousness is accepted
with him.*   And Gal. iii. 7, *They which are of faith, the same
are children of Abraham.*   Jerome says, *It is not the sons of
the saints, who obtain the places of the saints, but those who
perform their works.*   This is an effective argument against
the impudence of the Romanists, who measure a member
of the Church by this point alone, viz. that he does or does
not adhere to the Papal chair.   But Christ asks not whether he adhere to this or that national church, but to the
true faith ? not whether he be a Romanist, but whether he
be renewed and sanctified ?   In the spiritual state, whether
a man be a Greek or a Jew is not regarded ; much less whether he be a Greek or a Romanist.

Circumcision nor uncircumcision.] As in the business of
salvation the difference of nations affords neither prerogative nor prejudice ; by similar reasoning the difference of
ceremonies and external observances is of no moment.
Circumcision was in the Jewish church the chief religious
rite : it was used, therefore, to express the observance of
all the legal rites, and uncircumcision argued the neglect
of them.   The Apostle, then, affirms, that neither the observation nor neglect of all the outward ceremonies is of
any moment to Christians ; but that internal renovation
and true holiness contain the sum of our salvation.

The Christian is not commended to God by the observance of certain ceremonies or external traditions ; neither
is he alienated from God by the mere omission of the same.
So Paul constantly teaches : Gal. vi. 15, *In Christ Jesus
neither circumcision availeth any thing, nor uncircumcision, but
a new creature.*   Rom. xiv. 2, 3, *One believeth that he may
eat all things ; another who is weak eateth herbs.   Let not him
that eateth despise him that eateth not ; and let not him which
eateth not judge him that eateth.*   He lays down the same
rule as to the observance of days in vers. 5.   But more
clearly in 1 Cor. viii. 8, *But meat commendeth us not to God,*

for neither if we eat are we the better : neither if we eat not are we the worse. It is, then, a wretched thing to condemn some for meat and drink's sake, or to arrogate to ourselves holiness on account of abstinence from them.

What is said of circumcision, of meats, and of the observance of days, ought to be applied to all observations placed in external things. For these of themselves neither render men more acceptable to God by their observance ; nor less acceptable to him from their omission : We must not, then, trifle about these things, but strive for mortification and sanctification.

Hence the Monks are convicted of foolish pride, who account themselves superior to all other Christians by reason of these externals ; such as abstaining from certain meats, and shutting up themselves in convents, and (in one word) observing some rule of outward ceremonies invented by men. But if in Christ circumcision and uncircumcision make no difference, then the eating of flesh or fish, the living in convents or cities, and wearing frocks and hoods, has nothing in it that regards the salvation of Christians.

Barbarian or Scythian.] The former expressions seem particularly directed to the Jews, who considered themselves more acceptable and agreeable to God than others from the prerogatives of their nation and their ritual observances. The present are directed at the Greeks, who, refined by the knowledge of philosophy and the liberal arts, despised other nations, and considered them almost as brutes in comparison with themselves. The Apostle, therefore, says, this barbarism is no hindrance to those engrafted in Christ and truly renewed and sanctified. He mentions the Scythians by name, since they were accounted the most fierce of all barbarians; as if he had said, Not even the most barbarous barbarism should be any ground of prejudice against those who are enlightened by faith and renewed by the Spirit of God. Epiphanius,* almost in the very begin-

---

* Epiphanius, Bishop of Salamis, in Cyprus, in the fourth Century. He was born about the year 332, at a village in the neighbourhood of Eleutheropolis, in Palestine, and appears to have been educated in Egypt, where he imbibed the principles of the Gnostics. At length he left those heretics,

ning of his first book against the eighty heresies, calls barbarism Scythism; and says, that barbarism flourished in the ten first generations of the world, afterwards that Scythism prevailed from the flood to the destruction of the tower of Babel. But I confess that I do not clearly understand the reason of this distinction; that the Scythians are so joined to the Barbarians, I think is for the sake of amplification, and not of distinction: which also seemed the case to Ambrose, who writes that the Scythians are distinguished from other Barbarians in this place because they surpassed the rest in rudeness of manners.

No pious and holy man is to be esteemed nothing worth, because he is of unpolished manners and destitute of literary attainments. It is not elegance of manners but innocence of life, not erudition but faith, which commends us to God. *Ye see your calling, brethren, how that not many wise men after the flesh, not many mighty, not many noble are called. But God hath chosen the foolish things of the world to confound the wise,* 1 Cor. i. 26. So Augustine heretofore exclaimed, *The unlearned arise and seize on heaven; and lo, where we with our heartless learning wallow in the mire of flesh and blood!* Confess. lib. 8. cap. 8. A barbarian ignorance of other things is no hindrance to one who knows Christ,

---

and becoming an ascetic, returned to Palestine, and adopted this discipline of Hilarion, the founder of Monachism in that country. Epiphanius erected a Monastery near the place of his birth, over which he presided till he was elected to the See of Salamis, in 367. In 391 he commenced a controversy with John Bishop of Jerusalem, relative to the opinions of Origen, which Epiphanius condemned. In the course of this dispute, as in others in which he was involved, he displayed more zeal than charity or prudence; particularly when in the height of his resentment against the favourers of Origen, he sent word to the Empress Eudoxia, who requested his prayers for her son Theodosius, who was ill, that the prince should not die, provided she would discard the heretics who enjoyed the imperial patronage. Epiphanius died in 402 or 403, on returning from Constantinople to Cyprus. He was a man of great learning, but deficient in judgment and accuracy. His work entitled " Panarion," against heresies, is reckoned as a piece of Ecclesiastical history; but the carelessness or ignorance of the author as to facts and opinions, deducts much from its authority. The best edition of the writings of Epiphanius is that of Petavius, Paris, 2 vols. folio; reprinted at Cologne, in 1682.—*Gorton.*

and lives after his law : but even an angelic knowledge of
all things profits nothing to one who lives impurely, and
knows not Christ : for *in Christ there is neither Barbarian
nor Scythian,*

Bond nor free.] All these expressions have the same import, and signify, that a high or low station in the world
is not to be considered by a Christian as if the one were
nearer, the other farther from salvation. The condition of
slaves among the antients was most unjust and wretched :
they esteemed slaves as only animated tools, which their
master could use as he pleased ; yea, they claimed to themselves the power of life and death over them as over their
cattle. Notwithstanding this vile and abject condition,
the Apostle says there is no difference between the slave
and his master as far as concerns salvation : For the slave,
if he be renewed after the image of God, is acknowledged
as a son ; his master, if he remain wicked and impure, is
rejected as a spurious offspring.* Now what is said of
slavery and freedom is applicable to the noble and the ignoble, the rich and the poor; in one word, to all the different conditions of mortals in this world. For truly says
Jerome, *Our Religion knows nothing of the persons and conditions of men, but regards their souls.* And Lactantius,
Instit. lib. 5. cap. 15, *No one is poor in the eye of God, but
he who lacks righteousness ; no one rich unless he abound in
virtues ; no one, lastly, great, unless he be good and innocent,*
&c. But we must here beware lest we consider the Christian Religion as confounding political order, and the various ranks of men. The Apostle does not say that bond
and free are not to exist in this world : but that these dis-

* Is this representation of Slavery under heathenism centuries ago, more
remarkable than in this age of the extension of professed Christianity ?
Will it not be a matter of greater surprise to the world a few centuries
hence, that it was upheld in a corresponding existence, if not worse in regard to the treatment of the Slave, by Christian Britain in the nineteenth
Century ? Is the reasoning applied to the case in reference to the soul and
eternity less applicable *now* than it was formerly ? Let any one peruse but
half the Reports of the condition of things in our West Indian possessions
elicited by Parliamentary investigations, and the Reports of the Missionaries, say for the last ten years, and then judge.

tinctions are not found in Christ, or in a spiritual state of salvation. He who here affirms, that in the new man *there is neither bond nor free*, in 1 Tim. vi. 1, commands *servants who are under the yoke, to count their own masters worthy of all honour, that the name of God and his doctrine be not blasphemed.* This also Augustine teaches in these words, Expos. in Epist. ad Rom. propos. 72, *It behoves us as far as this life is concerned, to be subject to powers ; but as to our believing in God and being called to his kingdom, we need not be subject to any man who would divert us from it.*

Thus far it has been shewn, in opposition to this false and vain presumption of many, that external circumstances of any kind can avail nothing without this internal renewing of the heart: and that no condition, however vile and abject, forms an objection, if the Spirit of God be present regenerating and purifying the heart from sin. To this error the Apostle again opposes a true judgment, which he expresses more affirmatively in these concluding words, BUT CHRIST IS ALL AND IN ALL.] What the Jews hoped for from the privilege of their nation and the sign of the covenant, the Greeks from their philosophy, princes and great men from their dignity ; all these things, and others far more excellent, the man that is born again enjoys in Christ. On the other hand ; whatever blemish there may be thought, in being sprung from Gentile or Barbarian, in being born in uncircumcision, or in any low condition or mean station ; all these things are divested of all disgrace and dishonour through Christ living in the renewed ; and, consequently, this renewed state is of the utmost value. For *Christ* (regenerating them and uniting himself with the renewed) *is all* that which is necessary to salvation ; *in all,* namely, in all the faithful who are thus sanctified and united to Christ. He is all things to them, *meritoriously :* for since they become one mystical person with Christ, he imparts to them the merit of his passion, death, obedience, and righteousness ; and thus *he is made* to them *of God wisdom, righteousness, sanctification, and redemption, 1 Cor. i. 30.* He is all things to them *efficaciously ;* for whatever they possess or can do, as regards spiritual life and obtaining salvation, they possess from Christ and can do by him. *And I live, yet not I, but Christ liveth in me,* Gal. ii. 20 ; and 1 Cor. xv. 10, *But by the grace of God I am what I am : and his grace which was bestowed upon me was not in vain ; but I laboured more abundantly than they all ; yet not I, but the grace of God which was with me.* It can, therefore, want no more explanation, but stands plainly before us, that Christ is all things in all the regenerate.

Corollaries.

1. Christ and his Spirit renewing us is not esteemed of sufficient value by us, unless we esteem this *new man* of such great value, that we consider all other things, which men generally think make them honourable or despicable, as nothing in comparison.

2. Here the pride and vanity of those who glory in any earthly dignity is put down ; since any one of the regenerate is more noble and more free than they ; and is more nearly allied to God, and like him who is the fountain of honour.

Thus far on that part of the Apostle's admonition which respects the laying aside our vices : the other, which refers to the exercise of virtues, remains to be treated ; to this he had fortified and paved the way by shewing that they had not only put off the old man, but had put on the new.

Verses 12, 13.

Put on therefore as the elect of God, holy and beloved, bow-
els of mercies, kindness, humbleness of mind, meekness,
long-suffering.
Forbearing one another, and forgiving one another, if any
man have a quarrel against any : even as Christ forgave
you, so also do ye.

In the former part of the general exhortation, the Apostle advised the putting off and casting away of all vices, as
members of the old Adam. We now come to the second
part of the exhortation ; in which he exhorts the Colossians to put on and exercise all virtues ; and this part is
extended as far as verse 18.

This last division of the Apostle's exhortation consists
of three parts. In the first he excites to those virtues
which immediately regard our neighbours ; and whether
they be miserable and need our aid ; or wicked and injurious to us ; or in any other case, as expressed in vers. 12,
13, 14, 15. In the second he calls them to the study,
knowledge, and use of the Divine word ; by the ministry
of which we are instructed and taught in the above virtues ;
see vers. 16. Thirdly, and lastly, he prescribes to the
Colossians an universal rule to be observed on all occasions, in vers. 17.

With respect to the verse which we have in hand, three
things are to be considered : the agreement of this exhortation with what went before ; the preliminaries to the exhortation, and the exhortation itself.

1. First, it is proper to observe the agreement or dependence which the illative particle *therefore* intimates to
us. This word requires us to look back to the 10th verse,
where the Apostle states that they *had put on the new man ;*
whence he here infers, *therefore put on bowels of mercies,*
&c. As if he had said, They who have put on the new

man, ought to put on all his members, and all his properties : but these virtues are as the members and properties of the new man ; therefore, are to be put on by you
who have put him on. He uses the same argument before,
when from the circumstance of their having put off the
old man, he inferred, *Mortify therefore its members, fornication, uncleanness,* &c.

Corollaries from this inference.

1. We must seek to make the new man entire and perfect in all his members : for as the natural body appears
deformed if deprived of an eye, a hand, or a foot, or any
other of its members; so it is with the spiritual man, if he
lack any of his parts.

2. They have little or no sense of spiritual life, who do
not perceive, or perceiving do not grieve for, or grieving
for do not endeavour with all their might to amend and
supply, this mutilation of the new man.

3. Scarcely will an individual be found who, as far as
respects this new man, is not a monster either from deficiency or superabundance of limbs : I mean wanting in the
members he ought to have, or supplied with those he should
be without. But if we would attend to the Apostle, we
shall understand, that from the fact of our having put off
the old Adam, and put on the new man, we are bound to
suffer any inconvenience which may occur in either respect.
Thus much of the illative particle *therefore.*

2. *As elect of God holy and beloved.*] We here come,
secondly, to the preliminaries, or the reason on which the
exhortation is grounded, why these virtues should be
adopted by the Colossians. This is drawn from what is *fit*
and *honourable :* for these three attributes by which their
condition is described, prove them to be bound to these
virtues and to holiness of life. Let us consider them
apart.

As elect of God.] This may be understood either of an
eternal or temporal election, by which Christians are separated from the filth of the world to serve God according
to the precepts of the Gospel. And I consider the Apostle means this latter election ; which yet, if it be effica-

cious, presupposes the former one. But whether he means this or that, he speaks precisely to the purpose. For the consideration of our gratuitous election before the foundations of the world were laid, ought not to induce us to sloth, but influence us with eagerness to perpetual holiness of life; since God hath chosen us to this end : as it is said in Ephes. i. 4, *he hath chosen us in Christ, before the foundation of the world, that we should be holy*, &c. The same applies to temporal election, whereby we are called into the Church, and separated for a peculiar people of God; for this privilege also obliges us to cultivate holiness. This is a stipulation God makes with the Israelites, Deut. xxvi. 18, *The Lord hath avouched thee this day to be his peculiar people, that thou shouldest keep all his commandments.* So also Christ stipulates with a Christian, 2 Tim. ii. 19, *The Lord knoweth them that are his : And let every one that nameth the name of Christ depart from iniquity.* Let, then, every one who believes himself elect of God, live as the elect of God.

Those, consequently, who prate about their eternal election, and boast of their Christian profession, while in their deeds and in their manner of life they shew themselves neither elect nor Christians, are here reproved : but as the lazy Greeks made a profession of philosophy, so do these men of their Christianity : *it was all talk and no doing.* But we ought not to become like the idle philosophers ; for as Tertullian gravely argues, Apologet. cap. 46, *What analogy is there between the philosopher and the Christian ? the disciple of Greece and of Heaven ? the trader for an empty name, and for life ? the artificer of words and of deeds ?*

Holy.] That is by baptism and the sanctification of the Spirit. In the administration of baptism itself, Christians are consecrated to God ; they are renewed after the Divine image by the internal operation of the Spirit : in each respect they are called *holy ;* by each they are bound to a holy life. For whatever is consecrated to God, should in some way participate in the Divine holiness. Hence that passage of Levit. xi. 44, *Ye shall be holy, for I am holy ;* and Chap. xx. 26, *Ye shall be holy unto me : for I the Lord*

*am holy, and have severed you from other people that ye should
be mine.* Being then by baptism separated and consecrated
to God, we ought to put on all virtues, and exercise perpetual holiness of life.

Besides, what things are consecrated to God, are not to
be applied to any purpose, but always to be used according to the Divine will; which is seen plain enough in temples, vessels, and other inanimate things : How much
more, then, should this be attended to in men consecrated to
God by baptism? Now it clearly appears that *the will of
God* is *our sanctification,* 1 Thess. iv. 3: whence Nazianzen
calls baptism, *the covenant of a more holy life with God;* and
Peter, 1 Epis. iii. 21, *The answer of a good conscience towards
God.* Inasmuch, then, as we are holy by baptism, we
ought to lead a life holy and adorned with virtues.

Wherefore that internal operation of the Holy Spirit, in
which all true Christians participate, requires the same
from them even as it were in its own right. For the operation of the Spirit brings new life ; new life brings new
strength ; and these require new manners and actions.
Hence arises that exhortation of the Apostle to the regenerate and sanctified, Rom. vi. 19, *Now yield your members
servants unto righteousness unto holiness.* Now, that is, since
the Holy Spirit hath inspired holiness, so walk as *holy.*
Thus much of the second attribute.

And beloved.] This is the third attribute, by mentioning
which he would excite the Colossians to put on and exercise the virtues. Now he does not speak of the love of
the eternal benevolence, with which God embraced the elect
before the foundations of the world ; for notwithstanding
this love, they are accounted among rebels and enemies to
God prior to their effectual calling and regeneration. Rom.
v. 10, and Ephes. ii. 12. He speaks, then, of the love of
friendship, by which God receives into the number of his
children the elect, when actually converted and grafted into
Christ ; as in John i. 12, *But as many as received him* (Christ)
to them gave he power to become the sons of God. They,
therefore, who are beloved after this manner, ought as the
beloved to put on all the virtues which are agreeable to
God ;

1. Because it behoves one beloved mutually to love God : but the proof of love is the exercise of virtue ; *If ye love me, keep my commandments,* John xiv. 15.

2. Because it behoves one beloved to frame himself to the likeness of God who loves him : for as love arises from a similitude of dispositions, so does enmity arise from their dissimilitude.

Corollaries.

1. They who do not cultivate virtue and holiness, are not only impure but sacrilegious ; since they pollute by a disorderly life, their bodies and souls, which were sacred to God.

2. It is but folly for one to presume that he is loved of God, or that he loves God, who neglects to put on the ornaments of virtue : since they are at once signs of the Divine love towards us, and of ours towards God. For God always adorns those whom he loves by infusing virtues and gifts ; and they who love God worship him and honour him by the exercise of virtue. So much of the arguments which the Apostle uses as preliminaries to the exhortation itself.

3. We now come, in the last place, to the matter of the exhortation contained in these words, *Put on bowels of mercies, kindness,* &c. Here it is proper to consider the act of putting on, and the things or virtues so put on.

Put ye on.] This is a figurative expression taken from garments. But since in things spoken metaphorically we are not to suppose a similitude in all respects, it will not be foreign to the matter if we briefly note in what respects virtues are like garments, and in what they are unlike.

They are like : 1. Because as garments adorn the body ; so do virtues the soul. 2. Because as he who is stript of his clothes appears base and mean in the eyes of men ; so does the man stript of virtues, to God, to angels, and to pious men. 3. Because as clothes are not derived from the human body ; so true virtues are not of the will of man, but the gift of God. Hence that definition of the Schoolmen, *Virtue is that good quality of the mind which constitutes a virtuous life, and which God works in us,* Albert, lib. 5.

cap. 5 ; and Prosper is of the same opinion, De vita contempl. lib. 3. cap. 1 and 16, *Virtues are neither sought after
nor possessed without the gift of God.*

Virtues and garments differ : 1. Because the latter are
daily put on and off; but it is sinful to throw aside virtues
once put on. 2. Because garments do not become better,
but worse from daily wear; but virtues continually augment and strengthen by exercise. 3. Because we can procure clothes by our own efforts ; but virtues cannot be
obtained but by the gift of another, namely, God.

Here it may be asked, Why he bids the Colossians to
put on virtues, when it is said that true virtue is infused
into the human mind by God; and why, too, does he bid
them to put on what he had before said that they had put
on ?

I answer, it is clear from what preceded, that he addresses those whom he presupposes to be regenerate, holy,
and endowed with infused virtues ; and, therefore, to *put
on bowels of mercies, kindness,* &c. denotes nothing more
than daily to advance and exercise in their lives the virtues
impressed upon their hearts by the Holy Spirit. But now,
although it is the work of God alone to infuse into the heart
spiritual gifts and virtues proceeding from grace, yet, human co-operation is required in the exercise of them: See
for instance Paul, in 1 Cor. xv. 10, *By the grace of God I
am what I am, and his grace which was bestowed upon me was
not in vain, but I laboured more abundantly than they all; yet
not I, but the grace of God which was with me.*

As to the other part of the objection, it may also be
added ; the elect and holy who have put on virtues and
gifts by the life-giving aid of the Holy Spirit, both can
and ought to put on the same more and more; which, indeed, they are said to do, when they endeavour that these
gifts of the Spirit may be confirmed and augmented by
use and exercise. For although the power of increasing
does not agree very well with the clothing of the body,
yet it does with these garments of the mind. As Peter
says, in 2 Epis. iii. 18, *Grow in grace and in the knowledge
of the Lord.* These things may suffice concerning the act

of putting on : It follows that we notice the virtues themselves to be put on.

*Bowels of mercies, kindness, humbleness of mind, meekness,
long-suffering.*] He begins with those duties which we owe
when in prosperity to our neighbours in adversity. And,
in the first place, the Apostle requires us to put on *bowels
of mercies,* that is, the real inward and unpretended affection of condoling with another's woe. The phrase is a
Hebraism, which the Apostle frequently uses, even in the
New Testament. And it is taken from the emotion, and,
as it were, concussion which is felt in the stomach, in deep
affections of the mind. Thus it is said of Joseph, Gen.
xliii. 30, *his bowels did yearn,* or were set on fire *towards his
brother.* So in Lamentations ii. 11, *My bowels are troubled,
my liver is poured on the earth for the destruction of the daughter of my people.* In the New Testament also the same
phrase is used : See Luke i. 78 ; Phil. ii. 1. The most
tender affection is, therefore, intended by the expression
bowels of mercies. The Apostle wisely begins with the expression of condolence ; because from hence flows the act
of relief; and because, as says Gregory, Mor. 20. 27, *It is
more to compassionate any one from the heart, than to give :
for he who gives what is external, gives what does not belong to his
own person; but he who gives compassion, gives somewhat of
himself.*

The chief objects of this compassion are persons who
have none to give them relief, as widows and orphans ; but,
in general, it comprehends all oppressed with misery,
whether the poor, prisoners, the sick, the afflicted, &c.

We have many motives or incentives to this affection of
mercy.

1. We have the express and oft repeated command of
God : Luke vi. 36, *Be ye merciful:* Rom. xii. 15, *Weep with
them that weep ;* and 1 Pet. iii. 8, *Be ye kindly affectioned,*
&c. Whence Gregory Nazianzen says, Orat. 16, *If thou
hast nothing, give but a tear; for pity is a great solace to the
afflicted.*

2. We have, besides, the examples of the prophets, of
Christ, and the Apostles, and, lastly, of all good men :

Jer. ix. 1; Matt. ix. 36; Luke xix. 41; 2 Cor. xi 29.
Hence that saying of the Poet, *The good are tear-abounding*
men.

3. We have, lastly, the conformity of nature, and the
possibility of suffering similar things. For nothing is more
agreeable to nature, than to be touched with the evils and
misfortunes of those who are partakers of the same nature
with us. This the Apostle points out, Heb. ii. 17, where
he says of Christ, that *it behoved* him *to be made like his*
brethren that he might be a merciful and faithful High priest.
The possibility of suffering similar evils, when seriously
considered, forces mercy from any man that is not destitute of feeling : For what has happened to some one may
happen to any one; which even Aristotle acknowledges,
Rhet. 2. cap. 18.

Hence we conclude,

1. The apathy (ἀπάθεια) of the Stoics must be exploded
by a Christian ; as not agreeing either with our natural condition or our supernatural regeneration.   Prosper, De vit.
contempl. 30, 31, well remarks, *We are not in fault for hav-*
ing affections, but for making a bad use of them.

2. Bowels of mercy are found in every regenerate person : he is therefore moved at the very first view of another's
misery.

3. They who, ere they can be excited to mercy, must
have much solicitation, bewailing, and clamour from the
afflicted, can lay claim to little or nothing of the spiritual
man : they who are not moved by these, have nothing human in them.

Kindness.] From the affection, the Apostle passes to
the act ; because the pity of the rich without kindness is
but the illusion of the wretched.   Augustine properly defines true pity to be, *compassion in our heart for another's*
distress, such as will lead us to assist where we are able. Thus
by compassion the mind grieves, says Gregory, *as the liberal*
hand shews this affection of grief.   Consequently, these two,
mercy and kindness, must always be joined together, as
James recommends, Chap. ii. 16, and John, 1 Epis. iii. 17.
Whatever they pretend, they who have their hands closed,

have their bowels of mercy closed too, or rather they have none. But we shall also adduce some motives for this *kindness* or *liberality.*

The first shall be what ought to prompt us to all good works, the command of God and our Lord. For it is not the case (as the vulgar vainly imagine) that works of justice alone fall under the precept, and works of mercy are left to our own will. God distinctly requires of us works of beneficence, and severely punishes their omission. *Break thy bread with the hungry,* Isa. lviii. 7. See Matt. xxv. 41, 42, &c.

Secondly, the duty of dispensing their wealth is imposed upon all the rich. Hence benevolence towards the poor is called *righteousness,* Prov. xi. 18. And they are reproached with theft by the Fathers, who, when they might, assist not the poor. Hence that charge of Basil : *The bread which you withhold is the bread of your servant ; the garment which you keep is the garment of the naked ; and the money you lay up is the money of the poor.* And Gregory Nazianzen, Orat. 16, says, *May it not be my unhappy lot to grow rich while the poor are in want, and I not succour them in their distress,* &c.

Thirdly, A reward is promised by God to those who are beneficent towards the poor : A reward, I say, both in this life and in the life which is to come. That it is in this life see Ps. cxii. 5, &c. Prov. xi. 25, and xxviii. 27. For that which is to come, see Matt. xxv. 34, Luke xiv. 14, Gal. vi. 9. The testimonies of the Fathers to this are very numerous ; and hence the exhortations to benevolence. *We lose all earthly things by keeping them ; we preserve them by giving,* says Greg. Hom. 17. in Evang. *It is gain to give to the poor,* says Basil, Serm. 1, in Avaros. *Why fearest thou to render everlasting thy frail and transitory goods, or to entrust thy treasures to God's safe keeping ?* asks Lactantius, lib. 6. cap. 12. And Jerom, ad Nepotian says, *I do not remember to have read of an unhappy death of any one who had liberally exercised the works of charity ; for such an one has many intercessors.*

Humbleness of mind.] The Apostle well joins this to *mercy* and *kindness;* since, as Augustine observes, *there are many who would more readily give all they have to feed the poor, than become beggars themselves before God.* Indeed it often happens, that works of charity and mercy give occasion for pomp and pride. In whatever condition we are, then, we have need to *put on humility:* In prosperity (that is, when we abound in temporal or spiritual riches), lest we become insolent towards God, as in the case of Uzziah, 2 Chron. xxvi. 16, and of the Israelites, Hosea xiii. 6; lest we despise and oppress our neighbour as did Haman, in Esther iii. 6; or the Pharisee, in Luke xviii. 11. For, as Gregory has remarked, *It is a rare thing for a person who is preeminent in many respects not to despise any one.* In adversity too; lest we murmur against God, as the Israelites did; or despond in mind under our afflictions.

The following reflections will engender humbleness of mind in us :—

1. If we consider that whatever good thing we have, it does not come from ourselves, but from God; that it is small, in comparison of the virtues we are without, and the sins with which we are beset; and that we have abused this little good in many ways.

2. If we reflect that it is an especial part of the image of the devil, to admire one's self; but a part of the image of Christ to be humble and lowly, Matt. xi. 29. Whence Augustine says, de Trinit. 4. 10, *The prince of pride brings to death the man who indulges pride; Christ the Lord of humility brings to life the man who obeys.*

3. If we observe how God is affected towards the humble; viz. in that he has respect to them before others, Isa. lxvi. 2; and beyond all others he adorns and enriches them more and more with his gifts, Matt. xi. 25; Psal. xviii. 27; Luke i. 52, 53. Parisiensis not unaptly calls the human heart *a spiritual vacuum.* And as nature does not suffer a corporeal vacuum, but rather impels some bodies into places not suited to their nature; so the grace of God does not allow of a spiritual vacuum in the heart of the humble, but sends streams of heavenly blessings to fill it.

4. If we remark what mind God bears towards the

proud : viz. that he accounts them his greatest enemies, and pursues them with his wrath even to destruction. *He destroys the house of the proud,* Prov. xv. 25; *God resisteth the proud,* &c. 1 Pet. v. 5. From which Gregory, on that passage 1 Sam. xv. 17, WHEN THOU WAST LITTLE IN THINE OWN EYES, says, *Thou wast great in mine eyes, because lowly in thine own : now art thou abased before me, because great in thine own sight.* Therefore how much any one is precious in his own eyes, by so much he becomes more base before God.

Lastly, if we bear in mind that pride is the poison of all virtues, and of all good deeds. Whence Augustine (on Ps. xciii.) concludes, *Humility in evil deeds is more pleasing to God, than pride in good ones.* He, therefore, who combines other virtues without humility, does but bear chaff against the wind. On this account God determined that it was better for his holy Apostle to be buffetted by Satan, than to be inflated by the sin of pride, 2 Cor. xii. 7.

Meekness, long-suffering.] These two virtues are the daughters of *humility,* of which we have the greatest need in adversity, and when we have business with morose, reproachful, and wicked men ; for they become as a shield to us. As to *meekness;* it is that virtue which renders a man manageable in common intercourse, and prevents him from being exasperated beyond measure and justice at the follies, stubbornness, and lighter faults of others, even when they tend to his own injury or disadvantage. It is such a moderator of passion, that it absolutely restrains what is unjust, and so tempers and softens what is just, that it is neither rashly excited, nor borne headlong beyond its proper limits. A humble-minded man ($\pi\rho\alpha o\varsigma$) is not badly described by Aristotle, Ethic. 4, 5, when he says that he is not driven headlong by unbridled passion, but *is angry so far, so long, and against the person right reason enjoins;* and, in a word, *is not given to revenge, but rather easy to be appeased.*

We must strive after this virtue on many accounts.

1. Because it resides not with the good and perfect, but among those who often sin, from infirmity and igno-

rance; which even we ourselves do. *It is but just*, therefore, *that one requiring pardon for his offences should in his turn grant it.* Which also the Apostle advises, Gal. vi. 1, *Brethren, if a man be overtaken in a fault, ye which are spiritual restore such an one in the spirit of meekness; considering thyself, lest thou also be tempted.*

2. Because it brings the greatest utility to us, in rendering life pleasant and tranquil : while the passionate and angry are daily driven to madness, by the injuries they give and receive on every side. *The meek*, says the Psalmist, *shall inherit the earth; they shall delight themselves in the abundance of peace.* Ps. xxxvii. 11.

3. Because it is a sign and an essential mark of the sons of God, and of those destined to eternal happiness. *Blessed are the peace-makers; for they shall be called the children of God*, Matt. v. 9.

4. Because we have exhibited to us a living model of meekness in God himself (Jonah iv. 2 ; Joel ii. 13); the Son of God (1 Pet. ii. 23); and, in fine, in all the servants of God ; as Moses (Num. xii. 3); David (2 Saml. xvi. 10, 11); Paul (1 Thess. ii. 7), *We were gentle among you, even as a nurse cherisheth her own children.*

Long-suffering, μακροθυμιαν.] This is not very different from the preceding virtue, unless that it seems to refer to injuries of a more grievous nature done to us by men, and severer calamities sent by God himself. Therefore we should not only bear with calmness and meekness, the follies, infirmities, and daily and customary injuries of men ; but even if we should be annoyed and oppressed, however bitterly and maliciously, we must bear it with a great and generous mind.

1. On account of the Divine Providence which orders and disposes all these things, and to which it is right for a servant of God to submit. This we find to have been done by Job, David, and Christ himself; who, when evil entreated by the wicked, patiently obeyed the will of God.

2. On account of the advantage derived therefrom. For griefs and injuries greatly conduce to cure the diseases of the soul ; to beat down pride, to extinguish the love of the

world, as well as to shake off spiritual lethargy. Besides, they shew forth the virtues of the pious and the glory of God, and augment the reward and crown promised to the saints : In one word, they always *work together for good to them who love God,* Rom. viii. 28.

3. On account of our consciousness of sin and demerit. For whatever evils are brought upon us by the malice of men, are permitted by the justice of God.   He would inflict far heavier if he treated us according to our deserts. So the godly have ever acknowledged; Nehem. ix. 33; Dan. ix. 8.

4. On account of the worth and excellence of affliction. For it is not reproach (as the vulgar think) to suffer for Christ, or be trampled upon by the wicked; but, on the contrary, honourable.   Whence says Peter, 1 Epis. iv. 16, *If any man suffer as a Christian let him not be ashamed; but let him glorify God on this behalf.* So the Apostles were animated; *they departed from the presence of the council, rejoicing that they were counted worthy to suffer shame for his name,* Acts v, 41.   *We should rejoice in afflictions,* says Parisiensis, *because we are received to the communion of the sufferings of Christ, as it were to drink in common of the royal cup.* In this sense also it is said in Philippians i. 29, *Unto you it is given in the behalf of Christ, not only to believe on him, but also to suffer for his sake.*

From what has been said of these two virtues we gather,

That they are not to be accounted happy nor men of fortitude, who in this world commit violence and oppress others, and do what they please against whom they please under the impulse of their fury and lust.   They are not happy; since this is both the signal and the cause of their future damnation, Phi. i. 28: nor men of fortitude; for this is the effect of the old and impotent Adam, and shews them to be destitute of the sanctifying Spirit and all its gifts and ornaments.

On the other hand, We infer from the foregoing; that they who bear with a meek spirit the injuries and reproaches of the wicked, are neither base nor miserable; but happy

and valiant, as endowed with the Spirit of God, covered
with his gifts as arms of defence, and by their means conquerors over all evil.

Vers. 13. *Forbearing one another, and forgiving one another, if any man have a quarrel against any : even as
Christ forgave you, so also do ye.*

In these words the Apostle shews the use and requires
the practice of the afore-mentioned virtues of meekness
and long-suffering. It is of little moment to have virtues,
if you neglect to exercise them when occasion offers. But
in this verse three things are to be remarked: 1. The actions required ; two for instance : the action of suffering,
forbearing one another ; the action of forgiving, *and forgiving one another.* 2. The object of these actions (viz. the
μομφη) i. e. *the just cause of complaint.* 3. The rule of these
our actions, viz. the example of Christ, *as Christ also hath
forgiven,* &c.

Forbearing one another.] Here is the first act of the
before-named virtues. Now he is said *to forbear* who,
though attacked and wounded either by words or deeds,
does not immediately rise up to inflict revenge ; but endeavours to overcome his enemy with mildness and to bring
him back to a proper mind.

However this forbearance under injuries is accounted
mean among the proud, yet by the wise it is esteemed the
best and most glorious way of conquest ; and that on many
accounts. For

1. He who bears injuries, overcomes and conquers himself, whilst he represses and restrains the desire for revenge
always boiling forth from our corrupt nature ; and binds
and confines that wrath, as it were a furious monster, lurking within him. This mode of conquest Solomon cele-

brates in Prov. xvi. 32, *He that is slow to anger is better than the mighty; and he that ruleth his spirit than he that taketh a city.* *To conquer oneself is the greatest of conquests,* says Plato.

2. He who forbears, conquers the very malice of his enemy. For when two contraries are in contention and conflict, that is said to conquer which draws the other into similarity with itself; that to be conquered, which is drawn or changed by the other. Therefore, like as we say water is overcome by fire, when it becomes warm ; and, on the contrary, to have overcome it, if, retaining its own cold, it can subdue the fire : so we say a Christian is overcome by a wicked man, as often as he, by the provocation of attack, is drawn into similar fury ; on the contrary, we may pronounce him to have conquered when he retains his own disposition, and, by bearing with the violence of the other, changes and mollifies his ferocity. See a beautiful example 1 Sam. xxiv. 17, &c.; where David, by forbearing, and refraining from revenge, so mollifies and changes Saul, that from breathing blood and slaughter, he melts into tears and entreaties, confesses his fault, and is compelled to acknowledge and extol David's innocence and meekness. Who does not here see the malice of Saul overcome, and the patience of David triumphing?

3. He who forbears, not only conquers, but conquers by lawful means, and those which God commands his soldiers to use. Now it behoves a soldier obeying the command of his general, not only to fight, but to do it with those arms, and in that manner which is assigned him. *No one receiveth the crown unless he strive lawfully,* 2 Tim. ii. 5. But hear the decree of our commander, Prov. xxiv. 29, *Say not I will do so to him as he hath done to me ; I will render to the man according to his work. Recompence to no man evil for evil,* Rom. xii. 17 ; and again, vers. 21, *Be not overcome of evil, but overcome evil with good.* So much for the act of forbearing.

And forgiving one another.] In this second act there is more contained than in the former. For there are some who sometimes bear injuries, because, forsooth, they can-

not avenge them, or because they do not think it expedient; yet in the mean time the injury is treasured up in their
memory, malice rages in their hearts, and a thirst for revenge burns. The Apostle, therefore, would have us, not
only bear an injury, but remove from our hearts the very
desire itself of revenge; nay, that we should cherish a love
for our most bitter enemies. Here applies the precept of
Christ, Matt. xviii. 35, *That every one forgive his brother
from his heart:* and Luke vi. 27, 28, *Love your enemies; do
good to them that hate you; bless them that curse you, and
pray for them that despitefully use you.* We read that all
this was religiously observed by Christians in the primitive
Church. *It is the custom of all to love their friends; of Christians alone to love their enemies,* says Tertul. ad Scap.
Hence we are instructed

1. That those are in error who think that the forgiving
of injuries and loving our enemies is matter of counsel and
not of precept: for the Apostle teaches us that this belongs to *all the elect of God, holy and beloved,* that is, to all
the regenerate.

2. They who forgive others profit themselves, yea, remove their own sins in some measure: whence in the Greek
the phrase is χαριζομενοι εαυτοις, *remitting* or *forgiving your
own selves.* And Jerome writes on Ephes. v. *What good one
does to another is laid up more for him who performs the deed,
than for him for whom it is performed.* And Christ most
plainly says, Matt. vi. 15, *If ye forgive not men their trespasses, neither will your heavenly Father forgive you your
trespasses.*

3. No one walks so cautiously, but that he sometimes
offends against his neighbour both in words and deeds.
Hence the Apostle says, *forgiving one another;* as if we all
had need of this mutual forgiveness. Thus much as to the
actions required; viz. *forbearing and forgiving.*

If any man have a quarrel against any.] Here we have
the object or matter about which *forbearing and forgiving*
is to be exercised, viz. *a quarrel,* that is, some just cause
of complaint.

Here we must remark that all the words are put indefinitely, and are therefore to be received universally, in this manner; *If any man,* that is, whoever in truth he may be, whether superior or inferior : *shall have a quarrel,* that is, any cause of complaint whatever, on account of any wrong done either in word or deed : *against any,* viz. whether friend or foe ; let him know that the duty of forbearing and forgiving is necessarily imposed upon him.

Corollaries.

1. If a *just cause* is not a sufficient ground for inflicting revenge, it is evident that they grievously offend who break forth into disputes and strifes for trifling and nugatory causes, nay, for those that are unjust and absolutely nothing. See Matt. xviii. 28.

2. Since the act of forbearing and forgiving is required from all towards all, the pride of the great and the rich is rebuked, who think themselves exempt from this duty : as if only the poor and weak were born to bear injuries, and the powerful and noble to inflict them. But the Scripture has not respect for nobility, power, or riches, but for fraternity, when it speaks of the forgiveness of injuries. See Matt. xviii. 21.

It is asked, If this duty of forbearing and forgiving be so necessary to a Christian, that it is not lawful for him in any way to repel an injury done to him, or to restrain or punish the person who offers it; but is bound *when he is smitten on one cheek to turn the other;* or *when his cloak is taken away to offer his coat also?* as Christ says, Matt. v. 39, 40.

We reply, That it is not by any means lawful for a private person by himself, and according to the dictates of his own will, to seek his own revenge; but it is sometimes lawful to do it by means of the magistrate and according to his judgment. Neither ought we to seek our revenge through the magistrate himself with an exasperated and corrupt mind, that is, with the passion of anger and hatred against our neighbour; but with a peaceful and meek mind, that is, from a zeal for righteousness, and a desire for the amendment of our neighbour: for it is better to lose any thing of this world, than to make a wreck of our patience

and Christian charity. On the other hand, that it is lawful
to seek the aid of the magistrate against those who do us
injury is evident hence; 1. Because God himself, who approves nothing contrary to charity, hath ordained magistrates and tribunals. 2. Because laws in all well organised
states are enacted for the repairing of injuries; which laws
would remain absolutely useless if it was unlawful to recur
to their assistance against evil-doers. 3. Because it is
profitable even to evil-doers themselves, that they should
be punished for their crimes, and that the plunder they
obtain by doing injury to others should be taken from
them : Hence it may sometimes happen, that charity requires us to take vengeance of the wicked : for *he is overcome with the advantage of victory on his side,* says Augustine, *from whom the liberty of doing injury is taken away.*
August. Epist. 5, ad Marcell. As to what our Saviour says
and the other similar passages of Scripture, we maintain
that they should be interpreted according to the context.
Thus, *when you shall be smitten on one cheek, turn the other,*
that is, rather than break out yourself into revenge, and
inflict the same injury upon another. We say, too, that
such passages are to be understood with this limitation :
Do so as often as the glory of God and the good of our
neighbour seems to require it. These, therefore, are necessary precepts (as the Schoolmen say out of Augustine,)
as far as the *preparation of the mind* is concerned; and they
are to be followed in the *outward act,* as often as the glory
of God and the good of our neighbour requires. See more
on this point in Augustine, Epist. 5, ad Marcellinum.

Even as Christ forgave you, so also do ye.] Supply the
word *forgive.* The example of Christ ought to have with
Christians both the force of an argument for persuasion
and of a rule for direction, as far as forbearing and forgiving are concerned; the force of an argument; because the
members ought to correspond to their head. A proud or a
feeble member is inconsistent with a head which is humble
and crowned with thorns. Hence by Christ himself and
his Apostles, the example of Christ is urged principally in
those things which relate to charity and the humility of his

sufferings. *If I have washed your feet, ye ought also to wash one another's feet: for I have given you an example,* John xiii. 14. *Christ hath suffered for us, leaving us an example,* 1 Pet. ii. 21. *He that saith he abideth in him, ought himself also so to walk, even as he walked,* 1 John ii. 6. The example of Christ has, moreover, the force of a rule in directing us, inasmuch as it contains the most perfect model of virtue. Hence Bernard says, *What have you to do with virtues, who are ignorant of the virtues of Christ? Where, I beseech you, will ye find true prudence, but in the doctrine of Christ? where true temperance, but in the life of Christ? Where true fortitude, but in the passion of Christ?* But let us evince this in our acts of forbearing and forgiving : in which we have a perfect rule for imitation, whether we regard what Christ bore and forgave, or from whom, or, in fine, in what manner he bore and forgave.

As to *what* he bore and forgave? It was curses, and those the most grievous and bitter: for he was called a glutton and a wine-bibber, a friend of publicans and sinners, one possessed of a devil, one using the assistance of dæmons, a madman, a blasphemer, an impostor ;* and, in fine, what not? He suffered evil entreatment too, being spit upon, being beaten with rods, lastly, being crucified. Yet all these so many and so great injuries he bore and forgave.

From whom? From the chiefs of the people, from the people themselves, from the ignorant, from the wicked, from strangers and from countrymen, from Jews and Gentiles; in short, being injured by every description of men, he bore with them all, he pardoned them all.

In what manner? Not from such infirmity as rendered him unable to resist; but from humility and voluntary obedience, which made him willing to suffer. Isa. liii. 7 ; Matt. xxvi. 53. Not with a treacherous and deceitful intention, meditating and seeking future vengeance ; but with a pure heart inflamed with love, intreating from God the Father a gracious forgiveness for his enemies ; Luke

* Matt. xi. 19 ; John vii. 20 ; Luke xi. 18.

xxiii. 34.   Such was the perfect bearing of injuries and
the forgiveness of Christ, of which the Apostle speaks in
saying, *As Christ has forgiven you, so also do ye.*   We ought
therefore, to compare ourselves with this example ; and
although we cannot attain to its perfection, yet we should
remember always to propose to ourselves its imitation.

We derive the following instructions ;

1. It behoves a Christian to be certain of the pardon of
his sins through Christ : since this pardoning is the rule
and measure of pardoning others ; but a rule ought to be
fixed and certain.

2. He who does not freely pardon others, never feels in
his heart the benefit of Christ pardoning his sins : neither
can he who has not resolved to forgive his neighbour, conclude that his own sins are forgiven of God.

3. In vain does the mind eager for revenge excuse its
own malice by the extent of the injury done, and by the
loss to the man's own character if revenge be neglected,
and other points of the like nature, by which men are accustomed to inflame themselves with revenge.   All these
considerations vanish if we attend to the rule laid down
by the Apostle, *As Christ hath forgiven you, so also do ye.*

4. It is, therefore, a diabolical opinion, which has possessed the minds of almost all those who lay claim to gen-
tility, that they cannot bear, even a reproachful word, without the loss of their honour and their reputation ; but are
under the necessity of seeking revenge in a duel, at the
manifest peril of their own lives, and a plain attack upon the
life of another.

This more than heathenish opinion can be refuted by
many arguments :

1. We pull down the very foundation of what we are
striving to build, by laying down this maxim.   It is not a
sign of a cowardly or ignoble mind, nor disgraceful or
mean in a Christian, to bear injuries, but to inflict them.
This was briefly proved above, when we were reasoning on
meekness, patience, and their acts : we will now add, that
this was even approved by the very heathens, especially the
wiser among them.   Socrates, as we find in Plato (in his

Gorgia) draws the conclusion, that every injury is dishonourable and infamous to *the inflictor* of it, not *to him who
suffers it ;* and that, as he says himself, *for the strongest and
most solid reasons,* σιδηροῖς καὶ ἀδαμαντίνοις λόγοις. Aristotle follows the same opinion in his Ethics 5. cap. 11, giving this
reason ; *To inflict an injury is the effect of dishonesty ; and
on that account dishonourable and infamous : but to suffer
one with equanimity is the effect of virtue, and therefore glorious.* Seneca, in that book where he professedly considers whether an injury can affect a wise man, writes ; *We
ought to despise injuries, and what I may call the shadow of
injuries, contumely, whether they fall deservedly or undeservedly upon us. If deservedly, it is not contumely, but judgment
given ; if undeservedly, it is for him who did the injury, and
not for me to be ashamed of it.* That we may not accumu-
late more from profane authors, we have the opinion of
Christ himself, Matt. v. 11, *Blessed are ye when men shall
revile you.*

2.   Should we grant that injury or contumely has been
cast upon us, and that to do this is criminal ; nevertheless
it by no means follows, that it is lawful to repel it by
means of a duel : and that for these reasons ;

1.   No one ought to be judge in his own cause ; and,
least of all, one who is disturbed with anger, violence, and
the passion of revenge. Tertullian, De patient. says, *What
have I to do with a passion, which I cannot govern through impatience?*

2.   Individuals do injury to God and his vicarious repre-
sentative, the magistrate, when they seek to revenge themselves by private means. *Vengeance is mine, and I will repay,* saith the Lord, Deut. xxxii. 35; and Rom. xiii. 14,
Paul says of the magistrate, *He beareth not the sword in
vain.* But he would bear it in vain, if it was allowed to an
individual to draw the sword at his own pleasure.

3.   Duellists would punish every injury with the same
punishment, namely, death ; which is not the judgment of
a generous man, but of a madman. Now every punishment inflicted by one possessed of all his faculties, ought
to be commensurate with the offence.

We shall conclude with the saying of Christ. Matt. xxvi. 52, *All they that take the sword shall perish with the sword;* that is, as Augustine interprets it, *Every one who without legitimate authority granted to him, or enjoining him so to do, shall arm himself against the life of any man, shall perish either by the sword of man, or that of Divine vengeance.* From all these reasons it appears clear, that they are absolutely madmen, who follow the opinions of the many, renouncing the doctrine of Christ : so that they may retain the name of Gentlemen, they do not fear the title of homicide ; and, finally, so that they may avoid a suspicion of false infamy, they leap into the very pit of hell itself. Thus much of those virtues which we practise towards such persons as are hostile and injurious to us : We next come to those which refer to all without distinction.

Verse 14.

Above all these things put on charity which is the bond of perfectness.

The Apostle has exhorted the Colossians to put on meekness and long-suffering, and also to exercise these virtues : now he proceeds to advise them to put on charity also, which is the root, parent, and mistress, as well of these, as of all other virtues. This verse has two parts : the exhortation to put on charity ; and the commendation of charity, which contains the force of an argument for putting it on.

Above all these things charity.]   First, let us consider this virtue of charity itself; secondly, its pre-eminence, or the prerogative which belongs to it. The Apostle speaks of charity towards one's neighbour ; this, however, is always to be understood to spring from love towards God. Now it is thus defined by Clemens Alexandrinus ; *The extension of benevolence with just reason to the advantage of one's neighbour.* Strom. 2. But I am better pleased with the following definition : *It is a virtue divinely infused, by which God is sincerely loved for his own sake, and one's neighbour for God's sake.* For it is the same virtue of charity, which causes us to love God, and one's neighbour under God and for God. This love of charity is distinguished from every vicious love on account of its *beginning.* For charity flows from God, as a gift infused by the Holy Spirit into human hearts. *Love is of God,* 1 John iv. 7. *God hath given to us the Spirit of love,* 2 Tim. i. 7. Whence Prosper, De vita contempl. 3. 13, says, *Charity is a regulated will united to God, enkindled by the fire of the Holy Spirit.* But all vicious and inordinate love arises from the fountain of innate concupiscence : such is the love of the avaricious, the ambitious, the lustful ; and, in one word, of all the wicked.

It is distinguished also on account of its *order and its object.* For charity arises from God whom it loves for himself : corrupt love springs from oneself. Charity proceeds to love one's neighbour for the Lord's sake ; corrupt love pretends to love one's neighbour, but pursues one's own advantage and pleasure. Therefore, they neither agree in order nor in object. But when it is said, Charity proceeds from God to one's neighbour, it is by no means to be restricted to relatives, kinsmen, or our familiar friends ; but is to be extended to men universally : for every man who is in want of our good offices, or our assistance, is our neighbour. Luke x. 36. Hence Augustine, on Psalm cxviii. Conc. 8, says, *Every man is neighbour to every man ; nor is the remoteness of family ties to be considered, where there is a common nature.* With this view the Schoolmen say, Neighbour is to be understood not from *nearness of blood,* but *fellowship in reason.* Aquinas, Quæst. disp. de char. art. 7. But since we enlarged on this virtue of charity when treating the fourth verse of the first Chapter, we shall pass by the rest, and proceed with its pre-eminence.

The Apostle intimates this prerogative of Charity when he says, ἐπὶ πᾶσι τούτοις, *above all these,* as the common translation renders it. In the figure the Apostle has taken up he seems to compare charity to some outward garment, which is worn over the others ; to which comparison, however, we must attend not in regard to the order, as though

charity was to be put on last of all the virtues before-mentioned ; but with regard to the comprehensiveness of the
similitude.

1. As an outer garment is generally wider and larger
than the rest ; so does charity exceed the before-mentioned
virtues.

2. As that garment which is worn outermost is generally more beautiful and costly than the rest; so does charity among the other virtues shine like the moon among
the stars.

3. As the ranks and degrees of men are generally distinguished by the outer garment; so charity serves to dis-
criminate the true disciples of Christ and sons of God from
false and pretended ones. So John xiii. 35, *By this shall
all men know that ye are my disciples, if ye have love one to
another.*

Calvin reads, *on account of all these things put on charity.*
The Greek word επι, signifies both *over* and *because of (super
et propter);* and either way serves to illustrate the excellence of charity. For if the Apostle has commanded them
on account of all these virtues also to put on charity, he
wished to shew that neither they nor their actions could
subsist without charity.

For first, they have their truth, and, consequently, their
value, from charity ; as the Apostle says, 1 Cor. xiii. 3,
*Though I bestow all my goods to feed the poor, and though I
give my body to be burned, and have not charity, it profiteth
me nothing.* Many marvellous properties are to be found
in men, says Prosper, *which without having the marrow of
charity, put on the appearance of piety, but have not its reality.*
Epist. ad Ruffin. de lib. arbit.

Secondly, they have their actions from charity : for in
those points which regard our neighbour, she is as it were
the mistress of the other virtues, and causes them as her
servants to perform her tasks. On this account their properties and actions are attributed to charity. *Charity is
long-suffering,* &c. 1 Cor. xiii. 4, *suffereth all things, believeth
all things, hopeth all things ;* vers. 7, ib. This is what the
Schoolmen mean when they tell us that charity produces

the actions of all the other virtues, not *elicitively*, but *imperatively*.

Thirdly, they have their firmness and alacrity from charity. Whence Gregory (in cap. 28. Jobi) says, *If any work be found destitute of charity, it is immediately taken away by the tempter.* And Aquinas (Quæst. disp. de charit. art. 2) remarks, that it is the peculiar property of charity, that *in exercising the other acts of virtue, charity forces us to act voluntarily, promptly, with delight, and with firmness.* On these accounts the Apostle assigns to charity the first place among the virtues, and admonishes us to put it on either above all these or on account of them all. We come now to that encomium or eulogy of charity expressed by the Apostle in these words,

The bond of perfectness] a figurative expression. For he calls it *a bond* from the similitude of the effect, since it joins and combines together things differing from one another; and from this connexion and conjunction springs perfectness. Some refer this *perfection* to the virtues, others, to the church. The former say charity is *the bond of perfectness* among virtues themselves; since he who hath charity hath all the other virtues, and practises them; which the following Scriptures hint at; Rom. viii. 8, *He who loveth his neighbour hath fulfilled the law.* Galat. v. 14, *All the law is fulfilled in one word, namely this, Thou shalt love thy neighbour as thyself.* Whence Cyprian says, *In love, are combined all the volumes of the Scriptures. In this all religion is consummated.* It is consequently called *the bond of perfectness,* since it joins and binds together the duties of all virtues : so that wherever true charity is, there is found the whole body and connexion as it were of all virtues. But when this sense is allowed, the Romanists fall upon us, and object ;

If charity be the perfect fulfilling of the law, then does it justify : for they who perfectly fulfil the law are justified by the works of the law, yet this is impossible according to the Apostle, Rom. iii. 20.

We reply, the fulfilling of the law may be considered in a twofold sense, concerning the parts of the righteousness

commanded, and concerning the degree. True charity fulfils the law in all its parts, but not in full degree. But
justification is not had from the law unless it be fulfilled in
both ways; each being included in the Divine command.
We add this also, That charity if it be itself perfect, brings
the perfect fulfilment of the law; for if the principle that
operates be imperfect in any respect, the operations flowing from it must also be imperfect. Now we have the testimony of Augustine to shew that charity is imperfect in
every mortal, Eqist. 29. ad Hiero. *Entire charity exists in
no individual as long as he lives here on earth: but that which
is less than it ought to be, partakes of sin: from this sin there
is no man free upon earth.* This also Aquinas acknowledges,
Quæst. disp. de charit. art. 10.

But there are others who refer this perfection to the
body of the church, and affirm that charity is the bond of
perfectness in the church, since it unites her members one
with another, and effects a community of mutual operations for the advantage and preservation of the whole. For
as the perfection of the natural body arises from the union
and connexion of the parts, so much so, that we account it
halt and imperfect if they be torn away or separated: so
the body of the church is considered perfect and entire, as
all its members are held together by the bond of charity;
but weak and imperfect if they should be drawn asunder
by quarrelling and malice. In this sense, therefore, charity may be called *the bond of perfectness.* For the Apostle
teaches, Rom. xii. 5, that the church is *one body;* and
again, in Ephes. iv. 16, that this body *increases,* as far as it is
*fitly joined together and compacted by that which every joint
supplieth, according to the effectual working of every part.*
Nothing, therefore, prevents our admitting charity, in both
respects, to be *the bond of perfectness.* These things being
explained, we must point out some general corollaries or
instructions which flow from the above.

1. We hence learn to examine our acts of beneficence
and mercy, in order to ascertain whether they flow from
charity or not. Many persons impose upon themselves,
and while they are dreaming that they perform acts of cha-

rity, are doing no more than works of vanity: we must, therefore, examine as to the moving principle, the order, the object, the intention, &c.

2. We may collect from the foregoing, that with however many virtues any one may seem to be adorned, he is not clothed as becomes a son of God or a true Christian, unless he shall have put on over the rest this garment of charity.

3. Hence also we see the reason why the before-mentioned virtues, *mercy, humility, meekness, long-suffering,* and others, appear so seldom in common life; namely, because their parent *charity* has perished, as it is said in Matt. xxiv. 12, *Because iniquity shall abound, the love of many shall wax cold.*

Hence, lastly, we perceive that they who break the bonds of charity, and afford occasion for schism, rend the integrity and perfection of their mother the Church, and, as it were, dislocate and tear her limb from limb. Thus much concerning charity.

Verse 15.

And let the peace of God rule in your hearts, to the which also ye are called in one body: and be ye thankful.

Ye have heard the Apostle's exhortation to put on charity. He now exhorts to two other virtues, which are daughters, and, indeed, handmaids of charity; for they daily attend upon their mother, and cherish and preserve her. One of these virtues he calls *peace,* the other is *gratitude.*

As to the former, three things occur to be observed,

1. Whence this peace hath its origin: viz. from God: *the peace of God,* &c.

2. What is its office, viz. to rule and preside in human hearts : βραβευέτω.

3. What motives we have to render this duty of peace; viz. two : the ordinance of God ; *to which also ye are called,* namely, by God : our mutual relation; because we are members *of the same body.*

The peace of God.] This peace is either internal, which we call peace of conscience ; or external and brotherly, which we may call the peace of friendship. That former is established between God and the conscience of every individual whenever by faith he apprehends Christ, and the remission of his sins for Christ's sake, and God reconciled and propitious to him. Hence says the Apostle, Rom. v. 1, *Being justified by faith, we have peace with God, through our Lord Jesus Christ*: and Ephes. ii. 14, *He is our peace.* This peace cannot have its origin from any other source than God : and hence it is named *the peace of God,* Phil. iv. 7, *The peace of God which passeth all understanding,* &c. The latter subsists among neighbours, and arises from charity ; and the Apostle has respect in this place principally to this. Now this peace especially denotes that affection of the heart which inclines it to love and seek concord, and to procure and preserve it by all means : although he may also design the external effect, that is, a peaceful state of all things among Christians, which is wont to arise from that peaceable inclination. This peace in either respect is also from God. That peaceable affection is by the inspiration of God ; and the effect, or that happy and peaceful course of all things in the Church, is from the blessing of God. Isa. xlv. 7 ; and lxvi. 12 ; Galat. v. 22.*

Let it rule in your hearts, Βραβευέτω 'εν ταῖς καρδίαις ὑμων.] Some render this, *let it bear the palm;* others more aptly (as it seems to me) *let it command, rule,* or *moderate.* For the Apostle would intimate, that this is the duty of this virtue, to act as an umpire or steward amongst the other

---

* The Translator is here so forcibly reminded of the beautiful and affecting Collect of our Church for the fifth Sunday after Trinity, that he cannot refrain from adducing it :—" Grant, O Lord, we beseech thee, that the course of this world may be so peaceably ordered by thy governance, that thy Church may joyfully serve thee in all godly quietness ; through Jesus Christ our Lord." May every Reader's heart respond—" Amen."

affections: for so the word Βραβεύειν signifies. When, therefore, (as is often the case) the unruly affections of wrath,
hatred, and revenge rise in our hearts, this *peace of God*
ought to discharge its office, that is, put an end to the
contentions, as the umpire of the games, take away the
occasions thereof, compose their tumultuous affections,
and restore all things to peace.

But it is also to be noted, that the Apostle does not
simply direct that *the peace of God should rule*, but that it
should *rule in our hearts;* in the heart, not in the mouth
only, not in the countenance. For many pretend to the
desire of peace in words and look, who inwardly cherish
wrath and hatred: *whose words are soft, whilst war is in their
heart; they are softer than oil, although they be drawn swords,*
as says the Psalmist, lv. 21. Nazianzen also, Orat. 12,
complains, *Peace is extolled by all, but it is followed by few.*
If then this peace truly flourishes in our hearts, and performs its office, it will incline and draw all to concord, as
well the offending as the offended: the offending, whilst it
keeps wrathful elation from them; the offended, whilst it
removes inexorable obstinacy from them : it makes the former humble, and ready to give satisfaction; the latter easy,
and kind to forgive. This is the office of this steward.

To the which ye also are called in one body, He now shews
what incentives we have to perform this duty of peace.

The former ; Because *we are called to peace :* i. e. Because Christ our Leader and Saviour has not only by his
auspices established peace between us and God ; but he
hath called Jews and Gentiles, and so the whole world, to
cultivate peace with one another, by having called them
into his Church. This is clear,

1. Because this peace is foretold in many places by all
the prophets. Is. ii. 4, and xi. 6, and lxv. 12; So Mich.
iv. 3 ; Zech. ix. 10.

2. Because this peace is enjoined upon all who are
called and chosen into the family of God, that is, the
Church, by the commands of God and of Christ. *Have
peace one with another,* Mar. ix. 50. *Let us follow after the
things which make for peace,* Rom. xiv. 19. *Endeavouring to*

keep the unity of the Spirit in the bond of peace, Ephes.
iv. 3.

3. Because this peace was observed and maintained by
the primitive Church with all earnestness. *The multitude
that believed were of one heart and of one soul.* Acts iv. 32.

4. Lastly, this peace being violated, subverts the
Church which Christ would have to be perpetual. *For a
kingdom divided against itself cannot stand :* but, like as when
many draw a cord in different directions, if it break, they
both fall the more heavily on either hand ; so when the
Church is agitated by strifes, detriment and loss come
upon all.

> ...... *Domestic rents the people's weal disturb ;*
> *Internal discords fail of peace abroad :*
> .... *For nought unsociable is firm.*
> Prudent. in Psychom.

Thus much of the former incitement derived from the appointment of God. But there is an additional incitement
to the cultivation of peace, because not only are we called
thereto by the Divine appointment, but we are moreover
bound to it by a certain mystical relation, which the Apostle denotes in these words,

In one body.] They who are citizens of the same repub-
lic, are mutually called upon and bound to keep the peace ;
yet are they only united in one body politically : but they
who are members of the Church, are united in one body
supernaturally and mystically, so that they all depend upon
one Head, and are quickened and informed* as it were by
one Spirit. This we are taught by the Apostle, Rom. xii.
4, 5, and 1 Cor. xii. 12, 25, 26, where he infers that there
ought to be no difference between the members of the same
body, but the greatest harmony of spirit and sympathy.

---

* Omnes—vivificentur et quasi informentur ab uno Spiritu.

.... " All alike *inform'd*
With radiant light, as glowing ir'n with fire."
Milton.

" This sovereign arbitrary soul
Informs, and moves, and animates the whole."
Blackmore.

Now, from what hath been said concerning the origin of peace, its office, and the incentives to it, these instructions arise :

From the Author God, *the peace of God.*

1. That the peace of God rules among all those in whom the God of peace dwells : and on the other hand, they who reject this peace of God, thrust out the God of peace himself. Thus speaks the Apostle, 2 Cor. xiii. 11, *Live in peace, and the God of love and peace shall be with you.*

2. Whatever of religion and holiness, therefore, schismatics pretend to, they promote the cause of the devil, not of God. For he is the author and the sower of discord : But the true God, is *the God of peace*, 1 Cor. xiv. 33.

3. A union, or rather a confederacy, to assail the godly, extinguish the Gospel, and disseminate errors, is not a a mark of the Church : because there is not among them the peace of God, but the peace of the devil ; such subsisted between Herod and Pilate ; such is preserved among the very devils. In vain do the Romanists, therefore, boast of this union as among the marks of their Church. These instructions are derived from the origin of peace.

From the office ; *rule in your hearts.*

1. This peaceable disposition ought to prevail in all others, and to exercise as it were a regal power over them.

1. They who are opposed to this, are to be seized, restrained, and as it were put in chains, as rebels against their king. Of this kind are wrath, envy, hatred, and the other pests of human happiness and tranquillity.

3. Let counterfeit benevolence, pretended love, hypocritical reconciliation, be far from a Christian man ; for charity and peace ought to hold the sway in his heart, not to play merely in his countenance or his words.

From the incentives ; *to the which also ye are called in one body.*

1. They who disturb the peace of the Church are unmindful of their vocation, and despisers of the Divine appointment. For they whom God hath called and gathered together into his Church, the same he commands to dwell together, as it were in unanimous brotherhood, in their paternal house.

2. However they, who are the cause and the heads of
factions and dissentions, flatter themselves, and seem to
themselves to be lords, they are of all men the most miserable, because they are most hateful to God.   *These six
things doth the Lord hate, yea, seven are an abomination to
him,* Prov. vi. 16.   Now Solomon puts in the seventh
place, *he who soweth discord among brethren,* vers. 19.

3. He who violates peace, is not only hurtful to others,
but to himself.   For no member of an uniform body is injured, but it occasions detriment to the whole : Since therefore, we are all members of the same body, he who tears
and injures another, does the same as if any one by his
own hand should beat and wound another member of his
own body.

4· They who are pleased at the discords and evils of
others, are either stupid members, or indeed not at all members of this one body, the head of which is Christ, and
into the society of which all the godly are called.   Thus
much concerning *peace.*

And be ye thankful.] This is that other virtue to which
the Apostle exhorts, namely, gratitude ; which Cicero
called, in Orat. pro Cn. Planc. not only *the greatest of all
the other virtues,* but *the mother of them.*   Now this gratitude is required as well in regard to God, as in regard to
men.

We ought to be thankful to God ; because without
gratitude there can be no spiritual blessings within us.
For since every spiritual blessing depends upon a certain perpetual influx of Divine grace, ingratitude is that
infernal bar which interrupts the flow and the course of the
Divine goodness.   Therefore we ought to be thankful, lest
we should be deprived of all our gifts.   But gratitude to
God is joined with peace in this place, because our gratitude towards him especially appears in this, if we cultivate
peace religiously ; ingratitude, if we violate it.   For as a
mendicant and vagrant taken into a royal family, shews
himself grateful, if he endeavours with all his might to
adorn and defend the royal house ; but on the contrary,
proves himself ungrateful, if he aims to fill the same with
enmities, and to rend it asunder by factions : so miserable

mortals and outcasts called and chosen into the Church
(which is the house of God), render themselves grateful to
God their Lord, by living in the same peacefully ; but appear as ungrateful by separating and rending it in pieces
with dissentions. On this account therefore, the Apostle
subjoined, *And be ye thankful,* namely, towards God, by
whom *ye are called into one body.*

But gratitude towards men is also required, that peace
may be kept inviolate : because troubles and enmities
sometimes arise, as well from kindnesses not duly repaid,
as from injuries inflicted. Which we perceive in the example of Nabal, 1 Saml. xxv. ; who by his ingratitude so
exasperated the mind of David, that unless the prudence
and humanity of Abigail had relieved him, that ungrateful
man and his whole family would have been ruined. The
Apostle truly thinks this the worst and most pernicious
vice, which he numbers with the worst and most pernicious
vices in 2 Tim. iii. 2.

Instructions ;

1. If we would have God to remain kind to us, we
ought to shew ourselves thankful to him, and grateful for
the benefits conferred upon us.

2. The best proof that we can give of our gratitude is
that we obey the Divine will. *The chief of gratitude,* says
Clemens, *is to do what is agreeable to the pleasure of God.*
Strom. 7.

3. Those benefitted by kindnesses, are bound by the
Divine command (if occasion offers) to return thanks to
their benefactors not in mere words, but in reality. We
have the example of Joshua towards the harlot Rahab,
Josh. vi. 23 ; of David towards the sons of Barzillai, 1
Kings ii. 7, &c. Therefore they are to be blamed, and
scarcely to be looked upon as men, who not only neglect
returning kindnesses to their friends from whom they have
received benefits ; but, lest they should seem to acknowledge that they owe any gratitude, load them oft-times
with injuries and reproaches. Such were the men of Kei-
lah towards David, 1 Saml. xxiii. 12. Such also was the
conduct of Hanun, 2 Sam. x. 4. Such that of the Jews

towards Christ himself. So many examples of this ingratitude occur in common life, that the poet was, not afraid to go so far as to say, *He whose life is preserved to him is naturally ungrateful*.

Vers. 16.

Let the word of Christ dwell in you richly, in all wisdom ; teaching and admonishing one another in psalms, and hymns, and spiritual songs, singing with grace in your hearts unto the Lord.

Because it would be an endless task to exhort to particular virtues and duties of piety one by one, the Apostle would make his address compendious: This could best be done, in referring them to an absolute and perfect rule of virtue and of every duty : that he therefore does by referring them to the word of Christ.

There are two parts in this verse. In the former he excites them to the study and knowledge of the Scriptures, *Let the word of Christ dwell in you richly*, &c. In the latter, to the due use of the same, *teaching and admonishing*, &c.

Let the word of Christ dwell in you richly, in all wisdom] In these words it is proper to observe,

1. The matter or object of our study to which we are called by the Apostle ; and that is *the word of Christ,* namely, the Gospel, or the doctrine of the Scriptures. The Gospel in a certain special manner is called *the word of Christ,* because it was revealed and preached by Christ himself clothed with flesh ; and because it reveals and declares to us that eternal decree of God concerning Christ our Saviour and Mediator: Luke iv. 18 ; Rom. i. 3. In either respect, both of author and of matter, the Gospel is called *the word of Christ.* But the whole Scripture

may also be called *the word of Christ* for the same reasons. For before his incarnation, Christ, by his Spirit, inspired the patriarchs and prophets; as it is said 2 Pet. i. 21, *The prophecy came not in old time by the will of man; but holy men of God spake as they were moved by the Holy Ghost.* Yea, the Λογος itself was the eternal Son of God, who under the old Testament appeared to Moses, and instructed and established him in sacred things; as Tertullian contends, De Trin. Advers. Jud. Advers. Marcion, et alibi. Moreover, the Scriptures of the Old Testament no less than those of the New, speak and testify concerning Christ: This the Saviour asserts concerning the Old Testament, *Search the Scriptures; for they are they which testify of me,* John v. 39. Therefore, the object of this our study is the whole word of God; because the whole word of God is *the word of Christ.*

2. We must observe the mode of exercise in this study of the Scriptures: which the Apostle most fully expresses in three words:

'Ενοικειτω, *Let it dwell in you*] that is, Do not suffer the word of God, as a stranger, to stand without; but let it enter into the chamber of your heart, and constantly abide in your minds, no otherwise than as domestics dwell in the house; yea, let it be no less known and familiar to you, than they are wont to be who dwell with you.

Πλουσιως, *richly,* or *abundantly*] that is, Do not only cull some little particle, but turn over the whole Scriptures, prophets, apostles, evangelists; in a word, receive the whole doctrine revealed from heaven. Besides, admit the whole within you; into the mind, the memory, the affections, the life: in fine, let there be no part of you in which the word of God does not dwell.

'Εν παση σωφια, *in all wisdom*] that is, If ye apply to the word of God, that from thence ye may seek and learn all saving wisdom; namely, perfect knowledge, as well of the things to be believed, as of those to be done, in what is ordained for life eternal. This, then, is to be the aim of our study, that we be instructed in all saving wisdom out of the storehouse of the Scriptures.

Hence we derive these instructions :

1. It is the duty of pastors to call and excite the people to the constant reading and meditation of the Scriptures : it is the duty of the people to obey such exhortations.

2. They grievously sin who excite Christian people to the knowledge of human traditions and fables ; in the mean time forbidding them, as a thing full of danger, the reading of either Testament, that is, of the Divine word.

3. The word of God ought not only to be publicly preached in the temples, but to be read and heard in private houses.

4. In the word of God is contained the treasure of all wisdom necessary to salvation.

5. All, even the laics, should labour to obtain an understanding and full knowledge of Divine things.

6. That implied knowledge* which the Papists would have to be sufficient for the laity, is the offspring of laziness, the mother of impiety, not of devotion.

Therefore, the decree of the Council of Trent, and received opinion of the Papists, by which they deny that the Scriptures ought to be had in the vernacular tongue, or that the study of the Scriptures is to be required from the laity, may be refuted from this passage : nay, they affirm, that it is more safe for them to be restrained from reading the Scriptures, and is sufficient for them to regulate their course of life by the direction of their Pastors alone.†

---

* Vide Vol. I. p. 354, § 1.

† So Molanus, in lib. De pract. theol. tract. 3. cap. 27. conclus. 2.

The decree of the Council of Trent referred to by our author, is the one passed at the fourth session, on the Rule of Faith ; from which it is evident that the unrestrained perusal of the Scriptures is regarded by the Romish Church as pregnant with danger. The fourth Rule of the " Congregation of the Index," framed upon the Spirit of the Decree, says, " It is mani-
" fest from experience, that if the Holy Bible, translated into the vulgar
" tongue, be indiscriminately allowed to every one, the temerity of men
" will cause more evil than good to arise from it."

To shew how faithfully the unchangeable Church adheres to such principles to the present time, it is deserving of notice here, that in 1816 Pope Pius VII., writing to the Archbishop of Gnezn, designates the Bible So-

But the contrary opinion (which is ours, and the same as the Apostles) we shall shew can be confirmed, the sources of our argument being indicated,

1. From the command of God, who commands the study of the Scriptures not only to the clergy but to the people, and so to all who live in the Church; Deut. xi. 18, 19.

2. From the intention of God; who would have the doctrine of salvation to be delivered in writing, to the intent that it might be accessible to all, John xx. 31, and Rom. xv. 4.

ciety a " most crafty device, by which the very foundations of religion are undermined," a " pestilence," and " defilement of the faith, most imminently dangerous to souls." Leo XII. in 1824, speaking of the same institution, says that it " strolls with effrontery throughout the world, con-
" temning the traditions of the holy Fathers, and, contrary to the well
" known *Decree of the Council of Trent*, labours with all its might, and by
" every means, to translate, or rather to pervert, the Holy Bible into the
" vulgar languages of every nation ; from which proceeding it is greatly to
" be feared, that what is ascertained to have happened to some passages,
" may also occur with regard to others; to wit, that by a perverse interpre-
" tation, the gospel of Christ be turned into a human gospel, or what is
" still worse, into the gospel of the devil." The Irish Roman Catholic prelates, to whom this was written, publicly avowed their full concurrence with the Pope's views, and charged their flocks to surrender to the Parish priests all copies of the Scriptures received from Bible Societies, as well as all publications disseminated by the Religious Tract Society. See the Encyclical Letter of Pope Leo the XIIth. pp. 16, 54—57. See also Cramp's Text Book of Popery, Chap. 3 ; a work which ought to be in the hands of every Protestant, especially of every Protestant Minister, in the present day.

Of the Author—John Molanus, to whom our Expositor refers on the point under consideration, little is recorded, although he was a voluminous writer. He was a Professor of Theology who flourished in the sixteenth Century at Louvain, dying in 1585, at the age of 52. He commenced his authorship by critical Notes upon the Martyrology of Usuardus, which was published at Louvain, in 1568, and soon went through seven editions. Du Pin enumerates 13 volumes or pieces of his; the one alluded to above by Davenant, being his last, and published the year of his decease. He was appointed Censor of Books by the Pope and the King, so that it is evident his abilities and exertions were in repute : but some of his pieces, especially his work De Imaginibus, prove him to have been, like many of the French writers of the Romish Church, almost a Protestant.

3. From the commendation of all those who have applied themselves to the reading of the Scriptures. The eunuch is commended Acts viii. 28 ; the Bereans, Acts xvii. 11 : yea, all are pronounced *blessed* who become assiduous in the study of the Scriptures, Ps. i.

4. From the case of the Apostles ; who, as they preached publicly the mysteries of salvation to the people, so also, by their Epistles, they recommended the whole doctrine to be read by the same. For it is most absurd for any one to say that what was heretofore written as much to the people as to the clergy, is not now proper to be read by the people. We may instance the Epistles to the Romans, Corinthians, Galatians, Ephesians.

5. From the utility and necessity of this study. By the reading of the Scriptures men are enlightened and converted, Ps. xix. 8, 9. They are directed as by the most faithful counsellors, in all the ways of life, Ps. cxix. 24. They are armed against the fiery darts of Satan, Ephes. vi.

6. From the unanimous consent of all the Fathers ; who exhort the laity to the private reading of the Scriptures, and testify that the Scriptures were publicly read in ecclesiastical assemblies, not in an unknown tongue, but in a language understood by the people. Justin Martyr, Apolog. 2. ad Anton. near the end, and Tertullian in Apologet. testify, that the Scriptures were publicly read to the edification and understanding of the people. And B. Rhenanus, in Annotat. to Tertullian's book De corona militis, says, *I wish that custom could be restored to us,* &c.*

---

* Beatus Rhenanus, a native of Schelestat, or Slestad, in Alsace, where he was born in the year 1485. He was one of those men of learning who do not embrace any particular profession, and whose only business is to cultivate the sciences, and do service to the learned world ; of the classical attainments of which he possessed a considerable share, and was likewise well skilled in Divinity. His favourite employ was correcting or explaining ecclesiastical or profane authors, several of the works of both which classes he published with notes or introductory prefaces, and which were in general much esteemed. Tertullian's treatises were the first he published, with annotations on the peculiar words and difficult phrases of that author, and prefaces to most of his pieces. But he distinguished himself most by a history of Germany, published in 1531, in 4to. and which Du Pin entitles " a

As to the private reading of the Scriptures : Jerome, ad
Demetriad. de virginit. servanda ; Chrysostom, Hom. 1, and
2 in Matt. and Hom. 3, de Lazaro, and Hom. 9, in Coloss.;
Augustine, Enarr. in Psal. 33, and Epist. i. ad Volusian.;
Damascenus, De orthod. fide, lib. 4. cap. 18.; Theodoret,
De curand. Græc. affect. lib. 8, not far from the beginning ;
all advise it.   To these I add two testimonies of Count
Mirandula :* the former is drawn from the Preface to his
Heptaplum; *All the Israelitish multitude, cobblers, cooks,
dealers, shepherds, servants, maidens, to all whom the law was
delivered to be read, could not bear the burden of the whole
Mosaic wisdom.*   The latter testimony is extracted from
his Exposit. orat. Domin.   *The Evangelical history ought to
be continually read by every Christian man.*

You may see the arguments, by which Bellarmin and
other Papists endeavour to take away the reading of the
Scriptures from the people, refuted by Whitaker of blessed
memory,† in 1 controv. De sacra Script. quæst. 2. cap. 11,

noble history." He wrote also a description of the provinces of Illyricum,
and a preface to Erasmus's works. He was a particular friend of Erasmus,
who entertained a high opinion of his attainments as a scholar and a critic,
and of his character as a man. He died at his native place, in the communion of the Romish faith, in 1547. Yet one of his pieces, de Primatu
Petri, is in the Index Libror. Prohib. of Benedict XIV., together with
his Annotations on Tertullian's works. He was opposed to the Court of
Rome's usurpation of temporal power.

    * See Vol. i. Note †, page 354.

    † Dr. William Whitaker, the justly celebrated Master of St. John's,
Cambridge, at the period when our Expositor commenced his College career,
and who first noticed Davenant's abilities and genius. He was a native of
Lancashire, and educated at St. Paul's School, whence he proceeded to Trinity College, Cambridge, of which he became a Fellow. He was afterwards made Professor of Divinity at Cambridge, and Chancellor of St.
Paul's Cathedral in 1579 ; but resigned this latter preferment on being appointed Master of St. John's. He displayed his learning by Greek Transla-
tions of the English Liturgy, and of Dean Nowell's Catechism, and in his
different College Theses and Lectures ; but still more in his zeal for the
doctrines of the Reformation, by various publications against Cardinal Bellarmin, the Jesuits Campion and Stapleton, and others. In the former it
might be questioned, whether he shewed himself more the pious Christian
or the learned Divine ; by the latter he became esteemed as one of the
most eminent Protestant Polemics of the age; proving himself extremely

and shewn to be altogether sophistical and nugatory : For
from the abuse of the Scriptures, they infer that the use
itself is to be denied to the people, in this manner,

1. Some of the laity, by reading the Scriptures, fall
into absurd heresies; some into contempt of the Scriptures; some, either into contempt of the saints, or a pernicious imitation of them, when they read of their adulteries, lying, and things of that kind : therefore, the laity
are to be restrained from the Scriptures.

If this kind of argument were good, God, Christ, and
the Apostles have sinned, who would have the word of
God proclaimed to all indiscriminately, notwithstanding
many abused them to their hurt, 2 Pet. iii. 16. Besides,
on this ground, the reading of the Scriptures should be denied equally to the clergy and the laity : for they also oft-
times shamefully abuse the Scriptures. For who does not
know that almost all the heresies have sprung, not from
the laity and seculars, but from bishops, presbyters, and
monks ? We have almost as many testimonies, as names
of heretics. Lastly, the argument is inconclusive; *many
laics have abused the Scriptures, therefore they are to be taken
away from them indiscriminately* : Let the abuse be taken
away ; or at least, let the Scriptures be denied to those,

---

well versed, and strongly armed, in all the points of the Roman Catholic
Controversy. Bishop Hall was an almost enthusiastic admirer of him:
" The honour of our schools (says he), and the angel of our church, learned Whitaker, than whom our age saw nothing more memorable. What
clearnesse of judgment, what sweetness of style, what gravity of person,
what grace of carriage was in that man ! Who ever saw him without reverence? or heard him, without regard ?" His works and his worth gained
him renown throughout Europe ; so that Cardinal Bellarmin, the champion
of Popery, though often foiled by his pen, honoured his picture with a place
in his Library ; and said, " He was the most learned heretic he had ever
read." His works were published collectively at Geneva, in 1610, in two
vols. folio : but any of his pieces detached, when to be met with, are worth
the purchase to a person engaged in the study of the Romish Controversy.
It was Dr. Whitaker who drew up the famous Lambeth Articles, intended
by Archbishop Whitgift, and several other Bishops and learned Divines assembled at Lambeth, to settle some points then strenuously controverted
by one Barret, and Peter Baro. His answer to Campion is in Pope Benedict's Index Prohibit. ; but none of his other works.

concerning whom it appears that they read with a perverted mind. For, as Tertullian rightly observes, lib. 1. adver. Marcion, *There is much difference between the cause and the fault, between the state and the excess. Not the institution of a good thing, but the misuse of it is to be reprobated.*

Bellarmin here adds two testimonies from the most noted of the Fathers.

One is of Basil; who checked the steward of the Emperor's kitchen, impertinently prating about dogmas of faith, with this rebuke, *It is thy business to provide porridge, not to serve up Divine eloquence.*

I answer; He did not recal him by the rebuke from the study or the reading of the Scriptures; but restrained his pride and folly, who, when he was unskilful, thought that he could teach and refute Basil, *the teacher of the world*, and determine concerning the most weighty controversies of theology. Who would not confess this was a just reproof?

The other is drawn from Jerome's epistle to Paulinus, where he thus writes:

...... *What is the duty of Physicians,*
Physicians undertake; artificers confine themselves to their work:
The knowledge of the Scriptures is alone what all claim to themselves, The prating old woman, the drivelling old man, the wordy sophist, all presume upon, twist, teach this, before that they know it, &c.

We answer, he does not reprehend the laity because they read the Scriptures; but blames all, of whatever rank, who presume to teach and interpret the Scriptures, and undertake as it were the theological office, when they are either altogether ignorant of the Scriptures, or have been only slightly conversant with the first principles of the same. We also confess this to be intolerable audacity. That this is the meaning of Jerome is plain, because elsewhere he commends every way the study and the reading of the Scriptures by the laity, and on this very passage of the Apostle which we have now under consideration, he thus writes; *It is here shewn that the laity ought not only to possess*

the word of Christ sufficiently, but even abundantly. These
remarks concerning the first part of this verse, in which
he excites to the study of the Scriptures, may suffice.

*Teaching and admonishing one another in psalms and hymns
and spiritual songs, singing with grace in your hearts unto the
Lord.*] In the preceding words he excited the Colossians
to the study and knowledge of the Scriptures; now he
shews the manifold use of scriptural knowledge.

1. The first use is, that Christians (even laics) should
mutually teach and instruct one another in things pertaining to the faith; and what knowledge they procured to
themselves from the Scriptures, they should employ to
edify their brethren when needful. For although the business of teaching publicly with authority rests upon ministers; yet the duty of teaching privately out of charity, is
incumbent upon every private person, to whom the faculty
and the occasion is granted of edifying others in faith and
religion. Thus parents are bound to teach their children,
Deut. xi. 19; Psal. lxxviii. 5. This is commended in Abraham, Gen. xviii. 19. So husbands should teach their wives;
*If the women will learn any thing, let them ask their husbands
at home,* 1 Cor. xiv. 35. This, in fine, every brother should
teach his brother: as we read Apollos was instructed in the
doctrine of the Gospel by Aquila and Priscilla, Acts xxviii.
26. *There is an inward desire in all,* says Clemens, *of generating its own: in natural men indeed of generating men
only; but in the pious and faithful of generating pious and
faithful men.* Now this is done by imparting to them the
doctrine of the Gospel. 1 Cor. iv. 15.

We hence learn,

1. That it behoves the laity, not only to aim at their
own edification, but also their neighbour's.

2. The Papists grievously err, who scarcely permit the
laics (especially those who are in a humble condition) to
speak about the Scriptures, and the things pertaining to
Religion; whereas Paul exhorts them mutually to *teach one
another* in these things.

3. A knowledge of the Scriptures is to be employed,
not out of vain ostentation, not for sophistical skirmishing,

not for ridiculous and profane trifling, but for our advantage and that of our brother. Thus much of the first use.

2. *Admonishing,* νουθετοῦντες.] This is the second use, and relates to manners. The Apostle, then, wishes that Christians imbued with the knowledge of the Scriptures, should from thence derive the rule of manners ; and (when it is necessary) advise their brethren according to it, about the exercise of virtues, the avoiding of faults, and breaking off their sins. For this duty of mutual admonition and correction devolves upon all the pious. *I will teach sinners thy ways,* &c. Psal. li. 13. *Thou shalt not hate thy brother in thine heart ; thou shalt in any wise rebuke thy neighbour, and not suffer sin upon him,* Levit. xix. 17 ; *If any man obey not our word by this Epistle,—yet count him not as an enemy, but admonish him as a brother,* 2 Thess. iii. 14, 15. They who neglect this even participate in other men's sins : For truly says Prosper, De vita contemplat. 3. 23, *I sin among all sinners, when from a certain cruel malignity of mind I do not reprove them whom I know to have sinned, or to sin.* The Schoolmen lay down many conditions of legitimate correction. In correcting or admonishing another, they require aptitude for correction, meekness in correcting, a certain knowledge of the fault, a probable hope of the amending of the offender, suitability of the time, and weight of offence. But the Scriptures require before all other things, charity and meekness in instructing and admonishing brethren. *If any one be overtaken in a fault, ye who are spiritual restore such a man in the spirit of meekness,* Gal. vi. 1. To this that rule of Augustine in Expos. epist. ad Gal. has respect: *The office of reproving another's sin is never to be undertaken, unless our conscience shall clearly answer before God, that we do it from love : for whatever you shall say with bitterness of spirit, is the attack of one who punishes, not the charity of a corrector.*

Corollaries.

1. A true Christian not only directs his own ways according to the commands of God, but, as far as in him

lies, those also of his brethren. That diabolical speech of
Cain, (Gen. iv. 9) therefore, never comes into his mind;
Am I my brother's keeper?

2. That haughtiness which is wont to bear any correction or brotherly admonition with an evil mind, is to be rejected ; for it is the direct road to destruction, as Solomon
forewarns, Prov. xxix. 1.

3. These mutual admonitions are more grateful to the
godly and prudent, than flatteries are to fools : *He that re-
buketh a man, afterwards shall find more favour than he that
flattereth with the tongue,* Prov. xxviii. 23. Thus much of
the other use of the Scriptures, in admonishing.

3. *In psalms, and hymns, and spiritual songs, singing,* &c.]
This is the third use of the Scriptures, and regards the celebration of the Divine name, and our mutual comfort.
Some join these words, *psalms, and hymns, and spiritual
songs,* with those preceding, *teaching and admonishing one
another.* But others, and with not less probability, with
those following, *singing unto the Lord,* namely, *in psalms,*
&c. The point is of little moment: For if they are referred to the preceding, they are not to be understood as
though the materials of teaching and admonishing were to
be derived from psalms and hymns alone ; but the Apostle
thereby wished to intimate, that even when we mean to
promote hilarity, we ought to be mindful of mutual edification and utility.

As to the understanding of the words themselves : *psalms*
(as it seems to Jerome) are what treat of morality, and
shew what is to be done, and what avoided ; *hymns,* what
set forth the greatness and the majesty of God, and extol
his goodness and his works ; *songs* or *odes,* those which ar-
tificially unfold the harmony of the world and the order of
all creatures. Beza on this passage speaks somewhat dif-
ferently : he calls *psalms* whatever verses are written with
various arguments (which among the Hebrews are termed
mizmorim) : he calls those *hymns,* which contain the praises
of God only (which the Hebrews call *tehillim*) ; those *songs*
or *odes,* which are peculiar and more artificial, which also
embrace the same praises, but in a certain form more au-

gust than psalms or hymns (which the Hebrews call *schi-rim*). The Apostle would have us to entertain and promote our hilarity by these, according to that direction of St. James, v. 13, *If any be merry, let him sing psalms.* But in these psalms and hymns, or songs of believers, four conditions are required :—

1. That they must be *spiritual*] and that in a twofold respect; as well in regard to the origin, as in regard to the matter. As to the origin : like as Moses, David, and others, under the impulse of the Holy Spirit, composed and sang their hymns, psalms, and songs; so we, whether we sing the same or others, ought to do it by the influence and direction of the Holy Spirit. That the psalms and hymns of the godly flow as it were from the primary author, is gathered from Ephes. v. 18, 19, *Be not drunk with wine,* says the Apostle, *but be filled with the Spirit: Speaking to yourselves in psalms, and hymns, and spiritual songs,* &c. As though he had said, As wine is wont to excite the drunkards to foolish, silly, and lascivious airs ; so does the Spirit inspire the godly to psalms, and hymns, and spiritual songs. We have examples in the New Testament, of the blessed Virgin, Zacharias, and Simeon : and also in the primitive Church, certain of the holy fathers composed hymns, remains of which we retain even to this day. These psalms, hymns, and songs are also *spiritual* as to the matter : For they treat of spiritual things, relating to the glory of God and our salvation ; not of secular, vain, and earthly matters. This is the first condition.

2. They must be sung with *grace.*] Some explain grace in this passage to mean *gratitude,* or *thanksgiving,* The word *grace* is sometimes taken in this sense. In 1 Cor. xv. 57, *But thanks,* χαρίς, *be to God, who giveth us the victory ;* and in 2 Cor. ii. 14, *But thanks,* χαρίς, *be to God, who always causeth us to triumph in Christ.* Gratitude is not improperly joined to songs; because we are for the most part moved to sing in joyous and prosperous circumstances, in which condition the affection of gratitude is binding and plainly necessary. But others explain these words *with grace, with a certain gracious affability, which conveys both pleasure and*

utility to the hearers : so that what Horace says concerning
poets, the same may be said of these spiritual songs,
They would both profit and delight.
In this same sense the word *grace*, χαρις, is sometimes taken,
as afterwards in Chap. iv. vers. 6, *Let your speech be always
with grace,* 'εν χαριτι; and in Ephes. iv. 29 ; Let your speech
be such, *as shall minister grace to the hearers.*

3. They must be sung *in their hearts*] that is, from the
inmost affection of the heart : for he does not exclude the
voice, but advises that the affection of the heart be always
joined with the voice. And rightly indeed is a certain ardent motion required in the heart itself by the Apostle : for
the action of singing declares as it were the internal exultation of the heart. He therefore acts the hypocrite, who
sings with the heart asleep. Hence the Royal Psalmist,
when he addresses himself to sing, not only tunes his
voice to the harp, but his heart in preference to either and
before either. *My heart is fixed, O God, my heart is fixed :
I will sing and give praise unto the Lord. Awake up my
glory ; awake, psaltery and harp,* &c. Psal. lvii. 7, 8. So
the blessed Virgin, Luke i. 46, 47, *My soul doth magnify
the Lord ; and my spirit hath rejoiced in God my Saviour.*
The exultation of the heart, therefore, preceded ; where-
upon the tongue brake forth into that divine song. Hence
Bernard, in his Serm. 52 De modo bene vivendi, says,
*When in the presence of God you sing psalms and hymns, re-
volve in your mind what you sing with your voice ; do not
think one thing, and sing another.*

4. They must be sung *unto the Lord*] namely, to Christ
the Saviour, our God and our Lord. The songs of Christians ought not to aim at promoting dissoluteness or gain ;
but to be employed in celebrating the praises of Christ the
Redeemer. We do not without cause celebrate Christ as
true God in hymns, when the heathen are accustomed to
extol their false and senseless gods, Jupiter, Neptune,
Apollo, and the rest, in hymns : in this retaining, indeed,
a right opinion, because they judged this spiritual worship
to be rendered to the divine nature ; but yet erring most
perniciously in that they enrolled these monsters of men in

the calendar of gods.   That there was a yearly custom of
the primitive church, to sing hymns in their assemblies to
Christ the Lord, is collected from that epistle of Pliny the
Second to the Emperor Trajan, which is still extant, Lib.
10. epist 97, in which he writes, *that the Christians were accustomed on a particular day to meet before light, and to sing
together by turns a hymn to Christ as God.*   Of which epistle, and also of the manner of the Christians in worshipping Christ, Tertullian, in his Apologet, and Eusebius in
Hist. eccl. lib. 3, cap. 30, make mention.   But here it is
proper to advise by the way, That when we assert that
Christ our Lord is to be extolled in hymns, we do not exclude the Father or the Holy Spirit, nay, we call them into
a participation of the same honour: for he who extols
Christ the Redeemer, at the same time extols both the
Father, who sent him to redeem the world ; and the Holy
Spirit, who renders this redemption efficacious to all the
elect and believers.

Corollaries.

1.   The custom of singing is useful, and is to be adopted in the assemblies of Christians, as well in public as in
private.   For it has (as you see) the approbation of the
Apostles ; and also that of the more antient Fathers ; of
Justin Martyr, in Quæst. a Gentibus positis, quæst. 107 :
of Augustine, Confess. lib. 9, cap. 6 and 7 ; and lib. 10,
cap. 33 : in which places this same seems to have been the
opinion of Ambrose and Athanasius.

2.   It is so to be performed, that they who hear may
from thence derive spiritual pleasure and edification.
Therefore, farewell to all nugatory, and much more to impure sons : farewell to the superstitious bawlings of the
Papists, who bellow out psalms in their temples, but in an
unintelligible language, and with so much noise and tumult, that if they should use a vernacular language, yet no
one would perceive what is sung by them.

3.   In singing psalms it ought to be the especial care of
a Christian, that his heart be rightly affected : they who
neglect this, may perhaps please men by an artificial sweetness of voice, but they will displease God by an odious

impurity of the heart. Against such, that saying of Bernard may be turned, De interiori domo, cap. 50, *You sing that you may please the people more than God: you tune the voice; tune the will: you keep the harmony of sounds, keep also the concord of manners.*

4. What things are done for cheerfulness and relaxation of the mind by Christians, ought to be of such a kind, as are agreeable to Christ and the Christian religion: we must therefore detest the madness of those who cannot be cheerful without the reproach of Christ and the ridicule of religion.

Vers. 17.

And whatsoever ye do in word or deed, do all in the name of the Lord Jesus Christ, giving thanks to God and the Father by him.

The Apostle in this verse annexes a clause to his general exhortation; in which is contained most wholesome advice, and most efficacious to regulate our life in holiness and the fear of God. But lest we should seem to follow no method in handling this verse, we shall propound two things to be considered : the matter to be regulated, or the object of the rule ; and the rule itself laid down by the Apostle.

1. *Whatsoever ye do in word or deed.*] You perceive here the matter about which that rule which presently follows ought to be exercised; namely, all our words, and all our deeds: In which distribution also even the thoughts of the mind are comprehended ; for there are those deeds of the inner man, no less than those which meet the senses of the outer man.

And first as to our discourse or our words, they all indeed (if we would wish to be accounted Christians) ought to be subject to a certain rule. For truly says James i. 26, *If any man seem to be religious, and bridleth not his tongue, this man's religion is vain.* Hence also the Psalmist, xii. 4, attributes an unrestrained tongue to those who have cast off all fear of God ; *They say, With our tongues will we prevail, our lips are our own; who is Lord over us?* Hence, lastly, it is that the tongue of the glutton is read of as being most bitterly tormented in hell; namely, because it was unwilling to be regulated and restrained in this world. For thus, observes Cyprian, Lib. 1. epist. 3, *Among all parts of the body, the mouth and the tongue of Dives endure the greatest punishment ; because forsooth by his mouth and his tongue he had most sinned.* Which also Gregory remarks, Moral 1. cap. 5, *Because at feasts babbling is mostly wont to issue, the punishment indicates the guilt, when he affirms that he who feasted splendidly every day, burned most in his tongue.* It is evident, therefore, that the tongue, or our discourse, must be conformed to a rule.

Now as to the works, whether external or internal; they ought without doubt to be conformed to his rule : for if we must speak according to rule, then much more must we work. The actions of all creatures are performed according to a prescribed rule : human actions, therefore, ought much more to be subject to rule. Those axioms are known and approved by all : *Every work of nature is the work of intelligence ; all nature works as if actuated by the mind of some infallible agent.* Yea, we see not only brute animals, but the very elements, perform as well as intermit all their operations at the command and the good pleasure of God their Creator. From which, as it were *à fortiori,* it is concluded, that all human actions must be directed after the rule of the Divine will. And thus much concerning the matters to be regulated ; which is whatever we do, in word, or deed. Now let us consider the rule proposed in this place.

2. And it consists in two particulars. The former advises how we should conduct ourselves towards Christ ; namely, so, that we do all things in his name. The latter, how to behave towards God ; namely, so as to give thanks in all things to God the Father. We shall discuss these two branches of the proposed rule separately.

Do all things in the name of the Lord Jesus Christ.] That
is said *to be done in the name of Christ,* which is done
through his assistance, according to his command and will,
and for the promotion of his glory. All these things the
Scripture is wont to comprise in this form of speaking,
and the Apostle in this passage seems to have wished to
comprise them all. For so this phrase is every where employed, as well in the Old as in the New Testament. Thus
Psal. xliv. 6, *In thy name will we tread under our enemies;*
that is, by thy help. Psal. xxxi. 3, *For thy name's sake
lead me,* &c. that is, for thy glory. Luke x. 17, *The devils
are subject unto thy name;* that is, by thy invocation; by
thy aid. Matt. xviii. 20, *Where two or three are gathered together in my name;* that is, by my command, imploring my
help, for my sake, to advance my doctrine and glory.
You see what it is *to do all things in the name of Christ:*
Now it remains, that we briefly shew, that all things are
to be thus done in the name of Christ.

As to good actions which are done immediately in reference to God and our salvation; it is certain, that nothing
can either be done, or said, or thought, that is good by
us, unless it be done in the name of Christ, that is, according to the will of Christ, and by the assistance and invocation of Christ, and for the glory of Christ. *I can do all
things,* says the Apostle, *through Christ who strengtheneth
me,* Phil. iv. 3, *We are not sufficient of ourselves to think any
thing as of ourselves,* 2 Cor. iii. 5. Most truly said Augustine, Soliloq, cap. 24, 25, *It is not of man to wish what he
can, or to effect what he may wish, or to know what he would
wish or would do; but the ways of man are directed by God.*
Now God governs us by Christ: we ought therefore to do
all things relying upon the grace and assistance of Christ
the Mediator.

This likewise is evident, That all our good actions must
be referred to the glory of Christ. For if they are done
with any other end, although they may seem good as to
the external appearance, yet they become bad on account
of the perverse intent : *For the end determines the quality in
morals,* say the Schoolmen. Hence John, Revel. v. 13,

Every creature which is in heaven, and on the earth, and under the earth, &c. *heard I saying, Blessing, and honour, and glory, and power, be unto him that sitteth upon the throne, and unto the Lamb for ever and ever.* Hither ought all our good actions to have respect ; otherwise, as Augustine has well said, contra Julian, lib. 4. cap. 3, *Whatever good is done, and is not done for the end for which it ought to be done, although it seems to be good in the performance, yet the final cause itself not being the right one, it is sin.*

But also those actions which are indifferent in their nature, yet ought to be done by Christians in the name of Christ, that is (as we have explained it) according to the will of Christ, and for the glory of Christ. For although any one may eat, drink, and perform other such like actions as an animal or a man, Christ being neither invoked nor thought upon ; yet he cannot do these things at all as becometh a Christian, unless by Christ.

The reasons are these ;

1. We have no right to these creatures unless in Christ : therefore he is guilty of theft who, receiving things belonging to another against the will of God, takes to himself, in his own name, the creatures to his use : For *all things are ours* when *we are Christ's,* 1 Cor. iii. 22, 23. Therefore, although a civil authority is acquired by other modes; yet that evangelical authority, which gives us the faculty of using the creatures without injury to God, depends upon Christ.

2. Because, although we might have a right to the creatures without Christ ; yet they are not blessed by God, nor sanctified to our use, without Christ. Therefore on this account there is need of invoking the name of Christ, and the influence of Christ with his Father. For what the Apostle says concerning meats, 1 Tim. iv. 5, *They are sanctified by the word of God and prayer,* that also is to be accommodated to all the other creatures : but the efficacy of prayer depends upon the name of Christ.

3. Because we are bound, even in things and actions indifferent in their nature, for instance, in food, and clothing, and other things of that kind, to retain that mode, and

yield to those circumstances, which accord with the Christian doctrine and profession : we ought not therefore to eat, nor drink, nor clothe our bodies, not to use relaxation and lawful pleasure, nor to labour or work in our vocation, for our own will and pleasure ; but at the will and for the pleasure of our Lord Christ. He who acts in this manner, acts in the name of Christ, and for the glory of God ; and he observes that Apostolic precept, *Whether ye eat or drink, or whatever ye do, do all to the glory of God :* 1 Cor. x. 31.

But here it may be asked, Whether a Christian is bound in every action expressly to implore the help of Christ, to flee to the grace and mediation of Christ, and, in fine, to regard the glory of Christ in actual thought in every business.

We answer, This actual contemplation, whether concerning the help, or the grace, or the glory of Christ, is not either possible or necessary to us for the condition of this life ; but it is necessary that there be in exercise a fixed and as it were a rooted purpose in our hearts, of depending upon Christ, and referring the actions of our whole life to Christ. But we must also add, That it is the best thing, as often as it can be done, to raise our thoughts actually to Christ in all our doings : moreover it is fit and necessary, that we do that as often as the nature of the action which we undertake and transact requires it ; as when the matter is of a sacred character, or of great importance to our salvation.

Instructions.

1. The vulgar are deceived whilst they judge it to be lawful to themselves to use food, clothing, speech, or any indifferent thing whatever of their own will : for all these things must be used according to rule ; otherwise, although there be no evil in the thing itself, yet there will be in the person using it.

2. They who desire to maintain a right course of life, and to order their actions well, ought to have respect to Christ as to their polar-star.

3. No action is to be attempted by us to the perform-

ance of which we dare not implore the aid of Christ, and
which we do not judge to be pleasing and acceptable to
God for Christ's sake, at least not to be displeasing and
abominable. Let the avaricious, the lustful, the drunken,
and indeed all the wicked, hence judge of their actions.

4. We should not attempt even good actions relying
upon our own strength, but resting upon Divine aid, and
the mediation of Christ.

5. They abuse the name of Christ, who employ it for
those things which tend to the reproach, not to the glory
of Christ. Here the Papists sin grievously, who are wont
to exercise all their superstitions, to obtrude all their errors in the name of Christ; they are not much unlike those
indeed, who assume the name of Christ when they do the
works of the devil. And thus much of the former part of
the rule.

Giving thanks to God and the Father by him.] This is that
other part of the Apostolic rule; in which we are advised
how it behoves us to conduct ourselves towards God the
Father. For the word *God* is to be taken personally in this
place, and the word *Father* is added exegetically. Therefore *to God* and *the Father* is the same, as if he had said,
to God who is the Father both of Christ and also our
Father in Christ. The same form of speaking is used in
Ephes. v. 30. But let us come to the point; Here are
three things to be observed: 1. That we are to give
thanks; 2. To whom they are to be given; 3. By whom.

1. As to the first; Thanks are to be given both in the
using of the creatures and in the success and issue of all
things. The enjoyment of the creatures requires thanks
from us as a debt; otherwise we are inferior to the brute
animals. Hence that remark of the Apostle, 1 Tim. iv. 4,
*Every creature of God is good, and nothing to be rejected, if
it be received with thanksgiving.* Moreover in every success
and issue of things, and every action of ours, thanks are
to be given; because all things co-operate for good to those,
who undertake lawful and honest things by invoking the
name of Christ. On this account, in Ephes. v. 20, he more
fully expresses this duty in these words, *Giving thanks to*

God always and *for all things.* Neither is this duty to be
performed on our own account only ; but we are bound to
give thanks to God also for benefits towards our brethren,
and so to the whole church. *We give thanks to God always
for you,* &c. says the Apostle, 2 Thess. i. 3. It is plain,
therefore, this duty of giving thanks is to be perpetual,
&c.

2. To whom are thanks to be given ?   *To God the
Father.*] It is usual in the Scriptures, to prescribe this
method as well of praying as of giving thanks, that each
act should be directed to the person of the Father. But
there is no other reason for this, than that the Father is
the fountain of Deity, from whom, as from its primary
author, all good things are derived to us, by the Son's mediation, and by the Holy Spirit working the same in us.
That, therefore, the order of nature and of operation may
be indicated, we invoke the Father as much as possible,
we give thanks expressly to the Father : yet neither the
Son nor the Holy Spirit is excluded from an alliance in this
honour, since the essence of the three Persons is the same.
We may even add that reason also ; that the name Father
affords us confidence in speaking with God : for when we
invoke God the Father of Christ, faith immediately conceives, the same is now also become our Father in Christ.

3. By whom ?   *By him ;* namely *Christ.*] By Christ the
Mediator, therefore, we ought both to invoke God, and
give thanks after that God shall have heard us calling upon
him ; for our thanks will not indeed be pleasing to God,
unless by Christ and for his sake. Therefore it is proper
to acknowledge, that there neither hath been any merit in
us for obtaining blessings from God the Father, unless by
Christ; nor is there any faculty within us of giving the
thanks that are due, unless by the same Christ.

Instructions.

1. They who do all things in the name of Christ, will
always have copious matter for giving thanks to God, whatever things may befal them.

2. We ought to acknowledge the blessing of God in all
those transactions which happen well to us, not to attri-

bute prosperous events to our own strength or counsels: for he never gives thanks with the heart, who *sacrifices to his own drag.* Hab. i. 16.

3. God the Father will not be invoked, praised, or worshipped, unless through Christ his Son and our Mediator: relying therefore upon his merit and favour with the Father, we ought to render all these our duties to God. They therefore err, who choose to themselves other Mediators to God the Father.

Thus we have explained the universal exhortation of the Apostle, which has respect to all Christians alike. Now a particular exhortation follows, which is directed to certain orders of men variously.

Vers. 18, 19.

Wives, submit yourselves unto your own husbands, as it is fit in the Lord.

Husbands, love your wives, and be not bitter against them.

The Apostle now enters upon a particular and domestic exhortation. And since, as Aristotle has rightly observed, Polit. i. 3, *there are three alliances* (or moral relations) *of which every house is composed,* of which the husband and wife constitute the first; the parents and children, the second; the master and servants, the third: the Apostle assigns precepts to all these; but he begins with *the nuptial state,* as the first and most worthy.

But it is to be observed that he requires the duty of the wife in the first place, although the husband obtains the more worthy place in the first alliance. A twofold reason may be assigned. 1. Because it is more difficult to perform the duty of subjection than of love: for to love and delight is pleasant; but to subject oneself and obey another, is for the most part troublesome and hateful. 2. Because the affection of the husband for the most part depends on the due subjection of the wife : for if she yield her subjection, unless he is dead to all moral sensibility, he cannot but return his love. But let us come to the words of the Apostle.

We have in this eighteenth verse, 1. A proposition ; 2. A limitation of the proposition. This is the proposition, *Wives ought to be subject to their husbands.* The limitation, or mode of subjection is, *As it is fit in the Lord.*

In the proposition itself we shall briefly treat these four things. First, what subjection is considered in a general point of view. Secondly, in what things this particular subjection of wives towards their husbands consists. Thirdly, what are the reasons impelling women to yield this duty of subjection. Fourthly, what may be the impediments or obstacles, that this bounden duty should not be performed by them : for both these ought to be known that they may be avoided and removed.

1. The subjection, then, of one creature to another in general, is nothing else, if it be considered on the part of God, than a Divine disposition, whereby the more imperfect are subordinate to the more perfect, that by this subjection the former may be perfected, governed, and preserved by the latter. If it be considered on the part of the creature subjected, then the virtue of subjection is its ready inclination to obey this ordinance constituted by God himself.

We see without this appointed subjection neither natural affairs, nor political societies, nay, not even the world itself could consist. All earthly and sublunary things are subject to celestial ones ; for since they are in their nature more imperfect and ignoble, they cannot attain to their perfection without this natural subjection. So in political societies, government and subjection are accounted not only among the things that are useful, but among the things plainly necessary.* Hence citizens are subject to magistrates, soldiers to their commanders, for their good

* Arist. Polit. i. 3.

and advantage more than that of those to whom they are
subject.

Corollaries.

1. The Author of the creatures would not have them to
be confounded through *disorder. For God is not the author
of confusion, but of peace,* 1 Cor. xiv. 33. They, therefore,
are repugnant to God, who would take away the order of
obeying and ruling.

2. It is not the mark of a base and abject mind, but of
a generous one, and one not deviating from the law of
creation, to be subject promptly and with a willing mind to
his superiors. Whence that saying of the Heathen, *The
government over the good is easy ; every man in proportion to
his depravity bears a ruler with a rude impatience.*

3. They who shake off the yoke of due subjection, are
blind to their own interest: for that old adage is true,
πειθαρχία 'ετὶ τοῦς ἐυπραξίας μητηρ, *Obedience is the mother of
prosperity.*

But we must no longer cleave to generals : let us come
to the particular subjection of wives. This, then, we say
consists in three things :

First, in the internal act of the heart; when the wife
acknowledges in her mind, that her husband is and ought
to be her head and governor, and that she is the inferior,
even on the mere ground that she is a wife, although in
birth, riches, virtue, and prudence, she excel her husband.
This submission of the heart is the fountain of outward
subjection ; without this, all subjection is either forced or
pretended. The Apostle seems to have had respect to this
inward disposition in Ephes. v. 33, *Let the wife reverence
her husband.* That pious Sarah possessed this is evident,
who called Abraham her husband *lord,* not from the flattery of custom, but from the wish of testifying this subjection, 1 Pet. iii. 6.

Secondly, this subjection of the wife consists in the
study of conforming her manners and affections, as much
as possible, to the manners and affections of her husband
in things indifferent and lawful : *For the dissimilitude of manners has no tendency to love,* says Aristotle, Oeconom. lib. i.

cap. 4. This is indeed difficult; but the more difficult it is, the more laudable; because all cherish their own manners, indulge their own affections, and hate the contrary:

The melancholy do the merry hate,
And witty minds despise the sad.

Horat. Epist. lib. i. ep. 18.

It is, therefore, laborious, to strip off as it were her own disposition, and put on another's. But this is necessary to the wife, and is before all other things to be commended in her. For as a mirror adorned with gems, and skilfully polished, is nothing, unless it express a true likeness of the person looking into it; so a wife, however endowed and beautiful, is nothing, unless she render herself conformable to the manners of her husband. This study of conforming herself to the disposition of her husband, I think the Apostle has respect to in 1 Cor. vii. 37, where he says, that the married woman *careth how she may please her husband.* She often and seriously thinks,

And turns her rapid thought, now here now there,

that she may find out the way of pleasing her husband: this is the most ready way, if she study to accommodate her manners and affections themselves, and frame them to his.

Lastly, this subjection consists in performing those duties and offices which are incumbent upon her. The first duty is, to love her husband religiously, to minister to him obligingly, and to be his help and solace in every condition of fortune: Gen. ii. 18. *Love your husbands,* says the Apostle, Tit. ii. 4. *She will do him good all the days of her life,* Prov. xxxi. 12. The duties connected with this are those of taking care of the family and children, and administering other domestic matters *according to the established laws,* as says Aristotle. On this account Paul bids wives *to love their husbands,* to be *keepers at home,* Tit. ii. 4, 5. And Plutarch relates, that the Egyptian women did not make use of shoes, that they might learn to keep at home, and be ready for domestic offices. All these things pertain to the subjection of the wife: which let it suffice to have discussed lightly: for it is not our purpose to discourse largely on each of these particulars.

3. We must now come, in the third place, to those reasons which ought to excite and impel all good and pious matrons to perform these duties of subjection.

1. The first is derived from the Divine appointment; which it is wicked for a pious mind to resist: for religious obedience does not discuss the commands of God, but performs them. But God most clearly has sanctioned this female subjection, Gen. iii. 16, *Thy desire shall be to thy husband, sub viri potestate eris,* in the Vulgate; *and he shall rule over thee.*

2. The second is derived from the natural imperfection of the woman: For by nature she is more infirm than the man, and more unsuited for her own government and protection. This both the sacred Scriptures and philosophy testify. Women are said to be *the weaker vessels,* 1 Pet. iii. 7. And Aristotle affirms, that *they have indeed the power to determine, but without authority;* and that it is the leading quality of the woman *to subserve,* not *to direct.* Polit. lib. i. cap. 8.

3. The third is derived from the order of creation. For the woman was created after the man, out of the man, and for the man. But the end for which any thing exists, is better and more noble than the thing itself. This is urged by the Apostle, 1 Cor. xi. 8, 9.

4. The fourth is derived from the transgression of the woman. For she being seduced, violated the Divine command, and allured her husband into a participation of her transgression: Now it is just, that from thenceforward the wife should hearken to her husband, because the husband was ruined by hearkening to the wife. The Apostle makes use of this argument, 1 Tim. ii. 14.

5. The fifth is derived from the disadvantage of refusing this subjection, and disturbing the Divine ordination. For as in physical things, the disturbance of natural order yields many and great disadvantages, storms, floods, and earthquakes; so by the order of the due subjection of the wife towards her husband being disturbed, brawlings and clamours are heard in the house, like thunder; their bosoms are shaken by fear and mutual suspicions, as by

earthquakes; in fine, their whole life is overwhelmed with miseries and tears, as with inundations. It would be easy to bring in more reasons; but we shall be content with these.

4, It now remains to shew, in the last place, the usual hindrances to this subjection, and in the way of advice lay down, not all, but some of the principal of those things which ought to be avoided.

1. The first is pride: which makes the wife think highly of herself and all things belonging to her, as her figure, her prudence, her family; on the other hand, to despise and disesteem her husband, as unworthy to command such a woman. To obviate this evil; 1. Let her remember, that the dignity of her husband and her own inferiority is not to be estimated from virtues, figure, nobility, or riches; but from the Divine ordination alone: The authority of the husband, and the subjection of the wife, is founded in this, which neither ought nor can be abrogated or changed from such accidental causes. 2. Let her also consider; that it is the veriest proof of folly and vanity, to presume upon her own worth and prudence: for all those things which are easily inflated are empty. 3. Lastly, let her also understand; that this motion of pride proceeds from the devil, who, as he incited Eve to eat that fruit forbidden by God by infusing this poison; so, by instilling the same poison into the daughters of Eve, he daily tampers with them to throw off the subjection prescribed by God.

2. The second is the defect of true and genuine love. For she studies not to please her husband, whose greatest displeasure is that she has got such a husband: on the other hand, true love is a perpetual monitor, and the best teacher of obedience. *Retain love,* says Augustine; *for all duties depend upon it; by it you will possess what you have learnt, and what you have not learnt.* If, therefore, love be wanting, the wife neither knows how to please her husband, nor cares about it. This evil will be avoided; 1. If parents would not compel their daughters to odious nuptials; but before they give them in marriage, to do what we read

in Gen, xxiv. 57, 58, was done to Rebecca. *Then they said,
We will call the damsel, and inquire at her mouth. And they
called Rebecca, and said unto her, Wilt thou go with this
man? And she said, I will go.* 2. If they would beware in
contracting matrimony, lest they choose husbands for the
sake of honour or riches, who, they are sure, do not love
them cordially. 3. Lastly, if after contracting marriage,
they carefully avoid even the most trifling occasions of offence : for as things cleaving together in the beginning are
rent asunder by any sudden blow ; so also is it with the
fresh love of those just united in marriage. But God also
should be constantly invoked, that he would pour the bond
of true and holy love into their bosoms : for lascivious and
vague love is what arises from the flesh alone ; chaste and
constant love draws its origin from the Holy Spirit.

3. The third is a foolish affectation of divers vanities.
For she cannot perform the domestic duties which respect
her conjugal subjection, who is wholly drawn aside by the
study of foibles most foreign to the office of a matron.
Hither I refer that immoderate desire of appearing in public, to see, and be seen ; which is ever found in connexion
with a dislike of household care. From this source also
springs extravagance in dress, painting the face, in short,
a sort of external theatric parade in the whole tenor of life,
Prov. vii. 10. They who are mad of this disease of vanity,
care neither for husband, nor children, nor family. As,
therefore, they would withstand this evil, let wives reflect,
that they should please not the eyes of the people, but of
the husband alone. For (as says Clemens, Pædag. 2.) *It
is dishonest to make the beauty of the body a man-trap.* It is,
as says Augustine, De doctr. Christ. 4. 21, more dishonest
*to meditate by adultery of the countenance, the adultery of
chastity.* If, therefore, they will study ornament, they
should hear Tertullian, De cultu fæmin. *Let them borrow
from simplicity, fairness of the skin, and from chastity the
blush of the countenance ; and let them hang in their ears the
pearls of the word.* But the Apostle also recals them from
these vanities to their true ornaments, in 1 Tim. ii. 9. *Let
the women adorn themselves in modest apparel, with shame-*

*facedness and sobriety, not with broidered hair, or gold, or
pearls, or costly array ;* &c.

As it is fit in the Lord.] These words contain either the
reason of the aforesaid injunction, or rather the limitation.
If the reason, they must be explained in this manner ; Be
subject to your own husbands, because Christ your Lord
has so commanded you, whose ordination it is just that
Christians should obey. But concerning this Divine ordination we have spoken. If, therefore, these words contain
a limitation, (which I rather approve) then they are to be
explained thus; Be subject to your husbands, not absolutely, and promiscuously in all things, but as far as God
permits, or as far as it is befitting women who are *in the
Lord,* that is, believers and Christians.

The occasion of this limitation springs from the circumstance, that many believing women were united to unbelieving husbands, whom they were bound to obey, so far as it
could be done, without the violation of their faith and the
Christian religion. For if an unbelieving husband should
attempt to compel his wife to an idolatrous worship, she
must resist, and be governed by that rule of Peter, Acts
v. 29, *We must obey God rather than man.* There is the
same reason, if the husband attempt to entice his wife into
any sin : for it is not fit that those who are in the Lord,
should obey in such things. The foundation of this exception is, That all authority and superiority is derived
from God; and subordinate to the Divine authority : The
command of the inferior power, therefore, does not oblige
us to obedience when it is contrary to that of the superior,
as Durandus well observes, lib. 2. dist. 39. qu. 5. That
saying of Gregory, therefore, is always to be retained, *The
wife should so please the will of her husband, as not to displease
the will of her Creator.*

Corollaries from this limitation.

1. Wives obedient to their husbands by this due subjection, render a submission grateful to God himself; because they are subject not only for their own sake, but
much more in the Lord and for the Lord's sake.

2. The wife is bound to her husband to be a companion

and help, in prosperity and adversity, in all household duties; but in no manner in sin.

3. It is the mark of imprudence and impiety, to choose
such a husband as seems likely to persuade his wife to
those things which are not fit in the Lord. They do this
who marry Papists, or any other heretics, and wicked
persons, without any difference, provided the hope of
riches shine upon them from it.—And thus much concerning the subjection of the wife and its limitation.

Vers. 19. *Husbands, love your wives, and be not bitter
against them.*

It is prudently said by Chrysostom, *The scales should
always be equally poised in exhortations.* This Paul has accurately observed in this whole exhortation. In the foregoing verse he cast into one scale the duties of wives:
now he places in the other the duties of husbands also; so
that both should be equal in weight, neither the one being
more than duly depressed, nor the other raised above what
is meet. Therefore to come to the explication of the
words: The duty of husbands is expressed in these words;
by a precept enjoining *love;* by an injunction forbidding
bitterness.

1. First we must explain the precept, *Husbands, love
your wives.*] The word for *love* must be referred as well to
the passion as to the effect: Which is manifestly gathered
from Ephes. v. 25, where the love of Christ towards the
Church is proposed for an example to husbands; *Husbands,
love your wives, as Christ also loved the Church, and gave
himself for it.* 'Ηγάπησε, he *loved,* indicates the affection;
Παρέδωκε, he *gave himself,* demonstrates *the effect* of the
love.

In the first place, then, the Apostle requires the affection of love, namely, that the husband love his wife in

heart and mind. For this internal affection of love gives
the heart itself to the thing loved, which is the most precious and first gift, and that, in fine, in which all other
gifts are given when occasion requires : for love is diffusive
of its good. It is not badly said by Aristotle, Rhet. 2. 8,
*Love is the wishing to any one what it conceives to be good for
the sake of that one, and not for its own; and it is the endeavouring to accomplish this, as far as it can.* Therefore he requires such an affection in the heart of the husband. But
because we cannot thrust our eyes into the hearts of men,
to see the internal affection, external effects are required
in testimony of love : for the proof of love is the exhibition of its operation. Let us come to this.

The love of the husband ought chiefly to express itself
in three effects.

First, it is shewn herein, that he lives freely and cheerfully with his wife in his own house ; he is delighted
with her presence and company; he suffers himself to be
torn from her for any long time only by necessary
causes, and then thinks himself to be cast elsewhere and
to be thrown hither and thither, and at home with his wife
to rest as in the wished-for haven. For although married
persons ought to be so prepared in mind, that, if it be necessary, the one can bear absence from the other with
equanimity ; yet it is not to be allowed that the husband
should hate or be weary of the company of his own wife,
or willingly be elsewhere than with her ; for true love is
mostly delighted with the presence of the beloved, and is
tormented as it were by the absence of the same. This effect of love we see in Christ towards his Church : for he
never deserts her, or leaves her alone : but performs what
he promised Matt. xxviii. 20, *I am with you always even
unto the end of the world.* Thus, then, ought the husband
also to be animated towards his wife, to be with her constantly unto the last breath of his life. This Solomon requires from all pious and good husbands in Prov. v. 18, 19,
*Rejoice with the wife of thy youth. Let her be as the loving
hind and pleasant roe ; let her breasts satisfy thee at all times,
and be thou ravished always with her love. And why wilt*

*thou, my son, be ravished with a strange woman and embrace
the bosom of a stranger?* Yea, Aristotle himself considers
it injustice in the husband, if he despise his wife, and indulge unlawful pleasures elsewhere : and he calls that undivided society of life, and due benevolence which the husband is bound to yield towards his wife, *a pious and most
holy dwelling together, and dignified station of marriage.* The
opinion, therefore, or rather impiety, of the Emperor
Ælius Verus, is to be rejected ; who is wrong in having
affirmed, that the wife was a title *of dignity,* not *of pleasure :* as though wives should be satisfied that husbands
condescended to honour them by contracting marriage with
them ; and in the mean time it might be allowed the husband to follow pleasures, or rather iniquity, out of matrimony, at his own discretion. Thus much of the first
effect of love.

The second duty of love is, to direct and instruct his
wife to his utmost in all those things which relate to the
passing through this life well, or to the attaining eternal
life. On this account the husband is called *the head of the
wife* in sacred learning : that, as the body is directed by
the head, so the wife should be directed by the husband to
the common good of both. Aristotle writes, Oecon. l. 8,
that *by a prudent husband nothing should be neglected of
those things which tend to the instruction of his wife :* and he
alleges the cause ; namely, that she herself by being well
informed may be capable of instructing her children. This
also in Xenophon, in his Oeconomics, Ischomachus, whom
that sweet writer proposed as an example of a good husband, as Cyrus, of a good king, says that he carefully did.
Therefore he himself says, that he taught his wife, what
might suffice for those cares which related to her office ;
and for this end, first sought from God, both that he himself might teach those things which would be best for
either, and especially that she might learn the same. This
duty of love (as you may perceive) was not concealed even
from the heathen themselves, particularly as far as it relates to this life. But the sacred writers also extend this
care of the husband to the other life : for he ought even

in the business of religion, and in those things which regard her eternal salvation, to instruct his wife. For this
maxim is a sign of true love, to take care that his wife
may rightly worship God together with himself in this life,
whereby they may together enjoy God in the life to come.
On this account, Paul, in 1 Cor. xiv. 35, refers the wife to
the husband as to a domestic tutor; *If the wives would learn
any thing, let them ask their own husbands at home.* Therefore the husbands ought to direct their wives in things
earthly and secular; because they are co-partners in all
earthly things: they ought also to instruct them in divine
and heavenly things; because they are co-heirs of heavenly
blessings, *heirs together of the grace of life,* as Peter says,
1 Epis. iii. 7.

The third and last effect of love is, to provide his wife
with all necessary things. And in this respect it behoves
the husband to imitate the care and providence of Christ:
for he would have nothing wanting to his Church, which is
either necessary or conducive to its welfare, as to clothing,
food, and life: so the husband ought to acquire by his labour, and communicate to his wife out of love, whatever
either the necessity or dignity of her person shall require.
He who is not concerned about this duty, subjects himself
to that heavy censure, *If any man provide not for his own,
and especially for those of his own house, he hath denied the
faith, and is worse than an infidel,* 1 Tim. v. 8. Hence we
may conjecture what is to be thought of those monstrous
guttlers, who not only provide not for their family, but
dissipate the things which were well provided, in play, in
drinking, and harlots; the wife and children in the mean
while pinched, and all but perishing for want and hunger.
Neither the love of the husband, nor the faith of the Christian appears in these things: for whom that which they are
wont to allege is no excuse, that they consume what is
their own; for neither Divine nor human laws permit any
one to abuse his goods through lust. Besides, the wife
ought to be a partaker of all the goods which belong to
the husband, no less than she is compelled to be a partaker in all his ills. And thus much of the three effects of

love : which, the better to commend, we shall add a necessary caution by way of appendage.

He who is desirous of performing his duty in loving his wife, should beware of the vulgar error in choosing : Let him think from the beginning in entering upon matrimony, to choose, neither *by the eyes alone*, nor *by the fingers alone*, as Plutarch says, in Conjug. præcep.

They are said to marry *by the eyes alone*, who in choosing a wife regard chiefly her external form and beauty. That love, which rests upon so unstable a foundation, can in no way be firm and constant. Neither do I so intend this saying, as though it was unlawful to choose a modest woman from her face; (for we see the most religious and chaste patriarch Jacob to have preferred Rachel to Leah) but to be understood that external beauty is not especially, or by itself, to be sought after in marrying, but so far as it is the beauteous dress of a beauteous mind. *Virtue is more agreeable where it appears in a beautiful person,* says Virgil, Æn. lib. v. l. 344. Therefore, let the first enquiry be as to manners : If they are found to be good, and worthy of commendation, then beauty should not be slighted; which is not improperly called by Tertullian, *felicity of body, an accession to the plastic hand of the Divinity,* and *the genteel apparel of the soul.* The opinion of Solomon in this matter is to be remembered, Prov. xxxi. 30, *Favour is deceitful, and beauty is vain; but a woman that feareth the Lord, she shall be praised.*

Now they are led into matrimony *by the fingers,* who only regard what the wife shall bring in money; if the dowry satisfies, they are little or not at all solicitous about probity or piety. These are worse than the before-mentioned : for they respect beauty, that is to say, the good in the person; these, money, namely, the good apart from the person. Therefore, the love of the former is light; that of the latter, plainly nothing: for they seek not a wife, but a money-porter : after that they have laid their claws upon the money, they regard not of a straw the porter. But it is the character of the pious and the wise to prefer the wife to the money, rather than the money without the wife;

and to regard that in choosing a wife, which may and ought especially to induce them constantly to love the wife. And thus we have explained to you the precept which enjoins love: Now we must proceed to the injunction, which forbids bitterness.

2. *Be not bitter against them.*] The word is a metaphor, drawn from unpleasant and bitter food, by the taste of which men are offended. By this expression therefore, the Apostle intimates, that the conversation of the husband towards his wife ought to be pleasant and kind; not unsavoury and harsh: Yea, (as says Ambrose in Hexæm. 5. 7.) although *naturally he may be rigid, yet he ought to mitigate it by the very contemplation of marriage.* Which also was the opinion of the heathen: For (as Plutarch relates) *they who did sacrifice at the rites of Juno, took out the gall of the victim, and threw it away, signifying by the ceremony, that it was not fit that bile and bitterness should enter into the married state.*

The bitterness here prohibited is wont to shew itself in three things: the affections, the words, and actions.

1. First, in the very affections of husbands. For as far as the affections are bitter, they who are exasperated against their wives for light causes, and failures however small, both begin from thence either to hate them, or at least remissly and languidly to love them. They who are affected in this manner, although they neither do nor say any thing evil against their wives, yet often render the fellowship of the conjugal state unpleasant and disagreeable. That this bitterness is to be avoided, is gathered,

1. From the precept itself of loving their wives, which is imposed upon husbands: For it does not admit that exception, If they shall be, or whilst they shall be free from all faults: For God, who gave this precept of loving the wife, knew well that no mortal is free from his faults and imperfections: Therefore by this truly impossible condition being added or understood, the precept would be superfluous (and ridiculous). As, then, the wife is bound to obey her husband, notwithstanding his many imperfections; so also the husband is bound to love his wife. If

for light causes he even remits the affection of love, it must be ascribed to bitterness.

2. This also is plain from the example of Christ, who is proposed as an example to husbands by the Apostle. For he is not wont to hate or despise his church for her many faults and sins; but he rather studies to amend and cover her sins, whilst no odium is cast upon her person: Such ought to be the affection of the husband towards his wife. No fault or sin of the wife ought then to extinguish that matrimonial affection, unless it be of that kind as to extinguish and dissolve matrimony itself: for the wife remains, whilst matrimony continues, one flesh with her husband : *But no one never hated his own flesh, but nourisheth and cherisheth it, even as the Lord the Church,* Ephes. v. 29.

3. From the confession of the very heathen. For Aristotle himself, imbued with the light of nature, saw that the husband ought not for any fault immediately to alienate his mind from his wife ; but, as he says, Oecon. i. 8, he should forgive willingly *little faults,* τά μέν μικρὰ τῶν πλαισμάτων, although they should be voluntary ; but even if through ignorance she should offend in those which are of greater moment, he should be satisfied to have advised and instructed her, not to have hated her. And thus you see all bitterness is to be banished afar off from the very mind and affection of the husband.

2. Secondly, this bitterness seems to be placed in bitter, contumelious, or any other words opposed to conjugal love. For a tender mind is wounded no less by bitter words, than the body is by sharp weapons : Hence words are sometimes compared by the Psalmist to darts and swords. Psal. lv. It does not therefore become the husband to wound his wife by these swords. (Arist. Rhet.) As to contumelious words, they are most foreign from duty and from matrimonial love. For the design of contumely is, that one may rejoice in the disgrace of him who is treated contumeliously : but it is barbarous to rejoice in the disgrace of his own wife. But neither is that bitterness of passionate men to be suffered, which breaks out into hard words, and threats, although there may be no

intention either of contumely or injury. For if any one
who is angry with any brother, and breaks forth into bitter
words, *shall be guilty of hell fire*, Matt. v. 22, then how
much more he who does so against his wife? Therefore,
that all bitterness may be banished from the wedded state,
let that precept in Prov. v. 18, be kept in remembrance :
Rejoice with the wife of thy youth : not *strive, revile, threaten ;*
but *rejoice.*

3. Thirdly, Bitterness, and that the most bitter, is
found in the actions ; namely, when the husband, plainly
unmindful what the conjugal relation is, shews himself a
tyrant, and treats his wife as his servant. The very institution of marriage repels this bitterness : For God gave not
Eve to Adam as a servant or a slave, but for a companion
or help-meet. *Thou art not a lord, but a husband ; thou hast
not got a maid-servant, but a wife : God would have thee the
guide of the inferior sex, not the tyrant,* says Ambrose,
Hexæm. 5. 7. But this tyranny is exercised over the wife
in many ways :

1. When she is removed from all domestic rule, and is
degraded as it were to the rank of a maid, even perhaps
subjected to one of them. But the institution of marriage,
in which the wife is taken to the supreme administration of
the family under her husband, opposes this. Whence Xenophon calls the wife *the guardian of the domestic laws ;* and
Aristotle says, that she is *to preside over the inmates.* Moreover, the sacred Scriptures assign this to her, Prov. xxxi.
27 ; Tit. ii. 5. Although, therefore, it ought to be pleasant to the wife to obey her husband ; yet it is bitter if he
compel her to be subject to his own servant, or if he do
not suffer her to preside. Abraham was unwilling to be
bitter in this respect against Sarah, and on that account
cast out the bondmaid from his house, who began to be
disobedient and troublesome to her mistress ; as you may
gather from Gen. xvi.

2. It is a branch also of this tyranny, when those things
which pertain either to her necessity or even to her dignity
are denied or taken away by the husband. For she, by
virtue of the matrimonial contract, ought to be a partner

with the husband of all his goods: It is therefore injustice
if he consume on himself more than his circumstances allow, and in the mean time withdraws from his wife what is
just and good. This is esteemed bitterness in the doer,
and it necessarily savours of bitterness to the sufferer : *For
all persons deprived of their proper privileges are deeply grieved,*
says Aristotle, Œconom. i. cap. 8.

Lastly, It is the height of this bitter tyranny, to act
cruelly towards the wife by stripes or blows ; which we do
not read that any one among the heathen did, unless he
was drunk or mad. Hence the civil law permits the wife
*to avail herself of a divorce, if she can prove that her husband
has beaten her :* and it gives as a reason, *that blows are foreign to a state of freedom,* Cod. lib. 5. tit. 17. De repudiis;
and in Novell. constit. 117. For no superiority whatever
gives the power of coercing the inferior by blows. If two
persons enter into a league of friendship on the condition
that the younger shall obey the elder, and be directed in
all things by his wisdom and discretion; he is bound to
obedience by virtue of this contract : but if he refuse to
do that, he cannot be forced to his duty by blows. The
same must be said with regard to the matrimonial contract : for in this the husband and wife agree to a certain
amicable fellowship in life, so that the wife is to be subject to her husband, and directed by him ; but as a companion, not as a slave ; by advice, not by stripes.*

Aristotle gives this reason ; because *it is not fit to instil
such fear into the wife, which may be injurious both to respect
and love :* but that servile fear which is instilled by blows is
subversive of both.

Neither is it fit that any one should exercise power over
another by constraint supported by no law; but that power

---

* It is one of the glories of Christianity that it gave woman her proper
place in society. Under the Jewish dispensation, woman was perpetually
reminded that she was first in the transgression. In republican Athens,
man was every thing, and woman *nothing.* In most heathen countries she
is little more than a slave. It is in Christian nations she has been raised to
an equality with man. It is Christianity that has conferred upon her liberty
and heaven.

of chastising a wife by stripes is supported by no law either Divine or human.

Finally add, That is not to be done which cannot be done without sin, and what always derives its origin from this sin of bitterness. For although parents often chastise their children from love; yet both the experience and conscience of every one will testify, that no one proceeds to beat his wife except from anger, bitterness, or hatred; all which are unlawful things, and diametrically opposite to the matrimonial state. Therefore, let all bitterness be done away.

So far we have spoken of the duty of wife and husband. In the next place the duty of children and parents follows; among which the second domestic relation is placed.

Vers. 20.

Children, obey your parents in all things: for this is well-pleasing unto the Lord.

We have said that the second domestic relation subsists between parents and children : therefore the Apostle endeavours now to imbue these with wholesome instructions in this place. And as he began in that relation ordained to be prior, from the duty of the wives; so now he begins from that of children (as I conceive) for the same reasons, or at least not much unlike. The Apostle, then, follows this order; both because children oftener fail in the duty of obedience, than parents in that of love; as because this duty of obedience rightly discharged, cannot but draw parents to the discharge of their duty. But let us come to the words.

We have in them a precept; Children, *obey your parents,* &c. and the reason of the precept; *for this is acceptable to the Lord.*

In the precept three things are to be noted : To whom
it is given ; Concerning what matter ; and to what extent.
1. *Children*] In these words we perceive to whom this
precept is proposed. The translator has rendered it, *children.* But this Greek word (τα τέκνα) is evidently of more
latitude, for it denotes *young,* or *offspring* in general. It
therefore extends to sons and daughters, yea, to grandchildren ; for both according to the Scriptures, and according to lawyers, in the appellation of *children,* grandchildren
are comprehended ; as when the Jews are called *the children of Israel,* &c. Therefore, whoever is the τέκνον of another, on this very account he hath one to whom he owes
honour and obedience.

Observations.

1. No age exempts a child from duty to his parents ;
because the indissoluble foundation of duty remains always, even in their more advanced age.

2. No dignity of office frees from this debt : For although a magistrate is on political grounds more honourable than a private person, yet a son, on the ground of
having derived his origin from him, is always inferior to
his father. *And Joseph went up to meet Israel his father,*
&c. Gen. xlvi. 29. Therefore, whoever is a son, neither
by age, nor by station, nor riches, in fine, by no mode
whatever can he be exempt from this filial duty. But what
is it ?

2. *Obey your parents.*] Here we have the matter of the
precept, namely, obedience to be rendered to parents.
The Greek word ὑπακούετε, comprises two things ; a humble
promptitude in receiving the orders of another, and a
cheerful obedience in executing the same. Therefore it
pertains to this obedience, to do what parents order, to
learn what they teach, to correct and amend what they reprove, and, in one word, to perform all outward deeds
which may testify the internal affection of reverence and
submission.

The Apostle could have said *Honour,* as it is said in the
decalogue ; but he preferred, *Obey ;* namely, in order to
restrain that vice under which children mostly labour. For

many yield reverence and honour to their parents, who yet
fail to render obedience in the course of their life.

But we must also observe that he says, not to *fathers,*
but to *parents;* for in this word both parents are included;
and that properly too: for a son derives his origin from
both; therefore to both, that is, both father and mother,
he owes obedience and reverence.   Vide Prov. xxiii. 22.

In this very word *parents,* is implied the most powerful
argument, yea, many arguments, which ought to impel
children to obedience.   For as soon as the epithet *parents,*
sounds in the ears of a child, he calls to mind that they
are the persons from whom he has received his origin, his
support, and education.   If he has derived his origin, or
his bodily existence from them, then he ought by the law
of nature to be subject to them: If his food and sustenance, then he is bound to it by the moral debt of gratitude or justice.   Lastly, if his instruction and discipline,
then he is constrained to yield this obedience on account
of his own advantage.

Instructions.

1.   The desire of honouring parents is pretended in
vain, where the duty of obedience is not shewn, Matt. xxi.
30.

2.   He who despises his parents is not only to be reckoned to have thrown off piety, but also nature: for nature enjoins the offspring to submit to the parent; which
is observed in storks, and proposed to be imitated in men
by Ambrose, Hexæm. 5. 16.

3.   Contumely is fixed upon God himself, when parents
are not honoured: for whatever parents are, they have the
likeness of God, who is the supreme Father, and from
whom all paternity is derived.   *Of Him is the whole family
in heaven and earth,* Ephes. iii. 15.   Hence Laciantius,
Instit. lib. 5. cap. 19, calls God himself, our *true* and supreme *Father;* but he also adds, and earthly parents are
instruments of our existence under God.   These subordinate
parents ,therefore, cannot be contemned, without God also
being contemned.

4.   They who strive at pleasing their parents, the same

are for the most part pious towards God: for as Hugo de
St. Victor has well said, De sacram. lib. 1. cap. 7, *this paternity is to us the sign and image of the divine paternity ; so
that the human heart may learn by that principle which it sees,
what it owes to that principle from which it is derived, and
which it does not see.* Thus much concerning the matter of
the precept; Now let us discuss its breadth and latitude.

3. *In all things.*] The Apostle appears to extend filial
obedience to all things which are enjoined by parents,
without excepting justice and equity : for universal and
absolute obedience is due to God alone. But the limitation and explication of this charge may be obtained from
Ephes. vi. 1, where he expresses what remains to be understood in this place ; *Children, obey your parents in the Lord,*
that is, as far as it is allowed by God; or, as we may gather from the words immediately following, *obey in all
things,* in which, for example, this your obedience may be
pleasing to God. For, as Aquinas has laid down, Qu. disp.
de consc. art. 4, *We must not obey an inferior power against
the command of a superior.* By the expression *all things,*
therefore, in this place, we must understand, not all things
absolutely, but all things lawful and honourable. Hence,
therefore, we infer,

1. We must obey parents in things good and pious, as
well in regard to the thing commanded, as to the person
himself giving the command.

2. In things general and indifferent in their nature, it
behoves children to obey their parents. For although the
things prescribed be free and indifferent in their nature ;
yet obedience, when the parental command is interposed,
is not at one's pleasure, but under a mandate. For truly
and wisely was it said by Gerson, De relig. perfect. part.
3, *In things indifferent we must especially confide in the judgment of a superior ; since he tells us in the place of God what
is expedient and what is proper.*

3. Although the injunctions of parents may seem harsh
and unjust, yet if they contain nothing of impiety they
must be obeyed, especially by children not yet set free
from parental authority. We have a remarkable example

in Isaac, who withheld not his obedience to his father even unto death, Gen. xxii. 9, and in Christ himself, in his submission to his parents, Luke ii. 51.

But here a question may arise concerning married children, or those called to the administration of Church or State, whether they are still bound to obedience to parents, and how far?

We answer, That filial obedience is perpetual, and is to be rendered even to the last breath of life: which is manifest from the command itself, *Honour thy father, that thou mayest live long upon the earth.* Therefore, so long as we live here, so long is the obedience of honour due to parents; but not in the same manner and degree. Children, then, living in the paternal house, and under the paternal power, are bound to yield reverence, obedience, and assistance to their parents, and that in matters of domestic care, or in other matters according to their command and will. If parents would have them to remain at home, and aid them in household duties, they ought not to refuse; as is plain from the parable of the two sons, Matt. xxi. 28. If they wish to employ their labour to accomplish some outer business, in this also they must obey, Tob. v. 3. But as to married children, or those called to administer the Church or State, the case is different. For although all these are yet bound to revere, obey, and even to render assistance when occasion offers; yet they are not bound, as before, to dwell with them, nor to labour at the domestic business of their parents; because now they have their own and more weighty business.

With respect to married children this is plain; because the husband from the Divine ordination ought to leave his father and his mother to cleave unto his wife, Gen. ii. 24. Which we must not understand abstractedly, but comparatively, and in respect of individual fellowship and cohabitation: for he ought to labour for the support of his family, Gen. xxx. 30.

Now as to those who have undertaken ecclesiastical duties; they cannot be recalled by the authority of parents to the performance of their earthly business. For if a father cannot recal his son from the army of his earthly king by any authority with which he is invested, how much less from this sacred army? Nay, they who have put their hands to this work ought not to look back to that which they have left, Luke ix. 62.

The reason is similar in regard to those who discharge public offices: for it is just that private concerns yield to public ones. To conclude in a word: A son can never be freed from the duty of honouring and succouring his parents; but he may from the duty of dwelling with them, and administering their domestic affairs. And so far respecting the precept itself.

For this is well pleasing unto the Lord.] In these words is contained the reason or inducement, than which no other more efficacious can be presented to pious minds, to discharge that duty of obedience. For he does not say, *This your duty will be useful to you, or grateful to your parents;* but *it will be well-pleasing to Christ himself your Lord,* whom it is your happiness to please. But how does it appear that obedience towards parents is a thing so pleasing to Christ our Lord, and to God our Father?

It appears chiefly from two considerations: From even a temporal, and as it were an extraordinary reward, annexed to that command of honouring parents; which is urged by the Apostle in Ephes. vi. 2, Being *the first command with promise.* And also from temporal punishment, which is to be inflicted by the ordination of God upon the violaters of his command, which see in Deut. xxi. 18, &c. Neither was it concealed from the heathen themselves, that the life of those who conducted themselves piously and dutifully towards their parents was prolonged by the Divine gift. Whence that remark of the Greek poet; *Be assured that by honouring your parents you will flourish in the world:* and another to the same purport; *You will live long enough, if you sustain the old age of your parents.* They, therefore, acknowledge this to be *well-pleasing* to God. But they also have even declared that contempt of parents should be restrained by the severest punishments; *A wronging of parents or of the gods is to be expiated with a like judgment,*

says Valerius. Which also was agreeable to Plato; as you
may see in 11 De legibus.

Instructions.

1. It behoves the faithful in every good work, especially to respect the Lord himself. If our actions are well-
pleasing to him, it matters not much what men think of
us, or with what mind they may receive them.

2. Children, by obeying their parents out of a pure
heart, offer a service most pleasing to God himself by this
their obedience, and receive a reward from him; as is
clear from the example of the Rechabites, Jer. xxxv. 18.

3. He who by his contumacy provokes the anger and
curse of his parents against himself, calls down the anger
and the vengeance of God in like manner against him.
Abimelech is an example in Judg. ix. 56.

4. Hypocrites are much deceived, who under a pretence of piety towards God, neglect the duties of piety
and obedience towards parents: as though sacrifice was
more pleasing to God than either obedience or mercy. But
Christ most clearly refutes this error, in Matt. xv. 4, 5,
&c. The Papists have renewed this error of the Pharisees
by maintaining, That it is lawful for children, even in opposition to their parents, to profess religion, that is, to
enter a monastery; which kind of life being undertaken,
they cannot be subject to their parents, since they are
bound by a Divine and natural law. Let us see therefore,
what they think of this matter; and what we must think
according to the word of God.

Aquinas, Q. 2. qu. 88. art. 9, concludes, *after the years
of puberty, children may bind themselves by a religious vow
without the consent of their parents.* This is also the common opinion of the Papists, and is defended by Bellarmin
in lib. 2. De monachis, cap. 36, where he thus decides,
*That it is lawful for children, against the will of their parents,
to leave their home, and enter upon a monastic life, provided
they shall have reached the years of puberty, and the parents
are not in such poverty but that they may live without their
help.* It is decided that boys shall be accounted of the
age at fourteen; girls, at twelve. But on the contrary, we

shall prove that it is not lawful that this should be done against the will of the parents. For ;

1. To do any thing whatever not commanded by God, but in manifest violation of a command, is impious and rash : But for any one to bind himself to a monastic life does not come under the Divine precept ; and to resist parents, when they enjoin that upon us which is either good or is not unlawful, is a manifest violation of a Divine command : Since, therefore, it is good and lawful to profit their parents, and to serve them in their domestic cares, children, whilst not yet free, ought not to desert their parents against their will.

2. To offer to God what is another's, and that against his will, is opposed to virtue : But the power over children belongs to parents, whilst they are under their keeping, so that they cannot of their own will withdraw themselves from their parents, and betake themselves whither they wish : therefore they cannot vow to enter a monastery against the will of their parents. Hither applies that declaration in Numb. xxx. 3, 5, *If a woman shall have vowed in her father's house in her youth ; if her father shall have disallowed her, her vow shall be void.*

Neither is that reply of Bellarmin and Aquinas of any weight, who say, that before the years of puberty, i. e. (as they interpret it) before the twelfth year, a damsel cannot vow against the consent of her parents : but afterwards she may, because she is free in all those things which relate to her person : for the context opposes it ; which enacts this law concerning every woman remaining in her father's house, that is, under the care of her father, whether she be twelve years old, or more.

3. What it is rash to do without the advice or not with the approbation of parents, that it is impious to do against their consent and remonstrances : But it is the part of rashness, if a youth of sixteen, or a damsel of fifteen, shall resolve about their mode of life without the knowledge and approbation of their parents, especially in entering upon that kind of life, which by a certain necessity calls them off from yielding submission to their parents ; for it

is the duty of pious children, first to go to their parents,
to enquire both whether they may, and whether they wish
to do without their help and assistance : If, therefore, they
ought not to do this without the advice of their parents,
much less so against their will.

4.   We have the authority of the Council of Gangra,
cap. 16. tom. 1, *Whatever children separate from their parents under pretence of Divine worship, neither pay them due
reverence, let them be anathema.*   Bellarmin endeavours to
restrict it to those alone who forsake parents that are
needy, and betake themselves against their consent into
monasteries.   But this answer is of no weight.   For first,
the words of the Council are general ; *Whoever separate
from their parents,* without the gloss of Bellarmin, *placed in
extreme want.*   Secondly, it is not the part of a modest
child, when he hears his parent saying that he cannot do
without his assistance, and remonstrating against his pro-
posal to enter a monastery, yet to decide in opposition to
it.   Lastly, it is harsh to restrict the obedience of children
to the extreme poverty only of their parents.

5.   Basil in Quæst, largely explained, quæst. 15, plainly
asserts, *that children are not to be received into monasteries
unless they shall be offered by their parents.*   Bellarmin
answers, that is to be understood of children under age
alone ; that is, males before their fourteenth year, and females before their twelfth, are not to be received without
the consent of their parents ; but after this age they may
enter although the parents should be unwilling.   But Basil does not distribute children in that place, into adults
and those under age ; but into 'εϱημα γονέων, καὶ ὑπὸ γονεῖς
ὄντα, *those who are destitute of parents, and those whose parents are yet living, and have the care of their children.*   He
denies that the latter are to be received without the consent
of their parents.

Now let us proceed to solve the arguments of Bellarmin.   He opposes it by passages of Scripture, testimonies
of the Fathers, and of Councils, and by moral reasons.

1.   He brings that passage of Scripture out of Gen.
xii. 1, as it is in the version of the Vulgate, *Get thee out of*

thy country, and from thy kindred, and from thy father's house, unto a land that I will shew thee. Therefore it is lawful to leave parents against their will, and to enter a monastery.

I answer, In no respect does it meet the case. Abraham was now married, and his own master, not under the protection of his father; Abraham had a special command; it does not appear that Abraham's parents opposed him, nay, it appears, Gen. xi. 31, that his father consented to his journey ; not, indeed, to enter a monastery, but to go into the land promised by God : But we contend respecting children still living under the paternal care, who have not a special command from God, and yet forsake their parents against their will, and betake themselves to a monastery. The cases are altogether dissimilar.

2. From Deut. xxxiii. 9, *Who said unto his father and to his mother, I know you not ; and to his brethren, I am ignorant of you : these have observed thy word, and kept thy covenant.* To which he joins that passage, Matt. x. 37, *He that loveth father or mother more than me, is not worthy of me.*

I answer ; The former passage speaks of the Levites, who drew the sword at the command of God against the idolaters, without any distinction of relationship, as you may see in Exod. xxxii. It therefore proves no more, than that they were worthy of commendation, who, to preserve the worship of God, and execute the command of God, had respect neither to relative, nor any human concern. What has this to do with those, who against the command to honour their parents, forsake them, that they may practise a superstitious worship in monasteries ? That other passage does not say, *He that loveth father or mother more than cloister or hood,* but *more than Christ :* therefore it makes nothing to the point. If we cannot obey Christ and parents, then we must forsake parents : but lawful obedience is not opposed to religion, but is a religious work, and pleasing to God.

3. From Psalm xlv. 10, *Forget thy people, and thy father's house ; so shall the king greatly desire thy beauty.*

Therefore, in order to serve God, it is lawful and commendable to renounce parents, and flee into a monastery.

I answer, The conclusion does not follow from these premises, unless when we cannot at the same time obey both. But these words are spoken in a literal sense concerning the daughter of Pharaoh, who could not at the same time remain in Egypt with her father, and obey her husband Solomon: they are understood in a mystical sense concerning Christ and his spouse the Church, who cannot retain her innate corruption and please Christ. But children are not compelled by this kind of necessity to enter monasteries, and desert their parents.—He brings certain other testimonies of Scripture, but so foreign to the purpose, that I am ashamed to be occupied in refuting such idle attempts : Let us come then to the Fathers whom he quotes.

1. I unite them all under one testimony, that of Theophylact, as the same answer may be accommodated to them all. Thus, then, speaks Theophylact,* on John xix. *It behoves them not to obey parents opposing piety :* and Gregory, Hom. 37, on the Evang.: *Those adversaries whom we meet in the way of God, let us know nothing of them, by hating and avoiding them :* and Augustine, Epist. 38, ad Lætum, says, that he ought to be drawn from the perfect way, neither by the command nor the entreaties of his mother.

---

* The Theophylact here mentioned, and who flourished in the eleventh Century, is to be distinguished from a writer and a Bishop of the Greek Church, of the same name, who lived in the seventh Century. The Father to whom reference is made as above, was Archbishop of Acris, in Bulgaria. He was a native of Constantinople, whose great reputation for Theological attainments induced Maria, the empress of Michael Ducas, to urge him to accept the See of Acris, in a province then nearly barbarous. He zealously employed himself to diffuse Christianity in his province, and wrote several works of such excellence as to rank him among the principal of the ecclesiastical writers of the period. He was living in 1071, but the exact time of his death is unknown. His principal work is " Commentaries upon the four Gospels, the Acts of the Apostles, and the Epistles of St. Paul." He also wrote " Commentaries on the four minor Prophets." Of these works several editions have been published in Greek and Latin, and in Latin alone. His " Epistles," in number seventy-five, will be found in the Bibliotheca Patrum. From the references here made to him and others, we have some instructive specimens of the way in which the Roman Catholic advocates corrupt or pervert the Fathers.

I answer: All these are distorted by the very bad faith of Bellarmin; who, if he had looked into his authors, could not but perceive that they never even dreamt about entering monasteries against the will of parents. I approve that saying of Theophylact, namely, *That parents opposed to piety are not to be obeyed;* but, however, they must be obeyed by children when they exact the duties of piety; and this is what we maintain. The words of Gregory have respect to that saying of the Saviour, Luke xiv. 26, *If any man come to me and hate not his father and his mother, he cannot be my disciple.* Therefore, they relate equally to all Christians, not to monks alone. But Gregory in that place best interprets himself, who immediately adds these words to those which are adduced by Bellarmin: *Quasi per odium diligitur, qui carnaliter sapiens dum prava nobis ingerit, non auditur.* Gregory, therefore, means no more, than that parents, when they act wickedly towards their children, are not to be heard: which no one in his senses would deny. As to Augustine, He does not say that Lætus could enter a monastery against the will of his parents, whilst under their guardianship: nay, he no where indeed ever asserts in that epistle that he was a monk; but he shews that he was a preacher of the Gospel, and ought not to be led away by earthly cares from the office he had undertaken. *The duty,* says Augustine, *of preaching the Gospel hurries thee along; the celestial trumpet impels the soldier of Christ to the battle, whilst his mother keeps him back:* then a little after; *Thy Mother the Church, is the mother of thy mother: she requires thy just and due assistance,* &c. Therefore what Augustine urges is true, That a preacher of the Gospel ought not to be recalled from the office he has undertaken, not even by the intreaties of his mother: what Bellarmin infers, that a boy may not be prohibited from entering a monastery, not even by the command and authority of his parents, is false.

Two testimonies are cited from Jerome; one from his first Epistle to Heliodorus, in these words, *Although a grandson may hang upon his neck, although thy mother with dishevelled hair and her garments rent, may present the paps*

*which sucked thee, although thy father may prostrate himself
across the threshold, proceed trampling upon thy parent, and
with tearless eye flee forth to the banner of the cross. It is the
genius of piety alone to be cruel in this matter.* It is lawful
therefore for sons to follow Christ even against the will of
their parents.

This Epistle, which was written by Jerome when a youth,
and more of a rhetorician than a theologian, is of no
great authority to determine a controversy of theology.
But yet I answer; what Jerome says may be admitted, that
he must fly to the standard of Christ even by trampling
upon parents, if he can no otherwise get thither: yet I
deny that the standard of Dominic or Francis is to be approached in this manner. I add also, that children placed
under the power of their parents, may follow Christ, although they do not desert their parents. If, then, Jerome
would have the standard of Christ to be found no otherwise than in a monastic life, we unhesitatingly reject Jerome as in error: if this be not his meaning, he affords
nothing for confirmation to Bellarmin. And it is plain this
is not his meaning: for whereas Monasteries are for the
most part erected near cities and towns, Jerome calls Heliodorus into the desert, and expressly writes, *That a monk
remaining in his own country cannot be perfect.* Therefore,
the Papistic Monasteries should be deserts, if the opinion
of Jerome is to be allowed.

I come to another testimony drawn from Jerome's epistle 47. *If any one should reproach you that you are a Christian, or that you are a virgin, and for not caring to have forsaken
your mother in order to live in a monastery among virgins;
you are not to regard it: such detraction is your praise, that
cruelty is your piety: for you prefer him to your mother whom
you are commanded to prefer to your own life.*

I answer, We do not condemn the resolution to live a
virgin in those to whom the gift of continence is given by
God; neither do we even blame those, who, the better to
maintain this their resolution, flee as much as possible
from the world, and join themselves to those who follow
the same manner of life: But we deny that this virgin to

whom Jerome writes, betook herself to a monastery against
the consent of her parents, or could do so without violating filial duty : upon which the hinge of the controversy
turns. Jerome says, *for not caring to have forsaken your mo-*
ther in order to live in a monastery ; but he does not add, *against*
her will and consent ; nay, he plainly asserts, that the virgin
was consecrated by the will of her mother, and he exhorts
her by this argument to avoid the suspected company of
some young man or other, and that she would live with
her mother, provided she was unwilling for her to remain
in a monastery.

Ambrose, says Bellarmin, *in* 3. *De virginibus, speaking of*
those who profess it against the consent of their parents, does
not reprove them, but their parents, who endeavoured to pre-
vent their profession, whom he declares to be worse than Gen-
tiles. In proof of which he adduces these words of Ambrose ; *There* (that is, among the Gentiles) *they are with-*
drawn from marriage by rewards ; shall they be here compelled
to marry by injuries? there it is made violence to take them
away ; shall violence be done to them here lest they enter upon
it? &c.

What Bellarmin premises of his own is false, that Ambrose spake of those virgins who offered of themselves
against the will of their parents, and reproved their parents, not them. For Ambrose speaks of a certain father
who had vowed the virginity of his daughter; which paternal vow when the daughter wished to fulfil, and to profess her virginity according to the ceremonies customary at
that time in the church, a certain lover, by the favour of
her mother (as we may conjecture) sought to marry the
damsel, and hindered her profession by force. Ambrose,
therefore, interposed his authority ; he pronounced it not
lawful for any one to compel this virgin to marry against
her will, devoted to God by her father, as well as by her
own consent. Therefore Bellarmin shews nothing else
from this place, than that it was not lawful to compel a
virgin to marry by force ; which we may concede, without
any injury to our defence.

Next Bernard is introduced, who in Epist. 111, thus writes in the name of Helias the monk to his parents, who desired to draw him home to them from the monastery, *God is the sole cause whereby it is not lawful to obey parents. For he declares, He that loveth father or mother more than me is not worthy of me;* &c.

I answer, It is true, We must not obey parents against the will of God: but it is false which Bernard supposes, That children cannot serve God, unless they forsake their parents and betake themselves into a monastery. And to speak freely what I think, Bernard errs most grievously in this whole Epistle, by writing as though there was no religion, no salvation, out of a monastery : since, on the contrary, every thing which really pertains to religion may be performed by any Christian whatever without becoming a monk ; but many things which pertain to charity, cannot be performed by monks unless they come out from the monastery.

Bellarmin opposes to us Gregory of Tours,* who commends Leobardus and Pappula, because both against the will of their parents embraced the monastic life : therefore it is not only lawful but laudable to do this.

I answer, Gregory of Tours is not of so much authority with us, that we should admit whatever he may have praised as commendable. We therefore oppose the 16th Chapter of the Council of Gangra, where the same thing which

---

* St. Gregory of Tours, as he is commonly called ; otherwise George Florence, a Gallic Historian and Divine ; born of illustrious parentage in Auvergne, in 544. After finishing his studies under Avitus, Bishop of Clermont and successor to Gregory's Uncle Gallus, he was ordained a Deacon, and acquired celebrity as a preacher. In 573 he was chosen Bishop of Tours : and discharged the duties of his episcopate with such zeal and faithfulness, as to be looked upon as one of the greatest ornaments of the church of Tours. In 578 he was present at the Council of Paris, and he was subsequently employed as an ambassador by Gontran, king of the Burgundian Franks, and by his Nephew, Childebert II., king of Austrasia. He made a pilgrimage to Rome in 594, and died there, or after his return to his diocese, in 595. He wrote a History of France in ten Books, and eight Books of the miracles and lives of the Saints ; besides other works inserted in the " Bibliotheca Patrum." It is from his Lives of the Saints most probably that the case adduced is borrowed.

was commended by Gregory of Tours, is condemned, as we have before shewn. But, in order that it may be understood how inconsiderately he has extolled this and that, we shall add what Bellarmin conceals from this same history, that Leobardus not only himself entered a monastery against the will of his parents, but against his faith pledged to a virtuous damsel to marry her; and Pappula herself, not only unknown to and against the will of her parents, but, moreover, assuming the habit of a man, entered the monastery, and carried herself in it as a man for thirty years. At the Council of Gangra, Cap. 13, an anathema was pronounced against every woman on this very account who should assume the male attire.* Away, therefore, with the commendation of Gregory, which is diametrically repugnant as well to the decree of a grave Council, as to the interdict of God himself.

* This Council of Gangra, in Paphlagonia, was held about the year 370. It was assembled in reference to the errors of one Eustathius, but a different person from the Bishop of Sebastea of that name. Under pretence of leading a more perfect and austere life, he established such practices as were considered contrary to the laws of the Church. His errors were condemned in twenty Canons drawn up by this Council. which have been placed in the Code of the Canons of the Universal (the Roman) Church. The concluding words of the Fathers of this Council are too remarkable not to be cited here, and especially as worthy of observation in the present day. They are thus given by Du Pin. " We ordain these things not to conclude those " who would, according to the advices of Holy Scripture, exercise them- " selves in the Church by these practices of continence and piety, but " against those who use these kinds of austerities for a pretence to satisfy " their ambition, who despise those who lead an ordinary life, and who in- " troduce innovations contrary to Scripture and the ecclesiastical laws. We " admire virginity when it is accompanied with humility ; we praise absti- " nence which is joined with piety and prudence ; we respect that retire- " ment which is made with humility ; but we also honour marriage. We " do not blame riches when they are in the hands of persons that are just " and beneficent ; we esteem those who clothe themselves modestly, with- " out pride and affectation, and we abhor uncivil and voluptuous apparel : " We have a reverence for churches, and we approve the assemblies which " are there made as holy and useful : we do not confine piety to houses. We " honour all places built to the name of God ; we approve the assemblies " which are kept in the Church for the public good. We praise the Lar- " gesses which the faithful give to the Church to be distributed among the " poor. In a word, we wish and desire that these things may be observed

In the last place, Chrysostom is cited, who in the end of lib. 3, against the censurers of a Monastic life, thus speaks to parents, *If you shall oppose it, your children, if they should be endued with distinguished virtue, although you should be unwilling they may arrive at this monastic philosophy, they will enjoy eternal pleasures; but yon will heap to yourselves infinite torments.* This testimony I have deferred to the last place, because it appeared the most valid.

But I answer, It appears from that book of Chrysostom that all things at that time were most corrupt both in city and town, so that he says they deserved to have fire and brimstone rained upon them no less than Sodom and Gomorrha. Hence he takes the occasion of exhorting parents to send their young children and as yet not corrupted by the common contagion, into seclusion among the Monks, in whose schools there was somewhat of piety and the Christian Religion: not that they should be perpetually bound over and above the will of their parents, by I know not what rules, as it is now done; but that, being well grounded in piety and religion, they might reverence their parents, and be to them both a comfort and greater help through their whole life. These things being largely explained, at length he subjoins the words adduced by Bellarmin; *Your children, if they should be endued with distinguished virtue, although you should be unwilling they should arrive at this monastic philosophy,* &c. He does not say, *should become monks against your will, and wholly forsake you;* but *shall arrive at this monastic philosophy,* that is, shall learn Religion and Christian piety, which then flourished particularly among the monks. This is the meaning of

" in the Church, which we have learned from the Scripture and the Tradi-" tion of the Apostles." Du Pin. Cent. iv. p. 268.

On the sense of this last sentence, and the proper acceptation of the term Tradition, so grossly abused by the Modern Church of Rome, the Translator would take occasion to refer his Readers to an instructive and able publication of the Rev. James Phelan, entitled, The Catholic Doctrine of Tradition as opposed to that of the Church of Rome. Dublin, 1829; and noticed in the Protestant Journal for August, 1831. The more learned Reader and Controversialist will not omit to study Archbishop Laud's Conference with Fisher the Jesuit.

Chrysostom; which will be evident to every one reading the book itself; in the whole of which not even the smallest word is found, which proves a solemn undertaking of a monastic life against the will of their parents. But if that could be proved on account of those times, in which religion and the true study of Christianity flourished mostly among the monks, it does not make for the praise of the popish Monks, among whom idleness, lust, and superstition reign ; but true piety and religion are driven into exile. So much for the Fathers.

Certain Canons of the Councils are even brought forward by Bellarmin.

1. From the tenth Council of Toledo,* and the last Chapter, in which it is decreed, *that it concerns parents, not to dedicate their children to Religion sooner than their fourteenth year ; but afterwards it shall be lawful for children, even against the will of their parents, to enter a monastery by their own devotion.*

I answer, We are not bound by the authority of this Council, because it is opposed by better Councils : By the third Council of Carthage,† cap. 4, in which it is ordained, that virgins are not wholly consecrated before their twenty-fifth year : and although it opposes the Council of Gangra, a Canon of which we have before cited, prohibiting children from deserting their parents by a religious pretext. Lastly, it also opposes the opinion of all the Papists, and of Bellarmin himself : For that Canon (as it

---

* This Council was held in the year 656. It ordained seven Canons, and its proceedings were subscribed by the Metropolitans of Toledo, Seville, and Braga, with 17 Bishops, and 5 Bishops' deputies.

† This Council, according to Du Pin, was held in the year 397, under the Consulship of Cæsarius and Atticus. It ordained 50 Canons, most of which had been passed at the Council of Hippo, in the year 393. Several of the Canons of this Council are curious and remarkable. The 18th affirms, that none shall be ordained Priest, Bishop, and Deacon, unless they have converted all those who lived in the house with them. The 26th forbids the Metropolitan to assume the title of Prince of the Priests, or the Sovereign Priest, and declares, That no other name ought to be given him but that of Bishop of the First See.—The Church, at that time, seems to have been jealous of the rise and usurpation of spiritual pride and power. Alas ! how many little priests would be Sovereign priests if they could.

is extant in the edition of Surius and Binius) does not say
that after the fourteenth year children may enter upon a
monastic life against the will of their parents, but after the
tenth year it shall be lawful for them to do it. Bellarmin
saw that this was contrary to his argument, and did not
square with his distinction concerning children under age
and adults; therefore, in conformity with his own Jesuitical integrity, he adds four to the number.

2. He quotes from the Council of Tribur,* the 24th Canon, in these words, *If a damsel shall have assumed to herself the sacred veil of her own accord before her twelfth year,*

---

* This was an important Council, numerously attended, and remarkable
for the character of some of its Constitutions. It was held in the year 805,
under King Arnoldus, at his palace called Tribur, situated near Mentz.
The Archbishops of Mentz, Cologne, and Treves attended it, with nineteen German Bishops. It passed 58 Canons, several of which were confir-
matory of many of those novelties and superstitions with which the Church
now began to abound, and with which it was afflicted, and brought into a state
of bondage issuing in the subsequent dark age. The Canon referred to
above is thus stated by Du Pin : " The four and twentieth imports, that a
Maid, who had taken the Veil by her own desire, and without any constraint, before she is 12 years old, is obliged to retain her virginity, if she
hath worn that habit for a year and a day, and nobody may take her out of
the Monastery."

The Doctors and Fathers of the Church of Rome are in the present day
vehemently incensing the popular clamour against Tithes. The 13th and
14th Canons of this Council had respect to them, as existing and claimed by
her in those days. After the 13th had laid down the division, and appropriation ; the 14th goes on " to preserve the Tithes to the ancient Churches,
and annexes the Tithes of new broken-up lands to them; but if new houses
be built four miles from other Churches, in a wood, or other place, and a
Church be built there by the consent of the Bishop, they may put in a
Priest and give him the new Tithes." Thus was established, in this part of the
Church, that system which the church of Rome had been labouring, for three
preceding centuries, to establish throughout her growing empire. And we further see, from the decrees of this Council, how far Papal Supremacy had begun
to extend its grasp. The thirtieth Canon appoints, " that in memory of St.
Peter, the Holy Roman and Apostolic See ought to be honoured, it being just,
that that Church, which is the Mother of the priestly dignity, should be the
Mistress of Ecclesiastical order, so that 'tis fit, that men bear and endure the
yoke she lays upon them, although it be almost insupportable!! Nevertheless 'tis ordered, that if any Priest or Deacon be accused of carrying forged
Letters from the Pope to stir up any troubles, or lay any snares for the ministers of the Church, the Bishop may with due respect to the Pope, stop
his proceedings, till he hath written to the Holy See."

*her parents and tutors may make that act void if they wish.
But if at a more advanced age, a youth, or a young woman,
chooses to serve God* (namely, in a monastic life), *it is not in
the power of the parents to forbid it.*   Hence Bellarmin infers, that it was lawful for children to enter a monastery
after their twelfth year against the will of their parents.

I answer, the former part of the Canon is corruptly
cited, the latter is forged.   For that whole sentence, *But
if at a more advanced age,* and what follows, are not the
words of the Council, but assumed by Gratian, hence Bellarmin brings forward this Canon.   For Gratian, Caus. 20,
qu. 2, can. *Puella,* cites this in the same manner in which
Bellarmin has done : but those last words, in which the
whole force of the argument lies, are not found in the volumes of the Council themselves.   Nor is this new to Gratian, whom all know to be a famous interpolater of the
Councils who have compared that farrago of decrees with
the councils themselves.*   Bellarmin's moral reasons remain now to be solved.

1.   *It is lawful for children, against the will of their parents, to contract matrimony ; therefore, it is lawful for them
to profess continence against their will.*

I answer, Children sin if in contracting matrimony
they defer not this honour to their parents, and suffer
themselves to be directed by them : and they likewise sin
who desert them against their will, to lead a monastic life.
Although it must be conceded, That whatever is good and
pious in a monastic life may be practised by children, even
if their impious and profane parents gainsay it : for instance, they may preserve perpetual continence, if they
have that gift from God ; they may give themselves up to
prayer ; they may subdue their appetite for flesh by moderate fasting ; because these things are not opposed to
due obedience : but they cannot withdraw themselves from
the paternal roof against the will of their parents, and
place themselves in that state of life in which they are un-

* Vide Note, Vol. i. p. 285.

able to assist and sustain their parents ; because this is opposed to the Divine command.

2. *It is lawful for a man, against the will of his wife,
after the period of the marriage contract, to betake himself to a
monastic life ; therefore it is much more lawful for a son to do
that against the will of his father.*

I answer, That it is lawful by the canonical and anti-
christian law ; but by the Divine law it never was lawful :
for matrimony, from the moment of contract, is true and
confirmed matrimony, although not consummated. This
very contract, therefore, transfers the power of the husband's own body to his wife, and the wife's to the husband :
the husband therefore cannot against the will of the wife,
defraud her of her right. What the Schoolmen pretend,
that the monastic profession is a spiritual death, and that
by this death marriage is dissolved no less than bodily existence, is so ridiculous, that it needs no refutation : for to
die spiritually to the world and sin, is the duty of all
Christians, not of the monks only.

3. *Every free-born child after the years of puberty has his
own right, as far as pertains to those things which relate to
his person and condition ; therefore he may use this right, and
enter a monastery against the will of his parents.*

I answer, Children after the years of puberty do not
immediately so become their own masters, that they may,
without sin, neglect the counsel, throw off paternal rule,
or slink away from home at their own pleasure. Nay, we
constantly see in the Scriptures, that pious children, even
after their fourteenth year (which is fixed as the mark of
puberty) obey their parents, and yield to their commands,
even in those things which relate to their person : as Jacob
did in choosing a wife, and Isaac before him : So virgins
did not take to themselves husbands without paternal approbation : Exod. xxii. 17 ; Deut. vii. 3 ; 1 Cor. vii. 36. It is
therefore false, and contrary as well to Divine as to human laws, which Bellarmin takes for granted, That every
damsel after her twelfth year, and every youth after his
fourteenth year, may, against the will of their parents, de-

termine on these things which relate to their person and
condition. And if they may, yet this should always be
done with true obedience, and the honour due to parents,
which compels them to forego a cloistered life.

4. *We must obey God rather than men; But God requires
a perfect life in all things in general,* Matt. xix., *and in particular, by internal inspiration he calls certain persons: therefore if parents oppose, they are not to be listened to.*

Answer, Bellarmin plainly dotes, who binds perfection
to a cloister and a hood. We place the perfection of a
Christian life in faith and charity, not in ceremonies or monastic rules. And we say with Gerson, *That religious performances, are improperly and abusively, and perhaps arro-
gantly called a state of perfection.* We therefore answer to
the argument, That all Christians ought to aim at spiritual
perfection, neither must parents be listened to, if they
endeavour to hinder the progress of their children in
faith and charity: but if they direct their children to
continue under their control, to remain with them at
home, to obey them in domestic duties, I affirm that lawful commands of this kind cannot be contemned without
the violation of the Divine command, and the work of
perfection is more excellent to obey parents in the fear of
God, than to subject themselves to monastic traditions.

Vers. 21.

Fathers, provoke not your children to anger ; lest they be discouraged.

We have treated of the obedience of children. Now lest parents should suppose that they might do any thing they pleased by the power vested in them over their children, the Apostle would also advise even them not to abuse this their authority. And this verse consists of two parts : the former contains a prohibition ; the latter, the cause of the prohibition.

Fathers, provoke not your children.] By this prohibition he would restrain the paternal power within its limits : And here let us consider the act prohibited and the persons. *Provocation* is prohibited : Now this provocation arises from a manifold abuse of paternal power.

1. If it shall have denied or withdrawn from children those things which are rightly due to them, such, for instance, as food, clothing, and education corresponding with the rank and means of their father. And this, indeed, is so heavy a sin, that the Apostle did not fear to declare, that *he who should not provide for his own, had denied the faith, and was worse than an infidel,* 1 Tim. v. 8. But neither (which is often the case) must there be sin on the other side : which they commit, who spoil their children by more dainty food, more splendid clothing, and a better education than is needful. And our age truly is more in danger from this evil, than from too much severity towards children.* That remark of Quintilian, lib. i. cap. 2, is well suited for us. *I wish we ourselves did not ruin the manners of our children. We spoil them immediately in their infancy by delicacies. That soft education which we call indulgence, destroys all the vigour both of mind and body. What will he not*

---

* What would Davenant have thought and said in the present day ?

do when come to man's estate, who has crawled in purple in his
childhood.   He cannot yet utter his first words, and is already
a connoisseur in colours ; he already insists upon a purple dress.
We form their palate before that the mouth is formed, &c.

2. Children are provoked, if parents endeavour to load
them with impious and unjust commands. That was impious of Saul when he commanded Jonathan to seize and
bring David his friend, guiltless of any crime, that he
might be put to death, 1 Sam. xx. 31.   Hence we read,
vers. 34, that Jonathan was inflamed with grief and anger.
That was likewise impious of Herodias, who ordered her
daughter (to whom Herod had promised to give whatever
she might ask) to ask the head of John the Baptist, Matt.
xiv. 8. But we do not read that this dancing daughter was
offended at the impious command of her mother, because
she equalled her mother in impiety : if she had had any
piety, she would have grieved at it. But again, I call that
an unjust command, if a father, impelled by no necessity,
should endeavour by his authority to compel his son to
servile deeds, and unworthy of a free man. For the condition of children is one thing, that of slaves another.
Among children, a father holds not a tyrannical, but a
kingly rule ; Therefore he ought to use their labour as a
good king uses the labour of citizens, not as a master
abuses the labour of servants. This Aristotle himself has
noted, Polit. i. 7 : and viii. 2.

3. It pertains to this provocation, when parents being
seized with anger, rashly revile and wound their children
when they do not deserve it, with contumelious and unbecoming language.   For contumely has a certain sting,
which it is very difficult for even prudent persons to endure. Saul also provoked his son Jonathan with this kind
of injury, 1 Sam. xx. 30, where he breaks forth in these
words, *Thou son of the perverse rebellious woman, do not I*
know that thou hast chosen the son of Jesse to thine own con-
fusion, and unto the confusion of thy mother's nakedness ?
What could be said more bitter to provoke a son than that
in order to reproach him he even reviles his own wife as a
common prostitute ?

4. Children are provoked, when parents, out of wantonness and fury, beat and chastise them with unjust or immoderate stripes and punishments. I call that unjust chastisement, for which there is not a legitimate cause. Thus Saul even wished to strike his son with a javelin, for no other reason than that he had taken upon himself the defence of David, who was absent and innocent, 1 Sam. xx. 33, *Wherefore Jonathan arose from the table in fierce anger,* vers. 34. But chastisement is immoderate, when the severity of punishment exceeds the weight of the crime. Therefore it is provided for by Divine authority, that those who have authority over others, should not act with arbitrary cruelty towards criminals. *If the wicked man be worthy to be beaten, the judge shall cause him to lie down, and to be beaten before his face, according to his fault, by a certain number of stripes,* &c. Deut. xxv. 2, 3. And thus we have briefly demonstrated from what causes the provocation prohibited arises.

Corollaries.

1. Parental rule is not absolute, or unlimited; but must be conformed to nature and reason, and above all, to the Divine law.

2. It is proper to govern children with gravity and prudence : but it is not proper to exasperate them by bitterness and cruelty. For they are more likely to be kept within the bounds of duty by liberality and forbearance, than by fear and tyranny. *Fear does not keep a person long in the path of duty,* says Cicero.

3. Although it is not lawful to provoke and exasperate children, yet it is proper to instruct them, to chide them mildly, and to chastise them. That what is not expressly laid down in this place, is yet to be understood, is gathered from Ephes. vi. 4, *Fathers, provoke not your children to wrath: but bring them up in the nurture and admonition of the Lord.* For instruction and chastisement of offending children falls under the Divine command, and it makes for the advantage of those who are corrected. Prov. xxiii. 13, 14.

Hitherto we have considered the act prohibited. Now

let us examine in one or two words, what relates to the consideration of the persons.

Two persons are here marked out : he, or they to whom this interdict is given of not using provocation ; those are *fathers :* and they concerning whom, or on whose behalf it is given ; and these are the *children* of those fathers.

First, we must observe in this personal designation why the Apostle should not have retained a word which he used in the foregoing verse, when he gave the precept concerning the obedience of children : for there he speaks of *parents,* that is, of father and mother conjointly ; here he speaks of *father* alone. He seems to do this, because children often offend in defect of obedience towards their mothers ; therefore when he prescribes concerning obedience, it was very necessary to include mothers : but mothers seldom offend towards their children by too much severity ; therefore it was sufficient to have fathers alone restrained by this interdict. For too much indulgence is the sin of mothers, not cruelty, which scarcely happens in a father, unless he is void of all paternal affection.

Secondly, it is proper to observe that argument which is implied in the term *father.* For when he says, *Fathers, provoke not,* it is as if he had said, Do not what ought to be most foreign from the person and office of a father. The very name *father,* bespeaks clemency and mildness. Hence that saying of the poet,

He was gentle, as a Father.

And here earthly fathers have before them for their imitation an example of their heavenly Father, who is never so wrath against his children, but he is mindful of his paternal clemency, as it is in Psalm lxxxix. 31, &c. *If they break my statutes and keep not my commandments, Then will I visit their transgression with the rod, and their iniquity with stripes ; Nevertheless my loving kindness will I not utterly take from him, nor suffer my faithfulness to fail,* &c.

Thirdly, we must also notice that argument which is implied under these words, *your children.* For what else is this, than as if he had said, Afflict not your flesh, your blood, your bowels, your own selves, by any injury. For *a child is something of the father*, as Aquinas says, Qu. disp. de pecc. orig. art. 8; and by the authority of Aristotle, *his own beloved*. It is therefore against the inclination of nature itself, that a father should aim to wound and provoke his own children, whom it behoves him to love and cherish.

But neither must we omit that this consideration of the persons ought also to incline the children themselves to patience and equanimity, when harshly and cruelly treated : for the cruelty of the father towards his child is a heavy sin, but the wrath and fury of a child towards his father is excessively monstrous. Hence Cicero, in his oration for Cluentius, said, that *children should not only conceal the injuries of their parents, but bear them with equanimity*. And thus far we have explained the prohibition itself : Now let us consider the cause of the prohibition.

Lest they be discouraged, or *lest they become faint-hearted*.] The cause of the prohibition is derived from the disadvantage of provocation. And its great disadvantage is shewn : for when children are treated in this manner by parents, for the most part they fall under *discouragement*.

This *discouragement*, αθυμια, comprises three evils : 1. That heaviness and sadness of mind into which that cruelty of their parents is wont to plunge their children, especially pious children. Hence oftentimes diseases spring, and sometimes their premature death. For *as a moth hurteth a garment, and a worm, wood; so does sadness the heart*, Prov. xxv. 20. Therefore, parents must strenuously guard against this disadvantage, lest they should seem to have begotten children only for the purpose of having persons on whom they might inflict torment. And that paternal goodness of God is to be imitated, who would have obedience shewn to himself from his children with alacrity and joy, not with sorrow and distress : The same disposition ought to prevail in earthly parents.

2. This *discouragement* comprises that dejection and stupidity of mind, which makes them fearful, and unfit to enter upon any work. For children are terrified by the cruelty of their parents, and finding that themselves and

all their duties are disagreeable and hateful to them, at length they are cast down in mind, they venture to try or attempt nothing, but they become inactive and torpid. And parents should especially beware not to sink their children to this : for children are as the hands and arms with which the old age of parents should be defended ; they are the feet and legs whereby they must be sustained. Therefore as any one would deservedly be accounted mad, who should occasion such numbness to his legs and arms by any narcotic medicament, that they might become in a manner useless to him : so are those parents to be accounted not far from insane, who by their severity and cruelty, so beat and render their children stupid, that they can neither be of any help to their parents nor themselves.

3. This *discouragement* brings in its train (especially in those who are not of a very good disposition) a certain desperate contumacy. For when they perceive that all hope of pleasing is done away, they also on the other hand cast off all hope of pleasing ; yea, sometimes assume to themselves a boldness in displeasing, and a wantonness of provoking their parents. This, indeed, is the height of impiety in a child ; but yet the father must beware not to occasion this impiety by his cruelty. For repeated cruelty does not whet the minds of children to perform their duties, but recals and withdraws them from it. And thus much of the duty of parents.

Vers. 22, 23.

Servants, obey in all things your masters according to the
flesh; not with eye-service, as men-pleasers; but in sin-
gleness of heart, fearing God:
And whatsoever ye do, do it heartily, as to the Lord, and
not unto men.

The duties of wives and husbands, of children and parents, have been explained: There remain these of servants and masters; which being explained, nothing will be
wanting that pertains to domestic instruction. He begins
with servants. As to what pertains then to these, the Apostle
does three things: 1. He gives a precept of obedience;
2. He teaches the mode of obeying; 3. He adds certain
stimuli, or incentives to obedience, vers. 24, 25.

In the first place the precept is to be explained, which
is contained in these words,

1. *Servants, obey in all things your masters according to*
the flesh.] The occasion of this precept seems to spring
from the circumstance, that servants converted to Christianity, thought themselves to be exempt from the yoke of
servitude. Which opinion, full of error, the devil without
doubt instilled into the minds of men, that thence he
might render the Christian religion odious among the heathen, as a disturber of order. This error perhaps had
some colour; If masters embraced the Christian religion
together with their servants, it was unjust that they should
still hold them as slaves whom they were bound to account
as brethren: if Masters still adhered to paganism, when
their servants were converted, it seemed much more unjust
that he who had been delivered and redeemed from the
power of the devil, should nevertheless remain in bondage
to a pagan man, who himself remained a slave to the
devil. These things seemed to have an air of probability;

but notwithstanding, the Apostle gives a contrary precept; in which every word hath its weight to demonstrate the equity and even the necessity of the precept.

Servants. He addresses Christians, and yet he still calls them servants; Δουλοι.] This word does not denote such domestics as we now employ; who are in reality free and free-born, although they serve others for hire : but it denotes such as the ancients used ; who were either taken in war or bought, and on that account were wholly in the power of their masters.

Concerning the foundation of this servitude, whether it be just or violent, I shall not contend : yet it appears to have been allowed and established by the law of Nations. Hence Aristotle asserts, Polit. i. 3, that servants of this kind were nothing else than ὄργανα ἔμψυχα, *certain animated instruments of their masters.* And even among the sacred writers these servants are reckoned among the goods and possessions of their masters, Job. i. 3 ; and the servant is called in Exod. xxi. 21, *the money* of his master. The Apostle therefore shews by this very name, that they were bound to obedience : and on that account he adds his command,

Servants, obey in all things.] This precept was proposed in these same words to children, vers. 20, and, as it was then said, involved two things ; humility in receiving the commands of another, and alacrity in executing the same : for these two are intimated under this one word ὑπακουειν. But what he adds, *in all things,* that is to be restricted to things lawful and honest, and those which regard the duty of servants : for if a master shall order his servant to do any thing which is either contrary to piety or foreign from the duty of a servant, he is not bound to obey; because his master ought not to command such things. Rightly, therefore, has Jerome put in this exception, IN ALL THINGS; *namely,* says he, *in which the lord of the flesh does not command contrary to the Lord of the spirit.* Therefore, the Apostle does not include impious and unlawful obedience, when he enjoins them to obey *in all things,* but he forbids divided and arbitrary obedience according to the will of servants themselves.

Your masters according to the flesh.] This title also, equally as the preceding one of *servants*, shews the equity of the precept. For as the epithet *servant* admonishes of the performance of obedience to another, so the name *master* points out the obedience due from him to that other. But that addition *according to the flesh*, signifies that this lordship or power of man over man, is only temporal, and in things external and temporal, but does not extend to the soul and the conscience. This difference of Divine and human authority Christ observed in Matt. x. 28, *Fear not them which kill the body, but are not able to kill the soul: but rather fear him which is able to destroy both soul and body in hell.*

Instructions.

1. The Christian religion does not subvert political order; nay, it does not deprive Heathen masters of their legitimate authority over Christian servants. Therefore the Anabaptists err, who think all authority to be opposed to Evangelical liberty, even of Christians over Christians.* The Papists err, who would have it that the authority of kings over their subjects is dissolved by heresy; for if notwithstanding paganism, a master remained a master of Christians according to the flesh, then a king also will remain the king of his subjects.

2. The Christian religion frees from the yoke of human servitude that which is the best and most excellent thing in man, namely, the spirit and the conscience. See Gal. v. 1. They therefore err who would rule the minds and consciences of men by virtue of any superiority and human lordship; for they are masters *according to the flesh*, not *according to the spirit*. They also err who believe or obey doctrines or commands of superiors in spiritual things pertaining to salvation, not thinking or seeking from God whether or not they proceed from their own in-

* This was a doctrine peculiar to the Anabaptists at the period of the Reformation.—Translr.

ventions. The common people among the Papists labour under this error, who yield a blind faith and obedience to their prelates, as if they were the lords of the faith of Christians. Compare 1 Pet. v. 3, and 2 Cor. i. 24.

3. Christians may and ought to submit themselves according to the flesh (i. e. in things external, doubtful, and temporal) even to the unjust commands of those who are masters *according to the flesh*. Thus Augustine, in Expos. epist. ad Rom. propos. 74, *We must not resist magistrates, although they unjustly take away from us temporal things.* And Peter, 1 epis. ii. 18, *Be subject to your masters, not only to the good and gentle, but also to the froward.* And thus much concerning the precept and the necessity of obeying : Let us now proceed to the manner.

2. The manner of obeying is described by the Apostle, both negatively and affirmatively ; Negatively, he shews the diseases of servants, from which a Christian should be free : Affirmatively, he prescribes certain precautions opposed to the aforesaid diseases.

Not with eye-service, as men-pleasers.] He touches a disease too familiar to servants, and also its cause. The disease he calls *eye-service,* i. e. obedience *under the eye.* They fall under this disease, who, when their master is present and beholding them, sedulously and strenuously perform their duty ; but are idle when he is absent and knows nothing of their proceedings, and (what is worse) they waste and consume their master's substance. Such a servant is described in Luke xii. 45, who said in his lord's absence, *My lord delayeth his coming ;* and thereupon exercised tyranny over his fellow servants, but he himself *eats, and drinks, and is drunken.* This is a disease which should be banished far away from Christian servants. Now he points out the cause or fountain of this disease, when he forthwith subjoins,

As men-pleasers.] He is called *a man-pleaser,* who proposes this scope or end only to himself, to be praised by men, and to please them; in the mean time being no ways solicitous whether he shall effect this by true and lawful obedience, or by counterfeit and pretended means : therefore, when his inspector is absent, he desists from his work. That servant who is thus resolved to please his master, has no respect in his doings for integrity of conscience, nor the advantage of his master; but then only pretends to be diligent and industrious in performing the business of his master when he perceives that it will answer his own end. Servants of this kind are like actors on the stage. For as comedians, who act in order to please, and study to please that they may thereby obtain benefit, do not mount the stage unless when the people are beholding and looking on: so these *men-pleasers* move not a hand to labour, unless when they have their masters beholding and applauding them. And thus much concerning the disease of *man-pleasing*, and its origin, namely, a fraudulent purpose of pleasing. The remedies opposed to it follow.

But with singleness of heart, fearing God.] These words have a manifest antithesis to the afore-mentioned vices. For singleness of heart is opposed to deceitful *eye-service;* the true fear of God, to the fraudulent purpose of pleasing men. Therefore, having banished those vices, he would have these contrary virtues to rule. He who serves his master to the eye, seems to have two hearts : one dutiful and pious, which excites him to due obedience in his master's presence ; the other an undutiful and impious one, which impels him to idleness and fraud when his master is absent. But he who obeys *with singleness of heart*, has one heart alone, and ever the same, which moves him to perform his duty, whether his master be inspecting him or not; because he judges the chief fruit of duty is duty itself. Therefore he should be said to labour and work in *singleness of heart*, who does it having excluded deceit, hypocrisy, and all disguise of an evil intention under an honest appearance, and who desires to appear the same that he is, and to be the same that he appears. But to this simplicity he joins,

Fearing God.] As the study of deceitfully pleasing men can produce nothing else than *eye-service;* so the true and genuine fear of God always produces simplicity and sincerity. As, therefore, the cause is connected with the

effect, he places the fear of God with singleness of heart:
and rightly indeed; For he who fears or respects men
alone, will be changeable and inconstant in discharging
any office, because he is directed by an uncertain rule: for
indeed the fear of man is inconstant, inasmuch as it is incited whilst he is present, it vanishes on his being absent:
but the fear of God is constant and firm in the bosoms of
the pious, because God is always present to them, and
never ought or can be imagined as absent. *I am a God at
hand, and not a God afar off,* Jer. xxiii. 23. This was not
unknown to the poet, who said, *God seeth thee being near
at hand.* We have a remarkable example of the fear of
God in Joseph: who, when he was solicited to commit
adultery by his mistress herself whilst his master was absent and unconscious, would not hearken to her; but repelled her shamelessness by these words, *How can I do
this wickedness, and sin against God?* If he had been only
a *man-pleaser,* he both could and without doubt would
have done it: but because he feared God the Supreme
Lord, he could not wrong his earthly lord by this injury.
Such are all they who obey their masters *with singleness of
heart, fearing God.*

Vers. 23.   *And whatsoever ye do, do it heartily, as to the
Lord, and not unto men.*

The Apostle proceeds still in describing the manner of
lawful obedience: and he adds another condition, namely,
that all the duties of servants should be performed, not
only *in singleness of heart* and *the fear of God,* but also *from
the heart:* and he immediately subjoins the reason; namely,
because they serve the *Lord,* i. e. Christ, *not men.* Let us
therefore consider, first, the condition requisite in all the
obedience of servants; secondly, the reason of the condition required.

Whatever ye do, do it heartily, εκ ψυχης.] Two things are
implied in this one word :

1. That servants willingly and cheerfully do what things
are commanded by their masters, not compulsorily and
unwillingly. And, indeed, it is very probable, that certain Christian servants, obeyed their masters rather from
the necessity of their condition, than from the will, especially unbelieving masters. The Apostle, therefore, endeavours to cure this evil, when he bid them to do all things,
not from necessity, but *from the heart, heartily.* We do
any thing *heartily,* when the mind desires and rejoices that
that should be done which the hand does. On the contrary, when the mind murmurs and resists, although the
outward act may be performed, yet it is done rather from
the body than from the mind. For, as Prosper rightly
said, *If any thing be done against the will, it is done rather
for thee than that thou doest it.*

2. By this word it is also signified, that servants ought
to obey their masters μετ' ἐννοίας, that is to say, not only
should they be well disposed to the execution of the work,
but even possess benevolence of spirit towards the commander of the work. And these for the most part are connected together; for no one performs the work imposed
upon him cheerfully, except he who strives and reverences
him who commanded the work. And this is expressly laid
down in Ephes. vi. 7, μετ' ἐννοίας δουλεύοντες, *with good will
doing service. No one obeys better than he who renders obedience from love,* says Ambrose. Thus much for the condition : Let us now come to the reason of this condition.

2. *As to the Lord, and not unto men.*] That is, as those
who serve the Lord rather and more especially than men,
even in such compliances as are rendered to men : for
the use or utility of the works has respect to men ; the
mind of the doer first and especially to God. Therefore,
the negative particle in this place is not used absolutely,
as though it were wicked to serve men, or to respect men
whilst serving them ; but it is corrective and diminutive, shewing that it behoves us to regard the Lord
Christ more and first in those compliances, than earthly

masters themselves. There is a well known rule in the exposition of the holy Scriptures, *In comparisons that is often denied which is not to be excluded, but only postponed to another :* as in Mar. ix. 37, *Whosoever receiveth me, receiveth not me, but him that sent me ;* i. e., he rather receiveth the Father who sent me, than I who am sent; because he receiveth me by that grace. So in this place, *to the Lord, and not unto men,* i. e. to the Lord Christ, more than to men ; because for the sake of Christ you serve them.

But why in these lower and external observances are they said to obey the Lord more than men, whose commands they are, and whom alone they profit?

First, because they who obey are more the servants of Christ than of earthly masters. For earthly masters buy their servants for silver and gold ; Christ buys them with his precious blood : they redeem the body alone, and that for another service ; Christ redeems both soul and body for perpetual liberty. They must therefore especially serve Christ.

Secondly, because they obey earthly masters only at the appointment of Christ; therefore they rather obey Christ than them ; not unlike as inferior servants who obey a steward, yet are said more to obey their master, at whose will they yield to his steward: he is opposed, if he shall order the contrary to his master.

Thirdly, because Christ himself hath declared that he wishes his servants to obey their masters, and this he strictly commands in his word : and he himself also in his wise governance and by his authority, hath ordained some to service and others to dominion. Whilst faithful servants have respect to all these things, they are rightly said to *serve the Lord and not men.*

But now, that this is the most valid reason why they should do all things heartily, is gathered from hence, because this supreme Lord, that is to say, Christ, can both inspect the heart, and he is wont to regard the heart, more than the external act : It behoves the person therefore who desires to please him, to do all things *heartily.* Now let us collect the instructions in one view.

1. A Christian servant is not satisfied to please his earthly master, unless at the same time also he may please his supreme Lord, namely Christ.

2. Whatever work and external compliance may seem laudable; yet it is counterfeit and hypocritical when it is referred to a bad end.

3. In all the duties of our vocation we must study rather to preserve a good conscience, than to obtain human approbation.

4. A defect in all the observances of men towards men, arises from a defect of fear and reverence towards God.

5. They alone are judged truly to fear God, who are employed among men in a single and honest heart; on the contrary, they who carry themselves subtily and deceitfully towards men, are impious and treacherous against God.

To conclude therefore; This is the manner of Christian obedience, that a faithful man so act in all the duties of his vocation as if there was no other being in this world besides himself and God; for when he hath his eyes so fixed in every work on God, he will not dare to obtrude those compliances upon men which he knows to be odious and disagreeable to God the searcher of hearts. Thus much concerning the precept and the manner of obedience.

Vers. 24, 25.

Knowing that of the Lord ye shall receive the reward of the inheritance, for ye serve the Lord Christ:
But he that doeth wrong shall receive for the wrong which he hath done: and there is no respect of persons.

In these two verses are contained two incentives to the aforesaid obedience, derived from those considerations by which mankind are especially moved; namely, from the reward, and the punishment: that is to say, from the promise of a reward, in the former verse; from the threat of a punishment, in the latter verse.

As to the former verse, we have in it, 1. The promise of the reward itself; *Knowing that of the Lord ye shall receive the reward of the inheritance.* 2. The confirmation of the reward promised ; *for ye serve the Lord Christ.*

In this promise we may observe, first, the Author or Bestower of the reward promised, namely, Christ; *Knowing that of the Lord ye shall receive.*

The Apostle rightly and prudently would have those servants to expect a reward from Christ. For earthly masters give food and clothing to their slaves, whether bought or taken in war : they thought not any other reward to be due to them more than to their beasts. *Food is the slave's wages,* says Aristotle, Oecon. i. 5. The Apostle, therefore, consoles these servants,* that although they are neglected by their earthly masters, yet they have a heavenly master a munificent rewarder, who will not suffer them to be destitute of a reward, if from the heart they obey their masters, and as it becomes pious men and Christians. Therefore he joins that word ειδοτες, *knowing*, or *taking it for certain :* because it is wicked even to doubt concerning the reward which Christ himself has undertaken to bestow : for however men are accustomed to withhold and deny the reward engaged for, yet Christ neither ever will do so, nor can he. Thus much of the Author or Promiser of the reward.

Secondly, let us observe the quality of the reward signified by this addition, ἀνταπόδοσιν τῆς κληρονομιας, *the reward of the inheritance.* These things seem to be incongruous : for *a reward* is paid to labourers ; *an inheritance* is given to children. But the Apostle would indicate, that he is not speaking of any temporal reward, which should correspond in equal value to their work ; but of that eternal reward of blessedness, which surpasses far and wide all the worth of human works or duties.

---

* The reader will bear in mind, that the word *servants* is used here for *slaves*, δουλοι, in conformity with the authorised version of the Bible.

This celestial reward, therefore, is called *merces, hire or wages;* not because men are able to merit it by the excellence of their works, but because it bears a resemblance to a reward in certain other circumstances.

1. As hire is not given except to labourers and workmen ; so the heavenly kingdom is not given to the indolent, but to those striving in their vocation.

2. As hire is not wont to be given except after the works are finished ; so life eternal is not bestowed unless after the course of this life is ended.

Now in two other respects the heavenly reward is unlike hire.

1. Hire is given according to the merit of the workman ; but the heavenly reward is given from the grace and liberality of the bestower, Luke xvii. 10.

2. Hire is proportioned to the labours for which it is bestowed; but the heavenly reward hath no proportion to our services for which it is a reward ; for *finite hath no proportion to infinite.* Therefore this same reward is called *an inheritance,* because it pertains to the pious and faithful by right of sonship. And by this word he comforts Christian servants : For as they could not receive any reward from their earthly masters, who looked upon them as slaves ; yet they are to receive *an inheritance* from God, who accounts them as sons : and it behoves them to expect this *reward of the inheritance.*

Concerning this inheritance due to believers by right of adoption, the Apostle thus speaks in Rom. viii. 15, *Ye have received the Spirit of adoption whereby we cry Abba, Father. And if children, then heirs ; heirs of God, and joint heirs with Christ ;* vers. 17.

Corollaries.

1. No vocation is so mean and abject, to which a reward is not promised by God, if only men conduct themselves piously in the same. We are not, therefore, to consider how honourable our vocation may be ; but labour rather, that whatever in truth it may be (so that it is lawful and honest) it may be discharged well by us, and with a good conscience. Hence that counsel of the Apostle, 1 Cor.

vii 20, *Let every man abide in the same calling wherein he was called ; For he that is called in the Lord, being a servant, is the Lord's free man ;* vers. 22.

2.   It is not proper to fix the eyes or the mind upon those light rewards which are promised by men to those doing well ; but it behoves us always to regard that eternal reward which God the Father has promised to his obedient children.   Thus Paul in discharging his vocation, regards not the reward of human favour or glory, or of earthly gain, but that Crown *which the Lord shall give to all those loving his appearing*, 2 Tim. iv. 8.

3.   They sin who leave off to do well, or at least act languidly and remissly, on account of the ingratitude and iniquity of men : for it is sufficient for the godly man to know that he shall receive the reward of the inheritance from Christ ; with which he ought to be content, although in the mean while he is neglected and evil intreated by men.

4.   They also err who attribute this reward of blessedness to their merits.   For although it is given to the labourers, yet not for the excellence of their works, but by right of adoption, as was before said and proved.   But now adoption excludes merit, if it be rightly defined by Lawyers.   *Adoption*, says Durandus, lib. 3. dist. 10, qu. 2, *is the gratuitous taking of a person to a participation of an inheritance, to which inheritance he had no right.*   And thus much concerning the promise of the reward : The confirmation of the promise follows.

For ye serve the Lord Christ.]   This concerning their reward being received from Christ himself avails to confirm the hope of servants.   For the work and the reward are related ; Therefore, equity demands that for whom the work is done, from him the reward should be expected.   It will seem scarcely credible, that they who discharged the meanest offices among men here on earth, should be said on this very account to serve Christ himself, who sits in the heavens most glorious and by no means needing human service.   But the reason is manifest (as we have largely explained in the foregoing verse,) namely, that whatever

duties are performed to men according to the direction and
at the command of Christ, and on account of the appointment and for the glory of Christ, they are judged to be offered and rendered to Christ himself. For *he serves God,
who for the sake of God serves men*, as Jerome has rightly
observed on this passage. This Christ himself shews,
Matt. xxv. 40, 45, *Inasmuch as ye have done it unto one of
the least of these, ye have done it unto me ; Inasmuch as ye did
it not to one of the least of these, ye did it not to me.* He
speaks in this place concerning alms-deeds, as far as they
are done or denied to men ; but it ought to be extended to
all the works of obedience commanded by God : for when
these are rendered to men, they are rendered to God who
commanded them to be done ; when denied to them, they
are deemed as denied to God himself. And that rightly
too : for he who, being commanded by God to obey men, refuses to yield to human authority ; if he had power would
also shake off the Divine government.

Corollaries.

1. No service is dishonourable in which men conduct
themselves well and faithfully : for they who are such, serve
Christ himself, which is the height of dignity and honour.

2. No honour, no authority screens a wicked man from
ignominy and disgrace : for they who are of that character
serve the devil, which is the abyss of infamy and misery.

3. They who, being placed under the rule of others, are
unwilling to serve, are not only rebels against men, but
against God and Christ. Hence that reproof of God himself against the Israelites wishing to shake off the government of Samuel, *They have not rejected thee, but they have
rejected me*, 1 Sam. viii. 7.

4. We ought not to obey any mortal among those who
are opposed to the will of Christ : For it is unjust and foreign to reason that those should be obeyed against the
will of Christ, whom we obey for Christ.

And thus much of the former incentive, derived from the
promise of a reward : It remains to treat of the other, taken
from the threat of punishment.

Vers. 25. *But he that doeth wrong, shall receive for the
wrong which he hath done : and there is no respect of
persons.*

In the foregoing verse the Apostle had encouraged servants to perform their duty properly, by proposing a reward to them : Now he stimulates them to the same duty
by threatening a punishment. But there are two parts of
this verse. The first contains a commination, or threatening of punishment to all who shall fail in their duty ; *He
that doeth wrong,* &c. The latter contains an anticipation
of an implied objection, which seems to lessen the certainty of the punishment threatened ; *And there is no respect of
persons.*

*He that doeth wrong, shall receive for the wrong which he
hath done.*] Some think this punishment threatened to
wicked masters for the comfort of servants : as though the
Apostle had said, If your masters shall be unjust and
wicked, let not your minds be dejected, do not neglect to
perform for them whatever is in your power ; but leave
your revenge to God, who will avenge whatever injuries
shall be done to you.

Imperious and impious masters are accustomed to wrong
their servants in many ways. Sometimes they defraud
them of their clothing, food, or due wages ; Sometimes
they load and urge them by labours beyond their strength ;
sometimes they afflict them with reproaches and unjust
stripes : almost all which things happened to the people of
God in the Egyptian servitude ; Exod. v. For wrongs of
this kind, let not servants rise against their masters through
impatience or anger, or leave the tasks imposed upon them
through idleness, says the Apostle. Whoever, in fine, he
shall be who does these wrongs to his servant, he shall receive from God himself for the wrong which he hath done :
that is, he shall feel vengeance and punishment corres-

ponding to his iniquity. We have a sample of this Divine vengeance upon the Egyptian oppressors; whom God afflicted with much heavier punishments than they were able to afflict their Israelitish servants: and upon Saul, who is punished in his posterity for the wrong done to the slaughtered Gibeonites, 2 Sam. xxi.

Other interpreters refer this commination to servants themselves: as though the Apostle had said, If the expectation of the heavenly reward cannot inflame you to fulfil your duty; this at least should excite you, that God himself will punish, either your contumacy, or your idleness. For contumacious servants, who déspise their masters and regard them not of a straw, do wrong to them, as far as they do not pay them due obedience and reverence: the slothful and deceitful also are deemed to wrong their masters, because they either do not yield them due submission, or not with that faith and sincerity of heart with which they should have done. If, then, servants, by these or any other means, do wrong to their masters, they shall receive for the wrong done: that is, they shall be punished for their dishonesty by God, the judge and avenger. We have on record the example of Gehazi, 2 Kings v.

But I think with Jerome that both interpretations should be united; as well because the Apostle addresses all generally, as especially because he has placed this commination between the duties of servants and masters, that it may extend to both, and that equally. Thus, then, I explain the words of the Apostle; *He that doeth wrong;* whether he be the master, by afflicting his servant unjustly; or the servant, by despising or defrauding his master; each *shall receive for the wrong which he hath done*, that is, shall be severely punished by the Supreme Lord God according to the weight of his sin.

Instructions.

1. In all sin (although men may indulge the hope of impunity, yet) it is determined by God himself that the punishments which impend over sinners shall be inflicted. And what can it profit to have avoided the avenging hand of men, and to fall into the hands of the living God?

2. Earthly masters, with whatever power they may be armed, cannot safely or with impunity trample upon those subjected to them: for themselves also are subject to God; and *every sovereignty is under a still higher Sovereignty*, says Seneca.

3. In dealing with subjects or servants, they who are set over them ought always to consider, whether what they do is of that nature, that it may also be cleared from the charge of wrong by God the Judge : for an account must be rendered at his tribunal.

4. They are the most miserable of all mortals, who mostly afflict others by miseries : for they themselves shall receive for all those wrongs which they have done. They, therefore, doat who think themselves happy in this power of doing wrong. Thus Sylla obtained the surname of *Felix*, even because he could with impunity murder his innocent fellow citizens at will.

5. They who are under the rule and the power of others, ought to be induced by no wrongs to neglect their duty : but rather to continue at their duty, and leave their revenge to God. Thus much of the commination.

And there is no respect of persons.] There is in these words an anticipation of a lurking objection. For it might be objected on the part of masters, Who shall call us to account for evil intreating a servant ? Servants were accounted as nothing. It is understood, according to the opinion of Lawyers, that no wrongs could be done to servants. But suppose that we are arraigned ; we shall either escape through favour, or we shall avoid it by power, or we shall bribe the judge himself by money. The Apostle meets these notions ; and affirms, that the rule of Divine and of human justice is not the same. Human tribunals are very much like a spider's web : they enfold the powerless and weak ; but the mighty and the rich break through by main force. But that Supreme Judge is not terrified by power, nor turned aside by favour, nor bribed by the money of the wicked : there is at his tribunal *no respect of persons*. This is well depicted by Job, xxxiv. 19, *He accepteth not the persons of princes, nor regardeth the*

rich more than the poor : for they all are the work of his hands.
Upon this passage Ambrose writes in Ephes. vi. *The Lord*
is the just Judge ; he discerns causes, not persons.

But it might also be objected on the part of servants,
What? if we do not obey these earthly masters heartily ;
can it therefore be thought that God himself will avenge
them upon us wretches? It is sufficient that we have experience of miseries in going through life under these hard
and imperious masters; we may expect compassion from
God rather than punishment. The Apostle cuts off this
vain hope also in these persons, and denies that God is any
other than just and good, or can favour the poor out of
compassion, or withhold from the rich out of envy what is
their due. Nay, he hath even removed this *respect of per-*
sons by that broad law in Exod. xxiii. 3, *Thou shalt not*
countenance a poor man in his cause; and Levit. xix. 15, *Ye*
shall do no unrighteousness in judgment : Thou shalt not re-
spect the person of the poor, nor honour the person of the
mighty. There is, therefore, *no respect of persons* with God,
who, as the poet (Phocylides) rightly said,

> *Distributes just rights to every one, and warps not judg-*
>   *ment to favour.**

Instructions.

1. Not only those wrongs which are done to kings and
the great, but those to subjects and servants, have God
alike for their avenger.

2. We must therefore equally avoid both, that we may
not sin in either; since both will equally subject us to Divine vengeance.

3. It behoves those who act for God upon the earth, to
imitate this Divine justice, and, laying aside all *respect of*
persons, render what is due to every one. Well said Archytas, *that the judge amd the altar are the same : for we flee*
to either as often as wrong is done to us.† Therefore, that a

* Phocylides, a Greek Poet and Philosopher; a native of Miletus, who
flourished about 540 years before the Christian æra. The poem which is
extant and goes by his name, is accounted not genuine by some critics.

† Archytas of Tarentum, a soldier, a mathematician, and a celebrated
philosopher; eminent alike for his valour and his wisdom. He was repeat-

Judge may be a sanctuary, he ought to protect the poor and men of the lowest estate, as well as the rich and great.

edly chosen general of the Tarentines, and was Plato's instructor, it is said, in geometry. He was one of the first who applied the theory of mathematics to practical purposes, and gave a method of finding two mean proportionals between two given lines, and thence the duplication of the cube, by means of the conic sections. Many marvellous stories are related of his skill in mechanics, such as his constructing a wooden pigeon which could fly, &c. He flourished about 400 years before the birth of Christ, and after acquiring great reputation both in his legislative and military capacity, and being distinguished equally for his modesty and self-command, he was shipwrecked in the Adriatic sea, and his dead body thrown upon the Apulian coast. Horace has finely alluded to this fate of Archytas, in his lib. i. od. 28 :

> *Te maris et terræ numeroque carentis arenæ*
> *Mensorem cohibent, Archyta,*
> *Pulveris exigui prope littus parva Matinum*
> *Munera ; nec quidquam tibi prodest*
> *Aërias tentâsse domos, animoque rotundum*
> *Percurrisse polum, morituro !*

A treatise on the Universe, ascribed to him, and from which probably our Expositor cites the above passage, has been twice printed, at Leipsic, 1564, and at Venice, 1571, both in 4to.

END OF THE THIRD CHAPTER.

CHAP. IV.—Vers. I.

Masters, give unto your servants that which is just and equal; knowing that ye also have a Master in heaven.

This verse, which is placed the first of this fourth Chapter, seems to me to be separated from the foregoing Chapter unadvisedly and without any just grounds. It is referred therefore to the preceding Chapter by Chrysostom, Aquinas, Hugo,* Illyricus,† Musculus,‡ Zanchius, and others : and that it pertains to it, both the matter itself, which is plainly the same with the eight preceding verses, viz. the arrangement, proclaims; as well as the matter of the following verse, which is plainly new, and therefore could more properly be the beginning of a new Chapter. We shall explain this verse, then, as a portion of the for-

---

* For notices of these three characters, the Reader will consult Vol. i. p. 3 and 111 ; 33 ; and 195 : or the Index for their respective names.

† ILLYRICUS (MATHIAS FLACIUS), a Lutheran Divine, born at Albano, in Istria, in 1520. He studied at Venice, Basil, and Tubingen, and made an open profession of the doctrines of the Reformation. This procured him the friendship of Luther and Melancthon, although he subsequently had a dispute with the latter on the subject of concession to the Romanists, which difference of opinion, as usual, produced considerable enmity. He then removed to Magdeburgh, where he wrote several works, and commenced the collection of an Ecclesiastical History, denominated " The Centuries of Magdeburgh." In 1557 he became professor of Divinity and Hebrew at Jena, but gave up his chair in consequence of a quarrel concerning Original Sin, with Strigelius, another distinguished Divine and Reformer, of Wittemberg. He then removed to Ratisbon, and lastly to Frankfort, where he died in 1575. His principal works are, " Varia Doctorum Piorumque Virorum de Corrupto Ecclesiæ Statu," 1557 ; " Clavis Scripturæ," 2 vols. folio ; " Catalogus Testium Veritatis," folio.

‡ MUSCULUS (WOLFGANG), a celebrated German Divine and Reformer, was the son of a Cooper, and was born at Dieuze upon Lorraine, in 1497. His parents could give him no education, and he went about begging from door to door by singing, until his talents attracting the notice of a Convent of Benedictines, they offered to receive him into their Order, which he ac-

mer Chapter. Now it consists of two parts : In the former he sets forth to masters their duty ; *Masters, give unto
your servants that which is just and equal.* In the latter he
adds a stimulus to perform the same ; *knowing that ye also
have a Master in heaven.*

Masters.] Having explained the duty of servants, he
would advise masters likewise of their duty : because nothing is more pernicious than a tyrannical master; nothing
is more easy than to abuse command. Whence Plato says,
it is the best specimen of true justice, *if any one abstain
from wounding those whom he may easily injure.* I subjoin
his very words, being worthy of observation : Διάδηλος ὁ
Φύσει καὶ μη πλαστῶς σέβων την δίκην, μισῶν δὲ ὄντως τὸ ᾿αδικον ἐν
τούτοις των ἀνθρωπων εν οἷς αὐτῷ ῥάδιον ᾿αδικεῖν. De legib. 6.
Therefore, lest the Apostle should either seem to have neglected servants, or to have let masters go free of all law,

cordingly entered, and applying himself to study, he both made rapid
progress and became a good preacher. About the year 1518, he embraced
Lutheranism, which he supported with great zeal : this, as may be supposed, created him a great many enemies. However, nothing dismayed,
he made an open profession of his Religion : but he was ere long compelled to
flee, and took refuge at Strasburg in 1527. Here he soon afterwards publicly married ; but having no provision whatever, he was obliged to send
his wife to service in a Clergyman's family, and bind himself apprentice to
a weaver, who shortly dismissed him on account of his religious principles.
In 1531 he removed to Augsburg, where, on the expulsion of all the priests
and monks in 1537, he was made minister of the church consecrated to the
Holy Virgin, which he held until 1548, when Charles V. having entered
the city, and re-establishing popery, Musculus found it necessary to retire
to Switzerland, where, in 1549, he was invited by the Magistrates of Berne,
to the Professorship of Divinity. He died at Berne in 1563. Musculus
was a man of great learning and application, and considerable master of the
Greek and Hebrew languages. He translated the " Comment of St Chrysostom upon St. Paul's Epistles ;" the second Volume of the " Works of
St. Basil;" the " Scholia of the same Father upon the Psalms;" the " Ecclesiastical Histories of Eusebius, Socrates, Sozomen, Theodoret, Evagrius,
and the History of Polybius." He also published " Comments upon some
parts of both the Old and New Testaments," and was the author of some
original works both in Latin and German, particularly his " Loci Com-
munes," or " Common Places ;" which, with other of his Tracts, were
published in England during the reign of Elizabeth, in conjunction with
the writings of the principal Foreign Reformers.

he bound them also by his precepts. Let us proceed to
the precept itself: of which there are two members:

1. *Give unto your servants that which is just.*] τὸ δίκαιον,
that which is just, in this place includes whatever is due to
servants from legal obligation, or according to positive
laws; and excludes whatever is contrary to the same.
Aristotle, Œcon. i. 5, lays down three things as necessary
and due to servants, *their work, their sustenance, their correction.* We shall add also a fourth, viz. *their wages,* which
is due to our servants, because they are not slaves, as
they were formerly among the antients. It pertains therefore to the justice of masters to render all these things to
their servants according to due measure: it is the part of
injustice, or at least of folly, if they deal otherwise with
them. For instance, in enjoining work upon a servant, he
observes justice who neither imposes immoderate labour,
nor suffers him to grow stupid in ease and idleness: So in
allowing them sustenance, he who neither withholds necessary or convenient food, nor suffers them to indulge gluttony or drunkenness: In applying correction, he who does
not inflict punishment upon them with a cruelty exceeding
the extent of the fault, nor yet allows them to commit any
crime with impunity: In rewarding them, he who is neither
so sparing, that they cannot thereby procure for themselves
necessaries; nor so lavish, as to yield them matter for dissoluteness. The Greek Scholiast thus expresses the whole
point; *It is justice and equality to repay servants for their labour, and to supply them with an abundance of all those things
necessary for them.* The other branch of this precept follows:

2. *Give unto your servants that which is equal.*] In the
Greek it is τὴν ἰσότητα, *equality* or *equability.* Which word
we must not take in that sense, as if it were incumbent upon masters to give to their servants the same honour, the same obedience, which they exact from them.
For well spake Plato, τοῖς ἀνίσοις τὰ ἴσα 'ἄνισα, &c. *To give
equal things to unequals is inequality.*

This word ἰσότης, *equal,* therefore, does not designate the labours themselves, or the duties of servants and masters, which are different and plainly the reverse : but it refers to the mind and the manner of acting ; which in each ought to be equal by a certain proportionate analogy. For instance ; Servants are commanded to obey their masters in singleness of heart and the fear of God : now masters give them *that which is equal* when they rule them piously and religiously. Servants are commanded to obey their masters from the heart and with good will : masters repay them for their services, when they rule their servants with mildness and a sort of paternal affection. Therefore, that we may bring the difference of these words *just* and *equal* in this place, under a brief view : That is called *just* which the law requires, or what is due to servants from legal obligation : that is called *equal* which Charity and Christian lenity requires, or what is due to them from moral obligation. Of this *equity* or *equability*, these are the especial duties :

1. To esteem a servant as a partaker of a like nature, and moreover of the same grace ; not to look down upon them with a haughty spirit as some are wont to do. For although *master* and *servant* are words expressive of a distinct condition, yet *man* and *man* are names of the same nature. Whence that saying of Philo,* De spec. leg. *For-*

---

* PHILO, surnamed Judæus, in order to distinguish him from several other persons of the same name, was a Jew of Alexandria, descended from a noble and sacerdotal family, and pre-eminent among his contemporaries for his talents, eloquence, and wisdom ; and equally as well versed in the doctrines of the Greek Philosophers, as in the peculiar tenets of his own people. The partiality which he felt for the Platonists, seems indeed to have caused much confusion in his mind, through his attempts to amalgamate their philosophy with the Mosaic laws and institutions, and renders it difficult to decide how far his opinions preponderated in favour of either. It has been thought that he embraced Christianity before his death ; but the evidence for this assertion does not appear to be sufficient : for though living about our Saviour's time, and probably for some years after his crucifixion, yet there is no reason to believe that he ever visited Judea. Still, as he visited Rome, first in the reign of Caligula, to defend the cause of the Alexandrian Jews, who had been charged with disaffection to the Roman sovereignty—and again in the time of the succeeding emperor, he *might* have learnt something of the important events transacting in that

tune hath distinguished masters from servants ; both, however, have one common nature. And to this St. Paul had respect when he directed Philemon to receive back Onesimus, then become a Christian, *Not now as a servant, but above a servant, a brother beloved.* Philemon, 16.

2. So to act with servants in all things, that that should not be in force,—*Let my will stand for a reason ;* but let the master be ready to hearken to them and yield, as often as reason and truth shall require it. Job professes that he had rendered this equity to his servants ; and, unless he had done so, would have been obnoxious to the Divine anger : *If I did despise the cause of my man-servant or of my maid-servant, when they contended with me ; What then shall I do when God riseth up ; and when he visiteth what shall I answer him ?* Job xxxi. 13, 14.

3. To have some regard to human infirmity, and to treat servants debilitated by disease or old age, or any other cause, mildly and compassionately ; to cherish and take care of them kindly and affectionately. On this account the Romans seem to me to have termed the master *pater familias,* the *father of the family,* because he ought to embrace all in his family with paternal care and love, as mutually confiding in his fidelity and protection.

4. To give faithful and deserving servants, even beyond the agreement for wages, certain rewards over and above : For when they, by fidelity and love towards their masters,

early period of the Christian epoch ; and it is remarkable that his writings contain many sentiments concerning the Logos, or Word, which bear so close a resemblance to those of the Apostle John, and others so allied to the language of St. Paul, as both to exhibit and illustrate the sense of the Hebrew, or at least of the Septuagint version of the Scriptures, and lay some ground for the idea of his possessing some insight into Christianity. The late Mr. Bryant has collected the passages of Philo concerning the Logos, in his work entitled, " The Sentiments of Philo Judæus concerning the Λογος, or Word of God ; together with large extracts from his writings, compared with the Scriptures on many other particular and essential Doctrines of the Christian Religion." For further information on this interesting subject the Reader is referred to the more enlarged and minute details given in Mr. Horne's " Introduction to the Critical Study," &c. vol. ii. edit. 5, pp. 303, 304. For further particulars of the Life of Philo, let him consult Cave ; and Du Pin ; and Moreri.

shall have shewn themselves more than servants; *equality* requires that their masters by liberality and munificence should shew themselves more than masters. *Let thy soul love a good servant ; defraud him not of liberty, neither leave him to want,* Eccles. vii. 21.

Instructions :
From the fact, that even masters are subject
to rule.

1. A prudent dispenser of the word ought to instruct, admonish, and reprove, not only servants, or subjects, or men of the lowest rank ; but masters, magistrates, and likewise those who have submitted themselves to the yoke of Christ.

2. However it is usual for superiors to complain of the vices of their subjects (and that justly ;) yet for the most part they are tainted with no less faults : it is incumbent therefore upon both not so much to exaggerate the faults of another, as each to reform his own.

From that precept of giving servants what is *just :*

1. He is an unjust and wicked master who treats his servants after his own rule, not that of the Divine will : for the will of God is the rule of justice, and always prescribes a golden medium ; the human will verges to extremes. Hence said Plato, epist. 9, *A moderate service is what pleases God ; an immoderate one what is required by the cupidity of man.**

---

* Had our Expositor lived in the present day, we should in all probability have had some suitable illustration and admonitions on a point which he has not treated : for what topic of interest and importance connected with the subject in hand, or growing naturally out of his text, has he not discussed ? But the condition of slaves was not known in his time, nor, as it has since existed, could have been foreseen. The violation of human liberty in injured Africa, and the horrors of a middle passage had not been discovered. The system which he has but touched had not been fully developed : the sound of the slave-whip—the details of shooting excursions—the moanings of separated parents and children, husbands and wives—and the shrieks and groans of mutilated innocence and female torture, had not been heard on this side of the Atlantic. The exclusion of Missionary efforts and Religion from those dragged from their homes, and with nought besides to comfort them, had not been reported in England ; and a thousand other abominations contrary to Christian piety, practised upon the unoffending

2. But those are here to be blamed who offend on either side against that rule of justice which we have described from the beginning. Many think that they are provident and frugal, whilst they tame their servants with labours and stripes, and wear them out with hunger and fastings : Some, on the other hand, boast of their kindness for their servants, because they permit them to run abroad in idleness, and to waste their days in drunken banquetings. But neither practise *that which is just.*

From the precept of giving that which is *equal,*

1. A Christian master ought not only to consider what is the law or custom of humanity, but above all, what charity and Christian usage enjoin him to give his servants. If he shall not have performed the former, he acts unjustly even according to the judgment of men ; if he has not discharged the latter, he acts wickedly and cruelly in the sight of God.

2. The law of analogy, or *equity,* ought to prevail among all orders of men : and whatever superiors require from their dependants, they ought, equally, if not in kind, yet in analogy, to compensate the same. Thus much as to the precept.

Knowing that ye also have a Master in heaven.] Here he adds the inducement to the observance of the precept. And this is twofold : One consists in this, that they should know that they also have a Master ; *knowing that ye also have a Master.* The other, that they should know what manner of Master they have—*in heaven.*

Knowing that ye also have a Master] i. e. *Holding, believing, considering* that ye likewise and your servants are subject to a Master. This consideration is a sharp stimulus to render justice and equity to servants, because it strikes at injustice and iniquity. For on this account it is masters think to do what they please with servants, because

Negro, had not been brought to light. In a word, the subject of West Indian Slavery had not been investigated ; the wrongs of an injured mass of human beings, as existing in the British Colonies, and the claims of *justice* and *equity* on their behalf, had not come under consideration, nor been echoed through a land of professing Christians.

they imagine that they alone are servants only, that themselves are absolute masters, and nothing else but masters. They are commanded, therefore, to know and remember, that they also are servants of the same supreme Master, and on that account fellow-servants with their servants : Now it is far from reason, that a servant, although a little more honourable, should act unjustly and tyránnically with his fellow servants; because he would not like that God himself should act in the same manner towards him.

Ye have a Master in heaven.] By this expression he would indicate what sort of a Master masters themselves also have ; viz. *an heavenly* one, i. e. just, almighty, omniscient, in one word, GOD. This consideration also very much conduces to repress the injustice of masters. For they behave themselves haughtily towards their servants, because for the most part they have not the power of resisting them, and because they appear to have no judge or defender, who might avenge the wrongs offered to them. The Apostle, therefore, bids masters themselves to bear in mind that they have a Master, and that not a mortal, but an heavenly one, who will not suffer them to abuse with impunity the authority delegated to them over their servants. The subjects then to such a Master, ought religiously to obey him in all things, and to observe justice and equity.

First, because this heavenly Master is omniscient, so that nothing can be concealed from him which is done rashly and unjustly. Now it is the extreme of audacity, whilst the heavenly Master is looking on, to treat fellow-servants inconsiderately and cruelly. For that wicked servant mentioned in the Gospel dared not to afflict his fellow-servants until he saw his master was gone into a far country. Since, however, this heavenly Master is never absent from us, it is never safe to act frowardly.

Secondly, because this heavenly Master is holy and just, and hates all injustice. Earthly masters, indeed, sometimes either countenance the wickedness of servants, or at least wink at it; because they themselves are equally wicked : but there is no hope that he can please the heavenly

Master who dares to violate justice and equity. *The wicked and his ungodliness are both alike hateful unto God,* Wisd.
xiv. 9.

Thirdly, because this Master in heaven, is Almighty : he
therefore can punish that which he hates ; nor can any one
pluck himself out of his hands.   He is the Ruler over all,
neither stands in awe of any man's greatness : and *a stronger than the strongest shall bring a sore trial upon the mighty,*
Wisd. vi. 7, 8.   Let masters, then, think of these things :
that they have a Master ; that they have a Master in heaven, i. e. all-seeing, a hater of all injustice, and almighty :
and this shall constrain them to render justice and equity
to their servants.

Hence learn,

1.   That the faithful and godly should so carry themselves towards their inferiors, as always to remember that
they have a higher Master.

2.   That it is too much the custom among men of power and appointed to high station, to forget this supreme and
common Master.

3.   This forgetfulness is the origin of all injustice and
iniquity : as is evident in Pharaoh, Exod. v. 2, *I know not
the Lord ; I will not let Israel go.*

4.   We therefore should perpetually think what a Master
we have in heaven, that this very thought may be a stimulus to excite us to equity, and a restraint to keep us from
injustice and tyranny.

5.   It behoves us to treat our servants with that clemency
which we desire that our heavenly Master may use towards
us.

And thus ye have an explication of this economical exhortation, as it were, of the Apostle ; which we have referred to the third Chapter.   Now let us proceed to the
exposition of the last Chapter.

EXPOSITION

OF

THE FOURTH CHAPTER.

I PREMISE a few things concerning the argument of this Chapter; afterwards I shall proceed direct to the explication of the context Therefore, after having delivered the domestic precepts, which are accommodated to individuals according to the varied condition of the persons, the Apostle reverts to certain general exhortations, which he propounds to all in common. To these he immediately subjoins an honourable mention of Tychicus and Onesimus, by whom this Epistle was sent to the Colossians. At length he salutes by name those of the many pious persons who then dwelt at Rome, and commands this Epistle to be publicly read in the Church, and so concludes it.

The principal divisions of this Chapter are three :
> Exhortations,
> Commendations,
> Salutations.

He exhorts to three things :
> Perseverance in prayer ; in verses 2, 3, 4.
> Wisdom in conversation ; vers. 5.
> Discretion in speech ; vers. 6.

He commends to them two eminent men,
> Tychicus, vers. 7, 8 : Onesimus; vers. 9.

As to the rest of this Epistle, almost the whole is taken up with salutations, and a few occasional additions.

Let us come to the context.

Vers. 2, &c.

*Continue in prayer (*or, apply with all earnestness*) and
watch in the same with thanksgiving, &c.*

In this verse and the two following, he stirs up the Colossians to that most divine and useful work of *prayer.* In
treating which, it is not my intention to explain this trite
subject of prayer ; but only to expound those things which
are expressly touched by the Apostle in the context itself.
Now these in general are two : 1. Certain conditions requisite in the persons themselves who pray, in this second
verse. 2. Certain and very necessary materials of special
prayer, or causes of praying, vers. 3, 4.

Three conditions are enumerated in this place :
    Earnest perseverance,
    Cautious watchfulness,
    Pious gratitude :
Of each in their order.

Continue in prayer, Τῇ προσευχη προσκαρτερεῖτε.] This
Greek word is derived from κάρτος, which with one letter
transposed is the same as κράτος, that is, *strength, earnestness, victory.* Hence καρτερειν, *to endure with fortitude,* or
strenuously to persevere, and προσκαρτερειν, to apply with ardour and assiduity to any difficult and laborious thing,
until you shall have brought it to the wished-for end, and
shall have obtained the victory, as it were. Προσκαρτερησις,
therefore, involves these two things : a certain earnest intention of mind, and as it were struggle, whilst occupied
in prayer ; and an assiduous frequency in prayer : *with all
prayer and supplication in the Spirit,* Ephes. vi. 18.

As to this earnestness, or intention of mind ; it is indeed
very necessary on many accounts :

1. Because the occasions for prayer of this kind are
such as ought greatly to excite the human mind to perform

this work seriously and with the whole strength. For the magnitude of our intention is always wont to correspond, at least, it ought to correspond, to the magnitude of the business which is undertaken: But now, as says Parisiensis, De Rhet. divin. cap. 38, *there is no business that can be compared with that of obtaining pardon, grace, and glory: but these are things which in an especial manner are sought by prayer.* Therefore, to seek such great and good things frigidly, perfunctorily,—in a way of duty merely,—what else is it but to mock God?

2. Because those dead and sleepy prayers, which are uttered with a mind either wandering or benumbed, neither reach heaven, nor can move God to hear. For our prayer stands instead of a messenger between us and God; but if a messenger shall either loiter, or sleep by the way, he will neither reach the end of his journey, nor effect the business entrusted to him. Hence says Cyprian, De orat. Dom. *With what effrontery dost thou require to be heard of God, when thou dost not thyself hear the sounds of thy own voice?*

3. This intention of mind and fervour of spirit in prayer is required, because the heart, inflamed with this spiritual heat, immediately grows soft and is dilated, and becomes more apt and capable for receiving the Divine gifts. And I think this was the cause that the Egyptian Brethren should have wished to use *the most brief and rapid ejaculations in prayer;* namely, *that their intention should not vanish and be blunted through delays,* as says Augustine, De orando Deo, ad Probam. Epist. 121. cap. 10.

4. This intention and ardor of mind is most especially desirable even on the account, that it is a most sure sign of a pious and devoted mind; as, on the other hand, a cold and sleepy prayer is a mark of a carnal mind, and one rivetted to earthly things. Thus says Chrysostom, lib. 1, De orando Deo, *When I see any one not diligent in prayer, it is forthwith clear to me, that he can possess nothing exalted in his mind: again, where I behold any one earnest and very persevering in prayer, I conclude that he is endowed with all virtue and piety.*

5. Because this ardent desire, upon the testimony of Scripture, breaks forth in the prayers of all the saints. Jacob by this effort of fervid prayer, when he wrestled with God himself, came off conqueror, Gen. xxxii. 28. Moses by this same tied up as it were the hand of God, nor suffered him to destroy the rebellious Israelites. On account of this earnestness, David every where calls prayer his *cry.* In a word; This intention and fervour has ever greatly availed to the effectual obtaining of the object prayed for, as the Apostle James testifies, v. 1, *the effectual fervent prayer of a righteous man availeth much.* What is that fervent prayer, ενεργουμενη δεησις, but prayer excited, actuated, and as it were quickened, by some influence of the Spirit?

And thus much of the earnestness, or intention of mind, which is required in the act itself of prayer, and intimated by this word προσκαρτερείτε, *continue* or *apply with all earnestness, in prayer.*

But it is said, by this word προσκαρτερειτε is further intimated the assiduity or frequency of this exercise ; which ought to be such and so continual, that in that respect we are commanded in the holy Scriptures *to pray always.* Christ himself teaches his disciples by a parable, *that we ought always to pray, and not to faint,* Luke xviii. 1. *Pray without ceasing,* says the Apostle, 1 Thess. v. 17. Which places are not to be taken in that sense, as though, leaving and renouncing all other concerns, we should only be occupied in and cleave to prayer: but as Augustine has rightly observed, that charge, PRAY WITHOUT CEASING, *is to be received thus soberly, that certain seasons of prayer should not be omitted in any day.* De hæres. ad Quodvultdeum, hær. 57. Psallianorum seu Euchitarum. For he is deemed never to cease from his work, who works when he can and ought. This perseverance of prayer then, does not require an uninterrupted, but a frequently repeated act of prayer: that is to say, we should not lay aside the desire of prayer, either by the weariness of expectation, or the despair of obtaining, or for any other cause whatever; but we should invoke God frequently, and frequently plead with him, even when he seems to have shut his ears to our prayers. And this is the meaning of the Greek phrase.

It is not my intention here to shew how often every day, or at what hours we should pray: but we must shew that we ought to be occupied very often, yea, very frequently, in this exercise. As to the point of time, it is fit that we consult the Spirit and the occasion.

Inducements for the frequency of the exercise of prayer.

1. Our prayer ought to be constant; 1. Because we have constant and infinite causes for prayer. For whatever good we have, or desire to have; whatever evil we either suffer, or deserve to suffer, or fear; all these things supply matter for prayer. The blessings which we have excite to prayer; because in this manner God is to be honoured on account of the benefits received: the blessings which we want stir up to prayer; because they are to be looked for from God alone. The evils which we suffer call to prayer; because they can be removed by God alone: the evils which we fear; because by Him alone can they be banished. Hence the holy Fathers named prayer, *the sacrifice of the Christian, the key of heaven, the supply of want, the scourge of the devil,* &c. We have an example of the constancy of prayer in Eusebius, lib. 2. cap. 23.

2. Because constancy and importunity is the most efficacious means of obtaining what we seek; as Christ has taught us in that parable, Luke xviii.; and has also shewn in his own dealing towards the Canaanitish woman importunately beseeching him, and urging her prayers again and again, Matt. xv. Hence Gregory, in Psal. vi. Pœnitent. says, *God would be asked, would be compelled, would be conquered as it were by importunity: this violence is good, wherewith God is not offended, but placated.*

3. Because this perseverance in prayer greatly contributes to the declaring, increasing, and strengthening our faith. For it is the property of a proud and disdainful petitioner, to suffer no delays, and immediately to draw back from prayer on account of any adjournment. Hence that speech, 2 Kings vi. 33, *What should I wait for the Lord any longer?* But on the other hand, David, in Psal. v. 3, says, *In the morning will I direct my prayer unto thee and will look up.*

Faith then will not immediately draw back, but abide as it were in hope, and wait until it shall seem good to God to grant its request.

Instructions regarding the intention arising from these considerations.

1. Whereas we are excited by the Apostle to intensity and fervour of mind in prayer, we must conclude, that we are by nature frigid and torpid in this exercise, so that we can scarcely abstain from sleep unless we have a monitor and one to arouse us. The drowsiness of Apostles themselves testifies this, Matt. xxvi. 40.

2. We must therefore beseech God to impart to us the Spirit of prayer: for flesh and blood neither knows nor can understand the true and just ground of prayer without the teaching and inspiration of the Spirit. Hence that declaration in Rom. viii. 2, *We know not what to pray for as we ought,* &c.

3. Hence we clearly deduce, that the prayers of those persons are of none, or of little moment, who by no sense, no understanding of those things which are uttered, mutter forth their daily prayers, that they may be only said thereby to have prayed. But they might have learnt even from this place, that prayer is not a mere matter of duty, but a serious and laborious concern, in which it behoves us to be instant, not to sleep.

The Papists, therefore, deserve every odium, who would have a Christian people to hear public prayers in an unknown tongue, and also to babble their private prayers in an unknown tongue; as though they only desired to render a most divine and useful thing ridiculous, unfruitful, and becoming parrots more than men. We shall briefly glance at this error.

It is clear, that there is required in serious prayer both a consideration of those things which we ask of God, and an ardent desire of the same. Cyprian, De orat. Domin. thus writes concerning consideration, *Let every carnal thought be banished; neither let the mind think (in prayer) of any thing else than that alone for which it is praying.* Concerning the desire, Parisiensis, De Rhetor. Div. cap. 28, thus expresses himself, *The desire of obtaining what is sought is the voice of prayer; without this, prayer is dumb.* But now neither the thought, nor the desire of those things which are asked, is found in those who do not understand what they ask from God.

Paul condemns those prayers which are not understood; who concludes that we cannot say *Amen* to the prayers which are not understood, 1 Cor. xiv. 16. Augustine hath condemned it; who, in his book De magistro, cap. i. thus writes, *The people ought to understand the prayers of their priests, that they may have their attention fixed upon God by a common feeling.* Even the very Papists themselves among whom there was any thing of mind or firmness, have censured this error of the Romanists. Parisiensis, De Rhetor. Divin. c. 38, where he compares prayer to a messenger, says, *It is reckoned among the follies of that messenger, that he neither cares nor thinks of those concerns except this alone, that he offers a petition to God, and is altogether ignorant what it contains, and what is sought by it.* *And these things are manifest in all those praying persons, who mutter with their lips alone, understanding nothing whatever of those things which the words of their prayers signify.* And in Cap. 40, where he calls prayer *the calf of the lips,* he thus writes, *The flesh of that calf is the perceptions and considera-tion of those things which are signified by the words of prayer; the marrow is the pious intention of the person praying; the hairs of that calf are the external vocal sounds.* *They slay the sacrifice therefore, and defraud God of the better part of the calf, who either understand not, or care not about the signi-fication of the words.* Thus far Parisiensis. John Gerson, al-though involved in the error of the Roman church, denies this to be necessarily the case as far as regards the illite-rate; yet he voluntarily confesses that the conversion of the heart to God at the time of prayer, all things consi-dered, is more laudable if it be done according to the words and the meaning of the prayer. Lastly, Cajetan is convicted of error by the theologians of Paris, in having written that it is better that prayers should be said in the vulgar and known tongue, than in the Latin which is not

understood. But how does he defend himself? *I have not
written*, says he, *that it is better, but that it is* BETTER FOR
THE EDIFICATION OF THE CHURCH ; *neither have I written*
PRAYERS, *but* PUBLIC PRAYERS, WHICH ARE SAID IN
THE HEARING OF THE PEOPLE ; *and this I have founded
upon the doctrine of St. Paul,* 1 Cor. xiv. These things are
from Cajetan in answer to certain articles put forth in the
name of the Paris divines ; which work is found after the
third part of Aquinas. I will not dwell any longer on the
refutation of this most absurd error, which does away as it
were the very soul of prayer: for rightly said Athanasius,
in orat. 16, against Maximus the philosopher,* *to dispute
about things more clear and more manifest than the sun, is
nothing else than to suggest evil things to men defending the
cause of dishonesty and impudence.* Thus much concerning
the intention or fervour of persons praying.

Instructions referring to constancy or perseverance.

1. This exhortation itself to perseverance in prayer dis-
closes the depravity of our nature, which causes us to
cleave too much to carnal things and pleasures ; but, on
the contrary, on that account to be sluggish and grow
weary in spiritual things. For nothing is more pleasant to
a healthy soul than to pour forth its desires into the bosom
of its heavenly Father ; which, nevertheless, we are not
able to do without weariness.

2. We must above all things take care not to be drawn
away at any time from this so necessary exercise of prayer
by our pleasures, our business, or any other hindrances.
For like as if you should cut the nerves, you would leave
the whole body without motion and strength as a huge
trunk ; so if you set aside prayer (which Chrysostom calls
the nerve of the soul) you render the man altogether
maimed and feeble, and without any spiritual motion. And
here the eminent example of Daniel is set before us, who
could not be restrained from prayer even for one day,

* MAXIMUS TYRIUS, a celebrated philosopher of the second century, a
native of Tyre, in Phœnicia, whence he took his name, and who appears
to have adopted the principles of the Platonic school, with an inclination to
scepticism.

either by the royal edict, or the risk of death ; as may be seen, Dan. vi. 11.

3. Hence we may infer the misery of the ungodly and unbelievers : who, as they are void of faith and the love of God, cannot indeed pray, except for form's sake, much less can they *continue in prayer.* But what is more miserable than he who cannot hold any commerce with the very fountain of blessedness ?

4. Hence appears the happiness of the godly and faith‧ ful : who as they enjoy fervent and persevering prayer as an inexhaustible treasure, can never want any thing which is necessary and beneficial for them. For *if ye being evil, know how to give good gifts unto your children, how much more shall your Father which is in heaven give good things to them that ask him ?* And thus much of fervor and perseverance.

2. *Watch in the same.*] Here we have another attendant of just and legitimate prayer, namely, watchfulness. And we may refer this watchfulness either to what are properly called vigils, that is, to the stated and customary watches of the night; or to the vigils called so metaphorically, that is, the constant watchings of a Christian mind: yea, it may be allowed us to join both advantageously.

As to those nightly vigils; it is clear, that the Christians of the Apostle's times, on account of the cruelty of the pagans, were often compelled by a kind of necessity to nocturnal assemblies, when they would either preach the gospel, or offer public prayers to God ; as is manifest from Acts xii. 12, and xx. 7, and in other places. Moreover, for the sake of exciting solemnity and devotion, when the Emperors were converted to the Christian religion, and their affairs were settled and flourishing, they retained the custom of the vigils, and most especially celebrated them when the anniversary of the festivals approached. Hence the sermons of the Fathers upon the vigils of the Nativity, the vigils of Easter: we also read even now of the custom upon the vigils of the martyrs. Now they spent these vigils in the word and prayers, and prepared themselves beforehand in this manner for the

more holy observation of the feast, and the participation
of the Lord's supper. We shall bring some testimonies of
the Fathers. Tertullian, in 2 lib. ad uxorem, shews that
Christian women ought not to marry heathen husbands,
by the argument derived from these vigils : *What heathen,*
says he, *would willingly bear that his wife should go from his
side to these nocturnal convocations ? Who will carelessly allow her to pass her night in the Pascal solemnities ?* Before
they assembled at the vigils that they were accustomed to
sit up in the night, Athanasius also proves, Apol. ad Con-
stadt. where he complains that they were oppressed by the
Syrian president, for whilst they were intent upon prayer,
he sent his soldiers among them. Nazianzen mentions
these vigils, in Orat. 27, and Orat. 2. in Julian: and Bernard, on the vigil of St. Andrew, says, *He is an unworthy
man who does not observe the appointed abstinence of the vigil
with solemn joy.*

Now, besides these public vigils assigned to the public
assemblies of Christians, we may also observe that pious
and holy men sometimes spent sleepless nights in private
devotion, or applied most earnestly to prayer. Thus David
frequently affirms, that he even ceased not in the night
from prayer, Ps. xxii. 2, and lxxvii. 6. So Paul and Silas
shut up in prison, called upon God in the middle of the
night, Acts xvi. 25.

Concerning those public vigils which necessity brought
upon the Church, we mention that one; the reason thereof ceasing, they are now not improperly done away by
our Church : for that they would be liable to many disadvantages and dangers, no wise man will deny, who has surveyed the manners of this age. Moreover it is gathered
from Canon 35 of the Council of Eliberis,* that many in-

---

* This was the third Council of the Church in the fourth Century (for
the Council of Sinuessa, said to have been assembled on the alleged apostasy
of Marcellinus, ought not to be admitted in the number of Councils) said
to have been held at Eliberis or Elvira, now Granada, in Spain, about the
year 305. It passed 81 Canons touching such a variety of matters that it
is supposed to have adopted several antient codes, or to have drawn into
one collection the Canons of the preceding Councils of Spain. The Canon

conveniences arose from thence in the antient church;
where the women were debarred from these vigils, because
that under the cloak of prayer, they committed secret
wickedness. And the abuses at the vigils of the martyrs
which had almost been the usage and the law, are censured
in Augustine. See De morib. eccles. cathol. cap. 34. epist.
64, and in many places in his Sermons.

Now as to the devotion of private persons, who, not
being content with daily prayer, even watch in the night;
it is indeed truly laudable, if it be destitute of superstition, and arises out of zeal for the Divine name, and
finally be employed when there seems great and just cause
to exact this vigilance. David, yea Christ himself, furnishes us with an example for this watchfulness, Matt.
xxvi. 38, 39. Paul also imitates his Master in this matter,
2 Cor. vi. 5. Nor are these vigils only laudable, but they
are also delightful to the pious ; as Augustine truly says,
De bono viduit. cap. 21, *Vigils in as far as they do not injure the health, if spent in praying, singing, or reading, are
converted into spiritual pleasures.*

Hitherto we have spoken concerning vigils properly so
called. It remains that we treat those so termed metaphorically and figuratively, that is, the vigils of the mind;
which are plainly necessary, not only in our prayers, but
in our whole life, and therefore ought to be perpetual.
Now I say that the mind is vigilant or watchful, when no
ways asleep in sin and worldly things; but always lively
expects the day of death and the coming of Christ, and
tastes beforehand, as it were, future glory in hope and a
sure faith. He who keeps his mind prepared in this man-

referred to by our Expositor is given in these words :—" We have thought
fit to hinder women from spending the night in the Cemeteries, because
oftentimes under pretence of praying they commit in secret great crimes."
This Council has been mostly celebrated for condemning all use whatever of
pictures in Churches ; a decisive proof in itself, if proof were wanting, that
the use of images was then unknown in the Christian Church. " We
would not," says the 36th Canon, " have pictures placed in Churches, that
the object of our worship and adoration should not be painted on the walls."
The 34th Canon prohibited also the use of lighted candles in the Cemeteries
of the dead, that the spirits of the saints might not be disturbed.

ner, he lives in perpetual watchfulness; he who neglects this vigilance of mind, he, although he may pass days and nights in prayer, is, notwithstanding, judged to sleep. To this vigilance of mind Christ calls us in

Mark xiii. 35, 36, *Watch, for ye know not when,* &c.

Rev. iii. 2, *Be watchful,* &c.

Rev. xvi. 15, *Blessed is he that watcheth, and keepeth,* &c.

Paul,

1 Cor. xvi. 13, *Watch ye; stand fast in the faith,* &c.

1 Thess. v. 6, *Let us not sleep, but let us watch,* &c.

Peter,

1 Epis. v. 8, *Watch, because your adversary,* &c.

It therefore behoves us to observe these vigils, if we wish either ourselves or our prayers to be acceptable to God.   Hence Augustine, Serm. 23, in Evang. Matt. *Watch in heart, watch in faith, watch in charity, watch in good works.*   And Bernard, in vigil. Petri et Pauli; *Vigils are proposed for this end, that we may awake, if we shall have slept in any sin.*   Yea, as Cyprian speaks, De orat. Domin. *All godly men ought, even when they sleep with their eyes, to watch with their heart.*   As it is written of the person of the Church, *I sleep, but my heart waketh,* Cant. v. 2.

Instructions.

1. Hence is inferred the sottishness of our age: For we, as often as we assemble for public prayers or the preaching of the word, thereupon sleep in open day; whereas our forefathers in the primitive church, passed even whole nights without sleep with alacrity, that they might enjoy these spiritual exercises.

2. Our impiety and vanity is also inferred: For vigils among us are scarcely destined to any thing but wickedness or foolishness.

3. We may also conclude: That he raises his voice in vain to God in prayer, who sleeps in the conversation of his life: For God requires no less, nay, much more watchful minds than eyes, from those invoking his name.

4. The prayers of the ungodly and impenitent are accounted dreams rather than desires; because they are recited whilst the heart sleeps in sin.   Thus far of watchfulness.

With thanksgiving.] We come to the last condition which is required in persons praying, and in prayer itself, namely, gratitude, and thanksgiving flowing from thence. And rightly indeed is thanksgiving coupled with prayer: For in praying, whether we have respect to benefits already received, or look forward to those to be received, whether we consider those deferred, or altogether denied; on all these accounts we are bound to give thanks.

1. It is just that those seeking and expecting new benefits should shew themselves grateful on account of those before received: because, as even Aristotle rightly and wisely observed, Ethic. 9, *A return is required to preserve friendship:* but to God we have nothing that we can return except gratitude, Ps. cxvi. 12, *What shall I render unto the Lord for all his benefits towards me? I will take the cup of salvation,* &c.

2. We ought to shew ourselves grateful for benefits received; because in vain does he ask new benefits who shews himself unmindful of those supplied; *The hope of the unthankful shall melt away as the winter's hoar frost,* Wisd. xvi. 29.

3. Thanks are even to be given for those deferred, yea, for those denied. For when those things which we seek are deferred, it is done that they may be conferred at the most advantageous time for us; that we may esteem them more when bestowed: when they are altogether denied, it so happens, because God knew that those things would be hurtful to us which we judged for our advantage; on the contrary, that those would be as useful, which seemed to us to be bitter and unpleasant. This is what Chrysostom intimates, when he says, that *we must thank God, not only for manifest benefits, but for more hidden ones, which are afforded us unsolicited and in opposition to our desires.* Of this kind are sickness, poverty, persecution, and almost all those things which are commonly thought hard to be endured. And among these and the like, the opinion of Augustine, in Epist. Joan. tract. 6, is to be received, who asserts, that the pious and faithful, when they are not heard according *to their will,* yet are heard *to their safety.*

On these grounds, therefore, it is manifest, that thanksgiving, inasmuch as it is a tribute due to God on many accounts, is never to be intermitted.

Hence we are taught,

1. That almost all men are more prone to ask and to complain, than to be thankful.

2. That those ungrateful men are wholly unfit to offer unto God the sacrifice of prayer.

3. That good and evil are not to be measured by our sense, but must be left to the judgment of God our Father : for here is the fountain of ingratitude, that we do not believe those things to be best for us which are sent by God. The old poet was not undeservedly praised by Plato, in Alcibiades, lib. 2, because he had prescribed to his friends this form of prayer,

> *O Jupiter, grant to us thy blessings whether we pray for*
> *them or withhold our prayers,*
> *And repel from us all evils even though we pray for*
> *them.*

4. That we must not be rash or angry, if those things should be denied us which we desire; but rather give thanks to God the Father, who lovingly and prudently denies us hurtful things, even when they are foolishly and inconsiderately sought by us.

5. That nothing can happen to the pious and faithful, for which they may not and ought not to give the most deserved thanks ; according to that injunction of the Apostle, 1 Thess. v. 18, *In all things give thanks.* Thus much for the condition of legitimate prayer.

Vers. 3, 4.

*Withal praying also for us, that God would open unto us a
door of utterance, to speak the mystery of Christ, for
which I am also in bonds :*

That I may make it manifest, as I ought to speak.

Many things are to be prayed for from Almighty God,
both on our own account and that of others : but the
Apostle, passing by other things, excites the Colossians
to seek one great and necessary thing, namely, the propagation and increase of the Gospel.   And that very justly
too : for when this celestial light has diffused itself, and
penetrates the hearts of men, all other blessings of God
are added to them without asking.   Matt. vi. 33.

In these two verses two things are to be observed generally : For whom we must most especially pray ; What on
their account is to be earnestly sought from God.

For whom ?   *For us*]   That is, For me and the other
faithful ministers of the Gospel.

What is to be sought ?
- The faculty, liberty, efficacy of preaching ; *A door of utter-ance.*
- The use or exercise of this fa-culty ; *To speak the mystery of Christ,* &c.
- The proper manner of exercis-ing the same ; *as I ought to speak.*

Withal praying also for us.]   In the preceding verse (as
you have heard) he excited the Colossians to constant
prayer : Now he teaches that it behoved them to remember, not only themselves, but also their brethren, and especially ministers.   Thus in 2 Cor. i. 11, the Apostle says,
that he trusted for Divine assistance, the Corinthians

helping together with him to propitiate God by prayer. Nor is it without cause they who desire the increase of the Gospel from the heart, are excited to pray for the Apostles and other ministers; because a good and faithful minister is the public treasure of the Church, and therefore to be loved and cared for by all who love or care for the edification of the Church.

Hence let us observe,

1. That it is the duty of all the pious, assiduously and earnestly to pray to God for pastors and ministers of the Gospel.

2. That they who do not love them even for their vocation alone, although they have nothing else worthy of their love, have little of the Christian mind; they who vex and harass them, are plainly of a diabolical spirit. 1 Thess. v. 12, 13.

3. They who are in a low station, and of less sanctity, nevertheless may and ought to pray for them who are in a more eminent station, and endowed with greater sanctity: For the Apostle himself not only did not despise the prayers of the people of Colosse, but importuned them to a still greater degree. Hence says Augustine, in Psal. xxxviii. *The Apostle prays for the people; the people pray for the Apostle: all the members pray for themselves; The Head intercedes for all.*

4. To pray God for others we have no need of the mediatorial intercession of any one, but of mutual charity and necessity. Augustine speaks admirably on this head, cont. epist. Parmen. lib. 2. cap. 8, where he reprehends Parmenianus,* because he had said that a bishop is a mediator between the people and God : and he forthwith adds, *All Christians commend themselves to one another's prayers. But he for whom no one mediates, but he himself for all, he is the only and true Mediator.* See more in the same, tom. 7.

5. That the Papists vainly and foolishly, in those dumb prayers of the living, endeavour to ground that mediato-

---

* This was a schismatical African bishop, elected by the Donatists, after Donatus, their chief, in 350 ; he wrote several things in defence of his heresy, which were refuted by Optatus and Augustine.

rial and meritorious intercession of dead saints for the
church militant. For the living do not offer meritorious
prayers to God for the living, but only suppliantly unite
their prayers with those of their brethren. But whoever
does this on another's account, does not set himself up as
an intercessor properly so called, or as the advocate of
another; but only joins suppliantly in the same petitions.
Therefore, whatever may be determined about the universal prayers of the church triumphant for the safety of the
church militant, it should ever be remembered, that Christ
is the only Mediator both of redemption and of meritorious intercession with God the Father. Thus much of the
persons.

That God would open unto us a door of utterance.] Here
he proceeds to shew what he most especially wished that
they should ask from God on his account and that of other
ministers, namely, that he would open a door of utterance
to them. Christ, in Luke xxi. 15, calls this faculty, *a
mouth and wisdom: I will give you a mouth, and wisdom,
which all your adversaries shall not be able to gainsay nor resist.* And wisely indeed does the Apostle require this door
of his soul to be opened by God; because he alone illuminates the minds of men in this knowledge of Divine things,
he alone furnishes the gifts requisite for the discharge of
such an office. He opened a door of utterance to Moses,
who was by nature *slow of speech, and of a slow tongue,*
Exod. iv. 10. And in the same place he manifestly claims
this prerogative to himself, vers. 11, 12: *Who hath made
man's mouth? Have not I the Lord? Now therefore go, and
I will be with thy mouth, and teach thee what thou shalt say.*
So also Paul refers his faculty to the gratuitous gift of
God, 2 Cor. iii. 5, 6, *Not that we are sufficient of ourselves,
but our sufficiency is of God: who hath made us able ministers,* &c. Hence Clemens, Strom. 1, says, *There is one
teacher both of the preacher and of the hearer; he who supplies the fountain even of the sense and of the word:* Ἐις ὁ
διδάσκαλος, καὶ τοῦ λέγοντος καὶ τοῦ ακρωμένου, ὁ επιπηγάξων καὶ τὸν
νοῦν καὶ τὸν λόγον.

Instructions.

1. Nothing more salutary can be sought from God on

behalf of others, than that they may be qualified for the duties of their calling by the Divine bounty.

2. This is one cause why so many unlearned persons invade the ecclesiastical office, that the people do not with their whole heart seek from God able ministers : for he it is who gives to the Church apostles, teachers, evangelists, fitted for the work of the ministry. See Ephes. iv.

3. No one relying upon the strength of his natural abilities, or his erudition, ought to undertake this office of an evangelist, but to depend upon Divine grace and the Divine benediction.

4. Even they who are furnished with the greatest gifts, should notwithstanding daily seek from God, that the same gifts may be given, preserved, increased to them. Thus the Apostle, to whom was given an extraordinary knowledge of the gospel by special revelation, yet requests that prayer should be offered even for himself, that a door of utterance may be opened unto him more and more.

2. Since God is intreated to open a door of utterance to ministers, we may understand, that he gives them the liberty of preaching the Gospel, and opens as it were the way, when all obstacles are removed which the world and the devil are wont to oppose to the preaching of the Gospel. For it is the custom of Satan and his minions to gnash at the manifestation of the Gospel, and to employ all their arts to shut out this saving light; but God on the other hand interposes his authority, restrains the wicked and their leader, the devil, and against their will and resistance, opens the door to the preachers of his Gospel.

In the first publication of the Gospel this was most manifest, when almost the whole world conspired to close the door of gospel utterance ; but God, notwithstanding, opened so wide a door for it, that by means of a few fishermen it was diffused through the whole earth like lightning ;* as the Apostle testifies Col. i. 23. This the Fathers were always accustomed to allege against the heathen, and by this wonderful spread of the Gospel, to prove that its

---

* Matt. xxiv. 14.

truth flowed from God. Thus Clemens, Strom. 7, near the end, says; *The Grecian philosophy, if any magistrate prohibited it, immediately died away ; but our doctrine, even from the first preaching of it, kings, generals, and magistrates, with all their satellites, forbad ; nevertheless it does not droop like human doctrine, but flourishes the more.* How was this, unless because, by the faithful earnestly praying for it, God opened to it a door that it might go forth even in spite of its enemies ? Moreover, God, upon the pious constantly intreating for it, sometimes inclined the hearts of princes, not only not to oppose the Gospel, but to succour the ministers, and promote the progress of the Gospel. Thus he influenced Constantine, and after him Theodosius, and many other emperors, so that, renouncing paganism, they embraced the Christian religion. So in our age, and that of our ancestors, he influenced many princes, so that rejecting and extirpating Papistical superstitions, they opened a door for the Gospel by their own authority. On these accounts Paul rightly advises the Colossians, to pray that God would open a door of utterance to himself and the rest of the ministers of the Gospel : for this regards the power of God.

Instructions.

1. Ministers endeavour in vain to spread the Gospel, if God open not to them a door of utterance, and remove external obstacles out of the way.

2. It is the duty of every godly man, not only to ask of God, that he would extend the free course of the Gospel ; but also to exert all his own energies to do so himself.

3, They are therefore to be detested who cast any hindrance in the way of the word and its ministers, and, as much as in them lies, shut and bar this door. In this class are to be placed tyrants, who persecute the ministers of the Gospel ; heretics, who attack the doctrine of the Gospel ; and false and mistaken politicians, who lay it down as a principle, that it is of no consequence whether a door be opened for true Religion or papistical supersti-

tion, only that they may enjoy external advantages ;* and,
lastly, Simoniacal patrons, who cheat the ministers of the
Gospel of their due stipend, and seize upon what they
ought to receive.

3. When God is invoked to open a door of utterance to
his ministers, we also pray that he would give the efficacy
to the word of the Gospel of penetrating the minds of
men, and would open the doors of the hearts in the hearers
of it. So Gregory understood this passage, writing on
Job xxxviii.; where these words are used, *Paul prayed for
a door to be opened by the Lord in the heart of his hearers to
the mysteries of the Gospel. For he had the thunder of the
word, but he prayed for a way to be opened to it; for he knew
that it was not in his own power to give the way to it.* Therefore the Apostle advises wisely, that God should be invoked to open the door of the hearts of men; because the
utterance of preachers obtains this grace from the Spirit,
the enlightening the understanding of the hearer, the in-
fluencing his affections, and, finally, the entering into and
healing the will : Thus truly said Aquinas, Q. 2. qu. 177,
art. 1, where he disputes about the grace of utterance.
And this the Scriptures often teach: for instance, in Acts
xvi. 14, where God is said whilst Paul was preaching, *to
have opened the heart of Lydia, that she might attend to the
things which were spoken;* and Ephes. i. 17, 18, where Paul
prays God that *he would give* the Ephesians *the Spirit of
wisdom and revelation, that the eyes of their understanding,
oculos cordium illorum, might be enlightened,* &c. and in all
the passages where faith is declared to be *the gift of God:*
For by faith the door of the heart is opened for the admission of the Gospel : therefore, he who gives faith opens the
door of the heart to the Gospel. And hence it is that
Augustine, De prædest. sanct. cap. 20, asserts, that this
prayer to which the Apostle excites the Colossians for

* While Christians in the present day have had to deplore the inapplica-
bility of a remark in the last explanatory section, they have lived to hear
the truth and witness the mischief of this latter one with a vengeance.

opening a door of utterance, is *a most evident proof that the beginning of faith itself is the gift of God.*

Instructions.

1. It is not in human power effectually to teach salvation to the hearts of men, but this is to be attributed to Divine power and grace. Thus the Psalmist, cxix. 18, *Open thou mine eyes, that I may behold wondrous things out of thy law;* and beautifully says Augustine, in Epist. Joan. tract. 3, *Think not that any man can learn any thing from man: if he be not within who can teach, our babbling is vain. Teachers and admonitions are as helps from without; he who teaches the heart hath his throne in heaven.* See 4, De doctr. Christ. cap. 16. And Aquin. Quæst. disp. de magist.

2. Many open the door of their ears to the Gospel, who in the mean time have the door of the heart shut and barred. See Isa. vi. 9; Mark viii. 18.

3. Prayer to God for the opening of the heart must always be coupled therefore with the hearing or reading of the word. For there is *little light, whether in the hearing or reading the word, which prayer does not enlighten,* as speaks Parisiensis, De Rhet. Div. cap. 30.

And thus ye have explained, what it is *to open a door of utterance to ministers:* namely, to give them a suitable faculty for performing this office; to give free course to the Gospel, by removing external obstacles; and, finally, to give efficacy to the same, that it may enter and penetrate the hearts of the hearers.

To speak the mystery of Christ for which I am also in bonds.] The Apostle has taught the people that it behoved them to ask from God, to give a door of utterance to ministers, that is, the faculty, liberty, and efficacy of preaching: Now he adds, that they must further ask, that it may be granted them to draw out these gifts into use and practice. For it often happens, that when God has given a remarkable faculty to many, when he has vouchsafed peaceable times for propagating the Gospel, when, in fine, he has made the undertaking of their ministry effectual in the hearts of men, yet, through indulgence and avarice, through envy and vanity, they have at length laid aside

the desire and the care of speaking the mystery of Christ.
Thus Demas forsook the ministry, 2 Tim. iv. 10. They
who become indolent and avaricious, stifle the gifts bestowed upon them, and for the most part cast aside the
office of preaching the Gospel : they who become turbu-
lent or vain, preach to be sure, but yet in such a manner
that these latter sow discords, the former, nonsense, whilst
neither speak the mystery of Christ, that is, urge not the
doctrine of salvation offered to all who believe and repent
through faith in Christ crucified : And this is that mystery
which Paul determined alone to know and to preach, 1
Cor. ii. 2. Ye perceive, therefore, how necessary it is to
pray, that ministers after they are furnished with all necessary helps, should exert these gifts conferred upon them
in preaching the mystery of Christ.

Instructions.

1. We must pray not only that learned ministers may
be given to us, but further, that they may be encouraged
daily by God to discharge their office with alacrity and
constancy : for the declension from labour to indolence is
easy.

2. Ministers often fail in the work of their vocation,
because the people fail in the duty of prayer for them to
God. For most truly said Gregory ; *Because the people are*
evil, utterance is taken away even from good teachers, Hom.
12. upon Ezek. on those words of the prophet, Chap. iii.
26, *I will make thy tongue cleave to the roof of thy mouth,*
and thou shalt be dumb : for they are a rebellious house.

3. Whereas Paul is urgent that they should pray to
God, not that he might obtain the honours or the riches of
this world, but that he might speak and preach the Gospel ; we infer from thence, that nothing is to be so desired
by a pious minister, as the exercise of his ministry ; nothing to be so bewailed, as to be kept back from this
work.

4. When he adds, *to speak the mystery of Christ,* he
shews that they are but little mindful of their office, who
having the faculty and the opportunity of preaching, yet
rather affect to pass off their own wit, than to preach the

mystery of Christ. The people should desire to hear nothing else, the minister should preach nothing else, than the mystery of Christ, that is, the doctrine of salvation obtained through Christ.

For which 1 am in bonds.] These words are inserted by the way, but not unnecessarily : for they have their use, whether you look to the people, or the pastors.

1. They excite the people to love this Apostle, who, for the sake of the edification of the Church sustained so many afflictions.

2. They also stir them up to prayer for his liberation, who shews himself so desirous of their salvation, even in bonds.

3. Lastly, they excite to a true estimation of this treasure, namely, the Gospel; for the sake of which, the Apostle refuses neither bonds nor death itself.

Corollaries.

1. It is the duty of all the godly, not to shew that they are unmindful of ministers, as often as they sustain persecution for the sake of the Gospel; but to help them by their counsel, their assistance, and their prayers.

2. It behoves us to love, yea, to honour ministers afflicted for the sake of piety in a greater degree. For crowns and chains of gold do not more adorn the great ones of the world, than bonds and chains do the ministers of God : forasmuch as to suffer for Christ is the distinguished honour, with which only eminent soldiers are wont to be presented by their General. Thus in Philip. i. 29, we read : *For unto you it is given in the behalf of Christ, not only to believe in him, but also to suffer for his sake.*

Now if you regard Paul himself and other pastors, the aforesaid words have indeed their scope and utility. For they shew that Paul was not deterred from duty by these bonds or other inconveniences, but rather was thereby inflamed with a greater desire of discharging his duty ; for which cause he desires their prayers so ardently.

Corollaries.

1. It behoves ministers to love their office and to value it much, not only when the Gospel flourishes, but when

both they and it are despised and trampled upon by the ungrateful and wicked.

2. They are unworthy men in this spiritual army who are reckoned slothful in it, and weary of their labour; who soon grow tired or ashamed of their function, and bring their ministry to be hated or despised in the world.

3. Hence we infer, that although preachers of the Gospel may often be subdued and afflicted, yet the Gospel itself can never be either bound or extirpated: for as Chrysostom says, *as they cannot enchain the rays of the sun, so neither can they those of the Gospel. The word of God is not bound,* 2 Tim. ii. 9.

Vers 4. *That I may make it manifest, as I ought to speak.*

In the last place, he wished it also to be urged in the prayers of the godly, not only that ministers might and should preach the word, but that they might do it as they ought, that is, in a suitable and the best manner. For in all duties which are rendered to God, not the mere action, but the mode of doing it is even mostly regarded. Hence that saying of Luther (as I conceive) *That adverbs have the force of verbs with God,* that is, that the Mode of doing any thing, which is designated by *adverbs,* makes more for the praise or shame of the doer, than the action itself, which is expressed in that place by the term *verb.* For as in natural things the form is more becoming than the matter, so in morals the manner is more commended than the action itself. Hence Cyprian (De sing. cler.) says, *That is not holy which appears holy, except it be performed in a holy manner.* But to come to the words themselves; this little clause, *as I ought,* embraces many things in its compass: we shall be content with these three.

1. He ought to preach the word of God freely or confidently. I think we must put this in the first place, be-

cause the Apostle, in Ephes. vi. 20, (where these things are accurately described) expressly mentions this παρρησίας, or liberty of speaking. Neither can the legitimate preaching of the word consist without this liberty; because the end of preaching is, *to cast down and subvert every thing that exalts itself against the Divine truth, or will, by the spiritual weapons of the Gospel,* as says the Apostle, 2 Cor. x. 5.

Therefore, we ought not to preach smooth things, and, from a certain cowardly fear, withhold salutary ones : but those errors and sins which especially reign even in and among the greatest, are to be reproved. So God commands, Isa. lviii. 1, *Lift up thy voice like a trumpet, and shew my people their transgressions.* Thus the prophet Hosea freely censured the vices of the princes and priests, Chap. v. 1. Well and piously said Prosper, De vita contempl. lib. 3. cap. 23, *We ought to be more willing to restrain their enmities, who are unwilling to be amended, than to incur the displeasure of God whilst we flatter sinners.* For *they cure and heal those bitters, although they exasperate the passions,* as Clemens rightly remarks in Protrept.

Neither ought we, either in the doctrines themselves, or in the forms and modes of speaking, to accommodate ourselves to the errors of others to the prejudice of known truth : which timorous persons often do against their conscience, especially among those whom they imagine to incline some little towards the Popish errors. But this is opposed to that liberty which is required in Christian ministers; who ought not only to retain the very substance (so to speak) and possession of the truth, but even to defend its remote bounds and confines as it were. Hence the Apostle commands us to retain, not only *sound doctrine,* but also *the form of sound words.* And prudently does Gerson advise theologians *to avoid extraneous terms in the doctrine of truth,* part. 1. De exam. doctr. consid. i. For that oft repeated saying of Jerome is true, *Heresy arises from words inappropriately used.* Thus much of this παρρησια—this liberty of speaking.

2. We ought to preach the word of God constantly and diligently. So says the Apostle, Rom. xii. 7, He *to whom*

the ministry is committed, let him *wait on his ministering;
he who is a teacher, on teaching :* and 2 Tim. iv. 2, *Preach the
word ; be instant in season, out of season,* &c.

We ought not, therefore, to be withdrawn from discharging this office, either on the ground of our own advantage,
or of pleasure and ease ; nay, it ought to be the most desired and fruitful gain to a minister, that by his constant
labour he may win souls to Christ; this ought to be his most
delightful and acceptable pleasure, that by his ministry he
daily renders many pleasing and acceptable to God the
Father by Christ, as the Apostle insinuates, 2 Cor. ii. 2,
Col. i. 28. Some one of the Roman emperors formerly
said, that *an emperor ought to die standing ;* we should no
less boldly declare, that *a minister of the word ought to die
preaching.* Thus much of sedulity or diligence.

3. A minister ought to speak the word of God sincerely
and faithfully. It concerns this fidelity not to tack human
figments to the Divine word, and to thrust those things upon
the people as dogmas necessary to salvation. 1 Cor. xiv. 1.
For the Apostles themselves were dispensers of the mysteries of God, not maintainers of their own inventions ;
they helped, were not lords over the faith of Christians.
And the successors of the Apostles in the ministry, if they
would shew themselves faithful, ought to propagate Apostolic doctrine, not to draw out a new one : *If we or an
angel from heaven preach any other Gospel unto you than that
which we have preached unto you, let him be accursed,* Gal. i. 8.
This was the opinion of all the pious Fathers : who, although they admitted the authority of the Church in determining rites, yet thought that in matters of faith it
should be bound to the rule of the Scriptures alone, and to
add any thing to this rule they thought to be perfidious.
I will add some testimonies from the Fathers, because the
perfidious Tridentines have thrust so many dogmas upon
the Church, and that under an anathema, most of which
(by the confession of Papists themselves) have not a firm
foundation in Scripture. Hilary, lib. 6, De Trin. upon
those words HEAR HIM, says, *I will hear by all means, nor
will I hear any one else except him who hears him, or teaches*

him : and lib. ad Constant. he advises, *not to overstep the immutable constitution of the Apostolic faith, lest our faith should change with time, and not continue that of the unchangeable Gospel.* And Athanasius, De consiliis ; *If you are disciples of the Gospel, walk in the Scriptures : if you wish to invent any thing different to the Scriptures, why do you enter the lists with us, who cannot endure to hear what is not in them ?* Tertullian, De anima, cap. 1, says ; *Who shall reveal what God hath concealed ? It is better to be ignorant with God on our side because he has not revealed, than to flatter ourselves with the false knowledge which the presumption of man imparts.* Jerome, in Titus i. observes ; *Without the authority of the Scriptures prating is not to be credited.* Augustine frequently teaches, *that no one is to be bound to believe human authority without the foundations of Scripture ;* as in Epist. 19 to Jerome, and Epist. 48 to Vincent Donatist. These things may suffice to open the perfidy of the Papists.

It also concerns this fidelity, not to withhold from the people any part of the doctrine of salvation. For God gives this in command to all his ministers ; *Ye shall not add unto the word which I command you, neither shall ye diminish from it,* Deut. iv. 2. *If any man shall take away from the words of the book of this prophecy, God shall take away his part out of the book of life,* Rev. xxii. 19. And Paul on this account, when he endeavours to shew how faithfully he had conducted himself in the ministry, says, *I am pure from the blood of all men,* because he had withheld nothing from them, but *had declared the whole counsel of God,* Acts xx. 26, 27. Here, therefore, the Papists greatly sin, who plead often for the worship of images, the sale of indulgences, and the observance of their traditions ; but concerning justification by faith in the blood of Christ, and other fundamental doctrines of the Gospel, they are more dumb among the people than fish. Those also among ourselves sin, who do not endeavour to imbue their people with a knowledge of all those things (at least summarily) which are necessary to be believed or done for the attainment of salvation.

Lastly, it concerns this fidelity, so to apply doctrines, warnings, and reproofs, that they may be useful to the hearers, not that they may be vain or pernicious. For arguments true and useful in their own nature, sometimes become hurtful, when they are not set forth or applied in their place. And indeed rightly writes Augustine, De bono persever. lib. ii. cap. 21, *It is the character of a treacherous physician so to make up useful medicine, that it shall not do harm, or at least no good.* And in this matter it is usual and almost customary for most ministers to deviate, and not to speak as they ought. For nothing is more usual, than among the great and noble to proclaim smooth things to the people ; among the rude and common people, to bring crimes against the noble, the magistrates, and bishops. For what end, unless that all may be rendered curious and inflated with enquiring into and censuring the faults of others, but stupid and indifferent in judging and correcting their own ?

But we must pray and labour not only to preach the Gospel, but to do it *as it ought* to be done by all ministers, that is, freely, diligently, faithfully. Thus much for the first part of this exhortation.

Vers. 5.

Walk in wisdom toward them that are without, redeeming the time.

The foregoing exhortation to fervent and constant prayer having been explained, we proceed to the other, which excites the Colossians to a wise and circumspect conversation. And in treating this, there are three things to be observed.

1. The duty imposed ; *Walk in wisdom.*
2. The persons towards whom this duty is especially to be discharged ; *toward them that are without.*

3. The certain primary business of this requisite wisdom ; *redeeming the time.*

Walk in wisdom.] To walk in wisdom is to do all things cautiously and circumspectly, as men are wont to do when they perceive that they are beset on every side with difficulties and dangers : for danger is the whetstone of wisdom. Believers in those days lived in the midst of heathens ruling over Christians themselves, and serving idols and dæmons : there was need therefore of remarkable and precise wisdom, so to keep the middle course between Scylla and Charybdis, as neither to confirm the pagans themselves in their idolatries and impiety, nor seem to oppose government and lawful power.

There are then, as it were, four primary reasons of imposing this duty in this place.

1. To look well not to cast any spot of disgrace upon that God whom they worshipped, and the religion which they professed, by living badly. For it is presumed, that servants conform themselves to the disposition of their masters. Hence the pagans, as soon as they saw wickedness committed by Christians, spake against the God himself whom they worshipped, and imputed the wickedness of private men to our religion. This was charged to the adultery of David by the prophet, 2 Sam. xii. 14, *Thou hast given occasion to the enemies of the Lord to blaspheme.* Paul alleges this against the Jews, Rom. ii. 23. *Thou that makest thy boast of the law, through breaking the law dishonourest thou God? For the name of God is blasphemed among the Gentiles through you.* In fine, this Apostle employs this as a special incentive to integrity of life, 1 Tim. vi. 1, *That the name of God and his doctrine be not blasphemed.* Cyprian graphically describes the insult and blasphemy of unbelievers bursting forth on this account; whose words I transcribe out of his book De dupl. martyr. *Behold they who boast that they are redeemed from the tyranny of Satan, who preach that they are dead to the world, nevertheless are overcome by their lusts as well as we, whom they affirm to be yet held under the dominion of Satan. What does baptism profit them ? What does the Holy Spirit profit them,*

*by whose will they say they are governed? Why have
they the Gospel, the Gospel, continually in their mouth, when
their whole life varies from the precepts of the Gospel?* Thus
far Cyprian. Therefore let this primary business of wisdom be, so to walk, that our life may be an ornament, not
a disgrace to the Christian profession.

2. To beware that we do not so gratify the heathen and
ungodly, as to inflict a wound upon our consciences, by
communicating in any manner in their superstitions. For
it is the character of an idle, and moreover of an impious
mind, to be led away from the Divine direction even in the
slightest degree in the business of Religion, and to pass
over to the adversaries' camp : neither is it the conscience
of the Christian only, sinning in this manner, which it
wounds, but it hardens the mind of the pagan also in his
superstition who witnesses it. Hence this communication
with idolaters is strictly prohibited in both Testaments.
Thus in Exodus xxxiv. 15, *Thou shalt not make a covenant
with the inhabitants of the land ; when they go a whoring after
their gods and do sacrifice unto them, and one call thee, thou
shalt not eat of his sacrifice.* In 2 Cor. vi. 15, 16, it is
urged, *What communion hath light with darkness? and what
concord hath Christ with Belial? or what part hath he that
believeth with an infidel? and what agreement hath the temple
of God with idols?* In Ephes. v. 11, we are enjoined to
have no fellowship with the works of darkness.

And here it is worth while to consider the severity of the
antient Church towards those who incurred the least suspicion of committing idolatry, although they had done so
being compelled to it through danger of death. Diocle-
tian, Licinius, Julian, and other idolatrous emperors,
partly by fear, and partly by rewards, endeavoured to induce Christians to offer incense to their idols ; as may be
seen in Eusebius, Hist. eccl. lib. 8. cap. 3, and De vita
Constant. lib. 1, cap. 47; and in Nazianzen, Orat. 1. in
Julian. It might not seem perhaps of great moment to any
one, to throw a few grains of incense into the fire, at the
command of the emperor : but because this was done in
honour of the idols, severe decisions were passed against

them by the Church; which may be seen in the eight first canons of the Council of Ancyra.* Tom. i. Concil. p. 293. How great a wound they inflicted upon their consciences who did this, may be gathered from that narration which we have in Nazianzen, Orat. 1, in Julian. *Some Christians were led by the gifts and subtilty of Julian to offer incense; but being presently chastised by others, and brought to penitence, they returned to the emperor; they cried out, that their hand had sinned, not their mind, that they were Christians; they insisted that he would lop off the hands which they held out to offer the incense, and that (if he wished) he might cast them into that fire which they had polluted by their idolatry.* This perturbation of conscience follows every act of idolatry in the godly : in the ungodly and carnal for the most part, obduracy succeeds, and at length an entire falling away to idolatry. Let this, therefore, be the second business of walking wisely, carefully to beware not to bring guilt upon the conscience by any idolatrous communication.

3. The third is, that they should not rashly endeavour by external force to abolish idols or idolatrous rites, since they had neither the call nor the power of aiming at such things : for this is not *to walk in wisdom,* but to act madly without any reason. Indeed, a wise man will attempt to throw down idols placed in the hearts of pagans, sooner than in temples; if he takes a contrary course, he seems to perform not so much a work of wisdom as of sacrilege. God himself prescribed this wisdom to all the godly, in Deut. vii. 1, 5; *When the land shall be given into your power,......ye shall destroy their altars, and break down their images, and cut down their groves,* &c. Hence says Augustine, De verb. Dom. secun. Matt. serm. 6, *It is the part of furious Circumcelliones† to be cruel where they have not the*

---

* This Council was held in the year 314.

† These were a set of men who sprang up amidst the religious commotions occasioned by the heresies that infected the Church in the fourth Century, especially that of the Donatists. " These unhappy commotions," says Mosheim, Vol. i. p. 406, " gave rise to a horrible confederacy of desperate ruffians, who passed under the name of Circumcelliones. This fu-

power. WHEN THE LAND SHALL BE GIVEN INTO YOUR POWER, YE SHALL DESTROY THEIR ALTARS. *Where the power is not given us, ye shall not do it. For we do it before we have thrown down the idols in their hearts.* Therefore, God requires this from them who are under the power of idolaters, namely, that they should not pollute themselves with the superstitious worship of the idols; but he does not require, that they should attempt to hinder or abolish their idolatry by external force. *Ye shall see in Babylon gods of silver, and of gold, and of wood borne upon shoulders. Beware therefore that ye be in no wise like to strangers, neither be ye afraid of them, when ye see the multitude before them and behind them, worshipping them: but say ye in your hearts, O Lord, we must worship thee.* Baruch vi. 4, &c. in that Epistle which is attributed to Jeremy. Finally, I add the example of Paul; who, when he walked among the numerous idols of Athens, did not attempt to pull them down with his hands, or to shatter them with hammers, but with reason and argument. See Acts xvii. 16, &c. to the end.

4. The last business of wisdom is, not to refuse even to unbelievers and pagans, the obedience due to them, whether by Divine or human right. Christ commanded this to all his disciples, Matt. xxii. 21, *Render unto Cæsar the things which are Cæsar's, and unto God the things that are*

---

rious, fearless, and bloody set of men, composed of the rough and savage populace, who embraced the party of the Donatists, maintained their cause by the force of arms, and overrunning all Africa, filled that province with slaughter and rapine, and committed the most enormous acts of perfidy and cruelty against the followers of Cæcilianus. This outrageous multitude, whom no prospect of sufferings could terrify, and who, upon urgent occasions, faced death itself with the most audacious temerity, contributed to render the sect of the Donatists an object of the utmost abhorrence; though it cannot be made appear, from any records of undoubted authority, that the bishops of that faction, those, at least, who had any reputation for piety and virtue, either approved the proceedings, or stirred up the violence of this odious rabble." Africa was the theatre of the most bloody scenes, owing to the excesses of these wretches during a great part of Constantine's life. For a further account of the Circumcelliones the learned reader may consult Witsii Miscellanea Sacra, Vol. i. pp. 607—10, 4to. Lug. Bat. 1736.

God's. Paul preached this, Rom. xiii. 1, *Let every soul be subject unto the higher powers.* Peter himself advised to this, 1 Epis. ii. 13, *Submit yourselves to every ordinance of man for the Lord's sake; whether it be to the king, as supreme, or unto governors as sent by him,* &c. But all these concerning whom Christ, Paul, and Peter spake, were in that age heathens and idolaters. It is, therefore, the duty of a Christian walking wisely, even to honour heathens and unbelievers invested with power, to pay them tribute, to yield them obedience, and to do all those other things to which they are bound by laws not opposing the Divine laws. So Augustine, Quæst. V. et N. Test. quæst. 35, says, *The king is always to be honoured, if not for his own sake, yet on account of his station;* and De civit. Dei, lib. 5, cap. 19, *The power of ruling is not given to the wicked, unless by the Providence of the Most High God, when he judges human affairs worthy of such masters;* and cap. 21, *He who gave the kingdom to a Christian Constantine, he also gave it to an apostate Julian.* If even he gave the kingdom to an unbeliever, men may not withhold their obedience on account of infidelity.

2. Now, in the second place, we must speak more distinctly concerning the persons towards whom it behoves us to exercise this wisdom. And they are called *them that are without.* Under which title he denotes all not as yet admitted into the Church; as also in 1 Cor. v. 12, *What have I to do to judge them that are without?* For the Church is as a certain spiritual house: hence they who have enlisted their names under Christ, are accounted the *servants of faith:* they who have not done so, are judged to be *strangers* and *foreigners* from this family of the faithful.* Wisdom is indeed to be exhibited in our walk towards our brethren, and in like manner towards all men ; but special mention is made of them that are without in this place, because there is special difficulty in that respect. And the Apostle designated (as it is said) heathens and pagans by this word, on account of the circumstances

---

* See Gal. iv. ; Ephes. ii. 12, 13.

of those times : but inasmuch as we do not now live among
them, we must use this wisdom towards heretics, towards
the profane, and atheists, who usurp indeed the name of
Christians, but nevertheless are altogether strangers to the
true and living Church of Christ. These persons, then,
are to be considered, either as they preside over or as they
are subject to true and orthodox Christians.

When they preside and govern, we shall walk wisely towards them if we shall have performed those things which
were explained above by us.

When they are subject, and yet are frequently conversant among the orthodox, lest they should be thorns in
their eyes, there is need of manifold wisdom, both in public magistrates, and in private Christians.

1. The magistrate must exercise his wisdom towards
the learned, who are as standard-bearers and leaders of the
heretical faction. And it consists in this, to take care
most diligently not to hold conversations upon religion
with the more unlearned and simple orthodox : for although
they may have the *head of the dove,* yet all have *the tail of
the scorpion,* as says Bernard, Epist. 196. There is the
same reason concerning the books of heretics ; from the
reading of which the unlearned and unstable are to be restrained, lest they should be corrupted by the leaven of
their errors and heresies. See Gal. v. 9.

2. It pertains to this wisdom of the magistrate, to take
care that heretics, the unlearned, and those seduced by
others, be mildly and wisely informed and instructed by
learned and pious men, who shall be judged fit for this
business.

3. It behoves a pious and wise magistrate to employ
a double care towards all these strangers promiscuously :

First, to compel them by fines and punishments, at least
to attend the outward means of religion, namely, to be
present at prayers, and preaching, and the celebration of
the sacraments. Augustine frequently teaches this: In
Epist. 48, he confesses that he was of a contrary opinion,
but afterwards found by experience, that the terror of the
laws and medicinal trouble are very necessary to the de-

praved and indifferent minds of many. You may find more
in Epist. 50, and Epist. 204, ad Donat. et contra 2 Epist.
Gaudentii, lib. 2. cap. 17. This is the first care. Secondly, that they may not be permitted to exercise superstitious rites, both contrary and repugnant to true religion.
For in this kings serve God as kings, if by virtue of their
royal power they command good things, and prohibit the bad,
not only things which pertain to human society, but also those
which pertain to Divine Religion, says Augustine, Contra
Cresconium grammat. lib. 3, cap. 51. Augustine has also
similar remarks in Epist. 50. Thus much concerning the
wisdom of the magistrate towards heretics and all who are
without the pale of the orthodox church.

As to what belongs to private persons, especially the
rude and unlearned ; this is their chief wisdom towards
them that are without, to converse with them so far only
as natural, moral, or civil right requires ; not to enter into
any intimate friendship with them, not to desire any alliance, as many are wont. For wisely says Tertullian, advers.
Valentin., *As vices bred elsewhere are wont to put forth and*
infuse their poison into members that are near to them ; so the
vices of the wicked are derived to those who associate with them.
Hence to mix in marriage, or enter into friendship with idolaters, and to cleave to their errors, are judged as connected and consequences to one another by God himself,
Josh. xxiii. 12. Thus much as to the persons towards
whom this wisdom is to be exercised.

Redeeming the time.] In these words is expressed a particular and certain special business of this wisdom : concerning which a few things are to be added separately.
Redeeming the time, Καιρὸν ἐξαγοράζεσθαι, is nothing else
than to make the most difficult and inconvenient seasons,
and adverse to our salvation, advantageous and oppor-
tune. Such were the times when Christians lived in the
midst of the cruelties of idolaters; such also are now,
when we live in the midst of the seductions of heretics,
and profane scoffers of God and Religion. How, then,
shall the godly be able to find *a seasonable time* in this *un-*
seasonable one? No otherwise, truly, than by redeeming

this opportunity of serving God, and consulting their salvation, which so many disadvantages seemed to oppose. But it is redeemed for the most part at a great price :

Sometimes with the contempt and rejection of all honours and secular pleasures. For always a difficulty, ofttimes even ignominy and punishment, deter Christians from the path of salvation. Of this unseasonableness he makes a seasonable time to himself who, for the sake of religion and righteousness, thinks it a noble thing to despise the pleasures and delights of the world, to sustain contumely and punishments : this the Apostles and martyrs did in the primitive Church. See Acts v. 41.

Sometimes by the renouncing riches and all external good. For it was the custom of tyrants to strip and spoil the true worshippers of God of all their goods. As often as this happened, it allowed them to retain only the life of faith, all things else were exposed to their will ; just as travellers were wont to give all their stores to robbers, and only bargained for their life. This Augustine has taught us, in Epist. ad Rom. propos. 74, *We must not resist magistrates, although they should unjustly take from us all our temporal goods. Ye took joyfully the spoiling of your goods,* Heb. x. 34.

Sometimes at the expence of this life. For frequently the fierceness of persecution was so great, that not only was it a penal, but a capital crime to embrace the true Religion. Such times there were to Christians under many heathen emperors ; Such also were the times of Mary to us ; there are such times still to all the orthodox and godly under the empire of the Scarlet Whore. They who fall on these bitter times, might make blessed times of them, namely, by redeeming the occasion and opportunity of glorifying God by the voluntary pouring forth of their blood. See Acts xxi. 13. In a word; he is said *to redeem the time,* who submits himself to conditions however unjust (so that they are not unlawful) that he may cleave to God, and retain saving faith and a good conscience.

Instructions.

1. Such is the power of ungodliness and the fury of the

devil, that the godly can indeed only filch a little of the time which they consecrate to God and their salvation, unless it be redeemed for the most part at a great cost.

2. No times, however, are so adverse to the godly, and hindered by such difficulties, but the wise, who know how to redeem time, can find opportunity for glorifying God and promoting their salvation.

3. It is the part of a wise and magnanimous Christian, not to be deterred from faith or piety because the days are evil; but rather to be excited by these evils and disadvantages to constancy in the Divine worship, and the profession of the true faith : For to every business of this life, one time is convenient, another inconvenient; but for promoting the business of the future life, there is no time which may not be convenient to one who walks wisely.

Vers. 6.

Let your speech be alway with grace, seasoned with salt,
that ye may know how ye ought to answer every man.

The exhortation that preceded was to perseverance in prayer, and wisdom in conversation : This last member of the Apostolic exhortation excites to the use of discretion in speaking.

There are two members of this verse : 1. The exhortation itself; *Let your speech be alway with grace, seasoned with salt :* 2. The amplification of the exhortation ; *that ye may know how ye ought to answer every man.*

In the exhortation itself these three things must be considered : What, How long, In what manner.

1. If it be inquired what that is concerning which the Apostle labours so much in directing and instructing us ; It is *Your speech.*] This it is which he endeavours to direct as it were to a certain rule By which word, although

he seems especially to have respect to that converse which is held with infidels and pagans, yet he has respect also generally to whatever discourse Christians have with one another.

Instructions.

1. It is not sufficient to order our life and actions well, unless we at the same time regulate our words and discourse religiously. For Christians must not only live, but speak according to rule. *If any one among you seem to be religious and bridleth not his tongue, that man's religion is vain,* Jas. i. 26. Therefore away with that excuse plainly of a licentious poet,

We have a wanton escutcheon, but a chaste life.

Neither the life nor conversation is allowed to be indecorous in pious men.

2. Not only is there danger of guilt and damnation from wicked actions, but it is also incurred from wicked speeches ; because we are bound to useful speech and seasoned with grace; as shall be shewn presently. And hence the Apostle calls a wicked tongue *an unruly evil,* and declares that it is *full of deadly poison,* Jas. iii. 8. *Death and life are in the power of the tongue,* says Solomon, Prov. xviii. 21. Chrysostom, Hom. 2, in Matt. observes, that most men bring injury upon themselves by their tongues. And Cyprian, lib. 1, epist. 3, notes, that among all the parts of that rich man concerning whom we have a parable in Luke xvi., the mouth and the tongue suffered the most bitter torments, *because he had sinned more with the tongue and the mouth.*

3. It is the mark of a perfect and complete Christian, to manage his discourse and his tongue rightly. Hence, after the injunction concerning perpetual prayer and a wise conversation, the Apostle subjoins, in the last place, as the height of perfection, the government of the tongue : For, says he, *if any one offend not in word, the same is a perfect man, and able also to bridle the whole body.* James iii. 2. Ye thus have what it is which is to be regulated.

But for how long must we employ this care of our speech?

2. *Always,* says the Apostle. Not that we must always speak ; for there is a time to be silent : but that when we speak, we must always take care to speak as we ought.

Here, therefore, they are to be reproved, who only speak soberly and religiously before ministers or other grave men, or when they suffer from disease ; whilst in their banquets or private conversations, they think they may make use, as by a peculiar privilege, of any obscene or foolish expressions.

3. *Let it be with grace seasoned with salt.*] How our speech is to be rightly regulated, is now, in the third place, shewn ; namely, if it be in a manner seasoned with grace as with salt. Hence Tremellius translates the passage a little more freely, *Let your speech be with grace, and as if it were seasoned with salt.* By *grace* and *salt* in this place we must understand that pious and religious prudence flowing from the Holy Spirit, which first directs the heart, then the tongue of the man to utter speech as he ought. This gift of grace is likened to salt on two accounts :

1. Because as salt extracts the noxious humours from meats, and banishes all putrescency from them : so the grace of heavenly wisdom represses idle and useless language in the discourse of the godly ; and it altogether removes and takes away from them wicked, obscene, and impure language. *Let no corrupt communication proceed out of your mouth,* &c. Ephes. iv. 29.

2. Because as salt not only dries up the superfluous and noxious humours of meats, but makes them much more fit to be digested, and wholesome for nutriment ; so the salt of wisdom operates, not only that the discourse of Christians be not idle or noxious, but becomes more suited and useful for edification. For what is said of Solomon, Eccl. xii. 10, may be extended in a degree to all the godly, *He sought to find out acceptable words, and that which was written was upright, even words of truth.*

Instructions.

1. No discourse of Christians ought to be insipid : but

that is deemed as unsavoury, which is either hurtful, or no ways profitable.

2. It is not sufficient to season our speech with any kind of salt, but we must do it with the salt of wisdom. Therefore let that salt of satirical virulence be discarded, with which it is too much the custom with the petulant to season, or rather to embellish their conversation. Neither let us very much indulge those jocular saltings with which men of politer wit are delighted in a wonderful manner. For although I would not decide with Ambrose, that *all raillery is abhorrent to ecclesiastical rule,* and is, on that account, to be declined; yet I would affirm that the commendation of a Christian does not depend upon it; and therefore he must labour only for the salt of wisdom in his conversation.

3. They are altogether destitute of this salt, to whom it is customary and pleasant to blab out words corrupting to the mind or the affections of the hearers: for it is the property of salt to restrain corruption, not to produce it.

They corrupt the mind and judgment, who disseminate heretical, false, or ambiguous discourses, either inclining to Popery, or any other heresy. For words of this kind either impel the unskilful and unstable into error, or at least leave them doubtful in the faith.

They corrupt the will and affections, who belch forth obscene, profane, or irreligious sayings; whereby atheistical men attempt nothing else than to tear away from others also by this contagious discourse, the piety and fear of God which they themselves have cast off. But all these have not salt in themselves; but consumption, putridity, and poison, which they labour to infuse into all others.

Thus much concerning the exhortation itself; about which we have spoken the more briefly, because we have treated the same matter at the eighth verse of the preceding chapter.

That ye may know how ye ought to answer every man.] In these words he amplifies the aforesaid exhortation, by indicating the cause for sound and discreet speech, and the use of it.

That ye may know] Tremellius translates it, *And know ye.* In which words the Apostle shews the very cause or fountain of sound speech, namely, the knowledge drawn from the word of God, laid up in the mind of the speaker. For sound speech does not produce our knowledge; but knowledge causes us to use sound speech. Therefore, although in the order of nature knowledge precedes discreet speech; yet in the order of cognizance and manifestation, speech precedes and indicates knowledge. And hence it is that the Apostle in the former passage wrote, *Let your speech be seasoned with salt,* and then subjoined, *that ye may know,* &c. that is, that thence it may be manifest that ye are endowed with that distinguished knowledge which becomes Christians.

How ye ought to answer every man.] In these last words we have the fruit, the use, or application, as well of knowledge, as of wise speech; namely, *that it may be answered to every one even as it is fit:* That is, to unbelievers and pagans requiring a reason of our faith, constantly and prudently, lest we would expose our religion to ridicule; to heretics impugning the true faith, vigorously and bravely, that we may not suffer even the least particle of Divine truth to be overthrown; that we may impart saving doctrine to the ignorant, and to those enquiring after the ways of the Lord; that we may administer comfort to the afflicted, and those groaning under the burden of a wounded conscience; in a word, that to all, desiring our discourse on any account whatever, we may speak wisely and with profit.

Corollaries.

1. All Christians (under whatever title, whether Clerics or laics) must endeavour to obtain that knowledge of religion and divine things, which may guide them to render a reason of their faith. *Be ready always to give an answer to every man that asketh you a reason of the hope that is in you,* &c. 1 Pet. iii. 15.

2. Not only is this required from well instructed Christians; but even that they may abound in knowledge and speech, if not in more artificial, at least fruitful, and ac-

commodated also to the edification and various advantages of the brethren. This Paul extolled in the Corinthians, 2 Epis. viii. 7, *Ye abound in every thing, in faith, in utterance, in knowledge,* &c.

3. They are deservedly to be blamed, who do not apply themselves to sacred learning, which alone is wont to imbue the minds of men with this art of speaking wisely. For that salt is hidden in the word : and thence all wisdom is to be derived, which may be salutary either to the possessor himself, or to others. Hence the Apostles, being instructed in the Divine word, are called *The Salt of the earth,* Matt. v. 13. In which form of speaking, that which is the property of the Divine Word, is transferred to the persons to whom the administration of it is committed.

4. We may hence infer the cause, why almost all places every where echo with silly and insipid discourses; namely, because most men are destitute of this salt of the doctrine of the gospel, and of spiritual wisdom, whence every well seasoned speech flows.

5. Hence you will perceive with how great wickedness the Romanists surround themselves, who take away the salt of the Divine word from the people : for by that same act they impose upon themselves the necessity as it were both of thinking and speaking foolishly, to whom God gives it in command both to acquire knowledge and speech seasoned with salt to promote the advantage of their neighbours. But to those to whom either the health or the utility of their brethren is a matter of care, it behoves them to season both their mind and their speech with the salt of the Divine word : for *every one is bound to know that,* says Gerson, part. 2. in Regul. moral., *without the knowledge of which he cannot fulfill the command, and avoid sin.*

And thus we have dispatched the three-fold apostolical exhortation. Now we must pass on from the exhortations to the second part of this Chapter, namely, to the Apostolic encomiums and commendations which he bestows upon certain distinguished men.

Vers. 7, 8, 9.

*All my state shall Tychicus declare unto you, who is a be-
loved brother, and a faithful minister, and fellow-
servant in the Lord.*

• *Whom I have sent unto you for the same purpose, that he
might know your estate, and comfort your hearts;*

*With Onesimus, a faithful and beloved brother, who is one
of you. They shall make known unto you all things
which are done here.*

The Apostle proposed some very useful and very necessary exhortations in the six foregoing verses: Those having been explained, there now remains only the commendations of certain particular men, and salutations from
sundry persons. Perhaps these matters may seem of less
moment to some persons; but yet they are not to be made
light of: For that rule of Chrysostom is to be approved by
all, *Proper Names, although they may be recited alone in the
Scriptures are not to be despised,* Hom. 4. in Gen. *For like
as if any one should find dry herbs, having neither fragrance
nor colour that was pleasing, disposed in the officinal of the
physician; however mean may be their appearance, will yet
guess that some virtue and remedy is concealed in them: so in
the pharmacopœia of the Scriptures, if any thing occurs which
at first sight may seem to be despised by us, yet may we determine of a certainty, that there is some spiritual utility to be
found in it; because Christ, the Physician of souls, we may
suppose, would place nothing insignificant or useless in his pharmacopœia,* as Origen has admirably said, in Hom. 8, in
Levit. Let us now come to the point, and discuss in their
order, as well these commendations as the salutations following them.

    In these three verses, then, which we have recited, is
contained the second division of this Chapter; which is

employed to commend two distinguished men, by whom
this Epistle was transmitted to the Colossians. Now three
things are to be considered in these as it were commendatory letters :

1. The persons sent; namely, Tychicus, and Onesimus.

2. The causes of the
   mission ;
   $\left\{\begin{array}{l}\end{array}\right.$
   1. To make the affairs of Paul
      known to the Colossians.
   2. To know and look into the
      affairs of the Colossians.
   3. To comfort the hearts of the
      Colossians.

3. The commendations of the Missionaries :

   Of Tychicus; which are opened in the 7th
   verse.

   Of Onesimus ; which are opened in the 9th
   verse.

We must begin with the persons; and first with Tychicus : He was of Asiatic origin, and clave to Paul as his
companion in passing through Macedonia, and afterwards
preceding him, he awaited him at Troas, Acts xx. 4. In
the Synopsis which passes under the name of Dorotheus,*
he is said to have been the first Bishop of Chalcedon.
But the credit of this must rest with this author. It is
certain and clear, that he was a pious man, and endowed
with remarkable gifts, and employed the same to propagate the Gospel and edify the Church.

---

* DOROTHEUS flourished A.D. 303, according to Cave (Hist. Lit. Tom.
1, pp. 163. Ed. 1740), a very obscure person, of whom, therefore, the
more is said. And first, he is not some other persons who have borne his
name. Then the Roman and Greek martyrologies have decorated him with
more honours than he deserves. He is said to have written many Ecclesiastical Commentaries, and particularly *Synopsis de vita et morte Prophetarum,
Apostolorum, et Discipulorum Domini,* contained in the *Bibliotheca Patrum ;* of
the fabulosity of which Cave was convinced by a Greek fragment sent him
by his friend Dodwell, and which is given at length, occupying five pages,
with about two of commentary by the Literary Historian. The writer of
the fragment asserts that Dorotheus wrote in Latin, and that *he* translated
the work into Greek. Cave thinks it wonderfully probable, that a Greek,
and a Bishop of Tyre, in Phœnicia, should write in Latin ! In fact, it
almost appears, that, although a Latin and a Greek work are extant and
visible enough, the alleged author may be classed with the *Entia,* not
Rationis, but *Imaginationis.*

As to the causes of his mission; the first is gathered
from these words, *All my state shall he declare unto you :*
that is, he shall shew you all things about which you
ought to be informed. Paul was separated from the Colossians by a long distance, inasmuch as he was imprisoned at Rome, and, as it were, destined to the lions : On
account of their love, therefore, towards such an Apostle,
they desired doubtless to know how he did, what sufferings
he was labouring under, what danger threatened him, what
hope of deliverance there appeared, and other things of
the kind. Therefore, willing to satisfy this so becoming a
desire, he deputed Tychicus and Onesimus, who might
make all these things known to them.

Hence we may observe,

1. It becomes well-instructed Christians to desire a
knowledge of the prosperity or misfortune of their pastors, and to be kindly affected, and even ready to render
them assistance when occasion arises.

2. Pious pastors, even afflicted and imprisoned, so
conduct themselves, that it may be useful to the Church
to know what they do. So this great Apostle cast into
prison at Rome, and bound in chains, notwithstanding
*received all that came in unto him, preaching to them the king-
dom of God, and teaching those things which concern the Lord
Jesus Christ with all confidence,* Acts xxviii. 30, 31. It is no
wonder, therefore, if he who could do such remarkable
things under his confinement, should wish his affairs to be
known to them.

3. A Christian people, therefore, is to be blamed, to
whom it is no pleasure to see the prosperity of their ministers ; neither feel any sympathy in looking upon their miseries : who only care about their own things, but with
regard to their ministers, what they want or what they
suffer, they are no ways solicitous about. The Colossians
were otherwise minded, who earnestly desired to know all
Paul's concerns.

4. Ministers also are to be reprehended, who do not so
conduct themselves in every condition and fortune, that it
may be well for their people to know what they do and
what they suffer. Of this class are they, who in pros-

perity give themselves to ease; but under the cross despond
through indolence of mind, or through impatience rage
against God and men, and in the mean time are intent
upon no good thing. It is not to be desired that all the
affairs of these men should be made known to the people,
as what would be rather a scandal to them than a comfort.

That he might know your estate.] This was the second
cause why Paul would send Tychicus to the Colossians.
He desired not only that they might be informed about
his state, but that himself also should be informed about
their state. But the Apostle had respect most especially
to the things pertaining to their spiritual state: For he
desired to know how they were rooted in the faith, how
they agreed together in love, how they observed discipline
and order, and, in one word, how they adhered to their
Christian profession. This knowledge is very necessary to
the pastor: because the state of the people being little
understood, he cannot apply to them fitly and suitably
either his doctrine, or reproof, or consolation; as a physician cannot his medicines, unless he first inquire into
the state of the sick man.

Many things are here to be observed and imitated by us
ministers.

1. Let us observe the paternal love of Paul towards the
people; who, imprisoned and appointed to death, was yet
more solicitous about the affairs of others than about
his own life. If he cared less for his own life than the
spiritual edification of a Christian people, then it behoves
us to prefer the public good of the Church which we serve
to our own pleasure and private advantage.

2. Let us observe the diligence of the Apostle, who
was not satisfied to disseminate the Gospel by his preaching and by his letters, but thought it even his duty to inquire into the life and conversation of men, and, as much
as he could, to furnish himself with particular knowledge
of each individual. Thus every minister ought to labour,
not only in feeding his flock, but also in inquiring into and
discerning their manners.

3. Hence let us observe the wisdom of Paul: For he

undoubtedly makes the Colossians much more solicitous about regulating their life properly, whilst he intimates that he was so solicitous to know the same. There is no doubt but even amongst ourselves, all in whom there is the least spark of shame and honesty, would live more holily, if pastors, according to their office, would endeavour to know the manners and course of life of individuals.

And comfort your hearts.] This is the last cause whereby Paul was impelled to send Tychicus. They needed consolation in a twofold respect :

1. Because, as it is very likely, they were much grieved on account of Paul's being imprisoned, of whose death, by the well known cruelty of Nero, who then ruled, they could not but daily expect the sad tidings. Tychicus, therefore, relieves the minds of the Colossians, by relating to them that this eminent Apostle not only lived and was well, but even preached the Gospel freely in his bonds.

2. They needed consolation in respect of their own infirmity : For it is too much the case to shrink from a profession of the Gospel through impending danger. For the devil and the flesh, impatient of the cross, are wont to suggest to the minds of men, that it is folly to embrace that doctrine which kings endeavour to extirpate by punishment, which the wise men of the world endeavour to subvert by various schemes. The Apostle, therefore, in order to meet this evil, and confirm them in the faith against persecutors and against seducers, sent Tychicus to establish them, and exhort them that they should not be moved by these afflictions, but be ready after his example to suffer any thing for the Gospel. See 1 Thess. iii. 2.

Hence we may learn,

1. To acknowledge the inbred evil of our nature, which causes us all to be dejected in mind as often as we perceive the cross and affliction to threaten the profession of the Gospel : for we are as that stony ground, which *receives the word with joy, but when tribulation ariseth for the word's sake is forthwith offended,* Matt. xiii. 20. Therefore, it behoves us to withstand this evil, to lift up our hearts, and to confirm them by spiritual comforts. For *this our light*

*affliction which is but for a moment, worketh for us a far more
exceeding and eternal weight of glory,* 2 Cor. iv. 17.

2. A minister of the word ought not only to shew himself a pattern of constancy and fortitude in suffering, but
also to animate and strengthen others by building up,
consoling, and preparing them by all means to endure the
cross with joy. Thus, in time past, Tertullian, Cyprian,
and other pious pastors, for this end armed the Christians
to submit to martyrdom by their writings : so in the days
of Mary, our ministers of the Gospel consoled the hearts
of their people by letters and exhortations. They, therefore, are wholly unmindful of their duty, who despise
their brethren groaning and labouring under any cross
whatever, whose hearts they ought to comfort and strength-
en. Thus much for the causes of the mission.

*A beloved brother, and faithful minister, and fellow-servant
in the Lord.*] Ye have heard the causes of the mission :
Now let us come to the commendation of the person sent,
whom the Apostle, not only in this place, but also in
Ephes. vi. 21, honours with the same remarkable commendations. As to the present encomium, it consists of
three members : which we shall notice the more briefly,
because we have spoken in the seventh verse of the first
Chapter concerning them.

1. He calls Tychicus *a beloved brother.*] All Christians
were wont mutually to call one another by this name, according to the saying of Christ, Matt. xxiii. 8, *One is your
Master, and all ye are brethren.* But yet it is to be supposed
that Paul did it in this place, not only because of the
common custom, but because of his singular love towards
this man deservedly most beloved. Hence learn,

1. That brotherly love among all Christians ought to
be strong, but especially among ministers of the word. *I
command you that ye love one another,* said our Lord. John
xv. 17. Hence says Tertullian, De patient. *Love is the
chiefest bond of faith, and the treasure of the Christian name.*

2. They who bear hatred or envy towards their brethren, especially towards fellow ministers, possess nothing
of the candour of Paul, nothing of Christian charity : for

that saying of the Apostle, 1 Thess. iv. 9, agrees in all the truly pious, *Concerning brotherly love ye have no need that I write unto you,* &c.

2. He is called *a faithful minister.*] A double eulogy is contained in these two words : he is extolled from his honourable office, because *a minister ;* and from the faithful execution of the same, because *faithful* in the ministry.

A Minister] namely, of Christ : for he speaks not of any abject ministry, but of the ministry of the Gospel. He is therefore named *a minister* for the sake of honour. Hence learn,

1. That they are not to be reckoned among Christians who despise men, otherwise not at all to be despised, on the sole ground that they have undertaken the office of a minister. For if to be a Christian, is a glorious thing ; then to be among Christians the leader of a faithful people, the interpreter of the Divine will, a preacher of heavenly things, is by far the most glorious. Hence Paul, in 1 Tim. v. 17, assigned a double honour to the ministers of the word, *let them be especially counted worthy of double honour who labour in the word and doctrine.*

2. That they are foolishly modest and unworthy the ministry, whom the profane folly of others either causes to be ashamed or to repent of so honourable a vocation. Paul was otherwise animated, who thought that he honoured Tychicus by this title of *a Minister,* and commended him to the Colossians ; and who professed concerning himself, *I am not ashamed of the Gospel,* &c. Rom. i. 16. And Gregory Nazianzen, Orat. 7, says, that *it is more excellent to serve God in the sacerdotal office, than to bear the pre-eminence among earthly kings.*

3. That they also even sin on the opposite side, who endeavour to transform this spiritual ministry into a temporal empire. This the Romanists do, who constitute their Pope, not a minister of the Gospel, but a temporal monarch of the whole world. Thus much of the office.

Faithful.] This adds much to the commendation of Tychicus. For inasmuch as the ministry itself is to be ho-

noured, although in a wicked man ; yet dishonesty or infidelity in the discharge of this ministry, is wont, not only
to alienate our minds from the minister himself, but to
cast a stain even upon the ministry also.

This fidelity, which is commended in Tychicus, consists
in two things : in that he always exercised his ministry
both to promote the glory of God, and to advance the edification of the people of Christ.

Hence we are instructed,

1. They thrust themselves in vain into the ministry,
who in discharging the same do not prove themselves faithful ; nay, it is pernicious both to their own welfare and that
of others : neither shall they receive the prize destined to
teachers, but *that woe* directed against those who preach
not the gospel.

2. It behoves pious Christians to reverence their ministers, of whatever sort they are ; but highly to love the
faithful, and to bear them in their eye (as they say), yea
(as the Galatians did Paul) *to receive them as angels, or as
Christ Jesus himself,* Gal. iv. 14.

And fellow-servant in the Lord.] This is the last particular of the eulogium of this man. Now he calls him *a fellow-servant in the Lord,* because both served the same Lord,
namely Christ, by the preaching of the Gospel : they
therefore could not lightly esteem Tychicus, among whom
Paul was in honour, who acknowledged him for his fellow-
servant.

Observations.

1. It is the common duty of all ministers, to honour
their companions in the same ministry as much as they
can, and to render them well-pleasing and acceptable to
their people ; not to excite hatred towards them.

2. It becomes those who are appointed to a more eminent station, not to despise inferior ministers, but to esteem and treat them as their fellow-servants. Thus Paul
from his Apostolic eminence does not despise or depress
Tychicus, much inferior to himself ; but rather exalts him,
and puts him as his equal, by calling him *a fellow-servant.*

3. The Roman pontiff is not the true successor either

of Paul or of Peter,* who not only would rule over all the Clergy and the whole Christian world, but even in a regal manner over kings and emperors themselves : so far is he from treating his fellow-ministers as fellow-servants.—Thus far concerning Tychicus.

> Vers. 9.   *With Onesimus, a faithful and beloved brother, who is one of you. They shall make known unto you all things which are done here.*

The commendations of Tychicus being explained, the Apostle proceeds to his testimony also to Onesimus as equally to be honoured : For when, indeed, each was joined in the embassy, he thought each should also be joined in the commendation.

As to the person himself ; This Onesimus (as most conjecture) was the same whom Paul had made a true Christian of a runaway slave.   And hence it is that in the Epistle to Philemon, vers. 10, he glories that *he had begotten him in his bonds.*   Whence Jerome, writing against the errors of John of Jerusalem, says, *We read that Onesimus, renewed amidst the bonds of Paul, was taken from a slave to be a deacon.*

Observations.

1.   We should despise no one for his former misdeeds, after he shall have come to his right mind.   This Onesimus was once contemptible, useless, and a runaway slave ;

---

* The Second Section of the Decrees concerning Prohibited Books in the Index Romanum of Benedict XIV. art. 11. p. xxxiv. contains a particular condemnation of *persons* who shall dare to maintain that St. Peter and St. Paul are to be united as heads of the Roman Church, without subjecting the *latter* to St. Peter ; notwithstanding the testimonies of the Fathers, as Irenæus, Epiphanius, and Chrysostom, and of the historian Eusebius, to their being joint-founders of the Italian Church.   The sensitive jealousy of the Apostate See upon this head is curious and significant.

but after that he yielded himself to Christ, he did not become despised of Paul, but he sends him to the Colossians with Tychicus an illustrious man, upon the same occasion of honour.

2. They therefore sin grievously, who love rather to reproach the truly converted for their former evils, than to congratulate them upon renewed health. But here we ought to imitate God himself, who is wont to estimate the dignity or utility of men, not from their past condition which they shall have cast off, but from the present which they have put on. See Ezek. xviii. 22. Thus much of the person.

He sends this Onesimus to the Colossians commended by a threefold title.

1. That he was *a faithful brother*] i. e. not only a Christian, but a true and genuine Christian: for many have assumed that name to themselves who have denied the thing itself. Hence that mention *of false brethren,* Gal. ii. 4; and that animated description of the same 2 Tim. iii. 2—4, &c. But this Onesimus was not such an one: who had not only put on the name of a Christian brother; but had performed in all things, and towards all, the duty of a faithful, true, and Christian brother. Hence we may observe,

1. It should be the endeavour of all to answer to their name and profession: For to be called and thought a Christian, a divine, faithful, or any thing of that kind, and not to be so truly, renders him a laughing-stock, does not contribute to his honour, who is loaded with false titles. Hence the angel at the Church at Sardis is censured, because *he had a name to live when he was dead,* Rev. iii. 1. For as Tertullian shrewdly says, advers. Marcion, *He to whom nature denies what is implied in the name, is mocked by the name.*

2. They are to be loved by all the pious, and (as they say) to be embraced with both arms, who are faithful, as well in their Christian profession, as in their special vocation. For, in the words of Tertullian, *as jewels obtain favour for their very rarity; so a faithful brother, a faithful*

magistrate, a faithful minister, because such are seldom found, ought to be of the highest value among all.

3. Nothing is more pernicious or more dangerous to the Church, than those perfidious brethren who feign religion, when they despise it in their heart. Paul thought these false brethren to be robbers, pagans, yea, worse than all storms and shipwrecks : Hence when he would write a catalogue of his dangers, he cites in the last place the dangers which he had undergone among false brethren, as greater than all the rest, 2 Cor. xi. 26.

2. Onesimus is commended because he had been *beloved*] Namely, by the chief Apostle Paul, who was not accustomed to receive any into intimate friendship except they were most worthy of his love. Therefore the Apostle wished them to infer hence, that this man was endowed with remarkable virtue and piety, and therefore to be beloved, as by the Colossians themselves, so by all good men.

Observations.

1. It is a sign of a good and pious Christian to be dear to and beloved by his pastor ; and on the other hand, of an impious and profane person, to be hateful to the same.

2. It becomes a pious and prudent minister, to embrace those with a peculiar affection before others, whom he sees to be endued with remarkable piety. For however he is bound to take care of and to love the whole flock committed to him, yet they ought to have the pre-eminence in his love, who by holiness and probity of manners excel others : For these are *the joy* and *crown* of his ministry. Phil. iv. 1.

3. It ought to be the care of all believers, to be approved and deservedly beloved by their pastors, for their known faith and probity. They who care little about this, for the most part despise religion itself.

3. *Who is one of you.*] Lastly then, the Apostle wishes also by this consideration to render Onesimus more acceptable to the Colossians, because he was sprung from Colosse, that is to say, of their people and a countryman. For although this does not make much for the praise of

this man, yet it conduces something to inflame the Colossians with the love of him : for what is a person's own and is peculiar to him, is wont to be more loved by every one.

Observations.

1. It is proper to treat them with peculiar affection, to whom we are more near and bound in any peculiar respect; for example, if they should be of the same blood, affinity, or country with us, or of the same society.

2. That affection, therefore, is vicious, which in many begets contempt, or at least, a neglect of their own, namely, because they are of our kin. For as in things, so also in persons ; the things which are produced at home are nearest to dis-esteem, but all distant and foreign things are extolled with wonderful encomiums. Christ himself experienced this folly of his own countrymen, and seriously complained of it, Matt. xiii. 57, *A prophet is not without honour, save in his own country and in his own house.* And thus much of the person extolled, and of his commendation. Now as to the cause why he also had been sent to the Colossians together with Tychicus, this he shews in these last words ;

They shall make known to you all things which are done here.] Now he had said concerning Tychicus, *All my state shall he declare unto you :* But because men are wont not so firmly to believe a single witness, he would make them more certain of all his affairs by the testimony of two, that there might be no room left for doubt. It is not necessary to explain this in more words, because we have spoken of this same occasion at the seventh verse.

We have now finished the two former parts of this Chapter ; the first of which consisted in exhortations; the other in commendations : The third and last part remains, which is taken up with salutations.

Vers. 10, 11.

*Aristarchus my fellow-prisoner saluteth you, and Marcus,
sister's son to Barnabas, (touching whom ye received
commandments: if he come unto you, receive him.*

*And Jesus, which is called Justus, who are of the circumci-
sion. These only are my fellow-workers unto the kingdom of God, which have been a comfort unto me.*

We come now to the last part of this Chapter, which
contains scarcely any thing else besides certain compli-
mental salutations sent from different persons : In running
through which, because they are easy of explanation, we
shall be the more brief. For we ought not either to load
a plain text with too laboured a comment, or, as though
we held it not worthy of our consideration, wholly to pass
it by.

Three things, then, are here to be done by us. 1. We
must speak concerning this duty of salutation generally.
2. We must explain so much concerning the persons sending them as will tend to shew who they are. 3. Lastly, we
must speak of those eulogiums which Paul after his manner annexes in praise of every one.

Saluteth you.] As to this first thing then ; this Greek
word Ασπάζεται signifies either *to embrace,* which friends are
accustomed to do when they return from a distance ; or *to
salute,* as we are used to do those whom we meet by word of
mouth, and absent friends by letters, as well in our own
name as that of other persons. Now this *salutation* is the
auspicious prayer of health and happiness from its author
God, out of a benevolent mind.

The forms of salutation are various ; but all agree in
this, that we salute him whom we wish all joy and prosperity from God. Christ himself most commonly was accustomed to use this form, *Peace be to you ;* Luke xxiv. 36;

John xx. 19; which he also prescribed to his disciples, Luke x. 5. The Angel used this to Mary, which also was the manner of the Gentiles, *Hail, The Lord is with thee,* Luke i. 28.

But now when we salute absent persons by letters, the forms of the antients were in the beginning of their Epistles, *grace, prosperity ;* at the end, *farewell.* But the Apostles in each case, instead of these obsolete salutations, employed that more holy and august mode, *Grace be with you, and peace from God our Father, and from the Lord Jesus Christ ;* or at least one like to it and equivalent. Therefore *to salute,* under whatever form it be done, is to wish these blessings to another from God the fountain of all good things.

That this duty of kindly saluting others is not to be neglected by a pious and Christian man, but is to be performed as well to those present as to the absent (when occasion offers) is manifest in different ways :

1.   From the command of Christ our Saviour ; who bids us to perform this duty, Matt. x. 12, *Into whatsoever house ye enter, salute it,* &c.

2.   From the example of Paul and of the saints; who (as is plain both in this place, as well as in almost all his Epistles) was not accustomed to be unmindful of these salutations.

3.   From their use and manifold utility : For they not only express and declare the mutual charity which ought to flourish among Christians, but they nourish and increase it. Moreover, when they flow from a heart purified by faith and inflamed with love, they are acts pleasing to God, and bring down the wished-for blessing (as often as sought) upon the brethren. Lastly, if they are designedly neglected, it either argues hypocrisy, or that love is very cold and languishing; from even the suspicion of which it behoves all Christians to be free.

But here it may be objected; these salutations seem to be prohibited, as idle ceremonies, and to be held in contempt by those who are engaged. When Elisha sent his servant to raise the son of the widow, he forbad him either to salute others, or to answer those saluting him, 2 Kings iv. 29.　Christ himself also, when he sent his disciples to preach, said, *Carry neither purse, nor scrip, nor shoes; and salute no man by the way,* Luke x. 4.　If it be frivolous to salute those whom we meet with words, then it will also be frivolous to salute absent persons by letters.

We answer, that these phrases are tropes and hyperboles; and that the force of the words is this, to forbid us to contrive by the way, or to do any thing which may retard the business we have undertaken.　Both, therefore, would mean, that we must even abstain from salutations, if perchance they might hinder the execution of the office consigned to us; but absolutely to forbid these duties of humanity, was not either the mind of the prophet, or of the Saviour, in the words cited.　Hence observe,

1.　That external duties of humanity, which make for the increase of charity, are diligently to be performed by pious men.　Hence Augustine blamed the inhumanity of those who neglected these things: *If any one should not salute him whom he may meet, he will not be accounted a man by the traveller, but a post, or a statue of Mercury.*　Serm. 42. de sanctis.

2.　That they are to be performed not only in conformity with mere custom, but from love and true charity. For he incurs the guilt of a hypocrite and liar, who salutes him by word to whom from his soul he wishes not health and prosperity.　So Judas saluted Christ, whom he went about to kill, *Hail, Master!*　Matt. xxvi. 49.

3.　That they sin, who would have this duty of Christian charity to serve their pride and ambition.　So the Pharisees of old, whom on this account the Saviour rebukes, because *they loved salutations in the market places:* so the great ones among the heathen, who exacted this from their dependents.　Hence the poet (Mart. lib. 3, epig. 36) complains of Fabian; he commands (says he) more than what is just,

> *Horridus ut primo semper te manè salutem,*
> *Per mediúmque trahit me tua sella lutum.*

4. That they both act basely, who seek their own advantage by works of charity, and instead of the duty of salutation perform one of adulation. In this they sin, who neglect others, and by these offices of humanity court the great alone, and those from whom they expect gain. But they who are truly godly and Christians, act otherwise: They render all these things, not out of false pretence, not for empty pride, not for deceitful craft, but as expressive of the true charity and mystical union which there is between the faithful.

Aristarchus.] This Aristarchus was a Macedonian, born at Thessalonica, the inseparable companion of Paul, and partner of almost all his dangers. He travelled together with the Apostle through Macedonia, Greece, and Asia, and accompanied him even to Rome. Hence in Acts xix. 29, he is called, *Paul's companion in travel.* And in xx. 4, he is mentioned among those who accompanied the Apostle into Asia. Lastly, in the Epistle to Philemon, ver. 24, he is placed among the number of those who ministered to the Apostle imprisoned at Rome.

Therefore, in praise of this distinguished man that one circumstance is alleged, that he was *the fellow-prisoner* of Paul. Which word properly denotes his being overcome and taken by the sword, and therefore the slave of his conqueror by right of war. But the expression is figurative. For Paul calls himself a captive, not because he had become a captive by right of war, but because he had been treated as a captive and slave by the adversaries of the Gospel, by being thrown into prison and loaded with chains. But now he calls Aristarchus *his fellow-prisoner,* or (as Ambrose reads it) *the companion of his captivity,* because for the love of Paul he had scarcely ever departed from his side; but was with him, and ministered to him, even in prison and bonds.

Hence infer,

1. That there is nothing more glorious to the faithful, than to suffer persecution for the sake of righteousness and the Gospel. Hence Paul was not ashamed either of

his captivity or bonds, but by way of honour calls himself
and this Aristarchus also fellow-prisoners.

2. That they are to be accounted, both by the judgment of God himself, and of the Church, companions of
the same sufferings with prisoners and martyrs, who are
wont to aid them and bear the burden and heat out of charity : for in this respect this Aristarchus is deemed the
fellow-prisoner of Paul. This much of Aristarchus.

And Marcus] Called also *John,* in Acts xii. 12. He had a
pious and religious Mother, Mary of Jerusalem : in whose
house the Apostles and other Christians were accustomed
to meet for prayer, preaching, and other spiritual exercises ; as may be gathered from the same place. Mark
was esteemed the most celebrated as well for many other
things, as especially for being the writer of a Gospel, which
he had learnt from Peter, as Eusebius writes, lib. 2. Hist.
eccl. cap. 24 ; and Irenæus, lib. 3, advers. hæres. cap. 1.

Hence also he deservedly obtained an illustrious name in
the Church of God, because he moreover helped the apostles in preaching : for Eusebius, lib. ii. cap. 16, writes,
that the churches through all Egypt were founded chiefly
by his labour. Dorotheus in his Synopsis relates, that he
was first Bishop of Alexandria, and was there honoured
with the crown of martyrdom under Trajan. Jerome also,
in his Catalogue of Ecclesiastical writers, states that he
was buried in the same city.

When, or by whom he was converted to the Christian
faith, is not expressly stated in the Scriptures : but it is
very probable that he was converted by Peter. The following considerations make this credible : 1. Because Peter
was wont to frequent the house of his mother for the sake
of prayer and preaching, as was before shewn from Acts
xii. Therefore it is very likely that he was enlightened
by him. 2. Because the antients, viz. Irenæus and Eusebius, relate, that he derived the Gospel history from Peter.
Hence Irenæus calls him *the disciple of Peter.* 3. Because
Jerome, in Isa. lxv. broadly affirms, that *Paul converted
Timothy, Luke, and Titus ;* but *Peter,* this *Evangelist Mark.*
This Peter himself also seems to have indicated clearly

enough, in Epis. 1. cap. v. vers. 13, where he calls this
Mark *his Son :* yet he was not his natural, but his spiritual son, begotten by the seed of the word.   But now let
us examine those things which are hinted by the Apostle
himself.

In the first place, then, he dignifies this Mark by a surname ; *Sister's son to Barnabas.*] This Barnabas was an old
and celebrated disciple of Christ, as appears from Acts
i. 23 (see also iv. 36) ; where, when a consultation was
held about choosing another in the vacant place of the
traitor Judas, this Barnabas, or Barsabas, and Matthias,
were appointed candidates of this apostolic dignity.   But
in Acts xi. 24, he is distinguished by a brief but remarkable eulogy, *He was a good man, and full of the Holy Ghost
and of faith.*   Therefore it was honourable to Mark to be
so nearly related to such a man.

Secondly, Mark is also dignified by the testimony and
command of Paul himself.   For the Apostle (as it seems)
had commanded the Colossians before, that they should
receive this Mark honourably, if he should at any time
visit them : which is more expressly stated in some copies,
where it is read δέξασθαι, not δέξασθε, *ye received a commandment, to welcome him,*   So Ambrose regards it : and Calvin
prefers this reading, as what plainly indicates what that
command had been.

But it may be enquired, what reason or necessity was
there for this command.   Did Mark need commendatory
letters ?   Or, if Paul had not given this in command,
would he have been rejected by the Colossians, if at any
time he had gone to preach to them ?

We answer, It appears from Acts xv. 38, that some displeasure had happened between Paul and Mark, from the
circumstance that Mark had left him in Pamphylia, and
had not continued his companion in the office of preaching.   This perhaps had been made known to the Colossians : he might, therefore, have been accounted for a deserter, unless Paul, rendered in a manner more content,
had commanded them about receiving him.   For howsoever he had departed from Paul, yet it is very likely he

had not in the mean time ceased from the office of preaching, but had preached in other places.   Hence conclude,

1.   That the relatives of distinguished men are on this
very account to be honoured, if they are not themselves
degenerated.

2.   That upright and industrious ministers are to be
commended diligently to all by those who preside in the
Churches.

3.   If there shall be a slight error in any matter, that
ought not to occasion a lasting prejudice to the offender;
after he shall have amended himself.

4.   Ministers ought not to exercise lasting enmities;
but if at any time any cause of anger shall happen between
them, as soon as it can be done, all remembrance of it
should be obliterated from their minds.   Thus Paul, who,
heretofore displeased, had rejected Mark, being now reconciled, commends the same man to the Colossians, and
most diligently guards against his being rejected by them.

Vers. 11.   *And Jesus, which is called Justus; who are of*
the circumcision: These only are my fellow-workers unto
the kingdom of God, which have been a comfort unto
me.

This verse connects with the foregoing, in which the
Apostle had saluted the Colossians in the name of Aristarchus and Mark; in the third place he adds this illustrious man.   We have here to consider, 1. The person in
whose name he salutes the Colossians, *Jesus Justus;* and,
2. The commendations which he bestows upon him, not
individually, but common to him with Mark and Aristarchus.

Now these three are
extolled,
{
From their nation; because they
were Jews.
From their work; and that of a
twofold kind, { preaching,
comforting.
}

Jesus who is called Justus.] It is likely that he was the person who welcomed Paul into his house at Corinth, when he was rejected by the other blaspheming Jews. For thus Luke writes, Acts v. 5—7. *When Paul preached that Jesus was Christ, the Jews which dwelt at Corinth opposed themselves, and blasphemed; but he shook his raiment, and said unto them, Your blood be upon your own heads; and he entered into a certain man's house named Justus, one who worshipped God, whose house joined hard to the synagogue.*

This surname seems to have been assigned him, because he had been always most observant of justice and equity. We read that this same surname was given to some others, as to James Alphæus, who is called James Justus; concerning whom Eusebius has many things, lib. 2. cap. 1, and 23. This surname is also affixed to Barsabas, Acts i. 23. As to this Jesus Justus; there is neither any mention made (that I recollect) elsewhere in the Sacred Scriptures, nor does any thing occur in Eusebius; unless this be the same Justus whom he reckons third Bishop of Jerusalem, lib. 3. Hist. eccl. cap. 29. Thus much of the person.

Who are of the circumcision.] He now conjointly extols both this Justus and those two named above. And they are commended from their nation, namely, that they were sprung from Jewish parents; which is marked by the adjunct *of the circumcision.* And this so much the more contributes to their praise, because the rest of the Jews for the most part, as well at Rome, as in other places, were most bitter enemies of the Apostles and of the Christian religion: yea (as Justin Martyr, in his Dialogue with Trypho, writes) *The Jews were they who every where stirred up the heathen against the Christians, uttering the most odious lies against us and our Religion.* They, therefore, are here deservedly praised, who not only had cast off this inward malice of the Jewish race against Christ, but had put on Christ himself, and promoted the Christian Religion together with Paul and the other believers.

Here observe; It is not always safe in the business of Religion to follow the major part, or obstinately to retain national opinions. For they who were of the circumcision,

for the major part opposed Christ, and superstitiously contended for their ceremonies : yet these three persons feared
not to forsake the errors of their nation.

These only are my fellow-workers unto the kingdom of God.]
He now begins to commend them from their most commendable work, to which they had diligently applied
themselves with the Apostle; namely, the furtherance of
the Gospel.

Now he calls the Gospel *the kingdom of God*, because by
this men are introduced into the kingdom of God ; namely,
the kingdom of Grace in this life, that they may hereafter
be introduced into the kingdom of glory in the life to
come. It is not unusual in the Scriptures for the propagation of the Gospel and the erection of the Christian
Church to be called *the kingdom of God*. And this form of
speaking has respect to those two promises heretofore
made concerning the spiritual kingdom of the Messiah,
who was about to erect a Divine and spiritual kingdom by
the sceptre of the Word, and to administer it in the hearts
of believers. Hence that record in Matt. iv. 23, *And Jesus
went about all Galilee, preaching the Gospel of the kingdom ;*
and in Mark iv. 11, *Unto you it is given to know the mystery
of the kingdom of God*; and that of John, Matt. iii. 2,
Repent ye; for the kingdom of heaven is at hand. These
alone, then, of the Jews that were at Rome remained as
helpers of Paul in promoting and administering this spiritual kingdom.*

Corollaries.

1. Although very many every where draw back from
their duty, yet it becomes the pious minister to persevere,
even alone, in propagating the Gospel.

2. Nothing can be thought more honourable than this
office of the Gospel minister. For if they are to be accounted honoured who administer earthly kingdoms under
earthly kings, with how much more honour are they to be

---

* " This is generally and justly urged, as absolutely conclusive against
the traditions of the papists, that the Apostle Peter was at this time bishop
of Rome, where he resided twenty-five years !" Scott, in loc.

treated who conduct the spiritual kingdom under Christ, the spiritual King.

3. Nothing can be more miserable or more mad than the enemies of the Gospel : because they oppose the kingdom of God itself, which they cannot overcome ; and, as if they endeavoured to establish the kingdom of Satan, which will be overturned, together with all the favourers of it.

Which have been a comfort unto me.] Παρηγορειν, signifies either *to exhort*, or *to comfort.* The Apostle therefore intimates, that these three men in each respect, as well in the work of exhorting, as of comforting, proved themselves constant fellow-helpers : They exhorted him to endure the cross patiently; they comforted him by visiting him, by condoling with him, by ministering to his necessities ; finally, they omitted nothing which could smooth or mitigate that miserable condition of Paul now in prison.

Instructions.

1. The wisest and the best of men under the cross need the exhortations and consolations of the godly. This the royal Prophet confesses, and in Ps. lxix. 20, bitterly complains that all had failed in this duty to him ; *I looked for some to take pity, but there was none ; and for comforters, but I found none.*

2. It is a singular mark of the godly and truly faithful, to assist the afflicted, both by word and deed, and thus by the diligent employ of every duty, to refresh and comfort them. Thus Paul describes true saints ; *Distributing to the necessity of saints ; Rejoicing with them that do rejoice, weeping with them that weep,* &c. Rom. xii. 13, 15.

3. They, therefore, have nothing of Christian charity in them, who regard not the miseries and griefs of others, so that they themselves enjoy ease and pleasure. Of this sort were those at whom Amos directs his most pungent reproof, vi. 4, &c. *Ye lie upon beds of ivory, and stretch yourselves upon your couches,* &c. *but ye are not grieved for the affliction of Joseph.*

And so far the salutations and commendations of those three who were *of the circumcision,* that is, of the Jews :

Three others follow from among the Gentiles ; Epaphras,
Luke, and Demas.

Vers. 12.

*Epaphras, who is one of you, a servant of Christ, saluteth
you, always labouring fervently for you in prayers, that
ye may stand perfect and complete in all the will of
God.*

Epaphras saluteth you.] Let us consider the person himself, and what things are attributed to this person in this
place, whereby he is rendered more acceptable and commendable to his Colossian brethren.

This Epaphras was the Minister of the Colossians, and
sent at this time to the Apostle, to refer to him the state
of that Church, to assist him in his ministry, and learn
his opinion about the controversies with which that Church
was agitated. For so the Churches were accustomed to
resort to the Apostles as oracles, even at the remotest distance. For this purpose it is most likely Epaphras was
sent. Of the praises of Epaphras we have spoken at the
seventh verse of the first Chapter. We shall therefore now
notice those only, which are here expressly alleged by the
Apostle, in order that he might procure for him more kindness and esteem among the Colossians.

He is commended to
them in a threefold
manner :

{
From being their countryman ;
one of you.

From his eminent office ; *a servant
of Christ.*

From his sincere love towards
them ; *always labouring fervently
for you,* &c.
}

1. *Who is one of you.*] That is, your fellow-citizen,
born and educated among you, and finally given and devoted to your advantage. This especially conduces to

conciliate love for him. For *all love* (as the Schools express it) *is founded in some communication or participation of the same thing :* therefore, they who are participants of the same country and city, are united together as by a certain closer bond of love. For as their native soil is used to be dear to all, so it renders all things which spring from it even more dear to the wise and sober.

Corollaries.

1. They are deservedly to be blamed as vain and *void of natural affection,* who despise their own kindred and all their home concerns, being in the mean time addicted beyond what is just and good, to things and persons foreign to the house.

2. They who by a participation of country and city, or any like cause, are united with us, all other things corresponding, ought to be more dear than strangers. Hence says the Apostle, 1 Tim. v. 8, *If any provide not for his own, and especially for those of his own house, he hath denied the faith, and is worse than an infidel.*

2. *A servant of Christ.*] Now he extols him from the dignity of his office. For by *a servant of Christ,* he does not denote a Christian in general ; but one appointed to a more eminent place in this service of Christ, namely, to that distinguished and sacred function of the ministry of the Gospel. For although we are all servants of Christ, yet this appellation is frequently attributed by way of eminence to the ministers of the word. Thus Paul, in Rom. i. 1, describes himself as *a servant of Jesus Christ :* so James, Chap. i. vers. 1 ; and so the other Apostles.

Hence a Christian people may learn,

1. That Ministers are not to be despised as ministers, but under Christ their Lord, are to be acknowledged as set over other Christians, according to that word of the Apostle, *We intreat you, brethren, to know them who labour among you, and are over you in the Lord,* 1 Thess. v. 12. Therefore ministers serve their Lord Christ; but in Christ they are set over others, or at least ought to be preferred to them from dignity of office.

2. Ministers also may hence learn, what is most espe-

cially required from them in the discharge of this sacred
ministry: Not to please men; *If I please men,* says the
Apostle, Gal. i. 10, *I should not be the servant of Christ*:
not to be studious to promote their own advantage or
honour; but to prove themselves the servants of Christ.
Now he serves Christ the best, who chiefly labours that he
may bring very many to the knowledge and obedience of
Christ.

3. *Always labouring fervently for you in prayers, that ye
may stand perfect,* &c.] Lastly, he desires that Epaphras
may be rendered acceptable to the Colossians from his remarkable love towards them. This he sets forth and proves
in a twofold manner: by its effect, in this verse; by his
testimony, in the thirteenth verse.

Now here three things occur to be observed: 1. The effect itself of love; *prayer.* 2. The manner of the prayer;
which is expressed *by always labouring fervently.* 3. The
matter of the prayer; *that ye may stand perfect and complete
in all the will of God.*

1. As to the first, namely, the effect of love; true love
cannot flourish towards any one in the heart, without putting itself forth in some work. For among all the affections, love is the least accustomed to be inactive: which
is no less true of holy and chaste, than of that inconstant
and lascivious love, of which the poet speaks,

> *Sed malè dissimulo; quis enim celaverit ignem,*
> *Lumine qui semper proditur ipse suo?*

But now among the many operations of sincere love, none
is more useful to the beloved, none more accordant to the
minister, than this prayer whereby he pleads for the protection of God, and keeps off the plots and power of their
spiritual foes from his flock. And on this account, although the Apostle could have named many other effects,
from which he could have proved the love of Epaphras towards the Colossians, yet he wished chiefly to insist upon
this work of prayer.

---

* ....But I dissemble badly;
For who can e'er that fire conceal,
Which by its own light itself betrays?

Hence let us observe,

1. The especial duties of a minister; namely, to teach his flock, and to pray for it: For *prayers are the weapons of the priest*, as Ambrose heretofore remarked. *We will give ourselves to prayer, and to the ministry of the word*, Acts vi. 4.

2. The duty lies upon the minister, not only of praying publicly for the people committed to him, but privately, and that even mostly as often as he shall happen to be absent from his flock; this we are taught by this example of Epaphras. Thus much concerning the effect itself, namely prayer: Now concerning the mode.

2. *Always labouring fervently.*] In these words he shews of what kind was this prayer of Epaphras for the Colossians; namely, constant, and also fervent. That word *always*, παντοτε, indicates the constancy: as though Paul had said, that the distance of place had not induced forgetfulness of his flock in the mind of Epaphras; but that he, though then dwelling at Rome, was no less mindful of them in his daily prayers, than when present with them he looked on them personally. But that word *labouring fervently*, αγωνιζομενος, which intimates a contest, and as it were a wrestling with God himself, shews earnestness and fervor. For as Jacob of old wrestling with God would not let him go, without the blessing sought from him; so this godly minister strove daily with God, and urged him in a manner more vehemently to bless the Colossians.

Hence observe, it is the duty of a pious minister, not out of form or custom, but from real inward love, to pray God for the welfare of his flock. But of this we have spoken in the second verse.

3. *That ye may stand perfect and complete in all the will of God.*] This is the matter, or sum of the prayer: and here he desires for them three chief blessings; a true and perfect knowledge of the Divine will, true and perfect obedience to it, and final perseverance in each: for this is the meaning of the phrase ινα στητε, *that ye may stand.* As to the two former; both are implied and contained in that petition, *that ye may stand perfect and complete in all the will of God.* For no one is perfect and complete in all the will

of God, except he who both knows the will of God, and
studies to perform it with all his might. For the will of
God is, that we may know those things which he has revealed for our salvation; it is also the will of God, that
we should do those things which he commands to be done
in obedience to him. Of the knowledge of the Divine
will the Apostle thus speaks in Ephes. v. 17, *Be not un-*
wise, but understanding what the will of the Lord is. Of
obedience to it, the Saviour, in Matt. vii. 21, says, *Not*
every one that saith unto me Lord, Lord, shall enter into the
kingdom of heaven, but he that doeth the will of my Father
which is in heaven. And these are two great blessings.
The third blessing which he supplicates for the Colossians
is perseverance in the aforesaid perfection. And rightly
indeed : for he alone *who shall have persevered* in good, *shall*
be saved, Matt. xxiv. 13. *All your past actions go for nothing*
if what you began has not been brought to perfection, says
Cyprian, De bono patient.

Instructions.

1. We should pray God for those to whom we wish
well, not that they may have either the riches or the honours of this world, but knowledge and obedience to the
Divine will.

2. We must beware that we are not contented with
either bare and useless knowledge, or a certain blind obedience : for neither will render us *perfect and complete in the*
will of God.

3. Perseverance in good is a special gift of Divine
grace: For *if it were from man, we should not be obliged to*
seek it from God, says Augustine, De corr. et grat.

But here a doubt arises, about the knowledge and fulness of the Divine will: For since Epaphras prays that the
Colossians may stand *perfect in all the will of God,* it may
be asked, whether a perfection of this kind can fall to the
Christian in this life ?

It is answered, That absolute perfection is not to be
found in our pilgrimage here ; yet we must always attempt
and aspire after it, Christ being the author, who teaches
us to pray, *Let thy will be done in earth, as it is in heaven.*

What is therefore found in the saints, is a certain imperfect perfection, as well of knowledge as of obedience. But this includes a knowledge of the will of God sufficient and necessary for their state here, the purpose and desire to fulfil and perfect it, and constant progress in faith and godliness. Therefore it excludes brutish ignorance, hypocrisy, obstinacy, gross negligence, and those other evils which oppose the Divine will. Concerning this, Augustine, Cont. duas Epist. Pelag. lib. 3. cap. 5, writes, *There is a certain perfection according to the measure of this life, and it is to be ascribed to this perfection, that any one knows that he is not yet perfect.*

Vers. 13.

For I bear him record, that he hath a great zeal for you, and them that are in Laodicea, and them in Hierapolis.

That which in the former verse he demonstrated from the effects, he now endeavours to confirm by his own testimony; namely, that Epaphras was most desirous of their benefit and salvation: as though he would say, What was before said by me, that Epaphras, on account of his singular love, always laboured earnestly for you in prayer, I would not have you think that I affirmed it from uncertain conjectures alone, but that I declared it to you from most certain knowledge.

We shall here notice three things; the witness himself; the testimony exhibited to Epaphras; the cause of giving the testimony.

1. *For I bear him record.*] The witness, who testifies the love and desire of Epaphras towards the Colossians, is the most substantial and powerful beyond exception, namely, Paul himself. Hence we may observe,

1. It is the duty of those who preside over the Church,

when occasion offers, to honour and commend by their
testimony, all those whom they perceive to have discharged
their ministry honestly and faithfully.

2. To pay attention to ministers, that they may in
every way render clear and evident to all, that love and
care for the flock, by which they deserve so honourable a
testimony.

2. But now what was this testimony of Paul exhibited
to Epaphras? *That he hath a great zeal for you*, &c. The
Greek word for *zeal* is derived from a word which signifies
to grow hot, or *to boil up* as water being heated is wont to
do. The Apostle therefore would intimate, that this love
in Epaphras was no languid and ordinary love, but a fervent and vehement one, as well towards his Colossians,
as also towards the Laodiceans and Hierapolitans their
neighbours.

As to these cities ; Pliny, Hist. Nat. lib. 5. c. 29, calls
Laodicea, *a most celebrated city*, and writes that it was *situated upon the river Lycus*, and formerly called *Diospolis*.
Hierapolis was near to this. In the year after the death
of Paul, historians write, that both Colosse and Laodicea
were destroyed by an earthquake. And for many ages
afterwards it appears that the whole country of Asia Minor, in which these Churches formerly flourished, was
seized and subverted by Mahometan superstition and
Turkish tyranny.

Corollaries.

1. The fervor of charity, and zeal for the salvation of
their brethren, ought to grow strong in all Christians, but
especially in ministers; of this, Paul himself afforded an
illustrious example, Rom. ix. 3. For the coldness of love
shews the abounding of iniquity. Matt. xxiv. 12.

2. This love, and this desire of promoting the salvation of others, not only extends itself to that particular
Church in which we live, but to all those other churches
of Christ, with which we are joined in the unity of the
faith and of the Spirit. What therefore Paul said through
apostolical authority, that every one may say from Christian charity, *The care of all the Churches cometh upon me*

daily, 2 Cor. xi. 28. For it behoves us to testify our desire and love for all, at least by praying for them.

3. Although the Church of God is perpetual, yet the household of the Church in particular places or countries, is not certain, fixed, and perpetual. That is perceived from hence, because these celebrated churches mentioned in this place, have long since passed away.

4. Therefore we should avoid their example, lest through contempt of the Gospel, or our lukewarmness, the same should happen to us which God, having long since threatened to these Asiatic Churches, it is plain has already done. For thus he addressed the Church at Ephesus, Rev. ii. 4, 5, *Thou hast left thy first love ; except thou repent, I will remove thy candlestick out of its place.* He also threatened the Laodicean Church in the same manner, Chap. iii. 16, *Because thou art lukewarm, I will spew thee out of my mouth.*

But let us come to that which, in the last place, we proposed to explain, namely, why Paul took such diligent care that the Colossians should have a clear view of the love of Epaphras : for it is not credible that the most prudent Apostle would confirm a matter of small moment so religiously with his testimony.

This then was done, 1. That he might procure for Epaphras the greatest possible kindness and the highest respect among his people. For it is natural to men, to love and make much of those whom they consider to be desirous of their's before that of others. But it behoves a people to be affected in this manner towards faithful pastors : *Let those who rule well, be accounted worthy of double honour,* 1 Tim. v. 17.

2. Paul acted so seriously, that he might consult the benefit of the Churches themselves. For the greater favour and veneration the teachers are in, the greater benefit is wont to result to the hearers : for they willingly attend to his instruction, of whose desire and love towards themselves they have no doubt.

3. Whilst he narrates the desire of Epaphras for the welfare of these Churches, he thereby hoped, that he

might render every one among them more solicitous about
his own salvation. For shame will not suffer him to sit
idle who sees another labour in his concerns so earnestly.
For these reasons, therefore, the Apostle made known to
these churches the desire of Epaphras; and for the same
reasons it behoves all ministers to take care, that their desire also for procuring the salvation of their people should
be known.

Vers. 14.

Luke, the beloved physician, and Demas, greet you.

As to these two persons; he who is named in the first
place (if we believe the antient Fathers) is that celebrated
Evangelist, *whose praise is in the Gospel throughout all the
Churches;* and who *was chosen by the brethren, as the companion of Paul's travels,* 2 Cor. viii. 18.

That this Luke was by profession a physician, by birth
a native of Antioch; that he lived single eighty-four years,
and at length was buried at Ephesus and translated under
Constantine to Constantinople, is gathered from the Synopsis of Dorotheus, and Jerome's Catalogue.

The Apostle in this place bestows upon him no other
eulogium, than that he calls him *the beloved physician.*
Whilst he acknowledges that he was *beloved* to himself,
he affords a testimony to his virtue and piety: for the
Apostle was not accustomed to bestow special and familiar
love, except on account of faith and integrity clear and
illustrious. He is called *a physician* from the art which he
had before exercised; so Matthew the Apostle is also
called after his conversion *a publican,* Matt. x. 3. For
*from a physician of bodies, he was now made a physician of
souls; whose writings as often as they are read in the Churches,
so often Divine prescriptions are offered to men;* as Jerome
well remarks, in Epist. ad Philem. Some have doubted,

whether he who is in this place called *the physician*, was
the same with Luke the Evangelist; and seem rather to
incline to the contrary opinion, upon the weight of this
one argument, that the Apostle had bestowed upon him
no honourable title. But this conjecture is too slender to
set aside the common opinion which we derive from the
more antient Fathers, Jerome, Ambrose, Theodoret, and
almost all the rest. Neither is it necessary, that as often
as mention is made of noted men, so often they should be
signalized by some honourable title. Add to this, that it
appears from the antients, that this Evangelist was at first
a physician; nor can another person of his name be found
in Ecclesiastical history who was a *work-fellow* with Paul,
and *a companion* of his travels. Thus much of Luke.

And Demas.] This Demas in the Epistle to Philemon,
is reckoned among the companions and fellow-helpers of
Paul, vers. 24. *There salute thee, Marchus, Aristarchus,
Demas, Lucas, my fellow-labourers.* But the same person, in 2 Tim. iv. 10, is accused, because *he had forsaken
Paul, having loved this present world, and departed into Thessalonica.* Dorotheus, in his Synopsis, shews the cause,
that is to say, to become there an idolatrous priest. He
had perhaps observed that ministers of the Gospel, like
soldiers, were at once oppressed by labour and want; he
therefore betook himself to exercise the priesthood among
the idolatrous heathen, where a greater hope of tranquillity and profit shone upon him. The Apostle dignified him
by no title; therefore it is not necessary that we should
say more about him: we shall only elicit these observations;

1. That many greedily embraced the Gospel at the beginning, whom nevertheless afterwards either the fear of
persecution or the love of the world hurried away.

2. That the root of true faith and piety never was in
the hearts of those persons; according to that saying of
John, 1 Epist, ii. 19, *They went out from us, but they were
not of us; for if they had been of us, they would have continued with us,* &c. So Cyprian writes, Lib. 1. epist. 3, *That
the Church which believes in Christ, never departs from him;*

and that they are the Church who continue in the house of God.

3. Hence we gather what they are, who, having abandoned their ministry, flee from us to the Papists, to become Baalitish priests: namely, they are such as this Demas was, whom either envy, or the love of the world, that is, the desire of honour or riches, besotted.

Vers. 15.

Salute the brethren which are in Laodicea, and Nymphas, and the church which is in his house.

Because Paul wished this Epistle to be transmitted to the Laodiceans, and publicly read in their church, he prudently judged that they also should be saluted, lest it should seem that there was either little remembrance of, or little kindness in his mind towards them. For it is wise and useful to declare our love and good will towards those to whom we can communicate it, whom we would endeavour to instruct and direct by our exhortations or our advice ; because all are wont more readily to obey those, by whom they believe that they are loved.

Salute the brethren which are in Laodicea.] This general and promiscuous salutation, has respect to all who had assumed the Christian name and profession in that city. Hence we may observe,

1. That brotherly love and affection ought plainly to flourish among all Christians. The philosophers of old said, *that a wise man was a friend to a wise man, although unknown :* But we may say, that a Christian is a brother to a Christian, although unknown; yea, he is more united than any friend or brother : for there ought to be *one heart and one soul* of all believers. Acts iv. 32.

2. That this brotherly love is not only declared by words, but by services, as often as brethren, even they

who live in remote churches, need our assistance. For to salute one by word as a brother, and, when occasion offers, not to promote the welfare of a brother, is the work of derision rather than of love.

And Nymphas.] Now he joins a special salutation, on account of the special and distinguished piety of this man, as may be gathered from the following verses. For it is right to assign extraordinary honour to those, whose virtue appeared and shone in the Church surpassing all others.

In the Commentaries which pass under the name of Ambrose, a comical error has found its way : For they have transformed this pious and renowned man into a woman : For thus he is there treated of ; *He esteems Nymphas more dear than others, whose whole house he even salutes. For she is said to have been so devoted, that her whole house was marked by the sign of the cross.* But since the Greek is την κατ' οἶκον αὐτοῦ, not αὐτῆς, I cannot believe that Ambrose, or any other Greek scholar could err so childishly. In my opinion therefore, those latter words have been taken into the text by some ignorant and lazy Monk, who, according to the custom of his age, as soon as he heard the name Church, dreamed about painted crosses. Both the manifest barbarism of the words, as well as the entire want of likelihood of the thing itself, induces belief in this conjecture. For in that first and golden age of the Christian Church, the Cross of Christ depicted not upon walls, but in their breasts, indicated their devotion : neither is it probable that any wise man would, by painting this sign of the cross through his whole house, openly betray himself and others who were accustomed to assemble in his house, to the heathen at that time raging, and the Christians for the most part holding their sacred assemblies in the night. But this perhaps is too much about a thing of no great moment ; only I wished to vindicate Ambrose from the impertinences of some obscure fabricator of absurdities. Let us proceed.

And the Church which is in his house.] These words may be explained in a twofold manner : For they denote either the assembly of Christians who were accustomed to meet in the house of this distinguished man, for exercising sacred duties, that is, for prayer, for preaching the word, and the celebration of the sacrament; or they denote his private family, which for its religious sanctity merited this illustrious name of *Church,* Rom. xvi. 5.   So Theodoret thinks, who thus writes on this passage, *He made his private family a Church, adorning it with piety and religion.* Neither do I perceive that any disadvantage follows, if we unite both, and say, that the house of this man was called *a Church* by the Apostle, as well because the congregation of the faithful was accustomed to assemble in his house, as because he instructed all his domestics piously and in a Christian-like manner, and trained them daily in religious exercises.

Instructions.

1.   Every collection of believers, although on account of its smallness they may be included within the walls of a private house, and although on account of the fury of their enemies, they meet in nocturnal assemblies, is a true Church, and a living member of the universal Church.

2.   The Papists therefore err, who acknowledge no Church unless that which has sovereignty, and ever before the eyes of the world.   For sometimes the rage of persecution does not suffer the Church to move in the public sight of all, but compels her to slink as it were into private retreats.   *She flees into the wilderness,* Rev. xii. 6.   So aforetime, when the Arians ruled, Athanasius and the rest of the orthodox Christians were compelled to retire into corners.

3.   It is incumbent upon every head of a family, so to instruct and train his domestics in true Religion, that his house may deservedly obtain the name of *a Church.*   The pious Patriarch Abraham did this, of whom God himself testifies, Gen. xviii. 19, *I know him, that he will command his children and his household after him, to keep the way of the Lord, and to do justice and judgment.*   So Joshua, *As for me and my house, we will serve the Lord,* Josh. xxiv. 15.

4.   They are therefore unworthy the name of Christians, who (with respect to Religion) take not any care of their

domestics, but suffer their houses to be so polluted by rioting and drunkenness, that they may more truly be called taverns than Churches.

Vers. 16.

And when this Epistle is read among you, cause that it be read also in the Church of the Laodiceans; and that ye likewise read the Epistle from Laodicea.

He enjoins a threefold command upon the Colossians in this verse: One concerning this Epistle being published in the Church of the Colossians: *When this Epistle is read among you:* The other about transmitting the same to their neighbours the Laodiceans; *let it be read in the Church of the Laodiceans.* The third concerning the reading of some other Epistle, which he had received from Laodicea; *And that ye likewise read the Epistle from Laodicea.*

1. *When this Epistle is read among you.*] As to the first; The Apostle wished this his Epistle to be published and read in a usual assembly of the whole Church, that all might know it. Hence we derive two Corollaries:

1. That the Sacred Scriptures were not written for the end that they should be the peculiar property of a few of the clergy; but that they should be open to the whole Christian people, and should be known of all. Hence that the ordinary reading of the Scriptures obtained in the primitive Church, (1 Thess. v. 27,) and that in a language understood by the people, is clear from Justin Martyr, in Apolog. 2; from Tertullian, in Apologet.; and from other Fathers. Which custom B. Rhenanus, in Annotat. ad Tertull. De Corona militis, wished to be restored to the Papal church.*

2. That they err who deny that the reading of the

* Vide p. 134 of this Vol. and Note.

Scriptures itself conduces to the edification of a Christian people in faith and charity, unless there be added at the same time an illustration and exposition of them by a preacher. Far be it from us to detract from the utility or necessity of preaching; nevertheless, we assert with the Psalmist, concerning the word of God read studiously and devoutly, *The law of the Lord is perfect, converting the soul: the testimony of the Lord is sure, making wise the simple,* Psal. xix. 7.

2. *Cause that it be read also in the Church of the Laodiceans.*] This is the second command of the Apostle, in which the Colossians are ordered to communicate this Epistle to the Laodiceans.

A twofold reason may be offered for this command: One; because the doctrine of this Epistle is general, and on that account was not to be reserved for the private use of one Church, but to be communicated to the whole Church of God; but first to the neighbours of the Colossians, who having read the autograph, could take copies of it, and diffuse them through the whole Church of God.

The other reason is; Because (as it is very likely) this Church on account of its vicinity, was opposed in the same manner as the Church of Colosse, by those Jewish and philosophical seducers : therefore, lest there should be a necessity for a new Epistle, the Apostle would have this made common to both.

Hence observe, That among all the Churches of God, but especially among neighbouring ones, there ought to be a communication of spiritual benefits; so that if one Church should have any thing that might contribute to the edification of another, it should not grudge to impart it.

3. *And that ye likewise read the Epistle from Laodicea.*] We have in these words the last particular of the Apostolic command; which enjoins that a certain Epistle sent from Laodicea should be read in the Church of the Colossians. It is probable that the Laodiceans had written to Paul concerning the state of their affairs, and that the Epistle contained something in it which was very useful to be known by the Colossians : Hence the Apostle ordered it to be read by them.

But concerning this Epistle, Commentators have entertained very different opinions. Theophylact would have
the first Epistle to Timothy to be understood, which is
reported to have been written from Laodicea. Marcion the
heretic thinks the Epistle to the Ephesians to be indicated ;
the title of which he dared impudently enough to interpolate, and to write upon it *to the Laodiceans.* Vide Tertull.
advers. Marcion, lib. 5.

Some of the advocates for the Papacy (among whom is
Stapleton*) think that some Epistle was written by the
Apostle to the Laodiceans, which yet the Church by its
authority would not admit into the canon : and by this argument he attempts to prove that the canonical authority

---

* STAPLETON, *Thomas,* was born at Henfield, in Sussex, in 1535, and
educated at Canterbury and Winchester Schools, and New College, Oxford.
In Mary's reign he obtained a Prebend of Chichester, but on Elizabeth's
accession he retired with his parents to Louvain, whither, after an excur-
sion to France and Italy, he returned, and made great progress in his studies. In 1569, Allen invited him to Douay, to found there his English se-
minary of idolatry and rebellion. He prosecuted this work so acceptably
that he was elected their Professor of Divinity, took his degree of Doctor, and
was made afterwards Canon of the Collegiate Church of St. Amatus. He
had a great affection for the Order of Jesuits, and became a novice in it.
But he subsequently forsook them, and accepted an invitation to his old
station, Louvain, and the Professorship there, and obtained the lucrative
dignity of Dean of Hilverbeck. He became eminent as a Controversialist on the side of the Romish Church, in favour of which he was an indefatigable writer ; and at his death in 1598, he left a number of pieces, which,
together with his preceding works, were published collectively, at a great
expence, by the booksellers of Paris, in four thick vols. folio : 1620, the
contents of which are particularized by Dodd. This mass of learning
has been denominated CORPUS CONTOVERSIARUM. The renowned Cardinal Bellarmin is said to have been indebted to him for what he published concerning the Church, Tradition, and Scripture. Clement the
VIIIth was so much delighted with the productions of this zealous advocate, that he ordered them to be read daily in times of his refection, and
invited him to Rome with a design to confer on him the place of Pro-
tonotary, and, as some say, to make him Cardinal. All that is impor-
portant, however, in his " vast stores," has been well and ably refuted by
the justly celebrated Dr. Whitaker and others, (vide Note p. 135 of the
present vol.) ; and from the specimen here given by our Expositor, it may
be seen how easily the cobweb sophistry of the most renowned and best
educated champions of Popery is swept away, and all its pretty mechanism
reduced to a *modicum* of dirt. He who would have more of this writer
may consult Dodd's Church History, &c. Vol. ii. pp. 84, et seq.

of the Scriptures rested upon the judgment of the Church; which thus could exclude the writings of the Apostles themselves from the number of the sacred books. The ambiguity of the Latin version, which gives the passage thus, *Eam quæ Laodicensium est vos legatis, and that ye read that which is of the Laodiceans ;* and the bold dishonesty of a certain impostor, who put forth a certain forged epistle under the title of *Paul to the Laodiceans,* have given occasion to this error. But I answer, that no one ever accounted that epistle for a genuine Epistle of Paul, except Stapleton, and those like him, who are used to scrape together from every quarter arguments to set the authority of the Church above the Scriptures. Œcumenius in this place observes, He has not said *that* TO *the Laodiceans, but that* FROM *Laodicea,* which Theodoret also had observed before him. As to that which Stapleton (relying upon this passage) desires to hold for a genuine Epistle of Paul; I wonder at the impudent stupidity of the man, since that has already been rejected by all the Fathers who have mentioned it. Theodoret in this place, calls it a *fiction* and *forgery.* Jerome in his Catalogue of Ecclesiastical writers, where he reckons up all Paul's Epistles, at length subjoins these words, *Some read and to the Laodiceans ; but it is exploded by all.* Lastly, the 2d Nicene Council, Act 6. says, *Among the Epistles of the divine Apostle a certain one is spoken of to the Laodiceans, which our Fathers have reprobated as another man's.* That opinion, therefore, is consonant both to the Greek context and to truth, which we have propounded from the beginning; that an epistle from the Laodiceans to Paul was here meant, not one on the contrary part. And the opinion of Stapleton is to be detested, who determines that it was an Epistle of Paul himself, which all the Fathers have rejected as a forgery and unworthy of attention : Nor is the conclusion more sound, which he would deduce therefrom ; namely, that the Church had authority to exclude from the canon a true and genuine Epistle of the Apostle Paul. Thus much of the threefold command of the Apostle.

In those two verses which remain, he bids them to admonish Archippus to fulfil his ministry ; and, introducing a mention of his bonds, he subscribes his salutation with his own hand.

Vers. 17.

And say to Archippus, Take heed to the ministry which thou hast received in the Lord, that thou fulfil it.

The Apostle adds a new command about admonishing Archippus, to shew himself watchful and diligent in the discharge of his ministry.

Say to Archippus.] Some think this Archippus was only a deacon in the Church of Colosse ; conjecturing it perhaps from hence, that in this place he is ordered *to fulfil the ministry,* την διακονιαν, *which he had received.* But this is weak : For the words διακονος and διακονια are oftentimes taken for any service in the Gospel, so that the office of the Apostleship itself is called διακονια; *I magnify mine office* την διακονιαν, Rom. xi. 13. *Thou shalt be a good minister,* Καλος διακονος, *of Jesus Christ,* 1 Tim. iv. 6. *Whereof I was made a minister,* διακονος, Ephes. iii. 7. That, therefore, is more true which Jerome writes in Epist. ad Philem. namely, that this Archippus was either *a bishop* or at least *a teacher* in the Church of Colosse. But now in the absence of Epaphras (who was his colleague in this evangelical office) he must labour the more diligently therein, that he might supply the place of both. But he (it is very likely) on the contrary began to grow languid in his duty, and therefore needed admonishing. Hence the Apostle wrote, *Say to Archippus, Take heed to the ministry,* &c. Hence we may observe,

1. That even good ministers sometimes grow indifferent to their duty, and need a spur.

2. If private admonition does not suffice, they must be rebuked, by the whole Church, or by some public person in the name of the whole Church.

Take heed to the ministry which thou hast received in the Lord, that thou fulfil it.] The Apostle would have Archippus to be admonished carefully to weigh the following three things.

1. What he had received; *the ministry*] i. e. The Gospel ministry, than which nothing is more sublime, nothing more useful ; and therefore there is nothing to be handled more faithfully and diligently.   So the whole company of the Apostles judged, Acts vi. 4, *We will give ourselves continually to prayer and to the ministry of the word.*

2. From whom he had received this ministry ; *In the Lord*] i. e. *by the Lord,* as the Greek Scholia expound it. Therefore by the authority of Christ, who called him to this office, he would have this Archippus to be excited to discharge it diligently and faithfully.   For if Christ himself laid this office upon ministers, doubtless he will both look for and require an account of the administration of the office from them.   *Woe is unto me,* says the Apostle, 1 Cor. ix. 16, 17, *if I preach not the Gospel! For if I do this thing willingly, I have a reward ; but if against my will, a dispensation of the Gospel is entrusted to me.*

3. For what end he had received this ministry ; *That he might fulfil it.*] This, therefore, ought always to be the care of ministers, not so much to obtain honour, as to execute the labour of the ministry ; not so much that he might be dignified with that honourable office, as that he might fulfil its duties.   So Paul also admonished his son Timothy, 2 Tim. iv. 5, *Do the work of an Evangelist, make full proof of thy ministry.* But what is it *to fulfil the ministry ?* It is to do all those things which devolve upon a minister, and which conduce to the salvation of men and the furtherance of the kingdom of Christ.   Of this kind are all those things which are enumerated by the Apostle in the same Chapter [to Timothy], *Preach the word, be instant in season, out of season; reprove, rebuke, exhort,* and the like.   These are the things about which Archippus was to be admonished.

Hence observe, It is necessary for the minister who desires rightly to discharge his duty, often and seriously to consider, what ministry he has received, by whom it was imposed and committed to him, and lastly, what end Christ had in entrusting him with it.

Vers. 18.

*The salutation by the hand of me Paul. Remember my
bonds. Grace be with you. Amen.*

In this last verse of this Epistle, the Apostle does three
things. 1. He shews that he himself had written his usual
salutation with his own hand. 2. He introduces a mention of his bonds, which he inserts by way of parenthesis.
3. He adds the salutation of his own hand, which he had
just mentioned.

The salutation by the hand of me Paul.] That is, In order
that you may understand that this Epistle, although written by my amanuensis, is yet genuine, and dictated by me,
I affix at the end my usual salutation written with my own
hand, which you very well know. This was done prudently by the Apostle in his Epistles, lest any one at any
time should obtrude a forged Epistle upon the Church in
his name; which he himself intimated 2 Thess. iii. 17,
where he says, that this salutation written with his own
hand, is *the token in every Epistle,* namely, a sign whereby
fictitious epistles could be known from true and genuine
ones. The Greek Scholia do not seem rightly to have explained what Paul intended by this *salutation, which is the
token in every Epistle.* For they say that he subscribed
with his own hand, τὸ, Ἀσπάζομαι ὑμᾶς. ᾒ τὸ, Ἔρρωσθε. ᾒ τι
τοιοῦτον; *I salute you; Farewell; or such like.* But it is
manifest, the Apostle calls a salutation, that prayer for
grace which he subjoins in the same place; *So I write,* says
he, *The Grace of our Lord Jesus Christ,* &c. And thus
also in this place by *salutation* he understands that last
word, *Grace be with you,* as Theodoret, Chrysostom, and
Ambrose have rightly noted.

But before he subscribed that salutation, by a parenthesis as it were, on a sudden he introduces a mention of
his bonds: *Remember,* says he, *my bonds.*] This perhaps

he deferred to the end of the Epistle, with the idea that thereby he should fix it deeper in their minds. And he would have them to bear in mind his bonds on four accounts;

1. That from hence they might derive an example of patience and Christian fortitude, if the like thing should happen to vex and afflict them for the profession of the Gospel. For who would refuse to suffer for the Gospel, when he called to mind, that this celebrated Apostle for the profession of it, had passed great part of his life in bonds?

2. That they might hence take occasion to pray for such a man oppressed with such miseries and griefs. For nothing is more bitter to the afflicted, than for them to suspect that all men cast off all concern for them; nothing on the other hand is more desirable, than that they should understand that other persons have at least a remembrance of their afflictions, and desire from their hearts their deliverance.

3. That they might hence conjecture, how the Gospel should be esteemed; on account of which the Apostle neither refused to undergo ignominy, nor imprisonment, nor death itself. Doubtless it was a great treasure, to retain which all other things were renounced with a ready and willing mind.

4. That from hence a care should be revived within them of comforting and assisting the Apostle by all those duties of Christian Charity which we are bound by the command of Christ to exhibit towards our afflicted brethren. And these are the reasons on account of which we ought always to remember those who suffer persecution for righteousness' sake. Now let us come to the salutation.

Grace be with you.] This is that salutation always subscribed with the Apostle's own hand to his Epistles, as it respects the sense, although not always in the same words. Neither is it wonderful if this most brave setter-forth of Divine grace, wished this prayer for saving grace to be the mark of his Epistles, whence they might distinguish the genuine from spurious ones. For that he might shew the sum of our salvation to depend upon the grace of God alone, he was wont to begin his Epistles with this same prayer, as well as to conclude them by it, *as if fortifying the faithful on every side by the wall of Divine grace,* as says Chrysostom. Now by *grace* he understands the paternal favour of God accepting us in Christ the Mediator, and all spiritual blessings which are used to flow to us from this favour of God. Therefore, in this single word *grace* is contained that great fund of blessings which are promised to believers and exhibited in the Gospel.

That last word *Amen,* is derived, as is known, from the Hebrew word AMAN, which in Hiphil signifies *to believe;* in Niphal signifies *to be firm, stable, faithful.* It is therefore a particle of confirmation and certification ; and *when it is attached to a prayer, it is as it were its seal,* as Jerome observes. By this word, then, the Apostle shews the certain persuasion of his heart, that God would hear this his prayer, and bestow his grace abundantly upon them. Thus it behoves us to repose a sure faith in God, as often as we seek any thing from him, especially when we desire to obtain the gifts of saving grace; which, by seeking faithfully from God the Father for his Son's sake, shall be bestowed upon us by the Holy Spirit copiously and freely.

FINIS.

GENERAL INDEX

OF

SUBJECTS IN THE EXPOSITION.

C

Carthusian Monkery, not a state of perfection, I. 326.

Ceremonies, may be instituted by the Church, and with what cautions, I. 401, 402; 522; are not to be multiplied, 402; 467; 529; whether the observance or the neglect is in itself of any or no consequence, II. 91; Ceremonies of the Jews, I. 478, 472. Christian liberty in regard to all, 480; the legal ones were acknowledgments of human guilt, 461; shadowed forth the grace of Christ, 489; and the very substance in Christ, 492; abrogated by Christ, and why, 404; in what manner, 465, 466; for what time, and how far they might be observed after the passion of Christ, 405.

Charity, what it is, II. 118; preeminent among the graces, ibid.; how it fulfils the law, 121; participates with others in all things, I. 57; 372; how it differs from a vicious affection, II. 119; is like a garment, 120.

Charity, among neighbours, especially in loving the saints, I. 74, though unknown, 102; II. 297; towards strangers and enemies, I. 109: devils and the lost not objects of it, 77; the rule of in judging, viz. *presuming any thing to be good till the contrary appears,* I. 22; the rule in acting, viz. *what ye would not should be done to you, do not you to another,* how to be understood, II. 43.

Chastisement of the body by acts of mortification, examples of it, I. 539; errors of those who sin in this respect, 541; how far these exercises may and ought to be employed, 542, 543.

Chastisements, not inflicted upon the faithful by God as satisfactions for sin, 288.

Children, what ought to be the obedience of to parents, II. 169—172; such obedience yields to piety towards God, 179—183; are not to be brought up effeminately, nor treated harshly, 190—192; are as parts of their parents, 193, 194; evils of severity towards them, 194, 195.

CHRIST, that he might be the Me-diator, ought to be God-man, I. 163, 164; it behoved him to be God that he might teach salvation, 409, 410; and that he might be the author of salvation, 410, 411; in what manner he is one person, 415—420; yet not every where as man, 421; II. 13; is the Lord of all things, even as man, I. 35; the cause of the creatures, 187; the Creator of the world, 188; the end of all things, 203; the first-born of every creature, and in what sense, 184, 185; the first-born from the dead, and in what sense, 222—223; he first rose, 223; the author of our resurrection, 224, 225; hath a fulness of grace, 229; and why, 231; he alone hath it, 231; is the channel of grace by the efficacy of operation, the benefit of intercession, and the merit of his passion, 35; he infuses grace, as man, instrumentally, 212; all grace is from him, 514; he is the way to God; he alone could and ought to reconcile us, 239; how he hath redeemed us, 166, 167; how he is the Mediator of angels, 244—246; how he is the head of angels, 427.

Christ, the sympathy of in our afflictions, 272; our support in trials, II. 15; what knowledge was in Christ, I. 362; He alone is the head of the Church, I. 17, 18; 126; and that as to both natures, 210, 211; even of the antient church, 211, 212; in what respects he is called the head of the Church, 212, 513—516; of what Church he is the head, 218.

is the only meritorious intercessor, II. 238, 239.

Christ is the object of faith, I. 62; the principal and special object, ibid.; and the adequate object of faith, because he justifies, 61—63; he dwells in us by faith, 316.

Christ, is the image of the Father as God, both as God and as man, 173; the exemplar or model of the creatures, 188.

is as a tabernacle, 410—412; the conqueror of the devil on the cross, 473—475.

how he sits at the right hand of God, as God, II. 12, 14; and as man, 12, 13.

312   GENERAL INDEX.

Christ must be served faithfully, I.
36; II.148.
his appearing and manifestation
threefold, II. 25 ; coming to judgment will be soon and sudden,
28 ; our life, and how, See Life.
Christ, put for the Church of
Christ, I. 272.
Christian, as to the name is nothing,
I. 23, 443, 445; serving any
other than God is guilty of sacrilege, 23; living in sin is a walking
monster, 443.
Christian, the true, ought always to
advance, 116, 380, 381; II. 9,
86; is like a fruitful tree, I. 127;
in what respects, 129.
is dead to sin, the world, and
the flesh, II. 16; in what manner, ibid.; he grows in faith daily,
and how, I. 350, 351; does all
things in the name of Christ, II.
146.
is in Christ through faith and
the Spirit, I. 316; ought to imitate Christ, II. 10, 115.
Christian, his enemies, I. 133;
469.
his life ought not to be a scandal
to the Gospel, II. 251; his conversation is in heaven, II. 6, 7.
Christians, ought to teach, and admonish, and restrain one another,
II. 138, 139; are called *saints in
Christ*, and why, I. 20, 22 ; *faithful* in Christ, 24 ; *brethren in
Christ*, and why, 26.
are brethren among themselves,
ibid. ; II. 270, 297, 348 ; therefore live in concord, I. 26; and
united, 348, 349.
Church, whence it is called, I. 217;
of what Church Christ is the head,
218 ; hypocrites are not members
of the Church, 219—221, 515;
the Church is as the family of
God, 294, 295 ; receives all things
from Christ, 514 ; increase of the
Church, what, 516 ; how the
whole is united to Christ, and the
members of it with one another,
513—515.
Church hath the power of ordaining
external rites, I. 401.
may consist of manifold divisions,
218; each particular one may fall,
12, 20 ; II. 293.
a domestic family may be a
Church, II. 299.
Circumcision, internal what it is,

I. 448 ; the Christian excels the
Jewish in three things, 434; its
author, and the instrument of it,
438 ; ought to be total, 439.
Jewish what it signified, 460;
chief among their ceremonies,
433.
Circumcision, put for the Jews
themselves, I. 451.
Citizenship, a bond of love, II.
288.
Colosse, where situated, see Preface, lxxi ; overturned by an
earthquake, II. 293.
Comfort, what it comprises, I. 345,
346.
Commendation, conduces to perseverance, I. 374.
Commodus, base deeds of that Emperor, II. 95.
Communication, or impartation,
proper, I. 364 ; 414—417.
not to be had with the ungodly
or superstitious, II. 252.
of benefits should be mutual, 301.
Communion of saints, in what it
consists, I. 289.
Compassion, what, II. 104.
Conclusion concerning faith, where
there is only one proposition of
the Scriptures, I. 47.
Concord, see Peace.
the concord of love arises from
agreement in faith, I. 348.
Concupiscence, its first motions are
sins, II. 48.
threefold : natural, carnal, and
spiritual, 49.
Conservation of all things wholly
from God, I. 203.
Consolation, spiritual, does not exist without love, I. 342 ; Papists
confess the same when they appeal to their consciences, 347.
all strengthened by the gratuitous promises, 346.
Conversation of a Christian ought
to be on heavenly things, II. 5—
7.
Corruption natural, in the understanding, will, and affections, I.
452 ; compared to a state of darkness, 156.
Covetousness, a vice partly spiritual
and partly carnal, II. 51.
how a covetous man is said to be
an idolater, ibid.
the greatness of the sin, 52.
Creation and preservation alike the
act of God, I. 204.

Festivals to be observed by Christians, and how, 485, 486.
cautious in the observance of them, 486.
Figurative or parabolic expressions not lies, II. 79.
Flesh, put for original corruption, I. 436.
Forgiveness of injuries, yields advantage to the person forgiving, II. 112.
of sins, how the phrase is to be understood, I. 49; what the act includes, 457; is the property of God alone, 458.
Fornication, what it is, and how it differs from adultery, &c. II. 38.
not regarded as a crime among the heathen, ibid.; yet disapproved of by some of the wiser, 42; the heinousness of the sin demonstrated, 39, 40; not to be tolerated in a Christian State, 45; opposed to charity in many respects, 43; favoured by the Papists, 44; wherefore reckoned among things indifferent by the Apostle, 41.
Fortitude, Christian, in what it consists, I. 132; whence derived, 134; our need of it, ibid.; true, from God alone, 136; how it differs from patience, 137.
Free-will does not fit or dispose us for grace, I. 90; 149; 453. Vide Merits.
Friends, who are such, 250, 251.

G.

Glory future, the twofold array of soul and body, II. 25, 26;
the hope of, a consolation in all adversities, 29.
Glory of Christ, ought to be the end of all our actions, II. 146, 147.
vain-glory to be avoided by Ministers, I. 103.
God, the author and end of all things, I. 199; the preserver of all things, 203—208; acts to a special end, 199; to be loved for himself alone, 70; not to be worshipped through any image, 182.
is the Father of Christ, I. 56. Vide Father.
how he is invisible, 180; unknown, 181; an object of dread out of Christ, 179; omnipresent, II.201; in a threefold manner, I. 415.

how he is said to be angry, II. 54; is not a respecter of persons, 91; 211; his righteousness in punishing, 56; in how many ways he is blasphemed, 69.
God, his efficiency by his Ministers, I. 8; his philanthropy shewn in appointing them, 9; prevents us, 89; is the fountain of all grace, as he is our Father, 32—34; communicates grace by his Son, 35; the first author of reconciliation, 235; the author of our quickening, 455, 456; the author of salvation by fore-ordaining it, and by effectually calling to it, 145, 146.
God alone ought and could save us, 154.
hated by sinners, and in what manner, 250.
Grace, and peace, the Apostolic salutation, I. 29; why joined, ibid.; why grace is put first, 31; the practice of St. Paul in reference to this, II. 308.
Grace, denotes three things, I. 29; II. 308; all derived from God, I. 301; as our Father, 32, 34; through his Son, in a threefold manner, 351.
efficacious, the property of the elect alone, 146—148; 367; sending it only not found to move the will, 453; necessity of it on account of corrupt nature, 147, 453; fulness of grace, what, 230; our duty to grow in it daily, 116; II. 49.
Gratitude, duty of, I. 128.
See Thanksgiving.

H.

Hand, the right, of God, what it means, and what to sit there, II. 12—14.
Hand-writing of Ordinances, what, I. 461—463; how made void and abrogated, 465, 466.
Hatred, mutual between God and sinners, I. 250; perfect, in what it consists, and how evinced, I. 76, 77.
Head, what required to constitute headship, I. 215, 216; 511—513.
of the Church, Vide CHRIST.
Hearers should have general doctrines applied to them, I. 248; 319, 320.

M.

Magistrates, are all from God, II. 254 ; to be obeyed even if heathens and idolaters, 198 ; 254.

Malice, what, II. 66.

Man, naturally dead as to spiritual things, I. 451 ; prone to every evil, II. 65.

old, what, and how put off, 83 ; the members of 34, 36.

new, what, 84 ; his members, 98.

Men all, comprehended under *every creature*, I. 264.

Mark, who, II. 281, 282 ; converted by Peter, ibid. ; wrote the Gospel taught him by Peter, ibid. ; first Bishop of Alexandria, ibid.

Marriage, evil of unequal or improper, I. 159 ; contracted against the will of parents, is sin, 187 ; confirmed from the moment of contract, 188.

Martyrs, their sufferings make no satisfaction for others, I. 277, 279 ; festivals of, appointed for the worship of God alone, 487.

Mary, how said to have been full of grace, 232.

Masters, responsibility of, I. 211 ; II. 221 ; duties and obligations in regard to their servants, II. 216—220.

Meats, no distinction of to Christians, I. 480, 481 ; 521—523 ; what there was formerly among the Jews, 478 ; what was signified by those forbidden, 490.

Mediator, ought to be God-man, I. 163 ; the alone Mediator, as well of Redemption as of meritorious intercession, is Christ, ibid.

Meekness, the duties of and motives to, II. 107, 108.

Members of the old man, what, II. 34, 35.

Mercy to be shewn on the calamities of others, 103.

Merits of no man extend beyond his own person, I. 280 ;

none of congruity before grace, 90 ; 149 ; 259 ; nor of condignity after grace, 124 ; 149 ; 279.

Might, spiritual, in what exercised and what it effects, I. 132—134.

Mind, See Understanding.

Ministers ought to await a call, I. 29 ; their call twofold, ibid. ; yea, threefold, 268 ; order ought to exist

among them as among unequals, 296 ; to be attached to certain places and people, 298 ; when absent from their flock, more solicitous about it, 344 ; ought never to be wholly absent, 373.

all their sufficiency from Christ and his Spirit, 330 ; II. 239—241 ; their efficacy for the salvation of mankind, I. 8 ; are not to be slothful, 7, 8 ; 298 ; 341 ; are as centinels, 389 ; what considerations excite them to diligence, 104, 105 ; II. 305 ; in what their fidelity consists, I. 105 ; II. 248 ; in what their duty in preaching consists, I. 318 ; ought to teach both the Law and the Gospel, but in different ways, 319, 320 ; in the discharge of their duty must act impartially towards all, 321 ; to defend the Gospel and their fellow-ministers, 340 ; should reprove the vices of all, II. 247 ; not accommodate their statements to the errors of their hearers, ibid. ; ought not to affect eloquence, I. 105 ; should apply general doctrines, 248 ; preach the word freely and boldly, II. 246 ; constantly and diligently, 247 ; sincerely and faithfully, adding nothing to it, nor withholding any thing, 248, 249 ; fitly and suitably to their hearers, 250.

Ministers, their dignity, I. 104 ; 293 ; II. 271 ; 288 ; ought not to decry or depreciate one another, I. 101 ; II. 272 ; should endeavour to maintain a good repute, I. 101, 102 ; ought to be humble, 103 ; must not be immodest or vulgar, II. 74 ; are not lords of our faith, I. 268 ; but *ministers* only, 293 ; should not only preach to, but also pray for their people, I. 31 ; 113 ; 289 ; constantly and earnestly, 113, 114 ; II. 290 ; ought to enquire into the life and manners of every one committed to their care, II. 268 ; particularly to esteem the more pious, 275.

Ministers, what things afford them joy, I. 373 ; should especially rejoice in the spiritual welfare of their flock, I. 54 ; 340 ; should warn their people against seducers, 389.

how they absolve from sins, I. 286 ; ought to be animated to en-

dure the cross, I. 270; 292; 329;
II. 245 ; and to exhort others to
constancy under it, II. 269.

on what accounts they may declare their labours, I. 338, 339 ;
should be prayed for by the people, I. 238; that they may be
useful, 242; competent and diligent, II. 244.

Ministers' doctrines not to be received without examination, I.
388 ; 538.

Mode of acting sometimes of more
importance than the action, II.
246.

Monachism is not a state of perfection, I. 326 ; II. 92.

Monasteries, ought not to be entered by children against the consent of their parents, II. 174—
186.

Monks, the Carthusian, abstain from
meat, I. 481.

of Palestine, their austerities,
539.

Mortification what, and what things
required to it, II. 31, 33; Christ
the author of a threefold mortification, I. 444; quickening joined
to mortification, 442, 445 ; ought
to extend to all sins, 439, 457 ;
admits of degrees, 442 ; in this
respect differs from natural death,
II. 33; how they who are dead
unto sin ought still to mortify
themselves, 34 ; how far the renewed are dead unto sin, 16; how
any one can abolish sin in this
life, and how not, I. 440 ; the
mortification of a Christian perpetual, laborious, and hazardous,
II. 37.

Mortification of the flesh by external exercises; with examples of
it, I. 539, 540 ; how far such exercises may and ought to be undergone, 542, 543 ; errors of those
who sin in this respect, 541.

Multitude tends to confirm the
minds of believers, I. 94, 95.

not a mark of the Church, 516,
517.

Mystery, what it signifies, I. 300 ;
taken for the sum of Evangelical
doctrine, 356 ; for the calling of
the Gentiles, 300, 502.

Mysteries to be believed, not discussed, 303, 304.

N.

Name of Christ, what it is to do
any thing in the, II. 146.

Name, the origin not so much to be
regarded as the use, I. 3 ; without
the reality avails nothing, I. 10,
23 ; 100 ; 443 ; II. 274.

Nations, no distinction of with God,
II. 90.

Nature, our's good at the creation,
I. 250 ; corrupt, incapable of spiritual things, 146 ; is not disposed
for grace, 453 ; II. 60 ; is alienated from God, I. 249 ; at enmity
with God, and God an enemy to
it, 250, 251.

Natural corruption, pervades all the
faculties of the soul, 452, 453:
man thereby dead as to spiritual
perceptions, 450 ; explained by
parts, 451, 452; all prone to
every evil on account of it, II.
65.

Negations in comparisons, their peculiar use, II. 203.

Neighbour, who is our's, and how
the object of our love, I. 72.

New-Moon, the festival of among
the Jews, what it signified, I.
492.

Newness of life, 444, 445.

Nobility commends no one to God,
II. 94, 95.

Nourishment of the body of Christ,
what it signifies, I. 513, 514.

O.

Obedience, see Subjection.

blind, not good, I. 122 ; 534,
535.

Obedience of wives towards their
husbands, II. 151 ; of children
towards their parents, 168 ; of servants towards their masters, 196.

Obscenity in language to be avoided,
73.

Omniscience, does not appertain to
the human nature of Christ, I.
363—365.

Onesimus, a deacon, II. 273.

Opportunity to be embraced, I. 305 ;
II. 257, 258.

Order, what it is, 295, 296 ; various significations of, I. 374,375 ;
encomiums of it, 375 ; all things
done of God by order, II. 56.

ought to exist among the Minis-

tian monks, 225; should be offered to God alone, and why, I.
505—507; he alone is to be entreated for grace, 33.

Prayer, who they are that can confidently pray to God, 36; success
of in the Scriptures. II. 226.

Preaching the word, how it is the
instrument of producing faith, I.
86; the Gospel was preached
through the whole world, and
how, 91—93; how ministers
ought to preach, II. 246—250.

Presence of God, threefold, I. 415.

Present in Spirit, what, II. 372.

Pride, to be discarded, II. 156.

Procrastination not to be yielded to,
I. 99.

Properties of the Divine Nature not
communicated to the human, I.
364, 365.

Psalms, Hymns, and Spiritual Songs,
how they differ, II. 140.
in what manner to be used by
Christians, 141—144; antiquity
of the custom, 143.

Q.

Quickening of sinners the work of
omnipotence, and twofold, I. 455,
456.

R.

Reason natural, discovers not the
objects of faith, I. 391; See Philosophy.

Reconcile, meaning of the term, 234,
245; how angels may be said to
be reconciled to God, 244, 246;
430; how all creatures, 247.

Reconciliation twofold, 254, 255;
the primary author of our's, God;
the proximate agent, Christ, 234.
is made to the whole Trinity, but
said to be to the Father on two
accounts, 237, 238; Christ alone
could effect it, 239; hath reconciled us to himself, ibid.
its accomplishment through death
the most suitable and consistent
mode, 241, 242, and by the death
on the Cross, 243.

Redeemer, our's ought to be God
and man, I. 163; 409, 410.

Redemption four modes of effecting
it, I. 166; all redeemed by
Christ, the elect alone in Christ,
163, 164.

Redemption, obtained by Christ
alone, 171; our's in this life not
complete, and why, 165; not to
be contemplated without gratitude, 144; what the redeemed
were, and what they become, 154,
155.

Redeeming the time, what it imports, II. 257, 258.

Regeneration, necessarily precedes
the resurrection, I. 222.
precedes glory, II. 27.

Religion what it is, I. 503.
does not subvert political order,
II. 198.

Remission of sins, what, I. 457;
gratuitous, ibid.; universal, 458;
how the article in the Creed is to
be understood, 48, 49; guilt being
remitted the punishment is remitted, 278, 288; 457; to remit
sins peculiar to God, 458, 459;
how assigned to ministers, 286;
459; assured to believers, 37;
may be doubted of by them, but
not as believers, 49.

Renewed, their sins hateful to God,
but not themselves, 126,127.

Reputation to be guarded and preserved, I. 102.

Resurrection, Christ the first fruits
of it, 224; the threefold author
of our's, 225, 226; the Father
raised Christ, and yet he raised
himself, 448.

Resurrection spiritual as well as bodily, 224, 225; Christ arose from
the dead and quickens us from sin
by the same Almighty power, 446,
447; II. 10.
of Christ to be exhibited in our
life, 445; II. 7.
our's is twofold, and both effected
by Christ, II. 10; our spiritual
resurrection ought to be a copy of
Christ's bodily resurrection, 11;
is wrought in us by virtue of the
resurrection of Christ, 10.
the confidence of Christians, 29.

Revenge, how far it is lawful and
disallowed to a Christian, II. 113,
14.
by duel is not lawful, 116, 117.

Revilers of the Ministry warned, 1.
104.

Righteous we are so by the imputation of Christ's righteousness, I.
424.

Righteousness of God in punishing,
II. 55, 56.

S.

Sabbath, why instituted and what it
signifies, I. 491, 492.

Sacraments without Christ are of no
avail, 436, 437; are tenders of
grace, but only to Believers, 24;
447, 448; in themselves there is
no grace, nor in the *opus operatum*,
436, 446; nevertheless the external signs not to be despised, 437.

Saints, their infirmities illustrated
by various similitudes, 133; derive help from God, 134; their
works are not perfectly good, 145
—149; perform no works of supererogation, 279; are not to be
worshipped, 487.

Saints, what constitutes their true
life, see Life.

Salt of speech what, II. 261.

Salutation what it is, and its forms,
II. 277; how necessary, 278; in
what sense forbidden, 279; of
Paul, 306; of the Hebrews, I.
29; of the Apostles, 30.

Sanctification, what, I. 20, 21; 456;
twofold, 258; threefold, 259, 260;
all from Christ, see Holiness.

Sanctification accompanies justification, I. 457.

is effected by degrees in this life,
II. 102.

Satisfaction for our sins made by
Christ alone, I. 287; 459; to that
the Papists themselves resort
when consulting their consciences,
347; none made by us either in
doing or suffering, 457.

Schoolmen, obtrude their vagaries
for articles of faith, I. 305; 357,
358.

Scriptures, are believed on their
own authority among the faithful,
I. 6; are not confirmed by the
authority of the Church, 355,
500; are the sole rule of faith,
267; 423; 499—501; II. 246;
are perspicuous, I. 306; eloquent,
336; are the word of Christ in a
twofold manner, II. 130, 131;
their efficacy in changing men's
manners, I. 96; are to be read
diligently, 266, 353; by the Laity,
122; 266; II. 132; 263; objections to the practice answered, II.
136; how used in the primitive
Church, 300; are like a pharmacopœia, in which nothing is insignificant or useless, 265; impiously

compared by Hermanus to the fables of Æsop, I. 355.

Scythians thought to have been the
worst of barbarians, II. 92.

Seducers beguile men in two ways,
I. 368, 369.

Servant of fortune is not a distinction of nature, II. 217, 218.

deceitful and contumacious towards his earthly master, will be
punished by the Supreme Lord,
210.

Servants, their condition formerly,
197; four things necessary to a
servant, 216; ought to obey their
masters, 197; should serve heartily, for they serve Christ, 202,
207; whom we must serve faithfully as the Lord of all, I. 35, 36.

Serve, to serve God more easy than
to serve man, II. 221.

Service, eye, what, II. 199.

Simon the Cyrenian did not suffer
in the place of Christ, I. 257.

Sin, all to be avoided, I. 130, 134;
438; 459; II. 64; whence its
first motions spring, and what they
are, II. 48, 49; what it is to live
in it, II. 19, 20; 60, 62.

is a pleasant poison, I. 454; is
contagious, II. 257; provokes God
to inflict punishment, II. 54—56;
its enormity manifested by the
magnitude of the ransom, I. 163;
456; the body of sin, what, 438;
members of it what, II. 34, 35;
how it is dead in the renewed, II.
10.

Sin, original is not the mere privation or destitution of original
righteousness, I. 452, 453; II.
37; how it infects the whole man,
ibid.

Sins are the chains of the devil, I.
474; different kinds of, II. 49, 51.

Sinners are alienated from and enemies to God, I. 249, 250; are
dead, 450; are homicides, 454.

Singing an antient custom, useful,
and how to be employed, II. 143.
See Hymns.

Slanderers, a lesson for them, I. 102.

Slavery, no ground of distinction as
it regards men, with God, II. 94;
see Servants.

Soul, put for the whole person, I.
416.

Speech, the salt of, what, II. 261.

Spirit, to be present in, what it is,
I. 372.

Spirit Holy, is like a treasurer, I. 21.
why not called an image, 176.
Spiritual things should always be
contemplated, II. 6, 7; are especially to be preferred and desired,
I. 32; especially by ministers,
104; how far they may be known
naturally, 393.
Stedfast, what it signifies, and especially with regard to faith, 376.
Stephen, how he was full of grace,
232.
Strangers to be loved and how, I.
74; the evil of cherishing them
more than our own kindred, II.
276, 288.
Strengthening, spiritual, how necessary and effective, I. 132—134.
Subjection, what, how useful and
obligatory, II. 152.
of a wife towards her husband, in
what it consists, 153.
Succession local, of no avail without
succession of doctrine, I. 20.
Sufferings of others claim our sympathy, II. 108; 286.
of believers, see Afflictions.
of Christ, satisfactory, &c. see
Passion.
of the Cross, the best means
adapted for our redemption, I.
242; 474.
Superiors to be obeyed in things indifferent, II. 171.
Superstitious observances, I. 400.

T.

Tabernacles, feast of, why instituted and what it signified, I. 491,
492.
Temples are due to God alone, 507;
are dedicated by Papists to the
worship of angels and saints, ibid.
Testament Old, is the New under a
veil; the New is the Old revealed,
I. 493.
Thanksgiving what, I. 54; to whom
especially due, 55; reasons for it,
II. 235; should be always joined
with prayer, I. 58; II. 235; due
to God even for the use of the
creatures, II. 147.
evils of neglecting it, I. 129; II.
236.
Theology, not opposed to, but above
Philosophy, I. 394.
Theologians employ philosophy on
many accounts, 395.

Things above, what are so called,
II. 6.
on the earth described, 8; why
not to be sought after, 9.
Timothy who, and why called a brother by Paul, I. 5, 6.
circumcised by St. Paul, I. 405.
Tongue must be restrained and regulated, II. 260.
Traditions are not necessary, I. 265;
322; 346, 347; how far to be
observed in external things, and
how far not, 401, 402.
Traditions human, are not parts of
Divine worship, 534, 544; have
the appearance of wisdom, and
how, 530; to be rejected. See
Scriptures as the rule of faith.
Trinity, defined, I. 178; the works
of ad extrà indivisible, 5. 35, 55;
136, 145, 153; 209; 235—239;
414.
Triumph, description of Christ's
over the demons, I. 468;
upon the cross, 474.
Tychicus, first bishop of Chalcedon,
II. 266.

U.

Ubiquity does not attach to the human nature of Christ. I. 421; II.
13.
Unbelievers, none of their works are
good, I. 60.
Uncircumcision, various significations of, I. 451, 452.
Uncleanness, what meant by it, II.
46.
Understanding, necessity of in order
to decide in questions of moment,
I. 120, 121.
Understanding, our's naturally dark,
I. 252; in matters of faith altogether blind, 304; 452; how enlightened, 120.
Union, personal, in Christ what, I.
415; does not establish the ubiquity of his body, 419, 421.
mystical, is effected by faith and
the Spirit, 426; importance of it,
II. 23.

V.

Vices are contagious, II. 257; the
chains of the devil, I. 474; should
be abandoned by the Christian,
II. 63; with promptitude, 64; and
in toto, 65; and spiritually, 64.

INDEX OF QUESTIONS

INCIDENTALLY AND BRIEFLY DETERMINED IN THE WORK.

INDEX

OF

SUBJECTS AND WORKS

INCIDENTALLY GLANCED AT

IN THE NOTES.

INDEX

OF

PASSAGES OF SCRIPTURE

EXPLAINED BY THE WAY.

(The Translator has greatly amplified this Index, conceiving, that as many texts of Scripture, not noted in the Original Index, are yet illustrated by the connexion in which they stand in the work, it would prove useful to give them a place here. Also, in this Index are included a few texts discussed in the Dissertation on the Death of Christ.]

THE END.

ERRATA.

Page 42, § 3, line 4, for 11, read 2.

   261, before § 3, read—But says the Apostle, *Let your speech always,*
   &c.

Pp. 269 and 271, in the head line read—Vers. 7, 8.

Page 325, Note, line 2, for *Levins*, read *Lerins*.

IN VOL. I.

In the Life, page xi. line 12, in some copies, the comma should be after
   major ; and for *honore*, read *ponere.*

Page 123, line 4 of the middle section, the reader will be so good as
   insert, after *vocation*—1 Thess. II. 12, *Worthy of God ;*—and in
   the following quotation to read—*worthy of the Gospel.* Also, on

Page 170, dele last line of the Note, and read—to which Garner added a
   fifth Volume in 1684.

Page 547, for " *those Editions*" twice, read—this Edition.